# South America

*Caribbean Sea*

PANAMA

Maracaibo
**Caracas**
TRINIDAD

Medellín

VENEZUELA
*Orinoco*

GUYANA

Georgetown
Paramaribo
Cayenne

**Bogotá**
(Sánta Fé)

*GUIANA HIGHLANDS*

SURINAME
*French Guiana*

Cali

COLOMBIA

Quito
**ECUADOR**
**Guayaquil**

*Negro*
*Japur*
*Branco*

*Marajó I.*

Belém

**Fortaleza**

*Marañón*

*Amazon*
Manaus

A
N

*Juruá*
*Ucayali*

*Purus*
*Madeira*
*Tapajós*

*Xingu*

*Tocantins*

*São Francisco*

**Recife**
(Pernambuco)

**Lima**

P E R U

D
E
S

B  R  A  Z  I  L

**Salvador**
(Bahia)

**BOLIVIA**

La Paz

Brasília

*BRAZILIAN HIGHLANDS*

Sucre

*Paraguay*

**Belo Horizonte**

C
H
I
L
E

**PARAGUAY**

*Paraná*

**São Paulo**
**Rio de Janeiro**

Asunción

*Pacific*

*Paraná*

**Pôrto Alegre**

**Córdoba**

*Ocean*

*Uruguay*

URUGUAY

Valparaíso
**Santiago**

**Rosario**

**Buenos Aires**
Montevideo

Concepción

**ARGENTINA**

*Atlantic*

Bahía Blanca

*Ocean*

## FOR REFERENCE ONLY

CHAVEZ HIGH SCHOOL
LIBRARY
HOUSTON, TEXAS

*PATAGONIA*

Punta Arenas

*Falkland Islands*
(Islas Malvinas)

*Tierra del Fuego*

500 miles
805 kilometers

# LATIN
# AMERICAN
# HISTORY
# AND CULTURE

# ADVISORY BOARD

# ENCYCLOPEDIA OF

# LATIN AMERICAN HISTORY AND CULTURE

Barbara A. Tenenbaum

*EDITOR IN CHIEF*

Georgette Magassy Dorn
Mary Karasch
John Jay TePaske
Ralph Lee Woodward, Jr.
*ASSOCIATE EDITORS*

## VOLUME 1

**Charles Scribner's Sons**

**MACMILLAN LIBRARY REFERENCE USA**

SIMON & SCHUSTER MACMILLAN

NEW YORK

SIMON & SCHUSTER AND PRENTICE HALL INTERNATIONAL

LONDON   MEXICO CITY   NEW DELHI   SINGAPORE   SYDNEY   TORONTO

An imprint of Simon & Schuster Macmillan
866 Third Ave.
New York, NY 10022


**Library of Congress Cataloging-in-Publication Data**

Encyclopedia of Latin American history and culture / Barbara A.
   Tenenbaum, editor in chief ; associate editors, Georgette M. Dorn
   . . . [et al.].
      p.    cm.
    Includes bibliographical references and index.
    ISBN 0-684-19253-5 (set : alk. paper). — ISBN 0-684-19752-9 (v. 1
 : alk. paper). — ISBN 0-684-19753-7 (v. 2 : alk. paper). — ISBN
 0-684-19754-5 (v. 3 : alk. paper). — ISBN 0-684-19755-3 (v. 4 :
 alk. paper). — ISBN 0-684-80480-8 (v. 5 : alk. paper).
    1. Latin America—Encyclopedias.   I. Tenenbaum, Barbara A.
 F1406.E53   1996                         95–31042
 980'.003—dc20                           CIP


5  7  9  11  13  15  17  19  V/C  20  18  16  14  12  10  8  6

PRINTED IN THE UNITED STATES OF AMERICA

# EDITORIAL STAFF

# CONTENTS

# PREFACE

THE *Encyclopedia of Latin American History and Culture* strives to organize current knowledge of the region for the literate and curious public. It is the product of a mature field and contains the original work of 832 scholars from more than twenty different countries ranging from the United States to Uruguay to South Africa to Israel.

Our understanding of Latin American history and culture was greatly enriched by the most recent decade of scholarship, which has presented a vast array of new questions for study. Originally we had thought that surely 3,000 entries would be sufficient; the present volumes contain 5,287, almost twice as many. The additions demonatrate our concern that history and culture be covered as widely as possible to reflect the way Latin Americans of all classes understand their world. Thanks to these new insights, we have included entries about cultural phenomena ranging from cuisines to religions to sports.

The *Encyclopedia* was the brainchild of our publisher, Karen Day, who had spent large parts of her childhood in Latin America. She recognized that classrooms in the United States were becoming ever more inclusive of the Western Hemisphere as a whole and more interested in the history and culture of Latin America in particular. She gave us carte blanche to include important cultural figures by gently insisting on an entry for the popular Brazilian singer Roberto Carlos.

In developing the *Encyclopedia*, I had the privilege of working with four extraordinarily talented scholars with a wide array of interests, accurately reflecting the vast nature of the region and the task at hand. In alphabetical order, Georgette Magassy Dorn, Chief of the Hispanic Division at the Library of Congress, who grew up in Argentina, brought the passion of a generalist both to the work as a whole and to her Southern Cone speciality; she also provided a crucial knowledge of literature. Mary Karasch of Oakland University constantly kept us in line with her insistence on social issues and the importance of Brazil. John J. TePaske of Duke University not only assumed responsibility for the Andean region but gave us valuable guidance on the colonial period as well. Ralph Lee Woodward, Jr., of Tulane University conceived of and assigned the entries for both Central America and the Caribbean with rare good humor and perspective. In addition to serving as Editor in Chief, I was responsible for Mexico and the Spanish Borderlands as well as for general economic coverage.

From the very beginning we made several decisions that have molded and guided the work. We agreed that Brazil, the largest and most populous nation, would be accorded appropriate treatment in all entries concerned with Latin America as a whole, and that the Portuguese Empire would likewise be adequately covered. Also, we were determined to include the history of all areas of the Western Hemisphere that had once been part of the Spanish Empire, thereby erasing the arbitrary divide that has separated the history of the Spanish Borderlands that are now part of the United States from the rest of Latin America. However, we decided that the non-Spanish-speaking islands of the Caribbean would be covered with single country essays, with the significant exception of Haiti. We divided the proposed 1.8 million words into 300,000 per region with an additional 300,000 for general entries like "Colonial Medicine," "Family," or "Income Distribution." No entry was to have fewer than 100 words since we decided that any entry that could be done in fewer words was not worthy of inclusion. We also insisted that the history of the region be seen as a comprehensive unit from the dawn of time to the present. These decisions were not taken lightly; often we disagreed among ourselves, making the production of the work an interesting intellectual enterprise in its own right.

After we had settled on these basic outlines, we turned to our predecessors. I compiled a list of all the entries in such pioneering works as Michael Rheta Martin's *Encyclopedia of Latin American History* (1956, rev. ed. 1968) and Helen Delpar's superb *Encyclopedia of Latin America* (1974). There were marked differences in coverage; the first encyclopedia was devoted mostly to political and legal questions, while its successor was much more wide-ranging, including lengthy essays on various economic issues and short biographies of cultural figures. The various editors reviewed the lists and added and subtracted subjects based on recent events and changes in historical perspective. We all consulted with other scholars to make sure that our increasing specialization had not blinded us to important figures and trends in the regions to which we had dedicated our scholarly lives. During this period we decided to develop an advisory board to oversee our choices: Margaret E. Crahan (Hunter College), Richard Graham (University of Texas at Austin), Louis A. Pérez, Jr. (University of North Carolina at Chapel Hill), Jamie E. Rodríguez O. (University of California, Irvine), and Susan M. Socolow (Emory University). These advisors had an extremely difficult task searching for omissions from our prepared list. Since 1990, I have also scoured indices from other compendiums as well and consulted university librarians (most notably those from Shippensburg University, Dr. Signe Kelker and Berkley Laite), public librarians, scholars from other fields, and even the general public.

It soon became apparent that each of us had a different philosophy regarding the assignment process. It is a tribute to the universe of those who study Latin America that few scholars declined to write contributions when asked. Of course, the fact that both Georgette Magassy Dorn and I had routine access to the extraordinarily rich collections of the Library of Congress helped at every juncture along the way. In addition we benefited from relatively recent technological and political changes. It is doubtful that we could have included all of our contributions without fax machines. Further, political events conspired in our favor since the *Encyclopedia* was conceived in February 1990, shortly after the collapse of the Berlin Wall. In the ensuing years, it has profited from the muting of the kinds of ideological controversies that might have created difficulties in the search for objectivity. As we neared press time, the *ELAHC* set an important record: *every* assigned entry was received—yet another tribute to the diligence and dedication of the members of our field. On a sad note, several of our contributors passed away during the five years of preparation; they include James Cochrane, Warren Dean, Arthur Ennis, Heidy Fogel, Sheldon Liss, Richard Mazzara, Martha Robertson, and Roberto Valero.

In a work of this kind, it is customary to thank the editorial staff who helped push the project to completion, but the tributes registered here are more than just the obligatory mention. The ever unflappable Managing Editor, John Fitzpatrick, shepherded the manuscript from beginning to end, despite all manner of difficulties. We worked with the nicest Assistant Editor in publishing today, Leroy

Gonzalez, who soothed contributors and editors alike with aplomb. Once entries were received, our Copy Chief, Brenda Goldberg, managed a vast array of tireless and meticulous fact checkers all over the country, who bombarded the authors with countless inquiries, large and small, to make the text as accurate as possible. In particular, they insisted on the most accurate dates of birth and death yet found, prompting discussions of the differences between primary and secondary sources, phone calls to the subjects of biographies and their families, and the like. In most cases, the contributors answered all the queries and returned the manuscripts. When that was impossible, those of us at the Library of Congress filled the gap, especially J. David Dressing of Tulane University, who moonlighted at the Library with unselfish dedication, checking entries and translations in their final stages. Once the manuscripts went into type, Brenda Goldberg served as our "eagle eye," ever on the lookout for mistakes that had somehow crept into the text. Our thanks also to Pembroke Herbert and Sandi Rygiel of Picture Research Consultants, and Martha Davidson for their invaluable assistance in finding just the right illustrations, and to Deasy GeoGraphics, which produced our maps.

BARBARA A. TENENBAUM
*Specialist in Mexican Culture*
*Library of Congress*

# USING THE ENCYCLOPEDIA

This encyclopedia contains nearly 5,300 separate articles. Most topics appear in English alphabetical order, according to the word-by-word system (e.g., Casa Rosada before Casals). Persons and places generally precede things (Roosevelt, Theodore, before Roosevelt Corollary). Certain subjects are clustered together in composite entries, which may comprise several regions, periods, or genres. For example, the "Slavery" and "Mining" entries contain separate articles for Brazil and Spanish America. "Art" embraces separately signed essays on pre-Columbian, colonial, nineteenth-century, and modern art, as well as folk art.

NATIONAL TOPICS are frequently clustered by country, under one or more of the following subheadings:

> *Constitutions*
> *Organizations* (administrative, cultural, economic, labor, etc.)
> *Political Parties* (listed under the English name and including former
>      revolutionary movements that have entered the political system)
> *Revolutionary Movements*
> *Revolutions*

Note that an event with a distinctive name will be found under that term, whereas a generic name will appear under the appropriate country. Thus, the Chibata Revolt appears under *C* and the Pastry War under *P*, but the Revolution of 1964 appears under "Brazil: Revolutions."

MEASUREMENTS appear in the English system according to United States usage. Following are approximate metric equivalents for the most common units:

> 1 foot = 30 centimeters
> 1 mile = 1.6 kilometers
> 1 acre = 0.4 hectares
> 1 square mile = 2.6 square kilometers
> 1 pound = 0.45 kilograms
> 1 gallon = 3.8 liters

BIOGRAPHICAL ENTRIES (numbering nearly 3,000) are listed separately in an appendix in volume 5, where a rough classification is offered according to sex and field(s) of activity.

CROSS-REFERENCES appear in two forms: SMALL CAPITALS in the text highlight significant persons, concepts, and institutions that are treated in their own entries in the encyclopedia. *See also* references at the end of an entry call attention to articles of more general relevance. Cross-referencing is selective: obvious sources of information (such as most country, state, and city entries) are not highlighted. For full cross-referencing consult the index in volume 5.

ENCYCLOPEDIA OF

# LATIN
# AMERICAN
# HISTORY
# AND CULTURE

**ABAD Y QUEIPO, MANUEL** (*b.* 26 August 1751; *d.* 15 September 1825), bishop of Michoacán (1810–1814) and acute social commentator on late colonial Mexico. The illegitimate son of a noble Asturian family, Abad y Queipo was born in Santa María de Villarpedre, Asturias, Spain. He studied at the University of Salamanca for ten years before emigrating to the Americas, where he received a doctorate in canon law from the University of Guadalajara in 1805. He served in Michoacán from 1784 to 1814, rising through the ecclesiastical hierarchy to become acting bishop (unconfirmed by captive King Ferdinand VII) in 1810. An exemplification of the enlightened clergyman, Abad y Queipo strove to improve local economic conditions, in one instance by promoting the production of raw silk. He also advocated social reforms, such as the abolition of tribute, and he criticized many Bourbon policies, notably the INTENDANCY SYSTEM and the sequestration of pious funds.

Abad y Queipo, however, always favored reform within the imperial system. In 1810, when the rebellion led by his old friend Miguel HIDALGO Y COSTILLA broke out, he excommunicated the insurgent leader and unceasingly preached the social and economic evils of civil war. Nonetheless, he was suspected of harboring dangerously liberal views, and the restored Ferdinand VII recalled him to Spain in 1814. Abad y Queipo was fi-

nally confirmed as bishop of Michoacán but was never allowed to return to Mexico. In 1822 he resigned his hard-won bishopric to become bishop of Tortose. He also served in the provisional junta of 1820, which rekindled Ferdinand's doubts about the cleric's political loyalty; this led in 1824 to his arrest and imprisonment in the monastery of Sisla, where he died.

LILLIAN ESTELLE FISHER, *Champion of Reform: Manuel Abad y Queipo* (1955); HUGH M. HAMILL, JR., *The Hidalgo Revolt: Prelude to Mexican Independence* (1966); NANCY M. FARRISS, *Crown and Clergy in Colonial Mexico: The Crisis of Ecclesiastical Privilege* (1968).

R. DOUGLAS COPE

**ABADÍA MÉNDEZ, MIGUEL** (*b.* 5 June 1867; *d.* 15 May 1947), Colombian president (1926–1930). Born in La Vega de los Padres (now Piedras), Tolima, Abadía was sent to Bogotá for his education. He attended various private schools and received his doctorate in law in 1889 from the Colegio del Rosario. He became a publicist for Conservative Party ideals and was editor of several Bogotá newspapers. He also taught history and law. Abadía's energy, dedication, and deserved reputation for probity won him election to several congresses. An expert in constitutional law, he served as minister in the cabinets of several Conservative regimes before becoming president in 1926. During his presidency, the last of the "Conservative Hegemony," there was further irresponsible borrowing abroad to support the country's infrastructure. The economic downturn at the end of the 1920s brought increasingly violent confrontations with newly organizing labor in the petroleum fields (Santander) and the bloody repression of the banana workers' strike (Magdalena, November–December 1928). These episodes in turn provoked further civil unrest, including popular and student demonstrations and deaths (8–9 June 1929) in Bogotá. As a result, Abadía was forced to fire his war minister and others, and the Conservative Party fragmented. His political life was over. He died at La Unión, Cundinamarca, after five years of severe mental illness.

TERRENCE B. HORGAN, "The Liberals Come to Power in Colombia, *por Debajo de la Ruana:* A Study of the Enrique Olaya Herrera Administration, 1930–1934" (Ph.D. diss., Vanderbilt University, 1983), pp. 18–56; IGNACIO ARIZMENDI POSADA, *Presidentes de Colombia, 1810–1990* (1989), pp. 225–227.

J. LEÓN HELGUERA

*See also* **Colombia: Political Parties; Great Banana Strike.**

**ABAJ TAKALIK,** a Preclassic MESOAMERICAN site on the lower Pacific slope of southwestern Guatemala in the modern department of Retalhuleu. Several hundred pieces of sculpture document the evolution of styles from earliest ground or incised features on otherwise unshaped boulders, through monumental OLMEC sculpture like that of the Veracruz–Tabasco Olmec heartland, to portrait stelae with long-count Maya-like numerals and inscriptions in glyphs perhaps ancestral to both central Mexican and MAYA glyphs.

The settlement was occupied as early as the third millennium B.C., and after its development consisted of numerous earthen mounds arrayed on wide terraces cut into the sloping hillside. The mounds occasionally have adobe brick or facings of stone cobbles, but no masonry architecture.

The sculptured monuments include many Olmec-style pieces covering the full range of Olmec art, if one includes a possible corner from a large rectangular altar. Monument 23 is a typical Olmec colossal head. Late Preclassic "potbelly" sculpture (Monument 40) ties this area to the northern lowlands. Later, Maya portrait stelae appear without evolved precedents at the site. Their long-count dates, 7.16.0.0.0–7.16.19.17–19 on Stela 2 and 8.3.2.10.5 and 8.4.5.17.11 (A.D. 126) from Stela 5 (ca. 38–18 B.C.) are among the very earliest recorded long counts known. The portrait stelae are possible early evidence of the growing permanence of dynastic rule in the Maya area. Stela 5 shows a personage holding a ceremonial serpent, a motif of ruling power seen on later stelae elsewhere as the two-headed serpent bar.

Abaj Takalik is an early transitional site with precursors of the Olmec influence, pure Olmec, and very early Maya traits.

JOHN R. GRAHAM, "Discoveries at Abaj Takalik, Guatemala," in *Archaeology* 30 (1977): 196–197; JOHN R. GRAHAM, R. F. HEISER, and E. M. SHOOK, "Abaj Takalik 1976: Exploratory Investigations," in *Studies in Ancient Mesoamerica, III,* University of California Archaeological Research Facility Contribution no. 36 (1978), pp. 85–114.

WALTER R. T. WITSCHEY

**ABALOS, JOSÉ DE,** intendant of the province of Venezuela (1776–1783). Born in La Mancha, Spain, Abalos was chief official of accounting and of general administration on the island of Cuba and chief accountant in the province of Venezuela. When the intendancy of Venezuela was created by royal decree on 8 December 1776, he was appointed to the office of intendant by order of King CHARLES III.

By order of the crown, Abalos developed a program of instruction for the workings of the intendancy, which can be considered the first organic law for the administration of finance in Venezuela. While serving as intendant, he promoted numerous initiatives for the economic and commercial benefit of the province. He was inflexible in the collection of taxes; intervened in and confronted the COMPAÑÍA GUIPUZCOANA; offered credits to landowners; stimulated the diversification of crops; reactivated the mining industry; fought contraband; and established the state monopoly on playing cards, spirits, and tobacco. By the time of his retirement from the post in 1783, Abalos had brought about important advances in the reorganization of the royal finances and in the recuperation of the economy of the province of Venezuela.

For Abalos's influence on the colonial Venezuelan economy, see EDUARDO ARCILA FARÍAS, *Economía colonial de Venezuela* (1946). See also P. MICHAEL MC KINLEY, *Pre-revolutionary Caracas: Politics, Economy, and Society, 1777–1811* (1985); MARÍA TERESA ZUBIRI MARÍN, "José Abalos, primer intendente de Venezuela, 1777–1783," *Boletín Americanista* (Barcelona) 30, no. 38 (1988): 287–297.

INÉS QUINTERO

**ABASCAL Y SOUZA, JOSÉ FERNANDO** (*b.* 3 June 1743; *d.* 31 July 1821), viceroy of Peru (1806–1816). A native of Oviedo in northern Spain, Abascal pursued a military career and first visited America in 1767 as a junior officer assigned to the garrison of Puerto Rico. Following service in Spain, he returned to the empire with the 1776 expedition to the Río de la Plata, which captured the outpost of Sacramento on the eastern bank of the river from the Portuguese and established a new viceroyalty governed from Buenos Aires. After further service in Santo Domingo and Havana, he went to Guadalajara (Mexico) in 1799 as president of the *audi-*

*encia* (tribunal of justice). Appointed viceroy of the RÍO DE LA PLATA, Abascal was transferred to Peru before he was able to take up his position in Buenos Aires; wartime complications delayed his arrival in Lima until 1806.

Abascal's fame derives primarily from his firmness in repressing conspiracies against continued Spanish rule in Peru during the period 1809–1810 (at a time when his counterparts in other viceregal capitals were meekly acquiescing to the demands of creole revolutionaries), and in raising expeditionary forces to put down the early independence movements in Chile, Ecuador, and Upper Peru (Bolivia). A firm royalist and absolutist, he obstructed the implementation in Peru of the Spanish Constitution of Cádiz, promulgated in 1812. Although disturbed in 1814–1815 by a serious insurrection in Cuzco, Peru remained a bastion of royalism when Abascal retired to the peninsula in 1816.

VICENTE RODRÍGUEZ CASADO and GUILLERMO LOHMANN VILLENA, eds., *Memoria de gobierno del virrey Abascal* (1947); TIMOTHY E. ANNA, *The Fall of the Royal Government in Peru* (1979).

JOHN R. FISHER

**ABASOLO, MARIANO** (*b*. ca. 1783; *d*. 14 April 1816), Mexican insurgent leader. A native of Dolores, in 1795 Abasolo entered the regiment of the Queen's Provincial Dragoons at San Miguel el Grande. He joined Miguel HIDALGO in Dolores when the priest led an uprising against the colonial regime in September 1810. Abasolo became a colonel in the insurgent forces and eventually rose to the rank of field marshal. On 28 September 1810 he besieged Guanajuato and demanded its surrender, but he did not participate in the sack of the city. After the insurgents' defeat at Calderón Bridge in January 1811, he fled north with Hidalgo. He refused to remain in command of the troops when the principal insurgent leaders decided to continue to the United States. Captured at Acatita de Baján on 21 March 1811, Abasolo was taken to Chihuahua, where during his trial he denied all responsibility for the insurrection. Because of his denials and his wife's efforts he was condemned to perpetual exile rather than to death. He died in the fortress of Santa Catalina in Cádiz, Spain.

JOSÉ MARÍA MIQUEL I VERGÉS, *Diccionario de insurgentes* (1969), pp. 2–3; HUGH M. HAMILL, JR., *The Hidalgo Revolt*, 2d ed. (1970); LUCAS ALAMÁN, *Historia de Méjico*, vol. 1 (1985); and CARLOS MARÍA DE BUSTAMANTE, *Cuadro histórico de la Revolución Mexicana*, vol. 1 (1985).

VIRGINIA GUEDEA

*See also* **Allende, Ignacio.**

**ABBAD Y LASIERRA, ÍÑIGO** (*b*. 17 April 1745; *d*. 24 October 1813), author of the first history of Puerto Rico, *Historia geográfica, civil y natural de la Isla de San Juan Bautista de Puerto Rico* (1788). Born in Lérida, Spain, Abbad was educated at the monastery of Santa María la Real in Nájera, Spain. A Benedictine, he went to Puerto Rico in 1772 as confessor to the bishop Manuel Jiménez Pérez. He died in Valencia, Spain.

In the nineteenth century, Abbad's history underwent two editions, in 1831 and 1866. The latter edition, corrected and annotated by the Puerto Rican scholar José Julián Acosta, is still considered a valuable source of information. In 1959, the University of Puerto Rico reissued Abbad's work with an introduction by the historian Isabel Gutiérrez del Arroyo.

Information on Abbad can be found in KENNETH R. FARR, *Historical Dictionary of Puerto Rico and the U.S. Virgin Islands* (1973); ESTHER M. MELÓN DE DÍAZ, *Puerto Rico: Figuras, apuntes históricos, símbolos nacionales* (1975); and ADOLFO DE HOSTOS, *Diccionario histórico bibliográfico comentado de Puerto Rico* (1976).

OLGA JIMÉNEZ DE WAGENHEIM

**ABBOTTSVILLE,** an EASTERN COAST OF CENTRAL AMERICA COMMERCIAL AND AGRICULTURAL COMPANY immigrant settlement founded in Guatemala (1840) near the Polochic River port of Panzós. The company expected, through Abbottsville and a deep-water entrepôt at SANTO TOMÁS on the Gulf of Honduras, to dominate the commerce of an extensive hinterland.

Abbottsville was planned as the internal base for the agricultural and commercial empire the company expected to develop within Guatemala. It was intended to serve as a reception center for laborers and for immigrant colonists who came to claim acreage they had purchased in the company's inland agricultural settlements, as the collection point for exported produce, and as a distribution center for imported merchandise. Cancellation of the company's charter by the Guatemalan government deprived the town of function, and it was abandoned in 1844.

The role of Abbottsville in the colonization scheme of the Eastern Coast of Central America Commercial and Agricultural Company is laid out fully in WILLIAM J. GRIFFITH, *Empires in the Wilderness: Foreign Colonization and Development in Guatemala, 1834–1844* (1965), and from limited sources in PEDRO PÉREZ VALENZUELA, *Santo Tomás de Castilla. Apuntes para la historia de las colonizaciones en la costa atlántica* (1956).

WILLIAM J. GRIFFITH

**ABC COUNTRIES,** a name applied to the nations of Argentina, Brazil, and Chile during the period preceding World War I. Following the settlement of boundary disputes between Argentina and Chile in the early years of the twentieth century, these nations, along with Brazil, as the region's dominant economic and cultural powers, sought to establish a political alliance to mediate regional and hemispheric disputes. This effort was solidified with the so-called ABC Treaty of 1915, which followed the successful arbitration of a conflict between the United States and Mexico.

The ABC countries further advanced their role in inter-American diplomacy through mediating disputes between Colombia and Peru and, unsuccessfully, between Paraguay and Bolivia over the CHACO region. The coalition dissolved in 1917 as a result of Brazil's entry into the Allied effort against Germany.

While the direct results of the ABC Treaty were short-lived, the alliance between its three nations demonstrated their own international aspirations as well as the potential for inter-American diplomacy in this century.

DONALD M. DOZER, *Latin America: An Interpretive History* (1962).

JOHN DUDLEY

**ABENTE Y LAGO, VICTORINO** (*b.* 2 June 1846; *d.* 22 December 1935), Paraguayan poet. Abente published his first poems in his native town of Murguía, in the province of La Coruña, Spain. He went to Asunción in 1869, where he saw firsthand the sacking of the capital during the WAR OF THE TRIPLE ALLIANCE. Profoundly shaken by the devastation and ruin, he began to write poems reflecting human solidarity in the face of total destruction while harboring a deep faith in man's ability to recover and rebuild. Having developed a fondness for its land and people, he decided to remain in Paraguay and become a citizen. Abente was the first poet on record to sing of the Paraguayan woman in "Kygua Verá" (Lustrous Comb) and of her role in Paraguayan history in "La sibila paraguaya." He published most of his poems in Asunción dailies.

HUGO RODRÍGUEZ-ALCALÁ, *Historia de la literatura paraguaya* (1971), pp. 34–35; VICTORINO ABENTE, *Antología poéticas* (1984).

CATALINA SEGOVIA-CASE

**ABERTURA,** the policy of political liberalization or "opening" to democracy in Brazil initiated by the government of General João Batista FIGUEIREDO in 1979. With *abertura*, the military regime planned to implement democratic reform under the careful supervision of state political strategists in order to provide a more permanent means of support for the national security state. The forces of liberalization unleashed by the Figueiredo government, however, soon swept the military regime out of power.

The first stage in the *abertura* process was the passage of the Amnesty Act of 1979. This law revoked the imprisonment and banishment orders for persons convicted of political crimes by past regimes. Later that year, the Party Reform Bill allowed the creation of numerous opposition parties—a measure meant to divide the government's opponents. Nevertheless, it established the most open political system that Brazil has seen in over a decade.

Another major step in the *abertura* process occurred in November 1980 when Congress passed an executive-proposed constitutional amendment that reintroduced the direct election of state governors and all federal senators. Threatened by the progress of the *abertura*, military hard-liners initiated a series of bombings to thwart the liberalization process. Although it spread fear, the campaign of violence did not halt the decline of the hard-liners' influence.

The power of the National Renovation Alliance (ARENA), the regime's party, also began to wane. Opposition groups made key gains in the 1982 elections, and opponents of the military government organized a campaign for direct presidential elections (*diretas*) that gained vast popular support but fell short of securing the two-thirds' majority of senators needed to amend the Constitution. The end of the military regime came on 15 January 1985, when a majority of government party members joined forces with the opposition to elect Tancredo NEVES, Brazil's first civilian president since 1964.

MARIA HELENA ALVES, *State and Opposition in Military Brazil* (1985); THOMAS SKIDMORE, *The Politics of Military Rule in Brazil, 1964–1985* (1988); ALFRED STEPAN, *Rethinking Military Politics* (1988).

MICHAEL POLL

*See also* **Brazil: Amnesty Act; Brazil: Political Parties.**

**ABIPÓN INDIANS,** people who were a branch of the Guaycuruan linguistic family who lived in nonsedentary bands between the Río Salado and the Río Pilcomayo in northeastern Argentina. The Abipones hunted wild game; harvested vegetable foods, such as carob bean, coconuts, and dates; and after 1600, seized thousands of cattle and horses from the Spaniards. The language resembled those of the MOCOBÍ and Toba Indians, each differing from the others much as the Romance languages of Europe do. The societies of these three tribes also shared similar cultural characteristics. In the 1750s the Abipones comprised three bands: the Rïïkahés, of the plains of the southern Chaco; the Nakaiketergehés, a woodland people; and the Yaaukanigás, once a separate riverine people whose original identity was lost after a conquest. The Abipones were immortalized in the famous *Historia de Abiponibus equestri, bellicosaque Paraguariae natione* (1784) by Martin DOBRIZHOFFER, a Jesuit missionary and gifted ethnologist who served with the Abipones in the 1750s and 1760s and wrote his work of comparative anthropology in exile in Vienna.

Like the Mocobís, mounted Abipones raided Spanish farms, ranches, missions, and interprovincial commerce. In peacetime they traded with merchants and rural peoples of the upper Río de la Plata region. After 1640, however, they intensified attacks on Spanish persons and property. Around 1750, the changing Chaco ecology, the increase in violence among native peoples, and the loss of Indian access to cattle because of new practices of corrals and guards for livestock caused the

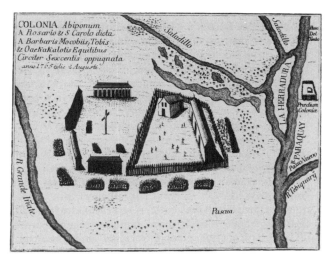

Siege of Rosario (Paraguay) during a raid. Drawing by Martin Dobrizhoffer. Reproduced from Martin Dobrizhoffer, *Historia de Abiponibus equestri bellicosaque Paraguariae natione* (Vienna, 1784). COURTESY OF HARVARD COLLEGE LIBRARY.

Abipones, who numbered about 5,000, to join Catholic MISSIONS. The first Riĩkahé group settled in the San Jerónimo mission of Santa Fe in 1748. Jesuits also helped Abipones establish three more missions, and a fifth Abipón mission was founded after the expulsion of the Jesuits. When independence destroyed the missions, Abipones, many of whom were sedentary cultivators and herders, settled down between the Río Salado and Río Bermejo west of the Río Paraná, but quite a few Abipón men joined the armies of José Gervasio ARTIGAS and later fought under other leaders in post-Independence Platine conflicts. In the 1850s, Italian Franciscans founded new missions for the Abipones in Santa Fe. After these missions were secularized in 1912, the Abipones slowly lost their tribal identity as they joined rural and urban lower classes of the provinces of Santa Fe, Chaco, and Formosa in Argentina.

MARTIN DOBRIZHOFFER, *An Account of the Abipones: An Equestrian People of Paraguay*, 3 vols., translated by Sara Coleridge (1822; repr. in 1 vol. 1970); ALFRED MÉTRAUX, "Ethnography of the Chaco," in *Handbook of South American Indians*, vol. 1, edited by Julian H. Steward (1946), pp. 197–300; JAMES SCHOFIELD SAEGER, "Another View of the Mission As a Frontier Institution: The Guaycuruan Reductions of Santa Fe, 1743–1810," in *Hispanic American Historical Review* 65, no. 3 (1985): 493–517.

JAMES SCHOFIELD SAEGER

*See also* **Indians.**

**ABOLITION OF SLAVERY.** *See* **Slavery.**

**ABRANCHES, GIRALDO JOSÉ DE.** *See* **Inquisition: Brazil.**

**ABREU, DIEGO DE** (*d.* 1553), conquistador and early settler. Abreu was born in Seville, Spain, and came to the Río de la Plata with the expedition of Pedro de MENDOZA in 1536. After the original settlement of Santa María del Buen Aire was abandoned, and after Mendoza's death earlier that year, Juan de Salazar y Ezpinosa founded Asunción in 1537. When Alvar Núñez Cabeza de Vaca, the second *adelantado* of the Río de la Plata, and the settlers of Asunción came into open conflict over how the settlement should be run, Abreu supported Nuñez. He later protested the naming of Domingo Martínez de Irala as governor and was sent to prison. He escaped, and led a group of loyalists against Martínez. When Martínez left Asunción on an exploratory trip in 1547, Abreu demanded that his successor, Francisco de Mendoza, surrender command. Abreu had Mendoza imprisoned and executed. When Martínez returned in 1549, Abreu abandoned the governorship he had assumed by force and fled inland. He wrote a detailed report of these disputes in 1548. Abreu never returned to Asunción and died in an Indian hamlet.

RICARDO LEVENE, *A History of Argentina* (1963).

NICHOLAS P. CUSHNER

**ABRIL, XAVIER** (*b.* 1905; *d.* 1990), Peruvian poet and critic. A leading member of Peru's avant-garde movement from the mid-1920s, Abril helped introduce surrealism and other modernist movements in Peru and Latin America, particularly with his contributions, both poetry and criticism, to *Amauta*, the leading cultural journal of the period.

His early poetry, usually ascribed to surrealism, is collected in *Hollywood* (1931) and *Difícil trabajo: Antología 1926–1930* (1935). In these books of verses and short prose, oneiric images of natural elements and human anatomy present a self in the process of fragmentation, and a desire for reintegration.

Abril's literary criticism includes studies of the work of Stéphane Mallarmé and the Peruvian poet José María EGUREN; he is best known for his works on the poetry of César VALLEJO: *Vallejo: Ensayo de aproximación crítica* (1958), *César Vallejo o la teoría poética* (1962), and *Exégesis trílcica* (1980).

Abril's focus on literary criticism, particularly his writings on Mallarmé, seems to coincide with a shift in his poetry to a more controlled use of imagery. Another factor in this change is the influence of Spanish medieval and Golden Age poets, which is reflected in his use of more conventional poetic forms, including traditional meters. Although this shift is apparent in his third collection, *Descubrimiento del alba* (1937), it is the determining element of his later poetry, which is marked by abstract symbolism.

LUIS MONGUIÓ, *La poesía postmodernista peruana* (1954), pp. 158–160; *Creación & Crítica* no. 9–10 (1971); WASHINGTON DELGADO, "La calle, la locura, el hogar y el mundo," in *Dominical (El Comercio)*, 3 February 1980: 12; RICARDO GONZÁLEZ-VIGIL,

*Poesía Peruana: Antología general*, vol. 3, *De Vallejo a nuestros días* (1984), pp. 65–67 and 471–472; JAMES HIGGINS, *A History of Peruvian Literature* (1987), p. 170.

JOSÉ CERNA-BAZÁN

**ACÁ CARAYÁ CAVALRY,** a famed escort regiment of the Paraguayan army. Established by Francisco Solano LÓPEZ in the period just prior to the WAR OF THE TRIPLE ALLIANCE (1864–1870), the Acá Carayá saw service in that conflict as a presidential guard unit and, later, as a shock force against the Brazilians. The regiment was distinguished by colorful uniforms and metal helmets adorned with the tails of howler monkeys (from which the unit earned its Guaraní appellation, meaning "monkey heads"). The Acá Carayá saw renewed service during the CHACO WAR (1932–1935) with Bolivia. The regiment remains a featured attraction of military parades during Independence Day and other national holidays in Paraguay.

LEANDRO APONTE B., *Hombres, armas y batallas* (1971); CHARLES KOLINSKI, *Historical Dictionary of Paraguay* (1973), p. 2.

THOMAS L. WHIGHAM

**ACADEMIA DE LA LENGUA Y CULTURA GUARA-NÍ,** Paraguay's leading institution dedicated to the study and promotion of the national Indian language, Guaraní. Founded in 1949 by ethno-botanist Guillermo Tell Bertoni, the Academia draws its inspiration from an earlier institution, the Sociedad de Cultura Guaraní (founded in 1920). The goals of the current institution include organizing classes in Guaraní, supporting literary efforts in that language, hosting regular sessions of the international Congreso de la Lengua Tupí-Guaraní, and helping to formulate government policy toward language use, especially insofar as education and the standardization of orthography are concerned.

Academia members have included such poets, playwrights, artists, and linguists as Marcos Morínigo, Branislava Susnik, Pablo Alborno, and Grazziella Corvalán. Though their work tends to be read only by specialists at present, the growing popular acceptance of the value of the Indian tongue can little be doubted. This is seen, for example, in the number of television programs and theater presentations in Guaraní. The Paraguayan government has also responded to these developments, albeit in a haphazard fashion, by publishing some of its official documents in Guaraní in addition to Spanish. The philosophy faculty of the National University of Asunción offers a degree in Guaraní, and it is now a required subject in the nation's secondary schools.

CHARLES J. KOLINSKI, *Historical Dictionary of Paraguay* (1973), p. 2; TADEO ZARRATEA and FELICIANO ACOSTA, *Avañe'e* (1981).

MARTA FERNÁNDEZ WHIGHAM

*See also* **Guaraní Indians.**

**ACADEMIA DE SAN CARLOS,** the first art academy in the New World and the principal Mexican artistic institution of the nineteenth century. Through the Academia de San Carlos, formally opened in 1785, the Bourbon administration implanted academic neoclassicism and dealt a definitive blow to the guild system of artistic production in New Spain. Teachers and materials, particularly an important collection of plaster casts of classical works, were sent from Spain. Closed between 1821 and 1824, the academy functioned fully again only after 1843, when it was reorganized. There were European teachers, annual exhibitions, scholarships to send the best students to Europe, and new plaster casts. In addition, a permanent collection of both Mexican and foreign paintings was formed. Under various names (Academia Imperial, Escuela Nacional de Bellas Artes, Academia Nacional de Bellas Artes) the academy continued; it promoted art with nationalist themes and, in the early twentieth century, assimilated artistic renewal. A student strike in 1911–1913 and an experiment in painting outdoors (*escuelas al aire libre*) accompanied the entry of the academy into the modernist movement. In 1929, with Diego RIVERA as director, the academy became part of the Universidad Nacional Autónoma de México with the name of Escuela Nacional de Artes Plásticas. As such, it continues today.

JUSTINO FERNÁNDEZ, *El arte del siglo XIX en México* (1967); JEAN CHARLOT, *Mexican Art and the Academy of San Carlos, 1785–1915* (1962).

CLARA BARGELLINI

*See also* **Art; Universities.**

**ACADEMIA LITERARIA DE QUERÉTARO,** a group of persons discontented with the colonial regime that formed in the city of Querétaro, Mexico. It included Corregidor Miguel DOMÍNGUEZ and his wife, Josefa ORTIZ DE DOMÍNGUEZ; military men such as Ignacio ALLENDE, Juan ALDAMA, and Mariano ABASOLO; clergymen; lawyers; and others, such as the brothers Epigmenio and Emeterio González. At the invitation of Allende, Miguel HIDALGO, curate of Dolores, attended on various occasions. Several members of the group met secretly to conspire against the colonial regime and to plan a popular uprising to apprehend peninsular Spaniards and confiscate their wealth to finance the movement.

The conspirators, who sought to obtain the support of military units, gathered arms and ammunition. They proposed to establish an emperor and some dependent kingdoms. The plot was denounced to the colonial authorities on 13 September 1810, leading to the arrest of several conspirators. Hoping to prevent his wife from notifying the rest of the conspirators, Domínguez, as a magistrate, locked her in their house. But Doña Josefa managed to alert Allende, and he in turn told Hidalgo what had happened. Consequently, Hidalgo launched the uprising on 16 September 1810.

HUGH M. HAMILL, JR., *The Hidalgo Revolt*, 2d ed. (1970); LUCAS ALAMÁN, *Historia de Méjico*, vol. 1. (1985); and CARLOS MARÍA DE BUSTAMANTE, *Cuadro histórico de la Revolución Mexicana*, vol. 1 (1985).

VIRGINIA GUEDEA

**ACADEMIAS,** series of ongoing literary and scientific meetings in eighteenth-century Brazil. The first academy was created in 1724 and was called Academia Brasílica dos Esquecidos (Brazilian Academy of the Forgotten). Begun under the patronage of Viceroy Vasco Fernandes César da Meneses, it lasted until 1725. The historian Sebastião de ROCHA PITA and other notables in Bahian society belonged to this academy.

Until the end of the eighteenth century, almost thirty academies existed in colonial Brazil. After the 1772 reform of the University of COIMBRA, where the Brazilian elite studied, these meetings became more scientific and less literary, but in either case the Brazilian academies were not so firmly established as their European counterparts. In Brazil scholars met in various towns and cities of the captaincies and wrote memoirs and proposed subjects for discussions, but their activity remained sporadic. For instance, when the count of Valadares assumed the government of the captaincy of Minas Gerais, an academy meeting took place 4 September 1768. Cláudio Manuel da Costa (1729–1789) read a poetic work he had written especially for the event.

A more organized academy was the Academia Brasílica dos Renascidos (Brazilian Academy of the Reborn), founded in Bahia in 1759, which lasted only six months. In 1772 the viceroy, the Marqués of Lavradio (ca. 1729–1790), supported in Rio de Janeiro an "assembly or academy" whose purpose was to study the three realms of nature. It was composed of medical doctors, surgeons, botanists, chemists, and some amateurs (*curiosos*). However, the most important contribution by Brazilian-born scientists and scholars to the study of natural history and agriculture was due not to the local academies but to the well-established Royal Academy of Sciences in Lisbon.

JOÃO LÚCIO AZEVEDO, *Novas Espanáforas: Estudos de história e literatura* (1932); JOSÉ ADERALDO CASTELO, ed., *O movimento academicista no Brasil, 1641–1820* (1969–1978); MASSAUD MOISÉS, *História da literatura brasileira*, vol. 1, *Origens, barroco, arcadismo* (1983).

MARIA BEATRIZ NIZZA DA SILVA

*See also* **Brazilian Academy of Letters.**

**ACAPULCO,** a port city of about 900,000 inhabitants (1990), has long been recognized as having the finest natural harbor on Mexico's Pacific coast. Its great harbor notwithstanding, Acapulco's role in the nation's economic geography has been defined more by its isolation from the central plateau by the rugged mountains of the state of Guerrero. The area was settled by the Spaniards in the 1530s as a site primarily for building ships to explore the Pacific coast. The first ships, built in 1532, traded and explored south to Peru and north to the Colorado River. Acapulco played an important role during the colonial period as New Spain's major Pacific port, and in 1565 the first MANILA GALLEON entered its protected bay. The annual galleons from the Philippines carried silks, jades, ivory, perfumes, and incense from the Orient, products that were traded for silver in Peru and Mexico, and ultimately reached to Spain.

Because of its hot, oppressive, and unhealthful climate, however, Acapulco remained a small settlement despite its importance. At the beginning of the nineteenth century, it had only about 4,000 permanent inhabitants, a large proportion of whom were blacks or mulattoes. The city's population rose as high as 9,000 to 12,500, however, during the annual two-week *feria*, referred to by the nineteenth-century German explorer Alexander von HUMBOLDT as "the most renowned fair of the world." The *feria*, associated with the arrival and departure of the galleon, drew large numbers of merchants southward along the "China Road" to the port.

Acapulco was described as a squalid place, but it was protected by Castle San Diego, built in 1616, and, after 1776, by Fort San Diego. With the end of the Manila galleon in 1815 and the subsequent independence of Mexico, Acapulco settled into relative obscurity as its mule trail fell into disuse. With no railroad across the mountains that separate Acapulco from the interior, the port lost its domination of commerce to Manzanillo, which was farther north along the coast and was the terminus of a rail line to Guadalajara and Mexico City.

Acapulco, however, was destined for a very different role. In 1927 an automobile road to the city was opened, and the first resort hotel was built on the beach in 1938. Miguel ALEMÁN, as president of Mexico, promoted the further development of tourism in Acapulco with the completion of a paved four-lane highway in 1955. Acapulco rapidly developed into a major resort area. Its unchecked growth, however, has created problems with water and sewage, severe pollution of the bay, and a general deterioration of the ecology. Overcrowding has caused a housing shortage and resulted in a sprawl of squatter settlements up the mountain slopes surrounding the bay. New resorts opened along the Pacific and Caribbean coasts of Mexico in the 1970s and 1980s, but Acapulco, with its dry winter and multiracial population, has remained a popular destination for both Mexican and foreign tourists.

WILLIAM L. SCHURZ, *The Manila Galleon* (1939), esp. pp. 371–384; JAMES CERUTTI, "The Two Acapulcos," in *National Geographic* 126 (December 1964): 848–878.

JOHN J. WINBERRY

*See also* **Tourism.**

**ACARAY RIVER**, affluent stream in eastern Paraguay that after a 108-mile course, joins the PARANÁ RIVER 6 miles upstream of the mouth of the IGUAÇÚ River. In 1968 a hydroelectric plant was built, with the assistance of Italian engineers, near the settlement of Hernandarias. The 45,000-kilowatt output feeds the capital city of Asunción, and secondary lines supply border towns in Brazil and northeastern Argentina. Expansion in 1976 enlarged production to 240,000 kilowatts.

HUGO G. FERREIRA, *Geografía del Paraguay* (1975).

CÉSAR N. CAVIEDES

**ACEVAL, BENJAMÍN** (*b.* 1845; *d.* 25 July 1900), Paraguayan statesman and educator. Though born in Asunción, Aceval spent most of his youth in Argentina, where he finished his law studies in 1873. He returned to Paraguay a year later in order to assume the post of justice minister in the Juan Bautista Gill government. In 1875 the same government sent him to Washington, D.C., where he presented Paraguay's claims to the CHACO REGION to President Rutherford B. Hayes, who had agreed to act as arbiter in Paraguay's land dispute with Argentina. Hayes upheld the Paraguayan claim, and Aceval returned to Asunción a much celebrated man. In 1877 he founded the Colegio Nacional of Asunción, with a subsidiary campus in Villarrica, and in 1886 he helped organize the Biblioteca Nacional. He continued to hold various ministerial and diplomatic posts until the end of the century. In 1887 he arranged a border treaty with Bolivia that provided a generous solution to the Chaco dispute but was rejected by the Paraguayan legislature, leaving the question open until it was resolved by war in the 1930s. Aceval died in Asunción.

HARRIS G. WARREN, *Rebirth of the Paraguayan Republic: The First Colorado Era, 1878–1904* (1985); CARLOS ZUBIZARRETA, *Cien vidas paraguayas*, 2d ed. (1985), pp. 217–218.

THOMAS L. WHIGHAM

**ACEVEDO DÍAZ, EDUARDO INÉS** (*b.* 1851; *d.* 18 June 1921), Uruguayan journalist and novelist, born in Montevideo. Connected from early on with his country's National (or Blanco) Party, Acevedo Díaz took up arms on three occasions between 1870 and 1897 to participate in revolutionary movements. As a journalist, he wrote tough polemics concerning party struggles in such periodicals as *La Democracia*, *La Razón*, and *El Nacional*. Due to his political militancy, he was imprisoned and exiled on several occasions, and it was during his exile in Argentina between 1876 and 1895 that he wrote his most representative works, the historical novels *Brenda* (1886), *Ismael* (1888), *Nativa* (1890) and his famous *Soledad* (1894), a series that would be completed in 1914 by *Lanza y sable*.

Acevedo Díaz is considered to be the first Uruguayan novelist as well as the founder of the historical novel in Uruguay. His entire work can be seen as an investigation into the origin of nationality, yet his effort occurred in the framework of the modernizing process carried out by the ruling class between 1870 and 1920. This process entailed the formation of a modern state, which required for its legitimacy the building of a nationalist sentiment in order to lend cohesion to the community. The work of Acevedo Díaz, like that of his contemporary Juan ZORRILLA DE SAN MARTÍN (*La leyenda Patria* [1879] and *Tabaré* [1888]), were significant contributions to this effort.

ALBERTO ZUM FELDE, *Proceso intelectual del Uruguay*, vol. 1 (1930); EDUARDO ACEVEDO DÍAZ, *La vida de batalla de Eduardo Acevedo Díaz* (1941); WALTER RELA, *Eduardo Acevedo Díaz* (1967); EMIR RODRÍGUEZ MONEGAL, *Vínculo de sangre* (1968); ARTURO SERGIO VISCA, "Eduardo Acevedo Díaz," in *Diccionario de literatura Uruguaya*, vol. 1 (1989).

MARÍA INÉS DE TORRES

**ACEVEDO HERNÁNDEZ, ANTONIO** (*b.* 1886; *d.* 21 September 1962), one of the founders of modern Chilean THEATER and the originator of social theater. His first plays date back to 1913–1914, a period in Chile marked by the influence of European theater and the Spanish *comedia*. His primary preoccupation as a dramatist was to define the creative options of an autochthonous theater that could express the social problems and existential dilemmas of the marginated strata—campesino sectors and lower-class urban settlements—of a society in the process of capitalist modernization.

A man of humble origins, Acevedo Hernández was forced to make a living moving from place to place working various jobs, such as farmhand, manual laborer, office worker, and free-lance journalist. This rich and diverse living experience became the main thematic source for his dramas and *comedias*. He wrote approximately thirty plays that include a variety of forms ranging from *sainetes* and *comedias* to political and social theater, and even biblical dramas. Durán Cerda provides a useful classification of Acevedo Hernández's plays. His most important works are *Arbol viejo* (1930; The Old Tree), which presents the dramatic conflict between the ancestral wisdom of the campesino's world and the changing values fostered by urban society, and *Chañarcillo* (1933), an epic drama of miners' struggles for social justice in nineteenth-century Chile. In his autobiography *Memorias de un autor teatral* (1982; Memories of a Playwright), Acevedo Hernández describes his literary formation through an intimate account of the conflicts and challenges he was forced to confront in order to stage his works. He died in Santiago.

JULIO DURÁN CERDA, *Panorama del teatro chileno, 1842–1959* (1959), pp. 56–62; JUAN VILLEGAS, "Teatro chileno y afianzamiento de los sectores medios," in *Ideologies and Literature* 4, no. 17 (1983): 306–318.

J. A. EPPLE

**ACHÁ, JOSÉ MARÍA** (*b.* 8 July 1810; *d.* 29 January 1868), president of Bolivia (14 January 1861–28 December 1864). After coming to power via a coup, Achá shared power in a three-man junta from 14 January until 4 May after which he became constitutional president.

Achá's presidency was marked by intense internal political agitation. His chief of police of La Paz, Plácido Yáñez, was responsible for Bolivia's worst political massacre on 23 October 1861. Yáñez arrested and then executed more than seventy political opponents, among whom was former president Jorge CÓRDOVA. Yáñez was later lynched by a mob. Known as the "Massacre de Yáñez," this episode detracted from Achá's positive accomplishments in the areas of economic and administrative reforms. Achá's administration also faced Chile's first attempts at expansion on the Bolivian coast, actions that eventually precipitated the WAR OF THE PACIFIC (1879–1884), the conflict in which Bolivia lost its coastal area.

Acha's political career, which included an unsuccessful attempt to overthrow the government of Manuel Isidoro BELZÚ (1850), was ended by a military coup led by Mariano MELGAREJO.

JULIO ARGUEDAS DÍAZ, *Los generales de Bolivia* (1929); MOISÉS ALCÁZAR, *Sangre en la historia* (1956); ALCIDES ARGUEDAS, *La dictatura y la anarquía*, in *Obras completas*, vol. 2 (1959).

CHARLES W. ARNADE

**ACONCAGUA,** at 22,834 feet, the highest mountain of the Western Hemisphere. It is located in the ANDES of western Argentina at 33 degrees south latitude. The Aconcagua River springs at its foot and flows in an 84-mile course into the Pacific Ocean. Considered the beginning of historical Central Chile, the well-irrigated valley was settled by Indians and Spaniards. Wine, fruits, tobacco, flax, and vegetables are grown for domestic consumption and export. Major centers in the valley are San Felipe, Los Andes, and Quillota. Not far from the river's mouth, in Chile, are the sister cities of VALPARAÍSO and VIÑA DEL MAR, both of which are connected with MENDOZA (Argentina) by an electric railway and a paved road.

CÉSAR N. CAVIEDES, *Geomorfología del Cuaternario del valle del Aconcagua, Chile Central* (1972).

CÉSAR N. CAVIEDES

**ACORDADA,** an enforcement and judicial agency established in New Spain provisionally in 1710 and officially in 1722. Staffed by a salaried captain-judge and a small group of subordinates, it drew its unsalaried agents from landholders, merchants, and their retainers who concentrated on property crimes, notably banditry. Initially operating in rural areas, it extended its jurisdiction to cities in 1756. In 1772 the Juzgado de Bebidas Prohibidas, charged with suppression of illegal intoxicants, came under its supervision. The organization maintained its own prison and sentenced offenders with little interference. It was extinguished by the Constitution of 1812's prohibition of independent judicial organizations.

ALICIA BAZÁN ALARCÓN, "El Real Tribunal de la Acordada y la Delincuencia en la Nueva España," *Historia Mexicana* 13, no.

Snowfields on Aconcagua. CARPENTER COLLECTION, LIBRARY OF CONGRESS.

3 (1964): 317–345; COLIN M. MAC LACHLAN, *Criminal Justice in Eighteenth Century Mexico: A Study of the Tribunal of the Acordada* (1974).

COLIN M. MacLACHLAN

**ACORDADA, REVOLT OF,** an insurgency following the Mexican election of 1828. After a heated campaign in which the function of the church, the status of Spaniards, mass politics, and secret societies played an important role, the moderate YORKINO (York rite Mason) Manuel GÓMEZ PEDRAZA won the presidential election of 1828. But on the night of 30 November, several hundred officers and men barricaded themselves in the building of the Acordada in Mexico City, demanding that the elections be annulled and all Spaniards expelled from the country. Fighting between government forces and the rebels erupted on 2 December. The following day the defeated presidential candidate General Vicente GUERRERO joined the insurgents. On 4 December, president-elect Gómez Pedraza resigned and fled the country rather than precipitate a bloody civil war. Nevertheless, mass demonstrations continued in the capital, ultimately resulting in a riot that destroyed the PARIÁN, the city's principal market.

ROMEO R. FLORES CABALLERO, *Counterrevolution: The Role of the Spaniards in the Independence of Mexico, 1804–38*, translated by Jaime E. Rodríguez O. (1974), esp. pp. 116–120; MICHAEL P. COSTELOE, *La Primera República Federal de México, 1824–1835* (1975), esp. pp. 198–206; LORENZO DE ZAVALA, *Ensayo histórico de las revoluciones de México desde 1808–hasta 1830,* vol. 2 (1985), esp. pp. 77–111.

JAIME E. RODRÍGUEZ O.

**ACOSTA, JOSÉ DE** (*b.* September or October 1540; *d.* 15 February 1600), Spanish Jesuit historian. Born in Medina del Campo, Acosta joined the Jesuit order while young and went to Peru in 1571. He lived there for fourteen years, and in Mexico City for one, before returning to his native Spain in 1587. His *Historia natural y moral de las Indias* (A Natural and Moral History of the Indies) was published in Seville in 1590. Widely read by educated Spaniards and quickly translated into most important European languages as well, Acosta's *Historia* enjoyed immediate success. Like other similar texts, the *Historia* places the entire American continent within a universal and providential Christian framework, implying a divine role for Spain as a conquering power. Many features of the natural American world, as well as indigenous religions, cultures, and governments, are described in great detail, making Acosta's work an invaluable source of information. Today it is considered by literary scholars and historians to be an elegantly written, classic example of sixteenth-century New World historiography.

A complete English translation by FRANCES LÓPEZ-MORILLAS of Acosta's *Historia natural,* with notes and introduction by Walter Mignolo, is presently in preparation. The best Spanish edition is JOSÉ DE ACOSTA, *Historia natural y moral de las Indias,* edited by Edmundo O'Gorman (1962). For a study of Acosta's ethnological method see ANTHONY PAGDEN, *The Fall of Natural Man: The American Indian and the Origins of Comparative Ethnology* (1982), pp. 146–200.

KATHLEEN ROSS

**ACOSTA, TOMÁS** (*b.* 1744; *d.* 1821), governor of Costa Rica from 1797 to 1810. Born in Cuba, Tomás Acosta is considered one of the most beloved and capable of Costa Rica's colonial governors. As early as 1805, he exposed the harmful effects of the tobacco monopoly on Costa Rica's economy and instituted policies designed to diversify agricultural production. Under the general aegis of the BOURBON REFORMS, Acosta removed some of the taxes from coffee production and greatly increased the growth of that important crop. His administration contributed to a growing sense of nationality among Costa Ricans in the pre-Independence era. Acosta, though a Spanish colonial official, was popular enough among Americans to have been considered as the intendant for Costa Rican economic affairs in 1812. He died in Cartago.

LIGIA MARÍA ESTRADA MOLINA, *La Costa Rica de don Tomás de Acosta* (1965); RALPH LEE WOODWARD, JR., *Central America: A Nation Divided* (1985); and THEODORE S. CREEDMAN, *Historical Dictionary of Costa Rica,* 2d ed. (1991).

KAREN RACINE

**ACOSTA GARCÍA, JULIO** (*b.* 23 May 1872; *d.* 6 July 1954), president of Costa Rica (1920–1924). As a nephew of Braulio CARRILLO (president 1834–1841) and a descendant of the conquistador Juan Vázquez de CORONADO, Acosta was well positioned for public life. He held many posts in the Costa Rican government, including delegate to the Constitutional Congress of 1902–1906, governor of his home province of Alajuela (1907), and consul to El Salvador (1912–1915) before winning the presidency in 1920. Acosta, a Liberal, served as Costa Rica's delegate to the Central American Unionist Party. He engaged troops in a border conflict with Panama. After his term he received many national and international awards and was the chief of Costa Rica's delegation to the United Nations organizational meetings in San Francisco in 1945.

ACADEMIA DE GEOGRAFÍA E HISTORIA DE COSTA RICA, *Homenaje al lic. Don Julio Acosta García* (1972); CARLOS MELÉNDEZ CH., *Historia de Costa Rica* (1979); HAROLD H. BONILLA, *Los presidentes* (1979).

KAREN RACINE

**ACOSTA LEÓN ÁNGEL** (*b.* 1932; *d.* 1964), Cuban painter. Born in Havana, Acosta León attended the famous San Alejandro school of painting and sculpture on a scholarship. He worked at odd jobs, including train conductor, to support himself while pursuing a career in the arts. In 1958 and 1959 he won prizes at expositions in Havana and received another award in 1959 from the National Salon. In 1960 Acosta León won a poster contest sponsored by the new National Institute of Industry and Tourism, and his oil painting *Carruaje* earned him a prize at the Second Pan-American Biennial in Mexico. Images of wheels and modern technology dominate Acosta's paintings; his major works are *Cafetera, Carro,* and *El circo* (all 1959), and *Carruaje* (1960).

GOVERNMENT OF CUBA, *Pintores cubanos* (1962); ADELAIDA DE JUAN, *Pintura cubana: Temas y variaciones* (1978).

KAREN RACINE

**ACOSTA ÑU, BATTLE OF,** one of the final engagements of the WAR OF THE TRIPLE ALLIANCE, fought on 16 August 1869. In the hill country some 45 miles east of Asunción, the retreating Paraguayan army of Francisco Solano LÓPEZ left behind a rearguard force of some 4,500 teenage boys, women, and old men, having ordered them to slow the advance of 20,000 Brazilian troops under the conde d'Eu. Purportedly wearing false beards in order to frighten their opponents, the boys put up a stiff and bloody resistance, but were overwhelmed by enemy cavalry. The battle, which Brazilian historians call "Campo Grande," has taken on the character of a national epic in Paraguay. Its immediate consequences, however, were minimal, as the Brazilians were soon able to resume their pursuit of López.

CHARLES KOLINSKI, *Independence or Death! The Story of the Paraguayan War* (1965); LEANDRO APONTE B., *Hombres, armas y batallas* (1971).

THOMAS L. WHIGHAM

**ACRE,** a Brazilian state sharing borders with Peru, Bolivia, and Amazonas. Although Brazil gave the little-known equatorial rain forest area to Bolivia in a treaty enacted in 1867, it was Brazilian, not Bolivian, SERINGUEIROS (rubber gatherers) who flooded into the area during the RUBBER boom. When Bolivia tried to establish its dominance over this 59,000-square-mile territory in 1899, Acreanos revolted and continued to rebel until 1902, when Bolivia and Brazil sent in troops. After a brief period of tension, Brazil's minister of foreign affairs, Barão do RIO BRANCO (1845–1912), skillfully negotiated a settlement giving Brazil the rubber-rich territory of Acre. Called the Treaty of PETRÓPOLIS, it was signed 17 November 1903. Although first attached to the state of Amazonas, Acre was converted into a federal territory in 1943 and became a state in 1962.

Most of Acre's residents worked gathering rubber from the forests and mingled with the 6,600 (as of 1988) Indians who lived there. In the 1970s, speculators and cattle ranchers infiltrated Acre via newly constructed roads, such as BR 364, BR 317, and the TRANSAMAZON HIGHWAY, which were part of the government's Operation Amazonia (1965) program. At the end of 1988, Acre was still the least populated (417,000 people) and developed state in Brazil. It had gained international notoriety, however, as a battleground between rubber workers and large landowners who clashed over control of the land.

CHICO MENDES, with additional material by TONY GROSS, *Fight for the Forest: Chico Mendes in His Own Words,* 1989; ANDREW REVKIN, *The Burning Season* (1990); SUSANNA HECHT and ALEXANDER COCKBURN, *The Fate of the Forest: Developers, Destroyers, and Defenders of the Amazon* (1990).

CAROLYN JOSTOCK

*See also* **Mendes Filho, Francisco "Chico" Alves.**

**ACUERDO** (*real acuerdo*), the regularly scheduled meeting of the judges of a tribunal (AUDIENCIA) with its president and crown attorney (*fiscal*) or attorneys to discuss matters of political administration. Exclusively at this meeting was correspondence from the king to be opened and read. When treasury officials were added to the group, the *acuerdo* was called a *junta de hacienda*. The decisions reached at an *acuerdo* were termed *autos acordados* and had the force of law. Through the *acuerdo*, the *audiencia* exercised its political authority. The legislative and administrative authority that emanated from the *acuerdo* gave the American *audiencias* significantly greater power than was exercised by their peninsular counterparts. Since the decisions were issued jointly by the region's chief executive and its *audiencia*, moreover, they carried considerable weight. The chief executive of the *audiencia* district was responsible for implementing the *acuerdo's* decisions.

*Recopilación de leyes de los reynos de las Indias,* 4 vols. (1681; repr. 1973), *libro* II, *título* XV, *leyes* xxiii, xxvi, xxvii, xxviii, xxx; CLARENCE H. HARING, *The Spanish Empire in America* (1947), p. 134; JOHN H. PARRY, *The Audiencia of New Galicia in the Sixteenth Century* (1948), pp. 8, 137–138.

MARK A. BURKHOLDER

**ADAMS–ONÍS TREATY (1819),** an agreement between Spain and the United States ceding the FLORIDAS to the latter. Also known as the Transcontinental Treaty and the Tratado de Cesión, the document was signed on 22 February 1819 by U.S. Secretary of State John Quincy Adams and veteran Spanish minister to the United States Luis de Onís y Gonzáles. The key provisions of the treaty ceded all territories held by the Spanish crown in the West and East Floridas to the United States and established a "transcontinental" boundary west of the Mississippi River that allowed the United States direct access to the Pacific Ocean. The line went north from the Sabine River; west along the Red River and Arkansas River, well above Santa Fe; then north and due west at 42° latitude, into the Oregon territory claimed by both the United States and Great Britain. Spain wanted the

United States to relinquish claims to Texas, which it did in Article 3. Spain also wanted the United States to withhold recognition of any Spanish American provinces that might revolt; however, such a proviso was not part of the final draft. The United States did agree to cancel up to $5 million in claims against Spanish citizens in Florida.

The U.S. Senate unanimously ratified the treaty on 24 February 1819, but the Spanish Council of State advised Ferdinand VII to send Francisco Vives to Washington to try to negotiate better terms. Nevertheless, the original version was finally approved by the U.S. Senate on 22 February 1821, and Mexico inherited Texas from Spain, "as delimited by the Transcontinental Treaty."

Negotiations between Adams and Onís were protracted, influenced strongly by a variety of considerations, including the invasion of the Florida territory by the U.S. general Andrew Jackson (1819), the intervention of the French minister Hyde de Neuville in discussions, and British-U.S. boundary disputes in the Northwest. Adams viewed the Pacific boundary as a major triumph for the United States; the historian Samuel Flagg Bemis asserts that "even without Texas the Transcontinental Treaty with Spain was the greatest diplomatic victory won by any single individual in the history of the United States."

PHILIP COOLIDGE BROOKS, *Diplomacy and the Borderlands: The Adams–Onís Treaty of 1819* (1939), which contains the text of the treaty; SAMUEL FLAGG BEMIS, *John Quincy Adams and the Foundations of American Foreign Policy* (1949) and *John Quincy Adams and the Union* (1965); ELENA SÁNCHEZ-FABRÉS MIRAT, *Situación histórica de las Floridas en la segunda mitad del siglo XVIII (1783–1819): Los problemas de una región de frontera* (1977), pp. 289–316.

LINDA K. SALVUCCI

**ADDITIONAL ACT OF 1834,** amendment to the Brazilian Constitution of 1824 that decentralized the system of government. The act created legislative provincial assemblies, elected regency, and abolished the Council of State. It gave provincial assemblies power to indict provincial presidents and magistrates; jurisdiction over civil, judicial, and ecclesiastical organizations; control of taxation, revenue, public education, public works, and police force; ability to create and abolish positions; and permission to contract loans. The autonomy given to provinces weakened the central government, fueled centrifugal forces, and nearly caused the dissolution of the state. Its interpretation in 1840 abolished the most decentralizing provisions and permitted political, administrative, and judicial recentralization.

RODERICK J. BARMAN, *Brazil, The Forging of a Nation, 1798–1852* (1988), pp. 160–216.

LYDIA M. GARNER

**ADELANTADO,** title often given to the leader of an expedition of conquest in medieval Castile and in the New World. The term *adelantado* was employed in medieval Castile for the military and political governor of a frontier province. The title was later used in the conquest and colonization of the Canary Islands and continued to be used in the conquest and colonization of the New World. Typically, an *adelantado* held the military title of captain-general and served as governor and chief magistrate over the men in the expedition. When a conquest was successful, the *adelantado* took over governance of the native population. In his contract (*capitulación*) with the crown, an *adelantado* normally received land for himself and the rights to assign land to his followers, to oversee the collection of revenues, and to administer justice. Sometimes he could assign native labor as well. The era of the *adelantados* came to an end as the crown sought to end the disruption and instability resulting from conquest and to establish tighter control over the New World. To accomplish this, the crown created AUDIENCIAS and, beginning in 1535, sent out viceroys with substantial authority. Many *adelantados,* however, had been granted extensive landholdings and had access to native labor. Although their formal political power was restricted by royal bureaucrats, they and their immediate heirs remained important members of the emerging colonial aristocracy. Although men titled *adelantados* were still leading conquests on the frontiers of the colonial world in the late sixteenth century, the era of the *adelantado* had ended by the 1570s.

CLARENCE H. HARING, *The Spanish Empire in America* (1947), pp. 22–25; LYLE N. MC ALISTER, *Spain and Portugal in the New World, 1492–1700* (1984), pp. 35, 63–64, 91, 97, 99, 137, 184, 312.

MARK A. BURKHOLDER

**ADELANTADO OF THE SOUTH SEA,** Vasco Núñez de BALBOA (1475–1519), Spanish explorer who claimed the Pacific Ocean for the Spanish crown. An enterprising youth, Balboa had sailed for the Caribbean in 1500 to trade in pearls. After several business failures, he fled to Darién, Panama, where the Spanish attempted to establish permanent settlements. Balboa got along well with the natives of the region and emerged as natural leader of his Spanish colleagues. In 1513, while searching for a wealthy tribe, he sighted the Pacific Ocean and descended to its shores to claim it for Spain. In reward, he was named governor of Darién and Adelantado of the South Sea. In 1519, however, Pedro Arias de ÁVILA (Pedrarias), representing jealous rivals, replaced Balboa as governor and had him beheaded.

KATHLEEN ROMOLI, *Balboa of Darién, Discoverer of the Pacific* (1953); CHARLES L. G. ANDERSON, *Life and Letters of Vasco Núñez de Balboa* (1941; repr. 1970); FREDERICK W. TURNER, "Visions of the Pacific," in *Southwest Review* 70 (1985): 336–349.

MICHAEL L. CONNIFF

**ADEM CHAHÍN, JOSÉ** (*b.* 27 October 1921; *d.* February, 1991), leading Mexican mathematician. A native of Tuxpan, Veracruz, Adem received his early education in his birthplace. He studied mathematics at the National University of Mexico from 1941 to 1945, after which he did graduate work at the Mathematics Institute (1946–1948). He traveled to the United States to complete a doctorate at Princeton University (1952). A researcher and educator, Adem taught at the National School of Engineering and Sciences and the National University, becoming a full-time researcher at the Mathematics Institute (1954–1961). His works on algebra have appeared in English. He directed the mathematics department at the National Polytechnic Institute from 1961 to 1973. He was a member of the National College, and received Mexico's National Prize in Sciences (1967).

JESÚS SILVA HERZOG, *Biografías de amigos y conocidos* (1980).

RODERIC AI CAMP

**ADEM CHAHÍN, JULIÁN** (*b.* 8 January 1924), leading Mexican geophysicist and specialist in atmospheric sciences. Adem obtained an engineering degree from the National University (1948) and his doctorate in applied mathematics from Brown University (1953), after which he completed advanced studies in atmospheric sciences in Stockholm (1955–1956). After serving as a full-time researcher at the Geophysics Institute, he became its director and then founded the Center for Atmospheric Sciences. Invited to be a member of the prestigious National College, Adem received Mexico's National Prize in Sciences (1976). Brother of mathematician José Adem Chahín, he is known for his discovery of a long-range predictive thermodynamic model.

*Colegio Nacional, Memoria,* vol. 8 (1974).

RODERIC AI CAMP

**ADMIRABLE CAMPAIGN,** a series of military engagements in the Venezuelan War of Independence. With operations in New Granada finished, Simón BOLÍVAR solicited the support of the government there for an invasion of Venezuelan territory to renew the fight for independence. The campaign began in New Granada on 14 May 1813 and ended in Caracas on 6 August of the same year. After crossing the summits of the Andes, he arrived in Mérida and from there continued to Trujillo, where he made his famous WAR TO THE DEATH speech on 15 June. He continued eastward, defeating his adversaries along the way, until the royal army capitulated in the city of La Victoria, not far from Caracas. The success, organization, and speed of the campaign allowed the republican forces to regain control of western Venezuela.

LINO IRIBARREN CELIS, *La Campaña Admirable* (1963), and UNIVERSIDAD DE LOS ANDES, *1813–1963: Mérida, Venezuela. Revista ''Libertador''commemoration del Sesquicentenario de la Campaña Admirable* (1963).

INÉS QUINTERO

**ADONIAS FILHO.** *See* **Aguiar, Adonias.**

**AFRANCESADO,** a person who collaborated with the regime of Joseph BONAPARTE during the War of Independence (1808–1814). In 1808, NAPOLEON lured CHARLES IV and his son, FERDINAND VII, into exile in France and placed his brother, Joseph, on the Spanish throne. During the ensuing War of Independence, Spaniards who cooperated with the new monarchy were termed *afrancesados* (or the Frenchified). The *afrancesados* were constitutional monarchists—though not wedded to one particular dynasty—who advocated moderate social and political reforms. There were several reasons for their collaboration with Bonaparte's regime. Some thought that resistance was a lost cause that encouraged anarchy and rebellion. They preferred French domination of Spain to repression or dismemberment and considered Joseph's regime a lesser evil. Others hoped that the Napoleonic system and the enlightened Constitution of Bayonne (1808) would generate reform from above. Those with secure jobs also argued for cooperation with the French, especially in occupied zones. Recent historians have portrayed the *afrancesados* as misguided and confused conformists.

HANS JURETSCHKE, *Vida, obra y pensamiento de Alberto Lista* (1951); MIGUEL ARTOLA, *Los afrancesados* (1953); JOAN MERCADER RIBA, *José Bonaparte, rey de España, 1808–1813,* 2 vols. (1972); RAYMOND CARR, *Spain, 1808–1975,* 2d ed. (1982), esp. pp. 110–115.

SUZANNE HILES BURKHOLDER

*See also* **Wars of Independence.**

**AFRICA, CUBAN INTERVENTION IN.** *See* **Cuban Intervention in Africa.**

**AFRICA, PORTUGUESE.** Portuguese contacts in Africa began with the earliest navigation beyond Cape Bojador in 1434. An early period of raiding was replaced after 1456 by more peaceful contacts with the African states of the coast. Factories were established at Arguin Island in 1448 and at Elmina (São Jorge de Mina) in 1482, and colonies were established on the uninhabited offshore islands of CAPE VERDE (1462) and SÃO TOMÉ (1472). After the successful rounding of the Cape of Good Hope in 1848 the Portuguese established posts at Sofala in 1505, Kilwa, and Mombasa.

The diplomatic efforts of Portuguese navigators and the later settlers of the offshore islands resulted in substantial influence on the adjacent coastline. Portugal established close relations with the African kingdoms of Jolof, Kongo, and Benin in the late fifteenth century. In Kongo especially these contacts resulted in the adoption of Christianity and literacy in Portuguese. The small Nigerian kingdom of Warri became Christian in 1580, and several small states in Sierra Leone also converted in the early seventeenth century.

Under King SEBASTIAN, Portugal sought to develop a colonial presence on the coast, especially in areas where trade and diplomacy had been most successful. In the 1570s Portuguese forces established a colony in ANGOLA and extended its control inland about 60 miles by 1620; at the same time Portuguese forces conducted a less successful series of operations in what would eventually become Mozambique against the kingdom of the Mwene Mutapa. The colonists of the Cape Verde Islands also sought to establish control on various posts along the coast of modern Guinea-Bissau, although these did not result in any significant territorial gains. After 1620 there were no more initiatives of this sort, although gains made by local initiative extended Angola slightly. In Mozambique local settlers managed to secure land grants from local rulers, which they registered as property of the Portuguese crown and received back as *prazos* (feudal estates), although in many ways they were more like independent petty rulers than Portuguese subjects.

A much more serious attempt to extend Portuguese control in Africa began in the 1850s and continued through the period of the "scramble for Africa," roughly from 1880 to 1920. The nuclei of the colonization were long-established groups of settlers or subjects in Angola, Mozambique, and the mainland across from the Cape Verde Islands, which became Guinea. These local settlers, the Afro-Portuguese, were a combination of mestizos and culturally Lusitanized Africans who owned land or held lower offices in the colony. Afro-Portuguese often pioneered the expansion, but metropolitan interests took over the resulting expanded colony in the late nineteenth century. As a result the holders of the Mozambican *prazos* had to be conquered by metropolitan armies, while the Angolan Afro-Portuguese protested in their press what became a significant loss of rights.

Portuguese colonial policy focused on making Angola a center for Portuguese colonization, and the central highlands region in particular received thousands of colonists. There was less colonization in Mozambique, which was given over to large concession companies or to supplying contracted labor for South African mines. In Guinea concessions obtained what little profit Portugal received from the small colony.

Officially, Portugal had a "civilizing mission" in Africa, and its policy stressed assimilation, whereby Africans would be granted the rights of Portuguese when they had absorbed Portuguese language and customs. However, the government provided little in the way of educational opportunities to make the assimilation policy effective. Most educational and social services were provided by underfinanced Catholic church missions or foreign missionaries, who were often subject to persecution.

After 1926 the New State dictatorship sought to tie the colonies more closely to the needs of Portugal, envisioning the metropole and its colonies as a cooperative zone, but one that worked to the benefit of the Portuguese of the metropole and colonies. These trends became more effective after the Second World War, when a wave of settlers and foreign capital flooded into the colonies. By the 1950s a number of African dissident groups had developed, sometimes in alliance with local groups of Afro-Portuguese. Government repression led to revolt, and by 1965 there were strong anticolonial guerrilla movements in all three colonies. In 1974 a revolution in Portugal, provoked in large part by the military demands of the antiguerrilla activities in the colonies, overthrew the dictatorship and set in motion the process that resulted in the granting of independence to all the African colonies in 1974–1975.

JOHN THORNTON

*See also* **Portuguese Empire.**

**AFRICAN-BRAZILIAN CULTURAL AND POLITICAL ORGANIZATIONS.** During the colonial era religious brotherhoods were created with the assistance of Catholic clergy. These BROTHERHOODS, often open to slaves as well as free persons, provided more than simply religious education to members, offering a range of financial and medical services for people of color that were unavailable elsewhere. They also made loans, offered insurance, and guaranteed their members proper burials. One of their most important functions was providing assistance in buying the freedom (*carta de alforria*) of those members who were slaves. Religious brotherhoods flourished in the late seventeenth and eighteenth centuries. Some, like Our Lady of the Rosary (Nossa Senhora do Rosário), had branches throughout the Portuguese territories in Africa, the Atlantic islands, the New World, and Portugal. Among the largest were the brotherhoods of the Rosary, Santa Ephigenia, and São Benedicto. These brotherhoods continue to be active in Brazil today.

The African population of Brazil was concentrated in the North and Northeast during most of the slave era, but in the nineteenth century the SLAVE TRADE flourished in southeastern Brazil to provide labor for the coffee plantations. The prospect of abolition prompted plantation owners to search for replacements for their slave labor. By the time of abolition in 1888, a government-sponsored program of European immigration had flooded both the rural and urban labor markets with new workers. Many Afro-Brazilians sought opportunities in the growing industrial cities, only to confront housing, employment, and other forms of racial discrimination. In São Paulo, where blacks were a small minority of the population, Afro-Brazilians formed a number of social and recreational clubs out of which eventually emerged a national movement for racial equality.

The Afro-Brazilian social clubs of São Paulo created between 1900 and 1920 used membership dues to finance small newspapers for the dissemination of club news. By the early 1920s a black press was active in the capital of São Paulo. Newspapers such as *Clarim da Alvorada* and *Progresso* began to advocate racial equality and circulate political ideas, including information from the Chicago *Defender* and Marcus Garvey's *Negro World*.

In 1926 the Centro Civico Palmares in São Paulo became the first Afro-Brazilian organization to develop a platform of advocacy for integration and equality for Afro-Brazilians, beginning with its efforts to integrate the police force of São Paulo. Increased racial consciousness and activism in São Paulo eventually led to the creation of the Frente Negra Brasileira in 1931, the first national Afro-Brazilian advocacy organization. It identified and fought instances of racial discrimination in São Paulo and more than twenty branch cities across Brazil. The Frente combined its activism with vocational training, basic elementary education, voter registration, and artistic and recreational activities. It was forcibly closed by President Getúlio VARGAS in 1937 when he banned all political parties under the ESTADO NOVO regime.

Although Afro-Brazilian political activity was curtailed after 1937, cultural organizations continued to flourish. In southern Brazil, small Carnival associations known as *cordões de* SAMBA soon evolved into the larger *escolas de samba*. These predominantly black social organizations quickly spread across the nation, eventually popularizing CARNIVAL in mainstream Brazilian culture. In the Northeast, Filhos de Gandhi (Sons of Gandhi), founded in the 1940s, began a new era of Afro-Brazilian group participation in Bahia's Carnival after many decades of discrimination against African themes and musical forms. They utilized the *afoxé* rhythms of the Ijexá Afro-Brazilian religion in contrast to the European themes and music popular during the 1930s. These cultural pioneers led the way for previously marginalized Afro-Brazilian Carnival traditions to become an integral part of the national culture.

After World War II the black press of São Paulo began publishing a new generation of journals. Journals such as *Senzala* and *Alvorada* reflected a broader awareness of the conditions of other black communities around the world, particularly those in the United States. Also during the 1940s, Abdias do NASCIMENTO introduced theater as a new forum for the discussion of racial issues with the creation of the Teatro Experimental do Negro (Black Experimental Theater).

The military coup of 1964 silenced many black journals, which were considered potential threats to national security. However, the liberation struggles in the Portuguese African colonies of Mozambique and Angola awakened a new international consciousness among Afro-Brazilian youth. Though radical blacks were persecuted by the government, an underground black consciousness movement grew throughout the 1970s and culminated in the creation of the Unified Black Movement (Movimento Negro Unificado—MNU). The MNU approved its charter on 20 November 1978, a date chosen to commemorate the anniversary of the murder of ZUMBI, the last ruler of PALMARES, a state founded by escaped slaves that flourished during the seventeenth century. Previously, most annual Afro-Brazilian celebrations had focused on 13 May, the anniversary of the abolition of slavery. The MNU argued that true abolition had not yet occurred, and established 20 November as the National Day of Black Consciousness. Zumbi became a symbol of the black consciousness movement, which for two years included every Afro-Brazilian organization in the country.

In the years following the creation of the MNU there was a resurgence in Afro-Brazilian cultural organizations. In the Northeast, Ile Aiye pioneered a new type of Carnival group known as the *bloco afro*. Each of these *blocos* chose themes in African and Afro-Brazilian history for their Carnival music and costumes, and some restricted membership to blacks only. Afro-Brazilian cultural traditions such as CAPOEIRA, a martial arts form of Angolan origin, moved from obscurity to public awareness when schools were established in major cities.

Simultaneously, Afro-Brazilians formed organizations to address social and economic problems. Community leaders such as Benedita da SILVA in Rio de Janeiro created a movement to improve conditions in the urban FAVELAS (slums), heavily populated by blacks. Other organizations emerged to promote awareness of racial discrimination, a problem often obscured by the government's promotion of Brazil as a "racial democracy." Some, like the Institute for the Study of Black Culture (IPCN), publicized cases of overt discrimination, while others concentrated on the study of social and economic issues and their impact on the black community. Benedita da Silva became the first black woman to serve in the national Congress, and spearheaded efforts to ensure greater Afro-Brazilian participation in politics. Today, the black consciousness movement incorporates social, cultural, political, and economic strategies to improve conditions for Afro-Brazilians.

FLORESTAN FERNANDES, *The Negro in Brazilian Society*, translated by Jacqueline D. Skiles, A. Brunel, and Arthur Rothwell (1969); ANANI DZIDZIENYO, *The Position of Blacks in Brazilian Society* (1971); MICHAEL MITCHELL, "Racial Consciousness and the Political Attitudes and Behavior of Blacks in São Paulo, Brazil" (Ph.D. diss., Indiana University, 1977); A. J. R. RUSSELL-WOOD, *The Black Man in Slavery and Freedom in Colonial Brazil* (1982); CLÓVIS MOURA, *Brasil: Raízes do protesto negro* (1983); PIERRE-MICHEL FONTAINE, ed., *Race, Class, and Power in Brazil* (1985); GEORGE REID ANDREWS, *Blacks and Whites in São Paulo, Brazil, 1888–1988* (1991); KIM D. BUTLER, "Up from Slavery: Afro-Brazilian Activism in São Paulo, 1888–1938," in *Americas* 49, no. 2 (1992): 179–206.

KIM D. BUTLER

*See also* **Race and Ethnicity; Slavery.**

**AFRICAN-BRAZILIAN EMIGRATION TO AFRICA,** a "return" of approximately 4,000 freed persons to Africa during the course of the nineteenth century. Although some émigrés were Brazilian-born, most had been taken as slaves from the YORUBA- and Fon-speaking areas of present-day Benin, Togo, and southwestern Nigeria during a period of widespread civil and religious warfare. Portuguese colonial law provided Brazilian slaves the opportunity to purchase their own freedom. Many Africans in Brazil participated in organized savings societies with the hope of returning to their homeland as free persons. The majority of émigrés left from BAHIA, a province engaged in direct trade with the African coast in tobacco and slaves, while a smaller number left from Rio de Janeiro. Large-scale emigration began after 1835 in the wake of an attempted rebellion led by African Muslims in Bahia's capital. Backlash against Africans prompted hundreds to risk their meager savings and even their lives in the transatlantic voyage.

Most émigrés were unable to return to their original homelands, instead forging new communities in the coastal cities of Ouidah and Grand Popo, where they became known as the "Bresiliens." Because the local populations had been long established in subsistence and commercial agriculture, the returnees carved their niche in skilled trades and commerce. From the 1830s through the 1850s, several Bresilien families accumulated substantial fortunes in the illicit SLAVE TRADE. They traded to Europeans in exchange for Bahian rum and tobacco, diversifying after the end of slavery to trade in palm products and other local goods. Returnees also engaged in skilled occupations such as carpentry, masonry, boat building and barbering. Some gained positions of prominence in society and politics. Less successful were those who settled in Lagos. They found themselves in competition with resident European traders and Yoruba freed persons released from the British protectorate of Sierra Leone. They did not speak English, they were Catholic rather than Protestant, and they rarely had the necessary capital to establish commercial enterprises. The Brazilians in Lagos became artisans, using the skills they had acquired as slaves. Some Central Africans returned to small communities in Benguela, Luanda, and the Cabinda coast.

J. MICHAEL TURNER, "Les Bresiliens: The Impact of Former Brazilian Slaves upon Dahomey," (Ph.D. diss., Boston University, 1975); MANUELA CARNEIRO DA CUNHA, *Negros, estrangeiros: Os escravos libertos e sua volta a Africa* (1985); MARY C. KARASCH, *Slave Life in Rio de Janeiro, 1808–1850* (1987); PIERRE VERGER, *Fluxo e refluxo do trafico de escravos entre o Golfo do Benin e a Bahia de Todos os Santos dos seculos XVII a XIX*, 3d ed. (1987).

KIM D. BUTLER

## AFRICAN BRAZILIANS: COLOR TERMINOLOGY.

Color is one of the crucial social variables of Brazil and constitutes one of the unique characteristics of Latin American culture. Like the terms "race" and "ethnicity," skin color is an imperfect concept used to identify people in Latin America. It is but one of the characteristics used. Other physical traits, such as hair and facial features like the shape of the nose, are also employed. In addition, an identification determined by physical appearance can be modified by such social variables as wealth and education.

Color terms utilized in Brazil describe the almost infinite shadings that result from race mixing among Indians, Europeans, and Africans, and among the mixtures themselves. During the colonial period, racist perceptions and medical notions combined to create multiple hierarchies. One was based on the idea that pure races were better than mixed races inasmuch as the latter, it was believed, contained the worst characteristics of the parents. The other, and more common, hierarchy was based on social usage that placed whites at the top of the social hierarchy and blacks or Indians at the bottom and arranged other groups by the degree to which they appeared white. "Purity of blood," which was used to describe whites of demonstrable European ancestry, was essential for entry into the highest stratum of society.

Race mixing is not unique to Latin America. But whereas other societies, such as that of the United States, have acknowledged a comparatively limited range of racially mixed groups, Latin American societies have historically recognized many differences. The result has been a plethora of racial identities, many of them conveying negative images. Over the years, hundreds of racial terms have been used in Brazil, but the most common have included *branco*, white; *branco da terra*, white of the land, a person whose whiteness was recognized only in a specific area; *moreno*, a light-skinned mulatto; PARDO or *mulato*, referring originally to the offspring of one white and one black parent; *mestiço*, MAMELUCO, or CABOCLO, an Indian-white mixture; *cafuzo*, a black and Indian mixture; *crioulo*, a Brazilian-born black; *negro* or *prêto*, a dark-skinned or African-born black; and *indigo*, Indian. Often the same term is applied to different groups in different parts of Brazil. *Cabra*, for example, was used to describe a very light-skinned mulatto, or a mixture of Indian, black, and white, or of Indian and black.

The existence of such a range of identified color groups is complemented by several other crucial characteristics. First is the mutability of such labels. Because part of the label is socially and culturally defined, a person's identity can change over time. Second, the existence of such fine gradations prevents an objective definition of such labels. While during the colonial period efforts were made to describe and define each possible combination, in reality this process was a failure. Instead, the labeling is often done by the observer on the basis of the relationship of the personal characteristics of the observer and the observed. The result is the imprecise definition of groups. This ambiguity has served effectively to prevent political organizing around racial identification.

Such ambiguity does not mean the absence of prejudice. Rather, it points to color-conscious societies in which the phenotypical appearance and culture of individuals is extremely important. Thus the differences among people make it difficult to redress social injustices.

CHARLES WAGLEY, "On the Concept of Social Race in the Americas," in *Contemporary Cultures and Societies of Latin America,* edited by Dwight B. Heath and Richard N. Adams (1965), pp. 531–545; MARVIN HARRIS, "Referential Ambiguity in the Calculus of Brazilian Racial Identity," in *Southwestern Journal of Anthropology* 26 (Spring 1970): 1–14; ROBERT M. LEVINE, *Race and Ethnic Relations in Latin America and the Caribbean: An Historical Dictionary and Bibliography* (1980); THOMAS M. STEPHENS, *Dictionary of Latin American Racial and Ethnic Terminology* (1989).

DONALD RAMOS

*See also* **Race and Ethnicity.**

**AFRICAN–LATIN AMERICAN RELATIONS.** Relations between Africa and Latin America from the sixteenth through nineteenth centuries centered on the transatlantic SLAVE TRADE, in which an estimated 10 million Africans were shipped to Hispanic and Portuguese America. The consequences of this trade and the contributions of Africans and their descendants to the demographic, economic, and sociocultural makeup are discernible with greater or less prominence throughout Latin America. Brazil, Cuba, Colombia, Panama, Venezuela, and the Dominican Republic have a strong African presence. Ecuador, Peru, Costa Rica, Nicaragua, and Honduras have populations of African descent who came from the English-speaking Caribbean following emancipation and independence. Argentina, Chile, Bolivia, Paraguay, and Mexico once had African slaves and populations of African descent, although evidence of their presence is not so visible today.

A major turning point in relations between Africa and Latin America followed the formal European colonialism in Africa and the establishment of diplomatic relations between African countries and, principally, Brazil and Cuba in the 1960s. Tracing its historical connections back to the transportation of more than 3 million Africans into Brazil and the subsequent return of Brazilians of African descent to West Africa in the nineteenth and twentieth centuries, Brazil took pride in what it saw as its exemplary race relations and promotion of African cultural and religious traditions. In the 1970s and 1980s Brazil's trade relations with Africa and willingness to dispatch engineers and other needed development personnel to Africa were often explained in these terms. Brazil sold its products to Africa and bought petroleum and natural gas from African countries. Brazil has also competed with some African countries in the production of cocoa and coffee, for example, but this has not jeopardized cooperative efforts. The Brazilian government began awarding scholarships to African students in the early 1960s.

Some of the same historical and cultural links underpin Cuba's relations with Africa. An energetic pursuit of internationalism and solidarity with "progressive" regimes and movements worldwide has brought Cuba to Africa in a number of capacities—educational, technical, and military. Perhaps most notable was Cuba's dramatic entry into the Angolan independence struggle in 1975 at the request of the Popular Movement for the Liberation of Angola (MPLA), supported by the then Soviet Union. The Cuban military presence turned the tide in favor of the MPLA and resulted in the routing of South African forces, which had entered the fray on the side of the National Union for the Total Liberation of Angola (UNITA).

Whether or not Cuba's African policy was self-generated or a function of a grand Soviet design for Africa has often been debated. Cuba has provided scholarships for students from several African countries for studies at the university and pre-university levels. With better access to higher education, Afro-Cubans have entered the sphere of diplomacy and the senior levels of the armed forces in ways that are not so discernible in Brazil.

To date, relations between Africa and Latin America have been largely nonreciprocal: Latin America has generally initiated proposals and Africa has responded to them.

Latin American and African countries have formal relations regarding the cocoa and coffee trades, OPEC membership, and the non-aligned movement. In the early 1960s Brazil established relations with African countries as part of a conscious shift away from its traditional identification with the West. Yet, paradoxically, Brazil unfailingly abstained from voting on United Nations resolutions condemning Portuguese colonialism in Africa. Following Angolan independence, however, Brazil became one of the first countries to recognize the MPLA regime. In post-colonial Portuguese-speaking Africa, Brazilian commercial and cultural activities have acquired a higher profile than those of Portugal.

Political and economic problems in Cuba in the late 1980s and early 1990s make it difficult to predict a continuation of its high profile policies of the recent past. And Brazil's political and economic problems, especially its foreign debt and inflation, and shifts in foreign policy objectives in the late 1980s have caused a scaling down of its African policies. It is reasonable to expect that the future will bring more initiatives from the African side.

JOSÉ HONÓRIO RODRÍGUEZ, *Brazil and Africa* (1965); WAYNE SELCHER, *The Afro-Asian Dimension of Brazilian Foreign Policy, 1956–1972* (1974); WILLIAM LEOGRANDE, *Cuba's Policy in Africa, 1959–1980* (1980); JUNE BELKIN and CARMELO MESA-LAGO, eds., *Cuba in Africa* (1982); PAMELA FALK, *Cuban Foreign Policy: Caribbean Tempest* (1986); CARLOS MOORE, *Castro, the Blacks, and Africa* (1988); GEORGE FAURIOL and EVA LOSER, eds., *Cuba: The*

*International Dimension* (1990); PEDRO PEREZ and JEAN STUBBS, *AfroCuba: An Anthology of Cuban Writing on Race, Politics, and Culture* (1993); MICHAEL L. CONNIFF and THOMAS J. DAVIS, eds., *Africans in the Americas* (1994).

ANANI DZIDZIENYO

## AFRICAN–LATIN AMERICAN RELIGIONS

### Overview

Between 1492 and 1870, at least 10 million Africans, representing hundreds of ethnic groups, were carried as slaves to the islands of the Caribbean and the Atlantic coasts of South, Central, and North America. Many thousands more were taken after the close of legal slavery or induced to emigrate as indentured servants. Despite the harshness of life both in slavery and after emancipation, they were more or less able to reconstruct a cultural identity on the basis of the elements of the African cultures that they carried with them and the social environments in which they found themselves.

Among the many cultural skills that Africans brought to the Americas were patterns of spiritual beliefs and practices that varied with each ethnic group. Some of the slaves were trained priests and priestesses of African spirits who carried with them powers of enchantment and healing. Thrown into the maelstrom of Atlantic slave societies, they found these skills to be valuable in meeting the challenges of plantation and urban life. In most cases the specific ethnic context of the beliefs and practices was lost, but in others sufficient numbers of Africans from the same region were able to reconstitute themselves as "nations" within the multiethnic societies to which they were taken. Through these nations, or communities, African beliefs and practices were preserved and developed in dialogue with the non-African traditions in their milieu.

The most influential African peoples in Latin America came from the coastal and forest zones of western Africa. Particularly notable were the Ashanti and Fanti peoples of present-day Ghana and Côte d'Ivoire (Ivory Coast); the Ewe- and Fon-speaking peoples of present-day Togo and Benin; the Hausa, Yoruba, and Ibo peoples of present-day Nigeria; and the many interrelated peoples of the former Kongo kingdom of present-day Zaire and Angola. Depending upon the conditions that members of each group encountered in the Americas, they were able to preserve more or less complex patterns of their spiritual beliefs and practices. Factors such as racial and ethnic demographics, agricultural and mercantile systems, and opportunities for manumission or escape all influenced the transplantation of African religions in the Americas.

Perhaps the most significant factor in the development of these traditions was the established European religion of a particular region. In the Roman Catholic colonies of Spain, Portugal, and France, slaves were baptized as a matter of law, and in some regions, par-

ticularly urban areas, the Catholic church actively supported slave rights and manumission. The Catholic church also accepted a wide variety of ethnic ceremonials as legitimate supplements to the orthodox sacraments. The Protestant churches of the British and Dutch colonies, by contrast, did not legislate the baptism of slaves and lacked the political power to influence their legal or social status. Slaves and free blacks came to accept Christianity through nonconforming Baptist and Methodist churches, which emphasized local leadership, biblical foundations, and personal conversion.

The social and religious factors stemming from these European religious traditions were crucial in determining the ways in which the African religions developed in their particular milieus. While there are many exceptions, as a broad general rule, Africans and their descendants in Catholic regions developed religious institutions alternative and parallel to Christianity, such as CANDOMBLÉ in Brazil, VODUN (vodou, voodoo) in Haiti, or SANTERÍA in Cuba. In the Protestant regions, however, they created alternative forms of Protestant Christianity, such as Revival in Jamaica or the Spiritual Baptists of Trinidad. This dialogue of religious elements either by juxtaposition in Catholic regions or reinterpretation in Protestant regions has been the primary focus of researchers who see in African-derived traditions models for understanding culture change. More recently, researchers have looked to the traditions for light on issues of the multiple meanings of symbols and the coexistence of plural identities.

In the Latin American world, African religious traditions have been particularly influential in areas of intensive eighteenth- and nineteenth-century sugar production. The African-derived traditions of Haiti, northeastern Brazil, and Cuba have shaped the national cultures of those countries, and their emigrants have established the traditions in other Latin- and English-speaking countries. Perhaps the most famous of the traditions, Haitian vodou, owes its reputation to the role of devotees in the slave revolt that overthrew the French colonial authorities of Saint Domingue and established the "black republic" of Haiti in the midst of slaveholding colonies and the newly independent United States. Tales of voodoo barbarism were revived during Haiti's occupation by U.S. Marines in the twentieth century and continue to serve to discredit black spirituality in that country and elsewhere. Vodou means simply "spirit" in the Fon language of enslaved Dahomeans brought to Haiti in the eighteenth century, and the tradition centers on cultivating the spirits' protection and inspiration in meeting the harsh challenges of the lives of the Haitian poor.

In Brazil, particularly the Northeastern city of Salvador da Bahia, the African-derived traditions are called *Candomblé*. Due to Brazil's relative proximity to Africa, a thriving reciprocal trade brought not only slaves but free Africans to Bahia. In the late eighteenth and early nineteenth centuries, they established a number of houses of worship based on the African traditions of the houses' founders. The prestige of these early houses formed the model for the veneration of African spirits throughout Brazil. While the old Bahian houses pride themselves on the purity of their African liturgies, others have wedded elements of their practices to European and Amerindian ideas, thus creating thousands of variants known collectively as Umbanda. It is largely through Umbanda's popularization of *Candomblé* that African spirits known as orishas (ORIXÁS) are popular throughout the country. The festival of Iemanjá, the maternal spirit of the oceans, is attended by hundreds of thousands on the beaches of Rio de Janeiro and millions of others throughout the country.

Africans in Cuba, like those in Brazil and to a lesser extent in Haiti, were able to maintain ethnic identities through religious organizations. The most widespread tradition is often called *Santería,* a name deriving from the correspondences developed between the spirits of the Yoruba people and the Catholic saints. Kongo practices form the basis of another tradition, known alternately as *Palo* or *Mayombe.* The secret religious societies of the Efik and Ejaham peoples have been transplanted to Cuba, where they are known as *Abakua.* While these traditions never achieved the approval of the wider society, their influence in festivals and popular music brought elements of their spiritualities to every sector of the Cuban population.

The traditions of Haiti, Brazil, and Cuba are only the best-known of African-Hispanic traditions. All the countries of the Atlantic littoral have produced more or less developed spiritualities that have their origin in Africa. The Haitian, Brazilian, and Cuban traditions have become most important because they have been studied by scholars and because emigrants have carried these traditions to other countries, where they often act as models for a renewed African consciousness. Haitians have taken vodou to the Dominican Republic and the United States; Brazilians have established *Candomblé* houses in Argentina; and Cubans have taken *Santería* to the United States, Puerto Rico, Mexico, Venezuela, and Colombia.

An extraordinary bibliography with nearly 6,000 entries may be found in JOHN GRAY, comp, *Ashé: Traditional Religion and Healing in Sub-Saharan Africa and the Diaspora, a Classified International Bibliography* (1989). Other important studies include MELVILLE J. HERSKOVITS, *The New World Negro: Selected Papers in Afroamerican Studies* (1966); ROGER BASTIDE, *African Civilisations in the New World,* translated by Peter Green (1972); ANGELINA POLLAK ELTZ, *Cultos afroamericanos* (1972); LEONARD E. BARRETT, *Soul-Force: African Heritage in Afro-American Religion* (1974); GEORGE EATON SIMPSON, *Black Religions in the New World* (1978); ROBERT FARRIS THOMPSON, *Flash of the Spirit: African and Afro-American Art and Philosophy* (1983); KORTRIGHT DAVIS and ELIAS FARAJAJÉ-JONES, eds., *African Creative Expressions of the Divine* (1991); and JOSEPH M. MURPHY, *Working the Spirit: Ceremonies of the African Diaspora* (1994).

JOSEPH M. MURPHY

*See also* **Slavery; Syncretism.**

## Brazil

A culturally diverse population, Brazilians also practice a variety of different faiths, several of which are rooted in the history of African slaves brought to work on Brazilian sugar plantations beginning in the sixteenth century. West African YORUBA and Dahomean peoples retained impressive segments of their religious beliefs and practices through syncretization with Catholic cultural elements. Bastide notes that on the special Catholic saints' days that were observed by plantation owners, Africans secretly celebrated their own deities. An example is the Yoruba deity Ogum, god of iron and patron of blacksmiths forging iron weapons and farm tools. In some regions of Brazil, Africans clandestinely worshipped Ogum under the guise of celebrating St. George, who was depicted in paintings, lithographs, and figurines on a white horse while slaying a dragon with a long iron sword. Cultural SYNCRETISM proceeded along two lines. First, the Yoruba *orixás* (deities) and Catholic saints were both structural intermediaries between a high and remote Olorun (God) and ordinary people on earth. Second, cultural items such as the iron weapons linking Ogum and St. George brought together *orixá* and saint. Over time the link between iron farm

Candomblé in Bahia. Cultos, Brazil, 1962. ORGANIZATION OF AMERICAN STATES.

tools and Ogum weakened in Brazil in that the slaves had no concern for the profitability of the master's plantation. The iron weapons retained as cultural elements, however, would serve as important symbols in the ongoing war, both real and psychological, between master and slave.

Yoruba beliefs and practices comprise a common cultural pattern running through most African Brazilian religions. However, each African Brazilian religion has been differentially shaped by the larger Brazilian milieu, which also included Central African religious traditions, indigenous shamanistic beliefs and practices, and a type of spiritualism known as Kardecismo. Furthermore, worshippers were not restricted to persons of African descent, and membership generally reflects the ethnic composition of a particular locale. African Brazilians dominate CANDOMBLÉ in Salvador, Bahia, while in the southern cities of São Paulo and Pôrto Alegre, European Brazilians comprise 50 percent of the members in the UMBANDA religion.

*Candomblé* During the latter part of the slave era and after emancipation in 1888, African Brazilians more openly practiced Candomblé in urban religious centers. Two Yoruba-influenced religions emerged: Candomblé in Salvador and Xangô in Recife. A closely related Dahomean-influenced religion known as TAMBOR DAS MINAS developed in São Luís.

Each religious center is led by a *mãe de santo* (mother of saint) or a *pai de santo* (father of saint). According to Wafer, their initiates are divided into two categories: those who go into trance and are possessed by deities, and those who do not. Of the latter, the males are called *ogãs* and the females are known as *equedes*; they work in special supporting roles that, in part, help provide financing and labor for the religious center and its celebrations in exchange for ritual protection and opportunities to dance along with the deities.

A religious center recognizes each deity during its annual cycle of celebrations. While dancing to polyrhythmic drumming and Yoruba songs and words in the more conservative religious centers, spirit mediums known as "horses" are possessed by the various deities in all practices of Candomblé. An important part of each celebration is feeding the honored deity as well as those who come to observe and enjoy the beautifully costumed deities and their dancing. After the main part of the celebration, the deities take their leave, and the "horses" are possessed by childlike spirits known as *erê*. Although spirits of the dead are an important part of many African Brazilian religions, it is rare that Candomblé in its more conservative form has anything to do with them. Instead, *eguns* (spirits of dead ancestors) are dealt with in the cult of Egum.

*Batuque* The Batuque religion in Belém is an independent religious system, which Leacock and Leacock say deserves recognition in its own right. Although African origins are present, Batuque has been "Brazilianized" far more than Candomblé. An early form of

Batuque was brought to Belém at the time of the Amazon rubber boom (1890–1913). It probably included cultural elements from the Dahomean influence in São Luís, generalized Yoruba religious traits, folk Catholicism, Brazilian and Iberian folklore and history, and indigenous Brazilian shamanic traits from the Pajelança of Pará and the Catimbó cult of northeastern Brazil.

Members of Batuque refer to the supernatural beings that possess them as *encantados*. They include a variety of spirits of the dead as well as deities, but not Catholic saints. Saints are said to live in the sky, while the *encantados* live in *encantarias* deep in the forest; under rivers, lakes, and the sea; and even in underground cities directly beneath human cities.

*Umbanda* Umbanda is another highly Brazilianized religion with Central and West African, pre-Columbian indigenous, folk Catholic, and spiritist origins. It is practiced primarily in southern Brazil, especially in Rio de Janeiro, São Paulo, and Pôrto Alegre. It is also found in nearly all major urban areas.

Umbanda apparently evolved out of Macumba in the 1920s. According to Bastide, Macumba was in part an outgrowth of the introduction of Yoruba deities into the earlier Central African Bantu cult known as Cabula. Congolese and Angolan religious traditions were present in Macumba and later in Umbanda, as, for example, in the use of the name Zambi for the high god, instead of the Yoruba name Olorun. Also, Central African beliefs in possession by spirits of the dead were retained in Macumba. This helped set the scene for the diffusion of Kardecist spiritist beliefs related to spirits of the dead, supernatural fluids, and "passes" to remove evil fluids from sick and troubled individuals. The new sociocultural mélange became Umbanda. According to Karasch, the frequent changes in symbols, beliefs, and rituals in Umbanda as it spread throughout Brazil was part of the flexibility that characterized Central African religions brought by slaves to southern Brazil.

Brown, in describing the "whitening" of Umbanda, notes that many early leaders of Umbanda were middle-class professionals, mostly European Brazilians. They were unhappy with the "highly evolved" Kardecist spirits who gave long-winded lectures on doctrine. They enjoyed the curing rituals of the African and Indian spirits in Umbanda but did not care for animal sacrifices, drinking, and the drumming and dancing often associated with what they regarded as the more primitive forms of Umbanda rituals. These "low" features were dropped from Pure Umbanda. During the 1950s some African Brazilians reacted to Umbanda Pura by decrying the de-Africanization of Umbanda. Differences in religious beliefs and practices to some extent reflected different social and racial sectors. Today these divisions within Umbanda maintain a relatively peaceful coexistence.

OCTAVIO DA COSTA EDUARDO, *The Negro in Northern Brazil* (1948); SETH and RUTH LEACOCK, *Spirits of the Deep: A Study of an Afro-Brazilian Cult* (1972); ESTHER PRESSEL, "Umbanda in São Paulo: Religious Innovation in a Developing Society," in

*Religion, Altered States of Consciousness, and Social Change,* edited by Erika Bourguignon (1973); ROGER BASTIDE, *The African Religions of Brazil* (1978); MARY KARASCH, "Central African Religious Tradition in Rio de Janeiro," in *Journal of Latin American Lore* 5 (1979): 233–253; CHESTER E. GABRIEL, *Communications of the Spirits: Umbanda, Regional Cults in Manaus, and the Dynamics of Mediumistic Trance* (1980); PATRICIA B. LERCH, "An Explanation for the Predominance of Women in the Umbanda Cults of Pôrto Alegre, Brazil," in *Urban Anthropology* 11 (1982): 237–261; DIANA DEGROAT BROWN, *Umbanda: Religion and Politics in Urban Brazil* (1986); JAM WAFER, *The Taste of Blood: Spirit Possession in Brazilian Candomblé* (1991); JÚLIO BRAGA, *Ancestralidade afrobrasileira: O culto de Babá Egum* (1992).

ESTHER J. PRESSEL

See also **Candomblé; Music and Dance: Popular; Syncretism; Umbanda.**

**AFRICANS IN HISPANIC AMERICA.** People of African descent live in all of the former Spanish colonies in the Americas. With few exceptions, they are the descendants of African slaves who were first brought to the Americas in 1502. African slavery finally ended in Spanish America in 1886, when Cuba became the last society to abolish it. A century later, the legacy of slavery remains apparent in all of the former slave-holding societies. Individuals who claim African ancestry are struggling everywhere for self-definition and a secure place in the lands of their birth.

Although blacks are a part of the human landscape everywhere, it is difficult to determine their demographic distribution. This is due to the fact that census data in most societies do not include the population's "racial" or ethnic heritages. The process of miscegenation, in addition, has occurred to such an extent that it complicates the task of "racial" identification. Some persons, reflecting a variety of complex historical and psychological factors, will not readily acknowledge that they are of African descent. These difficulties notwithstanding, we may cautiously divide the former Spanish possessions into three groups in accordance with the presumed size of their populations of African descent.

The first group consists of those societies where Afro-Latinos comprise one-third or more of the population. This is especially the case in the three Caribbean islands—Cuba, the Dominican Republic, and Puerto Rico. As much as 80 percent of the population of the Dominican Republic may be of African descent. Between one-third and two-fifths of Puerto Rico's population can claim African ancestry. In 1981 the Cuban census

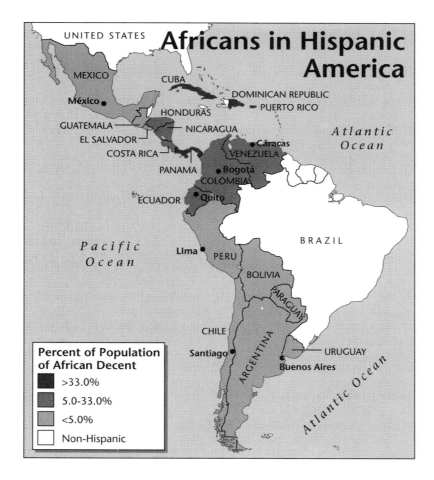

**Africans in Hispanic America**

Percent of Population of African Decent
- >33.0%
- 5.0-33.0%
- <5.0%
- Non-Hispanic

showed that 34 percent of the population was of African ancestry, a figure widely acknowledged by specialists as low. Taken together, the population of these three polyglot societies is approximately 18 million, of which 8 to 10 million may be of African descent. It should not be difficult to understand why this is the case. These islands, particularly Cuba, had been the recipients of sizable numbers of African slaves between the sixteenth and nineteenth centuries. With the exception of Panama, none of the societies of Central and South America fall into the first group. Many of the Afro-Panamanians are descendants of immigrants from the British Caribbean who came to help construct the Panama Canal and the railroad during the late nineteenth and early twentieth centuries.

The second category of former Spanish colonies consists of those with African-derived populations of between 5 and 30 percent. These include Nicaragua, Costa Rica, Honduras, Venezuela, Ecuador, and Colombia. Although most of these people are descendants of the African slaves who worked in those societies, a fairly high percentage of the Afro-Venezuelans and Afro–Costa Ricans are immigrants from the West Indies and their progeny.

The third group comprises societies where less than 5 percent of the population is of African descent. In Argentina, Chile, Bolivia, Uruguay, and Paraguay, the presence of blacks is negligible. They comprise a slightly higher proportion of the population in Mexico, Peru, Guatemala, and El Salvador.

It is important to underscore this demographic variation because there is a rough correlation between the size of the black population and its impact on the larger society. In addition, politicians in societies with large black populations, such as those in the Caribbean, cannot ignore their presence and are compelled to treat them as significant interest groups. Consequently, blacks in those societies are able to influence the political culture to a far greater extent than are their counterparts who constitute a smaller share of the body politic elsewhere. Nevertheless, in countries such as Colombia and Ecuador, the peoples of African descent have wielded some degree of power in those areas and regions where their number is not inconsequential. These areas include the Esmeraldas district in Ecuador, and Buenaventura on the Pacific coast of Colombia.

Afro-Latin Americans do not constitute a monolithic group. They possess, for example, phenotypes ranging from very black at one extreme to Caucasoid at the other. There are class divisions, religious differences, and distinctions between those who are native to a particular society and those of foreign birth. Some individuals, regardless of the country in which they reside, will deny the African part of their heritage because of its association with slavery and the unhealthy impact that racism has had on their personhood. These persons have internalized a societal zeitgeist that ascribes a lesser human worth to those who share an African ancestry. Con-

sequently, they are likely to define themselves in national terms such as "Cuban," "Mexican," or "Peruvian," and to eschew any "racial" identification. There is, of course, no incompatibility in simultaneously acknowledging a national as well as a "racial" or "ethnic" origin. The seeming rejection of one's "racial" heritage reflects the continuing salience and pernicious effects of a racist ideology that has never disappeared from the Spanish American landscape.

Racial prejudice, however, has never operated with the same overt and unrelenting malevolence in Spanish America as it has in the United States. Racial segregation never became official policy anywhere, but institutional barriers to equality and social justice were omnipresent. The relative absence of racist legislation has frequently led to the erroneous conclusion that Hispanic societies are essentially color blind. But there are undeniable systemic obstacles to the advancement of Afro-Latinos everywhere, and social prejudice directed at them remains an inescapable fact of life. Some observers maintain that the Spanish American variant of racism has had a more damaging impact on its victims than its more virulently expressed counterpart in the United States. One American noted in 1963, after a visit to Puerto Rico, "the Latin American system knows more about how to discriminate against the Negroes and make them like it than North Americans."

Under the circumstances, any assessment of the Afro-Latino condition must be made in the context of a racial zeitgeist that limits their possibilities and, in varying degrees, debases them as persons. Scholars have often noted that the adage "money whitens" is used in popular discourse in some societies and have mistakenly concluded that this indicates that an individual's position in society is largely a function of economic circumstances and not of "racial" heritage. The racism that underscores this adage, however, is obvious because it suggests that whiteness represents the societal standard. The depiction of Afro-Latinos in textbooks, comics, literature, and in private and public discourse is frequently negative, thereby demonstrating the pervasiveness of a racism that refuses to die.

The complex interplay of race and class in Spanish America has resulted in a disproportionate share of blacks occupying the lowest ranks of the social order. Poverty almost always wears a black face, or at least a brown one. This is the consequence of the survival of the structural and racial barriers to the advancement of blacks and Indians, who traditionally have been excluded from the elite groups. Cuba probably represents an exception to this pattern. The revolution effected fundamental changes in the country's social, economic, and political systems, as a result of which Afro-Cubans experienced an improvement in their condition. The Castro regime also tackled, with some success, the problem of institutional racism. The prejudice that undergirds and legitimizes social relations in Cuba, however, has been far more resistant to change. In addition, Afro-

Cubans are less likely than Caucasians to be appointed to positions of real power in the government.

Despite the enormity of the problems they confront, Afro-Latinos have struggled to create a livable space for themselves. There are examples of individuals who have held and continue to hold elective office, usually at the local level, in the Dominican Republic, Puerto Rico, Colombia, Venezuela, and elsewhere. Others have acquired a fair amount of real estate in Costa Rica, the Dominican Republic, and the coastal areas of Ecuador, Colombia, Venezuela, and Peru. Afro-Latinos, however, are still more likely to be found in service positions everywhere or to be unemployed. Although the professions have never been legally closed to them, at least in recent years, few persons have had the resources to acquire the requisite training. Contemporary Cuba stands alone in providing free education to those with the necessary aptitude, regardless of "racial" ancestry.

If the impact of Afro-Latinos on the political systems in which they live is not significant in most societies, the same cannot be said of their cultural influence. Linguists readily acknowledge the continuing impact of African languages on the vocabulary of Spanish and the ways in which it is spoken in societies, such as those of the Caribbean, that imported large numbers of slaves. African musical instruments, such as the marimba and the drum, still enjoy wide appeal. Similarly, musical styles, dance, culinary tastes, and art forms reflect, in varying degrees of vigor, African influences.

The problems that Afro-Latinos confront are similar, in many respects, to those that bedevil other peoples of African descent in the diaspora. Overwhelmingly poor, largely excluded from positions of political power, and invariably the victims of a systemic racism, hope is a luxury for many of them. Some still cling to vestiges of an African past; others welcome integration into the body politic. Those who constitute insignificant minorities in many countries face the prospect of being absorbed by the larger groups. In time, their more numerous counterparts in other societies may see the barriers to their progress weaken, if not disappear entirely.

FRANKLIN KNIGHT, *The African Dimension in Latin American Societies* (1974); ROBERT BRENT TOPLIN, ed., *Slavery and Race Relations in Latin America* (1974); LESLIE B. ROUT, JR., *The African Experience in Spanish America, 1502 to the Present Day* (1976); REID ANDREWS, *The Afro-Argentines of Buenos Aires, 1880–1900* (1980); RICHARD GRAHAM, ed., *The Idea of Race in Latin America, 1870–1940* (1990); WINTHROP R. WRIGHT, *Café con Leche: Race, Class, and National Image in Venezuela* (1990); MICHAEL L. CONNIFF and THOMAS J. DAVIS, *Africans in the Americas: A History of the Black Diaspora* (1994).

COLIN A. PALMER

*See also* **Race and Ethnicity; Slave Trade; Slavery.**

**AGACE INDIANS.** *See* **Payaguá Indians.**

**AGENCY FOR INTERNATIONAL DEVELOPMENT** (AID), a U.S. government organization created in 1961 to unify previously separate economic assistance activities. In the early 1990s it became known by the acronym USAID. Its program composition has shifted over time to reflect changes in executive and congressional priorities, U.S. foreign policy interests, and lessons learned about the processes of economic growth, poverty alleviation, and democratic development.

One of AID's first major undertakings was to implement U.S. economic assistance in Latin America and the Caribbean (LAC) under the ALLIANCE FOR PROGRESS, which stressed economic growth, social change, and democratic political development. LAC economic growth accelerated during the 1960s, and health and education indicators improved significantly. But progress in reducing poverty was less than hoped for, partly because political resistance to redistributive measures (through tax reform, agrarian reform, and comprehensive economic planning) exceeded expectations. Moreover, AID's efforts to stimulate democratic political development yielded disappointing results.

Concern about poverty led the U.S. Congress in 1973 to pass the "New Directions" legislation, calling for AID

Young Guatemalan girl of African descent. LATIN AMERICAN LIBRARY, TULANE UNIVERSITY.

23

to "give highest priority to undertakings submitted by host governments which directly improve the lives of the poorest of their people and their capacity to participate in the development of their countries." Some resulting programs were successful, but many were administratively cumbersome and had unexpectedly high costs per beneficiary.

The LAC-wide economic crisis of the 1980s, and its perceived threats to U.S. interests, resulted in a sharp expansion of AID assistance to the region, from $340 million annually in fiscal years 1977–1979 to $1.6 billion annually in fiscal years 1985–1987.

AID's objectives for LAC in the mid-1990s are to support sustainable development through programs that (1) contribute to broad-based economic growth, (2) build democracy, (3) promote smaller and healthier families, and (4) protect the environment. Since the early 1980s AID has emphasized the importance of economic policy reforms for achieving faster economic growth, now widely regarded as critical for reducing poverty. AID also believes that economic liberalization—by reducing or eliminating subsidies benefiting mainly middle- and upper-income groups—will result in more equitable economic growth, help strengthen political democracy, and free resources for targeted assistance to the poor. AID's economic assistance to LAC in fiscal year 1992 was approximately $1.3 billion, but by fiscal year 1994, it had fallen to about $700 million.

A balanced, thoughtful, and analytical critique is JUDITH TENDLER, *Inside Foreign Aid* (1975). An informative article with a good historical perspective and many references is ROLF H. SARTORIUS and VERNON W. RUTTAN, "The Sources of the Basic Human Needs Mandate," *Journal of Developing Areas* 23 (April 1989): 331–361. AID's annual *Congressional Presentation* discusses current policies and strategies, and provides details on country programs.

CLARENCE ZUVEKAS, JR.

**AGIOTISTA,** derogatory term used in nineteenth-century Mexico to describe those who made short-term loans to governments at very high rates of interest, usually assessed monthly rather than yearly, and often paid directly from tariff collections at the ports. The practice began in 1827 when Mexican treasuries, unable to borrow from abroad, started to rely on merchants for enough cash to meet a portion of their payrolls. Given their low creditworthiness, Mexican governments accepted loans whose face values were comprised of virtually worthless debt paper as well as cash. When tax collections shrank, *agiotistas* also received debt paper, forcing many into bankruptcy. It would appear that the practice ended in 1867 with the restored republic, but it is equally likely that it assumed different forms until banking achieved a firm foothold at the end of the nineteenth century.

CIRO F. S. CARDOSO, ed., *Formación y desarrollo de la burguesía en México: Siglo XIX* (1978); BARBARA A. TENENBAUM, *México en*

*le época de los agiotistas, 1821–1857* (1985) and " 'Neither a Borrower nor a Lender Be': Financial Constraints and the Treaty of Guadalupe Hidalgo," in *The Mexican and Mexican American Experience in the Nineteenth Century*, edited by Jaime E. Rodríguez O. (1989).

BARBARA A. TENENBAUM

**AGRAMONTE Y LOYNAZ, IGNACIO** (*b.* 23 December 1841; *d.* 11 May 1873), Cuban general. Agramonte is known to Cubans as a man of irreproachable behavior in both his public and his private lives. His gallantry as a cavalry commander is legendary. Few Cuban military feats against Spanish forces are better known than the daring rescue of his friend, Colonel Julio Sanguily, from the Spanish column that had captured him.

Agramonte, born in Camagüey, in central Cuba, was a distinguished lawyer and cattle farmer who became one of the insurgent leaders in his region when the TEN YEARS' WAR (1868–1878) broke out. He espoused the radical liberal ideas that were supported by many Camagüeyans but were in opposition to the conservative views of the head of the revolt, Carlos Manuel de Céspedes. When the vicissitudes of war forced Céspedes to come to terms with the Camagüeyans, they hastily drafted a constitution for the insurgent provisional government. Agramonte was one of the two authors of this constitution, which was a solemn manifestation of Camagüeyan liberalism.

Agramonte's relationship with Céspedes, who had been proclaimed president of free Cuba, continued to be marred by serious conflicts, some of them of a personal nature. But the two men succeeded in burying their differences, and Céspedes finally put Agramonte in command of the insurgent forces in Camagüey, where he developed into an exceptional military leader, quickly becoming the soul of the rebellion. After Agramonte was killed by a stray bullet while deploying his troops, his body fell into the hands of the Spaniards, who took it to the city of Camagüey, where they put it on display. Later the body was cremated, and Agramonte's ashes were scattered to the wind.

There are no English sources available on Agramonte. See CARLOS MÁRQUEZ STERLING, *Ignacio Agramonte, el Bayardo de la revolución cubana* (1936); and JUAN J. E. CASASÚS, *Vida militar de Agramonte* (1981).

JOSÉ M. HERNÁNDEZ

**AGRARIAN REFORM.** From the Spanish conquest to the late twentieth century, private and governmental institutions have tried to institute agrarian reform in Latin America. The extent to which calls for agrarian reform have been voiced over the past 500 years is perhaps the best evidence of the failure of all reform efforts, with a few notable exceptions. While pressures on the land in Latin America have been no greater than in other regions of the world, the fact that such a large proportion of the population still derives all or part of its subsistence from the land has pushed the issue of agrarian reform to the forefront throughout the region. The United States, for example, has its own history of forcibly evicting its indigenous and small farming population from the land. Yet the consequences of consolidating increasing amounts of arable land into fewer and fewer hands has not had the same result as in Latin America, because unlike Latin America the U.S. economy, for the most part, has been able to provide employment to those evicted. In Latin America, however, the eviction of peasants has only swelled the ranks of the unemployed in urban centers. It is for this reason that throughout the history of Latin America, various political movements have called for agrarian reform.

The first efforts at agrarian reform were carried out almost as soon as the Spanish established their empire in the New World. The first land grabs of the Spanish conquistadors in the Caribbean led to the virtual extinction of the Indian population and the monopolization of land by the conquistadors. This in turn resulted in the emergence of LATIFUNDIA (the concentration of large tracts of land in the hands of a few Spanish landlords) and *minifundia* (the division of the remaining lands among peasants into parcels not large enough to provide subsistence), which ultimately led the Spanish crown to introduce land reform. The NEW LAWS OF 1542 abolished the *encomienda,* recognized the autonomy of the Indian community, and prohibited Spaniards from occupying the Indian lands or living in Indian villages. Encroachments on Indian lands, however, continued throughout the colonial period, and in the eighteenth century the BOURBON REFORMS sought once again to enforce agrarian reform. In Brazil, the Portuguese crown grants, *sesmarias,* were extended to a few privileged settlers who dominated the good coastal lands for sugar production. As in Spanish America, colonial Brazil set the pattern of *latifundia* for the few and *minifundia* for the many.

After independence from Spain, most Latin American governments embarked on classical liberal notions of agrarian reform, which argued that Indians and Latino peasants would be better off if all farmers owned their own individual parcels of land and were free to partition and sell it according to the dictates of the free market. Under this formula, lands traditionally controlled by the corporate Indian community were often divided up and sold, only intensifying the earlier trend of land concentration. Throughout Latin America during the latter half of the nineteenth century, land was concentrated in this way as Latin American countries advanced fully into capitalist market relations. In Mexico, for example, both Benito JUÁREZ and Porfirio DÍAZ oversaw and approved of the concentration of land by the Mexican upper class and foreign interests as the correct, free-market road to economic advancement. This model was followed in other Latin American countries to varying degrees. In Brazil the government ceased granting lands in *sesmarias* in the mid-nineteenth century and sought instead to sell lands through the General Bureau of Public Lands, established in 1854. This resulted in further concentration of ownership.

Land concentration, however, led to landlessness and rural unemployment for many Latin American peasants, which in turn led to political unrest. The Mexican Revolution of 1910 was in part a response to the free-market policies so cherished by Porfirio Díaz and his CIENTÍFICOS. The monopolistic control of huge tracts of land, as well as foreign ownership of the mineral resources, mobilized millions to demand a nationalist strategy for land distribution. In the wake of the MEXICAN REVOLUTION, agrarian reform was written into the Constitution of 1917. Encompassed in the EJIDO program, the Mexican government sought to redistribute lands to the small- and medium-sized peasant farms. In practice the goals of the *ejido* program were never fully realized. At its peak, during the rule of Lázaro CÁRDENAS (1934–1940), substantial redistribution of land was carried out, so that the proportion of landless peasants went down from 68 percent of the rural population in 1930 to 36 percent in 1940. After 1940, however, landlessness among rural dwellers steadily increased at the same time that the land became concentrated more and more in the hands of private large landowners. Technological advances only widened the gap between large landowners and *ejidatarios,* since the former had more capital to purchase advanced machinery, seeds, and fertilizer. In Brazil, which had no agrarian reform comparable to Mexico's *ejido* program, pressures on land were released by expansion westward into Brazil's vast interior. Brazilian strongman Getúlio VARGAS (1930–1945, 1950–1954) encouraged westward expansion, since only 4 percent of Brazil's land was under cultivation as late as 1945. The opening up of western land helped reduce land concentration somewhat and vastly increased the number of farms.

Other Latin American countries experienced similar opposition to the concentration of land in the hands of the wealthy and growing problems of landlessness among the rural poor. In Central America, elite control of arable land caused widespread unrest. In El Salvador, for example, where in the early 1990s virtually all of the prime farmland was controlled by the elites and where over 70 percent of the peasants had no land at all, decades of conflict between peasants and large landowners over land control and distribution have yet to end. The *matanza* (slaughter) of the 1930s, in which an estimated 30,000 Salvadoran peasants were killed, was due largely to struggles between peasants and the elite over the land. In the 1980s further conflicts over land resulted in the estimated deaths of over seventy thousand, most of them peasants and small farmers. And while a truce was reached in 1992, the pressures on land promised to give rise to even more fighting. In Brazil, President João GOULART's call for the immediate expropriation of all large and medium landholdings adjacent

Nicaraguan campesino family. JIM WHITMER / STOCK, BOSTON.

to highways, rail lines, and public projects as a beginning to agrarian reform was one reason that the Brazilian middle class and military backed his overthrow in 1964 and replacement with a military dictatorship.

Efforts to legislate agrarian reform have proved unsuccessful, and in Latin America it has usually been forced through by revolutionary upheavals, as was the case in Mexico. In the Bolivian Revolution of 1952, peasants mobilized and expropriated farmlands while workers seized control of the mines. In both Cuba and Nicaragua, agrarian reform was achieved only after prolonged revolutionary struggles. On the other hand, in Peru a left-leaning military dictatorship that came to power in 1968 oversaw the breakup of farmland controlled by Peru's traditional landed elites. Yet while agrarian reform in Peru resulted in the diminished power of the traditional landed oligarchies, it did not benefit the majority of the peasant class. Despite promises, Peru's peasants still lacked access to arable lands in the 1990s. This had two negative consequences: malnourishment still plagued one-quarter of Peru's population and a greater part of its peasant population, and landlessness gave revolutionary organizations such as the Shining Path a base of support among many of Peru's peasants. As a result of increased government repression (over thirty thousand had died in Peru's civil war by 1994), Shining Path was weakened but not defeated by 1995. In Brazil, pressures on land led to open conflict in the countryside, and the 1994 Workers' Party candidate for president, Luis Inácio da SILVA, or Lula, called for a radical redistribution of land. Despite Lula's defeat in the election, calls for land redistribution had strong support among Brazil's poor. In Mexico, efforts to end the *ejido* program written into the 1917 Constitution were one stated reason for a guerrilla uprising in the southern state of CHIAPAS on 1 January 1994. As of November 1994, Zapatista guerrillas still held isolated

positions in Chiapas in hopes of pressuring the government to institute agrarian reform.

In two Latin American countries agrarian reform advanced further than elsewhere. In the wake of both the Cuban and Nicaraguan revolutions, radical land reform was carried out with mixed results. In Cuba the large sugar and tobacco *fincas* were taken over by the revolutionary Cuban government, while only the smallest landholdings were left in the hands of individual owners. Programs of education, health, and housing, however, transformed the Cuban countryside, and to this day the regime of Fidel CASTRO enjoys considerable support among Cuba's rural workers. Cuba's state-run agricultural industries, however, were noted for their waste and inefficiency in both production and distribution. To stimulate the agricultural sector, the Castro government periodically (most recently in 1994) allowed for independent farming and market sales of goods produced by private farmers. In the past this policy has resulted in more efficient production and better distribution of agricultural commodities, but the downside, for the Cuban government, is that independent farmers and merchants who accumulate land and capital are considered a threat to the Cuban government's state-run economy. With the end of Soviet aid and the severe crisis in the economy, the Cuban government was forced to allow independent small farming and farmer's markets, both of which could strengthen the small business class in Cuba, which in turn could represent a real threat to Castro's rule.

After the revolution of 1979 in Nicaragua, the Sandinistas expropriated lands owned by the Somoza family and its supporters. These lands were converted into collective farms, as were much of Nicaragua's previously uncultivated lands. This program aroused resentments among Nicaraguan peasants, who supported the revolution in hopes of receiving their own parcels of land. In response to a growing guerrilla movement in the countryside, the Sandinistas enacted one of the most comprehensive land reforms in Latin America. Beginning in the mid-1980s collectivization was deemphasized and peasants were granted individual tracts of land. To prevent latifundization the Sandinista government denied landholders the right to sell or divide up their land, thereby ensuring that land given to peasants would not later be sold off to large landowners. With the defeat of the Sandinistas in the 1990 elections, however, efforts have been revived to return expropriated lands to their former owners. Despite its political popularity, Sandinista land reform was unable to revive Nicaragua's agricultural sector. A ten-year civil war and a vigorous embargo by the United States ensured that Nicaragua's economy, including its agricultural industry, would stagnate throughout the 1980s. While land redistribution won the support of many peasants, it also angered urban dwellers, who suffered through constant scarcity of basic goods. After the elections of 1990, the conservative-dominated Nicaraguan legislature voted to turn back virtually all of the land reforms enacted by the Sandinistas during their rule.

ANDREW G. FRANK, *Capitalism and Underdevelopment in Latin America* (1969); CELSO FURTADO, *Economic Development of Latin America: A Survey from Colonial Times to Fidel Castro,* translated by Suzette Macedo (1970); FERNANDO HENRIQUE CARDOSO, "Dependency and Development in Latin America," in *New Left Review* 74 (1972): 83–95; RODOLFO STAVENHAGEN, *Social Classes in Agrarian Societies,* translated by Judy Adler Hellman (1975); Alain De Janvry, *The Agrarian Question and Reformism in Latin America* (1981).

MICHAEL POWELSON

*See also* **Agriculture.**

**AGREGADO,** a term referring to a wide variety of dependent individuals or, literally, "retainers." In Brazil's colonial period *agregados* could be freed slaves, free servants, or poor relatives who resided with a host family of slaveowners or peasants. For peasants, *agregados* usually worked as servants or extra laborers; for slaveowners, *agregados* typically were dependent kin or the families of freed slaves. In the nineteenth century, *agregados* came to denote the following that supported a wealthy landowner in local elections. Such *agregados* received favors, such as land, in return for votes. This patron-client bond maintained the hegemony of the landowners after Brazilian independence.

ENI DE MESQUITA, "O papel do agregado na região de Itú—1780–1830," *Coleção Museu Paulista* 6 (1977): 13–121; RICHARD GRAHAM, *Patronage and Politics in Nineteenth-Century Brazil* (1990).

ALIDA C. METCALF

**AGRESTE,** a term associated with northeastern Brazil, designating a transitional zone between the coastal *zona da mata* and the interior backlands (SERTÃO). Rainfall is one aspect of this intermediary position: the *agreste* receives an annual average of 30 to 43 inches—considerably more than the arid and semiarid *sertão* but less than the humid *zona da mata.* The *agreste* first emerged during the later nineteenth century as an area characterized by polyculture and a large number of independent small holders. This zone traditionally has served as a refuge during times of drought and as a commercial intermediary between the backlands and the coast.

KEMPTON EVANS WEBB, *The Changing Face of Northeast Brazil* (1974); MANUEL CORREIA DE ANDRADE, *The Land and People of Northeast Brazil,* translated by Dennis V. Johnson (1980).

GERALD MICHAEL GREENFIELD

**AGRICULTURE.** In 1994 agriculture was the primary occupation of just under one-third of all working Latin Americans. Because of rapid urbanization since the mid-1950s, the percentage of the Latin American labor force engaged in agriculture has steadily declined. Despite this, the agricultural sector still employs more people than any other single industry. In addition, agricultural products (including livestock) still constitute the major export commodity for more than half of all Latin American countries, making agriculture arguably the most important Latin American industry.

Historically agriculture has defined Latin American economies and social relations. For most of the history of the region, the vast majority of Latin Americans have been a part of the agricultural sector. Latin American agriculture can be divided into four distinct types that roughly correspond to historical phases: (1) pre-Columbian indigenous agriculture, (2) semi-feudal hacienda agriculture, (3) precapitalist plantation agriculture, and (4) modern commercial agriculture.

PRE-COLUMBIAN INDIGENOUS AGRICULTURE
According to recent data, seed cultivation appears to have begun in Mesoamerica by 7000 B.C. The first domesticated plants were probably avocados and CHILI peppers. Corn, or MAIZE, became a major food source in Mesoamerica and in South America between 3000 B.C. and 2000 B.C. Finally a kind of village life centered around the cultivation of corn appeared by 2000 B.C., and was well-established in Mesoamerica by 1200 B.C. The development of farming—a lengthy process of some five thousand years—is sometimes referred to as the "agricultural revolution."

The "triad" of Mesoamerican agriculture—corn, beans, and squash—developed from these beginnings and provided a nutritionally balanced diet for many pre-Columbian peoples. In addition to these basic staples, many other plant crops, combined with small game, and fish in coastal regions, eventually made up the New World diet. Most important among the other plant crops were POTATOES, tomatoes, chili peppers, fruits, and MANIOC (cassava), a potato-like root high in starch and calories. Prior to European contact, native Americans had very few domesticated animals. They raised small hairless dogs and turkeys, and in the Andean regions they cultivated guinea pigs. All of these traditional foods are still part of the Latin American diet, and many of them have become standard Old World fare as well.

The most common farming technique in early agriculture was "slash and burn" or *milpa* agriculture. Land was completely cleared of all vegetation and seeds were planted. Because of the harsh effects of the sun and rain in tropical and semitropical climates, the soil was generally exhausted within one or two years. This forced the early farmers to move about continually to find new land. During these early stages agriculture was unable to support large populations in one fixed place over a long period of time. Consequently, farmers eventually developed methods of agricultural preservation and expansion. The development of irrigation systems is considered to be the second phase in the agricultural "revolution" of the Americas.

IRRIGATION, through terracing in highland regions, the construction of ridged fields, and the establishment of CHINAMPAS (floating gardens in shallow lakes) allowed the same piece of land to support more and more people. This in turn permitted population growth, and with it the beginnings of political organization and social stratification. Enhanced agricultural methods thus led eventually to the highly advanced Maya, Aztec, and Inca civilizations encountered by the Spanish.

## FEUDAL HACIENDA AGRICULTURE

When the Spanish and Portuguese arrived in the Americas in the late fifteenth century, they radically changed the economic, social, and physical landscape. In addition to precipitating a disastrous decline of the indigenous population, the newcomers also had a drastic effect on the vegetation of the New World by their introduction of European plants and livestock.

Old World grains, fruits, and vegetables such as wheat, barley, oranges, lemons, pears, chick-peas, onions, and salad greens were brought in by the first Spanish settlers. Europeans also introduced tropical products from the Canary Islands, such as SUGARCANE and BANANAS, to the New World. The most significant ecological change, however, was the introduction of LIVESTOCK. Cows, horses, sheep, goats, pigs, and donkeys reproduced with amazing rapidity, and within a century there were more European animals in the New World than there were indigenous people. This livestock, particularly cattle, required large tracts of land, much of which had previously been used for the cultivation of traditional crops by indigenous people. Thus the introduction of European agriculture signified the first shift of land away from indigenous farmers and their traditional farming techniques.

In order to exploit indigenous labor for both mining and agriculture, the Spanish crown instituted the ENCOMIENDA system. This arrangement distributed indigenous peoples (and their land) to Spanish settlers (*encomenderos*), who in exchange for free use of their labor were legally obligated to protect the natives and train them in the Christian faith. Because of the abuses committed by the *encomenderos,* and the subsequent decline in the indigenous population (individuals were literally worked to death in many cases), the *encomienda* system was outlawed in 1542 and officially abolished in 1549; however, it was replaced by other systems of forced labor which were equally brutal, and often not as closely supervised as the *encomienda* system had been.

By the beginning of the seventeenth century, a semifeudal system of great estates, called HACIENDAS, came to dominate the Spanish American landscape. Haciendas (FAZENDAS in Brazil) were mixed ranches on which both farming and livestock raising were conducted, and they were worked by resident peons, usually of mestizo (mixed) ancestry, who through a combination of tribute laws, forced labor laws, and hereditary debt were confined to their hacienda in a system of virtual vassalage.

In the feudal tradition, labor was performed in exchange for use of a plot of land or in-kind payments of food, and economic efficiency was not a priority. Haciendas were the major food source of the newly emerging urban areas they surrounded, and they produced both European and traditional crops and livestock.

## PLANTATION AGRICULTURE

In addition to the primarily feudal system of the haciendas, great PLANTATIONS which produced agricultural commodities for a European market also developed during the colonial period. These large plantations, generally thought of as a precapitalist phenomenon, usually produced with greater economic efficiency than did haciendas. They became increasingly dependent upon African slaves for labor as the Indian population declined and withdrew into isolation.

Plantations produced a wide variety of export products, among which were INDIGO, a blue plant dye, and COCHINEAL, a red dye from an insect that breeds in the nopal cactus. Also exported from American plantations were agricultural commodities such as CACAO (the basic ingredient of chocolate), TOBACCO, COFFEE, and sugarcane. Sugar was the most profitable and widespread of the early plantation products.

Sugarcane was introduced onto American soil by Christopher Columbus on his second voyage in 1493. Sugar requires very large tracts of flat land and many laborers for profitable cultivation, and subtantial outlays of capital for refining. Thus it has historically been associated with very wealthy men, including Hernán Cortés, the conqueror of Mexico, who was one of the first sugar planters in the New World. The Portuguese colony of Brazil became the world's leading sugar producer by the late sixteenth century. Portugal had already developed sugar in its African colonies, and the Portuguese imported massive numbers of African slaves to work the Brazilian plantations. Eventually sugar became intimately connected with the African slave trade.

It is important to keep in mind that hacienda agriculture and plantation agriculture are not mutually exclusive terms and do not necessarily refer to mutually exclusive farming operations. Most agricultural estates in Latin America combined elements of both feudalism and capitalism. Hacienda and plantation agriculture, combined with the remnants of traditional (subsistence) agriculture, defined the agricultural landscape throughout the colonial period and well into the nineteenth century.

## MODERN COMMERCIAL AGRICULTURE

Independence from Spain and Portugal in the early nineteenth century brought few immediate changes to the social, economic, and physical landscape of Latin America. However, by the late nineteenth century, with liberal-positivist dictators in power in most of Latin America, the consolidation of huge tracts of land called

*Coffee.* Oil on canvas by Cândido Portinari. MUSEU NACIONAL DE BELAS ARTES, RIO DE JANEIRO; PHOTO BY J. S. RANGEL.

*latifundios* began in an attempt to develop export agriculture to its fullest advantage. Although the LATIFUNDIA system was seen as being key to the economic development of the region, economic inefficiency usually characterized these estates. Often only a small portion of the land was actually cultivated. Landowners consolidated enormous holdings primarily as a means of controlling the rural labor force.

During the late nineteenth and early twentieth centuries, land was frequently stolen from small farmers who were producing for a local market or for basic subsistence. This transfer of land forced many formerly self-sufficient peasants onto latifundios for lack of other alternatives. This was in many ways a logical strategy for large landholders in countries which were ''land rich'' and ''labor poor.'' Despite substantial growth in export earnings, ''progress'' was purchased at very great social cost. The historian E. Bradford Burns has referred to this phenomenon as ''the poverty of progress,'' because growth in the export sector was achieved with a drastic decline in food production for local consumption. This trend greatly impoverished the masses of Latin America, and more often than not the feudal relationship between peasant and landowner was maintained through a series of new forced labor laws and systems of DEBT PEONAGE.

In addition, the tendency during this period was for governments to encourage production of only one, or at the most two, commodities. This dependence on one export commodity for economic viability is called monoculture. Many Latin American countries developed monoculture economies during this period—often being dependent on one crop for more than 50 percent of their gross national product. This situation, which persists into the present, makes a country's economy, and thus its population, much more vulnerable to international market conditions.

The coffee industry grew at an enormous rate during the Liberal period and became a monoculture in Central America, Colombia, and Brazil. Also important after the mid-nineteenth century were WHEAT and cattle HIDES in Argentina and Paraguay, and HENEQUEN and COTTON in Mexico. The FRUIT INDUSTRY in the Caribbean islands, Central America, Colombia, Venezuela, Ecuador, and Brazil began to grow in economic importance in the early twentieth century. Improvements in ocean transportation allowed a wide variety of fruits to be exported, of which bananas were most important.

Often the development of these industries required new outlays of capital for modernization (particularly true for the sugar refining process) and for improved transportation facilities and infrastructure. Many U.S.

and European companies made investments in Latin American agriculture. The United States was most heavily involved in the sugar and fruit industries of the Caribbean Basin (Central America, the Caribbean, and the coasts of Venezuela and Colombia), and by the mid-twentieth century U.S. companies owned substantial shares in the agro-industry of the region.

Also by the mid-twentieth century, the impoverished peasant sector began to react to the high social costs of modernization. Improvements in rural health care decreased infant mortality and sparked rapid population growth, leading to rural unemployment. At the same time new industrialization schemes provided the hope of urban employment. These factors, combined with the exploitative conditions of the countryside, prompted massive rural-to-urban migration.

Other peasants mobilized politically to demand AGRARIAN REFORM and economic and social justice. Agrarian reform involves the transfer of land (particularly uncultivated land) from the latifundio, to small and medium-sized holdings. "Economic and social justice" simply refers to a decent standard of living and freedom from political repression, fear, and exploitation. Because of the inequitable circumstances in rural Latin America, the countryside became the setting for revolutionary movements, notably in Cuba and Nicaragua. But the demands of peasants have faced stiff political and economic opposition in most of Latin America, and where agrarian reform has been attempted, it has not alleviated rural poverty to any significant degree. The unwillingness of Latin American landholding elites to allow meaningful agrarian reform is the root of much of the political unrest in Latin America today.

Largely as a response to the Cuban Revolution, the United States through its AGENCY FOR INTERNATIONAL DEVELOPMENT (USAID) promoted rural development and reform in the 1960s and 1970s. Latin American investors were encouraged to diversify their agricultural base in an attempt to decrease the tendency toward monoculture, and peasants were encouraged to organize both producer and consumer cooperatives. In politically turbulent regions such as Central America, loans were made available for local entrepreneurs who were interested in nontraditional export crops such as cattle, cotton, cacao, flowers, lumber, and shrimp. In the long run, this development scheme had a negative effect on rural equity and social unrest because more land was transferred from small producers to larger landholders. Again, as during the Liberal period, many perceived that this land was literally stolen from peasants. In addition, many of the crops that were encouraged by the USAID were capital intensive and did not require a large labor force. Thus their expansion did not create new employment opportunities in rural areas. At the same time members of peasant cooperatives were often suspected of having communist sympathies, and consequently were persecuted by reactionary military regimes.

Contemporary Latin American agriculture combines

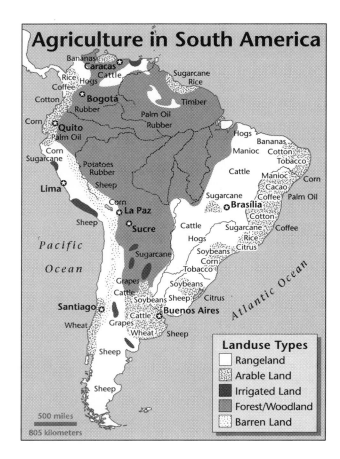

elements of pre-Columbian, hacienda, plantation, and modern commercial agriculture. Many Latin American peasants still farm the traditional *milpa* of corn, especially in highland regions which are not suitable for commercial crops. Since the 1960s, however, it has become increasingly difficult for peasant families to subsist in traditional agricultural communities. Consequently, many peasants have been forced into seasonal migration. Typically they work part of the year on their own subsistence plot—growing traditional products such as corn, beans, and squash—and for the remainder of the year they hire themselves out as temporary laborers on large commercial plantations. The feudal social relationships, as well as the economic inefficiency of the hacienda, still persist in many countries, and the modern commercial plantation is clearly the descendant of the colonial plantation.

RODOLFO STAVENHAGEN, ed., *Agrarian Problems and Peasant Movements in Latin America* (1970); ALFRED W. CROSBY, JR., *The Columbian Exchange: Biological and Cultural Consequences of 1492*, 3d ed. (1976); ROGER BURBACH and PATRICIA FLYNN, *Agribusiness in the Americas* (1980); E. BRADFORD BURNS, *The Poverty of Progress: Latin America in the Nineteenth Century* (1980); ALAIN DE JANVRY, *The Agrarian Question and Reformism in Latin America* (1981); MURIEL PORTER WEAVER, *The Aztecs, Maya, and Their Predecessors: Archaeology of Mesoamerica*, 2d ed. (1981); ROBERT WILLIAMS, *Export Agriculture and the Crisis in Central America*

(1986); JOHN SUPER, *Food, Conquest, and Colonization in Sixteenth-Century Spanish America* (1986); H. J. VIOLA and CAROLYN J. MARGOLIS, eds., *Seeds of Change: a Quincentennial Commemoration*, (1991).

RACHEL A. MAY

**AGUARDIENTE DE PISCO,** a grape brandy distilled in several Pacific Coast valleys of Andean South America. Made from grapes of quality too poor for wine, the brandy was developed by seventeenth-century planters. Distillation resulted in a clear brandy with a sweetish flavor and strong aftertaste, which, along with its alcohol content, made it a popular beverage for festive occasions. It combined well with fruits, and lime quickly became the favorite. Historians are uncertain why the brandy was labeled *pisco*. Local legend holds that Pisco Valley (Peru) landowners turned to distillation of grapes for brandy because they failed at making wine, thus giving *aguardiente de Pisco* a lead for brand recognition. For a time wine and brandy were both made in the Pisco region, but after Chilean wines captured foreign markets in the early nineteenth century, vineyard owners turned solely to brandy. Thereafter distilling *aguardiente de Pisco* moved to the upriver Pisco plantations, where cotton cultivation did not prevail. Shipped on muleback in teardrop-shaped clay casks, corked at the spherical end, it soon reached markets throughout Peru. Many travelers remarked favorably on the drink, and numerous popular legends arose regarding the proper way to imbibe it and its aftereffects. *Pisco* has become an item in the tourist trade and the foreign market only to the degree that the "*pisco* sour," a frothy blend of *pisco*, egg white, lime juice, and salt, has achieved popularity as an exotic drink.

NICHOLAS P. CUSHNER, *Lord of the Land: Sugar, Wine, and Jesuit Estates of Coastal Peru, 1600–1767* (1980), pp. 126–128; VINCENT PELOSO, "Succulence and Sustenance: Region, Class, and Diet in Nineteenth-Century Peru," in *Food, Politics, and Society in Latin America*, edited by John C. Super and Thomas C. Wright (1985), pp. 45–64.

VINCENT PELOSO

**AGUASCALIENTES, CONVENTION OF** (10 October–10 November 1914), a gathering of the military participants in the MEXICAN REVOLUTION after the defeat of Victoriano Huerta. It originated in a meeting called by Venustiano CARRANZA on 1 October 1914 in Mexico City, but after moving to the Teatro Morelos in Aguascalientes ten days later, it quickly developed a momentum of its own that departed from Carranza's objectives.

Few major military leaders attended as delegates, the principal exception being General Álvaro OBREGÓN. General Francisco VILLA attended long enough to sign the flag displayed on the podium, but left negotiations to his representatives, principally Roque González Garza. The Zapatistas, supporters of Emiliano ZAPATA, did not send delegates until another of Villa's representatives, General Felippe ÁNGELES, invited them to come. After their arrival on 26 October, the combined representatives of Villa and Zapa were able to dominate the deliberations of the convention. In an attempt to reconcile all factions, on 2 November, the convention voted to ask for the resignations of both Villa and Carranza and to name a new provisional president. Carranza then disavowed the convention, though Villa himself never resigned. General Eulalio GUTIÉRREZ took the provisional presidency. Within the week, most delegates loyal to Carranza, including Obregón, had left Aguascalientes.

A few weeks later, fighting broke out again between Carranza's followers, still designated as Constitutionalists, and the troops and supporters of Villa and Zapata, who took the name of Conventionists. Although the Zapatista forces did not remain allied with the Villistas for long, the failure of the Aguascalientes Convention led to the most bloody phase of the Revolution as generals Obregón and Villa led the forces of the two factions in battle during most of 1915. The Constitutionalists ultimately triumphed, with Villa's forces reduced to guerrilla activity by the end of December 1915.

ROBERT E. QUIRK, *The Mexican Revolution, 1914–1915: The Convention of Aguascalientes* (1960); LUIS FERNANDO AMAYA, *La soberana convención revolucionaria, 1914–1916* (1966); LINDA B. HALL, *Alvaro Obregón: Power and Revolution in Mexico, 1911–1920* (1981), pp. 76–94.

LINDA B. HALL

**AGUAYO, MARQUÉS DE** (marqués de San Miguel de Aguayo y Santa Olalla; *b.* ca. 1677; *d.* 9 March 1734), rancher, military governor of COAHUILA and Texas. Born in Spain to a landed family of Aragon, Aguayo married Ignacia Xaviera Echeverz Subiza y Valdés, heiress to the marquisate of San Miguel de Aguayo, through whom he acquired his title. In 1712 the couple moved to Coahuila, where Aguayo took over the administration of the family estates, increasing holdings by over 3 million acres by the time of his death.

Aguayo served as governor of Coahuila and Texas from 1719 to 1722. In 1716 he had provided livestock to the Domingo Ramón expedition, which established the permanent occupation of Texas. Three years later, in response to a French attack on the Spanish in east Texas, Aguayo offered to mount an expedition to drive the French out. Receiving a viceregal commission to raise five hundred men, he proceeded in 1720 to San Antonio and then to Los Adaes (present-day Robeline, La.), where he restored the abandoned presidio and missions. He also founded Presidio de los Texas, near present-day NACOGDOCHES, and Presidio Bahía del Espíritu Santo (now Goliad, Texas). Soon after his return to Coahuila, Aguayo resigned the governorship, citing poor health. PHILIP V rewarded Aguayo for his services in Texas by naming him field marshal in 1724.

ELEANOR CLAIRE BUCKLEY, "The Aguayo Expedition into Texas and Louisiana, 1719–1722," in *The Quarterly of the Texas State Historical Association* 15, no. 1 (July 1911): 1–65; VITO ALESSIO ROBLES, *Coahuila y Texas en la época colonial*, 2d ed. (1978); CHARLES H. HARRIS III, *A Mexican Family Empire: The Latifundio of the Sánchez Navarros, 1765–1867* (1975).

JESÚS F. DE LA TEJA

**AGÜERO ROCHA, FERNANDO** (*b.* 1918), Nicaraguan Conservative Party leader (1960–1972). Agüero assumed the leadership of a revived Conservative Party in 1960. The party's platform not only was anti-Somoza but also favored a "democratic revolution." Agüero stressed the need for economic and social reforms to prevent a Communist takeover in response to Somoza's entrenchment. In early 1963 he announced that the Conservative Party would boycott the forthcoming elections because the Somozas controlled the election machinery. True to Agüero's accusations, René SCHICK GUTIÉRREZ, the Somoza's handpicked successor, won the presidency.

In the presidential election of 1967, Anastasio SOMOZA DEBAYLE was a candidate himself. The opposition, consisting of Conservatives, Independent Liberals, and Christian Democrats, formed the National Opposition Union, (UNO) and coalesced behind their candidate Agüero. Somoza won by a three-to-one margin, prompting Agüero to charge Somoza with election fraud, claiming that ballot boxes were seized from Granada (an opposition center) and that intimidation at the polls and violation of voting secrecy were commonplace.

The unrest and scandal stemming from Somoza's election led to elaborate plans for his cession of the presidency without relinquishing his power. In 1971, the Kupia-Kumi Pact, arranged between Liberals and Conservatives, provided that Somoza would step down in favor of a three-man junta, comprised of two Liberals and one Conservative. Agüero joined the junta, calling the pact a "national solution," although he still opposed Somoza. The junta, commonly referred to as "The Three Little Pigs," split the opposition. Somoza controlled the junta and the National Guard; thus, the junta wielded no real authority. This lack of power was seen clearly in the aftermath of the 1972 earthquake, when Somoza appointed himself head of a national emergency council with special powers.

Agüero opposed Somoza's rule by decree, so Somoza removed him from the junta. By this time, Agüero had lost the popular backing of students and had been removed as Conservative Party leader anyway. In addition, Agüero's cooperation with Somoza resulted in the alienation and disillusionment of younger Conservatives and others, thereby splintering the Conservatives.

BERNARD DIEDERICH, *Somoza and the Legacy of U.S. Involvement in Central America* (1982); WALTER LA FEBER, *Inevitable Revolutions: The United States in Central America* (1984), esp. p. 163; JOHN A. BOOTH, *The End and the Beginning: The Nicaraguan Revolution*, 2d ed. (1985).

SHANNON BELLAMY

*See also* **Nicaragua: Political Parties.**

**AGÜEYBANA II** (*d.* 1511), nephew of Agüeybana I and next in line to rule the political confederacy of Boriquén (Puerto Rico) when the Spaniards took over the island in 1508. Agüeybana was of the Taino culture. Given in *encomienda* to the settler Cristóbal de Sotomayor, Agüeybana II led a revolt against the Spaniards in 1511. He succeeded in destroying their settlement and killing Sotomayor, but also lost his own life in the struggle to defeat the Spaniards.

Information on Agüeybana II appears in most history books on Puerto Rico as well as in CESARIO ROSA NIEVES and ESTHER MELÓN, *Biografías Puertorriqueñas: Perfil histórico de un pueblo* (1970).

OLGA JIMÉNEZ DE WAGENHEIM

**AGUIAR, ADONIAS** (Adonias Filho; Aguiar Filho; Adonias; *b.* 27 November 1915; *d.* 4 August 1990), Brazilian novelist. Set largely in the author's native state of Bahia, Adonias Filho's fiction blends the social themes of the regionalist novel of the 1930s and early 1940s with the existential and metaphysical concerns of the psychological novel that began to emerge at the same time. Such works as *Memórias de Lázaro* (1952), *Corpo vivo* (1962), and *O forte* (1965) juxtapose multiple levels of time and space in a dense, poetic, elliptical style, creating a dreamy atmosphere in which human beings fulfill their frequently tragic destinies.

THOMAS DEVENY, "Narrative Techniques in Adonias Filho's *Memórias de Lázaro*," in *Hispania* 63, no. 2 (1980): 321–327; FRED P. ELLISON, "The Schizophrenic Narrator and the Myth of Renewal in *Memórias de Lázaro*," in *From Linguistics to Literature: Romance Studies Offered to Francis M. Rogers* (1981).

RANDAL JOHNSON

**AGUILAR, JERÓNIMO DE** (*b.* ca. 1490; *d.* 1531), colonist and translator. Born in Écija, Spain, Aguilar was aboard a ship proceeding from Darién to Santo Domingo in 1511. When it struck shoals off Jamaica, he was among twenty men who escaped in a longboat that drifted to the east coast of the Yucatán Peninsula. The local cacique soon sacrificed thirteen of the men, but seven, including Aguilar, escaped into the territory of another ruler, who maintained them as servants. When Cortés's expedition arrived in 1519, Aguilar was one of only two Spaniards still surviving; the other chose to remain among the MAYAS. Aguilar, fluent in Spanish and Maya, proved invaluable as a translator for CORTÉS. Unable to speak NAHUATL, the language of the Aztecs, he teamed up with Cortés's mistress Doña Marina (MALINCHE), who spoke Nahuatl and Maya, to translate from Nahuatl to Spanish once the expedition reached the Aztec Empire. Rewarded with an ENCOMIENDA after the Conquest, Aguilar died without marrying.

ROBERT HIMMERICH Y VALENCIA, *The Encomenderos of New Spain, 1521–1555* (1991); HUGH THOMAS, *The Conquest of Mexico* (1993).

JOHN E. KICZA

**AGUILAR, MARTÍN DE** (*d.* January 1603), Spanish mariner, explorer of the Californias. Aguilar began his career of exploration as a sailor on the expedition of Sebastián VIZCAÍNO in the Gulf of California (June–November 1596). Subsequently he was an ensign on Vizcaíno's voyage that charted the coast of the Californias in 1602–1603. Next he served on the frigate *Tres Reyes,* the crew of which explored, made soundings, and obtained provisions along the coast to Monterey. From 17 December 1602 to 3 January 1603 he provisioned the *Tres Reyes,* which sailed north from Monterey. Separated from the flagship *San Diego* north of Point Reyes on 5 January, the *Santo Tomás* was forced beyond Cabo Blanco, Oregon. Aguilar discovered a large, raging river thought to be the Strait of Anián.

Aguilar and his pilot, Antonio Flores, died at sea; the pilot's aide, Esteban López, returned to Navidad, Jalisco, on 28 February 1603. The torrential river, first named the Santa Inés, was subsequently named the Martín de Aguilar (and was also known as the Antón Flores).

W. MICHAEL MATHES, ed., *Californiana I: Documentos para la historia de la demarcación comercial de California, 1583–1632* (1965); and *Vizcaíno and Spanish Expansion in the Pacific Ocean, 1580–1630* (1968).

W. MICHAEL MATHES

*See also* **Explorers and Exploration.**

**AGUILAR, ROSARIO FIALLOS DE** (*b.* 29 January 1938), Nicaraguan novelist. Born in León, Nicaragua, Aguilar has lived her entire life in the same city except for her studies in the United States (1955–1956) and a brief period in Costa Rica during the turmoil of the Sandinista revolution. Her first novel, *Primavera sonámbula* (1964), is the story of a young woman tottering between sanity and insanity. *Aquel mar sin fondo ni playa* (1974) tells the haunting story of a stepmother's guilt and her rejection of a severely retarded child. *Siete relatos sobre el amor y la guerra* (1986) is a collection of stories linked thematically by the Sandinista fight to oust the dictatorship of Anastasio Somoza. Her 1992 novel, *La niña blanca y los pájaros sin pies,* re-creates the lost female voices of the Spanish conquest of Central America. While Aguilar denies she is a feminist writer, her novels all center around women, maternity, and the consequences of rejecting motherhood, the Latin American social imperative for women. The Latin American literary critic Raymond Souza called her "one of the best-kept secrets in contemporary Spanish American fiction."

Aguilar's fiction is treated at length by RAYMOND D. SOUZA in *La historia en la novela hispanoamericana moderna* (1988) and "Novel and Context in Costa Rica and Nicaragua," *Romance Quarterly* 33, no. 4 (1986): 453–462. See also the interview of EDWARD W. HOOD with Aguilar, "Una conversación con Rosario Aguilar," in *South Eastern Latin Americanist* 37, no. 2 (1993): 15–21.

ANN GONZÁLEZ

**AGUILAR VARGAS, CÁNDIDO** (*b.* 12 February 1888; *d.* 19 March 1960), Mexican revolutionary, Constitutional, Convention leader, and politician. From modest origins in rural Veracruz, Aguilar signed the first revolutionary program in Veracruz, the Plan of San Ricardo, in 1910. A supporter of Francisco MADERO, he became a Constitutionalist in 1913 and was governor of his home state from 1914 to 1917. He was a deputy to the Constitutional Convention of 1917, of which he was elected first vice president, a position he used to publicize progressive issues. He served as secretary of foreign relations under Venustiano CARRANZA (1918), to whom he remained loyal until 1920. Aguilar went into exile in the early 1920s, after the rebellion led by Adolfo DE LA HUERTA, but returned to political activity as a federal deputy and senator in the 1930s and 1940s. He was expelled from the Mexican Revolutionary Party in 1944 for exposing corruption. He retired from the army as a division general. He spent his last years in self-imposed exile in El Salvador and Cuba and died in Mexico.

MIGUEL A. PERAL, *Diccionario biográfico mexicano* (1944), pp. 5–6; and RODERIC A. CAMP, *Mexican Political Biographies, 1884–1934* (1991), pp. 1–2.

RODERIC AI CAMP

**AGUILERA MALTA, DEMETRIO** (*b.* 24 May 1909; *d.* 29 December 1981), Ecuadorian novelist and playwright. Hailing from the Andes mountains and the coast, respectively, Jorge ICAZA (1906–1979) and Aguilera Malta are the two best-known Ecuadorian fiction writers. The latter's fiction spans several decades, beginning with *Don Goyo* (1933) and ending forty years later with *El secuestro del general* (1973). Early on, Aguilera Malta co-published a set of short stories, *Los que se van* (1931), that focused on problems of economic and ethnic exploitation of the coastal lower classes. His other novels take up many themes, among them, problems of economic development, the CUBAN REVOLUTION, the travels of Vasco de BALBOA, and indigenous beliefs and customs. An intriguing, well-crafted novel, *Siete lunas y siete serpientes* (1970) adeptly meshes legend, witchcraft, and modern superstition with the machinations of a local, lustful political boss bent on governing with an iron hand. In this work Aguilera Malta blends magic and realism to make an ironic commentary on Ecuadorian politics. In *El secuestro del general*, Aguilera Malta uses wordplay and irony to capture the way in which the power of language can sway and subjugate people to the absolute power of dictators. Language, myth, legend, fantasy, and concepts of power are the basic ingredients of the fictional worlds of Aguilera Malta.

GERARDO LUZURIAGA, *Del realismo al expresionismo: El teatro de Aguilera Malta* (1971); ANTONIO FAMA, *Realismo mágico en la narrativa de Aguilera-Malta* (1977); CLEMENTINE CHRISTOS RABASSA, *Demetrio Aguilera-Malta and Social Justice* (1980).

DICK GERDES

**AGUIRRE, JUAN FRANCISCO DE** (*b*. 1758; *d*. 17 February 1811), Spanish colonial naval officer and major geographer of Paraguay. Born in Asturias, Spain, Aguirre was a graduate of the Spanish Royal Naval Academy. He fought in several campaigns and was commissioned a lieutenant before being sent to South America in 1784. As part of the Madrid Treaty of 1750, Spain and Portugal had decided to readjust their frontiers in the Platine basin. To prepare the way for the arrival of Spanish and Portuguese border commissioners, Aguirre was dispatched to Paraguay. He spent twelve years in the colony, mapping its rivers and assembling a vast array of information in the form of a diary.

With the one possible exception of Félix de Azara's *Viaje*, Aguirre's work constitutes the most detailed extant account of life in eighteenth-century Paraguay. Aguirre was a keen observer. He visited almost every community in that isolated quarter of the empire and made a thorough study of its people and history. Since much of the original documentation from this period has been lost, Aguirre's diary remains one of the few reliable sources available to modern scholars. He was particularly interested in Paraguayan Indians, and the ethnographic materials included in the diary fill a major gap between the works produced by early Jesuit writers and those of the modern era.

After leaving Paraguay in 1796, Aguirre went first to Buenos Aires and then back to Spain, where he finished his naval career as a captain during the Napoleonic Wars. When the French invaded Spain, Aguirre went into hiding in the province of Asturias, where he died.

JUAN FRANCISCO DE AGUIRRE, "Diario de Capitán de Fragata, in *Revista de la Biblioteca Nacional de Buenos Aires* 17–20 (1949–1951); EFRAÍM CARDOZO, *Historiografía paraguaya* (1959), pp. 435–442; JACK R. THOMAS, *Biographical Dictionary of Latin American Historians and Historiography* (1984), pp. 84–85.

THOMAS L. WHIGHAM

**AGUIRRE, JULIÁN** (*b*. 28 January 1868; *d*. 13 August 1924,), Argentine composer and pianist. Born in Buenos Aires, Aguirre spent his formative years in Spain. At fourteen, he enrolled in the Madrid Royal Conservatory, where he studied composition with Emilio Arrieta, piano with Pedro Beck, harmony with José María Aranguren, and fugue with Cató. He was awarded first prize in piano, harmony, and counterpoint. In Madrid the celebrated Spanish composer Isaac Albéniz heard his music and predicted a brilliant career for the young musician. Aguirre returned to Argentina in 1886 and made a name for himself by giving concerts around the country. He spent a year in Rosario studying and experimenting with folk music before settling in Buenos Aires, where he played an important role in the artistic and musical life of the city. His early works drew their inspiration from European styles and forms, but from 1889 on, when he joined with Alberto WILLIAMS and others to create a distinctive nationalist style, his compositions for voice and piano—especially the *tristes* for piano—are based on the folk tunes, rhythms, and harmonies of his native Argentina.

Considered one of the best Argentine composers of his generation, Aguirre was also active in the field of music education, holding administrative and academic positions (professor of harmony) at Williams Conservatory. He founded the music department of the Athenaeum of Buenos Aires (1892) and the Argentine School of Music (1916). He wrote more than sixty piano pieces, two of which, the popular *Huella* and *Gato*, were orchestrated and performed by Ernest Ansermet in 1930. The remarkable *Rapsodia criolla* for violin and piano is a seminal work in the development of an Argentine nationalist style. Aguirre's output of nearly a hundred works includes chamber pieces, voice and piano works, and numerous songs and choral works, many for children. He died in Buenos Aires.

J. F. GIACOBBE, *Julián Aguirre* (1945); RODOLFO ARIZAGA, *Enciclopedia de la música argentina* (1971); GÉRARD BÉHAGUE, *Music in Latin America* (1979); *New Grove Dictionary of Music and Musicians*, vol. 1 (1980).

SUSANA SALGADO

**AGUIRRE, LOPE DE** (*b*. 1518; *d*. 27 October 1561), self-proclaimed rebel leader of ill-fated descent of the Amazon River. Few sixteenth-century Spanish explorers have secured the notoriety of Lope de Aguirre. He was a soldier from Oñate, in the province of Guipuzcoa, Spain, who joined the Pedro de URSÚA expedition to the Amazon. Aguirre was one of the instigators of a plot to assassinate Ursúa, and at first supported Fernando de Guzmán to replace the slain Ursúa. As the group traveled against great odds downstream, discipline disintegrated, Indian carriers were abandoned, and an increasing number of men were killed in brawls. Aguirre captained Guzmán's militia, heading fifty Basque harquebusiers. Paranoid, filled with delusions of grandeur, he cowed followers and massacred Guzmán and all others suspected of disloyalty.

Challenging the authority of king and church, Aguirre argued that the land belonged to the conquerors. His unrealistic goal was to descend the Amazon, sail northwestward until he could attack Spanish authorities in Peru frontally, then assume the land's administration. Shortly after he reached the Venezuelan coast, however, royal supporters surrounded his encampment. He killed his own daughter to prevent her capture. His was one of the bloodiest and most controversial expeditions of the Age of Discovery.

JOSÉ ANTONIO DEL BUSTO DUTHURBURU, *Historia general del Perú*, vol. 2, *Descubrimiento y conquista* (1978); JOHN HEMMING, *Red Gold: The Conquest of the Brazilians* (1978).

NOBLE DAVID COOK

**AGUIRRE, NATANIEL** (*b.* 10 October 1843; *d.* 11 September 1888), Bolivian writer and politician. Born in Cochabamba, Aguirre was an important political figure during the period of the WAR OF THE PACIFIC (1879). He was a firm believer in liberal ideas and a great defender of federalism. But Aguirre's importance comes from his literary work. He is the author of plays, short stories, and a historical novel, *Juan de la Rosa: Memorias del último soldado de la Independencia* (1885), which is his most important work and is considered the national novel of Bolivia. He also wrote historical books and diverse political treatises.

*Juan de la Rosa* is the story of the uprising of COCHABAMBA between 1810 and 1812, at the beginning of the War of Independence. Its narrator and protagonist is a twelve-year-old boy who participates in the events leading to the emergence of nationalism in the future Republic of Bolivia. In this novel, Aguirre endorses the main ideas of liberalism and tries to blend them with the vital force of the MESTIZO (mixed-blooded) population, which is portrayed as the protagonist of these early battles.

PORFIRIO DÍAZ MACHICAO, *Nataniel Aguirre* (1945); WALTER NAVIA ROMERO, *Interpretación y análisis de "Juan de la Rosa"* (1966); JOSÉ ROBERTO ARZE, Prologue to *Nataniel Aguirre*, 2d ed., by Eufronio Viscarra (1969); ALBA MARÍA PAZ SOLDÁN, "Una articulación simbólica de lo nacional: *Juan de la Rosa* de Nataniel Aguirre," (Ph.D. diss., University of Pittsburgh, 1986).

LEONARDO GARCÍA PABÓN

**AGUIRRE CERDA, PEDRO** (*b.* 6 February 1879; *d.* 25 November 1941), president of Chile (1938–1941). Born to a modest family in Pocuro, a village in Aconcagua Province, Aguirre Cerda graduated from the University of Chile with degrees in pedagogy and law. A member of the Radical Party, he served in the Chamber of Deputies from 1915 to 1921 and in the Senate from 1921 to 1924. He also held ministries in the administrations of Juan Luis SANFUENTES and Arturo ALESSANDRI PALMA. He was elected president in 1938 as the candidate of the Popular Front, a coalition of the Radical, Socialist, Communist, and Democratic parties and the Chilean Labor Confederation, narrowly defeating Conservative candidate Gustavo ROSS. Rightist strength in Congress and Aguirre Cerda himself, who had parlayed law and politics into a personal fortune, assured that Chile's first government of the working and middle classes would not pursue radical objectives. Aguirre Cerda had originally opposed the Popular Front concept, which originated in Moscow as an anti-Fascist strategy; Chile's was the only Popular Front government elected in Latin America.

As president, Aguirre Cerda vetoed the efforts of his Marxist allies to unionize agricultural workers, thus preserving the overrepresentation of landowners in Congress. He faced the rebuilding of the south-central provinces in the wake of the devastating 1939 earthquake centered in Chillán. Among his major achievements were the founding of the Chilean Development Corporation (CORFO), the state agency charged with fostering industrialization, establishing the minimum wage for urban workers, reforming education, and recognizing Chilean territorial claims in Antarctica. A genuinely popular president, Aguirre Cerda died unexpectedly after less than three years in office.

JOHN REESE STEVENSON, *The Chilean Popular Front* (1942); ALBERTO CABERO, *Recuerdos de don Pedro Aguirre Cerda*, 2d ed. (1948); and ALBERTO BALTRA CORTÉS, *Pedro Aguirre Cerda* (1960).

THOMAS C. WRIGHT

*See also* **Chile: Political Parties.**

**AGUIRRE Y SALINAS, OSMÍN** (*b.* 1889; *d.* unknown), president of El Salvador (1944–1945). A career military officer, Osmín Aguirre y Salinas was a member of the junior officers' clique which deposed President Arturo ARAÚJO in December 1931, establishing military control of El Salvador. During the regime of General Maximiliano HERNÁNDEZ MARTÍNEZ he was governor of the departments of Cuzcatlán, La Paz, and Usulután and chief of staff of the National Police, rising to the rank of colonel.

His brief tenure as president was part of the tumultuous era that followed the overthrow of Hernández Martínez. Fearing the fragmentation of the nation, an army coup removed Hernández Martínez's successor, the defense minister, General Andrés I. Menéndez, from the presidency in October 1944, installing Aguirre y Salinas. The Salvadoran Supreme Court declared his tenure unconstitutional, and the United States, which considered his regime profascist, withheld recognition.

Aguirre y Salinas maintained power despite protests, conducting elections during January 1945 installed the official candidate, General Salvador CASTAÑEDA CASTRO. Aguirre y Salinas's career ended when he led an unsuccessful coup against his handpicked successor.

There are no detailed studies of this era. The only Salvadoran publications are partisan pamphlets.

KENNETH J. GRIEB

**AGUSTÍN, JOSÉ** (*b.* 19 August 1944), Mexican novelist born José Agustín Ramírez Gómez. In his novel *La tumba,* a youth-centered narrative rejecting middle-class morality and the clichés of nationalism, and celebrating pleasure and self-exploration, Agustín uses street slang to create a lively, ironic narrative voice. With its publication in 1964, Agustín (together with Gustavo SAINZ) founded the literary movement known as "La Onda." In what is perhaps his best novel to date, *Se está haciendo tarde (final en laguna)* (1973), Agustín engages in a self-critique of the potential narcissism and alienation of such individualistic quests. In *Ciudades desiertas* (1982), based on his experiences in the University of Iowa's International Writing Program, the author advocates a return to the family and monogamy and to Mexican national culture, while lampooning the sterility of life in the United States. This reconciliation is extended to the family in *Cerca del fuego* (1986), in which the author attempts to fuse anti-imperialist and Jungian discourses.

As the preeminent enfant terrible of his generation, Agustín has maintained an irreverent, independent leftist stance (from his participation in the Cuban literacy campaign to his attacks on Mexican literary mafias and censorship). His history of contemporary Mexico, *Tragicomedia mexicana 1: La vida en México de 1940 a 1970* (1990), reflects this position.

MARGO GLANTZ, "La onda diez años déspués: ¿Epitafio o revalorización?" in her *Repeticiones: Ensayos sobre literatura mexicana* (1979), pp. 115–129; JUNE C. D. CARTER and DONALD L. SCHMIDT, *José Agustín: Onda and Beyond* (1986); CYNTHIA STEELE, "Apocalypse and Patricide: *Cerca del fuego* (1986), by José Agustín," in her *Politics, Gender, and the Mexican Novel, 1968–1988: Beyond the Pyramid* (1992), pp. 110–142.

CYNTHIA STEELE

**AGUSTINI, DELMIRA** (*b.* 24 October 1886; *d.* 7 July 1914), Uruguayan poet. Born in Montevideo, Agustini was a member of the Uruguayan group of writers of 1900—together with Julio HERRERA Y REISSIG, María Eugenia Vaz Ferreira, Alberto ZUM FELDE, and Angel Falco—and an innovative voice in Spanish American poetry. During her short life she published *El libro blanco (Frágil)* (1907), *Cantos de la mañana* (1910), and *Los cálices vacíos* (The Empty Chalices, 1913). The *Obras completas,* published posthumously in 1924, includes unpublished poems possibly belonging to a projected volume entitled *Los astros del abismo* (The Stars of the Abyss), which included a group of poems entitled "El rosario de Eros." Her early poetry, published in literary magazines, was very well received and showed the influence of *Modernismo.* In her later collections, she developed a more personal style and a voice that departs steadily from the canonical modernist poetics to which she subscribed. The language and imagery of her poetry was acclaimed for its erotic nature, an important foundational feature in Spanish American feminine poetics.

Agustini lived with her parents in Montevideo and spent long periods in Buenos Aires. Although she was well known in the cultural and social life of Montevideo, she was not an active member of the intellectual groups of her epoch. In 1913 she married Enrique Job Reyes, a common man with no intellectual interests, with whom she had had a long and formal relationship. She left him after a short period and returned to her parental household for comfort.

There are several unexplained mysteries regarding Agustini's short life. She was killed by her former husband, who then killed himself. This tragic event brought to Agustini's biography considerable sensationalism, which has colored the critical studies of most literary historians. It is fair to say that her life and her poetry are characterized by contradictory features that deserve much attention.

EMIR RODRÍGUEZ MONEGAL, *Sexo y poesía en el 900 uruguayo* (1929); CLARA SILVA, *Genio y figura de Delmira Agustini* (1968); DORIS T. STEPHENS, *Delmira Agustini and the Quest for Transcendence* (1975); LUZMARÍA JIMÉNEZ FARO, *Delmira Agustini: Manantial de la brasa* (1991).

MAGDALENA GARCÍA PINTO

**AIDS.** *See* **Diseases.**

**AIZENBERG, ROBERTO** (*b.* 22 August 1928), Argentine painter and printmaker. Born in Villa Federal, province of Entre Ríos, Aizenberg studied architecture at the University of Buenos Aires, receiving a degree in 1954. He later studied painting with Juan Battle Planas. Aizenberg achieved a level of maturity quite early in life. His images relate to the subjective world of the unconscious and continue the surrealistic tradition exemplified in Argentina by Battle Planas. He received the Palanza Prize (Buenos Aires, 1967) and the Cassandra Foundation Award (Chicago, 1970).

VICENTE GESUALDO, ALDO VIGLIONE, and RODOLFO SANTOS, *Diccionario de artistas plásticos en la Argentina* (1988).

AMALIA CORTINA ARAVENA

**ALAGOAS,** a state of northeastern Brazil. Encompassing 11,031 square miles, Alagoas has a population of 2,420,400 (1990 est.), composed overwhelmingly of individuals of mixed racial descent. The capital is Maceió. Along the coast, the climate is hot and humid; in the interior, hot and dry. To the west is Paulo Alfonso Falls, once regarded as one of the world's great falls but now used for hydroelectric power so that little water passes over the falls except during the rainy season. Industrialization is proceeding slowly, but the state remains primarily an agricultural region, where cotton, sugar, rice, tobacco, beans, and other crops are raised. Industries revolve around these products, textile manufacturing and sugar refining being the most important.

Originally part of the captaincy of PERNAMBUCO, the area that is now Alagoas was occupied by the Dutch in the early 1600s. Its forests and rugged interior offered havens to QUILOMBOS (communities of runaway slaves), among the most notable of which was PALMARES. As Portuguese-Dutch conflicts disrupted plantations, Palmares burgeoned, to the point of developing its own sophisticated governing structure and even maintaining a standing army. The Palmares resisted both the Dutch and the Portuguese until concerted Portuguese efforts finally destroyed the community in 1694.

Alagoas became an independent captaincy in 1817, a province of the Brazilian Empire in 1823, and a state of the republic in 1889.

CARA SHELLY

**ALAKALUF** (also spelled Alcaluf, Alacalufe; Kaweshkar or Kaweshrar in recent usage), maritime inhabitants of the fjords, archipelagos, and canals in the Chilean region south of the peninsula of Taitao approaching the Strait of Magellan. The Alakaluf are related linguistically to the YÁMANA (Yaghanes). Scholars dispute their origins; some claim Paleolithic roots; others argue that Alakaluf are descendants of peoples arriving in 6000–5000 B.C. (the Archaic period).

Early European explorers referred to these groups as Fuegians. Alakaluf bands maintained traditional subsistence patterns of hunting, gathering, and fishing by canoe until the mid-nineteenth century, when European colonization of the region and contact with whalers hastened their demise through disease and assimilation. As of 1990 fewer than 100 Alakaluf lived in the small community of Puerto Edén on the east coast of Wellington Island in Chile.

JUNIUS BIRD, "Antiquity and Migrations of the Early Inhabitants of Patagonia," in *Geographical Review* 28 (April 1938): 250–275; RICHARD SHUTLER, JR., ed., *South America: Early Man in the New World* (1983), pp. 137–146; MUSEO CHILENO DE ARTE PRECOLOMBINO, *Hombres del sur: Aonikenk, Selknam, Yámana, Kaweshkar* (1987); OSVALDO SILVA G. *Culturas y pueblos de Chile prehispano* (1990), p. 17.

KRISTINE L. JONES

**ALAMÁN, LUCAS** (b. 18 October 1792; d. 2 June 1853), Mexican statesman and historian. Born in Guanajuato, Alamán studied in Mexico City at the School of Mines. In January 1814 he traveled to Europe, where he observed politics in the Cortes in Spain and in other nations, met leading officials and men of science and learning, and studied mining and foreign languages. He returned to Mexico in 1820, beginning his political career in 1821 when he was elected deputy to the Cortes

from Guanajuato. Alamán played an active role in the Spanish parliament, proposing programs to restore the mining industry as well as a project for home rule for the New World, taking Canada as its model.

In 1822, upon learning that Mexico had declared its independence, Alamán traveled to London, where he organized the Compañía Unida de Minas (United Mining Company), arriving in Mexico in March 1823. He served as minister of interior and exterior relations during the periods 1823–1825, 1830–1832, and 1853. Initially, he distinguished himself as a liberal and a strong critic of the Vatican for failing to recognize his nation's independence. As a result of the increasing radicalization of politics in the later 1820s, however, he became a conservative and a supporter of the church as the one institution that could help maintain order.

During his term as minister of the interior from 1830 to 1832, Alamán gained notoriety as an authoritarian but also as a strong fiscal conservative. He devoted much of his effort to rebuilding the nation's economy, particularly the mining and the textile industries. He founded the BANCO DE AVÍO, the hemisphere's first development bank, and served as director of the ministry of industry from 1842 to 1846. He also reorganized the Archivo General de la Nación and founded the Museo de Antigüedades e Historia Nacional.

In his later years, Alamán became a champion of conservatism and advocated the return to monarchy. He is best known for his writings, particularly his *Disertaciones sobre la historia de la República Méjicana . . . ,* 3 vols. (1844–1849), and his *Historia de Méjico desde los primeros movimientos que prepararon su independencia en el año 1808, hasta la época presente,* 5 vols. (1849–1852), a magisterial work that remains the best and most distinguished account of the epoch.

MOISÉS GONZÁLEZ NAVARRO, *El pensamiento político de Lucas Alamán* (1952); CHARLES HALE, *Mexican Liberalism in the Age of Mora, 1821–1853* (1968), esp. pp. 11–38; JAIME E. RODRÍGUEZ O., *The Emergence of Spanish America: Vicente Rocafuerte and Spanish Americanism, 1808–1832* (1975), esp. pp. 167–178, 179–228, and "The Origins of the 1832 Revolt," in JAIME E. RODRÍGUEZ O., *Patterns of Contention in Mexican History* (1992); JOSÉ C. VALADÉS, *Alamán: Estadista e historiador* (1977).

JAIME E. RODRÍGUEZ O.

**ALAMBERT, ZULEIKA** (b. 1924), Brazilian Communist Party leader and feminist activist. Born in the port city of Santos, Alambert joined the Brazilian Communist Party (PCB) during the political ferment that accompanied the end of World War II and the ESTADO NÔVO. She was elected to São Paulo's state legislature for the PCB at the age of twenty-four. When the party was banned in 1947 she went underground until 1954.

Alambert served as a member of the overwhelmingly male-dominated central committee of the Moscow-line PCB. Several years after the establishment of a military dictatorship in Brazil in 1964, she went into exile in Chile.

Following Salvador ALLENDE's overthrow in 1973, she left Chile for France, where she participated in the organization of the European Committee of Brazilian Women. Returning to Brazil after almost ten years in political exile abroad, she, like some other female activists, encountered difficulties in channeling gender-specific claims through male-dominated political party organizations. She left the PCB and in 1986 published a theoretical criticism of Communist understandings of the "woman question." She served as president of São Paulo's State Council on the Status of Women, and then as special adviser to subsequent council presidents.

ZULEIKA ALAMBERT, "Zuleika Alambert, Dezembro de 1978," in *Memórias das Mulheres do Exílio*, edited by Albertina de Oliveira Costa, Maria Teresa Porciuncula Moraes, Norma Marzola, and Valentina da Rocha Lima (1980), pp. 48–68.

JUNE E. HAHNER

*See also* **Brazil: Political Parties.**

**ALAMO, BATTLE OF THE.** On 6 March 1836, Mexican troops under General Antonio López de SANTA ANNA, stormed the Alamo, on the edge of San Antonio, Texas, killing or executing all of its defenders (over 180 men) and taking heavy casualties. The battle ended a thirteen-day siege of the former Franciscan mission, which had served most recently as a barracks and fortification for soldiers from the Flying Company of Alamo de Parras (1801–1825).

For Santa Anna, it had seemed essential to take the Alamo quickly, so that he could march deeper into Texas and quash an insurrection—one of several provincial rebellions against his centralized dictatorship. The defenders of the Alamo, commanded jointly by Lieutenant Colonel William Barret Travis and James Bowie, believed that significant reinforcements would come to their aid and they could defend the site. Their miscalculation and the disaster that followed helped rally Texans, who defeated Santa Anna at the decisive battle of San Jacinto on 21 April 1836 amid cries of "Remember the Alamo."

Of little military significance, the battle for the Alamo has remained important for its symbolic dimensions. Wartime propaganda and Texas enthusiasts turned the Alamo's Anglo-American defenders, including David ("Davy") Crockett, into heroic martyrs, celebrated in prose, poetry, and cinema, and the battle site itself into a national shrine. At least seven Texas Mexicans also fought to the death alongside the Anglos, but memory of their role was obliterated by the anti-Mexican passions of the battle's aftermath and largely forgotten until Mexican Americans began to become a prominent political and intellectual force in American life in the 1970s.

Few scholars have examined this battle, but there are many popular accounts, most of the older ones highly romantic. JEFF LONG, *Duel of Eagles: The Mexican and U.S. Fight for the Alamo*

(1990), offers a sprightly and unrelentingly unsentimental view, and up-to-date guidance to sources. For the mythic Alamo, see SUSAN PRENDERGAST SCHOELWER, *Alamo Images: Changing Perceptions of a Texas Experience* (1985), a smart, handsomely illustrated work. For the often overlooked Mexican side, including Santa Anna's self-defense and criticism by his officers, see CARLOS E. CASTAÑEDA, ed. and trans., *The Mexican Side of the Texas Revolution* (1928).

DAVID J. WEBER

**ALARCÓN, MARTÍN, DE** (flourished 1691–1721), governor of COAHUILA (1705–1708) and governor of Coahuila and TEXAS (1716–1719). Alarcón's expedition, in 1718 and 1719, to aid Spaniards on the Neches River in east Texas and monitor the French who entered Texas from Louisiana, led to the founding of the Mission San Antonio de Valero (the ALAMO) and a *villa* (a Spanish town) at present-day San Antonio. These institutions became the nucleus of Spanish influence in the province of Texas. Before his service in northern New Spain, Alarcón was a soldier of fortune in Oran; he also served in the Spanish navy and was a sergeant major in the Guadalajara militia of New Spain (1691) and an *alcalde mayor* (a local appointed magistrate) and captain of Jacona and Zamora (Michoacán).

FRITZ LEO HOFFMANN provides the most thorough information about Alarcón; see especially the introduction to his translation of Fray Francisco Céliz, *Diary of the Alarcón Expedition into Texas, 1718–1719* (1935), pp. 18–27, and "Alarcón, Martin de," in *The Handbook of Texas*, vol. 1, (1952), p. 24. Also: OAKAH L. JONES, JR., *Los Paisanos: Spanish Settlers on the Northern Frontier of New Spain* (1979), pp. 41–42.

ADÁN BENAVIDES, JR.

**ALASKA.** *See* **Pacific Northwest.**

**ALBA, BERNANDO DOMÍNGUEZ.** *See* **Sinán, Rogelio.**

**ALBÁN, LAUREANO** (*b.* 9 January 1942), Costa Rican poet. Born in Santa Cruz de Turrialba, Costa Rica, Albán is best known for the poetry he wrote after leaving Costa Rica for Spain in 1978. That is especially true of *Herencia del otoño* (1980; *Autumn's Legacy*, 1982) winner of Spain's coveted Adonais Prize for poetry and the Costa Rican Prize for literature. *El viaje interminable* (1983; *The Endless Voyage*, 1984) was awarded the First Prize of Hispanic Culture by the Ministry of Spanish Culture. Albán's dedication to poetry began at fifteen when he and the Costa Rican poet Jorge Debravo formed the Turrialba group. In the 1960s he created the Costa Rican Writers Circle, published his first book of poems, *Poemas en cruz* (1962), and went on to establish the transcendentalist literary movement with his wife, the poet Julieta Dobles, and two younger Costa Rican poets, Ronald Bonilla and Carlos Francisco Monge. His English translator, Frederick Fornoff, describes his view of poetry as "a vehicle through which the poet carries his audience beyond the limited, circumstantial nature of human experience to the world of transcendent intuition that is universally confirmable through and only through poetry." Alban's work has been translated into French and Hebrew as well as English. He published *Infinita memoria de América* in 1991 and *Los nocturnos de Julieta* the following year.

ARNOLDO MORA RODRÍGUEZ, "La poesía religiosa de Laureano Albán," in *Káñina* 9, no. 1 (1985): 81–86; FREDERICK FORNOFF, "La poética de ausencia en Laureano Albán," and AMPARO AMOROS, "Una metafísica del mito originario: La poesía de Laureano Albán," in *Iberoamericana* 53 (1987): 138–139, 331–361; JUAN MANUEL MARCOS, "La poesía de Laureano Albán" in *Hispanofila* 32, no. 94 (1988): 69–77.

ANN GONZÁLEZ

**ALBERDI, JUAN BAUTISTA** (*b.* 29 August 1810; *d.* 19 June 1884), Argentine diplomat, political philosopher, and constitution maker. Perhaps Alberdi's most salient trait was that he did not fit the usual image of the Latin American nation builder. He was a sullen and somewhat timid man who spent most of his adult life away from his native land and who was devoid of eloquence and leadership qualities. Yet because he had a powerful mind and an acute sense of reality, Alberdi was able to influence his contemporaries to such an extent that he is rightly considered one of modern Argentina's founding fathers. The constitution of 1853 is essentially a reflection of his political creed, and it was his ideas that largely prevailed when the process of national unification culminated in 1880 and the country began to transform itself into one of the wealthiest and most dynamic in Latin America. At this time, too, Argentina was on the way to becoming the most Europeanized nation in the region as a result of an uninterrupted flood of immigration. This was a key development with which the name Alberdi is inextricably associated.

HISTORICAL SETTING

This remarkable statesman was born the same year that the Argentine independence movement began. At that time the total area of the new nation (more than a million square miles) was populated by fewer than 400,000 people. For this reason, and because the population centers were isolated and remote from one another, Argentines referred to their land as the "desert." Long little-regarded by Spain, it had developed along a pattern of disunity. Originally it had been settled from different and unrelated points in the neighboring territories, and it had been further divided by the political and economic systems imposed by the metropolis. As a consequence, Argentina had grown up as a polarized colony. On the one hand, there was the port city of Buenos Aires, which after its opening to transatlantic trade late in the eigh-

Juan Bautista Alberdi. ARCHIVO GENERAL DE LA NACIÓN, BUENOS AIRES.

teenth century, was economically and culturally oriented toward Europe. On the other, there were the cities of the interior, which had remained satellites of other colonial economies such as that of present-day Bolivia. This cleavage reflected not only conflicting interests, but also diverse social arrangements and life-styles.

By setting up a "national" government in 1810 without first consulting the provinces, the PORTEÑOS (people of the port city of Buenos Aires) further complicated the situation and so paved the way for the period of internal strife and anarchy that followed. Buenos Aires wanted unity, but only if the provinces accepted its supremacy. The provincial caudillos, for their part, rejected centralization under *porteño* rule, favoring instead local autonomy under a loose federal system. Total disintegration might have been Argentina's fate had it not been for the rise of a strong man, Juan Manuel de ROSAS, who governed with an iron hand between 1829 and 1852. He paid lip service to federalism, because in that way he would not have to share the income generated by the Buenos Aires customhouse with the provinces. But Rosas exercised authority over the country as a whole, more so than anyone before him. He also symbolized the traditionalist, nativist reaction that set in

against the liberal and "exotic" ideas of Bernardino RI-
VADAVIA, who had attempted to modernize the country
during the previous decade.

EARLY YEARS

Alberdi arrived in Buenos Aires from his native Tucumán in 1824. He was a weak, poor youngster who
had lost both parents. But he had family connections
and had been awarded a scholarship to study in the
College of Moral Sciences of the University of Buenos
Aires, recently founded by Rivadavia. Young Alberdi's
ambition was to become a lawyer.

Alberdi indulged in too much outside reading, however, and for this reason was a poor student; it took him
a long time to achieve his professional goal. But the
delay gave him the opportunity to witness the emergence of Rosas, develop personal contacts with him and
other caudillos, and most importantly, join the "generation of 1837," a group of intellectuals largely born after
1810. These young men were strongly influenced by
romanticism, the new literary and political movement
that Esteban ECHEVERRÍA had introduced from France in
1830. They formed a literary salon in June 1837, at one
of whose meetings Alberdi read his first important paper, an attempt to interpret Argentine reality in terms of
romantic ideology. On this occasion he also dismissed
Rivadavia as doctrinaire and proclaimed that Rosas's
power was legitimate.

Nevertheless, when Rosas's dictatorship tightened
shortly afterward, the salon had to go underground (under the name "May Association"), and its members later
had to seek refuge in Montevideo, Uruguay. Here Alberdi was finally able to obtain his law degree and begin
a profitable practice. Having turned against the dictator
like most of his colleagues, he became involved in the
literary warfare that the exiles waged for the liberation
of their country. In addition, he supported the military
campaign of the Uruguayan anti-Rosas faction and its
French allies. But these activities led nowhere, and he
felt increasingly disappointed. When a victorious pro-
Rosas Uruguayan army laid siege to Montevideo in
1843, he realized that he had no taste for the life of a
soldier. Alberdi left for Europe, where he met Argentina's most illustrious exile, General José de SAN MAR-
TÍN, the hero of national independence. Upon returning
to the Americas, Alberdi chose Chile as his haven, settling there in April 1844.

ALBERDI AND NATIONAL ORGANIZATION

By this time Alberdi was a man of note among Argentine exiles. His articles and pamphlets were well known,
and his analyses and political opinions were widely
commented upon and discussed. He had the opportunity to put them to work when, in 1852, a coalition led
by provincial caudillo Justo José URQUIZA ousted Rosas
and called a convention to draw up a new constitution.
Alberdi wrote a book especially for the occasion, commonly called *Bases*, which rapidly turned into the most

influential of its time. It was the convention delegates'
chief source of information on constitutional matters.

Unsurprisingly, therefore, the new constitution, promulgated on 25 May 1853, largely followed Alberdi's
recommendations. Seeking to reconcile Argentina's
warring factions, it provided for a federal system of
government similar to that of the United States, but it
also included significant adaptations to Argentina's peculiar needs. According to Alberdi, Argentina had to set
aside "its ridiculous and disgraceful mania for the heroic" and move forward along the path of material
progress. It had to promote the advance of learning and
instruction in general, build railroads and navigable canals, attract foreign capital, and encourage and facilitate
the colonization of the lands of the national domain.
Above all, there was Alberdi's most celebrated aphorism, "to govern is to populate." Argentina had to promote IMMIGRATION (especially of hardworking Anglo-
Saxons) in order to transform the "desert" into a source
of wealth and abundance. All of this required writing
into the constitution the fundamental principles of economic liberalism, which the delegates did, including a
remarkable bill of rights guaranteeing liberty, equality,
the right to work and trade, and the civil rights of aliens.

NATIONAL UNIFICATION

Another feature of the constitution was the stipulation
that Buenos Aires should be the capital of the republic
and that the income from customs was to belong to the
nation. This was unacceptable to Buenos Aires, and as a
result Argentina now split into two separate states: the
city of Buenos Aires and its province and the inland AR-
GENTINE CONFEDERATION. Urquiza remained as head of
the latter, and Alberdi broke with his own Buenos Aires
associates—including Domingo F. SARMIENTO and Bartolomé MITRE—in order to serve him through a diplomatic mission to Europe, to which he went without
setting his foot in the territory of the confederation. He
spent seven years as a diplomat and a writer, defending
the integrity of Argentina against Mitre's policies. To
him, *mitrismo* was *rosismo* in disguise, just as Rosas's dictatorship had simply been a prolongation of colonial
practices.

In 1861 Mitre's forces defeated the Confederation at
Pavón; Alberdi lost his position the following year. But
although he remained in Europe, Alberdi did not retire
to private life; rather, he continued to write about Argentine problems, albeit not always accurately, as was
the case with the Paraguayan War (1865–1870). The criticisms that he directed against the Buenos Aires government on this occasion showed that he was not well
informed; furthermore, he was dubbed a traitor to the
fatherland. Because of this, and because he had to con-
template how his enemies rose to power while he aged
perceptibly in exile, he lived through bitter days. This is
clearly reflected in his writings, wherein he began to
justify his actions with an eye on posterity.

By the late 1870s, however, things began to change in

the distant fatherland. There was an upsurge of provincial opposition to *porteño* domination, and a native of Tucumán, Nicolás AVELLANEDA, was elected president. Alberdi's followers thought that the time was ripe for his political comeback and elected him to congress. He arrived in Buenos Aires in 1879. By this time, however, he was a tired man of sixty-nine who could not even read his own speeches. Therefore, he could not give a good account of himself. But he was able to witness the triumph of his ideas about national unification, for it was during his Buenos Aires sojourn that the port city finally became part of the Argentine federal republic as its capital, as the 1853 constitution had called for.

LAST YEARS
Defeat did not silence Alberdi's critics, who fiercely opposed the diplomatic appointment that the Argentine government proposed to bestow upon him in 1881. It was obvious that his compatriots would never give him the wide recognition that he deserved. Disillusioned and disappointed, Alberdi expatriated himself, living again in France. He died there three years later, surrounded by a few friends. He had never married.

In 1889, by popular request, his remains were brought back to Buenos Aires, where they were buried in an impressive ceremony. The most prominent representatives of the local and national government were not present.

On Alberdi's ideas, see JOSÉ LUIS ROMERO, *A History of Argentine Political Thought* (1963). On Alberdi himself, most of the literature is in Spanish. The best biographical study is JORGE M. MAYER, *Alberdi y su tiempo* (1963). For a scholarly edition of Alberdi's most important work, see Mayer's edition of *Las "Bases" de Alberdi* (1969).

JOSÉ M. HERNÁNDEZ

*See also* **Argentina: Constitutions; War of the Triple Alliance.**

**ALBERNI, PEDRO DE** (*b.* 1745; *d.* 11 March 1802), Spanish soldier and explorer. Alberni, a native of Tortosa, Catalonia, joined the Barcelona-based CATALONIAN VOLUNTEERS in 1767. Following the Sonora Expedition of 1767–1771 in Mexico, he served in Jalisco and Nayarit, where he married Juana Vélez of Tepic. In 1782, Alberni was promoted to captain of the First Company of Catalonian Volunteers. Between 1789 and 1793 he commanded his unit on several expeditions to the Pacific Northwest. He established a Spanish base for the expeditions at Nootka Sound on Vancouver Island. As troop commander, Alberni assigned Catalonian Volunteers to assist in the mapping of the Spanish claim to the coast of Alaska and the PACIFIC NORTHWEST prior to the Nootka Sound Convention that led to Spain's loss of the area. He made friends with the Nootka Indians and compiled a small dictionary of 633 words in their language and their Spanish equivalents. While military commander of California, Alberni died at Monterey and was buried at Mission Carmel. Port Alberni on Vancouver Island is named for him.

JOSEPH P. SÁNCHEZ, *Spanish Bluecoats: The Catalonian Volunteers in Northwestern New Spain, 1767–1810* (1990).

JOSEPH P. SÁNCHEZ

**ALBERRO, FRANCISCO DE,** governor and commander in chief of the province of Venezuela (1677–1682). Alberro was appointed to both posts by the royal decree of 11 August 1675 after he gave 28,000 pesos to meet the needs of the monarchy. This marked the beginning of a series of appointments that were made in exchange for monetary gifts to help meet the colonial administration's economic needs. While in office he enforced the royal decree abolishing the use of Indians as personal servants. He also promoted wall-building and fortification projects in the cities of La Guaira and Caracas, both undertaken simultaneously after the French pirate François Grammont's attack on the port of La Guaira in June 1680.

At the end of Alberro's term, his successor, Diego de Melo Maldonado, convoked a trial of residence, as was the custom. In voluminous records Alberro is accused of abuse of power, illegal money collecting, unwarranted seizures, and carelessness and negligence in the performance of his duties.

On colonial administration, see JOSÉ GIL FORTOUL, *Historia constitutional de Venezuela*, vol. 1, 4 (1954), and GUILLERMO MORÓN, *Historia de Venezuela*, vol. 1 (1971).

INÉS QUINTERO

**ALBERTO, JOÃO** (*b.* 16 June 1897; *d.* 26 January 1955), prominent Brazilian political figure. As a young artillery officer, Alberto participated in the PRESTES COLUMN that traversed Brazil's interior during much of the 1920s. Alberto eventually broke with Prestes, joining the Revolution of 1930 that brought Getúlio VARGAS to power. Appointed federal intervenor in São Paulo by Vargas in 1930, Alberto served less than a year in the post. In 1932 he was appointed chief of police in the Federal District, where he created the special police to repress groups and individuals opposed to Vargas. Alberto was elected to the National Constituent Assembly the following year as a representative from Pernambuco, affiliated with the Social Democratic Party (PSD). In 1935 Alberto entered the diplomatic service, discharging various duties in Europe and the Americas until 1942. With Brazil's entry in the Second World War, Alberto led the Coordenação da Mobilização Econômica, a newly created superministry tasked with wartime economic planning and industrial-policy formulation. Following the progressive weakening of Vargas's ESTADO NOVO in 1944, Alberto once again led the Federal District police forces, until Vargas was removed from power in 1945. Vargas's return to the presidency in 1951 occasioned

Alberto's return to government service in various positions, most prominently as the Brazilian representative to the General Agreement on Tariffs and Trade.

THOMAS E. SKIDMORE, *Politics in Brazil, 1930–1964* (1967); ISRAEL BELOCH and ALZIRA ALVES DE ABREU, eds., *Dicionário histórico-biográfico brasileiro, 1930–1983* (1984).

WILLIAM SUMMERHILL

**ALBIZU CAMPOS, PEDRO** (*b.* ca. 12 September 1891; *d.* 21 April 1965), president of the Puerto Rico Nationalist Party in the 1930s and figurative head of the island's struggle for independence. Albizu Campos was born in Ponce, the illegitimate son of a black mother and a white, Spanish father. He excelled in his studies as a young man, obtaining a scholarship to attend college in the United States. While at Harvard, he was drafted to serve in the U.S. army, where he was placed in a segregated regiment. He returned to Harvard Law School after the war and obtained his degree in 1923.

Back on the island that year, Albizu became active in the Nationalist Party, founded in 1922. In the final years of the decade, he traveled to several Latin American and Caribbean countries, advocating the cause of Puerto Rican independence before government leaders and thus internationalizing "the colonial question." Upon his return, he took over a divided movement that weakly opposed the U.S. presence on the island, began to criticize the nature of existing relations between Puerto Rico and the United States, and committed himself to end U.S. colonial domination through the use of force. Under Albizu's leadership (he was elected president in 1930), the Nationalist Party of the 1930s was pro-Hispanic, militant, and violent. Its membership reached nearly 12,000.

The activities of the Cadets of the Republic, the paramilitary arm of the Nationalist Party, led to frequent clashes with government authorities. In 1936 chief of police Francis Riggs was shot to death, and shortly thereafter two nationalist supporters were seized and killed by police. Albizu and seven others were arrested in connection with the assassination and accused of conspiring to overthrow the government of the United States. The court sentenced Albizu to imprisonment in a federal penitentiary, where he remained until 1947.

In a climate of economic uncertainty following the Depression and political persecution promoted by U.S. colonial authorities, violent confrontations continued in the late 1930s. The "Ponce Massacre" gained the most notoriety, as 21 persons, including 2 policemen, were killed in what had been planned as a peaceful march. The commotion arose when Nationalists, shortly after Albizu's conviction, decided to hold a parade in Ponce, despite the last-minute revocation of their permit to march. The demonstrators apparently carried no arms, although a shot provoked the police into firing at the crowd. An American Civil Liberties Union investigation concluded that the ensuing violence was the result of extremist agitation and lack of police restraint.

Albizu returned to the political scene as Puerto Rico debated the benefits of permanent association with the United States, following the approval of Public Law 600, the precursor to local self-government. In 1950 from the mountain town of Jayuya he was involved in the declaration of independence. In a simultaneous move, police headquarters and the Puerto Rican governor's residence were attacked, as was Blair House, the temporary home of the U.S. president in Washington. Albizu was again arrested and found guilty of attempted murder, illegal use of arms, and subversion. Governor Luis MUÑOZ MARÍN granted him conditional freedom in 1953.

In 1954 three young nationalists fired their guns at U.S. representatives while the House was in session, wounding six people. Again, Albizu was jailed, until declining health required his transfer to a hospital in 1964. Governor Muñoz pardoned him on 15 November 1964; he died shortly thereafter. Although many have rejected Albizu's glorification of violence to achieve the lofty ideal of independence, his unequivocal actions and fiery rhetoric have inspired nationalists of all persuasions for many decades.

FERNANDO PICÓ, *Historia general de Puerto Rico* (1988); LUIS A. FERRAO, "Pedro Albizu Campos, el Partido Nacionalista y el catolicismo, 1930–1939," in *Homines* 13, no. 2 (1989) and 14, no. 1 (1990): 224–247; CARLOS RODRÍGUEZ-FRATICELLI, "Pedro Albizu Campos: Strategies of Struggles and Strategic Struggles," in *Centro de Estudios Puertorriqueños Bulletin* 4, no. 1 (1991–1992): 24–33; RUTH VASSALLO and JOSÉ ANTONIO TORRES MARTINÓ, *Pedro Albizu Campos: Reflexiones sobre su vida y su obra* (1991); MARISA ROSADO, *Las llamas de la aurora: Acercamiento a una biografía de Pedro Albizu Campos* (1992).

TERESITA MARTÍNEZ-VERGNE

**ALBUQUERQUE,** city of 602,000 inhabitants (metropolitan region, 1993) at the foot of the Sandia Mountains in the Middle Rio Grande Valley of central New Mexico. Francisco Cuervo y Valdés, then governor of New Mexico, founded Albuquerque in the spring of 1706, naming the new *villa* for Francisco Fernández de la Cueva Enríquez, duke of Alburquerque, then viceroy of New Spain. (The extra *r* in the city's original spelling gradually disappeared with the arrival of Anglo settlers in the mid-nineteenth century.) The first settlers were 35 families, totaling 252 people, from the capital of Santa Fe about 60 miles to the north. In 1752 the population was 476, and it had reached only 763 by 1776.

Like the other *villas* in New Mexico, Albuquerque was a farming and ranching settlement on the far northern frontier of the Spanish Empire. Their distance from the viceregal administration and culture in Mexico City obliged them to forge a tightly knit, self-sufficient traditional culture, elements of which grace the New Mexican cultural landscape to this day. Following the

MEXICAN-AMERICAN WAR (1846–1848), the city became a part of the United States and began to establish commercial relations with the eastern United States. The arrival of the Atchison, Topeka, and Santa Fe Railway (which bypassed the rival city of Santa Fe) in 1880 solidified Albuquerque's position as the most important Borderlands city of the region. Between 1890 and 1900, the population nearly doubled, reaching 6,326.

RICHARD E. GREENLEAF, "The Founding of Albuquerque, 1706: An Historical-Legal Problem," in *New Mexico Historical Review* 39, no. 1 (1964): 1–15; OAKAH L. JONES, JR., *Los Paisanos: Spanish Settlements on the Northern Frontier of New Spain* (1979), esp. pp. 109–167; MARC SIMMONS, *Albuquerque: A Narrative History* (1982).

J. DAVID DRESSING

## ALBUQUERQUE, ANTÔNIO FRANCISCO DE PAULA

(*b.* 1797; *d.* 1863), Brazilian imperial statesman, senator, and Liberal politician. Albuquerque was educated in Germany and began his career in the military, serving in Mozambique, in Macao, and in the 1824 revolt in PERNAMBUCO. He retired with the rank of lieutenant colonel in 1832. Albuquerque represented his home state, Pernambuco, in both the Chamber of Deputies and the Senate. He ran unsuccessfully for regent in 1835 and 1838. Albuquerque served in eight different cabinets: as minister of the treasury in 1830, 1831, 1832, 1846, and 1852; as minister of the empire, in 1832 and 1839; as minister of justice in 1839; as minister of war in 1844; and as minister of the navy in 1840, 1844, and 1846. He was appointed counselor of the state in 1850 and was awarded the title of viscount.

MIGUEL ARCHANJO GALVÃO, *Relação dos cidadãos que tomaram parte no governo do Brasil no periodo de março de 1808 a 15 de novembro de 1889* (1894), pp. 15–27; *Nôvo dicionário de história do Brasil* (1971), p. 37; RODERICK J. BARMAN, *Brazil: The Forging of a Nation, 1798–1852* (1988), pp. 180–181, 198–199.

JUDY BIEBER FREITAS

## ALBUQUERQUE, MATIAS DE

(*b.* 1595; *d.* June 1647), governor and CAPITÃO-MOR of PERNAMBUCO (1620–1626), thirteenth governor-general of Brazil (1624–1627), superintendent of war in Pernambuco and inspector and military engineer for the captaincies of the north (1629–1635). Born in Lisbon and baptized in the church of Loreto, Albuquerque was the younger son of Jorge de Albuquerque COELHO, third lord-proprietor of Pernambuco, and his second wife, Dona Ana, daughter of Dom Alvaro Coutinho, commander of Almourol. Later in life he changed his baptismal name, Paulo, to Matias in honor of his guardian, his father's first cousin, Matias de Albuquerque, viceroy of India (1591–1597), who was himself childless and named Matias as his heir. In 1604, after a papal dispensation was obtained because he was underage, young Albuquerque received a knighthood in the Order of Christ. In 1619, having served three

years in North Africa, the Mediterranean, and the Straits of Gibraltar at his own expense, he was summoned to Madrid.

In March of 1620 Albuquerque was named governor and *capitão-mor* of his brother's (Duarte de Albuquerque Coelho) CAPTAINCY of Pernambuco, Brazil, and arrived there the following day. Three urgent problems awaited him in his new post. The first was the restoration of donatarial authority after almost a half-century of absenteeism on the part of the second, third, and fourth lords-proprietor of Pernambuco and after the last four governors-general had resided in his family's captaincy instead of in BAHIA, the Brazilian capital. Second, there was the need to supply men, foodstuffs, and materials for the expanding Portuguese presence in northern and northeastern Brazil. Last, old defenses had to be rebuilt and new ones erected, and the local militias had to be trained to protect Pernambuco from threats of a Dutch attack. When the DUTCH WEST INDIA COMPANY seized Bahia along with the governor-general, Diogo de Mendonça Furtado, in 1624, Albuquerque was named thirteenth governor-general of Brazil. From Pernambuco he helped wage war against the Dutch until the joint Spanish-Portuguese armada of 1625 succeeded in recapturing the Brazilian capital in May of that year. As governor-general, he continued to coordinate efforts to supply Bahia, put down Indian revolts in the interior of the northeast, and prevent Dutch reinforcements from establishing themselves in Baía de Traição in the neighboring captaincy of Paraíba.

On 18 June 1627, Albuquerque departed from Pernambuco for Portugal. During the next two years, while he was in that kingdom and in Spain, he penned a number of important memorials to the crown on such varied topics as navigation in the Atlantic and Brazil's fortifications, sugar industry, and lack of coinage. Because of reports of plans of another Dutch attack on Portuguese America, Albuquerque was sent back to Brazil in 1629, arriving there on 18 October. This time, he was given a new post, free from the control of the governor-general—that of superintendent of war in Pernambuco and inspector and military engineer for the captaincies of the north. Four months later, on 15 February 1630, the Dutch West India Company's force of approximately sixty-seven ships and 7,000 men attacked Pernambuco. By 3 March they had control of the towns of Olinda and Recife and the adjoining island of Antônio Vaz. Albuquerque rallied his outmanned and outgunned forces, and for the next two years, from his strategically located headquarters at the Arraial do Bom Jesus three miles away from both Olinda and Recife, he kept the Dutch, who were superior in numbers, hemmed in and unable to profit from the captaincy's rich sugar plantations. He was attempting to follow the successful policy that had enabled the Portuguese to recover Bahia from the Dutch in 1625.

But this time no Spanish-Portuguese armada arrived to challenge Dutch control of the sea. With the desertion by April 1632 of several important Brazilian soldiers and the arrival of substantial reinforcements from Europe, the Dutch soon expanded up and down the coast of Pernambuco and other captaincies to the north. The Portuguese fought back, but to little avail. By the end of 1634, the Dutch controlled the coast from Rio Grande do Norte to the Cape of Santo Agostinho, and a great number of Portuguese settlers had made peace with them. In 1635, Porto Calvo, the Arraial do Bom Jesus, and Fort Nazaré were captured, and much of the surrounding rich sugar land was in Dutch hands. Albuquerque and over 7,000 Portuguese settlers, their families, and slaves were forced to retreat to the southernmost part of the captaincy to what is now the state of Alagoas. In late 1635, Dom Luis de Rojas y Borgia, a former governor of Panama, landed with 2,500 soldiers in Alagoas, replacing Albuquerque as head of the forces fighting the Dutch. Albuquerque continued by land to Bahia before returning to Portugal in 1636. Blamed for the loss of Pernambuco, he was imprisoned in the Portuguese border town of Castelo da Vide. In late 1640, his place of incarceration was moved to Lisbon's Castelo de São Jorge. Soon after the acclamation of the Duke of Bragança as King JOÃO IV on 1 December 1640, Albuquerque was freed.

He pledged his loyalty to Portugal's new monarch and, because of his military background, was made a member of the newly established Council of War and given the post of *mestre de campo general* (commander in chief) of the army that was being raised to defend the Alentejo. In that province he continued to train the Portuguese troops and help with the fortifications. He was also active in the early fighting and was given the post of commander of the troops (*governador das armas*) in the Alentejo, the first of three times he held that position. However, Albuquerque was soon imprisoned again, suspected of treason because his brother, the fourth lord-proprietor of Pernambuco, had been in Madrid when the Portuguese revolution began and remained there and because Albuquerque was a close relative of several of those involved in the conspiracy of 1641 against King João IV. Eventually his innocence was established, and he was restored to full honors and made a member of the Council of State. On 26 May 1644, he led Portuguese troops to victory at the battle of Montijo in Spanish Extremadura—the first significant Portuguese victory in a war that lasted almost thirty years, until peace was finally signed in 1668. Soon after his victory, Albuquerque was named the first count of Alegrete. At about that time, he married Dona Catarina Barbara de Noronha, sister of the future first count of Vila Verde. They had no children. Albuquerque retired from active duty late in 1646 and died the following year.

HELIO VIANNA's pioneering *Matias de Albuquerque* (1944) has been updated by FRANCIS A. DUTRA, *Matias de Albuquerque: Capitão-mor de Pernambuco e Governador-Geral do Brasil* (1976). Details of the struggle between donatarial authority and cen-

tralized government are found in FRANCIS A. DUTRA, "Centralization vs. Donatarial Privilege: Pernambuco, 1602–1630," in *Colonial Roots of Modern Brazil,* edited by Dauril Alden (1973). Defense problems are discussed in FRANCIS A. DUTRA, "Matias de Albuquerque and the Defense of Northeastern Brazil, 1620–1626," in *Studia* 36 (1973): 117–166. A valuable contemporary account of Portuguese America during Albuquerque's first tour of duty in Brazil is Franciscan FREI VICENTE DO SALVADOR, *História do Brasil 1500–1627,* 5th ed. (1965). The Dutch campaigns of the 1630s are described by Albuquerque's brother, an eyewitness and fourth lord-proprietor of Pernambuco, DUARTE DE ALBUQUERQUE COELHO, *Memorias Diarias de la Guerra del Brasil por discurso de nueve años empeçando desde el de M.D.C. XXX* (1654). Also useful for understanding Brazil during this time period is AMBRÓSIO FERNANDES BRANDÃO's classic account, *Diálogos das Grandezas do Brazil* (1618). There is a second edition of this title edited by JOSÉ ANTÔNIO GONSALVES DE MELLO (1966); a good English translation is entitled *Dialogues of the Great Things of Brazil,* translated and annotated by Frederick Holden Hall, William F. Harrison, and Dorothy Winters Welker (1987).

FRANCIS A. DUTRA

**ALCABALAS** (sales taxes), first imposed in Spain in 1342, in Mexico in 1574, and later in the sixteenth century in other areas of the Spanish Indies. Initially all goods were taxed at 2 percent of their sale price, but in 1632 another 2 percent was added for the empirewide Union of Arms. In 1635 the tax was increased in Mexico by still another 2 percent in order to finance the Spanish Main fleet (Armada de Barlovento). Although the rate fluctuated periodically in times of financial exigency and was widely differentiated after 1775, 6 percent prevailed in most areas of the Spanish Empire at the end of the colonial period. Certain items were exempt from the sales tax, including arms, dowries, booty, medicine, paintings, books, corn, and grain; clerics, Indians, and certain regions of the Indies were also exempt.

Until the beginning of the eighteenth century, *alcabala* collection was in semiprivate or private hands, normally those of the cities or the merchant guild (CONSULADO), whose officials periodically contracted with viceregal authorities on the amounts to be paid to the royal treasury for collection rights. In Peru in 1724 and Mexico in 1764, however, royal treasury officials began collecting sales taxes directly. By 1800 *alcabalas* generated close to 600,000 pesos annually in Peru and 2.5 million in Mexico.

*Recopilación de leyes de los reynos de las Indias,* 4 vols. (1681; repr. 1973); libro VIII, título XIII; FABIAN DE FONSECA and CARLOS DE URRUTIA, *Historia general de Real Hacienda,* vol. 2 (1849).

JOHN JAY TEPASKE

**ALCALDE,** a local magistrate. *Alcaldes ordinarios* were municipal magistrates normally elected each January 1 for a one-year term by the town council (CABILDO or AYUNTAMIENTO). Cities had two *alcaldes;* small towns normally had one. Although elected by a *cabildo, alcaldes* usually were not also *regidores* of the council.

*Alcaldes* were men of substance in the community. While many were native to the town, outsiders who married into prominent families could become *alcaldes*. Early *alcaldes* were routinely *encomenderos* or their relatives, but later *hacendados*, other property owners, and eventually merchants served.

*Alcaldes* exercised first-instance jurisdiction in civil and criminal cases within the municipality's boundaries, but they could not issue sentences of death or mutilation. Appeals from their decisions were heard by an *alcalde mayor* or *corregidor*, or by the AUDIENCIA within whose jurisdiction the town lay. Despite their judicial responsibilities, *alcaldes* were not required to have formal training in jurisprudence. In some cases *alcaldes* fulfilled nonjudicial responsibilities assigned by the *cabildo*.

CLARENCE H. HARING, *The Spanish Empire in America* (1947).

MARK A. BURKHOLDER

**ALCALDE MAYOR,** the chief administrator of a territorial unit known as an *alcaldía mayor*. *Alcaldías mayores* were provincial units of varying size and significance. The term was used most frequently in New Spain, where there were about two hundred of these units in the 1780s. In Peru similar provincial units were termed *corregimientos*.

The *alcalde mayor* had judicial, administrative, military, and legislative authority. Judicial appeals from his decisions were heard by an *audiencia*.

*Alcaldes mayores* usually were appointed for terms of three to five years. Originally the viceroys named most *alcaldes*, but in 1677 the crown started selling appointments, thereby greatly reducing the viceroys' patronage. The sales, moreover, resulted in the *alcaldes mayores* placing even more pressure on the native populations of their districts in order to recoup their investment and make a profit. Working closely with wholesale merchants, they routinely required the natives to purchase animals and merchandise from them (*repartimiento de mercancías* or *bienes*) at inflated prices, and in some cases they forced the natives to sell their produce to them at below market prices.

The abuses of the *alcaldes mayores* and their lieutenants led to their replacement in most parts of the empire by intendants in the late eighteenth century.

CLARENCE H. HARING, *The Spanish Empire in America* (1947); PETER GERHARD, *A Guide to the Historical Geography of New Spain* (1972).

MARK A. BURKHOLDER

**ALCARAZ, JOSÉ ANTONIO** (*b.* 5 December 1938), Mexican composer. Alcaraz studied at the National Conservatory in Mexico and then pursued postgraduate studies at the Schola Cantorum in Paris, the summer

courses for new music in Darmstadt, and the Opera Center in London. With his interest in music theater and mixed media, Alcaraz has composed some very significant works, including the aleatoric opera *Arbre d'or à deux têtes* for voice, piano, and toy instrument; an evening of theater music entitled *Qué es lo que faze aqueste gran roido, sol de mi antojo,* (1983); and a series of profane madrigals for voice and piano. *De Telémaco* for soprano, flute, and piano (1985); *Toccata* for piano (1957); *Otra hora de junio,* a two-voice madrigal (1988); *D'un inconnu* for violin and voice (1973); and *Cuanta consagración para tan poca primavera* (1981) and *Aubepine* (1984) for four mezzo-sopranos. His ballet *Homenaje a Lorca* (1963) received a prize from the University of the Theater of the Nations in Paris.

Alcaraz wrote *Hablar de música* (1982), *Suave teatro* (1984), and *Al sonoro rugir del telón* (1988). He founded the Micrópera de Mexico and the Opera de Cámara of the National Institute of Fine Arts (INBA).

*Pauta* (1982), p. 123; *X Foro internacional de música nueva* (1988), pp. 15, 44–45; *XIV Foro internacional de música nueva* (1992), p. 128.

ALCIDES LANZA

**ALCOHOLIC BEVERAGES.** Long before the Conquest, peoples of the Americas produced and consumed fermented beverages. These drinks became integral to the fabric of life, and withstood efforts to eliminate or replace them after the arrival of the Europeans. Some are still consumed today.

TRADITIONAL BEVERAGES
*Chicha* is a generic name for beverages made from grains or fruits. *Chicha* can be nonalcoholic, such as *chicha de quinoa*, which is simply a quinoa broth. But it is the fermented beverage that has had the most influence on Latin American history. Plantains, algarroba, palms, berries, cassava, sweet potatoes, and maize have been commonly used. The *chicha* from the Andean region is best known. To produce it, maize kernels were moistened, a diastase (often the saliva of women who chewed the kernels) and water added, and then the mixture was cooked. (*Masato*, or the common manioc beer of the Amazon region, was made in essentially the same way.) Malting (letting grains germinate after soaking), akin to the European method of beer making, was another method of fermentation. The alcoholic content of *chicha* varied from 2 to 12 percent, depending on the type of maize and the fermentation process. Twentieth-century Peruvian cookbooks present standard recipes for some of the more traditional *chichas*.

Pulque was the Nahuatl *octli*, the "honey water" common to the cultures of central Mexico. Pulque was also a ritual drink, associated with certain gods and ceremonial practices. As with *chicha*, the process of pulque production was simple. The stem of the maguey plant was cut, allowing the juice (*aguamiel*) to collect in the cavity of the plant. Traditionally this was extracted from the plant with a long tube, and placed in wooden or leather containers. The addition of already prepared pulque initiated the fermentation process, which could last from a week to a month. Variants of pulque (*pulque curado*) might include nuts, fruits, and herbs as sweeteners and flavorings. Frances CALDERÓN DE LA BARCA, perhaps Mexico's most famous nineteenth-century observer, wrote: "It is said to be the most wholesome drink in the world, and remarkably agreeable when one has overcome the first shock occasioned by its rancid odor." With distillation (a process introduced after 1492), the juice of the maguey also produced mescal and tequila, beverages that became increasingly popular in the nineteenth and twentieth centuries.

*Chicha* and pulque survived the Conquest and competition from imported beverages. They were admirably suited to the geography and culture of the Andes and Mexico. Ingredients were readily available and production was simple. This popularity was also due to their ceremonial use, as offerings to the gods to insure good harvests and to provide strength during battle. They were believed to have a range of magical and relating qualities that insured the continuation of the community and the culture. They were also valued for medicinal purposes, useful in combating infection and disease. The nutritional quality of *chicha* and pulque has been disputed since the sixteenth century, but modern nutritional analysis has demonstrated that both could, depending on ingredients used and the manner of preparation, contain significant amounts of protein, thiamine, riboflavin, niacin, vitamin C, calcium, and iron, in addition to other nutrients.

BEER

Europeans introduced their own beer—made from barley—soon after the Conquest, receiving licenses to manufacture it in Mexico as early as 1544. Despite early protection from the crown and efforts to limit consumption of Indian beverages, European beers made slow inroads in Latin America until the late nineteenth century, when a new wave of European immigration prompted changes in alcoholic consumption patterns. Regions receiving the largest numbers of immigrants experienced the most profound changes, but throughout Latin America, even those areas with dense indigenous populations, beer gradually became more popular. In Mexico in the twentieth century, the local and regional characteristics of beer have given way to uniform taste and quality as the three giant producers, La Cervecería Cuauhtémoc, Cervercería Moctezuma, and Cervecería Modelo, have dominated the industry. In Brazil, where beer has almost achieved the status of a national drink, the same process of centralization of production and distribution has occurred with the giant breweries of Brahmah, Antártica, and Kaiser.

Peruvian Indians in Cuzco drinking *chicha*. INSTITUTO AUDIO-VISUAL, INKA, CUSCO; PHOTO BY HORACIO OCHOA.

## WINE

Wine was the staple drink of the Spanish diet in the sixteenth century, and the preference for wine was carried to the New World. Despite the centrality of wine in the Iberian diet, however, it did not become the universal drink of Latin America. In Mexico, the production of wine had a sporadic history, as mercantilist legislation attempted to prevent its production. Disruptions in trade and the need for wine for religious and medicinal purposes led to occasional permission to grow grapes for wine, but it was not until the late nineteenth century that the industry developed in earnest. And it was only after World War II that Mexico developed a wine industry comparable to that of Peru, Chile, and Argentina. Peru, the center of Spanish civilization in South America, supported a flourishing wine industry in its coastal valleys. It hoped to maintain a monopoly of production and supply, but distribution problems led to the development of vineyards in other countries. Eventually, Chile, Argentina, and southern Brazil emerged as important producers. Wine, especially among the immigrant populations of the late nineteenth and early twentieth centuries, became common in the diet. Since the 1960s, wine production both for domestic consumption and for export has increased.

## CONSUMPTION AND ITS CONTROL

The introduction of distilled beverages had a profound impact on drinking habits in Latin America. High-alcohol spirits were substituted for low-alcohol traditional beverages and the more expensive European wines and beers. References to drinking habits from the sixteenth to the twentieth centuries suggest widespread indulgence, at least compared with what was deemed socially acceptable. Grape brandy, first imported from Spain, then produced at the successful vineyards established in Peru, Chile, Argentina, and Mexico, provided spirits for increasingly enthusiastic consumers. It did not, however, equal the popularity of *aguardiente,* known generally as *cachaça* or *aguardente* in Brazil, a spirit made from distilling the juice of sugarcane. The addition of citrus and other flavorings to the beverage helped create variety. Sugar, wherever it was grown in Latin America, was the basis for alcohol production. In the case of the Caribbean, sugar—and its products of molasses and rum—became one of the foundations of trade patterns linking New England, Europe, West Africa, and Latin America. The Spanish islands (and Venezuela) soon became known for light, dry rums, while the English islands produced heavier, darker rums.

Drinks made from these spirits have entered the global cocktail lexicon, and taken their place among martinis and manhattans as popular beverages. Two of the most favored are daiquiris, a drink of Caribbean origin, made from rum, fruit juice, and sugar, and margaritas, made from tequila, lemon or lime juice, sugar, and salt. A rival in taste if not in popularity is the pisco sour, a Peruvian concoction of pisco (a grape brandy),

citrus juice, and sugar. Brazilian cocktails have not yet achieved the international reputation of margaritas, daiquiris, and pisco sours, but caipirinhas and batidas, made from AGUARDIENTE, fruit juice, and sugar are worthy contenders.

Widespread use (and concern about abuse) of alcoholic beverages in colonial society led to attempts to regulate their production, distribution, and consumption. As early as 1529, the Spanish crown considered banning the production of pulque, the prelude to a succession of laws that sought to limit or ban certain types of alcoholic beverages. In some cases the crown's economic motive was clear; in other cases it was hidden behind laments over the moral decay of society. By the eighteenth century, cane brandy had come under as much attack as the local beverages of *chicha* and pulque. It was the "demon rum" of the colonies that was blamed for most social problems. Excessive drinking disrupted family life, slowed economic production, and caused a range of medical problems. Indians and mestizos drank the most, but Spaniards as well consumed excessive amounts of cheap cane brandy.

In Mexico, *chinquirito,* a type of cane brandy, was widely consumed, though it was only one of a dozen or so "prohibited beverages." Extremists argued that high mortality rates in the Indian population were largely due to excessive consumption of *chinquirito.* Compared with this noxious drink, some officials thought that the traditional pulque was "innocent, healthful, medicinal, and necessary." Produced in small stills throughout central Mexico, *chinquirito* prompted a century-long effort to curtail its production, distribution, and consumption. The trade in *chinquirito* had reached a level that negatively affected the wine and brandy producers of Andalusia. As fewer wines and spirits were transported across the Atlantic, taxes shrank and the maritime capacity of Spain was reduced.

At stake in the regulatory effort was control over a vast economic activity. In Mexico City alone there were over 1,500 shops, known by many different names, selling alcoholic beverages. The potential for taxing and licensing income was substantial. One eighteenth-century solution was to centralize control through the awarding of monopolies for production and distribution. Here the administrative history of spirits finds comparison with that of tobacco, meat, and other colonial products. In Colombia, this included the regulation of anise, which was the most popular local flavoring for *aguardiente.* As with other monopolistic efforts, success was often elusive. The availability of ingredients and the simple, inexpensive technology required for production undermined the most thorough legislation.

The political explanation for the control of alcoholic beverages invariably pointed to the social and health problems related to drinking, even though medical thought continued to argue in the late eighteenth century that alcohol was important for health, especially in hot regions. One important issue, from the sixteenth through the twentieth century, was excessive drinking among Indians, blacks, and *castas*.

Alcoholic consumption among Indians before the Conquest was associated with religious ceremonies; the availability and distribution of alcoholic beverages was controlled by politics and custom. After the Conquest, drinking became more widespread, leading to accusations by Europeans that drunkenness was extensive among Indians. By the late eighteenth century, there were carefully articulated theories explaining Indian susceptibility to alcohol due to "natural temperament," though consumption was at times regulated in Indian communities by social and religious customs that curtailed widespread alcoholic abuse.

The concern over Indian drinking intensified in the late nineteenth and early twentieth centuries. From Mexico to Bolivia, Indian drinking was equated with character and genetic weaknesses. Alcoholism among Indians was referred to as a grave national problem, and began to call forth the efforts of political reformers and educators. It was said to weaken countries economically, physically, and morally. More progressive interpretations, evident by the end of the nineteenth century, saw Indian alcoholism as another attempt by ruling groups to enslave the Indian. Education promised hope for eradicating alcoholism, and the new schools of revolutionary Mexico in the 1920s initiated campaigns to combat drinking, emphasizing the detrimental effects of excessive pulque consumption. When this did not work, reformers considered enacting plans similar to the Volstead Act, which ushered in prohibition in the United States. Nevertheless, consumption of fermented and distilled beverages continued, often to an extent that troubled the national conscience. The physical and psychological dependency on *chicha* and pulque, as well as on the new beverages introduced after 1492 has been singled out as the cause of everything from crime to malnutrition.

Pre-Conquest alcoholic beverages have retained their cultural significance into the twentieth century. Methods of preparation and rituals of consumption remained intact following the introduction of European beers and wines, though cheap, distilled beverages, especially cane brandy, have provided a popular alternative to the traditional beverages since the early sixteenth century.

Introductions to the history of pulque and *chicha* can be found in OSWALDO GONÇALVEZ DE LIMA, *El maguey y el pulque en los códices mexicanos* (1956); MARIO C. VÁZQUEZ, "La chicha en los paises andinos," *América Indígena* 27 (1967): 265–282; A. PAREDES, "Social Control of Drinking Among the Aztec Indians of Meso-America," in *Journal of Studies on Alcohol* 36, no. 9 (1975); 1139–1153; and C. MORRIS, "Maize Beer in the Economics, Politics, and Religion of the Inca Empire," in *Fermented Food Beverages in Nutrition*, edited by Clifford F. Gastineau, William J. Darby, and Thomas B. Turner (1979), pp. 21–35. GILMA LUCIA MORA DE TOVAR provides a thorough institutional history of cane brandy in *Aguardiente y conflictos sociales en la Nueva Granada durante el siglo XVIII* (1988). For comparisons with Mexico, see GILMA LUCIA MORA DE TOVAR, *El aguardiente de cana en México, 1724–1810* (1974). The social history of drink-

ing is presented in WILLIAM B. TAYLOR, *Drinking, Homicide, and Rebellion in Colonial Mexican Villages* (1979); MICHAEL C. SCARDAVILLE, "Alcohol Abuse and Tavern Reform in Late Colonial Mexico City," in *The Hispanic American Historical Review* 60, no. 4 (1980): 643–671; and JOHN C. SUPER, *Food, Conquest, and Colonization in Sixteenth-Century Spanish America* (1988).

JOHN C. SUPER

*See also* **Wine Industry.**

**ALCORIZA, LUIS** (*b.* 1920), Mexican film director. Born in Badajoz, Spain, into a theatrical family, Alcoriza performed in various plays as a child. After the fall of the Spanish Republic in 1939, the Alcoriza family immigrated to Mexico, where Luis continued his acting career in films in the 1940s. He also worked as a screenwriter for director Luis BUÑUEL on the acclaimed films *El gran calavera* (1949), *Los olvidados* (1950), *El bruto* (1952), *El* (1952), and *El ángel exterminador* (1962). He made his directorial debut in 1960 with the film *Los jóvenes.* Throughout the 1960s, Alcoriza directed a number of noted pictures, which constitute the most important film productions of the era: they include *Tlayucan* (1961), *Tiburoneros* (1962), *La puerta* (1968), and *Mecánica nacional* (1971), for which he received the Mexican film academy award, the Ariel, for best director. Other Alcoriza films include *Las fuerzas vivas* (1979) and *Lo que importa es vivir* (1987).

LUIS REYES DE LA MAZA, *El cine sonoro en México* (1973); E. BRADFORD BURNS, *Latin American Cinema: Film and History* (1975); CARL J. MORA, *Mexican Cinema: Reflections of a Society: 1896–1980* (1982); and JOHN KING, *Magical Reels: A History of Cinema in Latin America* (1990).

DAVID MACIEL

**ALCORTA, DIEGO** (*b.* November 1801; *d.* 7 January 1842), Argentine philosopher, physician, and politician. Born in Buenos Aires and educated there at the Colegio de la Unión del Sur and the University (1823–1827), Alcorta was more successful as an educator than as a politician. He was a founder of the Sociedad Elemental de Medicina in 1824 and became one of the pioneering surgeons of the Hospital de Hombres in 1828, a year after completing his medical studies. Also named principal professor of philosophy at the university that year, he dominated the philosophy department for fourteen years. An entire generation of writers and intellectuals had their first brush with European liberal writings under Alcorta's tutelage. His favorite texts came from the French Enlightenment, a reflection of the vogue for rationalism and utilitarianism in Buenos Aires in the 1820s. Among his students were Juan Bautista ALBERDI, Juan María Gutiérrez, José MÁRMOL, Felix Frías, and Vincente Fidel LÓPEZ, the shining lights of the Generation of 1837. As a deputy in the Chamber of Representatives, Alcorta voted in 1832 against the reinstatement of the caudillo Juan Manuel de ROSAS as governor of Buenos Aires. In 1833 he became vice rector of the University of Buenos Aires, but was ousted by Rosas supporters a year later. This did not prevent him from helping to write a blueprint constitution, which was dismissed in the emerging caudillo order as too liberal. Alcorta died in Buenos Aires.

CARLOS I. SALAS, *Apuntes biográficos del Dr. Diego Alcorta* (1889); JUAN MARIA GUTIÉRREZ, *Origen y dessarrollo de la enseñanza pública superior en Buenos Aires* (1915).

JEREMY ADELMAN

**ALDAMA Y GONZÁLEZ, IGNACIO DE** (*d.* 19 June 1811), Mexican insurgent leader. A lawyer who engaged in commerce, Aldama became magistrate of his native San Miguel el Grande. His brother Juan had joined Miguel HIDALGO, who launched an armed rebellion against the colonial regime on 16 September 1810. When Hidalgo reached San Miguel at the end of that month, Aldama signed an accord recognizing the authority of the insurgent leader. He subsequently joined the insurgent forces, eventually attaining the rank of field marshal. In February 1811, when Hidalgo and other insurgent leaders decided to retreat to the United States in search of aid, Aldama was sent, in the company of Friar Juan Salazar, as ambassador to Washington. Both men were captured in San Antonio Béjar, along with 100 bars of silver. Taken to Monclova, Aldama was tried and condemned to death. After submitting a disavowal of his actions, he was shot.

JOSÉ MARÍA MIQUEL I VERGÉS, *Diccionario de insurgentes* (1969), 15–16; HUGH M. HAMILL, JR., *The Hidalgo Revolt*, 2d ed. (1970); LUCAS ALAMÁN, *Historia de Méjico*, vol. 1 (1985); and CARLOS MARÍA DE BUSTAMANTE, *Cuadro histórico de la Revolución Mexicana*, vol. 1 (1985).

VIRGINIA GUEDEA

*See also* **Allende, Ignacio.**

**ALDAMA Y GONZÁLEZ, JUAN DE** (*b.* 3 January 1774; *d.* 26 June 1811), Mexican independence leader and co-evolutionary of Father Miguel Hidalgo. A Mexican creole *hacendado* anxious for recognition and social improvement, Aldama joined the Regimiento de Dragones Provinciales de la Reina, based in San Miguel el Grande, during the 1795 reorganization of the army of New Spain. Beginning service as a lieutenant, he had been promoted to the rank of militia captain by 1808. Involved in the Querétaro conspiracy (1810), Aldama traveled to the town of Dolores to inform Father HIDALGO and Captain Ignacio ALLENDE that the plot had been exposed. He was present during the first moments of the Hidalgo revolt, when prisoners were liberated from the Dolores jail and the district subdelegate was arrested.

From the beginning, Aldama attempted to maintain moderation among the rebels and opposed excesses such as property destruction and violence against Spaniards. Following the rebel capture of Guanajuato and the occupation of Valladolid, Morelia, he was promoted to lieutenant general. After the rebel defeat at Puente de Calderón (17 January 1811), Aldama retreated north with other principal rebel leaders. He was captured on 21 March 1811 and tried by royalist court-martial at Chihuahua. Despite his claims that he was a minor participant, Aldama was condemned to death and executed by firing squad.

LUCAS ALAMÁN, *Historia de México desde los primeros movimientos que prepararon su independencia en el año de 1808 hasta la época presente*, 5 vols. (1849–1852; repr. 1942); HUGH M. HAMILL, *The Hidalgo Revolt: Prelude to Mexican Independence* (1966); BRIAN R. HAMNETT, *Roots of Insurgency: Mexican Regions, 1750–1824* (1986).

CHRISTON I. ARCHER

*See also* **Mexican Independence, War of.**

**ALDANA, JOSÉ MARIA** (*b.* 1758; *d.* 7 February 1810), Mexican composer and violinist. Aldana began violin lessons while a choirboy at the cathedral in Mexico City. In 1775 he joined the cathedral orchestra but relinquished that post in 1788 when duties as violinist at Mexico City's Coliseo theater, begun two years earlier, conflicted. In 1790 he was named the Coliseo's orchestra director, a position he held concurrently, after 1808, with leadership of the Mexico City choir school. Compositions such as his vesper psalms for the Office of the Dead and other sacred and secular works (*Boleras nuevas*; *Minuet de variaciones*) place Aldana among the best native composers of his day.

ROBERT STEVENSON, *Music in Mexico: A Historical Survey* (1952).

ROBERT L. PARKER

**ALDEIAS,** Indian village settlements also known as *reduções*. *Aldeias* were Indian villages organized as MISSIONS by the regular clergy or colonial governors of Brazil. They were self-sufficient economic units that included the mission proper and the agricultural fields surrounding it. These mission villages stretched along the coast from the Amazon to the interior of southern and central Brazil. In Spanish America they were known as *reducciones*. Defeated Indians were often gathered into segregated fortified missions to facilitate conversion, pacification, and civilization. White merchants were not allowed into the *aldeias* without a special license. The missionaries tried to protect the Indians from mistreatment and enslavement by the white settlers, who disdained manual labor.

The most successful *aldeias* were established after 1549

by the Jesuits in Brazil. Since the Jesuits were few in number, the creation of permanent villages facilitated mass conversion. A handful of missionaries usually gathered scattered tribes into an *aldeia,* with a church, school, dormitory, kitchen, and warehouse, usually leaving one or two brothers behind to preside over these Christian settlements. To facilitate conversion of the entire tribe, evangelization usually aimed at converting the *caciques* (chiefs) and shamans first. The missionaries mastered the Tupi language, writing a dictionary, grammar, and catechism. The protection and gifts, as well as the religious ritual and music, offered by the Jesuit missionaries attracted the Indians. By 1655 the JESUIT ORDER was given complete control over all the Indian *aldeias* in Brazil.

Because of the threat of disease and enslavement, the missions were isolated from white settlements. For over two hundred years the Jesuits fought against Indian enslavement with the support of the crown. This resulted in white rebellion and Jesuit expulsions in 1662 and 1684. By the mid-seventeenth century the Jesuits had to compromise with the white settlers' desire for Indian labor by allowing a contract labor system for up to six months. The Jesuits began to arm their mission villages to protect the Indians from the slave-hunting expeditions (*bandeiras*) from São Paulo. In 1759 the Jesuit order was expelled from Brazil by order of the marquis of POMBAL. With the expulsion of the Jesuits, the larger *aldeias* fell under the control of the secular clergy, who incorporated the missions into the parish system; others were placed under secular directors until they were all disbanded by the end of the century.

Life was regimented in the *aldeias;* the ringing of bells summoned the Indians to pray, hear mass, study, and work in the fields. The Indians were often forced to accept Christianity and to perform manual labor for the missionaries. The congregation of the Indian tribes often facilitated the spread of diseases, such as smallpox and measles, which decimated whole tribes. Nonetheless, the *aldeias* provided a safe haven for many small tribes and helped to ensure Portuguese settlement and control of Brazil.

JOHN HEMMING, *Red Gold: The Conquest of the Brazilian Indians, 1500–1760* (1978); E. BRADFORD BURNS, *A History of Brazil,* 2d ed. (1980); JOHN HEMMING, *Amazon Frontier* (1987).

PATRICIA MULVEY

**ALEGRE, FRANCISCO JAVIER** (*b.* 12 November 1729; *d.* 16 August 1788), historian of the JESUITS in New Spain, latinist, and literary critic. A Jesuit priest and teacher born in Veracruz of Spanish parents, Alegre is best known for his *Historia de la Provincia de la Compañía de Jesús de Nueva España.* In this four-volume work, Alegre chronicles the history of Jesuit missionary activity in New Spain from their arrival in 1572 to shortly before the suppression of the order in 1767. Alegre was known

to be a brilliant teacher and writer with broad interests. He wrote several poetic works as well as a prodigious multivolume treatise on theology, *Institutionum theologicarum,* published posthumously in 1789. After the Jesuits of New Spain were banished to the Papal States in 1767, Alegre, along with several of his colleagues, lived the rest of his life in Italy and made a living as a tutor and librarian. One of the more original works of this period is his *Arte poético del Mon. Boileau,* a translation and extensive commentary on Nicolas Boileau's *L'art poétique,* published posthumously by Joaquín García Icazbalceta in 1889. This is an early instance of literary criticism from a decidedly Latin American perspective.

See ERNEST J. BURRUS and FELIZ ZUBILLAGA's critical edition of Alegre's *Historia de la Provincia de la Compañía de Jesús* (1956), esp. pp. 1–32 for a bio-bibliography. ALLAN FIGUEROA DECK studies Alegre as a precocious literary critic in *Francisco Javier Alegre: A Study in Mexican Literary Criticism* (1976).

ALLAN FIGUEROA DECK, S.J.

**ALEGRÍA, CIRO** (*b.* November 1909; *d.* February 1967), Peruvian novelist, essayist, and politician. A relative of the Argentine novelist Benito LYNCH, in his youth, Alegría had as his first-grade teacher the *mestizo* César VALLEJO, one of the most important Latin American poets of the twentieth century. Alegría lived for some time on his paternal grandfather's estate in Marcabal Grande, where he familiarized himself with the indigenous culture, camping with the natives at the edge of the jungle and listening to their tales.

Alegría was active in the American Popular Revolutionary Alliance (Alianza Popular Revolucionaria Americana—APRA), for which he was imprisoned in 1932–1933. Forced into exile from 1934 to 1960, he returned to Peru and was elected to the Peruvian Chamber of Deputies in 1963. While in exile Alegría lived and wrote in Santiago, Chile, winning prizes for his first three novels: *La serpiente de oro* (1935; The Golden Serpent), *Los perros hambrientos* (1938; The Hungry Dogs), and *El mundo es ancho y ajeno* (1941; Broad and Alien Is the World), which was honored by its American publisher Farrar and Rinehart. It subsequently was translated into twelve languages. In the 1940s Alegría lived in the United States, where he taught at several universities.

Revealing his concern for the marginalized members of Peruvian society, particularly the indigenous population, Alegría's novels demonstrate considerable artistic merit and are of great testimonial value. According to Mario VARGAS LLOSA, *Broad and Alien Is the World* is "the point of departure for modern Peruvian narrative literature and its author [is] our first classic novelist." Alegría cared little about novelistic structure and form, but was able to re-create with great skill the experiences and dialogue of indigenous peoples, achieving at his best considerable lyrical intensity.

ANGEL FLORES, *The Literature of Spanish America* (1966–1969), vol. 4, pp. 245–258; EMIR RODRÍGUEZ MONEGAL, *Narradores de esta América* (1969), pp. 166–174; EILEEN EARLY, *Joy in Exile: Ciro Alegría's Narrative Art* (1980).

KEITH McDUFFIE

*See also* **Literature: Spanish America; Peru: Political Parties.**

**ALEGRÍA, CLARIBEL** (*b.* 1924), Salvadoran writer. An outstanding poet, Alegría pioneered feminism as well as the modernization of the Central American novel with her masterpiece, *Cenizas de Izalco* (Ashes of Izalco, 1965). Her later works have been recognized for their testimonial writing about Salvadoran women.

Although she was born in Nicaragua, Alegría was taken to El Salvador at age one. She was only seven when the MATANZA (massacre) of 1932—in which dictator Maximiliano HERNÁNDEZ MARTÍNEZ assassinated 30,000 peasants in the space of a month—took place. She swore that one day she would write down everything she had witnessed. She studied at Georgetown University in Washington, D.C., during the late 1940s and became one of the first Central American women to obtain a university degree. While in Washington she married Darwin Flakoll, with whom she wrote *Cenizas de Izalco,* which initiated a shift from poetry to narrative as the basic Central American literary form. Flakoll also translated this work in 1989. In the 1950s they moved to the small town of Deyá on the island of Majorca, Spain. They lived next to the English poet Robert Graves, and shared an expatriate life with well-known artists and writers. In 1980 Alegría moved to Nicaragua, where she worked on behalf of the Salvadoran people. She also cowrote with Flakoll her testimonial narrative about women, *No me agarrarán viva: La mujer salvadoreña en la lucha* (1983), translated by Amanda Hopkinson as *They Won't Take Me Alive: Salvadoran Women in the Struggle for National Liberation* (1984).

Besides *Cenizas,* her books include *Sobrevivo* (1978), winner of the Casa de las Américas Award; *Álbum familiar* (1984), translated by Amanda Hopkinson as *Family Album* (1991); *Pueblo de Dios y de mandinga* (1985); and *Luisa en el país de la realidad* (1987), translated by Flakoll as *Luisa in Realityland* (1987).

MARÍA B. DE MEMBRENO, *Literatura de El Salvador* (1959); MANLIO ARGUETA, *Poesía de El Salvador* (1983); JOSÉ CORONEL URTECHO, *Líneas para un boceto de Claribel Alegría* (1987); SANDRA BOSCHETTO and MARCIA MC GOWAN, eds., *Claribel Alegría: An Anthology of Critical Essays* (1994).

ARTURO ARIAS

**ALEGRÍA, FERNANDO** (*b.* 26 September 1918), Chilean writer and scholar. Born and raised in Santiago, Chile, he moved to the United States in 1940. His creative works (fifteen novels and four volumes of short stories) have centered primarily on the historical reality of his native country, but have also focused on the relationships and divergences between the Latin American and North American cultures. He began his academic career as professor of Latin American literature at the University of California, Berkeley (1947–1967), and later taught at Stanford University, where in 1990 he was awarded an endowed chair in the humanities.

Three thematic concerns dominate Alegría's narrative work. The first is the literary representation of the founding fathers of Chile's social history, found in the biographical novels *Recabarren* (1938), *Lautaro, joven libertador de Arauco* (1943; Lautaro, A Young Liberator, 1944), and *Allende* (1989). The second distinctive theme is the reevaluation of the historical and cultural experience of the Generation of 1938, developed in *Mañana los guerreros* (1964; Tomorrow the Warriors) and the autobiographical novel *Una especie de memoria* (1983; A Type of Memoir). Finally, he has written a trilogy focusing on the picaresque misadventures of Chileans who come to work in the United States where they are later forced to confront their true identities vis-à-vis the contradictions of American society: *Caballo de copas* (1957; *My Horse González,* 1964), *Amerika, Amerikka, Amerikka* (1970; *The Funhouse,* 1986), and *La rebelión de los placeres* (1990; The Rebellion of the Placeres).

JUAN ARMANDO EPPLE, *Para una fundación imaginaria de Chile. La literatura de Fernando Alegría* (1987); NICOLÁS KANELLOS, ed., *Biographical Dictionary of Hispanic Literature in the United States* (1989), pp. 6–13; HELMY GIACOMÁN, ed., *Homenaje a Fernando Alegría* (1972).

J. A. EPPLE

*See also* **Literature.**

**ALEIJADINHO** (Antônio Francisco Lisbôa; *b.* ca. 1738; *d.* 18 November 1814), Brazilian architect and sculptor. Born in the provincial capital of Villa Rica do Ouro Prêto, Aleijadinho was a product of colonial Brazil, where the baroque and rococo art and architecture of MINAS GERAIS was a vehicle of nativist expression; here Saint Michael the Archangel appeared in a profusion of Indian feathers, and a dark-skinned Virgin Mary was portrayed as a MESTIZO. Contributing to this nativism was Antônio Francisco Lisbôa, known as Aleijadinho (the Little Cripple), whose prolific and distinctive work as an architect, sculptor, and decorator of Mineiro churches is emblematic of the era.

Aleijadinho was the son of Manuel Francisco Lisbôa and a slave named Isabel; he had two full siblings. The year Aleijadinho was born, his father married another woman, by whom he had four legitimate children. Although his father recognized Antônio Francisco as his son, gave him his name, and brought him into his profession of builder and artisan, little documentation illuminates their relationship. His father may have learned his craft from family members in Portugal, because his brother, Antônio Francisco Pombal, was also an architect who built Mineiro churches; on their mother's side they were presumably related to the celebrated Portuguese architect João Antunes. In addition to working under his father's direction, Aleijadinho was taught design by the painter João Gomes Baptista.

Aleijadinho executed his first pieces in wood and stone at age fourteen and worked steadily at his craft until close to his death in Ouro Prêto at the age of seventy-six. He made effective use of Brazil's native soapstone, which is relatively easy to carve when freshly cut. He often worked in conjunction with the painters Francisco Xavier Carneiro and Manoel da Costa Ataíde.

The church was the center of Mineiro social life and Aleijadinho's main patron. Eighteenth-century Portuguese church architecture was influenced by that of Bavaria and Austria, in part due to the cultural interchange resulting from the marriages of King JOÃO V (reigned 1707–1750) and the Marquês of POMBAL to Austrian princesses. The Austrian-Bavarian influence is apparent in the churches of Minas, particularly those designed and decorated by Aleijadinho. Although Aleijadinho never left Brazil, printed engravings gave him a familiarity with European forms.

While Aleijadinho's body of work is immense, and he is known to have contributed to many projects as a subcontractor, his documented work is concentrated in Ouro Prêto, Sabará, São João del Rei, and Congonhos do Campo. His most important works are the churches of São Francisco in Ouro Prêto and São João de Rei, Nossa Senhora do Carmo in Sabará, and Bom Jesus de Matosinhos in Congonhos. This last church is a pilgrimage site graced by Aleijadinho's magnum opus, sixty-six wooden life-size figures that comprise an incomplete set of the stations of the cross (1796–1799) and twelve remarkable soapstone statues of the Old Testament prophets (1800–1805), arranged in a dramatic, ballet-like way on the entry terrace.

Much of this work was done under the handicap of a debilitating and painful disease that has been variously described as leprosy, syphilis, or a viral influenza contracted in 1777. It caused scarring, crippling, progressive loss of movement, and disfigurement, and gained for him the name by which he is best known. He lost his toes, his hands atrophied and shriveled, and he had to be carried to his work sites, where curtains shielded him from casual views. He executed the Congonhos prophets with chisel and mallet strapped to the stumps of his gnarled hands.

Details of Aleijadinho's life are provided by his mid-nineteenth-century biographer, Rodrigo José Ferreira Brêtas, who obtained information from Aleijadinho's daughter-in-law, Joana Francisca Lopes, in whose home the artist spent his last days. Among the known facts of Aleijadinho's personal life is that he had a son with a

The prophet Baruch. Sculpture by Aleijadinho, at the church of Bom Jesus de Matinhos (1796–1805). BENSON LATIN AMERICAN COLLECTION, UNIVERSITY OF TEXAS AT AUSTIN.

slave named Ana; Manuel Francisco Lisbôa was born circa 1775 and followed his father's profession.

More than a dozen Mineiro towns and Rio de Janeiro claim to possess statues, retables, pulpits, altars, doorways, windows, fountains, and buildings attributed to Aleijadinho. Some of the many items ascribed to him may have been done by his assistants and students. His most distinctive works are undoubtedly his sculptures, which Aleijadinho infused with his own suffering. Art historian Pál Kelemen wrote, "Aleijadinho carried Brazilian Rococo to its fullest flowering. . . . A rare human story lives in his masterpieces; his gift was genius."

No more modern definitive biography of Aleijadinho exists. Researchers should begin with RODRIGO JOSÉ FERREIRA BRÊTAS, *Antônio Francisco Lisbôa—O Aleijadinho,* in *Revista do Arquivo*

*Público Mineiro*, vol. 1 (1896): 163–174. The premier work by a great authority on Baroque art is GERMAIN BAZIN, *Aleijadinho et la sculpture baroque au Brésil* (1963). For the Latin American context see PÁL KELEMEN, *Baroque and Rococo in Latin America* (1967). A brief study that tackles some of the questions of authenticity of attributed works and has an abbreviated version of Brêtas is SYLVIO DE VASCONCELLOS, *Vida e obra de Antônio Francisco Lisbôa, O Aleijadinho* (1979). In a similar vein are DELSON GONÇALVES FERREIRA, *O Aleijadinho* (1981); FERNANDO JORGE, *O Aleijadinho: sua vida, sua obra, seu génio*, 6th rev. ed. (1984); and MYRIAM A. RIBEIRO DE OLIVEIRA, *Aleijadinho: Passos e Profetas* (1985). For an excellent photo essay on his magnum opus, see HANS MANN and GRACIELA MANN, *The Twelve Prophets of Aleijadinho* (1967). For Aleijadinho's place in Mineiro culture see the classic by ALCEU AMOROSO LIMA, *Voz de Minas*, 2d rev. ed. (1946). Those seeking fuller listings of sources should consult the fine bibliographies by James E. Hogan (Librarian, College of the Holy Cross), "Antônio Francisco Lisbôa: 'O Aleijadinho': An Annotated Bibliography," in *Latin American Research Review* 9, no. 2 (1974): 83–94; and "The Contemporaries of Antônio Francisco Lisbôa: An Annotated Bibliography," in ibid., 138–45.

FRANK D. McCANN, JR.

**ALEM, LEANDRO** (*b.* 25 February 1842; *d.* 1 July 1896), theoretician and founder of the Argentine Radical Party (Unión Cívica Radical—UCR). Profoundly opposed to the arranged politics of the ruling oligarchy in late-nineteenth-century Argentina, Leandro Alem founded and led the Unión Cívica (UC) between 1890 and 1896. Against a backdrop of economic depression, in 1890 Alem and his associates rebelled against the government and forced the resignation of President Miguel JUÁREZ CELMAN. But elements of the ruling elite succeeded in co-opting many of those affiliated with the Unión Cívica. Alem broke with the UC, created an intransigent splinter group, the Unión Cívica Radical, and played at revolution for the next five years. He failed, however, to generate the popular support necessary to challenge the government. In 1896 the UCR was a minor faction on the margin of the political spectrum. Frustrated and despondent, Alem committed suicide in 1896.

Born in Buenos Aires, Alem attended schools in his native city. His tumultuous public life began in 1868 in an independent political club called Equality, whose members advocated ethical and moral politics and EFFECTIVE SUFFRAGE (votes not compromised by corruption). In 1871 he entered the politics of Buenos Aires Province, and in 1874 he was elected a national deputy. A defender of provincial rights, Alem vigorously opposed the federalization of the city of Buenos Aires and warned against a dangerous centralization of politics.

Increasingly isolated, Alem resigned from Congress and assumed a new role as the intellectual leader of discontented pockets of the elite who were frozen out of national politics. Together with Aristóbulo del VALLE and Hipólito YRIGOYEN, Alem in 1877 formed the short-lived Republican Party, which was dedicated to federalism and to civic honesty rather than corrupt and arranged politics. In 1889 Alem and others organized the Unión Cívica de la Juventud (Youth Civic Union), which in 1890 evolved into the Unión Cívica as it attracted wider support.

Alem was a primary leader in "El Noventa" ('90), an armed insurrection against the government in July 1890 that brought down the regime of President Juárez Celman, although the rebels failed to take power. A shaken government was forced to guarantee total amnesty to the rebels. As one politician stated: "The revolution is conquered, but the government is dead." But it was the politics of accommodation that deprived Alem of a victory. During 1891 the UC split into the National Civic Union (UCN), led by Bartolomé MITRE, and Alem's faction, the UCR. Mitre's UCN soon reached an arrangement with the oligarchy and won participation in the political process. Alem preached "relentless struggle," which became the motto of the UCR.

The UCR emerged in the 1890s as a party of vague ideals motivated more by emotion than by a carefully developed program. It was Alem who erected the two great principles of radicalism: an ethical conception of politics and a federal form of government. The UCR continued to flirt with revolution. In 1893 Alem led an insurrection in the province of Santa Fe and identified the party with the demands of agricultural colonists. Failure to generate a revolution on a broader scale precipitated division and crisis in party ranks and severely weakened the UCR. A bitter Alem surveyed the wreckage of the party in 1896 and predicted: "The conservative members of the Radical Party will go along with Don Bernardo [de Yrigoyen]; other Radicals will become socialists or anarchists; the Buenos Aires rabble, led by that perfidious traitor, my nephew Hipólito [Yrigoyen], will come to an agreement with Roque SÁENZ PEÑA, and we intransigents, will go to hell (José Luis Romero, *A History of Argentine Political Thought*, pp. 216–217). Alem had lost both influence and authority, which likely contributed to his suicide later in the year.

In a larger historical context, Leandro Alem not only led disaffected members of the elite but also represented traditional popular elements that earlier in the century had identified with the dictator Juan Manuel de ROSAS. Alem was a link between the federalism and populism of the early and mid-nineteenth century and the later reforms of Hipólito Yrigoyen and, some would argue, Juan Domingo PERÓN.

GABRIEL DEL MAZO, *El radicalismo: Ensayo sobre su historia y doctrina*, 3d ed. (1957), chaps. 1 and 2; JOSÉ LUIS ROMERO, *A History of Argentine Political Thought*, translated by Thomas F. McGann (1963), chap. 8; DAVID ROCK, *Politics in Argentina, 1890–1930: The Rise and Fall of Radicalism* (1975), chaps. 3 and 4; and RICHARD J. WALTER, *The Socialist Party of Argentina, 1890–1930* (1977), pp. 7–9.

PAUL GOODWIN

*See also* **Argentina: Political Parties.**

**ALEMÁN VALDÉS, MIGUEL** (*b.* 29 September 1900; *d.* 27 September 1983), president of Mexico (1946–1952). Alemán represents a notable political generation in twentieth-century Mexico. He was the first civilian to hold the presidency for a full term after a series of revolutionary generals, a feat that marked the beginning of the dominance of the professional politician in Mexico. His administration is remembered for the young, college-educated politicians appointed to his cabinet; for corruption in high office; for an emphasis on state-supported industrialization; for the reform of the government-controlled party, the Institutional Revolutionary Party (Partido Revolucionario Institucional—PRI); for the decline in the number of military officers in political office; for additions to the National University; and for increased ties between politicians and business elites. Alemán produced one of the two most influential political groups in contemporary politics (the Alemanistas), one that influenced decision making through the 1970s.

Alemán was born in the small rural community of Sayula, Veracruz, on Mexico's east coast, the son of a farmer who became a general during the Mexican Revolution (1910–1920). He studied in various towns before moving to Mexico City to enroll at the National Preparatory School. Alemán continued his studies at the National Autonomous University, where he received his law degree in 1928. Although he initially practiced law, specializing in labor disputes, he soon entered the political arena.

Alemán's first post was as an adviser to the Secretary of Agriculture and Livestock (1928–1930); he subsequently was appointed a judge of the Superior Court of the Federal District from 1930 to 1934. At the age of thirty-four, he represented his home state in the Senate, and two years later he achieved national recognition by winning election as governor of Veracruz (1936–1939). Before completing his term of office, Alemán was appointed head of General Manuel ÁVILA CAMACHO's presidential campaign in 1939. Following Ávila Camacho's successful bid for the presidency, Alemán was named minister of internal affairs (1940–1945), a position that he used to set his career on a course toward the presidency in 1946.

After leaving government, Alemán directed Mexico's tourism agency from 1961 until his death. He became a major figure in business circles, developing holdings in print and electronic media, including Televisa, Mexico's largest television network. The president's son, Miguel Alemán Velasco, has continued to be an important figure in Mexican television.

GEORGE S. WISE, *El México de Alemán* (1952); MIGUEL ALEMÁN, *Miguel Alemán contesta* (1975); LUIS MEDINA, *Civilismo y modernización del autoritarismo, historia de la Revolución mexicana* (1979).

RODERIC AI CAMP

*See also* **Mexico: Political Parties.**

**ALENCAR, JOSÉ MARTINIANO DE** (*b.* 1 May 1829; *d.* 12 December 1877), Brazilian writer, playwright, poet, and statesman. He was born in Messajana, state of Ceará, in northern Brazil. In 1850 he graduated from law school and founded the academic journal *Ensaios Literários*, of which he was the editor. Between 1851 and 1855, Alencar contributed to *Ensaios Literários* and other academic journals and also worked as a journalist on several daily newspapers. Most of his political career occurred between 1859 and 1877.

Alencar is considered to be one of the founders of Brazilian narrative writing. He cultivated Indianist and urban novels and introduced some of the most significant techniques observed in the Latin American narrative. As a romantic writer and an artist, he sought to underscore nationalistic themes and undermine Eurocentric aesthetics, which were so prevalent at the time. Before Alencar, Brazilian letters were characterized by gongoristic classicism. which also dominated Portuguese literature. In all of his work, Alencar demonstrated an acute concern for language and the establishment of a true Brazilian linguistic expression, one devoid of all Portuguese influence.

Some of his most significant works are *O marquês de Paraná* (1856), an autobiographical piece; *O guarani* (1857), an interpretation of Brazilian colonial history in which he depicts the relationship between native Brazilians and the Portuguese colonizers; *O demônio familiar* (1857), a two-act comedy; *A noite de São João* (1857), a musical comedy, with music by Elias Lobo; *As asas de um anjo* (1860), a comedy in one prologue, four acts, and one epilogue. His novel *Lucíola* was first published in Paris in 1862. *As minas de prata* (1862, 1865–1866) is another historical novel.

The novel *Iracema* (1865), subtitled by Alencar "the myth of Ceará," is considered to be his chief work. Its leitmotiv is the beauty of Brazil. It is seen as the most nationalistic of his books, a work that has merited translations in several languages and is acclaimed as one of the world's most important classics of romantic literature. Alencar's narrative displays the Portuguese language as it was spoken in the Americas, with its own dynamic linguistic expressions, and with creative images and symbols that capture in great detail the unique beauty of Brazil. It is a romantic love story between an Indian princess, Iracema, and the white Martim; from their love is born Moacyr, whose name means "the son of pain." Iracema is also considered to be the first heroine of the Brazilian novel, for her death is depicted in the narrative as the sacrifice of her love for Martim. Alencar died in Rio de Janeiro.

CLAUDE HULET, *Brazilian Literature*, vol. 1 (1974); ACADEMIA CEARENSE DE LETRAS, *Alencar 100 anos depois* (1977); ASSIS BRASIL, *O livro de ouro da literatura brasileira* (1980); RENATA MAUTNER WASSERMAN, "Re-Inventing the New World; Cooper and Alencar," in *Comparative Literature* 36 (1984): 130–152; MARÍA TAI WOLFF, "Rereading José de Alencar: the Case of *A Pata da Gazela*," in *Hispania* 71 (December 1988): 812–819; LAURA LYNN

FRANKLIN, "Indianism in *Atala* of Chateaubriand and *Iracema* of José de Alencar: A reappraisal" (Ph.D. diss., George Washington University, 1989); GUSTAVO PÉREZ FIRMAT, *Do the Americas Have a Common Literature?* (1990), esp. p. 394.

ROSÂNGELA MARIA VIEIRA

*See also* **Literature.**

**ALESSANDRI PALMA, ARTURO** (*b.* 20 December 1868; *d.* 24 August 1950), president of Chile (1920–1925 and 1932–1938). Educated at the University of Chile as a lawyer, he entered politics as a candidate of the Liberal Party (PL). A bombastic orator and tireless campaigner, he served in the Chamber of Deputies, in the Senate, and as a cabinet minister. Running on a reformist ticket, he was elected president in 1920. Alessandri had the bad luck to become president when Chile was suffering from a massive economic dislocation caused by the postwar collapse of the nitrate market.

Alessandri hoped to introduce numerous economic and social reforms, but his political opposition refused to pass his legislative program. Caught between widespread social unrest and an entrenched parliamentary opposition, Alessandri's reforms languished. The president found an unexpected ally in disaffected field-grade army officers who, distressed by their own wretched economic situation and the nation's suffering, intimidated the legislature into passing the reform package.

While initially pleased with his newfound support, Alessandri discovered that the officer corps was demanding that the legislature resign. Aware that he could not control them, Alessandri quit in January 1925, and a conservative military junta began to rule. When it became clear that the junta would attempt to elect a conservative to the presidency, junior army officers seized power and requested Alessandri to return. Upon doing so in March, Alessandri, ruling under the newly written Constitution of 1925, managed to pass certain reformist legislation. He resigned a second time in October, when he realized that he could not control the minister of war, Carlos IBÁÑEZ DEL CAMPO, who would seize power in 1927.

Alessandri went into exile, joining the various plots to overthrow Ibáñez. After the dictator's fall, in 1931, Alessandri returned to Chile, where he unsuccessfully ran against Juan Esteban Montero Rodríguez for the presidency. In 1932, following the collapse of the Montero administration and the Socialist Republic, Alessandri became president for a second term.

Due to widespread unrest and the collapse of the economy, Alessandri's second term of office was only slightly less turbulent than his first administration. He nonetheless managed to govern the nation, stimulating the economy by encouraging the creation of national industries and supporting the construction of public and private housing. His brutal suppression of an abor-

tive Nazi coup in 1938 alienated many people, contributing to the defeat of Gustavo Ross Santa María, Alessandri's candidate for the presidency.

An energetic and dynamic individual, Alessandri remained active in Chile's political life, serving as president of the Senate. A forceful leader, he may best be remembered as the man who appealed to the lower classes and who, using the powers provided by the 1925 Constitution, restored order to Chile and led it out of the Great Depression.

RICARDO DONOSO NOVOA, *Alessandri, agitador y demoledor. Cincuenta años de historia política de Chile*, 2 vols. (1952–1954); ARTURO ALESSANDRI PALMA, *Recuerdos de gobierno*, 3 vols. (1967); ROBERT J. ALEXANDER, *Arturo Alessandri. A Biography*, 2 vols. (1977); PAUL W. DRAKE, *Socialism and Populism in Chile, 1932–1952* (1978); BILL ALBERT, *South America and the First World War: The Impact of the War on Brazil, Argentina, Peru, and Chile* (1988), pp. 286–287, 311–312.

WILLIAM F. SATER

**ALESSANDRI RODRÍGUEZ, JORGE** (*b.* 19 May 1896; *d.* 31 August 1986), president of Chile (1958–1964). The son of former president Arturo ALESSANDRI PALMA, Jorge was an engineer who entered politics in 1926. An industrialist, he served as a senator and, later, as cabinet minister in the government of Gabriel GONZÁLEZ VIDELA. A man without clearly defined political ideas, the conservative Alessandri became president in 1958, barely defeating his left-wing opponent, Dr. Salvador ALLENDE, in a bitterly contested election.

As a minority president, Alessandri attempted to revive the Chilean economy by stimulating the domestic industries, particularly the construction sector, and encouraging the American copper companies to increase production. His government was one of the first to institute a modified agrarian reform program. After some initial success, Alessandri's economic program foundered because the sluggish domestic economy could not satisfy consumer needs. When imports soared, Alessandri had to devalue the Chilean currency, precipitating another devastating round of inflation that led to widespread political unrest. Rather than expanding the role of the state, the austere Alessandri unsuccessfully attempted to cure Chile's deep-seated socioeconomic problems using traditional methods.

In 1970, supported by the conservative National Party (PN), Alessandri again opposed Salvador Allende for president. This time, unlike 1958, Allende triumphed, largely because his opposition was divided between Alessandri and the Christian Democrat, Radomiro Tomic.

JAMES F. PETRAS, *Politics and Social Forces in Chilean Development* (1969), 104–107; BARBARA STALLINGS, *Class Conflict and Economic Development in Chile: 1958–1973* (1978).

WILLIAM F. SATER

**ALEXANDER VI, POPE** (*b.* 1 January 1431; *d.* 31 October 1503), pope (1492–1503). The Spaniard Rodrigo de Borja, the future Alexander VI, is notorious for his immorality and corruption. He fathered four illegitimate children and bribed other cardinals to elect him pope. As a protégé of King FERDINAND II OF ARAGON, Alexander issued a number of papal bulls sanctioning Spain's conquest and colonization of the New World. The papal bull of 1493 fixed the demarcation line of the future American empire along a circle which passed 100 leagues (3 nautical miles) west of the Cape Verde Islands and set the stage for the Treaty of TORDESILLAS (1494). Alexander also confirmed the new Spanish territories as a papal fief held by the crown (1493), granted the crown all tithes levied in the New World (1501), and charged the monarchs with christianizing the native populations. The responsibility for conversion was linked to Alexander's conferring upon Ferdinand and ISABELLA the title "the Catholic kings" (*los reyes católicos*) (1494).

JOHN H. ELLIOTT, *Imperial Spain, 1469–1716* (1963), esp. pp. 52–100; JOHN H. PARRY, *The Age of Reconnaissance* (1963).

SUZANNE HILES BURKHOLDER

**ALEXANDER, EDWARD PORTER** (*b.* 26 May 1835; *d.* 28 April 1910), American diplomat. Following distinguished service as a Confederate artillery and engineering officer during the Civil War, Alexander successfully adapted to civilian life in business, railroading, and rice planting in Georgia and southern California. In 1897 President Grover Cleveland appointed him as arbitrator of the Costa Rica–Nicaragua boundary dispute under the terms of the Convention of San Salvador (27 March 1896). Alexander spent three years in Central America, mostly in San Juan del Norte (Greytown), Nicaragua, and rendered several decisions leading to a temporary agreement between the two states in 1900. Alexander's role in this affair reflected the rising U.S. presence in the diplomatic affairs of the isthmus.

DOUGLAS SOUTHALL FREEMAN, "Edward Porter Alexander," in *Dictionary of American Biography* (1928), vol. 1, pp. 164–166; RALPH LEE WOODWARD, JR., "Las impresiones de un general de las fuerzas confederadas sobre Centroamérica en los años finales del siglo XIX," in *Anuario de estudios centroamericanos* 4 (1979): 39–66.

RALPH LEE WOODWARD, JR.

*See also* **United States–Latin American Relations.**

**ALEXIS, JACQUES STÉPHEN** (*b.* 22 April 1922; *d.* April 1961), Haitian novelist, story writer, essayist, and physician. Son of historian, novelist, playwright, and diplomat Stéphen Alexis, Jacques Stéphen was born in Gonaïves during the American occupation of Haiti. Successor to the Marxist nationalism of Jacques ROUMAIN, he eventually emerged to become the compelling exponent of his own lyrically infused, proletarian-identified vision of a uniquely Haitian "marvelous realism." Initially educated at the College Stanislas in Paris and the Institution Saint-Louis de Gonzague in Port-au-Prince, Alexis took an early, active part in Haitian avant-garde cultural and political life. A member of the Communist Party at sixteen, he later also wrote regularly, as Jacques la Colère, for the radical journal *La Ruche*. With René DEPESTRE and other members of its editorial staff, he directly contributed to the success of the Revolution of 1946, which brought down the government of Élie LESCOT. While pursuing his medical studies in Paris, Alexis moved in radical, left-wing, surrealist, existentialist, and Antillean négritude circles. Thereafter, he traveled through Europe, the Middle East, Russia, and China. Returning to Haiti in 1954, Alexis published *Compère général soleil* (1955), the novel that established his reputation as one of his country's most important writers of fiction. *Les Arbres musiciens* (1957), *L'espace d'un cillement* (1959), and *Romancero aux étoiles* (1960), a collection of short stories, followed in quick succession to confirm that original assessment.

Representing a formal and thematic convergence between literary realism, Afro-Antillean cultural nationalism, Marxist anticolonialism, and a universalizing art that "is indissolubly linked to the myth, the symbol, the stylized, the heraldic, even the hieratic," Alexis's fiction strives for "a new balance . . . born of singularity and antithesis" (J. S. Alexis, "Of the Marvelous Realism of the Haitians," *Présence Africaine* [English edition], nos. 8–10 [1956]: 265). Extending the legacy of Jacques Roumain, it enlarges the settings, formal daring, thematic range, and visionary reach of the Haitian peasant and working-class novel. His influence among contemporary writers continues to be felt near the end of the twentieth century and is particularly evident in René Depestre's *Le mât de cocagne* (1979) and Pierre Clitandre's *Cathédrale du mois d'aout* (1982).

Radical opposition to the François DUVALIER regime forced Alexis to leave Haiti clandestinely in 1960. Attempting to land secretly at Mole Saint Nicholas a year later as part of a small guerrilla group, Alexis was apprehended, imprisoned, and finally stoned to death by his captors. In addition to published novels, stories, and essays bearing witness to his passionate devotion to Haiti's common folk and a historical materialist critique of essentialist versions of négritude, he left behind two unpublished works in progress, *L'Eglantine* and *L'Étoile absinthe*.

*Europe: Revue Mensuelle* 49, no. 501 (January 1971), is largely devoted to an assessment of Alexis and the literature of Haiti. See also J. MICHAEL DASH, *Jacques Stéphen Alexis* (1975), and DAVID NICHOLLS, *From Dessalines to Duvalier: Race, Colour, and National Independence in Haiti* (1979).

ROBERTO MÁRQUEZ

**ALFARO, RICARDO JOAQUÍN** (*b*. 20 August 1882; *d*. 23 February 1971), a Panamanian statesman who served as minister to the United States (1922–1930; 1933–1936), foreign minister (1946), and provisional president (1931–1932). A tireless advocate of Panamanian rights in the Canal Zone, Alfaro negotiated the HULL–ALFARO TREATY (1936) and served as an adviser during the treaty negotiations with the United States in 1947. He also protested the continued U.S. occupation of defense sites after World War II until the U.S. withdrawal in 1948. Alfaro presided over the 1932 presidential campaign with fairness and honesty, a rarity in Panamanian politics. Subsequently, he served as a member of the International Court of Justice at The Hague (1959–1964).

RICARDO J. ALFARO, *Medio siglo de relaciones entre Panamá y los Estados Unidos*, new ed. (1959); WALTER LA FEBER, *The Panama Canal: The Crisis in Historical Perspective* (1978); MICHAEL CONNIFF, *Panama and the United States* (1991).

THOMAS M. LEONARD

**ALFARO DELGADO, JOSÉ ELOY** (*b*. 25 June 1842; *d*. 28 January 1912), president of Ecuador (interim 1896–1897, constitutional 1897–1901, interim 1906–1907, constitutional 1907–1911). Born in Montecristi, Manabí, Alfaro began his political career as a partisan of General José María Urvina, leading revolts in 1865 and 1871 against the conservative regime of Gabriel García Moreno (1869–1875). When the movements failed, he fled to Panama, where he developed a successful business and married. He subsequently used his wealth to finance liberal publications and insurrections against conservative governments in Ecuador and to support liberal causes throughout Latin America. By 1895, when he returned to Ecuador to lead the liberal forces, Alfaro had an international reputation as a revolutionary. With the support of wealthy coastal exporting interests, Alfaro's forces defeated the government troops. Alfaro convened a constituent assembly that wrote a new liberal constitution and elected him president. The liberals would retain power for the next three decades.

Despite a commitment to liberal principles, including the creation of a secular, activist state, Alfaro's political style was authoritarian and personalist. Until his death in 1912, he sought to maintain power by any means and was a principal cause of the political turmoil that characterized Ecuador in this period. He failed in his effort to prevent the inauguration of his successor Leonidas Plaza in 1901, but managed to oust Lizardo García, who took office in 1905. As in 1896, Alfaro convened the 1906 constituent assembly to legitimize his usurpation of power.

During Alfaro's second constitutional term, the Quito and Guayaquil Railroad was inaugurated, and real property held in mortmain by religious orders was nationalized. These accomplishments were partly eclipsed by Alfaro's harsh repression of political opponents and lack of respect for civil liberties.

Failing to prevent the inauguration of Emilio Estrada as his successor on 31 August 1911, Alfaro once again fled to Panama. However, when Estrada's untimely death in December 1911 unleashed a civil war, he returned from Panama to participate in the unsuccessful insurrection against the government. The public damned Alfaro and his supporters as unprincipled opportunists willing to destroy the nation to gain their ends and demanded that the rebels be punished. Alfaro was taken to Quito for trial. A mob burst into the prison and murdered the prisoners, including Eloy Alfaro.

LUIS ROBALINO DÁVILA, *Orígines de Ecuador de hoy*, vol. 7, pts. 1–2 (1969); LINDA ALEXANDER RODRÍGUEZ, *The Search for Public Policy: Regional Politics and Government Finances in Ecuador, 1830–1940* (1985), esp. pp. 46–49; FRANK MACDONALD SPINDLER, *Nineteenth Century Ecuador* (1987), esp. pp. 147–210.

LINDA ALEXANDER RODRÍGUEZ

*See also* **Ecuador: Constitutions; Political Parties; Revolution of 1895.**

**ALFARO SIQUEIROS, DAVID** (also Siqueiros; *b* 29 December 1896; *d*. 6 January 1974), Mexican artist. Muralist, painter, printmaker, theoretician, labor organizer, soldier, and Communist Party leader, Siqueiros not only produced a sizable and influential body of political-artistic theory but was the most technically innovative of the *tres grandes,* the Big Three of the Mexican School, begun in 1922 with Diego RIVERA and José Clemente OROZCO. After returning in 1922 from studies in Europe, Siqueiros, along with Rivera and Xavier Guerrero, organized the Syndicate of Technical Workers, Painters, and Sculptors and began to publish the artist newspaper *El Machete* (1924).

In the search for materials and methods that could be used for outdoor murals that would be legible to spectators in transit, Siqueiros was the first artist, from 1932 on, to employ industrial synthetic paints (Duco or pyroxilyn, vinylite, etc.), an electric projector to transfer images onto the wall, and a spray gun (with stencils) to paint murals. He also used surfaces such as damp cement, masonite, and plywood, as well as more traditional grounds. He invented polyangular perspective, often on curved walls, to activate filmically a static surface. He also used blowups of documentary photographs as contemporary visual sources and *esculto-pintura* (sculptural painting). His painting style was dramatic and exuberant, even baroque, with simplified solid images thrusting forward, illusionistic destructions and re-creations of space (floors, walls, and ceilings), and the building up of surfaces with granular materials.

Far from being merely a formalist innovator, Siqueiros employed these means to strengthen and make more powerful his political content, an approach he called *pin-*

*El Coronelazo* (self-portrait) by David Alfaro Siqueiros. CENIDIAP / INBA.

*tura dialéctico-subversiva* (dialectic-subversive painting).
He championed monumental rather than easel painting,
street murals, collective artistic teams, a scientific and
psychological knowledge of artistic tools and forms,
multiple and portable paintings rather than unique ones.
He wrote to Anita Brenner, explaining that ''what we
seek is not only technique and style in art that sympa-
thizes with revolution, but an art that itself is revolutionary.''

BERNARD S. MYERS, *Mexican Painting in Our Time* (1956);
RAQUEL TIBOL, *Siqueiros: Introductor de realidades* (1961), and
*David Alfaro Siqueiros* (1969); MARIO DE MICHELI, *Siqueiros*
(1968); ORLANDO S. SUÁREZ, *Inventario del muralismo mexicano*
(1972).

SHIFRA M. GOLDMAN

**ALFONSÍN, RAÚL RICARDO** (*b.* 13 March 1926),
president of Argentina (1983–1989). The son of a local
storekeeper, Alfonsín was raised in Chascomús, Buenos
Aires Province. His maternal great-grandfather was an
Irishman named Richard Foulkes, who married Mary
Ford, daughter of a family of FALKLAND ISLANDS kelp-
ers. Staggeringly different from most British residents of
South America, Don Ricardo became a passionate Argentine patriot fighting alongside the famous Radical
leader Hipólito YRIGOYEN in the abortive revolution of
1905. With such family traditions, Alfonsín grew up
fiercely opposed to electoral fraud, dictatorship, and
corporatism. But it was only after Ricardo BALBÍN's

Raúl Alfonsín at independence celebration, Buenos
Aires, 9 July 1985. REUTERS/BETTMANN ARCHIVE.

death in September 1981 that he attained power in the Radical Party by winning the presidency (his first government post) in October 1983. The Radicals, who normally polled about 25 percent, got 51.7 percent, while the Peronists, with 40 percent, suffered their lowest vote and first ever defeat. The Alfonsín government introduced heterodox economic shock treatment, dubbed the Austral Plan, organized the first human rights trials in Latin America, and withstood three military uprisings. Defeat came in the shape of a civilian challenge. The Peronist Carlos Saúl MENEM captured 47 percent in the May 1989 election, reducing Alfonsín to an opposition figure once again.

PABLO GIUSSANI, *Los días de Alfonsín* (1986); JIMMY BURNS, *The Land That Lost Its Heroes: The Falklands, the Post-War, and Alfonsín* (1987).

ROGER GRAVIL

**ALGARROBO,** a tree that grows in desert and semiarid regions of mountains, plains, the CHACO, at the edges of mountainous rain forests, and in pampean woodlands. Various species exist: *Prosopis alba, Prosopis alba* of the panta variety, *Prosopis nigra, Prosopis chilensis*, and *Prosopis hassleri.* Many societies refer to the algarrobo simply as "the tree." Since very ancient times it has been a source of construction material, fuel, ingredients for food and drink, and forage for animals. A flour made from its legumes (carob beans) is used to make a kind of cake (*el patay*) known for its high nutritional value and long preservation. The same legumes are used to prepare a fermented beverage called *aloja.* The algarrobo's wood is very strong and can be polished to a beautiful luster.

H.L. D'ANTONI and O.T. SOLBRIG, "Algarrobos in South American Cultures, Past and Present," in *Mesquite, Its Biology in Two Desert Ecosystems*, edited by B. B. Simpson (1977).

JOSÉ ANTONIO PÉREZ GOLIÁN

**ALGUACIL MAYOR,** the chief constable of an AUDIENCIA or sheriff of a municipality. By the late sixteenth century he purchased the position for life, was able to bequeath it to an heir upon payment of the requisite tax, and received a portion of the fines he imposed. His responsibilities included executing court orders, arresting suspects, and maintaining public order. Since he could name assistants throughout the *audiencia* district, he enjoyed substantial patronage. The position could be very lucrative, but initially it was expensive; in 1611 a purchaser of the post in New Spain paid 115,000 pesos for it.

The *alguacil mayor* of a municipality also bought his post and held it for life. The responsibilities and patronage were similar to those of the *audiencia* counterpart but on a municipal scale. In addition, the *alguacil mayor* was usually entitled to participate in the city council's deliberations.

CLARENCE H. HARING, *The Spanish Empire in America* (1947); JOHN H. PARRY, *The Sale of Public Office in the Spanish Indies Under the Hapsburgs* (1953).

MARK A. BURKHOLDER

**ALHÓNDIGA,** the massive, fortresslike granary of Guanajuato constructed by Intendant Juan Antonio RIAÑO to store sufficient grain to supply the city for a year. When Riaño received word that the rebel forces of Father Miguel HIDALGO were approaching the city of Guanajuato, he ordered the granary prepared for a lengthy siege. Gathering coin, silver bars, and other valuables, the royalists became the target not only for the rebel forces but also for the plebeians of the city. On 28 September 1810, Riaño was killed in the first assault and the rebels overwhelmed the defenses, sacked the building, and massacred about 300 European Spaniards, CREOLES, and royalist militiamen. In 1811, following the executions of the rebel leaders Hidalgo, Ignacio ALLENDE, Juan ALDAMA, and Mariano JIMÉNEZ, their heads were placed on display in iron cages on the corners of the *alhóndiga*, where they remained until MEXICAN INDEPENDENCE in 1821.

LUCAS ALAMÁN, *Historia de México desde los primeros movimientos que prepararon su independencia en el año de 1808 hasta la época presente*, 5 vols. (1849–1852; repr. 1942); CARLOS MARÍA DE BUSTAMANTE, *Cuadro histórico de la Revolución Mexicana*, 3 vols. (1961); HUGH M. HAMILL, *The Hidalgo Revolt: Prelude to Mexican Independence* (1966).

CHRISTON I. ARCHER

**ALLENDE, IGNACIO** (*b.* 25 January 1769; *d.* 26 June 1811), Mexican independence leader and corevolutionary of Father Miguel HIDALGO. Born to a wealthy landowning family, Allende joined the militia of San Miguel el Grande as a lieutenant and was promoted in 1797 to captain. He participated in the meetings of CREOLE societies that plotted for MEXICAN INDEPENDENCE, favoring independence under King FERDINAND VII or some other member of the Spanish royal family. When the regime discovered the Querétaro conspiracy in September 1810, Allende went to the town of Dolores to assist Father Miguel Hidalgo, who later named him captain-general of the American armies.

Many historians point to Allende's military background, but it should be remembered that he was a militia officer who had not commanded significant forces. A creole, he experienced difficulties with a rebellion that exploded rapidly into a mass movement dominated by Indians and MESTIZOS. During and after the bloody occupation of Guanajuato, Allende attempted to restore order and to halt atrocities against Spaniards, uncontrolled pillaging, and other excesses. At Valladolid, Morelia, he ordered his troops to use force against insurgent looters. On many occasions, he opposed Hidalgo's apparent willingness to sanction violence as a means to attract supporters to the revolutionary cause.

After the battle of Monte de las Cruces (30 October 1810), Hidalgo rejected Allende's belief that the capital should be occupied, and the insurgents began the peripatetic wanderings that led to the occupation of Guadalajara. Even before the disastrous rebel defeat at Aculco (7 November 1810), many Indians and mestizos abandoned the rebel army. Allende was present in Guanajuato, but he did not play a major role in the battle of 25 November 1810 that resulted in the second major rebel defeat. Following the royalist victory at the battle of Puente de Calderón on 17 January 1811, the insurgent chiefs replaced Hidalgo, naming Allende supreme commander. Retreating to the north, Allende decided to regroup the insurgent forces in the United States. However, on 21 March 1811, the senior rebel commanders were surprised by treachery and captured north of Saltillo. Allende was taken prisoner, tried by court-martial at Chihuahua, and executed by firing squad.

LUCAS ALAMÁN, *Historia de México desde los primeros movimientos que prepararon su independencia en el año de 1808 hasta la época presente*, 5 vols. (1849–1852; repr. 1942); CARLOS MARÍA DE BUSTAMANTE, *Cuadro histórico de la Revolución Mexicana*, 3 vols. (1961); HUGH M. HAMILL, *The Hidalgo Revolt: Prelude to Mexican Independence* (1966); JOHN TUTINO, *From Insurrection to Revolution in Mexico: Social Bases of Agrarian Violence, 1750–1940* (1986).

CHRISTON I. ARCHER

**ALLENDE, ISABEL** (*b.* 2 August 1942), Chilean novelist, born in Peru, where her father was a member of the diplomatic corps. After her parents separated, she was brought up in an old labyrinthine house surrounded by stories that eventually influenced her first novel, *La casa de los espíritus* (1982; *The House of the Spirits*, 1985), a work that brought Isabel Allende immediate international recognition. The novel is a melodramatic account of a patriarchal family saga whose story runs parallel to Chile's history in the twentieth century. Translated into several languages, it achieved remarkable success throughout the Western world.

From 1967 to 1974, Allende worked as a journalist for *Paula*, a woman's magazine in her native Santiago. In 1973 her uncle, Chilean president Salvador Allende, was assassinated by the Chilean military during a coup d'état that ousted his Socialist government. In 1975, fearing for her life, Isabel left Chile and went into exile. She settled with her family in Caracas, Venezuela, where she continued to practice journalism.

In *The House of the Spirits* she highlights the independent nature of the female characters, whose lives become increasingly entangled in the political process of their country, assumed to be Chile but never actually named. Her second novel, *De amor y de sombra* (1984; *Of Love and Shadows*, 1987), centers around a historical

event, the discovery of the remains of a group of victims of a massacre by the military regime in a mine at Los Riscos, Chile. The novel can be interpreted as a denunciation of the military regime that ousted President Allende's government. Beginning with her third novel, *Eva Luna* (1987; *Eva Luna*, 1988), Allende's attention shifts from Chile's contemporary reality to a broader setting, where storytelling from a female viewpoint becomes the focus of her fiction. In 1989, after moving to California, she published *Los cuentos de Eva Luna* (*The Stories of Eva Luna*, 1991), tales told by the title character of her previous novel. Later works include *El plan infinito* (1991; *The Infinite Plan*, 1993) and *Paula* (1994, trans. 1995). In 1994 she was awarded the Orden al Mérito Gabriela Mistral by the Chilean government.

MARCELO CODDOU, *Los libros tienen sus propios espíritus* (1987), and *Para leer a Isabel Allende* (1988); MAGDALENA GARCÍA PINTO, *Women Writers of Latin America* (1991).

MAGDALENA GARCÍA PINTO

**ALLENDE GOSSENS, SALVADOR** (*b.* 26 July 1908; *d.* 11 September 1973), president of Chile (1970–1973). Born in Valparaíso of an upper middle-class family, Allende studied in the public schools and graduated from the University of Chile with a medical degree in 1932. He was an active Mason throughout his adult life.

Allende was attracted to socialist doctrine during his youth. He participated in university politics and in 1933 was a founding member of the Socialist Party. He was elected to the Chamber of Deputies in 1937, and he served as minister of health (1939–1942) in the Popular Front government of Pedro AGUIRRE CERDA. His long career in the Senate began in 1945 and continued until 1969. As a senator, he gained a reputation as an expert in parliamentary procedure and rose to the presidency of the Senate (1965–1969). Allende held various offices in the Socialist Party, serving twice as secretary-general.

Allende ran for the presidency of Chile four times. In 1952 he garnered only 5.4 percent of the vote. In 1958 and 1964 he ran as the candidate of the Popular Action Front (FRAP), which was founded in 1956 to unite the Communist, Socialist, and smaller leftist parties. With coalition support, Allende received 28.9 percent of the vote in 1958; he lost to Jorge ALESSANDRI RODRÍGUEZ by only 33,500 of 1,236,000 votes cast. The leftward movement of Chilean politics in the wake of the CUBAN REVOLUTION (1959) raised expectations of an Allende victory in the 1964 presidential election. To prevent that possibility, the rightist Conservative and Liberal parties broke their alliance with the Radical Party and threw their support to reformist Christian Democrat Eduardo FREI. After an intense campaign featuring Central Intelligence Agency (CIA) financing and scare tactics equating Allende with Fidel CASTRO, Frei won with 55.6 percent of the vote to Allende's 38.6. Throughout the Frei administration,

Allende was the most visible spokesman of the opposition Left and advocate of more vigorous reform.

The 1970 presidential election offered Chileans clear choices. Reacting to Frei's reforms, the Right reorganized as the National Party and selected former president Jorge Alessandri as its candidate. The Christian Democrats ran Radomiro TOMIC of the party's left-center bloc. Allende was the candidate of Popular Unity (UP), a new coalition of the Socialists and Communists and four non-Marxist parties, including the historic Radical Party. Allende won a close race: he received 36.5 percent of the vote to Alessandri's 35.2 and Tomic's 28.0. After two months of U.S.-orchestrated attempts to block congressional ratification of the popular election and to foster a military coup, Salvador Allende took office on 3 November 1970.

Allende's election fixed the world's attention on Chile, which would provide the laboratory for testing the question: Is there a peaceful road to socialism? Allende had promised to move Chile rapidly toward socialism through the acceleration of agrarian reform and extensive nationalization in key economic sectors. His first year in office was highly successful in meeting these goals and in building popular support. Thereafter, mounting problems began to plague his government, compounding the difficulties imposed by opposition control of Congress and the judiciary. By the end of 1971, accelerating inflation, the exhaustion of foreign currency reserves, and disinvestment in the private sector had weakened the economy. Meanwhile, the Christian Democrats and the National Party formalized an anti-UP alliance, the Nixon administration stepped up its destabilization campaign, and critical divisions within the UP and Allende's own Socialist Party began to surface.

Although the pace of reform rose dramatically under the UP, popular expectations rose faster, resulting in widespread extralegal worker occupations of haciendas and factories. Torn between his legal obligations and hiscommitment to the *pueblo,* Allende vacillated on the wave of takeovers; he lost crucial middle-class support by appearing soft on the rule of law. The opposition struck a major blow in an October 1972 "bosses' strike." Called by the *gremio* (GUILD) movement, a broad coalition of business and professional groups, the strike paralyzed the economy, revealed the government's vulnerability, and forced Allende to bring military officers into his cabinet. From this point forward, confrontation escalated and much of the opposition embraced the goal of overthrowing the government.

Despite the growing polarization and the rise of violence, Allende achieved an impressive record of reform. Under his administration, the traditional rural estate virtually ceased to exist, the state took control of the "commanding heights" of the economy, and progress was made in income redistribution. The final test of UP popularity was the March 1973 congressional election. The UP received 44 percent of the vote, down from the 49.7 percent it had won in the April 1971 municipal

Salvador Allende greeting miners during the first anniversary of the nationalization of the copper mines, 12 July 1972, Santiago, Chile. LA NACIÓN.

elections but still 7.5 points above the 1970 presidential vote tally. Nonetheless, the UP's failure to achieve a congressional majority and the opposition's failure to attain the two-thirds majority necessary to impeach the president signaled three and a half more years of conflict before the 1976 presidential election. A second *gremio* strike took place in July and August 1973. With the country in chaos and the government near collapse, the military staged a coup on 11 September. Salvador Allende, *compañero presidente* to Chile's poor, committed suicide in the MONEDA PALACE while it was under military attack. The overthrow and death of Allende marked the end of the transition to socialism and the beginning of a lengthy military dictatorship.

SALVADOR ALLENDE, *Chile's Road to Socialism,* edited by Joan Garcés and translated by J. Darling (1973); STEFAN DE VYLDER, *Allende's Chile: The Political Economy of the Rise and Fall of the Unidad Popular* (1976); ARTURO VALENZUELA and J. SAMUEL VALENZUELA, eds., *Chile: Politics and Society* (1976); PAUL E. SIGMUND, *The Overthrow of Allende and the Politics of Chile, 1964–1976* (1977); ROBERT J. ALEXANDER, *The Tragedy of Chile* (1978); OSVALDO PUCCIO, *Un cuarto de siglo con Allende: Recuerdos de su secretario privado* (1985); and SERGIO BITAR, *Chile: Experiment in Democracy* (1986).

THOMAS C. WRIGHT

*See also* **Chile: Political Parties; United States–Latin American Relations.**

**ALLENDE-SARÓN, PEDRO HUMBERTO** (*b.* 29 June 1885; *d.* 17 August 1959), Chilean composer. Allende was born in Santiago and studied composition at the National Conservatory in Santiago (1899–1908). He studied piano and violin, the latter under the guidance of Aurelio Silva. Early in his career he taught violin and general musical subjects in secondary schools and later taught composition and harmony at the National Conservatory. He was a key figure in revitalizing the music education system in Chile, both at the primary and secondary school levels. After a trip to Europe in 1910–1911, Allende was elected to the Chilean Folklore Society. In recognition for his research and compositional efforts, as well as for his contribution to music education, in 1945 he received the Premio Nacional de Arte, becoming the first composer to be so honored.

Allende was the first important figure to promote Chilean musical nationalism by integrating in his works the songs and dances of the ARAUCANIAN and MAPUCHE Indians as well as MESTIZO folk music, which he orchestrated in a lavish French impressionist style. He wrote *Paisaje chileno* for chorus and orchestra (1913); *Escenas campesinas chilenas* (1913–1914), a symphonic suite; *La voz de las calles* (1919–1920), a symphonic poem; *Tonadas de carácter popular chileno*, for piano (1918–1922); *Concerto sinfónico* for cello and orchestra (1915); *Luna de la media noche* for soprano and orchestra (1937); Violin Concerto (1940); and *La Cenicienta* (Cinderella, 1948), a chamber opera for children.

Allende's writings include *Metodología original para la enseñanza del canto escolar* (1922); *Conferencias sobre la música* (1918); "La música popular chilena" in *Art populaire*, from the First International Congress of Popular Art, Prague (1928); and "Chilean Folk Music," in the *Bulletin of the Pan American Union* (September 1931).

JOHN VINTON, ed., *Dictionary of Contemporary Music* (1974), pp. 7–8; GÉRARD BÉHAGUE, *Music in Latin America: An Introduction* (1979); p. 179; *New Grove Dictionary of Music and Musicians* (1980).

ALCIDES LANZA

**ALLIANCE FOR PROGRESS,** a policy inaugurated in 1961 by President John F. Kennedy as a ten-year $20 billion cooperative effort to bring political stability and representative government to Latin America. Events in the late 1950s brought the United States to the realization that within Latin America the economic, social, and political disparities that divided the region's peoples served as breeding grounds for revolution. In response, the United States designed development programs that climaxed with the Alliance for Progress Charter, signed by all members of the ORGANIZATION OF AMERICAN STATES, except Cuba, at Punta del Este, Uruguay, on 17 August 1961. The Alliance hoped to bring political stability and representative government to Latin America through economic reform by providing funds to improve the infrastructure for industrialization (such as roads and dams) and by collaborating in private investment projects. Economic and social justice was encouraged by changing the inequitable tax systems and by providing for schools and health care facilities. The policies were formulated within the context of the Cold War because both the U.S. and Latin American leadership feared that Communist-inspired Fidelismo would spread from Cuba to other parts of the hemisphere. The Alliance sought to deter the Communist appeal by supporting social reform and economic growth that would create political stability.

Under the Alliance for Progress, Latin American armed forces placed a new emphasis on counterinsurgency, which included civic action programs, such as literacy training, teaching of technical skills, opening new land, building schools and highways, improving sanitation and health facilities, and other projects useful to civilians. It also shifted emphasis from defense against offshore incursions to internal security. Enthusiasm for the Alliance quickly waned. By 1963 military governments had come to power in several Latin American countries, diminishing the hope for democracy, and in some countries the military lost interest in the civic action programs, using counterinsurgency training only to suppress political opposition. In the United States, President Lyndon B. Johnson was less committed than Kennedy to democratic reform and favored private over public investment. Plagued by the war in Vietnam, the costs of the Great Society, and civil violence at home, and reassured by the apparent inability of Fidel Castro to encourage revolution elsewhere, the United States gave less attention to Latin America in the late 1960s. When Richard M. Nixon assumed the presidency in 1969, he noted that the Alliance was a concept with great promise that had not achieved its economic and social objectives, and when Congress terminated it in 1972, the AGENCY FOR INTERNATIONAL DEVELOPMENT (AID), which had administered most of the Alliance programs, agreed.

HERNANDO AGUDELO VILLA, *La revolución del desarrollo: Orígen y evolución de la Alianza para el Progreso* (1966); WILLIAM D. ROGERS, *The Twilight Struggle: The Alliance for Progress and the Politics of Development in Latin America* (1967); JEROME LEVINSON and JUAN DE ONIS, *The Alliance That Lost Its Way: A Critical Report on the Alliance for Progress* (1970); ARTHUR M. SCHLESINGER, JR., "The Alliance for Progress: A Retrospective," in *Latin America: The Search for a New International Role*, edited by Ronald G. Hellman and H. Jon Rosenbaum (1975).

THOMAS M. LEONARD

**ALMAFUERTE** (*b.* 13 May 1854; *d.* 28 February 1917), pseudonym of Pedro Bonifacio Palacios, Argentine poet and journalist. Born in San Justo in Buenos Aires province, Almafuerte was self-taught. Raised by an aunt in Buenos Aires, he remained in the capital, living in poverty and solitude.

Almafuerte cultivated an extravagant persona that bespoke his commitment to exemplifying attributes and values of a mystical, unsettled, and contradictory self-identity that transcended established middle-class conventions. To be sure, during this period Buenos Aires remained relatively sedate alongside its European models. Yet, Almafuerte was able to project a complex, idiosyncratic persona that gave him a unique status among the writers of the period as something of a prophet concerning the impact on the solitary individual of the multiple tensions of a society undergoing vertiginous modernization. In this sense, Almafuerte may be read as an antiphony to the vast sociopolitical undertaking of the Generation of 1880, who sought to impose a liberal hegemony on Argentine society.

In the worldly and often aggressively profane (or, at least, decidedly materialistic) context of the Generation of 1880, Almafuerte aligned himself with a traditional, humanitarian Christian sentiment that is reflected in titles like *Evangélicas* (1915), *Cristianas y Jesús, El drama del Calvario, Cantar de cantares, Lamentaciones* (1906), and *El misionero* (1905) and in the didactic, sermonizing tone of many of his compositions. Yet, despite this sort of catechistic focus, the structure of his poetry frequently reflects the innovative exercises of the more urbane and sensual modernists.

ROMUALDO BRUGHETTI, *Viva de Almafuerte, el combatiente perpetuo* (1954); ENRIQUE LAVIÉ, *Almafuerte* (1962); MARTA MORELLO-FROSCH, "Almafuerte: Ética y estética a contrapelo de la historia," in *Cuadernos hispanoamericanos* 296 (1975): 420–427; DAMIÁN FERRER, *Perfil de Almafuerte* (1980).

DAVID WILLIAM FOSTER

**ALMAGRO, DIEGO DE** (*b.* ca. 1475; *d.* 8 July 1538), conqueror of Peru and Chile. Almagro, illegitimate son of Juan de Montenegro and Elvira Gutiérrez, was born in Almagro, in New Castile. His first years were economically and socially difficult ones, and in 1514 he left for the Indies in search of fortune. He participated with some distinction in minor discoveries in Castilla del Oro and became a close associate of Francisco PIZARRO, another dynamic social-misfit soldier of fortune. With some financial assistance from cleric Hernando de LUQUE, who may have been representing a silent partner, the two men began making plans to explore South America's west coast, widely believed to be the seat of an empire of great riches.

Pizarro set sail southward from the Isthmus of Panama in the first expedition of 1524; Almagro, responsible for maintaining supplies, followed behind, covering much the same route and suffering hardships similar to those of the Pizarro group. In an encounter with the cacique (chief) of Las Piedras, Almagro lost an eye at Pueblo Quemado. On the second expedition (1526), which was jointly planned with Pizarro, neither the leaders nor their men got along well. When Almagro returned to the isthmus for more troops and supplies, he inadvertently carried notice of the discontent. When

the governor of Panama got wind of the situation, he recalled both men. In the meantime, Pizarro was able to secure enough evidence of wealth to convince the official that a third and more massive attempt was warranted.

At this juncture Pizarro returned to Spain and procured an agreement with the crown that made him chief commander of the expedition, leaving Luque as bishop of Tumbes. Almagro, who received relatively minor offices in the north, remained on the isthmus ill, perhaps with syphillis, as Pizarro started the third expedition near the end of 1530. By the time Almagro and his men were able to reach Pizarro at CAJAMARCA, the INCA ruler ATAHUALPA had already been captured and much of the wealth allocated to Pizarro's men. Almagro did secure appointment as the chief commander of New Toledo, about 520 miles south of Pizarro's New Castile, and marched into Cuzco (Peru) on 15 November 1533.

Convinced that vast cities and wealth lay to the south, and perhaps encouraged by the duplicitous Pizarrists who wanted to be rid of him, he organized an expedition and marched southward on 3 July 1535. The group passed Lake Titicaca, crossed with great hardship and

Diego de Almagro. Anonymous grabado from Antonio de Herrera, *Historia general de las Indias, Islas y Tierra Firme del Mar Océano en VIII décadas, 1292–1554* (Madrid, 1601–1615). LIBRARY OF CONGRESS.

loss of life through frigid Andean passes, and entered Chile at Copiapó. The expeditionary force marched as far south as the Maule River in south-central Chile, but found no indication of the expected treasures. Instead, the Europeans were attacked by fierce Indian fighters who had eluded Inca rule.

Almagro and his men gave up and returned to Peru via the desert coastal route. The soldiers passed through what became Arequipa and marched into Cuzco on 8 April 1537, shortly after Pizarro supporters had broken the siege led by MANCO INCA. Almagro and his men occupied Cuzco, believing it to be within the jurisdiction of New Toledo. Almagro, to ensure his control, imprisoned Francisco's brothers, Hernando and Gonzalo Pizarro, while Friar Francisco de BOBADILLA, a suspected Pizarrist, began negotiations to effect a peaceful settlement of the territorial dispute. Gonzalo Pizarro escaped jail, and Almagro freed Hernando on the condition that he return to Spain. Hernando, however, fielded a Pizarrist army that met and defeated Almagro on 6 April 1538 at Salinas, near Cuzco. Fearing an uprising of Almagro's supporters, Hernando Pizarro ordered him executed in his cell. He was buried in Cuzco's MERCEDARIAN church.

Almagro's illegitimate mestizo son, Diego de Almagro, the Younger, born in Panama in 1520 (his mother was Ana Martínez, a native of the isthmus), would later head a movement to overthrow Pizarrist domination of Peru. After the assassination of Francisco Pizarro in Lima on 26 June 1541, he governed Peru briefly, but fell to the king's forces, led by Governor Cristóval Vaca de Castro, on 16 September 1542 in the battle of Chupas, near Huamanga. He was captured and executed in Cuzco. Only twenty-two years old when he died, he was buried alongside his father in the Mercedarian church.

ROLANDO MELLAFE and N. MEZA VILLALOBOS, *Diego de Almagro* (1954); JOSÉ ANTONIO DEL BUSTO DUTHURBURU, *Diego de Almagro* (1964).

NOBLE DAVID COOK

**ALMAZÁN, JUAN ANDRÉU** (*b.* 12 May 1891; *d.* 9 October 1965), Mexican politician. Almazán, a general, was an important figure during and immediately following the Mexican Revolution (1910–1920). Noted for his candidacy in the Mexican presidential election of 1940, Almazán represented the Revolutionary Party of National Unification (Partido Revolucionario de Unificación Nacional—PRUN) in opposition to the government candidate, General Manuel ÁVILA CAMACHO, who was chosen to succeed President Lázaro CÁRDENAS. The campaign generated considerable electoral violence, and some observers expected Almazán to lead a rebellion against the government after losing. Instead he went into exile in Panama, Cuba, and the United States. He returned to Mexico in 1947, and was a businessman until his death in Mexico City.

JAMES W. WILKIE, *México visto en el siglo XX* (1969); ALBERT L. MICHAELS, *The Mexican Election of 1940* (1971); RODERIC A. CAMP, *Mexican Political Biographies, 1935–1981* (1982), p. 16.

RODERIC AI CAMP

*See also* **Mexico: Political Parties.**

**ALMEIDA, JOSÉ AMÉRICO DE** (*b.* 10 January 1887; *d.* 10 March 1980), a leading Brazilian social novelist of the 1930s. Almeida was an important figure in both Northeastern and national Brazilian politics until his death. A strong supporter of Getúlio VARGAS's 1930 revolution and a minister in Vargas's government, his own presidential candidacy was thwarted by Vargas's coup in 1937. Later he served as governor of his home state of Paraíba. These and other episodes of his political life were described in his memoirs *Ocasos de sangue* (1954).

Influenced by POSITIVISM and Euclides da CUNHA's *Os sertões*, Almeida wrote *A Paraíba e seus problemas* (1923), which documents his sociopolitical concerns about his state and region. Although he wrote three novels with similar economic and social themes and the same poetic style, *A bagaceira* (1928; *Trash*, 1978) is recognized as his most important work. A pioneering regionalist work within the nationalist ideology of Brazilian MODERNISM, *A bagaceira* is primarily a literary exemplification of beliefs and ideas he expressed in *A Paraíba e seus problemas*. In this poetic novel replete with regionalist expressions, he describes the effects of the periodic droughts on the people of the Northeast and, specifically, the conflict between the *sertanejos* (frontiersmen) and the *brejeiros* (marshmen). Today, however, the novel is considered more of a monument of that period than a vibrant work of literature.

R. L. SCOTT-BUCCLEUCH, "Translator's Foreword," in *Trash* (1978).

IRWIN STERN

**ALMEIDA JÚNIOR, JOSÉ FERRAZ DE** (*b.* 8 May 1850; *d.* 13 November 1899), Brazilian painter best known for his *caipira* paintings. Born in Itú, São Paulo, Almeida Júnior enrolled in the Imperial Academy of Fine Arts in 1869. A disciple of Vítor MEIRELES, Almeida Júnior specialized in drawing and historical painting. Between 1871 and 1874 he won seven student painting awards. In 1874 he obtained the gold medal in historical painting, entitling him to compete for the academy's European travel award competition. Although he declined, he did accept a monthly stipend to travel in Europe offered by the emperor, PEDRO II, who took an active interest in supporting talented young artists.

In Paris he studied with French academic artists and entered several Salon exhibitions. When he returned to Rio in 1882, he organized an exhibition to show the eight paintings he had completed while in Europe. They included religious paintings, figure studies, genre paintings, and a new category, *caipira* painting. His *O Derrubador brasileiro,* the first in a series of *caipira* paintings, expanded the narrow thematic options then available to historical and genre painters. It remained faithful to the traditional academic aesthetic canons but depicted a scene in the daily life of the common people from the interior of the state of São Paulo. These paintings helped bring into focus the important historical role of the Brazilian backwoodsmen. His other *caipira* compositions include *Caipiras negaceando, Caipira picando fumo, Pescando, Amolação interrompida,* and *Caipira pitando.*

GASTÃO PEREIRA DA SILVA, *Almeida Júnior: Sua vida e sua obra* (1946); MARCOS ANTÔNIO MARCONDES, *Almeida Júnior: Vida e obras* (1980).

CAREN A. MEGHREBLIAN

**ALMEIDA, LUIS DE.** *See* **Lavradio, Marquês do.**

**ALMEIDA, MANUEL ANTÔNIO DE** (*b.* 17 November 1831; *d.* 28 November 1861), Brazilian novelist. Almeida is famous for a single text, the novel *Memórias de um sargento de milícias,* which was serialized in 1853 and published in two volumes in 1854–1855. It was rediscovered, after 1922, by the modernists, who celebrated it for its detailed and quite realistic descriptions of urban life in Rio de Janeiro in the years just before Independence in 1822—descriptions that include a broader range of social types than any other Brazilian novel of its time—and for its entertaining and highly unsentimental vision of life. Some critics endeavored to classify Almeida's *Memórias* as an early example of the realist novel in Brazil, but clearly its literary roots can be traced to such eighteenth-century British works as Henry Fielding's *Tom Jones.* It has also been suggested that the nineteenth-century Brazilian novel would have developed along quite different lines had Almeida not died in a shipwreck in 1861, but there is no evidence that he produced any prose fiction between 1853 and his death.

*Memoirs of a Militia Sergeant,* translated by Linton L. Barrett (1959); ANTÔNIO CÂNDIDO, ''Dialética da malandragem,'' in *Revista do Instituto de Estudos Brasileiros* 8 (1970): 67–89; JOHN M. PARKER, ''The Nature of Realism in *Memórias de um sargento de milícias,''* in *Bulletin of Hispanic Studies* 48 (1971): 128–150.

DAVID T. HABERLY

**ALMOJARIFAZGO,** a tax, of Arab origin, on the maritime trade of Andalusia. The *almojarifazgo* was charged on Seville's trade with America from 1543, constituting thereafter the principal duty on imperial commerce until its abolition in 1778. Initially levied at 2.5 percent on exports and 5 percent on imports, its rates were equalized at 5 percent in 1566 and thereafter varied, as did the practice of granting exemptions for particular products or regions. It was also charged on most intercolo-nial as well as transatlantic trade. The issue of determining the values of commodities in order to calculate the *almojarifazgo* was never resolved satisfactorily, and its collection thus provided much scope for fraud.

CLARENCE H. HARING, *The Spanish Empire in America* (1947), esp. pp. 261–263; ISMAEL SÁNCHEZ-BELLA, *La Organización financiera de las Indias, siglo XVI* (1968), esp. pp. 238–247.

JOHN R. FISHER

**ALMONTE, JUAN NEPOMUCENO** (*b.* 1803; *d.* 1869), regent of Mexico's Second Empire (1863–1864). The illegitimate child of José María MORELOS Y PAVÓN—a leader of Mexico's independence movement—Almonte was awarded the rank of brigadier general before the age of thirteen by the Congress of Chilpancingo. In 1815 he was part of the commission sent by Morelos to the United States, the first of many diplomatic posts he would hold. After serving as part of a commission to establish the border between Mexico and the United States (1834), Almonte fought against the rebellion in Texas at the battles of the ALAMO and SAN JACINTO, where he was captured. Freed in 1836, Almonte served as minister of war (1839–1841) before returning to the United States as ambassador in 1842.

When the United States admitted Texas as a state, Almonte returned to Mexico to support the war effort. Originally a federalist, he became a conservative and a monarchist. He served as Mexico's minister to London and later to Paris. After the republican forces won the War of the REFORM (1858–1861), Almonte openly sought European intervention to establish a monarchy in Mexico. He returned to Mexico with the support of the French army in 1862 and was selected as one of the executive triumvirate of the Council of Notables and later regent. Emperor MAXIMILIAN gave Almonte various honors, including a cabinet post, before naming him as the Mexican Empire's representative to Napoleon III (1866). On the fall of the Second Empire, Almonte remained in Paris, where he died.

ALBERTO MARÍA CARREÑO ESCUDERO, *Jefes del ejército mexicano en 1847* (1914); ALFRED JACKSON HANNA and KATHRYN ABBEY HANNA, *Napoleon III and Mexico: American Triumph over Monarchy* (1971); *Diccionario Porrúa de historia, biografía y geografía de México,* 5th ed. (1986).

D. F. STEVENS

**ALOMÍA ROBLES, DANIEL** (*b.* 3 January 1871; *d.* 17 July 1942), Peruvian ethnomusicologist and composer. Born in Huánuco, Alomía Robles was sent as a child to Lima to study solfège with Cruz Panizo and piano with Claudio Rebagliati. From 1892 to 1894 he studied medicine in San Fernando. While doing research on the Campas Indians, he was encouraged by a Franciscan friar to study aboriginal music. He eventually dedicated more than twenty years of his life to the subject. His research took him to remote regions of Ecuador and Bolivia, where he collected and classified folk materials. In 1910 he gave a celebrated lecture on Andean melodies at the University of San Marcos in Lima. Alomía Robles's wife, the pianist Sebastiana Godoy, assisted in the harmonization of native music. Although he became a noted composer, he is best known for his research on Indian music. He died in Lima.

RODOLFO HOLZMANN, "Catálogo de las obras de Daniel Alomía Robles," in *Boletín Biblioteca Universidad Mayor de San Marcos* 13 (1943); GÉRARD BÉHAGUE, *Music in Latin America* (1979); *New Grove Dictionary of Music and Musicians*, vol. 1 (1980).

SUSANA SALGADO

**ALONSO, AMADO** (*b.* 13 September 1896; *d.* 26 May 1952), Argentine writer and literary critic. Born in Lerín, Navarra, Spain, Alonso directed the Institute of Philology at the University of Buenos Aires from 1927 to 1946, a position that allowed him to exercise considerable influence on the introduction of European formalism and stylistics into Argentina, and from there into Latin American literary and linguistic scholarship. In 1938 Alonso, along with Pedro HENRÍQUEZ UREÑA, published *Gramática castellana*, one of the classic structuralist analyses of the Spanish language. The *Gramática*, designed to be used in secondary-school courses, had numerous reprintings in subsequent decades. Alonso authored many important studies on Iberian and Latin American literature, including early studies on Jorge Luis BORGES. His most important text, however, remains *Poesía y estilo de Pablo Neruda* (1940), probably the first full-length monograph on a Latin American poet to be written from the point of view of formalist stylistics, in addition to being one of the earliest studies on the Chilean poet. In 1945, Alonso translated into Spanish Ferdinand de Saussure's *Curso de lingüística general* (1945), one of the founding texts of modern linguistics. Whether writing specifically about poetry or exploring the poetic dimension of prose, Alonso exemplified the importance accorded by the literary criticism of the period to the questions of the specific qualities of literariness.

DIEGO CATALÁN MENÉNDEZ PIDAL, *La escuela lingüística española y su concepción del lenguaje* (1955); EMILIO CARILLA, *Estudios de literatura argentina, siglo XX*, 2d ed. (1968), pp. 163–172; LAURENCE SAMUEL JOHNSON, "The Literary Criticism of Amado Alonso and His Principal Disciples" (Ph.D. diss., Columbia University, 1970).

DAVID WILLIAM FOSTER

**ALONSO, MANUEL A.** (*b.* 6 October 1822; *d.* 4 November 1899), Puerto Rican essayist, story writer, and poet. Son of a Spanish captain posted in Caguas, Alonso received his early education there. He went on to study medicine in Barcelona, Spain. Returning as a doctor in 1849, he assumed his place in colonial Puerto Rican society as one of the group of moderate liberal reformers that identified an authentic national purpose with the ascendency of the island's progressive white creole elite. As a writer, he was the first to give effective literary expression to its programmatic outlook and its defense of the existence of a distinctly Puerto Rican nationality. While studying in the Catalán metropolis, he joined other Puerto Rican students in compiling, contributing to, publishing, and sending home the *Aquinaldo puertorriqueño* (1843, 1846; Puerto Rican Christmas Carol), the *Album puertorriqueño* (1844; Puerto Rican Album), and *El cancionero de Borinquén* (1846; Puerto Rican Songbook) now generally regarded as the catalytic events promoting a self-consciously Puerto Rican literature.

After 1849, Alonso quickly emerged as the island's signal *costumbrista*, its preeminent writer on local idiosyncrasy, particularly peasant folkways, creole custom, lore, and traditions. Published in 1849, and in an expanded two-volume edition in 1882–1883, Alonso's signature collection of lyric vignettes and ethnographic prose sketches, *El jíbaro*, gave the titular metaphor of the independent rural mestizo peasant symbolic currency as the emblematic representation of the popular ethos and the recalcitrant obstacle to the creole elite's presumptively more enlightened, entrepreneurial notions of national progress. Impressively synthesizing the colonial, ethnic, and interclass drama of a historically evolved local culture during a crucial period of transition, *El jíbaro* established Alonso as the key figure of a nascent insular tradition of short narrative, literary criticism, and the essay of cultural commentary. After later visits to Spain (1858–1861 and 1866–1871), Alonso returned to Puerto Rico, serving in his later years as editor of the liberal reformist periodical *El agente* and as medical director of the Asilo de Beneficencia.

MODESTO RIVERA Y RIVERA, *Concepto y expresión del costumbrismo en Manuel A. Pacheco (El Gíbaro)* (1952), and *Manuel A. Alonso: Su vida y su obra* (1966); JOSEFINA RIVERA DE ÁLVAREZ, *Diccionario de literatura puertorriqueña*, vol. 1 (1970), pp. 49–52.

ROBERTO MÁRQUEZ

**ALONSO, MARIANO ROQUE** (*b.* 1792?; *d.* 1853), Paraguayan consul (1841–1844) and military figure. Alonso emerged during the hectic months following the September 1840 death of José Gaspar Rodríguez de FRANCIA, Paraguay's first authoritarian dictator and leader of the country since 1814. Francia had left no formal provision for a successor, and when he died, power devolved to the four chiefs of the Asunción barracks, who proved to be ineffectual and corrupt administrators. In January 1841, they were replaced by a triumvirate headed by a sergeant and two former alcaldes of the city. This regime was itself displaced within a month by Alonso, then a junior officer with many years of service but with little real authority or talent. Evidently feeling himself inadequate to the task of governing, he made a fateful decision to appoint as his secretary Carlos Antonio LÓPEZ, a noted attorney from the interior. Alonso needed the latter's help in organizing a national congress that would create and legitimize a new government. When the congress met in March 1841, however, Alonso played the role of subordinate to López, and agreed to join with him in a two-man consular regime authorized by the congress. After the consuls took office, Alonso in effect abdicated his position, preferring to return to the barracks and the company of rustic soldiers like himself. He made sure that his military colleagues refrained from further interference in politics. This show of support brought him many rewards from López, who continued to favor him with a substantial annual pension after the consulate was replaced by a presidential regime in 1844.

In his later years, Alonso lived quietly on his cattle ranch in the interior, where he died in 1853.

CHARLES J. KOLINSKI, *Historical Dictionary of Paraguay* (1975), p. 217; JOHN HOYT WILLIAMS, *The Rise and Fall of the Paraguayan Republic, 1800–1870* (1979), pp. 103–105.

THOMAS L. WHIGHAM

**ALONSO, RAÚL** (*b.* 24 January 1924; *d.* 31 July 1993), Argentine painter and printmaker. Born in Buenos Aires, the son of the distinguished Spanish artist Juan Carlos Alonso, Raúl was self-taught. In 1958 he traveled to Europe and settled in Paris for a while. He exhibited around the world. He was invited to the Universal Exhibition in Brussels and to the Ibero-American Biennials in Mexico City, São Paulo, Valparaíso, Cali, and Punta del Este. In 1991 he had a show at the Hammer Gallery in New York. He received several awards, including the honor prize at the National Salon (Buenos Aires, 1975). He illustrated several books, among them *The Ten Commandments, Amatoria,* and *Borradores.* Alonso's paintings combine nature and imagination, appealing not only to the mind but also to the emotions of the viewer.

VICENTE GESUALDO, ALDO BIGLIONE, and RODOLFO SANTOS, *Diccionario de artistas plásticos en la Argentina* (1988).

AMALIA CORTINA ARAVENA

**ALPACA.** *See* **Llama.**

**ALSINA, ADOLFO** (*b.* 14 January 1829; *d.* 29 December 1877), Argentine politician. Alsina was born in Buenos Aires, the only son of Valentín ALSINA and Antonia Maza. He received his early education in Buenos Aires and Montevideo, and a law degree from the University of Buenos Aires in 1854. After the battle of CASEROS, he wrote articles attacking the commander, Justo José de URQUIZA, and plotted his assassination. As a member of the Liberal Party, to which his father belonged, he helped defend Buenos Aires when it was besieged by Urquiza. He subsequently fought at the battle of

CEPEDA, was one of the *porteño* (Buenos Aires) deputies denied admission to the congress that met in Paraná, and participated in the battle of PAVÓN.

In 1862 Alsina was elected deputy to the national Congress. During an internal party dispute over a proposal to federalize the city of Buenos Aires, he and his followers broke with the Liberal Party to form the Autonomista Party. The party, which consisted of important *estancieros*, Federal Party intellectuals, José HERNÁNDEZ, and Leandro ALEM, had little support outside the province of Buenos Aires. In 1866 Alsina became governor of Buenos Aires, with Nicolás AVELLANEDA as his minister of government. Among the accomplishments of his administration was the separation of the office of justice of the peace from that of the military commandant.

In 1867, Alsina was Domingo SARMIENTO's running mate in the latter's successful bid for the presidency. His relations with Sarmiento were never harmonious, but he did support Sarmiento's decision in 1870 to punish Ricardo LÓPEZ JORDÁN (h) for the assassination of Urquiza. He again was a candidate for the presidency in 1874, and in the congressional elections of that year he won in Córdoba and La Rioja but not in Buenos Aires, which his partisans controlled, because Sarmiento sent national troops to supervise the elections. Lacking support, Alsina withdrew his candidacy and endorsed the man Sarmiento had selected as his successor, Avellaneda, and his own supporter, Mariano Acosta, for the vice presidency.

President Avellaneda appointed Alsina his minister of war and the navy. Alsina was responsible for the suppression of the Revolution of 1874, a pro-Bartolomé MITRE movement, and for the campaign that built a new frontier line of forts from Carhué to Laguna del Monte and to Trenque Lauquén. He hoped to minimize Indian resistance to the advance by incorporating some tribes into the national guard, but as a precaution he supplied the national army with revolvers and telegraph lines. In 1877 he furthered the policy of "conciliation" by persuading Mitre to stop his partisans from starting a revolution; he was planning another advance of the frontier line when he died in Buenos Aires.

JACINTO R. YABEN, "Alsina, A.," in *Biografías argentinas y sudamericanas*, vol. 1 (1938), pp. 118–122; YSABEL F. RENNIE, *The Argentine Republic* (1945), pp. 111, 115, 120–125, 139; JOSÉ LUIS ROMERO, *A History of Argentine Political Thought*, translated by Thomas F. McGann (1963); VICENTE OSVALDO CUTOLO, "Alcina, A." in *Nuevo diccionario biográfico argentino, 1750–1930*, vol. 1 (1968), pp. 100–101; RICARDO LEVENE et al., "Historia de las presidencias: 1862–1898," in Academia Nacional de la Historia, *Historia argentina contemporánea, 1862–1930*, vol. 1 (1965), sec. 1, pp. 257–263.

JOSEPH T. CRISCENTI

**ALSINA, VALENTÍN** (*b.* 16 December 1802; *d.* 6 September 1869), Argentine politician. Alsina was born in Buenos Aires, the son of Juan de Alsina and María Pastora

Ruano. He studied at the University of Córdoba, where Gregorio Funes was one of his teachers, and received his law degree in Buenos Aires. From 1824 to 1827 he contributed articles to *El Nacional* and *El Mensajero Argentino* and was undersecretary of foreign affairs in the government of Bernardino RIVADAVIA. Alsina supported General Juan LAVALLE's revolution of 1 December 1828, and briefly served in his government. In 1829 he was the director of the public library in Buenos Aires. He was persecuted by Buenos Aires Governor Juan Manuel de ROSAS and was kept a prisoner aboard the lighter *Sarandí* until Colonel Enrique Sinclair, a relative, and Dr. Manuel Vicente MAZA, his father-in-law, arranged for his escape to Colonia in 1835. His wife, Antonia Maza, and their small child, Adolfo, fled from Buenos Aires with the help of Sinclair's friend Ricardo Haines, an Englishman. The family was reunited in Montevideo, where Alsina became a member of the Argentine Commission, which had as its aim the overthrow of Rosas. The commission sent his brother, Juan José Alsina, to represent it; he was later replaced by his relative, Governor Pedro Ferré of Corrientes. Unlike many members of the commission, Valentín Alsina never believed that Lavalle and his Ejército Libertador would overthrow Rosas.

In 1843 Alsina participated in the defense of Montevideo, then besieged by Manuel ORIDE, by enrolling in the Argentine Legion. His function was to contribute anti-Rosas articles to the local newspapers *El Moderador, El Nacional, El Grito Argentino,* and especially to *El Comercio del Plata.* In 1843 he wrote his famous "Notes" to the first edition of Sarmiento's *Civilización i barbarie,* (1845), in which he maintains that terror first appeared in Buenos Aires with Rosas.

In 1852 Alsina was appointed minister of government by Vicente López y Planes, governor of Buenos Aires. As minister he restored to their rightful owners the properties Rosas had confiscated. He represented the extreme wing of the Unitarian Party, opposing national organization and the Acuerdo de San Nicolás because representation in congress would be based on population. Elected governor of Buenos Aires Province 30 October 1852, Alsina made Bartolomé MITRE his minister of the interior, annulled the land grants Rosas had made to the veterans of the Indian campaigns and civil wars, organized an invasion of Entre Ríos, and appointed Hilario Lagos and Cayetano Laprida to the departmental posts of military commandant. When Lagos and Laprida revolted on 1 December 1852, he resigned as governor.

In 1853 Alsina was president of the Court of Justice, and in 1854 he was twice elected senator but did not serve. From 1855 to May 1856 he was minister of government and foreign affairs in the administration of Pastor Obligado. In 1857 he was again elected governor of Buenos Aires Province, approved the return to Buenos Aires of Rivadavia's remains, and evidently became involved in a plot to assassinate the military commander Justo José de URQUIZA. The legislature forced Alsina to resign after the provincial forces were defeated by the confederation armies at the battle of CEPEDA. Three days later Buenos Aires and the Argentine Confederation signed the Pact of San José de Flores (11 November 1859), which was mediated by Francisco Solano López, whereby Buenos Aires agreed to join the confederation after a provincial convention examined the Constitution of 1853. Alsina participated in that convention.

In 1862, after the battle of PAVÓN, he was elected a senator of the national Congress that met in Buenos Aires and refused the presidency of the Supreme Court. That year he was entrusted with the task of writing the provincial rural code that became law in 1865. As the temporary president of the Senate, he proclaimed the election of Bartolomé MITRE and Marcos Paz as president and vice president in 1862, and of Domingo SARMIENTO and of his son Adolfo ALSINA as president and vice president in 1867. He died in Buenos Aires.

ESTANISLAO S. ZEBALLOS, "Apuntes biográficos del doctor Valentín Alsina," in *Revista de derecho, historia y letras* 10 (1901): 171–175; ADOLFO SALDÍAS, *La evolución republicana* (1903); RAMÓN J. CÁRCANO, *De Caseros al 11 de septiembre (1851–1852)* (1918); YSABEL F. RENNIE, *The Argentine Republic* (1945), pp. 80, 84, 86–87, 89–90, 103; HAROLD F. PETERSON, *Argentina and the United States, 1810–1960* (1964); JACINTO R. YABEN, *Biografías argentinas y sudamericanas,* vol. 1 (1968), pp. 125–129; VICENTE OSVALDO CUTOLO, *Nuevo diccionario biográfico argentino, 1750–1930,* vol. 1 (1969), pp. 104–106; JOSEPH F. CUSCINTI, ed., *Sarmiento and His Argentina* (1993); TULIO HALPERÍN-DONGHI et al., eds., *Sarmiento: Author of a Nation* (1994).

JOSEPH T. CRISCENTI

**ALSOGARAY, ALVARO** (*b.* 22 June 1913), Argentine economist and political leader. A disciple of Ludwig von Mises and an ardent defender of the social market economy, Alsogaray has been one of Argentina's leading conservatives in the postwar period. He was born in Esperanza, in the province of Santa Fe, and first held public office as under secretary of commerce and then as minister of industry (1955–1956) during General Pedro ARAMBURU's government. As Arturo FRONDIZI's economics minister (1959–1962), Alsogaray implemented a conservative, market-oriented reform program, unsuccessfully attempting to control inflation by reducing the public payroll and privatizing a number of deficit-ridden STATE CORPORATIONS. From 1966 to 1968 he was Argentina's ambassador to the United States. In 1983 Alsogaray founded the Union of the Democratic Center (UCD), a conservative party whose economic program has largely been implemented by the Peronist government of Carlos Saúl MENEM (1989–).

JUAN CARLOS DE PABLO, *Los economistas y la economía argentina* (1977); GARY W. WYNIA, *Argentina in the Postwar Era: Politics and Economic Policy Making in a Divided Society* (1978).

JAMES P. BRENNAN

*See also* **Argentina: Political Parties.**

**ALTAMIRANO, IGNACIO MANUEL** (*b.* 13 November 1834; *d.* 13 February 1893), Mexican writer. Born in Tixtla, Guerrero, Altamirano learned Spanish and studied at the Instituto Literario de Toluca, a school for the education of indigenous scholars. Journalist, bureaucrat, statesman, and diplomat, Altamirano supported liberal causes in Mexico during the years of the REFORM, the FRENCH INTERVENTION, and thereafter. He founded the review *El Renacimiento* (The Renaissance), which lasted for one year (1869), in order to advocate and foment a national literary culture. His series of articles, *Revistas literarias de México* (Literary Reviews of Mexico [1868–1883]), constitutes the first serious attempt to produce a systematic history of Mexican LITERATURE since Independence. In his criticism, he viewed the novel as the ideal genre for educating readers and establishing a national literary culture. His narrative production includes a collection of novellas, *Cuentos de invierno* (Winter Tales [1880]); and three novels, *Clemencia* (1869), *La navidad en las montañas* (Christmas in the Mountains [1871]), and *El Zarco* (written between 1886 and 1888, published posthumously in 1901). After years of public service as a teacher in Mexico and as a consul in Spain and France, Altamirano died in San Remo, Italy.

CHRIS N. NACCI, *Ignacio Manuel Altamirano* (1970); LEDDA ARGUEDAS, ''Ignacio Manuel Altamirano,'' in *Historia de la Literatura Hispanoamericana*, vol. 2, *Del neoclasicismo al modernismo*, edited by Luis Íñigo Madrigal (1987) pp. 193–201.

DANNY J. ANDERSON

**ALTAR DE SACRIFICIOS,** a modest Formative and Classic-Period MAYA site at the strategic junction of the Usamacinta and La Pasión rivers on the modern Mexico-Guatemala border. It is readily linked to the larger YAXCHILÁN, downstream, and to SEIBAL, upriver on La Pasión. Ceramic evidence (the Xe Ceramic Complex, about 900–700 B.C.) shows that Altar was occupied quite early. A 12-foot-high platform facing a plaza has been dated to the Middle Formative Period and demonstrates the early construction of civic-ceremonial architecture. Dated stone monuments at Altar begin with Stela 10, 9.1.0.0.0. (A.D. 455) and close with Stela 22, 10.1.0.0.0 (A.D. 849).

In addition to its early occupation, the site is noteworthy for providing ceramic evidence, as does nearby Seibal, of occupation by foreigners (Putun or Mexicanized Mayas) moving up the Usamacinta and La Pasión rivers during the Terminal Classic Period.

A tomb excavated beneath Structure A-III at Altar provides evidence for several additional lines of thought regarding both political relationships and other factors involved in the Classic Maya collapse. The fully extended elite internment included the Altar Vase, which illustrates a funeral rite dated to A.D. 754. The scenes show ritual dancing and sacrifice ceremonies by six individuals, including, apparently, ruling elite from three other sites. The vase also shows a young woman committing ritual suicide (by cutting her throat with a flint knife). A similar (or the actual) knife was recovered near the vase itself. The skeletal material from Altar dated to the Late Classic Period also indicates increasing nutritional deficiencies near the time of the Classic Maya collapse.

LEDYARD A. SMITH, *Excavations at Altar de Sacrificios: Architecture, Settlement, Burials, and Caches* (1972); GORDON R. WILLEY, *The Artifacts of Altar de Sacrificios* (1972); RICHARD E. W. ADAMS, ''Maya Collapse: Transformation in the Ceramic Sequence at Altar de Sacrificios,'' in *The Classic Maya Collapse*, edited by T. P. Culbert (1973), pp. 21–34.

WALTER R. T. WITSCHEY

**ALTEPETL,** a term derived from *in atl, in tepetl* (''the water, the mountain'') denoting the provincial unit, or regional state, of pre-Hispanic NAHUA society. By definition, each *altepetl* had a ruler, land base, marketplace, and temple dedicated to a patron deity. The *altepetl* was subdivided into smaller districts (groups of four, six, and eight were common) known as CALPULLI or TLAXILACALLI, which enjoyed political representation and gave tribute services by means of a rotational system. After the Spanish invasion, institutions such as the ENCOMIENDA and parish were based directly on the *altepetl*, known later as a pueblo, which generally continued to be governed by indigenous elites.

Excellent discussions of *altepetl* structure before and after the Conquest can be found in JAMES LOCKHART, *The Nahuas After the Conquest: A Social and Cultural History of the Indians of Central Mexico, Sixteenth through Eighteenth Centuries* (1992), and JAMES LOCKHART, FRANCES BERDAN, and ARTHUR J. O. ANDERSON, trans. and ed., *The Tlaxcalan Actas: A Compendium of the Records of the Cabildo of Tlaxcala (1545–1627)*, (1986). Though he barely mentions the term *altepetl*, CHARLES GIBSON's monumental study *The Aztecs Under Spanish Rule: A History of the Indians of the Valley of Mexico, 1519–1810* (1964) provides an invaluable study of the evolution of the indigenous corporate entity.

ROBERT HASKETT

**ALTIPLANO,** the largest plateau in the ANDES mountains. This historically important region lies in contemporary southern Peru and Bolivia. Starting in the region of Lake Titicaca, the altiplano extends southward in an opening between two branches of the southern Andes, at an average altitude of about 12,500 feet. Most of the area is Bolivian national territory and includes the cities of La Paz, Oruro, and Potosí. The altiplano contains important agriculture lands, pasturage, and mineral deposits and, according to Herbert Klein, was the site of ''the domestication of the staple products of Andean civilization,'' particularly the POTATO, and of ''the American cameloids: the llama, ALPACA, and vicuña.''

The altiplano was home to a number of indigenous societies, most notably the AYMARA, who were incorporated into the Inca empire in the fifteenth century. Under

Alpaca grazing on the altiplano in Peru. © H. GOHIER / PHOTO RESEARCHERS, INC.

Spanish rule, the altiplano's indigenous peoples were forced into settlements that were subject to heavy tribute and labor obligations to the colonial state, in particular labor for the *mita de minas* for the silver mines at Potosí, the most profitable mining area in the sixteenth-century empire. The altiplano communities resisted these demands, most overtly in a series of eighteenth-century uprisings. Although silver production declined in the late colonial period, the altiplano remained an important economic zone, particularly after the rise of tin mining in the late nineteenth and early twentieth centuries. The altiplano's mining unions and agricultural communities have played major roles in contemporary Bolivian politics.

HERBERT S. KLEIN, *Bolivia: The Evolution of a Multi-Ethnic Society* (1982) especially pp. 3–26.

ANN M. WIGHTMAN

*See also* **Silver Mining.**

**ALTUN HA,** a minor but surprisingly rich Maya center located in Belize, approximately 35 miles north of Belize City. The site comprises a central ceremonial precinct and main reservoir surrounded by residences and minor temples.

The site was settled by about 200 B.C., when major construction, including the first ceremonial structure, was begun. By A.D. 1, the focus of construction had moved to the east, to what would become the site's central precinct. Constructed near the main reservoir about A.D. 100 was a temple that became a focus of ceremonial life until about A.D. 250.

During the Classic period (A.D. 300–900), intensive construction began in the central precinct, culminating in a group of temples and elite residences that were organized into plazas and erected on an artificial platform. The northern plaza appears to have been the primary ceremonial center until A.D. 550. At this time a lavish burial, containing shell ornaments, pearls, jade, pottery, stingray spines, and ceremonial flints, was placed within the western temple's core. Residential and minor ceremonial-center construction was expanded around the fringes of the central precinct.

After A.D. 550, construction activity shifted southward, forming the unusual central precinct with two plazas and a border of temples on the south. One of seven rich Late Classic period (A.D. 550–800) tombs in the easternmost temple of the south plaza included a giant carved jade head of the god Kinich' Ahau. Construction declined during the period, becoming poorer in quality and ending by A.D. 800. Apparently a great part of the middle and lower classes remained at the site even after major rebuilding and maintenance of temples had ceased, as is shown by traces of occupation in the Postclassic period (A.D. 900–1300) found in reused Classic period structures at the site center and its hinterlands.

DAVID M. PENDERGAST, *Altun Ha: A Guidebook to the Ancient Maya Ruins*, 2d ed., rev. (1976), and *Excavations at Altun Ha, Belize, 1964–1970*, vol. 1 (1979).

KATHRYN SAMPECK

**ALVARADO, ANTONIO** (*b.* 1938), Panamanian abstract painter. Although he studied under the figurative painter Alberto DUTARY (*b.* 1932), Alvarado's early works showed a keen awareness of international trends such as abstract expressionism. A UNESCO grant in 1969 allowed him to travel to Japan, where he was influenced by oriental art, Zen, and Buddhism.

In his drawings, serigraphs, and bright acrylic paintings, Alvarado experiments with reducing art to its essential forms, and his work ranges from precise, hardedge paintings like *Homenaje a Varèse* (1972) to such strong gestural compositions as *Buda No. 120* (1981). In the 1970s, he held the position of director of the Department of Visual Arts of Panama's Instituto Nacional de Cultura.

GILBERT CHASE, *Contemporary Art in Latin America* (1970); DAMIÁN BOYÓN, *Artistas contemporáneos de América Latina* (1981).

MONICA E. KUPFER

**ALVARADO, LISANDRO** (*b*. 19 September 1858; *d*. 10 April 1929), Venezuelan ethnologist, linguist, naturalist, and historian. At the age of twenty, Alvarado traveled to Caracas to study medicine at the University of Caracas; where he came in contact with the positivist and evolutionist ideas that were in vogue in Latin America in the latter part of the nineteenth century. The tenets of these schools of thought would serve as a guide to his diverse intellectual activities. Alvarado conducted investigations in the areas of ethnography, linguistics, and history and studied ancient and modern cultures, traveling throughout the country as part of his research. He was proficient in several languages and was one of the first Venezuelans to study the indigenous customs and languages of the country's aboriginal groups. Alvarado was a regular member of the academies of medicine, language, and history. His major works include: *Sobre las guerras civiles del país* (1894) and *Glosario de voces indígenas de Venezuela* (1921).

PASCUAL VENEGAS FILARDO, *Lisandro Alvarado* (*1858–1929*) (1973); PEDRO GRASES, *Obras completas*, 7 vols. (Caracas, 1953–1958), *La obra lexicográfica de Lisandro Alvarado* (Caracas, 1981); CESIA ZIONA HIRSHBEIN, *Historia y literatura en Lisandro Alvarado* (Caracas, 1981).

INÉS QUINTERO

*See also* **Positivism.**

**ALVARADO, SALVADOR** (*b*. 1880; *d*. June 1924), military leader of the MEXICAN REVOLUTION and social reformer. Alvarado, the son of a printer, was born in northwest Mexico. After opposing the PORFIRIATO in the anarcho-syndicalist Mexican Liberal Party (Partido Liberal Mexicano—PLM) and participating in the brutally suppressed workers' strike at CANANEA in 1906, he transferred his allegiance in 1909 to the more moderate, broader-based movement of Francisco I. MADERO. His organizational and tactical skills elevated him rapidly in the military hierarchy during the revolutionary campaigns against Porfirio DÍAZ and Victoriano HUERTA. In 1914, Madero's successor, the Constitutionalist leader Venustiano CARRANZA, promoted him to division general. Then, following a brief stint as military commandant of the Federal District, he became Carranza's proconsul for the conquest and administration of the state of Yucatán.

Subduing a powerful regional oligarchy with his 7,000-man army in March 1915, Alvarado immediately attempted to make Yucatán a model of what the Mexican Revolution could accomplish, to transform the region into a social laboratory. His three-year governorship (1915–1918) was characterized by an effective blend of populist reform and authoritarian military rule. Buoyed by a swell in HENEQUEN revenues generated by World War I, Alvarado established more than a thousand new schools, the majority of them in remote, previously untouched hamlets and hacienda communities. He enforced an earlier, moribund decree "freeing" the debt peons who worked in slavelike conditions on the henequen estates and attempted to redress labor abuses through state-run tribunals. Under Alvarado's aegis, Mexico's first feminist congresses were convened, and special feminist leagues were organized. Alvarado was also responsible for the creation of a small but powerful urban labor movement, based in Mérida, the state's capital, and in Progreso, its principal port. In 1916, seeking to institutionalize his regional movement, Alvarado incorporated the workers and campesinos into a nascent state party, the Socialist Workers' Party (Partido Socialista Obrero). Its name was changed a year later to the Socialist Party of Yucatán (Partido Socialista de Yucatán). Many now regard it as a forerunner of Mexico's present-day corporatist edifice, the Institutional Revolutionary Party (Partido Revolucionario Institucional—PRI).

Carranza removed Alvarado as governor in 1918; although Alvarado harbored presidential aspirations, he never regained the renown he had known as Yucatán's revolutionary caudillo. In 1924, with fellow Sonoran Adolfo DE LA HUERTA and an important segment of the Mexican army, he rebelled against Carranza's successor, Alvaro OBREGÓN SALIDO, and was killed by Obregonistas in El Hormiguero, Chiapas, in June 1924.

FRANCISCO J. PAOLI BOLIO, *Yucatán y los orígenes del nuevo estado mexicano: Gobierno de Salvador Alvarado, 1915–1918* (1984); GILBERT M. JOSEPH, *Revolution from Without: Yucatán, Mexico, and the United States, 1880–1924*, rev. ed. (1988).

GILBERT M. JOSEPH

**ALVARADO XICOTENCATL, LEONOR** (*b*. 22 March 1524; *d*. 1583), the first prominent *ladina* (child of Spanish and Indian parents) born in Guatemala.

Daughter of the conquistador Pedro de ALVARADO and of Luisa de Xicotencatl, a Tlascalteca Indian princess, doña Leonor was born at Utatlán, the capital of the

Quiché, and was brought up by her godparents. Alvarado arranged her marriage to his friend and chief lieutenant, Pedro de Portocarrero, about 1541. She escaped death when a mudslide resulting from a flood and earthquake covered the capital at Almolonga and killed her stepmother, doña Beatríz de la Cueva, in 1541.

After the death of Portocarrero in 1547, doña Leonor married Francisco de la CUEVA, the brother of her stepmother. From this marriage were born the children who were Pedro de Alvarado's descendants in Guatemala. Her second husband died in 1576, and doña Leonor died seven years later, at the age of fifty-nine. Her remains were buried in the Cathedral at Santiago (now Antigua Guatemala), beside those of her father and her stepmother.

JOSÉ MILLA, *La hija del adelantado*, 4th ed. (1936), a novel; ADRIAN RECINOS, *Doña Leonor de Alvarado, y otros estudios* (1958).

DAVID L. JICKLING

**ALVARADO Y MESÍA, PEDRO DE** (*b.* 1485?; *d.* 29 June 1541?), a leader in the Spanish conquests of Mexico, Central America, and Ecuador. Born in Badajoz to a family of the minor nobility, Alvarado came to the Americas around 1510. He was a member of the Juan de GRIJALVA expedition to the Gulf coast of Mexico, and then accompanied Hernán CORTÉS as his chief lieutenant on his conquest of central Mexico (1519–1521). He was in charge of the garrison in TENOCHTITLÁN (Mexico City) during the events that led up to the disastrous Spanish withdrawal from the city (the NOCHE TRISTE) and played an outstanding role in the final siege and Spanish victory.

Known to the native peoples as "Tonatiuh" (the Sun), Alvarado was sent south by Cortés in 1523 with an army of 429 Spaniards and some 20,000 Tlaxcalans and other Indian allies. He led the Spanish conquests of SOCONUSCO, Guatemala, and El Salvador, and pushed into Honduras, where he met conquistador groups coming from Nicaragua. His two letters of *relación* to Hernán Cortés are the only extant and immediate eyewitness accounts of the campaign. In all these events he showed his customary bravery, impetuousness, and cruelty.

After the Conquest he ruthlessly suppressed a major Cakchiquel revolt, and founded the first two Spanish capitals, Almolonga and Ciudad Vieja. (The latter was destroyed in 1541 by an avalanche of water and mud that killed his second wife shortly after he himself had died.) He seized the best *encomiendas* and slave *cuadrillas* for himself, his five brothers, and other relatives and associates. Many of his Indian slaves were put to work on gold panning or shipbuilding. At one time he allegedly owned 1,500 branded native slaves who worked in the gold fields.

Alvarado dominated much of Central America for about seventeen years (1524–1541). His life after he became governor of Guatemala was marked by ambition and restlessness. His frequent absences and predatory return visits were disruptive. Each new expedition deprived the region of Spaniards, native auxiliaries, and supplies.

Leaving his brother Jorge in charge, Alvarado returned to Spain via Mexico in 1526–1527 to defend himself against charges of wrongdoing. While there, he married Francisca de la Cueva, a member of the high nobility, won his case, and was named governor and captain-general of Guatemala. His new wife died in Veracruz (1528) during the return journey to Guatemala.

Alvarado immediately began to plan an expedition to the South Seas but was diverted from it by news of the wealth won in Peru by Francisco PIZARRO and Diego de ALMAGRO. Against royal orders, he set off for Quito in 1534, again leaving Jorge as lieutenant governor. This time he took some 500 Spaniards and 2,000 native auxiliaries with him. Penetrating inland, Alvarado met Almagro. Potential conflict turned to negotiations when Alvarado realized that his men were tired, and that some of them were being induced to change sides. He finally agreed to turn over most of his men, ships, and equipment in return for 100,000 gold pesos. After his return to Guatemala (1535) he complained to the crown about Almagro's conduct, and his anger was increased by the discovery that some of the payment he had received consisted of adulterated and even falsified coinage.

Again facing accusations, this time from Mexico, Alvarado boldly set off from the coast of Honduras to

Pedro de Alvarado y Mesía, 1808. Known as the "Guatemala Portrait." ORGANIZATION OF AMERICAN STATES.

plead his case in Spain (1536). There, on 22 October 1538, Charles V absolved him of all blame, and reappointed him as governor of Guatemala for seven more years. Charles also obtained a papal dispensation so that Alvarado could marry Beatríz de la CUEVA, his deceased wife's sister.

Alvarado had been absent for over three years when he returned to Santiago de Guatemala in 1539. On his way from the coast he took over the governorship of Honduras from Francisco de Montejo and moved its main city inland to Gracias a Dios. In Guatemala he vigorously set about finding places for the large entourage that he and his new wife had brought from Spain. He also began to build ships and to collect men and supplies for yet another voyage of discovery to the Spice Islands.

He sailed with the new expedition in 1540, leaving Francisco de la CUEVA in charge. This time he took 850 Spaniards and many Indians with him. The fleet stopped for supplies at a port in Jalisco, where Alvarado met Viceroy Antonio de MENDOZA, made a series of agreements with him, and joined in the suppression of a native revolt in Nueva Galicia. In late June 1541, during a skirmish, he was crushed to death by a falling horse.

WILLIAM R. SHERMAN, "A Conqueror's Wealth: Notes on the Estate of don Pedro de Alvarado," in *The Americas* 26 (1969): 199–213; ADRIÁN RECINOS, *Pedro de Alvarado, Conquistador de México y Guatemala*, 2d ed. (1986).

MURDO J. MACLEOD

**ÁLVAREZ, JUAN** (*b.* 27 January 1790; *d.* 21 August 1867), president of Mexico (1855–1856). The orphaned son of a landowner in Santa María de la Concepción Atoyac in coastal Guerrero State, Álvarez joined the insurgent army of José María MORELOS Y PAVÓN in 1810. After independence Álvarez commanded militia forces in Guerrero and participated in several federalist revolts of the 1820s and 1830s. He is best known for his strong relationship with Guerrero's peasantry. During widespread peasant revolts in the 1840s he mediated land claims and reduced taxes. He simultaneously recruited the peasant rebels for federalist movements and the war against the United States. His efforts and political connections led to the creation in 1849 of the state of Guerrero, of which he was the first governor. In 1854–1855 Álvarez led the Revolution of Ayutla against the conservative government of Antonio López de SANTA ANNA. This movement began the period of the REFORM. Álvarez retired to Guerrero after a brief stint as president from October 1855 to September 1856. He remained politically active and supported the Liberal governments of Benito JUÁREZ against both the Conservatives and Maximilian's empire. He died at his hacienda on the Guerrero coast.

Álvarez was most important as a champion of the incorporation of Mexico's peasant masses into the polity of the young nation-state. Advocating universal male suffrage and municipal autonomy, he utilized the fundamental similarities between the peasant tradition of annual elections for village office and the basic tenets of popular sovereignty common to nineteenth-century political ideologies in Mexico and elsewhere. In promoting this model of state formation, Álvarez differed from both conservatives and many prominent liberals.

CLYDE G. BUSHNELL, "The Military and Political Career of Juan Álvarez, 1790–1867" (Ph.D. diss. University of Texas, 1958); DANIEL MUÑOZ Y PÉREZ, *El general don Juan Álvarez* (1959); FERNANDO DÍAZ DÍAZ, *Caudillos y caciques: Antonio López de Santa Anna y Juan Álvarez* (1972).

PETER GUARDINO

**ÁLVAREZ, LUIS HÉCTOR** (*b.* 25 October 1919), Mexican politician and opposition party leader. A native of Ciudad Camargo, Chihuahua, Álvarez received part of his education in El Paso, Texas. A businessman, he was first employed in the textile industry, after which he became director of the Río Bravo Industrial Company (1957). Selected by the National Action Party (PAN) as its presidential candidate, he opposed Adolfo LÓPEZ MATEOS in the 1958 presidential election. Although he remained out of the national political limelight for many years, he won election as mayor of Chihuahua in 1983. Upon completion of his term, he became president of the PAN in 1986. Under his leadership PAN ran its most successful presidential campaign, with Manuel CLOUTHIER as its presidential candidate, in 1988.

*Hispano Americano*, 2 December 1957; DONALD V. MABRY, *Mexico's Acción Nacional: A Catholic Alternative to Revolution* (1973); ABRAHAM NUNCIO, *El PAN* (1986).

RODERIC AI CAMP

*See also* **Mexico: Political Parties.**

**ÁLVAREZ, MANUEL** (*b.* 1794; *d.* 5 July 1856), fur trapper, merchant, and government official in NEW MEXICO.

The life of Álvarez, a native of Abelgas, Spain, exemplifies the tremendous opportunities that existed in New Mexico during the first half of the nineteenth century for an enterprising and well-connected immigrant.

In 1818 Álvarez emigrated to Mexico; in 1823 he moved to Cuba after Mexican independence unleashed anti-Spanish sentiment. There he obtained a U.S. passport and sailed to New York, planning to work his way back to Mexico. By 1824, Álvarez had joined a trading group in Saint Louis and had reached New Mexico, where he became friends with Charles Bent. There he opened a store to sell goods imported from Missouri.

The contacts and commercial ties that Álvarez built during the 1820s enabled him to take up fur trapping in 1829, when Mexican authorities expelled all Spanish residents from the country. By 1831, Álvarez worked for the American Fur Company as the leader of a team of forty fur trappers hunting in an area that is now part of Yellowstone National Park. Álvarez managed his store in Santa Fe from a distance until 1834, when he returned there, his Spanish origin no longer a problem.

While claiming Mexican citizenship, Álvarez used his U.S. passport to gain an appointment as U.S. consul for Mexico, based in Santa Fe. Forced loans that American merchants made to the New Mexican officials during the 1837 revolt in Taos and Río Arriba, and losses to Americans resulting from the Texan expedition against Santa Fe in 1841, prompted American claims for reimbursement. Even though he never received complete confirmation of his post, Álvarez represented these petitions to the New Mexican governor and Mexican officials. His success in this role came from his relationship with Governor Manuel ARMIJO, based in part on the information that Álvarez and Bent provided about Apache and Texan movements of concern to New Mexico.

Upon the U.S. declaration of war against Mexico in 1846, the Americans sent ''spies'' to speak to Álvarez. He appears to have provided reports about affairs in New Mexico and advice on how to proceed with its occupation. Álvarez met with Governor Armijo and probably contributed to his decision not to oppose Colonel Stephen Watts KEARNY and his force when it arrived to occupy SANTA FE. Although his friend Charles Bent served as interim governor of New Mexico until his murder during the 1847 revolt against the Americans, Álvarez received no post in the administration.

In the wake of the military government imposed on New Mexico after the revolt of 1847, Álvarez began to use his political skills in defense of the Spanish-Mexican population of the territory. He came to lead a political party, arguing against the propensity of military rule to ignore the civil rights of the population and advocating immediate statehood for New Mexico in order to bring back civilian rule. After a brief stint as editor of one of the early New Mexican newspapers in order to gain support for the statehood faction, Álvarez won the post of lieutenant governor alongside Congressman William Messervy in the election of 1850. Because Messervy had to spend most of his time in Washington, D.C., lobbying for statehood, running the state fell to Álvarez. Opposition from the army and the territorial party hampered the new government's ability to function. Soon after, the Compromise of 1850, admitting California to the Union as a free state and organizing New Mexico and Arizona into a single territory, made the position of the Statehood faction untenable.

Álvarez was never again involved as prominently in the affairs of the territory, and withdrew to his commercial ventures during the last years of his life. His ambition, and his service as an advocate for various American and Spanish-Mexican constituencies, wove him into the fabric of the critical events of New Mexican history bridging the Mexican and American periods. He died in Santa Fe.

HOWARD ROBERTS LAMAR, *The Far Southwest, 1846–1912: A Territorial History* (1966); DAVID J. WEBER, *The Taos Trappers: The Fur Trade in the Far Southwest, 1540–1846* (1971); JANET LECOMPTE, *Rebellion in Rio Arriba, 1837* (1985); THOMAS E. CHÁVEZ, *Manuel Álvarez, 1794–1856: A Southwestern Biography* (1990).

ROSS H. FRANK

*See also* **New Mexico.**

**ÁLVAREZ ARMELLINO, GREGORIO CONRADO** (*b.* 26 November 1925), Uruguayan military leader and president (1981–1985). Álvarez played an important role from 1973 to 1985, when the armed forces governed the country. The press, including that of the Left, had already popularized the figure of ''Goyo'' Álvarez, a commanding officer with a nationalist orientation and sympathies toward the leftist militarism of Peruvian General JUAN VELASCO ALVARADO. Álvarez was appointed president by the military regime in 1981. He became one of the elements most opposed to the move toward democracy in Uruguay. After the election of Julio María SANGUINETTI to the presidency, the political parties refused to accept the transfer of power directly from General Álvarez. The president of the Supreme Court of Justice had to intervene as a transitional leader in order for the restoration of democracy to be completed.

ANGEL COCCHI, *Nuestros partidos*, vol. 2 (1984); MARTIN WEINSTEIN, *Uruguay: Democracy at the Crossroads* (1988).

JOSÉ DE TORRES WILSON

**ÁLVAREZ BRAVO, LOLA** (*b.* 3 April 1907; *d.* 31 July 1993), Mexican photographer. A pioneering modernist photographer, Álvarez Bravo's career spanned six decades. Born in Lagos de Moreno, Jalisco, she studied photography in the 1920s under the tutelage of Manuel ÁLVAREZ BRAVO, to whom she was married from 1925 to 1949. While some of her early imagery bears relation to his, by the 1930s she had developed a distinct pictorial language that evinces her deep interest in the cinema as well as her empathy for the Mexican people. Her oeuvre includes photographs documenting everyday urban and rural life; these compositions often emphasize the ironic, humorous, or poetic aspects of mundane events. Other bodies of work include landscapes, still lifes, portraits of Mexican artists and intellectuals, and innovative photomontages. Álvarez Bravo was active as a teacher, documentary photographer for governmental agencies, exhibition curator, and director of the prestigious Galería de Arte Contemporáneo in Mexico City (1951–1958), which mounted important exhibitions featuring the artists of the Mexican School. She died in Mexico City.

The most comprehensive study is CENTRO CULTURAL/ARTE CONTEMPORÁNEO, *Lola Álvarez Bravo, fotografías selectas 1934–1985* (1992). See also LOLA ÁLVAREZ BRAVO, *Recuento fotográfico*

(1982), which contains conversations with the artist and extensive illustrations; OLIVIER DEBROISE, *Lola Álvarez Bravo, reencuentros* (1989); *Lola Álvarez Bravo, the Frida Kahlo Photographs* (1991); ELIZABETH FERRER, "Lola Álvarez Bravo: A Modernist in Mexican Photography," in *History of Photography* 18, no. 3 (1994): 211–218.

ELIZABETH FERRER

*See also* **Photography.**

**ÁLVAREZ BRAVO, MANUEL** (*b*. 4 February 1912), Mexican photographer. Self-taught in the art of photography, Álvarez has practiced the profession since 1923. In the 1930s, he began to capture on film the works of the Mexican muralists and other scenes of Mexican cultural life. Soon after his first exhibition, in 1932, his photographs were discovered by the international art community. Álvarez Bravo has exhibited his work in museums and galleries all over the world. He was awarded the National Prize for Art in 1975, and has been the recipient of numerous other national and international awards for photography. He is a member of the Mexican academy of arts.

Álvarez Bravo uses black and white film; his themes are creativity and beauty, and he is known for his portraits of famous as well as common people, and urban and rural scenes of a changing Mexico. He is one of the most renowned Latin American photographers.

LUIS REYES DE LA MAZA, *El cine sonoro en México* (1973); E. BRADFORD BURNS, *Latin American Cinema: Film and History* (1975); CARL J. MORA, *Mexican Cinema: Reflections of a Society: 1896–1980* (1982); and JOHN KING, *Magical Reels: A History of Cinema in Latin America* (1990).

DAVID MACIEL

**ÁLVAREZ DE PINEDA, ALONSO** (*d*. 1520), sailor. Little is known about Álvarez de Pineda, except that he was captain-general of the first European expedition to navigate systematically the entire coastline of the Gulf of Mexico from the Florida Keys to the Yucatán Peninsula. The voyage resulted in a hand-drawn map showing the peninsula of Florida as part of the mainland, not an island, as had been believed. The voyage also located the mouth of the Mississippi River (Río del Espíritu Santo), with its great discharge of fresh water.

Made in 1519, the voyage was sponsored by the governor of Jamaica, Francisco de GARAY, who sought knowledge of the lands between those Juan Ponce de León had reached in 1513 (west of the Florida Peninsula) and the region west of Cuba (Yucatán and Central America). He also hoped to find a passage to the "South Sea" (the Pacific Ocean), discovered by Vasco Núñez de Balboa.

An early (ca. late 1530s) navigational guide that must have incorporated Álvarez de Pineda's information is PAULINO CAS-

TAÑEDA, MARIANO CUESTA, and PILAR HERNÁNDEZ, *Transcripción, estudio y notas del "Espejo de navegantes" de Alonso Chaves* (1983). See also ROBERT S. WEDDLE, *Spanish Sea: The Gulf of Mexico in North American Discovery, 1500–1685* (1985), esp. pp. 95–108.

JERALD T. MILANICH

**ÁLVAREZ GARDEAZÁBAL, GUSTAVO** (*b*. 31 October 1945), Colombian writer. A native of Tuluá, Valle, he studied chemical engineering at Medellín's Universidad Pontificia. About 1963 he published parts of his first novel, *Piedra pintada* (1965), and was expelled from the university. Álvarez returned to Valle and continued to write fiction. The VIOLENCIA in Valle remained a major theme of his work, but after 1977 his novels reflected other currents as well, including opposition to the Gran Cauca elite. Álvarez taught at the Universidad del Valle (Cali) and was elected in 1978 to the municipal councils of Cali and of Tuluá. Recognized as Valle's major writer, he was a Guggenheim fellow in 1984–1985 and has won numerous other awards. His novels include *La tara del papa* (1971); *Cóndores no entierran todos los días* (1972); *Dabeiba* (1973); *El bazar de los idiotas* (1974); *El titiritero* (1977); *Los míos* (1981); and *Los sordos ya no hablan* (1991).

RAYMOND L. WILLIAMS, comp., *Aproximaciones a Gustavo Álvarez Gardeazábal* (1977); RAYMOND L. WILLIAMS, *The Colombian Novel, 1844–1987* (1991); DAVID C. FOSTER, *Handbook of Latin American Literature*, 2d ed. (1992), p. 210.

J. LEÓN HELGUERA

**ALVAREZ MARTÍNEZ, GUSTAVO** (*b*. 12 December 1937; *d*. 26 January 1989), Honduran general, chief of the armed forces. When Honduras resumed a civilian government in January 1982 with the election of Roberto Suazo Córdova to the presidency, the military coalesced under the leadership of Colonel Alvarez Martínez, appointed by the national assembly as commander in chief of the armed forces. Leading the armed forces as a "third party" of hard-liners in the Honduran political spectrum, Alvarez Martínez centralized and modernized the command structure, a feat that earned him a promotion from colonel to brigadier general. Then, with President Suazo Córdova, he forged a united front that stressed military subordination to the constitution as well as an alliance between the armed forces and the Liberal Party of Honduras. However, fellow officers, annoyed by his "high-handedness," ousted Alvarez Martínez and split decisively with Suazo in 1984. Five years later, the general was assassinated in Tegucigalpa by six men, an act for which the Popular Liberation Front claimed responsibility.

JAMES A. MORRIS, *Honduras: Caudillo Politics and Military Rulers* (1984); JAMES DUNKERLEY, *Power in the Isthmus: A Political History of Modern Central America* (1988).

JEFFREY D. SAMUELS

**ALVEAR, CARLOS MARÍA DE** (*b.* 25 October 1789; *d.* 2 November 1852), Argentine soldier and politician. Alvear, born in Misiones, was the son of a Spanish naval officer and a creole mother. After service in the Peninsular War he returned to Buenos Aires in 1812 with José de SAN MARTÍN and other patriots to play a leading role in the military and political organization of independence. As president of the Assembly of the Year XIII (1813), he influenced its policy in the direction of liberal reform. The capture of Montevideo from the Spanish in 1814 strengthened Alvear's military base, and he was appointed supreme director of the UNITED PROVINCES OF THE RÍO DE LA PLATA to restore stability to the revolutionary government. His tendency toward dictatorship and centralism caused his overthrow and exile after less than four months in office (April 1815).

Alvear subsequently changed political direction and joined forces with the Littoral caudillos in an attempt to overthrow the Buenos Aires government and establish a federal system. But the caudillos' success at CEPEDA (1820) failed to secure him the governorship he desired. He was recalled to office by Bernardino RIVADAVIA and, while minister of war, fought a successful military campaign against Brazil at Ituazingó early in 1827. He retired to private life until Juan Manuel de ROSAS appointed him minister to the United States in 1838. He died in New York.

THOMAS B. DAVIS, JR., *Carlos de Alvear: Man of Revolution* (1955); TULIO HALPERÍN DONGHI, *Politics, Economics, and Society in Argentina in the Revolutionary Period* (1975).

JOHN LYNCH

**ALVEAR, MARCELO TORCUATO DE** (*b.* 4 October 1868; *d.* 23 March 1942), Argentine political leader and president (1922–1928). Born into a prominent landed Buenos Aires family, Alvear became involved in the political reform activities of Leandro ALEM and the Radical Civic Union (UCR) as a law student at the University of Buenos Aires. Alvear supported the UCR's 1893 uprising, but in the wake of its failure and the UCR's declining fortunes, he undertook a self-imposed exile in Europe and was not present at the time of the Radicals' 1905 rebellion. Despite this, Alvear maintained close contacts with Hipólito YRIGOYEN and other prominent Radicals and was elected to Congress in 1912.

As Yrigoyen's ambassador to France (1916–1920), Alvear had his first serious differences with the Radical leader, specifically in his opposition to Argentina's neutrality in World War I. Alarmed by labor protests and the oligarchy's increasing hostility to his government, Yrigoyen chose Alvear as his successor, seeing his aristocratic credentials as an asset and his lack of a solid base within the party as leaving him open to manipulation. As president, Alvear tried to solve the problem of the national debt, a legacy, in large part, of Yrigoyen's patronage practices.

During Alvear's presidency, Yrigoyen's rivals within the UCR organized a separate party, the Antipersonalist Radical Civic Union, though Alvear himself was not a promoter of the *antipersonalista* movement. After the 1930 coup, he was forced into exile in Brazil but returned to assume control of the party, supporting its policy of electoral abstention until 1935 and then serving as the leader of the Radicals' loyal opposition to the nondemocratic governments of the period, losing as the 1937 Radicals' presidential candidate in an election characterized by widespread fraud.

FÉLIX LUNA, *Alvear* (1974); DAVID ROCK, *Politics in Argentina, 1890–1930: The Rise and Fall of Radicalism* (1975); LUIS A. ALEN LASCANO, *Yrigoyenismo y antipersonalismo* (1986).

JAMES P. BRENNAN

*See also* **Argentina: Political Parties.**

**ALVES, FRANCISCO** (Francisco de Morais Alves; *b.* 19 August 1889; *d.* 27 September 1952), Brazilian singer and songwriter. Alves was born in Rio de Janeiro and raised in the Saúde district of São Paulo. He began his musical career in 1918 as a singer in the João de Deus-Martins Chaves Circus. The following year, Alves made his first recording with an interpretation of ''Pé de anjo'' (Angel's Foot) and ''Fala, meu louro'' (Speak, My Parrot), both by SINHÔ. He continued singing and recording while driving a taxi and occasionally performing in the circus or musical theater. In 1927 Alves began recording at the Odeon, where he took the stage name Chico Viola. Subsequently, he became a great success performing in CARNIVAL celebrations, with the sambas ''A Malandragem'' (Gypsy Life) in 1928, ''Amor de malandro'' (A Scoundrel's Love) in 1930, ''Se você jurar'' (If You Promise) in 1931, and ''Sofrer é da vida'' (Life Is about Suffering) in 1932. At the Odeon, Alves made the first electronically produced record in Brazil with his interpretation of Duque's ''Albertina'' and ''Passarinho do má'' (Bad Little Bird) in 1927. In 1952 Alves was killed in an automobile accident; his funeral was attended by thousands. Known as the *rei da voz* (king of voice), Alves recorded the most 78 rpm LPs of any Brazilian singer: almost 500 records.

MARCOS ANTÔNIO MARCONDES, ed., *Enciclopédia da música brasileira: Erudita folclórica popular* (1977).

LISA MARIC

**ALVES BRANCO TARIFF** (1844), Brazil's first post-Independence tariff reform. Named for the finance minister of the time, the tariff raised import duties from an across-the-board rate of 15 percent ad valorem to 20 percent for cotton textiles and 30 percent for most other goods. Duties for a few agricultural products such as tobacco, tea, and hemp were set at 40 to 60 percent. The tariff was enacted after negotiations to renew the Anglo-Brazilian commercial treaty of 1827 became entangled in diplomatic disputes over Brazil's failure to halt the slave trade and Britian's refusal to lower duties on Brazilian sugar and coffee. Sometimes described as protectionist, the tariff was chiefly a fiscal measure intended to increase government revenues, which came overwhelmingly from customs receipts. Falling short of the more consistently protectionist proposals made in 1843 by a parliamentary commission, it had scarcely any adverse effects on British trade with Brazil. More important for the development of domestic industry was an 1846 decree eliminating all taxes on imported machinery.

As a result of both the 1844 increase in tariffs and the general growth in foreign trade, government revenues nearly doubled between 1845 and 1855. An even more liberal tariff schedule superseded the Alves Branco tariff in 1857.

NÍCIA VILELA LUZ, *A luta pela industrialização do Brasil* (1961); LESLIE BETHELL, *The Abolition of the Brazilian Slave Trade: Britian, Brazil, and the Slave Trade Question, 1807–1869* (1970).

B. J. BARICKMAN

*See also* **Slave Trade, Abolition of.**

**ÁLZAGA, MARTÍN DE** (*b.* 1757; *d.* 11 July 1812), Argentine merchant and political figure. A Basque of humble origins, Álzaga probably arrived in Buenos Aires in 1769. After serving a ten-year clerkship with the prominent merchant Gaspar de Santa Coloma, Álzaga launched his own mercantile career in 1780, becoming a successful merchant, a leading figure in the local *cabildo* (town council), and a spokesman for those merchants who worked to preserve the Spanish monopoly trade. Dismayed by the liberal trade policies enacted by Viceroy Santiago de LINIERS Y BREMOND, and convinced that Liniers was an agent of the hated French, Álzaga and his followers attempted a royalist coup d'état on 1 January 1809, which was defeated by an increasingly radicalized militia led by Cornelio de SAAVEDRA.

After independence in 1810, Álzaga continued to represent the concerns of Spanish loyalists. In July 1812 he again led a coup against a creole government that he viewed as inimical to the interests of Spain. No more successful than three years earlier, Álzaga and his followers were arrested by the government, now under the leadership of Bernardino RIVADAVIA, and were executed.

ENRIQUE UDAONDO, *Diccionario biográfico colonial argentino* (1945), pp. 65–67; ENRIQUE WILLIAMS ÁLZAGA, *Dos revoluciones* (1963) and *Martín de Álzaga en la reconquista y en la defensa de Buenos Aires, 1806–1807* (1971).

SUSAN M. SOCOLOW

**ALZATE Y RAMÍREZ, JOSÉ ANTONIO DE** (*b.* 21 November 1737; *d.* 2 February 1799), prominent figure in the Mexican Enlightenment. Born in Ozumba (modern state of Mexico), Alzate studied at the Colegio de San Ildefonso, where he received a bachelor's degree in theology in 1756, the same year he took holy orders. From an early age, Alzate was also deeply drawn to secular studies, including mathematics, physics, astronomy, and the natural sciences; his wide-ranging interests earned him the sobriquet the "Pliny of Mexico." Alzate carried out his own research, such as conducting astronomical observations to determine the latitude of Mexico City. However, he made his greatest scientific contribution as an author and editor, promoting new scientific knowledge and the worldview of the Enlightenment through a series of publications, culminating in the *Gazeta de literatura de México* (1788–1795). Though sometimes marred by polemics, this journal informed readers of the latest scientific advances in both Europe— Alzate had become a member of the Royal Academy of Sciences in Paris in 1771—and the Americas. Alzate translated foreign materials and himself contributed numerous articles in which he described Mexico's rich natural and human resources and pointed out the practical benefits of new scientific methods for Mexican economic development.

CLEMENT MOTTEN, *Mexican Silver and the Enlightenment* (1950); BERNABÉ NAVARRO B., *Cultura mexicana moderna en el siglo xviii* (1964); ELÍAS TRABULSE, *El círculo roto: Estudios históricos sobre la ciencia en México* (1982).

R. DOUGLAS COPE

**AMADO, JORGE** (*b.* 10 August 1912), perhaps the most widely known and most popular of all Brazilian novelists. A major figure of the generation that developed the social "novel of the Northeast" in the 1930s, Amado has been writing for six decades, completing more than twenty novels. His work has been translated into at least thirty languages and has inspired many films, television series, and even popular songs. A recipient of numerous international awards, Amado was elected to the Brazilian Academy of Letters in 1961.

From the 1930s until the 1950s Amado was both a political activist and a writer. He was a member of the Aliança Nacional Libertadora (1935) and the Brazilian Communist Party, of which he was an elected federal congressman during its brief period of legality (1945–1947). Because of his political activities, he spent several periods in exile. The trilogy *Os subterrâneos da liberdade* (1954) re-creates, in novelistic form, the political struggles against Getúlio VARGAS's authoritarian Estado Novo in the 1930s and 1940s.

Amado's literary production ranges from novels marked by social protest and denunciation, especially during his "proletarian" phase of the 1930s—for example, *Cacau* (1933), *Suor* (1934; *Slums*, 1938), *Jubiabá* (1934; *Jubiabá*, 1984)—to those notable for the colorful, humorous, and often picaresque chronicles of the political customs and sexual mores of Brazilian society; these latter often have memorable female protagonists, for exam-

Jorge Amado greets his mother on his arrival from the USSR in 1952. ICONOGRAPHIA.

ple, *Dona Flor e seus dois maridos* (1966; *Dona Flor and Her Two Husbands*, 1969), *Tereza Batista, cansada de guerra* (1972; *Tereza Batista, Home From the Wars*, 1975), and *Tieta do Agreste, pastora de cabras* (1977; *Tieta the Goat Girl*, 1979). Many critics have pointed to *Gabriela, cravo e canela* (1958; *Gabriela, Clove and Cinnamon*, 1962) as the dividing line between Amado's politically engaged narratives and his more exuberant, picturesque, populist tales that exalt the freedom to live and love outside the confines of bourgeois morality. The short *A morte e a morte de Quincas Berro d'Água* (1959) ingeniously and satirically contrasts bourgeois and "popular" culture and values.

Amado's novels and his occasional short narratives typically deal with different aspects of his home state, focusing primarily on the city of Salvador or the cacao region of southern Bahia. Novels such as *Terras do sem-fim* (1943; *The Violent Land*, 1945), *São Jorge dos Ilhéus* (1944), and *Tocaia Grande: A face obscura* (1984) re-create struggles for control of rich cacao lands, combining political intrigue and intertwined love affairs.

Those works set in Salvador often focus on the life and culture of the city's predominantly black lower classes, frequently portrayed as living in a sort of harmonious primitive communism (*Capitães de areia*, 1937) and spiritually sustained by the values of the Afro-Brazilian religion CANDOMBLÉ. Amado's praise of miscegenation and Afro-Brazilian culture reaches its high point in *Tenda dos milagres* (1969; *Tent of Miracles*, 1971).

Amado's idealization of the lower classes has drawn harsh criticism from those who see him as exploiting,

rather than celebrating, their culture. But his defenders have argued that his insistent focus on the poor, even if vitiated by the use of "exotic local color," has made him an eloquent spokesman for the downtrodden and the oppressed in Brazilian society.

MARIA LUISA NUNES, "The Preservation of African Culture in Brazilian Literature: The Novels of Jorge Amado," in *Luso-Brazilian Review* 10, no. 1 (Summer 1973): 86–101; WALNICE GALVÃO, "Amado: Respeitoso, respeitável," in her *Gatos de outro saco: Ensaios críticos* (1976), pp. 13–22; FRED P. ELLISON, "Jorge Amado," in his *Brazil's New Novel: Four Northeastern Masters* (1979), pp. 81–108; ALFREDO WAGNER BERNO DE ALMEIDA, *Jorge Amado: Política e literatura* (1979); BOBBY J. CHAMBERLAIN, "Salvadore, Bahia, and the Passion According to Jorge Amado," in *The City in the Latin American Novel*, edited by Bobby J. Chamberlain (1980).

RANDAL JOHNSON

**AMADOR, MANUEL E.** (*b.* 25 March 1869; *d.* 1952), one of Panama's first modern artists, creator of the national flag (1903). Amador occupied the public posts of minister of finance (1903–1904) and consul in Hamburg, Germany (1904–1908) and in New York City, where he lived from 1908 to 1925. Later, he worked as an auditor in Panama's Contraloría General (1926–1940).

Amador produced most of his oeuvre between 1910 and 1914, and after 1940. His style of vigorous drawing, gestural brush strokes, and somber colors reflected the lessons of German expressionism and the American artist Robert Henri (1865–1929). He painted landscapes and still lifes, but his main subject was the human figure, as exemplified by *Cabeza de Estudio* (1910) and *Rabbi* (1948). The University of Panama holds an important collection of his drawings, watercolors, and prints.

RODRIGO MIRÓ, *Manuel E. Amador: un espíritu sin fronteras* (1966) and "Lewis, Amador, Ivaldi," in *Revista Lotería*, no. 219 (May 1974): 72–80.

MONICA E. KUPFER

**AMADOR GUERRERO, MANUEL** (*b.* 30 June 1833; *d.* 2 May 1909), physician and politician, first president of Panama (1904–1908). Born in Turbaco, Colombia, Amador Guerrero was a member of a distinguished Colombian family. In 1855 he began studying medicine and became a successful physician. Beginning his political career as a Conservative, he was named president of the department of Panama in 1867, but a revolution prevented him from assuming the post. After a year in exile, he returned to become chief physician of the Panama Railroad. In 1903 he traveled to the United States to secure support for the independence movement. (French engineer Philippe Jean BUNAU-VARILLA arranged for financial and military support for the cause in return for an appointment as ambassador to the United States.) The price Amador paid for support was the unfavorable HAY–BUNAU-VARILLA TREATY of 1903, which dominated U.S.-Panamanian relations for years to come. Amador became the first president of the independent republic of Panama in 1904 and immediately embarked on a vigorous public-works program. His term ended a year before his death.

MANUAL MARÍA ALBA C., *Cronología de los gobernantes de Panamá, 1510–1967* (1967), pp. 249–254; DAVID G. MC CULLOUGH, *The Path Between the Seas: The Creation of the Panama Canal, 1870–1914* (1977), pp. 341–402; EDUARDO LEMAITRE, *Panamá y su separación de Colombia* (1980), pp. 480–558.

SARA FLEMING

**AMAPÁ,** a Brazilian state that once guarded the Amazon delta against foreign invasion via the Atlantic Ocean. The seventeenth-century Portuguese showed no interest in this strategic area on the northern seaboard until France occupied land adjacent to it. In 1637, the future Amapá became Costa do Cabo Norte, the first captaincy that was clearly west of the line drawn by the Tordesillas Treaty of 1494. Sixty years later, the French invaded Costa do Cabo Norte, but Portugal forced their withdrawal. After the Portuguese dissolved Costa do Cabo Norte in the mid-eighteenth century, the French once again encroached on the area between the Amazon and Oyapock rivers. The ongoing border conflicts with France were not resolved until the twentieth century, when Brazil and France turned to an impartial arbitrator, Walther Hauser, president of Switzerland. Hauser awarded Amapá to Brazil on 1 December 1900, after which it became part of the state of Pará. The federal government detached the area in 1943 and created the territory of Amapá (54,161 sq mi). On 1 January 1990, Amapá became a state.

Since it is in Amazonia, RUBBER gathering was and still is important in Amapá. The Bethlehem Steel Company has mined and exported most of the magnesium, which was discovered in 1945. Prospectors have extracted alluvial gold from the rivers in Amapá since the 1970s, and other residents have farmed, mined coal, and cut timber. By 1990, over half of its 252,000 inhabitants resided near the capital city, Macapá, which rests on the equator.

LESLIE BETHELL, ed., *Colonial Brazil* (1987); DAVID CLEARY, *Anatomy of the Amazon Gold Rush* (1990); SUSANNA HECHT and ALEXANDER COCKBURN, *The Fate of the Forest: Developers, Destroyers, and Defenders of the Amazon* (1990).

CAROLYN JOSTOCK

**AMAPALA, TREATIES OF (1895, 1907).** The first of these agreements was signed in Amapala, Honduras, on 20 June 1895 and created a confederation known as the "República Mayor de Centro América," which was later changed to "Los Estados Unidos de Centro América." Within three years this union was defunct due to a revolution begun in El Salvador. The official dissolution of the first treaty took place on 30 November 1898.

In 1907, the second Treaty of Amapala ended a conflict between Honduras and Nicaragua, and reflected the tone of the MARBLEHEAD PACT of July 1906. The latter had recognized the interests of the United States in the region and had created the CENTRAL AMERICAN COURT OF JUSTICE. The court had its first test the following summer, when Nicaragua complained that Guatemala and El Salvador had instigated a revolutionary movement in Honduras. The ensuing conference ended hostilities, complied with the court's orders, and fueled hopes that a new spirit of peaceful coexistence would replace the characteristic interventionism of nineteenth-century Central America.

MICHAEL RHETA MARTIN, *Encyclopedia of Latin American History;* revised edition by L. Robert Hughes (1968); THOMAS L. KARNES, *The Failure of Union,* rev. ed. (1976); NICARAGUA: MINISTERIO DE RELACIONES EXTERIORES, *Documentos oficiales referentes a la guerra entre Nicaragua y Honduras de 1907, y la participación de El Salvador* (1907).

JEFFREY D. SAMUELS

**AMAR Y BORBÓN, ANTONIO** (*b.* March 1742; *d.* 26 April 1826), viceroy of New Granada (1803–1810). Amar y Borbón had a distinguished career in Spanish military service before becoming viceroy of New Granada in 1803. A conscientious ruler, he was generally well liked during the first part of his administration. After 1808, however, he faced creole demands for the establishment of American juntas to assume rule during the captivity in France of King FERDINAND VII. When such a junta was created in Quito (1809), he was unable to suppress it, in part because he had to deal with the same demands in Bogotá. He first sought to head off the junta movement there, while the viceroy of Peru saw to Quito. But as conditions in Spain deteriorated further with further French advances, a junta was formed in Bogotá on 20 July 1810. Largely as a figurehead, the viceroy was made a member and then deposed five days later. Expelled from the colony, he returned to Spain and remained there until his death.

ROBERT L. GILMORE, "The Imperial Crisis, Rebellion and the Viceroy: Nueva Granada in 1809," in *Hispanic American Historical Review* 40 (Feb. 1960): 1–24; MARIO HERRÁN BAQUERO, *El virrey don Antonio Amar y Borbón* (1988); CARMEN PUMAR MARTÍNEZ, "La narración perdida de Amar y Borbón sobre los sucesos de julio de 1810: Una historia diferente," in *Boletín de historia y antigüedades* 76, no. 766 (1989): 689–704.

DAVID BUSHNELL

**AMARAL, ANTÔNIO JOSÉ AZEVEDO DO** (*b.* 1881), Brazilian journalist. Born in Rio de Janeiro, Amaral earned a degree from Rio's Faculdade de Medicina in 1903, but he soon established himself in CARIOCA journalism, writing for *Jornal do Commercio, A Notícia,* and *Correio da Manhã.* Expelled from England for his pro-German reporting in 1916, he returned to Brazil.

After becoming the editor of the *Correio da Manhã*, he went on to edit *O País* and founded *Rio-Jornal* (1918) with João do RIO and *O Dia* (1921) with Virgílio de Melo Franco. A translator of the corporativist Mihail Manoilesco, Amaral is most noted for the rightist nationalism of his own essays, which made him an influential spokesman for the nationalist authoritarianism and statist industrialization of the ESTADO NÔVO era.

AZEVEDO AMARAL's works include *Ensaios brasileiros* (1930), *O Brasil na crise atual* (1934), *A aventura política do Brasil* (1935), and *O estado autoritário e a realidade nacional* (1938). Other helpful sources are A. GUERREIRO RAMOS, *A crise do poder no Brasil* (1961); ASPÁSIA B. ALCÂNTARA, "A teoria política de Azevedo Amaral," in *Revista DADOS* 2/3 (1967); JARBAS MEDEIROS, *Ideologia autoritária no Brasil, 1930–1945* (1978); and BOLIVAR LAMOUNIER, "Introdução," to AZEVEDO AMARAL, *O estado autoritário e a realidade nacional*, 2d ed. (1981).

JEFFREY D. NEEDELL

*See also* **Salgado, Plínio; Vargas, Getúlio; Viana, Francisco José de Oliveira.**

**AMARAL, TARSILA DO** (*b.* 1 September 1886; *d.* 17 January 1973), Paulista artist and salon leader whose paintings, sculpture, drawings, engravings, and illustrations helped to define, inspire, and stimulate the Brazilian modernist movement, especially the *Pau Brasil* (Brazilwood) and *Antropófagia* (Cannibals) avant-garde submovements. Her works are known for their cubist forms, Brazilian colors and themes. *A negra, A caipirinha, Abaporu, Floresta, Antropófagia,* and other works were shown at galleries and museums in Paris, London, Argentina, Chile, and Brazil from 1922 until 1970. Amaral also wrote poems and articles and illustrated books and periodicals. Other writers and composers dedicated works to her, and she was the subject of a film, books, articles, and interviews.

Amaral grew up on the family *fazenda* and attended *colégios* in Santana, São Paulo, and Barcelona. After her 1906 marriage to André Teixeira Pinto, she settled in São Paulo, where she studied sculpture with Zadig and Mantovani, and design and painting with Pedro Alexandrino and Georg Fischer Elpons. In Paris in the early 1920s Amaral attended the Académie Julian and studied at the studios of Émile Renard, Pedro Alexandrino, André Lhote, Albert Gleizes, and Fernand Léger.

She joined the "Grupo dos Cinco" (with Anita MALFATTI, Mário de ANDRADE, Oswaldo de ANDRADE, and Menotti del Picchia) in 1922. With other Brazilians, including Lucília Guimarães Villa-Lobos, Heitor VILLA-LOBOS, Victor Brecheret, and Emiliano DI CALVALCANTI, Amaral traveled annually between Europe and Brazil until 1928. In 1930 she briefly became diretora-conservadora of the Pinacoteca do Estado (State Painting Museum) in São Paulo. In 1931 she exhibited at the Moscow Museum of Modern Western Art, which bought one of her works (*O pescador*). Recognized by

retrospective exhibits in Rio (1933, 1969), São Paulo (1950–1951, 1969), and Belo Horizonte (1970), Amaral's work is widely reflected in the literature on Latin American art and culture.

MARTA ROSSETTI BATISTA, *Brasil. Vol. 1, Tempo Modernista—1917/29: Documentacão* (1972); ARACY A. AMARAL, *Tarsila—Sua Obra e Seu Tempo*, 2 vols. (1975); MARY LOMBARDI, "Women in the Modern Art Movement in Brazil: Salon Leaders, Artists, and Musicians, 1917–1930" (Ph.D. diss., University of California at Los Angeles, 1977).

MARY LUCIANA LOMBARDI

**AMARANTH,** an annual herb with tiny seeds (genus: *Amaranthus*; family: Amaranthaceae) that includes fifty to sixty species, the most nutritious of which are the grain amaranths. Three species utilized in the Americas are *A. hypochondriacus* in northwestern and central Mexico, *A. cruentus* in southern Mexico and Central America, and *A. caudatus* in the Andes. Growing from 1 to 10 feet tall, with broad, colorful leaves, the plant bears up to half a million seeds on each seed head. The grain and the leaves are sources of high-quality protein, while the leaves, eaten like spinach, are rich in vitamins and iron. Once toasted, boiled, or milled, the seeds may be eaten in cereals, baked as a flour in breads, popped like popcorn, and made into candies. The Mexicans mix honey or molasses and popped amaranth into a sweet they call *alegría* (happiness).

Domesticated in the Americas, pale-seeded amaranth dates from 4000 B.C. in Tehuacán, Puebla. Archaeologists have also located amaranth in 2,000-year-old tombs in northwestern Argentina. Before A.D. 1500 the core regions of amaranth cultivation were in Central Mexico, Peru, and northwestern Argentina. Additional pockets were in Ecuador, Guatemala, southern and northwestern Mexico, and the North American southwest. By 1519 amaranth was a major food crop subject to tribute in the Aztec Empire. Each year the AZTECS filled eighteen granaries with the ivory-white seeds (*huauhtli*). They utilized the plant as a toasted grain, for greens, and as a drink. They also popped it. Although an important part of the Aztec diet, amaranth was banned by the Spanish because of its ritual use. In the early sixteenth century, the Aztecs celebrated a feast in honor of their patron deity, HUITZILOPOCHTLI, whose statue made of amaranth dough they paraded through the streets of TENOCHTITLÁN. Returning to the temple, the priests broke the statue into pieces, consecrated it as the bones and flesh of Huitzilopochtli, and distributed the pieces in a "communion" ceremony. Other deities were also represented by amaranth dough, while the Tepanecs and TARASCANS used it to form images of birds and animals.

In spite of Spanish prohibitions, the Indians of Mexico and Guatemala continued to plant amaranth and to make statues with the dough. Over time it was even assimilated into Christian rituals, being used to make rosaries. Indian farmers in the Andean highlands of

Peru, Bolivia, and northwestern Argentina also cultivated amaranth, and the colonial Spanish recorded that red and white amaranth seeds (*bledos*) were a very common food of the Indians, of which they made candies. Due to its antiquity in the Andes, it is known by various names: *kiwicha, achis, achita, ckoito, coyo,* or *coimi* in Peru; and *coimi, cuime, millmi,* or *quinua millmi* in Bolivia. Daniel K. Early notes that amaranth is making a comeback in Peru and Mexico.

JONATHAN D. SAUER, "The Grain Amaranths: A Survey of Their History and Classification," in *Annals of the Missouri Botanical Garden* 37, no. 4 (1950): 561–632, and "Grain Amaranths," in *Evolution of Crop Plants,* edited by N. W. Simmonds (1976), pp. 4–7; JOHN N. COLE, *Amaranth from the Past for the Future* (1979); DANIEL K. EARLY, "The Renaissance of Amaranth," in *Chilies to Chocolate: Food the Americas Gave the World,* edited by Nelson Foster and Linda S. Cordell (1992), pp. 15–33.

MARY KARASCH

**AMAT Y JUNIENT, MANUEL DE** (*b.* 1704; *d.* 1782), viceroy of Peru (1761–1776). Born in Varacisas into a noble Catalan family, Amat pursued a military career in Europe and North Africa until becoming captain-general of Chile in 1755. In Santiago he promoted higher education and public order, but his efforts to subdue the Araucanian Indians were unsuccessful.

As viceroy of Peru, Amat oversaw with ruthless efficiency the expulsion of the Jesuits in 1767, and, superficially at least, undertook a major overhaul of defenses, fortifying ports and organizing militia companies throughout the provinces. Although public revenues expanded considerably in this period, Amat's viceregency was pervaded by corruption, according to his many critics, including Antonio de ULLOA (1716–1795), who served under him as governor of Huancavelica, in south-central Peru. Following his return to Barcelona in 1777, the aged bachelor married a young Catalán, leaving for both her and posterity the splendid Palacio de la Virreina, now a museum.

VICENTE RODRÍGUEZ CASADO and F. PÉREZ EMBID, eds., *Memoria de gobierno del virrey Amat* (1947); JOSÉ CRUCES POZO, "Cualidades militares del virrey Amat," in *Anuario de Estudios Americanos* 9 (1952): 327–345; LEON G. CAMPBELL, *The Military and Society in Colonial Peru, 1750–1810* (1978), esp. pp. 21–68.

JOHN R. FISHER

**AMAUTA,** a Quechua word designating an ancient adviser to the INCA nobility; a wise and noble man, interpreter of the firmament and religious issues, keeper of knowledge. In modern Peru, during the Indianist (*indigenista*) revival of the 1910s and 1920s, the word became a symbol for the group of radical intellectuals, politicians, and artists headed by socialist José Carlos MARIÁTEGUI, founder of the journal *Amauta.* This journal was published in thirty-two issues between September 1926 and September 1930. Contributions by the most important Peruvian progressive figures of the time, including

Víctor Raúl HAYA DE LA TORRE (until his political break with Mariátegui in 1928), José SABOGAL, Jorge BASADRE, and Martín Adán, as well as by foreign intellectuals, made *Amauta* a major source for analysis of Peruvian national problems with an international perspective.

JESÚS CHAVARRÍA, *José Carlos Mariátegui and the Rise of Modern Peru, 1890–1930* (1979).

ALFONSO W. QUIROZ

*See also* **Indigenismo.**

**AMAZON BASIN, ARCHAEOLOGY.** The archaeology of the Colombian Amazon Basin is concentrated in the Caquetá River in the region of Araracuara and La Pedrera and in the Amazon River in the region close to the city of Leticia, Colombia. The research done in these areas has focused on the identification of pottery traditions and on the study of the early human adaptations to the forest environment. The first studies defined the existence of an early pottery tradition related to the Barrancoid ceramics (2000 B.C.), whose occurrence may be the result of migrations from the central or lower Amazon. The pottery is characterized by simple forms with

Cover for an early issue of José Carlos Mariátegui's journal *Amauta,* 1927. HARVARD COLLEGE LIBRARY.

incised decoration. A second pottery tradition is characterized by an elaborate polychrome pottery whose origin is presumed to be at the mouth of the Amazon River (Marajoara complex) or in the northern Andes.

The studies geared toward the understanding of human adaptations to the tropical forest of the Amazon are focused on the existence of soils arising from intentional human enrichment (anthropic soils). However, the origin of these rich organic soils sometimes called *terra preta* is in debate. Most of the existing evidence indicates that *terra preta* soils are formed by natural processes related to fires, flooding, and other factors that affect the soil's chemical composition. The objective of the research conducted in this area is to understand if the Amazon Basin sustained large-scale societies in the past.

For a more descriptive review of the archaeology of the Amazon Basin see LEONOR HERRERA, ''Amazonía colombiana,'' in Alvaro Botiva Contreras, et al., *Colombia prehispánica* (1989). For a detailed study on the Araracuara region, see SANTIAGO MORA C. et al., *Cultivars, Anthropic Soils and Stability* (1991). A good review of the archaeological problem surrounding the debate on ancient productivity of *terra preta* soils and population density is presented in THOMAS P. MYERS, ''Agricultural Limitations of the Amazon in Theory and Practice,'' in *World Archaeology* 24, no. 1 (1992): 82–97.

AUGUSTO OYUELA-CAYCEDO

*See also* **South America: Pre-Colombian.**

**AMAZON PACT (1978).** The Treaty for Amazon Cooperation provides a framework for collaboration on economic development, conservation, and use of natural resources among the countries of Amazonia. Signed on 3 July 1978 by Bolivia, Brazil, Colombia, Ecuador, Guyana, Peru, Suriname, and Venezuela, the pact was designed to curtail foreign influence by giving member nations the exclusive responsibility for the development of the Amazon region. The member countries could not sustain the isolationist purpose of the pact, however, because their development projects required substantial external financing. In 1989, facing a virtual boycott on foreign lending until environmental standards for Amazonian projects were improved, the pact members created permanent committees on natural resources and the environment. These committees have taken the initiative in developing projects that meet the environmental demands of international financiers. The current collaboration among the member states under the Amazon Pact has laid the groundwork for more ambitious regional projects, including economic integration.

MARIA ELENA MEDINA, ''Treaty for Amazonian Cooperation: General Analysis,'' in *Land, People, and Planning in Contemporary Amazonia*, edited by F. Barbira-Scazzocchio (1980), pp. 58–71; MICHAEL J. EDEN, *Ecology and Land Management in Amazonia* (1990); JUAN DE ONÍS, *The Green Cathedral: Sustainable Development of Amazonia* (1992).

MICHAEL A. POLL

**AMAZON REGION,** the South American area formed by the Amazon River basin. It measures about 2.3 million square miles (6 million sq km), and covers parts of Brazil (more than half of its total area), Bolivia, Peru, Ecuador, Colombia, Venezuela, Guiana, Suriname, and French Guyana.

ENVIRONMENT
The region is the richest ecosystem in the world. It contains about 20 percent of the total available fresh water on earth and includes the Amazon, known as the River Sea, the world's largest river in terms of water volume and drain basin, and some one thousand tributaries. About 10 percent of the world's living species, many of them yet to be studied, can be found in the region. Its magnificent rain forests cover both the vast and unflooded uplands (*tierras firmes*, in Spanish; *terras firmes*, in Portuguese) and the inundated and swampy lands near its major rivers (in Spanish, *várzeas*; in Portuguese, *igapós*).

The Amazon offers an amazing diversity of natural products, many with economic value, including cacao, coca, guaraná, manioc, nuts, palm hearts, plants used as medicines or in the composition of medicines, rubber, spices, tropical fruits, oils, and different kinds of wood. The region is also rich in minerals. Its soil, however, is poor, with only 6–7 percent of it being appropriate for conventional agricultural production.

COLONIAL HISTORY
When the conquistadores arrived in the Amazon region, the area was inhabited by Indians. The many indigenous groups had distinct and sometimes sophisticated cultures, living along the rivers, trading with one another, and sustaining themselves by hunting, fishing, and gathering in the forest. Great civilizations had once flourished at Santarém and on Marajó Island.

The first white man reported to have entered the region was the Spaniard Vicente Yañez Pinzón. The TORDESILLAS TREATY, signed in Europe in 1494, granted control of the Amazon region to Spain, but the area was already the object of attention from Portugal, Holland, England, and France, all of which were eager to exploit its riches.

Indeed, the region fired the imagination of Europe, for many Europeans believed that El Dorado, a mythical kingdom full of precious metals, was hidden in the Amazon, and some actually organized expeditions to search for it. The name of the Amazon River and its surrounding region was also derived from a myth: in 1541 the Spanish explorer Francisco de ORELLANA, the first European to descend the river from the Andes to the Atlantic, reported that he had been attacked by women warriors, much like the Amazons of the Greek myth. Since his time the word ''Amazon'' has designated both the region and its major river.

The English, Dutch, and French penetrated the Amazon from the north, establishing a few trading posts that assured them sites for their future colonies of British, Dutch, and French Guiana. After the slave trade was introduced in this region, its rain forests frequently served as a refuge for fugitive black slaves.

The Spanish entered the Amazon from the Andes, the Portuguese from the Atlantic. Both counted on the work of Catholic MISSIONARIES. These missionaries, especially Jesuits, Capuchins, Franciscans, and Dominicans, gathered the Indians in places where they could be christianized and used to extract products of commercial value, such as spices and medicines, to be exported to Europe. Indian labor was also exploited by the *encomenderos,* who had authorization from the Spanish crown to do so.

Spain and Portugal, aiming to maintain control over an area coveted by other European nations, established outposts, sent out settlers and military personnel, and constructed forts around which towns grew up. In 1750, by the terms of the Treaty of Madrid, based on the *uti possidetis* principle (whoever had it, possessed it), Spain ceded to Portugal the eastern part of the Amazon region from the Atlantic to the junction of the Madeira River. In 1759 the marquis of POMBAL, minister of King José I of Portugal, expelled the Jesuits from the area and made an abortive attempt to develop commercial agriculture under state control, via the General Company of Pará and Marahão.

Since the beginning of the eighteenth century, when the sciences developed greatly in Europe, the Amazon region has been regularly visited by European scientific expeditions. In 1736 the expedition of the French mathematician Charles-Marie de la Condamine identified local species, such as RUBBER, quinine, and curare. He also measured depths, falls, and speeds of the Amazon River. Condamine's expedition was followed, among others, by expeditions led by Prussian Alexander von HUMBOLDT (1799–1804), the Austrians Spix and Martius (1817–1820), and the Swiss Louis Agassiz (1865).

Despite visits by missionaries, adventurers, *encomenderos,* armies, and scientists, and the efforts of a few settlers, the Amazon region remained basically an Indian territory until modern times. Most of it continued to be unknown, unexplored, and untouched by white people when Spain and Portugal withdrew from South America at the beginning of the nineteenth century.

NATIONAL HISTORY

Settlement of the Amazon region by non-natives progressed slowly until the last decades of the nineteenth century, when a rubber boom prompted substantial changes in the area. Rubber had been in great demand since 1839, when Charles Goodyear discovered how to stabilize and vulcanize it, thereby making it commercially useful. The richest *Hevea* trees on earth were in the Amazon region, especially in the area where Brazilian and Bolivian territory meet. Large numbers of migrants moved to the region to work as rubber tappers. They extracted the liquid from the rubber trees, transformed it into huge balls of rubber, and sold them to local trading posts. At these posts they bought, at exorbitant

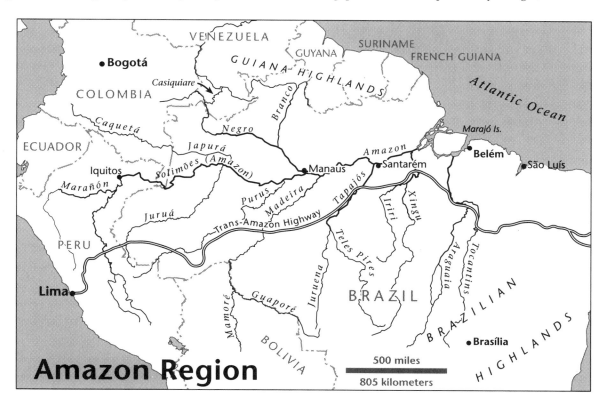

Amazon Region

prices, the products they needed to live. The rubber was then transported to the trading houses at the Brazilian ports of Belém and Manaus, where it was exported.

Rubber was responsible for creating the local millionaires, the "rubber barons," during a time of frenetic activity and luxury. The magnificent Manaus Opera House remains a symbol of those days. But the lust for rubber also caused a serious border dispute between Bolivia and Brazil. Moreover, it attracted foreign capital to the area, especially to trade houses and to charter companies, such as the Bolivian Syndicate. Foreign capital was also applied to the construction of railroads, such as the Madeira–Mamoré Railway (finished in 1912), linking Brazil and Bolivia.

From the beginning of the twentieth century, however, Amazon rubber faced—and lost out to—competition from the Malayan plantations. By the 1910s the Amazon rubber boom was finished, leaving few lasting benefits for the region. From then on, the activity was carried on only by the descendants of the earlier migrants, poor rubber-tappers reduced to debt peonage. The only exception was the attempt made by the automobile magnate Henry Ford, who planted rubber trees between 1927 and 1945 across 2.5 million acres he owned in Pará, Brazil. Ford's failure, due to lack of knowledge about local conditions and to diseases among the plants, helped to carry on the legend that the Amazon destroys those who attempt its conquest. Indeed, in 1967 Daniel Keith LUDWIG started the Jari Project, a huge agro-industrial complex in Pará. In 1981, after facing several problems, Ludwig gave up and sold the enterprise to a Brazilian conglomerate.

CONTEMPORARY HISTORY

In the second half of the twentieth century the Amazon region has known the most dramatic transformation of its entire history. Its population has increased at unprecedented levels, due to massive migration. The original Indian population, however, has dropped dramatically, due to diseases, conflicts with the settlers and ranchers, and disorganization of their way of life. From an original 2 to 5 million in 1500, the Amazon Indian population is now estimated to have shrunk to 150,000 to 200,000 people.

Recent migrations to the Amazon have been the result of socioeconomic changes in other regions, such as the increase of land and income concentration and urban poverty. Migrations have also been stimulated by the Brazilian federal government, which launched programs to attract homesteaders and formulated policies of tax exemptions and subsidies to attract companies and businesses. Brazil has been the only country in the region to carry on an explicit state policy aimed at integrating the Amazon into the national economy.

The Amazon has been crossed by an extensive network of roads and highways, such as the pioneer Marginal Forest Highway (1948), linking Santa Cruz, Bolivia, to Caracas, Venezuela, and the four highways that unite different parts of the Amazon with Brazil's capital, Brasília. These highways serve as economic axes: a great number of cities, towns, and hamlets have sprung up beside them, transforming the once-rural Amazon population into an increasingly, and in the case of Brazil, predominantly, urban population.

An assemblage of economic activities has marked the current occupation of the region. Agroforestry has shown itself to be productive and not environmentally damaging. Agriculture, carried on mainly by homesteaders, has remained a source of frustration, due to the inadequacy of soil and to ignorance about local conditions. The traditional Indian crop of coca, since associated with the international traffic of drugs, has penetrated into the forests of Colombia, Bolivia, and Peru. It has produced local fortunes, but has also increased social tensions. Cattle ranching, developed mainly on large estates, increased dramatically during the 1970s in the Brazilian Amazon, as a response to federal incentives. This activity, together with wood cutting, has been responsible for high rates of deforestation. State and private exploration of the rich Amazon mineral reserves, especially gold, manganese, cassiterite, iron, and copper, has been intense since the 1960s.

The recent large-scale occupation of the Amazon, due to its environmental consequences, has made exploitation of the region an international issue. It has brought together a large number of actors whose interests do not always match, including entrepreneurs, environmental groups, government and nongovernment organizations, *fazendeiros*, homesteaders, Indians, land speculators, missionaries, national and transnational corporations, peasants, politicians, professionals, traders, and wage laborers. The main challenge for the future of the Amazon seems to be creating a balance between economic progress, social justice, and ecological preservation.

JOHN H. HEMMING, *Amazon Frontier: The Defeat of the Brazilian Indians* (1935; rpt. 1987); BERTHA BECKER, *Geopolítica da Amazônia* (1982); MARIANNE SCHMINK and CHARLES H. WOOD, *Frontier Expansion in Amazonia* (1984); SUE BRANFORD and ORIEL GLOCK, *The Last Frontier—Fighting over Land in the Amazon* (1985); STEPHEN G. BUNKER, *Underdeveloping the Amazon: Extraction, Unequal Exchange, and the Failure of the Modern State* (1985); GHILLEAN T. PRANCE and THOMAS E. LOVEJOY, eds., *Amazonia* (1985); CARLOS MORA and CARLOS E. ARAMBURU, *Desarollo Amazônico: Una perspectiva latinoamericana* (1986); LUIS E. ARAGÓN and LUC J. A. MOUGEOT, *Migrações internas na Amazônia* (1986); WARREN DEAN, *Brazil and the Struggle for Rubber* (1987); JOSÉ DE SOUZA MARTINS, *Caminhada no chão da noite* (1989), pp. 67–96; SUSANNA HECHT and ALEXANDER COCKBURN, *The Fate of the Forest* (1990); ANTHONY SMITH, *Explorers of the Amazon* (1990).

JANAÍNA AMADO

*See also* **Environmental Movements; Explorers and Exploration; Forests;** and individual cities and states.

The Amazon River. © NADEAU / PHOTO RESEARCHERS, INC.

**AMAZON RIVER,** the world's largest river. The Amazon is 3,900 miles long (exceeded only by the Nile), discharges an average 7 million cubic feet per second, and drains more than 2.5 million square miles. It arises in Peru, drops down the eastern slopes of the Andes, and then flows east through Brazil to the Atlantic Ocean. Its depth varies from 66 to 660 feet within Brazil, and its width ranges up to 7 miles (near where it is joined by the XINGU RIVER). Throughout much of its lowlands plain, the Amazon is actually a labyrinth of waters, fed and interconnected by some 11,000 large and small tributaries. A northwestern tributary, the Rio NEGRO, is joined to the ORINOCO basin by the swampy CASIQUIARÉ CANAL.

The lowlands basin is bounded to the north by the GUIANA HIGHLANDS and to the south by the BRAZILIAN HIGHLANDS. Thus the river and its tributaries are forced into a narrow course for their last several hundred miles before reaching the sea. This creates a daily tidal bore (the *pororoca*) up to 16 feet high, which makes navigation hazardous.

Due to the enormous size of the Amazon, the first Europeans in the region called it the River Sea. Today, Brazilians call it the Amazonas only to its junction with the Rio Negro; above there it is known as the Solimões. Spanish Americans refer to the section west of Iquitos as the MARAÑÓN. The lowlands constitute the world's largest rain forest, renowned for its incredibly rich biological diversity.

Because the drainage lies in the Northern and Southern hemispheres, the Amazon experiences two rainy seasons, in February and July. The floodwaters rise as much as 50 feet over dry-season levels. The main course of the river, fed by Andean tributaries, carries vast quantities of silt and organic matter. For this reason, the natives called it white water. The Negro, however, drains lowlands, is relatively free of silt, and picks up a dark, acidic character from mangrove roots along its course. Its waters were called black by the Indians. When they meet near MANAUS, the white and black waters swirl and intermingle for nearly 30 miles before blending.

In 1500 and 1501, explorers Vicente Yáñez PINZÓN and Amerigo VESPUCCI sailed across the Amazon's mouth, which straddles both the equator and the Tordesillas Line. At that time an estimated 2.4 million natives lived in the basin.

The Spanish government claimed the river, based on the TREATY OF TORDESILLAS. This claim was reinforced by the first exploration, carried out by a Spaniard. In 1541–1542, Francisco de ORELLANA took command of an expedition organized by Gonzalo PIZARRO and sailed down the Amazon, claiming it for Spain. Because the South Atlantic lay within Portugal's sphere, however, the Portuguese gradually gained jurisdiction. Spain annexed Portugal in 1580, so the matter seemed moot.

In 1637–1639 the Portuguese captain Pedro Teixeira, with secret orders to secure the area for his government, led an expedition up the Amazon. When Portugal declared its independence from Spain in 1640, the Amazon remained under its control.

In 1750 Spain and Portugal signed the TREATY OF MADRID, which recognized Portugal's effective occupation of the southern Amazon basin. It designated the PARAGUAY, Guaporé, Mamoré, and MADEIRA rivers as an international boundary. Over the next century and a half, Portugal (and later Brazil) managed to annex more territory in the northern and western Amazon basin.

HILGARD O'REILLY STERNBERG, *The Amazon River of Brazil* (1975); JOHN HEMMING, *Red Gold* (1978) and *Amazon Frontier* (1987); GORDON MAC CREAGH, *White Waters and Black* (1985);

ROGER D. STONE, *Dreams of Amazonia* (1985); ANTHONY SMITH, *Explorers of the Amazon* (1990).

MICHAEL L. CONNIFF

*See also* **Brazil: Geography.**

**AMAZONAS,** Brazil's largest state. Occupying some 602,000 square miles in the heart of the vast tropical AMAZON REGION, Amazonas is entirely lowlands, much of it flooded for months at a time and most of it covered with tropical rain forest. The main physical features are the NEGRO and Solimões rivers, which flow together to create the AMAZON RIVER.

When the region was first explored by Europeans in the 1540s, it was densely populated by native peoples. Gradually the native population declined, due mostly to diseases new to the area. By the 1630s, when Portuguese military expeditions established a permanent presence there, the natives were already disappearing. In 1669 the Portuguese built a small fort near the confluence of the Negro and Solimões/Amazon rivers, focus of a settlement called São José do Rio Negro, that gradually grew into the modern city of MANAUS. By the 1730s, the Portuguese had mostly dislodged the Spanish from the central Amazon. These territorial gains were legalized in the TREATY OF MADRID of 1750 (confirmed in the 1777 TREATY OF SAN ILDEFONSO).

For most of the colonial era, the Portuguese administered the central Amazon from Belém and São Luís, Maranhão. In 1755, however, the region was designated the captaincy of São José do Rio Negro in order to promote economic exploitation. In the ensuing years, merchants and adventurers in São José mounted great Indian slaving expeditions. The town also became the gathering point for animals and plant materials destined for export.

Amazonas became a separate province in 1850 (and a state after 1891). São José was designated a city and gained its modern name shortly afterward. From then on, Manaus was the center of a boom in natural RUBBER exports, stimulated by Charles Goodyear's development in 1839 of the vulcanization process for hardening rubber. The boom peaked in the early years of the twentieth century, when incredible profits accumulated in the hands of local merchants. Before the bubble burst, city fathers erected a sumptuous opera house to show off their wealth. Today Manaus has more than a million inhabitants, a busy deep-water port, a free-trade zone, and a great variety of exports.

ARTUR REIS, *Estado do Amazonas* (1978); LEO A. DESPRES, *Manaus* (1991).

MICHAEL L. CONNIFF

**AMBROGI, ARTURO** (*b.* 19 October 1875; *d.* 8 November 1936), Salvadoran writer. Born in San Salvador, the son of an Italian-born Salvadoran army general, Ambrogi edited several literary reviews in San Salvador in the 1890s before traveling widely in South America, where he was much influenced by intellectuals in Chile and Uruguay, particularly by Rubén DARÍO in Buenos Aires. He became one of the leading Salvadoran modernist and impressionist writers of the early twentieth century, especially with his lyrical *Manchas, máscaras y sensaciones* (1901) and *Sensaciones crepusculares* (1904), *El libro del trópico* (1907), *El tiempo que pasa* (1913), and *Sensaciones del Japón y de la China* (1915). His frequent travels throughout the world are strongly reflected in his work, which also contains much folklore.

ARTURO AMBROGI, *Marginales de la vida* (1912); JOSÉ GÓMEZ CAMPOS, *Semblanzas salvadoreñas* (1930); LUIS GALLEGOS VALDÉS, *Panorama de la literatura salvadoreña del período precolombino a 1980* (1987), esp. pp. 115–130.

RALPH LEE WOODWARD, JR.

**AMEGHINO, FLORENTINO** (*b.* 18 September 1854; *d.* 6 August 1911), Argentine geologist and paleontologist. The son of Italian immigrants, Ameghino was born at Luján in Buenos Aires Province. As a boy he was an avid collector of bones and fossils, and he continued this avocation while working as a schoolteacher and storekeeper. He never received formal scientific training, but his reputation as a man of learning spread, especially after he traveled to Paris in 1878 with part of his collection. He ultimately published almost two hundred articles and monographs, corresponded with foreign specialists, and served as museum director in La Plata and Buenos Aires. Ameghino won greatest notoriety for his hypothesis that humankind originated in and spread from South America. This was not generally accepted, yet he is recognized as a tireless investigator and a pioneer of Argentine SCIENCE.

JOSÉ BALBINI, *Historia de la ciencia argentina* (1949), pp. 92–98; JOSÉ GABRIEL, *El loco de los huesos* (1940).

DAVID BUSHNELL

**AMÉLIA, EMPRESS** (Amélia Augusta de Leuchtenberg; *b.* July 1812; *d.* January 1873), empress consort of Brazil (1829–1831). Milan-born daughter of Eugène de Beauharnais, Napoleon's stepson, and the Bavarian duchess of Leuchtenberg, Amélia became the second wife of Emperor PEDRO I of Brazil in 1829. A young woman of rare beauty and sensitivity, Amélia appeared in Rio de Janeiro at a critical time for the Brazilian monarchy—a time of recrimination over the loss of Uruguay, governmental deadlock, financial crisis, nativist ferment, and growing public dissatisfaction with the emperor.

Amélia's arrival in Rio was predicated on the banishment of Pedro's mistress, the marchioness of Santos, which cleared the way for the emperor's reconciliation with José Bonifácio de ANDRADA E SILVA, a bitter foe of the marchioness. Empress Amélia joined Andrade in advising Pedro to appoint a new cabinet headed by the marquis of Barbacena, who had been her escort from Bavaria to Brazil. The Barbacena ministry smoothed the emperor's relations with parliament and probably prolonged his reign. Pedro's dismissal of Barbacena a year later set off the chain of events that led to the abdication and exile of Pedro and Amélia in April 1831.

From Brazil they went to Paris, where Amélia bore the former emperor a daughter, Maria Amélia, and served as guardian of his eldest daughter, Maria da Glória, when Pedro left for Portugal to secure the Portuguese throne for Maria da Glória. Amélia rejoined Pedro in Lisbon in September 1833, a year before his death. She devoted most of the rest of her life to charity work in Portugal.

MARIA JUNQUEIRA SCHMIDT, *A segunda imperatriz do Brasil* (1927); LIGIA LEMOS TÔRRES, *Imperatríz dona Amélia* (1947).

NEILL MACAULAY

**AMENÁBAR, JUAN** (*b.* 22 June 1922), Chilean composer. Born in Santiago, Amenábar was introduced to music by his father, a cellist and member of the Bach Society. At age thirteen he entered the Catholic Conservatory, where he studied harmony with Lucila Césped and choral techniques with Luis Vilches. In 1940 he enrolled at the University of Chile to study civil engineering. He attended the composition classes of Jorge Urrutia Blondel from 1948 to 1952 at the National Conservatory of Santiago. Amenábar joined the National Society of Composers (1953) and while chief of the music programs at Radio Chilena (1953–1956) he promoted contemporary Chilean composers and started to experiment with electronic music. From 1954 to 1957 he organized the concerts of the music department at the Catholic University in Santiago, where he founded the experimental sound workshop. His *Los peces* (1957), a study on the Fibonacci series, was the first tape composition made in Latin America. In 1958 he took electronic music courses given by Werner Meyer-Eppler at the University of Bonn. Upon his return to Chile, he worked with José Vicente ASUAR in the creation of an electronic music studio at the University of Chile.

Amenábar has taught composition and has served as president of the National Association of Composers. In addition to electronic music, he has written religious choral music, incidental music for theater and films, chamber music, and piano and organ pieces. He has also written and published musicological essays about new musical techniques, music for movies, folk music, etc.

JOHN VINTON, ed., *Dictionary of Contemporary Music* (1974); *New Grove Dictionary of Music and Musicians*, vol. 1 (1980); GÉRARD BÉHAGUE, *Music in Latin America* (1979); *Composers of the Americas*, vol. 17 (1971), p. 15.

SUSANA SALGADO

**AMERICA,** the term used since 1507 to describe the lands of the Western Hemisphere, derived from the Florentine navigator and explorer Amerigo VESPUCCI. Vespucci sailed to the New World with the Alonso de Ojeda expedition in 1499 and his many descriptive letters of the New World to Pier Francesco de'Medici and Piero Soderini were translated and circulated throughout Europe. The letters came to the attention of a circle of scholars working on an update of Ptolemy's *Geography* in the monastery of Saint-Dié in the Vosges Mountains of what is today Alsace-Lorraine. Vespucci's news of the discovery of a new continent inspired them to christen the new lands "America," which they did in a 1507 edition entitled *Cosmographiae introductio.* In that volume, cartographer Martin Waldseemüller prepared a map that for the first time identified the New World as "America." His map was copied by others, and the name quickly took root throughout Europe.

JOHN BOYD THACHER, *The Continent of America, Its Discovery and Its Baptism: An Essay on the Nomenclature of the Old Continents* (1971); GERMÁN ARCINIEGAS, *Amerigo and the New World: The Life and Times of Amerigo Vespucci,* translated by Harriet de Onís (1978).

J. DAVID DRESSING

**AMERICAN ATLANTIC AND PACIFIC SHIP CANAL COMPANY,** a North American firm owned by Cornelius Vanderbilt and associates that successfully negotiated an exclusive canal concession with Nicaragua on 27 August 1849. Assisted by Ephraim George SQUIER, representative for the United States government, the company agreed to build, at its own expense, a canal across the Nicaraguan isthmus open to vessels of all nations and to provide support services of rail and carriage lines. Debate over canal privileges and Nicaraguan rights of sovereignty and property heightened tensions between British and North American interests in the region, and resulted in the passage of the CLAYTON–BULWER Treaty in 1850. Plans for eventual construction were thwarted by both inadequate financing and geographical barriers.

GERSTLE MACK, *The Land Divided, History of the Panama Canal and Other Isthmian Canal Projects* (1944), esp. 184–185, 188–190; DAVID I. FOLKMAN, JR., *The Nicaragua Route* (1972), esp. 18, 33, 35–37.

D. M. SPEARS

**AMERICAN REVOLUTION, INFLUENCE OF.** The American Revolution influenced Latin America because it was the first modern movement of anticolonialism. Drawing its ideology from the Enlightenment, it manifested a deep faith in the ability of people to advance their rights.

As the SEVEN YEARS' WAR ended (1763), the balance of power shifted in England's favor at the expense of the French and Spanish Bourbons, thus setting the scene for the period (1775–1825) that Herbert Eugene Bolton has called "the greater American Revolution," during which most European powers lost their colonies. Americans shared a keen resentment of Europeans for their obsession with the balancing of power, which often coincided with the loss of American lives and money. President George Washington underscored this dislike for European entanglements in his Farewell Address.

From the mid-1760s, England expected its colonists to participate in and help pay for the defense buildup. When the colonists resisted, the North American struggle for independence began; Spanish Americans likewise complained of increased levies and resorted to insurrection. In 1781, José de ABALOS, a Spanish official in Venezuela, noted the "vehement desire for independence" among South Americans influenced by the success of the North Americans. A. R. J. Turgot warned the Bourbons in 1776 that the American Revolution stood for anticolonialism in the New World—a fact that Spain could no longer ignore.

Turgot's message registered in Spain, where CHARLES III (1759–1788) introduced governmental reforms to produce greater defense revenues. "Free" trade conducted through Spain (1778) and the adoption of the INTENDANCY SYSTEM also were meant to stop British threats. The opening of new ports and the formation of merchant guilds overseas attracted American capital for regional economic development. The Bourbons also sponsored measures favoring laissez-faire, among which were the publication of the *Informe de la ley agraria* (Agrarian Report) of 1795 and the 1807 recommendation to study political economy in the universities, using Adam Smith's *Wealth of Nations* as a text. Documenting conclusions from varied sources, the Agrarian Report cited figures from the United States—a convincing example of what a free economy could contribute to national prosperity. It also underscored economic "federalism" by stressing the advantage of regional production rather than Bourbon centralization. Although the Portuguese-Brazilian context differed, the Marquês de POMBAL's reforms had the same effect: regional economies under the Brazilian elites expected to align themselves with Europeans, as long as the relationship was one of equality.

To provide this equality, the Iberians promoted "federative" monarchies in accord with the regional economic structures. This type of commonwealth relationship, however, failed in practice through lack of trust between Europeans and Americans. Through this monarchical reform, however, Latin Americans were exposed to two models: the republican United States and the Iberian constitutional projects. They preferred the hemispheric model because of its remarkable success by 1808.

The Spanish world was fascinated with events in North America from the outset, and the contacts were many. Spain was well aware of the possibility of furthering anticolonialism among its subjects. Thus, the choice was made not to resort to censorship; instead,

Spanish subjects were permitted to read freely about the American Revolution in books and periodicals. Spanish Americans thus were able to study the debates that were held in Philadelphia, the minutes of sessions in England (Parliament) and America, and the list of grievances. In short, Latin Americans were fully exposed to the American Revolution and the subsequent establishment of the prosperous United States republic.

Francisco de MIRANDA, having served as a Spanish officer in the American Revolution, subsequently witnessed the young nation's transition from war to peace (1783–1784). He recorded his impressions in a diary and gained the close friendship of the nation's key leaders. From 1785 until his return to his native Venezuela in 1810, Miranda tried to secure England's help for his projects to emancipate Venezuela. His greatest contribution was the propaganda sent from London—bundles of documents and letters that specified revolutionary procedures as well as the type of government that should be emulated: that of the United States of America.

The most influential writer for Miranda on behalf of Britain's assistance with Latin America's emancipation, and especially as an advocate of the American model, was "William Burke," who reflected the ideas of two great English reformers: James Mill and Jeremy Bentham, Miranda's close friends. From 1810 to 1812 James Mill was the principal organizer of Burke's editorials in Venezuela. These writings offered an excellent analysis of the American Revolution and the successful growth of the United States from 1787 to 1810. Among other things, they provided a review of Alexander Hamilton's financial program; the first full version of "Western Hemisphere idea," the promotion of inter-Americanism; and an account of the development of a Spanish American political unit (March 1811) that would join with the United States in guiding the destiny of the Americas.

WILLIAM SPENCE ROBERTSON, *The Life of Miranda,* 2 vols. (1929); CHARLES CARROLL GRIFFIN, *The United States and the Disruption of the Spanish Empire, 1810–1822* (1937); HARRY BERNSTEIN, *Origins of Inter-American Interest, 1700–1812* (1945); JOSÉ DE ONÍS, *The United States as Seen by Spanish American Writers, 1775–1890* (1952); ARTHUR PRESTON WHITAKER, *The Western Hemisphere Idea: Its Rise and Decline* (1954); MARIO RODRÍGUEZ, "The Impact of the American Revolution on the Spanish- and Portuguese-Speaking World," in *The Impact of the American Revolution Abroad,* edited by Richard B. Morris (1976), pp. 100–125; *La revolución americana de 1776 y el mundo hispánico: Ensayos y documentos* (1976); "The First Venezuelan Republic and the North American Model," in *Revista interamericana de bibliografía* 37, no. 1 (1987): 3–17; and "William Burke" and Francisco de Miranda: The World and the Deed in Spanish America's Emancipation (1994). For Portuguese America, see KENNETH R. MAXWELL, *Conflicts and Conspiracies: Brazil and Portugal, 1750–1780* (1973) and "The Generation of the 1790s and the Idea of Luso-Brazilian Empire," in *Colonial Roots of Modern Brazil,* edited by Dauril Alden (1973), pp. 107–144. See also E. BRADFORD BURNS, "The Intellectuals as Agents of Change and the Independence of Brazil," pp. 211–246; EMILIA VIOTTI DA COSTA, "The Politics of

Emancipation of Brazil'', pp. 43–48; and A. J. R. RUSSELL-WOOD, ''Preconditions and Precipitants of the Independence Movement in Portuguese America,'' pp. 3–40; all in *From Colony to Nation,* edited by A. J. R. Russell-Wood (1975).

MARIO RODRÍGUEZ

**AMERICANOS.** *See* **Confederates in Brazil and Mexico.**

**AMERICO DE FIGUEREIDO E MELO, PEDRO** (*b.* 29 April 1843; *d.* 7 October 1905), Brazilian painter. Americo's artistic career began at a young age. At the age of nine he was chosen to accompany the naturalist Louis-Jacques Brunet on a scientific mission through Northeastern Brazil. Soon after his return from the expedition, he moved to Rio, and in 1855 enrolled in the Imperial Academy of Fine Arts. By 1858 his artistic capabilities had captured the attention of the emperor PEDRO II, who personally awarded him a European travel stipend. In Europe, Americo studied painting with such masters as Ingres and Horace Vernet. But his interests and talents extended beyond the fine ARTS. He wrote a criticism of Ernest Renan's *Life of Jesus,* for which he received a commendation from Pope Pius IX, and obtained a doctorate from the University of Brussels in natural science and applied physics. When he returned to Brazil in 1864, he wrote a novel entitled *Holocausto.* The same year he won the competition for professor of figure drawing at the academy.

Although Americo lived a good part of his adult life in Europe, he nevertheless left an important artistic legacy in Brazil. Alongside Vítor MEIRELES, Americo was instrumental in producing visual images, which official institutions of the Second Empire sponsored and prized. His artistic repertory includes religious and allegorical compositions as well as court portraits and historical paintings. His most important historical paintings include two military paintings depicting battles from the WAR OF THE TRIPLE ALLIANCE, the 1872 *Batalha de Campo Grande* and the 1879 *Batalha do Avaí,* and his 1888 homage to Brazilian independence, *Grito do Ipiranga.*

*Arte no Brasil,* vol. 1 (1979), pp. 543–550; DONATO MELLO JÚNIOR, *Pedro Americo de Figueiredo e Melo, 1843–1905* (1983); CAREN MEGHREBLIAN, ''Art, Politics, and Historical Perception in Imperial Brazil, 1854–1884'' (Ph.D. diss., UCLA, 1990).

CAREN A. MEGHREBLIAN

**AMÉZAGA, JUAN JOSÉ DE** (*b.* 28 January 1881; *d.* 21 August 1956), president of Uruguay (1943–1947). Amézaga was born in Montevideo. After receiving his law degree in 1905, he was a professor of philosophy, director of the Labor Office, twice a representative for the department of Durazno, minister of industry, ambassador to Argentina (1916), adviser on secondary education, president of the State Insurance Bank (1918), and attorney for the Central Railroad of Uruguay. Amézaga was elected president as Uruguay emerged from a decade of institutional changes initiated in 1933 by President Gabriel TERRA's coup d'état and culminating with the coup of his successor, General Alfredo BALDOMIR, in 1942. Greatly influenced by international trends, Baldomir guaranteed free elections and a restoration of democracy. From that new electoral process, the Colorado Party and Amézaga emerged triumphant by promoting BATLLISMO, the ideology based on the political, economic, and social ideas of the former president, José BATLLE Y ORDÓÑEZ. With its exports of meat and wool, Uruguay prospered economically during World War II. And Amézaga's election guaranteed that Uruguay would be aligned with the Allied cause during the war.

Amézaga was the author of numerous legal texts, including *Enseñanza del derecho civil* (1908) and *Un capítulo de historia internacional* (1942).

ARTURO SCARONE, *Uruguayos contemporáneos* (1937); BENJAMIN NAHUM et al., *Crisis política y recuperación económica, 1930–1950* (1984); JUAN CARLOS PEDEMONTE, *Los presidentes del Uruguay* (1984).

JOSÉ DE TORRES WILSON

*See also* **Uruguay: Political Parties.**

**AMORIM, ENRIQUE** (*b.* 25 July 1900; *d.* 1960), Uruguayan writer and educator. Born in Salto and educated in Buenos Aires, Amorim was named minister of education and foreign affairs of Uruguay in 1918. His early and most highly regarded novel, *La carreta* (1931), reveals the writer's attraction to the Criollista movement as well as the intimate knowledge, gained as a child, of the customs, problems, and people of the countryside. His participation in militant activities of the Communist Party influenced Amorim's socially oriented writing during the 1930s and 1940s. Later novels, such as *Corral abierto* (1956), *Los montaraces* (1957), and *La desembocadura* (1958), continued to display the essential characteristics of his fiction: a dialogue between humans and the land, a strong ethical flavor, rural characters or themes, and a novelistic structure resembling multiple short stories. He focused above all on the new consciousness of the rural people, as seen in *El caballo y su sombra* (1941) (translated into English as *The Horse and His Shadow,* 1943) and in *La victoria no viene sola* (1952). Amorim also excelled as a poet, literary critic, movie scriptwriter, and film critic.

K. E. A. MOSE, *Enrique Amorím, the Passion of a Uruguayan* (1972); V. DE LÓPEZ BRENDA, *Enrique Amorím: Panorama lexicográfico de ''La carreta''* (1984); LEONARDO GARET, *La pasión creadora de Enrique Amorím* (1990).

WILLIAM H. KATRA

**AMPARO, WRIT OF,** constitutional action that originated in Mexico and since has been adopted by several other Latin American nations. As authorized by Articles 103 and 107 of the Mexican Constitution of 1917, presently in force, the *amparo* (literally, "protection") permits any private individual or group to seek federal judicial relief from a broad range of official abuses of rights guaranteed by Articles 1–29 of the Constitution, Mexico's Bill of Rights.

The writ was first established under the leadership of Manuel Crescencio REJÓN by the Yucatán Constitution of 1841, by federal statute in the Reforms Act of 1847 (spearheaded by Mariano Otero), and constitutionally by the liberal Federal Constitution of 1857. The *amparo* bears the influence of U.S. legal practice, especially judicial review, the Bill of Rights, and the Anglo-American writ of habeas corpus, as revealed to Latin America at large through translations of De Tocqueville's *Democracy in America* (1855). It also derives from Spanish sources, including ancient *fueros* (special privileges) and the procedures of the royal courts of Castile and Aragon and various special tribunals of colonial Spanish America, and from the French judicial appeal of *cassation*, the Constitutional Senate of 1799, and the Declaration of the Rights of Man. The *amparo* is thus of hybrid origin.

In Mexico, the writ has become the sole judicial instrument for correcting constitutional violations by legislators, executive officials, and judges, both federal and local. According to the eminent jurist-scholar Héctor Fix Zamudio, the remedy now has at least five major constitutional control functions and procedural forms. It is used as an emergency procedure to protect fundamental human rights such as life, liberty, and physical safety (usually while the petitioner is under confinement by local police or courts) and is brought first to the federal district courts as with the Anglo-American habeas corpus, federal removal, prohibition, and injunction procedures. It is also employed as an appeal to "finalize"— that is, review and reverse—mistaken interpretations of federal or state codes by lower courts or any administrative tribunal. Known as the judicial, cassation, or "direct" *amparo*, it is comparable to the U.S. writ of *certiorari* or, more so, the French *cassation*. Constituting some 80 percent of all Mexican *amparo* cases, it is brought directly to one of the four chambers of the federal Supreme Court (criminal, administrative, civil, or labor) or, if a case of lesser importance, to one of the Collegiate Circuit Courts. In addition, Mexicans use the *amparo* as a remedy against abuses by executive agencies and bureaucrats. This administrative, or "indirect," *amparo* is first brought to federal district courts; as such it is comparable to the Anglo-American petitions for injunction, declaratory judgment, and mandamus. Appeals may then be taken directly to the Supreme Court when the issue is of "transcending national importance" (giving the High Court *certiorari*-like discretion to hear the case). *Amparo* has been used as a method to challenge unconstitutional (per Article 27) official confiscations of the land and water rights of small individual, communal village, and *ejido* farmers. In these "agrarian" *amparos*, formal procedural requirements may be waived for petitioners. Finally, as the only vehicle that can challenge the validity of a legislative statute, the "constitutionality" *amparo* (*amparo contra leyes*) approaches United States–style judicial review. But this last use of the procedure is limited in effect, rarely successful, and procedurally cumbersome; for example, only the full 21-member Supreme Court can issue a negative declaration, which applies only to the parties-litigant (*inter partes*), not broadly, or *erga omnes*. As with all *amparo* decisions, however, five consecutive judgments of the court do bind all state and federal courts and administrative tribunals as precedent (*jurisprudencia*).

The *amparo* is used across the socioeconomic spectrum in Mexico, as evidenced by the crushing amount of caseloads in the federal courts with *amparo* jurisdiction. It now serves, with certain limits on its application to major government policies, as the principal guardian of the national legal order, from edicts of the president to the smallest *municipio*. In various forms, the writ has been adopted constitutionally by Argentina, Bolivia, Chile, Costa Rica, Ecuador, El Salvador, Guatemala, Honduras, Nicaragua, Paraguay, and Venezuela.

RICHARD D. BAKER, *Judicial Review in Mexico: A study of the Amparo Suit* (1971), is the only book on the *amparo* in English, but is dated in several important respects. A seminal counterpart in Spanish is IGNACIO BURGOA, *El juicio de amparo*, 24th ed. (1988). Comprehensive articles in English include: HÉCTOR FIX ZAMUDIO, "A Brief Introduction to the Mexican Writ of Amparo," in *California Western International Law Journal* 9, no. 2 (1979), and "The Writ of *Amparo* in Latin America," in *Lawyer of the Americas* 13, no. 3 (1981); CARL E. SCHWARZ, "Judges Under the Shadow: Judicial Independence in the United States and Mexico," in *California Western International Law Journal* 3, no. 2 (1973), and "Rights and Remedies in the Federal Trial Courts of Mexico and the United States," in *Hastings Constitutional Law Quarterly* 4 (1977).

CARL E. SCHWARZ

*See also* **Judicial Systems.**

**AMPÍES, JUAN DE** (*d.* 8 February 1533), Spanish conquistador. Ampíes played an important role in the process whereby Spain established itself in the New World. In 1511 he became the first royal factor on the island of HISPANIOLA. An advocate of a peaceful Conquest, he defended the Indians on the Los Gigantes Islands (today Curaçao, Aruba, and Bonaire) and was partly responsible for their being declared *indios guaitiaos* (friendly Indians). When the Indians who inhabited CUMANÁ (the coastal region of northeastern Venezuela) put to death the missionaries who had come to evangelize the area, Ampíes opposed the use of retaliatory measures against them. When the first peaceful colonizing activities were undertaken with Indians considered to be friendly—activities that were consistent with the doctrines promoted by Fray Bartolomé de LAS CASAS— Ampíes was assigned in 1520 to populate Los Gigantes with a group of Caquetío Indians. He later established contact with the inhabitants of the South American mainland and was able to gain their confidence.

In 1526 Ampíes bought some captured Indians on Hispaniola and then freed them and made use of a commercial expedition to return them to their homelands. This gesture led to the organization of an expedition under the leadership of his son, whose object was to create a permanent settlement on the mainland. The result was the founding of Coro on 26 July 1527. Because of an agreement with the House of WELSER banking firm, however, Ampíes had to abandon the settlement of Coro in 1528 and limit his authority and jurisdiction to the island territories.

See the translation by Jeannette Johnson Varner of the classic eighteenth-century work by JOSÉ OVIEDO Y BAÑOS, first historian of the province of Venezuela, titled *The Conquest and Settlement of Venezuela* (1987). More specific is DEMETRIO RAMOS PÉREZ, *La fundación de Venezuela: Ampíes y Coro, una singularidad histórica* (1978).

INÉS QUINTERO

*See also* **Conquistadores.**

**AMPUDIA Y GRIMAREST, PEDRO DE** (*b.* 1805; *d.* 1868), Mexican military officer and minister of war (1859–1860). Born in Havana, Cuba, Ampudia arrived in Mexico in 1821 as a lieutenant in the retinue of the last viceroy of New Spain, Juan O'DONOJÚ. He joined the Army of the Three Guarantees and supported the PLAN OF IGUALA for Mexican autonomy and independence. Ampudia fought against the Spanish holding the fort of San Juan de Ulúa in the harbor of Veracruz, and later against the rebels in Texas. He served as governor of the state of Tabasco (1843–1844). During the war with the United States (1846–1848), Ampudia directed the defense of Monterrey and fought under General Antonio López de SANTA ANNA at the battle of Angostura. Ampudia also served during the war as governor of the state of Nuevo León, and he held that office again during several months in 1854. Elected to the Constituent Congress of 1856–1857, Ampudia fought on the republican side during the War of the REFORM; during the Second Empire, he served MAXIMILIAN.

ALBERTO MARÍA CARREÑO ESCUDERO, *Jefes del ejército mexicano en 1847* (1914); CHARLES L. DUFOUR, *The Mexican War: A Compact History, 1846–1848* (1968); *Diccionario Porrúa de historia, biografía y geografía de México*, 5th ed. (1986).

D. F. STEVENS

**AMUNÁTEGUI ALDUNATE, MIGUEL LUIS** (*b.* 11 January 1828; *d.* 22 January 1888), Chilean historian and public figure. Born and educated in Santiago, and one of the numerous disciples of Andrés BELLO, Amunátegui was a brilliant member of a brilliant Chilean generation. A devoted Liberal, he was eight times elected to the Chamber of Deputies and also served in the cabinet during the presidencies of José Joaquín PÉREZ, Aníbal PINTO, and (briefly) José Manuel BALMACEDA. In 1875 he was offered the chance to become the "official" candidate for the presidency. The government's control over elections would have ensured his triumph, but he declined.

Among the great nineteenth-century Chilean historians, Amunátegui can be ranked as second only to Diego BARROS ARANA. His chief works were *La reconquista española* (1851), *La dictadura de O'Higgins* (1853), *Los precursores de la independencia de Chile* (3 vols., 1870–1872), and *La crónica de 1810* (3 vols., 1876). His numerous other writings cover a range from philology to the Chilean frontier dispute with Argentina. His two-part work on the latter theme, *Títulos de la República de Chile a la soberanía y dominio de la extremidad austral del continente americano* (1853, 1855), was the first to give coherent shape to Chile's territorial claims.

SIMON COLLIER

**ANÁHUAC,** a term from the Nahuatl *atl* (water) and *nahuac* (near) that usually refers to Mexico City (once surrounded by large lagoons) and, by extension, to the Valley of Mexico, the central highlands, and the Mexican nation, particularly in conjunction with the region's pre-Hispanic heritage. Originally, however, a reference to the water's proximity might also have implied the seacoast, warm lowlands inhabited by the Aztecs' trading partners. Alonso de Molina, in his classic Nahuatl dictionary, defines the modified term *anauacayotl* as "things that are brought from neighboring lands." Anáhuac was also the destination of the legendary ruler-god QUETZALCOATL when he left Tula, heading east.

NIGEL DAVIES, *The Aztecs: A History* (1973), pp. 12, 333; ALONSO DE MOLINA, *Vocabulario en lengua castellana y mexicana y mexicana y castellana*, 4th ed. (1977), pt. II, p. 6.

STEPHANIE WOOD

**ANARCHISM AND ANARCHOSYNDICALISM.** Anarchism and anarchosyndicalism—ideologies that sought to replace existing political orders with a collective society based upon the needs of workers—were the most important currents to influence the LABOR movement from its origins to 1930. Anarchists undertook much of the early organizing and propaganda and acted as individuals. Anarchosyndicalism, which replaced anarchism as the most widely held position among workers, reached its maximum influence in the early twentieth century. By the 1930s, however, both ideologies lost ground, although a few adherents still existed. The appeal of anarchism, in particular, stemmed partly from the fact that small firms or artisanal shops dominated most manufacturing sectors. Pressured by the emergence of modern larger production units, artisans looked for ways to survive and better their lives. Later, anarchosyndicalism proved attractive as a means to combat the emerging capitalist economy that threatened to marginalize artisans and subordinate workers to industrial discipline with low wages. Countries where large groups of southern European immigrants lived tended to have stronger anarchist and anarchosyndicalist movements because many new arrivals (some fleeing persecution at home) carried these ideologies with them. Vibrant organizations that espoused one of these doctrines first emerged in Argentina, southern Brazil, and Uruguay.

Anarchism took both a collective and an individualistic form. It gathered strength in Mexico's highly artisanal economy after 1860. Before 1900, immigrant members of the First International, based in Europe, founded short-lived sections in several large Latin American cities. By 1900, however, anarchism in some forms had appeared almost everywhere in Latin America. Anarchists differed concerning which strategies and tactics to pursue. Many saw trade unions as inherently reformist and chose to work through small affinity groups to win workers and others to the cause. Anarchists agreed that they should build a revolutionary movement to destroy the state and create a new society, but they often disagreed upon its shape. Independent artisans tended to favor a society composed of small producers, each governing a particular area of production. Occasionally anarchists joined unions just to recruit people. Some workers practiced "propaganda by the deed" and perpetrated individualist acts, such as the killing of Buenos Aires's police chief in 1909 for his role in the massacre of workers on May Day that year. Proletarian violence in the face of bourgeois violence, anarchists argued, justified such deeds.

Anarchosyndicalism played an even larger role in Latin America, but differences emerged among its followers. Its main objective was to adapt anarchist principles to the conditions of an emerging industrial capitalism. It spread rapidly, and after 1900 organizations pledged to it formed wherever a labor movement existed. Both a revolutionary and proletarian doctrine, anarchosyndicalism attempted to overcome the ineffectiveness of anarchist practice. Although theory and practice varied considerably over space and time, direct action formed one central feature. Workers relied on strikes, sabotage, or boycotts rather than gains through the institutions of the capitalist state. The proletariat was not to participate in political parties because voting just legitimized the system. Anarchosyndicalists undertook to destroy the state, not to control or reform it. Trade unions could act as vehicles of struggle and as the nucleus of the new society, which some envisioned as a free association of free producers gathered into unions that would govern through a large federation. Even union organization created controversy. Some saw unions as minorities of militants and argued against enrolling everyone regardless of whether or not they identified as working class or saw employers as the enemy. Others

warned that union bureaucracies weakened revolutionary militancy, and they opposed paid officials, permanent staff, or strike funds. In general, anarchosyndicalists turned to organizing on an industrial rather than craft basis (anarchists generally favored the latter). These groups would join local, provincial, national, regional, and eventually international federations. National groupings formed in several countries, and continental conferences met, uniting workers in given trades and in these federations. All persuasions of anarchists maintained extensive international contacts. Members of the U.S. anarchosyndicalist Industrial Workers of the World, for example, founded branches in Chile after 1910.

Anarchosyndicalists sought to destroy the state through the revolutionary general strike, which either became an armed confrontation of the masses against the forces of repression representing capital or else took place peacefully when all workers dropped their tools and walked away from their jobs. In theory they discredited strikes for limited objectives, but in practice supported them because they believed that understanding came through struggle. In reality, most anarchosyndicalist unions negotiated with the state, although some did not. Both anarchists and anarchosyndicalists published newspapers, edited books, and ran cultural programs for workers and their families, offering an alternative lifestyle. The strongest anarchosyndicalist organizations emerged in Argentina and Brazil, but they also exercised influence over workers and the labor movement through at least the 1920s in Chile, Cuba, Mexico, Peru, Uruguay, and elsewhere. The widespread failure of revolutionary general strikes eventually led workers to follow less radical strategies and seek limited gains.

The appearance of Communist parties after 1917 and the growing strength of syndicalism doomed both anarchist currents either to disappear as an important force or else to play a decidedly secondary role. The last great movements in which anarchosyndicalists played a leading part occurred around World War I. The defeats suffered in the São Paulo (1917) and Montevideo (1919) general strikes, for example, helped discredit anarchosyndicalism, as did the severe repression after the SEMANA TRÁGICA (1919) in Argentina. Nevertheless, in the 1920s anarchosyndicalist unions still proved influential in Bolivia and Ecuador, in the broad social movement that overthrew the Cuban dictator Gerardo MACHADO in 1933 and in rural strikes in the Argentine Chaco and Patagonia. After 1930 anarchism and anarchosyndicalism declined as significant forces. There remained, however, individual workers and specific unions that still espoused each of them. Gradual economic development doomed these doctrines, which once spoke to the needs of workers and artisans caught in the initial stages of capitalist development.

General overviews of the early period of the Latin American labor movement are found in HOBART A. SPALDING, *Organized Labor in Latin America* (1977), chaps. 1 and 2, and MICHAEL

HALL and HOBART A. SPALDING, "The Urban Working Class and Early Latin American Labour Movements, 1880–1930," in *The Cambridge History of Latin America,* vol. 4, edited by Leslie Bethell (1986), reprinted as "Urban Labor Movements" in *Latin America: Economy and Society, 1870–1930,* edited by Leslie Bethell (1989) (see especially the bibliography, which surveys the field). Among the leading country studies of anarchism and anarchosyndicalism are JOHN W. F. DULLES, *Anarchists and Communists in Brazil, 1900–1935* (1973); ANGEL QUINTERO RIVERA, *Workers' Struggle in Puerto Rico: A Documentary History* (1976); GUILLERMO LORA, *A History of the Bolivian Labour Movement, 1848–1971,* translated by Christine Whitehead, edited and abridged by Laurence Whitehead (1977); JOHN M. HART, *Anarchism and the Mexican Working Class, 1860–1931* (1978); JACOV OVED, *El anarquismo y el movimiento obrero en Argentina* (1978); PETER BLANCHARD, *The Origins of the Peruvian Labor Movement, 1883–1919* (1982); PETER DE SHAZO, *Urban Workers and Labor Unions in Chile, 1902–1927* (1983).

HOBART A. SPALDING

**ANAYA, PEDRO MARÍA DE** (b. 1794; d. 21 March 1854), president of Mexico (1847, 1847–1848). A career military officer, Anaya served as deputy in the Mexican Congress (1829–1830) and as a senator (1844–1845). He was appointed minister of war in 1845 by President José Joaquín de HERRERA. He was substitute president for Antonio López de SANTA ANNA from 2 April 1847 to 20 May 1847 and later that year was elected interim president, serving from 13 November 1847 until 8 January 1848. As defender of the convent of Churubusco on the southern outskirts of Mexico City during the war with the United States, Anaya was forced to surrender by U.S. General David E. Twiggs. When Twiggs occupied Churubusco and asked him where the munitions were, Anaya answered, "Si hubiera parque, no estarían ustedes aquí" ("If we had any munitions, you would not be here"). Anaya served as minister of war in 1848 and again in 1852, and was governor of the Federal District in 1849. He was serving as director general of the Post Office at his death in Mexico City.

ALBERTO MARÍA CARREÑO ESCUDERO, *Jefes del ejército mexicano en 1847* (1914); CHARLES L. DUFOUR, *The Mexican War: A Compact History, 1846–1848* (1968); JOSÉ MARÍA MIGUEL I VERGÉS, *Diccionario de insurgentes* (1969); *Diccionario Porrúa de historia, biografía y geografía de México,* 5th ed. (1986).

D. F. STEVENS

**ANCASH,** Peruvian department northeast of Lima known as Huaylas before 1839, when it was renamed Ancash (Quechuan for "blue"). The capital city of Huaraz (population 50,000 in 1990) stands at 10,000 feet above sea level. The department's highland region features the impressive Callejón de Huaylas, a canyon formed by the river Santa and flanked by the White and Black ranges of the Peruvian Andes. This region has been struck by devastating earthquakes and subsequent landslides, especially in 1941, 1962, and 1970. In the latter, approximately 70,000 people died, including most of the inhabitants of the cities of Yungay and Ranrahirca, who were buried by an avalanche from the northwest side of the Huascarán, the highest mountain of the Peruvian Andes.

Tourist sites include the towns of Caraz, Carhuáz, and the pre-INCA center of Chavín. The major industrial city is the port of Chimbote (1990 population 325,000), powered by the Santa hydroelectric complex.

FÉLIX ALVAREZ-BRUN, *Ancash: Una historia regional peruana* (1970); ANTHONY OLIVER-SMITH, *The Martyred City: Death and Rebirth in the Andes* (1986).

ALFONSO W. QUIROZ

**ANCHIETA, JOSÉ DE** (b. 19 March 1534; d. 6 September 1597) Jesuit missionary. An early Jesuit missionary known as the "Apostle of Brazil," José de Anchieta was skillful in teaching and evangelizing the native Indians. Of Spanish origin, he was born in Tenerife, in the Canary Islands, and studied at the University of Coimbra, where he entered the Society of Jesus as a brother in 1551. In 1553 he arrived in Brazil, where he taught at the Jesuit College of São Paulo. He was an accomplished writer and linguist. A master of Latin grammar and prose, he was one of the first missionaries to learn the TUPI language of the Indians well enough to write a Tupi grammar to augment the Jesuit missionary endeavors in Brazil. He served as the secretary to Manuel da NÓBREGA, the leader of the first group of Jesuit missionaries in Brazil. He was responsible for the founding in Brazil of the Jesuit educational system based on the *ratio studiorum,* which emphasized classes in Latin, grammar, philosophy, mathematics, cosmography, and astronomy. In 1577 he made solemn profession as a priest in the JESUIT ORDER.

While Manuel da Nóbrega was working in northern Brazil, Anchieta concentrated his efforts on founding *aldeias,* or fortified missions, in the southern captaincies of São Vicente, Rio de Janeiro, and Espírito Santo. He founded a third regular college in 1554 in São Paulo, where he was a zealous teacher. He also composed a great number of hymns, sacred songs, plays, and a poem in praise to Our Lady. In 1563 he worked with Manuel da Nóbrega in a pacification mission among the TAMOIOS, who were allied with the French and attacking settlements in Santos and São Vicente. After serving as a teacher and missionary, he was appointed Jesuit provincial of southern Brazil from 1578 to 1587.

A saintly and dynamic missionary, Anchieta spent forty-four years laboring in South America, despite a painful back injury which often incapacitated him. His letters and sermons give glowing accounts of the natural beauty of Brazil and are an excellent chronicle of early Brazilian history. Various miracles were attributed to him and he is called the "miracle worker" of Brazil.

SERAFIM S. LEITE, *História da Companhia de Jesus no Brasil,* vol. 2 (1938); CHARLES R. BOXER, *Salvador de Sa and the Struggle for*

*Brazil and Angola (1602–1686)* (1952); SERAFIM S. LEITE, *Novas paginas da história do Brasil* (1965); HELIO VIANNA, *História do Brasil colonial* (1975); JOHN HEMMING, *Red Gold: The Conquest of the Brazilian Indians* (1978).

PATRICIA MULVEY

**ANCÓN, TREATY OF (1883),** an agreement between Chile and Peru ending Peru's participation in the WAR OF THE PACIFIC. The treaty ceded Tarapacá to Chile, allowing Santiago to occupy the provinces of TACNA and ARICA for a period of ten years. Santiago annexed Tarapacá subject to outstanding claims of foreign creditors. The agreement also called for a plebiscite to take place in 1893 in the two provinces; the winner could retain the two provinces, and the loser would receive $10 million in silver pesos.

Because it did not specify the procedures under which the plebiscite should occur, the treaty failed to settle the issue of the ownership of Tacna and Arica. Santiago successfully resisted attempts by the Pan-American movement and the United States to settle this boundary issue until, in 1929, it signed an agreement with Lima. In return for retaining control of Arica, Chile constructed some port facilities in Tacna, paid Lima $6 million, and returned Tacna to Peruvian control. Thus, the Ancón agreement, while ending the formal state of war, did not completely resolve the territorial disputes arising from the 1879 war.

WILLIAM J. DENNIS, *Tacna and Arica: An Account of the Chile-Peru Boundary Dispute and of the Arbitrations by the United States* (1931); ROBERT N. BURR, *By Reason or Force: Chile and the Balancing of Power in South America, 1830–1905* (1965), 160–164.

WILLIAM F. SATER

**ANDAGOYA, PASCUAL DE** (*b.* 1495; *d.* 1548), early Spanish explorer and chronicler of the Conquest. Andagoya arrived in the Caribbean in 1514 with Pedrarias Davila (Pedro Arias de ÁVILA), and in 1521 he became governor of Panama. The following year he led a group to explore to the south. Andagoya sailed down the Pacific coast to the San Juan River of southern Colombia, where, suffering from an injury and virtually out of supplies, he turned back. Andagoya returned with tales of great riches to the south. Inspired by these tales, Francisco PIZARRO utilized the information uncovered by Andagoya in subsequent forays south. In 1537 Andagoya became governor of the Pacific coast region of Colombia. However, his rival Sebastián de Belalcázar brought charges against him, believing that Andagoya had encroached on his domain. Andagoya was jailed and sent to Spain. According to some accounts, he died in Cuzco, Peru, in 1548; others maintain that he never returned to the New World.

As an explorer Andagoya enjoyed a special reputation for his humane regard for the natives. He is most remembered for his lively account of the deeds of con-

quest, *Narrative of the Proceedings of Pedrarias Davila in the Provinces of Tierra Firme or Castilla del Oro, and of the Discovery of the South Sea and the Coasts of Peru and Nicaragua* (translated by Sir Clements Markham, 2d ed. 1978).

Beyond Andagoya's own writings, the early Spanish exploration, conquest, and settlement of Panama and Colombia are covered in CARL ORTWIN SAUER, *The Early Spanish Main* (1969). Two classic works capture much of the flavor of the times: SIR CLEMENTS MARKHAM, *The Conquest of New Granada* (1912); and FREDERICK ALEXANDER KIRKPATRICK, *The Spanish Conquistadores* (1934).

RONN F. PINEO

*See also* **Balboa, Vasco Núñez de.**

**ANDEAN PACT.** The Cartagena agreement of May 1969 established the Grupo Andino or Andean Common Market. The pact sought to integrate the economies of Colombia, Ecuador, Peru, Bolivia, and Chile. Venezuela joined in 1973, and Chile withdrew in 1976. The primary objective of the Andean Pact was to promote regional industrialization. To this end, it adopted several innovative strategies: the elimination of internal constraints on trade, the formation of a common external tariff, the development of sectoral programs, and the strict regulation of foreign investment.

Initially the Andean Group's efforts at cooperation produced substantial increases in regional trade and industrial growth. By the 1980s, however, these positive trends were reversed. The policy of substituting local industrial products for imports was costly. Internal economic inequalities were intensified. Owing to the fragility of Andean economies and the international economic crisis, regional trade declined. Andean economic integration also suffered setbacks due to conflicts of national interest over tariffs, a boundary war between Ecuador and Peru, and failures to enforce Pact policies. Despite making some progress in achieving economic unity, the Andean Pact has yet to overcome structural problems and deep-seated regional conflicts.

ROGER W. FONTAINE, *The Andean Pact: A Political Analysis* (1977); LYNN KRIEGER MYTELKA, *Regional Development in a Global Economy: The Multinational Corporation, Technology, and Andean Integration* (1979); CIRO ANGARITA and PETER COFFEY, *Europe and the Andean Countries: A Comparison of Economic Policies and Institutions* (1988).

STEVEN J. HIRSCH
ALFONSO W. QUIROZ

**ANDERSON IMBERT, ENRIQUE** (*b.* 12 February 1910), Argentine critic, literary historian, fiction writer, and influential teacher. Born in Córdoba, he studied philology and literature at the University of Buenos Aires with Pedro HENRÍQUEZ UREÑA and Alejandro KORN. His novel *Vigilia* (1934) was awarded the Buenos Aires Municipal Prize for Literature. He wrote essays, fiction, and articles for major Argentine journals, such as SUR, and was literary editor of the newspaper *La Vanguardia.* After teaching at the University of Tucumán (1940–1947), he went to the United States, where he taught at the University of Michigan until 1965, returning briefly to Argentina in 1955 to teach at the universities of Buenos Aires and La Plata. From 1965 to 1980 he was the Victor Thomas Professor of Hispanic Literature at Harvard University. Since then he has divided his time teaching at various universities in Argentina, serving as president of the Argentine Academy of Letters, lecturing, and, primarily, writing creative fiction. In 1954–1961 he published his best-selling two-volume book on literature, *Historia de la literatura hispanoamericana* (Spanish-American Literature: A History, 1963).

Julio CORTÁZAR considered Anderson Imbert one of the most important short-story writers of Latin America. The author of more than thirty books of essays, fiction, and criticism, Anderson was awarded the Mecenas Prize in 1990 for *Narraciones completas.* He has written definitive critical essays about Henrik Ibsen, Domingo SARMIENTO, Rubén DARÍO and George Bernard Shaw. His major works of fiction included *El grimorio* (1961), *El gato de Cheshire* (1965), *La locura juega al ajedrez (1971), Evocación de sombras en la ciudad geometrica* (1989); his works of criticism include *Mentiras y mentirosos en el mundo de las letras* (1992) and *Teoría y técnica del cuento* (1979). An excellent selection of Anderson's short stories is translated into English in *Woven on the Loom of Time* (1990).

HELMY F. GIACOMÁN, ed., *Homenaje a Enrique Anderson Imbert: Variaciones interpretativas en torno a su obra* (1973); RUBÉN AMÉRICO LIGGERA, *De espejos, fantasmas y esqueletos: Ensayos sobre la obra literaria de Enrique Anderson Imbert* (1990).

GEORGETTE MAGASSY DORN

**ANDES,** chain of mountains stretching over 4,500 miles, from the island of Trinidad (11 degrees north latitude) down to Cape Horn (57 degrees south latitude). Surpassing the Himalayas, Alps, and Rocky Mountains in average height, it is the largest and highest mountain chain in the world. At the widest point (Arica, Chile, to Santa Cruz, Bolivia) the chain is 460 miles wide: the whole western Alps, from Cannes to Vienna, would fit across this segment. ACONCAGUA (22,834 feet) is the highest summit of the Americas, and many high peaks, most of them volcanoes, rise above 20,000 feet. The stretch of the Andes from Venezuela to Bolivia is the most densely populated mountain region of the world. In this area the most advanced Indian cultures of the continent developed. The lifting of the Andes began in the Cretaceous Period, 130 million years ago, and is still in progress.

PEDRO CUNILL, *La América andina* (1981); and HÉCTOR MIRANDA, *Historia de Los Andes* (1989).

CÉSAR N. CAVIEDES

**ANDRADA, ANTÔNIO CARLOS RIBEIRO DE** and **MARTIM FRANCISCO RIBEIRO DE,** Brazilian statesmen and younger brothers of José Bonifácio de ANDRADA. Children of a merchant of Santos, they all graduated from Coimbra University and entered gov-

The Peruvian Andes. ORGANIZATION OF AMERICAN STATES.

ernment service. All three were self-assured, quarrelsome, unscrupulous, and vindictive when crossed, confusing personal and family advancement with the public interest.

Antônio Carlos (*b.* 1 November 1773; *d.* 5 December 1845), then a royal judge, gave support to the 1817 revolt in Pernambuco, suffering three years' imprisonment. Elected from São Paulo to the Lisbon Cortes in 1821, he took the lead in asserting Brazil's rights. Martim Francisco (*b.* 27 June 1775; *d.* 23 February 1844) served as minister of finance in the cabinet headed by José Bonifácio from 1822 to 1823. The three brothers sat in the Constituent Assembly and, following the dismissal of José Bonifácio and Martim Francisco as ministers, launched a campaign of opposition to PEDRO I that contributed to the violent dissolution of the Constituent Assembly in November 1823. Deported to France, the brothers did not return from exile until 1829. After Pedro I's abdication in 1831, the brothers tried by various means, legal and illegal, to secure control of power. They were involved in the abortive coup of April 1832 and in the Caramurú movement for Pedro I's restoration. In 1834 and again in 1838 Antônio Carlos unsuccessfully sought election as regent. He and Martim Francisco played a leading part in securing the premature declaration of PEDRO II's majority in July 1840. The two brothers dominated the first cabinet appointed by the emperor, but their ambition and highhandedness brought about their dismissal from office in February 1841. Antônio Carlos, the most energetic and domineering of the three brothers, became a leader of the new Liberal Party, securing election to the Senate prior to his death.

RODERICK J. BARMAN

**ANDRADA, JOSÉ BONIFÁCIO DE** (*b.* 13 June 1763; *d.* 6 April 1838), statesman and geologist, known in Brazil as the patriarch of independence. A native of Santos, São Paulo, and the eldest of the Andrada Brothers, José Bonifácio settled in Portugal after graduating in 1788 from Coimbra University. In 1790 the Portuguese government sent him on a mission to study scientific topics in northern Europe. During a decade's absence, he established himself as an expert on minerals and mining. In 1801 he was appointed to several government posts in Portugal. The multiplicity of his new responsibilities and his impatient, imperious character reduced his effectiveness as a bureaucrat. Following the French invasion of Portugal in 1807, he did not accompany the government to Brazil but played a notable role in organizing resistance. His subsequent career in Portugal was stultifying. In 1819 he finally secured permission to retire to Santos, still drawing most of his salary.

The revolution that began in Pôrto in 1820 drew José Bonifácio to the center of Brazilian politics. He played a key role in the provisional government of São Paulo and publicly advocated the continuance of the kingdom of

José Bonifácio de Andrada. ICONOGRAPHIA.

Brazil created in 1815. When the prince regent, Dom Pedro, decided in January 1822 to defy the Cortes and to stay in Rio, José Bonifácio was the logical choice to serve as the prince's chief minister and adviser. José Bonifácio's self-confidence, energy, and determination were indispensable during the next year and a half in establishing the prince's authority within Brazil. The flow of events forced José Bonifácio, not originally an advocate of political independence, to accept that outcome in September 1822. He preserved for the new emperor PEDRO I the traditional powers of the Portuguese monarchy.

José Bonifácio's very successes undercut his position. As the new nation state was consolidated, so his talents became less indispensable and his domineering character less tolerable. Intrigues at court achieved his dismissal as minister in July 1823. José Bonifácio and his brothers, as members of the Constituent Assembly, sitting at Rio since May, went into opposition, denouncing the Portuguese-born faction at court and thereby attacking the emperor himself. The outcome was the violent dissolution of the Assembly in November 1823 and the exiling to France of the Andrada brothers until 1829.

On his return, José Bonifácio again became a favored advisor of PEDRO I. When the emperor abdicated on 7 April 1831, he named José Bonifácio to be his son's guardian (*tutor*). Although the new regime refused at first to recognize this nomination, the legislature voted in June to make José Bonifácio guardian. His handling of his position was not successful. PEDRO II and his sisters did not flourish physically or psychologically. José Bonifácio used his position for political purposes, being involved in plots to overthrow the regime. The government forcibly removed him as guardian in December 1833. José Bonifácio spent his remaining years in quiet retirement on Paquetá Island, Rio de Janeiro.

OCTAVIO TARQUINO DE SOUSA, *História dos fundadores do império*, vol. 1, *José Bonifácio* (Rio de Janeiro, 1957).

RODERICK J. BARMAN

**ANDRADE, CARLOS DRUMMOND DE** (*b.* 31 October 1902; *d.* 17 August 1987), considered Brazil's most important twentieth-century poet. Drummond (or "The Master," as he is best known) was an active poet and writer through several literary generations—from MODERNISM through CONCRETISM—and influenced many contemporary Brazilian poets. Born in Minas Gerais and intimately associated with that state in his poetry, Drummond spent most of his life in Rio de Janeiro where, like many other Brazilian writers, he earned his living as a bureaucrat—in the education ministry—and a journalist. He contributed poetry to major literary reviews and translated many of the classic writers of

Carlos Drummond de Andrade. ICONOGRAPHIA.

French and Spanish literature. He also wrote hundreds of *crônicas* (journalistic sketches) about daily life that reveal a genuine, kind soul.

Drummond was not an original member of the group that "founded" Brazilian modernism in São Paulo in 1922. Nevertheless, under their influence, he, along with other contemporary young *mineiro* (that is, of Minas Gerais) writers (e.g., Emílio Moura [1901–1971]), founded *A Revista*, the leading literary review of *mineiro* modernism in 1925. It was not until his 1928 collaboration on Oswald de ANDRADE's journal *Revista de Antropófagia* (Review of cannibalism) that he attained national acclaim. His poem "No meio do caminho" (In the middle of the road) established the characteristics he pursued in all his poetry: a rejection of traditional forms and structures; a conversational tone and a highly colloquial language reflecting actual Brazilian speech; and an interest in everyday affairs of life, often from a satirical point of view.

Collections of poems published in the 1930s and early 1940s reflected contemporary political upheavals. He debated leftist ideologies and antibourgeois sentiments in *A rosa do povo* (1945), but the volume ends on a note of a search from within for resolution of these dilemmas. Later collections would turn to his sense of isolation from his small-town roots and a growing displeasure with big-city life. *A vida passada a limpo* (1959) reviews his perennial interests within a new light. Here, the elegy on the destruction of Rio's Hotel Avenida assumes several levels of symbolic meaning: society's change, the "endurance" of a work of art (be it one of architecture or poetry), and the role of the artist. Among his other important collections are *Lição das coisas* (1962), which includes experimental concretist verse, and *As impurezas do branco* (1973), which examines modern technology.

Drummond was a friend of the American poet Elizabeth Bishop, who spent some twenty years in Brazil. His reputation in the United States was a consequence of her translations of his works, often published in the *New Yorker*, and also of later translations by Mark Strand, among others. Drummond's influence on modern Brazilian poetry has been immense.

Collected translations include *The Minus Sign*, translated by Virginia de Araújo (1981), and *Travelling in the Family*, translated by Thomas Colchie et al. (1986). IRWIN STERN, "A Poet for All Brazilians," in *Review* 32 (1984): 16–17, offers a brief critique. RICARDO LOBO STERNBERG, *Carlos Drummond de Andrade and His Generation* (1986) and *The Unquiet Self: Self and Society in the Poetry of Carlos Drummond de Andrade* are the major studies in English.

IRWIN STERN

**ANDRADE, GOMES FREIRE DE** (*b.* 11 July 1688; *d.* 1 January 1763), governor and captain-general of southern and western Brazil. A member of a distinguished family whose roots trace back in Galicia before 711, the year of the Moorish invasion, and in Portugal since the fourteenth century. For centuries the Freire de Andrades contributed senior officials to Portugal's army, navy, church, and civil service. Andrade, named after an uncle who served as governor of Maranhão during the BECKMAN REVOLT, was born in Jeromenha, situated between Vila Viçosa and Badajóz. He attended the University of Coimbra and became fluent in French and Spanish. Along with his father, he served in the WAR OF THE SPANISH SUCCESSION, after which he retained an appointment in a cavalry unit stationed in the capital. In 1733 he was appointed governor and captain-general of the captaincy of Rio de Janeiro, a post he retained until his death. It was the first of many administrative units for which he became responsible. By 1748 he governed all of western and southern Brazil, including Minas Gerais, Goiás, Mato Grosso, São Paulo, Santa Catarina, and Rio Grande do Sul. Among his notable responsibilities were the settlement of coastal Rio Grande do Sul, the definition of Brazil's southern boundary in accordance with the TREATY OF MADRID (1750), commander of Portuguese forces in Rio Grande do Sul during the GUARANÍ WAR (1752–1756), and the expulsion of the Jesuits (1760) from lands under his jurisdiction. Andrade never married; he died in Rio de Janeiro after an extended illness.

CHARLES R. BOXER, *The Golden Age of Brazil, 1695–1750: Growing Pains of a Colonial Society* (1962); ROBERT ALLAN WHITE, "Gomes Freire de Andrade: Life and Times of a Brazilian Colonial Governor, 1688–1763" (Ph.D. diss., University of Texas, 1972).

DAURIL ALDEN

**ANDRADE, JORGE** (*b.* 1922; *d.* 1988), Brazilian playwright. In his theater Jorge Andrade was the sensitive historian and understanding judge of a fast-disappearing society. He became in every sense the first completely successful modern Brazilian playwright, doing for São Paulo what the novelists and dramatists of the Northeast and Érico VERÍSSIMO in the South have been accomplishing for their regions, for Brazil, and for the world since the 1930s.

*A moratória* (1954), a play in three acts with two sets, demonstrates the dramatist's great maturity. The subject is essentially a continuation of that of *O telescópio* (1951), both chronologically and thematically, but reflects the considerable development of the author as a person and artist. Here, the slow, painful, and somehow inconclusive passage from one era to another is emphasized more sharply. Simultaneous use of two sets, one the *fazenda* in 1919, the other a city apartment in 1932, requires superior technical skills as well as literary sophistication for full realization and appreciation.

Employing carefully selected situations, emotions, and language, which appear simple and natural without naturalistic triviality, the author solves the age-old problems of classical tragedy with Flaubertian preci-

sion. The entire, balanced action turns on the past and its influence on the present through the use of graphic reminiscences that join the two times and places for the author and spectator, whereas the characters must rely on memory alone. With a view of both the past (1919) and the fictional present (1932), we in the actual present are afforded unique historic and dramatic perspective. Transitions from hope to despair on one level, underscored ironically or fatalistically on the other, grip the audience emotionally.

Having vindicated through its ancestors a society whose demise he had begun to record, Jorge Andrade now turned to another class of that society, the tenant farmers. *A vereda da salvação* (published 1957; produced 1964) has as its point of departure a tragic example of religious fanaticism in Minas Gerais, the details and analyses of which the playwright studied most carefully. During a long period of revision, Andrade reconsidered the events, the criticism of his work, and his own meditations on the human condition. More than ever, the new *Vereda da salvação* is neither *mineiro* nor *paulista*, but Brazilian and universal. In fact, it has enjoyed long successful runs in Poland.

The collection *Marta, a árvore e o relógio* (1970) is a very interesting anthology from several points of view. Not only does it contain two new plays, but it also presents Jorge Andrade's major works in a historico-fictional chronology, rather than in the chronology of their writing, to create his full cycle of São Paulo. Thus, the newest play, *As confrarias*, is the first in the collection, and *O sumidouro*, long in progress and the second newest, is the last. The other eight are inserted between these two in more or less fictional order and not in the order in which they were written. The title is comprised of symbols that recur throughout the series of plays.

Having in every way explored everything possible in the world of coffee barons and São Paulo and having realized that censorship made it virtually impossible to stage anything serious on current matters in Brazil, Jorge Andrade turned to television after 1970. When he did create another play, *Milagre na cela* (1977), which dealt with political oppression and torture, his public could receive it only in published form.

LEON F. LYDAY and GEORGE WOODYARD, *Dramatists in Revolt: The New Latin American Theater* (1976), pp. 206–220.

RICHARD A. MAZZARA

*See also* **Literature: Brazil.**

**ANDRADE, MÁRIO DE** (*b.* 9 October 1893; *d.* 25 February 1945), Brazilian writer. Mário Raul Moraes de Andrade was a man of multiple talents and immensely varied activities. From a relatively modest background, especially compared with his modernist counterparts, he was born in São Paulo and, after graduating from the Ginásio Nossa Senhora do Carmo, studied music and piano at the Conservatorio Dramático e Musical in São

Paulo, and was professor of piano. Widely acknowledged as the leading figure—or "pope"—of the Brazilian modernist movement of the 1920s, he was arguably Brazil's most important and versatile literary personage during the first half of the century. He was involved in almost all of the literary, artistic, and cultural movements of the period. He wrote novels, short stories, and poetry; he was a literary, art, and music critic and theorist; he was also a musicologist, a folklorist, and an ethnographer. As director of São Paulo's Department of Culture from 1935 to 1938, he fostered many activities that promoted the development of modern social science in Brazil.

One of the governing concepts of Andrade's cultural and artistic activity, along with his insistence on freedom of artistic expression and experimentation, is what has variously been called his "sense of commitment" or his "quasi-apostolic consciousness." Especially important in this regard is his extensive research into the specific characteristics of Brazilian speech and popular culture, research intended to help forge a more authentic cultural identity. Andrade conceived of nationalism as the first step in a process of self-discovery that would eventually contribute to universal cultural values, to the extent that it was authentic and faithful to itself. His ultimate goal was the integration of Brazilian culture into universal culture, not the closure implied by the more xenophobic currents of nationalism that also found expression within the Brazilian modernist movement. Andrade recognized the difficulty of creating an authentic national culture in a country permeated by European values and standards. He expressed this theme as early as 1922 in the poem "Inspiração," which opens the collection *Paulicéia desvairada* (*Hallucinated City*), when he wrote: "São Paulo! comoção de minha vida . . . / Galicismo a berrar nos desertos da América!" (São Paulo! tumult of my life . . . / Gallicism crying in the wilderness of America!). In "O trovador" in the same volume, he wrote, "Sou um tupi tangendo um alaúde!" ("I am a Tupi Indian strumming a lute!").

Andrade's artistic answer to this dilemma was to use popular forms of expression structurally—not merely ornamentally—in elite cultural forms. He began by systematizing errors committed in everyday speech as a means of capturing an authentically national social and psychological character through language itself. By bringing those errors into educated speech and writing, he hoped to help in the formation of a Brazilian literary language. His interest in popular culture as a means of understanding Brazil evolved into the systematic study of Brazilian folklore and the re-creation of popular forms on an erudite level. Knowing and incorporating the foundations of Brazilian popular thought, he felt he could help lead Brazil to self-knowledge and contribute to its passage from nationalism to a universal level in the higher arts. The 1928 novel *Macunaíma*, which David Haberly has described as both an etiological myth of national creation and an eschatological myth of national destruction, represents the artistic culmination of Mário de Andrade's research in Brazilian folklore and popular forms of expression.

THOMAS R. HART, "The Literary Criticism of Mário de Andrade," in *The Disciplines of Criticism: Essays in Literary Theory, Interpretation, and History,* edited by Peter Demetz (1968), pp. 265–288; HAROLDO DE CAMPOS, *Morfologia do Macunaíma* (1973); JOAN DASSIN, *Política e poesia em Mário de Andrade* (1978); RANDAL JOHNSON, "Cinema Novo and Cannibalism: *Macunaíma*" and "*Lesson of Love,*" in *Brazilian Cinema,* edited by Randal Johnson and Robert Stam (1982), pp. 178–190, 208–215; DAVID T. HABERLY, *Three Sad Races: Racial Identity and National Consciousness in Brazilian Literature* (1983), pp. 123–160; JOÃO LUIZ LAFETÁ, *Figuração de intimidade: Imagens na poesia de Mário de Andrade* (1986).

RANDAL JOHNSON

*See also* **Modernism.**

**ANDRADE, OSWALD DE** (*b.* 11 January 1890; *d.* 22 October 1954), Brazilian writer and intellectual. As a theoretician of Brazil's social and aesthetic modernization, Andrade was a leading contributor to the Brazilian modernist movement in the arts and culture, initiated formally by the MODERN ART WEEK held in February 1922 in São Paulo, which he helped to plan. His principal modernist contributions are the "Manifesto da poesia pau Brasil" (1924; Brazilwood Manifesto), whose ideas inspired the cubistic geometrism and "constructive innocence" of Tarsila do AMARAL's canvases of the mid-1920s—and the "Manifesto antropófago" (1928; Cannibal Manifesto), which led to the founding of a national vanguardist movement whose model of "devouring assimilation" of foreign influence under the totem of the cannibal tribes who devoured Europeans was summarized in the aphorism "Tupy or not Tupy, that is the question." The *Antropofagia* movement—again paralleled in the plastic arts by Amaral's paintings—created a paradoxical telluric and vanguardist model for resolving the dialectic between national and foreign cultural influences.

Andrade's early years reflect the transition from Brazil's belle époque aesthetic to modernism. A graduate of São Bento Seminary and the Largo de São Francisco Law School, Andrade began his literary career as a journalist and contributor to fin-de-siècle and premodernist magazines (*O Pirralho, Papel e Tinta*), in which he introduced Italo-Paulista dialect. With Guilherme de Almeida he wrote two plays in French in 1916. His premodernist life is fictionalized in *A trilogia do exílio,* later published as *Os condenados,* and in the collective diary *O perfeito cozinheiro das almas deste mundo.* During the 1920s he spent much of his time in Paris with Amaral and her circle. Influenced by cubism and the poetic prose of Blaise Cendrars, his early modernist work includes two "inventions" combining fragmented poetry with prose, *Memórias sentimentais de João Miramar* (1924) and *Serafim Ponte Grande* (1933); the poetry collection *Pau Brasil* (1925); and the two manifestos.

Andrade also wrote expressionistic drama (*O homem e o cavallo; O rei da Vela; A morta*), followed by the social mural novels in the series *Marco-Zero*. His works after 1945 include poetry (''Cântico dos cânticos para flauta e violão'') and essays on literature, culture, and philosophy addressing utopian themes. In the 1960s his work began to receive critical reevaluation, culminating in the current recognition of his texts as foundations of Brazil's literary and intellectual modernity.

Oswald de Andrade is included in the UNESCO Archives Series on Latin American writers (to appear in Portuguese and English). Introductions to his life and works may be found in HAROLDO DE CAMPO, ed., *Oswald de Andrade: Trechos escolhidos* (1967); K. DAVID JACKSON, ''Rediscovering the Rediscoverers,'' in *Texas Quarterly* 19, no. 3 (Autumn 1976): 162–173; JORGE SCHWARTZ, ed., *Oswald de Andrade* (1982); MARIA AUGUSTA FONSECA, *Oswald de Andrade* (*1890–1954*): *Biografia* (1990).

K. DAVID JACKSON

**ANDREONI, JOÃO ANTÔNIO** (pseud. of André João Antonil; *b.* 1649; *d.* 13 March 1716), Jesuit administrator and author of a seminal study of the economic roots of early eighteenth-century Brazil, *Cultura e opulência do Brasil por suas drogas e minas* (1711). Born in Tuscany and educated in law at the University of Perugia, he entered the Society of Jesus on 20 May 1667 and came to Bahia, Brazil, in 1681. There, after serving as secretary to Antônio VIEIRA, he became Vieira's rival and leader among German- and Italian-born Jesuits serving in Brazil. A proficient Latinist and a keen administrator, he held a succession of posts in the Society of Jesus, from minister of novices to rector of the college at Bahia, and served both as provincial Visitor and as provincial. Unlike Vieira, he sided with the settlers in their efforts to obtain Indian labor and, again unlike Vieira, he was anti-Semitic. But he is best known for his unique and outstanding treatise concerning the sources of Brazil's wealth—sugar, tobacco, gold, and cattle. He died in Bahia.

SERAFIM LEITE, *História da companhia de Jesús no Brasil*, 10 vols. (Rio de Janeiro, 1938–1950); ANDRÉE MANSUY, ed., *Cultura e opulência do Brasil por suas drogas e minas* (Paris, 1965).

DAURIL ALDEN

*See also* **Jesuits.**

**ANDRESOTE** (Andrés López Del Rosario), the *zambo* leader of the rebellion in Venezuela against the COMPAÑÍA GUIPUZCOANA of Caracas in 1730–1733. Andresote dealt in contraband in the region of Yaracuy, mocking the controls which the Compañía Guipuzcoana sought to place on the commerce of the province of Venezuela. To protect his interests, the director general of the *compañía* ordered his arrest. Andresote and his followers clashed violently with the authorities and representatives of the *compañía* in their effort to continue their contraband operations with the island of Curaçao. Troops were sent from Caracas to put down Andresote's group, but when they failed to accomplish this in 1732, the commander in chief of Venezuela vowed to combat him personally. Andresote fled in 1733 to Curaçao, where he died a short while later.

TULIO FEBRES CORDERO, *La Rebelión de Andresote* (*Valles del Yaracuy, 1730–1733*) (Caracas, 1952), and CARLOS FELICE CARDOT, *La Rebelión de Andresote* (*Volles de Yaracuy, 1730–1733*) (1957).

INÉS QUINTERO

**ANDREVE, GUILLERMO** (*b.* 1879; *d.* 1940), Panamanian journalist, intellectual, and politician. Andreve was one of the most influential liberal leaders in Panama in the early twentieth century. He held many government positions. He was a member of the National Assembly, secretary of public education, secretary of government and justice, and an ambassador in Latin America and Europe. Andreve wrote on many subjects, and his writings are an important source for the study of Panamanian politics in the 1920s. In his writings Andreve dwells on the inadequacies of the laissez-faire structure created by nineteenth-century liberalism and advocates a more interventionist state for Panama.

''Escritos de Andreve,'' in *Revista lotería*, nos. 282–284 (August–October 1979); JORGE CONTE PORRAS, *Diccionario biográfico ilustrado de Panamá*, 2d ed. (1986).

JUAN MANUEL PÉREZ

**ANDUEZA PALACIO, RAIMUNDO** (*b.* February 1843; *d.* 17 August 1900), president of Venezuela (1890–1892). Andueza began his political and military activity after the FEDERAL WAR (1859–1863) as aide-de-camp and secretary to the president of the Republic, Marshal Juan Crisóstomo FALCÓN (1863–1868). Having ties with the Liberal Party, he carried out important, and sometimes divisive, public duties during the administrations of Antonio GUZMÁN BLANCO (1870–1877) and Francisco LINARES ALCÁNTARA (1877–1878). After a brief period of exile, Andueza returned to Venezuela and became one of the political leaders of the Partido Liberalismo Amarillo (Yellow Liberalism Party).

With the end of the hegemony of Guzmán's policies during the administration of Dr. Juan Pablo ROJAS PAÚL (1888–1890), the Federal Council elected Andueza president for the 1890–1892 term. In an atmosphere of conflict between militarists and those favoring civilian rule, he declared himself a defender of the trend toward civilian rule and appointed a cabinet composed primarily of civilians. His administration is seen as having been blessed by a period of economic boom. Andueza saw the completion of various public projects begun before his regime and fostered a politics of clientele, with the object of creating a broad base of support that would allow him to remain in power. From within the state legislatures, he promoted a constitutional reform that included, among many other amendments, the lengthening of the presidential term from two to four years. Congress refused to launch this constitutional reform immediately, but the president declared that the new statute was in effect. The immediate result was the beginning of the Legalist Revolution led by General Joaquín CRESPO, who put an end to Andueza's term of office. When Crespo died in 1898, Andueza returned from exile and again took up political activity, becoming minister of foreign affairs under General Cipriano CASTRO, who became president in 1900.

MANUEL ALFREDO RODRÍGUEZ, *Andueza Palacio y la crisis del liberalismo venezolano* (1960), and RAMÓN J. VELÁSQUEZ, *La caída del liberalismo amarillo: Tiempo y drama de Antonio Paredes* (1977).

INÉS QUINTERO

*See also* **Venezuela: Political Parties.**

**ANGEL, ALBALUCÍA** (*b.* 7 September 1939), Colombian novelist. Angel is one of Colombia's most important writers since Gabriel GARCÍA MÁRQUEZ. Following an independent narrative style, she has produced four distinct novels. *Los girasoles en invierno* (1970) is an experiment in radical feminism, and *Dos veces Alicia* (1972) plays on the Lewis Carroll text of *Alice in Wonderland.* The later novels delve into deeper issues of Colombian history and cultural values. *Estaba la pájara pinta sentada en el verde limón* (1975), her most significant novel, deals with the period of Colombian history known as La Violencia (1948–1956) and intriguingly reconstructs the era through two parallel but opposing perspectives: on the one hand, the unseen violence perpetrated by a young female adolescent who is not allowed to leave her house, and on the other, the quoted firsthand descriptions of actual grotesque political killings as reported in journals and books.

*Misiá Señora* (1982) looks at the relationship of a daughter, mother, and grandmother. Through erotic imagery, soliloquy, and monologue, the novel captures what was once the ideal of femininity, which encompassed sensuality, decency, courage, inner strength, and a feeling of fulfillment. The four novels show not only the author's search for innovation through language and theme and creativeness in her early period but also her successful later efforts to transform the literary act into a profound social and cultural commentary on her native land.

DICK GERDES, ''*Estaba la pájara pinta sentada en el verde limón*: Novela testimonial/documental de 'La Violencia' en Colombia,'' *Revista de Estudios Colombianos* 2 (1987): 14–19; *Manual de literatura colombiana*, vol. 2 (1988).

DICK GERDES

**ÁNGELES, FELIPE** (*b.* 13 June 1869; *d.* 26 November 1919), Mexican revolutionary. A well-educated career soldier, Ángeles was in France when the revolution broke out in 1910. He returned to Mexico in 1912. Sharing Francisco MADERO's liberalism, Ángeles soon became one of the new president's closest confidants within the military. Ángeles was arrested because of this association after the February 1913 coup that brought Victoriano HUERTA to power, but he was soon able to join the Constitutionalists in their fight against the Huerta regime. Within this camp he quickly found his most important revolutionary role as Pancho VILLA's close advisor and played a large part in the fighting that would eventually lead to Huerta's downfall. In 1914 Ángeles helped bring the Villistas and the Zapatistas together in an alliance against the followers of Venustiano CARRANZA. But after Villa lost the big battles of CELAYA and León de las Aldamas in 1915—often ignoring the tactical advice of Angeles in the process—Ángeles fled the country in exile to the United States. Always ambitious, he tried to rejoin the revolutionary struggle by leading a small band of soldiers across the border into Chihuahua. In 1919, he was captured there and executed by forces loyal to Carranza.

FEDERICO CERVANTES, *Felipe Angeles y la revolución de 1913. Biografía (1869–1919)*, 2d ed. (1943); ALVARO MATUTE, ed., *Documentos relativos al General Felipe Angeles* (1982); ALAN KNIGHT, *The Mexican Revolution*, 2 vols. (1986).

SAMUEL BRUNK

**ANGELIS, PEDRO DE** (*b.* 29 June 1784; *d.* 10 February 1859), essayist and scholar. Bernardino RIVADAVIA, former president of Argentina (1826–1827), persuaded Angelis, an Italian intellectual living in Paris, to take up residence in Buenos Aires and help develop the cultural life of the new nation. Angelis arrived in 1827 and became co-editor of Rivadavia's official paper, *La crónica política y literaria de Buenos Aires.* He also founded the Ateneo (an intellectual society) and edited the *Gaceta mercantil.* In 1828 Angelis edited the Latin text *Cornelli Nepotis . . . vitae excellentium imperatorum* for the university.

He attained prestige in the Argentine literary world and served Rivadavia's cause as well as that of Juan Manuel Ortiz de ROSAS. During the second Rosas dictatorship (1835–1852), Angelis became fascinated with history and began collecting original historical documents, many of which he included in his six-volume work *Colección de obras y documentos relativos a la historia antigua y moderna de las provincias del Río de la Plata. Ilustrada con notas y discertaciones* (1836–1837). He served as head of the government printing office and was head archivist. In 1852 Angelis sold his collection of over twenty-seven hundred books and twelve hundred manuscripts to the government of Brazil, where today they can be consulted in the National Library (in Rio de Janeiro) under *Colección de Angelis.*

RICARDO CAILLET-BOIS, RAFAEL ALBERTO ARRIETA, and DO-MINGO BUONCORE, eds., *Historia de la literatura argentina*, vol. 6 (1960), pp. 27–32. ELÍAS DÍAZ MILANO, *Vida y obra de Pedro de Angelis* (1968).

NICHOLAS P. CUSHNER

**ÂNGELO, IVAN** (*b.* 1936), Brazilian novelist, short story writer, and journalist. Born in Minas Gerais, Ângelo began his literary career in 1956 in Belo Horizonte, Minas Gerais, as an editor of the literary journal *Complemento*. Three years later he published a collection of short stories, *Homem sofrendo no quarto*, for which he was honored with the Prêmio Belo Horizonte. In 1966 he moved to São Paulo and began a career with the newspaper *Jornal da Tarde*, becoming editor in chief in 1984. Ângelo's very successful and highly political novel *A festa* (1976) details, in a fragmented style, life in Brazil under military rule in the early 1970s. *A Casa de vidro: Cinco histórias do Brasil* (1979) is a critical investigation of Brazilian society. A collection of dynamic short stories, *A face horrível* (1986), reveals the author's commitment to facing the social issues affecting the country.

EMIR RODRÍGUEZ MONEGAL, "Writing Fiction Under the Censor's Eye," in *World Literature Today* 53 (Winter 1979): 19–22; CANDACE SLATER, "A Triple Vision of Brazil," in *Review: Latin American Literature and Art* 32 (January–May 1984): 13–15; ROBERT E. DI ANTONIO, "The Confluence of Mythic, Historical, and Narrative Impulses in Ivan Angelo's *A Festa*," in *International Fiction Review* 14 (Winter 1987): 18–22; NELSON H. VIEIRA, "Ivan Angelo," in *Dictionary of Brazilian Literature*, edited by Irwin Stern (1988); pp. 29–30.

GARY M. VESSELS

**ANGOLA,** former Portuguese colony and independent country in west central Africa since 1975. Angola was one of Brazil's major trading partners before 1850 and homeland of many enslaved Africans imported into Latin America. The meanings of "Angola" have changed over time. "Ngola" first referred to the ruler of Ndongo, then to the hinterland of Luanda, and finally to the region from Cape Lopez to Benguela in southern Angola. Africans identified as "Angolans" in Latin America generally came from the Portuguese-controlled central region of Angola, in particular the capital Luanda and the Kwanza River valley, and the region between and to the east of Kasanje. Major populations include the Kongo of northern Angola, the Mbundu in the center, the Lunda-Chokwe to the east, and the Ovimbundu and Ngangela in southern Angola.

PHILIP D. CURTIN, *The Atlantic Slave Trade* (1969); MARY C. KARASCH, *Slave Life in Rio de Janeiro, 1808–1850* (1987); JOSEPH C. MILLER, *Way of Death* (1988).

MARY KARASCH

*See also* **Africa, Portuguese; Slavery; Slave Trade.**

**ANGOSTURA, CONGRESS OF,** convoked by Simón BOLÍVAR in order to place the patriot regime in Venezuela on a formal legal footing. At the opening session, held at the Orinoco River port of Angostura (today Ciudad Bolívar), on 15 February 1819, Bolívar delivered a major address in which he warned against imitation of Anglo-American institutions and called for a new constitution featuring a hereditary Senate and a "moral power" with special responsibility for education and morals. The Congress failed to act on these two suggestions but did produce a Venezuelan constitution and confirmed Bolívar as supreme commander.

The Congress had token representation of New Granadans, in line with Bolívar's strong commitment to union with the neighboring colonies. In December 1819, following the patriots' victory at Boyacá, the Congress formally proclaimed the union of all the former Viceroyalty of New Granada as the Republic of [Gran] Colombia. The Congress dissolved on 19 July 1820.

VICENTE LECUNA, comp. and HAROLD A. BIERCK, JR., ed., *Selected Writings of Simón Bolívar*, 2 vols. (1951), vol. 1, pp. 173–197, for Bolívar's address; GERHARD MASUR, *Simon Bolivar*, rev. ed. (1969), chap. 19.

DAVID BUSHNELL

**ANGUILLA,** the northernmost of the LEEWARD ISLANDS in the Caribbean. Settled by the British in 1650, the small, 35-square-mile island successfully repelled attacks by CARIB Indians in 1656, a contingent of Irishmen in 1688, and French marauders in 1745 and 1796. From the seventeenth to the nineteenth century, Anguilla attempted to develop a plantation economy, but failed because of inadequate rainfall. Remnants of the invasion forces and the subsequent introduction of slaves are seen in the ethnic mixture of the population. The estimated seventy-five hundred inhabitants are predominantly of African descent, with some European, especially Irish, blood.

In 1825, Anguilla became more closely linked politically to neighboring SAINT KITTS, in whose House of Assembly an Anguilla representative was seated. In 1871 Anguilla, along with Saint Kitts, became part of the Leeward Island Federation. Dominated historically by Saint Kitts, Anguilla petitioned unsuccessfully for direct rule from Britain. No political change occurred, however, until 1967, when Saint Kitts, Nevis, and Anguilla were granted self-government as an associated state of the United Kingdom. Anguilla seized the opportunity to launch a final offensive for separation from Saint Kitts. Attempts at mediation failed, and in 1969, British security forces invaded. In 1980, Anguilla successfully separated from the associated state, becoming a British dependent territory. In 1982, a new constitution, providing for self-government, was approved.

CENTRAL OFFICE OF INFORMATION FOR THE GOVERNMENT OF ANGUILLA, *Anguilla: The Basic Facts* (1979); COLVILLE L. PETTY, *Anguilla: Where There's a Will There's a Way* (1984).

D. M. SPEARS

**ANHANGUERA.** *See* **Bandeiras.**

**ANÍSIO, CHICO.** *See* **Chico Anísio.**

**ANNALS OF THE CAKCHIQUELS,** also called the *Memorial of Sololá,* are an account of KAQCHIKEL (Maya) history from their immigration to Guatemala through the Spanish invasion and up to the seventeenth century, compiled by two members of the Xajil royal lineage, Francisco Hernández Arana and Francisco Díaz.

The *Annals* present a charter for the future mapped out in the past. Following this charter, the Kaqchikel rose from subservience in Tulán to hegemony in Guatemala. Spanish arrival, and the concomitant wars and pestilence, brought social and economic disruption, followed by community restructuring. Subsequently the *Annals* list lineage births and deaths, land purchases, and church activities. Implicit in the charter, and explicit in current political rhetoric, is foreshadowed ethnic resurgence.

The preinvasion part of the document is linguistically and culturally "pure," eschewing loanwords and recording practices out of favor with the Spanish church and civil laws. Although the *Annals* evince less accommodation than the K'iche' (Quiché) POPOL VUH, it may be argued that the emphasis on lineage status and politics, in both the preinvasion and postinvasion sections, is partially a response to Spanish policy of awarding cacique privileges: tribute and work levies, as well as land titles.

DANIEL G. BRINTON, trans., *The Annals of the Cakchikels* (1885, repr. 1969); ROBERT M. CARMACK, *Quichean Civilization: The Ethnohistoric, Ethnographic, and Archaeological Sources* (1973), 47–50.

JUDITH M. MAXWELL IxQ'ANIL

**ANTARCTIC FRANCE.** *See* **French Colonization in Brazil.**

**ANTARCTICA.** In contrast to most North Americans, who tend to think of Antarctica as a remote and isolated continent, many Latin Americans, especially those in the SOUTHERN CONE, view Antarctica as relatively close and linked to the South American mainland through geology, geopolitics, and history. The tip of the Antarctic Peninsula is only about 600 miles from Tierra del Fuego, and two South American nations, Argentina and Chile, have made formal claims of sovereignty to portions of Antarctica. Furthermore, the 1947 RIO TREATY (Inter-American Treaty of Reciprocal Assistance) defines the security zone of the Americas as extending to the South Pole and includes the sectors claimed by Argentina and Chile. Thus, there is reason to speak of a "South American quadrant" of Antarctica extending from the Greenwich Meridian (0° longitude) to 90° west longitude.

No human being had seen Antarctica until early in the nineteenth century, when, within a few short years, British, Russian, and U.S. sailors reported discovering it. There is also a suggestion (unfortunately without documentation) that sealers operating out of Buenos Aires might have seen Antarctica as early as 1817.

During the so-called heroic period of Antarctic exploration in the early twentieth century, the southern nations of Latin America supported expeditions from Europe and the United States by providing them with supplies and assisting in rescue efforts when necessary. Two noteworthy efforts were the Argentine rescue of a Swedish expedition in 1903 and that of Sir Ernest Shackleton's crew by the Chileans a decade later.

By the late 1940s seven nations had made sovereignty claims to Antarctica, three of which (Argentina, Chile, and Great Britain) overlapped in the South American Antarctic quadrant. The nationalistic regime of Juan Domingo PERÓN in Argentina stressed the linkage between the Argentine Antarctic claim and the effort to recover Las Malvinas (FALKLAND ISLANDS). Tensions between Great Britain and Chile were exacerbated to the point that there were numerous diplomatic protests and at least one shooting incident.

To defuse Antarctic tensions, a group of twelve nations proposed a program of scientific cooperation (the International Geophysical Year, 1957–1958), and out of this effort grew the Antarctic Treaty (signed 1959; in force since 1961), which ensures that a demilitarized Antarctica is preserved for scientific study. The treaty does not permit new or expanded sovereignty claims, but does not require nations with preexisting claims to abandon them.

More than forty nations have signed the Antarctic Treaty, and almost half of these maintain permanent or temporary scientific stations on the ice. These include Argentina, Chile, Brazil, Uruguay, Peru, and Ecuador; Colombia and Cuba have also signed the treaty and have sent personnel to Antarctic bases of other countries.

Tensions over international competition for Antarctic resources, especially mineral deposits, were eased in October 1991 at a special meeting in Madrid, when the treaty members signed a "Protocol on Environmental Protection." The protocol confirms that Antarctica should be a special natural reserve dedicated to peace and science; a key provision bans mining activity in Antarctica for at least fifty years.

The sovereignty claims of Argentina and Chile remain in place, although there have been recent suggestions that the South American quadrant of Antarctica be subject to some form of condominium control by the group of six South American nations with bases in Antarctica.

PHILIP J. QUIGG, *A Pole Apart* (1983); DEBORAH SHAPLEY, *The Seventh Continent: Antarctica in a Resource Age* (1985); PETER J. BECK, *The International Politics of Antarctica* (1986); JACK CHILD, *Antarctica and South American Geopolitics: Frozen Lebensraum*

(1988); CARLOS J. MONETA, ed., *La Antártida en el sistema internacional del futuro* (1988); M. J. PETERSON, *Managing the Frozen South: The Origin and Evolution of the Antarctic Treaty System* (1988); READER'S DIGEST, *Antarctica*, 2d ed. (1990).

JACK CHILD

**ANTEQUERA.** *See* **Oaxaca.**

**ANTEQUERA Y CASTRO, JOSÉ DE** (*b.* 1693; *d.* 5 July 1731), governor of Paraguay (1721–1725) and leader of an anti-JESUIT uprising. In 1724 Antequera led Paraguayan forces into battle against a Jesuit-trained GUARANI militia from the missions who sought to remove him from office. Born in Panama, Antequera was the son of a Spanish bureaucrat. Educated first by Jesuits, he earned his licentiate in arts and doctorate in law in CHARCAS and Lima and went to Spain to seek employment. He became a member of the Order of Alcántara and secured an appointment for several years as protector of the Indians for the Audiencia of Charcas, where his father had once been a judge (*oidor*). As acting prosecutor (*fiscal*) in 1720, he took sides in a feud between Paraguayans and Jesuits that reached the *audiencia*. He undertook a judicial review of an unpopular governor, Diego de los Reyes y Balmaceda, an ally of the Jesuits, and simultaneously got the *audiencia* to name him next governor of Paraguay, a common but technically illegal combination, although the viceroy confirmed the appointment.

After Antequera arrived in Paraguay in 1721, he removed Reyes from office, took a Paraguayan mistress, and befriended an opponent of the Jesuits, José de Ávalos y Mendoza. In retaliation, the Jesuits had the viceroy reinstate Reyes, although he never again served. In 1722 the Jesuits helped Reyes flee to Corrientes, infuriating Paraguayans and from there threatening Antequera. The latter insisted that the Jesuits accept him as governor. Antequera argued that the dispute was a matter of justice, not government, and that the *audiencia*, not the viceroy, had jurisdiction. The *audiencia* agreed until 1724, when an aggressive viceroy, José de ARMENDÁRIZ, challenged the Charcas judges. He ordered an army of mission Guaranis led by Baltasar García Ros, lieutenant governor of Buenos Aires, to depose Antequera, but 3,000 Paraguayans with Antequera destroyed the smaller Guarani force in August 1724 at the Tebicuary River. They then expelled the Jesuits from Asunción.

Antequera's victory made his position untenable. The viceroy, the Jesuits, officials in Buenos Aires, and the new bishop of Paraguay, José de Palos, opposed him. His former colleagues in Charcas cut him adrift, and in 1725 he fled to Córdoba, where Franciscans sheltered him, and then moved to Charcas. He was apprehended and sent to Lima. From 1726 to 1731, he was jailed at the viceregal court, where he prepared his defense. Renewed rebellion in Paraguay in 1730 caused the viceroy to demand that the Audiencia of Lima find Antequera guilty of heresy and treason, and the judges complied. They ordered his execution and that of his principal lieutenant, Juan de Mena. The sentence was so unpopular that it provoked a riot in Lima, and the viceroy's troops shot Antequera on his way to the gallows. Four decades after Antequera's death, King Charles III, who had expelled Antequera's Jesuit enemies from Spain in 1767, posthumously exonerated Antequera. In Asunción, Antequera's legacies were the spirit of rebellion and José Cañete, his natural son and father of the noted jurist Pedro Vicente Cañete. Antequera's memory is honored by streets named for him in Asunción and Lima.

*Colección general de documentos que contiene los sucesos tocantes á la segunda época de las conmociones de los Regulares de la Compañía en el Paraguay y señaladamente la persecución que hicieron a don Josef de Antequera y Castro* (1769); JAMES SCHOFIELD SAEGER, "Origins of the Rebellion of Paraguay," in *Hispanic American Historical Review* 52, no. 2 (1972): 215–229, and "Institutional Rivalries, Jurisdictional Disputes, and Vested Interests in the Viceroyalty of Peru: José de Antequera and the Rebellion of Paraguay," in *The Americas: A Quarterly Review of Inter-American Cultural History* 32, no. 1 (1975): 99–116; ADALBERTO LÓPEZ, *The Revolt of the Comuneros, 1721–1735: A Study in the Colonial History of Paraguay* (1976).

JAMES SCHOFIELD SAEGER

**ANTICLERICALISM** was both a widespread attitude and a deeply ingrained sentiment among Latin America's intellectual and political elites who viewed organized religion, especially the Roman Catholic church, as a threat to the state and an obstacle to social change. Although anticlericalism reached its zenith in the nineteenth century, it had its roots in the eighteenth and perdured as a powerful force well into the twentieth. It was an attitude shared by both conservatives and liberals, although not always for the same reasons.

Conservative anticlericalism was rooted in the struggle of the enlightened Catholic monarchs of Europe and their liberal advisers to reform the church and to subordinate it to the crown's interests. Charles III, influenced by the count of Aranda, Pedro Rodríguez de CAMPOMANES, and others, represented the apogee of regalism, the Spanish form of Gallicanism. Both doctrines claimed that the king had the right to exercise temporal authority over the church, including the power to name bishops and collect tithes. The marquis de POMBAL, with the full approval of the Portuguese crown, led the way by expelling the JESUITS from both Portugal and Brazil in 1759. These governing elites believed that in order for their nations to be great once again, they must modernize themselves. To do so would involve, most of all, reforming the church, which in Spain, Portugal, and the New World had come to resemble the church as it had been on the eve of the Reformation. The eighteenth-century church in the Hispanic-Lusitanian world had

TRES ÉPOCAS

PARTIDO LIBERAL

MINISTERIO DE JUSTICIA

PLAN DE TUXTEPEC

AYER

HOY

MAÑANA.

Anticlerical political cartoon in the Mexican newspaper *El Hijo del Ahuizote*. BENSON LATIN AMERICAN COLLECTION, UNIVERSITY OF TEXAS AT AUSTIN.

acquired enormous properties held in mortmain; monasteries and convents were overpopulated; and a tradition-laden clergy was a source of frequent scandal. Many of the reform measures that the newly independent states in Hispanic America enacted to limit the number of the clergy or to reduce church wealth were in fact modeled on earlier BOURBON REFORMS.

The regalist tradition, fashioned in Spain and Portugal, resurfaced in one way or another in every one of the new republics. Simón BOLÍVAR, although not unfriendly to the church, sought to impose restraints and controls on it. But other leaders, such as José Gaspar Rodríguez de FRANCIA in Paraguay and Guzmán Blanco in Venezuela, subjected the church to harsh scrutiny and did not hesitate to expel or even to execute priests, confiscate church property, and curtail clerical influence in every way possible. Even where conservatives considered the church an ally, they nonetheless viewed with suspicion any independent activity on its part. They resented any outside influence on the church, which meant especially the pope. In Brazil, relations between Dom PEDRO II and the church, with the exception of a clash with the bishops (1873–1875), were in general rather harmonious, and the church survived the monarchy relatively unscathed.

Liberals shared with the conservatives the belief that the church should be subordinate to the aims of the newly independent states. In this sense most Latin American liberals were essentially regalists in their treatment of the church. But unlike the conservatives, they also wanted a more open, democratic society based on law. For this reason they, like liberals in Europe, considered the church, with its landed estates, special privileges, and extraordinary influence in society as the primary obstacle in the way of implanting republican ideals and bringing about social change. The liberals were influenced by the criticism the philosophers of the ENLIGHTENMENT had leveled at organized religion, by the example of Protestant Europe and America, and by certain liberal doctrines within Catholicism itself that called for church reform. In particular, the ideas of the Gallicanist Abbé de Pradt and other European thinkers who proposed the creation of a national church freed from the tutelage of Rome, were well received by Bolívar, Bernardino RIVADAVIA in Argentina, and certain liberals in Peru.

Liberal anticlericalism mirrored the same phenomenon in Europe, but given Latin America's slower development, it arrived in the New World in smaller dosages and in differentiated phases. In general, three distinct phases can be discerned: an incipient but rather tepid anticlericalism at the time of Independence; a more aggressive mid-century anticlericalism, which coincided with the rise of liberal capitalism; and in the latter part of the century a more socially minded and openly antireligious anticlericalism, which reflected the influence of POSITIVISM.

In general, most liberals at the time of Independence were neither antireligious nor desirous of destroying the church. Rather, they sought to control it, reform it, and place it at the service of the new republics. Many of the first liberals were priests who supported the reforms. Singled out for reform from the beginning, however, were the religious orders. The liberals, not unlike the Protestant reformers, viewed religious life as an aberration in the history of Christianity. Also, given the fact that there were far more Spanish missionaries among the religious than among the secular clergy before Independence, the former were more readily associated in the public mind with the colonial past. Early on in Mexico, Peru, Gran Colombia, and Argentina, liberals enacted laws that severely limited the number of religious and that placed them under the control of the local bishops. The Jesuits in particular were the *bête noire* of the liberals, who had the newly returned Society of Jesus expelled from many of their countries.

As the century wore on, in Europe liberal hostility toward the church increased, and the church in turn, especially during the pontificate of Pius IX (1846–1878), assumed a more defiant attitude toward liberalism. In Latin America a second generation of liberals, determined to bring about social reform and influenced by utilitarian philosophies, became considerably more outspoken in its criticism of the church. In Chile, Francisco BILBAO, essayist and politician, equated Catholicism with absolutism. In Peru, Francisco de Paula GONZÁLEZ VIGIL was excommunicated for championing the cause of freeing both the church and governments from the influence of the Roman Curia.

By mid-century, liberal minorities in Peru, Colombia, and Mexico had declared open war on the church's wealth, properties, and privileges, especially the ecclesiastical FUERO. In Mexico the church decried the Reform Laws of Benito JUÁREZ and welcomed MAXIMILIAN's rule. Liberalism in Mexico in particular made control of the church a cornerstone of its reformist thrust. The strong anticlerical articles in the Constitution of 1917 reflected the liberals' perception of the church as both a conservative and an antinationalist force. In a similar way, in Ecuador toward the end of the century José Eloy ALFARO DELGADO swept aside all of the church's privileges, which had been created in Gabriel GARCÍA MORENO's time, and opened the door to Protestant missionaries.

Finally, in the latter part of the nineteenth century, anticlericalism entered a third phase by assuming the mantle of positivism and scientific progress. Intellectuals such as Manuel GONZÁLEZ PRADA in Peru went beyond denouncing church privileges; they attacked religion itself. González Prada, like other pro-Indian advocates, singled out clerical influence on the indigenous population as one of the principal reasons for Latin America's backwardness. In universities and avant-garde circles, intellectuals accused the clergy of maintaining women, children, and the lower classes in ignorance by appealing to their emotions and catering to their superstitions.

The greatest number of anticlerical laws in Latin America were enacted in the decade of 1880–1890. These laws called for obligatory civil marriage, the end of clerical control of the civil registry, the secularization of cemeteries, the end of the church's monopoly over public charities, and in some cases the laicization of education. Separation of church and state, unrestricted tolerance for non-Catholics, and the right to divorce were measures that only gained acceptance in most countries in the twentieth century.

Anticlericalism was an attitude most prevalent among the emerging capitalistically oriented middle and upper classes, usually centered in the capital and port cities. These classes were especially receptive to innovative and radical ideas from Europe. Masonic lodges in particular became the nerve centers of hostility toward the church. Anticlericalism, by way of contrast, was much less observable among the traditional upper-class families of the rural interior or the urban lower middle classes, for whom Catholicism was perceived as a source of stability. In general, anticlericalism was not a common attitude among the lower classes, least of all the Indians and blacks.

As a psychological phenomenon, anticlericalism can be explained in part as an expression of the liberals' frustration over the survival of the colonial mentality and its tenacious hold over the majority of Latin Americans long after Independence, and the subsequent lack of social progress that resulted from that influence. For many liberals and social reformers, hostility toward the church became the principal mode of rejecting that colonial past. Anticlericalism was also primarily a masculine attitude. Most women, even the wives of leading liberals, continued to practice their religion as in colonial times. Insofar as liberalism stood for freedom and the use of reason, Catholicism symbolized passive submission to authority and dogma.

In time classical liberalism was superseded by reform ideologies and thinkers with a more subtle and sophisticated view of religion and social change, and anticlericalism began fading away. Most important, since the Second Vatican Council, the church has undergone a historic reform and renewal, relieving some of the old sources of antagonism.

On regalism in Bourbon Spain see RICHARD HERR, *The Eighteenth-Century Revolution in Spain* (1958) and JOHN LYNCH, *Bourbon Spain, 1700–1808* (1989). An overview of church-state conflicts can be found in J. LLOYD MECHAM, *Church and State in Latin America: A History of Politico-Ecclesiastical Relations*, 2d ed. (1966). To understand the intellectual background of anticlericalism see LEOPOLDO ZEA, *The Latin American Mind*, translated by James H. Abbot and Lowell Dunham (1963). On González Prada and other Peruvian anticlerics see JEFFREY KLAIBER, *Religion and Revolution in Peru, 1824–1976* (1977). On anticlericalism in Mexico see ROBERT E. QUIRK, *The Mexican Revolution and the Catholic Church, 1910–1929* (1973).

JEFFREY KLAIBER, S. J.

*See also* **Catholic Church; Masonic Orders.**

**ANTIGUA,** largest of a three-island unit in the Leeward Islands that, along with Barbuda and Redonda, comprises the independent state of Antigua and Barbuda.

Although the island was sighted during Columbus's second voyage to the Caribbean in 1493, geography and a lack of natural resources, including a limited supply of fresh water, conspired to deter sustained, permanent settlement by both the indigenous peoples of the region, the Arawaks and the CARIBS, and the conquering Spanish. Unguarded and unexploited for over a century, Antigua was seized by an English expedition in 1632. Initially populated by small-scale subsistence and tobacco farmers, the island became a producer of sugarcane in the 1660s, a change that, with the subsequent introduction of African slaves, completely transformed the nature of the colony. By 1700 Antigua had developed into a traditional plantation society comprised of large estates, a small European planter class, and large numbers of slave laborers.

Full integration into the British mercantile system as

a sugar producer provided Antigua with a secure, stable market into the nineteenth century. By the 1830s, however, as abolition and free trade became imperial policy, this flourishing dependence had begun to collapse. Acceptance of crown colony status in 1868 by the island elites preserved the basic features of colonial life, though growing numbers of bankrupt sugar estates and newly formed free villages of ex-slaves heralded the eventual stagnation of plantation society.

As the old planter and bureaucratic elite declined in numbers and influence in the early decades of the twentieth century, Antigua's long-oppressed lower classes began to mobilize. Inspired by the labor movements and pan-Africanist ideology that swept through the Caribbean in the years following World War I, local blacks formed the Antigua Trades and Labor Union (ATLU) in 1939 to promote political, economic, and social reforms. In the years that followed, as Britain began its long process of decolonization, the ATLU and its political wing, the Antigua Labor Party (ALP), under the leadership of Vere Bird, came to dominate island politics.

Having guided Antigua to independence in 1981, Bird became its first prime minister and proceeded to set up a personalist regime based on extensive corruption and nepotism, before passing power to his son, Vere, Jr., in 1994. With the almost total elimination of agro-exports from its economy, the island and its government have become reliant upon U.S. capital and tourism, thereby perpetuating Antigua's traditional dependent status.

HENRY PAGET, *Peripheral Capitalism and Underdevelopment in Antigua* (1985); FRANKLIN W. KNIGHT, *The Caribbean: The Genesis of a Fragmented Nationalism*, 2d ed. (1990); ROBERT CORAM, *Caribbean Time Bomb: The United States' Complicity in the Corruption of Antigua* (1993).

TIMOTHY P. HAWKINS

**ANTIGUA (LA ANTIGUA GUATEMALA).** The appellation came into being several years after devastating earthquakes in July and December of 1773 forced Spanish crown officials, over church and local opposition, to move the capital of Spanish Central America from Antigua, then known as Santiago de Guatemala, to the present site of Guatemala City.

Capital of the AUDIENCIA of Guatemala from 1541 to 1773 (for all but several short periods) and the most important city of the region, Antigua was conceived out of natural disaster. Santiago en Almolonga, its predecessor, was founded in 1527 on the lower northern slopes of the dormant Agua volcano. As the first permanent capital of Guatemala it lasted but fourteen years. In early September 1541, after three days of heavy rain, a mudslide exploded down the steep slopes of Agua, largely destroying the settlement's Spanish core.

Within months of the destruction of the old city (known as Ciudad Vieja), and after much debate, local authorities decided on a location in the Panchoy Valley,

about 3 miles north of Santiago en Almolonga. By late 1541, the city's *cabildo* (city council) had begun to supervise laying out the new city.

All of the Indian slaves and many *naborias* (dependent servants) held by the city's Spanish *vecinos* (citizens) were freed in 1549–1550 by order of the *audiencia* president, Alonso LÓPEZ DE CERRATO, as part of his efforts to enforce the NEW LAWS, promulgated by Spain in 1542. Angry at losing their labor force to emancipation, Santiago's Spanish *vecinos* were further incensed when the religious orders persuaded large numbers of these freedmen and their families to establish barrios in the shelter of their monasteries, on the perimeter of the Spanish city.

Thus, within a decade of its founding, Santiago had a Spanish core abutted on three sides by Indian communities. It was a microcosm of the Spanish ideal of "two republics," whereby Spaniards and Indians lived and worked beside each other while maintaining separate statuses and social identities. However, because the Indians, highly vulnerable to Old World diseases, began to decline drastically and were seen as incapable of hard labor, small numbers of African slaves were introduced into Spanish Central America before 1550. Confined at first to rural mines and sugar plantations, black, and later MULATTO, slaves were brought to Santiago's Spanish households.

Due to the shortage of Spanish women, the Spanish community absorbed a number of Indian women. It also admitted some *casta* (mixed) offspring, especially legitimate children of both sexes and illegitimate mestizas (female offspring of Indian–Spanish unions). MESTIZOS not taken into the Spanish community either retained the *casta* status or entered the Indian group.

By the 1560s and 1570s, free *castas*, free blacks, and even poor Spaniards began to spill into the Indian barrios adjoining the Spanish city. Such intrusions led to Indian displacement, Indian–*casta* unions, and an increased likelihood of either Indian Hispanization or flight to rural areas to escape both tribute payment and the onerous labor obligations associated with Indian tributary status. These factors, combined with the impact of epidemic disease, resulted in the decline of Indian tributary populations and barrio self-rule.

Santiago in the late seventeenth and eighteenth centuries was a large urban center of over 30,000 inhabitants. It had a large multiethnic artisan population and served as a center for both the distribution of imported trade goods and the collection and sale of Indian tribute items for crown and individual *encomenderos* (recipients of Indian tribute). Santiago also served as an entrepôt for the export trade in CACAO, HIDES, TOBACCO, and INDIGO.

Antigua has enjoyed a varied existence since its destruction in 1773. During the late eighteenth century (and later), its colonial ruins served as a source of architectural details (doors, grills, etc.) for the buildings of the new capital and elsewhere; its crumbling walls, as a

The Cathedral of Antigua, Guatemala, ca. 1907. LATIN AMERICAN LIBRARY, TULANE UNIVERSITY.

source of saltpeter for making gunpowder. In the early nineteenth century, Antigua was one of Guatemala's main centers of COCHINEAL production. By the 1850s, the city and its fertile surrounding lands began to be intensively devoted to COFFEE production.

Despite the post-1773 dismemberment of Antigua's colonial architectural heritage and the important role of coffee cultivation, the city in recent decades has been recognized by regional and international bodies as a cultural monument worthy of preservation. Set amid spectacular natural surroundings, its numerous colonial ruins, public buildings, and houses rebuilt in the colonial style have made Antigua a tourist center and a magnet for a sizable resident foreign community.

Important and accessible studies on Antigua's architectural history are SIDNEY DAVID MARKMAN, *Colonial Architecture of Antigua Guatemala* (1967); and VERLE L. ANNIS, *The Architecture of Antigua Guatemala, 1543–1773* (1968). Antigua's social and population histories are analyzed in CHRISTOPHER H. LUTZ, *Santiago de Guatemala, 1541–1773: City, Caste, and the Colonial Experience* (1994). Important aspects of the city's sixteenth- and seventeenth-century socioeconomic and political elite history are covered in PILAR SANCHIZ OCHOA, *Los hidalgos de Guatemala: Realidad y apariencia en un sistema de valores* (1976); and STEPHEN A. WEBRE, "The Social and Economic Bases of Cabildo Membership in Seventeenth Century Santiago de Guatemala," (Ph.D. diss., Tulane University, 1980). The destruction and move of the capital city are described in MARÍA CRISTINA ZILBERMANN DE LUJÁN, *Aspectos socioeconómicos del traslado de la Ciudad de Guatemala (1773–1783)* (1987). MANUEL RUBIO SÁNCHEZ, *Monografía de la ciudad de Antigua Guatemala* (1989), is one of the few studies to adequately consider the city's history

after the 1773 earthquake and the move of the capital to what is now Guatemala City.

CHRISTOPHER H. LUTZ

**ANTILLES.** *See* **Caribbean Antilles.**

**ANTIOQUIA,** a department in northwestern Colombia comprising an area of 24,600 square miles. In 1985, the department had a population of 3,828,000, concentrated in the temperate valleys of the Central and Western Cordilleras. The capital of Antioquia is MEDELLÍN, the second largest city in Colombia. Named after the Syrian city of Antioch, the department has played a leading role in the economic development of Colombia, and its people, known as *paisas*, are sometimes said to constitute a "race" different from that of other Colombians.

Little is known about Antioquia's indigenous population, which may have numbered as many as 600,000 at the time of the arrival of the first Spaniards under Jorge de Robledo, who founded Santa Fé de Antioquia in 1541. Early settlers were lured by reports of gold in the area, especially the lode at Buriticá and the placers of the Nechí and Cauca rivers. Gold MINING, sustained by the labor of African slaves, remained a mainstay of the local economy throughout the colonial period, eventually being supplemented by commerce, stock raising, and agriculture. The region experienced considerable economic growth in the late eighteenth century, a development that some historians attribute to reforms introduced by Juan Antonio MON Y VELARDE, a judge of the Bogotá AUDIENCIA (high court), who conducted a VISITA (official investigation) of Antioquia from 1782 to 1785.

Between the eighteenth and twentieth centuries, Antioqueño colonizers established many new settlements to the south and southwest of the original province. This process of expansion is prominent in the myth of Antioqueño distinctiveness, although colonization was probably not as egalitarian as was once believed. Part of the territory colonized by the Antioqueños was detached from the department to form the new department of Caldas in 1905. Its capital, Manizales, was founded by Antioqueños in 1848.

In the twentieth century, Antioquia and Caldas became major coffee producers, accounting for 36 percent of Colombia's total output by 1914 and 47 percent by the late 1950s. Antioquia also became Colombia's principal industrial center with the establishment of large factories producing textiles, apparel, and other consumer goods. The department's economic growth was spurred by improved transportation, notably completion of a railroad in 1929 linking Medellín with the Magdalena River at Puerto Berrío and extensive road construction afterward.

Numerous explanations have arisen to account for the entrepreneurial skills of the Antioqueños as well as their propensity to colonize. Some have attributed these qualities to the Basque ancestry of early settlers in the region. Others have stressed habits derived from their experience in mining or have argued that gold mining and associated commerce generated the capital necessary for investment in industry. By the late twentieth century, however, Antioquia's economic primacy had diminished as other regions industrialized.

JAMES J. PARSONS, *Antioqueño Colonization in Western Colombia*, rev. ed. (1968); KEITH H. CHRISTIE, "Antioqueño Colonization in Western Colombia: A Reappraisal," in *Hispanic American Historical Review* 58 (1978):260–283; JAIME SIERRA GARCÍA, *Cronología de Antioquia* (1982); ANN TWINAM, *Miners, Merchants, and Farmers in Colonial Colombia* (1982).

HELEN DELPAR

**ANTOFAGASTA,** largest province of the Norte Grande region and the most vast territory of continental Chile, with 50,578 square miles. The 407,409 (1992) inhabitants live in an extremely arid environment dotted with only a few river and piedmont oases. The region's major urban area, Antofagasta (population 218,754), is located on the coast and has been the main port for the exportation of minerals extracted from the interior of the

*Horizontes* by Francisco A. Cano, 1913. Considered a symbol of Antioquia. BOLSA DE VALORES, MEDELLÍN, COLOMBIA.

province. Calama on the Loa River (population 109,645) is the second major center and thrives on the activities of CHUQUICAMATA—the largest open-pit copper mine in the world. Other settlements are the port of Tocopilla and the fishing town of Mejillones.

Most of the province of Antofagasta became part of littoral Bolivia after the country was instituted by Simón Bolívar in 1825. It was thinly occupied by Bolivia and largely settled by Chilean guano gatherers and miners. The WAR OF THE PACIFIC (1879–1884) resulted in Bolivia's loss of this region to Chile and the beginning of an active exploitation of the rich nitrate deposits and metal mines of the interior by Chilean-Anglo-American companies. Today the region's economy is supplemented by modern fisheries, most of them owned by Chileans.

INSTITUTO GEOGRÁFICO MILITAR, "La Región de Antofagasta" in *Geografía de Chile,* vol. 23 (Santiago, 1986).

CÉSAR N. CAVIEDES

*See also* **Mining; Nitrate Industry.**

**ANTONIL, ANDRÉ JOÃO.** *See* **Andreoni, João Antônio.**

**ANTÔNIO CONSELHEIRO.** *See* **Conselheiro, Antônio.**

**ANTUÑANO, ESTEVAN DE** (*b.* 1792; *d.* 1847), Mexican industrialist. One of Mexico's first modern industrialists, Antuñano was born in Veracruz into a Spanish immigrant family. He was educated in Spain and in England, where he became familiar with industrial production. In the 1830s he led the modernization of the textile industry in Puebla, setting up Mexico's first mechanized spinning factory, La Constancia Mexicana, which produced cotton yarn on Arkwright spindles powered by the waters of the Río Atoyac. By the early 1840s, he owned four such factories in Puebla.

An enlightened entrepreneur, Antuñano recognized that the mechanization of spinning deprived women and children of employment and tried to alleviate the problem by turning La Constancia into a model experiment in the employment of family labor. He provided both housing and health care for his workers. Unfortunately, wages were low and people worked eleven to sixteen hours daily.

A vigorous propagandist, who authored over sixty pamphlets, Antuñano had a vision of national development. He wanted to see the traditional manufacturing center of Puebla wrest control of northern Mexican markets, then dependent on contraband. Trade with the north would revitalize Mexico's central cities and agricultural districts. Silver exports would bring in foreign exchange. His vision floundered on the realities of the scarcity of raw cotton and currency, the persistence of contraband, and national disintegration. Antuñano died

Estevan de Antuñano. Anonymous. BENSON LATIN AMERICAN COLLECTION, UNIVERSITY OF TEXAS AT AUSTIN.

of natural causes during the U.S. Army's occupation of the city of Puebla. A French merchant, to whom he owed money, acquired most of his properties.

MIGUEL A. QUINTANA, *Estevan de Antuñano,* 2 vols. (1957); JAN BAZANT, "Industria algodonera poblana de 1803–1843 en números," in *Historia Mexicana* 14 (July-September 1964): 131–143; GUY P. C. THOMSON, *Puebla de los Angeles: Industry and Society in a Mexican City, 1700–1850* (1989).

MARY KAY VAUGHAN

**ANTÚNEZ, NEMESIO** (*b.* 1918; *d.* 19 May 1993), Chilean artist, whose work is characterized by optical and psychological effects achieved by means of perspective distortions and geometric configurations. Antúnez's work has been classified as surrealist, due to the unusual effects resulting from his manipulation of space. He studied architecture at Catholic University in his native Santiago from 1937 to 1943 and at Columbia University in New York City in 1945. A fellowship enabled him to study with Stanley W. Hayter of Atelier 17 in New York in 1947. In 1950 he followed Hayter to Paris.

After returning to Chile in 1953, he organized *Taller 99*, an artists' collective. In the late 1950s his work anticipated op art effects, with an emphasis on expression. He executed a mural, *Heart of the Andes*, at the United Nations (1966). A characteristic presentation of space in Antúnez's painting consists of rectangular boxes telescoping out of one another as though suspended in a void. Seemingly transparent planes and figures are used to create the illusion of endless expanses of space. Minuscule anthropomorphic figures often populate these spatial configurations (e.g., *New York, New York 10008*, 1967). His work consolidates the heritage of geometric art and surrealism, two strong movements in the art of Latin America.

Antúnez held several administrative posts, including director of the Museum of Contemporary Art, University of Chile, Santiago (1961–1964), cultural attaché at the Chilean embassy, New York City (1964–1969); director, National Museum of Fine Arts, Santiago (1969–1973).

LOWERY S. SIMS, "New York Dada and New World Surrealism," in Luis Cancel et al., *The Latin American Spirit: Art and Artists in the United States, 1920–1970* (1988), pp. 174–175.

MARTA GARSD

**ANZA, JUAN BAUTISTA DE** (*b.* 1736; *d.* 19 December 1788), military officer, governor of New Mexico (1778–1788). One of the most effective instruments of the BOURBON REFORMS on the northern frontier of New Spain, Anza was born at the presidio of Fronteras (Sonora), where his father, a member of the landowning-military-merchant elite, served as commander. While captain at Tubac (present-day southern Arizona), young Anza led an exploring party overland to southern California in 1774, and in 1775–1776, by the same route, he escorted the colonists who founded San Francisco. Appointed governor in 1777, Anza rode personally with the combined Hispano-Indian force that defeated Cuerno Verde, the Comanches' leading war chief, in New Mexico in 1779. His diplomacy resulted in treaties and alliances, first with the COMANCHES in 1786, and then with the Utes, Jicarilla APACHES, and NAVAJOS. A generation of relative peace ensued, with steady growth of the Hispanic population and unprecedented territorial expansion. Anza died in Arizpe (Sonora).

Anza is deserving of a new biography. Older works include: HERBERT E. BOLTON, *Outpost of Empire* (1931), and ALFRED B. THOMAS, *Forgotten Frontiers: A Study of the Spanish Indian Policy of Don Juan Bautista de Anza, Governor of New Mexico, 1777–1787* (1932).

JOHN L. KESSELL

**ANZOÁTEGUI, JOSÉ ANTONIO** (*b.* 14 November 1789; *d.* 15 November 1819), officer in the Venezuelan Emancipating Army. Anzoátegui was on the pro-independence side from the beginning of the independence movement in 1810. In his birthplace of Barcelona, Venezuela, he stood out as a leader of the SOCIEDAD PATRIOTICA DE CARACAS who was in favor of emancipation. Anzoátegui took part in the Guiana campaign of 1812, and when the First Republic fell, he was imprisoned in the vaults of La Guaira.

Anzoátegui returned to war in 1813 and fought in numerous battles. He helped Simón BOLÍVAR take the city of Bogotá in 1814; participated in the two Los Cayos expeditions financed by Alexandre Pétion, president of Haiti; was present at the taking of Angostura in 1817, in the Los Llanos campaign of 1818, and in the campaign for the liberation of New Granada in 1819. Bolívar placed him in charge of operations in Santa Marta and Maracaibo, but his death prevented him from carrying out his mission. For his military actions, he was decorated with the Order of the Liberators of Venezuela and the Boyacá Cross.

ESTEBAN CHALBAUD-CARDONA, *Anzoátegui (general de infantería)* (1941); FABIO LOZANO Y LOZANO, *Anzoátegui: Visiones de la Guerra de Independencia* (1963); and CARLOS SÁNCHEZ ESPEJO, *Vida útil y gloriosa* (1970).

INÉS QUINTERO

**APACHES,** twelve linguistically related tribes which occupied an extensive territory in present-day Arizona and New Mexico. They combined hunting and gathering with small-scale agriculture. Initially attracted to the material benefits of the Spanish MISSIONS, they subsequently rejected the regulation of their lives and the attempt to suppress their traditional religion and its practice. They launched a general uprising in 1677, initiating a century of hostility that halted the extension of the northern frontier of the Viceroyalty of New Spain. The Bourbon crown's expansion of presidio garrisons and initiation of subsistence rations in the 1770s brought generally peaceful relations into the 1820s, with a substantial growth in the Hispanic population south of Apache-dominated areas.

The gradual dissolution of the presidio garrisons for want of material support, and the attempt by state officials in the early 1830s to force the Apaches to become sedentary workers in order to receive subsistence rations, led to a renewal of the periodic, devastating Apache raids. The frontier countryside was slowly depopulated. Though U.S. annexation after 1848 carried with it the promise of controlling Apache incursions, for nearly three decades the United States limited itself to protecting the settlements on its side of the border. Only in the 1880s, when the U.S. and Mexican governments reached an agreement on mutual border crossing were the Apache raids ended, with the remnants of the tribes permanently restricted to reservations.

JOHN UPTON TERRELL, *Apache Chronicle* (1972); JOHN L. KESSELL, *Friars, Soldiers, and Reformers: Hispanic Arizona and the Sonora Mission Frontier 1767–1856* (1976); DAVID J. WEBER, *The*

*Mexican Frontier, 1821–1846: The American Southwest Under Mexico* (1982); FRANCISCO R. ALMADA, *Diccionario de historia, geografía y biografía de sonorenses* (1983), pp. 56–63.

STUART F. VOSS

**APALACHEE**, a native people whose name was given to a Spanish mission province in northwest Florida and mistakenly given to the Appalachian Mountains. The Apalachee, associated with the late pre-Columbian Fort Walton archaeological culture, inhabited the region from the Aucilla River west to the Ochlockonee River. Throughout their history the Apalachee were farmers governed by a paramount chief and a hierarchy of village chiefs and officials. At the time of the first European contact (the Pánfilo de NÁRVAEZ expedition in 1528), they numbered about fifty thousand. Hernando de SOTO's army wintered at the Apalachee town of Anhaica for five months in 1539–1540. The resulting introduction of diseases and military conflict had a severe impact.

Beginning in 1633 Spanish Franciscan priests established missions in Apalachee. Nine to fifteen missions, most with several satellite villages, functioned throughout the remainder of the seventeenth century. When English raiders from the Carolinas, aided by native allies, destroyed the missions in 1703–1704, the Apalachee population, which by 1675 had stabilized at about eight thousand, was shattered. Survivors were enslaved or fled. A handful of Apalachee survived into the nineteenth century in Texas.

MARK F. BOYD, HALE G. SMITH, and JOHN W. GRIFFIN, *Here They Once Stood: The Tragic End of the Apalachee Missions* (1951); JOHN H. HANN, *Apalachee: The Land Between the Rivers* (1988); CHARLES R. EWEN, "Anhaica: Discovery of Hernando de Soto's 1539–1540 Winter Camp," in *First Encounters: Spanish Explorations in the Caribbean and the United States, 1492–1570,* edited by Jerald T. Milanich and Susan Milbrath (1989).

JERALD T. MILANICH

*See also* **Missions: Spanish America.**

**APARECIDA, NOSSA SENHORA DA** (Our Lady of Aparecida), the Virgin of Conception, is the patron saint of Brazil. She first appeared in 1717 as a terra-cotta image in the net of three poor fishermen in the Paraíba River between Rio de Janeiro and São Paulo. The 15-inch image is said to have miraculously provided large catches to supply the table for visiting Dom Pedro Miguel, then governor of São Paulo and Minas Gerais. A chapel built in 1745 was replaced by a church in 1852 and by a larger edifice in 1888. Pope Pius XI proclaimed Aparecida the patron saint of Brazil in 1930. Today, hundreds of thousands of pilgrims annually visit the Basilica of Aparecida in São Paulo, especially in May, October, and December.

Rubem César Fernandes views Aparecida as a weak national symbol for two major reasons. The first is Brazil's strong regionalism, based on geographic and historical differences. Other religious figures, such as Padre CÍCERO in the northeast and Nosso Senhor do BONFIM in Salvador, are evidence of this regionalism. Aparecida is recognized as the principal religious shrine in the south-central region, comprised by the states São Paulo, Rio de Janeiro, and Minas Gerais, whose importance in national politics may help explain why Aparecida was chosen as the national patron saint. The second reason Aparecida is considered a weak national figure is because the clergy and the majority of the faithful worship her in different ways. The pilgrims see themselves as depending on her protection in exchange for a promise, while the clergy views her more as a mediator and in terms of sacred mysteries.

LUÍS DA CÂMARA CASCUDO, *Dicionário do folclore brasileiro,* 2d ed. (1962), pp. 56–57; RUBEM CÉSAR FERNANDES, "Aparecida: Nossa rainha, senhora e mãe, saravá!" in Viola Sachs et al., *Brasil & EUA: Religião e identidade nacional* (1988), pp. 85–111.

ESTHER J. PRESSEL

**APOLINAR** (Pablo Livinalli Santaella; *b.* 23 July 1928), Venezuelan artist. Although born in the small town of Guatire, Apolinar has spent his life in Petare, near Caracas. His preference for religious themes derives from years spent in a Catholic boarding school. He became an artist in 1965, when he produced his first painting, *The Bolivarian Neighborhood.* Since then his works have combined a primitive style with religious intimacy. In 1967 three of his paintings were included in the First Retrospective of Twentieth-Century Venezuelan Primitive Art, at the Musical Circle Gallery in Caracas. In the early 1970s he began a series of very imaginative books, the *Biblioteca de Apolinar,* which were first exhibited in 1972. The artistic and thematic complexity of these books gained him immediate recognition and inclusion in the 1977 Creadores al Margen show at the Museum of Contemporary Art in Caracas.

DAWN ADES, *Art in Latin America* (1989), pp. 297, 338.

BÉLGICA RODRÍGUEZ

**APONTE-LEDÉE, RAFAEL** (*b.* 15 October 1938), Puerto Rican composer. Born in Guayama, Puerto Rico, where he was educated, Aponte-Ledée left Puerto Rico in 1957 to study with Cristóbal Halffter at the Madrid Conservatory. He remained in Madrid until 1964, when he left to begin studies with Alberto GINASTERA and Gerardo GANDINI at the Torcuato di Tella Institute in Buenos Aires. After returning to Puerto Rico in 1965, Aponte-Ledée moved to the forefront of the new music movements of the 1960s. In San Juan he cofounded the Fluxus group (1967) with Francis Schwartz. He also spent several years teaching music composition and theory at the University of Puerto Rico (1968–1973) and at the Puerto Rico Conservatory (from 1968).

Aponte-Ledée's works include *Tema y 6 diferencias* for piano (1963); elegies for strings (1965, 1967); *Presagio de pájaros muertos* (1966); *Impulsos . . . in memoriam Julia de Burgos* for orchestra (1967); *La ventana abierta* (two versions; 1968, 1969); *SSSSSS²* (1971); and *El palacio en sombras* for orchestra (1977).

ISABEL ARETZ, *América latina en su música* (1977); GÉRARD BÉHAGUE, *Music in Latin America* (1979).

SARA FLEMING

**APPLEYARD, JOSÉ LUIS** (*b.* 1927), Paraguayan poet. Born in Asunción, Appleyard studied law. He also taught literature and history at the Ateneo Paraguayo (Atheneum of Paraguay) and at the National University. He belongs to the poetry group that calls itself Academia Universitaria del Paraguay. Appleyard was awarded the First Prize in Poetry in 1943 and the Municipal Poetry Prize of Asunción in 1961. He is an aesthetic and nostalgic poet, with an oeuvre firmly rooted in the Paraguayan land and culture. In *Los monólogos* (1973) and *La voz que nos hablamos* (1983) he explores the "third language of Paraguay," the mixture of Spanish and Guaraní. Among Appleyard's lyrical works are *Tomando de la mano* (1981), *El labio y la palabra* (1982), *Solamente los años* (1983), and *Las palabras secretas* (1988). Other works by Appleyard are *Entonces era siempre* (1946); *El sauce permanece* (1947); and *Imágenes sin tierra* (1964).

*Diccionario de autores iberoamericanos* (1982).

WILLIAM H. KATRA

**APRA/APRISMO.** *See* **Peru: Political Parties.**

**APURÍMAC,** a major river draining the southern Peruvian Highlands into the Amazon basin. The Apurímac is one of the principal headwater tributaries of the AMAZON RIVER and forms a nearly impassable natural boundary. In Inca times the river was spanned by a rope suspension bridge made famous in modern times by the American writer Thorton Wilder in the novel *The Bridge of San Luis Rey.* The Incas held the river to be sacred and its name, Apurímac, can be translated from Quechua as "Great Oracle" or "Revered Speaker."

BURR CARTWRIGHT BRUNDAGE, *The Empire of the Inca* (1963) and *The Lords of Cuzco: A History and Description of the Inca People in Their Final Days* (1967).

GORDON F. McEWAN

**ARAB–LATIN AMERICAN RELATIONS**

HISTORY
The first links between Latin America and the Middle East were made through immigration. Arab immigration began in the mid-nineteenth century and intensi-

fied after World War I. According to Omar el Hamedi, president of the Congress of Arab Peoples, some 15 million Latin Americans are of Arab descent. President Carlos Saúl MENEM of Argentina is a prominent example of Arab assimilation into Latin American society. Arab immigrants called for the extension of diplomatic recognition to the newly independent Syrian and Lebanese states after 1945. However, there was little diplomatic interaction between Latin America and the Middle East until the 1960s, when, after helping to found the Organization of Petroleum Exporting Countries (OPEC), Venezuela worked closely with Arab oil exporters, and Cuba's new revolutionary government attempted to solidify contacts with the more radical Arab governments and groups. In the 1970s some Arab countries launched a diplomatic offensive in Latin America as elsewhere in an effort to line up support against Israel in the United Nations (UN), and many Latin American nations began to identify with the third world movement. Economic relations increased after the rise in oil prices in 1973–1974 as nations such as Brazil and Argentina realized they could offset trade deficits with Arab oil producers by increasing their exports to them and sought to attract investment. The Sandinista victory in Nicaragua in 1979 brought increased relations with Arab nations and Iran, and the breaking of relations with Israel.

CULTURAL RELATIONS
Since 1974 annual Arab–Pan-American congresses have been attended by officials from Arab countries as well as by Latin Americans of Arab descent. The first congress established an Arab–Pan-American Federation of Arab Communities in Latin America. Committees of friendship with Arab countries, such as the Arab-Uruguayan Friendship Association, exist in a number of Latin American countries as do joint cultural institutions. Arab countries have encouraged the furthering of Arab studies at universities, and cultural exchange programs have been developed in cooperation with the Arab League and the Organization of American States (OAS). The Arab League publishes Spanish- and Portuguese-language journals and has financed the publication of translated Arab books. Saudi King Faisal donated $100,000 for the construction of the first mosque in Buenos Aires.

POLITICAL RELATIONS
Egypt, Lebanon, Algeria, Iraq, Syria, and Libya are, in decreasing order of importance, the Arab countries most heavily represented in Latin America. The Palestine Liberation Organization is represented in seven countries, and the Western Saharan Polisario in three. The Arab League has four missions—in Brasilia, Buenos Aires, Santiago, and Mexico City. Egypt, Morocco, and Saudi Arabia have observer status in the OAS. Since the Iranian revolution, Iran has sought to expand its relations in Latin America. Brazil and Venezuela have had the longest diplomatic representation in the largest number

of countries of the Middle East, with Argentina, Mexico, and Cuba also having extensive diplomatic representation in the region.

Membership in the Group of Seventy-Seven and the Nonaligned Movement and in the UN provides opportunities for gaining mutual support on issues of importance. Representatives of the 115 developing nations that are members of the Group of Seventy-Seven assemble to coordinate policies prior to major UN meetings. Latin American nations with membership in the Nonaligned Movement have taken the most consistently pro-Arab stance. In 1975 Arab nations succeeded in obtaining the support of Brazil, Mexico, Cuba, Grenada, and Guyana for a UN resolution condemning Zionism. This was repealed in 1991, with Cuba the only Latin American nation voting in opposition. During the 1970s, Augusto Pinochet's Chile and the military regime in Argentina sought to prevent the Arab world from supporting international condemnation of their human rights record. Argentina succeeded in obtaining support against Britain for its stance on the Malvinas (FALKLAND ISLANDS) from all the Arab nations with the exception of Oman. During its conflict with the United States, Nicaragua was able to obtain Arab support for resolutions in the UN and for winning a seat on the Security Council in 1982.

MILITARY RELATIONS

Cubans have been involved in training Palestinian guerrillas and in combat operations in the Middle East. Cuban military personnel were sent to Syria and the Republic of Southern Yemen and assisted pro-Marxist guerrillas in Oman as well as Eritrean separatists until Cuba transferred its support to the Marxist government in Ethiopia. Some Sandinistas trained in Palestinian camps and participated in operations in both the Middle East and Europe. Later, Palestinians as well as Libyans worked with the Nicaraguan armed forces in training in the use of Soviet-bloc weapons. Libya and Algeria supplied tanks and other arms. Saudi Arabia in turn funded the purchase of light arms and planes for use against the Sandinista government.

Chile sold both Iran and Iraq cluster bombs during the Iran-Iraq war. Iraq provided missiles to Argentina in the Malvinas war and helped to fund development of a medium-range guided missile. However, during the Gulf War, Argentina sent two warships, the only Latin American nation to participate in the coalition against Saddam Hussein. Brazil, the world's sixth largest arms exporter, sells one-third of its weapons to the Middle East. Although Brazil's largest customer, in 1989 Iraq defaulted on weapons bills and after the invasion of Kuwait, Brazil agreed to honor the UN embargo.

ECONOMIC RELATIONS

Until the Iran-Iraq war disrupted supplies, Brazil imported half of its oil from Iraq, financed largely through arms sales. Braspreto, the overseas subsidiary of the state oil company, has drilling concessions in Saudi Ara-

bia, Libya, Egypt, Iraq, and Algeria. After the UN embargo on Iraq, Iran replaced that country as Brazil's leading foreign supplier of crude oil and became an important market for Brazilian manufactures and technology. Argentina has not depended as much as Brazil on oil imports from the Arab world, but has succeeded in selling agricultural as well as industrial products there, with Egypt, Saudi Arabia, and Iran being the largest customers. Argentine scientists have assisted Iranian nuclear research since 1976. The Libyan Arab Foreign Bank joined with Argentine capitalists to form a Libyan Argentine Investment Bank and with a variety of other sources to form the Arab Latin American Bank with headquarters in Lima. Iran helped Peru finance the Trans-Andean pipeline and with Venezuela established a jointly owned maritime oil transportation company.

There have been frequent diplomatic exchanges to promote trade between the two regions. Since the breakup of the Soviet Union, this is especially important for Cuba, due to the long-standing U.S. embargo.

ROGER W. FONTAINE and JAMES D. THEBERGE, eds., *Latin America's New Internationalism: The End of Hemispheric Isolation* (1976), esp. pp. 172–196; EDWARD S. MILENKY, "Latin America: New World or Third World in International Affairs?" in *Europa-Archiv* (1977); EDY KAUFMAN, YORAM SHAPIRA, and JOEL BARROMI, *Israel–Latin American Relations* (1979); FEHMY SADDY, ed., *Arab–Latin American Relations: Energy, Trade, and Investment* (1983); "Arab League takes closer look at region; Syro-Lebanese & Palestinian immigration no longer ignored," *Latin America Weekly Report*, 23 April 1987; DAMIAN J. FERNÁNDEZ, *Cuba's Foreign Policy in the Middle East* (1988); DAMIAN J. FERNÁNDEZ, ed., *Central America and the Middle East: The Internationalization of the Crises* (1990); JOANN FAGOT AVIEL, "Arab-Iranian Relations with Nicaragua," in *Review of Latin American Studies* 3, no. 2 (1991).

JoAnn Fagot Aviel

*See also* **Nicaragua: Political Parties—Sandinista National Liberation Front.**

**ARACAJU,** capital of the state of SERGIPE in Brazil. With a population of about 400,000 (1989 est.), Aracaju is a port city and regional industrial center located on the Rio Sergipe approximately 6 miles from the coast. Although founded in 1855, Aracaju follows a grid pattern, a model unusual among Brazilian cities. Agricultural products such as HIDES, COTTON, and SUGAR dominate the commerce of the port; local industry centers on the processing of these and other agricultural products. Small-scale offshore oil drilling began in the late 1970s.

Cara Shelly

**ARADA, BATTLE OF** (2 February 1851). José Francisco BARRUNDIA, Doroteo Vasconcelos, José Dolores NUFIO, and other Central American liberals sought to oust Guatemalan caudillo Rafael CARRERA, but Guatemalan troops resisted the raids of their "National Army" in

1850. After Barrundia was elected president of the Representación Nacional at Chinandega, Nicaragua, on 9 January 1851, the group plotted a new invasion, even though the Chinandega Diet refused to sanction it. They entered Guatemala on 22 January 1851 with the intention of taking Guatemala City. Skillfully outmaneuvering his enemy, Carrera routed them at San José la Arada, south of Chiquimula, in the most stunning victory of his military career. Remnants of the National Army straggled into Honduras and El Salvador, pursued by Carrera, who carried out a deliberate campaign of reprisal until the Salvadoran government came to terms on 17 August 1853.

His victory at Arada brought Carrera enormous prestige and assured his return to the Guatemalan presidency and establishment of an authoritarian dictatorship. Arada ended the efforts of Barrundia and the middle-state liberals to reorganize the federation and destroyed Salvadoran pretensions of leadership of a new federation.

PEDRO ZAMORA CASTELLANOS, *Vida militar de Centro América* (1924); JOSÉ N. RODRÍGUEZ, *Estudios de historia militar de Centro-América* (1930), pp. 218–223; MANUEL RUBIO SÁNCHEZ, *El Mariscal de campo José Clara Lorenzana* (1987), pp. 47–71; RALPH LEE WOODWARD, JR., *Rafael Carrera and the Emergence of the Republic of Guatemala* (1992).

RALPH LEE WOODWARD, JR.

**ARAGON,** northeastern region and former kingdom of Spain united with Castile through the marriage of FERDINAND II and ISABELLA I.

The states of Catalonia, Aragon, and Valencia composed the crown of Aragon, which in the thirteenth and fourteenth centuries acquired a commercial empire in the Mediterranean. Aragonese prosperity was eclipsed in the fifteenth century by plague, civil war, and a financial crisis which led to a decline in trade and industry. Although the marriage of the "Catholic kings" (1469) united the crowns of Castile and Aragon, the three Aragonese states retained separate courts (*cortes*) and distinct feudal privileges (FUEROS), which limited the Castilian monarch's ability to raise armies and taxes. When the Aragonese sensed an infringement on their traditional liberties by the Spanish crown, they characteristically rebelled (1591–1592, 1640–1652). In the War of the Spanish Succession (1701–1714) Aragon supported the Archduke Charles of Austria, and consequently PHILIP V abolished its political privileges (1716) as punishment for supporting his rival claimant to the Spanish throne.

GERALD BRENAN, *The Spanish Labyrinth* (1943), esp. pp. 87–130; JOHN H. ELLIOTT, *Imperial Spain, 1469–1716* (1963), esp. pp. 17–43, 273–280, 317–353; RAYMOND CARR, *Spain 1808–1975*, 2d ed. (1982), esp. pp. 1–78; HENRY KAMEN, *Spain, 1469–1714: A Society of Conflict* (1983, 2d ed. 1991) esp. pp. 9–15, 139–144, 235–240.

SUZANNE HILES BURKHOLDER

**ARAGUAIA RIVER,** a waterway that rises southwest of Goiás in Brazil and flows northward, forming the natural border between the states of Goiás and Mato Grosso and Tocantins and Pará, and covering a distance of 1,366 miles. It joins the TOCANTINS RIVER at Bico do Papagaio. Midway through its course, the Araguaia separates into two branches that enclose the island of Bananal, the largest fluvial island in the world. Its basin covers 150,000 square miles. Without a firm riverbed, the Araguaia is long and shallow and includes many lakes with broad, white-sand beaches. During the summer, it floods well beyond its banks. Navigation is difficult, and until recently human habitation along the river has been scarce.

During the seventeenth century, explorations and raids out of São Paulo and Belém reached as far as the Araguaia in search of Indians from the various tribes in the region: Caiapó, Javaé, Carajá, Chambioá, Crixá, Xavánte, and Apinagé. The mining industry in Goiás and Mato Grosso during the eighteenth century did not contribute to the growth of the area's population. In the nineteenth century, the government of Goiás tried to encourage the formation of settlements in order to make navigation to the Pará possible. To this end military detachments were established at Leopoldina (today Aruaña), São José, and Santa Maria (today Araguacema), but the effort was not successful. It was not until the 1960s that true habitation of the valley occurred, aided by new means of communication as well as farming and ranching projects. Owing to the Araguaia's abundance of fish and to its beaches, tourism has developed into a growing industry.

DALÍSIA ELISABETH MARTINS DOLES, *As comunicações fluviais pelo Tocantins e Araguaia no século XIX* (1973); COUTO DE MAGALHÃES, *Viagem ao Araguaia*, 7th ed. (1975).

LUIS PALACÍN

**ARAMAYO FAMILY,** a wealthy silver and tin dynasty of the nineteenth- and twentieth-century Bolivian oligarchy. The first members in the New World were a Spanish silver miner, Diego Ortiz de Aramayo, from Navarre, and a Chichas landowner, Francisco Ortiz de Aramayo. Francisco's son, Isidoro Ortiz de Aramayo, was the father of José Avelino, born on 25 September 1809 in Moraya, a small town in the province of Sud Chichas. A mining industrialist, writer, and public servant, José Avelino founded the tin dynasty. A self-made man and a mining innovator, he bought silver mines in POTOSÍ and, with European associates, began mechanizing Bolivian silver mining. As a writer and national deputy, he opposed the crude military despotism of Manuel Isidoro BELZU, Mariano MELGAREJO, and Agustín MORALES. At his death in Paris on 1 May 1882, he reportedly left more debts than riches to his descendants.

On 23 June 1846, José's son Félix Avelino was born in Paris. In the family tradition he became a mining industrialist, writer, and noted diplomat. In 1901, while serving as Bolivia's ambassador to London, he gave an Anglo-American company, the Bolivian Syndicate of New York, concessionary rights to the rubber-rich Acre region to prevent further Brazilian encroachments. War ensued, however, and Bolivia ceded the territory to Brazil in the 1903 Treaty of Petrópolis. As part of Félix Avelino's modernization of the family tin and bismuth mines, he incorporated the Aramayo, Francke Company in London in 1906. Before his death in 1929, he passed control to his son Carlos Víctor, who internationalized family holdings by founding the Compagnie Aramayo des Mines de Bolivie in Geneva in 1916.

Carlos Víctor was born in Paris on 7 October 1889, and died there in April 1981. One of Bolivia's three tin barons (with Simón PATIÑO and Mauricio HOCHSCHILD), he epitomized the Aramayo dynasty's zenith. Critics charged that the family's wealth, second in the country, benefited neither the state nor the Indian mine workers. Although their share of national tin output averaged only 7 percent, the Aramayos exerted enormous political influence. Carlos Víctor bankrolled the Republican Party and owned La Paz's reactionary newspaper, *La Razón.* He successfully plotted with Hochschild and Patiño against reformist governments of the 1930s and 1940s, but failed to prevent revolution and expropriation in 1952.

ERNESTO O. RÜCK, *Centenario de Aramayo* (1909); ADOLFO COSTA DU RELS, *Félix Avelino Aramayo y su época, 1846–1929* (1942); DAVID FOX, *The Bolivian Tin Mining Industry* (1967); ALFONSO CRESPO, *Los Aramayo de Chichas, tres generaciones de mineros bolivianos* (1981).

WALTRAUD QUEISER MORALES

*See also* **Tin Industry.**

**ARAMBURU, PEDRO EUGENIO** (*b.* 21 May 1903; *d.* ca. 1 June 1970), president of Argentina (1955–1958). During the 1950 coup against Juan D. PERÓN, General Aramburu remained on the sidelines. But menaced by a ''Bring Back Lonardi'' movement and by Perón's possible return from exile, he led the 13 November 1955 coup against President Eduardo LONARDI. After Lonardi's death Aramburu implored the United States to force Perón out of Latin America. When Peronist-inclined officers mutinied in July 1956, Aramburu ordered them killed in the first wave of political executions in twentieth-century Argentina.

Aramburu's régime reversed Lonardi's conciliation and launched a suppression of Peronism by declaring its functionaries ineligible for public service. In economic policy Aramburu was rigid on wage control, encouraged foreign investment, and denationalized Argentina's Central Bank in favor of membership in the World Bank and International Monetary Fund. With this course set, in 1958 he called elections. Even with Peronist candidates forcibly excluded, Aramburu lost the presidency to Arturo FRONDIZI. In July 1963 Aramburu again ran unsuccessfully for president, this time on the Argentine People's Union ticket. With resentment over the 1956 shootings and his concealment of Eva PERÓN's corpse still smoldering, the Montoneros, leftist Peronists, kidnapped and shot him in Timote, Buenos Aires Province.

LUÍS BERTONE DES BALBES, *Cronología militar argentina, 1806–1980* (1983).

ROGER GRAVIL

**ARANA, FELIPE DE** (*b.* 23 August 1786; *d.* 11 July 1865), Argentine landowner and official. Born in Buenos Aires to a merchant family, Arana took a law degree in Chile, then returned to Buenos Aires to participate in the revolution of May 1810. He was president of the House of Representatives in 1828 during the first government of Juan Manuel de ROSAS and was appointed minister of foreign affairs when Rosas returned to office in 1835. His policy was nationalist in tendency, and he negotiated treaties (1840 and 1850) that ended French intervention in the Río de la Plata. But Arana had few ideas of his own, and on domestic as well as foreign policy was little more than a mouthpiece of Rosas. During the terror of 1840–1842 he was deputy governor of Buenos Aires.

H. S. FERNS, *Britain and Argentina in the Nineteenth Century* (1960); ERNESTO H. CELESIA, *Rosas: Aportes para su historia*, 2d ed., 2 vols. (1968–1969).

JOHN LYNCH

**ARANA, FRANCISCO J.** (*b.* 1905; *d.* 18 July 1949), chief of the armed forces of Guatemala (1945–1949). A leader of the October revolution of 1944, Arana became a member of a three-man revolutionary junta that supervised the transition to the democratic and reformist government of Juan José ARÉVALO in March 1945. As Arévalo's chief of the armed forces, he suppressed a number of attempted coups by right-wing landowners and reactionary officers. Entertaining presidential ambitions of his own, he eventually courted the right-wing opposition to the revolution by promising to curb the growing influence of communism. The other presidential aspirant, Colonel Jacobo ARBENZ GUZMÁN, another hero of the 1944 revolution, pursued a left-wing agenda with the support of leftist labor unions. Political rivalry between Arana and Arbenz intensified in the summer of 1949. Arana was allegedly plotting the takeover of the government when he was shot resisting arrest by partisans of Arbenz. The suppression of the revolt that followed Arana's assassination cleared the way for Arbenz's election in 1950.

PIERO GLEIJESES, *Shattered Hope: The Guatemalan Revolution and the United States, 1944–1954* (1991); RICHARD H. IMMERMAN, *The CIA in Guatemala: The Foreign Policy of Intervention* (1982).

PAUL J. DOSAL

**ARANA, JULIO CÉSAR** (*b.* 1864; *d.* 1952), a Peruvian businessman who exploited rubber and other jungle products in the Putumayo River lowlands of northeastern Peru. By 1903, after some twenty years of work, he had set up the largest natural rubber-gathering business of the era. He controlled Amazon lands totaling 25 million acres, importing men from the British Caribbean colonies as overseers and workers and using members of local tribes as actual rubber gatherers. The company demanded that the workers meet daily quotas. Many were beaten, and some were murdered if they did not comply. News of enslavement and terror in the rubber camps eventually reached human rights groups. An international scandal developed after British diplomat Roger Casement witnessed the abuses in 1910 and reported that the native population had been reduced by four-fifths. Pressure from the United States and England in 1910 led the Peruvian government to force Arana to stop the worst abuses, and his power declined as the natural rubber boom ended.

FREDRICK B. PIKE, *The Modern History of Peru* (1967), p. 194; THOMAS M. DAVIES, JR., *Indian Integration in Peru: A Half Century of Experience, 1900–1948* (1974).

VINCENT PELOSO

**ARANA OSORIO, CARLOS** (*b.* 17 July 1918), president of Guatemala (1970–1974). Born in Barbareña, Santa Rosa, Arana pursued a military career. Graduating from the Escuela Politécnica in 1939, he rose rapidly as a military officer, achieving the rank of lieutenant colonel in 1952. During the presidency of Julio César MÉNDEZ MONTENEGRO (1966–1970), he directed a counterinsurgency campaign that earned him the title "Butcher of Zacapa." Allegedly head of the MANO BLANCA (White Hand), a right-wing terrorist organization, he was implicated in the plot to delegitimize the left by kidnapping archbishop Mario Casariego in 1968.

In 1970 Arana was elected president in a campaign marked by violence and fraud. His presidency was characterized by repression and economic nationalism. State planning produced marked increases in public investment and economic growth. Since leaving office he has remained politically influential through the CAN (Central Auténtica Nacional).

GEORGE BLACK, *Garrison Guatemala* (1984); MICHAEL MC CLINTOCK, *The American Connection*, Vol. 2, *State Terror and Popular Resistance in Guatemala* (1985); JAMES DUNKERLEY, *Power in the Isthmus: A Political History of Modern Central America* (1988).

ROLAND H. EBEL

**ARANGO, DÉBORA** (*b.* 1910), Colombian artist. Born in Medellín, Arango studied with Eladio Vélez in the Medellín Institute of Fine Arts, from 1933 to 1935, first displaying her works in 1937. Her bold and expressive use of color and contrast, often of exaggerated human forms, inspired heated debate over the morality of herself and her work, especially from the Roman Catholic church in Bogotá. Indeed, Arango's innovative and vibrant oil and watercolor paintings of provocative nudes shocked many sectors of Colombian society in the 1940s.

Arango then turned to social criticism, often from a feminist perspective, focusing upon such themes as prostitutes and popular culture. Her work of the late 1940s and 1950s, which retained its highly political and anticlerical character, much in the style of the caricaturist Ricardo Rendón (1894–1931), placed her in the vanguard of Colombian abstract art. In the 1950s, Arango traveled to England and Paris, where she added ceramics to her repertoire. She became professor at the Institute of Fine Arts in 1959.

SANTIAGO LONDOÑO, "Paganismo, denuncia y sátira en Débora Arango," in *Boletín Cultural y Bibliográfico* 22, no. 4 (1985): 2–16.

DAVID SOWELL

**ARANGO Y PARREÑO, FRANCISCO DE** (*b.* 22 May 1765; *d.* 21 March 1837), Cuban statesman, economist, and sugar planter. Educated in Cuba and Spain, Arango y Parreño graduated with a degree in law and spent his life in public service, including representing the city of Havana to the court in Spain and as one of two representatives from the island to the CORTES OF CÁDIZ. In 1792 he wrote the *Discourse on the Agriculture in Havana and Ways of Developing It* that called for development of the SUGAR INDUSTRY, utilizing massive slave labor, a position he modified after the Haitian Revolution. He returned to Cuba and, with the cooperation of Governor Luis de las Casas, shifted the focus of the island's economy to development of sugar. He also co-owned one of the five largest plantations on the island. He served as director of the Economic Society in 1795 but believed its function less important than that of the *consulado*, of which he was also a member. He contributed articles to the *Papel Periódico* favoring government intervention to develop the sugar industry and hinder the Spanish monopolies. His writings and his defense of Cuba in Spain helped form the liberal Cuban mind of the period. The major effect of his policies on the island, however, was the growth of the sugar industry, and its benefit to those who are now referred to as the sugarocracy.

Arango's life and work are examined in detail in RAMIRO GUERRA Y SÁNCHEZ, et al., eds., *A History of the Cuban Nation*, vol. 3, translated by Raoul L. Washington (1958); MANUEL MORENO FRAGINALS, *The Sugarmill: The Socioeconomic Complex of Sugar in Cuba 1760–1860*, translated by Cedric Belfrage (1976); and W. W. PIERSON, JR., "Francisco de Arango y Parreño," in *Hispanic American Historical Review* 16 (November 1936): 451–478.

JACQUELYN BRIGGS KENT

**ARANHA, OSWALDO** (*b.* 15 February 1894; *d.* 27 January 1960), Brazilian politician and diplomat. Aranha was part of the clique from Rio Grande do Sul that came to national prominence after the Revolution of 1930. A close friend of Getúlio VARGAS, Aranha was one of the architects of the Revolution of 1930. He served successively as minister of justice and minister of finance in the Provisional Government (1930–1934) and helped Vargas establish national authority by turning the blame for Brazil's economic crises away from the elite classes. From 1934 to 1937 Aranha served as Brazilian ambassador to the United States and became convinced that Brazil should ally itself with the United States, not with Germany. In 1938 he became foreign minister and moved Brazil into a clear pro-Allied role first as a supplier of raw materials, and later as a supplier of troops who fought in Italy.

Although often identified as a "liberal" member of the ESTADO NOVO, Aranha viewed race, ethnicity, and class as determinants of intelligence and success, and he shaped Brazil's immigration laws to attract urban professionals at the expense of rural laborers. From 1947 to 1948 Aranha served as president of the General Assembly of the UNITED NATIONS, where he increased Brazil's international presence and is best known for presiding over the partition of Palestine. In 1953 Aranha was appointed minister of finance in the democratically elected Vargas government. Aranha withdrew from public life following the suicide of Vargas in 1954 but remained an active member of the Partida Trabalhista Brasileiro until his death.

FRANK MC CANN, *The Brazilian–American Alliance, 1937–1945* (1973); STANLEY HILTON, *Brazil and the Great Powers, 1930–1939; The Politics of Trade Rivalry* (1975); BORIS FAUSTO, *A revolução de 1930* (1986).

JEFFREY LESSER

*See also* **Brazil: Revolutions.**

**ARAUCANA, LA,** Spanish epic poem in thirty-seven cantos and three parts (Part 1, 1569; Part 2, 1578; Part 3, 1589), written by Alonso de ERCILLA Y ZÚÑIGA (1533–1594). Its stanzas (in ottava rima) narrate the warfare between the invading Spaniards and the Araucanians of southern Chile from the arrival of the conquistador Pedro de VALDIVIA to the years 1557–1558, at which point Ercilla was a soldier in Chile. The poem follows the course of events very closely, though with a number of imaginative flourishes. By 1632 no less than eighteen editions of the epic had appeared, a tribute to its widespread popularity. *La Araucana* was praised by Cervantes in *Don Quixote* and was admired by Voltaire. It was the first book to bring Chile to the attention of Europe, and in Chile itself it is regarded as a national classic.

The sixth stanza of Canto 1, beginning *"Chile fértil provincia y señalada / En la región antártica famosa"* (Chile,

fertile province / located in the famous southern region) can be recited by most educated Chileans. The classic modern study of the poem is a five-volume work (1910–1918) by Chilean scholar José Toribio MEDINA.

F. RAND MORTON, *Notes on the History of a Literary Genre: The Renaissance Epic in Spain and America* (1962); ALONSO DE ERCILLA Y ZÚÑIGA, *La Araucana,* edited by Olivo Lazzarín Dante (1977).

SIMON COLLIER

*See also* **Literature.**

**ARAUCANIANS** (*Araucano* in Spanish), historical term used to refer to indigenous peoples in the southern cone exclusive of Tierra del Fuego and Patagonia. The etymology of the word "Araucanian" is unclear, but it was used in the earliest Spanish observations of the native inhabitants in southern Chile (see, for example, Pedro de VALDIVIA's letters and chronicles and Alonso de ERCILLA Y ZÚÑIGA's epic poem *La Araucana*). Some believe the word derives from the terms used by the Inca (*Aucas* or *Promaucas,* from the Quechua *purem,* "wild enemy," and *auka,* "rebel") to refer to the southern peoples they were unable to conquer. The term *Araucano* (sometimes *Auca*) was used by colonial and military officials in documents and literature to refer to native inhabitants encountered in the southern colonial frontier (Chile and Argentina). Scholars continue to use the term, although there is growing preference for the MAPUCHE (*mapu,* meaning "land," and *che,* "people," in Mapundungun), the name used by the people to refer to themselves.

The Araucanian world in the sixteenth century encompassed the valleys and coasts, and transcordilleran highlands of the southern Andes, ranging south of the Bío Bío River to the northern regions of Chiloe along the western slopes of the cordillera and extending into the eastern precordillera to the headwaters of the Río Chubut and Río Colorado.

A common language encoded shared cultural understandings about social organization and religious beliefs and linked the Araucanians. An exogamous kinship system allowed the expansion of Araucanian family groups, which were loosely organized according to specific territorial claims. Each individual kin group, though related to other groups by shared linguistic and ceremonial forms, retained autonomy. The autonomous decision-making power of each kin leader was maintained over the centuries, even though at different times the Araucanians joined together to form bands, tribes, and even confederations in their attempts to maintain cultural and political independence.

The Araucanians resisted the incursion of the Inca in the mid-fifteenth and early sixteenth century, and their experience prepared the Araucanians to resist the Spaniards as well. While it is possible that earlier contacts between individual Araucanians and Spanish explorers may have gone unrecorded, the first sustained encounter began with the arrival of Pedro de Valdivia and the founding of Concepción in 1550 near the Bío-bío River. There followed over three centuries of warfare and resistance to Spanish conquest on the part of the Araucanians.

Araucanian experience in maintaining a defensive frontier against Inca and Spanish forces in the fifteenth and sixteenth centuries also prepared them militarily and technically to expand their activities into the south and to the east in the late eighteenth and nineteenth centuries. In this process, the exogamous nature of Araucanian social relations facilitated the incorporation of neighboring peoples, including the linguistically and culturally related PEHUENCHES (fifteenth–seventeenth centuries) and later the more distantly linked PAMPAS (also called Puelche) and TEHUELCHES (eighteenth–nineteenth centuries), bands of the Gününa këna linguistic family which had roamed the pampas and southern Patagonian steppes for millennia.

When Araucanians and Pehuenches from the cordillera began to send hunting and raiding parties (MALONES) into the pampas east of the cordillera (late seventeenth–eighteenth centuries), they came into conflict with the CREOLE ranching interests there. When competition with Chilean colonists for control of fertile land in southern Chile accelerated in the early nineteenth century, increasing numbers of Araucanians

moved from the eastern cordilleran highlands and pre-cordillera to settle in permanent encampments in the Argentine pampas. In this epoch, the Araucanians enjoyed a cultural and economic renaissance, expanding their material and ceremonial base through raids and alliances to coalesce into powerful intertribal confederations.

Traditionally, the Araucanians have been treated as interesting but marginal forces in the historiography of both Chile and Argentina. Because primary archival sources tend to be located either in Chile or in Argentina, knowledge of the Araucanian world prior to their ultimate military conquest in the late nineteenth century tends to be colored by nationalistic concerns. The story of Araucanian military resistance to Spanish conquest was recast by creole independence leaders in the nineteenth century as emblematic of a Chilean nationalism. Public statuary in Santiago immortalized as a national hero LAUTARO, the Araucanian warrior held responsible for Valdivia's capture and death in 1553, at the same time that government policies of "pacification" eroded Mapuche lives and property in the south. On the other side of the cordillera, the Araucanians traditionally have been viewed as invading hordes who plagued the expansion of the southern Argentine frontier in the eighteenth and nineteenth centuries, although in Argentina, too, the Araucanians on occasion have

Araucanian/Mapuche Indians of southern Chile. COLLECTION OF ELYN KRONEMEYER.

been cast as symbols of independence and nationalism, as exemplified by the first MONTONEROS in the early nineteenth century.

More recent analytical approaches to Araucanian history, which have led to a reassessment of the role of the Araucanians, tend to view them as significant actors who participated in fundamental ways in the history of both Chile and Argentina.

JULIAN H. STEWARD, ed., *Handbook of South American Indians,* vol. 2 (1946), pp. 687–766; LOUIS FARON, *The Hawks of the Sun: Mapuche Morality and Its Ritual Attributes* (1964); BERNARDO BERDICHEWSKY, "Araucanians," in *Encyclopedia of Indians of the Americas,* vol. 2 (1974); PATRICIA J. LYON, ed., *Native South Americans* (1974), pp. 327–342; JUDITH EWELL and WILLIAM BEEZELEY, eds., *The Human Tradition in Latin America: The Nineteenth Century* (1989), pp. 175–187; JOSÉ BENGOA, *Historia del Pueblo Mapuche: Siglos XIX y XX* (1985); LEONARDO LEÓN SOLIS, *Maloqueros y Conchavadores en Araucanía y las Pampas, 1700–1800* (1990).

KRISTINE L. JONES

**ARAUJO, ARTURO** (*b.* 1878; *d.* 1 December 1967), president of El Salvador (1 March–2 December 1931). Arturo Araujo's presidential campaign and brief presidency revealed fundamental changes that had occurred in Salvadoran politics by 1930. Himself a member of the landowning oligarchy, Araujo was educated as an engineer in England and returned to El Salvador with pro-union sentiments and admiration for the British Labour Party. In June 1918, Araujo was the keynote speaker at the First Workers' Congress, held in the western town of Armenia, where he received the title of Benefactor of the Working Classes in General for his efforts on their behalf. The next year, Araujo made an unsuccessful bid for the presidency, then attempted to come to power through an invasion from Honduras in 1922. When Pío Romero Bosque declined to name his successor in the elections of 1930, Araujo and the Partido Laborista won with a platform based on Alberto MASFERRER's nine-point *mínimum vital* program. He guaranteed adequate food, clothing, housing, education, and work for all Salvadorans and held out the promise of agrarian reform to the dispossessed rural population. However, government corruption and the Great Depression prevented the fulfillment of these campaign planks, and Araujo was overthrown in a coup engineered by his vice-president, General Maximiliano HERNÁNDEZ MARTÍNEZ. Araujo's failed experiment with labor-based appeal resulted in fifty years of direct military rule in El Salvador and the elite's deep distrust of popular politics.

JULIO CONTRERAS CASTRO, *De cómo fue traicionado el presidente ingeniero Arturo Araujo por Maximiliano Hernández Martínez* (1944); THOMAS P. ANDERSON, *Matanza: El Salvador's Communist Revolt of 1932* (1971); RAFAEL GUIDOS VÉJAR, *El ascenso del militarismo en El Salvador* (1980).

KAREN RACINE

*See also* **El Salvador: Political Parties.**

**ARAUJO, JUAN DE** (*b.* 1646; *d.* 1712), Spanish composer active in Peru and Bolivia. Araujo was born in Villafranca de los Barros, Extremadura. He studied music in Lima, first with his father, and later at the University of San Marcos. It is possible that TORREJÓN Y VELASCO may have been Araujo's music teacher during the 1660s. For a while Araujo worked as choirmaster in churches in Panama, but around 1672 he was back in Lima, where he was ordained a priest and designated choirmaster of the cathedral of Lima, where he served until 1676. After spending some time in the area of Cuzco, in Peru, he traveled to Bolivia, where in 1680 he was appointed chapelmaster of the cathedral of La Plata, a position he retained until his death. In La Plata (now Sucre), one of the most influential and wealthy cities of the Viceroyalty of Peru, Araujo substantially expanded the musical library of the cathedral with Spanish and European religious music. He also formed several important boy choirs and during some celebrations conducted works for ten voices. He composed a number of pieces, including several religious works: a Passion, two Magnificats, three Lamentations, a Salve Regina, as well as religious hymns and other choral works, most of them now in the archives of the Sucre Cathedral and the seminary of San Antonio Abad in Cuzco. In more than 106 *villancicos* and *jácaras,* Araujo displayed a vivid wit in his adept utilization of the polychoral technique. The texts of the *villancicos* are taken from Spanish baroque poetry, usually accompanied by a harp. The collection of *villancicos* is now preserved at the Archives of the Musical Section of the Museo Histórico Nacional of Montevideo, Uruguay.

ROBERT STEVENSON, *The Music of Peru* (1960); LAURO AYESTARÁN, "El barroco musical hispano-americano, los manuscritos de la iglesia de San Felipe Neri (Sucre, Bolivia), existentes en el Museo Histórico Nacional del Uruguay," in *Yearbook of the Interamerican Institute of Musical Research, Tulane University,* vol. 1 (1965); *New Grove Dictionary of Music and Musicians,* vol. 1 (1980).

SUSANA SALGADO

**ARAÚJO LIMA, PEDRO DE.** *See* **Lima, Pedro de Araújo.**

**ARAWAKS.** *See* **Caribs.**

**ARBENZ GUZMÁN, JACOBO** (*b.* 14 September 1913; *d.* 27 January 1971), president of Guatemala (1951–1954). Born in Quezaltenango to a Swiss immigrant father and a Guatemalan mother, Arbenz completed his military education in 1935 at the Escuela Politécnica, where he excelled in athletics. In 1939 he married the daughter of a wealthy Salvadoran planter, María Cristina Vilanova, who was alleged to have Communist sympathies.

Arbenz participated in the movement to overthrow President Jorge UBICO in July 1944, going into exile when he became disillusioned with Ubico's successor, General Federico Ponce Vaides. He joined the October Revolution against Ponce and became a member of the triumvirate that conducted the elections of December 1944, which brought Juan José ARÉVALO to power.

Named minister of defense by President Arévalo, Arbenz began to maneuver to succeed him. He also used his position to obtain the necessary bank loans to enable him to become a wealthy landowner. Faced with formidable political opposition from armed forces chief Major Francisco Javier ARANA, Arbenz conspired with Arévalo to have him assassinated while investigating an illegal arms cache on 18 July 1949. This provoked a military uprising that was put down when Arbenz distributed arms to students and workers. Now the undisputed head of the Revolution and backed by a coalition made up of the military, many peasants, the trade unions, government employees, and a number of centrist and left-wing parties (named the Unidad Nacional), he was overwhelmingly elected president in November 1950.

Although perceived in the United States as either Communist or under Communist influence, the Arbenz regime can best be understood as populist and nationalist. Arbenz's economic policies were directed toward creating a modern capitalist nation. In his inaugural address, President Arbenz stated that his economic policies would stress private initiative, but with Guatemalan capital in the hands of Guatemalans. To achieve that end, he adopted the proposals of the World Bank to begin construction of an Atlantic port and highway to compete with the port and railroad owned by the UNITED FRUIT COMPANY; he also built a hydroelectric plant to compete with the U.S.-owned power plant.

Arbenz's populism was reflected in his support for the newly formed National Confederation of Guatemalan Campesinos (CNCG)—which gradually came under Communist influence—and its campaign to increase agricultural wages. Most important was the enactment of the famous Decree 900, the agrarian reform law that was designed to expand domestic purchasing power and put unused land under cultivation. Under the law, idle land on holdings above 223 acres could be expropriated and distributed to peasants for lifetime usufruct. Owners were to be compensated through twenty-five-year bonds for an amount equal to their self-declared tax valuation for 1952 and paid for by the peasants at a rate of 3 to 5 percent of their annual production. Under the program some one hundred thousand peasants received 1.5 million acres, for which the government issued over $8 million in bonds.

The United Fruit Company, which had only 15 percent of its land under cultivation, was particularly hard hit: 400,000 of its more than 550,000 acres were expropriated for $1,185,115—the amount of its own valuation for tax purposes. The company declared that the property was worth at least $16 million.

The agrarian reform law, the perceived radicalization of the peasantry by the now Communist-led CNCG, and the growing influence of a small cadre of Communists such as José Manuel FORTUNY, Carlos Manuel Pellecer, and Víctor Manuel GUTIÉRREZ, galvanized both upper- and middle-class opposition, even from many of the individuals and groups that had originally supported the Revolution. Intense lobbying by the United Fruit Company and the fear that Guatemala might become a Communist "bridgehead" in the Americas galvanized the Eisenhower administration into making common cause with the opposition, now led by the exiled Colonel Carlos CASTILLO ARMAS and General Miguel YDÍGORAS FUENTES. When a shipment of arms from Czechoslovakia arrived in Guatemala in May 1954, the CIA helped Castillo Armas invade from Honduras. Abandoned by the army, Arbenz resigned the presidency on 27 June. U.S. Ambassador John Puerifoy dictated a settlement that resulted in Castillo Armas assuming the presidency on 8 July. Arbenz went into exile, living in Cuba, Uruguay, France, Switzerland, and finally Mexico, where he died.

Jacobo Arbenz Guzmán delivers inaugural address, 15 March 1951. AP/WIDE WORLD.

JAMES DUNKERLY, *Power in the Isthmus: A Political History of Modern Central America* (1988); MANUEL GALICH, *¿Por qué lucha Guatemala? Arévalo y Arbenz: Dos hombres contra un imperio* (1956); PIERO GLEIJES, *Shattered Hope: The Guatemalan Revolution and the United States* (1991); JIM HANDY, "Resurgent Democracy and the Guatemalan Military," in *Journal of Latin American*

*Studies* 18 (1986): 383–408; RICHARD H. IMMERMAN, *The CIA in Guatemala: The Foreign Policy of Intervention* (1982); STEPHEN C. SCHLESINGER and STEPHEN KINZER, *Bitter Fruit: The Untold Story of the American Coup in Guatemala* (1982, 1983); RONALD M. SCHNEIDER, *Communism in Guatemala, 1944–1954* (1958).

ROLAND H. EBEL

**ARBITRISTAS,** a diverse group of seventeenth-century peninsular and creole innovators who propounded ideas aimed at the reform of the political, social, and economic life of Spain and the Indies. They included some serious economic and political thinkers, inventors of useless gadgets, and even a few charlatans (e.g., alchemists).

These *arbitristas*, who usually shared a common faith in empiricism, compiled detailed information on each problem before devising a solution, however impractical. They had no common ideology or program and most often attempted to repair existing institutions. Given the hierarchical political system in the Spanish Empire during the seventeenth century, they looked to the existing political leadership to sponsor their projects. In Spain, the *arbitristas* tended to flock around the chief minister of King Philip IV, the conde-duque de OLIVARES. *Arbitristas* in the Indies usually sought the patronage of the viceroy and turned their attention to pressing colonial problems: American Indian relations, the output of precious metals, corruption, fiscal innovations, and moral rejuvenation.

An excellent survey of the *arbitristas* in Spain is J. H. ELLIOTT, "Self-perception and Decline in Early Modern Spain," *Past and Present* 74 (1977): 41–61. For the *arbitristas* in the Indies see FRED BRONNER, "Peruvian *Arbitristas* Under Viceroy Chinchón, 1629–1639," *Scripta Hierosolymitana* 26 (1974): 34–77.

KENNETH J. ANDRIEN

**ARBOLEDA, CARLOS** (*b.* 1929), Panamanian sculptor and painter. Arboleda studied at the San Marcos Academy in Florence, Italy (1949–1954), and at the Real Academia de Bellas Artes in Barcelona, Spain (1955–1960). Upon his return to Panama, he became professor of sculpture at the Escuela Nacional de Artes Plásticas (1961–1964). He was the founder of and a teacher at the Casa de la Escultura, later renamed Centro de Arte y Cultura (1964–1990).

Although his early works included neoclassical nudes in marble, like *Serenidad* (1950), Arboleda also worked in wood, stone, ceramics, and metal, developing a less academic, more symbolic mature style. His talent is most outstanding in sculptures with indigenous themes such as *Piel Adentro*.

ROSA MARTÍNEZ DE LAHIDALGA, *Carlos Arboleda, pintor y escultor panameño* (1974); M. KUPFER, *Encuentro de Escultura* (1987).

MONICA E. KUPFER

**ARBOLEDA, JULIO** (*b.* 9 June 1817; *d.* 12 November 1862), Colombian poet, politician, and presidential claimant (17 August–12 November 1862). Born to a family of aristocrats in Timbiquí, Cauca, he studied at Stoneyhurst College in England (1831–1834) and the University of Popayán (1837–1838). He lost part of his wealth while serving in the WAR OF THE SUPREMES (1839–1841). A gifted orator and an elegant essayist, Arboleda served as congressman (1844–1846). He opposed President José Hilario LÓPEZ in the press, was jailed, and led a revolt against López (1851). Fleeing to Peru, he remained in exile there until November 1853, when he was elected to the Senate. Back in Bogotá, in 1854 he escaped from the dictator José María MELO, against whom he had campaigned. Elected president designate [stand-in] in 1857, 1858, 1859, and 1860, Arboleda won the presidency (1860) for the 1861–1865 term but was not sworn in. During the Liberal revolution led by his uncle, Tomás Cipriano de MOSQUERA, he fought at Santa Marta (November–December 1860), moved his forces across Panama, and reached Pasto in May 1861. A year of bitter civil warfare that wracked southern Colombia ensued. Arboleda routed an invading Ecuadorian army (July 1862), and was killed at Berruecos (Nariño) four months later. Although Arboleda was celebrated for his literary genius, his greatest work, the epic poem *Gonzalo de Oyón*, survives only in fragments.

DANIEL ZARAMA, *Don Julio Arboleda en el sur de Colombia* (1917); CARLOS ARTURO CAPARRISO, *Arboleda* (n.d.); J. LEÓN HELGUERA and ALBERTO LEE LÓPEZ, "La exportación de esclavos en la Nueva Granada," in *Archivos* (Bogotá), 1, no. 2 (1967): 447–459; GERARDO ANDRADE GONZÁLEZ, *Prosa de Julio Arboleda: Jurídica, política, heterodoxa y literaria* (1984).

J. LEÓN HELGUERA

**ARCE, ANICETO** (*b.* 17 April 1824; *d.* 14 August 1906), president of Bolivia (1888–1892). Born in Tarija to an important merchant family, Arce was the largest shareholder of the Huanchaca Company, the most prosperous silver mining company in late-nineteenth-century Bolivia. He became one of the leaders of the Conservative (or Constitutionalist) Party and one of the most effective presidents of Bolivia during the period of hegemony of the Conservative oligarchy (1884–1899). He helped capitalize the Huanchaca Company through close association with the sources of Chilean capital. During the WAR OF THE PACIFIC (1879–1884), Arce favored a peace treaty with Chile, but he was exiled. His competition with Gregorio PACHECO in the 1884 elections, in which both candidates tried to outspend the other, signaled a new oligarchical electoral style. When Arce became president in 1888, he sponsored the building of a rail network that tied the Bolivian silver mines to the Pacific coast. He also improved the road system, reformed the military, and fostered the exploration of the Chaco frontier. According to a controversial biography by Ramiro Condarco Morales, Arce attempted to reform the hacienda labor system and bring Bolivia into the industrial age rather than, as other authors asserted, exploit the country for his personal profit. He died in Sucre.

The most recent and sympathetic biography is RAMIRO CONDARCO MORALES, *Aniceto Arce* (1985). See also ALIPIO VALENCIA VEGA, *Aniceto Arce* (1982). An excellent history of the Huanchaca Company and Arce's role in silver mining is ANTONIO MITRE, *Los patriarcas de la plata: Estructura socioeconómica de la minería boliviana an el siglo XIX* (1981). HERBERT S. KLEIN, *Bolivia: The Evolution of a Multi-Ethnic Society* (1982) deals with many facets of Arce's life and influence.

ERICK D. LANGER

*See also* **Bolivia: Political Parties.**

**ARCE, MANUEL JOSÉ** (*b.* 1 January 1787; *d.* 14 December 1847), the first constitutionally elected president of the UNITED PROVINCES OF CENTRAL AMERICA. Born in San Salvador to a CREOLE family, he studied at the University of San Carlos in Guatemala but did not graduate. Much influenced by Doctor Pedro MOLINA and Father José Matías DELGADO, Arce participated in the Salvadoran insurgencies of 5 November 1811 and 24 January 1814, the latter of which resulted in his imprisonment until 1818. He led the Salvadoran forces who opposed Central American annexation to Agustín de ITURBIDE's Mexican Empire until his defeat at San Salvador by General Vicente FILÍSOLA on 7 February 1823, when he went into exile in the United States.

After Central American independence from Mexico (1 July 1823), Arce returned in February 1824 to join the governing junta of the new republic, serving briefly as provisional president. After a heated electoral campaign in 1825, the federal congress elected him Central American president over José Cecilio del VALLE by a vote of 22 to 5 (even though del Valle had won a plurality of 41–34 in the electoral college, only one vote short of the required majority). Arce's deals with conservative legislators cost him support among his liberal supporters, and his attempts to strengthen the Central American federation by interventions in the state governments led to the civil war of 1827–1829. Frustrated and disillusioned, he turned over power to his conservative vice president, Mariano Beltranena, on 14 February 1828. When Francisco MORAZÁN triumphed in the war, Arce went into exile in Mexico, where he wrote his memoirs, a valuable historical source for the 1820s.

Arce attempted to return to power in 1832, but, defeated at Escuintla by federal forces under the command of General Nicolás Raoul, he retreated to Soconusco, where he engaged in agriculture for several years. In 1843 he returned to El Salvador but soon was forced to flee to Honduras. In 1844 he appeared again in Guatemala, where he raised a force with the intention of ousting General Francisco MALESPÍN from power in El Salvador. Malespín dealt him another military defeat in May of that year, preventing Arce's return to his native

Manuel José Arce. ORGANIZATION OF AMERICAN STATES.

land until after Malespín's death in 1846. Arce died a year later, impoverished, in San Salvador.

See RAMÓN A. SALAZAR, *Manuel José Arce* (1899), and MANUEL JOSÉ ARCE, *Memoria del General Manuel José Arce* (1830, several subsequent editions), Arce's memoir. A useful short sketch is VÍCTOR JEREZ, "El General D. Manuel José Arce," in *San Salvador y sus hombres* (1967), pp. 53–57; also useful is ROLANDO VELÁSQUEZ, *Carácter, fisonomía y acciones de don Manuel José Arce* (1948). PHILIP FLEMION, "States' Rights and Partisan Politics: Manuel José Arce and the Struggle for Central American Union," in *Hispanic American Historical Review* 53, no. 4 (1973): 600–618, provides a detailed examination of the intrigue surrounding Arce's presidency. His "Manuel José Arce and the Formation of the Federal Republic of Central America" (Ph.D. diss., University of Florida, 1969) contains a more extensive account of his career.

RALPH LEE WOODWARD, JR.

**ARCE CASTAÑO, BAYARDO** (*b.* 21 March 1949), Nicaraguan leader and member of the Sandinista National Directorate. Arce was born in Managua. His father's career as a journalist led him to become a reporter for *La Prensa* while a student at the National Autonomous University in León. He came into contact with the Sandinista National Liberation Front through his work at the newspaper and joined the Student Revolutionary Front in 1969. Arce was responsible for rural logistical support in the northern highlands from 1974 to 1976. He belonged to the Prolonged Popular War faction of the Sandinistas. Tomás BORGE chose Arce to be his representative on the unified Sandinista National Directorate in March 1979.

After the fall of Anastasio SOMOZA in 1979, Arce became head of the Sandinista political commission. He greatly influenced the September 1979 meeting of the Sandinista leadership that set forth its short-term strategies in the "Seventy-two-Hour Document." In May 1980 he became president of the Council of State. As a leading radical theorist, Arce gave a speech in 1984 rejecting the need for elections and endorsing a one-party state. He organized the Sandinista presidential campaigns in 1984 and 1990. In 1993 Arce became president of the editorial council of the newspaper *Barricada*.

GABRIELE INVERNIZZI et al., *Sandinistas: Entrevistas a Humberto Ortega Saavedra, Jaime Wheelock Román y Bayardo Arce Castaño* (1986); DENNIS GILBERT, *Sandinistas: The Party and the Revolution* (1988).

MARK EVERINGHAM

*See also* **Nicaragua: Political Parties.**

**ARCHAEOASTRONOMY.** *See* **Astronomy.**

**ARCHAEOLOGY.** The discovery of the New World by Christopher COLUMBUS set the stage for a clash of cultures unprecedented in history. Great civilizations centered in Mexico and Peru were found, but within a few decades, these testaments to human achievement lay in complete ruin. The natural questions arising from that experience—who were the indigenous inhabitants of this unfamiliar environment, and where did they originate?—laid the foundations for the archaeological study of the Western Hemisphere. From 1492 until the present day, archaeologists have been patiently studying the remains and monuments of those cultures and the many that preceded them by surveying, excavating, analyzing, and extrapolating from everything they have left behind. The interest of the general public in their findings is enormous; recent breakthroughs in the decipherment of Maya hieroglyphic writing and discoveries of ever older, bigger, and wealthier sites both in Mesoamerica and in the Andean region generate headlines around the world. Further, some scholars are beginning to elaborate general chronologies of New World history that see the pre-Columbian and post-Columbian events as a long continuum and turn to anthropological, environmental, and sociological findings as keys to its study.

EMERGENCE OF ARCHAEOLOGY

Although interest in the New World past began in 1492, four centuries passed before the discipline of archaeology started to catch up with international curiosity. In the meantime, many chose to speculate based on texts compiled by ethnographer friars like Bernardino de Sahagún; chronicles such as those by Bernal DÍAZ DEL CASTILLO and Pedro CIEZA DE LEÓN; or the defenders of the indigenous peoples like Bartolomé de LAS CASAS and GARCILASO DE LA VEGA. Others preferred to make judgments based on later travelers' accounts, such as that by Alexander von HUMBOLDT. Latin Americans themselves, like Carlos de SIGÜENZA Y GÓNGORA in seventeenth-century Mexico, excavated at TEOTIHUACÁN and gathered artifacts and manuscripts about the pre-Columbian past. In the next century the creole patriot Francisco Antonio de FUENTES Y GUZMÁN extolled the glories of the Maya past in Guatemala.

During these centuries, the intellectual public was fascinated by questions posed by findings in the New World such as the relationship between the mounds left in the present-day United States and the great civilizations of the Aztecs and Incas; which was older, the New world or the Old; and how societies different from those depicted in the Bible could have possibly existed. One explanation of the mounds offered by Benjamin Smith Barton in 1787 proposed that they had been built by Danes, who, after spending time in the United States, traveled to Mexico and became the TOLTECS. From 1831 to 1848, Edward King, Viscount Kingsborough, published a nine-volume set, *Antiquities of Mexico*, dedicated to proving that the indigenous peoples of Mesoamerica were descended from the ten lost tribes of Israel.

Archaeology as it is known today ostensibly began in the former Spanish colonies with the opening of national museums in Mexico (1824) and Peru (1826). In 1827 and 1828, Constantine Rafinesque published in the *Saturday Evening Post* the first attempts at deciphering the glyphs left by the Maya. The discipline of archaeology began to separate science from speculation only in the 1840s. In that decade, American travel writer John Lloyd STEPHENS and English artist Frederick Catherwood undertook the first serious explorations in the Maya area, notably COPÁN, PALENQUE, and UXMAL, publishing *Incidents of Travel in Central America, Chiapas, and Yucatan* (1841) and *Incidents of Travel in Yucatan* (1843), which became best-sellers. That decade also saw the foundation of the Smithsonian Institution (1846) and the discovery of the Maya ruins at TIKAL (1848). The U.S. diplomat Ephraim G. SQUIER traveled to Central America in the 1850s, exploring ruins there. Meanwhile, from 1838 to 1842 the Swiss explorer Johann Jakob Tschudi traveled to Chile and Peru, visiting the Temple of the Sun at PACHACAMAC, the ruins at CHANCAY, and sites high in the Andes. From 1863 to 1865 Squier systematically explored the most notable ruins of Bolivia and Peru and developed the first relative chronology for the area. The French Abbé Charles Étienne BRASSEUR DE BOURBOURG found the sixteenth-century text of Bishop Diego de LANDA, *Relación de las cosas de Yucatán,* and pointed out the immense importance of the POPOL VUH of the K'ICHE' MAYA. In 1869, railroad construction workers unearthed a rich pre-Hispanic burial ground at Ancón on the Peruvian central coast. The geologists Wilhelm Reiss and Alphons Stübel, the first to work at this site, conducted systematic excavations in Peru in 1874–1875. The Mexican Congress forbade French archaeologist Désiré Charnay from exporting his Yucatán finds in 1880. Two years later, the British scientist Alfred Maudslay explored the Maya site of YAXCHILÁN in Guatemala and shipped several important pieces to England, where they ultimately came to reside in the British Museum. In 1899–1904 he published the monumental *Biologia Centrali Americana* with four volumes devoted to archaeology, including his work on Yaxchilán and Copán in Honduras.

In the 1890s there were major excavations throughout Latin America. The Peabody Museum of Harvard University sponsored the first important large-scale excavation at Copán, and the Mexican government funded the work of Leopoldo Batres and his team at Teotihuacán and elsewhere. From 1892 to 1896, German-trained Max Uhle worked in Peru and Bolivia after a thorough study of Inca and other pottery styles, some of which had come from the Centeno Collection in Cuzco that had been sold to the Ethnographic Museum in Berlin. Denied government permission to work at TIWANAKU in 1895, Uhle conducted stratigraphic excavations at the site of Pachacamac on the Peruvian coast south of Lima. Working layer by layer, he observed that the Peruvian Tiwanaku culture (now recognized as HUARI) had held sway there before the Incas. During the next decade, in coastal excavations, Uhle found artifacts of MOCHE (North Coast) and NASCA (South Coast) consistently below levels that contained pottery with Tiwanakoid influence, prompting him to propose a six-period sequence in Andean history: Primitive Coastal Fishermen, Protoid Cultures, Tiwanaku Culture, Tiwanaku Epigonal Styles, Local Cultures, and Inca Empire. He later excavated in Chile and Ecuador.

Latin Americans, too, were interested in using stratigraphy, the determining of historical order through the examination of sites layer by layer. In Argentina, Juan B. Ambrosetti used the method at Pampa Grande in the northwest; Luis M. Torres made valuable contributions to the archaeology of the Paraná delta; and Félix F. Outes became the leading expert on the archaeology of the Pampas-Patagonia. According to Ignacio BERNAL, this methodology came to Mexico through the establishment of the Escuela Internacional de Arqueología y Etnología, inaugurated on 20 January 1911, which trained such future archeologists as Alfonso CASO and Manuel GAMIO, whose work in the Valley of Mexico in 1912–1915 demonstrated the existence of a pre-Teotihuacán culture. But at that time the stratigraphic method led to identification of pottery only according to the large-scale "civilization" it belonged to, not in terms of phases within that culture. In 1917 Gamio dug shafts under the volcanic lava of the Pedregal in southern Mexico City and found pottery and other evidence of a civilization that had existed be-

fore Teotihuacán—CUICUILCO—which later came to be known as the Formative cultures of the Valley of Mexico.

MESOAMERICA

Interest in the Maya continued in two areas. The epigraphers who studied Maya writing had been hard at work deciphering codices and inscriptions. In 1905 Joseph T. Goodman published his correlations between the Christian and Maya calendars, and in 1906 Eduard Seler and Ernst Förstemann, known as "the father of Maya hieroglyphic research" determined the double-column glyph order. Meanwhile, other Maya specialists excavated sites. From 1914 to 1955, the Historical Division of the Carnegie Institution in Washington, D.C., directed by Sylvanus G. Morley, dominated work and publications on Maya areas, often marginalizing views with which it disagreed.

Beginning in 1928, George Vaillant, working for the American Museum of Natural History, excavated at Zacatenco and other sites in the Valley of Mexico. Together with Samuel Lothrop, he developed the "Q complex theory" that the tropical forest or lowland Maya civilization arose in part from a Central American culture. Alfred Kidder's work at KAMINALJUYÚ indicated that the Guatemalan highlands might be a possible source for Maya lowland civilization. Roughly contemporaneously, Oliver Ricketson at the Maya site of UAXACTUN and Caso at the ZAPOTEC center of MONTE ALBÁN had determined general sequences. Nevertheless, Maya and Central Mexican archaeology remained divided even though a consensus was developing that saw a commonality among the regions with monumental sites throughout Mexico and northern Central America.

Still, debate raged over the antiquity of the Maya versus the OLMEC. In 1938 Matthew Stirling discovered a stela at the site of Tres Zapotes with an inscribed date earlier than any known for the Maya area. After expanding his research to other Olmec sites, he concluded that an Olmec civilization situated in tropical Tabasco and southern Veracruz had preceded that of the Maya. This view was seconded by Miguel COVARRUBIAS in Mexico. Eventually radiocarbon analysis from the sites of LA VENTA and SAN LORENZO verified the priority of Olmec culture, although controversy continued over whether and to what degree Olmec culture had influenced the development of the Maya.

During the 1940s and early 1950s, Mexican and U.S. archaeologists began working more closely, bringing greater sophistication to earlier concentration on description. This led to a number of projects, notably that at Tikal sponsored by the University of Pennsylvania from 1956 to 1969. However, the magnificence of Mexican and Central American sites contributed to the emphasis on their flamboyant and artistic qualities at the expense of more scientific considerations. Further, their importance for the development of tourist revenue propelled Mexican archaeology into much greater stress on restoration and reconstruction rather than detailed settlement studies and the recovery of data that would permit the reconstruction of ancient social, political, and economic systems. This problem came to a head with the discovery of the TEMPLO MAYOR remains during the construction of the Mexico City subway system in the 1960s and was further complicated by growing nationalist rhetoric throughout Latin America concerning foreign direction or participation in excavations.

In the 1950s Sylvanus G. Morley and J. Eric S. Thompson, author of a dictionary of Maya glyphs, developed and popularized an analysis of Maya society as ruled by priests; pacific; dominated by slash-and-burn agriculture, and featuring ceremonial centers unoccupied except at certain ritually determined times of the year. Despite the multitude of stelae depicting figures with weapons and standing on nude, trussed prisoners, and the 1946 discovery of murals at BONAMPAK filled with scenes of battles and sacrifices, Morley and Thompson persisted in fostering an identification of the "pacific" Maya with classical Greece and the "bloodthirsty" Aztecs with imperial Rome.

But this analysis could not withstand subsequent discoveries. In 1952 Yuri Knorozov revealed that the Mayas used phonetic as well as pictographic and logographic signs. In 1958 Heinrich Berlin identified an emblem glyph associated with each individual Maya site. Alberto Ruz's discovery in 1959 of a chiefly burial at Palenque spurred further research into the possibility of kings as rulers rather than priests. In 1960 Tatiana Proskouriakoff was the first to devise a chronological sequence of Maya rulers based on monumental texts for the site of Piedras Negras, Guatemala; David Kelley published his sequence for QUIRIGUA in 1962, and Proskouriakoff followed for Yaxchilán in 1963–1964.

In the 1970s Michael Coe identified and described the Primary Standard Sequence found around the tops of many Maya vases and noted that scenes painted on the objects often depicted events in the *Popol Vuh*. Also in the 1970s, Dennis E. Puleston and Alfred H. Siemens published photos showing evidence of intensive agriculture at Maya sites, and population estimates speculated that DZIBILCHALTÚN in northern Yucatán might have held a population of 50,000 during Classic times, as had Tikal. Although Dzibilchatun and Tikal were much smaller than Tenochtitlán, with an estimated population of 150,000 to 200,000, some still argue that those cities contained 10,000 more inhabitants than Seville at the time of the Conquest, almost a century later.

In the 1980s Linda Schele and others popularized a view of the Maya performing elaborate blood rituals in the museum exhibit and catalog "The Blood of Kings" and the popular book *A Forest of Kings*. At the same time, David Stuart, Stephen Houston, Nikolai Grube, and others have combined Knorozov's findings with those of Proskouriakoff and Michael D. Coe, and have been able to use phonetic, historical, and syntactical approaches to read even the signatures of individual artists on their beautifully painted pots.

The currently "accepted" pre-Columbian chronology for Mesoamerica is as follows:

| | |
|---|---|
| 1,500–900 B.C. | Early Preclassic or Early Formative |
| 900–400 B.C. | Middle Preclassic or Middle Formative |
| 400 B.C.–A.D. 200 | Late Preclassic or Late Formative |
| 250–900 | Classic |
| 900–1200 | Early Postclassic |
| 1200–1519 | Late Postclassic |

PERU

Archaeology in Peru advanced considerably in the twentieth century as well. In 1911–1912 Yale professor Hiram BINGHAM discovered and excavated the highland site of MACHU PICCHU near Cuzco. Peruvian studies continued after World War I with the work of Julio TELLO and Rafael Larco Hoyle. Tello worked on both the highlands and the coast, was publicly funded, and trained many students; Larco tended to focus his research on the North Coast and to use his own resources. Both were concerned with the origins of Andean culture, and they shared the need to show that Peru, rather than Mexico, had been the progenitor of civilization in the New World. Based on his work at CHAVÍN DE HUÁNTAR, Tello argued that an early Chavín culture originated in the Amazonian tropical forest and spread through the Andean highlands before moving to the unoccupied coastal valleys; Larco was convinced that it was a coastal culture on the basis of his discovery of Chavín material at the North Coast site of CUPISNIQUE. In 1948 Larco proposed that Tiwanakoid pottery had been distributed from Huari.

In the 1920s, Luis E. Valcárcel began his work by studying the Inca fortress of SACSAHUAMAN, near Cuzco. He chose to bypass the debate on origins and concentrated instead on the reconstruction of the entire sequence of central Andean prehistory, extending it back to the Preceramic Period. John H. Rowe began his work in that same area around Cuzco in the 1940s, ultimately tracing the sequence to earlier settlements as far back as Chavín. The discovery by Junius Bird of a Preceramic occupation before a pre-Chavín and then a Chavín one at the North Coast site of Huaca Prieta in 1946 galvanized coastal research into the origins question once more.

Also in 1946, the first multi-institutional project was begun in the Virú Valley, on the principle that one area could serve as a microcosm for the entire country and that its location on the North Coast gave it access to a previously worked-out ceramic sequence. The project featured detailed aerial and on-site mapping of all sections of the valley to show that the way people arranged themselves across the local landscape reflected the relationship between land, technology, and political and social culture. Wendell C. Bennett (Yale University);

Archaeologists at work, Chan Chan, Peru. ANTHRO-PHOTO FILE.

William Duncan Strong, James A. Ford, and Clifford Evans (Columbia University); Gordon R. Willey (Smithsonian Institution); Junius Bird (American Museum of Natural History); and Donald Collier (Chicago Museum of Natural History) conducted fieldwork and published the most thorough chronological and cultural sequences yet available for the entire Andean region.

Bennett and Strong, as well as other archaeologists, pursued traditional cultural stratigraphy to establish chronological sequences in the Huari in the Central Highlands and Cahuachi on the South Coast. Until the 1960s, Frederic Engel and E. P. Lanning, among others, demonstrated the existence of a number of early sites that showed evidence of the origins of public architecture. In 1956, Emilio Estrada discovered the site of VAL-DIVIA, later excavated by Clifford Evans and Betty Meggers. They concluded that Valdivia produced pottery dating to circa 3000 B.C., preceding the accepted date of introduction of pottery in Peru by a thousand years.

During the 1960s, Japanese investigators began to excavate in Peru, working on a major effort to test Tello's theory of Chavín origins, producing spectacular results at KOTOSH; Yoshitaro Amano studied the Chancay Valley and established a museum in Lima to preserve his impressive collection of artifacts. Also, at this time, Peruvian archaeologists developed an interest in ethnobotany and an ecological focus. Richard MacNeish headed the largest collaborative project in the late 1960s, the Ayacucho Archaeological-Botanical Project, which brought together scholars from the United States, France, Mexico, and Peru in fields such as archaeozoology, microbiology, and paleontology. Its results extended the

chronology for the Andes back several thousand years through carbon-14 dating. The University of San Marcos and governmental agencies in Peru created a project to study Chavín de Huántar once more, led by Luis G. Lumbreras and Hernán Amat.

Although these projects emphasized stratigraphic analysis, John Rowe and his students worked on stylistic variants within sites. In collaboration with Rowe, Dorothy Menzel and others established the chronological sequence for the ICA Valley that remains in use today. Lanning and Engel noted the importance of the *lomas* as a vital factor in sustaining preagricultural sedentary life on the Central Coast; subsequently Michael Moseley proposed that the Peruvian maritime habitat provided the coastal populations with the conditions necessary for corporate labor, an idea still hotly debated. Archaeology also successfully integrated information from ethnohistorical sources as John V. Murra and John Rowe investigated the Inca province of Huánuco and the Inca capital of Cuzco, respectively. From this research Murra developed his theory of verticality, stressing the relationships between those who live at different altitudes in the Andes.

During the 1970s other archaeologists looked at sources of food supply, the development of camelid domestication in the Andes, urbanism, the early state, and the cultural significance of climatic fluctuations owing to EL NIÑO. At the same time, there was a renewal of large-scale projects headed by Peruvians and foreigners. These included the Harvard CHAN CHAN–Moche Valley Project, the San Marcos–Michigan Junín Project, the Volkswagen Institute–Riva Agüero Project, and the Huari

Urban Prehistory Project. Attention still focused on Chavín; excavations by Richard Burger showed that the site had been occupied first during the Initial Period and that the Early Horizon occupation was not as early as previously thought for the north highlands. He later excavated at Huaricoto, in the central Peruvian highlands, with Abelardo Sandoval, finding evidence of a ceremonial tradition previously uncovered by Seiichi Izumi at Kotosh and by Terence Grieder at Galgada. At the latter site, Grieder showed that the highland tradition dated to preceramic times and that the architects of Chavín de Huántar drew inspiration from an equally ancient coastal tradition. Thomas Pozorski at CABALLO MUERTO, and Rogger Ravines at GARAGAY, on the North and Central coasts of Peru, respectively, have shown examples of this coastal ceremonial tradition.

Stratigraphic and radiocarbon evidence show that monumental architecture characterized the settlement of the Central Coast of Peru during the Initial Period. On the North Central Coast, work by Thomas and Sheila Pozorski has traced the development of impressive public architecture at PAMPA DE LAS LLAMAS-MOXEK from the end of the Preceramic Period through most of the Initial Period. Toward the end of the Initial Period this local architectural tradition was merged with the Central Coast concept of monumentality in the construction of the neighboring ceremonial site of SECHÍN ALTO, the largest such site ever constructed in Peru. In northwestern Argentina, Alberto Rex González stratigraphically studied cave sites in the provinces of San Luis and Córdoba. He was the first to create a chronological integration of northwestern Argentine and north Chilean archaeological sequences, as the Austrian Oswald F. A. Menghin had done for the Late Pleistocene peoples in the Argentine south. Evidence from remains in Chile showed that both the Tiawanaku and Inca empires had spread there.

OTHER REGIONS

At the same time researchers in other areas came to question the dominance of Peru in the formation of the earliest South American cultures. It is now generally accepted that a number of regional cultures developed in the highlands and along the coast of Peru and Ecuador, and that the development of Andean civilization was promoted through the interregional exchange of resources and ideas. For example, Allison Paulson has shown that sites like Valdivia and others on the Ecuadoran coast exchanged shells with sites like CERRO NARRÍO in the highlands, and that this exchange network expanded into Peru during the period from 1800 to 900 B.C. In 1961 Gerardo Reichel-Dolmatoff discovered an equally ancient ceramic site at PUERTO HORMIGA in northern Colombia; later Lanning led a team that discovered an earlier pottery culture in lowland Ecuador. Donald Lathrap, following his research in the upper Amazon (the Ucayali River) in Peru, concluded that the Amazon was a rich riverine environment capable of supporting the development of complex society. He saw

the early ceramic sites in northern South America as evidence for the tropical forest mother culture that Tello had hypothesized. Although archaeologists are excited by these finds, the general public was more interested in the Moche gold from the tombs found in the late 1980s at the Peruvian site of SIPÁN.

Major breakthroughs came later for regions lacking spectacular monumental remains. Archaeology developed slowly in Brazil, despite Meggers and Evans's finds in MARAJÓ, Mexiana, and Caviana in the late 1940s. In 1955 the French team of José Emperaire and Annette Laming began work on local shell middens (SAMBAQUIS). In Rio Grande do Sul, Eurico Miller developed the first typology for stone projectile points dating from 4000–2000 B.C. in that area. In 1965 the Smithsonian Institution and the Conselho Nacional de Pesquisas agreed on a five-year plan to investigate a region extending from the mouth of the Amazon to the Uruguayan border. They divided each state and systematically numbered all recorded sites, mapped them, collected from the surface, and stratigraphically tested them when possible.

By the final meeting in 1973, more than 1,500 sites had been investigated in Pará, Rio Grande do Norte, Bahia, São Paulo, Minas Gerais, Rio de Janeiro, Guanabara, Paraná, Santa Catarina, and Rio Grande do Sul. The results permitted the development of a general time-space framework for the coastal strip. During that time a joint French-Brazilian effort worked in the LAGÔA SANTA region and the Northeastern state of Piauí. In 1974 the Instituto de Arqueologia Brasileira created the Centro de Pesquisas Arqueológicas, which subsequently supported work on hundreds of sites in Amazonia. Also in the 1970s, the Brazilian government passed a law requiring archaeological salvage where the environment will be affected by construction, prospecting, and other activities.

The currently accepted chronology for South America is as follows:

| | |
|---|---|
| ?–2500 B.C. | Preceramic |
| 2500–1800 B.C. | Late Preceramic |
| 1800–900 B.C. | Initial Period |
| 900–A.D. 1 | Early Horizon (Chavín) |
| A.D. 1–A.D. 600 | Early Intermediate |
| 600–1000 | Middle Horizon |
| 1000–1476 | Late Intermediate |
| 1476–1532 | Late Horizon (Inca) |

Archaeological investigations require government support and relative political calm. Starting in the late 1980s, many foreign researchers who had gained valuable experience working on sites in Peru became frightened by the apparently growing power of the Sendero Luminoso political movement. Consequently, some shifted their focus to other South American venues such as Ecuador and Argentina. It is to be expected that these regions will soon show interesting results and make archaeological debate even more exciting.

A comprehensive overview of archaeology can be gleaned from GORDON R. WILLEY and JEREMY A. SABLOFF, *A History of American Archaeology*, 3d ed. (1993). For works on Mesoamerica, see IGNACIO BERNAL, *A History of Mexican Archaeology*, translated by Ruth Malet (1980); and JAIME LITVAK KING, "Mesoamerica: Events and Processes, the Last Fifty Years," in *American Antiquity* 50, no. 2 (1985): 374–382. For works in South America, see RICHARD P. SCHAEDEL and IZUMI SHIMADA, "Peruvian Archaeology, 1946–1980: An Analytic Overview," in *World Archaeology* 13, no. 3 (1982): 359–371; BETTY J. MEGGERS, "Advances in Brazilian Archaeology, 1935–1985," in *American Antiquity* 50, no. 2 (1985): 364–373; LUIS G. LUMBRERAS, *The Peoples and Cultures of Ancient Peru*, translated by Betty J. Meggers (1974).

RICHARD DAGGETT
BARBARA A. TENENBAUM

**ARCHILA, ANDRÉS** (*b.* 24 December 1913), Guatemalan violinist and musical conductor. Archila was the son of Andrés Archila Tejada, director of a well-known marimba band. Recognized as a prodigy and violin virtuoso, Archila studied at the Santa Cecilia Academy in Rome. After returning to Guatemala in 1944, he promoted the organization of the National Symphony Orchestra, of which he was conductor until 1959, when he moved to the United States. For more than twenty-five years he was third violin in the National Symphony Orchestra as well as associate director of the Washington Symphonic Orchestra in Washington, D.C. He also founded and played first violin in the Pan American Union String Quartet.

JOSÉ A. MOBIL, *Historia del arte guatemalteco*, 9th ed. (1988), p. 353; *Crónica* (Guatemala), 15 June 1990, p. 81; CARLOS C. HAEUSSLER YELA, *Diccionario general de Guatemala*, vol. 1 (1983), p. 88.

RALPH LEE WOODWARD, JR.

## ARCHITECTURE

### Architecture to 1900

The European discovery of America presented Spain and Portugal with an unprecedented opportunity to introduce new ideas, customs, objects, architecture, and cities there. Iberian occupation of the territory was tied directly to the process of converting the Indians to Christianity that began with the discovery itself, and the church as an institution made the biggest initial contribution to the new American architecture.

European conquest did not proceed evenly throughout the vast American territory. For a half century following Columbus's voyages, European settlement was centered in the Caribbean, where the Spanish imposed architectural styles with features ranging from Gothic to Renaissance to Mudejar. The architecture that resulted was characterized by a varying synthesis of native and imported influences that depended on the experience, education, and cultural background of its designers and artisans.

Forts developed into complexes that blended medieval and Renaissance plans, as exemplified by El Morro in Puerto Rico, built at the end of the sixteenth century. With the founding of Havana in 1514, the center of Spanish activity began to shift away from Santo Domingo. Havana's fortified nature influenced its life and development, but the need for military severity blended with a certain local architectural flair to define Havana's individuality, a process of adaptation to local conditions repeated for other cities in the New World. For example, when the Cathedral of Santo Domingo was completed in 1541, it used a Gothic floor plan, but without its accompanying solidity and horizontality, and contained a plateresque main portico featuring carving in plaster and stone, all of which exemplified spontaneous local adaptations.

The religious orders established their presence not only in the quality and quantity of their buildings, but also through their labors in the organization of new settlements and the consolidation of existing ones. As in the Caribbean, a synthesis of European theories and practices developed, with architectural works of marked Gothic influence in the sixteenth century and pronounced Renaissance influence in the seventeenth. It was during the sixteenth century that the great Mexican cathedrals were constructed. The Cathedral of Mexico City was begun in 1563, but not completed until 1813. Modifications of its original plan resulted in a church with the central nave higher than the two lateral ones and with a cupola and two towers at the front. It is a building of great proportions, in which the characteristic synthesis of many architectural styles from the plateresque to the neoclassic is meticulously expressed.

In addition to the more than 200 traditional churches and convents constructed in less than a century, New World circumstances often led Spaniards to build fortified convents and open chapels. The former were solid and introverted buildings with battlements that created the image of a spiritual fortress and made them seem even more alien when set against the backdrop of the countryside. The open chapel, which had European roots, was particularly popular in Mexico. It combined the Spanish impulse toward conversion with the indigenous reverence for nature by placing altar and fountain in a limited space.

Functionally, churches and convents alluded directly to known European styles. Nonetheless, the preponderance of indigenous craftsmen and laborers involved in their construction often influenced their stylistic outcome. This is most evident in changes made to the portals of the churches. Because of the value that indigenous peoples attached to exterior space, and the ways they used it, the portal became a representative, symbolic, and instructional element of great importance, incorporating native themes and styles of workmanship and decorative representation.

In South America, the Conquest and expansion proceeded slightly after that of Mexico. The numerous cloisters built in the city of Quito, Ecuador, founded in 1534,

Jesuit church of San Martín, Tepotzotlán, Mexico. MIGUEL
ANGEL ROCA / HORACIO GNEMMI.

were of imposing proportions and had grandiose and
ingenious solutions, in which once again Indian crafts-
manship provided silent witness to his presence.

Although the Spanish and Portuguese effort to build
new cities did not meet strong opposition, they were
created by combining European architectural thought
with the environmental and human factors specific to
each site. That mixture was demonstrated in the city of
Puebla de los Angeles in Mexico, founded in 1532,
which established an ordered, urban plan.

The 1573 Planning Ordinances of Philip II introduced
urban planning criteria that both capitalized on acquired experience and sought to standardize future settlements. Although Renaissance thought inspired the
plans for the new cities, their appearance differed
greatly from that of ideal European cities, approximating more nearly the criteria and proposals of the Roman
architect Vitruvius in his treatise on city planning, *De
architectura*, favored by architects of the Italian Renaissance. Three principal elements characterized the grid
layout of the new American cities/administrative centers: the street, the blocks of buildings, and the plaza.
That link of spatial structure and administrative func-

tion led to the emergence of new urban traits such as the
possibility of growth within the same grid and a formal
link to the surrounding territory. This allowed for a
gradual urban expansion into the surrounding rural
space.

The central point of reference in Spanish American
cities was the plaza, which helped to integrate their
political and religious functions. The straight lines of
the streets defined the characteristic image of the urban
landscape, and the importance of buildings was gauged
by their proximity to the plaza. To the general plan
proposed by the ordinances were added all the modifications and variations that practicality, experience, and
necessity demanded.

This process continued until the eighteenth century,
but the founding of major cities—many of which were
to become capitals, such as Mexico City, Caracas,
Bogotá, Lima, and La Paz—took place in the sixteenth
century. Those that followed continued with the original policies and adopted the same regular plan. Also,
previously established centers grew and developed in
the eighteenth century. The only exception to the planning style of the ordinances was that of the JESUITS in
their Guaraní Indian missions. Yet there were also irregular and superimposed cities that demonstrated the
synthesis of two cultures, with the indigenous providing a basis for the Spanish. Cuzco, Peru, is an example
of new architectural language expressed amid the huge,
severe walls of the Incas, thus signifying the confrontation between two opposing conceptions of the world.

In contrast to the Spanish, early Brazilian urban settlements were largely shaped by Portuguese policies of
focusing on strategic coastal sites. São Salvador da Bahia de Todos os Santos (commonly called Bahia),
founded in 1549, marked the beginning of a period of
city building. Institutions defining an ordered style did
exist here, but they were without the marked rationality
of the Renaissance-Spanish style, and allowed planners
and designers more creative freedom. The Portuguese
selected a suitable and convenient site to build the humble fortified port of Bahia, which thanks to its Afro-
Brazilian population would develop a colorful syncretic
aspect unlike any other city in Spanish America.

THE BAROQUE
From 1650 until the latter eighteenth century, Latin
America adopted an architectural style with a manner
and language that, despite regional variations, demonstrates numerous stylistic commonalities. During this
period, the church modified European baroque to capitalize on previous architectural experiences and create
new vistas, while at the same time buildings established
a more harmonious relationship with the city. Each region introduced its own original variants. Since the
Conquest, the Mexican indigenous population had appropriated and mastered interior space and produced a
body of professionals that included few Europeans.
Mexican buildings exhibited a riotous expanse of color

often supplemented by extravagant polychrome plasterwork, the mingling of curved and straight forms, and highly original tilework. Portals acquired more richness and volume, and in many cases their ornamentation dominated the entire church facade. During this period, the Mexicans developed the *estípite,* a pilaster shaped like a truncated upside-down pyramid. The use of this ornament became characteristic of a new style, churrigueresque, often termed "estípite baroque." The Jesuit church of San Martín Tepotzotlán, shown here, demonstrates the combination of a more Europeanized intricately carved white facade that leads into a graceful tower with a completely decorated and sensuous interior. El Sagrario in Mexico City, Santa Prisca in Taxco, and Santo Domingo and San Francisco Acatepec in Puebla are a few more examples of the baroque during this period.

The Andean baroque, by contrast, began in Cuzco during the period 1651–1669 with the construction of the Cathedral and La Compañía church, shown here. It was followed in Lima from 1657 to 1675 with the con-

struction of the new Church of San Francisco. Cuzco regained its architectural authority under the leadership of Bishop Manuel de Mollinedo (1673–1700), and its style predominated in more than fifty churches from Belén and San Pedro in Cuzco itself to the church in the town of Asillo near Lake Titicaca. Finally, the baroque reached its apogee in Lima from 1700 to 1740 with the Torre Tagle Palace and the churches of San Agustín and La Merced.

In Brazil, religious architecture evolved energetically in the seventeenth and eighteenth centuries, especially in Bahia, where churches had a sole nave, usually with a wooden roof. Although the styles continued to be European, the valuable decorative elements reflected the exuberance of the population. These buildings were notable for the large interiors designed to accommodate the entire community, and combined with a sense of sculpture, they brought a new element to the urban landscape.

After 1750, Minas Gerais was the center of Brazilian development. In the last decades of the century, ALEI-

La Compañía church, Cuzco, Peru. LIBRARY OF CONGRESS.

131

Cathedral and City Hall, Córdoba, Argentina. ORGANIZATION OF AMERICAN STATES.

JADINHO (Antônio Francisco Lisboa) made his unique contribution. Aleijadinho brought sculpture nearer to architecture with such force and mastery that his work became a style unto itself. The facade of the church of São Francisco de Assis, designed in 1774, and built in Ouro ·Prêto, is testimony to the management of space and other changes that Aleijadinho brought to architecture. In this church the oval towers recede, yet they remain visually and materially integrated by an undulating cornice that traverses the entire facade. Sculpture plays an important role in linking the facade with the interior using the altarpiece, the pulpit, and the ceiling of painted wood to provide a distinctive spatial and optical effect.

Architecture in Paraguay and the region of the Guaraní Indians followed a different course, shaped by the availability of abundant supplies of wood. The site chosen for each church with its perimetrical gallery, and the spatial value of the plaza as atrium and cemetery, endowed the building with multiple meanings, as demonstrated by the eighteenth-century San Roque Church in Yaguarón. The use of a gallery, created in response to the demands of the climate, replaced the idea of the facade.

The Jesuit mission settlements in Argentina, Brazil, Paraguay, and Bolivia, infused with the charisma and spirit of the Order, developed a sense of coherence and spatial balance unique in urban America. A small group of priests and a significant number of indigenous people joined forces to contribute their respective visions and versions of reality. The architecture—from simple sheds to elaborate churches—consciously grew out of indigenous communal life, combining simplicity with dignity. Skilled woodworking resulted in balanced buildings of marked horizontality in which technological solutions were readily seen, clearly distinguishing them from buildings that made use of alternative solutions. Their buildings were simple, but not lacking in such details as pulpits and Solomonic columns. Their refined painted murals lent them an artistic value not ordinarily apparent from the pronounced rationalism of the structure.

The Cathedral of Córdoba, Argentina, begun at the end of the seventeenth century, represents an important moment in the history of architecture in that country and in all of America. Of great volume and harmonious proportions, the Cathedral always tends toward the horizontal, its cupola and the two towers of the facade adding character to the solid and stony presence. Exterior ornamentation is concentrated on the cupola and the towers, which are rendered with special grace and ingenuity. The serene and static interior space was "altered" with overwrought ornamentation added in the nineteenth century.

## THE ARCHITECTURE OF INDEPENDENCE

Spanish professors introduced the neoclassical style to Latin America at the ACADEMIA DE SAN CARLOS, created in Mexico in 1785. In the beginning, the introduction of neoclassicism represented a decision and aspiration to follow similar trends in Europe, and it confronted its followers with a style that many did not hesitate to refer to as consolidated archaisms. The period signified, above all, the beginning of the end of the baroque style. The novelty and freshness of neoclassicism suited the spirit of independence that was spreading throughout Latin America. In Mexico City, for example, many buildings dating from as early as the sixteenth century were torn down by government decree to make way for the more simplified style. European architects led the way almost everywhere, from Manuel TOLSÁ in Mexico City (the School of Mines), Domingo de Petrés in Bogotá (the Cathedral), Joaquín Toesca in Santiago (La Moneda Palace and the Cathedral), and Próspero Catelin in Buenos Aires (the Cathedral).

Following Independence, many Latin American nations suffered crises of organization and identification.

Italy, France, England, and the United States variously contributed ideas, capital, and immigrants, each of which left a pronounced stamp on regional development. Neoclassicism may have replaced the baroque, but as in Europe, it was followed by the neo-Gothic. In the Americas, both neoclassicism and the neo-Gothic lacked the ideological content they possessed in their European environments, and relied on their merely symbolic aspects. It wasn't until after 1870, however, that changes initiated decades earlier began to affect the urban landscape.

As in Europe, academic posture was confronted by a romantic one, and functional traditionalism also found its niche. During the late nineteenth century, there was a notable increase in the quality and quantity of new architectural themes and forms of expression which were displayed in the many theaters, libraries, government buildings, railroad stations, prisons, and exhibition centers constructed at that time. Construction activity was not equal in all Latin American countries; Argentina boasts many important works during this period, not only in Buenos Aires, but in La Plata and Córdoba as well. The TEATRO COLÓN and the Congressional Palace, built between 1892 and 1906 in Buenos Aires, testify to this notable period of architectural history.

The new cities founded in the nineteenth century covered a wide range of styles, but almost all were affected by high levels of European immigration. In Argentina, an important pole of attraction, towns grew around rail-

Salón de los pasos perdidos, Palacio de Justicia, Córdoba, Argentina. MIGUEL ANGEL ROCA / HORACIO GNEMMI.

roads and agricultural communities. Out of sheer practicality, the grid layout was widely adopted, and immigrant artisans and laborers often added varied interpretations and combinations. La Plata, founded in 1882 as the capital of the province of Buenos Aires, is a typical example. The traditional grid was superimposed, with an irregular web of plazas at major points of intersection. A monumental axis crosses the city, and public buildings serve as points of attraction, interest, and reference. The structure of this city is completed by the green in the streets and in the great park at the foot of the axis. The city had a large European population, whose architectural influence is evident in the neo-Gothic cathedral and in the neoclassic Museum of Natural Sciences.

Haussmann's Paris served as a model for numerous urban reconstructions complete with new buildings. Mexico City, Lima, Havana, Asunción, Bahia, and Buenos Aires, among others, acquired during the second half of the nineteenth and the beginning of the twentieth centuries boulevards, promenades, and parks, along with infrastructural works and the first low-income housing projects, such as those built in Buenos Aires in 1885.

By the beginning of the twentieth century, the modernist spirit had arrived in the art world, which began to feel the rejection of academe in architecture. The alternative to academe was art nouveau, whose diffusion in Latin America was not widespread. In countries where it found a home, such as Brazil, Mexico, and Argentina, only its formal features were preserved, and in some cases only its decorative elements.

The Nationalist Restoration movement, which had few concrete results, was nonetheless important as the first attempt to create an American architecture with its own theoretical corpus. It also implied the need for the study and valuation of an architectural heritage. Argentina provided much theoretical substance for this movement, and interesting and representative works were created in Peru. Carlos Noel, Angel Guido, Juan Kronfuss, Alejandro Christophensen, and Pablo Hary are some of the names associated with the Nationalist Restoration movement.

The third anti-academe alternative that arose during the first three decades of the twentieth century was that of art deco, whose geometrization and simplification, along with the use of reinforced concrete, opened the way to modern architecture.

LEOPOLDO CASTEDO, *A History of Latin American Art and Architecture from Pre-Columbian Times to the Present* (1969); JORGE HARDOY et al., *Colóquios sobre urbanización en América desde su origen a nuestros días*, 4 vols. (1970–1978); GRAZIANO GASPARINI, *América, barroco y arquitectura* (1972); JAVIER AGUILERA ROJA and LUIS J. MORENO REXACH, *Urbanismo español en América* (1973); DAMIÁN BAYÓN, *Sociedad y arquitectura colonial sudamericana* (1974); MARCELLO CARMAGNANI, *América latina de 1880 a nuestros días* (1975); MICHAEL RAGON, *Historia mundial de la arquitectura y el urbanismo modernos,* vol. 1 (1979).

HORACIO GNEMMI

## Modern Architecture

The ideology of modern architecture in Latin America has its roots in European cultural, social, economic, and political influences, which serve as a backdrop for an eclectic architectural praxis through the twentieth century. At the programmatic base of the modern movement lie the ideals of democracy, creative liberty, social equality, constructive rationality, progress, and confidence in science and the scientific method to produce a physical reality that safeguards humankind and society and reinvents the city.

However, ideas that have been transplanted to a different culture often are fragmented and rarely retain the charge they obtained in the ideological process or the clarity of the debate and framework from which they sprang. What come through are particularities, like messages from another world. This must be how concepts such as Renaissance, baroque, neoclassicism, and eclecticism arrived in the Americas, where they were transmuted, recycled, and reinterpreted. The reception and interpretation in the United States of the same movement was quite different, reflecting a different level of industrialization, modernization, and debate over urban life and the model city.

Modern architecture entered Latin America via native students who were educated in the United States and Europe in the 1930s, returned to their countries, and, through their practice and teaching, promoted a wealth of experience. Examples are Carlos Villanueva in Venezuela and Emilio Duhart in Chile, as well as a few Spanish expatriates, such as Felix Candela in Mexico and Antonio Bonet in Buenos Aires.

There are three recognizable periods of modern architecture in Latin America. In the decade 1930–1940, modernism was introduced. The period of 1940–1965 was marked by the rationalist architecture of Le Corbusier, which often mixed with nationalist sentiments in Mexico, Brazil, and Venezuela. During this time important infrastructural projects such as hospitals, schools and universities, and housing complexes were completed. In 1965–1980 there developed a desire for heritage, texture, and tradition as well as the adoption of new techniques and technologies, sometimes in opposition to each other and sometimes synthesized. This period witnessed experimentation in the design and construction of housing, commercial centers, banks, and other institutions. For much of Latin America the 1980s constituted a "lost decade" in terms of economic and architectural growth.

In Latin America, some architects opted for poor, vernacular technologies; others for craft-oriented ones (especially in Colombia). Brick architecture, inspired by the European brutalism of the 1960s, was popular into the 1990s. Concrete brutalism, also from Europe, passed through several design phases between 1960 and 1990. The high expense of metal technologies in Latin America forced a transformation in the use of this material

Banco de Londres, Buenos Aires. MIGUEL ANGEL ROCA / HORACIO GNEMMI.

that cut costs while retaining its advantages in storage and speedy construction. Architectural decisions throughout Latin America resulted from a blend of personal preferences and global conditions, and this reflected the variable and difficult conditions in the region for so many years.

ARGENTINA

With the development of a pure rationalism by Antonio and Carlos Vilar, Jaime Roca in the 1930s followed the suggestive work of Sánchez, Lagos, and de la Torre to build the impressive Kavanagh Building, the only tower capable of overcoming the hills of Buenos Aires in the form of stepped stone, which calls to mind the front of the Plaza de San Martín in Buenos Aires. In the 1940s the group consisting of Bonet, Juan Kurchan, and Jorge Ferrari Hardoy recovered rationalism, though introducing a certain dimension that is psychological, plastic, freer. In the 1950s Alfredo Agostini made his appearance. His association with Santiago Sánchez Elía and Federico Peralta Ramos produced the most interesting works of the decade, as did Mario Roberto Alvarez, who erected the magnificent San Martín Theater. The 1960s was the decade of Clorindo Testa, who is best

known for his Bank of London and South America, completed in 1966, which is the most important example of Latin American brutalism and one of the most significant architectural achievements in Latin America in the latter half of the twentieth century. It is a plaza-building surrounded by harmoniously conceived and executed screens, which call to mind the English sculptures of Henry Moore or Barbara Hepworth, enclosing a space covered with jutting, internal trays. The 1970s to 1990s witnessed the unfolding of various groups who, within rationalism, made impressive designs and accepted the technological challenge by returning to geometry. M. Baudizzone, J. Erbin, J. Lestard, A. Varas as well as Flora Manteola, Javier Sánchez Gómez, Josefina Santos, Justo Solsona, and Rafael Viñoly, who by their banks and by ATC stand out in the 1970s.

A worthy alternative of the 1960s was "casablancism," with its use of modest materials, which established itself as an alternative to the dominant rationalism. This line with interruptions continued in worthy nationalist and populist lines such as those of Moscato and Schere. Díaz developed a brick architecture that continued to some extent the brutalism of the 1960s.

BRAZIL

Modern architecture appeared in Brazil in a 1922 model in São Paulo and in Gregori Warchavchik's 1925 "Manifesto on Functional Art," in which he simultaneously embraces the modern and the indigenous. In 1930 the revolution of Getúlio Vargas permitted a natural dialogue between those in power and architects, moved by similar ideological bases, social backgrounds, and objectives. Lúcio COSTA headed the new architecture in Brazil and in 1931 became the director of the School of Fine Arts.

In 1929, Le Corbusier briefly visited Buenos Aires, São Paulo, and Rio de Janeiro. His enormous impact was evident in his second trip in 1936, when he succeeded in defining the governing lines of the Ministry of Education and Health with his students and disciples Costa, Oscar NIEMEYER, Ernani Vasconcellos, and Carlos Leão. This work introduced a new, formal, and urban order in the center of Rio and promoted an integration of the arts with the murals of Cândido PORTINARI.

In 1939, the Brazilian pavilion at the New York World's Fair was designed by Costa and Niemeyer. Between 1940 and 1950, Niemeyer undertook projects in Pampulha, Belo Horizonte, and Ibirapuera. In all of them he demonstrated a rationalist and reductivist language with few pure elements of great impact and spatial distinction in tension. The decorative value of his work, and of the entire Brazilian school, was lauded in 1950 by Walter Gropius, founder of the Bauhaus, as an original contribution to modernism and sharply criticized by the Swiss architect Max Bill for its formalism lacking content.

Alvorada Palace (Palace of Dawn), Brasília. ORGANIZATION OF AMERICAN STATES.

But this architecture of representation quickly established itself internationally and transformed Brazil at a very early date into a strong source of ideas. In 1955, Juscelino KUBITSCHEK, governor of Minas Gerais, was elected president of Brazil. A strong ally of architects, he promoted discipline in Belo Horizonte and in the shoreline park in Rio, where Alfonso Eduardo Reidy accomplished his second masterpiece, Pedrogrulho, an apartment complex in which a sort of crescent of duplexes are spread out on a hillside with access halfway up and with a social and sports center at ground level. In the shoreline park, drawn up by Roberto BURLE MARX, Reidy erected the Museum of Modern Art, an authentic paradigm of the formal, structural, and conceptual values of Brazilian architecture.

Kubitschek decided to move the capital to the interior in an attempt to balance the development of the country, which had spilled out along the coast, its back to the profound interior of mostly tropical rain forest. Five possible locations were suggested in an initial study, from which the current site of Brasília was chosen. Niemeyer was named director of architecture and urban planning. On his suggestion, a national contest of designs for the project was undertaken in 1956, and an international jury selected the plan of Lúcio Costa. His simple, schematic layout was reminiscent of early Roman cities, with axes running north-south and east-west, crossing at a center, represented in Brasília by the bus station. The project reflected this historical dimension only in this one point, since overall it was a triumph of progressive city planning, in which isolated segments were tied together by such devices as freeways and landscaping. The small east-west cross streets contain huge super blocks of apartment buildings, while located along the large axis are the ministries and other government buildings.

As a result of the anti-Brasília debate and the influx of influences from Italy and the United States, after 1965 Brazilian architecture found a renewed interest in tra-

dition and preservation that was combined in the 1980s with the creative, formal planning in the work of SESC Pompeya by Lina Bo Bardi. Important figures and works in the 1970s included Mendes da Rocha in São Paulo, Asis Reis in his offices in Bahía, and Guedes in his São Paulo homes. They take from their institutions the concrete seen in brutalism and explore new formalizations and specializations. São Paulo, transformed into the industrial capital of Latin America, exhibits a dynamism and productive wealth that is reserved compared to developments in Rio. The critique of Brasília as a model class-based, capitalist city, with abstract zoning, served as a reformulation of interventions like that of Guedes in Bahía, but the coherence and the formal, ideological exemplariness of Brasília remain unquestionable.

MEXICO

There are three general stages in Mexico. The rationalist stage, which lasted until the 1940s, is characterized by an integration of the arts and a reaction to asceticism. The best examples of this period are Juan O'Gorman's Central Library in Mexico City's University City, which is covered with murals, and the diverse buildings in which José Clemente OROZCO and David Alfaro SIQUEIROS participated.

After the 1950s an architecture developed that recognized tradition—pre-Columbian, Spanish colonial, and republican—with emphasis on grand scale, the relationship between architecture and landscape, and the use of natural materials and living colors. Pedro RAMÍREZ VÁZQUEZ in the Museum of Anthropology, Juan Legorreta in his hotels, and the factories of Casas are representative. González de León and A. Zabludowsky express in their magnificent work these same values while adding a structural consciousness that Félix Candela established in the local architectural debate, combining the value of expression with technological research.

COLOMBIA

Colombian architecture after the adoption of modernism has sought to synthesize the new with the traditional, such as in the use of an old material—brick—by the upper classes in the church-styled houses of Bogotá in the 1930s. Along with an excellent work force and a constant adaptation of the international ideas, Colombia has developed an architecture of great and homogenous identity.

Thus, Rogelio Salmona approached the expressionist sensibility of Alvar Aalto between 1965 and 1972 in the Residencias del Parque, which calls to mind the Romeo and Juliette district in Stuttgart of Hans Scharoun, and its interior patios, which remind one of Runcorn and certain images of the Italian Tendenza. The Guest House of Cartagena is one of the great works of Latin America in recent years. Forero in Medellín developed along a similar route in his redesigned patio houses and galleries with nooks.

The examples these four countries provide illustrate that the people we call Latin Americans share a similar colonial history but differ in much else. Each country demonstrates varying attractions to modernism and tradition. Thus, Brazilians, influenced by their geography and the tropics, produced a more synthetic architecture, strong statements of culture against a dreamlike landscape, while the Argentines creatively approached time and space on the limitless pampa, deeply influenced by the European diaspora, to create a profound and authentic identity.

LEONARDO BENÉVOLO, *History of Modern Architecture,* 2 vols. (1971); "Arquitectura Latinoamericana y Argentina," essays in *Summa* (1972–1990); JORGE GLUSBERG, *Miguel Angel Roca* (1981), *Seis arquitectos mexicanos* (1983), and *Breve historia de la arquitectura Argentina,* 2 vols. (1991); ENRIQUE BROWNE, *Otra arquitectura en América Latina* (1988); GEOFFREY BROADBENT, *Emerging Concepts in Urban Space Design* (1990).

MIGUEL ANGEL ROCA

**ARCINIEGA, CLAUDIO DE** (*b.* before 1528; *d.* 1592/93), the most important architect of sixteenth-century New Spain. Originally from Burgos, Spain, Arciniega was in the city of Puebla from 1554 to 1558; in 1559, the viceroy, Luis de VELASCO, called him to Mexico City and appointed him *maestro mayor de las Obras de Cantería de la Nueva España.* His 1559 monument commemorating the death of Emperor Charles V is known through an illustrated contemporary publication. In a sober Renaissance style sometimes called "purist," it provides some idea of what his many other works, known only through documents, may have been like. Arciniega was involved in most of the important construction projects of his time in Mexico City, including the cathedral (of which he was the first architect), the viceregal palace, and the churches of the principal religious orders. He also was called upon to give opinions about the cathedrals of Puebla and Pátzcuaro, the fortifications of Veracruz, and

the mines of Taxco. In Mexico City elements in the cathedral and the facade of the Church of San Antonio Abad are ascribed to him or to his followers.

GEORGE KUBLER, *Mexican Architecture of the Sixteenth Century* (1948); MANUEL TOUSSAINT, *Claudio de Arciniega, arquitecto de la Nueva España* (1981).

CLARA BARGELLINI

*See also* **Architecture.**

**ARCINIEGAS, GERMÁN** (*b.* 6 December 1900), Colombian writer, diplomat, and political figure. Born in Bogotá of Basque descent, Germán Arciniegas became one of Latin America's most colorful and well-known writers. From an early age, he exhibited a talent for combining politics and journalism. In 1921, while attending the law faculty of the National University in Bogotá, he founded the journal *Universidad,* at which time he also attended a discussion group that included future Colombian reform leader Jorge Eliécer GAITÁN. In 1924 Arciniegas received an appointment to the faculty of sociology and continued to write for several newspapers and reviews throughout the next decade. He was director of *La revista de las Indias* in 1938 and *El Tiempo* in 1939. Both positions brought Arciniegas into collaboration with Latin America's leading intellectuals.

In 1939 Arciniegas was appointed Colombian chargé d'affaires in Buenos Aires. It was an exciting time to be in that city, and while there Arciniegas met with and was influenced by the community of exiles from Spain, a distinguished group that included José Ortega y Gasset, Ramiro de Maetzu, Ramón Pérez de Ayala, and also with the Argentines Alfredo PALCIOS and Victoria OCAMPO. Arciniegas was also influenced by the cultural elitism of José Enrique RODÓ, and he corresponded with such intellectual figures as Stefan Zweig, Alfonso REYES, and Gabriela MISTRAL.

Arciniegas was recalled to Colombia to serve as minister of education in 1941–1942, a position he held for a second time from 1945 to 1946. While in office he founded the Popular Library of Colombian Culture and a museum of colonial artifacts, both designed to enhance the public's awareness of Colombian history and culture. When domestic politics made it uncomfortable for Arciniegas to remain in Colombia, he relocated to the United States for a series of professorships at major universities: the University of Chicago (1942, 1944); the University of California at Berkeley (1945); and Columbia University (1943, 1948–1957).

In 1959 Arciniegas resumed his diplomatic career when he was named ambassador to Italy; the next year he was transferred to Israel, where he received an honorary degree from the University of Tel Aviv. He also became ambassador to Venezuela in 1967 and in the 1970s acted as Colombia's emissary to the Vatican. Arciniegas continued his editorial work throughout his life: he was the original force behind *La Revista de América* and subsequently donated his papers and books to the National Library in Bogotá.

Arciniegas has been a controversial figure, eliciting both praise and criticism. His hostility to Spain and the Conquest, coupled with his economic interpretation of history, have led many critics to condemn him as a spokesman for Moscow, but a closer reading reveals that Arciniegas's true vision of America was as a democratic continent free from the fanaticism of Europe. He glorified the nationalist and democratic spirit of America and praised the triple virtues of independence, democracy, and republicanism, an attitude that has appeared in the hundreds of books and articles he has written during his lifetime. Among his most notable works are: *Amerigo and the New World: The Life and Times of Amerigo Vespucci,* translated by Harriet de Onís (1955); *América es otra cosa: Antología y epílogo de Juan Gustavo* (1992); *Germans in the Conquest of America: A Sixteenth-Century Venture,* translated by Angel Flores (1943); *America in Europe: A History of the New World in Reverse,* translated by Gabriela Arciniegas (1986); *Biografía del Caribe* (1945); *Bolívar y la revolución* (1984); and *El caballero de El Dorado, vida del conquistador Jiménez de Queseda* (Caracas, 1959).

FEDERICO CÓRDOVA, *Vida y obras de Germán Arciniegas* (1950); PEDRO GONZÁLEZ BLANCO, *Against Arciniegas: A Blunt Criticism* (1956); and ANTONIO CACUA PRADA, *Germán Arciniegas: Su vida contada por el mismo* (1990).

KAREN RACINE

**ARCOS, SANTIAGO** (*b.* 25 July 1822; *d.* September 1874), Chilean radical. The son of a Spanish father and a Chilean mother, Arcos was born in Santiago but grew up in Paris, where in 1845 he met his friend Francisco BILBAO (1823–1865). In 1847 he traveled in the United States (part of the time with the Argentine writer and politician Domingo Faustino SARMIENTO [1811–1888]) and from there went to Chile (February 1848). With Bilbao and others he formed the radical SOCIEDAD DE LA IGUALDAD (Society for Equality) in April 1850. When the society was suppressed in November 1850, he was deported to Peru, from where he set out to visit the California goldfields. Back in Chile in 1852, he wrote (in prison as a subversive) his classic *Carta a Francisco Bilbao* (first printed in Mendoza, Argentina), an acute analysis of the defects of Chilean society. For this, he was swiftly banished to Argentina. In the 1860s he settled in Paris, where he remained for the most part. With the onset of fatal illness, he committed suicide by throwing himself into the Seine.

GABRIEL SANHUEZA, *Santiago Arcos, communista, millonario y calavera* (1956); CRISTIÁN GAZMURI, "El pensamiento político y social de Santiago Arcos," in *Historia* 21 (1986): 249–274.

SIMON COLLIER

**ARDEN QUIN, CARMELO** (*b.* 1913), Uruguayan abstract artist. Born in Rivera, Uruguay, Arden Quin was educated in Catholic schools in Brazil. He converted to Marxism in 1930 and began to study art in 1932. In 1935 he met the influential constructivist artist Joaquín TORRES GARCÍA in Montevideo. Moving to Buenos Aires three years later, Arden Quin studied philosophy and literature, and soon joined that city's artistic avant-garde, which included Edgar Bayley, Gyula KOSICE, Tomás Maldonado, and Lidy Prati. By the early 1940s, Arden Quin's early cubist style had given way to a geometric abstraction that tentatively rejected the convention of a rectangular frame by employing irregular and cut-out supports for paintings and collages; he pursued this direction in his art throughout the remainder of the decade, as did others in his milieu. He also experimented with sculptures and paintings with movable components, such as his *Coplanal* (1945), a square relief with manipulable geometric figures at each corner.

Along with Kosice and Rhod Rothfuss, Arden Quin was one of the chief contributors to the single issue of the review *Arturo,* published in 1944, and with them he initiated the GRUPO MADÍ in 1946. He and the sculptor Martín Blaszko left the group in 1948, and Arden Quin moved to Paris, where he began to associate with some of the leading figures of European abstract art, including Jean Arp, Auguste Herbin, Michel Seuphor, Constantin Brancusi, Serge Poliakoff, and Nicolas de Staël. One-man exhibitions of Arden Quin's art were held at the Galerie de la Salle, Saint-Paul de Vence, in 1978 and at the Espace Latino-Américain, Paris, in 1983.

MARI CARMEN RAMÍREZ, "Re-positioning the South: The Legacy of El Taller Torres-García in Contemporary Latin American Art," and FLORENCIA BAZZANO NELSON, "Carmelo Arden Quin," in Mari Carmen Ramírez, ed., *El Taller Torres-García: The School of the South and Its Legacy* (1992), pp. 260–261, 348–349; ELIZABETH FERRER, "Carmelo Arden Quin," in Waldo Rasmussen et al., eds., *Latin American Artists of the Twentieth Century* (1993), p. 372.

JOSEPH R. WOLIN

**ARDÉVOL, JOSÉ** (*b.* 13 March 1911; *d.* 7 January 1981), Cuban composer. Born in Barcelona, Ardévol began composing as a boy. His father, Fernando Ardévol, conductor of Barcelona's Chamber Orchestra, instructed him in piano, composition, and conducting. At nineteen he studied conducting with Hermann Scherchen in Germany. In 1930 he moved to Cuba, where he taught history and aesthetics at Havana Municipal Conservatory (1936–1941); he also taught composition in the universities of Havana (1945–1950) and Oriente (1949–1951). Ardévol founded the Chamber Orchestra of Havana (1934), conducting it until 1952, and helped found the Grupo de Renovación Musical (1942), of which he was the spokesman and leader. He was very much committed to the CUBAN REVOLUTION, directing an underground group called the National Music Committee. In 1959 he was appointed director of the radio orchestras of the Ministry of Education and subsequently national director of music. He also served as editor of the musical magazine *Revolución* and as professor of composition at the Havana Conservatory (1965) and the National School of Music (1968). Ardévol's early music reflects a neoclassical influence mixed with nationalism; by the 1940s he had changed toward serialism and atonality, influenced by Anton von Webern. His works include *Música de cámara, Tres Ricercari, Suites cubanas,* several concerti and other orchestral works, plus a considerable amount of chamber and vocal music. He won the Cuban First National Music Award six times (1938–1953) and the International Ricordi Symphonic Award (1949). His *Música para pequeña orquesta* was a commission that premiered at the First Inter-American Musical Festival in Washington, D.C. in 1958. He died in Havana.

*Composers of the Americas*, vol. 1 (1955); ALEJO CARPENTIER, *La música en Cuba*, 2d ed. (1961); GÉRARD BÉHAGUE, *Music in Latin America* (1979); *New Grove Dictionary of Music and Musicians*, vol. 1 (1980).

SUSANA SALGADO

**ARENA.** *See* **El Salvador and Brazil: Political Parties.**

**ARENALES, JUAN ANTONIO ÁLVAREZ DE** (*b.* 13 June 1870; *d.* 4 December 1831), military and political leader of the Independence era. Born in Spain, Arenales entered on a military career that in 1784 took him to South America. He served in Upper Peru (later Bolivia) where he demonstrated a special interest in the welfare of the Indian population. His involvement in the 25 May 1809 revolution at Chuquisaca led to his arrest and imprisonment, but he escaped to collaborate first with Manuel BELGRANO in his campaigns in the Argentine Northwest and Upper Peru and then with José de SAN MARTÍN in his attempt to liberate Peru. Returning to Salta, where he had married, he became governor in 1823. Arenales sought to emulate the enlightened reformism of Bernardino RIVADAVIA and the Unitarist faction and also participated in the final mopping up of royalist resistance in Bolivia. However, in the general backlash against the UNITARISTS' effort to impose a centralist constitution, Arenales was deposed as governor early in 1827. He died in exile in Bolivia.

JACINTO R. YABEN, *Biografías argentinas y sudamericanas: Perú en 1821*, vol. 1 (1938), pp. 165–173.

DAVID BUSHNELL

**ARENAS, REINALDO** (*b.* 16 July 1943; *d.* 7 December 1990), Cuban novelist, short story writer, poet, and essayist. Arenas was born in Perronales, a rural area in Oriente Province. His early experiences living in the country in a house full of what he terms "semisingle" women [as depicted in his novels *Singing in the Well* (1982) and *The Palace of the Very White Skunks* (1991)]

shaped much of his work and character, as did the friendship and guidance of writers Virgilio PIÑERA and José LEZAMA LIMA when he was a young man. Although Arenas received little formal schooling as a child, his mother taught him to read and write, and he began writing while very young. In 1959 he joined Fidel Castro's rebel forces, and after the fall of the government of Fulgencio Batista he studied agrarian management in the Oriente town of Holguín and in Havana. His increasing disenchantment and unwillingness to compromise with the new Cuban regime, along with the unabashed homosexuality evident in both his life and his work, caused him to run afoul of the Castro government. Although both his novels *Singing in the Well* (1982) and *Hallucinations* (1971) received some attention in Cuba, he was persecuted, imprisoned, and censored there, even as his work was being published and acclaimed abroad. In 1969 *Hallucinations*, which had been smuggled out of Cuba, was honored in France as one of the best foreign novels. In 1980 he joined the MARIEL BOATLIFT and left for the United States, where he settled in New York City until taking his own life in the final stages of AIDS.

Arenas's work takes the lyrical, ornate, baroque style of Cuban literary tradition and applies it to the themes of rebellion, repression, and the dehumanization that the subjugation of human beings brings upon both victims and perpetrators. Using the specific situations that he lived and knew intimately, he explores the universality of slavery and oppression. Particularly successful examples are his long poem *Leprosorio* (1990) and his novels *Arturo, la estrella más brillante* (1984) and *El asalto* (1991). Shortly before his death he finished his autobiography, *Antes que anochezca* (1992; translated as *Before Night Falls*, 1993). His work has been translated into many languages.

PERLA ROZENCRAIG, *Reinaldo Arenas: Narrativa de transgresión* (1986); ROBERTO VALERO, *El desamparado humor de Reinaldo Arenas* (1991).

ROBERTO VALERO

**ARENAS CONSPIRACY,** a plot to restore Spanish rule in Mexico that was uncovered on 19 January 1827 in Mexico City. The instigator of the plot, a "royal commissioner," was never identified. First arrested was a Spanish friar, Joaquín Arenas, who revealed the conspiracy while attempting to recruit a military commander for the cause. The plan called for the arrest of President Guadalupe VICTORIA and General Vicente GUERRERO on 20 January, the restoration of all Spaniards to their colonial posts, and amnesties and rewards for all who cooperated in the restoration of monarchical government. Only a part of the leadership, including the Spanish generals Gregorio Arana, Pedro Celestino Negrete, and José Antonio Echávarri, was discovered. In the Federal District, Puebla, and Oaxaca, at least sixteen individuals were arrested, five of whom were friars. Fourteen were executed between April 1827 and September 1829, including General Arana and five friars, thus circumventing corporate FUEROS. The trials became a *cause célèbre*, dividing the two major political parties, the Scottish-rite and York-rite Masons (YORKINOS and ESCOCESES), with the latter taking the offensive against the Spaniards. The plot spurred the effort of 1827–1834 to expel Spanish-born males from Mexico.

The major sources are JAIME DELGADO, *España y México en el siglo XIX*, vol. 1 (1950), pp. 357–375; JOSÉ MARÍA BOCANEGRA, *Memorias para la historia de México Independiente, 1822–1846*, vol. 1 (1892), pp. 414–440; JUAN SUÁREZ Y NAVARRO, *Historia de México y del general Antonio López de Santa Anna*, vol. 1 (1850), pp. 79, 390–395, 417–436, 704–722; and ROMEO FLORES CABALLERO, *Counterrevolution: The Role of Spaniards in the Independence of Mexico, 1804–1838*, translated by Jaime E. Rodríguez O. (1974).

HAROLD DANA SIMS

**AREQUIPA,** a city and department in southern Peru. Founded by Spaniards in 1540, Arequipa became a commercial center during colonial times and the second city of modern Peru.

The city of Arequipa lies on the banks of the Chili River, 7,700 feet above sea level and approximately 60 miles from the Pacific coast. Towering over the city is the volcano Misti (18,990 feet high), a snow-covered, picturesque cone. The region is extremely arid, but irrigation has allowed agriculture to flourish in the Arequipa Valley.

Andean peoples inhabited the valley long before the arrival of the INCAS, despite the assertion of Garcilaso de la Vega that Inca Mayta Cápac found the valley unpopulated. The need for pasturage and agricultural products induced Andean ethnic groups to send colonists into the valley. Aymara and even earlier peoples lived along the river. They were still there when the Inca armies arrived. The Incas may have forcibly resettled other peoples to Arequipa as *mitmaqs* (colonizers) for political purposes, but they called all the groups in the valley *mitmaqs* for propaganda, to discredit the existence of early cultures and civilizations.

In 1535, Spaniards first arrived in the region, marauding outward from Cuzco, the Inca capital that had just fallen to the conquistadores. Two years later, Diego de ALMAGRO and his expedition passed through on their return from Chile. By 1539 some Spaniards had received *encomiendas* (grants of Indian labor and tribute) in the valley. The first Spanish attempt to establish a settlement in the region, however, was in 1539 at Camaná on the coast. When that locale proved hot and disease-infested, they received permission from Francisco PIZARRO to move inland and founded Arequipa on 15 August 1540.

An oasis in the desert expanses of southern Peru, Arequipa quickly became an agricultural and commercial center. As president of the AUDIENCIA (high court) of Lima, Pedro de la GASCA created the *corregimiento* of Arequipa in 1548, the first province in the region. At about the same time a branch (*caja real*) of the royal treasury opened in the city. Residents used light volcanic sillar for construction, and Arequipa soon became known as the "White City." Arequipa distributed merchandise from Lima throughout southern Peru and was a stopping point for traders on their way to the mining camps of Upper Peru. Using the nearby port of Quilca, Arequipa transshipped the royal treasure on its passage from Potosí to Lima.

View of Arequipa, Peru, with Mount Misti. LIBRARY OF CONGRESS.

Around 1600, however, Arequipa's fortunes suffered a prolonged, albeit temporary, setback. The port of Arica became the southern conduit to Upper Peru, to the detriment of Arequipa's commercial life. Volcanic eruptions and earthquakes in 1600 and 1604 devastated the city and its farmlands. (The region is geologically unstable and has suffered severe tremors on many occasions.) The neighboring Vitor Valley, where many residents had vineyards, was particularly hard hit and took several years to recover. At roughly the same time, Arequipa, which had been perhaps the first great Peruvian wine producer, lost the Lima market to vintners around Ica and Pisco. But Arequipan wines retained their dominance in Upper Peru. The rich farmlands generally yielded a surplus of foodstuffs such as wheat, corn, and potatoes, and abundant flocks allowed the development of a significant textile industry. In 1612 it became the episcopal seat of the Arequipa diocese, with jurisdiction over all of southern coastal Peru.

The 1700s brought new prosperity to Arequipa. Local vintners began distilling *aguardiente* (brandy) from their surplus wine and made large profits from its sale in Upper Peru. The Proclamation of Free Trade (1778) increased commercial activity, although higher royal fiscal exactions caused a short-lived rebellion in January 1780. When CHARLES III established the Peruvian intendancies in 1784, the intendant of Arequipa received jurisdiction over all the provinces of southern coastal Peru. By the 1790s Arequipa was the second largest city in the viceroyalty, with a population of 22,030. It was a royalist stronghold during the wars for independence. Pumacahua and his Indians invaded Arequipa in 1814 and killed the intendant, but they were able to hold the city only briefly.

Despite its royalist sentiments, however, Arequipa's economic interests lay less with Lima than with Upper Peru, and following independence Arequipa became a chief opponent of Lima's attempts at political centralization. Foreign commercial interests flocked to Arequipa, attracted by its economy and the access it offered to Bolivia. Arequipa's wine and brandy trade declined, replaced by wool exports. By 1876 railroads linked Arequipa with the coast and with Cuzco via Juliaca, and a Bank of Arequipa opened in 1872. The city has remained a bureaucratic, commercial, and agricultural center, attracting ever greater numbers of migrants from the sierra. Its population in 1990 was 117,734, with 921,160 in the department.

GERMÁN LEGUÍA Y MARTÍNEZ, *Historia de Arequipa,* 2 vols. (1912–1914); VICTOR M. BARRIGA, *Memorias para la historia de Arequipa,* 4 vols. (1941–1952); GUILLERMO GALDOS RODRÍGUEZ, *La rebelión de los Pasquines* (1967); ALBERTO FLORES-GALINDO, *Arequipa y el sur andino: Ensayo de historia regional (siglos XVIII–XX* (1977); ALEJANDRO MÁLAGA MEDINA, *Arequipa: Estudios históricos,* 3 vols. (1981–1986); KEITH A. DAVIES, *Landowners in Colonial Peru* (1984); KENDALL W. BROWN, *Bourbons and Brandy: Imperial Reform in Eighteenth-Century Arequipa* (1986).

KENDALL W. BROWN

**ARÉVALO BERMEJO, JUAN JOSÉ** (*b.* 10 September 1904; *d.* 7 October 1990), president of Guatemala (1945–1951). Born in Taxisco, Santa Rosa, he graduated from the Escuela Normal in 1922. After working for the Ministry of Education, he spent the duration of the UBICO administration in voluntary exile in Argentina, where he completed his doctorate in philosophy in 1934. The leaders of the October Revolution of 1944 brought him back to campaign for the presidency, which he won overwhelmingly in December 1944.

Arévalo took office on 15 March 1945 with a broad, and ultimately contradictory, populist agenda: to pursue economic development while defending economic nationalism; to create a stable democratic order while greatly increasing political participation; and to expand social welfare while encouraging industrialization. Unable to achieve all of these objectives, the Arévalo administration, nevertheless, changed the legal and institutional structure of the country. Among its major accomplishments were a social security law (1946) guaranteeing workmen's compensation, maternity benefits, and health care; a labor law (1947) legalizing collective bargaining and the right to strike, and mandating a minimum wage (although peasant unions were forbidden); the Social Security Institute (IGSS), which built hospitals and clinics throughout the country; the National Production Institute (INFOP), which provided credit and expertise for small producers; and the creation of a national bank and a national planning office. Foreign investments were to be left intact but subject to government regulation. In 1949 the Congress enacted the Law of Forced Rental, which allowed peasants to rent unused land on large estates. The government also began to distribute lands confiscated from their German owners during World War II.

Arévalo's populist coalition began to unravel early in his administration. Among the causes were the establishment of diplomatic ties with the Soviet Union on 20 April 1945, the emergence of Communist leadership in the Confederación de Trabajadores de Guatemala (Víctor Manuel GUTIÉRREZ GARBÍN) and the Partido de Acción Revolucionaria (José Manuel FORTUNY), the creation of the Communist-oriented Escuela Claridad (1946), and the passing of a Law on the Expression of Thought (1947) that expanded the definition of sedition to include anything urging "disregard of the laws or authorities."

The final blow to the legitimacy of the Arévalo administration was his connivance with his handpicked successor, Captain Jacobo ARBENZ, in the assassination of Arbenz's conservative presidential rival, Major Francisco Javier ARANA, on 18 July 1949. The assassination touched off a military rebellion that was put down by students and workers armed by Defense Minister Arbenz. However, stimulated by the "minute of silence" demonstrations commemorating the assassination, many students and professionals joined the conservative opposition. In all, President Arévalo had

Juan José Arévalo Bermejo on his inaugural day. LIFE
MAGAZINE, © TIME WARNER, INC.; FRANK SCHERSCHEL.

to contend with over twenty coup attempts against his
government.

Although he left Guatemala at the end of his presidency and Arbenz was overthrown in 1954, *arevalismo*
remained an important current in Guatemalan politics
and was greatly feared by the supporters of the counterrevolution of 1954. His 1962 announcement (from
Mexico) that he would once again run for the presidency in 1963 precipitated the demand that a "preven-
tive coup" be launched by the army. On 29 March he
secretly crossed the Mexican border, precipitating
the overthrow of the YDÍGORAS FUENTES government.
The military government that followed canceled the
elections, thereby ending his bid for the presidency. He
returned to Guatemala City in the 1980s, where he lived
until his death.

JUAN JOSÉ ARÉVALO, *The Shark and the Sardines* (1961), *Anti-
Kommunism in Latin America: An X-Ray of a Process Leading to a
New Colonialism* (1963), and *Escritos Políticos y Discursos* (1953);
ARCHER BUSH, *Organized Labor in Guatemala, 1944–1949* (1950);
PIERO GLEIJES, *Shattered Hope: The Guatemalan Revolution and
the United States* (1991); STEPHEN SCHLESINGER and STEPHEN
KINZER, *Bitter Fruit: The Untold Story of the American Coup in
Guatemala* (1982, 1983); RONALD M. SCHNEIDER, *Communism in
Guatemala, 1944–1954* (1958); LEO A. SUSLOW, *Aspects of Social
Reforms in Guatemala, 1944–1949: Problems of Planned Social
Change in an Underdeveloped Country* (1950).

ROLAND H. EBEL

*See also* **Guatemala: Political Parties.**

**ARÉVALO MARTÍNEZ, RAFAEL** (*b.* 25 July 1885; *d.*
1975), one of Guatemala's foremost literary figures. Born
in Guatemala City, Arévalo Martínez attended the Colegio de Infantes, a school where children of the rich and
the poor studied side by side. Along with other fathers of
Guatemalan literature, such as Miguel Ángel ASTURIAS,
Enrique GÓMEZ CARRILLO, and Máximo Soto-Hall,
Arévalo Martínez is credited with introducing modernism to twentieth-century Guatemalan literature. Influenced by two of Latin America's foremost modernist
poets, Rubén DARÍO and José MARTÍ Y PÉREZ, Arévalo
Martínez exhibits the development of a distinct, yet confident, Latin American consciousness in his novels and
poetry.

The ability of Arévalo Martínez to combine aesthetic
concerns with a social commitment is undoubtedly his
largest contribution to contemporary Latin American
prose and poetry. Throughout his long literary career,
his unique literary style balanced his personal search for
identity with a need to discover his place in society.
Among Arévalo Martínez's outstanding works are his
1915 masterpiece, *El hombre que parecía un caballo* (The
Man Who Looked Like a Horse), which remains one of
the finest pieces of literature in the first quarter of the
twentieth century; the psycho-zoological utopian classics, *El mundo de los maharachíasa* (The World of the
Maharachías [1939]) and *Viaje a Ipanda* (Journey to Ipanda [1939]); and his critical historical study of the Estrada
Cabrera administration, *¡Ecce Pericles! La tiranía de Manuel Estrada Cabrera en Guatemala* (3d ed., 1983).

MARÍA A. SALGADO, *Rafael Arévalo Martínez* (1979).

WADE A. KIT

**ARGENTINA.** [Coverage begins with a three-part survey of Argentine political history. There follow a variety
of entries on specialized topics: **Civil Code; Commercial Code; Constitutions; Federalist Pacts; Geography;
Movements** (Federalists and Unitarists); **Organizations**
(civic, cultural, labor, etc.); **Political Parties;** and University Reform.]

### The Colonial Period

FIRST SETTLEMENTS
The discovery and conquest of colonial Argentina was
accomplished without the flamboyant personalities of
Hernán CORTÉS or Francisco PIZARRO and without the
bloodshed that characterized other Spanish conquests
in America. Indian population density was thin near the

contact points of Asunción, Córdoba de Tucumán, and Buenos Aires, and the lack of precious-metal mines eliminated the possibility of widespread Indian SLAVE-labor abuses. Spanish exploration thrust north from the Río de la Plata estuary to Asunción and south from Peru, terminating on the fertile plain of what is today central Argentina. East of this plain were the floodplains of the Paraná; west were the Andes Mountains; and north, the Chaco Desert. Further north were the rocky mountain passes to Bolivia and Andean Peru.

Initial Spanish occupation of Tucumán was sporadic. In 1537 the expedition of Pedro de MENDOZA and Domingo de IRALA landed in the Río de la Plata estuary and advanced north to found Asunción, preferring to settle there rather than Buenos Aires. The Diego Rojas expedition of 1542–1544 into northwest Argentina resulted in no permanent settlement. Spanish advances from Peru ran into stiff Indian opposition. Towns were founded and *encomiendas* granted, but often they were abandoned. By the third quarter of the sixteenth century, a string of towns ran through the interior, from Salta to Córdoba, the latter of which was not permanently settled until 1573.

Governor Jerónimo Luis de Cabrera set out from his capital of Santiago del Estero with 100 Spaniards and forty carts full of supplies, as well as herds of cattle and farm animals to establish a settlement close to Buenos Aires. The group traveled more than 240 miles to the banks of the Río Primero, where they founded Córdoba de Tucumán on 6 July 1573. It was a superb site for serving the future trade routes that would cross the territory, far enough removed from the possible administrative restrictions of Buenos Aires, and blessed with an ideal climate and not too many Indians.

It was not long before Córdoba became the preeminent settlement of the Spaniards. The bishop built a cathedral, and by 1585 the town had 150 *vecinos* (householders) living in one-story mud-brick houses while the surrounding Indian population of 6,000 was organized to do manual work. In 1580 Juan de GARAY founded Buenos Aires for a second time. Even though it had an enormously wide estuary, the strict economic policies of the Spanish government severely restricted trade, leaving Córdoba the major settlement.

By 1600 the Spanish settlements were fixed. North of the Río de la Plata estuary were the major towns of Santa Fe and Asunción; in the center of the plains were the string of towns from Córdoba north to Salta, which was just below the entrance to the Andean passes to Peru. The central string of settlements that ran from Buenos Aires to Peru fell under the economic domination of Peru. The Portuguese of Brazil were the dominant force in Buenos Aires and along the eastern rim of the settlements.

ADMINISTRATION

The enormous expanse of land in the Río de la Plata made government and defense difficult. Nine hundred miles separated Asunción from Mendoza, and there were a thousand miles between the Andes foothills beyond Salta and Buenos Aires. Towns could not easily band together to ward off Indian attacks. In 1617 PHILIP III declared that the Plata region would form two *gobernaciones,* one whose capital was in Asunción and the other in Buenos Aires. In these two cities (there were 212 Spanish householders in Buenos Aires in 1620) a governor would represent the crown. The designation of a governor in the Spanish Empire reflected the instability of an area, one which still had not controlled the surrounding Indians. So the governor was a military man, a *gobernador y capitán-general,* and not until well into the eighteenth century did Buenos Aires, Córdoba, or Asunción have an AUDIENCIA to serve as a court for major cases and to advise the governor. With the exception of the years 1661–1671, the Audiencia of Charcas had jurisdiction over the Río de la Plata. Only in 1785 was an *audiencia* established in Buenos Aires.

Colonial governors in the Río de la Plata had reputations for implementing get-rich-quick schemes and then returning to Spain, Mexico, or Lima as quickly as possible. The opportunities for wealth in the contraband trade of Buenos Aires were innumerable. Governor Diego de Góngora, who died in 1623, was found guilty of profiting from contraband slave trading and his estate fined 23,000 ducats in 1631. One would think that such a concern with recouping the purchase price of the governorship and of turning a profit had a major effect on the quality of administration, but perhaps it did not. John H. Parry concluded that it did not, but his data were primarily from Lima and Mexico City. Perhaps a port city like Buenos Aires offered too great a temptation.

In a major administrative reorganization of the Río de la Plata in the eighteenth century, required by increased trade and economic prosperity, CHARLES III created a VICEROYALTY which separated the Río de la Plata from Peru in 1776. Six years later, the INTENDANCY SYSTEM was inaugurated for greater financial centralization and unification. Eight intendancies were founded—Buenos Aires, Córdoba, Salta, Potosí, Charcas, Cochabamba, La Paz, and Paraguay—with four *gobiernos*—Montevideo, Misiones, Chiquitos, and Moxos—which were headed by military governors. The intendant, appointed directly by the crown, acted as fiscal officer, chief justice, and military commander. The geographical divisions imposed by the intendancy system in the Río de la Plata formed the basis of the national boundaries of Uruguay, Paraguay, Argentina, and Bolivia after independence.

THE COLONIAL CHURCH

The close relationship between the CATHOLIC CHURCH and the Spanish government resulted in both cooperation and friction. In the Río de la Plata both religious orders and secular clergy were present in significant numbers. DOMINICANS, FRANCISCANS, JESUITS, CARMELITES, Premonstratensians, and secular clergy attended to parish duties, but the religious orders were given the special mandate of working on Indian MISSIONS. However, the frontiers of the Río de la Plata were frequently aflame with Indian insurrections, and the few Indian groups that did survive Spanish policy were not receptive to Christian proselytization.

Church influence in the Río de la Plata was more evident in towns and cities, where Spanish and MESTIZO populations gradually increased in number. Church and state were bound by an agreement called the PATRONATO REAL. In recognition of its defeat of the Muslims in Spain and its discovery of America, the Spanish government provided financial support for the establishment of the church in America. In exchange the government had the right to appoint bishops and approve clergy for the Indies.

The two institutions, church and state, became dominant forces in Spanish America. The placing of the church edifice in the center of a city or town was symbolic of the influence and pervasiveness of the institution. The clergy controlled morals, public and private behavior, reading materials, education, and, most important of all, the cleric's own self-image as the gatekeeper of heaven. The Holy Office of the INQUISITION was established in Buenos Aires (ca. 1580), and although it did not have jurisdiction over the Indians, it served as an arm of the controlling and sometimes arbitrary religious conformity. Religion was a link with the mother country and must have provided the Spanish colonists a measure of familiarity and comfort. On the other hand, the all-pervasive nature of Spanish Catholicism became bitterly resented by intellectuals, and there developed a peculiar form of ANTICLERICALISM that carried past the period of independence and well into the nineteenth century.

The controversial Jesuit reductions of northern Argentina and Paraguay stand as an example of the contradictions inherent in the Spanish missionary effort not only in the Río de la Plata but in all of Spanish America. In the reductions the Jesuits strove mightily to develop an economically independent complex of mission towns. However, in the process they became the economic and spiritual patrons of the Indians. They refused to allow Spanish merchants to enter the mission towns; they controlled the production and sale of YERBA MATÉ; they encouraged the enormous expansion of herds of cattle; they developed a nation within a nation. The balance, however, went awry. The Jesuits were convinced that their goals were just and the means appropriate, but the state and its mercantile arm were not. The state looked upon the church as its creation, and vice versa. An uneasy truce resulted.

Colonial art and architecture achieved their greatest level of accomplishment within the religious domain. The massive Jesuit churches of Misiones province, with their baroque statuary and detail, were easily matched by the constructions of Santa Catalina and Jesús María near Córdoba. However, the Río de la Plata as a whole was not as financially affluent as Peru or Mexico, a situation reflected in the simplicity of its civil and religious architecture.

THE COLONIAL ECONOMY

The economic history of colonial Argentina did not begin with the GAUCHO or the pampas, even though the politics of wheat and cattle have defined the economic structure of Argentina in modern times. Long before the gaucho became the symbol of the Argentine cattle range or the Indians were cleared from the pampas, a tradition of cereal farming and cattle raising had taken root. This agro-pastoral tradition had several wellsprings: the Río de la Plata area just west of Buenos Aires; the Asunción–Entre Ríos–Corrientes triangle, which specialized in cattle; and the Córdoba–Tucumán region, which had a mix of farming and cattle raising.

Hindered by sporadic but violent Indian wars, economic expansion was slow on these three frontiers. Between 1580 and 1790 there were flare-ups that had devastating effects on the lives and property of Spanish settlers. In 1589 an especially brutal Indian raid on San Miguel del Tucumán destroyed houses and cattle. In 1664 Governor Alonso de Mercado y Villacorta wrote that the Mocobí and Chaco Indians had been active for the previous thirty years, attacking the towns of Esteco, Salta, Jujuy, and Tarija de Santa Cruz de la Sierra. Almost twenty years later, Governor Fernando de Mendoza lamented the sorry state of Tucumán caused by Indian raids and the expenditures made to resist the Calchaquí incursions. Fighting with the Mocobí continued through 1700 and well beyond. During the period 1740–1780, the conquest of the Chaco became an obsession, and peace came only after 1776. The Mocobí chiefs accepted gifts of clothes, a fortress for the Indians, ranches, farms, and cattle on the occasion of a peace settlement.

The Indian wars disrupted the flow of cattle along the major routes to the HACIENDAS as well as to the precious-metal mines in Andean Peru. Supplying Andean Peru with mules and cattle had become the major economic activity of Tucumán. Mules were wintered and fattened in Salta, then transported overland to Peru. The mule trade to Peru started around 1600; the significant trade, half a century later. Between 1657 and 1698 over 73,000 mules were shipped from Salta, and an annual average of 2,000 to 7,000 was maintained throughout the eighteenth century.

Two major factors influenced the economic development of Buenos Aires and the towns that ran north to Asunción. One was the desire of the Spanish government that Buenos Aires surpass Lima as a major port of entry. This led to a series of restrictive import laws and the erection of a customhouse in Córdoba to prevent the flow of goods from Buenos Aires to Lima and vice versa. The other major factor was the considerable presence of Portuguese merchants in Buenos Aires during the sixteenth and seventeenth centuries. They illegally imported SUGAR and slaves, and exported HIDES, tea, and cloth supplied by large cattle ranches along the Paraná River near Santa Fe and Corrientes. No matter what the Spanish government did, it could not stem this flood of contraband. Colônia do Sacramento on the Río de la Plata estuary, which Portugal claimed as a trading base, was a continual irritant between the two nations for a hundred years.

In the first half of the eighteenth century, treaties with the French and British permitted the unloading of slaves in Buenos Aires and the export of hides and agricultural goods. Buenos Aires grew, its population increasing to over 20,000 by 1776, and silversmiths, masons, shop-keepers, and builders plied their trades in the burgeoning city.

The export of hides from Buenos Aires became a major economic activity after 1700. They were in great demand by European armies for shelter and clothing. By this time wild herds of *cimarrón* cattle, which had propagated and spread through the pampas, were hunted by bands called VAQUERÍAS. The government issued licenses for their capture. Tallow and hides were the only two by-products sought from cattle. Between 1700 and 1725, an estimated 75,000 hides a year were exported from the port of Buenos Aires, and many more were illegally shipped and never recorded. Gradually the acquisition of rangeland and the exploitation of cattle through ranching replaced the *vaquerías*. Ranching encouraged the movement of the Spanish population west and southwest from Buenos Aires, but Indian resistance prevented any meaningful penetration of what is today known as the pampas. Jesuit reductions on the southwest frontier, similar to those of Paraguay, were unsuccessful. Jesuit ranches around Córdoba sent large quantities of hides to Buenos Aires for sale and eventual export. In return, imported and local goods such as sugar, TOBACCO, RICE, and cloth, were shipped to central Argentina.

However, land was of little use without laborers. In the Río de la Plata, the *conchabado,* the black slave, and the peon were the three major categories of labor. The *conchabado* served on an estate or ranch for a lengthy period of time. He contracted (*se conchabó*) with the owner for months or years. The peon was hired for a day or two, or at most for a harvest. In the sixteenth century a bitter dispute arose between crown and colonists over the use of native labor. Those Indians who were available in Tucumán were forced to serve as domestic help or to work on farms, tend cattle, or weave blankets and cotton goods which were often shipped to Peru for sale. Francisco de Alfaro was sent from Charcas to investigate, and his recommendations to the crown (the *Ordenanzas*), published in 1611, put an end to the dispute. Alfaro advised severely limiting the use of Indians for personal service. As a result, there was an increase in black slave labor. Between 1588 and 1610 an estimated 561 blacks valued at 149,195 pesos were sold in Córdoba alone. Independent slavers brought blacks to Buenos Aires through 1702, when the French took over the slave trade, only to be supplanted by the British South Sea Company in 1715. After 1715 that company supplied an average of 4,800 slaves a year to America, and between 1715 and 1739, 8,600 to Buenos Aires. The Jesuits in Tucumán participated in these purchases; their ranches and colleges owned 3,164 slaves in 1767. These ranches and farms supported colleges as well as urban enterprises, a good example of social reality becoming appropriate, and thus moral.

The economic policies of the mother country hindered growth and development of local industries. The cattle industry grew almost by its own dynamic, and the meager supply of imported goods created a contraband trade that reduced confidence and drove a wedge between colonists and mother country.

BOURBON REFORMS

By the middle of the eighteenth century, society in the Río de la Plata region had evolved. Native-born Spaniards (CREOLES) were at the top of the social pyramid, followed by MESTIZOS, Indians, freed blacks, and black slaves. Among these, Indians and blacks were the most apt to form permanent unions, and most urban areas and towns had substantial black populations. The two largest cities were Buenos Aires and Córdoba, with urban and rural populations of around 70,000 and 30,000 respectively. Toward the third quarter of the century, Córdoba had over 200,000 people and Buenos Aires over 300,000.

Towns were constructed according to similar plans, with a plaza complex that included the church and government offices in its square and with the homes of the elite close to the center of the town. Houses were made of adobe. Beyond the towns were farms, and further out were the ranches and haciendas. The population that lived in these concentric circles emanating from the plaza always maintained links with the town. Local industries provided goods for consumption and sometimes for trade. The ox carts of Córdoba became the accepted means of long-distance hauling. A measure of self-sufficiency and economic specialization characterized this period. A series of uprisings involving Indian laborers, called the COMUNERO REVOLT, created a feeling of unease and ushered in a series of political and economic changes.

The Spanish version of the ENLIGHTENMENT provided the foundation for change. Essential alterations in the character and content of existing institutions were suggested, and to accomplish such a vast reform, the king had to reign supreme. The first step in implementing this program was the 1767 expulsion of the Jesuits from the Spanish domains because they were considered an obstacle to total royal power. Next came the institution of the intendancy system to restore fiscal and administrative strength to the flagging empire. More ports were opened in both Spain and America to eliminate, at least partially, the monopoly enjoyed by elite merchant groups. The decree of 2 February 1778, extending free trade to the Río de la Plata, meant that merchants from thirteen free trade ports of Spain could ship goods there. This measure provoked immediate opposition from the Lima merchants, who claimed that they would no longer have control of Andean Peru's economy.

The result of free trade for Buenos Aires was extraordinary. It began a period of affluence that lasted until 1810. Building construction, city lighting, improved docks, and technical improvements in general were evident. Immigration from Spain skyrocketed, and the 1795 inauguration of a chamber of commerce called the CONSULADO was indicative of the city's economic progress. The slave trade increased as more labor was needed for growing Buenos Aires industries. A sizable export trade in salted beef developed. The main beneficiary of the resurgence of the Río de la Plata was the city of Buenos Aires, which was the major urban market, the heart of the cattle economy, the financial capital, and the cultural center. The interior, led by Córdoba, was resentful that it did not receive what it perceived as its full share.

PRELUDE TO INDEPENDENCE

While free trade and general fiscal reforms were making the Río de la Plata a more pleasant place to live, external forces were weakening the Spanish hold on the region. A series of wars with Britain and France disrupted trade. Admiral Sir Home POPHAM and General William BERESFORD captured Buenos Aires in 1806, causing the viceroy to flee inland. A French-born Argentinian, Santiago de LINIERS Y BREMOND, organized a militia and eventually drove them out. The controlling merchant elite in Buenos Aires was split, one group favoring the monopoly traders and the other favoring more liberal

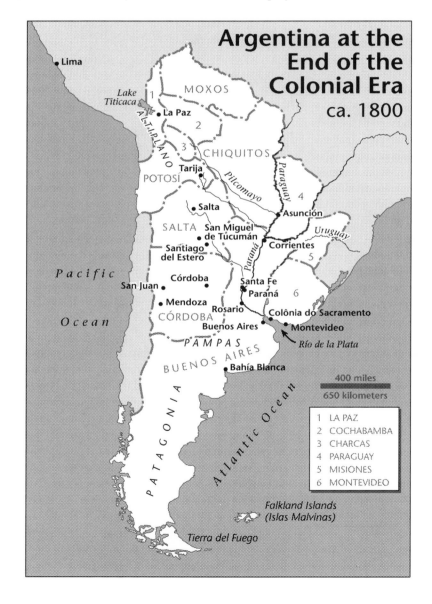

**Argentina at the End of the Colonial Era**
ca. 1800

1 LA PAZ
2 COCHABAMBA
3 CHARCAS
4 PARAGUAY
5 MISIONES
6 MONTEVIDEO

policies. When Seville fell to Napoleon's forces in 1810, signaling the collapse of Spanish rule in the Iberian Peninsula, motions for the formation of a new government were passed in a *cabildo abierto* (open town meeting) in Buenos Aires. The group championing free trade, led by Cornelio de SAAVEDRA and Mariano MORENO, assumed power. The independence movement had begun.

JOHN H. PARRY, *The Sale of Public Office in the Spanish Indies Under the Hapsburgs* (1953); JOHN LYNCH, *Spanish Colonial Administration, 1782–1810: The Intendant System in the Viceroyalty of the River Plate* (1958); GUILLERMO FURLONG CARDIFF, *Misiones y sus pueblos de Guaraníes* (1962); CEFERINO GARZÓN MACEDA, *Economía del Tucumán, Economía natural y economía monetaria, siglos XVI–XVII–XVIII* (1968); HORACIO C. E. GIBERTI, *Historia económica de la ganadería argentina* (1961); CIRO F. S. CARDOSO and HECTOR PÉREZ BRIGNOLI, *Historia económica de América Latina*, vol. 1, *Sistemas agrarios e historia colonial* (1979); JOHN FISHER, ''Imperial 'Free Trade' and the Hispanic Economy, 1778–1796,'' in *Journal of Latin American Studies* 13, pt. 1 (1981): 21–56; NICHOLAS P. CUSHNER, *Jesuit Ranches and the Agrarian Development of Colonial Argentina, 1650–1767* (1983); DAVID ROCK, *Argentina 1516–1982: From Spanish Colonization to the Falklands War* (1985), esp. pp. 1–78.

NICHOLAS P. CUSHNER

*See also* **Captain-General; Livestock.**

### The Nineteenth Century

As the nineteenth century began, the provinces that later comprised the Argentine Republic all belonged to the Viceroyalty of Río de la Plata, whose capital was Buenos Aires. The province of Buenos Aires, including the capital and its immediate hinterland, was enjoying rapid growth and rising prosperity. This was a result of the easing of overseas trade by late-colonial commercial reforms, the establishment of the viceroyalty in 1776, and the alteration of the trade routes to and from Upper Peru (modern Bolivia) to run through Buenos Aires rather than Pacific ports. The central province of Córdoba, whose capital was second in size only to Buenos Aires—with around 10,000 inhabitants as against nearly 50,000—felt mixed effects from these changes, as did the northwestern provinces of Tucumán and Salta. They benefited from the increase in traffic with Upper Peru, but some of their handicraft industries (such as the ponchos made by Córdoba artisans) suffered from the greater availability of European goods in the Buenos Aires market. Wine producers of the Mendoza and San Juan Provinces in the Cuyo area were likewise at a disadvantage. Much of the interior population, however, was dependent on little more than a subsistence economy, and was little affected by trade routes or trading policies.

Apart from handling silver shipments from Upper Peru and the return flow of imports paid for by the silver, Buenos Aires was shipping great quantities of hides from the surrounding pampa to the factories of the industrializing North Atlantic. Its status as an active port also gave it exposure to all manner of new ideas and fashions from Europe, resulting in an intellectual ferment that had its counterparts throughout the Spanish colonies but was more pronounced in Buenos Aires—certainly more so than in the Argentine interior. Then, in 1806, the Río de la Plata felt an external stimulus that aroused decidedly mixed reactions even in Buenos Aires, with its strong orientation to Europe and the North Atlantic.

The attack, although not authorized by the government in London, was a by-product of the Napoleonic Wars in Europe in which, at the moment, Spain was aligned on the side of France against Great Britain. Spain's colonies were thus enemy territory and Buenos Aires a potentially rich prize. It was easily taken by the invaders, who behaved with moderation and held out the prospect of unrestricted trade with Britain—an offer that was not unwelcome to export producers or to PORTEÑO (Buenos Airean) merchants not tied to metropolitan Spanish trading firms. Yet foreign occupation as such was an affront to the local population, which before the end of 1806 reacted strongly. The Buenos Aires militia, under the French-born officer Santiago LINIERS, proceeded to throw out the British forces. It also defeated a second British expedition that arrived early in 1807.

THE COMING OF INDEPENDENCE

The defeat of the British invasions by a largely creole militia gave a major boost to local pride and self-confidence as well as a fund of military experience on which to draw later. Liniers himself became acting viceroy of the Río de la Plata. In 1808, however, the Napoleonic invasion of Spain caused loyal Spaniards and colonials to shift to a British alliance. Liniers was suspect by virtue of his French origin, even though he professed allegiance to the rump government of Spanish resistance still holding out in southern Spain. A coup attempt against him in Buenos Aires was foiled, but in Montevideo, which also formed part of the viceroyalty, a junta headed by the local Spanish governor breathed defiance. Meanwhile, the arrival in Rio de Janeiro of CARLOTA JOAQUINA, sister of King FERDINAND VII, a captive of the French, became an added complication. The wife of the Portuguese prince regent, she invited Spanish Americans to recognize her as interim head of the empire. The idea proved attractive to a group of CREOLE professionals at Buenos Aires who felt that such an arrangement might well lead to de facto colonial autonomy.

In the end nothing came of Carlotista intrigues, and Liniers was replaced in late 1809 by a new viceroy sent out directly from Spain; Montevideo then returned to obedience. But the continuing decline of Spanish fortunes in the conflict with Napoleon triggered strong demands for the establishment of a governing junta in Buenos Aires, ostensibly to rule in the name of King Ferdinand until such time as he regained his throne. A junta was created on 25 May 1810 and promptly called on all parts of the viceroyalty to accept its claims. There was resistance in peripheral areas—Uruguay, Paraguay, Upper Peru—and a brief attempt at counterrevolution in Córdoba, led by Liniers, who was the hero of resistance against the British. But all the future Argentine provinces, with varying enthusiasm, recognized the Buenos Aires junta.

With the establishment of a revolutionary junta in Buenos Aires, Argentina had for all practical purposes achieved self-government. The junta itself, however, was soon torn by internal conflict between a radical activist group led by Mariano MORENO and a moderate faction identified initially with the militia officer Cornelio de SAAVEDRA. Moreno, one of the junta's secretaries, took a hard line against any who resisted its authority, while using its newspaper to disseminate the writings of Jean-Jacques Rousseau and to prepare public opinion for outright independence. The moderates, for their part, had more support in the interior; this proved decisive and led to the departure of Moreno to diplomatic exile (he died en route).

Factional strife would be a constant of the revolutionary scene, as junta followed junta over the next few years and other forms of government were tried as well. A constituent assembly that met in 1813 adopted a broad package of liberal reforms, including restrictions on the religious orders, abolition of the Inquisition, and elimination of titles of nobility and Indian forced labor; however, it proved unable to produce a constitution. Meanwhile, Paraguay was permanently lost to the jurisdiction of Buenos Aires, despite a military expedition sent to take control of it in 1811; Uruguay was fought over by Spanish loyalists, Uruguayan autonomists, agents of Buenos Aires, and Portuguese interlopers from Brazil; and a succession of Argentine armies sent to liberate Upper Peru met with temporary success and ultimate failure.

Thanks in part simply to its remoteness, Argentina was the only one of Spain's rebellious colonies that never experienced Spanish reconquest, even in the years 1815–1819, which in other theaters were the low point of the independence movement. During these very years the Argentine provinces experienced an interlude of relative stability under the administration of Supreme Director Juan Martín de PUEYRREDÓN, and in 1816 another constituent congress meeting in Tucumán declared formal independence at last. After moving to Buenos Aires, the congress adopted a first constitution in 1819, which remained largely a dead letter. Meanwhile, with the support of Pueyrredón, an army under the Argentine liberator José de SAN MARTÍN crossed the Andes into Chile in 1817, to begin the series of campaigns that ultimately took him to Peru.

Even while San Martín was successfully carrying the war across the Andes, the Portuguese were gaining control of Uruguay. Intermittent fighting with the royalists continued in the northwest and Upper Peru. But by 1820 the independence of Argentina proper was assured. At the same time, however, the precarious internal unity achieved under Pueyrredón dissolved, largely as a result of a widespread backlash against the centralism of the abortive 1819 constitution and the intrigues mounted by administration supporters to implant some form of constitutional monarchy.

As of 1820 each separate province took control of its own affairs, even though few of them had the human or material resources to do so with any chance of success. The principal exception was Buenos Aires, where Governor Martín Rodríguez and his chief minister, Bernardino RIVADAVIA, consolidated internal order; established a smooth-running provincial administration; and took such progressive steps as founding the University of Buenos Aires, creating a stock exchange, and reforming and simplifying the tax system. By suppressing several small monasteries and seizing church assets, they offended conservative traditionalists. They also sacrificed the interests of the interior by insisting that all foreign trade go through the port of Buenos Aires and by maintaining essentially a tariff primarily for revenue purposes to the detriment of domestic industries seeking protection.

Most key officials and supporters of the Buenos Aires government belonged to the so-called Unitarist faction whose name reflected its commitment to a centralized political system. Despite strong reservations in much of the interior, where opinion was basically federalist, a national congress convoked by Buenos Aires produced another centralist constitution in 1826, and Rivadavia became president of all Argentina under its terms. However, once again the adoption of such a constitution led to violent protest in much of the country. Worse, it happened at a time when war with Brazil over possession of Uruguay—which in 1825 had rebelled against Brazilian rule and rejoined Argentina—made national unity all the more important.

Recognizing his inability to impose the Unitarists' solution on the nation as a whole, Rivadavia resigned in mid-1827 and went into exile. Each province once more assumed full control of its affairs. Buenos Aires this time fell to the local faction of Federalists, led first by Governor Manuel DORREGO—until he was overthrown and murdered in December 1828 in an abortive comeback attempt by the Unitarists—and then Juan Manuel de ROSAS. The war with Brazil simply petered out, with Uruguay established under British mediation as an independent nation.

THE ROSAS ERA

Juan Manuel de Rosas, who dominated Argentina from 1829 to 1852, is one of the two most controversial figures of Argentine history, his only rival being Juan D. PERÓN. A wealthy rancher and successful exporter of hides and salt beef, Rosas's political ideal was the stability and tranquility of the colonial era. He felt little sympathy for the Unitarists' reform agenda and dismissed their brand of constitutional centralism as hopelessly impractical. Rosas chose to concentrate instead on protecting the immediate interests of Buenos Aires and his fellow ranchers. At the same time, he skillfully cultivated a wider base of popular support by presenting himself as a defender of traditional values while associating his enemies with unwelcome foreign influences.

Though Rosas assumed the governorship of Buenos Aires Province with dictatorial powers, he still found himself sometimes at odds with the provincial legislature. Therefore, in 1832 he resigned the office to assume leadership of a vast military campaign against the Indian peoples who still occupied much of the choicest land of the PAMPA and who, by their raiding parties, were making life precarious for the outermost creole settlements. He was brilliantly successful, pushing the Indian frontier southward to Patagonia and claiming for creole occupation great amounts of land that he divided among his followers or sold on easy terms. Rosas thereby laid the basis for the large-estate system in much of the best land of Argentina.

While Rosas was away, his wife and close adherents in Buenos Aires were stirring up trouble for the governors who succeeded him. The most extreme instance was the rise of a vigilante group known as the MAZORCA, which terrorized both Unitarists and lukewarm Federalists (that is, those not strictly beholden to Rosas: see under ''Argentina: Movements''). The upshot was that in 1835, the province welcomed Rosas back as governor, this time with the *suma del poder público*, or ''sum of public power,'' meaning that he was invested with supreme executive, legislative, and judicial authority. He did not dismiss the legislature or courts, but they now existed simply to do his bidding. Nor did he hesitate to apply terror as needed, whether by means of his official police and military apparatus or by unleashing the Mazorca against his foes. (It should not be forgotten, of course, that Rosas's enemies were not always squeamish about their methods, either.)

Rosas as governor curried favor with the church, but more in words than by action, for he did not return many of the church assets taken by Rivadavia, nor did he reverse the religious toleration that had been another of the Unitarists' achievements. He showed little interest in education but did build up an effective military, with whose help he extended his control beyond the confines of Buenos Aires province, forging alliances with Federalists of the interior and helping them overcome Unitarist or dissident Federalist rivals. He never attempted to create a full-fledged national government, much less issue a constitution. The other provinces of what was dubbed the Argentine Confederation merely delegated to him, as Buenos Aires governor, the right to act for all of them in matters of national security and foreign relations. Rosas was not much interested in how his provincial allies ran their own bailiwicks, only whether they gave unswerving allegiance to him as the leader of all.

Rosas's system had begun to take shape during his first governorship, but it was perfected only after 1835, and it withstood the test of repeated Unitarist conspiracies, including invasions launched from their Uruguayan base in exile. Rosas likewise withstood two efforts to unseat him by European powers in alliance with the Unitarists, the first in 1838 by France and the second in 1845–1848 by France and Great Britain combined. France was seeking redress for real or imaginary injuries suffered by her citizens; the British were angered at Rosas's insistence on keeping the Paraná River closed to foreign navigation and his meddling in Uruguay, where he allied with the Uruguayan Blanco Party in order to counter the Unitarist exiles. Both powers resorted to blockading the Argentine coast, but they were often at cross-purposes with each other and with the Unitarist exiles. Furthermore, they were not prepared to invest resources on the scale that would have been required to humble Rosas. Eventually, they withdrew without achieving their announced objectives. The British did not, however, withdraw from the FALKLAND ISLANDS, or Islas Malvinas, which they had taken by force in 1833, during Rosas's absence from the governorship.

Rosas was equally effective in defending the economic interests of the Buenos Aires ranchers, whose traditional cattle business was increasingly complemented by sheep raising for the export of wool. He decreed tariff protection for the artisanal industries of the interior provinces, but the policy was halfhearted, as his own agro-exporting class was best served by unhampered foreign trade. To cover military and other expenditures, he resorted to paper-money inflation, which hurt wage earners but not the ranchers whose exports were sold for foreign currency. Also, he kept the Paraná closed. However, the latter policy led to friction with his Federalist allies in the provinces upstream, while his general concentration on Buenos Aires interests tended to weaken his appeal nationally.

Once the threat posed by both Unitarist exiles and European powers had been dispelled, it seemed to many that the time had finally come to get the country properly organized with a federal constitution, yet Rosas still refused to do so. In response, one of his political allies, Justo José de URQUIZA—governor of Entre Ríos province up the Paraná River—set out to overthrow Rosas. He enlisted other disaffected Federalists, made peace with the Unitarists in Uruguay, and enlisted the help of Brazil, which had shared much the same grievances against Rosas as Britain and France. The culmination was the battle of Caseros, fought almost at the outskirts of Buenos Aires, in February 1852. Rosas's forces were defeated, and the dictator took ship for England, where he lived the rest of his life as an exile.

NATIONAL ORGANIZATION

Rosas had been the first Argentine leader to forge effective national unity. This achievement, along with his defense of national sovereignty against European intruders, largely accounts for the admiration he continues to receive from many Argentines. Yet he had to go before national unity could be institutionalized on a permanent basis, under the auspices of Urquiza, who called the constituent convention of 1853 that wrote the Argentine constitution which remains in force at the end of the twentieth century. It was federalist in structure but endowed the national authorities with extensive powers, including the right to "intervene" in a province under certain circumstances, deposing the governor in favor of a presidential "interventor"—a provision that would lend itself to frequent abuse in coming years. The constitution further incorporated a number of significant liberal reforms, among them the final abolition of SLAVERY in Argentina, and it committed the nation to a course of outward-oriented growth by such features as a clause expressly requiring the government to promote foreign immigration.

Buenos Aires Province refused to ratify the constitution and join the union. After Rosas's fall, it had come under the control mainly of returning Unitarist exiles who soon broke with Urquiza because of personal rivalries and because, in the last analysis, they wanted Buenos Aires to be the dominant partner in any new political arrangement. As a result, the authorities of the reorganized Argentine Confederation established their capital at Paraná, in Urquiza's home province, with Urquiza as president. They effectively opened the Paraná River to foreign trade and were able to bring some colonies of European immigrants to the interior provinces.

But the confederation also became bogged down in a continuing feud with the province of Buenos Aires, which proceeded to organize itself as an independent state. Thanks to its greater resources, this state became a model of progressive change, much as it had been in the 1820s. Domingo SARMIENTO, the future "schoolmaster president," presided over expansion of the provincial education system. Construction of the first Argentine railroad was begun in 1854, westward from the city of Buenos Aires into the adjoining pampa. Immigrants came to Buenos Aires, too, and most Argentine trade continued to flow through the port of the separatist province, despite the formal opening of the Paraná River.

The standoff between Buenos Aires and the confederation gave way in 1859–1861 to a series of armed confrontations. At first they favored Urquiza, but in the end the victory went to Bartolomé MITRE, governor of Buenos Aires and shortly to become president of a definitively united Argentina (1862–1868). Some revisions were made in the constitution to ease Buenos Aires's acceptance of it, but these were not substantial. On the other hand, some factions in the interior were still unprepared to accept the rule of a liberal PORTEÑO such as Mitre, who had to contend with repeated local uprisings that continued even after Argentina became involved, along with Brazil and Uruguay, in the WAR OF THE TRIPLE ALLIANCE against Paraguay (1865–1870). Argentina's primary role in the war was as a route through which Brazilian forces got to Paraguay, as the Brazilians did most of the allied fighting; yet the mere fact of being allied to Brazil, their traditional foe, rankled many Argentines. In the end Argentina settled in her own favor a dispute with Paraguay over territory in the Gran Chaco, but for Argentines their participation in the war has given rise to more historical recrimination than national pride.

Mitre was succeeded as president during the war by Sarmiento (1868–1874), who like Mitre faced scattered uprisings in the interior and like him did not hesitate at times to use brutal tactics against them. However, provincial malcontents were no match for a united national government that was able to purchase the latest military equipment and to move its forces across a steadily growing rail network. Thus, gradually internal peace was established. The government was often highhanded, brandishing the threat of arbitrary military impressment against unruly GAUCHOS, misapplying the constitution's intervention clause against uncooperative governors, and practicing widespread electoral fraud.

Moreover, political power was concentrated in a network of provincial bosses and members of a national mercantile, landowning, and professional elite, with little participation by popular elements. The principal organ of this loose coalition was the Partido Autonomista Nacional (PAN or National Autonomist Party), organized in time to elect Sarmiento's immediate successor, Nicolás AVELLANEDA (1874–1880). Yet the formal apparatus of constitutional government was maintained, and most civil liberties were respected. Property rights in particular were well protected. The system was thus basically liberal, in the nineteenth-century meaning of the term, even if not democratic, and it was well suited to the mission of fostering economic growth.

From the standpoint of state-building, there were still two important items of unfinished business. One was to incorporate into the effective national territory the southern regions, including most of PATAGONIA, that were still occupied by largely autonomous Indian groups. This was achieved in 1879–1880 by General Julio A. ROCA, Avellaneda's minister of war, in what Argentines called the CONQUEST OF THE DESERT. Much as happened in the western United States in the same years, the native people were either exterminated or herded into reservations, and the land was opened for white settlement. The other remaining problem was the relationship between the city of Buenos Aires and the national government. Its status as capital of both the nation and its wealthiest, most populous province led to continual tension between the authorities of one and the other; while the mere combination of Buenos Aires city and province created a unit so much stronger than the other provinces that the latter inevitably feared subordination to Buenos Aires's interests. The obvious solution was to detach the city as a separate federal district, which was finally done in 1880 in the aftermath of the

Plaza de Mayo, Buenos Aires, ca. 1880 ARCHIVO GENERAL DE LA NACIÓN.

government's triumph over the Patagonian Indians. Buenos Aires Province contested the move in a brief civil war, but to no avail. When Roca himself became next president (1880–1886), he ruled from a federal district.

ORDER AND PROGRESS

The consolidation of order was accompanied by a surge of social and economic modernization. One aspect of this was an impressive advance in public education, promoted not just by Sarmiento (who, among other things, imported women normal school teachers from the United States to show his fellow Argentines what a proper system of free public schools was like) but also by his successors. By the end of the century the literacy rate was approaching 50 percent, as against half that much when Sarmiento assumed the presidency.

To Sarmiento and his collaborators, education ideally should be laic rather than religiously oriented, and this too was achieved for schools under the national government's jurisdiction by a controversial law of 1884, passed during the Roca administration. The law took its place with other measures of the same decade establishing civil registry and civil marriage. The regime's support of secularization—while holding onto traditional state control over the church—led to a temporary rupture of relations with the Vatican but underscored its adherence to cultural and intellectual, if not always political, liberalism.

Most impressive of all was the pace of economic growth. In roughly the half century from the 1870s to World War I, the economy grew at a rate of about 5 percent annually—an achievement matched by no Latin American nation before or since. The growth was based mainly on a steady increase in the production and export of livestock products and grains. An emphasis on ranching was nothing new, though sales of jerked (dried and salted) beef dropped off sharply by the end of the century, even as fresh meat exports gradually increased. These involved both the sale of cattle on the hoof and refrigerated lamb or mutton. Hides remained another significant item in overseas trade, but WOOL became—and until the end of the century remained—the country's leading export.

Large-scale grain production was something entirely new. Until the 1870s Argentina was actually an importer of wheat and flour, whereas by 1900 wheat exports were a close second to wool. Previously, there had been no lack of suitable land, but crop farming was labor-intensive and population sparse. Massive European immigration, with over a quarter million persons entering the port of Buenos Aires in the record year 1889, provided the needed agricultural labor, even though not all went to the rural sector and by no means all stayed. Some, indeed, were *golondrinas* (swallows) commuting between Europe and Argentina to work the harvest season in both northern and southern hemispheres.

All this was accompanied by steady growth in transportation and other infrastructure. Most obvious was

151

the consistent advance of RAILROAD construction. Ultimately, it gave Argentina Latin America's largest rail network, stretching nearly 10,000 miles by 1900. Railroads reinforced political unity, and they allowed Tucumán sugar, for example, to be sold in a larger national market; even more importantly they tied all parts of the country to the port of Buenos Aires.

In the building and operation of railroads, foreign capital, technology, and equipment, from Great Britain above all, made an important contribution. Foreign investment likewise played a key role in financial services, with the establishment of branches of foreign banking firms. There was less direct foreign investment in incipient consumer-goods manufacturing, though many of the factories were started by immigrants or sons of immigrants. At least the land itself remained overwhelmingly in native hands, even if unequally distributed. In certain areas of agricultural colonization, landownership was rather widespread, but in the livestock sector and much of crop farming as well, the pattern was one of huge private estates, worked by wage labor or by tenants and sharecroppers.

The national government built some of the railroads in outlying areas unattractive to private investors. Its primary role, however, was to maintain order and to guarantee, if not the freedom to vote and have one's vote honestly counted, at least freedom of contract. This is what "Peace and Administration," the political slogan of Julio Roca, amounted to in practice. The same Roca, more than anyone else, set the tone for Argentine politics in the late nineteenth century. Both as president himself (including a second term from 1898 to 1904) and then as a power behind the scenes between presidencies, he proved a master manipulator who kept things running smoothly most of the time. To be sure, his immediate successor, Miguel JUÁREZ CELMAN (1886–1890), was forced to resign amid a financial crisis that he could not solve and had even helped to bring on through speculative mismanagement. But Carlos PELLEGRINI (1890–1892) then completed the presidential term while skillfully pulling the country out of the crisis.

A greater problem in the end was the exclusivism of the regime and the natural resentment of groups left out. The once free-living gauchos had been tamed by the advent of the sheep raising and a more modern military, and the rural population generally was either ignored or co-opted by the ruling machine. The urban working class, though it was beginning to form unions and its interests were defended by Latin America's first Socialist Party (established in 1896), was for the most part simply ignored. The professional middle class, however, was another matter. As Latin America's largest and best educated, it was fully conscious of its right to a larger voice and increasingly resentful of the regime's restrictive practices. The Unión Cívica Radical (UCR), or Radical Party as it came to be known, was founded in 1890 and had some success in channeling the middle-class discontent. In view of the prevalence of electoral fraud, the Radicals adopted a policy of boycotting elections and kept open the option of revolutionary direct action. Mainly they organized, grew in strength, and waited; they would finally win power in 1916.

The Radicals' message was a bitter condemnation of the existing regime as corrupt and undemocratic, devoted to all the vested interests while oblivious to the needs and desires of the population as a whole. The charges were often vague, but they contained a measure of truth. Revisionist historians of right and left would elaborate on them in succeeding years, giving the rulers of the period a somewhat tarnished image. More recently, as one thing after another went wrong in the Argentina of the late twentieth century under populist and military leadership alike, the elitist manipulators of the last quarter of the previous century earned some new respect. They did get things done, and they presided over a process of growth that made Argentina—for a time—Latin America's most developed country.

In addition to the treatment in general histories of Argentina, one may consult, for an interpretation of the independence period, TULIO HALPERÍN-DONGHI, *Politics, Economics, and Society in Argentina in the Revolutionary Period*, translated by Richard Southern (1975); on the early national era, MIRON BURGIN, *The Economic Aspects of Argentine Federalism, 1820–1852* (1946), JOHN LYNCH, *Argentine Dictator: Juan Manuel de Rosas, 1829–1852* (1981), and the classic historical polemic by DOMINGO F. SARMIENTO, *Life in the Argentine Republic in the Days of the Tyrants; or, Civilization and Barbarism* (1868; many later editions); on intellectual history and especially concepts of Argentine nationhood, NICLOAS SHUMWAY, *The Invention of Argentina* (1992); on the process of national organization, TULIO HALPERÍN-DONGHI, *Proyecto y construcción de una nación: Argentina, 1846–1880* (1980), and WILLIAM H. JEFFREY, *Mitre and Argentina* (1952); on the late nineteenth century, DOUGLAS W. RICHMOND, *Carlos Pellegrini and the Crisis of the Argentine Elites, 1880–1916* (1989); on economic and social history, JONATHAN C. BROWN, *A Socioeconomic History of Argentina, 1776–1860* (1979), JAMES R. SCOBIE, *Buenos Aires: From Plaza to Suburb, 1870–1910* (1974), and *Revolution on the Pampas: A Social History of Argentine Wheat, 1860–1910* (1964), RICHARD W. SLATTA, *Gauchos and the Vanishing Frontier* (1983), and MARK D. SZUCHMAN, *Order, Family, and Community in Buenos Aires, 1810–1860* (1987); and on British relations, HENRY S. FERNS, *Britain and Argentina in the Nineteenth Century* (1960).

DAVID BUSHNELL

### The Twentieth Century

The history of Argentina in the twentieth century turns on the problem of its place in the global economic order. Created in the final quarter of the nineteenth century as a "new" country—somewhat along the lines of Canada, Australia, South Africa, and New Zealand—a hundred years later it was still struggling unsuccessfully with the disappearance of those factors that had led to its emergence in the first place: the collapse of the British Empire, the rise of agricultural protectionism, and a western Europe increasingly turned inward.

One way of conceptualizing the entire sweep of the century is to consider what the country looked like to foreigners in 1914, and then to revisit it in 1944 and 1994. On the eve of the First World War, Argentina was one of the principal destinations of western European immigration and investment, and one of the chief beneficiaries of a relatively open international trading order. Between 1880 and 1914 the capital city of Buenos Aires had been remodeled to resemble Paris, but most of the principal buildings in the major provincial cities were also rendered in French beaux-arts style. Although located geographically in South America, the country faced east, in the sense that the major lines of communication had their terminus in Buenos Aires and other cities of the littoral (particularly Rosario, which was created as a major grain port). But it also looked across the Atlantic in cultural, culinary, and artistic fashions.

At the higher levels of society, an elite of ranchers-cum-lawyers and ranchers-cum-bankers took their cues from London and Paris, while a vast immigrant proletariat from Spain and Italy, as well as smaller complements from other countries, tended to regard Argentina as a temporary venue where they could attain the prosperity and well-being denied them by the exhausted countries they had left. They maintained as best they could their connections with their places of origin, particularly the Spanish and Italians, who constituted 80 percent of all foreign residents. Some men commuted back and forth (and probably maintained families in both places).

By some measures, Argentina ranked as one of the five or six wealthiest countries in the world in 1914. Probably the methodologies in use today would raise questions about the ranking, but certainly in terms of the overall value of trade, balance of payments, and prospects for future investment, the assessment was not overdrawn. Argentina on the eve of the First World War also possessed something that it has since lost—a sense of unbounded optimism, based on the nearly universal assumption that the boom years of 1880–1914 could be extrapolated indefinitely into the future. Certainly the notion of Argentina as a country located geographically in Latin America but not really part of it was justified by statistics: in the entire region no country except Uruguay (a lost Argentine province that resembles it in many ways) came close to it in prosperity, urbanity, sophistication, and well-being. And no country was more closely linked economically to the North Atlantic area.

Thirty years and two world wars later (in both of which the country had remained advantageously neutral), Argentina had consolidated much of that promise. It possessed an infrastructure that compared favorably with all but the wealthiest countries of western Europe. (While Greater Buenos Aires possessed a greatly disproportionate share of the nation's wealth and development, this was not regarded as a serious problem.) At the same time, the country as a whole had managed to

integrate large immigrant communities, whose children now spoke Argentine Spanish and thought of themselves as Argentines. It had, however, failed to achieve a working political consensus. After several unsuccessful attempts at political integration of a new middle class, by 1944 the armed forces, rather than civilian political parties, were the principal arbiters of the country's destiny. Whether in populist or conservative guise, a succession of generals stood at the country's helm for most of the time until 1982.

Argentina's exemplary prosperity at this point was due to the Second World War, which created an unlimited demand for foodstuffs and agricultural raw materials, particularly on the part of Great Britain, the country's principal customer and until lately its chief foreign investor. The intense need for Argentine products, and the inflated prices that the British were willing to pay for them, discouraged any serious thought about technological modernization in the countryside, and likewise postponed serious consideration of the role of industry, which grew in spite of, rather than because of, concrete government policy. The fate of the Pinedo Plan (1940), which attempted conscientiously to map out a program of balanced economic growth, is perhaps symptomatic: It fell victim to partisan politics and the firm conviction that "God is an Argentine," that is, that nature and a benevolent international environment would always provide.

The war left Britain virtually bankrupt, and Argentina was left to bank its hopes on a third world war, which never came. By the mid-1950s the country had entered into a gradual but persistent economic decline, which in turn introduced new tensions into the political fabric that exploded into near–civil war in the late 1960s and early 1970s. By 1994 the country seemed finally to have come to terms with the twentieth century, in the sense that it now saw its future largely in association with its South American neighbors, particularly Brazil and Chile, as well as with the United States as the principal power in the hemisphere and the world. Both changes were culturally wrenching, and Argentines resisted them as long as they could. But the consolidation of the European Common Market combined with the collapse of the Soviet Union, which had become the country's principal purchaser of cereals, left little choice.

This new development was buttressed by changing demographics. As a result of decades of economic stagnation and political conflict, one in ten Argentines now lived abroad, many in the very countries from which their ancestors had emigrated a hundred years before. But 1 million or more were also living in the United States and Canada. Meanwhile, Argentina's relative wealth continued to attract illegal immigration from poorer neighboring countries, particularly Bolivia and Paraguay, weakening its orientation toward Europe. Paradoxically, by the 1980s the invasion of popular culture from the United States acted as a social glue, perhaps the only one, binding younger Argentines of all social classes.

The promise of a closer association with the United States was slow to find fulfillment. For one thing, the two countries were competitive in major export lines, particularly cereals. For another, U.S. investment remained distrustful of Argentine political stability, and also U.S. corporations were forbidden by federal legislation to compete in a local environment where the basic instrument of negotiation was the gratuity offered under the table. Most of all, after the Cold War the United States was unsure of where Latin America as a whole—setting aside the particular problem of Argentina—fit in its overall design.

### 1900–1943

For the first thirty years of the century Argentina was often held up as a political exemplar for Latin America and indeed for much of southern Europe as well. It had in fact achieved a major transition to democracy through the implementation of universal manhood suffrage (SÁENZ PENA LAW, 1912), which in turn made possible the election of President Hipólito YRIGOYEN in 1916, the first such popularly chosen chief executive in all of South America. However, under Yrigoyen Argentina's political system was less competitive and open than it appeared at first glance. The new president regarded his Radical Party as the only legitimate repository of the national will, and himself as little less than indispensable for its actualization. Many of the traditional characteristics of Hispanic political culture—personalism, authoritarianism, sectarianism, as well as a syndicalist relationship with the labor movement—survived into the democratic period.

Though the Radical Party was originally organized to protest the promiscuous use of electoral fraud by the country's ruling elites, once in power Yrigoyen himself showed scant respect for the outcome of contests in which his party was defeated: He intervened to overturn the results of provincial elections more often than any previous government. Moreover, though Yrigoyen stepped down at the end of his first term in 1922, he quarreled with his handpicked successor, Marcelo T. de ALVEAR, who refused to do his bidding. The conflict between the two men split the Radical Party into "personalist" and "antipersonalist" wings, and although Yrigoyen managed to obtain reelection in 1928 as the candidate of the largest of the two rumps, he permanently alienated a large part of his former constituency, which, when the world crisis hit Argentina two years later, made common cause with his enemies and successfully overthrew both him and the existing political order.

Throughout the 1920s Argentina's conservative and provincial parties had struggled mightily to overturn the gathering hegemony of the Radical Party, but to no avail. By the middle of that decade many of Yrigoyen's critics were encouraged to dabble instead in antidemocratic ideologies imported from France and Italy. Argentine "nationalism" was a curious amalgam of clerical, militarist, xenophobic, and authoritarian sentiments rather than a coherent ideology. It also assumed many different forms. One was the Argentine Patriotic

League, whose followers specialized in breaking up labor demonstrations; another was the paramilitary "leagues," which trained on military bases during off-duty hours; yet another was a new clutch of newspapers and magazines that railed against the excess of "cosmopolitan" (e.g., immigrant) elements in Argentine life, as well as against British and American influence ("imperialism") in high places. In time Yrigoyen and the Radicals became the principal target of all these groups, and the Argentine army their chosen instrument.

The revolution of 1930 constituted, then, a temporary convergence of two movements. One was democratic but anti-Yrigoyen (Alvear himself, serving as ambassador to France, even gave the conspirators his tacit support). The other was not merely anti-Radical but committed to a new vision of the political order. General José Félix URIBURU, the leader of the coup that ousted Yrigoyen on 6 September, was a man of limited talents but firm authoritarian convictions. A combination of political naïveté and a worsening case of cancer forced his retirement in 1932 before he could complete his quasi-fascist project.

General Agustín P. JUSTO, Alvear's former war minister, struck a deal with the Conservative Party and the anti-Yrigoyen Radicals to hold new elections (in which he would be the presidential candidate), but with the important difference that the results would be predetermined by the Interior Ministry. Thus was born the "patriotic fraud," which effectively assured Conservative victories in the presidential contests of both 1932 and 1937, as well as in most races for congress and the provincial legislatures.

Former President Alvear returned from France in late 1930 expecting to be the victorious presidential candidate in new elections. Instead, he and his associates were temporarily exiled to the extreme Patagonian south. Some "antipersonalists" continued to support the Justo administration (the so-called CONCORDANCIA), but most returned to the parent Radical Party. With Yrigoyen's death in 1933, Alvear became its undisputed leader, a position he held until his death in 1942. His efforts to negotiate with President Justo to produce a more honest electoral system came to naught. His discussions with President Roberto M. ORTIZ (who took office in 1938) seemed to hold out more promise, but the latter resigned from office in 1940 due to ill health, and his replacement, Ramón S. CASTILLO, refused to carry the negotiations forward. The political stalemate was finally broken, somewhat unexpectedly, by a military coup in June 1943.

Both Radicals and (later) Peronists have referred to the 1930s as the "infamous decade." In so doing they are referring not merely to the systematic application of electoral fraud, but to a series of important changes in economic policy, the centerpiece of which is the ROCA-RUNCIMAN PACT, concluded with Great Britain in 1933. The treaty was Argentina's response to the threat of imperial preference, declared at the Ottawa Conference of 1932. In effect, it saved Argentina's place in British markets in exchange for preferential treatment for British exports in Argentina, accomplished through exchange control, new tariff walls against non-British goods, and a system of production and trade quotas. According to critics then and since, this effectively prevented Argentina from diversifying its economy, tying it instead to a semicolonial relationship to the United Kingdom.

In fact, however, whatever the intentions of its drafters, the pact had a very different effect. It helped Argentina to weather the world crisis better than most major countries (including the United States). And it even helped to promote the growth of Argentine industry, though in unintended and unexpected ways. The sudden introduction of commercial discrimination against American, German, and other products compelled Britain's major competitors to establish factories in Argentina, and by 1944 the country was producing a wide range of products, from light bulbs to textiles, formerly imported from abroad. This great leap forward was much accelerated by the Second World War, which deprived Britain of what advantages it had gained in 1933, since its industries were now utterly unable to service the Argentine market.

In many ways the Conservative antipersonalist administrations of the 1930s and early 1940s are among the best the country has ever experienced. Their accomplishments include a vast program of public works—hospitals, all-weather roads, ports, airports, and waterworks. They created a system of national parks and greatly extended the state railroads to the more remote provinces. They poured significant new investment into YPF, the state petroleum company. In contrast to the Perón regime and those that followed it, these parastatals were run along orthodox financial lines so that they did not constitute a drain on the budget.

Moreover, it was during this period that much of Argentina's modern social legislation was introduced, including the five-and-a-half-day work week, paid vacations, maternity leave, pensions for government employees, and indemnification for discharge from employment. The Justo administration also greatly increased the country's housing stocks by subsidizing low-cost dwellings.

## 1943–1966

The Conservatives failed, however, to anchor their accomplishments in the political realm. By 1943, in fact, it was clear that they also lacked a presidential candidate. President Castillo's decision to impose Senator Robustiano PATRÓN COSTAS of Salta provoked unhappiness throughout Concordancia ranks, but more to the point, it also led to unrest in the field-grade and flag ranks of the Argentine army. The military had been relatively quiescent since its return to the barracks in 1932, but by the early 1940s the army was rent with divisions and intrigues, which took the form of "lodges." One such group, the United Officers Group (GOU), was convinced that the Axis was about to win the war and concerned that Patrón Costas and the Conservatives (who were thought to be pro-British) might compromise the country's neutrality. This, at any rate, was the proximate cause of the revolution of 4 June 1943.

Between 1943 and 1946 Argentina's military men struggled both to provide programmatic definition for the new regime and to deal with the shifting currents of wartime politics. Three different flag-rank officers held the presidency during these years, each gradually ceding increasing power to Colonel Juan PERÓN, who became vice president in 1944 and a presidential candidate in 1946. Although hitherto unknown to the Argentine public, Perón was no stranger to military politics. He was an early member of the Argentine Patriotic League and had been an active conspirator in the revolution of 1930, for which he was rewarded with a position as aide-de-camp to the war minister and subsequently seconded to the Italian army, where he trained with Mussolini's Alpine troops.

A man of considerable charm, charisma, and tactical skills, Perón began building his political base within a few weeks after the coup of June 1943 by taking control of the Secretariat of Labor and Social Welfare. Within eighteen months he had turned it into a political machine dedicated to his own advancement, coopting labor leaders hitherto loyal to the Socialist and even Communist parties. It was Perón who finally realized Yrigoyen's dream of a syndicalist relationship with the labor movement, one that would outlast both his three presidencies and his person. At the same time, Perón was a master at the "sword and cross" rhetoric dear to Argentina's traditional and authoritarian right. The conjugation of the two produced a phenomenon hitherto unknown in Latin America—an enduring form of authoritarian populism.

The emergence of Perón in 1946 split the Argentine political community down the middle, dividing virtually all of the country's political forces. The new party attracted disaffected (or opportunistic) Conservatives, Socialists, Communists, and Radicals, although most of its actual cadres were recruited from the latter. Perón also benefited from the support of the Roman Catholic hierarchy, to whom he had promised not to abolish obligatory religious instruction in public schools (established in 1944).

A larger Radical remnant formed the bulk of the Democratic Union, the anti-Peronist coalition created for the 1946 elections, although it too drew support from the leadership of the Conservative, Radical, Socialist, and Communist parties. Its presidential candidate, José Tamborini, was a colorless career politician who proved no match for the dashing colonel and his fiancée, a small-time actress by the name of Eva Duarte ("Evita"), who became his wife—and much more—after the elections. Thus the elections of 1946 pitted "old" politics

against "new," with the Peronists winning a decisive 54 percent. Even so, the not negligible 46 percent that went to the opposition was the beginning of long-term polarization in Argentine politics.

The first Perón era (1946–1955) is generally divided into two periods. Up to 1951 the government benefited from the accumulated wartime surpluses of foreign exchange, as well as the high prices for agricultural products generated by the temporary collapse of the Western European economies. This allowed Perón to engage in boom-and-spend populism without producing inflationary pressures or requiring confrontations between different sectors of society. These happy conditions came to an end in 1952, reversing economic trends and forcing the president to take refuge in more orthodox policies. This in turn had the effect of neutralizing his primary constituency—the labor movement—while alienating the business community, agriculture, and important elements of Argentina's large urban middle class.

The untimely death of Eva PERÓN in 1952 was likewise a blow to the regime, since the president's wife acted as a kind of talisman and lightning rod for the opposition and was the idol of millions of working-class Argentines, particularly women. Without her pseudo-revolutionary discourse, the regime lost much of its "popular" mystique. A quarrel with the Catholic church—something against which Señora Perón would surely have counseled—eventually provoked conspiracies in the armed forces, the second of which led to Perón's overthrow in September 1955.

During Perón's first period of rule, the most salient feature of the regime seemed to be its authoritarian personalism, which some people mistook for fascism. In retrospect, it appears to have been a kind of Argentine New Deal, complete with government agencies that preempted much of the economic space formerly reserved to a handful of private businesses and agricultural enterprises. Certainly Peronism reshaped Argentine politics along more egalitarian lines, although in a rough-and-ready fashion: It created a modern labor movement, the most powerful in Latin America, and it gave women the right to vote. It continued the policies of the governments of the 1930s, delivering government services to long-neglected regions and social groups, although with a more specifically pointed political thrust. Like the New Deal, too, it often brandished the language of radical economic redress, while actually strengthening the power of the middle class even more than that of the labor movement.

However, these policies were not implemented in a particularly gentle way, and not always efficiently or honestly either. Loyalty to the leader, his wife, and their movement became the overarching criterion of civic virtue—and often, eligibility for government largess. As long as the government possessed the resources, it could prevail over the opposition in any electoral contest. But once it was forced to ask for sacrifice, and also to abandon its "anti-imperialist" banners (by negotiating an agreement with Standard Oil and seeking a rapprochement with the United States), it rendered itself vulnerable to attacks from both the left and the right.

The overthrow of Perón did not resolve any of the fundamental issues of Argentine politics. The coalition that produced the "Liberating Revolution" (September 1955) was as diverse as the one that had brought Perón to power in the first place, sometimes drawn from the same elements (the armed forces and the Catholic church) that had supported his election in 1946. The military saw the Liberating Revolution as an opportunity to purge Argentine public life of all Peronist influence, a sectarian exercise which took forms (such as total proscription of the party) that even many of its civilian supporters could not fully condone. Even at its lowest points, Peronism still counted for a third of the electorate, which maintained it as the largest single force in the country, and no one could hope to win a majority at the ballot box without its tacit support. The leader of the Radicals, Arturo FRONDIZI, surmised as much, and cleverly concluded a pact with Perón (now living in exile) by which the latter would instruct his followers to vote for Frondizi in the 1958 elections. In exchange, Frondizi would legalize the Peronists four years thence. The agreement assured Frondizi's election, but also his premature overthrow, since when he permitted the Peronists to run under their own names in the elections of 1962, the armed forces quickly deposed him.

In retrospect, the failure of the Frondizi presidency was probably the costliest episode in the country's political history. Frondizi sought both to integrate Peronism into the country's democratic life and at the same time to wean away many of Perón's followers to a more moderate and responsible form of populism-cum-nationalism. Unfortunately, the armed forces insisted upon regarding Frondizi himself as some sort of covert leftist, while a dissident faction of his own Radical Party (the so-called Radicals of the People) vehemently objected to any effort to end the proscription of the Peronist Party. These developments eventually canceled out the early achievements of Frondizi's administration—the attraction of new investment, particularly from the United States, and major initiatives in science and education.

Following Frondizi's overthrow, the military staged new elections in which Arturo ILLIA, the candidate of the Radicals of the People, limped into office with a mere 26 percent of the vote. (The Peronists, forbidden once again from presenting their own candidates, registered their protests with blank ballots.) Illia was an austere and honest politician, but clearly a minority president whose very presence in the CASA ROSADA was mortgaged to the goodwill of the military. This was a limitation with which he himself could not live, provoking a confrontation that led to his replacement by the commander in chief of the Argentine army, General Juan Carlos ONGANÍA, in June 1966.

## 1966–1973

Between 1966 and 1973 three different generals took turns trying to rule Argentina, none with much success. The purpose of the exercise, which General Onganía insisted on calling the "Argentine Revolution," was no longer to eradicate Peronism so much as it was to wait out the death of its leader, at which point elections could be safely convoked. This presupposed, however, that in the meanwhile the generals would be able to manage the Argentine economy with at least modest success. After two relatively good years, economic deterioration resumed, provoking popular disorder that climaxed in a general uprising in the province of Córdoba in May 1969. Moreover, the generals were beginning to quarrel amongst themselves. Former president General Pedro ARAMBURU (1955–1958), who had been talking to the civilian politicians, was kidnapped and murdered in 1970 under circumstances that suggest guerrilla collusion with the authorities.

By the early 1970s what most Argentines remembered about Perón's period of power was that the times had been better (which indeed they had). Even his "bad" period (1952–1955) seemed desirable by comparison. The overall effect was to re-Peronize important sectors of the middle class. This was politically significant because it suddenly pushed most Argentines into the Peronist camp. (The trade union movement and most unorganized workers—household servants, for example—had never wavered in their loyalty.) Moreover, the new generation of Argentine students had no personal memory of the Perón period, but was much impressed by family accounts and an accumulating "revisionist" literature that equated Peronism, which its enemies in the 1940s and 1950s likened to fascism, with "movements of national liberation" in the third world. This had the lethal effect of updating Peronism for a new generation captivated by the example of the Cuban Revolution and the anticolonial revolutions in Africa and Asia.

This ideological mutation was much encouraged by Perón himself. After brief sojourns in Paraguay, Panama, the Dominican Republic, and Venezuela, in the late 1950s he settled in Franco's Spain, where he perfected a confusing rhetoric that allowed all but the most intransigent anti-Peronists to assume that in the event of his return, their agendas would prevail. At the same time, the Perón residence in Puerta de Hierro became a place of pilgrimage for Argentine politicians of the most varied persuasions, each of whom left the encounter convinced that the former president's return was the sine qua non for Argentina's recovery as a great and prosperous nation.

Perhaps the most important aspect of the Peronist revival of the 1970s was the sudden adherence of young people of middle- and upper-middle-class origins, many of whom began their political careers in formations of the extreme right or extreme left. The two groups eventually hived off an urban guerrilla movement, which specialized in selective assassinations and

157

kidnapping of unsympathetic figures of the military regime. While he refused to take responsibility for these violent actions, Perón also refused to condemn them, cynically declaring that they were the inevitable result of "oligarchical" rule and "surrender to the forces of imperialism." In effect, the Peronist youth and its guerrilla cohorts convinced the generals, already beset with economic problems and growing popular discontent, that it would be better to return power to the civilians.

Perón was allowed to return briefly to Argentina in 1972, though forbidden from running for president the following year. His stand-in, Héctor CÁMPORA, won the race with 49 percent of the vote and assumed office in May 1973. Almost immediately, however, it became apparent that the real power in the new administration lay with the Peronist Youth and the more leftward elements of the party. Perón ordered Cámpora to resign, and his successor to convoke new elections for September. On that occasion Perón returned to power with nearly 62 percent of the vote.

### 1973–1994

Perón was seventy-eight years old and in problematic health. The selection of his third wife, María Estela Martínez (Isabel) de PERÓN, as his running mate was not particularly reassuring, since she was almost illiterate and possessed of far less native political talent than Eva Duarte. Although Perón returned to power on a wave of popular euphoria, he quickly became bogged down in the country's intractable economic problems. More to the point, he also became embroiled in a controversy with the Peronist Youth and other leftward elements of his coalition, who regarded Peronism in power as entirely too bland and conservative. By 1974 Perón had expelled these young people from the movement, and they resumed guerrilla actions against the government

they had done so much to install. After Perón's death later that year, they accelerated their violent activities, doing much to undercut the fragile credibility of Isabel Perón's succession.

Brief and inglorious, Isabel's tenure lasted as long as it did only because the military had decided to let things deteriorate until there was wide popular clamor for their return. When they finally overthrew her in March 1976, they not only decimated the tiny urban guerrilla movement, but engaged in a sweep that eventually resulted in the "disappearance" of some 9,000 persons, some of whom had links to terrorism or to the Left, but many more of whom were innocent victims. At incalculable human and moral cost, a semblance of order was restored in Argentina, and for a brief period (1978–1980) the country experienced a modest economic recovery. By 1981, however, huge government deficits and general mismanagement caused a revival of inflation—and of political activity. To neutralize both, in April 1982 President General Leopoldo GALTIERI decided to invade the Falkland (Malvinas) Islands, long under British occupation but claimed by every Argentine government for more than 150 years.

The recuperation of the Malvinas suddenly reversed the fortunes of the military government, but only briefly. Somewhat unexpectedly, the British (or rather, Prime Minister Margaret Thatcher) decided to dispatch an expeditionary force to retake the islands. By June contingents of the Royal Marines and the British army had defeated the Argentine occupation force, which did not put up much of a fight. The humiliation of the Argentine military was complete, and President Galtieri was forced to resign. The following year Radical Raúl ALFONSÍN, one of the chief critics of the military, was elected president.

Alfonsín's triumph was significant on two counts. It

Demonstration in the Plaza de Mayo for "Los Desaparecidos" (the missing), ca. 1980. © 1983 ENRIQUE SHORE / WOODFIN CAMP & ASSOCIATES, INC.

was the first time the Peronists had to go to the polls without Perón—and the first presidential election they had ever lost. The result was to provoke considerable soul-searching and subsequent attempts to modernize and renovate the party. Alfonsín's victory was also the product of considerable defection from other parties, including the Peronists and the small conservative parties. Radicalism remained the faith of only one out of four voters, and after a brief burst of personal popularity, the new president discovered his limits.

Because Alfonsín ended his term in 1989 several months ahead of time and in a rush of hyperinflation, it is easy to overlook his real accomplishments. He normalized the political scene; he brought the commanders in chief of the armed forces to trial for human rights offenses; he ordered an investigation of disappearances, which eventually documented their exact number and nature; and he successfully resisted two military uprisings, one sparked by the Left and one by the Right. He also provided Argentina with a new identity as a country at once "Western, nonaligned, and developing." During his rule Argentina was an avid participant in the councils of the nonaligned and a pointed critic of the United States in Central America and elsewhere.

Unfortunately, Alfonsín inherited a large foreign debt and a huge apparatus of money-losing government enterprises. A politician with no training in economics, he was by temperament inclined to seek ideological solutions to concrete problems. He wasted two years trying to divide the Western European countries from the United States on the debt issue, and for practical political reasons chose not to liquidate or reduce the size of the parastatals. (Had he chosen to do so, however, most likely he would have encountered serious resistance from the Peronists.) Eventually mismanagement—and the larger difficulties Argentina faced in a protectionist world—exacted its price. By 1989 the government had lost control of its own economic situation. There was a massive flight of capital, and the Argentine unit of currency lost value exponentially. In May the Radical candidate for the presidency, Córdoba governor Eduardo Angeloz, was defeated by Peronist Carlos Saúl MENEM. A seven-month transition period had been anticipated between administrations, but within days of Menem's election it was obvious that the Alfonsín government had lost the ability to govern. The inauguration date was accelerated so that Menem could immediately reassure the panic-stricken public.

Menem took office during one of the darkest moments of modern Argentine history. He had served two terms as governor of La Rioja, a small, poverty-stricken province in the northwest where he had put thousands of his friends and followers on the government payroll, compensating them with scrip redeemable only within provincial boundaries. This was hardly a reassuring preamble to his presidency, but almost from the moment of taking office he reversed course. In effect, Menem took the kind of measures to assure Argentine

economic stability that no government, including those dominated by the military, had ever dared to attempt. He also reversed age-old policies that discouraged foreign investment and saving, and most important of all, he proceeded to privatize Argentina's huge public sector. At the same time, he broke the back of the country's powerful labor movement.

Menem also tackled the military question head-on. He pardoned the six commanders in chief of the armed forces whom Alfonsín's courts had sentenced to lifetime reclusion for human rights offenses. This gave him virtually unlimited control of the armed forces, something no Argentine president since 1930 could claim to possess. It also permitted him to slash military budgets, greatly reducing the size of the armed forces, and eventually (in 1994) to eliminate conscription. One attempt to overthrow his government in December 1990 was easily turned aside; the sight of the rebels surrendering army headquarters in downtown Buenos Aires, ordered on their hands and knees by loyalist troops, underscored the low estate into which the praetorian forces in Argentine society had fallen.

By 1993 Argentines had repatriated more than $5 billion of the purportedly $50 billion worth of assets offshore. Foreign investment had returned to the country. The Argentine peso was placed on par with the dollar, a strict fiscal discipline that reduced inflation to single digits. At the same time, dismantling huge parastatals and privatizing essential government services (education, health) opened a new gap in Argentina between rich and poor, and badly frayed the fabric of what had once been Latin America's quintessential middle-class society. Nonetheless, Menem continued to hold the support of more than 40 percent of the Argentine public, while his opposition was divided and confused.

At this point the president decided to alter the Argentine constitution of 1853, which forbade consecutive presidential terms. Somewhat surprisingly, he was able to convince former president Raúl Alfonsín, his archenemy, to endorse the idea of a new charter. The result was to divide the Radical Party yet further, thus all but assuring Menem's reelection in 1995.

Two large questions hover over Argentina. The first is whether it will find a role in the world economy that provides the basis for sustained economic growth. While internal Argentine policies, such as unsound monetary practices, disincentives to agricultural and industrial productivity, and irresponsible administration of government resources, have undoubtedly inhibited economic development since the 1950s, it is still unclear whether even an open, liberal, and free-trading Argentina will find the kind of insertion that was available to it prior to 1930. Perhaps the most encouraging development has been the increasing economic coherence of other South American neighbors, particularly Chile and Brazil, which may over time provide a replacement for the European markets that once made possible an exemplary pattern of growth.

The second question is whether Argentina will fashion impersonal political institutions capable of guaranteeing pluralism and freedom, as well as the rights of property and an independent judiciary. It appears that personalism is still the operative political doctrine, with Menem (and his finance minister Domingo Cavallo) little less than indispensable to stability and order. While the Peronist Party has successfully made the transition to a modern political movement since the death of General Perón, it and its rival, the Radical Party, are both prone to extended periods of one-man rule. The survival of Alfonsín as the president of the Radical Party while Menem plots his reelection, suggests that the political development of Argentina continues to lag behind its other qualities as a nation, which include remarkable creativity, a capacity for adaptation, and a strong will to belong to the most modern community of nations.

EZEQUIEL MARTÍNEZ ESTRADA, X-Ray of the Pampa (1971); ALBERTO CIRIA, Parties and Power in Modern Argentina, 1930–1946 (1974); MARK FALCOFF, Prologue to Perón: Argentina in Depression and War, 1930–1945 (1975); DAVID ROCK, Argentina in the Twentieth Century (1975) and Authoritarian Argentina: The Nationalist Movement and Its History, Its Impact (1993); Reflexiones sobre la nación Argentina (1982); ROBERT D. CRASSWELLER, Perón and the Enigmas of Argentina (1986); SANDRA MCGEE DEUTSCH, Counterrevolution in Argentina, 1900–1932 (1986); CARLOS H. WAISMAN, From Military Rule to Liberal Democracy in Argentina (1987) and Reversal of Development in Argentina: Postwar Counterrevolutionary Policies and Their Structural Consequences (1987); PAUL LEWIS, The Crisis of Argentine Capitalism (1990); ROSENDO FRAGA, Argentina en las urnas, 1931–1991 (1992); SUSANA TORRADO, Estructura social de la Argentina, 1945–1983 (1992); RICARDO PIGLIA, Respiración artificial (1994).

MARK FALCOFF

See also **Argentina: Organizations, Political Parties; Falklands/Malvinas War.**

**ARGENTINA: CIVIL CODE,** a set of laws governing Argentine society in matters pertaining to family law, inheritance, the ownership of goods, and legal contracts and obligations. Congress, originally authorized to do so by the Argentine Constitution of 1853, on 6 June 1863 finally empowered the Argentine president to form special committees to draft civil, commerical, military, and penal codes. The civil code was the product of one man, Dalmacio VÉLEZ SARSFIELD, a jurist and legislator from the province of Córdoba who had been active in Argentine politics since the 1820s.

Vélez's vision of society was both patriarchal, in recognizing the husband's legal control and patria potestad (parental authority) over his children and the wife's lack of them, and individualistic, in allowing individuals to enter freely into contracts. The code Vélez wrote also reaffirmed concepts of marriage and divorce that were rooted in canon law, especially his stipulation that separation was the only solution to an irreconcilable marriage.

The Argentine government adopted Vélez's code by promulgating law No. 340 in September 1869. Since the civil code was put into effect in 1871, several major changes have transformed Vélez's vision of the Argentine family and society. Disputes between church and state led in 1888 to law No. 2393 sanctioning civil marriage. In 1919 another set of revisions, which transformed the legal status of minor children, was followed in 1948 by further changes in the form of law No. 13.252, which enabled Argentines to adopt children. Other revisions, incorporated in law No. 11.357 of 1926, removed many legal restrictions on women. Finally, in 1985, divorce and women's right to share in exercising patria potestad over their children became legal, thereby completing the civil code's recognition of the transformation of the Argentine family and replacing Vélez's patriarchal views.

JUAN CARLOS RÉBORA, La familia (boceto sociológico y jurídico, 2 vols. (1926); DONNA J. GUY, "Women, Family, and the Law in Nineteenth-Century Argentina," Journal of Family History 10, no. 3 (1985): 318–331; JULIO J. LÓPEZ DEL CARRIL, Patria potestad, tutela y curatela (1993).

DONNA J. GUY

**ARGENTINA: COMMERCIAL CODE,** the body of legislation that governs the business and legal practices associated with industry and commerce in Argentina. The original version, drafted in 1857 by Dalmacio VÉLEZ SARSFIELD and Eduardo Acevedo for Buenos Aires Province, was implemented there after 1859 and by 1862 had been put into effect throughout the country. The same body of law was also adopted by Paraguay, and most of it was implemented in Uruguay in 1865.

Since the commercial code was enacted well before the civil code went into effect in 1871, it contained many provisions that served as substitutes for civil law. This circumstance, as well as changes in late-nineteenth-century business practices, forced reconsideration of many aspects of the law. Accordingly, a major revision of the commerical code was enacted in 1889. Since that time, parts of the law have been subjected to various changes, notably in 1914, 1946, and 1963.

The role of the commerical code in Argentine economic development has been of critical importance. Since 1861 it has made it possible for foreign and domestic businesses to operate under a uniform code of laws. Such stability has been essential for the formation of modern corporations and for the creation of a system of banks and other credit institutions. The formulation and implementation of this code helped stimulate the economic modernization of Argentina.

Código de comercio con las referencias al código y la legislación complementaria (1975).

DONNA J. GUY

**ARGENTINA: CONSTITUTIONS.** Argentina was the last Latin American country, of those that obtained independence in the early nineteenth century, to adopt an effective national constitution, but the one finally adopted—in 1853—has proved to be Latin America's longest lasting. The first serious attempt to write a constitution came in 1813, when the Asamblea General Constituyente met in Buenos Aires for that purpose but was unsuccessful. It is remembered instead for its liberal reform legislation. Two years later a temporary frame of government, the Estatuto Provisional (Provisional Statute), was issued by a junta representing the city of Buenos Aires. It provided for the formal separation of powers and detailed the rights and responsibilities of citizenship, but was intended to last only until a new constituent congress could adopt a permanent constitution.

Not until 1819 was a constitution in fact issued. It established a highly centralized form of government and was drafted in such a way that it could easily be fitted out with a constitutional monarch, in case one should be recruited in Europe. Thanks both to its centralism and to its crypto-monarchism, the 1819 constitution aroused wide opposition; in much of the country it was a dead letter, and even in Buenos Aires and its immediate hinterland it proved ephemeral. The next Argentine constitution, that of 1826, met the same fate. Adopted under the auspices of the Unitarist party of Bernardino RIVADAVIA, it, too, was centralist and on that ground was soon repudiated by most of the Argentine interior.

Although efforts to impose a national constitution ended in failure, the individual provinces one after another adopted constitutions for their internal government. Some of these were clumsily drafted documents that only give a veneer of legality to the rule of local CAUDILLOS. Others, as in Córdoba and Corrientes, gave their provinces a systematic form of political organization and, though not always observed to the letter, were not simply ignored. One conspicuous exception was Buenos Aires, which not only failed to adopt a provincial constitution but also, during the long dictatorship of Juan Manuel de ROSAS (1829–1832, 1835–1852), obstructed efforts to draft a constitution for the nation as a whole.

The fall of Rosas created the conditions for national-level constitutional organization. Justo José de URQUIZA, who led the coalition that ousted Rosas, called a constituent convention that met in 1853 at Santa Fe and produced the first successful Argentine constitution. Incorporating the main features of a proposal drawn up by Juan Bautista ALBERDI (which in turn owed something to the United States constitutional model), it was broadly federalist in design, allotting the provinces substantial yet carefully defined powers in local affairs, while giving the national authorities extensive faculties to maintain order and to assist economic development. A clause that was later subject to frequent abuse allowed the federal government to "intervene" in a province when public order was threatened. Another article expressly called on the federal authorities to promote foreign immigration. The constitution gave Roman Catholicism official status as the religion of the nation but placed it under state control (*patronato*) and expressly gave toleration to non-Roman Catholics. A number of other liberal reform measures (for instance, the final abolition of SLAVERY) were included in the text of the constitution.

The province of Buenos Aires initially refused to ratify the 1853 constitution, organizing itself as an independent state with a constitution of its own. This act of secession reflected distrust of Urquiza in Buenos Aires and the fear that a federal government controlled by the interior provinces might adopt measures inimical to Buenos Aires interests. However, after a brief interlude of civil warfare, Buenos Aires agreed to enter the union. It insisted, as a condition, that the constitution be reformed so as to strengthen the autonomy of the provinces; this was done by a reform convention of 1860.

In reality, the federalist nature of the Argentine constitution was steadily undermined both by the abuse of the intervention clause and by the practice of granting financial subsidies from the national to the provincial treasuries. Yet the constitution remained generally in force until 1949, when the government of Juan D. PERÓN replaced it with a new charter that eliminated the prohibition of immediate reelection of the president and incorporated an elaborate set of social guarantees.

The 1949 constitution was revoked after Perón fell from power in 1955. The constitution of 1853 was then restored, although in 1957 it was amended to include a considerably briefer list of social guarantees. Many of its provisions were superseded by the military and civilian regimes that prevailed from the fall of Perón until the restoration of constitutional normalcy in 1983. It was never formally replaced, however, and since 1983 has been fully in effect.

LEO S. ROWE, *The Federal System of the Argentine Republic* (1921); AUSTIN F. MACDONALD, *Government of the Argentine Republic* (1942), chap. 7 and *passim*; SANTOS P. AMADEO, *Argentine Constitutional Law* (1943); ARTURO ENRIQUE SAMPAY, ed., *Las constituciones de la Argentina, 1810–1972* (1975); MIGUEL A. KMEKDJIAN, *Análisis pedagógico de la constitución nacional* (1983).

DAVID BUSHNELL

**ARGENTINA: FEDERALIST PACTS (1831, 1852),** de facto federalist alliances between the Argentine littoral provinces. After the collapse of the UNITARIST experiment in the 1820s, local caudillos took control of the provinces. Often seen as the opponents of legal rule, they were nevertheless concerned to forge a framework for reconciling interprovincial relations, because some rules had to be spelled out for relations with foreign governments, customs regulations needed enforcing, and, most important, peace had to be restored between

Buenos Aires and other provinces. Moreover, these governors were determined to counter the LIGA UNITARIA, which united the interior provinces in 1830 under General José María PAZ. On 4 January 1831, the governors of Entre Ríos, Santa Fe, and Buenos Aires (later joined by the governor of Corrientes) signed the first federalist pact. In a general sense, this accord served as the skeleton constitution for a decentralized federation of provinces and as the blueprint until the formal 1853 Constitution. The pact embraced the principle of free trade and self-governing provinces but left the issue of control over customs revenues simmering in ambiguity. In effect, Buenos Aires retained its grip over the primary source of the region's fiscal revenues.

This control by Buenos Aires eventually became a factor in bringing down the Buenos Aires caudillo Juan Manuel de ROSAS in early 1852. The victorious alliance, led by the Entre Ríos governor, General Justo José de URQUIZA, reinvoked the 1831 pact, and on 31 May 1852 a new federal pact was signed, this time involving most of the interior provinces. It gave sweeping powers to Urquiza as interim director but also called for a Constitutional Congress, which a year later approved a new constitution for the Republic. Buenos Aires, however, was loath to join the federation and be stripped of its grip over the customhouse, and eventually seceded from the new confederation. In 1861, after some amendments, Buenos Aires agreed to accept the 1853 Constitution. The federal pacts served as intermediate formulas until full constitutional rule could be consolidated.

JOHN LYNCH, *Argentine Dictator: Juan Manuel de Rosas, 1829–1852* (1981), esp. pp. 138–139; HAYDEL GOROSTEGUI DE TORRES, *Historia argentina: La organización nacional* (1972), esp pp. 19–31; DAVID ROCK, *Argentina, 1516–1982: From Spanish Colonization to the Falklands War* (1985; rev. ed. 1987), esp. pp. 104–120.

JEREMY ADELMAN

**ARGENTINA: GEOGRAPHY.** The Argentine Republic, the official name of the country located on the southeastern edge of South America, lies between 21.5 and 55 degrees south latitude. Natural boundaries in the east are the URUGUAY RIVER and the Atlantic Ocean; in the north, the PARANÁ and PILCOMAYO rivers; and in the west, the high summits of the ANDES. The 33,070,000 inhabitants (1991) live in a continental territory of 1,112,160 square miles, 85.7 percent of them concentrated in urban areas. The birthrate is 20.0 per thousand, infant mortality is 25.7 per thousand, and life expectancy is 71 years. There is a 95.3 percent literacy rate. The country is administratively organized into twenty-two provinces, the national Territory of Tierra del Fuego, and the Federal District of Buenos Aires.

Naturally well diversified, Argentina comprises ten major geographical regions: (1) the Platine front, the most densely populated segment, overlooking the RÍO DE LA PLATA estuary; (2) the Littoral, the provinces bordering on the Paraná and Uruguay rivers; (3) the northeast, composed of the provinces contiguous to Paraguay; (4) the northwest, including the rim lands of the Bolivian altiplano; (5) the Córdoban and Pampean sierras in the center of the country; (6) Cuyo on the eastern slopes of the Andes; (7) the PAMPA, comprising the central provinces; (8) Neuquén and northern Patagonia; (9) southern Patagonia; and (10) Argentine TIERRA DEL FUEGO.

The climate of the Platine front and most of the northeast is subtropical and humid, with rains peaking in the summer months, while the north and northwest share the aridity of the Paraguayan CHACO and the Bolivian ALTIPLANO, with sporadic summer rains swelling the few rivers of the region. Equally dry are the eastern margins of the Andes and the pampean sierras: most of the water in these regions comes from the melting of snow in the Andes. In the Andes of Neuquén, humidity crossing from the Pacific Ocean leads to greater precipitation and to a permanent snow cover that feeds numerous streams and piedmont lakes. The arid pampa and northern Patagonia receive little rain, being in the shadow of the Andes and thus deprived of the humidity of the southern winds. Southern Patagonia is a cold, wind-battered region with little rainfall in the winter. The Argentine segment of Tierra del Fuego is cold all year round but more humid than Patagonia owing to the westerly winds blowing in from the subantarctic Pacific.

In correspondence with this variety of climatic regions, the vegetation also varies remarkably. Subtropical forests and wetlands, with remnant stands of tropical species, abound in the Littoral and northeast. In the northern Chaco plains, shrubs and hardwoods are common, while evergreen forests arise nearer the Andean piedmont. In the northwest, thorny vegetation and dry shrubs grow in the few valleys that descend from the altiplano. The pampean sierras as well as the Cuyo piedmont are covered by hard scrub, dry grass, and halophytic shrubs; only near rivers have green oases developed. The core of the pampa and northern Patagonia is dominated by gramineous species favorable to the grazing of cattle and sheep. In Neuquén and along the foothills of the Patagonian Andes, there are rain forests similar to those on the wetter Pacific side of the Andes. In southern Patagonia as well as in Tierra del Fuego, only hard grasses and isolated shrub tussocks are able to weather the constant winds and cool temperatures.

In a country of open plains, with the exception of the northwest and the Andes, the early settlers found the territory well suited for ranching. This was also the main activity in the plains close to the Río de la Plata and Paraná rivers. Agricultural practices in the tradition of the peninsula, for example, concentrated irrigation of alluvial valley floors for purposes of horticulture and grain production, were applied only in the river oases of the northwest, in Cuyo, and in the pampean sierras, in the many areas where there had once been Indian agricultural communities. Here developed an agrarian aristocracy that was more conservative, thrifty, and daring than the ranching elites of the Río de la Plata. During colonial times, many settlements in the interior functioned separately from those on the estuary, their economic life concentrated on sugar plantations, grain production, and raising animals of burden for the mining settlements in Peru.

Only after independence (1816) and the tumultuous years that followed did the pastoral-agrarian economy that reigned during the republic's golden years arise. The old colonial SALADEROS (meat-salting establishments) became cattle ranches; wild horses roaming free in the pampa were replaced by stock kept behind barbed-wire fences; improved pastures resulted in a better quality of meat and a competitive beef-exporting industry. Agriculture also underwent a revolution. New immigrants planted cereal and industrial grains in the fertile soils along the Paraná River and the Río de la Plata estuary. By contrast, the traditional agricultural methods of the interior languished. As new waves of immigrants arrived, colonization advanced into the dry plains of the southern pampa and northern Patagonia, opening new fields for hard grains and specialized fruit orchards. The irrigated valleys at the foot of the Andes were transformed into fertile oases for fruit, vineyards, and vegetables.

These developments laid the foundations of a strong agrarian economy in Argentina capable of keeping the fiscal coffers filled by means of active exporting. The country attracted growing numbers of immigrants, most of whom were not interested in joining the agricultural labor force, becoming instead an "urban-industrial" working class that provided ancillary services to the expanding beef- and wheat-exporting activities of Argentina. Even in the 1990s, agricultural production makes up 34 percent of national exports, with only 12 percent of the economically active population engaged in agro-pastoral activities. Roughly 360 million acres are classified as arable land—65 million acres as farmland and the rest as natural and artificial pastures. The latter support 50.5 million head of cattle, 4.5 million hogs, and 27.5 million sheep. New contributions to the agricultural output of the country have been sorghum and maize, raised mostly for export, which make up 13 percent of total exports.

Industrial development is to a large degree indebted to the agrarian bases of the country. Meat and grain export, toward which the economy in Argentina has been oriented since the early twentieth century, demands an urban-industrial infrastructure to support transportation and shipping. This infrastructure is provided mostly by the cities on the waterfront: Buenos Aires, Rosario, Paraná, and Bahía Blanca. At the same time, food-processing establishments, packing plants, and grain mills have multiplied in the larger cities. The expansion of the urban population necessitated a growth in services, manufacturing, construction, and administration. The service sector of Argentina comprises 23.3 percent of the labor force, manufacturing 19.7 percent, construction 6.6 percent, and administration 13.5 percent. They contribute 18.3 percent, 32.8 percent, 6.4 percent, and 8 percent, respectively, to the gross national product.

The figures show that manufacturing has become the most efficient economic activity of the country. Nevertheless, the extreme reliance on the export of agricultural commodities, the low rate of reinvestment in other sectors of the economy, the high demand for consumer goods, the obligations of the state, and the maintenance of public administration and armed forces have imposed on the country a burden it has been almost unable to bear since the middle of the twentieth century. Although exports have dominated imports between 15 and 25 percent since 1960, large foreign loans had to be incurred. In 1987 a crisis point was reached when the nation had a negative payment balance of 4.2 billion dollars and an outstanding external debt of 56 billion dollars. Interest payments alone on this debt constituted 53 percent of the income from all exports. In 1988, the country's annual inflation rate reached 650 percent, and the rate of economic growth was reduced to −1.1 percent. Great improvements were made in the early 1990s.

The inoperative economic system of Argentina stood in stark contrast to its great natural and human resources. The regional variety of the country allows the production of a wide range of foods, and with an average daily calorie intake of 2,920 per person, the nation is the second best fed on the continent, just behind Uruguay. The oil, gas, and coal supplies of Patagonia assure that the country's energy needs are met; the nation produces 157,730,000 barrels of oil per year (1988) and needs to import only 13,463,000. Hydroelectricity is provided by numerous stations located in the Andes and along the Paraná and Uruguay rivers.

ALFONSO ARNOLDS, *Geografía económica argentina* (Buenos Aires, 1963); JAMES R. SCOBIE, *Argentina: A City and a Nation* (1971); TULIO HALPERÍN-DONGHI, *Argentina: La democracia de las masas* (Buenos Aires, 1972); FEDERICO A. DAUS, *Geografía y unidad argentina* (Buenos Aires, 1978); GUILLERMO A. TERRERA, *Geopolítica argentina* (Buenos Aires, 1983); MARIO QUADRI C., *La Argentina descentralizada* (Buenos Aires, 1986); JUAN ROCCATAGLIATTA, *Argentina hacia un nuevo ordenamiento territorial* (Buenos Aires, 1986); PATRICIO H. RANDLE, *Geografía histórica argentina (Buenos Aires, 1987)*; CARLOS REBORATTI, *Nueva capital, viejos mitos* (Buenos Aires, 1987); MARIANO ZAMORANO, *Argentina* (Madrid, 1988); and GEOFFREY E. FOX, *The Land and People of Argentina* (1990).

CÉSAR N. CAVIEDES

*See also* individual features and regions.

## ARGENTINA: MOVEMENTS

### Federalists

The Argentine Federalists were a post-Independence faction favoring a national organization allowing provincial autonomy, as against the tightly centralized system sought by the UNITARISTS. Strong Federalist sentiment in the interior provinces was already evident during the struggle for independence, inspired by resentment of the domineering ways of revolutionary leaders in the former colonial capital, Buenos Aires, and in some instances by differences of economic interest. The national constitutions of 1819 and 1826 proved abortive because much of the interior refused to accept their centralist orientation. Even in Buenos Aires itself there was an influential Federalist faction, led initially by Manuel DORREGO and later by Juan Manuel de ROSAS, who first became governor of Buenos Aires Province in 1829. Rosas implanted a personal dictatorship over all Argentina, but without abandoning the Federalist banner and without creating any formal national institutions.

The appeal of Federalists to local sentiment and to Argentine nativism (while depicting the rival Unitarists as beholden to European influence) won them wide popular support in the cities as well as the countryside. However, their most representative figures were large landowners and militia officers like Rosas, who forged close patron-client ties with the rural population of their respective provinces. After the formal adoption in 1853 of a federal-style constitution, Federalism soon ceased to be a distinct political movement.

MIRON BURGIN, *The Economic Aspects of Argentine Federalism, 1820–1852* (1946); TULIO HALPERÍN-DONGHI, *Politics, Economics, and Society in Argentina in the Revolutionary Period*, translated by Richard Southern (1975); JOHN LYNCH, *Argentine Dictator: Juan Manuel de Rosas, 1829–1852* (1981).

DAVID BUSHNELL

### Unitarists

The Unitarists, or *Unitarios* in Spanish, were a post-Independence faction that favored a centralized political organization with the provinces strictly subordinate to a strong national government. Their greatest strength was among professional and merchant groups of the city of Buenos Aires, although they had pockets of support in some interior provinces. Led by Bernardino RIVADAVIA as chief minister, they consolidated control of the province of Buenos Aires in 1821. Five years later they made him president of a united Argentina. He fell from power in 1827 when most of the interior refused to accept the Unitarist constitution of 1826. From 1829 to 1831, General José María PAZ created a network of pro-Unitarist local governments in the interior, based on his native province of Córdoba, but all attempts to revive the cause of Unitarism succumbed before the growing power of FEDERALIST dictator Juan Manuel de ROSAS.

Apart from their support of centralized government, which most of the country rejected, Unitarists promoted liberal reforms, inspired by European models, in socioeconomic and religious affairs. The resulting friction with more traditional elements, including the bulk of the clergy, as well as their identification in the popular mind with the narrow economic interests of the port city of Buenos Aires, further undermined their political position.

A classic expression of Unitarist ideology and a highly subjective history of their struggles is DOMINGO F. SARMIENTO, *Life in the Argentine Republic in the Days of the Tyrants; or, Civilization and Barbarism* (1868; many later editions). The best recent treatment in English is found in the biography of their nemesis by JOHN LYNCH, *Argentine Dictator: Juan Manuel de Rosas, 1829–1852* (1981). On Unitarist reformism, see David Bushnell, *Reform and Reaction in the Platine Provinces, 1810–1852* (1983).

DAVID BUSHNELL

## ARGENTINA: ORGANIZATIONS

### American Industrial Society for Machinery
### Sociedad Industrial Americana de Maquinarias—SIAM

The rise and decline of the industrial manufacturing concern SIAM Di Tella followed that of the Argentine economy. The company was founded in 1910 in Buenos Aires by three Italian immigrants, Torcuato DI TELLA and the Allegrucci brothers, to make a dough-kneading machine. Di Tella quickly became the driving force and the Allegruccis withdrew. After Di Tella died in 1948, his management team continued to run the company.

SIAM produced a wide assortment of machinery. After World War I it built gasoline pumps largely for the state-owned oil company, Yacimientos Petrolíferos Fiscales, and ran service stations. SIAM manufactured pumps with a license from a U.S. company, setting a pattern for most of its products. In the 1930s SIAM broke into consumer goods by manufacturing refrigerators. By the early 1960s SIAM was producing a full range of consumer goods, from irons and fans to motor scooters and cars, as well as industrial machinery and steel pipes. It had branches in Uruguay, Brazil, and Chile. It could claim that it was the largest locally owned manufacturing company in Latin America.

Changes in government policies and difficulties in raising capital brought down SIAM. The large number of foreign corporations permitted to build cars hurt SIAM's ability to compete. Lacking adequate capital for new investment, it maintained automobile production too long, thereby weakening the company. Similar problems existed with its other consumer goods products. By 1972, when the government took over SIAM for financial reasons, the firm owed taxes that amounted to 60 percent of its capital. It survived for the next decade largely by selling capital goods to state enterprises, but after the military coup of 1976, the government no longer favored local companies, thus dooming SIAM. When the government attempted to privatize SIAM in 1981–1982, there were no takers. The company had to be broken up.

THOMAS C. COCHRAN and RUBEN REINA, *Entrepreneurship in Argentine Culture: Torcuato di Tella and SIAM* (1962); JORGE SCHVARZER, *Expansión económica del estado subsidiario, 1976–1981* (1981); PAUL H. LEWIS, *The Crisis of Argentine Capitalism* (1990); TORCUATO S. DI TELLA, *Torcuato Di Tella: Industria y política* (1993).

JOEL HOROWITZ

### Argentine Civic Legion
### Legión Cívica Argentina–LCA

A right-wing paramilitary product of the 1930 revolution that installed General José Félix URIBURU in power, the Argentine Civic Legion arose in early 1931. Its first leader was Dr. Floro Lavalle, a medical doctor, landowner, and founding member of the Argentine Patriotic League; by 1933 Carlos Ribero, a former naval officer, became its head, followed by David Uriburu in the 1940s. The Legion absorbed other paramilitary groups that had been active in the coup and enlisted young aristocrats, Conservative Party members, civil servants (often coercively), military officers, upper-class women, and even schoolchildren. Its opposition to liberal democracy, partisan politics, leftism, and immigration, and its support for hierarchy, family, and religion won the favor of the Uriburu government, which gave it juridical personage and official recognition as its partner in creating order. It also allowed the Legion to use government buildings and services. The group received military instruction at army installations, and weapons and uniforms from the Ministry of War. When thousands of uniformed Legionarios paraded through Buenos Aires in April and May 1931, Uriburu praised the group for protecting the revolution against its enemies.

The Legion became a focus of controversy. Many, including some fellow right-wing nationalists, criticized its ties to the government, military, and Conservative Party. Its spying activities and repression of students suggested that the Legion was an official tool against opponents of the regime, or a means by which Uriburu could perpetuate his rule or bring Conservatives to power. Even potential sympathizers disapproved of recruiting women and children into a militarized organization.

After 1932 the Legion no longer enjoyed official ties to the government. Nevertheless, it continued to occupy government-owned buildings and carry out terrorist acts with impunity. By the mid-1930s it added opposition to Jews and imperialism, and support for state regulation of capital and labor, to its original goals. It did not hide its sympathy for European fascism and the Axis powers.

CARLOS IBARGUREN, *La historia que he vivido*, 2d ed. (1969); ALBERTO CIRIA, *Parties and Power in Modern Argentina*, translated by Carlos A. Astiz with Mary F. McCarthy (1974); SANDRA MC GEE DEUTSCH, *Counterrevolution in Argentina, 1890–1930: The Rise and Fall of Radicalism* (1986).

SANDRA MCGEE DEUTSCH

### Argentine Patriotic League
### Liga Patriótica Argentina—LPA

The Argentine Patriotic League was an antilabor organization that arose in 1919 and was particularly active until the mid-1920s. After World War I, the military and the middle and upper classes feared that the Russian Revolution might spread to Argentina. The general strike that burst into the SEMANA TRÁGICA (Tragic Week) of January 1919 confirmed their fears. During this week, self-styled civil guards and police attacked worker neighborhoods of Buenos Aires. Other bourgeois citizens formed defense committees against possible labor onslaught. Naval officers coordinated the civil guards and defense committees, giving them arms, vehicles, and military instruction.

After the Tragic Week, a group of naval and army officers invited prominent citizens, other officers, clerics, and society women to create a permanent organization to guard against labor disruptions and leftist views. These people founded the Argentine Patriotic League on 20 January 1919. The defense committees became the first "brigades" of the League; similar committees that had formed in other parts of the nation were incorporated. The League also organized brigades of property owners and strikebreakers in areas of labor strife. In addition, women in the larger cities formed their own brigades. On 5 April 1919 the brigades elected Manuel CARLÉS as League president. In the 1920s the League's core included about 820 women and 11,000 men. The majority of its female members and its leaders were upper-class, but the rank-and-file male activists were largely middle-class. A significant number of military officers also belonged to the League.

The League hoped to maintain the status quo through repression and social welfare activities. Male members began to undertake the first task by breaking strikes and attacking unions and radicals in the large cities. When rural strikes broke out from late 1919 to 1921, they shifted their focus to the countryside. For example, in PATAGONIA they helped the army kill over 1,500 striking ranch workers in 1921. Meanwhile, League men and women established factory schools, employment services, and other social programs. The League publicized the need for such programs and wider measures like social security to divert workers from the class struggle.

When the postwar labor activism ended in the early 1920s—partly thanks to the League—the organization faded from prominence. Yet it participated in the revolution of 1930 against President Hipólito YRIGOYEN

(1916–1922, 1928–1930) and remained in existence at least until the late 1970s.

OSVALDO BAYER, *Los vengadores de la Patagonia trágica*, 4 vols. (1972–1978); DAVID ROCK, *Politics in Argentina, 1890–1930: The Rise and Fall of Radicalism* (1975); SANDRA MC GEE DEUTSCH, *Counterrevolution in Argentina, 1900–1932: The Argentine Patriotic League* (1986).

SANDRA MCGEE DEUTSCH

### Argentine Rural Society
### Sociedad Rural Argentina

The Sociedad Rural Argentina is an elite corporate organization active in the promotion of ranching and the protection of ranchers' interests in Argentina. Founded in 1866 by ESTANCIA owners José and Benjamín MARTÍNEZ DE HOZ, Francisco MADERO, Jorge Temperley, Ricardo Newton, Mariano Casares, and Luis Amadeo, the society was initially chartered to promote ranching and agriculture in Argentina. Through publications, such as the *Anales de la Sociedad Rural Argentina* (which first appeared in 1867), contests, and exhibitions, it transformed cattle ranching into one of Argentina's leading export industries by the end of the nineteenth century. Its International Annual Exhibition, held since 1875 in Buenos Aires, remains a major event that attracts participants from throughout Argentina, the Americas, and Europe.

The society has also exerted its influence on Argentine politics, with many of its members holding leadership posts in provincial and national governments. It became particularly active during the years between the two world wars. Its support of conservative tax and commercial policies put it at odds with the Radical Party and its leader, President Hipólito YRIGOYEN, during his first administration (1916–1922). When the more conservative Marcelo T. de ALVEAR (1922–1928) succeeded Yrigoyen, the society, led by Luis Duhau, campaigned for government protection of the cattle industry.

During the 1930s, the society became more aggressive. It supported General José F. URIBURU's military *golpe* (coup), which ended Yrigoyen's second term in office in September 1930. It also called for government protection of ranching and the industry's export markets. Although economic and political changes have reduced its prestige, the society remains influential.

PETER H. SMITH, *Politics and Beef in Argentina: Patterns of Conflict and Change* (1969); HORACIO C. E. GIBERTI, *Historia económica de la ganadería argentina*, 3d ed. (1981).

DANIEL LEWIS

### Argentine Trade Promotion Institute
### Instituto Argentino de Promoción del Intercambio—IAPI

The Argentine Trade Promotion Institute was a government agency created to control the export of important products (chiefly grains and meat) and to purchase key goods abroad. The IAPI was established in March 1946 by the outgoing Edelmiro Farrell government at the suggestion of the advisers of Juan Perón. It was severely modified, stripped of much of its power, in the wake of Perón's fall from power in 1955 and abolished in April 1958.

A crucial economic tool of the Perón regime, IAPI countered efforts by the Allies to purchase food for Europe jointly and also eliminated the unpopular large grain-exporting firms. As a monopoly, IAPI could drive a hard bargain with purchasers of Argentine goods, as well as with producers. IAPI purchased at low prices from producers and sold at high prices. Profits were used to subsidize industrialization. After 1950 the need for more exports led IAPI to encourage greater production.

IAPI remains controversial. Most commentators believe it crippled the agriculture sector by paying low prices, thereby discouraging production and helping to create a balance-of-payments crisis. Charges of corruption were also made. The agency's defenders believe that producers' profits did not suffer as claimed and that IAPI produced higher prices for exports than the falling terms of trade would have permitted under other circumstances.

JOSÉ ALFREDO MARTÍNEZ DE HOZ (h.), *La agricultura y la ganadería argentina en el período 1930–1960* (1967); JORGE FODOR, "Perón's Policies for Agricultural Exports 1946–1948: Dogmatism or Commonsense?" in *Argentina in the Twentieth Century*, edited by David Rock (1975); SUSANA NOVICK, *IAPI: Auge y decadencia* (1986); PAUL H. LEWIS, *The Crisis of Argentine Capitalism* (1990).

JOEL HOROWITZ

### Federation of Argentine Workers
### Federación Obrera Argentina—FOA

Founded in 1901 after a compromise between anarchist and socialist labor leaders, the Federación Obrera Argentina (FOA) changed its name to Federación Obrera Regional Argentina (FORA) in 1904, becoming the representative of the anarchist branch of the Argentine labor movement. The socialists had left the federation in 1903 to form the Unión General de Trabajadores, taking about 1,800 affiliates, while the FOA retained around 7,600 members. By 1904, its membership had grown to 33,000. In 1905 the FORA declared its allegiance to "the economic and philosophical principles of anarcho-communism," rejecting any possible compromise with other ideological tendencies within the labor movement. Government repression of anarchist activism on the one hand, and the absorption of socialist organizations by the growing syndicalist movement on the other, led to a short-lived fusion of anarchist and syndicalist groups in 1914. In 1915 the FORA saw itself divided once again between the so-called FORA IX Congress, standing for the 1915 congress dominated by the syndicalists, and the FORA V Congress, standing for the 1905 congress, which had proclaimed the principles of anarcho-communism. The two federations remained divided until 1922, when the syndicalist FORA was absorbed by a new syndicalist-dominated organization, the Unión Sindical Argentina. A small hard core of devoted anarcho-communists remained at the FORA V Congress, although the influence of anarchism in the labor movement had become almost negligible. In 1930 the merger of the Unión Sindical Argentina, the socialist Confederación Obrera Argentina, and the remnants of the FORA gave birth to the Confederación General del Trabajo (CGT).

DIEGO ABAD DE SANTILLÁN, *La F.O.R.A.: Ideología y trayectoría del movimiento obrero revolucionario en la Argentina*, 2d ed. (1971); RUTH THOMPSON, "The Limitations of Ideology in the Early Argentine Labour Movement: Anarchism in the Trade Unions, 1890–1920," in *Journal of Latin American Studies* 16 (1984): 81–99; RONALDO MUNCK, with RICARDO FALCÓN and BERNARDO GALITELLI, *Argentina: From Anarchism to Peronism. Workers, Unions and Politics, 1855–1985* (1987).

EDUARDO A. ZIMMERMAN

### General Labor Confederation
### Confederación General de Trabajo—CGT

In 1930 union leaders, frustrated by bitter divisions between rival workers' organizations and concerned about labor's tenuous relationship with the state, joined forces and created the Confederación General de Trabajo (CGT). A fusion of the Socialist-controlled Confederación Obrera Argentina, the syndicalist-dominated Unión Sindical Argentina, and several autonomous unions, the CGT would experience major problems in compatibility and commonness of purpose throughout its history. Syndicalist-oriented unions demanded the pursuit of an apolitical course; Socialists wanted a working relationship with sympathetic political groups.

Communist-affiliated unions in the manufacturing and construction trades joined the CGT in 1936, thereby exacerbating the CGT's problems. In 1943 internal bickering resulted in a rupture of the organization into two factions. A new military government, which included among its leadership Juan Domingo PERÓN, took advantage of the weakened condition of a divided CGT. The Socialist and Communist factions were abolished, and the others, lacking powerful and independent leadership, fell under the control of Perón. CGT delight with Perón's pro-labor policies was offset by the concern of some unions with the growth of Perón's political power and the erosion of CGT independence.

In 1947 Perón, now president of Argentina, completed the consolidation of his power base in the CGT, which now became an appendage of the state with no independence. The CGT had grown powerful, from a membership of 500,000 in 1947 to 2.5 million in 1955. With Perón's fall the CGT returned to its adversarial role with government. In the 1990s destructive splintering continued to inhibit labor's ability to speak with one voice.

SAMUEL L. BAILY, *Labor, Nationalism, and Politics in Argentina* (1967), pp. 99, 151–192; HOBART A. SPALDING, JR., *Organized Labor in Latin America: Historical Case Studies of Workers in Dependent Societies* (1977), pp. 151–206; HIROSCHI MATSUSHITA, *Movimiento Obrero Argentino, 1930–1945* (1983), pp. 77–311; DAVID ROCK, *Argentina, 1516–1982: From Spanish Colonization to the Falklands War* (1985).

PAUL GOODWIN

*See also* **Labor and Labor Movements.**

### Liga Federal
### Liga Litoral
### Liga Unitaria

The Federal, Littoral, and Unitary leagues were political alliances during the independence and early national periods. The Liga Federal, also known as Liga Litoral and Liga de los Pueblos Libres (League of Free Peoples), was not created through a specific pact but came into being in 1814–1815 as Federalist leaders in the Argentine littoral provinces joined forces with each other and with the Uruguayan leader José Gervasio ARTIGAS in opposition to the *porteño* revolutionists who sought to enforce strict obedience to the central authorities in Buenos Aires. The caudillo José Eusebio Hereñú of Entre Ríos is credited with making the initial move. His province was ultimately joined by Santa Fe, Corrientes, Misiones, and Córdoba, all of which were represented at the Congress of Free Peoples meeting at Concepción del Uruguay, Entre Ríos province, in mid-1815. All proclaimed Artigas as "protector." The ultimate objective was an independent Argentina organized as a loose confederation of Platine provinces, which would have included what is now Uruguay. They did not achieve this aim, and Artigas's Uruguay fell to Portuguese occupation. The other provinces continued with varying success, and despite repeated internal dissensions, to resist the control of Buenos Aires. The Federalists' victory at the battle of CEPEDA (February 1820) led to the final collapse of the centralist regime, after which the league dissolved.

The Liga Unitaria (also known as Liga Militar), formed in August 1830, was based in the interior province of Córdoba, where the Córdoba-born Unitarist general José María PAZ had seized control the year before. By decisively defeating the leading Federalist caudillo of the Argentine interior, Juan Facundo QUIROGA, Paz was able to bring nine provinces, extending from Córdoba to the Bolivian border, into his orbit. They formed the Liga Unitaria to create a "supreme military power" that functioned in practice, under Paz, as a provisional national government. However, it still faced the bitter opposition of Buenos Aires governor Juan Manuel de ROSAS and his Federalist allies in the littoral provinces, and it quickly collapsed following the capture of Paz during a skirmish in May 1831.

The Liga Litoral (also known as Liga Federal and Liga

167

de los Pueblos Libres) organized expressly to combat the Liga Unitaria, had its origin in a series of separate understandings among the provinces of the littoral region that were allied with Buenos Aires. Their alliance was formalized in January 1831 by the signing of the Federal Pact, which, in addition to providing for military cooperation against the Unitarists, created an interprovincial "representative commission" and delegated to Rosas, the governor of Buenos Aires, authority to act in the name of all provinces in foreign relations. As the tide of civil conflict turned against the Unitarists, more provinces became signatories of the Federal Pact; eventually all signed it. While the "representative commission" never became effective, Rosas took advantage of his special role in foreign relations to secure his personal political control over the country. After the fall of Rosas in 1852, the Liga Federal ceased to exist.

ALBERTO DEMICHELI, *Formación constitucional rioplatense*, vol. 3, *Los pactos en el proceso de organización* (1955); JOHN STREET, *Artigas and the Emancipation of Uruguay* (1959), pp. 243–328; VICTOR TAU ANZOÁTEGUI, *Formación del estado federal argentino (1820–1852)* (1965); JOSÉ MARÍA PAZ, *Memorias*, vol. 2 (1968), chap. 16; JOHN LYNCH, *Argentine Dictator: Juan Manuel de Rosas, 1829–1852* (1981).

DAVID BUSHNELL

### Sociedad de Beneficiencia

The Sociedad de Beneficiencia was the major welfare-dispensing agency in Argentina in the nineteenth century. After the Independence Wars, the incipient Argentine government struggled to reassert order. In 1823, Government Minister Bernardino RIVADAVIA created the Sociedad de Beneficiencia to run the asylums, hospitals, and orphanages of Buenos Aires, in order to keep streets clear of the infirm, diseased, and homeless. Although it was proclaimed illegal during the period 1838–1852, when the dictator Juan Manuel de ROSAS considered it an arm of liberal Unitarists, the Sociedad became, by the late nineteenth century, Latin America's most extensive social welfare and public health institution. In particular in the 1860s, mainly as a result of casualties of the WAR OF THE TRIPLE ALLIANCE (1865–1870) and disease (such as the cholera epidemic of 1867–1868, and the outbreak of yellow fever in 1871), there was a proliferation of hospitals and clinics. One distinctive feature of the Sociedad was its control and management by women of the Buenos Aires elite. Its importance culminated with the establishment of the Rivadavia Hospital for Women in 1887. The directors came from the city's most prominent families and often bequeathed sizable sums upon their death.

The Sociedad became the most important means for women to participate in the public life of Buenos Aires. They used this position, however, to propagate traditional paternalistic and religious values. In 1880 President Julio A. ROCA made the Sociedad de Beneficiencia a national institution. Ultimately, its management of the medical system conflicted with the growing professionalization and male control of medicine, provoking bitter disputes in the 1890s. Furthermore, the city's rapid growth and pressing social problems led to the creation of parallel institutions, especially those controlled by immigrant mutual aid societies. The care of homeless children remained one of the Sociedad's most important tasks; it ran the foundling home, and the girls' and boys' orphanages. As spaces grew scarce, the Sociedad shifted to "fostering," the placement of homeless children with families or single persons. In 1946, President Juan Domingo PERÓN took over its activities and reorganized them under the Dirección Nacional de Asistencia Social, directed by his wife, Eva.

CARLOS CORREA LUNA, *Historia de la Sociedad de beneficia*, 2 vols. (1923); CYNTHIA J. LITTLE, "The Society of Beneficence in Buenos Aires, 1823–1900" (Ph.D. diss., Temple University, 1980).

JEREMY ADELMAN

### United Officers Group
### *Grupo de Oficiales Unidos—GOU*

There is some dispute on the exact meaning of the acronym GOU, which was one of several secret lodges of Argentine military officers. Robert Potash claims that it was originally formed by twelve members in February or early March 1943 as the Grupo Organizador y Unificador, and that an enlarged organization of nineteen members was formed in July as the Grupo Obra de Unificación. Others have asserted that the initials stood for Gobierno, Orden, Unidad, insinuating a connection with Franco's Spain. It is most commonly referred to as the United Officers Group. Although some members had been German-trained and sympathized with the Nazis, the organization was primarily concerned with military and economic competition with Brazil, industrialization, the acquisition of arms, and domestic political corruption.

On 6 June 1943, three days after a coup ousted Ramón CASTILLO, the GOU took over and installed General Pedro RAMÍREZ as president. The GOU placed its most prominent officers into high political and military positions. Bowing to U.S. pressure, Ramírez broke diplomatic relations with the Axis powers on 26 January 1944. His vice president, General Edelmiro FARRELL, condemning the break, replaced him in February. GOU member Colonel Juan D. PERÓN became Farrell's war minister and vice president. The GOU was dissolved on 23 February 1944.

ROBERT A. POTASH, *The Army and Politics in Argentina, 1928–1945* (1969); MARVIN GOLDWERT, *Democracy, Militarism, and Nationalism in Argentina, 1930–1966* (1972); ALBERTO CIRÍA, *Parties and Power in Modern Argentina, 1930–1946* (1974); RONALD C. NEWTON, *The "Nazi Menace" in Argentina, 1931–1947* (1992).

ROGER GRAVIL
CHRISTEL K. CONVERSE

### Yacimientos Petrolíferos Fiscales—YPF

Immediately following World War I, powerful international PETROLEUM companies moved into Argentina in an effort to secure the best oil properties. Concerned by their presence, President Hipólito YRIGOYEN created the YPF in 1922 as a state petroleum monopoly to ensure Argentine control over this vital resource. It was left to his successor, President Marcelo T. de ALVEAR (1922–1928), to invigorate the agency. To head the YPF, Alvear named Colonel Enrique Mosconi, under whose leadership it became symbolic of Argentina economic independence. In a different context, Mosconi's imprint can be discerned on the state oil companies of Bolivia, Brazil, and Uruguay. In the 1950s and 1960s Presidents Juan Domingo PERÓN and Arturo FRONDIZI, concerned about maximum productivity and economic development, undermined the idea of a state petroleum monopoly. Gradually, foreign petroleum companies were again invited to participate more fully in the exploitation of the nation's oil fields.

DAVID P. ROCK, *Politics in Argentina, 1890–1930: The Rise and Fall of Radicalism* (1975); CARL E. SOLBERG, *Oil and Nationalism in Argentina: A History* (1979), pp. 76–111.

PAUL GOODWIN

## ARGENTINA: POLITICAL PARTIES

### Antipersonalist Radical Civic Union
### Unión Cívica Radical Antipersonalista

In 1924 the Antipersonalistas in Argentina emerged as a separate political party when they broke ranks with the Radical Civic Union (Unión Cívica Radical—UCR) and its leader, Hipólito YRIGOYEN. The appearance of the Antipersonalistas reflected tensions that had typified Argentine radicalism since its birth in 1890.

Vincente C. Gallo, Yrigoyen's minister of the interior, led a dissident group within the UCR known as the "Azules," or "Blues," a faction that later became known as the Antipersonalistas. They represented the old elite wing of the party and actively worked against Yrigoyen from 1918 until the end of his term in 1922. Yrigoyen's successor in office, Marcelo T. de ALVEAR, was nominally an Antipersonalista but failed to pursue policies that would assure the survival of the party. A mass base never materialized because the Antipersonalistas were denied access to state patronage, thus lacking the political rewards and positions necessary to gain support. Establishment of a committee structure to organize recruitment in the provinces succeeded only in the province of Santa Fe. Alvear's own ties were with the province of Buenos Aires, and he never established a working relationship with the Antipersonalistas' Santa Fe base.

In order for mass-based politics to succeed, there was need of an administration committed not only to flexible and somewhat inflationary spending of state resources but also, for political purposes, to an expansion of the bureaucracy. Alvear, however, pursued a conservative fiscal policy, and the Antipersonalista influence never effectively spread beyond the borders of Santa Fe.

The Antipersonalistas ran candidates for the presidency in 1928, but Yrigoyen won in a landslide. In 1930 the Antipersonalistas supported the revolution that ousted Yrigoyen and then joined with conservatives who dominated Argentine politics until the military coup of 1943.

JOSÉ LUIS ROMERO, *A History of Argentine Political Thought,* translated by Thomas F. McGann (1963), pp. 224–225; ROBERT A. POTASH, *The Army and Politics in Argentina, 1928–1945: Yrigoyen to Perón* (1969), pp. 41 n., 47, 59–60; PAUL B. GOODWIN, JR., "The Politics of Rate-Making: The British-Owned Railways and the Unión Cívica Radical, 1921–1928," in *Journal of Latin American Studies* 6 (1974): 257–287.

PAUL GOODWIN

### Democratic Union
### Unión Democrática—UD

Formed in 1945, the Democratic Union of Argentina was a superficially united and diverse front of old-line political parties and interest groups opposed to the presidential candidacy of Juan Domingo PERÓN. Radicals José P. Tamborini and Enrique N. Mosca headed their ticket in elections scheduled for February 1946. The front's campaign, with its dated slogan, "For Liberty and Against Nazi-Fascism," failed to address the issues that concerned most of the electorate. Moreover, the UD was tainted because of links both to Moscow-oriented Communists and to the U.S. government. Perón won with 52.4 percent of the vote; the UD garnered 42.5 percent.

JOSEPH A. PAGE, *Perón: A Biography* (1983), chap. 16; ROBERT D. CRASSWELLER, *Perón and the Enigmas of Argentina* (1987), pp. 174ff.

PAUL GOODWIN

### Independent Socialist Party
### Partido Socialista Independiente—PSI

The Independent Socialist Party of Argentina was created in 1927 as the result of a power struggle within the mainline Socialist Party. The new party was led by mostly younger members with a more nationalistic, conservative orientation than the directors of its older predecessor. Entering national congressional elections for the first time in 1928, the Independents came in ahead of the mainline Socialists for second place in the city of Buenos Aires. Two years later they scored an even more impressive victory in a similar contest, besting both the Socialists and the representatives of the incumbent national administration, the Radicals (of the Unión Cívica Radical), to capture a majority of the congressional seats available.

In 1930 the Independents formed an important part of the conservative coalition that contributed to the overthrow of popularly elected President Hipólito YRIGOYEN (1928–1930). Party leaders Antonio de Tomaso and Federico Pinedo subsequently served as cabinet members under the conservative president Agustín P. JUSTO (1932–1938). A handful of other party members were elected to the national Congress and to the city council of Buenos Aires in the early 1930s. In Congress and on the council, the Independent Socialists usually allied with the conservative bloc on most major issues, although their opposition to the first mayor (*intendente*) of Buenos Aires appointed by Justo led to his forced resignation a few months after assuming office.

The death of Antonio de Tomaso, the party's main leader, in 1933, coupled with a growing popular reaction against the antidemocratic practices of the conservative regime with which the Independents were associated, caused the party to lose considerable electoral support. By 1936, the Independents were polling less than 3 percent of the total vote in national and local elections and by 1940 had virtually disappeared from the national political scene. While the Independents enjoyed some momentary influence, they are best remembered as one of several examples of recurring divisions within the mainline Socialist party and of the often ephemeral nature of the many short-lived parties and factions that have characterized much of Argentina's modern political history.

HORACIO SANGUINETTI, *Los socialistas independientes* (1981).

RICHARD J. WALTER

### Intransigent Radicals
### Movimiento de Intransigencia y
### Renovación—MIR

The Intransigent Radicals were a nationalist faction of the Radical Party which emerged during the 1930s in opposition to the undemocratic governments of the period and in repudiation of the more conservative Radical Party faction led by Marcelo T. de ALVEAR. Vindicating the *yrigoyenista* tradition, they were inspired in the 1930s and early 1940s by the governor of Córdoba, Amadeo Sabattini, who vigorously promoted economic nationalism, an interventionist state, and strict neutrality in World War II, a program encapsulated in the party's founding document, the 1945 Carta de Avellaneda.

Organized as the Movimiento de Intransigencia y Renovación (MIR) after 1945, the Intransigents lost a bitter power struggle with the more conservative faction of their party, the so-called unionists, in the selection of the Unión Democrática ticket chosen to run against Juan PERÓN in the 1946 election, but dominated the party during the Peronist government (1946–1955). In 1956 they established a separate party, the Intransigent Radical Civic Union (UCRI), which brought Ar-

turo FRONDIZI to power in the 1958 presidential election. Frondizi's drifting away from many of the party's principles, especially those concerning issues of economic nationalism, weakened the Intransigents' credibility.

Frondizi's ouster in a 1962 coup d'état and his establishment in 1964 of a separate political party, the Movement of Integration and Development (MID), effectively led to the Intransigent Radicals' demise. They ran as a separate party for the last time in the 1963 election won by the Radical Civic Union of the People (UCRP), though they were briefly resuscitated in the 1980s in the form of the Intransigent Party (PI), led by former *intransigente* governor of Buenos Aires, Oscar Alende. The PI was the most important left-of-center party during the first years of Raúl ALFONSÍN's Radical administration, though it too eventually disbanded.

MARCELO LUIS ACUÑA, *De Frondizi a Alfonsín: La tradición política del radicalismo*, vols. 1 and 2 (1985); CELIA SZUSTERMAN, *Frondizi and the Politics of Developmentalism in Argentina, 1955–62* (1993).

JAMES P. BRENNAN

### Justicialist Party
### Partido Justicialista

The Justicialist Party (formerly the Peronist Party) grew out of the electoral coalition that brought Juan D. PERÓN to power in 1946: the labor-based Laborista Party, the young nationalists of the Union of Radical Civic Renewal (Unión Cívica Radical Renovadora), and the right-wing Independent Centers (Centros Independientes). After the election Perón decreed their merger into the Sole Revolutionary Party (Partido Único de la Revolución), but that sounded too totalitarian, so the name was changed to Peronist Party (Partido Peronista). After Perón was overthrown in 1955, the party was outlawed; it eventually reappeared under the name Unión Popular, since no reference to Perón was permitted.

When neo-Peronists, who sought legalization by repudiating Perón, gained control of the Unión Popular in 1966, Peronist loyalists challenged them under the banner of the Justicialist Party, which is still mainline Peronism's official title. "Justicialism," a term coined by Perón himself, refers to his official ideology. In theory it seeks a middle way between democracy and authoritarianism, capitalism and socialism, individualism and collectivism. In practice it aims at what he called "the organized society," which essentially is a corporate state with representation based on government-controlled associations of employers, workers, and professionals.

Under the first Peronist regime (1946–1955) the party acted as an electoral machine, patronage vehicle, and control network. It had a hierarchical structure, with a supreme leader (Perón) at the top, a handpicked Superior Council just beneath him, and a spreading network of provincial (state), departmental (county), and neighborhood, and workplace organizations. Officers were appointed from above, and great emphasis was placed on obedience and discipline. The party also embraced a special trade union wing based on the General Confederation of Labor (Confederación General de Trabajadores; CGT) and the Feminist Peronist Party, which Evita Perón formed in 1949. There was also a leadership school to train future party elites. Though formidable on paper, the party actually had little real vitality, since Perón permitted his subordinates almost no initiative.

After Perón's fall the outlawed party was torn between neo- and orthodox Peronists until his return in 1973. After his death the following year, open warfare broke out between its right and left wings, with the latter eventually forming the Authentic Peronist Party (Partido Peronista Auténtico). When the military took power in 1976, it outlawed all parties.

The restoration of democracy in 1983 found the Justicialist Party weakened, divided, and somewhat discredited by its past, since many people blamed the Peronist government's mismanagement from 1973 to 1976 for bringing on military rule. Consequently, it lost the presidential elections to its main rival, the Radical Civic Union, although it still won control of the Senate and a majority of provincial governorships. During the next six years a reformist faction took control of the Justicialist Party and gave it a more democratic image. As a result, Justicialists won a majority of the gubernatorial and congressional elections in 1989 and saw their candidate, Carlos Saúl MENEM, elected president. In September 1991 the party increased its congressional majority by trouncing the Radicals in midterm elections.

PARTIDO PERONISTA, *Directivas básicas del Consejo Superior* (1952); GEORGE BLANKSTEN, *Peron's Argentina* (1953); ALBERTO CIRIA, *Perón y el justicialismo* (1971).

PAUL H. LEWIS

### National Autonomist Party
### Partido Autonomista Nacional—PAN

The Partido Autonomista Nacional (PAN) was a political party formed in 1874 as an amalgamation of the Partido Nacional, which represented a coalition of political leaders of the interior provinces, and the Partido Autonomista, which championed the local interests of Buenos Aires province against national encroachments. While there was initial friction within the party over specific issues, e.g., whether the city of Buenos Aires should be federalized, after the PORTEÑO autonomist revolt failed in 1880, both groups opposed the presidential reelection of Bartolomé MITRE. In order to thwart Mitre, Adolfo ALSINA of the Partido Autonomista abandoned his own candidacy and backed the Partido Nacional's Nicolás AVELLANEDA, who won as the candidate of the PAN.

For the next four decades the PAN controlled Argentina, with all presidents elected from its ranks. Although never a doctrinal party, it shared the POSITIVIST-tinged,

but still liberal, economic and political ideology that predominated in Argentina in the late nineteenth century. Provincial cattle raisers formed the backbone of the party, while bankers, merchants, and *porteño* landowners joined to enrich themselves. Political administration was centralized in the name of progress, and the early economic success and political stability of the party allowed it to rule on an authoritarian basis, with *comités* (committees) throughout the villages and towns of Argentina controlling affairs through appointed leaders.

The PAN remained a loose coalition of provincial "situations," as boss-dominated local power structures were known at the time, relying heavily on behind-the-scenes manipulation, of which the all-time master was Julio A. ROCA, elected president in 1880 and again in 1898. The PAN became a political machine directed from the CASA ROSADA, the residence of the president. The party used outright electoral and other forms of corruption, and PAN leaders dispensed jobs in the railroad and communication sectors through a system of patronage. These methods were effective, as attested to by the sheer duration of the party's national power.

The PAN became increasingly anachronistic as Argentina's rapid social and economic development led to demands for a more representative political system. After 1890 the party became defensive with the rise of the Unión Cívica and its radical faction. President Roque SÁENZ PEÑA (1910–1913), though from the PAN, formed a larger coalition to win election, and sponsored the electoral reform that allowed the Radical Party to gain power in 1916. The PAN persisted for a time in the form of various traditional factions loosely referred to as "the Conservatives."

CARLOS MELO, *Los partidos políticos argentinos* (1970), pp. 22–47; NATALIO R. BOTANA, *El orden conservador: La política argentina entre 1880 y 1916* (1977); DOUGLAS W. RICHMOND, *Carlos Pellegrini and the Crisis of the Argentine Elites, 1880–1916* (1989).

DAVID BUSHNELL
DOUGLAS W. RICHMOND

### Personalist Radical Civic Union
### Unión Cívica Radical Personalista

The Personalist Radicals, also known as Yrigoyenistas, were a faction of the Radical Civic Union Party (UCR) active from 1924 to 1933 and loyal to the Radical leader and former president Hipólito YRIGOYEN. Differences over fiscal policy and party organization led to a split in the Radical Party during the presidency of Marcelo de ALVEAR (1922–1928). As the 1920s came to a close, the dominant pro-Yrigoyen wing of the party buttressed its political position by arguing for the nationalization of the country's growing oil industry. The Personalists' control over Congress and the Radical Party machinery guaranteed the reelection of Yrigoyen in 1928.

Although they held a majority in the Argentine Congress, the Personalists accomplished little after 1928.

Economic crisis and political confusion contributed to the success of the Revolution of 6 September 1930 that overthrew the elected government. While the Radical Party would recover after World War II, Yrigoyen's death in July 1933 led to the Personalist wing's rapid disintegration.

DAVID ROCK, *Politics in Argentina, 1890–1930: The Rise and Fall of Radicalism* (1975); RICHARD WALTER, *The Province of Buenos Aires and Argentine Politics, 1912–1943* (1985).

DANIEL LEWIS

### Progressive Democratic Party
### Partido Demócrata Progresista—PDP

The PDP was founded on 14 December 1914 in Buenos Aires by Lisandro DE LA TORRE and other reform-minded conservatives who united to oppose what they perceived in Hipólito YRIGOYEN's demagogic populism. De la Torre, a fiery orator, was the ideal PDP presidential candidate for the 1916 election. He waged the first modern presidential campaign in Argentine history. The PDP platform spelled out a program of far-reaching reforms, such as separation of church and state, secular divorce, and popular election of all office holders on the municipal, provincial, and national levels. The ticket lost in a three-way race because many ambivalent conservatives did not support de la Torre.

Nonetheless, the party prospered in Sante Fé, de la Torre's province, for which it wrote a progressive constitution in 1921 that remained in effect until 1935. PDP members were active in municipalities and in the provincial government of Santa Fe. Luciano F. Molinas served as governor of the province from 1932 to 1936. Moving to the left of center politically, the PDP joined the Democratic Union in 1945 to oppose the candidacy of Juan D. PERÓN. PDP members such as Horacio Thedy and Eduardo de Cara served in Congress in the 1950s and 1960s. In 1972 the PDP joined with other small provincial parties to form the Federal Popular Alliance, and in 1982 it formed an alliance with the Democratic Socialist Party for electoral purposes. PDP theoretician Rafael Martínez Raymonda was Argentine ambassador in Rome from 1979 to 1981. Ricardo Molinas, son of the former governor of Santa Fe, served as an official of the judiciary, and Santa Fe's Alberto Natale began serving as deputy in congress in 1984.

ALBERTO A. NATALE, *Derecho político* (1979); RAFAEL MARTÍNEZ RAYMONDA, *¿Qué es el Partido Demócrata Progresista?* (1983); RICARDO F. MOLINAS, *El Partido Demócrata Progresista* (1983).

GEORGETTE MAGASSY DORN

### Radical Party
### Unión Cívica Radical—UCR

The Radical Party (UCR) emerged as a splinter of the Unión Cívica after an insurrection toppled the government of Miguel JUÁREZ CELMAN in 1890. Led by Leandro ALEM, the UCR refused co-optation by the ruling elite and adopted "relentless struggle" as its motto. Its rejection of compromise or participation in a political process it deemed corrupt left insurrection as the only path to power. In 1893, 1896, and 1905, UCR leadership attempted to spark revolution but in each case failed to generate broad-based support. The failed revolution of 1905, led by Hipólito YRIGOYEN, convinced the UCR to cultivate a following among the growing urban and rural middle class.

The electoral reform law of Roque SÁNEZ PEÑA, passed by Congress in 1912, provided for secret and compulsory suffrage for all males over eighteen. The UCR was the prime beneficiary of the legislation, and its candidate, Yrigoyen, was elected to the presidency in 1916.

Because of its broad and heterogeneous base, the ideology and policies of the UCR were at best nebulous. In the 1890s electoral reform was the party's only clearly defined demand. Passage of the Sáenz Peña law met this goal, and the UCR was left with a confused amalgam of ideas highly critical of the past and full of hope for the future. Author Manuel GÁLVEZ suggested that the party faithful appreciated the content of the ideas despite their lack of specificity. President Yrigoyen pragmatically interpreted UCR doctrine to suit the needs of power politics. While the UCR projected an image of virulent nationalism, in reality it took a moderate, rhetorical form, exercised to influence elections.

In 1924 a group of Radicals, dissatisfied with Yrigoyen's heavy-handed leadership, broke with the UCR and created a separate faction known as the ANTIPERSONALISTAS. This group supported the Revolution of 1930, in which the military cut short Yrigoyen's second term as president. As of 1930 the UCR had failed to solve the problem of political instability, in large part because its leadership could not devise policies to unite the diverse constituency it claimed to represent.

The UCR, persecuted by the conservative governments of the 1930s, returned to intransigence, boycotting the presidential election of 1931 and attempting a revolution in 1932 in the province of Entre Ríos. With Juan Domingo PERÓN's rise to power in the 1940s, many Radicals deserted the UCR and joined the Peronist-UCR Junta Renovadora. Revolution removed Perón from power in 1955, and the UCR again entered the political arena. In 1957 it split into two factions, the Unión Cívica Radical Intransigente (UCR Intransigent), led by Arturo FRONDIZI and the Unión Cívica Radical del Pueblo (UCR of the People), under the control of Ricardo BALBÍN. The terms of Radical presidents Frondizi (1958–1962) and Arturo ILLIA (1963–1966) were terminated by military coups.

In 1983 UCR candidate Raúl ALFONSÍN was elected president and prosecuted the military both for excesses committed during the DIRTY WAR (1977–1981) and its failure in the FALKLANDS/MALVINAS WAR against Great Britain. In 1989, beset by hyperinflation and spreading unrest, Alfonsín left office six months early and handed over the reins of power to the Peronist victor in the elections, Carlos MENEM.

JAMES R. SCOBIE, *Argentina: A City and a Nation,* 2d ed. (1971); DAVID ROCK, *Politics in Argentina, 1890–1930: The Rise and Fall of Radicalism* (1975); GUIDO DI TELLA, *Argentina Under Perón, 1973–76: The Nation's Experience with a Labour-Based Government* (1983); EZEQUIEL GALLO, ''Argentina: Society and Politics, 1880–1916,'' in *The Cambridge History of Latin America,* vol. 5, *c. 1870–1930,* edited by Leslie Bethell (1986), chap. 10; SUSAN CALVERT and PETER CALVERT, *Argentina: Political Culture and Instability* (1989), chap. 8.

PAUL GOODWIN

## Socialist Party
### Partido Socialista

Founded in the mid-1890s, the Socialist Party of Argentina was led by a mixture of middle-class professionals and skilled workers, whose goal was to establish a socialist Argentina through peaceful means. The party also sought to mobilize the nation's working class, which at the time was largely foreign born, as the main political force in the country. Its initial programs emphasized social reforms and social welfare, the promotion of political democracy, and measures such as separation of church and state and abolition of the armed forces. The Argentine Socialists did not, however, call for the abolition of private property.

The Socialists were the first political party in Argentina to advocate equal rights for women, especially the right to vote. Women were allowed and encouraged to participate in internal party affairs, where they could vote on candidate lists and other resolutions. A number of women associated with the party were well-known champions of women's rights, most notably Alicia MOREAU DE JUSTO, who was married to the party's founder.

Beginning in 1896, the Socialists participated consistently in the electoral process. After receiving only a handful of votes at first, the party steadily gained ground until by 1914 it had managed to elect several congressmen and a national senator from the federal capital of Buenos Aires. Building on these achievements, the Argentine Socialist Party became one of the two or three most important parties in the country and clearly the most influential and successful socialist Party in the Americas. Although its electoral fortunes fluctuated, the Socialist Party's representation in the national Congress was constant and significant, peaking with 43 of a total 158 national deputies in the early 1930s. At the same time, Socialists were also influential in municipal governments, especially in the cities of Buenos Aires and Mar del Plata, in the province of Buenos Aires. From these positions the Socialists initiated and enacted numerous measures based on their platform.

Despite these successes, the Socialists never approached the status of a national power. Beset by constant internal disagreement, they suffered numerous divisions. Because they failed to spread their message and organization to the interior of the country, their electoral support remained confined to the limits of the federal capital. Most fundamentally, when the Socialists proved unable to reconcile their international orientation with a powerful and growing sense of Argentine nationalism and projected an elitism which often seemed patronizing, they failed to develop solid backing from the nation's working classes, which flocked to the banner of Juan PERÓN and Peronism in the 1940s and 1950s.

Following World War II and the rise of Perón, the Socialist Party declined sharply in electoral support and political influence. Aside from the continued popularity and influence of a few notable party figures, the Socialist Party became something of a historical relic in the postwar era.

RICHARD J. WALTER, *The Socialist Party of Argentina, 1890–1930* (1977); JEREMY ADELMAN, ''Socialism and Democracy in Argentina in the Age of the Second International,'' in *Hispanic American Historical Review* 72, no. 2 (May 1992): 211–238.

RICHARD J. WALTER

## Youth Organization of the Radical Party
### Fuerza de Orientación Radical de la Joven Argentina—FORJA

Active in the 1930s, Argentina's ''Infamous Decade,'' the Youth Organization of the Radical Party argued for a nationalist rejuvenation of Argentine politics and society. The death of the former president and party founder Hipólito YRIGOYEN in 1933 and the participation of the Anti-Personalists in the CONCORDANCIA left the Radicals in disarray. Repression of opposition political organizations and their leaders by the Argentine government during the 1930s encouraged the formation of new factions and groups within radicalism. A group of activists who had unsuccessfully challenged Marcelo de ALVEAR for control of the Radical Party after 1931 met on 29 June 1935 and formed FORJA. Echoing Radicalism's traditional faith in democratic practices, the group blended the old with a reaction against the electoral fraud and conservative, self-serving economic policies of the ruling Concordancia. With numerous influential members, including Raúl Scalabrini Ortiz, Luis DELLEPIANE, Gabriel del Mazo, and Arturo JAURETCHE, the group's leaders called for the establishment of ''popular sovereignty'' and the ''emancipation'' of the Argentine people.

By World War II, FORJA's policies had become more nationalistic. While supporting the country's neutrality in the war, its leadership grew increasingly pro-Nazi, anti-British, and anti-American. In these respects, FORJA's platform anticipated nationalist elements in political movements that gained prominence in Argentina during the postwar era. By 1943, despite the literary talent of its leaders, the group had established few links with labor and the military. The military coup of 4 June 1943 and the rise of Juan Domingo PERÓN after 1944 pushed the organization to the sidelines of Argentine politics.

ARTURO JUARETCHE, *FORJA y la década infame* (1962); CRISTIÁN BUCHRUCKER, *Nacionalismo y peronismo: La Argentina en la crisis ideológica mundial, 1927–1955* (1987), pp. 258–276.

DANIEL LEWIS

## ARGENTINA: UNIVERSITY REFORM.

The university reform movement in Argentina began in Córdoba in 1918. There, in the country's oldest and most conservative university, student protests successfully effected major changes in the administration of that institution, including direct student participation in the management of university affairs and greater flexibility with regard to entrance requirements, class attendance, and course content. The aim of these reforms was to modernize the traditional, elite-dominated Argentine university, making its curriculum more attuned to contemporary issues and problems and opening its doors to more students of the middle and working classes.

The reform movement spread quickly to Argentina's other universities and eventually to much of the rest of Latin America. While a principal emphasis remained on educational change, reform also stimulated student interest and activism in broader political matters. One consequence of reform was the formation in 1918 of a national student group, the Federación Universitaria Argentina, which served to integrate similar federations at individual universities and articulate student interests nationwide. Soon, students and their organizations in Argentina and elsewhere in Latin America associated with the reform began to make pronouncements and take stands on a number of issues. Generally, they favored democracy over dictatorship, strongly opposed foreign investment and outside intervention in the region—especially on the part of the United States—and advocated improved conditions for the working classes. The students frequently resorted to strikes and demonstrations to support their demands.

Since 1918, the achievements of the university reform movement have provoked controversy in Argentina. There, periods of extreme student activism and influence have alternated with eras of severe repression during which universities have been taken over by national authorities and purged of unwanted professors and students, many of whom have suffered terribly in the process. Moreover, the effects of reform on the overall quality of education have undergone increasing scrutiny. What was once Latin America's finest system of higher education has since experienced serious deterioration. Nonetheless, students continue to be important participants in national life, and the principles of university reform still have considerable force and influence.

RICHARD J. WALTER, *Student Politics in Argentina: The University Reform and Its Effects, 1918–1964* (1968); VIRGINIA W. LEONARD, *Politicians, Pupils, and Priests: Argentino Education Since 1743* (1989).

RICHARD J. WALTER

**ARGENTINE CONFEDERATION,** designation used for Argentina during the dictatorship of Juan Manuel de ROSAS and the following period of national organization. Its original basis was the Federal Pact of 1831, which provided for a loose alliance of Federalist-controlled provinces against the rival Unitarists. Ultimately all provinces joined. The Confederation had no organs of its own but delegated to Rosas, the governor of Buenos Aires, authority to act on behalf of all provinces in matters of foreign relations, a mandate that he interpreted broadly. When the present national constitution was adopted in 1853, it retained the name Argentine Confederation for the more structured union that it created. A reform of 1860 substituted the name Argentine Nation.

JOSEPH T. CRISCENTI, "Argentine Constitutional History, 1810–1852: A Re-Examination," *Hispanic American Historical Review* 41 (1961): 367–412, esp. pp. 400–408; VÍCTOR TAU ANZOÁTEGUI, *Formación del estado federal argentino (1820–1852)* (1965); HAYDÉE GOROSTEGUI DE TORRES, *Argentina: La organización nacional* (1972).

DAVID BUSHNELL

**ARGUEDAS, ALCIDES** (*b.* 15 July 1879; *d.* 6 May 1946), Bolivian writer, politician, and diplomat. Born in La Paz, Arguedas studied in his native city, where he received a law degree, and in Paris. He served in Bolivian legations in Europe for twenty-five years. In these years he began to write for the press and, upon his return to La Paz, gained a measure of fame for his articles. In 1916 he was elected to the Chamber of Deputies, and in 1919 he became foreign agent in France and Spain. He also wrote historical novels, one of the earliest being *Pisagua* (1903), which dealt with the events of the WAR OF THE PACIFIC. His most highly regarded work, however, was his sociological study *Pueblo enfermo* (1909), in which he criticized his own people for defects in their character, brought on, he suggested, by their oppressive history. This theme carried over to other books, including his *Historia general de Bolivia* (1992). It was no wonder then that his works—novels, histories, articles—would all be controversial. At the same time, however, his histories have been praised by his countrymen and foreigners alike for the biting criticism of his nation's past.

CHARLES ARNADE, "The Historiography of Colonial and Modern Bolivia," in *Hispanic American Historical Review* 42 (1962): 333–384; DWIGHT B. HEATH, *Historical Dictionary of Bolivia* (1972), p. 25; JACK RAY THOMAS, *Bibliographical Dictionary of Latin American Historians and Historiography* (1984), pp. 98–99.

JACK RAY THOMAS

**ARGUEDAS, JOSÉ MARÍA** (*b.* 18 January 1911; *d.* 2 December 1969), Peruvian novelist, poet, and anthropologist. The most important Latin American writer of indigenous narrative, Arguedas, although born of white parents, saw indigenous culture from the inside, having been raised in his early years by Quechua Indians in various towns in the Peruvian Andes. He spoke Quechua before he learned Spanish. His mother died when he was three years old, and his father, an itinerant judge, was often away. Between 1931 and 1963 Arguedas earned degrees in literary studies and anthropology and held posts in various government cultural programs and museums of folklore and ethnology.

Arguedas admired the Spanish cultural heritage, but he feared its power to destroy the indigenous culture he valued so highly. In his folkloric and ethnological studies, Arguedas aspired to preserve the best of indigenous culture. He sought to attain a kind of cultural fusion, or *mestizaje*, in which the values of both of Peru's cultures could be joined. His novels and short stories reflect this most strikingly in their ability to re-create in Spanish the indigenous mentality and way of life.

In 1964 Arguedas became head of the department of ethnology and professor of Quechua at the Agrarian University. One day after his resignation, in December 1969, he shot himself. It was perhaps his doubt that *mestizaje* would ever be achieved—that in fact indigenous culture would not survive—which led to his suicide. Evidence for this exists in his final unfinished novel, *El zorro de arriba y el zorro de abajo* (The Fox from Above and the Fox from Below), published posthumously in 1970.

EARL M. ALDRICH JR., *The Modern Short Story in Peru* (1966); JEAN FRANCO, *An Introduction to Spanish-American Literature* (1969), pp. 253–254; JOSÉ MIGUEL OVIEDO, ed., *Homenaje a José María Arguedas, Revista Peruana de Cultura,* vols. 13 and 14 (1970); ANTONIO CORNEJO POLAR, *Los universos narrativos de José María Arguedas* (1973); JULIO ORTEGA, ed., *Revista Iberoamericana* 49, no. 122 [special issue devoted to Arguedas] (1983).

KEITH MCDUFFIE

**ARGÜELLES, HUGO** (*b.* 2 January 1932), Mexican playwright. Born in Veracruz, Argüelles studied at the School of Dramatic Arts of the Instituto Nacional de Bellas Artes (INBA) in Mexico City, where he later taught. He also founded the School of Fine Arts in Puebla. He won, among others, the Premio Nacional de Teatro in 1958 for his play *Los cuervos están de luto* (1958; The Crows Are in Mourning) and the Juan Ruiz de Alarcón award in 1961 for *Los prodigiosos* (1956; The Prodigies). His plays are characterized by black humor and a tone of mockery, capturing the essence of the Mexican spirit. Argüelles enjoys broad recognition for his extensive production of theatrical works, some of which he has successfully directed for television. Other major plays are *La dama de la luna roja* (1970; The Lady of the Red Moon), *El gran inquisidor* (1973; The Grand Inquisitor), *El cocodrilo solitario del panteón rococó* (1985; The Solitary Crocodile of Rococó Pantheon), and *Los gallos salvajes* (1986; The Wild Roosters).

HERIBERTO GARCÍA RIVAS, *Historia de la literatura mexicana,* vol. 4 (1974), pp. 478–479; EMILIO GARCÍA RIERA, *Historia documental del cine mexicano,* vols. 8 and 9 (1978), pp. 81–83, 233–235; MIRTA BARREA-MARLYS, ''Hugo Argüelles,'' in *Dictionary of Mexican Literature,* edited by Eladio Cortés (1992).

JEANNE C. WALLACE

**ARGÜELLO, LEONARDO** (*b.* 1875; *d.* 15 December 1947), Nicaraguan physician, writer, and politician. Born in León, the center of Nicaraguan liberalism, Leonardo Argüello participated in the revolutionary movement of 1911–1912. For his efforts Argüello was made a deputy in and the president of the Nicaraguan Congress. In 1925, Argüello was named minister of public instruction, a position in which he distinguished himself by attempting to broaden education to include the rural population and by allocating more money for schools and libraries. During the 1930s and 1940s, Argüello occupied himself with his writing but was brought from academic life back to politics in February 1947, when Anastasio SOMOZA GARCÍA arranged to have Argüello succeed him as president of the nation. Argüello, although already over seventy years old, did not prove to be the puppet that Somoza has anticipated, rather, he began to increase the participation of anti-Somocistas in the government. Three months into his term, Argüello was removed from office by a May 1947 coup led by Somoza's National Guard and forced into exile.

SARA BARQUERO, *Gobernantes de Nicaragua* (1937); and RALPH LEE WOODWARD, JR., *Central America: A Nation Divided* (1985).

KAREN RACINE

**ARGÜELLO, SANTIAGO** (*b.* 1791; *d.* 1862), Spanish military and civilian official in New Spain and Mexican California. Born at Monterey, California, he began his career as an officer in the Spanish army and later served the Mexican government until 1834. Described as tall, stout, and of fair complexion, Argüello was appointed *alcalde* of San Diego in 1836 and prefect of Los Angeles in 1840. He also served as administrator of the former mission at San Juan Capistrano from 1838 to 1840. Argüello's lands included Rancho Tia Juana, Rancho Trabuco, and the San Diego Mission estate, which were granted to him in 1829, 1841, and 1846, respectively. He and his wife, Pilar Ortega, of Santa Barbara, had twenty-two children, many of whom became influential in Mexican California society.

HUBERT HOWE BANCROFT, *History of California,* vol. 2 (1885); CHARLES HUGHES, ''Decline of the Californios: The Case of San Diego,'' in *Journal of San Diego History* 21 (1975): 1–31.

IRIS H. W. ENGSTRAND

**ARIAS, ARTURO** (*b.* 22 June 1950), Guatemalan novelist and literary critic. Born in Guatemala City, Arturo Arias is considered one of the leading representatives of the Guatemalan "new" novel. His first novel, *Después de las bombas* (1979; *After the Bombs*, 1990), narrates the mythical and carnivalesque story of a boy's search for his father during the political unrest that followed the Guatemalan counterrevolution of 1954. His second novel, *Itzam Na* (1981), which won the prestigious Cuban Casa de las Américas Award for best novel, is a combination of voices and written documents depicting the social and political alienation of bourgeois Guatemalan youth of the 1970s. His third novel, *Jaguar en llamas* (1989), deals with the indigenous side of Guatemalan history from the Conquest to the present and is his most ambitious work to date. In 1990 he published his fourth novel, *Los caminos de Paxil*, which also looks at contemporary Guatemalan political history in light of the Mayan past. Arias has also published a collection of short stories, *En la ciudad y en las montañas* (1975), and a collection of essays, *Ideologías, literatura y sociedad durante la revolución guatemalteca: 1944–54* (1979), which won the Casa de las Américas Award for essays; he coauthored the screenplay for *El Norte* (1983). In 1988 he was elected president of the Congress of Central American Writers. Arias has a doctorate in the sociology of literature from the École des Hautes Études en Sciences Sociales in Paris and teaches at San Francisco State University.

For a study of Arias's work, see the essays by DANTE LIANO, JUDY MALOOF, MARÍA ROSA OLIVERA-WILLIAMS, and ILEANA RODRÍGUEZ in *Cambios estéticos y nuevos proyectos culturales en Centroamérica*, edited by Amelia Mondragón (1994). See also FERNANDO ALEGRÍA, *Nueva historia de la novela hispanoamericana* (1986); SEYMOUR MENTON, *Historia crítica de la novela guatemalteca*, 2d ed. (1985); MARIO ROBERTO MORALES, "La nueva novela guatemalteca y sus funciones de clase," in *Literatura y crisis en Centroamérica: Ponencias*, by Ileana Rodríguez, Ramón Acevedo, and Mario Roberto Morales (1986); and JORGE CAMPOS, "Guatemala: La busca de la salvación en la droga y el viejo mundo indígena," in *Insula: Revista de Letras y Ciencias Humanas* 38 (1983): 11. Arias was interviewed by LISA DAVIS and SONIA RIVERA for "Guatemala: Hacia la victoria: Conversación con Arturo Arias y María Vázquez," in *Areito* 10 (1984): 32–35. Criticism by Arias includes his 1993 study, *Postmodernism and New Cultural Tendencies in Latin America*.

ANN GONZÁLEZ

**ARIAS, DESIDERIO** (*b.* 1872; *d.* 1931), military figure, politician, and president of the Dominican Republic (17 May 1916–June 1916). Born in Muñoz, Dominican Republic, Arias emerged as a key leader in the Liberal guerrilla movement led by Juan I. Jiménez in the 1910s. Assigned to the post of minister of war and the navy after Jiménez's election, General Arias consolidated his own power and moved against the president in a coup d'état in 1916.

Arias's coup and the civil disorder that followed pro-voked the United States to intervene, and Arias retired to private life under the watchful eye of the United States. Until the end of his life, Desiderio Arias played a role in his nation's political life as a symbol of the Liberal guerrillas. He died in a rebellion against President Rafael TRUJILLO MOLINA.

SUMNER WELLES, *Naboth's Vineyard* (1966).

TODD LITTLE-SIEBOLD

**ARIAS CALDERÓN, RICARDO** (*b.* 1933), Panamanian philosopher and intellectual and leader of the Christian Democratic Party (PDC) known for his honesty. In the 1980s, Arias Calderón became one of the leading opponents of the dictator General Manuel Antonio NORIEGA MORENO (1983–1989). In 1984, he ran for second vice president on a ticket headed by Arnulfo ARIAS MADRID in a coalition with the latter's Authentic Panameñista Party (PPA). With the death of Arias in 1988, the opposition to Noriega was thrown into chaos. In 1989, in preparation for the May elections, the Christian Democrats joined with the majority faction of the Panameñistas, headed by Guillermo Endara Paniza, and other political parties to form a broad anti-Noriega coalition called CivicADO (Democratic Alliance of Civic Opposition). With Endara heading the ticket, Arias Calderón ran for vice president. The candidate for second vice president was Guillermo Ford.

The Noriega government claimed victory in the elections, but the opposition's count as well as that of independent observers indicated just the opposite. The government later annulled the results. During a demonstration against Noriega's rule, Arias Calderón and the other candidates were beaten by the dictator's "dignity battalions." CivicADO took over the government after the 1989 U.S. invasion. On 17 December 1992, Arias Calderón resigned from the vice presidency under pressure from his own party because of disagreements with Endara and because Endara had lost a referendum on constitutional and other issues two days earlier. (The PDC had already pulled out other members from the coalition in April 1991.)

*Panama: A Country Report* (1989); *Latin American Weekly Reports* (8 January 1993), p. 8.

JUAN MANUEL PÉREZ

**ARIAS DE ÁVILA, PEDRO.** *See* **Ávila, Pedro Arias de.**

**ARIAS DE SAAVEDRA, HERNANDO** (Hernandarias; *b.* 1561; *d.* 1634), one of the greatest figures in Argentine history and the first CREOLE to hold public office in Latin America. He was born in Asunción to Captain Martín Juárez de Toledo, a close associate of Alvar Núñez CABEZA DE VACA, and María Sanabria, daughter of the ADELANTADO Juan Sanabria y Mencia Calderón. Following a common custom of the period, he was given his paternal grandfather's last name. From a very young age, Hernandarias participated in conquests and explorations and came in contact with important figures of the early history of the Río de la Plata region. He became known for his bravery and was severely wounded more than once.

In 1576, when he was only fifteen years old, he went to work for the governor of Tucumán, Gonzalo de Abrego. In 1577, he entered the service of Hernando de Lerma in Santiago del Estero, and three years later he accompanied Alonso de Vera y Aragón, cousin of the *adelantado* Juan Torres de Vera y Aragón, in a six-month cattle drive from Paraguay to Buenos Aires. In 1582, Hernandarias was with Juan de GARAY for the second founding of Buenos Aires. That year he married Garay's daughter, Jerónima Contreras. In 1588, he accompanied Juan Torres de Vera y Aragón in the founding of San Juan de Vera de las Siete Corrientes.

Hernandarias held public office a total of six times, three times between 1590 and 1597 as interim governor of the Río de la Plata, and another three times between 1597 and 1618 as governor. The first time he became governor he was only 29 years old. As governor, Hernandarias proved to be an enlightened administrator. He encouraged commerce among the different provinces; tried to curb the rampant contraband in the Río de la Plata region; protected the Indians and encouraged the creation of Jesuit MISSIONS in Paraguay; distributed land among Spaniards, creoles, and MESTIZOS; built schools, churches, and hospitals; and promulgated laws designed to improve the living standards of the population.

Hernandarias's policies created resentment among powerful Spaniards, particularly those engaged in contraband. In 1618, his enemies prevailed against him, and the new governor, Diego de Góngora, had him imprisoned and most of his property confiscated. His wife sought refuge with her brother, General Juan de Garay. Hernandarias's friends took his case to the crown, which sent the *juez pesquisador* (investigating judge) Matías Delgado Flores to investigate. Hernandarias was set free, and he was absolved of any wrongdoing in July 1624 by the OIDOR Alonso Pérez de Sálazar, who had been sent by the AUDIENCIA of Charcas. Hernandarias died in Santa Fe.

JUAN ESTEVAN GUASTAVINO, *Hernandarias* (1928); CARLOS MARÍA ARANGUREN, *Hernandarias* (1963); FRANCISCO JOSÉ FIGUEROLA, *Por qué Hernandarias* (1981).

JUAN MANUEL PÉREZ

**ARIAS MADRID, ARNULFO** (*b.* 15 August 1901; *d.* 10 August 1988), Panamanian politician and three-time president (1940–1941, 1949–1951, 1968). A medical doctor by profession and a graduate of Harvard Medical School, Arnulfo Arias was a controversial politician. Elected three times and overthrown on every occasion (the last time after just eleven days in office), Arias dominated Panamanian politics for fifty-seven years. He was highly nationalistic and anti-American. After joining the nationalistic organization *Acción Comunal* in 1930, he was leading it a year later in the revolution that overthrew the corrupt government of Florencio Harmodio AROSEMENA.

As a populist leader, Arias tried to ingratiate himself with the masses by promoting social revolution and using anti-establishment rhetoric. His platform was embodied in what he called *panameñismo,* translated as ''Panama for the Panamanians.'' His policies against the Chinese and West Indians, whom he stripped of citizenship, and others, such as requiring people in some professions to wear uniforms, made people uneasy. His first presidency constituted a small revolution, challenging the oligarchy and the United States. He promulgated a nationalistic constitution, created a social security system, gave women the right to vote, attempted a land reform program, and involved the state more actively in the economy. His enemies, the U.S. in particular, accused him of Nazi tendencies. Arias did not allow the U.S. to acquire more land for military bases with long-term leases and full jurisdiction as the U.S. had requested. Arias was trying to avoid the creation of other areas in Panamanian territory over which Panama would not have control. His nationalism and anti-Americanism put him on a collision course with the U.S., which in 1941 was involved in his overthrow. In the mid-1980s, Arias became the major figure opposing the dictator General Manuel Antonio NORIEGA. His followers came to power after the 1989 U.S. invasion and renamed his party the Arnulfista Party of Panama.

FELIPE JUAN ESCOBAR, *Arnulfo Arias* (1946); JORGE CONTE PORRAS, *Arnulfo Arias Madrid* (1980).

JUAN MANUEL PÉREZ

**ARIAS MADRID, HARMODIO** (*b.* 3 July 1886; *d.* 23 December 1962), Panamanian politician and president (1932–1936). Harmodio Arias was a prominent and highly respected politician in the 1920s and one of the leaders of the 1931 revolution that overthrew the government of Florencio Harmodio AROSEMENA. He and his brother Arnulfo became the leaders of a new and more nationalistic generation of middle-class Panamanians. He was very popular for his opposition to the ratification of the 1926 treaty with the United States. Harmodio became president in 1932 after one of the freest and most honest elections the country had seen.

He came from a modest family. In 1911, he earned a doctorate in law and political science at the University of London. In 1912, President PORRAS appointed him to a commission charged with drafting a legal code. He was a professor at the law school (1918–1920), deputy to the National Assembly (1920–1924), and Panama's representative to the International Court of Justice at The Hague and the League of Nations. As a member of the National Assembly, he staunchly defended national sovereignty. He also had a very successful law practice.

As president, Harmodio Arias attacked corruption and incompetence, for which he incurred the wrath of those accustomed to using the government for personal gain. He presided over an honest administration. In 1935, Arias founded the University of Panama. In 1936, he negotiated a new treaty with the United States that ended the latter's right to intervene in Panama's internal affairs. As the editor of *El Panamá-América*, he continued to be an influential voice in Panamanian politics after he left the presidency.

MÉLIDA RUTH SEPÚLVEDA, *Harmodio Arias Madrid: El hombre, el estadista y el periodista* (1983); PATRICIA PIZZURNO GELÓS, *Harmodio Arias Madrid y las relaciones internacionales* (1991).

JUAN MANUEL PÉREZ

**ARIAS SÁNCHEZ, OSCAR** (*b.* 13 September 1940), president of Costa Rica (1986–1990), awarded the Nobel Peace Prize in 1987 for designing a plan for peace in Central America. Arias Sánchez's father was an early follower of José FIGUERES FERRER and an active member of the National Liberation Party (PLN). His mother's family is part of the Costa Rican coffee elite that

Oscar Arias Sánchez. Guatemala City, 7 August 1987. JASON BLEIBTREU / SYGMA.

emerged during the nineteenth-century coffee boom. Arias Sánchez came to international prominence shortly after his inauguration in 1986 when he took bold initiatives to propel Central America into a peace process. His proposals for peace and stability in the region led to an agreement, signed in 1987, between Honduras, Guatemala, Nicaragua, El Salvador, and Costa Rica.

The Arias plan, or ESQUIPULAS II, established the framework for the pacification and democratization of Central America. It provided for the restoration of civil liberties, for amnesty for political prisoners, for free elections, and for genuine dialogue between governments and opposition forces. The plan contributed to the process that brought peace and free elections to Nicaragua and new hope for the eventual demilitarization of the region.

Even though Arias came to the international scene at a relatively young age, he had served a long apprenticeship in the highly competitive arena of Costa Rican party politics and in the rigorous intellectual environment of the University of Costa Rica (UCR). He received his law and economics degrees from the UCR, was awarded a master of arts degree in political science and economics from the London School of Economics (1967), and earned a doctor of philosophy degree from the University of Essex, England (1974). He joined the faculty of UCR in 1969 and served as a member of the ad hoc Commission of the National University (1972–1975). He was a director of the Costa Rican Technological Institute from 1974 to 1977.

Arias began his political career in the PLN and held high elected and appointed positions in the national government and in the party. He served as secretary to the president (1970–1972) during the last José Figueres Ferrer administration. From 1972 to 1977, he held a cabinet-level position as minister of national planning and economic policy. While serving as a member of the National Assembly (1978–1982), he also held other leadership positions. He was secretary of international affairs (1975–1979) and he was elected secretary general in 1979 on a reformist platform that brought a new generation of leaders to the fore. Arias ascended to the presidency chiefly by serving in positions of party leadership and in the administration of President Luis Alberto MONGE ÁLVAREZ. He won the PLN primary and then defeated Rafael Angel CALDERÓN FOURNIER in the general election.

Arias has received many awards and honorary degrees from universities in Europe, Central America, and the United States. Since his presidency he has lectured widely on the related questions of world peace and the environment, donating the proceeds from the lectures to the Arias Foundation, which was established to support research on these issues. He has also continued to be active in politics.

OSCAR ARIAS SÁNCHEZ, *Grupos de presión en Costa Rica* (1971), and *¿Quién gobierna en Costa Rica?* (1976); JOHN PATRICK BELL, "Political Power in Contemporary Costa Rica," in *Journal of*

*Inter-American Studies and World Affairs* 20 (1978): 443–454; SETH ROLBEIN, *Nobel Costa Rica* (1989).

JOHN PATRICK BELL

*See also* **Costa Rica: Political Parties.**

**ARICA,** a port city in Tarapacá Province, situated in the sparsely populated Atacama Desert of northern Chile. Throughout its history, Arica has been a commercial and transportation link, connecting Bolivia with the Pacific. The first Europeans to pass through the region were members of the Diego de ALMAGRO expedition. In 1565 the governor of Peru, Lope GARCÍA DE CASTRO, created Arica province (*corregimiento*), and five years later Spanish residents founded the town, San Marcos de Arica, with El Morro peak marking the entrance to the bay.

During colonial times Arica was a main conduit between Lima and the great SILVER mines of Upper Peru. Mercury for amalgamating silver ores was shipped to Arica, and then mule and llama teams carried it to Upper Peru. Returning teams brought silver from the mines. In the 1680s, however, piracy along the Pacific coast threatened the shipments, and teamsters began taking the mercury overland from Huancavelica, bypassing Arica altogether. The port continued to handle much of the merchandise sent by the merchant guild of Lima to Upper Peru. With the proclamation of intra-imperial free trade in 1778, Arica enjoyed renewed vigor as a commercial way station.

Upon independence from Spain, Arica was initially part of Peru and continued to be a conduit for Bolivia. Guano and nitrates brought Peru and Chile into conflict over the region. During the WAR OF THE PACIFIC (1879–1883), the city surrendered to the attacking Chileans on 7 June 1880 following a bloody siege, and Peru and Chile disputed ownership of the province until the Treaty of 1929 confirmed Chilean possession. Gustave Eiffel designed the cathedral. Connected by railroad with Tacna in Peru and La Paz, Arica has remained a free port for Bolivia.

VICENTE DAGNINO, *El correjimiento de Arica, 1535–1784* (1909); RÓMULO CÚNEO-VIDAL, *Historia de la fundación de la ciudad de San Marcos de Arica: Leyendas de Arica, Tarapacá y Atacama* (1977); LUIS ALBERTO GALDEMES ROSAS, *Historia de Arica* (1981).

KENDALL W. BROWN

**ARIDJIS, HOMERO** (*b.* 6 April 1940), Mexican writer. Like many of his contemporaries in Mexico, Aridjis has had a varied career, including journalism, diplomatic service, and teaching. Trained as a journalist, he was a member of a writing workshop directed by the noted Mexican short-story writer Juan José ARREOLA and was awarded fellowships by the Centro Mexicano de Es-

critores (Mexican Writers Center) and the Guggenheim Foundation.

Aridjis has written poetry and prose, much of it first published in Mexican literary journals and Sunday cultural supplements of newspapers and subsequently appearing in numerous collected works. His many volumes of poetry, among them *Antes del reino* (1963) and *Vivar para ver* (1977), focus on themes of love, life, and death, and are heavily charged with emotion. More recently he has attempted to create the "poema nuclear" (nuclear poem), modifying his use of language and including social and historical themes. As a prose writer of stories and novels, he combines narrative and poetic elements (*Mirándola dormir*, 1964, and *Perséfone*, 1967), autobiography (*El poeta niño*, 1971), and the historical (*1492, vida y tiempos de Juan Cabezón de Castilla*, 1985). Much of Aridjis's writing has been translated into English and other languages. In recent years, he has been actively involved with other intellectuals in the Grupo de los Cien (Group of 100), Mexico's foremost ecological movement.

MANUEL DURÁN, "Música en sordina: Tres poetas mexicanos. Bonifaz Nuño, García Terrés, Aridjis," in *Plural*, no. 8 (1972): 29–31; MERLIN H. FORSTER, "Four Contemporary Mexican Poets: Marco Antonio Montes de Oca, Gabriel Zaid, José Emilio Pacheco, Homero Aridjis," in his *Tradition and Renewal: Essays on Twentieth-Century Latin American Literature and Culture* (1975); FRANK DAUSTER, "Poetas mexicanos nacidos en las décadas de 1920, 1930 y 1940," in *Revista Iberoamericana*, 55, nos. 148–149 (1989): 1161–1175.

GABRIELLA DE BEER

**ARIEL,** an essay (1900) by the Uruguayan writer José Enrique RODÓ. The title alludes to a character in Shakespeare's *The Tempest* who in this short book becomes a symbol of the enlightening spirit with which the author aspires to enhance Latin American culture. Written in the aftermath of Spain's imperial collapse in the war of 1898 against the United States and addressed primarily to young Latin Americans, *Ariel* is both an idealistic call to cultural independence and a warning against the tendency toward utilitarian overconfidence that Rodó discerned in North American progressive materialism. *Ariel*'s format is a scholarly final lecture by old Próspero (another symbolic name from *The Tempest*), who exhorts his students as builders of the future to strive individually for standards of excellence. *Ariel* is less a social philosophy than a cultural manifesto, the elitist spirit and erudite style of which have often been defended or attacked by Latin American readers and writers as ARIELISMO.

LEOPOLDO ALAS ("Clarín"), prologue to *Ariel*, 2d ed. (1901); ROBERTO GONZÁLEZ ECHEVARRÍA, "The Case of the Speaking Statue: *Ariel* and the Magisterial Rhetoric of the Latin American Essay," in his *The Voice of Masters* (1985); CARLOS FUENTES, prologue to *Ariel* (1985), translated by Margaret Sayers Peden.

PETER G. EARLE

**ARIELISMO,** an idealistic quality of Hispanic American thought. The term is a neologism derived from José Enrique RODÓ's ARIEL (1900), an essay that advocates a harmonious synthesis of the finest attributes of Greco-Roman culture, the Judeo-Christian heritage, and modern (late-nineteenth-century) perspectives. In Latin American intellectual circles it has customarily been associated with elitism, spiritualist aesthetics, and high standards of excellence.

*Arielismo* has often been used to explain the contrast between refined intellectual activity and high culture on the one hand, and a more direct, pragmatic approach to Latin American problems on the other. Practical-minded critics of the tendency have recognized its value as a cultural ideal and educational stimulus but have considered its advocates to be out of touch with Latin America's most pressing political, social, and economic needs.

*Arielismo* has had few explicit defenders. However, important twentieth-century writings have shared or revised its spirit: among them, the Mexican Alfonso REYES's *Visión de Anáhuac* (1917), the Venezuelan Mariano PICÓN-SALAS's *Regreso de tres mundos* (1959), and the Dominican Pedro HENRÍQUEZ UREÑA's *Seis ensayos en busca de nuestra expresión* (1928). Its detractors have been more pointed in their reaction: see, for example, Alberto ZUM FELDE, *Proceso intelectual del Uruguay y crítica de su literatura* (1941), and Luis Alberto SÁNCHEZ, *Balance y liquidación del novecientos* (1941). In 1971 Roberto FERNÁNDEZ RETAMAR published *Calibán,* a socialist-oriented essay in which the leading roles in Rodó's work are reversed: now Próspero, the imperialistic magician, symbolizes the United States, and the uncouth Calibán is made over to represent a victimized Latin America.

MARTIN S. STABB, "The Revolt Against Scientism," in his *In Quest of Identity* (1967); JOSÉ MIGUEL OVIEDO, "Bajo las alas de Ariel," in his *Breve historia del ensayo hispanoamericano* (1991); JOHN A. CROW, "Ariel and Calibán," in his *Epic of Latin America,* 4th ed. (1992).

PETER G. EARLE

**ARISMENDI, JUAN BAUTISTA** (*b.* 1775; *d.* 23 July 1841), officer in the Venezuelan Emancipating Army. Arismendi was born in La Asunción on Margarita Island. At the commencement of the movement for emancipation from Spain, Arismendi took the pro-independence side and participated in the 1812 expedition to Guiana. He returned to Margarita Island following the expedition only to find it under the control of Coronel Pascual Martínez of the Spanish government. Arismendi's pro-independence leadership led to his arrest and imprisonment first in La Guaira and later on Margarita Island. During his imprisonment, Spanish authority was forcibly ousted and Arismendi was named governor of the island in 1813. That same year he traveled to Caracas to place himself in the service of Simón BOLÍVAR, who put him in charge of the Barlovento campaign.

Arismendi returned to Margarita Island in 1814 and was named its commander in chief. In 1819 he served as vice president of the republic for a short time. Two years later he led his own armed contingent in the battle of CARABOBO. He remained on Margarita Island and on more than one occasion during the Southern campaign resisted orders for his recruitment. In 1828 José Antonio PÁEZ appointed him second in command of the army, and in 1830 he was an active participant in the movement that dissolved GRAN COLOMBIA. Arismendi was elected senator in the National Congress for the province of Margarita in 1835 and was reelected in 1839.

MARIANO DE BRICEÑO, *Historia de la Isla de Margarita: Biografías del General Juan Bautista Arismendi y de la Señora Luisa Cáceres de Arismendi* (1885); HORACIO BIANCHI, *Juicio histórico sobre la vida y obra del General Juan Bautista Arismendi* (1941); and FRANCISCO JAVIER YÁNES, *Historia de Margarita y observaciones del General Francisco Esteban Gómez* (1948).

INÉS QUINTERO

**ARISMENDI, RODNEY** (*b.* 22 March 1913; *d.* 27 December 1989), leader of the Communist Party of Uruguay. Arismendi was born in the city of Río Branco in the department of Cerro Largo. He studied law in Montevideo, where he was a prominent student leader. During this period he joined the Communist Party, whose secretary general, Eugenio Gómez, had held the office since the party's inception. Arismendi took over for Gómez as secretary general in 1955 and held the office until 1989. As a journalist and director of the daily *Diario Popular,* he was forced into exile but was elected a representative to Parliament in 1946, and went on to serve a number of terms in the legislature. In 1973 Arismendi was imprisoned by the military regime and later deported; he lived for more than ten years in the Soviet Union. Returning to Uruguay in 1984, he was elected to the senate, an office he held until his death.

Arismendi was one of the principal pro-Soviet Marxist theorists in Latin America, publishing several books on ideological themes and playing an important role in the creation of the leftist FRENTE AMPLIO. After his death, he was replaced as secretary general of the Communist Party by Jaime Pérez, a former union leader.

MARTIN WEINSTEIN, *Uruguay: Democracy at the Crossroads* (1988); GERARDO CAETANO and JOSÉ RILLA, *Breve historia de la dictadura* (1991).

JOSÉ DE TORRES WILSON

*See also* **Uruguay: Political Parties.**

**ARISTA, MARIANO** (*b.* 1802; *d.* 1855), president of Mexico (1851–1853). Arista enlisted as a cadet in the Provincial Regiment of Puebla at the age of fifteen. In June 1821 he joined the Army of the THREE GUARANTEES under the leadership of Agustín de ITURBIDE to support the PLAN OF IGUALA for autonomy and independence for Mexico. Arista continued to serve in the army, reaching the rank of brigadier general. On 8 June 1833 he rebelled against the radical reforms of President Valentín GÓMEZ FARÍAS, calling on General Antonio López de SANTA ANNA and the army to preserve the FUEROS (prerogatives) and properties of the regular and secular clergy. Exiled to the United States in November 1833, Arista was able to return to Mexico only after the triumph of the Plan of Cuernavaca, which provided the basis for Santa Anna's formation of a more conservative government. Arista served as a member of various military commissions before being named commanding general of the state of Tamaulipas in 1839. In 1846, Arista was called to lead the Army of the North. On 8 May 1846, at Palo Alto, Tamaulipas, Arista's forces were defeated by a U.S. army contingent under General Zachary Taylor in the first major battle of the war. The next day Arista retreated and turned over command to General Francisco Mejía. Arista served as minister of war from 12 June 1848 to 15 January 1851, on which date he assumed the office of president. He resigned on 6 January 1853 and moved to Europe. He died aboard a British ship en route from Portugal to France, where he hoped to obtain medical treatment. He was buried in Lisbon; his ashes were returned to Mexico in 1880.

ALBERTO MARÍA CARREÑO ESCUDERO, *Jefes del ejército mexicano en 1847* (1914); CHARLES L. DUFOUR, *The Mexican War: A Compact History, 1846–1848* (1968); MOISÉS GONZÁLEZ NAVARRO, *Anatomía del poder en México, 1848–1853* (1977); *Diccionario Porrúa de historia, biografía y geografía de México*, 5th ed. (1986).

D. F. STEVENS

**ARISTIDE, JEAN-BERTRAND** (*b.* 15 July 1953), president of Haiti, 1991. Following a period of violence and instability, Aristide won a popular democratic election and became the youngest president in Haitian history, succeeding provisional president Ertha Pascal Trouillot on 7 February 1991. A charismatic Roman Catholic priest who strongly supported the theology of liberation, Aristide had strong backing from the black peasant masses. A Vodun priestess participated in the inauguration ceremony as Aristide took the oath of office in the creole language of the poor peasants. Well educated and dedicated to the welfare of the poor, Aristide was an outspoken critic of the DUVALIER dictatorship and of the TONTON MACOUTES, who continued to threaten him after the ouster of Jean-Claude Duvalier in 1986. The *macoutes*, along with the oppressive poverty of Haiti, presented formidable obstacles to the popular Aristide as he began his administration. Resistance to Aristide's military reforms led to his ouster by the army on 30 September 1991 in a coup led by Brigadier General Raoul Cedras. The imprisoned former leader of the *Tonton macoutes*, Roger Lafontant, was reportedly executed during the coup. Late in 1994 Aristide was returned to office following lengthy U.S.-sponsored diplomacy and

the virtual occupation of the country by an American military force.

*Aristide: An Autobiography,* translated by Linda Maloney (1993).

RALPH LEE WOODWARD, JR.

**ARIZONA,** a colonial territory of Spain (until 1821) and part of the Mexican state of Sonora (until 1853). JESUIT missions, slowly expanding north from Sinaloa after 1630, reached southern Arizona by 1700, led by the noted missionary Father Eusebio KINO. Until the cessation of hostilities with the Apaches in the 1770s, Hispanic population was limited to the missions of San Xavier del Bac and Tumacácori, and to the presidio of Tubac (moved to Tucson in 1776). Thereafter, the Hispanic population slowly expanded along the Santa Cruz valley and then east to the San Pedro valley, peaking at well over 1,000 in the 1820s. However, the breakdown of the presidial system (including cessation of gift rations to the APACHES) and of the missions (administered by the FRANCISCANS after the Jesuit expulsion of 1767) led to renewed Apache raiding after 1830 that forced a retreat of the Mexican frontier in southern Arizona. When U.S. troops occupied Tucson in late 1846, Mexicans remained only there and at Tubac. In 1848, Apaches forced the complete abandonment of the latter. Through purchase under the Treaty of La Mesilla (30 December 1853), southern Arizona was joined to the rest of Arizona as a territory of the United States.

JAY WAGONER, *Early Arizona, Prehistory to Civil War* (1975); JOHN L. KESSELL, *Friars, Soldiers, and Reformers: Hispanic Arizona and the Sonoran Mission Frontier 1767–1856* (1976); DAVID J. WEBER, *The Mexican Frontier, 1821–1846: The American Southwest Under Mexico* (1982).

STUART F. VOSS

**ARLT, ROBERTO** (*b.* 2 April 1900; *d.* 26 July 1942), Argentine writer. Born in Buenos Aires, Arlt's writing was one of the major critical (re)discoveries of the halcyon, countercultural period between the demise of Juan PERÓN (1955) and the military coup of 1966. One dimension of the interest in Arlt was a reaction against the emerging international monumentalization of Jorge Luis BORGES. Arlt evoked several components of Argentine culture that were judged to be absent in Borges: he was of immigrant extraction; he was unlettered and unencumbered by an immense bookish learning; his literature centered on the urban proletariat, with a heavy emphasis on the socially marginal, misfits, and the aberrant; he was unconcerned by coherent ideologies and, indeed, often seemed to relish the incoherent and the contradictory; and he exemplified the practice of literature, not as an intellectual pastime, but as gainful employment. While today it may seem specious to promote a categoric disjunction between Borges and Arlt, Arlt was championed as an authentic voice of all of the gritty aspects of the Argentine sociopolitical body that the aloof Borges—at least in his world-literature embodiment—seemed to deny. Moreover, in novels like *Los siete locos* (1929; *The Seven Madmen*, 1984), dramas written for the populist theater, such as *Trescientos millones* (1932), and in the hundreds of newspaper columns that constitute a veritable mosaic of the underbelly of the Buenos Aires proletariat and petite bourgeoisie in the watershed years of the Great Depression, Arlt moved the literary registers of Spanish away from the rhetorical and poetic models of modernism and other European standards (including ossified academic norms) toward the beginnings of a true urban colloquiality in Argentine literature, one perhaps less sociolinguistically authentic than it is emblematically authentic. He died in Buenos Aires.

DAVID WILLIAM FOSTER, *Currents in the Contemporary Argentine Novel* (1975), pp. 20–45; ADEN HAYES, *Roberto Arlt, la estrategia de su ficción* (1981); ENRIQUE GIORDANO, *La teatralización de la obra dramática, de Florencio Sánchez a Roberto Arlt* (1982); *Review* (Center for Inter-American Relations), no. 31 (1982), special issue devoted to Arlt; GERARDO MARIO GOLOBOFF, *Genio y figura de Roberto Arlt* (1988).

DAVID WILLIAM FOSTER

**ARMADA DEL MAR DEL SUR,** a small Pacific fleet designed by the Spanish crown to protect Spanish settlements along the Pacific coast of Tierra Firme (South America) and to convoy Spanish shipping in the Pacific. Its construction was originally prompted by the incursions of English, Dutch, and French traders and pirates, which began in the 1570s. Its most important convoy duty was accompanying the merchant fleet that carried Peruvian silver from Callao to Panama in Tierra Firme for the PORTOBELO fair and returned laden with European goods.

The armada normally consisted of between four and six warships—usually two to four galleons of 600 to 1,000 tons each and a similar number of smaller vessels of 80 to 100 tons. This nucleus was often supplemented in times of distress by various hastily converted merchant vessels.

Despite frequent complaints about poor quality and high costs, viceregal authorities relied on the colonial shipyards at Guayaquil to build the vessels. Given the crown's reluctance to support Pacific defenses, the viceregal treasury in Lima struggled to finance the construction and maintenance of this small defense force. As viceregal finances began to deteriorate by the late seventeenth century, however, the burden of defending

*Armada del mar del sur.* Anonymous. MUSEO NAVAL, MADRID.

the Pacific increasingly fell on private commercial interests.

The best survey is PABLO E. PÉREZ-MALLAÍNA and BIBIANO TORRES RAMÍREZ, *La armada del mar del sur* (1987). Two important articles are PETER T. BRADLEY, "Maritime Defence of the Viceroyalty of Peru (1600–1700)," in *The Americas* 36, no. 2 (October 1979): 155–175, and LAWRENCE A. CLAYTON, "Local Initiative and Finance in Defense of the Viceroyalty of Peru: The Development of Self-Reliance," in *Hispanic American Historical Review* 54, no. 2 (May 1974): 284–304. The best general surveys on Pacific defenses and foreign intrusions are PETER T. BRADLEY, *The Lure of Peru: Maritime Intrusion into the South Sea, 1598–1701* (1989), and GUILLERMO LOHMANN VILLENA, *Historia marítima del Perú*, vol. 4, *Siglos XVII y XVIII* (1973).

KENNETH J. ANDRIEN

**ARMED FORCES.** Armed forces, generally including a nation's army, navy, air force, and national police force, have been prominent in the political, social, and economic history of every Latin American country. Latin American nations emerging from the wars for independence had weak identities and ill-defined borders. Their militaries, however, had been forged into cohesive organizations by more than a decade of fighting. They and the Roman Catholic church emerged as the dominant institutions in most Latin American nations. The need to develop a national identity, to establish domestic order, and to protect these newly independent nations from external threats gave the region's armed forces serious responsibilities and privileged roles in politics as well as social and economic affairs. Imperial Brazil, too, had to rely on its military for defense during border disputes as well as during the WAR OF THE TRIPLE ALLIANCE.

The political role was sometimes enshrined in national constitutions, making the armed forces responsible for maintaining social order and for deciding when it was necessary to do so. This responsibility, in part, was the premise for many of the scores of military coups that have been prominent features of post-Independence Latin American history. Also, throughout the nineteenth century and to a lesser degree into the twentieth century, intraclass struggles over the sharing of national power raged between conservatives and liberals. Frequently, the opponents would solicit the support of elements within the army (the dominant service) or among the armed services. The CHILEAN REVOLUTION OF 1891, which pitted the Conservative Congress and the navy against Liberal President José Manuel BALMACEDA and the army is illustrative of this struggle.

The political and military history of each Latin American country is, of course, unique. For example, Peru, which became independent in 1824, did not have a civilian president until 1872. Mexico, with both military and civilian presidents in the nineteenth century, was wracked by regional rebellions from Texas to Yucatán, war with the United States, civil war, and the violent ouster of a foreign emperor. Brazil's first presidents following the overthrow of the emperor in 1889 were military men. Although only one Chilean president was overthrown by the military from 1818 until 1973 (the military coup against the government of Salvador ALLENDE), the prominence of Chile's military resulted from heroics in the War of Independence and in the WAR OF THE PACIFIC (1879–1883) as well as from the need to maintain the integrity of its historically contested more than 2,000-mile-long border with Argentina, Bolivia, and Peru.

By the end of the nineteenth century, German, French, and Italian military missions had arrived throughout Latin America, significantly increasing professionalism and leaving their own unique marks. The Bolivian army that fought the CHACO WAR (1932–1935), trained for the most part by a German mission headed by General Hans Kundt, paraded with spiked helmets. Following the disastrous War of the Pacific, Peru contracted with a French mission that was withdrawn during the early days of World War I. Nevertheless, they adopted the French campaign cap. Late in World War I, the United States entered the competition, and by 1939 most Latin American nations had a U.S. naval mission. Also by this time the United States had become very concerned with the influence of German and Italian military missions within the region, and forced them out.

Military professionalism spawned institutional interests separate from those of other national elites. The result was personalist military regimes in many Latin American countries. These regimes were typically created via military coups led by junior officers or by a senior officer who gradually eliminated his rivals. Although a coup may have been motivated by military perceptions that leaders were abusing the national interest or the military institution or both, it usually devolved into a dictatorship, headed by a military strongman in a business suit, that attempted to legitimize itself through rigged elections and the governmental involvement of various civilian interests. Regimes led by Colombia's Gustavo ROJAS PINILLA (1953–1957), Peru's Manuel ODRÍA (1948–1956), Venezuela's Marcos PÉREZ JIMÉNEZ (1948–1958), El Salvador's Maximiliano HERNÁNDEZ MARTÍNEZ (1931–1944), Nicaragua's Anastasio SOMOZA GARCÍA (1937–1956), and Cuba's Fulgencio BATISTA (1952–1959) are examples of personalist military governments. At the same time, post-Revolutionary Mexico managed to restrain its military and keep it firmly under civilian control, and Costa Rica abolished the military altogether, relying solely on a national police force to maintain order.

The intensification of Latin American military professionalism following World War II led to a different kind of involvement of its armed forces in national politics: "institutional" military governments. These regimes were formed by the military as an institution. Institutional military regimes in Latin America typically were headed by the chief of staff of the armed forces, with subordinates assuming cabinet-level and other impor-

Venezuelan cadets at attention. LIBRARY OF CONGRESS.

tant government posts. By the mid-twentieth century, institutional coups were led by commanders in chief, not insubordinate colonels, because Latin American military institutions had become larger and weapons were more powerful. Coups in countries with large military forces having powerful weapons required careful planning and the involvement of many individuals. This was the lesson learned by the Brazilians whose attempted coup failed in 1961 but succeeded in 1964.

Institutional military regimes sought to legitimize themselves through official military ideology and the forging of stable relationships with specific civilian interests, including economic technicians, private enterprises, and the official church. The broad military support linked to powerful civilian interests allowed institutional military governments to repress dissent and opposition by harsh means and to stay in power despite considerable unpopularity. The first institutional military government in Latin America was formed by the armed forces of Peru in 1962, in order to prevent the nationalist leader Víctor Raúl HAYA DE LA TORRE from assuming power. Institutional regimes were soon formed in Brazil (1964), Argentina (1966), Ecuador (1972), Uruguay (1973), and Chile (1973).

Ideology developed in military institutes of advanced study was key to the mid-twentieth-century role of Latin American armed forces in politics. Doctrines of national security were developed at institutions such as the Brazilian Escola Superior de Guerra, founded in 1949, and the Peruvian Centro de Altos Estudios Militares, founded in 1950. These doctrines asserted that communism threatened political order through subversion of national institutions, and that to defeat communism, it was necessary for the military systematically to play a larger role in national affairs. The institutional military governments that their ideology attempted to legitimize tried to weaken subversion through measures as diverse as populist social reform (Peru) and promotion of rapid economic growth (Brazil, Chile). In so doing, they gave themselves action agendas calling for long periods of military rule.

Professional education not only transformed the political roles of Latin America's armed forces; it also changed the basis of military seniority and the social status of officers. With few opportunities for armed combat and with personalistic coups more difficult to execute, educational performance became a key factor for military promotion. Influenced by European and North American professionalism, promotion to general officer came to require mid-career education, often on economic and social issues, and periods of study abroad. Increased education created a more self-confident military elite. Whereas turn-of-the-century Latin American officers were said to have been threatened by the sophistication of civilian leaders, increased education and broader experience, combined with control of the means of physical coercion, often made the military the intimidators. Typically recruited from the lower middle class and proud of

the social mobility that military service made possible, their new education, plus the discipline and hardship of traditional military training, created a separate and self-righteous consciousness among the military.

Continued prominence of the armed forces as an institution was strongly supported by the perception of Marxism as a threat to political order. Military contempt for civilian capabilities was reinforced by U.S. post–World War II policies aimed at preventing armed Communist takeovers such as that engineered by Fidel CASTRO in Cuba in 1959. Through the Military Assistance Program, the International Military Education and Training Program, and other facilities, the United States provided Latin American armed forces with external sources of funding, training, and material far out of proportion to that available to any other public- or private-sector institution. Both materially and as a source of international legitimation, this support strengthened the capacities of the armed forces in the political systems of the region.

The legitimacy of institutional military governments was undermined by a variety of factors. Military national security doctrine could not supplant the ideology of democracy, in which civilian rule is the norm and military government is an aberration. Harsh suppression of civil rights, poor economic policy management, allegations of corruption, and military adventurism combined to undermine public confidence in military leaders. With this backdrop, military disunity and civilian opposition contributed to a return to civilian rule from the Rio Grande to Tierra del Fuego, beginning with Ecuador in 1979 and culminating with Chile in 1989.

Despite returning to the barracks at the beginning of the 1990s, the armed forces continued to wield substantial political power in many Latin American countries. Within the public sector, the salaries, benefits, and terms of employment of military officers were relatively privileged. Although constitutionally subject to civilian authority, the armed forces continued to exert formal and informal veto power in many areas. Sometimes this power served to preserve mandated sources of material support, sometimes extralegal privilege, sometimes to maintain military conceptions of public order.

With the decline of communism as a threat and the breaking apart of the Soviet Union, the balance between civilian and military power in Latin America is beset by a need to redefine the mission of the armed forces. With force and budget reductions in North America and Europe, the broad-gauged and prominent political roles of Latin American armed forces have become increasingly anomalous. Historic border disputes; the continuation of insurgencies in Guatemala, Colombia, and Peru; and the need to patrol national boundaries suggest a focus on the traditional core role of the armed forces: defending national territorial integrity. In the late twentieth century there has been a dramatic shift in the prominence of the military. In 1979 military officers were chiefs of state in nineteen nations in Central and South America. At the close of 1991, all of these countries were led by civilians who had come to power in open elections. By March 1995, the armed forces did not dominate the government of any American or Caribbean country.

To trace the development of analysis of the armed forces in Latin America, one might begin with BENJAMIN RATTENBACH, *Sociología militar* (1959); EDWIN LIEUWEN, *Arms and Politics in Latin America* (1961); MORRIS JANOWITZ, *The Military in the Political Development of New Nations* (1964); and SAMUEL P. HUNTINGTON, *Political Order in Changing Societies* (1968).

Contemporary writings examining the nature of institutional military government and the evolution of civil-military relations include ABRAHAM F. LOWENTHAL and J. SAMUEL FITCH, eds., *Armies and Politics in Latin America*, rev. ed. (1986); ALAIN ROUQUIE, *The Military and the State in Latin America* (1987); ALFRED C. STEPAN, *Rethinking Military Politics: Brazil and the Southern Cone* (1988); AUGUSTO VARAS, ed., *La autonomía militar en América Latina* (1988); and LOUIS W. GOODMAN, JOHANNA MENDELSON, and JUAN RIAL, eds., *The Military and Democracy: The Future of Civil-Military Relations in Latin America* (1990).

LOUIS W. GOODMAN

**ARMENDÁRIZ, JOSÉ DE** (*b.* 1670; *d.* ?) marquis of Castelfuerte and viceroy of Peru, 1724–1736. A native of Rivagorza, Spain, Armendáriz pursued a military career from a young age, serving in Flanders, Catalonia, Naples, Portugal, and Villaviciosa. Captain-general of Guipúzcoa when named viceroy of Peru in 1723, he was probably the most distinguished Spanish military officer to serve in South America.

Armendáriz proved energetic and firm, unlike his predecessor, Fray Diego Morcillo, but was neither an innovator nor a reformer. He stepped up surveillance along the Pacific coast to reduce smuggling by foreign vessels and limited the duration of the Portobelo fairs to deter contraband. Armendáriz also devoted great energy to strengthening colonial defenses throughout the continent. He captured and executed José de ANTEQUERA, the former *oidor* (judge) of Charcas, who had installed himself as an independent governor of Paraguay. The execution touched off a serious tumult in Lima, which Armendáriz crushed. Because the guards killed two Franciscan partisans of Antequera in suppressing the uprising, the clergy harshly criticized the viceroy, but the crown fully supported him. He also acted swiftly and severely to defeat the mestizo rebellion of Alejo Calatayud in Cochabamba. Armendáriz attempted to curb the corruption of provincial governors (*corregidores*) and restrict the sale of *aguardiente* (distilled liquor), with little success.

Promoted in 1729 to captain-general, the highest Spanish military rank, Armendáriz received the great honor of membership in the Order of the Golden Fleece upon his return to Spain. He then commanded the regiment of royal guards.

"Relación del estado de los reynos del Perú que hace el Exmo. Señor Don José Armendaris, marqués de Castel-Fuerte,

á su sucesor el marqués de Villagarcía, en el año de 1736," in MANUEL A. FUENTES, ed., *Memorias de los virreyes que han gobernado el Perú*, vol. 3 (1859), pp. 1–369; J. A. DE LAVALLE, "La ejecución de Antequera," in *El Ateneo* 2 (1886): 23–35, 66–80; RUBÉN VARGAS UGARTE, *Historia general del Perú*, vol. 6 (1966), pp. 121–190.

KENDALL W. BROWN

**ARMENDÁRIZ, PEDRO** (*b.* 1912; *d.* 18 June 1963), Mexican actor. Born in Mexico City, Armendáriz attended school in San Antonio, Texas, and completed his studies at the California Polytechnic Institute. He worked as a journalist in the United States before returning to Mexico in 1934. Armendáriz debuted in the film *María Elena* (1935) and went on to appear in more than 100 movies. He was a leading actor with the famed team of director Emilio "El Indio" FERNÁNDEZ. Armendáriz's striking screen presence made him one of the most popular leading stars of Mexican cinema. His most memorable films are *Distinto Amanecer* (1943), *María Candelaria* (1943), *Maclovia* (1948), *La perla* (1946), and *Enamorada* (1947). He was also cast in several Hollywood films, including *Fort Apache* (1948) and *From Russia with Love* (1963). He died in Los Angeles.

LUIS REYES DE LA MAZA, *El cine sonoro en México* (1973); E. BRADFORD BURNS, *Latin American Cinema: Film and History* (1975); CARL J. MORA, *Mexican Cinema: Reflections of a Society: 1896–1980* (1982); and JOHN KING, *Magical Reels: A History of Cinema in Latin America* (1990).

DAVID MACIEL

**ARMIJO, MANUEL** (*b.* 1801; *d.* 1853), governor of New Mexico (1836–1846). Armijo's administration was notable mainly for its opposition to Anglo-American incursions. He sought to control the illegal activities of American trappers, and in 1841 he led the Mexican forces that defeated a group of Texans, led by General Hugh McLeod, who sought to conquer New Mexico. In 1846 Armijo led the Mexican army that opposed the invasion of the province by General Stephen W. KEARNY. In the face of superior U.S. forces, he abandoned the defense of the territory and fled to Mexico, where he remained.

RALPH EMERSON TWITCHELL, *The Leading Facts of New Mexican History*, 5 vols. (1911–1917), and *The Conquest of Santa Fe, 1846*, edited by Bill Tate (1967).

RICHARD GRISWOLD DEL CASTILLO

**ARNAZ, DESI** (*b.* 2 March 1917; *d.* 2 December 1986), Cuban bandleader, actor, and pioneer television producer. Born Desiderio Alberto Arnaz y Acha in Santiago de Cuba to an influential family, Arnaz and his father went into exile in Miami with the overthrow of President Gerardo MACHADO in 1933. Discovered there by Xavier CUGAT, he joined the Cugat band for a six-month tour. He then returned to Miami and, with his own band, introduced the conga line to the United States, and started a national dance craze. During the 1940s, he appeared on Broadway and made several feature films. While filming *Too Many Girls* in 1940, he met Lucille Ball, marrying her the same year. They were divorced in 1960.

Although popularly known for his role as Ball's husband in the television show *I Love Lucy*, his most important contributions came as the guiding force behind its production company, Desilu. His many innovations created the presentation and format of the situation (sitcom) comedy as it is known today and began the practice of "reruns." Desilu bought its own studio and became the most important independent production house in the industry, producing many of the successful 1950s television comedies. Arnaz retired in the early 1960s. He died in Del Mar, California.

Arnaz chronicled his own life through his divorce from Lucille Ball in his autobiography, *A Book* (1976). His contributions to the music industry are discussed in JOHN S. ROBERTS, *The Latin Tinge: The Impact of Latin American Music in the United States* (1979). Innovations to the television industry are discussed in WILLIAM BODDY, *Fifties Television: The Industry and its Critics* (1990).

JACQUELYN BRIGGS KENT

**ARNS, PAULO EVARISTO** (*b.* 14 September 1921), archbishop of São Paulo, Brazil (1970–). A Franciscan priest born in Forquilhinha, Santa Catarina, Arns was a relatively unknown figure until he was named auxiliary bishop of São Paulo in 1966. Like most of the hierarchy, Arns supported the 1964 military coup, but after being named archbishop in November 1970, he became a trenchant critic of the military government and one of Brazil's outstanding voices on behalf of human rights. A venerated public figure, Arns denounced the widespread use of torture. In January 1972 he created the Archdiocesan Justice and Peace Commission, which became known for its efforts to defend human rights. In his pastoral work, Arns supported CHRISTIAN BASE COMMUNITIES, which became controversial in the 1970s and 1980s because of some activists' support for the labor movement and the Workers' Party. In 1973, he was named a cardinal.

After becoming one of Brazil's most prominent public figures in the 1970s, Arns fell out of favor with the Vatican and was less visible in the 1980s. When John Paul II became pope in 1978, Arns and the archdiocese of São Paulo came under careful scrutiny. In 1980, the pope asked Arns to write a report explaining and defending the church's overt support for a major strike that had taken place that year. Four years later, the Vatican undertook an investigation of seminars in dioceses identified with LIBERATION THEOLOGY, including the archdiocese of São Paulo, which was admonished to avoid portraying Christ as a revolutionary. In 1989, the pope dismantled and subdivided the archdiocese, which had previously been the largest in the world in terms of its Catholic population. Arns remained archbishop of São Paulo, but it was now a smaller archdiocese, from which most of the poor areas where base communities had flourished were excised.

PAULO EVARISTO ARNS, *Em defensa direitos humanos* (1978); HELCION RIBEIRO, ed., *Paulo Evaristo Arns* (1989); W. E. HEWITT, *Base Christian Communities and Social Change in Brazil* (1991), esp. pp. 28–37.

SCOTT MAINWARING

*See also* **Catholic Church; Liberation Theology.**

**AROSEMENA, FLORENCIO HARMODIO** (*b.* 17 September 1872; *d.* 30 August 1945), a civil engineer and president of Panama (1928–1931). Arosemena presided over one of the most corrupt periods in Panamanian history. His only previous political involvement had been a brief period as a councilman in the Panama City government. He became president largely as a result of the manipulations of President Rodolfo CHIARI (1924–1928). He and his cronies lined their pockets and used their offices for their own personal businesses. He was overthrown on 2 January 1931 by the nationalistic organization *Acción Comunal*. It was the first time since its separation from Colombia that a constitutionally elected government of Panama had been overthrown.

WALTER LA FEBER, *The Panama Canal: The Crisis in Historical Perspective* (1978).

JUAN MANUEL PÉREZ

**AROSEMENA, JUAN DEMÓSTENES** (*b.* 24 June 1879; *d.* 16 December 1939), jurist, teacher, journalist, member of the Panamanian Academy of History, and president of Panama (1936–1939). Arosemena had a long history of public service. In 1912 he was named chief justice by President Belisario PORRAS, who appointed him governor of the province of Colón in 1922. He became secretary of foreign relations in the administration of Florencio Harmodio AROSEMENA (1928–1931).

In 1936 he was the candidate for president of the National Revolutionary Party, which his younger brother, Arnulfo, had helped to organize. He was elected with the backing of President Harmodio ARIAS MADRID (1932–1936). He died before his term expired and was succeeded by Augusto S. Boyd. Arosemena's regime was basically a caretaker government, paving the way for Arnulfo ARIAS's ascension to power in 1940.

MANUEL MARÍA ALBA C., *Cronología de los gobernantes de Panamá, 1510–1967* (1967); WALTER LA FEBER, *The Panama Canal: The Crisis in Historical Perspective* (1978); JORGE CONTE PORRAS, *Diccionario biográfico ilustrado de Panamá*, 2d ed. (1986).

JUAN MANUEL PÉREZ

**AROSEMENA, JUSTO** (*b.* 1817; *d.* 1896), Panamanian intellectual and statesman. At sixteen he was awarded a bachelor's degree in humanities from the College of San Bartolomé, Colombia. In 1837 he was awarded a doctorate in law by the University of Magdalena. Arosemena spent most of his life in government, serving as minister of foreign relations (1848–1849), speaker of the Chamber of Deputies of the Colombian Congress (1852), senator, president of the Constitutional Convention of Río Negro (1863), and the first president of the Federal State of Panama (1855).

He wrote extensively on law and politics and was a prominent exponent of European liberal ideas. He belonged to the radical faction of the Liberal Party, the Golgotha. Arosemena believed that freedom had to reach everyone in society and that this required sovereignty. He favored autonomy for the isthmus. Arosemena envisioned the potential economic benefits that could be derived from an interoceanic canal, but he warned against foreign domination. Although he admired the U.S. political system, he spoke against U.S. intervention in other countries, particularly after the MEXICAN WAR (1846–1848). His most important works are *Examen sobre la franca comunicación entre los dos océanos por el istmo de Panamá* (1846), *Estudios constitucionales* (1852), and *El Estado Federal de Panamá* (1855).

JOSÉ DOLORES MOSCOTE, *La vida ejemplar de Justo Arosemena* (1956); OCTAVIO MÉNDEZ PEREIRA, *Justo Arosemena*, 2d ed. (1970).

JUAN MANUEL PÉREZ

**AROSEMENA, PABLO** (*b.* 1836; *d.* 29 August 1920), Panamanian politician and president (1910–1912) and an ardent supporter of classical nineteenth-century liberalism. Arosemena held many important political posts during his long political life. He was attorney general, president of the Sovereign State of Panama in 1875 and 1885 (on both occasions overthrown by the Colombian army), and in 1880 he was elected second vice president to the Colombian presidency. Arosemena continued to be active in politics after Panama's separation from Colombia. In 1904 he became president of the National Constituent Assembly. He served as Panama's president from September 1910 to October 1912, having been appointed by the National Assembly to finish the term of José Domingo de Obaldía following his death. (Arosemena succeeded Carlos Antonio MENDOZA, who temporarily had assumed the presidency immediately following Obaldía's death.)

ERNESTO DE JESÚS CASTILLERO REYES, *Historia de Panamá*, 7th ed. (1962); GUSTAVO A. MELLANDER, *The United States in Panamanian Politics: The Intriguing Formative Years* (1971).

JUAN MANUEL PÉREZ

**AROSEMENA GÓMEZ, OTTO** (*b.* 19 July 1925; *d.* 20 April 1984), president of Ecuador (1966–1968). A native of Guayaquil who received his law degree from that city's public university, Arosemena entered local politics. Serving as president of the Guayas provincial electoral tribunal (1952) and then as a deputy in the National Congress, he became a prominent businessman as well as a lawyer. He was twice chosen as senator representing coastal commercial organizations. Originally a Liberal, Arosemena broke away to organize his personalistic Coalición Institucionalista Democrática (CID) on 2 February 1965. He was one of three CID members in the 1966 Constituent Assembly, where he made a pact with the Right and was chosen provisional president of the nation (November 1967).

Arosemena remained in office for twenty months, during which a new constitution was adopted and national elections were held. His government was cautious in the area of domestic policy, although Arosemena was outspoken in foreign affairs. Hostility to U.S. policy led him to withhold his signature from the official declaration adopted by the 1967 conference of hemispheric presidents in Punta del Este, Uruguay. He subsequently criticized the ALLIANCE FOR PROGRESS and after a public exchange with the U.S. ambassador, ordered his expulsion from Ecuador. Once out of office, Arosemena sought to build the CID, but with limited success. His party backed the rightist presidential candidate León FEBRES-CORDERO in the 1984 elections, then swiftly dissolved upon the death of Arosemena.

JOHN D. MARTZ, *Ecuador: Conflicting Political Culture and the Quest for Progress* (1972).

JOHN D. MARTZ

*See also* **Ecuador: Political Parties.**

**AROSEMENA MONROY, CARLOS JULIO** (*b.* 24 August 1919), president of Ecuador (1961–1963). Scion of a wealthy Guayaquil family, Arosemena received his law degree in 1945 from the University of Guayaquil and became active in Liberal politics. By the 1950s he was an ardent nationalist, loyal to José María VELASCO IBARRA. He was elected to the Chamber of Deputies in 1952 and 1958, and he became president of the Federación Nacional Velasquista in 1960. In the latter year he was the vice presidential candidate on the slate with Velasco and was swept to office by the Velasquista landslide victory.

Presiding over Congress in his role as vice president of the republic, Arosemena soon broke with Velasco and became an outspoken critic. When Velasco was overthrown in 1961, Arosemena, at age forty-two, succeeded him as president. A supporter of labor and an outspoken nationalist, he espoused moderate reforms while expressing sympathy for the CUBAN REVOLUTION. This position aroused traditional domestic interests and angered the United States. His public displays of drunkenness became increasingly frequent, and the opposition hardened. On 11 July 1963 Arosemena was overthrown by the armed forces, which set up their own junta.

Arosemena soon organized his personalistic party, the Partido Nacionalista Revolucionario (PNR), which carried his banner in elections for the 1966 Constituent Assembly and afterward. But the PNR was unable to generate significant popular support. By 1984 its congressional representation consisted of Arosemena himself, and since 1986 the PNR has been moribund.

MARTIN C. NEEDLER, *Anatomy of a Coup d'État: Ecuador 1963* (1964); JOHN D. MARTZ, *Ecuador: Conflicting Political Culture and the Quest for Progress* (1972).

JOHN D. MARTZ

*See also* **Ecuador: Political Parties.**

**AROSEMENA QUINZADA, ALBACÍADES** (*b.* 20 November 1883; *d.* 8 November 1958), Panamanian president (1951–1952). Arosemena was born in Los Santos. He was a cattleman and a businessman but was also very active in politics, having served as minister of the treasury, treasurer of the Panama City government, and ambassador to Spain and France. Arosemena Quinzada was president after the overthrow of Arnulfo ARIAS. His period in office was very chaotic, and he was unsuccessful in his attempts to calm the situation.

ALBACÍADES AROSEMENA QUINZADA. *Edición conmemorativa del centenario de su nacimiento* (1984).

JUAN MANUEL PÉREZ

**ARRAIS, MIGUEL** (*b.* 15 December 1916), governor of Pernambuco (1963–1964, 1987–1991), mayor of Recife (1960–1962), federal deputy (1991–1994), and populist figure in Northeastern Brazil.

Miguel Arrais was born into a rural middle-class family in the interior of Ceará. He eventually settled in Recife and graduated from law school in 1937. A government job and his family provided him with political connections and led to his appointment as finance secretary of Pernambuco in 1947. By 1955, he had joined the Frente do Recife, a reformist left-center coalition that reached out to rural workers. Arrais won election as mayor of Recife in 1960 and gained a reputation for courting poor voters with slum improvement programs.

In 1963 Arrais became governor of the state amid rising tensions throughout the country. He implemented a minimum wage for rural workers, expanded farm credit, and promoted unionization in the countryside. Although not an ally of President João GOULART, Arrais was accused of radicalizing politics in the Northeast and blamed for successive waves of strikes and lockouts. As a result, he was jailed for a year following the 1964 coup. He spent most of the period 1965–1979 in Algeria, representing petroleum exporters.

Arrais returned to Brazil in 1979 and three years later won election to Congress. Using his image as an elder statesman, he ran for governor in 1986 and took office the following year. He failed to make a large showing in the primaries for president in 1989 but was elected federal deputy that year. He was the leading candidate for governor of Pernambuco in 1994.

JOSEPH A. PAGE, *The Revolution That Never Was* (1972); GUITA GRIN DEBERT, *Ideologia e populismo* (1979); JOSÉ ARLINDO SOARES, *A frente do Recife e o governo do Arrais* (1982); ISRAEL BELOCH and ALZIRA ALVES DE ABREU, comps., *Dicionário histórico-biográfico brasileiro, 1930–1983* (1984).

MICHAEL L. CONNIFF

**ARRAU, CLAUDIO LEÓN** (*b.* 6 February 1903; *d.* 9 June 1991), Chilean pianist. Early recognized as a prodigy, Arrau became one of the most accomplished Latin American musicians of the twentieth century. As a youth from Chillán, Arrau was sent on a grant from the Chilean government to study at the prestigious Julius Stern Conservatory in Berlin under the tutelage of Martin Krause from 1912 until 1918. During his tenure in Germany he earned numerous honors, including the Liszt and Ibach prizes. Throughout the 1920s and 1930s Arrau toured Europe and the Americas before settling in the United States after the outbreak of World War II.

Arrau was known for his slow tempos and lack of ostentation, a style that emphasized the inherent beauty of the music rather than the skill of the musician. In 1935, Arrau played a series of recitals in Berlin featuring the complete keyboard works of Bach. After this performance, he announced that he would no longer publicly perform any Bach, as he felt the piano could not do the composer justice.

In later years, Arrau brought his talents to Japan, Australia, and Israel, and recorded distinctive versions of major works by Beethoven, Brahms, Chopin, and others. He received many honors, including the UNESCO International Music Prize, and was named a commander in the French Legion of Honor. The cities of Santiago and Chillán both contain streets bearing Arrau's name.

JOSEPH HOROWITZ, *Conversations with Arrau* (1982); INGO HARDEN, *Claudio Arrau* (1983).

JOHN DUDLEY

**ARREOLA, JUAN JOSÉ** (*b.* 21 September 1918), Mexican writer. Born in Ciudad Guzmán in the state of Jalisco, Arreola received the prestigious Premio Xavier Villaurrutía in 1963 for his only novel, *La feria* (The Fair, 1963). He has also written drama but is best known for his innovation in the short story and other short prose forms. His major collections of stories and prose pieces include *Varia invención* (Various Inventions, 1949), *Con-*

*fabulario* (Confabulary, 1952), *Palindroma* (Palindrome, 1971), and *Bestiario* (Bestiary, 1972). Together with writers such as José Revueltas and Juan Rulfo, Arreola's works move Mexican literature beyond a parochial consideration of nationalistic themes and address Mexican identity in the context of universal human truths and archetypes. Through the use of humor, satire, irony, fantasy, and linguistic playfulness, he has explored themes such as religiosity, the absurd, materialism, the commercialism of the United States, and relations between the sexes. He has also played an influential role in Mexican literature as the director of writing workshops and as the editor of two important literary series in the 1950s, *Cuadernos del unicornio* (The Unicorn's Notebooks) and *Los presentes* (Those Present).

YULAN M. WASHBURN, *Juan José Arreola* (1983); RUSSELL M. CLUFF and L. HOWARD QUACKENBUSH, "Juan José Arreola," in *Latin American Writers*, vol. 3, edited by Carlos A. Solé and Maria Isabel Abreu (1989), pp. 1229–1236.

DANNY J. ANDERSON

**ARRIAGA, PONCIANO** (*b.* 1811; *d.* 1 March 1863), Mexican politician and cabinet minister, "Father of the Constitution of 1857." Born in the provincial capital of San Luis Potosí, Arriaga was an ardent federalist and radical liberal. He used his oratorical and writing skills in the movements against President Anastasio BUSTAMANTE in 1832 and later against President Antonio López de SANTA ANNA. Arriaga was deposed as *regidor del ayuntamiento* (president of the city council) of San Luis Potosí and jailed for these activities in 1841, but the following year he was elected to represent his home state in the national Congress.

During the war with the United States (1846–1847), Arriaga helped to supply the Mexican army in Coahuila and Nuevo Laredo. He opposed the Treaty of GUADALUPE HIDALGO for conceding territory in order to gain peace. He served briefly (13 December 1852–5 January 1853) as minister of justice under President Mariano Arista. When Santa Anna regained the presidency, Arriaga was exiled. In New Orleans, he met Benito JUÁREZ, Melchor OCAMPO, and other liberals. With the triumph of the Revolution of AYUTLA (1854), Arriaga returned to Mexico and was elected to the Constituent Congress of 1856–1857. As president of the congress, he was one of the principal authors of the Constitution of 1857. During the War of the Reform (1858–1861), Arriaga supported the Juárez government and later served as republican governor of the state of Aguascalientes (1862–1863) and the Federal District (1863).

FRANCISCO ZARCO, *Historia del Congreso extraordinario constituyente de 1856–1857* (1898–1901, repr. 1956); JESÚS REYES HEROLES, *El liberalismo mexicano*, 3 vols. (1957–1961); RICHARD N. SINKIN, *The Mexican Reform, 1855–1876: A Study in Liberal Nation-Building* (1979); *Diccionario Porrúa de historia, biografía y geografía de México*, 5th ed. (1986).

D. F. STEVENS

**ARRIERO,** an indigenous, mulatto, mestizo, or humble Spanish man who, from the mid-sixteenth century on, managed four or five mules (and, less often, horses). Typically teamed up with other muleteers or assistants to form *recuas* (strings) of twelve to fifty animals, *arrieros* transported a great variety of goods, often grains, ten to fifteen miles a day, not infrequently along trade routes dating back to pre-Hispanic times. Arrieros earned anywhere from twenty-five pesos a year to ten times that amount, with variation corresponding largely to capital investment. Numerous regulations sought to govern arrieros, such as the kind of animals they used, how many animals, where they obtained grain to feed the animals, what goods they transported, and how much they charged. In Mexico, arrieros eclipsed *tlamemes* (pre-Conquest human carriers), facilitating a much expanded and less onerous interregional trade and transportation system.

Mexican arrieros have received greater scholarly attention than those of other parts of Latin America. ROSS HASSIG, *Trade, Tribute, and Transportation: The Sixteenth-Century Political Economy of the Valley of Mexico* (1985), is a most useful compilation of data. Biographies of muleteers include JOHN C. SUPER, "Miguel Hernández: Master of Mule Trains," in *Struggle and Survival in Colonial America*, edited by David G. Sweet and Gary B. Nash (1981); and RICHARD BOYER, "Juan Vásquez, Muleteer of Seventeenth-Century Mexico," in *The Americas* 37 (April 1981): 421–443.

STEPHANIE WOOD

**ARRIETA, JOSÉ AGUSTÍN** (*b.* 1803; *d.* 1874), Mexican painter. In an effort to explain the Mexicanism, the rustic provincialism, of Arrieta's work, it has been judged according to a single criterion, that of popular painting. It is often forgotten that as a student at the Academy of Fine Arts in Puebla under the direction of Julián Ordóñez and Lorenzo Zendejas, he was competent in genres typical of the academy, such as painting historical themes or representing the human figure, in full or in half, as well as torsos and heads. Although he was not a student at the ACADEMIA DE SAN CARLOS in Mexico City, he occasionally sent work there from 1850 to 1871.

Arrieta's extensive work stresses two themes: folkloric paintings and dining-room paintings or still lifes. He took pride in an impeccable technical control. His dining-room paintings, which became popular with collectors of rustic art, are full of allusions to European art in their details as well as in some elements of their harmonious composition. His folkloric paintings depict scenes inside homes as well as in public places, such as the street. His work is replete with subtle implications of popular culture.

FRANCISCO CABRERA, *Agustín Arrieta, pintor costumbrista* (1963); FAUSTO RAMÍREZ, *La plástica del siglo de la independencia* (1985).

ESTHER ACEVEDO

**ARRIETA, PEDRO DE** (*fl.* 1691–15 December 1738), Mexican architect. Born in Real de Minas, Pachuca, Arrieta passed the examination to become a master architect in Mexico City in 1691. Four years later he supervised the buildings of the Inquisition, and in 1720 he became *maestro mayor de la catedral y del real palacio,* the highest rank to which an architect in New Spain could aspire. Among the many public and private buildings ascribed to him are the Basilica of GUADALUPE (1695–1709); the remodeling of the Jesuit church of the Profesa, contracted in 1714 and completed in 1720; and the Palace of the Inquisition with its peculiar suspended arches (1733–1737). His work is classicizing in that he insisted on the use of columns and rejected the surface movement of the salomonic baroque with its characteristic spiral columns. Also characteristic of Arrieta's buildings are polygonal arches and narrative reliefs.

MANUEL TOUSSAINT, *Colonial Art in Mexico* (1967); HEINRICH BERLIN, "Three Master Architects in New Spain," in *Hispanic American Historical Review* 27 (1947): 375–384; MARÍA CONCEPCIÓN AMERLINCK, "Pedro de Arrieta, su origen y testamento," in *Monumentos históricos* 6 (1981): 27–32.

CLARA BARGELLINI

*See also* **Architecture.**

**ARRIVÍ, FRANCISCO** (*b.* 24 June 1915), Puerto Rican author, dramatist, and theater director. Arriví was born in San Juan and graduated from the University of Puerto Rico in 1938. From 1938 to 1941 he taught at Ponce High School, where his students staged his first plays. After his return to San Juan in 1941, he wrote, directed, and translated dramas and was active in the radio productions of the School of the Air until 1948. He studied drama at Columbia University in New York under a Rockefeller grant in 1949 and was programming director for the Puerto Rican government radio station for ten years. A tireless organizer, Arriví established the Tinglado Puertorriqueño experimental theater company and developed the theater program of the Institute of Puerto Rican Culture, which he directed from 1959 to 1970. He launched the institute's yearly festivals, among them Puerto Rican Theater, International Theater, and the Theater of Ponce. He was instrumental in the creation of the Fine Arts Center in Santurce as a forum for the performing arts in 1981.

In 1959 the Institute of Puerto Rican Literature honored Arriví's *Vejigantes* (Carnival masks, 1958), a powerful drama about racial identity in Puerto Rico, which formed part of a trilogy of plays on the same theme that Arriví entitled *Máscara puertorriqueña* (Puerto Rican masquerade, 1959–1960). Other famous plays by Arriví are *María Soledad* (1947), *Caso del muerto en vida* (The case of a man dead in life, 1951), *Club de solteros* (Bachelors' club, 1953), and *Cóctel de Don Nadie* (The cocktail of Mr. Nobody, 1964). Arriví has also published books of poetry and collections of essays on theater and literature, including *Areyto mayor* (An indigenous festival, 1966) and *Conciencia puertorriqueña del teatro contemporáneo, 1937–1956* (Puerto Rican awareness of contemporary theater, 1967).

FRANK M. DAUSTER, *Ensayos sobre el teatro hispanoamericano* (1975); JOSEFINA RIVERA DE ALVAREZ, *Literatura puertorriqueña: Su proceso en el tiempo* (1983); ESTHERVINDA ZACARÍAS DE JUSTINIANO, *Francisco Arriví: Bibliografía selectiva* (1986).

ESTELLE IRIZARRY

*See also* **Theater.**

**ARROYO ASENCIO,** a small river in Uruguay near Mercedes, in the department of Soriano. Its importance derives from the fact that from its banks originated the famous GRITO DE ASENCIO (28 February 1811), which marked the beginning of the revolution in the BANDA ORIENTAL, the old name for what is known today as Uruguay. Outstanding in this event were Pedro Viera and Venancio Benavídes, inhabitants of the area who organized their neighbors into an uprising against the government of Montevideo. Although he was not present, the influence of the caudillo José ARTIGAS, the future head of the revolution in the area, was significant.

BROTHER DAMASCENO, *Ensayo de historia patria,* vol. 1 (1950); JOHN STREET, *Artigas and the Emancipation of Uruguay* (1959).

JOSÉ DE TORRES WILSON

**ARROYO DEL RÍO, CARLOS ALBERTO** (*b.* 27 November 1893; *d.* 31 October 1969), president of Ecuador (nonelected 1939 and elected 1940–1944). Born in Guayaquil, Arroyo del Río studied law, entered private practice, and taught at the University of Guayaquil, eventually becoming rector in 1932. He became active in the Liberal Radical Party, serving as a member of the *Junta de Beneficencia,* secretary of the Municipal Council (1917–1918), and president of the Municipal Council (1921–1922). In 1922–1923 he represented Guayas Province in Congress, serving as president of the Chamber of Deputies in 1923. Elected senator in 1924, he actively opposed the revolution of July 1925 and the Ayora administration, and ten years later (1934–1935) led the congressional opposition to President José María VELASCO IBARRA that resulted in the dissolution of Congress.

When Aurelio Mosquera Narváez died in office on 15 November 1938, Arroyo del Río assumed executive power as president of the Senate and presided over an extraordinary congress that abrogated the Constitution of 1938 and reinstated the Constitution of 1906. He resigned on 28 May 1944 to run for president. He was elected and took office on 1 September 1940. The supporters of his leading opponent, Velasco Ibarra, charged that the election was fraudulent and attempted a coup.

The insurrection failed, and the leaders, including Velasco Ibarra and Carlos Guevara Moreno, were exiled.

Within a few months of Arroyo del Río's inauguration, Peru invaded territory claimed by Ecuador. In 1944, Arroyo del Río was removed from office as a result of the country's defeat in the 1941 border war with Peru, and Velasco Ibarra was recalled from exile to replace the discredited president. Arroyo del Río left the country, going first to Colombia, then to New York City; he returned to Guayaquil in 1948 to resume his legal practice. He remained the target of public attacks until his death.

OSCAR EFREN REYES, *Breve historia general del Ecuador,* vol. 2 (1957), esp. pp. 813–827; DAVID H. ZOOK, JR., *Zarumilla-Marañon: The Ecuador–Peru Dispute* (1964); ENRIQUE AYALA MORA, ed., *Nueva historia del Ecuador: Época republicana IV,* vol. 10 (1983), esp. pp. 105–108.

LINDA ALEXANDER RODRÍGUEZ

*See also* **Ecuador: Constitutions; Peru–Ecuador Boundary Disputes.**

**ARROYO GRANDE, BATTLE OF,** a major engagement in the Platine civil wars fought on 5 December 1842. In the midst of Uruguay's GUERRA GRANDE, the gaucho army of General Fructuoso RIVERA crossed into Argentine territory and campaigned successfully against the military forces of the Buenos Aires strongman Juan Manual de ROSAS. At the beginning of December 1842, however, Rosista troops under the command of General Manual ORIBE met Rivera's army at Arroyo Grande, on the right bank of the Uruguay River in Entre Ríos, and decisively defeated it, eliminating 3,000 men and capturing a wealth of munitions in the process. This victory made it possible for Oribe to carry the fight immediately onto Uruguayan soil, where his troops were soon besieging Montevideo. A very energetic participant in the Arroyo Grande struggle, under Oribe's command, was Justo José de URQUIZA, who at that time was only a minor Entrerriano cavalry officer, but who would soon be the most important political figure in the Littoral provinces.

TELMO MANACORDA, *Fructuoso Rivera, el perpetuo defensor de la república Oriental* (1946); *The Cambridge History of Latin America,* vol. 3 (1985), pp 645–647.

THOMAS L. WHIGHAM

**ARRUFAT, ANTÓN** (*b.* 14 August 1935), Cuban playwright and poet. Born in Santiago in Oriente Province, Arrufat studied in his native city as well as at the University of Havana. He has traveled to Czechoslovakia, France, Italy, and England and been very active in promoting literary activity in Cuba. He was editor in chief of the influential *Casa de las Américas* from 1960 to 1965 and has contributed to *Lunes de Revolución, Ciclón, Cuba en UNESCO, La Gaceta de Cuba,* and others. His work has

attained such national acclaim as the honorable mentions he received for his play *El vivo al pollo* in the Casa de las Américas competition in 1961 and for his collection of poetry *Repaso final* in the 1963 competition. In 1968 he won the coveted prize given by the Cuban Union of Writers and Artists (UNEAC) for his play *Los siete contra Tebas,* which established him as one of Cuba's leading playwrights and at the same time brought him into temporary disfavor with the Castro regime. After a decade or so of being relegated to the periphery, he was rehabilitated and has become active again. Arrufat remained in Cuba, where he began publishing and participating in cultural activities once again. His most recent work is a novel, *La caja está cerrada* (1984).

ROBERTO VALERO

**ART.** [Coverage includes **Pre-Columbian Art; The Colonial Era; The Nineteenth Century; The Twentieth Century;** and **Folk Art.**]

### *Pre-Columbian Art of Mesoamerica*

Mesoamerican art begins about 1500 B.C., when permanent objects of great craft and skill begin to be imbued systematically with religious and other meanings by their makers. Before that time, craftsmen made finely honed tools and other utilitarian works that have endured, but their religious and ritualistic objects have perished. This era of the union of craft and meaning in enduring, nonperishable works is also the era in which the first civilizations of MESOAMERICA arose, most notably the Olmecs of the Gulf Coast. By the end of the second millennium B.C., the OLMECS (a modern name; their name for themselves is lost forever), probably in pursuit of hard stones like jade for making sacred objects, had established trade routes that reached from modern Guatemala and Honduras to the Mexican states of MORELOS and GUERRERO. Roughly extending from fourteen to twenty-one degrees north latitude, and excluding the Caribbean islands, this region is called Mesoamerica (Middle America), and from about 1500 B.C. until the Spanish Conquest in 1521, it was an area of some cultural unity, sharing concepts of religion, the calendar, and cultural practices, such as the ballgame. Dramatically different art styles emerged, however, at different times and places.

OLMEC

The Olmec (ca. 1500 B.C.–ca. 400 B.C.) built sacred centers along the swampy rivers of the Gulf Coast. At both SAN LORENZO and LA VENTA in southeastern Mexico, millions of cubic feet of earth were formed into earthworks. La Venta exhibits the first known Mesoamerican pyramid, and its shape, a fluted cupcake, suggests derivation from the volcanoes of Central Mexico. Although radiocarbon dating has shown San Lorenzo to have been destroyed before the rise of La Venta, these and other centers of Olmec culture share forms and materials, including colossal portrait heads of their early rulers and altarlike thrones of imported basalt. Without obvious prototypes, the Olmec achieved the most naturalistic and plastic forms found in the New World, including basalt carvings of the human form (for example, the ''Wrestler,'' ca. 800 B.C.) and fine kaolin ''hollow baby'' sculptures.

WEST AND CENTRAL MEXICAN CULTURES

Both provincial and idiosyncratic styles merged in the highlands of West and Central Mexico and treated the human form, particularly in the ceramics of Tlatilco and Xochipala.

*West Mexican Cultures* From about 200 B.C. until about A.D. 500, peoples in West Mexico made monumental architecture and buried their dead in underground shaft tombs, following patterns that seem to be somewhat distinct from the rest of Mesoamerica. The Nayarit, Colima, and JALISCO traditions are best known through their hollow clay tomb sculptures: animated groupings of figures from Nayarit; hollow dogs and parrot vessels from Colima; and warriors with clubs from Jalisco.

*Central Mexican Cultures* At the end of the first mil-lennium B.C., new civilizations emerged in Central Mexico, in the MAYA region, OAXACA, and the Gulf Coast; their florescence in the first millennium A.D. is generally known as the Classic period. In central Mexico, the greatest city of its day arose at TEOTIHUACÁN, peaking in the fifth century with a population of about 250,000. The city plan focused on two colossal structures completed by about A.D. 200, the pyramids of the Sun and Moon, and followed by a rigid grid that encompassed all constructions, sacred, civil, or domestic. Religious buildings generally have alternating vertical and sloping planes called *talud-tablero,* but buildings of all sorts, including those with elaborate architectural ornament, were painted with brilliant stucco pigments, some with freehand images and others laid out with a template. Featured are devotional images of major deities, especially TLALOC, god of rain, agriculture, and war, and the great goddess, Spider Woman; these gods are also the subjects of the few surviving stone sculptures.

Teotihuacán artisans fashioned vast quantities of figurines, initially by hand, and then later in molds. They exported these and cylinder tripod vessels to the rest of Mesoamerica. Teotihuacán's decline and eventual demise, A.D. 650–800, may have disrupted Mesoamerica, leading to the end of the Classic period.

Openwork limestone relief from the Late Classic period (late eighth or early ninth century). Probably Chiapas or Tabasco, Mexico. FUNDACIÓN AMPARO, MUSEO AMPARO; PHOTO BY BOB SCHALKWIJK.

SOUTHERN MEXICAN CULTURES

*Oaxaca* In Oaxaca, the ZAPOTECS made hilltop MONTE ALBÁN their capital and, in front of their buildings, set up two-dimensional reliefs of rulers and their conquests. Three-dimensional figures attached to urns accompanied the noble dead into richly painted tombs set under palaces. Although the TOTONACS dominated the Gulf Coast, EL TAJÍN was probably built by the Huaxtecs. To the south, the Totonacs made life-size hollow ceramic sculptures of gods and humans, and the Aztecs later adopted the art.

*Maya Region* In the Maya region, both in the lowlands, at EL MIRADOR and CERROS, and in the highlands, at KAMINALJUYÚ, Abaj Takalik, and IZAPA (ca. 200 B.C.– A.D. 250), experiments in art, writing, and architecture led to uniform practices in the Classic (A.D. 250–900) at dozens of lowland sites. Highland stone stelae pictured rulers and gods and used a writing system to record names and dates. At lowland sites, each setback of pyramids was faced with a giant stucco mask.

At TIKAL, carved stelae with flat, linear images of rulers covered with ritual paraphernalia and accompanied by dates counted from a base date that can be correlated to the European calendar, were erected before A.D. 300. By 550, the end of the Early Classic, such monuments had been set up at UAXACTUN, COPÁN, YAXCHILÁN, CARACOL, and other sites. The union of ruler portraiture and glyphic historical narrative was unique to the Classic Maya. In a script that represents both the sounds and syntax of languages, these texts illuminate Maya art from a Maya point of view. Large structures housed royal tombs, shrines for ancestor worship. At both Tikal and RÍO AZUL, monochromatic paintings in red or black covered tomb walls, some with death dates and others with iconography of the underworld. Kings took rich offerings to the grave, including pots, jade masks and jewelry, sacrificial victims, perishable foodstuffs, and cloth. Stone ballcourts were included on most city plans.

During the fourth and fifth centuries, weaponry, fashions, and goods from distant TEOTIHUACÁN affected the Maya. Traditional quadruped and basal-flanged bowls gave way to cylinder tripods on which the Maya began to paint narrative scenes in bright stucco or earth-toned slips.

Widespread sixth-century warfare hindered the development of Maya art, but in the seventh century, city-states flourished. At PALENQUE, King Pacal the Great initiated interior wall sculpture with multifigural compositions. Before his death, he built the nine-level Temple of Inscriptions for his own memorial, and an interior staircase leads to his tomb. At Copán and QUIRIGUA, seventh- and eighth-century sculptures featured high relief, and portraits of Copán king 18 Rabbit achieve a plastic three-dimensionality. Tikal stone sculpture followed established canons, but the carved wooden lintels of funerary temples bear innovative imagery. Under kings Shield-Jaguar and Bird-Jaguar, Yaxchilán favored lintels recording marriage, bloodletting, and warfare.

To the north, King Chaac erected palaces at UXMAL with elegant proportions. At BONAMPAK, a complete program of paintings treats warfare, bloodletting, and dynastic succession; in subject and style it relates closely to contemporary paintings at CACAXTLA in Central Mexico, which in turn shared an eclectic style with XOCHICALCO and SEIBAL. In the ninth century, most Classic cities were abandoned.

About 900, at both TULA (in Hidalgo) and CHICHÉN ITZÁ (in Yucatán) new art forms emerged, including chacmool statues, atlantean supports, and serpent columns. Metallurgy arrived in Mesoamerica, and the Chichén Sacred Well (a natural sinkhole) received gold-disk offerings with repoussé designs. Colonnades flank many civil structures; at Chichén Itzá, a stone skull rack adjoins the largest ballcourt in Mesoamerica. Elaborate paintings at Chichén detail massive warfare, perhaps waged by a TOLTEC and Chichén alliance. Together, these two cities dominated all of Mesoamerica, and along their axis, both Toltec and Mayan iconography and ideology were shared and diffused until these cities were abandoned in the twelfth century. Poorly made architecture characterizes later architecture at MAYAPAN and TULÚM.

AZTEC

In Central Mexico, the AZTECS founded their island capital, Tenochtitlán, in about 1345. Politically and economically imperialistic, they dominated much of Mesoamerica at the time of the Spanish Conquest, and their wealth supported Tenochtitlán's development as a sacred center where architecture and sculpture replicated the cosmos and the gods. Dedicated to HUITZILO-POCHTLI, the Aztec sun god, and to Tlaloc, the main dual pyramid, or *Templo Mayor*, faced a round temple of QUETZALCOATL, the Feathered Serpent creator and wind god. The Aztec placed three-dimensional basalt sculptures inside religious architecture, including the beheaded COATLICUE with her necklace of hearts and hands. Round two-dimensional stones such as the dismembered Coyolxauhqui, sister of Huitzilopochtli, and the great Calendar stone recording the ages of mankind's destruction were placed flat on the ground or on the surface of a temple. At the same time, simple vegetal and animal forms were formed from hard, semiprecious stones. Aztec nobility dwelt near the sacred precinct in multistoried palaces. Canals replaced streets, and aqueducts brought fresh water from the mainland. Ruler portraits were carved into live rock at nearby Chapultepec, and pools and temples were formed of the live rock of mountains surrounding the Valley of Mexico.

Like most Mesoamericans, the Aztecs had quantities of screenfold genealogies, histories, and religious and divinatory texts. Some skilled scribes may have been foreigners, MIXTECS from Oaxaca, who also practiced metallurgy and featherwork in Tenochtitlán. Little Aztec gold survives, but Mixtec gold from a Monte Albán tomb reveals the skill in lost wax and filigree that the Aztecs admired.

Within a generation of the Spanish conquest in 1521, little art in the pre-Columbian tradition was being made. The Spanish sought native tribute lists, histories, and maps of New Spain through the 1580s, but by 1600, the elite tradition of native art and architecture had ceased in Mesoamerica.

MIGUEL COVARRUBIAS, *Indian Art of Mexico and Central America* (1957); MICHAEL D. COE, *America's First Civilization: Discovering the Olmec* (1968); RICHARD F. TOWNSEND, *State and Cosmos in the Art of Tenochtitlán* (1979); ESTHER PASZTORY, *Aztec Art* (1983); GEORGE KUBLER, *The Art of Ancient America*, 3d ed. (1984); MARY ELLEN MILLER, *The Art of Mesoamerica* (1986); LINDA SCHELE and MARY ELLEN MILLER, *The Blood of Kings: Dynasty and Ritual in Maya Art* (1986); MICHAEL D. COE, *The Maya*, 4th ed. (1987); MICHAEL KAN, CLEMENT MEIGHAN, and H. B. NICHOLSON, *Sculpture of Ancient West Mexico: Nayarit, Jalisco, Colima* (1989); LINDA SCHELE and DAVID FREIDEL, *A Forest of Kings: The Untold Story of the Ancient Maya* (1990).

MARY ELLEN MILLER

### Pre-Columbian Art of South America

The Inca Empire (A.D. 1438–1532), crushed by the Spanish invaders, was only the last of many pre-Hispanic cultures in the Central Andes (a geographical and cultural area that includes the Pacific Coast, highlands, and tropical lowlands of modern Peru as well as the Bolivian altiplano), each of which had contributed to a very long and distinguished tradition in the arts. This tradition included architecture, sculpture, and painting as well as textiles, pottery, and metalwork, classes of objects that occupied a paramount position in the symbolic life of the ancient inhabitants of the Central Andes.

#### CHAVÍN

One theme that runs throughout Andean cultural history is the intimate relationship between architectural monuments and their natural surroundings. This phenomenon is evident at the highlands center of CHAVÍN DE HUÁNTAR (the seat of CHAVÍN culture, ca. 850–200 B.C.), a ceremonial site built in a sacred geographical context. The site is located between two rivers whose waters originate from the melting snows of a sacred mountain; the river water was channeled through tunnels in the main temple to produce a rumbling, thundering sound that emanated from its interior. It is likely that mountain worship was a principal reason for the construction of Chavín de Huántar, and it may have motivated the design of later monuments (such as the NASCA LINES and Tiahuanaku [TIWANAKU] and Inca structures). In fact, the main building may have represented a real or cosmic mountain. Named the Castillo, it is a massive structure faced with cut granite blocks laid in horizontal rows of alternating widths. Inside, a labyrinth of stone-lined galleries, compartments, and ventilating shafts runs through the temple on several irregular levels.

The Castillo was adorned originally with dozens of stone sculptures, such as the Lanzón (14.77 feet tall), which resides in a small, dark chamber deep inside the temple. The Lanzón is carved to represent a costumed anthropomorphic figure with a feline mouth and serpent hair. The conjoining of diverse elements from the natural world in a single figure, combined with a mysterious and awesome setting, evokes an otherworldly experience. The Lanzón was most likely a cult object, perhaps symbolic of natural forces.

#### PARACAS

PARACAS culture (ca. 700 B.C.–A.D. 200) is at present best known through elaborately decorated textiles and well-made ceramic vessels. The largest scientifically documented group of Paracas textiles comes from a burial precinct called the Necrópolis on the Paracas peninsula. Among the hundreds of funerary bundles excavated there, several dozen contained dignitaries, each of whom had been wrapped in stunning woven garments. The brightly colored images of animals and of costumed human impersonators that are embroidered on these garments relay information about the worldview and social roles of the members of Paracas society. Other, more abstract designs likely encode information about ancestral relationships and community supernaturals. The Paracas cultural tradition included two styles of fineware pottery, one a postfire resin-painted ware and the other an extraordinarily thin, finely crafted monochrome ware modeled into animal and plant forms.

Few extensive architectural remains are known for NASCA culture (ca. A.D. 1–700). Of these, the most prominent is the ceremonial center of Cahuachi, with its forty mounds of varying sizes. The largest construction, the Great Temple, is a 66-foot-high stepped mound formed by encasing a natural rise with elongated, wedge-shaped adobes. Cahuachi's architectural forms were oriented to the spiritual world: the site has a natural spring that was a hallowed landscape feature, and a sunken court on top of one mound opens east toward a sacred mountain associated in local legend with water sources.

The most famous material remains of Nasca culture are gigantic desert markings. The Nasca geoglyphs, which include biomorphic figures, geometric designs, and straight lines, undoubtedly had multiple meanings; one of their functions may have been as ceremonial paths related to some sort of ritual process directed towards a mountain/water/fertility cult.

Nasca pottery is notable for its rich palette. Images were painted in many different colors of slip clay, which was fired on top of a solid-color ground. They illustrate creatures and plants, as well as human beings wearing facial masks and ritual costumes. Many of these images are similar to some of those embroidered on fabrics from the Paracas Necrópolis, but the use of polychrome slip-based pigments represents a major artistic and technological breakthrough in pottery making on the southern coast.

Embroidered mantle with bird impersonators. Early Intermediate period (A.D. 50–100), Paracas, Peru. © MUSEUM OF FINE ARTS, BOSTON.

## MOCHE

An important center of MOCHE culture (ca. A.D. 100–750) comprises two adobe structures in the form of truncated stepped platform mounds, the Huaca del Sol and the Huaca de la Luna (in the Moche Valley). Although only a portion of the original remains, the Huaca del Sol is a spectacular landmark, towering 130 feet above the desert plain at its highest point. Across a wide plain, the Huaca de la Luna sits on the steep lower slopes of a hill.

Almost all Moche structures were adorned with polychrome murals, such as one (now destroyed) at Pañamarca in the Nepeña Valley that depicted a religious procession of elaborately costumed figures carrying goblets. The same scene is known from painted depictions on Moche pottery, which carries a pictorial art rich in naturalistic detail. Moche potters also excelled in modeling vessels into realistic, commanding portraits of their rulers.

As shown most beautifully in the tombs of SIPÁN, Moche metalsmiths—the most sophisticated artists within the Andean metallurgical tradition—crafted masks, beads, and nose, ear, and headdress ornaments as well as bells and rattles for the elite to use as adornments and to display political power and social status and to communicate religious beliefs. They also developed ingenious procedures to impart the colors of gold and silver to objects actually made of alloys.

## TIAHUANACO/TIWANAKU AND HUARI

Confusion exists over the relationship of two principal polities, Tiahuanaco and HUARI, that thrived in the Central Andes during the period ca. A.D. 550–900. The cities were centers of power that, while culturally distinct in many respects, shared a religious iconography as well as the production of certain art forms (such as interlocked tapestry tunics and knotted hats). Some scholars believe that the earlier Pucara culture was the common heritage of these two, which could help explain the similarities in their art.

The original form of the buildings at Tiahuanaco is uncertain, but set within its palaces, temples, and plazas were impressive large stone sculptures. The so-called Gate of the Sun is a large single block of andesite incised with images of the principal figures in the Tiahuanaco belief system: a central, frontal figure dressed in an elaborate tunic, flanked by rows of staff-bearing human- and condor-headed attendants seen in profile.

The Huari empire extended throughout the highlands and coast of Peru. It boasted both administrative and ceremonial sites with large rectilinear structures, multistory buildings, and edifices with interior galleries and plazas. Tapestry tunics and four-cornered hats are two of its most spectacular artistic expressions; the predominant imagery features the same staff-bearing figures seen on the Gate of the Sun as well as geometric motifs. A limited number of recognizable subjects appear in Huari tunics, but iconography is overshadowed by color patterns. Huari culture is known also through monolithic sculptures and carved miniature figures.

## CHIMÚ

CHAN CHAN in the Moche Valley was the capital city of the CHIMÚ kingdom (ca. A.D. 1100–1476). The central core of monumental constructions contains ten huge adobe rectangular enclosures that were major administrative centers of the empire. These palace compounds are enriched with carved clay wall decoration: repeating figures of fish, crustaceans, birds, and anthropomorphs are arranged in bands and panels. Many of the same motifs appear in other media, such as woven garments. For example, pelicans are represented on a stunning set of garments made entirely of undyed white cotton; white birds are brocaded in a checkerboard design on white plain-weave and gauze fabric.

## INCA

Chimú metalworking also was highly developed and was so prized by the INCAS that they took objects and artisans to the capital when their king, PACHACUTI, vanquished the Chimú ruler Minchançaman. Pachacuti undertook the rebuilding of Cuzco, the political and religious capital of the Inca Empire, in what some scholars claim is the physical form of a puma, the animal that symbolized the Inca dynasty. The technically astounding stonework of Inca imperial architecture is evident in Cuzco's main temple, the Coricancha, with its foundations and freestanding buildings of perfectly cut and fitted basalt (much of this stonework was obscured originally by sheets of beaten gold). Inca rulers had palaces not only in Cuzco but also in the country. The sites of Pisac, Ollantaytambo, and MACHU PICCHU were royal estates developed by Pachacuti. His architecture focused on the contrast between built and natural form, often incorporating into a building site natural outcrops that were embellished and elaborated with walls, niches, and carving.

Like generations of Andeans before them, these last pre-Hispanic peoples embedded symbolic meanings in cloth. In Inca society, dress was a mark of identity and distinction (Inca royalty wore the most sumptuous woven garments), material was an important accessory to ritual, weavings were offered as a major sacrificial item, and cloth was exchanged during diplomatic negotiations. Fabric indeed had a social and sacred nature in the Andean world.

ALAN R. SAWYER, "Tiahuanaco Tapestry Design," in *Textile Museum Journal* 1, no. 2 (1963): 27–38; JOHN H. ROWE, "Form and Meaning in Chavín Art," in *Peruvian Archaeology: Selected Readings,* edited by John H. Rowe and Dorothy Menzel (1967); CHRISTOPHER B. DONNAN, *Moche Art of Peru: Pre-Columbian Symbolic Communication* (1978); JOHN H. ROWE, "Standardization in Inca Tapestry Tunics," in *The Junius B. Bird Pre-Columbian Textile Conference, May 19th and 20th, 1973* (1979); MICHAEL E. MOSELEY and KENT C. DAY, eds., *Chan Chan: Andean Desert City* (1981); ANN P. ROWE, *Costumes and Featherwork of the Lords of Chimor: Textiles from Peru's North Coast* (1984); JOHAN REINHARD, "Chavín and Tiahuanaco: A New Look at Two Andean Ceremonial Centers," in *National Geographic Research* 1, no. 3 (1985): 395–422; WALTER ALVA, "Discovering the New World's Richest Unlooted Tomb," in *National Geographic* 174, no. 4 (1988): 510–549; RICHARD L. BURGER, "Unity and Heterogeneity Within the Chavín Horizon," in *Peruvian Prehistory,* edited by Richard W. Keating (1988): 99–144; SUSAN A. NILES, "Looking for 'Lost' Inca Palaces," in *Expedition* 30, no. 3 (1988): 56–64; ANTHONY F. AVENI, ed., *The Lines of Nazca* (1990); ANNE PAUL, *Paracas Ritual Attire: Symbols of Authority in Ancient Peru* (1990), and *Paracas Art and Architecture: Object and Context in South Coastal Peru* (1991); RICHARD BURGER, *Chavín and the Origins of Andean Civilization* (1992); ANITA COOK, "The Stone Ancestors: Idioms of Imperial Attire and Rank Among Huari Figurines," in *Latin American Antiquity* 3, no. 4 (1992): 341–364; REBECCA STONE-MILLER, *To Weave for the Sun: Andean Textiles in the Museums of Fine Arts* (1992); RICHARD F. TOWNSEND, ed., *The Ancient Americas: Art from Sacred Landscapes* (1992); HELAINE SILVERMAN, *Cahuanchi in the Ancient Nasca World* (1993); WALTER ALVA and CHRISTOPHER DONNAN, *Royal Tombs of Sipán* (1993).

ANNE PAUL

*See also* **Mesoamerica.**

### The Colonial Era

The nature of colonization often dictates that art and architecture follow the forms and iconography of the colonizers. Although this was true in Latin America, varying local conditions made for differences from the colonizing countries as well as among the colonies themselves. The differences were not only in materials and techniques, as could be expected, but also in emphases and interests. Under these circumstances, European stylistic terms can be confusing and so must be extended by terms that reflect Latin American developments more accurately. Although much has been investigated, there still are large gaps in the knowledge of Latin American colonial art, so that serious interpretative studies are difficult, and superficial generalizations are too easily made.

ARCHITECTURE IN SPANISH AMERICA

A type of architecture common to all of Spanish America is the extensive system of coastal fortifications, many of which were designed in the sixteenth century by the Italian engineer Battista Antonelli. However, most of the art and architecture preserved from the early colonial era is concentrated in the monastic establishments. Especially in Mexico, where evangelization was inspired by humanist utopian ideas, monastic complexes often evolved into spectacular, monumental groups of buildings. Erected after the first conversions had been consolidated, the complexes consist of large atriums or enclosed sacred spaces in front of churches. They often were intentionally built on the sites of the indigenous religious structures they replaced. A cross is in the center of the atrium; chapels, called *posas,* are at the corners; and there is some sort of "open chapel" that served for outdoor liturgy, in which great numbers of Indians in the atrium could participate. Open chapels can be complex, separate structures, as was frequent in New Spain; they can be integrated into the church building in the form of balconies, as in Mexico and Peru; or they can simply be sheltered under overhanging roof extensions, as in New Granada.

The church building itself is usually a single nave, although basilican plans also exist. In Mexico sixteenth-century churches generally have one rather squat tower or a belfry wall (*espadaña*) and are vaulted, while in South America there are many examples with wooden roofs. The massive proportions and appearance of sixteenth-century churches in Mexico have given rise to the term "fortress church." Although protection from hostile Indians could be necessary in border areas, heavy walls have more to do with the presence of less-than-professional builders coupled with an abundant work force, and crenellations served not defense but a desire to make these buildings into symbols of the fortified City of God. Next to the church is the cloister, where the friars lived and where visitors could be accommodated.

Special mention must be made of San Francisco in Quito. In contrast with New Spain, where less than a generation after the Conquest enormous buildings were being erected, warfare in the Andean area made it impossible to build monumentally until the later sixteenth century. Thus San Francisco was not completed until around 1575. With its Italianate ornament and rustication, filtered through Flemish mannerist sensibilities, and a symmetrical facade between two towers, it is a seminal structure that influenced many later churches of the region.

Architectural styles in the sixteenth century included Gothic, Renaissance (in its plateresque and purist varieties) and Mudéjar. The use of treatises, especially of Sebastiano Serlio's illustrations, can be documented again and again in architectural details everywhere from the steps in front of San Francisco in Quito to the painted coffering of Mexican cloister walks and rooms. The architectural scheme for evangelization created in the sixteenth century continued to be used, with changes in building styles and ornament, throughout the colonial period in frontier areas.

The missions of the Jesuits in Paraguay, eastern Bolivia, northeastern Argentina, and southern Brazil form a separate group. Built between 1609 and the expulsion of the Jesuits from the Americas in 1767, most of the churches are spaces enclosed by curtain walls and supported by wooden columns, such as the eighteenth-century example at Yaguarón, Paraguay. At Trinidad, Paraguay, however, the church is a vaulted stone structure completed about 1740.

Just how much was preserved from the native cultures in artistic matters is still debated. In architecture, beyond certain techniques and materials, there is little. Adobe and *bejareque* (earth-and-stick) constructions and palm or grass roofs were retained, and are still used in many regions. In central Mexico something of the pre-Columbian tradition of stone carving manifested itself in a sixteenth-century style called *tequitqui*, in which European subject matter mingles with respect for the mass of the stone and some native motifs, as can be seen in atrium crosses, facades, and baptismal fonts. Also of native origin are the *quincha* vaults (plaster-coated webs of straw and reeds on wooden frames) of Peru.

Spanish settlements in the New World were generally built on a grid plan, with a cathedral or parish church and a plaza at the center—a scheme that was formalized in Spanish domains by ordinances. Civilized life for the colonist was city life, and much importance was given to regulated public spaces. In the early period most monumental residences were fortresslike, but the sixteenth-century houses of Diego Columbus in Santo Domingo and of Cortés in Cuernavaca have external loggias. Later palaces often have balconies and ground-level porticos. There are also hospitals, schools, and other public buildings. Usually the basic scheme is that of rooms around internal patios.

The cathedrals were being erected at the same time as the last cathedrals of Spain and generally depended heavily on European models and workmen. The first in the New World was the cathedral of Santo Domingo (1512–1541), built by Europeans (like most colonial structures in the Caribbean). Except for examples in that area, such as the wooden-roofed cathedral of Cartagena, most of the cathedrals of the rest of Spanish America are vaulted and follow similar schemes: rectangular plans with a nave and two side aisles and side chapels. Generally the facade is flanked by two towers. In elevation the older cathedrals of Santo Domingo, Mérida, and Guadalajara, as well as the cathedrals of Cuzco and Lima, are of the hall-church type: the roof is the same height over the nave and the aisles. After 1585, at the cathedrals of Mexico City and Puebla, the plans were more tightly centralized and the buildings were given a basilican elevation.

Cathedrals in Latin America, as elsewhere, often took very long to build and thus display a range of styles. Most were finished in the seventeenth century, by which time baroque elements and movement were evident. In ecclesiastical architecture this meant ornate sculpted portals with strong centralizing and ascending tendencies. Everywhere, though later and less frequently in South America, baroque architecture was marked by the use of the twisted salomonic column, initially introduced in RETABLOS (elaborate gilt wooden altarpieces). Some movement also occurs in plans: facades protrude into the spaces before them; niches in the interiors push out the walls.

The most variety in plans occurred in the eighteenth century, when circular and oval buildings were erected. During the seventeenth century, building types varying according to function and regional characteristics became established. Churches other than cathedrals were often built on the Latin cross plan, although the basilican plan also was used. Convent churches, in which the two entrances are at the sides of the nave rather than at the end (which is set aside for the nuns and opens only to the adjacent cloister), developed in New Spain. Sanctuaries often have a centralizing tendency, as at eighteenth-century Esquipulas in Guatemala, with its four corner towers. The dome, elevated on a drum (thereby adding drama to the mass of the building and directing light into the interior), proliferated in New Spain, where its many variations are proof of the presence of local architects and artisans.

In Cuzco and Lima, earthquakes in 1650 and 1656 were followed by extensive building campaigns that resulted in another important group of churches. San Francisco in Lima, the most coherent building of this group, is characterized by retablo portals whose multiple columns protrude and mass toward the center, where broken and curved pediments create a strong vertical movement. Other regional variants are defined to a great extent by technical and material considerations. Examples include the buildings with stucco and glazed tile decoration in the area of Puebla in New Spain and squat churches with broad, screen-type facades, resistant to earthquakes, in southern Mexico and Central America. In the highlands of Peru and Bolivia, centered at the Peruvian towns of Arequipa, Cajamarca, and Puno, is the "mestizo" architecture of the eighteenth century, characterized by low relief and overall portal carving.

PAINTING AND SCULPTURE IN SPANISH AMERICA
New World painting and sculpture developed from a European base. Although ingredients of colors, feather mosaics, *amate* (fig tree) paper, and sculptures of corn pith, maguey, and local woods were retained from pre-Columbian times, the new Christian subject matter and the forms that clothed it could come only from Europe. Traveling and resident European artists and works, notably prints, introduced the new iconography and styles. Even when pre-Columbian iconography is depicted, as in some Mexican sixteenth-century wall paintings and manuscripts, the style is European. The Flemish painter Simon Pereyns in Mexico and the Italian Jesuit lay brother Bernardo Bitti, who was also a sculptor and worked in Peru, are examples of European painters who introduced the mannerist style into the New World.

Local painters emerged, especially in New Spain, where the process of the Americanization of art seems to have been quicker, and the workshops they established continued for generations. The style of Francisco de Zurbarán was introduced partly through the importation of some of his works. By the middle of the seventeenth century Peter Paul Rubens, too, had found his way to the New World via prints and followers such as Diego de la Puente in Peru. Before the end of the century the softer style of Bartolomé Murillo had reached Latin America. In Mexico the paintings of Baltasar de ECHAVE ORIO, Luis JUÁREZ, and their descendants (Baltasar de Echave Ibía, Baltasar de Echave Rioja, and Jose Júarez), of Juan CORREA, and of Cristóbal de VILLALPANDO covered the seventeenth century. Gregorio VÁZQUEZ CEBALLOS was the most important seventeenth-century painter of New Granada and the only Latin American colonial painter who left a considerable number of drawings. Miguel de Santiago and Nicolás Javier Goríbar worked in Quito. The best painter of Peru was Melchor Pérez Holguín, whose work is concentrated in Potosí.

In Cuzco some painters, among them Diego Quispe Ttito, took a more European direction, while others de-

*Purísima Concepción* by Baltasar de Echave Ibía, 1622. Reproduced from Manuel Toussaint, *Pintura colonial en Mexico* (1965). PINACOTECA VIRREINAL, MEXICO.

veloped a style, now called the Cuzco school, in which gold patterning was applied especially to the clothing of religious figures, giving them a sumptuous and archaic character. Peculiar to the area, too, are paintings of richly robed Virgins, pyramidal in form. Representations of angels were very popular everywhere, and a special type emerged in the Andean highlands: angels dressed as soldiers and carrying rifles (*arcabuceros*). From the middle of the seventeenth century, in both Mexico and Peru, historical paintings appeared, and a consciousness of the differences that distinguish the New World from the Old emerged. Contemporary occurrences, notably processions, are depicted in a way that reveals the variety of local peoples.

In sculpture, carved wooden gilt and painted retablos were the principal decoration of churches. In the sixteenth century, they were generally executed by European artists in Renaissance style. Andalusian influence was strong in sculpture; European artists came to the

*Archangel with Musket.* Circle of the Master of Calamarca, Peru. Oil on cotton, late seventeenth century. NEW ORLEANS MUSEUM OF ART: MUSEUM PURCHASE.

New World, and European pieces, often figures of the Virgin, found their way there as well. The Europeans trained native artists, and their successors eventually developed retablo schemes and vocabularies of their own. These are among the most notable creations of the colonial period throughout Latin America.

In the seventeenth century, in accord with baroque tastes, retablo compositions acquired richness, with attention tending to concentrate on the center. The twisted salomonic column proliferated in New Spain after its introduction around mid-century. Important examples are the retablos of Santo Domingo in Puebla, of Meztitlán, and the three in the Capilla de los Ángeles in the cathedral of Mexico City. In South America mannerist scrolls and grotesques seem to have lasted longer into the seventeenth century than they did in New Spain; especially fantastic are the many carved pulpits. After around 1670, however, the salomonic column dominated retablo design. The retablo in the apse of the Compañía in Cuzco (ca. 1670) and that at Cocharcas are considered among the finest. In South America the carved ceiling is also of great importance. San Francisco

in Quito is an example of an interior lined with golden retablos and ornament and covered by a gilt carved ceiling.

Variety and imagination in supports and decorative elements continued into the eighteenth century. There also developed a tendency toward polychromy and an emphatic unification in design that drew attention to a single central image or group of images, and subordinated or even eliminated the rest in favor of elaborate, often theatrical, framing devices. The impact of the ephemeral decorations for processions and of stage sets for theater was probably considerable and is only beginning to be assessed. In New Spain the *estípite* was introduced around 1720 and became the identifying hallmark of a style, sometimes called CHURRIGUERESQUE, which includes rococo elements. As had happened with the salomonic column, it was first used on interior retablos and then moved to the exteriors, notably the facade of the Sagrario in Mexico City in the 1740s. However, unlike the salomonic column, the *estípite* was little used in South America. Rather, richness was enhanced there by further elaborations of earlier, ultimately mannerist forms in retablos and pulpits. The sculpted individual baroque figure acquired movement and often was part of a theatrical ensemble. These trends can be seen in winged Virgins of the Apocalypse of Quito. An urge toward lifelikeness is evident in the many figures made to be dressed in real clothing.

By the mid-eighteenth century it is possible to speak of neoclassical trends. In New Spain this signified a rejection of the *estípite* and a renewed interest in classical elements. In retablos there was a tendency to abstraction and rococo delicacy of ornament along with greater realism in the figures, which no longer were gilt but, rather, painted in naturalistic colors. In painting, a partial return to mannerist coloring mingled with rococo sweetness and simplified compositions, as in the work of Miguel CABRERA in Mexico City and Manuel de Samaniego in Quito. Concern among artists over their position and role coincided with these developments: Cabrera attempted to establish an academy and Samaniego composed a treatise on painting. A generalized secularization of culture is evident in the luxury of furniture and the decorative arts, in the proliferation of portraiture and domestic religious art, and in the increased interest in genre, exemplified in the *casta* paintings—representations of the racial mixes that made up Iberoamerican populations. An important factor in the taste for luxury goods was the commerce with the East, which brought to Spanish America great quantities of Oriental wares, on their way to Spain via Mexico. This contact with the East was the origin of the many ivory figures still to be seen, especially in Mexico.

With the establishment of the ACADEMIA DE SAN CARLOS in New Spain in 1785, academic neoclassicism formally entered the New World. Its introduction was accompanied by a fresh wave of artists from Europe who built severe monuments and buildings from California to the Southern Cone, among them Manuel TOLSÁ in New Spain, Antonio Bernasconi in Guatemala City, Domingo de Petrés in Colombia, Marias Maestro in Lima, and Joaquín Toesca in Chile. Neoclassicism also affirmed itself in sculpture and painting, notably in portraits, such as those by Rafael Jimeno in New Spain and by José Gil de Castro in Peru.

ART AND ARCHITECTURE IN BRAZIL
Brazil differs from the rest of Latin America in that the artistic relationship with the mother country was stronger, so much so that developments in Brazil were sometimes contemporary and complementary to developments in Portugal rather than derivative. Fortifications were as important as in the Spanish colonies, but urbanization tended to be more medieval in character, so that grid plans are the exception. As in Spanish America, church architecture concentrated talent and effort. Mannerist forms dominate seventeenth-century construction, as at São Benito in Rio de Janeiro (planned in 1617, built in 1670–1680) and in the Jesuit church (now cathedral) of Salvador, rebuilt between 1657 and 1672.

Most of what has been preserved is from the eighteenth century, when the typically Portuguese double-shell, elongated octagonal nave and elaborate *capela-mor* (presbytery) type of church architecture made its appearance. It was to dominate Brazilian colonial art; an early instance is Nossa Senhora da Glória do Outeiro in Rio de Janeiro (1714–1730). Later in the century, rococo curves were introduced into architectural plans and decorations. Although there are important examples of this in various places, such as in buildings by the Italian architect Antonio Giuseppe Landi in Belém, the best known instances are in Minas Gerais, beginning with Nossa Senhora do Rosário dos Prêtos in Ouro Prêto, built around 1785.

Sculpture and painting in colonial Brazil were often closely associated with architecture. As in Portugal, the typical retablo design of the seventeenth century was a series of ornamented concentric arches framing a tiered platform for the cult image. In the eighteenth century the earlier tight designs, like the one at São Francisco at Salvador (1723–1746), were transformed into more open and ascending compositions, exemplified especially in Minas Gerais. Much of the painting that is preserved is ceiling decoration, either within coffered ensembles, as at São Francisco at Salvador, or, after around 1740, in illusionistic compositions. Notable among these is the 1773 ceiling of A Conceição da Praia in Salvador, by José Joaquim da Rocha, and other numerous examples in Minas Gerais. Walls covered with painted tiles, a type of decoration that is ubiquitous in Portugal, also occurs in Brazil; an important example can be seen in the cloister at São Francisco, Salvador.

The flourishing of art in Minas Gerais corresponded to the inland shift in population and wealth of the eighteenth century. Patronage also changed. Art in the coastal cities and settlements had been produced for and often in monastic establishments, but in the interior, lay brotherhoods contracted a great number of works. As in Spanish America, rococo mixed with Oriental elements and there was a progressive secularization of culture, along with the introduction of neoclassical elements toward the end of the eighteenth century. The principal artist of this period in Minas Gerais was the crippled mulatto sculptor and architect Antônio Francisco LISBOA (O Aleijadinho, "Little Cripple"). Among his masterpieces are the Church of São Francisco at Ouro Prêto (1774–1794), a strikingly unified conception whose entrance protrudes between towers, complete with retablo and illusionistic ceiling decoration, and the sanctuary of Bom Jesus de Matozinhos at Congonhas do Campo (1796–1805), with its sculptures representing the passion of Christ and with twelve prophets carved in soapstone. Although the quality of Aleijadinho's work and his fame have overshadowed his predecessors and contemporaries, artists such as his uncle, the architect Antônio Francisco Pombal, the sculptor Francisco Javier de Brito, and the painters Bernardo Pires da Silva and Manoel da Costa Athaide, are only a few of the personalities who contributed to this last phase of Brazilian colonial art.

DIEGO ANGULO IÑIGUEZ, *Historia de arte hispanoamericano*, 3 vols. (1945–1956); PÁL KELEMEN, *Baroque and Rococo in Latin America* (1951); GEORGE KUBLER and MARTIN SORIA, *Art and Architecture in Spain and Portugal and Their American Dominions, 1500 to 1800* (1959); MANUEL TOUSSAINT, *Colonial Art in Mexico* (1967); RAMÓN GUTIÉRREZ, *Arquitectura y urbanismo en Iberoamérica* (1983); SANTIAGO SEBASTIÁN, JOSÉ DE MESA, and TERESA GISBERT, *Arte iberoamericano desde la colonización a la independencia*. Vol. 29, *Summa Artis* (1985); OCTAVIO PAZ, "Introduction," in *Mexico: Splendors of Thirty Centuries* (1990); SANTIAGO SEBASTIAN, *El barroco iberoamericano* (1990); DAMIÁN BAYÓN and MURILLO MARX, *History of South American Colonial Art and Architecture* (1992).

CLARA BARGELLINI

### The Nineteenth Century

The history of nineteenth-century Latin American art has two modes: one emphasizing continuity with European art, including the Eurocentric styles of the colonial viceroyalties, and another emphasizing change, fragmentation, and celebration of local values. The latter has tended to dominate, since the art history of the period has often been organized around political categories, stressing national schools, the break with the colonial past, and the emergence of popular art forms.

The nineteenth century in Latin America did indeed produce great changes, incessant wars and revolts, social upheavals, and both demographic and economic surges. Cities such as Caracas, Buenos Aires, Santiago, and Rio de Janeiro, which were just emerging at the end of colonization, would become important cultural centers by the twentieth century. Patronage also changed, from aristocratic to bourgeois, from centralized to highly dispersed, from religious to secular, with the emergence of a popular market for the arts becoming ever more important as the century progressed. It would, however, be a mistake to ignore the strong relationships of Latin American nineteenth-century art both to the previous viceregal traditions and to contemporary European art. Indeed, the history begins in the late colonial period, with the rise of neoclassicism and romantic art, so that the stylistic transition from the viceregal era to that of independence was initially quite smooth.

NEOCLASSICISM AND THE ACADEMIES

In Mexico, the establishment in 1785 of the ACADEMIA DE SAN CARLOS on neoclassical principles yielded a strong uniformity in "official" art from 1790, and in many ways it provides an archetype for Latin American art at the end of the colonial era and the early years of independence. Although the academy was in part an imposition of a centralizing Spanish Bourbon regime, it also responded to pre-existing local artistic and intellectual currents. By 1811, the younger academic artists, studying under the Valencian painter Rafael JIMENO Y PLANES (1761–1825), the sculptor-architect Manuel TOLSÁ (1757–1816), and their Mexican fellow-professors, were using the neoclassical style and historical allusions to promote liberal political ideas (Pedro Patiño Ixtolinque, *King Wamba Threatened by One of His Electors,* relief sculpture, 1817). The interplay of ancient European and Mexican themes would continue to be a hallmark of Mexican academic art, with pre-Hispanic history incorporated by mid-century into the mix of subjects, as in the work of Manuel VILAR (*Tlahuicole,* 1851), José María OBREGÓN (*The Discovery of Pulque,* 1869), and Rodrigo Gutiérrez (*The Senate of Tlaxcala,* 1875). Furthermore, the importance of the neoclassical architecture of Tolsá (School of Mines, Mexico City) and colleagues such as Francisco Eduardo TRESGUERRAS (Church of El Carmén, Celaya, 1802–1807) in setting the tone for the following century cannot be overstated. One should also note, however, the coexistence of romantic styles on a more personal basis, as in the works of the Mexican artist-patriot José Luis Rodríguez Alconedo (1762–1815).

Neoclassical taste was also established outside Mexico by official commissions and the importation of artists from Europe, most notably in Brazil, Argentina, Chile, and what would become Colombia. Again, architecture provides the best examples, as in the case of the works of Andrés Blanqui, an Italian Jesuit, and the Frenchman Prosper Catelin in Buenos Aires (Cathedral, finished 1823), of Fray Domingo de Petrés in Bogotá (*d.* 1811; Cathedral, Santa Fe de Bogotá), or, especially, of the Italian Joaquín Toesca in Chile (Santiago Mint, 1788–1799).

The Mexico City academy and its younger sibling at Puebla (in operation by 1812?; confirmed in 1819) were apparently the only official arts organizations founded in the Spanish viceroyalties during the colonial era (private drawing academies operated sporadically in a number of viceregal cities, including those founded in Lima by Javier Cortés around 1810 and by the Sevillian José del Pozo soon thereafter). By the 1840s, however, there were academies operating in Jalisco (by about 1830), Bogotá, Caracas (chartered 1826, in operation by the mid-1830s), Quito, Cuenca, Buenos Aires (privately from 1818; at the university from 1822), Santiago (by 1849), and perhaps elsewhere (the topic has not been properly studied). Oddly, Lima, which had been such an important viceregal center, continued to rely on private schools, to its great detriment; as we will see, Peruvian artists seeking academic training before 1919 often traveled to Quito or Buenos Aires.

In Brazil, the transfer of the court of Dom JOÃO VI to Rio de Janeiro led, in 1816, to the arrival of a group of mostly French artists and architects under the neoclassicist Joachim Lebreton, with a mandate to educate young Brazilians. An academy was begun soon after, and, in 1826, the Académia Imperial de Belas Artes, under the direction of the painter Jean-Baptiste DEBRET (a cousin of David; 1768–1848), moved to its sumptuous new neoclassical building designed by Auguste-Henri-Victor GRANDJEAN DE MONTIGNY (1776–1850), who also designed such important monuments as the Customs House. In Argentina, the teaching of the Swiss painter Johann Guth (in Argentina from 1817) and the Italian Paolo Caccianiga (from the late 1820s) at the university produced several generations of artists aware of both neoclassical and romantic values.

It is impossible to characterize the academies universally, since each organization reflected widely varying local patronage. In Brazil, the academy initially enforced a rigid French classicism, while Mexico City was more eclectic and the Puebla academy, responding to the ethnographic interests of its patrons, developed an important school of genre painting. At Mexico City, genre subjects were admitted in figure competitions early in the century, and landscape painting was an important part of the curriculum. In general, we may say that the academies were centers of continuity, if also of progress. A number of other constants may be cited: the academies were typically Eurocentric, inviting European artists to professorships and tending to suppress interest in the artistic values, if not the subject matter, of pre-Hispanic civilizations and indigenous social groups. The influence of Paris was mediated by that of Rome, particularly in Mexico and Buenos Aires, while Spanish artists often came from the Levant rather than from Madrid, yielding in both cases a more international and eclectic character. Finally, the academies were essential for keeping the Latin American artists abreast of technical developments and for providing a stable base for education and patronage in the midst of often chaotic political and economic situations. Many of the academies, especially in the first two-thirds of the century, maintained the racial openness that had already distinguished the arts in the viceregal era.

## HISTORY PAINTING

Nineteenth-century Latin America produced a surprising number of academic history painters of the first rank, almost none of them known outside the field. In Mexico, these include—in addition to the already mentioned Vilar, Obregón, and Rodrigo Gutiérrez—Juan CORDERO (1824–1884), Santiago Rebull (1829–1902), Felipe S. Gutiérrez (1824–1904), Félix PARRA (1845–1919), and Leandro Izaguirre (1867–1941). (A particular strength of the Mexican system was its program of sending young artists to Rome.) In Brazil, in addition to Lebreton, Debret, and their colleague Nicolas-Antoine Taunay (1755–1830), there are Vítor MEIRELES DE LIMA (1832–1903), Pedro AMÉRICO de Figueiredo (1843–1905), Rodolfo Amoêdo (1857–1941), and Manuel de ARAÚJO PÔRTO ALEGRE (1806–1879), an art historian and diplomat as well as a painter. The first half of the long career of Elyseu d'Angelo VISCONTI (1867–1944; also active in Europe) was dedicated to salon-style history painting; he turned to impressionist and postimpressionist works in the 1920s. In Chile and Peru, the Frenchman Raymond Quinsac Monvoisin (1790–1870; in America, 1845–1861) brought neoclassical principles but found his own style affected by romantic values. In Venezuela, Arturo Michelena (1863–1898) and Martín Tovar y Tovar (1828–1902) were among the many artists contributing to the artistic programs of the regime of Antonio GUZMÁN BLANCO.

## SCULPTURE

From the outset, the Mexican and Brazilian academies developed strong programs in sculpture, in part because of sculpture's role in the production of coinage and medals and its value as a communicator of public values, but also because drawing after sculpture was such an important aspect of the academic education. By the time of Alexander von HUMBOLDT's visit in 1803, the Mexico City academy had acquired a sizable collection of plaster casts after ancient and European works, many still in use today. Manuel Tolsá's activities as sculptor-architect and teacher thus began a century-spanning academic dynasty that included his students Patiño Ixtolinque (mentioned earlier) and José María Labastida (active 1830–1849) and their successors, the Catalán Manuel Vilar (1812–1869) and the Mexican Miguel Noreña (1843–1894), with a general trajectory from neoclassicism through romantic appropriation to symbolic realism. In Brazil, Auguste-Marie Taunay (1768–1824), who had accompanied his brother Nicolas in the Lebreton group, served as the first professor of sculpture, establishing the neoclassical style. He was succeeded by João Joaquim Alão.

## RELIGIOUS ART

The academies and their circles of patrons (including governments) in nineteenth-century Latin America quickly came to play the dominant role in patronage at the centers of power, replacing the Roman Catholic church. Indeed, if there is any one element that signals a break in Latin American culture at the time of Independence it is the collapse of centralized, "official" church patronage. In part due to liberal anticlericalism and the almost universal disestablishment of the church, the collapse was also in part aesthetic, since the new neoclassical principles were often at odds with significant aspects of viceregal religious art, such as the vast gilded RETABLOS (altarpieces). Similarly, with a few notable exceptions, officially commissioned polychromed sculpture became almost purely replicative at the centers of power after about 1830. Although the church hierarchy continued to commission the occasional large-scale painting, religious histories and even devotional pictures were as likely to be the product of academic competitions and the salons as of clerical interest. As a result, much of the best religious art of the nineteenth century was produced for provincial patrons—local parishes, family altars and so forth—by artists with little or no academic training. Polychromed statuary became a significant folk art form, as it remains even in the southwestern United States to this day. Similarly, the *ex voto*, which may be found well back into the viceregal era, moved into the center of art history, with literally thousands of examples, many of extremely high artistic quality, produced in almost every country.

## PORTRAITURE

The introduction of neoclassicism at the end of the colonial era meant that the straightforwardly realistic, classically simple bourgeois portrait, often at half-length, had already become dominant by about 1800; among its many virtues was the provision of a format in which provincial painters could express their genius even without benefit of academic training. We therefore see, occasionally in the same work, stylistic continuity and striking change, as the political and social forces unleashed at Independence are commemorated through portraiture by an extraordinarily wide range of artists.

Nonacademic masters have left an indelible image of the years of struggle for independence. The Peruvian José Gil de CASTRO ("El Mulato Gil"; d. ca. 1841), an officer in Bernardo O'Higgins's Chilean independence army, was active as a portraitist in Chile from 1814 to 1822 and thereafter in Argentina and Peru. His portraits of Bolívar and the other leaders of the independence movement are canonical, while his memorial portrait of *The Martyr Olaya* (1823) has come to sum up the entire era. In Mexico, José María ESTRADA (active ca. 1830–1865), who received provincial academic training in Jalisco, adapted both neoclassical formulas and viceregal traditions, such as the portrayal of deceased nuns, to his deceptively simple images, which can be at once naive and psychologically perceptive (*Don Francisco Torres* [*The Dead Poet*], 1849). That rural activity need not imply technical backwardness is best seen in the works of Hermenegildo BUSTOS (1832–1907), one of the finest portraitists of his century, who, in spite of describing himself as an "amateur," produced stunning evocations

*The Martyr Olaya* by José Gil de Castro, 1828. MUSEO DE HISTORIA DE LIMA; PHOTO BY DANIEL GIANNONI.

of the provincial bourgeoisie of west-central Mexico (*Don Juan Muñoz and Doña Juliana Gutiérrez*, 1868).

Academic portraiture may be said to have moved from a neoclassical mode, occasionally enhanced by romantic elements, in the first half of the century, to a reliance on the salon values of haute bourgeois European portraiture in the second half—although in both cases, French influence (including that of Franz Winterhalter) was often accompanied by contemporary Italian currents. In Mexico, one can cite Pelegrín CLAVÉ (1810–1880)—the Catalán artist who, with Manuel Vilar, had been called to Mexico in 1846 to restructure and revitalize the Mexico City academy—and Felipe S. Gutiérrez (*Señora Sánchez Solís*, about 1875). (In contrast, Juan Cordero's portraits occasionally extol the *mestizo* origins of his sitters, perhaps as a critique of the Eurocentric values of Clavé and his supporters at the academy.) In Colombia, the autodidact José María ESPINOSA (1796–1883) produced surprisingly refined neoclassical portraits, while, later in the century, Epifanio GARAY (1849–1903) adapted conventions learned in Paris both to portraiture and to history

subjects, achieving a vivid bravura realism. Their quieter counterpart in Venezuela was Martín Tovar y Tovar. In Argentina, the Italian Carlos Enrique PELLEGRINI (1800–1875), originally trained as an engineer, established portraiture on neoclassical realist principles from 1828; he was soon joined by Cayetano Descalzi (born in Italy, active in Argentina after 1830), who, like Pellegrini, initially benefited from the patronage of the dictator Juan Manuel de Rosas and his circle, and by the Argentine Ignacio Baz (1826–1887), who eventually had to flee Rosas's tyranny. The Taunay family, along with Debret and the short-lived José Correia de Lima (1814–1857), developed neoclassical and romantic portraiture in Brazil; their counterparts in Chile were Raimundo Quinsac Monvoisin (1790–1870), Alejandro Cicarelli (1811–1879, to Chile via Brazil, 1848), and Cicarelli's pupil, the polymath Pedro Lira (1845–1912), who adapted oil techniques gained from a study of the seventeenth-century Dutch masters. As with Garay in Colombia and Gutiérrez in Mexico, the salon style of late-nineteenth-century academic portraiture was developed to a high degree of refinement by Rodolfo Amoêdo in Brazil. In Peru, this category suffered from the lack of a local official academy, which in part caused the talented portraitists Daniel Hernández (1856–1932) and Francisco LASO (see Genre, below) to go to Rome and Paris for training and to remain abroad through much of their careers.

LANDSCAPE AND NATURALIST DESCRIPTION
Beginning in the mid-1700s, an important series of naturalist expeditions—Cook (Pacific, 1768–1776), MUTIS (northern Andes, 1784–1817), Humboldt (1799–1804), to cite only the best known—visited the Western Hemisphere or Pacific rim to record previously unclassified flora and fauna. As Bernard Smith has demonstrated, the artistic demands of these expeditions developed an empirical, realist style outside the aesthetic values of the academies, with immense importance for the future. To this we can add, with Stanton Catlin, that the necessarily New World subject matter of both the European and the American artist-recorders, including those who focused on human society as well as natural wonders, turned Latin American art away from dependence on European models and began to focus it on its own social and natural contexts.

Among the other new categories opened in Latin American art during the romantic era was landscape, which had been almost nonexistent in colonial art. Stimulus here came both from abroad, in the form of foreign artists who came in search of the picturesque or who were invited to teach at the academies, and from the national movements themselves, which produced patrons eager to see their independent homelands celebrated in art. Landscape was also affected by what Robert Rosenblum has called "the northern Romantic tradition" of England, Germany, and the United States, and so provided an important counterweight to neoclassical and academic influences. Among many itinerant European painters who came in search of *l'exotisme américain* were Thomas Ender (Austrian, 1793–1875; in Brazil, 1817–1818), Johann Moritz RUGENDAS (German, 1802–1858; active in Brazil, 1820–1823, Mexico, 1831–1834, Chile, Argentina, Peru, and Uruguay, 1834–1846), and Jean-Baptiste-Louis Gros (French, 1793–1870; in Mexico 1830s). In Mexico, landscape painting was established by Daniel Thomas EGERTON (English, *d.* 1842; in Mexico from 1830) and Eugenio Landesio (Italian, 1810–1879; in Mexico from 1855), the latter having been called to teach the subject in the academy. Each was influenced by Claude Lorraine, but while Egerton looked to Lorraine's romantic qualities through Turner's eyes, Landesio stressed the classical aspects derived from the Venetian Renaissance and the Bolognese school, which he couched in a *plein air* realism. The resulting combination of romantic engagement, classical composition, and realist technique found its brilliant fruition in the works of the internationally famous Jóse María VELASCO (Mexican, 1840–1912), who is rightfully considered among the greatest landscape masters of any period (*The Valley of México,* 1875). Landscape was established in Argentina by the polymath Prilidiano PUEYRREDÓN (1823–1870), and in Uruguay by Juan Manuel Besnes (1788–1865) and Juan Manuel BLANES (1830–1901; see Genre, below). Among its practitioners in Brazil (with a local tradition

going back to Post in the seventeenth century!) was Agostinho José da Mota (1824–1878). In Ecuador, landscape was introduced by Rafael Salas (1830–1906), perfected by Rafael Troya (1845–1921), and also practiced, in both oils and watercolors, by Joaquín PINTO (1842–1906), especially at the end of his career.

GENRE
Genre painting has strong roots in the colonial period (see the Mexican eighteenth-century *Castas*). In the nineteenth century, genre is dominated by *costumbrista* art, a sometimes contradictory blend of ethnographic realism and romantic celebration of the picturesque, often motivated by civic pride. (The movement affected literature as well as the visual arts.) Genre was thus closely allied with landscape and scientific illustration and often found official or academic as well as private support. As with landscape, visiting European painters made an important contribution and in many cases became residents, training or influencing artists born locally. In addition to Debret (in Brazil 1816–1824) and Rugendas, we may mention Frederick Catherwood (English, 1799–1854; in the Yucatán and Chiapas with the North American archaeologist J. L. Stephens, 1839–1841); Léon Gauthier (French; in Colombia 1850s), Claudio Gay (French, 1800–1873; in Chile 1843–1851), Adolphe

*Hacienda de Chimalpa* by José María Velasco, 1893. MUSEO NACIONAL DE ARTE, MEXICO.

d'Hastrel (French, 1805–1870; in Uruguay 1839–1841), Victor Patricio de LANDALUZE (Spanish, 1828–1889; in Cuba from about 1855), Conrad Martens (English, 1801–1871; in Uruguay 1833–1834; with Darwin to Valparaíso, 1834), Edward Walhouse Mark (English, 1817–1895; in Colombia 1843–1856), Edouard H. T. Pingret (French, 1788–1875; in Mexico 1852), and Emeric Essex Vidal (English, 1791–1861; in Argentina and Uruguay, 1810s).

At the same time, American-born painters and lithographers, encouraged by local patronage, embraced genre enthusiastically. As has already been noted, Puebla, Mexico, was an important center of *costumbrismo*, with José Agustín ARRIETA (1802–1874) the outstanding proponent of both genre and still life. In Mexico City, Felipe S. Gutiérrez blended academic composition with ethnographic realism, as in his *The Farewell*, which also alluded to the biography of the patron, the politician Felipe Sánchez Solís. Works such as *The Wake* (*El velorio*, 1889), by José María Jara (1866–1939), at once cater to and rise above the continued interest of the European salons in ethnic customs.

The best-known Peruvian *costumbrista* is the nonacademic Pancho FIERRO (1803–1879), whose lively watercolors and caricatures compare favorably with Goya's drawings. (Fierro also painted murals, which have not survived.) Another Peruvian painter, Francisco Laso (1823–1869), produced what is surely the most stylistically advanced work by a Latin American artist at midcentury, the strikingly modern *Dweller in the Cordillera* (*Indian Potter*), painted in Paris in 1853. Laso's severe yet sensitive image of an indigenous potter—hieratically frontal, silhouetted against an ambiguous light wall, shadowed by a large-brimmed hat, almost symbolist in his isolation—has more in common with the abstracted portraits of Whistler than with the genre pictures of his contemporaries in Latin America. As with certain works by Debret at the beginning, José Correia de Lima in the middle, and Rodolfo Amoêdo or José Ferraz de ALMEIDA Júnior (1850–1899; *The Guitarist*, 1899) at the end of the century in Brazil, Laso's image erases the distinctions between *costumbrismo* and traditional portraiture.

Perhaps because of romantic principles derived from the teaching of Guth and Caccianiga, in the area of the Río de la Plata genre and landscape were early fused. Along with Pueyrredón, the outstanding early exponent of *costumbrismo* in Argentina was the academy-trained painter and lithographer Carlos Morel (1813–1894), whose brilliant career was curtailed by shock-induced insanity in 1845; there was also the French-trained Juan León Pallière (1823–1887), who worked in Buenos Aires in the 1850s, occasionally in collaboration with Enrique Sheridan (Argentine, trained in Britain, ca. 1835–1860). Perhaps the most extraordinary of the southern artists was Juan Manuel Blanes, the Argentine-born Uruguayan who combined the sweep of the pampas landscape, genre, contemporary history, and allegory in images of

an almost symbolist effect (*Paraguay: Image of Your Desolate Country*, ca. 1880; *Review of Rio Negro by General Roca*, 1891). The allegorical use of the human figure, including indigenous types, was widespread at the end of the century, as in the cases of Amoêdo in Brazil or Felipe Gutiérrez and Jesús F. Contreras (see Impressionism, below) in Mexico.

GRAPHIC ARTS

The dominant means of expression in the graphic arts for the first half of the century is the archetypically romantic medium lithography, which was used by both visiting artists (such as Humboldt, Debret, and Egerton) and Americans as a means of distributing their images of *costumbrismo* and nationalistic landscape, as well as a vehicle for political cartooning and social satire, often influenced by Daumier. Among the many lithographers active in Latin America was the Englishman Joseph Skinner (active in Peru around 1805); the Italian Claudio LINATI (1790–1832; in Mexico from 1825), who first brought lithography to Mexico; and Linati's contemporary, the German Karl NEBEL (1805–1855; in Mexico from 1829), who preceded Catherwood in depicting pre-Hispanic monuments as well as *costumbrista* scenes. From the 1830s, a popular graphic tradition became in-

*Paraguay: Image of Your Desolate Country* by Blanes, 1880. COURTESY OF MUSEO NACIONAL DE ARTES PLÁSTICAS, MONTEVIDEO.

creasingly dominant, with audiences among both the bourgeoisie and the working classes. The most famous artist active in this sphere was the Mexican José Guadalupe POSADA (1851–1913), whose works have become such an important influence on modern artists. Although Posada's audience may not have been as uneducated as is sometimes assumed, his sources in popular art are clear, and his vivid, highly abstracted renderings in a wide variety of graphic media (including direct carving in type metal) had the effect of bridging the worlds of the bourgeois fine arts and the arts of peasants and working people.

ARCHITECTURE

Until mid-century, various local versions of the neoclassical style predominated; as late as 1854–1865 Pueyrredón's designs for Buenos Aires could maintain a basically neoclassical format. Eventually, architecture took up the romantic attitude: one finds Florentine Renaissance villas and even neo-Gothic structures, especially in Brazil, where the colonial use of tiles was often maintained in even the severest Tuscan design. After the 1850s, however, the influence of French urbanism under Baron Haussmann and Beaux-Arts eclecticism gradually predominated, as may be seen in Mexico City's Paseo de la Reforma or in the Alameda and other projects at Santiago de Chile initiated by François Brunet de Baines (called from France in 1849 to organize a school of architecture) and Benjamín VICUÑA MACKENNA, the superintendent of public works. (This trend continued in the twentieth century, as the Avenida Rio Branco in Rio de Janeiro [1903–1906] indicates.)

The policies of Porfirio Díaz in Mexico, which encouraged European and North American investment, also opened up Mexican architecture to international influence just at the time that rapid economic expansion made considerable new construction necessary. Ministry buildings (such as that now housing the National Museum of Art) were built in a modified Beaux-Arts style, while the use of boulevards, initiated under Maximilian in the 1860s, continued to be the norm. French influence was often tempered by Italian intervention, most notably in the work of Adam Boari at the turn of the century, including the Florentine Renaissance revival Post Office and the difficult-to-characterize Palace of Fine Arts, which was completed after 1919 by Antonio Muñoz and Federico Mariscal. A similar phenomenon may be seen in Buenos Aires, where economic expansion at the turn of the century led to the adoption of a neo-baroque Beaux-Arts mode in the works of Alejandro Christophersen (San Martín Palace) and Julio Dormal (final design for the Teatro Colón, 1905–1908). Many of the finest works of nineteenth-century architecture, however, are anonymous or not yet attributed, especially the many suburban villas, rural haciendas, and more modest urban dwellings of the new upper-middle class.

IMPRESSIONISM, SYMBOLISM, AND ART NOUVEAU

For the most part, the development of impressionist and postimpressionist European avant-garde styles is a twentieth-century phenomenon in Latin America. One should cite, however, the paintings of Martín A. Malharro (1865–1911), a precursor of the impressionists active by the 1880s in Argentina, and the symbolist or art nouveau aspects of the work of the Mexican Julio RUELAS (1870–1907) and his follower, Roberto MONTENEGRO (1885–1964), in both painting and the graphic arts. Mexican sculpture, especially in the hands of Jesús F. Contreras (1866–1902; influenced by Rodin) and his younger associates Agustín Ocampo and Fidencio Nava, carried a symbolist decadent mode into the first years of the new century.

GABRIEL GIRALDO JARAMILLO, *La pintura en Colombia* (1942); JOSÉ MARIA DOS REIS, *Historia da pintura no Brasil* (1944); ADRIÁN MERLINO, *Diccionario de artistas plásticas de la Argentina* (1954); P. M. BARDI, *The Arts in Brazil* (1956); JOSÉ PEDRO ARGUL, *Pintura y escultura del Uruguay* (1958); *Pintura venezolana 1661–1961* (1960); ANTONIO R. ROMERA, *Historia de la pintura chilena* (1960); BERNARD SMITH, *European Vision and the South Pacific, 1768–1850* (1960); YARA TUPYNAMBÁ, *Tres séculos e meio de pintura no Brasil* (1961); JEAN CHARLOT, *Mexican Art and the Academy of San Carlos* (1962); JULIO E. PAYRÓ, *23 Pintores de la Argentina, 1810–1900* (1962); JOSÉ MARÍA VARGAS, *Historia del arte ecuatoriano* (1964); STANTON LOOMIS CATLIN and TERENCE GRIEDER, *Art of Latin America Since Independence* (1966); JUSTINO FERNÁNDEZ, *El arte del siglo XIX en México* (1967); ALFREDO BOULTON, *Historia de la pintura en Venezuela*, 2 vols. (1968); LEOPOLDO CASTEDO, *A History of Latin American Art and Architecture* (1969); JOSEFA EMILIA SABOR, *Bibliografía básica de obras de referencia de artes y letras para la Argentina* (1969); GASPAR GALASZ and MILAN IVELIC, *La pintura en Chile desde la colonia hasta 1981* (1981); CARACAS, CONSEJO MUNICIPAL DEL DISTRITO FEDERAL, *Guzmán Blanco y el Centenario del Libertador, 1883* (1983); FAUSTO RAMÍREZ, *La plástica del siglo de la independencia* (1985); DAWN ADES, *Art in Latin America: The Modern Era, 1820–1980* (1989); FAUSTO RAMÍREZ, *Mexico: Splendors of Thirty Centuries* (1990).

MARCUS B. BURKE

*See also* **Architecture.**

### *The Twentieth Century*

Latin American art in the twentieth century reflected the same influences and styles that characterized European and North American art of the period.

EARLY YEARS

During the first two decades of the century, Latin American art absorbed the combined influences of Spanish realism (exemplified by Joaquín Sorolla and Ignacio Zuloaga), symbolism, and French impressionism. In Mexico, Saturnino HERRÁN (1887–1918) depicted the Mexican Indians in a nonidealized manner, while Joaquín Claussell (1866–1935) painted the native landscape with impressionist techniques. In Brazil, Elyseu d'Angelo VISCONTI (1867–1944) worked in an impressionist manner, and in Uruguay, Pedro Blanes Viale (1879–1926) produced luminous, sun-drenched landscapes.

Varieties of postimpressionism had a large following, including Armando REVERÓN (1889–1954) of Venezuela, Pedro FIGARI (1861–1938) of Uruguay, and Andrés de SANTA MARÍA (1860–1945) of Colombia. Reverón became the hermit of Macuto beach, where he painted "white" coastal scenes in which he reconverted, or purified, the colors of the spectrum through light back into white. Santa María explored the properties of distortion and artificial light in his interior scenes. Figari, also an essayist, diplomat, and lawyer, painted scenes of salon life in Buenos Aires, as well as the African ritual dances of Montevideo known as the CANDOMBLÉ, in bright flat colors and patterned compositions reminiscent of Édouard Vuillard in France.

MODERNISM

In its strictest sense, cubism had few followers in Latin America. The Mexican Diego RIVERA (1886–1957) was a cubist between 1913 and 1917. In Argentina, Emilio PETTORUTI (1892–1971) developed a highly personal version of synthetic cubism with delicately orchestrated colors. Yet, cubism and futurism exerted a major influence throughout Latin America as a basis for the innovations of the 1920s and after. More than just in cubism, Pablo Picasso was imitated in all of his stages, especially the work he produced in the 1920s and 1930s.

Throughout the 1920s, artists began to affirm their regional identities by applying a synthesis of cubism, futurism, and expressionism to local themes. An avantgarde emerged in Mexico, Cuba, Argentina, Chile, and Brazil. The major movement of the early 1920s was the Mexican mural movement. In 1921, after General Álvaro OBREGÓN had consolidated power as president, education minister José VASCONCELOS invited a dozen or so artists to paint murals on the walls of public buildings. Among the invited group, three stood above the rest: José Clemente OROZCO (1883–1949); Diego Rivera; and David Alfaro SIQUEIROS (1896–1974). In their premural careers, each artist had taken a different route. Orozco had earned his living as a political cartoonist while painting expressionist watercolors of brothel interiors. Rivera had been a bohemian in Paris, experimenting with the style of all the major movements from impressionism to cubism. Siqueiros, who had fought in the Revolution, was leaving behind the mild impressionism picked up at the Open Air school and was flirting with constructivist as well as futurist approaches to art. These muralists revived the ancient techniques of fresco and encaustic, and took revolutionary and indigenous themes as the subjects of their murals. Orozco's view was dark and dystopic, while Rivera and Siqueiros (both committed Communists) were painters of revolutionary hope. The mural movement in Mexico became associated with the Syndicate of Technical Workers,

*Antropofagia*. Oil on canvas by Tarsila do Amaral, 1929. PRIVATE COLLECTION, SÃO PAULO, BRAZIL.

Painters, and Sculptors, whose official organ was the newspaper *El Machete*.

In 1924 the Cuban painter Victor Manuel (1897–1969) introduced modern art in Cuba with the aid of the painters Eduardo Abela (1889–1965), Carlos ENRÍQUEZ (1900–1957), Fidelio PONCE DE LEÓN (1895–1949), and Amelia PELÁEZ (1897–1968) and the sculptor Juan José Sicre (1898–1974). These artists were supported by the essayist Jorge MAÑACH and the editorial staff of the *Revista de Avance*.

In Argentina, poets and painters banded together in 1924 to found the review *Martin Fierro*. The group included the painters Juan del Prete (*b.* 1897), Alejandro Xul SOLAR (1887–1963), and Emilio Pettoruti, as well as the writers Leopoldo LUGONES, Ricardo GÜIRALDES, and Jorge Luis BORGES. In Chile, the most Francophile of the southern countries, a group called Montparnasse was founded in 1928. It included the painters Camilo Mori (1896–1970) and Pablo E. Burchard (1873–1960).

The most revolutionary movement occurred in Brazil, where the painter Emiliano DI CAVALCANTI (1897–1976) and several poets organized the MODERN ART WEEK in São Paulo (1922). This was a week-long festival of the arts that included dance, poetry readings, and an art exhibition. Perhaps the greatest innovator within Latin American art of the 1920s was Tarsila do AMARAL (1886–1973). A native of São Paulo, Amaral had studied in Paris with Fernand Léger and André Lhote. Her mature style is one of colorful and bold forms. She was a founding member of the Pau Brasil movement in 1924, as well as of the anthropophagist movement in 1928. She collaborated with her husband, the poet Oswaldo de ANDRADE, in a series of paintings and poems in which native imagery is fused with that of modern industry. Both poet and painter were involved with the magazine *Klaxon*.

## SOCIAL REALISM

During the 1920s, there was a rejection of the Parisian avant-garde as well as an embrace of the aesthetics of the Mexican muralists in the Andean countries. In Peru, José SABOGAL (1888–1956) demonstrated a commitment to mural painting as well as to indigenous subject matter. In 1926, in La Paz, Bolivia, the National Academy of Fine Arts was founded and later directed by Cecilio Guzman de Rojas (1900–1950), a Bolivian painter trained in Spain who painted Indians in a symbolist style.

The Mexicans' call for a figurative and socially committed art was most influential in countries such as Peru, Bolivia, and Ecuador. Eduardo Kingman (b. 1913) and Oswaldo GUAYASAMÍN (b. 1919) were the main representatives of social realism in Ecuadorian painting. In 1933, Siqueiros traveled to Argentina, where the painters Juan Carlos Castagnino (1908–1971), Lino Spilimbergo (1896–1964), and Antonio BERNI (1905–1981) collaborated with him on a mural near Buenos Aires. Berni later became known for his large collages, made out of diverse materials salvaged from refuse, as well as for his iconographic characters Juanito Laguna, a poor slum boy, and Ramona Montiel, a prostitute. Through them, Berni expressed his social and political concerns. In Brazil, a nationalistic mural style was dominated by Cândido PORTINARI (1903–1961), who painted scenes of local customs and life among the poor with a less political emphasis than that of the Mexicans.

## CONSTRUCTIVISM, SURREALISM, AND ABSTRACTION

Alongside social realism, new avant-garde groups continued to emerge throughout Latin America in the 1930s and 1940s. In 1934 the Uruguayan painter Joaquín TORRES-GARCÍA (1874–1949) returned to Montevideo, where he founded the Association of Constructive Art as well as his workshop school. Among the artists who studied with the constructivist master were Julio Alpuy (b. 1919), Gonzalo FONSECA (b. 1922), and Washington Barcala (b. 1920) as well as Torres-García's two sons.

A touch of the fantastic had existed in Mexican art throughout the 1920s and 1930s in the paintings of Frida KAHLO (1907–1954) and Juan O'GORMAN (1905–1980). Surrealism was introduced in Latin America after the mid-1930s. André Breton visited Mexico in 1938, and the surrealist European painters Remedios VARA (1908–1963) and Leonora Carrington (b. 1917) sought refuge there from World War II in 1942. The painters Rodríguez Lozano (1900?–1970), Julio Castellanos (1905–1947), and others who were associated with the antimuralist group of poets "Los Contemporaneos" practiced a classicism tinged with surrealist as well as homoerotic overtones. In the mid-1930s, the Argentine Juan Battle-Planas (b. 1911) exhibited his paranoiac X rays in Buenos Aires. In 1939 the Orion group emerged, with the painters Luis BARRAGÁN (1902–1988), Vicente Forte (1912–1980) and Leopoldo Presas, who had affinities with the Italian metaphysical school. Raquel FORNER (1902–1989), another Argentine painter, went through a surrealist phase before devoting herself to themes of space travel in a vivid, expressionist style.

The Cubans Wilfredo LAM (1902–1982) and Mario CARREÑO (b. 1913) had affinities with surrealism. The Guatemalan modernist Carlos MÉRIDA (1891–1984) practiced a subtle geometric abstraction with roots in Maya pictographs. The Chileans Roberto MATTA (b. 1911) and Nemesio ANTÚNEZ (b. 1918) both studied architecture but later turned to a surrealist or metaphysical abstractionist type of painting. Surrealist variations found many adherents in Chile, including Rodolfo Opazo (b. 1935), Juan Gómez Quiros (b. 1939), Ricardo Yrrárazaval (b. 1931), and Guillermo Núñez (b. 1930). In Mexico, Rufino TAMAYO (1899–1991) represented a modernist opposition to the mural movement. His synthesis of pre-Columbian and cubist forms, his use of the colors of contemporary Mexican popular culture, and his call for an apolitical art had a profound effect on the younger generation of artists.

## PLURALISM AND THE POSTWAR PERIOD

After the mid-1940s, abstract art took a firm hold, with geometric tendencies becoming more prevalent in the east and informalist ones in the west. In Argentina, the Arte Concreto-Invención movement emerged under the leadership of Tomás Maldonado (b. 1922). Informal-

*Man Contemplating the Moon.* Lithograph by Rufino Tamayo, 1955. ART MUSEUM OF THE AMERICAS, ORGANIZATION OF AMERICAN STATES.

ist abstraction had its exponents in the work of the Argentines Sarah GRILLO (*b.* 1921) and José Antonio Fernández-Muro (*b.* 1920), the Uruguayan Carlos Paez Villaró (*b.* 1923), and the Brazilian Manabu MABE (*b.* 1924).

In the 1950s, a number of new artists emerged in Central America, Cuba, and South America. In Nicaragua, Armando MORALES (*b.* 1927) painted flat black-and-white abstractions endowed with mystical meanings before turning to a figurative, more metaphysical style. In Colombia, Alejandro OBREGÓN (1920–1991) developed a style derived from Picasso, Antoní Clavé, and informalism, while Enrique GRAU (*b.* 1920) painted homoerotic images of chubby male youths. In Ecuador, Manuel Rendón (1894–1982) initiated abstract painting, attracting followers in the younger artists Aníbal Villacis (*b.* 1927) and Enrique TÁBARA (*b.* 1930). The Bolivian María Luisa PACHECO (1919–1982) conjured up jagged Andean peaks in glowing textile colors, and the Peruvian Fernando de SZYZLO (*b.* 1925) painted abstraction in luminous glazes inspired by the poetry and religion of the INCAS. In Cuba, René PORTOCARRERO (1912–1986) and Mariano (1912–1990) and Cundo (*b.* 1914) Bermúdez painted neocolonial interiors, roosters, and dancers in a decorative expressionism.

INFORMALISM, NEOFIGURATION, AND GEOMETRY
The informalist tendency spread to sculpture in the 1940s and 1950s. The Argentine Libero Badii (*b.* 1916) was very much a part of this current. In the meantime, Francisco Zuñiga (*b.* 1917), a Costa Rican residing in Mexico, depicted the Indian woman in a monumental style derived from the Mexican muralists. In Cuba, Roberto Estopiñán (*b.* 1921) brought to his work a neofigurative sensibility that had much in common with the postwar work of Marino Marini in Italy and Henry Moore in Britain.

From the late 1950s and into the 1960s, a violent neofiguration spread throughout the Spanish-speaking Americas. José Luis Cuevas (*b.* 1932), Marcello Grassman (*b.* 1925), Julio Zachrisson (*b.* 1927), Carlos Alonso (*b.* 1930), and Hermengildo Sabat (*b.* 1934) practiced forms of neofiguration exclusively through the mediums of drawing and printmaking. In Colombia, Fernando BOTERO (*b.* 1932) started painting obese figures satirizing Colombian society. Jacobo BORGES (*b.* 1931) of Venezuela worked in an expressionist manner in which vividly colored figures swirled through the pictorial space. In Argentina, Luis Felipe NOÉ (*b.* 1933), Ernesto DEIRA (1928–1986), Rómulo MACCIÓ (*b.* 1931), and Jorge de la VEGA (1930–1971) made their appearance under the collective name of "Otra Figuración." These artists specialized in a colorful expressionist drip technique that depicted faces and monstrous creatures, reminiscent of the COBRA painters.

The Mexicans Gunther GERZSO (*b.* 1915), Vicente ROJO (*b.* 1932), and Manuel FELGUEREZ (*b.* 1928) all worked abstractly throughout the 1960s, the latter two favoring hard-edged compositions. Francisco TOLEDO (*b.* 1940) followed in Tamayo's footsteps, while adding a fantastic, erotic edge to his compositions. The Guatemalan Rodolfo Abularach (*b.* 1934) turned the human eye into a cosmic icon, first in highly detailed pen-and-ink drawings and etchings and later in oils. Marcelo Bonevardi (*b.* 1929), an Argentine, embedded polished wooden constructions in flatly painted metaphysical compositions on canvas. In Colombia, variations of constructivism and geometric abstraction were to be found in the work of sculptors Ramírez Villamizar (*b.* 1923) and Edgar NEGRET (*b.* 1920) and painters Omar Rayo (*b.* 1928) and David Manzur (*b.* 1929). The latter, however, eventually returned to figuration through a reinterpretation of Renaissance themes.

Venezuela and Argentina were the major producers of optical and kinetic art. Jesús Rafael SOTO (*b.* 1923), Alejandro OTERO (1921–1991), and Carlos CRUZ DIEZ (*b.* 1923) were the leading kinetic artists in Caracas. Otero, under the influence first of Paul Cézanne and later of constructivism, produced a series of coffeepots throughout the late 1940s. In the 1950s he began color rhythms, which consist of superimposed vertical bands painted in bright Duco colors. Soto, expatriated in Paris for many years, created his delicately orchestrated "vibrations" by suspending thin wires from frames or attaching squares to thinly striped canvas or wood panels, creating a rippling effect. Later Soto produced the "penetrables," environments made of densely packed translucent nylon tubes through which people could walk. Cruz Diez, also living in Paris, executed his "physichromies" by painting along perpendicular vertical strips attached to a flat surface instead of the surface itself. Argentines and Brazilians have explored plastic, metal, light, glass, and other materials in their optical and kinetic work. The leading Argentine artists working in this area have been Rogelio Polesello (*b.* 1939), Julio Le Parc (*b.* 1938), Eduardo MAC ENTYRE (*b.* 1929), Miguel Angel Vidal (*b.* 1928), and Ary Brizzi (*b.* 1930).

In the late 1950s and throughout the 1960s Puerto Rico produced some major artists in spite of the aggressive avalanche of pop culture from the United States. Julio Rosado del Valle (*b.* 1922) was a self-taught expressionist who moved between figuration and abstraction. Luis Hernández Cruz (*b.* 1936) was an abstractionist with constructivist tendencies who produced paintings as well as sculpture. Myrna Baez (*b.* 1931) was a printmaker and painter who worked with the human figure within a landscape context, while Lorenzo HOMAR (*b.* 1913) and Rafael Tufiño (*b.* 1922) were printmakers who were devoted to a social realist aesthetic. Undoubtedly, the island's greatest artist is the portraitist Pancho Rodón (*b.* 1934), whose artistic production consisted of devastating depictions of such Latin American luminaries as Borges, Múñoz Marín, Rulfo, and Rómulo Betancourt.

Critics as diverse as Julio Payro, Luis Cardoza y Aragon, Jorge Romero Brest, José Gomez Sicre, and Marta

Traba have documented the development of the visual arts in Latin America in the twentieth century. It is true that Latin America is responsible for no original "ism" in the twentieth century. Nevertheless, thanks to its firmly held aim of maintaining connection with its communities by means of visual messages charged with meaning, it has gradually produced an image bank of real importance to the region.

PAUL F. DAMAZ, *Art in Latin American Architecture* (1963); INSTITUTO DE CULTURA HISPÁNICA, *Arte de América y España* (1963); YALE UNIVERSITY ART MUSEUM, *Art of Latin America Since Independence* (1966); WALTER ZANNINI, *História geral do arte no Brasil* (1983); DAWN ADES, *Art in Latin America* (1989); FAUSTO RAMÍRES et al., *Mexico: Splendors of Thirty Centuries* (1990).

ALEJANDRO ANREUS

### Folk Art

Folk art is produced by an individual or group working together in response to the religious, ceremonial, cultural, and artisanal traditions of the particular ethnic or tribal group to which he or she or they belong. Called *arte popular, arte folklórico,* or *artesanías* (artisan goods) in Spanish and *artesenato* in Portuguese, the genre includes religious or ceremonial art and sculpture, toys, masks, pottery, basketry, TEXTILE arts, musical instruments, decorative items, equestrian gear, jewelry, and other objects that are both artistic and folkloric in nature. The folk artist is generally untrained in academic art, and uses at-hand materials. At its best and most traditional, folk art in Latin America is spontaneous, colorful, whimsical, thought-provoking, and crafted by skilled artisans. At its worst, the work—often derided as "airport art"—is the mass-produced degeneration of traditional folk art forms, produced by impoverished, unskilled workers responding to consumer demand from outside their cultural and economic circle.

Latin American folk art is sometimes indistinguishable from fine art produced in the region. In the opinion of the Bolivian art historian Teresa Gisbert, "The borders between folk art and 'fine' art in Latin America are highly imprecise, and more than imprecise, artificial."

In the pre-Columbian era, highly skilled metallurgists, weavers, ceramicists, jewelers, lapidaries, stonemasons, muralists, and other artisans created works of timeless beauty for political and religious elites, primarily in the urban centers of MESOAMERICA and the Andes. In the homes and villages of ordinary people, less well-trained artists created objects for their own needs and those of the common folk. Although many fine examples of elite art from this period have survived to the present, little of the pre-Columbian folk art created for the masses exists today, although its influence endures. Much of this work was made of highly perishable materials, such as straw, flowers, and wax.

The arrival of Europeans in the late fifteenth century had a major impact on the folk arts of Latin America. Diseases and mistreatment at the hands of the Iberian conquerors led to the extinction of many native groups and to the irretrievable loss of much knowledge and many artistic skills. Europeans destroyed much of the art, especially that made of precious metals and objects they considered idolatrous.

On the positive side, however, Europeans introduced new materials and technologies into the Americas. Artists were quick to incorporate such novelties as glass, sheep's wool, iron, cowhide, canvas, linen, paper, and silk into their art. Forged iron and steel tools meant improved techniques for working metal, wood, leather, and stone. The pottery wheel and glazing techniques revolutionized ceramic art. Domestic animals, the wheel, oceangoing vessels, written languages, and other imports from Europe led to better communication and transportation, as well as advances in mining, farming, marketing, and supply. The galleon trade between Acapulco and Manila, which began in 1570 and ended with Mexican Independence from Spain in 1821, brought additional new materials and artistic influences to the Americas from the Orient. The galleons, which also called at ports such as Lima and San Salvador de Bahia, introduced Latin America to such Asian influences as glazing techniques and forms in ceramics: silk and metallic threads in textile arts; incrustation of mother-of-pearl and tortoise shell in furniture; ivory carving for religious imagery; and lacquer techniques. Black slaves from Africa brought to many parts of Latin America other artistic techniques and cultural heritages. Their skills at working gold, silver and iron, as well as their textile art traditions, had a lasting impact on popular arts in those regions, where, even during slavery, blacks were allowed to practice their ancient arts. Within a short period after contact with Europe, Latin American folk art, while still an indigenous expression in most regions of the Americas, demonstrated nevertheless the impact of innovations and influences from Europe, Asia, and Africa.

As indentured servants, slaves, or apprentices, native and mestizo craftsmen learned new skills from master European craftsmen. Catholic clergy were also instrumental in instructing natives. They fostered and preserved the arts, although they often destroyed work they believed to be idolatrous. A select few pupils were taught at formal arts-and-crafts schools such as San José de los Naturales, founded in Mexico City by Pedro de GANTE about 1526; and the Franciscans' Colegio de San Andrés, founded in Quito in 1552.

During the three centuries of colonial rule, however, native artisans and their output were subjected to strict regulations and controls. Although Europeans appreciated native artistry, they resented the prestige that artisans enjoyed, and feared competition from them. For example, although natives were highly skilled at working metals, in 1550 Philip II of Spain forbade them to possess or work precious metals. Artisans also were not allowed to incorporate native constructs and designs in their work. In the isolated regions of the Americas and in private, however, indigenous people, mestizos, and blacks conserved ancient folk art traditions, passing cultural knowledge and skills from parents to children.

When most parts of Latin America declared their independence from Spain and Portugal in the first quarter of the nineteenth century, the folk arts in the new nations experienced an exuberant revival. Liberated from servitude to the Iberians, the people had more freedom to create objects for their own pleasure and use. Pre-Columbian themes, symbols and flags of the new nations, local flora and fauna, and other conceits previously forbidden by the Iberians appeared in religious and ceremonial art, silver, jewelry, equestrian gear, toys, ceramics, household goods, public art, clothing, textile arts, architecture, and popular painting. The trend continued throughout the political chaos of the nineteenth century, until the twentieth century, when the pervasiveness of a cash economy made increasing demands on people's time and energies. "Folk art occupies the brief interlude between court taste and commercial taste," wrote George Kubler. In those regions of the Americas where barter economies, poverty, and cultural conservatism still prevail, the traditional folk art phenomenon endures, primarily in the Andean highlands, rural Northeastern Brazil, and the Indian regions of Mexico, Guatemala, Panama, and the Amazon basin.

In the mid-twentieth century, when air travel, affluence, and consumerism began to bring tens of thousands of visitors from the Northern Hemisphere to all parts of Latin America, the folk arts underwent a new mutation. Artists who had produced works only for their own use and enjoyment, or for that of their traditional clientele, responded to the new market created by outsiders eager to purchase their work. Increasingly, upper- and middle-class Latin Americans, as well as foreigners, became interested in collecting folk art. The casual output of part-time artists and family workshops was rapidly supplanted by cottage industries producing folk art goods on a near industrial scale and to importers' specifications. By the late 1960s the employment of thousands of workers in the production and exportation of folk art from Latin America had become a burgeoning part of the economies of nearly all countries in the region.

The work itself was forever changed. Some of the folk artists, who traditionally work in anonymity, became famous personalities, showing their work in galleries and museums around the world and sharing art critics' columns with artists working in academic modes. The lines between folk art and fine art were blurred. Yet in the villages, alleys, markets, and workshops of Latin America, anonymous folk artists still hover over their workbenches, spontaneously fashioning ordinary materials into objects of delight and beauty, in the exercise of ages-old traditions and the enduring human need for artistic expression.

GEORGE KUBLER and MARTIN SORIA, *Art and Architecture in Spain and Portugal and Their American Dominions, 1500 to 1800* (1959); GEORGE MC CLELLAND FOSTER, *Culture and Conquest:* *America's Spanish Heritage* (1960); LILLY DE JONGH OSBORNE, *Indian Crafts of Guatemala and El Salvador* (1965); ELIZABETH BOYD, *Popular Arts of Spanish New Mexico* (1974); NELSON H. H. GRABURN, ed., *Ethnic and Tourist Arts: Cultural Expressions from the Fourth World* (1976); FRANCISCO STATSNY, *Los artes populares del Perú* (1979); AUGUST PANYELLA, *Folk Art of the Americas* (1981); and *Brazil: Arte do Noreste/Art of the Northeast* (1985); HENRY GLASSIE, *The Spirit of Folk Art: The Girard Collection at the Museum of International Folk Art* (1989); CHLOË SAYER, *Arts and Crafts of Mexico* (1990); MARTHA J. EGAN, *Milagros: Votive Offerings from the Americas* (1991); GLORIA FRASER GIFFORDS, *Mexican Folk Retablos* (rev. ed. 1992); MARION OETTINGER, *The Folk Art of Latin America: Visiones del Pueblo* (1992); LILIANA VILLEGAS and BENJAMIN VILLEGAS, *Artefactos: Colombian Crafts from the Andes to the Amazon* (1992).

MARTHA J. EGAN

*See also* **Manila Galleon; Slavery.**

**ARTIGAS,** department in northwestern Uruguay, 4,689 square miles in area with 69,200 inhabitants. Founded in 1852 on the bases of the settlement of San Eugenio, the city of Artigas has 35,120 inhabitants (1985). Located on the Quaraí River, it is the provincial capital. The region produces beef, hides, wool, and wheat, and entertains active trade exchanges with neighboring Brazil.

CÉSAR N. CAVIEDES

**ARTIGAS, JOSÉ GERVASIO** (*b.* 19 June 1764; *d.* 23 September 1850), Uruguayan caudillo and leader of the independence movement. Born into a prominent landowning family, Artigas received his early education in a school run by Franciscan friars in Montevideo. In his youth he developed a love for the common people and a firsthand practical knowledge of the country's resources by participating in the primary economic activity of the region—the roundup of unmarked cattle and the illegal sale of hides to Portuguese and British commercial agents. In 1799 he was appointed an official of the BLANDENGUES, a militia regiment centered in Montevideo, which was charged with protecting rural settlers against Indian raids and countering the smuggling activities of the Portuguese in present-day Brazil.

Artigas was an early enthusiast of the independence movement against the Spanish viceregal government first announced in Buenos Aires in 1810. The following year, as head of the rural militia in the BANDA ORIENTAL (literally, "East Bank," or today's Uruguay), he commanded a brilliant military triumph in Las Piedras (18 May 1811). Months later, he refused to abide by the armistice negotiated by the elitist Ruling Committee in Buenos Aires, which would have returned his province to the Spanish. His army's march into exile along the banks of the Ayuí River in Entre Ríos—referred to as El Exodo Oriental (the Exodus of the Orientals)—was joined by nearly 16,000 people who were largely from the lower classes. In no other region of the insurgent

José Gervasio Artigas. ORGANIZATION OF AMERICAN STATES.

provinces was the emancipation struggle waged with such a high degree of popular adhesion. Henceforth, Artigas's distrust of *porteño* (Buenos Aires) priorities would play a decisive role in his actions.

For the next decade, Artigas defended the territorial integrity of the Banda Oriental against military invasions and economic incursions by the Spanish, Portuguese, and British. Moreover, by providing firm leadership in the resistance to the centralist ambitions of Buenos Aires, he emerged as a defender of the confederation of provinces that included Entre Ríos, Córdoba, Corrientes, and Santa Fe. Styling himself the "Protector of Free Peoples," he issued a number of farsighted decrees from his military encampment at Purificación, near present-day Paysandú. Artigas's "Instrucciones del Año XIII," modeled upon the legal principles of the United States, set forth the tenets of a federal constitution to unite the provinces on an equal basis. His "Reglamento provisorio para el fomento de la campaña y seguridad de sus hacendados" (1815) aimed at subdividing large landholdings in order to create economic opportunity for the large class of "dispossessed" creoles, mestizos, zambos, and Indians, and at accelerating the resettlement of rural areas in order to restore regional prosperity. These measures, in addition

to the priority he gave to the defense of Banda Oriental territory at the expense of the struggle in the north against Spanish royalist forces, earned him the wrath of Buenos Aires's Dictatorial Party. Artigas's Federalist League, in contrast with the Buenos Aires leadership, demanded assemblies and congresses, not kings; a democratic order with the participation of the rural masses rather than a patrician society governed by an urban elite; and protection for local agriculture, industries, and arts rather than the domination of American markets by European trading companies.

Simultaneous with Artigas's defense of Banda Oriental autonomy was his objective of establishing a loose confederation uniting all the provinces of the former viceroyalty. Between 1814 and 1820 there was continual conflict in the region between the armies commanded by the Buenos Aires elite and what they called the "Anarchists of the Littoral"—that is, the caudillos of the provinces, who supported Artigas. On several occasions Artigas himself fought shoulder to shoulder with the plebeian soldiers of Santa Fe and Entre Ríos in order to repel armies sent from Buenos Aires. He also organized the region's defense against Portuguese invasions from the east. In 1816 his vastly outnumbered forces suffered defeats in San Borja, Ibiracoí, Carrumbé, India Muerta, Arapey, Arroyo Catalán, and Aguapey, which led to the Portuguese occupation of Montevideo in January 1817.

Approaching the new decade, Artigas continued his struggle against the Portuguese and the Spanish despite his troops' lack of arms and the decimation of his fighting ranks. Conflict and dislocation had claimed the lives of half of the region's 50,000 inhabitants. His program of land confiscations and levies fueled local resistance. In 1819 Artigas rejected the constitution promulgated by Buenos Aires on account of its monarchist orientation and the central role ascribed to that city for governance of the region. In January 1820, his army of 3,000 troops suffered heavy losses to Portuguese troops in the battle of Tacuarembó. Fructuoso RIVERA (later Uruguayan president), until then a trusted lieutenant, deserted his ranks weeks later by signing an armistice with the Portuguese. In the battle of CEPEDA in February 1820, Artigas's lieutenants, Pedro Campbell (of Irish ancestry), Francisco RAMÍREZ, and Estanislao LÓPEZ (strongmen of Entre Ríos and Santa Fe) inflicted heavy losses on the Buenos Aires army led by José RONDEAU, and ended for the time any pretense of *porteño* domination over the united provinces. The Treaty of PILAR, as negotiated by López and Ramírez with the leaders of Buenos Aires, created an important legal precedent for Argentina's future reconstruction according to federalist principles. Yet the intractable Artigas, who had no part in the negotiations, angrily accused Ramírez of treason for having made a pact with the enemy.

Artigas's military decline came rapidly. He led an army of 2,500—half of whom were mission Indians—in a series of inconclusive skirmishes against Ramírez, who then pulverized Artigas's troops in the battle of Avalos,

Corrientes, in 1820. Artigas fled to exile in Paraguay, where the dictator Dr. José Gaspar Rodríguez de FRANCIA kept him virtually a prisoner. Confined and in humble circumstances, Artigas lived in obscurity until his death thirty years later.

Nineteenth-century Argentine historians—most notably Manuel BELGRANO, Bartolomé MITRE, Vicente Fidel LOPEZ, and Domingo F. SARMIENTO—treated the legacy of Artigas in most disfavorable terms: he represented in their eyes the paradigmatic example of a despotic caudillo at the head of "barbarous" rural masses who were intent upon destroying urban civilization. However, beginning in the 1880s, revisionist Uruguayan writers began propagating a benevolent image of Artigas as "father of the country," a view that prevails to this day.

BARTOLOMÉ MITRE, Historia de Belgrano y de la Independencia Argentina, 2 vols. (1858–1859); EDUARDO ACEVEDO, José Artigas: Su obra civica, alegato historico, 3 vols. (1950); JOHN STREET, Artigas and the Emancipation of Uruguay (1959); HUGO D. BARBAGELATA, Artigas y la Revolución Americana (n.d.); VICENTE FIDEL LÓPEZ, "Appendix," in Historia de la República Argentina, vol. 4 (1883–1893; repr. 1964); WASHINGTON REYES ABADIE, OSCAR H. BRUSCHERA, and TABARÉ MELOGNO, Artigas: Su significación en la revolución y en el proceso institucional iberoamericano (1966); ALBERTO ZUM FELDE, Proceso histórico del Uruguay (Montevideo; 1987).

WILLIAM H. KATRA

See also **United Provinces of the Río de la Plata.**

**ARUBA,** an island in the southern Caribbean Sea, sixteen miles north of Venezuela, which forms with CURAÇAO and Bonaire the Dutch LEEWARD ISLANDS. Aruba was part of the federation of the Netherlands Antilles until 1986, when it became a self-governing country within the kingdom of the Netherlands. The island, famous for its magnificent beaches, has a tropical climate with a very low rainfall. It has an area of 69 square miles and a population of 64,052 (1991). In 1499 the Spanish explorer Alonso de OJEDA discovered Aruba, as well as CURAÇAO, and claimed it for Spain. When Johannes van Walbeeck seized Curaçao for the Netherlands in 1634, he also took possession of Aruba. Except for a few years early in the nineteenth century when it was occupied by the British, the island was until 1954 part of the Dutch colonial realm in the Caribbean, which was governed from Willemstad in Curaçao.

The island was too arid for agricultural development, and the DUTCH WEST INDIA COMPANY, which did not want it developed as a trading center, discouraged settlement of the island in the seventeenth and eighteenth centuries. Until the nineteenth century, the native Arawak Indians were the majority of the island's small population. When the British returned Aruba to the Dutch in 1816, the population was under 2,000. Thereafter, immigrants came from the other Leeward Islands to settle. Through intermarriage, the Indians lost their separate identity. Papiamento and Dutch are the principal languages.

Raising horses and sheep was the major occupation in the early years. In 1824 gold was discovered, and mining of this precious metal was of some importance for the rest of the century. The decision of the U.S. Standard Oil Company (now Exxon) to build refineries for its Venezuelan crude oil at St. Nicholaas on Aruba in 1929 brought quick economic development of the island. Laborers came from the other islands, boosting Aruba's population. The oil industry also gave the island a relatively high standard of living for the Caribbean. When the Netherlands Antilles became a self-governing federation of islands in 1954, Aruba participated in the government, situated in Curaçao, but the people of Aruba felt dominated by Curaçao. In 1971 the Electoral Movement of the People (MEP) was founded under the leadership of Gilberto (Betico) Croes, and it campaigned for severing all ties with Curaçao.

In 1983 the government of the Netherlands and of the Netherlands Antilles agreed to give Aruba a separate status in 1986, with the provision that it would become completely independent by 1996. In 1986 Aruba obtained its new status. It now has its own legislature, the Staten, and an executive that is formed by a cabinet under the leadership of a prime minister. The first prime minister was Henny Eman, leader of the Aruban Peoples Party (AVP), Betico Croes and his MEP having lost control of the government. In 1984 Exxon decided to close its oil refinery, thus creating for Aruba a severe economic depression. The island's economy recovered rather swiftly after 1988, primarily due to the sharp increase in tourism.

The MEP, under the new leadership of Nelson Oduber, regained its popularity. Oduber was able to form a coalition government in 1989 and replaced Eman as prime minister. The MEP did not favor complete independence and contemplated holding a referendum on this issue.

VERA M. GREEN, Migrants in Aruba: Interethnic Integration (1974); CORNELIUS GOSLINGA, A Short History of the Netherlands Antilles and Surinam (1979).

ALBERT GASTMANN

**ARZÁNS ORSÚA Y VELA, BARTOLOMÉ** (b. 1676; d. January 1736), Bolivian writer and historian. Born in Potosí of Spanish parents, Arzáns dedicated his life to the writing of his multivolume Historia de la villa imperial de Potosí, the most complex and fascinating text of the colonial period in Bolivia. Arzáns did not completely finish the work; his son Diego wrote the final 8 of its 322 chapters. The manuscript was lost for many years, and the first edition was not published until 1965.

In this work, Arzáns attempts to give a complete and detailed history of POTOSÍ, one of the most prosperous cities of the New World during the sixteenth and seventeenth centuries. It was founded in 1545 next to the

Mountain of Potosí, a rich silver mining site. In order to capture and convey the splendor and greatness of the city, Arzáns includes historical data, legends, short stories, Indian myths, descriptions of daily events, and details about various aspects of life in the city. The book is an exuberant and baroque depiction of Potosí, with history and fiction intertwined. The *Historia* is crucial to an understanding of Bolivia because of the historical, literary, and ideological information it provides; it can be seen to prefigure the nationalism in the country.

MARIO CHACÓN TORRES, *Documentos en torno a Bartolomé Arzáns Orsúa y Vela* (1960); LEWIS HANKE and GUNNAR MENDOZA, Introduction to *Historia de la villa imperial de Potosí*, 3 vols. (1965); LEONARDO GARCÍA PABÓN, *Espacio andino, escritura colonial y pensamiento andino: La historia de Potosí en la narrativa de Bartolomé Arzáns* (Ph.D. diss., University of Minnesota, 1990).

LEONARDO GARCÍA PABÓN

**ARZE, JOSÉ ANTONIO** (*b.* 13 January 1904; *d.* 23 August 1955), Bolivian intellectual and politician. Born in Cochabamba, Arze was the most influential Marxist intellectual and the leading leftist politician in Bolivia during the 1940s. In 1928 he helped found the National Student Federation (FUB), which demanded university reforms on the Argentine model. As the presidental candidate of the FUB in 1940, Arze received almost a fifth of the total vote. Thereafter, he was instrumental in organizing the first effective national leftist party, the Party of the Revolutionary Left (PIR), which rivaled in size and influence the National Revolutionary Movement (MNR) among the opposition parties of the 1940s. Arze again became a presidential candidate in 1951. He was a professor of sociology at the University of San Francisco Xavier in Sucre and founder of the Institute of Bolivian Sociology and its journal, the *Revista del Instituto de Sociología Boliviana*. The author of numerous books and translator of Louis Baudin and Georges Rouma, Arze influenced several generations of leftist politicians in Bolivia.

An excellent introduction to Arze and his times is HERBERT S. KLEIN, *Parities and Political Change in Bolivia: 1880–1952* (1969). Short summaries of Arze's life are available in GUILLERMO FRANCOVICH, *El pensamiento boliviano en el siglo XX* (1956), pp. 108–110, and VALENTÍN ABECIA BALDIVIESO, *Historiografía boliviana*, 2d ed. (1973), pp. 451–453.

ERICK D. LANGER

See also **Bolivia: Political Parties.**

**ASADO.** Huge herds of wild cattle roamed much of the pampa until the mid-nineteenth century. Inhabitants of the Río de la Plata, especially the equestrian GAUCHO, developed a fondness for beef, especially *asado*, which is roasted beef (or lamb or goat). The meat, often a side of ribs, is skewered on a metal frame called an *asador* and is roasted by placing it next to a slow-burning fire. Gauchos favored cooking *asado* with the wood of the que-

bracho tree because it smokes very little. *Asado*, accompanied by maté tea, formed the basis of the gaucho diet. The technique is still used today.

FÉLIX COLUCCIO, *Diccionario folklórico argentino*, vol. 1 (1964), pp. 27–28; RICHARD W. SLATTA, *Gauchos and the Vanishing Frontier* (1983), p. 76.

RICHARD W. SLATTA

**ASCASUBI, HILARIO** (*b.* 14 January 1807; *d.* 17 November 1875), Argentine poet, journalist, politician, and entrepreneur. His adventurous adolescence took him through Portugal, France, England, and Chile. In 1824 he reorganized an old printing shop in the provincial city of Salta, renaming it Imprenta de la Patria, and began publishing the *Revista de Salta*. Thus began his journalistic career, which he never abandoned. In 1825 Ascasubi began a second career, this time in the army fighting the *caudillaje* (bossism). As a lieutenant he was in charge of recruiting and tasted defeat in two battles. Under General Juan LAVALLE, the hero of the fight against the tyrant Juan Manuel de ROSAS, Ascasubi became captain. A prisoner during 1831–1833 in a pontoon in Buenos Aires, he escaped to Montevideo and set up a bakery, becoming rich enough to help Lavalle and the Argentine refugees. At the same time, he managed to continue pursuing his poetic interests, achieving fame with this ''gauchescos'' *trovos* (popular ballads) published later under the title *Paulino Lucero* (1872).

Ascasubi joined the armies successfully fighting the Rosas dictatorship and, as a lieutenant colonel in the ensuing period (1843–1852), performed various jobs while continuing his writing. From 1853 to 1859 he published *Aniceto el Gallo, Gaceta Joco-Tristona y Gauchi-Patriótica* (Aniceto the Rooster, Humorous-Sad and Gauchi-Patriotic Gazette). Although retired, Ascasubi was sent to France in 1860 to recruit for the Argentine army. In Paris he finished and published his main work, the lengthy *Santos Vega, o Los mellizos de La Flor* (1872), a narrative poem that depicts the PAMPA, the idiosyncrasies of its inhabitants and their customs, the intimate life within the ESTANCIA, and the mythological figure of the PAYADOR (singer).

Absorbed by the political events in his country, Ascasubi was not only a chronicler, but an exceedingly active participant. As a writer, he transmitted the everyday happenings, the anecdotes that humanize and draw us near to historical events. As a publisher, he established a number of important newspapers. As a businessman, he brought gas service to Buenos Aires, extended the railroad tracks, and helped erect the TEATRO COLÓN (1857).

MANUEL MUJICA LÁINEZ, *Vidas de El Gallo y el Pollo* (1966); DAVID LAGMANOVICH, ''Tres cautivas: Echeverría, Ascasubi, Hernández,'' in *Chasqui* 8, no. 3 (1979); 24–33.

ANGELA B. DELLEPIANE

See also **Gauchesca Literature.**

**ASIANS IN LATIN AMERICA.** In 1990 Alberto FUJI-MORI, son of Japanese immigrants, became president of Peru. His election underscores the fact that not only Europeans, but Asians as well, have immigrated in significant numbers to Latin America and contributed to the social, cultural, economic, and political development of the region. Every Latin American country has received some Asian immigrants in the nineteenth and twentieth centuries.

As early as the seventeenth century, *chinos de manila* were known in Mexico City, Cuba, and other parts of Spanish America, the result of the MANILA GALLEON trade between Mexico and the Philippines. However, organized, large-scale Asian immigration to Latin America, consisting almost exclusively of Chinese and Japanese, did not take place until the mid-nineteenth century. Most of the Chinese went to Cuba, Peru, Mexico, and parts of Central America, while the Japanese settled largely in Peru and Brazil, and a much smaller number in Bolivia. Whether forced or free, large-scale Asian movement to Latin America was part of the international labor migration of the late nineteenth and early twentieth centuries in the wake of the worldwide development of capitalism and imperialism, and specifically of the decline of slavery in Latin America.

The bulk of the early Chinese and Japanese immigrants worked under harsh agricultural labor conditions, gradually making the transition to independent agricultural or urban commercial activities. The relative prosperity experienced by Asian communities in the early twentieth century resulted in anti-Asian violence and persecution in all these countries, with the worst being the expulsion of the Chinese from northern Mexico during the Great Depression and the deportation and incarceration in the United States of Japanese Peruvians during World War II.

THE CHINESE IN PERU, CUBA, AND MEXICO

From 1847 to 1874 as many as 225,000 Chinese "coolies," under eight-year contracts, almost all male, were sent to Cuba and Peru, with 80 percent or more destined for the sugar plantations. In Cuba, then still a Spanish colony, the Chinese worked alongside African slaves, the chief source of plantation labor, while in Peru, where slavery was abolished in 1854, Chinese coolies supplanted black slaves. Scholars have viewed *la trata amarilla* (the yellow trade) as both a transition from slave to free labor and, even more, a modified form of slavery. Not disputed is the indispensability of Chinese labor to the maintenance of the plantation-based economies of both societies.

In Peru several thousand coolies also helped build the Andean railroad and worked in the offshore GUANO mines south of Lima. In the 1870s escaped coolies and free Chinese were among the pioneers who penetrated the Peruvian Amazon, building settlements, introducing trade activities and small-scale manufacturing, and cultivating rice, beans, sugar, and other crops.

In Cuba a small number in the nineteenth century were also employed in domestic service, cigarette factories, and other small manufacturing, as well as by the colonial government in large public-works projects. In the 1860s *chinos mambises* (Chinese freedom fighters) also joined fellow slaves and free blacks in the first armed struggle to overthrow Spanish colonial rule. As men who were neither slave nor free, neither black nor white, the Chinese coolies helped break down the racialist ideology of Cuba's plantation system.

While free Chinese migrants continued to enter Cuba and Peru in the first decades of the twentieth century, the numbers were not large, and both governments sought to limit further Chinese immigration in the face of local protest against perceived Chinese "excesses" in commercial activities. The gender imbalance from the coolie period was never sufficiently redressed, and subsequent generations were increasingly mestizoized. At the end of the twentieth century, Chinese Peruvians remained a visible minority, their presence captured by the ubiquitous *chifas* (Chinese restaurants). Since the CUBAN REVOLUTION of 1959, a large number of Chinese Cubans have left the island as part of the massive exodus of the Cuban middle class.

Free Chinese immigrants began entering Mexico at exactly the same time that the United States enacted Chinese exclusion and Porfirio DÍAZ took power in Mexico and promoted immigration along with development, particularly of the frontier region between northern Mexico and the United States. Instead of assuming laboring jobs in the mines and railroads, which were filled by Mexicans, the Chinese entered the new economic niche of local commerce and became truck farmers, small manufacturers, and, especially, small shopkeepers, forming in effect a ubiquitous petite bourgeoisie. They prospered even through the turmoil of the MEXICAN REVOLUTION, in part by provisioning the various revolutionary armies.

Numbering over 24,000, the Chinese had become the largest immigrant community in Mexico by 1927. Besides large colonies in Sonora and Baja California Norte, they had also settled in every state and territory except Baja California Sur and Tlaxcala. Not surprisingly, however, their relative success inevitably generated resentment and sporadic persecution, which culminated in 1929–1930 with the expulsion of the large Chinese colony of Sonora (state bordering Arizona) and subsequent nationalization of their businesses, spelling the decline of the Chinese throughout Mexico.

THE JAPANESE IN PERU AND BRAZIL

Japanese immigration to Peru and Brazil began in 1899 and 1908, respectively, and continued into the 1970s, with the high point (over 60 percent of the total) during the interwar decades of the 1920s and 1930s. Early Japanese immigration to Latin America resembled that of the Chinese in that the vast majority went as contract laborers, but the patterns soon diverged, with three distinguishing features. First, the Japanese contracts were of shorter duration, and the Japanese made a relatively quick transition from plantation labor to independent farming. Second, from the beginning the Japanese government acted to control and regulate migration through licensing immigration companies and protecting the migrants' rights and interests once overseas, including subsidizing immigrant colonization activities. Third, while men still outnumbered women, the Japanese government encouraged the migration of women, ensuring in turn the integrity of migrant families, the formation of new families, and the continuity of Japanese traditions in the adopted homelands.

By 1924 most of the Japanese in Peru had left the plantations for independent farming or for Lima and other cities and towns throughout the country, where they opened up a variety of small businesses in the service and food sectors. Large numbers of free immigrants continued to arrive until after the attack on Pearl Harbor in 1941. During the war, under pressure from the United States, a willing Peruvian government deported 1,429 Japanese citizens and residents to concentration camps in the United States, while confiscating

Japanese immigrant man with indigenous Peruvian wife. INSTITUTO AUDIO-VISUAL INKA, CUSCO, PERU.

Japanese-owned property and nationalizing Japanese businesses.

The Japanese community of Peru managed to recover from this act of infamy and to grow in the postwar years. As the largest immigrant community in Peru, they numbered 32,002 in 1966, almost evenly divided between men and women, with more than half living in Lima and the vast majority of them second, third, or fourth generation. Through reproduction and some continual immigration, the population had grown to over 50,000 by the early 1970s and has remained stable.

Japanese immigration to Brazil represents the largest and longest continuous flow of people from Asia to Latin America: a total of 237,466 migrated between 1908 and 1961. By the late 1970s the Japanese Brazilian population had grown to over 700,000 (three-quarters Brazilian-born), making it the largest Japanese community outside Japan and the most prosperous and successful Asian immigrant community in Latin America.

Always heavily concentrated in São Paulo city and state (90 percent in the late twentieth century), Japanese immigrants have made significant contributions to both the agricultural (rice, cotton, vegetables, and especially coffee) and, more recently, the industrial-commercial (manufacturing, shopkeeping, international trade) development of the country. They were also instrumental in the early colonization of the vast Amazon region. Although in the immediate postwar years the majority of Japanese Brazilians were a rural middle-class of small and medium landowners—having won the all-important concession to own and lease land—living in hundreds of Japanese settlements, they have become since the 1960s a highly educated, urban middle-class, active in Brazilian economic and political life.

By the late twentieth century the once prominent Chinese immigrant communities of Latin America had declined significantly, the result of absorption into the larger society by miscegenation or assimilation or departure by voluntary exodus or expulsion. In contrast, Japanese immigrants and their descendants in Brazil and Peru continued to grow in size and prominence, retaining their distinctive identity while also increasingly integrating into the national life.

ANITA BRADLEY, *Trans-Pacific Relations of Latin America* (1942); WATT STEWART, *Chinese Bondage in Peru* (1951); C. HARVEY GARDINER, *The Japanese and Peru, 1873–1973* (1975); DENISE HELLY, *Idéologie et ethnicité: Les chinois Macao à Cuba, 1847–1886* (1979); ROBERT J. SMITH, "The Ethnic Japanese in Brazil," in *Journal of Japanese Studies* 5, no. 1 (1979): 53–70; JAMES L. TIGNER, "Japanese Immigration into Latin America," in *Journal of Inter-American Studies and World Affairs* 23 (November 1981): 457–482; EVELYN HU-DEHART, "Coolies, Shopkeepers, Pioneers: The Chinese of Mexico and Peru (1849–1930)," in *Amerasia Journal* 15, no. 2 (1989): 91–116.

EVELYN HU-DEHART

*See also* **Mestizo.**

**ASIENTO.** The *asiento* was a contract granted by the Spanish crown to an individual or company allowing the holder exclusive rights in the SLAVE TRADE with Spain's American colonies; it constituted the principal legal means of supplying slaves to Spanish America. These monopolistic arrangements specified the number of *piezas de Indias* (standard slave units, each *pieza* being equivalent to a prime male slave) to be delivered annually, ports of entry, and lump sums and head taxes to be paid to the Spanish monarchy. The *asientistas,* holders of the *asiento,* rarely provided their full complement of *piezas de Indias* so that contraband trade in slaves and other goods flourished, often with the complicity of *asientistas* and their agents.

The *asiento* apparently emerged in the 1590s, although similar contracts date from the early 1500s. The Portuguese dominated the *asiento* until Portugal's assertion of independence in 1640 undermined the arrangements. Spain refused to offer commercial rights to "rebels," "heretics," or enemies—categories that seemed, in the mid 1600s, to encompass all possible contractual partners. Not until 1662 did the Spanish, striving to boost royal revenues, revive the *asiento.*

Because Spain lacked adequate commercial and maritime resources and access to the African coast, foreigners continued to dominate the trade. European powers so coveted the contract as an opportunity to penetrate the commerce of the Spanish empire, that the *asiento,* its actual fiscal importance greatly exaggerated, became an instrument of foreign policy and diplomacy. The contract fell to the Dutch in 1675, to the Portuguese in 1694, to the French in 1701, and, finally, to the English in the Peace of Utrecht (1713) as a spoil of war. The Anglo-Spanish agreement survived until 1750, but the monopolistic character of the *asiento* slowly passed into eclipse, and Spain abrogated the system in 1789.

COLIN PALMER, *Human Cargoes: The British Slave Trade to Spanish America, 1700–1739* (1981); JAMES A. RAWLEY, *The Transatlantic Slave Trade* (1981).

CARA SHELLY

**ASOCIACIÓN CRISTIANA FEMENINA (YWCA),** organization founded (London, 1855; United States, 1858; World YWCA, 1894) for the "temporal, moral, and religious welfare of young women who are dependent on their own exertions for support," with affiliates appearing throughout Latin America in the 1890s. Resident "Yankee teachers" and Englishwomen established a branch in Buenos Aires in 1896; the Mexican YWCA was founded by social reformer María Elena Ramírez. The YWCAs offered temporary housing for women travelers, aid to immigrant women and girls, and recreational and educational programs for young working women. The YWCAs were centers for the discussion of feminist ideas on secular (or progressive Protestant) education, woman suffrage, abolition of prostitution and the white slave trade, and health care and civil rights for women.

MARIFRAN CARLSON, *¡Feminismo! The Woman's Movement in Argentina from Its Beginnings to Eva Perón* (1988); WARD M. MORTON, *Woman Suffrage in Mexico* (1962).

FRANCESCA MILLER

**ASOCIACIÓN DE MAYO,** an Argentine literary group of the early nineteenth century. Following the 1810 separation from Napoleonic Spain and the May 1819 declaration of the Argentine Republic and in the context of the civil strife that led to the tyranny of Juan Manuel de ROSAS in 1835, Buenos Aires was fertile ground for an array of social, cultural, and literary activities inspired by French romanticism. The principal reference point for these activities was the Generation of 1837, its principal spokesperson was Esteban ECHEVERRÍA (1809–1851), and one of its major groups was the Asociación de Mayo. The French influence on figures like Echeverría, Juan María Gutiérrez (1809–1878), and Juan Bautista ALBERDI (1810–1884)—all prominent names in Argentine literary history—as well as on a first generation of students at the Universidad de Buenos Aires, which the country's first president, Bernardino de RIVADAVIA (elected 1826), had recently established, was evident in the fact that the Asociación's members had originally met between 1835 and 1837 in the salon of the wife of the French consul. In 1837, the group began to meet in the Librería Argentina de Marcos Sastre, where, as the Salón Literario, they pursued their reading and discussion of French cultural texts. It was at Echeverría's suggestion that in 1838 they began to identify themselves under the banner of Joven Argentina or the Asociación de Mayo, both denominations underscoring their commitment to considerations of foundational national identity in conformance with romantic ideological currents that extended beyond a strictly French base. (France was already an organized nation state; thus, the efforts at national sociocultural unity of a country such as Italy offered perhaps more precise reference points for these Argentine literati.) After considerable, if frustrated, efforts to influence the course of public and political events—Echeverría's 1846 *Dogma socialista* is the key synthetic document here—the exile imposed in 1839 by the defeat of Juan LAVALLE (1797–1841) and the confirmation of Rosas's dictatorial power disbanded the group definitively.

JUAN ANTONIO SOLARI, *Asociación de Mayo y dogma socialista* (1937); ANTONIO JUAN BUCICH, *Esteban Echeverría y su tiempo* (1938); *Antecedentes de la Asociación de Mayo, 1837–1937* (1939); RODOLFO A. BORELLO, "Mayo: Literatura y realidad," in *Universidad* [Santa Fe], no. 64 (1965): 175–206.

DAVID WILLIAM FOSTER

**ASPERO,** one of the largest known Cotton Preceramic Period settlements in Peru. Radiocarbon dates place the peak occupation between 3000 B.C. and 2500 B.C. Aspero is located just north of the floodplain of the Supe River on the Pacific coast of Peru. The site is about 5,350,000–7,150,000 cubic feet of ashy midden covering thirty acres. It has at least fourteen corporate labor platform mounds, the largest about 115 feet wide, 165 feet long, and 33 feet high.

The mounds are layers of rooms that were partially demolished and filled in to form an elevated base for new rooms. The rooms were not domestic but rather appear to have been used for ritual activity. Some were decorated with colored paint, clay friezes, and wall niches. In the larger mounds, the rooms were approached from a central stairway and were hierarchically arranged, that is, access to one was through another, with the inner rooms the most highly decorated.

Artifacts included twined cotton and bast fiber textiles, bags, and nets; reed baskets; gourd bowls; pecked-and-ground stone tools and bowls; carved wood, bone, and shell ornaments; and unbaked clay human figurines. Most of these figurines represented females, some pregnant. All but one were found in a cache sealed between two floors in one of the large mounds, where they appear to have been a symbolic dedicatory burial.

The subsistence economy was mixed, with the primary marine food sources—mainly small fish and shellfish—supplemented with fruits, peppers, legumes, and tubers such as achira (*Canna edulis*). While the beans, peppers, tubers, and some fruits were cultivated, most agriculture was directed toward producing raw materials for textiles (cotton) and containers (gourds). Maize was probably present in the latest levels, but it clearly was not an important food source.

MICHAEL E. MOSELEY and GORDON R. WILLEY, "Aspero, Peru: A Reexamination of the Site and Its Implications," in *American Antiquity* 38 (1973): 452–468; ROBERT A. FELDMAN, "Preceramic Corporate Architecture: Evidence for the Development of Non-Egalitarian Social Systems in Peru," in *Early Ceremonial Architecture in the Andes*, edited by C. B. Donnan (1985); ROBERT A. FELDMAN, "Preceramic Unbaked Clay Figurines from Aspero, Peru," in *The New World Figurine Project*, edited by Terry Stocker (1991).

ROBERT A. FELDMAN

*See also* **Archaeology.**

**ASPÍLLAGA FAMILY,** Peruvian plantation owners. The matriarch of the family, Catalina Ferrebú de Aspíllaga, migrated to Lima from Chile in the 1820s. Sons Ramón (d. 1875) and Antonio went into the family's transport business, which operated between Lima and Callao. As partners of financier Julián Zaracondegui, they purchased a large property on the northern coast, Hacienda Cayaltí. Ramón managed the plantation with his sons Antero (1849–1927) and Ramón (1850–1940) and eventually took control of it. Earlier they had purchased a cotton farm in the Pisco Valley, Hacienda Palto. They stocked both enterprises with indentured Asians, whom

they overworked with impunity. They then sank the profits into commercial urban real estate and developed close ties with English lenders. Younger brothers Baldomero and Ismael helped out, but the older sons Antero and Ramón ran the family business. The Aspíllagas became linked with other wealthy families of Lima through marriage, and they joined the prestigious Club Nacional.

In politics, the Aspíllagas helped organize the Civilista Party. The younger Ramón sat briefly in the national Chamber of Deputies. After 1906 Antero was elected to the Chamber of Deputies and then moved to the Senate, where he carefully guarded the interests of export planters. He lost as the candidate of the Civilista Party in the presidential elections of 1912 and 1919. On the eve of the ballot count in 1919, Augusto LEGUÍA, a contender for president, conspired with the army to nullify the vote, despite the fact that he probably would have won. Thereafter the family concentrated on its plantation and on mining and banking. Family members sat on the board of directors of the powerful Banco Popular, from which they received large low-cost loans in the 1930s. On the plantations they fiercely opposed all efforts to organize labor and became hated opponents of the American Popular Revolutionary Alliance (APRA), which tried to organize field workers into unions and teach them to read in night classes. The Aspíllagas supported Luís Sánchez Cerro for president in 1931 and General Oscar BENAVIDES thereafter. After World War II they withdrew from direct management of Hacienda Palto but continued in sugar despite shrinking returns. In 1968 the military reform government seized control of the Aspíllaga plantations, compensating the owners with government bonds.

DENNIS GILBERT, *La oligarquía peruana: Historia de tres familias* (1982); MICHAEL GONZALES, *Plantation Agriculture and Social Control in Northern Peru, 1875–1933* (1985), esp. pp. 29–32, 166–194.

VINCENT PELOSO

*See also* **Peru: Revolutionary Movements; Plantations.**

**ASSEMBLY OF NOTABLES,** Mexican council that offered the crown to Archduke MAXIMILIAN. On 16 June 1863, General Élie-Frédéric Forey ordered the establishment of a thirty-five-member Junta Suprema de Gobierno. This provisional junta appointed a three-man executive power, which consisted of Juan Nepomuceno ALMONTE, Mariano Salas, and Archbishop Pelagio Antonio de Labastida, and then designated the 215 members of an Assembly of Notables. The assembly met on 8–10 July in the building of the former Chamber of Deputies and included the Conservative Luis G. Cuevas, a former minister, and Pedro Escudero y Echánove, who had sat in the Constituent Congress of 1856–1857. Members tended to be moderates, though some, such as José Fernando RAMÍREZ and Manuel OROZCO Y BERRA, refused to participate. Rejecting both federalism and centralism, the assembly opted for "a moderated, hereditary monarchy as the form of government best suited to Mexico, with a Catholic prince" as emperor of Mexico. The assembly offered a vacant Mexican crown to Archduke Maximilian of Hapsburg. Should Maximilian decline the offer, the opinion of Napoleon III was to be sought.

The assembly was an attempt by the French, then in concert with leading Conservatives and moderates, to provide legitimacy for Maximilian's accession to the throne. The republicans, however, maintained that the Juárez administration, elected in 1861, was the legitimate government and that the assembly was illegal.

RAFAEL TAFOLLA PÉREZ, *La Junta de Notables de 1863* (1977); JOSÉ FUENTES MARES, *Juárez, Los Estados Unidos y Europa* (1983), pp. 358–363.

BRIAN HAMNETT

**ASSIS, JOAQUIM MARIA MACHADO DE.** *See* Machado de Assis.

**ASSUNÇÃO, LEILAH** (*b.* 1943), Brazilian playwright, author, and actress. Born Maria de Lourdes Torres de Assunção in Botucatu, São Paulo, Assunção holds a degree in education from the University of São Paulo and has studied acting, fashion design, literary criticism with Antônio CALLADO, and theater at the Teatro Oficina. Besides writing, she has acted in several plays and worked as a fashion model. In her theater Assunção reveals a humorous sensitivity for the middle class and their problems, and especially for women restricted in their environment and confronting a man's world. Although some of her works were censored in the years of military rule, Assunção's first play, *Fala baixo senão eu grito* (1969), a critical analysis of the heroine's life, won a Molière Prize. Margot Milleret describes *Boca molhada de paixão calada* (1980), perhaps Assunção's most political play, as depicting "a couple in their forties who re-create their past by acting out previous sexual encounters." Assunção is considered one of the most important playwrights in Brazil today, and is one of the few to live exclusively on the earnings from her writing, due in part to the popularity of her television scripts.

ALCIDES JOÃO DE BARROS, "A situação social de mulher no teatro de Consuelo de Castro e Leilah Assunção," in *Latin American Theatre Review* 9 (Spring 1976): 13–20; MARGO MILLERET, "Entrapment and Flights of Fantasy in Three Plays by Leilah Assunção," in *Luso-Brazilian Review* 21 (Summer 1984): 49–56; ELZBIETA SZOKA and JOE W. BRATCHER III, eds, *3 Contemporary Brazilian Plays in Bilingual Edition* (1988), esp. pp. 211–216; ANN WITTE, "Feminismo e anti-feminismo em Leilah Assunção e Millôr Fernandes," in *Dactylus* 9 (1988–1989): 15–20; MARGO MILLERET, "(Re)playing the Brazilian Dictatorship," in *Discurso literario: Revista de estudios iberoamericanos* 7, no. 1 (1990): 213–224.

GARY M. VESSELS

**ASTRONOMY.** In contrast with modern cultures, religious beliefs in indigenous societies in the Western Hemisphere propelled the development of astronomy. Archaeoastronomy consults written and unwritten sources for information about how these peoples thought about and observed the heavens within the con-

Observatory at Chichén Itzá. ORGANIZATION OF AMERICAN STATES.

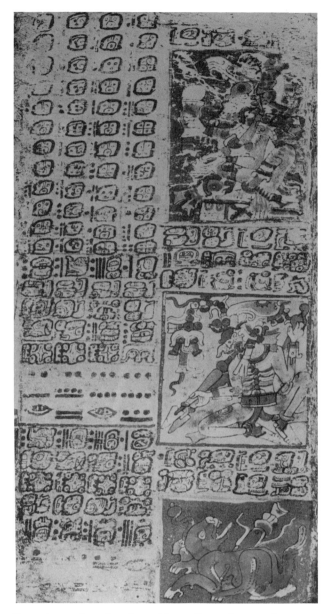

Page devoted to the planet Venus from the Dresden Codex, compiled and used by Maya priests for divinatory purposes. The codex also includes farmer's almanacs, lunar tables, and eclipse tables. SACHSISCHE LANDESBIBLIOTHEK, DRESDEN.

ical events occurring at the horizon, as did peoples in the Central Valley of Mexico, Andean peoples, and those who lived in the present-day U.S. Southwest. The Governor's Palace at UXMAL, for example, displays over 300 Venus glyphs, and the constructions at TEOTIHUACÁN show planning designed in accordance with a solar horizon calendar, as did those at TENOCHTITLÁN. Some suggest that the Caracol, built around A.D. 1000 at the site of CHICHÉN ITZA served as the astronomical observatory behind the written Venus calendar found in the Dresden Codex, which also includes an almanac showing that the Mayas could predict solar eclipses. Indeed, five of the sixteen surviving pre-Columbian codices include Venus almanacs used to regulate specific practices of warfare and ritual sacrifice.

Although it is harder to discern astronomical orientations among the indigenous peoples of the present-day U.S. Southwest and the Andean region, suggestive evidence abounds. The Casa Rinconada, from the eleventh-century Anasazi-PUEBLO cultures of Chaco Canyon, New Mexico, a huge circular kiva for worship, is perfectly aligned on the pole star and contains a special window, possibly designed to admit the light emanating from the summer solstice sunrise. In CASA GRANDE, Arizona, buildings contain accurate solar alignments at solstices and equinoxes, and the CHUMASH INDIANS of California carved their astronomical sightings into rocks.

Andean peoples, too, watched the skies for information about the future. Manuscripts produced after the Spanish conquest and on-site observations indicate that the Coricancha Temple (Temple of the Sun) in CUZCO possessed an astronomical orientation; opposite inner halls look out toward the June and December solstice sunrise and sunset positions, reflecting the Incas' dualistic, vertical view of the cosmos still held today. It is thought that the Incas built pillars along the Cuzco horizon to demarcate solar positions and provide information about when to begin planting at what altitudes. The desert plateaus of coastal Nasca, Peru, contain over 100 geometrical shapes known collectively as the NASCA LINES. Although some scholars have speculated that the lines were the remains of a horizon-based astronomy system, that view has been discredited. Nevertheless, modern Andean peoples believe that a sighting of a bright Pleiades constellation will yield good harvests, and Quechua speakers think the Milky Way (Mayu) continues the river system flowing through the Valley of Cuzco into the heavens.

text of their worldview as a whole. For example, the MAYAS emphasized the special relationship between the sun and Venus to which they assigned religious significance, whereas current astronomy arranges planets according to distances from the sun. It is likely that Andean and Mesoamerican peoples shared the belief that time flowed around the horizon, as Mexicans depicted on their calendar wheels. Scholars have discovered that the Mayas even constructed buildings in alignment with astronom-

ELIZABETH CHESLEY BAITY, "Archaeoastromony and Ethnoastronomy So Far," *Current Anthropology* 14 (1973): 389–449; ANTHONY F. AVENI, ed., *Archaeoastronomy in Pre-Columbian America* (1975), and *Native American Astronomy* (1977); BETH A. COLLEA and ANTHONY F. AVENI, *A Selected Bibliography on Native American Astronomy* (1978); ANTHONY F. AVENI, *Skywatchers of Ancient Mexico* (1980); RAY A. WILLIAMSON, ed., *Archaeoastronomy in the Americas* (1981); JOHN B. CARLSON, "Ancient Skies," *Humanities* 7 (1986): 24–28; JOHN B. CARLSON and W. JAMES JUDGE,

221

eds., *Astronomy and Ceremony in the Prehistoric Southwest* (1987); A. F. AVENI, ed., *World Archaeoastronomy* (1989); JOHN B. CARLSON, "America's Ancient Skywatchers," *National Geographic Magazine* 177 (1990): 76–107; RAY A. WILLIAMSON and CLAIRE R. FARRER, eds., *Earth and Sky: Visions of the Cosmos in Native American Folklore* (1992); CLIVE L. N. RUGGLES and NICHOLAS J. SAUNDERS, eds., *Astronomies and Cultures* (1993).

JOHN B. CARLSON

*See also* **Aztec Calendar Stone.**

**ASTURIAS, MIGUEL ÁNGEL** (*b.* 19 October 1899; *d.* 9 June 1974), Guatemalan writer and Nobel Prize winner (1967). His country's greatest writer in the twentieth century, Asturias was also one of the forerunners of Latin America's Boom literature of the 1960s, along with Jorge Luis BORGES of Argentina and Alejo CARPENTIER of Cuba.

Asturias was born in the old district of La Parroquia in Guatemala City and spent his early years there. His father, a lawyer, fearing persecution by dictator Manuel ESTRADA CABRERA (1898–1920), moved the family to the small town of Salamá, where they lived from 1903 to 1907. In this town the young mestizo (mixed Mayan and Spanish heritage) came into contact with the Mayan life-style, something that would mark him for the rest of his life.

In Guatemala City, Asturias completed his secondary education at the nation's top public institution, Instituto de Varones, and enrolled in the law school of the University of San Carlos in 1918. In April 1920 he became active in the overthrow of dictator Estrada Cabrera, emerging as a student leader after this epic struggle. As a result, he traveled to Mexico City with a student delegation and met Mexico's minister of education, José VASCONCELOS, a well-known philosopher on ethnic issues and miscegenation. Young Asturias was greatly influenced by his thinking. Asturias received his law degree in 1923 but never practiced. Already the author of poems, short stories, and essays, he left for Paris in 1924.

In Paris, Asturias studied ethnology under Georges Raynaud, a Mayanist, and came to rediscover his own Mayan roots as a result. He was also a correspondent for *El Imparcial,* one of Guatemala's leading newspapers, and traveled extensively throughout Europe. His first published book was *Leyendas de Guatemala* (Legends of Guatemala, 1930), in which the prehuman forces and creatures of Mayan myth are given new life, and Mayans are placed in that landscape.

In 1933 Asturias returned to Guatemala, then under the control of another dictator, General Jorge UBICO (1931–1944). Unable to make a living as a writer, Asturias was forced to work for the official newspaper, *El Liberal Progresista.* Later he founded the first radio news program in Guatemala, "Diario del Aire" (Radio newspaper, 1937).

Miguel Ángel Asturias. ORGANIZATION OF AMERICAN STATES.

In 1944, when the Ubico dictatorship was overthrown, Asturias fled to Mexico, where he published his best-known novel, *El señor presidente* (The President, 1946). Of this work, critic Gerald Martin says that it "exemplifies more clearly than any other novel the crucial link between European Surrealism and Latin American Magical Realism" (1989). It remains the single most famous Latin American "dictator novel."

One year later the new democratic government of Juan José ARÉVALO (1945–1951) named Asturias cultural attaché in Mexico. Three years later he was appointed ambassador to Argentina, where he published his masterpiece, *Hombres de maíz* in 1949 (translated as *Men of Maize* in 1975). Soon after, he began his ideological transition toward leftist politics. *Men of Maize* is considered by some critics to be the first unmistakable Magical Realist Joycean novel in Latin America, the most ambitious to this day, and perhaps the greatest of the twentieth century. According to Chilean critic Ariel Dorfman (1992), the contemporary Spanish American novel begins with its publication. It anticipates by fifty years many issues popular at the end of the twentieth century, such as ecology, feminism, global consciousness, and a defense of native peoples. Gerald Martin describes it as "a profound meditation on the history of Guatemala, contained within a symbolic history of Latin America since the conquest, contained within the history of humanity's passage from so-called barbarism to so-called civilization since the Greeks, contained within the novelist's own reflections on the human condition."

Asturias was ambassador to El Salvador in 1954 when the country was invaded by a mercenary army and the democratic process was interrupted. He went into exile in Argentina, then moved to Genoa, Italy, where he published his last truly memorable novel, *Mulata de tal* (1963), a work that, fusing the experience of Quetzalcoatl with that of Dante, anticipates Latin America's Boom literature.

In 1966 Asturias's old university friend Julio César MÉNDEZ MONTENEGRO was elected president of Guatemala and named Asturias ambassador to France. That same year Asturias won the Lenin Peace Prize, and the following year, the Nobel Prize for literature.

When General Carlos ARANA OSORIO gained control of Guatemala in 1970, Asturias resigned as ambassador and gave the Nobel Prize money to his son, Rodrigo, who apparently used it to found a guerrilla organization. Asturias died in Madrid and is buried in the Père-Lachaise Cemetery in Paris.

Asturias, essentially a novelist, also wrote poetry, plays, and journal articles. His books are *Leyendas de Guatemala* (stories, 1930); *Émulo Lipolidón* (play, 1935); *Alclasán* (play, 1940); *El señor presidente* (novel, 1946); *Sien de alondra* (poetry, 1949); *Hombres de maíz* (novel, 1949); *Viento fuerte* (novel, 1949); *El papa verde* (novel, 1954); *Weekend en Guatemala* (stories, 1955); *Soluna* (play, 1955); *Los ojos de los enterrados* (novel, 1960); *El Alhajadito* (novella, 1961); *Mulata de tal* (novel, 1963); *Clarivigilia primaveral* (poetry, 1965); *Letanías del desterrado* (poetry, 1966); *El espejo de Lida Sal* (stories, 1967); *Maladrón* (novel, 1969); *Tres de cuatro soles* (poetry, 1971); and *Viernes de dolores* (novel, 1972).

LUIS HARSS and BARBARA DOHMANN, "Miguel Ángel Asturias," in their *Into the Mainstream: Conversations with Latin American Writers* (1967); RICHARD J. CALLAHAN, *Miguel Ángel Asturias* (1970); ARIEL DORFMAN, "Myth as Time and Word," translated by Paula Speck, in *Review 75*, no. 15 (1975): 12–22; JEAN FRANCO, "Miguel Ángel Asturias," in *Latin American Writers*, vol. 2, edited by Carlos A. Solé (1989), pp. 865–873; GERALD MARTIN, *Journeys Through the Labyrinth: Latin American Fiction in the Twentieth Century* (1989), ARIEL DORFMAN, "Hombres de Maíz: El mito como tiempo y palabra" in Gerald Martin, ed., *Asturias's Hombres de Maíz: Critical Edition* (1992).

ARTURO ARIAS

**ASUAR, JOSÉ VICENTE** (*b.* 20 July 1933), Chilean composer and acoustic engineer. Born in Santiago, Asuar began his musical studies with Jorge Urrutia-Blondel (composition) and Juan ORREGO-SALAS (orchestration) at the Santiago Conservatory. From 1952 to 1958 he studied engineering at the Catholic University of Chile, continuing his education in Germany, at the Technical University of Berlin (1959–1960). While in Germany, he studied with Boris Blacher at the Berlin Hochschule für Musik (1959–1960) and with Jacques Wildberger at the

Baden Hochschule für Musik. He studied composition privately under Fritz Winckel and Werner Meyer-Eppler; at Darmstadt University he attended the summer seminars of Boulez, Ligeti, Stockhausen, and Maderna (1960–1962). Back in Santiago, Asuar was director of the electronic music studio (1958–1959) at the Catholic University. In 1960 he returned to Germany to organize an electronic music studio at Karlsruhe. In Caracas from 1965 to 1968, Asuar created and directed the first Venezuelan studio of electronic music. In 1969 he became director of the Department of Sound Technology at the University of Chile. The following year he was awarded a Fulbright grant to study computer music with Lejaren Hiller at the State University of New York at Buffalo.

Asuar has written works for instrumental ensembles, chamber and vocal music, and a considerable number of electronic music pieces. Some of his compositions are *Variaciones espectrales* (1959), *Encadenamientos* (1957), *Preludio a la noche* (1961), *Estudio aleatorio* (1962), *La noche II* (1966), and *Kaleidoscopio* and *Catedral* (1967). He has also written several essays about electronic-music techniques.

JOHN VINTON, ed., *Dictionary of Contemporary Music* (1974); GÉRARD BÉHAGUE, *Music in Latin America* (1979); *New Grove Dictionary of Music and Musicians*, vol. 1 (1980).

SUSANA SALGADO

**ASUNCIÓN,** capital city of Paraguay, founded 15 August 1537 (the Feast of the Assumption) by Juan de Salazar y Espinoza on the east bank of the Paraguay River, 956 miles upstream from the port of Buenos Aires, Asunción became the capital of Paraguay on 14 May 1811. As the center of the nation's political, economic, religious, and cultural life, Asunción dominates Paraguay's commerce, industry, and communications. It has a humid, subtropical climate with a mean temperature of 84°F during the summer (October through March) and an average rainfall of 50 inches, occurring primarily in December and January. By the seventeenth century, Asunción was overshadowed by Buenos Aires, with its more favorable commercial location. Demographic data suggest that Asunción's population surpassed 3,500 by 1565; 7,000 by 1800; 11,000 by 1846; 42,000 by 1900; 203,000 by 1950; 389,000 by 1972, and had exceeded 729,000 by 1990.

The town was laid out in a gridiron pattern with a central plaza containing the religious, governmental, and commercial institutions. Within Asunción the competition for commercial dominance between port and plaza was resolved in favor of the plaza. During its first three centuries, Asunción was a nearly economically self-sufficient frontier river town with a Spanish- and Guaraní-speaking MESTIZO population of limited class divisions. It was subject to indigenous attack as late as the 1740s. The city prided itself on the secondary and religious training available at the Real Colegio y Semi-

Downtown Asunción. © 1987 ULRIKE WELSCH / PHOTO RESEARCHERS, INC.

nario de San Carlos, which opened in 1783. Construction of public buildings and roads during the Carlos Antonio LÓPEZ administration (1844–1862) reflected increasing affluence. During the WAR OF THE TRIPLE ALLIANCE (1864–1870), however, Brazil captured, pillaged, and destroyed much of the city. The export of Asunción's wealth to Buenos Aires destroyed its development and slowed the nation's postwar commercial growth.

Renovated nineteenth-century buildings such as the 1843 cathedral; the government palace, built on the site of the former *cabildo* (city hall) and used by every president since Francisco Solano LÓPEZ (1862–1870); and the railroad station and theater, begun during the Carlos Antonio López administration, are landmarks of contemporary Asunción. The Pantheon of Heroes, a smaller version of the Invalides in Paris, was completed in 1937.

Initially connected to Buenos Aires by river and road and in the twentieth century by rail, and linked by road to Brazil and Bolivia, the city prospered. Beginning in the 1960s, Asunción expanded its telephone, water, sewage, and electrical power services. Since World War I, and in particular since the 1960s, better-paying jobs, modern conveniences, and kin in Asunción have attracted increasing numbers of rural migrants and some foreign immigrants. By 1990 the city accounted for 18 percent of the nation's total population. As in the nineteenth century, the region surrounding Asunción produces foods such as corn and rice as well as sugarcane and fruit for the city. Asunción exports tobacco, cotton, hides, meat, and timber to international markets.

Asunción controls the nation. Power resides primarily in the national executive. The judiciary, the two-chamber Congress, and all the public institutions have their headquarters in the city. Municipal government is weak, however, since the president traditionally appoints the mayor. The seat of the archbishop for this primarily Catholic country is Asunción. The city is home to the Universidad Nacional de Asunción (founded 1889) and the Universidad Católica "Nuestra Señora de la Asunción" (founded 1960) as well as the National Theater and a variety of museums.

DEPARTMENTO DE CULTURA Y ARTE, MUNICIPAL DE ASUNCIÓN, *Historia edificia de la ciudad de Asunción* (1967), provides a series of short sketches by various authors on different aspects of the city, with over half the material after 1870. MABEL CAUSARANO, *Asunción: Análisis histórico-ambiental de su imagen urbana: Álbum gráfico, 450 años* (1987), is a photo-album history of the city. HARRIS GAYLORD WARREN, *Paraguay and the Triple Alliance: The Postwar Decade, 1869–1878* (1978), esp. pp. 16–18 and 33–34, also provides descriptive material on the nineteenth century, while FULGENCIO R. MORENO, *La Ciudad de la Asunción* (1926, repr. 1968), concentrates primarily on colonial development, including political, demographic, economic, and social information. GEORGE F. MASTERMAN, *Seven Eventful Years in Paraguay* (1869), esp. pp. 32–34, provides an excellent description of Asunción in the nineteenth century and the wartime conditions of Paraguay, but his analysis of Francisco Solano López must be approached with caution.

VERA BLINN REBER

**ASYLUM** (Sp./Port. *asilo*) is a distinctive diplomatic and political practice employed primarily in Latin America and a major institution for human rights protection in the Western Hemisphere. Asylum may be defined as the right to offer protection to individuals suffering from political persecution. United Nations Resolution 2312 (XIII) of 1967 defines asylum to be a state's right, the concession of which does not constitute a hostile action toward the asylee's original territorial state.

Based on Roman law, the notion of asylum dates to pre-Christian times, although one of its greatest historical expressions has been through canon law. Asylum has evolved principally as a result of custom, rather than legal factors. In the nineteenth and twentieth centuries, the institution of asylum has become largely a Latin American practice. It grew there as a result of local political volatility which manifested itself in the recurrence of uprisings and revolutionary upheavals. Furthermore, for the young Latin American nation-states, concession of immunity in asylum cases implied diplomatic recognition by the major powers.

In modern usage, two types of asylum exist: internal and external. Internal asylum, more commonly referred to as territorial asylum, was the only type of asylum known until relatively recently. It is generally considered a consequence of territorial sovereignty. States grant this type of asylum to foreigners fleeing their own countries. Although a state possesses the right to not admit any person to its territory, no state, after providing a persecuted individual hospitality, may expel him or turn him over to a state which requests him.

External asylum is that granted on an extraterritorial basis and is permitted in legations, embassies, consulates, warships, and military camps. Diplomatic asylum, which applies to the former three locations, is the most common form of external asylum and may be conceded to nationals of the country in which the diplomatic entity is accredited and located. Diplomatic asylum arose when the European states began to maintain permanent representatives abroad and thus since the inception of diplomatic immunity.

EARLY EVOLUTION OF ASYLUM

Diplomatic asylum in Latin America dates to the late nineteenth century and stemmed from the political organization of independent states. Once the ascendency of anticlerical liberals eradicated religious asylum, and as states began to consolidate, the new governments perceived recognition as a significant priority. Thus, they did not breach the sovereignty of another nation's diplomatic premises. As a result, individuals persecuted for their political beliefs attempted to obtain asylum inside those premises.

Although the practice of asylum became relatively common in the first twenty-five years after Independence, its legal basis remained ambiguous, as reflected in early asylum treaties. In 1865 an agreement was signed in Lima regulating political asylum. In 1867 various European and American legations convened in Lima at a conference which recognized diplomatic asylum as a common practice in the region. The diplomats, however, did not claim that asylum represented a basic rule of international law, nor was it claimed to be a practice native to Latin America. The Lima conference also required that the practice of asylum not interfere with the sovereignty of the American people.

The Convention on the International Penal Law, adopted on 23 January 1889 by the First South American Congress on Private International Law at Montevideo, represented an affirmation of the conclusions of the former conference. The 1889 assembly reasserted the notion that asylum should be regulated through international law. It also recognized the diplomatic asylum of political offenders as a right permitted by the usage, conventions, or laws of the South American countries.

The Sixth International Conference of American States, held in Havana, resulted in the adoption of a Convention Fixing the Rules to Be Observed for the Granting of Asylum on 20 February 1928. The United States was the only American state expressing reservations about the doctrine of asylum. The Convention of Havana established several important principles of diplomatic asylum in Latin America. First, asylum may be conceded only in urgent cases and only for the time strictly necessary for the asylee to secure his safety. Second, asylees may not be disembarked in any part of their national territory nor anywhere near it. Third, as long as asylum lasts, asylees are not permitted to practice acts contrary to public security. Fourth, the right to asylum may be given to political delinquents only in diplomatic legations or military locations. Finally, the government of an asylee's national territory can demand that the asylee be removed from the territory as soon as possible, and the diplomatic agent that has agreed to grant asylum can demand the necessary safe-conducts for the asylee.

In 1933 the Seventh International Conference of American States, held in Montevideo, adopted a Convention on Political Asylum on 26 December 1933. This rather vague agreement permitted the state granting asylum to define the crime of the asylee as political. The significance of this treaty and the 1928 Havana Convention lies in their widespread acceptance. Treaties which declare asylum as a basic human right have not been embraced so inclusively. The Second South American Conference on Private International Law at Montevideo adopted a Treaty on Political Asylum and Refuge on 4 August 1939, revising the 1889 Montevideo treaty.

## HAYA DE LA TORRE CASE

On 28 March 1954, the Tenth Inter-American Conference held in Caracas adopted conventions on diplomatic and territorial asylum, partially as a result of the HAYA DE LA TORRE case between Colombia and Peru. The Caracas Convention defines territorial asylees as individuals who come from states in which they suffer persecution as a result of political convictions, ideas, or associations or for political crimes. In 1954, Caracas also hosted the Convention on Diplomatic Asylum, which asserted that each state may decide whether to grant or refuse asylum to any individual. The asylum-granting state also was responsible for stipulating the nature of an asylee's crime. It also established the principle of non-refoulement, or the proscription of forced return of an asylum seeker to a country of persecution. Finally, the Convention also expressed the boundaries of rights to freedom of expression, assembly and association. While guaranteeing them, it prohibited asylees from provoking or organizing against a sovereign state.

One of the most important cases in Latin American asylum history has been the Haya de la Torre case. In January 1949, Víctor Raúl Haya de la Torre, leader of the Peruvian APRA party, sought refuge in the Colombian embassy in Lima. Colombia argued that custom represented a sufficient legal foundation for asylum. Peru, on the other hand, historically has tended to reject this claim. The two countries carried the case to the International Court of Justice for clarification, because they could not agree on the interpretations of the 1928 Havana Convention regarding the determination of the nature of the asylee's crime and the obligation of a territorial state to concede the necessary safe-conduct.

Following a series of disputes regarding these issues, the International Court of Justice in 1950 produced a jurisprudential doctrine, concluding that Peru was not required to grant Haya de la Torre safe-conduct, that Colombia was not required to turn him over to Peruvian authorities but was required to put an end to the irregularly conceded asylum. After an asylum of five years, Peru issued Haya de la Torre a decree of exile from the country. Colombia agreed to turn him over to the Peruvian minister of justice for one hour for judgment before issuance of the exile decree. Peru reserved extradition rights and demanded that Haya de la Torre never be granted territorial asylum in Colombia. The Haya de la Torre case is important as an example of asylum acting as an impetus for jurisprudence. The involvement of the International Court of Justice as a juridical actor in an asylum case is significant.

## FAJARDO, CÁMPORA, AND HONECKER CASES

Two other relevant cases for the legal interpretation of asylum principles and asylum's institutional evolution are the Saúl Fajardo case in Colombia in 1952 and the Hector José Cámpora case in Argentina in 1976. From 17 March to 4 April 1952, the Colombian guerrilla Saúl Fajardo was sheltered in the Chilean embassy in Bogotá.

The two governments involved disagreed on the nature of Fajardo's crime, with Colombia declaring the asylum illegal because they considered Fajardo not a political delinquent but rather a common criminal. This case reflects the importance of the distinction between political and common crimes and the weight of political expediency.

Ex-president Hector Cámpora remained in the Mexican embassy for over three years as a result of the Argentine government's refusal to grant him a safe-conduct. The Cámpora case represents the first time an asylum had been so prolonged when the asylee was not charged judicially. With Cámpora were his son Hector Pedro and ex-secretary of the Peronist Movement, Juan Manuel Abal Medina. These individuals requested and were granted asylum in April 1976. In November 1979, ex-president Cámpora was allowed to go to Mexico, where he was diagnosed with a terminal illness.

The Argentine government, though recognizing the right of asylum and allowing it to function in other cases, refused to grant the safe-conducts necessary for these particular asylees to leave the country. The refusal resulted not from the existence of charges of common crimes, as in the case of Haya de la Torre. Rather, the Argentine government admitted that Cámpora was a political criminal but still refused him the safe-conduct. By late 1979, Mexico threatened to carry the case to the International Court of Justice, using the Haya de la Torre case as a precedent. In effect, the Argentine government denied the obligation of a territorial state to issue the safe-conducts. The Cámpora matter illustrates, first, that the Haya de la Torre case proved to be a precedent in the institution of asylum. Second, it shows that political expediency often shapes, and sometimes undermines, the operation of the institution.

An important contemporary case is that of Erich Honecker, former prime minister of East Germany, who was charged with manslaughter and misappropriation of state funds. Honecker fled his country in March 1991 and lived in the Chilean embassy in Moscow from December 1991 to July 1992. Some members of the post-Pinochet Chilean government, including the Chilean ambassador in Moscow, Clodomiro Almeyda, felt the country owed a debt to Honecker, who had provided asylum to many of Salvador Allende's supporters. Although the Chilean government announced in March 1992 that it would not grant asylum to Honecker, it allowed him to remain in the embassy until Russian authorities determined his future. In July the Chilean government asked Honecker to leave its Moscow embassy. Honecker's trial in Germany began in November 1992, but in January 1993 the German court, recognizing that Honecker suffered from terminal cancer, canceled the trial and allowed Honecker to travel to Chile.

## MASSIVE DIPLOMATIC ASYLUM

Although historically asylum has been determined on an individual basis, the establishment of military governments in Brazil, Argentina, Chile, Ecuador, Peru, Bolivia, and Uruguay in the 1960s and 1970s stimulated massive requests for asylum. Most asylees from these countries sought protection in Mexico, Venezuela, Costa Rica, and to a lesser extent, in Colombia.

The most relevant and visible case of massive diplomatic asylum in modern Latin American history is the case of Chile after the 11 September 1973 military coup in which President Salvador Allende was deposed. In the months following the coup, many embassies, including the missions of countries outside the region, admitted thousands of asylum seekers. Among the asylees were Hortensia B. de Allende, the wife of the assassinated president, who was asyled in the Mexican embassy; most of Allende's cabinet ministers; journalists, intellectuals, professionals, and bureaucrats associated with the deposed regime; and leaders of political parties and labor unions, along with other social activists.

In a different political and international context, another modern case of massive request for diplomatic asylum is that of the Cubans who stormed the Peruvian embassy in 1980 to request asylum. The Cuban government announced that any Cuban who wished to leave the country should go to the Peruvian embassy. More than 10,000 people appeared in three days. Although not all of those who requested asylum did so as a result of political persecution, Peru eventually granted asylum to 740 Cubans. The balance either decided to remain in Cuba or fled to the United States in the MARIEL BOATLIFT which the Peruvian embassy incident precipitated.

Until recently the overwhelming majority of exiles protected by asylum came from relatively prosperous sectors of society and from all sides of the ideological spectrum depending on the country and circumstance. Asylees were typically prominent politicians, skilled workers, social leaders, religious figures, university graduates, intellectuals, artists, businessmen, and women. With variations from case to case and country to country, this was the general profile of asylum seekers from Guatemala after an armed coup deposed the reformist government of President Jacobo Arbenz in 1954; from Cuba after 1959 when Fidel Castro took power and instituted revolutionary trials against thousands of people believed to be associated with the old regime; from Brazil, Argentina, and Uruguay during several years after the military seized power in 1964, 1966, and 1973, respectively; from Chile in 1973 after General Augusto Pinochet deposed the Allende government; and from Nicaragua after Sandinista guerrillas defeated the dictatorship of Anastasio Somoza Debayle in 1979. The social, political, or economic prominence of many asylum seekers accorded this international legal institution particular prestige and relevance in Latin America. Some countries, including Mexico, Venezuela, Costa Rica, and even the United States and Canada, have greatly benefited from often highly qualified, talented, and creative exiles.

REFUGEES

Political conflicts and revolutionary upheavals in South and Central America have increasingly been accompanied by a general decline in economic conditions as an exacerbation of social inequalities in the countries affected. These interrelated political and economic problems have stimulated waves of migrants seeking either safety and protection or employment and better economic opportunities in Latin American nations which are relatively more stable and developed, as well as in the United States, Canada, and Europe.

Although some of these migrants have applied for political asylum in diplomatic missions, the majority of them have left their country without diplomatic aid or protection. Few have applied for territorial asylum. A sizable proportion of migrants escaping political and economic problems in Latin America in the 1980s established residence in other countries or moved from one to another outside the legal protection of the asylum status. Instead, they were refugees using tourist visas and other temporary alien permits or were without documentation. Over time, these circumstances have created considerable confusion and overlapping between the cases of individuals fitting the classical definition of asylees, economic migrants, and the new phenomena of refugees legitimately concerned with their security as a result of membership in communities suffering political repression, such as ethnic groups or residents of areas affected by war and generalized violence.

As a consequence of the economic and political events of the 1980s in the hemisphere, the typical Latin American refugees are no longer persons who enter an embassy in search of protection, assured by their prestige and status of a friendly welcome and good treatment in the recipient country. Nor are they individuals capable of assuring their maintenance and economic well-being with little or no external support. During the past decade, and directly as a consequence of the political unrest, violence, and economic stagnation in Central America and the Caribbean, large numbers of peasants, unskilled workers, indigenous groups, and marginalized populations have sought protection and welfare assistance outside their country of origin. Migrating under very precarious conditions, their disadvantages are significant and their needs urgent. In contrast with the experience of most traditional exiles protected by the institution of asylum, many refugees of this new type have endured harsh conditions. They have often been perceived and isolated as active supporters of revolutionary movements posing a threat to the security of the host country or as social and economic burdens.

Diplomatic asylum has remained a crucial instrument of human rights protection, particularly at specific times of political crisis or as a mechanism to evade severe travel and migration restrictions imposed upon citizens, as in the case of Cubans storming the Peruvian embassy in Havana in 1980. A more diverse and complex migration process has emerged since 1980, however, extending the narrowly defined notion of asylum to the broader experience of refugees. Given its complexity and magnitude, the Central American and Caribbean refugee phenomena became a source of serious international controversy and a difficult political and economic responsibility for recipient countries and humanitarian organizations. Furthermore, the practical impossibility of clearly defining the borderline between political refugees and economic migrants has resulted in a more restricted application of asylum principles and tighter immigration controls on the part of recipient countries such as Mexico, Costa Rica, and the United States.

*Central America and the Caribbean*   The most significant waves of refugees in the hemisphere include Nicaraguans, Salvadorans, Guatamalans, Cubans, and Haitians. In 1981 indigenous people from the Atlantic coast of Nicaragua began entering Honduras from the Mocorón region, and in 1986 over 14,000 were in camps run by the United Nations High Commissioner for Refugees (UNHCR). They represented approximately half of the estimated 30,000 indigenous people from Nicaragua who, after the Sandinistas' seizure of power in 1979 and during the U.S.-sponsored anti-Sandinista civil war of the 1980s, escaped into the Miskito region of Honduras, were forcibly relocated, or joined the contra forces fighting the Sandinistas.

Simultaneously, 14,000 Nicaraguans, mostly peasants, crossed the border, either disaffected from the Sandinista regime or forced by the contras to the department of El Paraíso in Honduras, where they settled in camps under the protection of the Red Cross and the UNHCR. The Nicaraguans in El Paraíso represented part of a larger group of Nicaraguan peasants, mainly from the departments of Nueva Segovia, Jinotega, Esteli, and Madriz, in exile in Honduras. As many as 230,000 Nicaraguans also fled to Costa Rica in various waves. Only 30,000 of them were officially recognized as refugees by Costa Rican authorities.

The formal repatriation process of the Indians began in 1986. During 1987, 14,000 Indians repatriated with international assistance. By 1989, only 9,000 indigenous people were registered as refugees by the UNHCR in Honduras. All but a handful returned to Nicaragua after the elections of 1990, when the Sandinistas lost power to a coalition of opposition forces led by Violeta Chamorro. Most of the peasant refugees settled in the El Paraíso region in Honduras were repatriated to Nicaragua after 1989, and the return of refugees from Costa Rica also intensified after that year.

Between 1981 and 1985, 46,000 Guatemalan refugees entering the southern Mexican state of Chiapas, bordering on Guatemala, received refugee status. Initially, local peasant communities helped the refugees settle in camps run by the Catholic church. Later, the Mexican government and the UNHCR took charge of many of those camps. These officially recognized refugees constituted part of a much larger group of peasants, mostly Indians of several different ethnic and linguistic groups.

Guatemalan refugees being repatriated from Mexico. PHOTO BY DERRILL BAZZY.

These refugees were often victims of the counterinsurgency campaign launched by the Guatemalan army in the highlands of the country, an area heavily populated by the Maya-K'iche' Indians. By the end of 1992, only 8,000 Guatemalans exiled in Mexican camps had returned to their country. In 1993 massive repatriations of Guatemalan Indians started under the leadership of the 1992 Nobel Peace Prize winner, Rigoberta MENCHÚ, who was also an Indian refugee.

Between 1980 and 1986, Salvadorans suffering government repression or directly affected by the country's civil war emigrated in massive numbers to neighboring countries. Approximately 21,000 settled in internationally supervised refugee camps in Honduras. In 1987 refugees settled in Honduras began to return to El Salvador in large contingents. By 1990, without the explicit consent of the Salvadoran government, more than 16,000 had forced their return to their country in a series of very large convoys.

Cubans and Haitians have also left their countries in massive numbers, with the primary destination being the United States. Between 1959, when Fidel Castro took power, and 1980, almost 800,000 Cubans migrated to the United States. In 1980 more than 125,000 Cubans left their country in the Mariel boatlift. The Haitian "boat people" began migrating to the U.S. in large numbers in 1972, and by 1980 more than 1,000 a month were attempting the journey in boats that were often homemade and flimsy.

The examples of Cuban and Haitian immigration into the United States reflect the ambiguities involved in asylum and refugee policy, since one set of refugees, those abandoning Castro's Socialist Cuba, has been welcomed with open arms, while the other, fleeing the repression and poverty of Haiti's elite-dominated society, have been turned back. Cubans have been perceived as immigrating for political reasons, while Haitians have been said to seek improved economic conditions. The administration of U.S. president Jimmy Carter attempted to clarify the immigrant situation by creating the category "Cuban-Haitian entrant," which meant that these groups received federal aid and were allowed to remain in the country on a two-year trial basis but did not receive refugee status. This classification was applicable to entrants before 1 January 1981, but it did nothing to halt immigration or resolve the status of later immigrants, particularly Haitians, who continued to enter South Florida at a rate of 10,000 a year.

*Devising Solutions*   A refugee may be generally defined as "a person outside his or her country of origin, who is unable or unwilling to return there owing to a well-founded fear of being persecuted on grounds of race, religion, nationality, social group, or political opinion." This definition is based on the Convention Relating to the Status of Refugees of 28 July 1951 and the Protocol Relating to the Status of Refugees adopted on 31 January 1967. Although the concept of refuge stems from the tradition of territorial asylum, refugees do not necessarily ask for individual protection; rather, they may seek refuge as a result of persecution due to their membership in some type of group. Refuge is a central aspect of human rights issues.

The Office of the United Nations High Commissioner for Refugees, the foremost international agency responsible for refugees, was created by the United Nations General Assembly on 14 December 1950. It is nonpolitical and its statute brings within the mandate of the United Nations' authority those refugees covered by previous bilateral treaties as well as those resulting from both pre- and post-1951 events or conditions. Since the creation of the UNHCR, the 1951 Convention and the 1967 Protocol have been the principal instruments for international regulation of refugees.

The Cartagena Conference of Experts of 1984 conducted a comparative study of the refugee question in Central America and attempted to formulate a regional solution. Although it is not a legal mechanism, the Cartagena Declaration is significant as a proof of consensus within the region regarding refugees. The Declaration also expanded the definition of a refugee to include persons fleeing not because of specific persecution but rather as a result of more general violence.

The CONTADORA negotiations of 1984, followed in 1987 by the Esquipulas II peace accords, or the Procedure for the Establishment of a Firm and Lasting Peace in Central America, further attempted to define solutions to the refugee problem in Central America by requiring that the matter be addressed; the parties also agreed to seek international support in their efforts. In response, the International Conference on Central American Refugees, Returnees and Displaced Persons (CIREFCA) was created in 1989. The region's governments have been compelled to collaborate with the UNHCR and other international organizations. Rather than refuge remaining a bilateral question, therefore, it has become internationalized as third actors have begun to participate actively. The Central American conflict represents a turning point from the Haya de la Torre asylum case, since it implies that the refugee must not only be regulated but also administered by international institutions. Protection of the politically persecuted is now granted internationally rather than based on sovereign national rights.

S. PRAKASH SINHA, *Asylum and International Law* (1971); ATLE GRAHL-MADSEN, *Territorial Asylum* (1980); GUY S. GOODWIN-GIL, *The Refugee in International Law* (1983); DAVID A. MARTIN, ed., *The New Asylum Seekers: Refugee Law in the 1890s*, International Studies in Human Rights Series, vol. 10 (1988); KEITH W. YUNDT, *Latin American States and Political Refugees* (1988); F. MARKX-VELDJUIJZDEN, *The Right of Asylum: Selective Bibliography* (1989); MARY ANN LARKIN, FREDERICK C. CUNY, and BARRY N. STEIN, eds., *Repatriation Under Conflict in Central America* (1991).

ADOLFO AGUILAR ZINSER

*See also* **Emigration; Pan-American Conferences; United States–Latin American Relations.**

Atacama Desert, Chile. PHOTO BY MARCELO MONTECINO.

**ATACAMA DESERT,** interior region of southern Bolivia, northern Chile, and northwestern Argentina, 8,250–13,200 feet in elevation. Considered the driest desert of the world, the Atacama expands along a series of elongated, flat-bottomed basins, the remnants of shallow lakes of Quaternary Age. Today, on the floors of the desiccated lakes, borax, natural salt, and nitrate deposits are mined. Along intermittent watercourses fed by the icecaps of Andean volcanoes, pastoral communities of Atacameño Indians were established about 5,000 years ago. They were skilled woodcarvers and expert wool and ceramic artisans who traded with the INCAS and the AYMARA (TIAHUANACO) Indians to the north and the DIAGUITAS to the south. Several towns in the Atacama Desert, such as Peine, San Pedro de Atacama, and Lasana, still bear the strong cultural imprints of the old Atacameño culture.

The classic work on this region is ISAIAH BOWMAN, *Desert Trails of Atacama* (1924).

CÉSAR N. CAVIEDES

**ATACAMES,** the name assigned to the prehistoric culture occupying the ESMERALDAS coast during the Integration Period (A.D. 500–1531). Recent archaeological research of the Atacames type site has established three occupational phases: Early Atacames 1 and 2 (A.D. 700–1100) and Late Atacames (A.D. 1100–1526). The end point marks the first of Francisco PIZARRO's voyages of conquest down the coast of Ecuador.

Early ethnohistorical accounts, which report a densely populated coast, describe the town of Atacames as having over 1,500 houses laid out on a grid plan with streets and open plaza areas. Archaeological investigations conducted in the 1970s by the Spanish archaeologist José Alcina Franch and his colleagues confirmed these early descriptions, having documented a series of large habitation sites with mound groups and extensive cultural refuse all along the coast of Esmeraldas, including Atacames, Tonsupa, Balao, and La Tolita. Most mounds are long, low platforms that supported residential structures, while others are funerary mounds containing numerous urn burials or tall, chimney-type interments of stacked bottomless urns.

At the Atacames site, a progressive expansion in site size and complexity has been documented. The mounds vary considerably in size, from 420 to 5,520 square yards in area and from less than 30 inches to over 80 inches in height. Mounds are predominantly round throughout the sequence, but ellipsoid and irregular shapes occur as well. The overall site configuration experienced temporal shifts throughout the Integration Period, as on-site population levels continued to grow. By Late Atacames times, a regular grid pattern emerged with rows of mounds and open avenues running obliquely from the shoreline.

Atacames pottery is generally less decorated and more poorly crafted than that of the preceding Tiaone culture, although vessel forms remain diverse. These include a range of small olla forms, polypod bowl forms, as well as pedestal cups (*compoteras*) with anthropomorphic faces. Red-on-buff painting is the predominant decorative technique, with geometric designs executed in fine- to medium-width lines. Other pottery artifacts include spindle whorls with a large flat base and small conical top, cylindrical seals or stamps, and modeled zoomorphic whistles.

Also found in abundant quantities are a wide variety

of small beads (*chaquira*) used for bodily adornment. These were manufactured from a range of raw materials including lithics, shell, bone, and precious metals such as gold and copper. Shell beads seem to predominate, and those made from *Spondylus* were highly prized and widely traded. Other forms of bodily decoration characteristic of Atacames include dental mutilation and gold-inlaid teeth. The latter may have been the prerogative of high-status individuals.

The large size and internal complexity of towns such as Atacames, together with specialization in craft production and the deferential treatment of the dead, all suggest a fairly complex form of sociopolitical organization, very probably a stratified chiefdom. As was the case with the JAMA-COAQUE II settlements to the south, however, Atacames was probably succumbing to strong MANTEÑO domination prior to the Spanish Conquest and was an important port-of-trade in the coastal traffic in *Spondylus* shells, precious metals, and other sumptuary goods.

FRANCISCO DE XEREZ [1528], ''La relación Sámano-Xerez,'' in *Colección de documentos inéditos para la historia de España*, vol. 5 (1842), pp. 193–201; BETTY J. MEGGERS, *Ecuador* (1966); MERCEDES GUINEA BUENO, *Patrones de asentamiento en la arqueología de Esmeraldas (Ecuador)* (1983); ROBERT A. FELDMAN and MICHAEL E. MOSELEY, ''The Northern Andes,'' in *Ancient South Americans*, edited by Jesse D. Jennings (1983); MERCEDES GUINEA BUENO, ''Valoración de las evidencias de intercambio en la desembocadura del Río Esmeraldas: El problema cronológico,'' in International Congress of Americanists, *Relaciones interculturales en el área ecuatorial del Pacífico durante la época precolombina*, edited by Jean François Bouchard and Mercedes Guinea Bueno, BAR International Series 503 (1989), pp. 127–146; CÉSAR M. HERAS Y MARTÍNEZ and JESÚS ADÁNEZ PAVÓN, ''Chimeneas cerámicas: Un rasgo cultural de significación controvertida,'' in International Congress of Americanists, *Relaciones interculturales en el área ecuatorial del Pacífico durante la época precolombina*, edited by Jean François Bouchard and Mercees Guinea Bueno, BAR International Series 503 (1989), pp. 147–162.

JAMES A. ZEIDLER

**ATAHUALPA** (*b.* ca. 1498; *d.* 26 July 1533), INCA ruler at the time of the Spanish Conquest of Peru. Little accurate information exists about the life of Atahualpa—even his date and place of birth are uncertain. Some suggest he was born in the imperial center of Cuzco; others, that he was from Tomebamba (Cuenca, Ecuador). His father was HUAYNA CAPAC, the last undisputed ruler of TAHUANTINSUYU, the Inca Empire; his mother was a favorite secondary wife from the north. Huayna Capac died unexpectedly from smallpox that swept into the Andes ahead of the Spanish.

The Andean practice of succession was not based on primogeniture; any male child from the principal or from any of the secondary wives could become *último* Inca (ruler). The division of Cuzco into separate halves (*hanan* and *urinsaya*) with a divided government and the importance of the cults of the lineages (*panacas*) of previous Inca rulers complicated the question of succession. As he lay dying, Huayna Capac was repeatedly asked by elder advisers about the succession. It seems he favored his youngest child, Ninan Cuyochi, who, unfortunately, also contracted smallpox and died. Huayna Capac's second choice was probably HUASCAR, his son with Ragua Ocllo. Initially the Cuzco religious and political elite supported Huascar. Indeed, the Cuzco leadership proclaimed him heir after Huayna Capac's death. But as Huayna Capac shifted into and out of a coma in his last hours, he also named Atahualpa, a favorite from the north, who had promising military potential. Atahualpa, with the support of great military commanders, moved southward in an attempt to secure control of Tahuantinsuyu. Victorious, Atahualpa's forces captured Huascar outside Cuzco and imprisoned him. General Quizquiz went into Cuzco, attempting to obliterate completely the Huascar faction.

Such was the political scene in the realm when the handful of Spaniards under Francisco PIZARRO arrived on their third expedition of 1531. Atahualpa had left commander Rumiñavi in charge of Quito and Chali-

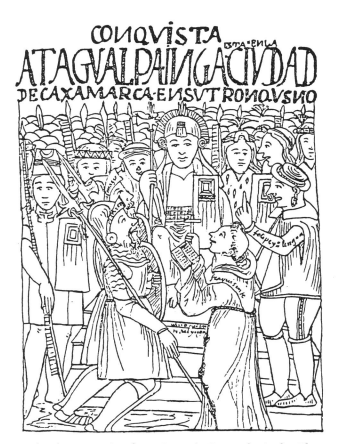

Atahualpa. Drawing from Guamán Poma de Ayala, *El primer nueva corónica y buen gobierno* (ca. 1615).
COURTESY OF THE ROYAL LIBRARY, COPENHAGEN.

cuchima in control of the central Andes while he, along with a few thousand troops, traveled to CAJAMARCA to rest and enjoy the thermal baths nearby. There he was captured by the Spanish on 16 November 1532. After realizing the European thirst for gold, Atahualpa offered, as ransom, to fill a room within two months with gold, and twice with silver. Pizarro and the other Europeans were astounded, as shipments slowly began to make their way into Cajamarca from throughout the realm. With the completion of the ransom (a total of about 13,420 pounds of 22½-carat gold and 26,000 pounds of good silver), the quandary of what to do with the Inca ruler increased. Atahualpa began to mistrust the promise of release and had probably ordered his commanders Rumiñavi and Chalicuchima to move toward Cajamarca. But the Spanish convinced Chalicuchima to enter Cajamarca and took him prisoner.

Ultimately, a group that included royal officials and the recently arrived Diego de ALMAGRO persuaded Pizarro that it was dangerous to keep the Inca captive and that he should be executed. The principal Atahualpa defenders, Hernando de SOTO and Hernando PIZARRO, were away at the time the mock trial took place. Atahualpa was charged with ordering while in jail the execution of his half brother and preparing a surprise attack against the Spaniards, charges for which he was found guilty and sentenced to die at the stake. Friar Vicente de Valverde succeeded in converting Atahualpa to Christianity, and therefore the Inca was garroted instead of burned. In later years myths evolved (the *Inkarrí* cycle) that he would return and usher in a new age during which the yoke of the invaders would be overthrown.

JOHN HEMMING, *The Conquest of the Incas* (1970); FRANKLIN PEASE, *Los últimos Incas del Cuzco* (1972).

NOBLE DAVID COOK

## ATAHUALPA (JUAN SANTOS)

**ATAHUALPA (JUAN SANTOS)** (*b.* 1710?; *d.* ca. 1756), leader of an indigenous rebellion in the jungles and mountain slopes of east-central Peru from 1742 to 1752. Not much is known about the early life of Juan Santos, who later took the name Atahualpa. He was born either in Cajamarca or, more likely, Cuzco; he learned Spanish and Latin while studying with the Jesuits. A Jesuit may have taken him to Spain and Africa.

In 1742 Juan Santos appeared in the mountains of Chanchamayo, declaring himself the descendant of ATAHUALPA, the Inca captured and murdered in 1533 by Francisco PIZARRO at the outset of the Spanish conquest of Peru. A charismatic leader, Juan Santos combined Christian and Andean messianism. Raiding from the jungles of the Gran Pajonal, his followers destroyed the region's Franciscan missions. Juan Santos aimed to drive the Spaniards out of Peru but was unable to mobilize the populous central highlands. Nonetheless, several military expeditions against his stronghold failed to defeat him, and the government finally established forts along the frontier to prevent him from invading the highlands. In 1752 Juan Santos's forces seized Andamarca, threatening Jauja, but quickly withdrew. His hostilities then ceased. He probably died in Metraro. His uprising reflected mounting indigenous resistance to the colonial system. Revolts in Tarma (1744) and Lima (1750) supported his call for insurrection, and even after 1752 rumors about the new Atahualpa disturbed Peru.

MARIO CASTRO ARENAS, *La rebelión de Juan Santos* (1973); STEVE J. STERN, "The Age of Andean Insurrection, 1742–1782: A Reappraisal," in *Resistance, Rebellion, and Consciousness in the Andean Peasant World, 18th to 20th Centuries,* edited by Steve J. Stern (1987), esp. pp. 43–63; ALONSO ZARZAR, *"Apo Capac Huayna, Jesús Sacramentado": Mito, utopía, y milenarismo en el pensamiento de Juan Santos Atahualpa* (1989).

KENDALL W. BROWN

**ATAIDE, TRISTÃO DE.** *See* **Lima, Alceu Amoroso.**

**ATENEO DE LA JUVENTUD** (Athenaeum of Youth), a Mexican literary and intellectual society, 1907–1914. Although founded as the Sociedad de Conferencias (Society for Lectures) in 1907 and known as the Ateneo de México (the Athenaeum of Mexico) after 1912, the group was christened the Ateneo de la Juventud in 1909 and it is by this name that it is generally known. Under the leadership of Antonio Caso and Pedro HENRÍQUEZ UREÑA, the society came to include such influential thinkers and writers as Alfonso REYES, José VASCONCELOS, and Martín Luis GUZMÁN. The Ateneo developed around the short-lived literary journal *Savia Moderna* (Modern Vigor, 1906), whose contributors attempted to depart from *modernista* writing and the influence of French literature. Eventually the society became a forum for questioning the official philosophy of POSITIVISM employed by the government of Porfirio DÍAZ for state administration and social regulation. By organizing annual cycles of lectures, the Ateneo proposed a political, social, and intellectual renovation of Mexican society through the public discussion and broad dissemination of knowledge. In 1912, after the start of the Mexican Revolution (1910), members of the group participated in founding the Popular University and assisted the minister of education, Justo Sierra, in establishing the School of Higher Studies in the National University of Mexico. Although the society disbanded in 1914, its influence was immense during Mexico's post-Revolutionary state-building decades of the 1920s and 1930s.

JUAN HERNÁNDEZ LUNA, ed., *Conferencias del Ateneo de la Juventud* (1962); JOSÉ ROJAS GARCIDUEÑAS, *El Ateneo de la Juventud y la Revolución* (1979); JAMES WILLIS ROBB, "Alfonso Reyes," in *Latin American Writers,* vol. 2, edited by Carlos A. Solé and Maria Isabel Abreu (1989), pp. 693–703; GABRIELLA DE BEER, "José Vasconcelos," in *Latin American Writers,* vol. 2 (1989), pp. 575–584, and "El Ateneo y los ateneístas: Un examen retrospectivo," in *Revista iberoamericana* 55, no. 148–149 (1989): 737–749.

DANNY J. ANDERSON

**ATENEO DEL URUGUAY,** a forum founded in 1877 for intellectuals in Uruguay. It reached its zenith in the 1880s. The Ateneo was romantic and spiritualist. It encouraged moderate rationalism, critically debated POSITIVISM and philosophical materialism, and rejected artistic realism. Born during the Lorenzo LATORRE dictatorship, it brought together a young, professional elite whose members possessed or were heirs to the liberal creed of the "principista" generation of 1870, who were now opposing militarism. From its ranks came politicians and polemicists like Julio HERRERA Y OBES, Joaquín de Salterain, and Carlos María Ramírez, who would succeed the militarists. It also provided early schooling for youths who, like José BATLLE Y ORDÓÑEZ, would succeed these men. It was eclipsed by new cultural movements toward the end of the nineteenth century, but would again become a political and intellectual rallying point in opposition to the dictatorship of 1933.

ALBERTO ZUM FELDE, *Proceso intelectual del Uruguay y crítica de su literatura*, vol. 1 (1930); ARTURO ARDAO, *Espiritualismo y positivismo en el Uruguay* and *La sección filosófica del Ateneo* (1950).

FERNANDO FILGUEIRA

**ATL, DR.** (Gerardo Murillo; *b.* 1875; *d.* 1964), Mexican artist and participant in the MEXICAN REVOLUTION. A native of Guadalajara, he became a noted landscape artist and volcanologist. After studying painting at Bellas Artes in Mexico City, he departed in 1896 for Rome, where he later received degrees in philosophy and law. His pseudonym, Dr. Atl (*atl* being the Nahuatl word for "water"), was suggested to him by the writer Leopoldo LUGONES in Paris in 1902, and he used this name on his works of art. Returning to Mexico, he hiked up Popocatépetl and Iztaccíhuatl, an experience that led to a lifelong interest, both scientific and artistic, in volcanoes.

After a second stay in Europe, Atl returned to Mexico in 1914 and joined the Constitutionalist movement under Venustiano CARRANZA. He became a member of the Revolutionary Confederation, a group of military and other Constitutionalist officials formed in 1914 that pressured Carranza to carry out social reforms. He was a close collaborator of General Álvaro OBREGÓN, and helped him attract the support of the CASA DE OBRERO MUNDIAL and other workers' groups in Mexico City during the Constitutionalist occupation in early 1915. After the Revolution, he returned to painting and authored several books, including works on art and volcanology.

A good biography is ARTURO CASADO NAVARRO, *El Dr. Atl* (1984). A beautiful edition of his work is GERARDO MURILLO,

*Dr. Atl: Pinturas y dibujos* (1974), with a prologue by Carlos Pellicer. Works in English include MACKINLEY HELM, *Modern Mexican Painters* (1941), pp. 1–20; and AGUSTÍN VELÁSQUEZ CHÁVEZ, *Contemporary Mexican Artists* (1937), pp. 45–55.

LINDA B. HALL

**ATLANTIC CHARTER,** a declaration of solidarity made by Great Britain and the United States on 14 August 1941. Prior to U.S. entry into World War II, President Franklin Delano Roosevelt met with Winston Churchill, the prime minister of Great Britain. Together the two leaders issued the Atlantic Charter, a broadly conceived statement affirming the two nations' solidarity in the face of impending threats to international security.

The Atlantic Charter cited the rights of all nations to self-determination and "the abandonment of the use of force" in international disputes. The charter was eventually approved by all members of the United Nations, including the countries of Latin America, for whom the charter's repudiation of aggression and insistence on unrestricted free travel on the seas bore particular significance.

DONALD M. DOZER, *Are We Good Neighbors?* (1959).

JOHN DUDLEY

**ATLANTIC ISLANDS, MIGRANTS FROM.** The Portuguese commonly moved inhabitants of Atlantic possessions (i.e., the AZORES and MADEIRA) to distant portions of their realm. This was expedient for two reasons: it solved the problem of overcrowding in geographic locales already overburdened with growing populations and simultaneously provided stable settlers for the more remote regions of the Portuguese Empire. On occasion, Portuguese settlers in North Africa also were resettled when their communities were threatened by the Moors. Relocation reached its height in the eighteenth century when *açorianos* (Azorians) were brought in large numbers to Brazil, but it continued into the early years of the nineteenth century.

After Brazil became independent in 1822, the Atlantic islanders fanned out through the English-speaking Caribbean, arriving in substantial numbers in British Guiana in the 1830s and 1840s and later on in Jamaica, Trinidad, Bermuda, and New England. Indeed, the exodus continues to the present; migration is an accepted pattern in the Azores, where limited economic opportunities foster it. Atlantic islanders' migration to Brazil in the eighteenth century, however, bears unique characteristics and deserves scrutiny. The distinguishing feature of this migration is that it was largely agricultural and *voluntary*. One might argue that the incentives were hard to refuse, but relocation to Brazil was a matter of choice for the most part.

The traditional immigrant from the *ilhas* (islands) was a farmer, content to remain on the soil. For eighteenth-century Brazilian administrators such an individual was deemed more desirable than local Brazilians, who were more likely to desert colonization schemes for the recently discovered gold fields. This was especially true in the Far South of Brazil, where efforts to secure the Platine area for the Portuguese had been tenuous since the founding in 1680 of COLÔNIA DO SACRAMENTO across the La Plata estuary from Spanish-held Buenos Aires. Between São Paulo and the fortress of Colônia one small community, Laguna, was the sole deterrent against Spanish aggression. Settlers had been enticed there by offers of free food before the first harvest and sufficient head of cattle to start a livestock business. While the Laguna experiment was successful, the program, initiated and supervised by engineer José da Silva Pais, was considered insufficient to secure the southern boundary. Moreover, it relied exclusively on Brazilian-born recruits. To keep control over the southern regions, therefore, the colonization plan was reformulated in the 1740s to include a massive resettlement of Azorian colonists, a move carefully detailed in a *regimento* (Royal Order) of 1747. The royal orders contained precise instructions on the physical layout of communities built for the Atlantic islanders; each new village was uniformly aligned, and building elements were spaced sufficiently distant from each other to allow for future growth while simultaneously preventing overcrowding. Atlantic volunteers, who were recruited as *casais* (married couples), were given a house as well as fresh fish each week, two cows, and a ewe.

By 1753 several Azorian communities had been established in Rio Grande do Sul and Santa Catarina. Although the numbers of settlers fell short of the anticipated 4,000 *casais,* at least 950 had settled by 1749, and in the following three years scattered groups continued to arrive. The settlers not only practiced agriculture but also played an important geopolitical role in securing the south for the Portuguese. After 1750, when the notion of *uti possidetis* dominated the boundary demarcations between the Spanish and the Portuguese, the Portuguese minister Alexandre de Gusmão could point to settlement in these new southern communities as a clear example of "effective occupation."

Atlantic island resettlement proved to be attractive elsewhere in Brazil. Indeed, colonial administrators begged for Atlantic colonists, who would not only stabilize a region but also provide models of behavior for the local populace, which was consistently denigrated by officialdom. In the Comarca of Porto Seguro, for example, Indian townships were located next to European settlers' communities, with both groups living in the same type of housing. In the far north, in Amapá, Portuguese administrators created São José de Macapá and Nova Mazagão with immigrant *casais* in order to stabilize the northern borders of the mouth of the Amazon River. Everywhere the Azorian was exalted as the type of settler who would bring prosperity to Brazil. The Portuguese prime minister, the Marquês de POMBAL,

counted on such infusions of Europeans to make possible his scheme of transforming the wilds of Brazil into a European settlement. Clearly the Portuguese felt a need to "civilize" Brazil, and the sturdy, no-nonsense Atlantic islander was seen as the key to this policy.

ROBERTA M. DELSON

**ATUSPARIA REVOLT** of 1885, the largest regional rebellion of primarily Indian peasant composition in nineteenth-century Peru. It was a direct consequence of the Peruvian civil war (1883–1885) between the Reds (a nationalist resistance movement led by Andrés CÁCERES) and Blues (a peace-with-Chile faction led by Miguel IGLESIAS) that followed the disastrous War of the Pacific (1879–1883). In their battles against the Blues, who then controlled the provincial government in the department of ANCASH, the rebels were at times led or aided by non-Indian Red militants. The revolt itself, however—which now bears the name of Pedro Pablo Atusparia, *alcalde ordinario* or district *varayoc* (headman) of the northern half of Huaraz province in 1885—was mobilized by subaltern Indian headmen, who fielded tens of thousands of their compatriots in siege warfare against Blue elements among the mestizo and creole population that dominated the valley towns of the Callejón de Huaylas.

Rebels burned the provincial treasury archive, which held the poll-tax registers. Indians considered the new poll tax to be illegitimate because it did not guarantee access to common lands, as the indigenous head tax had in earlier decades. The *varayoc* signed petitions protesting the postcolonial state's disregard for "Indian rights" and criticized its tendency to collapse into the "criminal projects" of warring caudillos. Rebels controlled the region for two months until Blue counterinsurgency forces from Lima put down the revolt in torrents of blood. After repression and the conclusion of the civil war, however, resistance continued; the poll tax was successfully boycotted until its official abolition in 1895.

The most comprehensive treatment of the Atusparia revolt is WILLIAM W. STEIN, *El levantamiento de Atusparia* (1988). It builds on CESAR A. ALBA HERRERA, *Atusparia y la revolución campesina de 1885 en Ancash* (1985). A more recent study that places the revolt in its historical context is MARK THURNER, "From Two Nations to One Divided" (Ph.D. diss., University of Wisconsin, 1993).

MARK THURNER

**AUCHMUTY, SAMUEL** (*b.* 22 June 1758; *d.* 11 August 1822), British general who distinguished himself as a commanding officer in the British army during several key battles with the Spanish in Argentina and Uruguay. Born in New York under British rule, Sir Samuel Auchmuty remained loyal to the throne and fought for the British during the American War of Independence. Auchmuty remained in the armed forces and served in

India, Egypt, and, beginning in 1806, Latin America, where he took part in the 1806–1807 British invasion at the Río de la Plata and then commanded the occupation of Montevideo, Uruguay. While in Latin America, Auchmuty also published an anti-Spanish newspaper, *La Estrella del Sur*, and fought in a failed attack on Buenos Aires in 1807. He died while serving in occupied Ireland.

WILLIAM W. KAUFMANN, *British Policy and the Independence of Latin America: 1804–1828* (1951).

JOHN DUDLEY

**AUDIENCIA,** a regional high court in Spanish America in the colonial era and the district under its jurisdiction.

Audiencias were the highest judicial tribunals in the Spanish colonies, enjoyed executive and legislative authority, and, in the absence of a region's chief executive, served as the executive on an interim basis. The first audiencia was established in 1511, and by 1606 there were eleven colonial tribunals: in Santo Domingo, Mexico City, Panama, Guatemala, Lima, Guadalajara, Santa Fe (New Granada), Charcas, Quito, Chile, and Manila. Panama's tribunal was abolished in 1751, but by the close of the colonial era there were additional tribunals in Buenos Aires, Caracas, and Cuzco. With the exception of Cuzco and Guadalajara, the audiencia districts became, with modest modifications, the territorial bases for nation-states after independence.

The Audiencias in 1650

**Viceroyalty of New Spain**
- Guadalajara
- Mexico
- Guatemala
- Santo Domingo

**Viceroyalty of Peru**
- Panama
- Santafé
- Quito
- Lima
- Charcas
- Chile

1000 miles
1610 kilometers

Each audiencia had a presiding officer, judges, and at least one crown attorney (*fiscal*). The sizes of the audiencias varied substantially, however. The early audiencias were small, consisting of a president, several judges who handled both civil and criminal cases, and one crown attorney. In 1568, the viceregal tribunals of Lima and Mexico were assigned additional judges to handle criminal cases (*alcaldes del crimen*); the remaining judges (*oidores*) specialized in civil cases. With the expansion of the courts in 1776, each audiencia had a regent who oversaw the overall operation of the tribunal, three or more *oidores,* and two *fiscales,* one for civil and one for criminal cases. The tribunals of Lima and Mexico also had several *alcaldes del crimen,* giving the courts a total of eighteen ministers each. Together, the American audiencias had one hundred ministers.

Audiencia judges and crown attorneys were required to be university-trained lawyers and at least twenty-five years of age when named to a court. Their appointments were for life or the pleasure of the king.

As the most professional branch of the royal bureaucracy and the most important civil institutions under their jurisdiction's chief executive, audiencias held prestige and power in judicial, legislative, and executive matters. Among their judicial responsibilities was first-instance jurisdiction for cases that related to the royal treasury and for certain cases that arose in the capital cities where they resided. As courts of appeal within their districts, audiencias exercised final authority in criminal cases and most civil suits.

The audiencias also had executive and legislative responsibilities. A district's chief executive received the audiencia's advice on all major questions; decisions reached through this consultation had the force of law unless disallowed by the Council of the Indies. In the executive's absence, the court assumed his duties and governed. Audiencias also were required to enforce royal laws, and to that end judges undertook periodic inspection tours within their districts. Judges also often sat with one or more corporate bodies in a colony, such as the merchants' guild.

Audiencias, then, possessed formidable powers. Their role in judicial affairs and in overseeing the implementation of royal legislation made their decisions important for the communities they served. Since appointments of audiencia ministers were for life or royal pleasure, the audiencias provided an element of continuity at the highest level. Incoming executives disregarded their advice only with peril. Armed with far-reaching authority, the audiencias were, always in theory and often in fact, an important check on other institutions of government.

Although the initial audiencia ministers were born in Spain, men born in the New World (creoles) began to receive audiencia appointments in 1585. From that year to 1687, creoles constituted 24 percent of all new appointees. In 1687, the crown began to sell audiencia appointments during periods of financial crisis and, as a result, Americans secured 44 percent of the appointments until 1750, most through purchase, and many in their district of birth. As a result of securing dispensations from legislation restricting local social and economic ties, many of these purchasers were deeply linked to their region of service, a circumstance that compromised their ability to provide impartial justice. When the crown stopped sales and began to reassert its authority over the courts in the early 1750s, the percentage of Americans who entered the courts dropped back to 24 percent. This change, which was most pronounced in the appointments immediately following the expansion of the courts' size in 1776, did not go unnoticed by creoles. With regard to the audiencias, their clamor for appointments was not, as was once thought, to gain entry into high positions, but rather to return to an era in which they had enjoyed frequent access to these powerful courts.

*Recopilación de leyes de los reynos de las Indias,* 4 vols. (1681; repr. 1973), *libro* II, *títulos* XV–XVIII; JOHN H. PARRY, *The Audiencia of New Galicia in the Sixteenth Century* (1948); JOHN L. PHELAN, *The Kingdom of Quito in the Seventeenth Century* (1967); GUILLERMO LOHMANN VILLENA, *Los Ministros de la audiencia de Lima en el reinado de los Borbones (1700–1821)* (1974); MARK A. BURKHOLDER and D. S. CHANDLER, *From Impotence to Authority: The Spanish Crown and the American Audiencias, 1687–1808* (1977), and *Biographical Dictionary of Audiencia Ministers in the Americas, 1687–1821* (1982).

MARK A. BURKHOLDER

**AUDIENCIA DE LOS CONFINES.** The NEW LAWS OF 1542 called for the creation of the Audiencia de los Confines, so named because it was to be situated at Comayagua, a village on the border of Guatemala and Honduras, where the court held its first session in May 1544. In May 1548 the second president, Alonso LÓPEZ DE CERRATO, arrived. He recommended the court's removal to Santiago de Guatemala (now Antigua), a much larger and more prosperous settlement that was less isolated. Although Gracias a Dios had only a few poverty-stricken residents, the AUDIENCIA had remained there for four years because Governor Alonso Maldonado and his colleagues profited illegally from local business affairs. In 1549 Cerrato moved the court to Santiago, where it occupied the bishop's residence.

At first, jurisdiction of the *audiencia* extended from Panama north to Yucatán and Tabasco, but soon those regions were removed from its district. In the 1560s the Audiencia de los Confines was abolished and a court was reestablished at Panama with administration by the Audiencia of Mexico. However, the *audiencia* in Guatemala was restored by 1570 with jurisdiction from Chiapas to Costa Rica. As the Audiencia of Guatemala, the court maintained this arrangement until the end of the colonial period.

For a discussion in Spanish, see MARIO GÓNGORA, *El estado en el derecho indiano, época de fundación (1492–1570)* (1951). Various aspects of the *audiencia* are dealt with in RALPH LEE WOODWARD, JR., *Central America, a Nation Divided,* 2d ed. (1985); MURDO J. MAC LEOD, *Spanish Central America: A Socioeconomic History, 1520–1720* (1973); and WILLIAM L. SHERMAN, *Forced Native Labor in Sixteenth-Century Central America* (1979).

WILLIAM L. SHERMAN

**AUGUSTINIANS,** a Roman Catholic religious order of priests and brothers named after the fifth-century bishop and saint Augustine of Hippo. The Order of the Hermit Friars of St. Augustine, as it is formally known, adopted Augustine's "rule" at the time of their founding by the Holy See in 1256. Classified as a mendicant order, members are known as friars; they are governed by an elected prior-general, who resides in Rome, and are organized throughout the world into regions called provinces, each governed by an elected prior-provincial. By the fourteenth century, the Augustinians were established in most parts of Europe. Later they expanded into Africa, Asia, and America, within the extensive colonial empires of Portugal and Spain. In addition to preaching and missionary activity, they engaged in many types of ministry, including higher education, writing, and patristic studies. Among their better known friars are Giles of Rome (ca. 1245–1316), Martin Luther (1483–1546), St. Thomas of Villanova (1486–1555), Luis de León (1527–1591), and Gregor Mendel (1822–1884).

On 7 June 1533 seven Spanish Augustinians, led by Francisco de la Cruz, arrived in Mexico City, where they established a large church and friary, San Agustín, which was to be the core of a new Augustinian province and the principal center of their activity in Latin America and, eventually, the Philippine Islands. Augustinian expansion in New Spain (Mexico) was rapid. By the end of the sixteenth century, the number of Augustinians, including both Spaniards and criollos, exceeded 600 friars, located in some seventy-two missions throughout central Mexico, extending from San Luis Potosí in the north to Oaxaca in the south. The growth in the region of Michoacán was especially notable, resulting in the creation of a second Mexican Augustinian province in 1602. The two administrative regions, the provinces of Mexico and Michoacán, continue to exist, and among their churches are several imposing historic monuments, some still occupied by Augustinian friars. Worthy of particular attention for art and architecture are the friaries of Acolman, Cuitzeo, Morelia, and Yuriria. The friary of San Agustín in Mexico City, however, no longer exists; its large church was confiscated in the nineteenth century and converted into the national library in 1884.

The leading Augustinian figure in colonial Mexico was Alonso de la VERA CRUZ, a sixteenth-century missionary, educator, writer of philosophical texts, canon lawyer, and administrator. Educated at the University of Salamanca, he was one of the founders and principal lecturers of the University of Mexico, established in 1553. Like his friend and associate Bartolomé de LAS CASAS, Fray Alonso was keenly interested in defending the rights of the native Indians, a goal he pursued in two of his series of lectures, *Relectio de dominio infidelium et iusto bello* and *Relectio de decimis* (in *The Writings of Alonso de la Vera Cruz,* edited and translated by Ernest Burrus, 1968–1976). His teachings met with opposition, especially from the archbishop of Mexico, Alonso de Montúfar, who denounced him to the INQUISITION. Recalled temporarily to Spain in 1562, Fray Alonso defended his views successfully, was regarded favorably by PHILIP II, and was therefore able to influence legislation aimed at removing abuses of the Indians. His interest in the native peoples was not merely academic, for he was an active missionary who spoke Tarascan, the language of Michoacán, and advocated full incorporation of the Indians into the sacramental life of the Catholic church.

Another prominent sixteenth-century Augustinian was Andrés de URDANETA, the mariner-turned-friar who is credited with discovering the eastbound route across the Pacific Ocean from Manila to Acapulco. Employed by the crown as a navigator, he also led the first group of Augustinian missionaries to the Philippine Islands in 1564–1565. Another early friar was Agustín Farfán, a physician who published the first medical handbook in Mexico, *Tratado de medicina* (1579). Two seventeenth-century authors of note were the historians Juan de GRIJALVA and Diego Basalenque.

Before the middle of the seventeenth century the Augustinians were to be found in most parts of the Spanish Empire. An extensive development took place in Peru, where the foundations of a new province began at Lima in 1551. The province of Peru was the base from which were organized the provinces of Quito, Ecuador (1573), New Granada (Bogotá, Colombia, 1575), and Chile (Santiago de Chile, 1595), as well as missions in the regions later known as Bolivia and Argentina. The Peruvian missions of the colonial period were grouped principally in the areas of Lima, Trujillo, and Cuzco, and their history has been recorded by two able seventeenth-century chroniclers, Antonio de la Calancha and Bernardo de Torres. A noted Augustinian in the more recent history of Latin America is Diego Francisco Padilla. A patriot and pamphleteer in the independence movement in Colombia, he was a member of the first junta of the revolutionary government in 1810.

The Augustinians, like all the older religious orders, went into severe decline in Latin America in the nineteenth century. Liberation from Spain and the accompanying wars and confiscations, often anticlerical as well as anti-Spanish, greatly reduced the numbers and influence of the friars. In the twentieth century, however, there has been a recovery, accomplished in part with the help of friars from western Europe, especially Spain, and from the United States. In 1990 the Augustinians were active in nearly every country of Latin

America, most notably in Mexico and Peru. Mexico had two provinces entirely composed of native-born friars, and Peru had four major mission areas, composed chiefly of foreign-born friars. Besides Mexico, full-fledged Augustinian provinces existed in Colombia, Ecuador, and Chile, and the number of friars in Brazil and Argentina also was considerable. As of 1988 the total number of Augustinians in fourteen countries of Latin America was 714.

For the general history of the Augustinians see *History of the Order of St. Augustine,* 4 vols. (1979–1989); and ROBERTO JARAMILLO, comp., *Los Agustinos en América Latina: Pasado y presente* (1987). Specialized studies include GREGORIO DE SANTIAGO VELA, *Ensayo de una biblioteca ibero-americana de la Orden de S. Agustín,* 8 vols. (1913–1931); AVENCIO VILLAREJO, *Los Agustinos en el Perú, 1548–1965* (1965); ERNEST BURRUS, *The Writings of Alonso de la Vera Cruz,* 5 vols. (1967–1975); MANUEL MERINO, ed., *Crónicas agustinianas del Perú,* 2 vols. (1972); NICOLÁS P. NAVARRETE, *Historia de la provincia agustiniana de San Nicolás de Tolentino de Michoacán,* 2 vols. (1978); ALIPIO RUIZ ZAVALA, *Historia de la Provincia agustiniana del santísimo Nombre de Jesús de México,* 2 vols. (1984); ARTHUR ENNIS, *Augustinian Religious Professions in Sixteenth Century Mexico* (1986).

ARTHUR J. ENNIS, O.S.A.

**AURY, LOUIS-MICHEL** (*b.* ca. 1788; *d.* 30 August 1821), French privateer during the Latin American Wars for Independence (1810–1821). Born in Montrouge, a Paris suburb, Aury grew up during the French Revolution and entered Napoleon's navy at an early age. In 1803 he left his warship at Guadeloupe to join French privateers. Seven years later, with the equivalent of several thousand dollars in prize money, Lieutenant Aury had achieved notoriety as a privateer. He suffered serious setbacks when U.S. officials in New Orleans confiscated his ship in 1810 and a Federalist mob in Savannah burned his ship to the water in 1811, episodes that embittered Aury toward the United States. In 1812 José Pedro Gual, representative of the Cartagena creole government, arranged for Aury to command a refitted privateer. The U.S. declaration of war against Britain had improved conditions for French privateers in America, and Latin American rebel governments had begun to issue patents to those who would carry their struggle against Spain to the high seas. Operating from Cartagena, Commodore Aury's fleet supported Simón BOLÍVAR by devastating Spanish shipping, but a bitter rivalry developed between Aury and the commander of Bolívar's Venezuela squadron, Luis BRIÓN.

After Cartagena fell to the Spanish late in 1815, Aury joined Bolívar in Haiti but refused to serve under Brión's command. Instead, he accepted a patent from Mexican rebels and in 1816 reorganized his fleet in New Orleans, in close association with merchants headed by Edward Livingston. With Aury, they supported General Xavier Mina, a young Spanish rebel who had organized his expedition in Liverpool and brought it to Baltimore with the cooperation of Gual. The New Or-

leans associates hoped to wrest Florida from Spain and to gain access to Mexico's silver mines. Aury established a government at Galveston only nominally connected with the revolution in Mexico. From Galveston he directed profitable privateering operations in the Gulf of Mexico, channeling the booty back to New Orleans. Mina arrived at the end of 1816, but Aury refused to support his plan for an overland invasion of Mexico, preferring to continue privateering or to make a seaborne assault on Tampico. Mina took most of the forces and invaded Mexico in April 1817, only to be captured by the Spaniards and executed in October 1817.

Aury, meanwhile, sailed to FLORIDA, arriving on 15 September 1817 at Fernandina, Amelia Island, where Gregor MAC GREGOR had established a Republic of Florida, which he turned over to Aury as the representative of the Mexican rebels. Aury began a lucrative commerce with Georgia in slaves and merchandise. These activities embarrassed the Spanish and French governments and were a nuisance to the United States. Thus, on 2 December 1817 President James Monroe ordered U.S. troops to suppress Aury's bases at Fernandina and Galveston. Aury, in collaboration with Gual, abandoned further pretense of operating under the authority of a nonexistent Mexican government and formed an independent Florida Republic on 9 December. Two weeks later U.S. forces took over Amelia Island and remained there until after Spain sold Florida to the United States in 1821.

Aury resumed privateering operations in the Caribbean. Again refusing to serve under Brión, he acquired patents from the governments of Chile and Buenos Aires and established a base at Old Providence Island in the western Caribbean. After a successful raid on Izabal, Guatemala, in May 1819, he plotted with José Cortés Madariaga, envoy of Chile and Buenos Aires to Jamaica, to liberate Central America. His privateering brought prosperity to Old Providence, but his efforts at a rapprochement with Bolívar failed, sabotaged by Brión, even after Aury petitioned Bolívar for incorporation of Old Providence into Gran Colombia. Aury undoubtedly felt his settlement would be more secure attached to Colombia than to distant Buenos Aires. His campaign in April 1820 to take the Spanish forts at Trujillo and Omoa, Honduras, failed, but Aury continued his privateering from Old Providence until a fall from his horse abruptly ended his life.

Aury's attacks on Spanish shipping contributed to the establishment of Latin American independence. Despite his strong commitment to republicanism inherited from the French Revolution, however, he was often suspected of placing his own interests ahead of those of the creole republics whose flags he flew.

GEORGE COGGESHALL, *A History of American Privateers and Letters of Marque During Our War with England* . . . (1856); LEWIS BEALER, *Los corsarios de Buenos Aires: Sus actividades en las guerras hispanoamericanas de la independencia, 1815–1821* (1937); L. E. DABNEY, "Louis Aury: The First Governor of Texas under the

Mexican Republic," in *Southwestern Historical Quarterly* 42, no. 1 (1938): 108–116; HARRIS G. WARREN, "Documents Relating to the Establishment of Privateers at Galveston, 1816–1817," in *Louisiana Historical Quarterly* 21, no. 4 (1938): 1086–1109; STANLEY FAYE, "Privateersmen of the Gulf and their Prizes," *Louisiana Historical Quarterly* 22, no. 4 (1939): 1012–1094, and "Commodore Aury," in *Louisiana Historical Quarterly* 24, no. 3 (1941): 611–697; HARRIS G. WARREN, *The Sword Was Their Passport: A History of American Filibustering in the Mexican Revolution* (1943); HAROLD A. BIERCK, *La vida pública de don Pedro Gual* (1947); MARTIN LUIS GUZMÁN, *Javier Mina, héroe de España y México*, 2d ed. (1955); CLIFTON B. KROEBER, *The Growth of the Shipping Industry in the Río de la Plata Region, 1794–1860* (1957); JAIME DUARTE FRENCH, *Los tres Luises del Caribe: ¿Corsarios o libertadores?* (1988).

RALPH LEE WOODWARD, JR.

*See also* **Piracy.**

**AUSTIN, MOSES** (*b.* 4 October 1761; *d.* 10 June 1821), founder of the American lead industry and father of Stephen F. AUSTIN. Reared in Connecticut, Moses Austin moved to Richmond, Virginia, in 1785 to manage a mercantile business. An entrepreneur, he revived the lead business, making considerable money before experiencing business reverses. He then moved to Spanish Upper Louisiana, where he received a land grant for his lead enterprise. He founded Potosi, Missouri, in 1798 and prospered until the War of 1812. Bankrupt by 1820, Austin saw his economic revival in establishing a colony in TEXAS, for which he secured permission from the Spanish government. His son, Stephen Fuller, established the colony after his father's death.

EUGENE C. BAKER, *The Austin Papers* (1924–1928) and DAVID B. GRACY II, *Moses Austin: His Life* (1987).

DAVID B. GRACY II

**AUSTIN, STEPHEN FULLER** (*b.* 3 November 1793; *d.* 27 December 1836), father of Anglo-American TEXAS. Born in southwest Virginia, Austin lived and attended school in Spanish Upper Louisiana, Connecticut, and Kentucky before beginning work at age seventeen in his father's mercantile and lead businesses in Missouri. He served in the Missouri territorial legislature, but demonstrated no special business acumen. Loyalty to his father, despite financial reverses, drew him into land speculation in Arkansas (1819) and law studies in Louisiana (1820).

In 1821, Austin determined to carry out his deceased father's plan to settle Anglo-Americans in Spanish Texas. He received or participated in five *empresario* contracts, his first one for 300 families being the only one fulfilled by any *empresario*. Until 1828, Austin was responsible for civil and military affairs of the Anglo-American settlements, an authority he exercised with a patience and tact that minimized friction between the settlers and the Mexican authorities until unrest led to the conventions of

1832 and 1833, which sought changes in unpopular laws and separate statehood within Mexico.

Returning from a trip to Mexico City, where he obtained many of the demands of the conventions of 1832 and 1833, Austin was arrested (1834) on suspicion of inciting insurrection and held in Mexico City for eighteen months. Back in Texas (1835), he supported opposition to the Mexican central government, and during the TEXAS REVOLUTION (1836) commanded troops, later serving as a commissioner to the United States. Defeated for president of the republic, he became secretary of state but died in office soon after.

EUGENE C. BARBER, *The Austin Papers* (1924–1928) and *The Life of Stephen F. Austin* (1925).

DAVID B. GRACY II

**AUTO, AUTO SACRAMENTAL,** a genre originating from a dramatic form developed especially in the thirteenth and fourteenth centuries, the *miracle* (France) or *auto* (Iberian Peninsula) presented episodes involving a miracle, usually the intervention of the Virgin Mary in favor of a poor sinner, commonly of the lower classes, guilty of some unpardonable crime before the law, human or divine. The theater of the early Renaissance in Spain (Juan del Encina) and Portugal (Gil Vicente) is essentially a stylized form of that of the Middle Ages, combining the religious and the profane with more realistic characterizations and dialogue. Whereas Encina's *autos* were no longer liturgical or ecclesiastical, Vicente continued the medieval tradition and introduced the allegory. In this genre he was a precursor of Calderón de La Barca, whose *autos sacramentales* epitomize the form in content and technique.

All variations were utilized in the New World by the JESUIT missionaries from Spain and Portugal. In their efforts to convert and colonize Indians in their MISSIONS, the priests not only followed Iberian models, but also incorporated much that they observed in native settings and culture, including language, in order to present the teachings of the church to their catechumens. These traditions have evolved to our day, with Ariano Vilar SUASSUNA as perhaps the chief proponent in Brazil in his *Auto da compadecida* and other works.

SÁBATO MAGALDI, *Panorama do teatro brasileiro* (1962).

RICHARD A. MAZZARA

**AUTO RACING.** *See* **Sports.**

**AUTOMOBILE INDUSTRY.** Motor vehicles first arrived in Buenos Aires in 1889, and in 1916 Ford Motor Company established assembly operations in Argentina. While Ford's move marked the beginning of automobile production in Latin America, several North American automakers already maintained distribution networks in major countries there. Throughout the first half of the twentieth century, U.S. firms, anxious to supplement slowing domestic growth, dominated the Latin American auto trade. Most began by distributing U.S.-built vehicles; some, such as Chrysler and Kaiser, proceeded to authorize licensing agreements, enabling local manufacturers to assemble their vehicles, while others, including General Motors, established subsidiary operations to assemble vehicles. In either case, early assembly operations were small-scale, designed to build vehicles from complete knockdown kits (CKDs) imported from the United States. The CKDs included virtually all the sheet metal and subassemblies required to produce a vehicle. Following Ford's lead, General Motors built an assembly plant in Brazil in 1925, and before long most of Detroit's major automakers had established assembly operations in the Mexico City area. Auto production stagnated during the Great Depression and World War II, however, and locally built vehicles remained a small portion of vehicles sold in Latin America. Vehicle shortages during the war prompted Latin American governments to end their dependence on imported vehicles, and resultant policies effected a resurgence in the industry. Thereafter, auto manufacturing expanded. In 1992 Brazil and Mexico produced 1.1 million vehicles each, as opposed to 9.7 million units in the United States. The prevalence of automobiles in Latin America still lags behind other industrialized nations, however. In the United States, for example, there was one vehicle for every 1.6 people in 1990; in Mexico, that ratio dropped to one for every 8.9, while in Brazil there was only one vehicle for every 12 people. Brazil and Mexico emerged as dominant producer nations, while Argentina, Chile, Peru, Colombia, and Venezuela played much smaller roles.

After 1945, governments in Brazil, Mexico, Argentina, and Chile supported the development of the automotive industry in order to end dependence on imported vehicles and to increase employment. They encouraged foreign investment, granted tax incentives to heavy industry, and levied high tariffs on imported finished vehicles while maintaining duty-free status for CKDs. Some imposed outright bans on imported vehicles. The incentives, coupled with a car-starved market, resulted in an influx of European manufacturers and renewed growth. During the 1950s, Córdoba, Argentina, became an important automotive center and was home to Fiat and Kaiser assembly plants. Argentina's inducements also attracted General Motors and Rambler. Córdoba became known for its militant labor force, which commanded higher wages; since labor costs in Brazil were lower, Volkswagen constructed its plant in São Paulo, and both General Motors and Ford chose Brazil for future expansion. In Mexico, no fewer than eleven auto firms were represented. By the late 1950s, more than twenty major European, North American, and Japanese manufacturers assembled imported components—far too many entrants to achieve efficiency in such a small market.

Governments realized that the goal of substituting domestic for foreign vehicles needed refinement: manufacturers were unable to achieve the economies of scale necessary to control costs and produce quality products at affordable prices. Since all major producers were foreign-owned and managed, the importation of the components of their vehicles created a drain on foreign exchange. Brazil took the first step by initiating content restrictions, which stipulated that an increasing portion of a vehicle's content must be locally produced. Argentina followed suit in 1958, and in 1960 Mexico not only enacted local-content laws but also rationalized the number of its auto manufacturers. Content laws challenged automakers in two ways: first, they became increasingly responsible for building a complex vehicle, not just a kit; second, they were now subject to the vagaries of local-parts supply, inflation, and infrastructure problems.

Prices of domestically produced vehicles were substantially higher than in Europe or North America owing to production inefficiencies, higher material and financing costs, and taxes. Latin America's markets languished. The large and rapidly growing market sought by the manufacturers remained limited by low incomes. During the 1970s governments and manufacturers began to look beyond domestic markets. They sought to capitalize on the region's low labor costs and believed increased export volume would both lower prices for the domestic market and alleviate trade imbalances. Despite major worldwide economic recessions in the 1970s and the 1980s and spiraling inflation, which eroded cost advantages, the Latin American automobile industry, particularly that of Mexico, reached new production records. While trade barriers and lackluster economies throughout the world have softened demand for new vehicles, the Latin American automobile industry is as vital as ever. South America's MERCOSUR Trade Agreement and the NORTH AMERICAN FREE TRADE AGREEMENT (NAFTA) are expected to stimulate exports by further eliminating trade barriers between producing nations.

DEEBE FERRIS, Ward's Automotive Yearbook (1962–1993); MOTOR VEHICLE MANUFACTURERS ASSOCIATION OF THE U.S., INC., Automobile Facts and Figures (1967–1992); JACK N. BEHRMAN, The Role of International Companies in Latin American Integration (1972); RHYS OWEN JENKINS, Dependent Industrialization in Latin America: The Automotive Industry in Argentina, Chile, and Mexico (1977), and Transnational Corporations and the Latin American Automobile Industry (1987); IAN ROXBOROUGH, Unions and Politics in Mexico: The Case of the Automobile Industry (1984), pp. 45–46; RICHARD S. NEWFARMER, ed., Profits, Progress, and Poverty (1985), pp. 205–207, 225; BERNHARD FISCHER et al., Capital-Intensive Industries in Newly Industrializing Countries: The Case of the Brazilian Automobile and Steel Industries (1988).

JANET M. PLZAK

**AVALOS, PACT OF (1820),** a last-ditch effort by José Gervasio ARTIGAS to save his ideal of a confederation, signed on 24 April 1820 in the small town of Avalos, Corrientes, Argentina. Only the provinces of Corrientes and Misiones joined Artigas, who represented the BANDA ORIENTAL, in the signing of the treaty.

Artigas's Federal League had been moribund since 23 February, 1820, the day Buenos Aires and two federalist CAUDILLOS signed the Pact of El Pilar in spite of his adamant opposition. Many of the federalist caudillos had been acting independently of Artigas because he was tied down fighting the Portuguese in the Banda Oriental, leaving them to their own devices in facing the ever present threat of Buenos Aires. The Pact of Avalos bound the signatories to fight for freedom and independence and allowed each province to elect its own governor and manage its internal economy. Artigas was again named the Protector of the Free Peoples, but he was already a beaten man, with no real power to influence events.

JOHN STREET, *Artigas and the Emancipation of Uruguay* (1959); LUIS NAVARRO GARCÍA, *José Artigas* (1987); MANUEL LUCENA SALMORAL, *José Gervasio Artigas: gaucho y confederado* (1988).

JUAN MANUEL PÉREZ

**AVELLANEDA, NICOLÁS** (*b.* 10 October 1837; *d.* 25 November 1885), president of Argentina (1874–1880). Avellaneda, a native of Tucumán, established a regime that completed the formation of modern Argentina by consolidating national order. He represents a continuation of liberal policies that were adjusted to appease provincial interests. A friend of Domingo SARMIENTO and the minister of religion, justice, and public instruction in Sarmiento's regime, Avellaneda became president by imposition. When Bartolomé MITRE, the defeated presidential candidate, led a revolt in 1874, Sarmiento headed the government forces and crushed Mitre. Avellaneda, however, could not mold the interior and the *porteños* into an effective coalition. He sought to curb Buenos Aires province, for example, by allowing European immigrants, but not Argentine citizens, to settle Patagonia.

Throughout the 1870s financial difficulties limited Avellaneda's presidency. He angered major exporters who depended upon European markets by defaulting on payment of Argentina's foreign debt. Because of budgetary constraints, there were few public works projects in the provinces. During Avellaneda's presidency, the first wheat was shipped from Rosario to Great Britain (1878). Agricultural production increased, as did immigration. In 1876 the government enacted the first comprehensive public land law, mainly to facilitate the settlement of European farmers. Wool production increased to 50 percent of the value of all Argentine exports. The gaucho population declined rapidly. Cultural life flourished, and education became more widely available. Avellaneda signed boundary treaties to settle disputes with Paraguay (following the WAR OF THE TRIPLE ALLIANCE), Brazil, and Chile.

The government federalized the city of Buenos Aires in 1880, a decision that provoked a bloody revolt in Buenos Aires Province. Avellaneda and Congress crumbled under the pressure of this event, but a nationalist junta eventually suppressed the rebellion. The traditional parties began to fade away, paving the way for the rise of the Partido Autonomista Nacional. As if to indicate the triumph of an evolving liberal system, the remains of José de San Martín were brought from France to Argentina.

Avellaneda's interest in education, land, and unification formed the basis for his writings. At one time he was an editor of the influential newspaper *El Nacional*. In addition to lecturing frequently, Avellaneda was a prolific writer of essays. He also produced a book, *Tierras públicas* (Public Lands, 1865). His collected writings, *Escritos y discursos* (1910), fill twelve volumes.

Avellaneda's early background is discussed in ALLISON W. BUNKLEY, *The Life of Sarmiento* (1952). MARK D. SZUCHMAN, *Mobility and Integration in Urban Argentina: Córdoba in the Liberal Era* (1980), is a cogent analysis of social changes in the interior. The decline of the gauchos is portrayed in RICHARD SLATTA, *Gauchos and the Vanishing Frontier* (1983). There is a deft analysis of the 1870s in DAVID ROCK, *Argentina, 1516–1987* (1987). For the beginning of the agricultural boom, see JAMES SCOBIE, *Revolution on the Pampas: A Social History of Argentine Wheat, 1860–1910* (1964).

DOUGLAS W. RICHMOND

*See also* **Argentina: Political Parties.**

**AVERÍA,** a Spanish tax on the Indies trade that covered the costs of providing armed protection for merchant shipping. First collected in 1521, the *avería* was administered by the CASA DE CONTRATACIÓN of Seville, working closely with the *consulado*. There was no fixed rate, the aim being to spread the costs of necessary defense over all commodities, although in 1644 PHILIP IV guaranteed that the maximum charge would be 12 percent of the value of cargoes. The ad valorem tax was abolished in 1660 in favor of an agreement that the principal merchant houses of Seville would contribute fixed sums toward the costs of defending the transatlantic fleets.

GUILLERMO CÉSPEDES DEL CASTILLO, *La avería en el comercio de Indias* (1945); CLARENCE H. HARING, *The Spanish Empire in America* (1947), esp. pp. 305–306.

JOHN R. FISHER

**AVIATION.** Beginning in 1910, Latin American, European, and U.S. aviators in small but growing numbers pioneered airplane flights in Latin America. In aviation's early barnstorming and aerial pathfinding phase, flying in Latin America was characterized by several factors that were natural consequences of the times: the relatively few Latin American aviators came from wealthy families, such as the Brazilian Alberto SANTOS-DUMONT, who in 1906 made the first airplane flight in Europe; and most planes were imported from Europe or the United States—the latter factor would persist indefinitely. As elsewhere, fatal accidents often occurred in the flimsy and underpowered planes of aviation's infancy.

Mexico was the site of several milestones in military aviation. Early in 1911 the regime of Porfirio Díaz, faced with spreading revolution, hired two French barnstormers to fly reconnaissance over rebel forces, the first known combat sorties of an airplane anywhere. As most factions in the revolution came to possess small numbers of planes, almost every facet of aerial warfare, if in microcosm and isolation, was recorded either preceding or concurrent with developments in World War I in Europe—besides reconnaissance, air-to-air combat, tactical air support, and the bombing of population centers occurred. Two noteworthy events occurred in 1914: a Constitutional plane piloted by Gustavo Salinas Carmiña scored a near miss on a Huertista warship off the west coast and U.S. Navy planes flew reconnaissance over Veracruz in the first use of aviation in a U.S. intervention.

In 1915 the Constitutionalists formed what was later the Fuerza Aérea Mexicana; it was soon conducting training, and manufactured a respectable number of airplanes of its own design after World War I restricted foreign supply. Argentina, Brazil, Chile, Cuba, and Uruguay created military air arms before or during World War I.

From 1919 on, most Latin American countries developed air arms with the aid of foreign military missions. They were equipped mainly with hand-me-downs from Europe and the United States, and their operations were for the most part noncombat: training, surveying, security watch. Like their army and naval counterparts, air officers sometimes engaged in volatile politics, a notable example being Marmaduke GROVE, who was briefly head of state in Chile in 1931. Periodically Latin American air arms engaged in aerial warfare after 1919; leading examples were operations of the air arms of both Bolivia and Paraguay in the CHACO WAR (1932–1935); operations of U.S.-equipped fighter squadrons from Mexico in the Philippines and from Brazil in Italy in World War II; and the gallant but doomed fight of the Argentine air force against the British in the South Atlantic War of 1982. Helicopters and strike aircraft have hunted guerrillas in the 1970s and 1980s.

Nonexistent until 1919, civil air transport in Latin America stemmed from the failure of surface transportation to blanket an often difficult and diverse geography. It was spurred by an international rivalry with martial implications and was fostered by nationalism.

The international rivalry pitted three non–Latin American groups against one another: Germans, who created airlines in South America, most notably So-

ciedad Colombo-Alemana de Transportes Aéreos (SCADTA), in Colombia in December 1919, the first lasting airline in the region; U.S. officials, fearing the implied threat to the Panama Canal, and private interests, recognizing a most fertile field for air transport, the latter launching Pan American Airways (1927), which with unprecedented government aid monopolized all U.S. international airline business until World War II; French private interests, whose heavily subsidized airline Aéropostale developed the world's longest route system, including routes in much of South America, by 1930. The rivalry featured three of the great pioneers in air transport history—Juan Terry Trippe of Pan American; Peter Paul von Bauer of SCADTA in Colombia; and French-born Marcel Boulloux-Lafont, who resided in South America. In the end, von Bauer secretly sold controlling interest in Depression-weakened SCADTA to Trippe (1931), and Boulloux-Lafont lost Aéropostale when the French government forced it into bankruptcy in 1931 by withdrawing its subsidy.

The Germans continued to present a threat until, with the outbreak of World War II, a wave of nationalizations quelled their activity.

Lines both domestic and international multiplied in the 1930s, some fading as others took to the sky. It was increasingly clear that air transport filled special needs in a region struggling to modernize, but also clear that airlines helped maintain the dependency imbalance. One line, Compañía Mexicana de Aviación (CMA), will serve to illustrate. It was founded in 1924 by U.S. entrepreneurs to fly payrolls to oil fields. With the help of some well-connected Mexicans, CMA added routes and diverse cargo. In 1929 it became a Pan American subsidiary in Mexican guise in order to carry PAA mail and cargo, something foreign lines could not do under Mexican law. CMA became truly Mexican after World War II, in a general trend to divest lines based in Latin America of foreign control, even though these lines still depended on outsiders for equipment such as the jets they began to acquire in the 1960s.

A number of Latin American air forces became involved in air transport. In 1929 Línea Aeropostal Santiago-Arica (later Línea Aérea Nacional, LAN) was founded by Comandante Arturo Merino Benítez as a division of the Chilean air force to carry mail and passengers, in part to counter the presence of PANAGRA, the jointly owned subsidiary of Pan American and the U.S. conglomerate W. R. Grace. It soon became a civil line, and ultimately the major Chilean domestic and international carrier. Other air forces, for example, Argentina's, developed transport divisions to serve sparsely settled areas, such as that from the Pampas to the Chilean border, that would not be profitable for a private-sector airline. Another dimension of Latin American air transport is that it is no longer the preserve of the well-to-do. After World War II it began to be more available to the less affluent with the rise of low-fare airlines. The pendulum had begun to swing.

Significant works covering one or more aspects of aviation in Latin America are WESLEY PHILLIPS NEWTON, *The Perilous Sky: U.S. Aviation Diplomacy and Latin America, 1919–1931* (1978); MARYLIN BENDER and SELIG ALTSCHUL, *The Chosen Instrument: Juan Trippe, Pan Am, The Rise and Fall of an American Entrepreneur* (1982); R. E. G. DAVIES, *Airlines of Latin America Since 1919* (1984).

One of the best reference works dealing with the world's air forces (including those of Latin America), their histories, and their current statuses is MARK HAMISH et al., *Air Forces of the World: Illustrated Directory of the World's Military Air Powers* (1979). The British periodical *Air International* has monthly updates on both military and civil aviation around the world.

Many Latin American countries have produced their own historical literature on their aviation. Those on Mexico include JOSÉ VILLELA GÓMEZ, *Breve historia de la aviación en México* (1971); and ENRIQUE SANDOVAL C., *Historia oficial de la fuerza expedicionaria mexicana* (1946), on the Mexican fighter squadron in the Philippines. In addition, the U.S. scholar Donathon C. Olliff is working on a history of aviation in Mexico that he has shared with this author.

WESLEY PHILLIPS NEWTON

**ÁVILA, ALONSO DE** (*b.* ca. 1539; *d.* 3 August 1566), leader of the so-called Cortés Conspiracy of 1565–1566. Ávila was a leading light of the second, native-born generation of *encomenderos* in Mexico. Less economically secure than their fathers, they grew increasingly resentful of the royal policies that progressively limited their power. They sought a champion in Martín CORTÉS, the conquistador's son and second marqués del Valle, who arrived in Mexico in 1563. Cortés soon clashed with the viceroy, Luis de VELASCO, and his pretensions to political influence increased when Velasco's death left an undersized, three-man AUDIENCIA as the highest authority in the colony.

In October 1565, Alonso de Ávila, Gil GONZÁLEZ DÁVILA (his older brother), and several other members of the colonial elite began actively plotting the overthrow of the government. They planned to assassinate the *audiencia* judges and other high officials and to proclaim Cortés king. But the marqués wavered, refusing explicitly to endorse the conspiracy. His indecision, along with the general indiscretion and ineptitude of the conspirators, allowed the *audiencia* to strike first. On 16 July 1566, the *audiencia* arrested the Ávila brothers and Cortés. After a brief trial, Alonso and Gil were condemned to death—a sentence clearly intended to deter any future conspirators. Both brothers were beheaded in Mexico City's central Plaza.

FERNANDO BENÍTEZ, *The Century After Cortés*, translated by Joan Mac Lean (1965); LESLEY BIRD SIMPSON, *Many Mexicos* (1966), esp. pp. 119–126; JORGE IGNACIO RUBIO MAÑÉ, *El Virreinato*, vol. 2, *Expansión y defensa: Primera parte* (1983), pp. 3–21.

R. DOUGLAS COPE

**ÁVILA, JULIO ENRIQUE** (*b.* 4 August 1892; *d.* 1968), Salvadoran poet and intellectual leader. A professor of chemistry and pharmacology, and later dean of the Faculty of Chemistry and Pharmacy at the National University of El Salvador, Ávila became known primarily as a literary figure. His first book, *Fuentes de alma* (1917), established him in the "modernist" school of Rubén DARÍO. Subsequent works, especially the poetic novel *El vigía sin luz* (1927) and an anthology, *El mundo de mi jardín* (1927), established him as one of the leading Salvadoran poets of his generation.

ALFONSO MARÍA LANDARECH, *Estudios literarios* (1959), pp. 114–139; LUIS GALLEGOS VALDÉS, *Panorama de la literatura salvadoreña del período precolombino a 1980* (1987), esp. pp. 209–216; DAVID ESCOBAR GALINDO, *Índice antológico de la poesía salvadoreña* (1987), pp. 256–257.

RALPH LEE WOODWARD, JR.

**ÁVILA, PEDRO ARIAS DE** (Pedrarias Dávila; *b.* ca. 1440; *d.* July 1531), Spanish soldier, governor of Panama (1514–1526) and of Nicaragua (1527–1531), and founder of Panama City (1519). Pedrarias was a member of a prominent noble family of Segovia; his uncle was an archbishop and his older brother was the count of Puñonrostro. He was perhaps of *converso* origins.

In his boyhood Pedrarias was a page in the court of Juan II of Castile and León (1406–1454). In later life he distinguished himself in the war against the Moors in Granada (1482–1492) and as a colonel of infantry fighting in North Africa (1508–1511). Physically imposing and athletic, Pedrarias was nicknamed "the jouster" and "the gallant." After another had declined the honor, he accepted an appointment as CAPTAIN-GENERAL and governor of Castilla del Oro in Darién (also known as Panama), offered in June 1513, despite his being seventy-three years of age.

Information had reached the king about the riches to be found in Panama, and owing to rumors of a great body of water to the south, a large fleet was organized under the command of Pedrarias. Among fifteen hundred or more passengers, the vessels carried a brilliant array of notables, including Pedrarias's wife, Isabel de Bobadilla y Peñalosa, the chronicler Gonzalo Fernández de OVIEDO Y VALDÉS, the historian Bernal DÍAZ DEL CASTILLO, and Hernando de SOTO. Altogether, it was perhaps the most distinguished passenger list of any fleet sailing to the New World. Pedrarias embarked for the Indies in April 1514 with orders to assume control of the colony; suspend the acting governor, Vasco Núñez de BALBOA; and to bring Balboa to justice on the charge of usurping authority from previous leaders.

The king learned of Balboa's discovery of the Pacific Ocean a few days after the departure of Pedrarias. Accordingly, the crown appointed Balboa ADELANTADO, but he was subject to Pedrarias. It took six months for the commission to reach Panama, and Pedrarias withheld the information from Balboa. Initial contact between the two men was cordial, and Balboa freely shared his knowledge of the land and people of Panama with Pedrarias. Balboa was acquitted in his judicial review, but because of his prestige and popularity, Pedrarias seethed with resentment and jealousy. To help relieve the tension, Bishop Juan de Quevedo arranged the betrothal of Pedrarias's daughter María to Balboa. The aging governor doubtless welcomed a good political match for his eldest daughter, who was in a convent in Seville.

Meantime, lieutenants of Pedrarias led predatory *entradas* in search of gold and slaves, undoing by their brutality much of the goodwill Balboa had established among the natives. Balboa continued his project to build ships to sail down the Pacific coast to explore the rich land of "Biru," of which Indians had spoken. His plans were interrupted when a companion betrayed him, charging that he planned to overthrow the authority of Pedrarias, to whom he was still subject. Balboa was also accused of being more interested in his Indian mistress than in his betrothed. Pedrarias, his parental pride wounded, saw the opportunity to be rid of his rival once and for all. Balboa, apparently innocent of the charge of treason, was found guilty, denied appeals, and beheaded along with three of his friends at Acla in January 1519.

That same year Pedrarias founded the city of Panama, on the south coast of the isthmus. Under his aegis Pascual de ANDAGOYA made an exploratory voyage in 1522 to investigate the great civilization that was said to exist to the south. Later, Pedrarias was a partner in the expedition of Francisco PIZARRO that led to his conquest of Inca Peru. In 1522 Pedrarias also dispatched lieutenants northward, and in 1523 Francisco HERNÁNDEZ DE CÓRDOBA, who was welcomed by local CACIQUES, founded the cities of León and Granada in Nicaragua. When he plotted with others and renounced the authority of Pedrarias, Hernández de Córdoba was arrested and executed in 1526. Despite mounting criticism of Pedrarias, he was appointed governor of Nicaragua in 1527.

His daughter María was married to Rodrigo de Contreras, a nobleman of Segovia and later governor of Nicaragua (1534–1544); another daughter, Isabella, became the wife of explorer Hernando de SOTO, the future governor of Cuba. His extreme cruelty to Spaniards and Indians alike notwithstanding, Pedrarias enjoyed powerful support, including that of the influential Juan RODRÍGUEZ DE FONSECA. With such friends back in Spain, as well as extraordinarily good luck, he served as a governor in Central America for seventeen years, a remarkable career for the times. In 1531, at age ninety, the bitter old man died in León. By then he had justly earned the nickname "the wrath of God," bestowed upon him by a contemporary chronicler.

The standard biography of Pedrarias is PABLO ÁLVAREZ RUBIANO, *Pedrarias Dávila: Contribución al estudio de la figura del "gran justador," gobernador de Castilla del Oro y Nicaragua* (1944), although it sees the subject in a more positive light than do most historians. Very convenient and useful are the 152 documents presented in the appendices. Also valuable is MARIO GÓNGORA, *Los grupos de conquistadores en Tierra Firme, 1509–1530* (1962). Showing Pedrarias in a very negative role is his contemporary antagonist, the chronicler GONZALO FERNÁNDEZ DE OVIEDO Y VALDÉS, *Historia general y natural de las Indias*, 5 vols. (1959); also critical of Pedrarias is the historian BARTOLOMÉ DE LAS CASAS, *Historia de las Indias*, edited by Agustín Millares Carlo, 3 vols. (1951). See also CARLOS MOLINA ARGÜELLO, *El gobernador de Nicaragua en el siglo XVI* (1949). In English, consult KATHLEEN ROMOLI, *Balboa of Darien: Discoverer of the Pacific Ocean* (1953), and CARL ORTWIN SAUER, *The Early Spanish Main* (1966).

WILLIAM L. SHERMAN

**ÁVILA CAMACHO, MANUEL** (*b.* 24 April 1897; *d.* 13 October 1955), president of Mexico (1940–1946), remembered for his moderate leadership and for his consolidation and refinement of the achievements of his predecessor, Lázaro CÁRDENAS. His administration was crucial in the final transition from military to civilian political leadership, and in tempering government attitudes toward the Roman Catholic church after he declared himself a believer. He also moderated the nationalism and anti-Americanism of the Cárdenas administration, which had been symbolized by the 1938 nationalization of oil, and allied Mexico with the United States during World War II. As president Ávila Camacho reversed socialist tendencies in public education, repealing constitutional amendments stipulating adherence to that philosophy of education.

Ávila Camacho was born in Teziutlán, Puebla, the hometown of his lifelong friend, the notable labor leader Vicente Lombardo Toledano. (One source claims, however, that his birthplace was Martínez de la Torre, Veracruz.) He was largely raised by his mother, Eufrosina Camacho, and received some preparatory schooling and business training, but instead of continuing his education he joined the Constitutionalists under General Antonio Medina in 1914. He remained in the army as a career officer, serving his mentor, Lázaro CÁRDENAS, as chief of staff in 1920. Three years later he commanded the 79th Cavalry Regiment in Michoacán, where he opposed the rebellion of Adolfo DE LA HUERTA. Promoted to brigadier general in 1929, he again fought under General Cárdenas against the Escobar rebellion, the last major uprising of disgruntled Revolutionary generals against the government. Between 1929 and 1934 he commanded several important military zones, and when Cárdenas reached the presidency in 1934, Ávila Camacho was appointed *oficial mayor* (executive officer) of the secretariat of national defense, after which he rose to subsecretary and, ultimately, in 1937, to secretary of that agency. He resigned his position 17 January 1939 to run for president on the government party ticket in a heated electoral campaign against Juan Andrew Almazán.

LUIS MEDINA, *Historia de la revolución mexicana*, vol. 20, *Del cardenismo al avilacamachismo* (1978), and vol. 21, *Civilismo y modernización del autoritarismo* (1979).

RODERIC AI CAMP

**AVILÉS, GABRIEL** (marqués de Avilés: *b.* 1735; *d.* 19 September 1810), viceroy of Peru (1801–1806). Like his predecessor, Ambrosio O'HIGGINS, Avilés served as captain-general of Chile (1795–1799) before his promotion to Peru, and also briefly as viceroy in Buenos Aires (1799–1801). Avilés played a prominent role in the repression of the TÚPAC AMARU rebellion (1780–1783), combining firmness as a military commander with denunciation of the social abuses and administrative corruption that had provoked the insurrection. Before his transfer to Chile—as field marshal and second marqués de Avilés—he served as governor of Callao.

During his vice-regency in Peru, Avilés promoted public health, repressed a conspiracy in Cuzco, and oversaw the incorporation into the viceroyalty of Mainas and Guayaquil (in present-day Ecuador). He remained in Peru for four years under his successor ABASCAL, but refused the offer of appointment as viceroy of the Río de la Plata following the May 1810 revolution. Shortly thereafter he left Lima for Spain, but died in Valparaíso, Chile.

CARLOS ALBERTO ROMERO, ed., *Memoria del virrey del Perú, marqués de Avilés* (1901).

JOHN R. FISHER

**AVIO,** a form of credit and investment used in MINING, but also employed in other forms of economic activity. In mining, the *aviador* (financier), who supplied the *avios,* furnished mine owners with cash, mercury, salt, and magistral (crushed copper pyrites) for the general purposes of mining or refining SILVER. When mine owners were unable to repay these debts because of floods, lack of labor, or exhaustion of veins, *aviadores* frequently acquired ownership of the enterprise. In the south of New Spain, merchants used *avios* to lend money to aspiring ALCALDE MAYOR candidates who needed substantial resources to purchase the post. In order to repay the loan, the *alcalde* or his lieutenant would force the indigenous people to purchase mules or luxury commodities for which they had to pay by producing COCHINEAL and COTTON.

Two sources on the *avios* in mining are PETER BAKEWELL, *Silver Mining and Society in Colonial Mexico-Zacatecas* (1971), and DAVID BRADING, *Miners and Merchants in Bourbon Mexico (1763–1810)* (1971). BRIAN HAMNETT's *Politics and Trade in Southern Mexico, 1750–1821* (1971) has a thorough discussion of the system of *avios* and *repartamiento* of merchandise.

EDITH COUTURIER

**AXAYACATL** (*b.* ca. 1449; *d.* 1481), AZTEC emperor from 1468/69–1481. The sixth Mexica TLATOANI (a "speaker" or ruler), Axayacatl ("Watery Visage") was the grandson of two previous rulers: MOTECUHZOMA I on his mother's side, and ITZCOATL on his father's side. According to one native history, he became ruler at age nineteen. His short reign was devoted to military campaigns. To the expanding Aztec empire he added Toluca, MALINALCO, and other Matlatzinca polities west of the Mexica capital of TENOCHTITLÁN; he also subdued the Tuxpan area on the Gulf coast. In 1473 a dispute between Axayacatl and his sister's husband Moquihuix, ruler of TLATELOLCO, Tenochtitlán's neighbor to the north, led to Tlatelolco's military defeat. In 1478 Axayacatl led a disastrous campaign against the TARASCANS in MICHOACÁN; native histories state that all but 200 of Axayacatl's 20,000 or more soldiers perished in the worst Mexica defeat until the Spanish conquest. Axayacatl was succeeded by his brother, Tizoc. Axayacatl's son, MOTECUHZOMA II (1466–1520), was ruling when CORTÉS invaded Mexico.

DIEGO DURÁN, *The Aztecs: The History of the Indies of New Spain,* translated by Doris Heyden and Fernando Horcasitas (1964); BURR CARTWRIGHT BRUNDAGE, *A Rain of Darts: The Mexica Aztecs* (1972); NIGEL DAVIES, *The Aztecs: A History* (1980).

LOUISE M. BURKHART

**AYACUCHO,** also known as Huamanga, the principal city (1981 population, 68,535) and capital of the department of the same name (1981 population, 523,821) in south-central highland Peru. Founded by Francisco PIZARRO on 9 January 1539 as San Juan de la Frontera, it was moved several miles to its present site on 25 April 1540 by Alonso de Alvarado. It is located about 9,025 feet above sea level on a small plain in an intermountain valley about 224 miles southeast of Lima. During the colonial period Ayacucho became a significant administrative center for the region, a way station on the major route from Lima to Cuzco almost equidistant from both cities, and the residence of miners from neighboring HUANCAVELICA and of local landowners.

On 9 December 1824, the nearby plain of Quinua was the site of the BATTLE OF AYACUCHO, which ensured the independence of South America from Spanish control. The city then entered an extended period of decline due to its isolation and limited natural resources, especially water. A railroad intended to link Ayacucho with central Peru and commemorate the centennial of the 1824 battle terminated at Huancavelica. The reopening of the colonial University of San Cristóbal de Huamanga (1677–1886) in 1959 and the completion of an all-weather highway to the coast near Pisco in 1968 revitalized the city. From 1961 to 1972 the population grew from 21,465 to 34,706, but the department remained one of the poorest in the country. In response to the activities of the Shining Path, an insurgent group that originated at Ayacucho in 1980, the city and most of the department have been under nearly continuous military control since late 1982. The combination of insurgent activity and military presence has contributed to high levels of violence, repression, and forced migration.

LUIS R. FOWLER, *Monografía histórico-geográfica del Departamento de Ayacucho* (1924); INSTITUTO NACIONAL DE ESTADÍS-

TICA, *Censos nacionales: VIII de población, III de vivienda, 12 de julio de 1981: Departamento de Ayacucho,* vol. 1 (1983); CARLOS IVÁN DEGREGORI, *Ayacucho 1969–1979: El surgimiento de Sendero Luminoso* (1900).

DAVID SCOTT PALMER

*See also* **Peru: Revolutionary Movements.**

**AYACUCHO, BATTLE OF,** the final battle of the Wars of Independence, which took place at the hacienda Ayacucho, near the city of Huamanga (later renamed Ayacucho), Peru, on 9 December 1824. Since Simón BOLÍVAR had been notified by the Colombian government that he could no longer command a Peruvian army, he appointed the thirty-two-year-old Bolivian general Antonio José de SUCRE to lead the liberation army. Although the royalists outnumbered their opponents by more than two to one, possessed superior artillery, and occupied the strategic heights overlooking the plains, Sucre was able to rally his forces with a desperate cavalry charge that routed the enemy and captured the Spanish commander, General José de LA SERNA. The royalists suffered 1,400 dead and 700 wounded, while total casualties on the patriot side amounted to 900. That evening all royalist forces in the sierra surrendered, followed shortly thereafter by those in Lima. Although a diehard Spanish force managed to hold out in the fortress at Callao until January 1826, Spanish power in South America was ended after more than three centuries of Spanish rule.

TIMOTHY E. ANNA, *The Fall of Royal Government in Peru* (1979).

PETER F. KLARÉN

**AYACUCHO, MARSHALS OF.** *See* **Marshals of Ayacucho.**

**AYALA, ELIGIO** (*b.* 1880; *d.* 24 October 1930), president of Paraguay (1924–1928) and educator. Born in Mbuyapey of humble parents, Ayala displayed considerable talent at an early age and rose rapidly in the ranks of the Partido Liberal. In the 1890s, he moved to Asunción, where he attended the Colegio Nacional and began teaching in 1904, giving courses in philosophy, civics, psychology, and logic. In 1908 he received a doctorate in law from the university.

At this time, Ayala embarked on a political career. He held office as attorney for the indigent, civil judge, and congressional deputy. After participating in the 1904 and 1911 revolutions as a Liberal stalwart, he left Paraguay and spent the next eight years in Europe.

Upon his return after World War I, Ayala dedicated himself to teaching and journalism. He regained his old congressional seat and in 1920 was appointed finance minister by President Manuel Gondra. Ayala quickly gained a reputation for honesty and level-headedness.

Eschewing the jingoism of many Liberals, he took a stand in favor of negotiations with Bolivia over the disputed CHACO REGION.

After serving as provisional president of Paraguay in 1923, he was elected to that office one year later. His administration brought the first spate of internal peace in more than twenty years. Bent on reforming the nation's archaic fiscal system, Ayala balanced the national budget, stabilized the currency, and paid off a considerable portion of the government's debt. With Paraguay's renewed access to international credit, Ayala purchased munitions for his fledgling army and two warships for the navy. His emphasis on the professionalization of the armed forces rescued the military from continued partisan strife and prepared it for the upcoming CHACO WAR, a conflict that Paraguay was unable to avoid after all. Indeed, in the last year of Ayala's administration there was a series of border incidents that overshadowed all the progress he had promoted.

In 1928 Ayala resumed the post of finance minister, this time in the government of his successor, José P. Guggiari. He also retained several key posts in the Partido Liberal. Two years later he was killed in Asunción, the victim of a tragic romantic involvement.

WILLIAM B. PARKER, *Paraguayans of To-Day* (1921); CARLOS ZUBIZARRETA, *Cien vidas paraguayas,* 2d ed. (1985), pp. 277–280; *The Cambridge History of Latin America,* vol. 5 (1986), pp. 475–496.

THOMAS L. WHIGHAM

**AYALA, EUSEBIO** (*b.* 15 August 1874; *d.* 4 June 1942), intellectual, statesman, provisional president (1921–1923), and president of Paraguay (1932–1936). Ayala studied law and wrote essays on history, political economy, and international law. In 1900, he obtained his law degree at the National University in Asunción, subsequently teaching in various disciplines. As a diplomat, he displayed a profound knowledge of the major boundary dispute that existed with Bolivia. On 20 August 1920, Ayala was appointed to President Manuel GONDRA's cabinet, but because of factional fighting, Gondra was forced to resign. Ayala replaced him in November 1921 as provisional president, only to resign in 1923 in the middle of a civil war. He was elected president in 1932, leading Paraguay through the CHACO WAR against neighboring Bolivia. After the defeat of the Bolivians, Ayala's government was toppled on 17 February 1936 by a military coup that had civilian support. In spite of his overthrow, Ayala has been regarded as one of the most capable national leaders of his generation.

PAUL H. LEWIS, *Paraguay Under Stroessner* (1980); RIORDAN ROETT and RICHARD SCOTT SACKS, *Paraguay: The Personalist Legacy* (1991).

MIGUEL A. GATTI

*See also* **Paraguay: Political Parties.**

**AYALA, JOSÉ DE LA CRUZ** (*b.* 1854; *d.* 29 January 1892), Paraguayan politician, journalist, and social critic. Better known by his pen name "Alon," Ayala was a Liberal firebrand who helped crystallize resistance to the Bernardino CABALLERO and Patricio ESCOBAR governments in the 1880s. Born in the interior town of Mbuyapey, Ayala witnessed the cruelties of Paraguayan politics as a child, when his father and older brother were assassinated in his presence. When he arrived in Asunción in 1877, he was already very much a confirmed rebel. He entered the Colegio Nacional, where he studied the Greek and Roman classics and received a bachelor's degree in 1882.

While at the *colegio*, Ayala cemented his friendship with the young historian Cecilio BÁEZ, who encouraged him to enter the then booming field of journalism. Following Báez's suggestion, he wrote for several newspapers, including *El Heraldo* and *La Democracia*. His editorial pieces, published pseudonymously, attacked the government's policy of selling public lands to foreign entrepreneurs. More generally, he denounced the corruption that had seeped into every level of the Paraguayan body politic. Deeply offended by Ayala's stinging criticisms, President Caballero had him drafted and sent to an isolated army outpost in the Chaco. Ayala managed to escape and, from hiding, smuggled out a series of letters (tellingly entitled *Cartas del infierno*), which appeared in opposition dailies, vexing Caballero and Escobar still further. In 1891 Ayala momentarily came out of hiding to join the Liberals in a civil war, but he was forced to escape to Argentina, where he died one year later.

HARRIS G. WARREN, *Rebirth of the Paraguayan Republic: The First Colorado Era, 1878–1904* (1985), pp. 64, 73, 81; CARLOS ZUBIZARRETA, *Cien vidas paraguayas*, 2d ed. (1985), pp. 205–207.

THOMAS L. WHIGHAM

**AYCINENA, JUAN FERMÍN DE** (*b.* 7 July 1729; *d.* 3 April 1796), first *marqués* of Aycinena. He has been called the most powerful man in the history of CENTRAL AMERICA. Born in Siga, Navarra, in July 1729, he emigrated to New Spain in 1748 and began his commercial career as a mule runner, principally in Oaxaca, before arriving in Santiago de Guatemala (today Antigua) in 1753 or 1754. Subsequently he became the leading indigo exporter, wholesale merchant, and creditor in the Kingdom of Guatemala, and perhaps its only millionaire. He acquired several estates, especially Salvadoran indigo plantations, many through foreclosure. He was among the leading *trasladistas,* or supporters of the transfer of the capital city after 1773 to GUATEMALA CITY, and a generous benefactor of church and state. In 1783 he acquired the only Castilian title in late colonial Central America. In 1794 he became the first prior of the Consulado de Comercio of Guatemala City. Married three times, his numerous offspring became the center of the "oligarchy" in late colonial and early republican Central America.

DIANA BALMORI, STUART F. VOSS, and MILES L. WORTMAN, *Notable Family Networks in Latin America* (1984), pp. 61–69; RALPH LEE WOODWARD, *Central America: A Nation Divided*, 2d ed. (1985), pp. 74–75.

RICHMOND F. BROWN

**AYCINENA, MARIANO DE** (*b.* 15 September 1789; *d.* 22 January 1855), chief of state of Guatemala (1827–1829). Aycinena was a leading figure in Central American independence. A younger son of Juan Fermín de Aycinena, first marquis of Aycinena, he was a patriarch of Guatemala's most prominent and powerful family in the late colonial and early republican era. As *síndico* (attorney general) of the *ayuntamiento* of Guatemala City, he helped lead the movement for independence. Afterward he promoted the annexation of Central America to the Mexican Empire of Agustín de ITURBIDE, with whom he had corresponded prior to independence. He became a leader of Central American conservatives in the early republic and an officer of the Consulado de Comercio while managing his family's international trading firm. He was involved in the negotiations that resulted in a British loan to Central America in 1824, the proceeds of which some contemporary politicians and later historians accused him of appropriating.

As chief of state of Guatemala during the presidency of Manuel José ARCE, Aycinena was a central figure of the civil war that disrupted the UNITED PROVINCES OF CENTRAL AMERICA from 1826 to 1829. Aycinena's faction was ultimately defeated by the forces of the Honduran general and unionist hero Francisco MORAZÁN. Exiled after the war, he returned to Guatemala in the late 1830s and lived there for the rest of his life. Although not a prominent participant in Guatemalan government during that time, he enjoyed informal influence through his family, whose members dominated government and society in the Conservative Era (1838–1871).

Modern assessments of Aycinena's role in the era of independence are in MARIANO RODRÍGUEZ, *The Cádiz Experiment in Central America, 1808 to 1826* (1978); and MILES WORTMAN, *Government and Society in Central America, 1680–1840* (1982). Guatemalan historian RAMÓN SALAZAR provides a bitter view in his *Hombres de la independencia* (1899).

RICHMOND F. BROWN

**AYCINENA, PEDRO DE** (*b.* 19 October 1802; *d.* 14 March 1897), Guatemalan minister of foreign relations (1854–1871) and interim president of Guatemala (1865). Aycinena was a principal minister and adviser to the Conservative regimes of Rafael CARRERA (1851–1865) and Vicente CERNA (1865–1871). Son of Vicente Aycinena, second *marqués* of Aycinena, younger brother of Juan José de Aycinena, and nephew of Mariano de Aycinena, he belonged to one of Guatemala's most prominent families. In 1836 he married his first cousin,

Dolores Aycinena y Micheo, daughter of José de Aycinena, Spanish Councilor of State and the Indies under Ferdinand VII. Their son Juan Fermín de Aycinena Aycinena was the eminent Guatemalan poet.

Graduating in civil and canon law from the University of San Carlos in 1821, Aycinena joined the Colegio de Abogados in 1823. He spent much of the 1820s in Europe representing his family's merchant house and returned to Guatemala to manage his family's affairs in the 1830s, following the family elders' expulsion after the civil war of 1826–1829. In the 1840s, with the return to Conservative rule in Guatemala (and most of his brethren to the country), he became involved in government. As foreign minister, he negotiated the controversial WYKE-AYCINENA TREATY of 1859, which acknowledged British rights to Belize. He also negotiated Spanish recognition of Guatemalan independence in 1863. He was briefly exiled following the Liberal Revolution of 1871 and returned to pursue law and commerce until his death in 1897, the last of the Guatemalan *serviles* (conservatives).

DIANA BALMORI, STUART F. VOSS, and MILES L. WORTMAN, *Notable Family Networks in Latin America* (1984), pp. 61–69. Further details may be found in ROBERTO ZECEÑA FLORES, "Biografías de Ex-Ministros de Relaciones Exteriores," in *Diplomacia y sociedad* (Guatemala City) 3 and 4 (November–December 1969): 18–19, and RAMIRO ORDÓÑEZ JONOMA, "La Familia Varón de Berrieza," in *Revista de la Academia Guatemalteca de Estudios Genealógicos, Heráldicos e Históricos* 9 (1987): 644–645.

RICHMOND F. BROWN

**AYCINENA PIÑOL, JUAN JOSÉ DE** (*b.* 29 August 1792; *d.* 17 February 1865), third marquis of Aycinena and titular bishop of Trajanópolis (1859). Juan José de Aycinena was the dominant figure of the conservative political faction in nineteenth-century Central America and the Guatemalan Republic, which he helped found. Born in Antigua Guatemala to a family of immense wealth and power, Aycinena trained as an attorney before entering the priesthood in 1817. Although a cleric, he was involved in virtually every area of Guatemalan public life. As a member of the Economic Society, he promoted the development of a Central American silk industry. Most important, he operated in the midst of Central American politics. A promoter of Central American independence from Spain (1821) and annexation to the Mexican Empire (1821–1823), Aycinena was sent into exile in the United States for most of the 1830s with his political faction's (and family's) defeat in the Central American civil war of 1827–1829.

A forceful advocate of constitutional monarchy and of a pronounced secular role for the Catholic church, Aycinena is perhaps best known for a series of political tracts written in exile in the early 1830s. The *Toros amarillos* (yellow-paged polemics) called for the dissolution of the UNITED PROVINCES OF CENTRAL AMERICA in the name of isthmian peace. Returning to Guatemala in 1837, Aycinena played a central role in the formal breakup of the United Provinces through his newspaper, *El Observador*, and as a delegate to the federal congress.

With the collapse of the federation, Aycinena exercised extraordinary power as Guatemala's minister of government, justice, foreign affairs, and ecclesiastical affairs (1842–1844). Subsequently, as vice president of Guatemala's Chamber of Representatives (1851–1865), as a councillor of state (1856–1865), and especially as rector of the University of San Carlos (1840–1854; 1859–1865), Aycinena helped set the tone of politics and society under Guatemalan strongman José Rafael CARRERA (1844–1849; 1851–1865). His biographer, David L. Chandler, asserts, no "single individual [was] more responsible . . . for the outlines of society and government that subsequently took shape in Guatemala. . . . Father Aycinena became the Conservative prophet of a new era."

DAVID L. CHANDLER, "Peace Through Disunion: Father Juan José de Aycinena and the Fall of the Central American Federation," in *The Americas* 46 (October 1989): 137–157; and *Juan José de Aycinena: Idealista conservador de la Guatemala del siglo XIX*, translated by Victoria Vázquez, Marina Vázquez, and Lucia Robelo Pereira (1989).

RICHMOND F. BROWN

**AYLLU,** the basic social unit in modern Andean Indian society. An *ayllu* today is a community that consists of a number of unrelated extended families living in a specified area and following common rules of crop rotation under relatively informal leadership. In ancient times there existed a social unit that basically corresponds to the modern *ayllu*, but its exact nature is unclear due to confusion and casualness of QUECHUA usage in the Spanish chronicles.

Modern anthropologists have often assumed that *ayllus* were clan groups, but there is no unequivocal evidence to prove this assertion. In the Spanish chronicles, the word *ayllu* was used in connection with several different concepts that can refer to lineages of the royal INCAS, a moiety, or the community groups referred to above. As John Rowe points out in his classic article on Inca culture, in Quechua the word *ayllu* seems to be a generic term for "kin group," and its specific reference was probably clarified by the context. Moreover, the modern definition of *ayllu*, and what evidence there is for defining the ancient *ayllu*, do not conform to the anthropological definition of clan, particularly in the respect that the *ayllu* seems to lack totemic association with any animal or plant. *Ayllus* were normally named for a person or place.

Under Inca rule, the *ayllu* is defined by Rowe as a kin group with theoretical endogamy, with descent in the male line, and lacking totemism. The *ayllu* owned a specific territory, and each member couple cultivated what they needed for their support. Each year the family plots or fields were redistributed to ensure the proper rotation of crops and that the needs of each family were met.

The best discussion of the meaning of *ayllu* in Inca times is in JOHN H. ROWE, "Inca Culture at the Time of the Spanish Conquest," in *Handbook of South American Indians*, vol. 2 (1946), pp. 183–330. Modern *ayllus* are discussed by BERNARD MISHKIN, "The Contemporary Quechua," and HARRY TSCHOPIK, JR., "The Aymara," in *Handbook of South American Indians*, vol. 2 (1946), pp. 411–470 and pp. 501–574, respectively.

GORDON F. McEWAN

*See also* **Indians.**

**AYLWIN AZÓCAR, PATRICIO** (*b.* 26 November 1918), leader of the Christian Democratic Party (PDC) and president of Chile (1990–1994). One of the original founders of the PDC, he served as the head of the National Falange as well as of the party itself. As the leader of the PDC's more conservative wing, the *oficialistas*, and later, as head of the entire party, he doubted the Allende government's (1970–1973) commitment to respect the nation's constitution. Aylwin increasingly came to believe that President Salvador ALLENDE could not be trusted and, following last-minute negotiations, demanded that the president appoint only military men to his cabinet as proof of his honest intent. When Allende complied only partially, Aylwin apparently sided with the pro-coup forces, believing that the military would restore democracy to the nation.

Following Allende's overthrow in 1973, Aylwin, particularly after the death of Eduardo FREI, slowly emerged as the PDC's most viable spokesman. As the head of Chile's most popular party and one of the leaders of the anti-PINOCHET forces, Aylwin became a leader around whom the various diverse parties could unite. In 1989 he managed to forge a coalition of seventeen disparate elements, defeat two opponents, and win the presidency with 55 percent of the vote.

Following his election, Aylwin created a coalition government in an attempt to retain widespread public support. His economic programs consisted of attempting to build on the momentum generated by the Pinochet administration while implementing new laws, and passing new taxes, to protect the working class.

Aylwin's principal problem following his election, as well as before it, was General Augusto Pinochet. The former dictator, although no longer president, still controlled the army. He was intent, moreover, on ensuring that the newly elected government would not punish the armed forces for their activities in overturning Allende or in the succeeding years. Aylwin, however, had to attempt to heal the nation while bringing to justice those who had committed abuses. Aylwin's election marked the return of Chile to its democratic traditions.

PAUL E. SIGMUND, *The Overthrow of Allende and the Politics of Chile, 1964–1976* (1977), 217–218, 220, 223; JULIO FAÚNDEZ, *Marxism and Democracy in Chile: From 1932 to the Fall of Allende* (1988), 235.

WILLIAM F. SATER

*See also* **Chile: Political Parties.**

**AYMARA.** Between approximately 1200 and 1500, at least twelve distinct Aymara-speaking kingdoms dominated the area of the Andean ALTIPLANO (high plateau) between Cuzco in present-day Peru and Potosí in present-day Bolivia. The origins of the Aymara language are not clear, but linguist Alfredo Torero believes that it may have developed in the area of HUARI (Wari) culture in the central highlands of Peru. Although the Aymara actually constituted one cultural and linguistic group, there was often fierce competition among them, and consequently the kingdoms were well fortified militarily.

The most basic social and economic unit among the Aymara was the extended family, which in turn belonged to larger groups known as *ayllus*. An AYLLU is generally understood to be a group of people who hold land in common and who trace their origins to one spiritual or legendary ancestor.

Above the *ayllu* level Aymara society had a dualistic structure that divided human communities into complementary halves. Each kingdom, as well as each village or settlement, was composed of two moieties, or *parcialidades*: a superior one, usually called *hanansaya*, and one of inferior status known as *hurinsaya*. This political division reflected a conception of the universe based on the unity of halves, or opposites. This dualism was symbolized by the male/female relation, and features of the physical world (rocks, mountains, bodies of water) were often conceived of as either male or female.

Each Aymara kingdom had two *kurakas*, or chiefs, one for each *parcialidad*; and on the district and village levels there were usually also leaders for both *hurinsaya* and *hanansaya*. *Kurakas* were responsible for allocating lands to *ayllu* members, ensuring that the proper religious rites were performed, and periodically redistributing some of the community's wealth. In return for performing these functions, *kurakas*, who generally had access to considerably more land than did commoners, had their fields tilled by *ayllu* members and received various other types of labor service as well. This labor for the leaders was viewed as a form of reciprocity by the common people for the generosity the *kurakas* demonstrated in redistributing the society's surplus.

The anthropologist John Murra was among the first scholars to show how agricultural "archipelagos" were used by the Aymara in order to make the best of the Andean region's varied geography. In this "vertical" system, agricultural lands with different altitudes and ecologies were utilized to produce a variety of crops. Most Aymara communities had their primary settlements on the sides of highland valleys or on the *altiplano*, where they were able to graze herds of llamas and

Studio photograph of an Aymara male. LIBRARY OF CONGRESS; PHOTO BY MAX T. VARGAS.

into their state system. The Aymara responded in a variety of ways to the invasions. Kingdoms in the area of Lake Titicaca eventually rose in revolt against increasing Inca demands for land and labor. Further south, Aymara leaders seem to have more readily cooperated with the invaders in return for certain concessions. For instance, the *kurakas* of the Charcas, Caracaras, Chuis, and Chichas were feasted by the Inca leaders, showered with gifts, and made officers in their armies. In general, the main burdens of Inca rule probably fell on the common people, who now, in addition to working the lands of their own *kurakas*, also had to do the same for the Inca leaders and spiritual cults.

The Inca imperial approach of building on pre-existing Andean social and political institutions, and the flexibility of the Aymara lords in cooperating with the new state, helped Aymara culture survive to experience the next invasion: that of the Spanish, which began in 1532. During the Conquest and Spanish colonial period Aymara people used a variety of strategies, ranging from revolt to alliances with the colonialists to skillful use of the colonial legal system, in order to survive domination and maintain fundamental aspects of their culture. Since political independence from Spain in 1825 the Aymara have continued as a distinct cultural and linguistic group despite attacks on their communal organizations and system of land tenure, the racism of the dominant mestizo society, and their economic exploitation as peasants and poorly paid workers.

In 1993 somewhere between 28 percent and one-third of the population of Bolivia continues to speak Aymara. Although throughout the nineteenth century and well into the twentieth most Aymara people were peasant farmers, now many are urban and have diverse occupations. There are Aymara industrial workers, truck drivers, business people, intellectuals, and professionals. Today Aymara political and cultural organizations have links with other Native American rights groups in Bolivia and other countries.

JOHN V. MURRA, "An Aymara Kingdom in 1567," in *Ethnohistory* 15, no. 2 (1968): 115–151, and *Formaciones económicas y políticas del mundo andino* (1975); NATHAN WACHTEL, *The Vision of the Vanquished* (1977); THÉRÈSE BOUYSSE-CASSAGNE, "L'espace aymara: *Urco et uma*," in *Annales,* 33, nos. 5–6 (1978): 1057–1080; MARTHA J. HARDMAN, ed., *The Aymara Language in Its Social and Cultural Context* (1981); FRANKLIN PEASE, "The Formation of Tawantinsuyu: Mechanisms of Colonization and Relationship with Ethnic Groups," in *The Inca and Aztec States, 1400–1800,* edited by George A. Collier, Renato I. Rosaldo, and John D. Wirth (1982), pp. 172–198; JOHN V. MURRA, "The Limits and Limitations of the 'Vertical Archipelago' in the Andes," in *Andean Ecology and Civilization: An Interdisciplinary Perspective on Andean Ecological Complementarity,* edited by SHOZO MASUDA, IZUMI SHIMADA, and CRAIG MORRIS (1985); XAVIER ALBO, ed., *Raíces de América: El mundo Aymara* (1988).

ANN ZULAWSKI

*See also* **Tiwanaku.**

alpacas, exploit salt deposits, and grow potatoes and quinoa. Lands in lower valleys provided vegetables, maize, coca leaf, cotton, tropical fruits, and vegetables.

It was through their *ayllus* that families obtained products grown in lowland zones that were more than several hours' walk from their base communities. *Ayllu*-held lands in distant regions were farmed by agricultural colonists (*mitimaes, llacturuna*) who were sent by the highland leaders for this purpose. Most ethnohistorians believe that because of the system of agricultural colonies the Aymara economy was able to function without markets or a medium of exchange. Products from lowland areas most likely were redistributed to community members by the *ayllu* leaders as a form of largesse.

After about 1440, the INCA—a Quechua-speaking ethnic group based in the Cuzco area—began to expand southward and to incorporate the Aymara kingdoms

**AYOLAS, JUAN DE** (*b.* 1539?), Spanish EXPLORER active in Argentina and Paraguay. Ayolas was born a HIDALGO in the Briviesca region of Spain. Thanks to his long-time friendship with Pedro de MENDOZA, he received a commission as *mayordomo* when the latter organized an expedition to explore the basin of the Río de la Plata in the early 1530s.

The voyage from Spain was not without its problems. Ayolas discovered a plot against Mendoza by dissident Spaniards while the small fleet was off the Brazilian coast. His quick action saved the ADELANTADO and placed Ayolas in a good position to play a major role in the exploration of the Plata.

After the founding of Buenos Aires in 1536, Mendoza chose his friend to lead a new expedition inland to find a viable route to the silver districts of Upper Peru (what he optimistically termed the *Sierra de la Plata*). Ayolas ascended the Río Paraná with three vessels and two hundred men. He received succor along the way from various groups of Guaraní Indians, especially in the vicinity of what would one day become the city of Asunción. Proceeding upriver from that point, he finally halted in February 1537 at a spot some 120 miles to the north. There he divided his men, leaving behind forty under the command of Domingo Martínez de IRALA and setting out on foot with the remaining 160 to cross the inhospitable CHACO region to Peru.

What occurred next is not entirely clear and is based exclusively on the testimony of a converted Chané Indian boy named Gonzalo. According to this eyewitness, after many tribulations, Ayolas and his party actually reached the Andes. He left a number of Europeans at an improvised camp in the hill country and, ferrying a quantity of silver taken from the resident INCAS, recrossed the Chaco to the Río Paraguay, where the exhausted Ayolas expected to find Martínez de Irala and the three vessels awaiting his return. Irala, however, had gone south after a year in order to find provisions and to repair his ships. While Ayolas pondered his next move, a large band of PAYAGUÁ Indians invited the weary Spaniards to take refuge with them, and then, at a prearranged signal, fell upon them and killed them to a man. Only the Indian boy Gonzalo escaped to report what he had seen to Irala. The latter campaigned hard against these same Payaguáes over the next few years, but he never recovered the bodies of his comrades.

HARRIS GAYLORD WARREN, *Paraguay: An Informal History* (1949), pp. 34–50; CARLOS ZUBIZARRETA, *Cien vidas paraguayas*, 2d ed. (1985), pp. 21–23.

THOMAS L. WHIGHAM

**AYORA CUEVA, ISIDRO** (*b.* 31 August 1879; *d.* 22 March 1978), president of Ecuador (nonelected 1926–1929 and elected 1929–1931). Born in Loja, Ayora studied medicine in Quito, did postgraduate work in Berlin, and completed an internship in Dresden. After returning to Ecuador in 1909, he developed a private practice and taught obstetrics at Central University, where he accepted the post of director of maternity (1917). Elected deputy of Loja in 1916 and president of the cantonal council for 1924–1925, Ayora was appointed rector of Central University and director of the Civil Hospital of Quito in 1925. On 10 January 1926 he became a member of the provisional governing junta and minister of social welfare, labor, and agriculture. On 1 April 1926 he accepted the position of provisional president.

Ayora concluded an agreement with Princeton economist Edwin W. KEMMERER to head an advisory mission whose purpose was to propose solutions to the nation's financial problems. In October 1926 the mission drafted laws to modernize and strengthen Ecuadorian financial institutions and procedures to eliminate budget deficits. Ayora, with the backing of the military, was able to enact most of the sweeping reforms proposed by the Kemmerer Mission.

Ayora was elected to the presidency in 1929 but suffered increasing public criticism for his policies, many of them based on the recommendations of the Kemmerer Mission. Public dissatisfaction mounted as internal conditions deteriorated in response to disruptions in the world economy. Critics blamed the Ayora government for exacerbating the nation's problems. When popular discontent erupted in mass demonstrations in Quito, Ayora resigned on 24 August 1931. He returned to his medical practice and remained active in professional organizations and administrative positions.

LINDA ALEXANDER RODRÍGUEZ, *The Search for Public Policy: Regional Politics and Government Finances in Ecuador, 1830–1940* (1985), esp. pp. 131–133, 137–164.

LINDA ALEXANDER RODRÍGUEZ

**AZAR, HÉCTOR** (*b.* 17 October 1930), Mexican playwright who founded the Centro de Arte Dramático (CADAC, 1975), a respected theater school. Azar, born in Atlixco, Puebla, studied in the United States under the direction of Max Reinhardt at Actors' Studio. His first plays (both 1958), *La Apassionata* and *El alfarero*, depicted social problems from a stylized point of view. *Olímpica* (1962), his best-known work, and *Inmaculada* (1963) are poetic dramas that deal mainly with feminine frustration. His collection of short pieces, *Juegos de azar* (1973), includes a religious mystery play, *La seda mágica*, and a Renaissance farce, *Doña Belarda de Francia*. A more traditional drama, *Los muros vacíos* (1974), contrasts with his later experimental works, such as the farcical trilogy *Diálogos de la clase medium* (1979–1986) and a poetic drama that pays homage to the Mexican painter Rufino TAMAYO, *Las alas sin sombra* (1980). His critical essays are collected in *Funciones teatrales* (1982).

MARÍA DEL CARMEN MILLÁN, "Prólogo," in *Los juegos de Azar* (1973); JACQUELIN EYRING BIXLER, "Zoon Theatrykon: Azar y la búsqueda teatral," *Texto crítico*, no. 10 (1978): 42–54.

GUILLERMO SCHMIDHUBER

**AZARA, FÉLIX DE** (*b.* 18 May 1746; *d.* 20 October 1821), scientist and writer. Spanish military man and enlightened scientist, Azara spent twenty years (1781–1801) traveling throughout the Viceroyalty of the Río de la Plata, gathering information about the area and conducting experiments. He was born in Aragon, and after studying philosophy at the University of Huesca, entered the Military Academy at Barcelona. Commissioned as *alférez* (ensign) in the Company of Engineers, he participated as an officer in the Algiers campaign of 1775. By 1781, with the rank of lieutenant colonel, Azara was in America to participate in the boundary commission charged with fixing the limits between the Spanish and Portuguese dominions in South America. Upon returning to Spain in 1802, Azara wrote scientific treatises as well as general descriptions of the area. Best known are *Descripción é historia del Paraguay y del Río de la Plata* (1847) and *Viajes por la América meridional* (1809).

ENRIQUE UDAONDO, *Diccionario biográfico colonial argentino* (1945), pp. 122–123.

SUSAN M. SOCOLOW

**AZCAPOTZALCO** (Place of the Ant Hill), the capital city of the Tepanecs and the dominant military and political power in the Basin of Mexico from the mid-fourteenth century through the first quarter of the fifteenth century. Located on the western edge of Lake Tetzcoco, Azcapotzalco's preeminence coincides with the reign of its greatest ruler, Tezozomoc. Under this ambitious and long-lived ruler, the Tepanecs successively conquered cities to the west, south, east, and finally north of the lake. Following Tezozomoc's death in 1426, the legitimate heir was deposed. In the revolt that followed, Azcapotzalco was conquered in 1428 by a coalition of forces led by Mexico TENOCHTITLÁN and TETZ-COCO, former tributaries of Azcapotzalco, and Tlacopán, its former ally. The political strategies and administrative policies of Tezozomoc's Tepanec Empire served as a model for the Triple Alliance that was subsequently formed by the victorious new powers. Present-day Azcapotzalco is a part of Mexico City.

NIGEL DAVIES, *The Toltec Heritage: From the Fall of Tula to the Rise of Tenochtitlán* (1987).

ELOISE QUIÑONES KEBER

**AZCÁRATE Y LEZAMA, JUAN FRANCISCO DE** (*b.* 11 July 1767; *d.* 31 January 1831), Mexican lawyer, writer, and leader of the struggle for Mexican independence. Azcárate studied jurisprudence and in 1790 became a lawyer of the Royal Audiencia. He taught courses at the University of Mexico and became a member of the Academy of Jurisprudence and the College of Lawyers. A distinguished lawyer, Azcárate was also interested in politics, becoming a member of the city council of Mexico City in 1803.

Azcárate played an important role during the imperial crisis provoked by Napoleon's invasion of Spain and the abdication of the Spanish monarchs, when the capital's city council, dominated by creoles, decided to promote autonomist interests. He was the author of the council's *representación* of 19 July 1808 to the viceroy against the recognition of any monarch but the legitimate one. An active participant in the meetings convened to discuss the creation of a governing junta, Azcárate was imprisoned during the coup d'état of 15 September. Freed in 1811, he rejoined the city council in 1814. He was a member of the governing junta in 1821 and one of the signers of the Declaration of Independence. Azcárate served in various diplomatic posts during the Augustín de ITURBIDE regime. In 1827 he was a member of the Committee of Public Education and the following year of the Tribunal of War and Marine.

ENRIQUE LAFUENTE FERRARI, *El Virrey Iturrigaray y los orígenes de la independencia de México* (1941); JOSÉ MARÍA MIQUEL I VERGÉS, *Diccionario de insurgentes* (1969), pp. 59–61; LUCAS ALAMÁN, *Historia de Méjico*, vol. 1 (1985); *Diccionario Porrúa de historia, biografía y geografía de México*, 5th ed., vol. 1 (1986), pp. 244–245.

VIRGINIA GUEDEA

**AZCÁRRAGA MILMO, EMILIO** (*b.* August 1930), prominent entrepreneur and chief executive officer of Televisa, Latin America's largest media network. He is the son of Emilio Azcárraga Vidaurreta, founder of Televisa, and Laura Milmo, members of prominent Mexican entrepreneurial families. Emilio Azcárraga Milmo and his family have a controlling interest in the Televisa media empire, which dominates Mexican programming. He became president of Televisa in 1973 and, according to *Forbes* magazine, had a net worth of $1 billion in 1991. Azcárraga bought out his partners, Miguel Alemán and Rómulo O'Farrill, in 1990, giving his family exclusive control of the business. He has continued the family policy of generous support of the arts. Azcárraga was president of Friends of the Arts in Mexico, a major sponsor of "Mexico: The Splendor of 30 Centuries," an exhibit that appeared in New York, San Antonio, and Los Angeles in 1990 and 1991.

MARJORIE MILLER and JUANITA DARLING, "El Tigre," in *Los Angeles Times Magazine*, 10 November 1991, pp. 24–26, 28–29, 51.

RODERIC AI CAMP

**AZCONA HOYO, JOSÉ SIMÓN** (*b.* 26 January 1927), president of Honduras (1986–1990). Born and raised in Honduras, José Azcona received his degree in civil engineering from the National Autonomous University in 1963. He studied and worked in Mexico, Costa Rica, and the United States intermittently during the 1960s and 1970s but maintained his ties to the Liberal Party in Honduras. He served in a variety of political positions, including congressional deputy (1982–1985) and minister of communication (1982–1983). Azcona broke with incumbent president Roberto SUAZO CÓRDOVA in 1985 and led a faction of the Liberal Party known as the Rodista Dissent Movement, after his mentor Modesto RODAS. Under a new electoral system, in which the two main parties alternate terms in power, Azcona won the 1985 presidential race even though he did not receive a plurality. Despite this successful transition of power between civilian presidents, the strength of the Honduran military grew during Azcona's administration. Although he was widely viewed as responsible and trustworthy, Azcona was a weak president faced with increasingly complicated domestic and foreign issues: the presence in his country of Nicaraguan contras, rapidly expanding U.S. involvement in the area, Salvadoran refugees, and the appearance of a guerrilla threat.

JAMES A. MORRIS, *Honduras: Caudillo Politics and Military Rulers* (1984); JAMES DUNKERLEY, *Power in the Isthmus* (1988); ROY GUTMAN, *Banana Diplomacy* (1988).

KAREN RACINE

*See also* **Honduras: Political Parties.**

**AZCUÉNAGA, MIGUEL DE** (*b.* 4 June 1754; *d.* 19 December 1833), Argentine military man. Born in Buenos Aires, the son and grandson of prominent Basque merchants (Vicente de Azcuénaga and Domingo Basavilbaso), Azcuénaga was related by blood or marriage to many of the more conservative Spanish monopoly traders in Buenos Aires. After studying in Spain, he returned in 1773 to the city of his birth as a commissioned military officer. Between 1776 and 1800 he served as a member of the *cabildo,* a colonel in the militia, and the chief of militia in Buenos Aires. He was especially active as the commander of a volunteer infantry battalion during the English invasions of 1806–1807.

A participant in the *cabildo abierto* (open town council meeting) of 23 May 1810, Azcuénaga was a fervent supporter of the end of viceregal rule. He served in the first independence government and was especially active in organizing the military forces of the new government. Dismissed from the government as the result of political intrigue, Azcuénaga later held a variety of posts, including *gobernador intendente* of Buenos Aires (1813), president of the War Commission, and Buenos Aires deputy to Congress (1818). He died in Buenos Aires.

ENRIQUE UDAONDO, *Diccionario biográfico colonial argentino* (1945), p. 125; BERNARDO GONZÁLEZ ARRILI, *Hombres de Mayo* (Buenos Aires, 1960), pp. 47–50.

SUSAN M. SOCOLOW

**AZEVEDO, ALUÍSIO** (*b.* 14 April 1857; *d.* 21 January 1913), Brazilian novelist. Aluísio Azevedo was the major figure of Brazilian naturalism, a movement influenced by the novels of Émile Zola and other European naturalists, but also firmly grounded in the social and historical context of Brazil at the end of the Empire period. Azevedo appears to have seen literature as a way to get ahead in life, and his first naturalist novel, *O mulato* (1881) was a scandalous success. He published three more naturalist novels, including his masterpiece, *O cortiço* (1890), but simultaneously turned out a number of romantic potboilers. Azevedo abandoned fiction after he was appointed to the Brazilian diplomatic corps in 1895, at the age of thirty-eight. While his works exhibit his gift for describing places, from the provincial city that is the setting for *O mulato* to the Rio de Janeiro slums in *O cortiço,* all Azevedo's novels are weakened by their improbable plots and stereotypical characters. His Brazilian contemporaries were shocked and titillated by the heavy-handed treatment of sexuality in Azevedo's novels—the English translation of *O cortiço,* published in 1926 as *A Brazilian Tenement,* had to be drastically censored for North American audiences— but today's critics view his works primarily as historical documents. While he and his contemporaries saw these works as innovative attempts to modernize and renew the Brazilian novel, the underlying themes of his naturalism are pessimism about Brazil's future and fear of all the changes that the future might bring: the family skeletons that abolition of slavery might uncover, the white population's prospect of increased competition from mulattos and immigrants, and the education and emancipation of women.

DOROTHY S. LOOS, *The Naturalistic Novel of Brazil* (1963); SÔNIA BRAYNER, *A metáfora do corpo no romance naturalista* (1973); LÚCIA MIGUEL-PEREIRA, *Prosa de ficção de 1870 a 1920,* 3d ed. (1973), pp. 142–159; JEAN-YVES MÉRIAN, *Aluísio Azevedo, vida e obra* (1988).

DAVID T. HABERLY

**AZEVEDO, FERNANDO DE** (*b.* 2 April 1894; *d.* 19 September 1974), Brazilian educator, editor, sociologist, and cultural historian. As city director of public education from 1926 to 1930, Azevedo led in the implementation of school reforms in Rio de Janeiro. Later he was secretary of education and culture in São Paulo. In 1934 he founded and then later directed the humanities faculty of the University of São Paulo. As editor of the Biblioteca Pedagógica Brasileira and Brasiliana series, he introduced new ideas and revived Brazilian classics.

Azevedo wrote on sports and physical education, classical Latin literature, educational sociology, and the sociology of sugar mills and railroads. His major work was *A cultura brasileira* (1943), published as a supplement to the 1940 census. This ambitious survey combines a social and psychological history of the development of the Brazilian people with an institutional history of the CATHOLIC CHURCH, the professions, literary and artistic achievements, and the sciences. It interprets Brazilian culture through the history of education from colonial times through the 1930s, calling for a unified system of public education to build national unity.

FERNANDO DE AZEVEDO, *História da minha vida* (1971), and *A cultura brasileira* (1943), translated by William Rex Crawford, under the title *Brazilian Culture* (1950); MARIA LUIZA PENNA, *Fernando de Azevedo: Educação e transformação* (1987).

DAIN BORGES

See also **Education**.

**AZEVEDO, THALES DE** (*b.* 26 August 1904), Brazilian social scientist and first director of the Instituto de Ciências Sociais at the Universidade Federal da Bahia. Thales Olimpio Góis de Azevedo was born in the city of Salvador, Bahia. He studied medicine and later anthropology and ethnography. Dedicated to the creation of a center for social sciences at Universidade Federal da Bahia, he was one of the authors of the proposal calling for the establishment of such a center. In 1961 the president of the university founded the Instituto de Ciências Sociais and appointed Azevedo the first director.

Azevedo's publications include *Gaúchos, notas de antropologia social* (1943); *Uma pesquisa sobre a vida social no estado da Bahia* (with Charles Wagley and Luís de Aguiar Costa Pinto, 1950); *Civilização e mestiçagem* (1951); *Les élites de couleur dans une ville brésilienne* (1953); *O catolicismo no Brasil* (1955); *Atualidade de Durkheim* (with Nelson Sampaio and A. L. Machado Neto, 1959); *Ensaios de antropologia social* (1959); *Social change in Brazil* (1963); *Cultura e situação racial no Brasil* (1966); *A evasão de talentos* (1968); *Integração intercultural* (1974); *Democracia racial, ideologia e realidade* (1975); *A religião civil brasileira: Um instrumento político* (1981).

FLORESTAN FERNANDES, *A etnologia e a sociologia no Brasil* (1958); KARL N. DEGLER, *Neither Black nor White: Slavery and Race Relations in Brazil and the United States* (1971); MÁRCIO MOREIRA ALVES, *A igreja e a política no Brasil* (1979).

ELIANA MARIA REA GOLDSCHMIDT

**AZORES**, an archipelago consisting of nine islands (Flores, Corvo, Terceira, São Jorge, Pico, Fayal, Graciosa, São Miguel and Santa María) and several islets in the North Atlantic, 800 miles off the coast of Portugal. First mentioned by the Arab geographer, Edisi in the twelfth century, the Azores were discovered by the Portuguese in 1427 during their voyages of discovery. These expeditions were financed by the MILITARY ORDER of Christ, which was headed by Prince HENRY THE NAVIGATOR. Initially the explorers visited the central islands and, to the east, Santa María and São Miguel. Twenty-five years later the western Azores were discovered by Diogo de Teive, a Madeiran sugar merchant and navigator.

The Azores played an important role in the exploration of and, later, the trade with the New World. COLUMBUS's ship, the Niña, visited Santa María in 1493 on its return from his first voyage to America. His crew was briefly detained by the islanders until Columbus could negotiate their release. Later, the Azores served as a post between Europe and the Americas where Portuguese ships would stop in order to pick up fresh food and water before continuing their journey across the Atlantic.

Woad, a dyestuff planted by the Flemish, who had established settlements there in the fifteenth century, was an important export until it was replaced by indigo from Brazil.

T. BENTLEY DUNCAN, *Atlantic Islands* (1972).

SHEILA L. HOOKER

See also **Explorers of Latin America**.

**AZTEC CALENDAR STONE,** the standard designation in the English-speaking world for the most famous pre-Hispanic carved stone monument, which in Mexico is more commonly known as the "Piedra del Sol." The Calendar Stone is an irregular mass of basalt, whose upper surface features an intricately sculptured disk over 11.5 feet in diameter. Buried about 264 feet west of the second doorway of the Viceregal Palace, it was discovered on 17 December 1790, while the Plaza Mayor (Zócalo) of Mexico City was being repaved. Set vertically into the southwest tower of the cathedral, it constituted a major tourist attraction until 1885, when it was removed to the Galería de los Monolitos of the Museo Nacional de México. In 1964 it was installed in the Sala Mexica of the new Museo Nacional de Antropología in Chapultepec Park.

This huge, once brightly polychromed stone, which functioned as one type of *cuauhxicalli* (eagle vessel), a receptacle for sacrificed human hearts and blood, was probably positioned horizontally on a stepped ceremonial platform. It is the most complex extant image of the solar disk, symbol of the celestial orb that constituted the pivot of the AZTEC cosmos.

Although other identifications have been proposed, the central *en face* human visage is almost certainly that of the diurnal solar deity, Tonatiuh, flanked by claws clutching human hearts. It occupies the center of a large, X-shaped symbol that constitutes, with its numerical coefficients, the date 4 Ollin (Movement). In the "wings" of the Ollin are the dates 4 Ocelotl (Jaguar), 4 Ehecatl (Wind), 4 Quiahuitl (Rain), and 4 Atl (Water), on which the four previous cosmogonic eras, or "suns," had terminated by different cataclysmic destructions. Adjoining the 4 Ollin, the date on which the fifth (current) sun would end, are three other dates, 1 Tecpatl (Stone Knife), 7 Ozomatli (Monkey), and 1 Quiahuitl, and an iconographic ensemble featuring the royal crown, *xiuhuitzolli*. Their correct interpretation continues to be controversial.

In the next concentric circle are the twenty day signs of the 260-day divinatory cycle, the *tonalpohualli*, com-

Aztec calendar stone. PHOTO BY LEE BOLTIN.

mencing at the top and proceeding counterclockwise. Edging this circle are eight solar ray elements, four of them partially covered by the next two concentric circles. Around the first of these circles are fifty-two quincunx images (small squares with a design in each corner and the center), each one symbolizing a year (*xihuitl*). Some of the images are covered by the ray elements. The second circle features stylized eagle feathers. The next concentric zone contains sets of four U-shaped elements that appear to represent sanguinary splatters, and, edging the outermost rim, sets of four parallel bars.

Encircling the disk, with tails at the top and heads at the bottom, are two typically compartmentalized *xiuhcoatl* (fire serpents) whose edging flame devices partially cover the sets of four bars. Peering from their gaping jaws are the profile faces of two deities, the sun god, Tonatiuh, on the right, and the fire god, Xiuhtecuhtli, on the left. At the top, between the *xiuhcoatl* tails, is the date 13 Acatl (Reed), the year of the creation of the present sun. On the narrow rim of the disk is carved a typical version of the "celestial band," featuring stellar images and stone knives that possibly symbolize solar rays.

The colossal size of the Calendar Stone, its superbly conceived concentric patterning, and its rich symbolic imagery have contributed to its worldwide renown—it has become the unofficial national emblem of Mexico. In the popular mind, it is the symbol par excellence of Aztec civilization.

The classic original study of the Calendar Stone, which also contains an account of the circumstances of its discovery, is ANTONIO DE LEÓN Y GAMA, *Descripción histórica y cronológica de las dos piedras que con ocasión del nuevo empedrado que se está formando en la plaza principal de México, se hallaron en ella el año*

*de 1790* (1792). Although in need of some modifications and additions, the most successful and comprehensive interpretation of the monument is still HERMANN BEYER, *El llamado "Calendario Azteca": Descripción y interpretación del cuauhxicalli de la "Casa de las Aguilas"* (1921; reprinted in *El Mexico Antiquo* 10 [1965]: 134–256). ROBERTO SIECK FLANDES reconstructed its original polychromy in his article "Cómo estuvo pintada la piedra conocida con el nombre de 'El Calendario Azteca?,' " in *Vigesimoséptimo congreso internacional de americanistas, Actas de la primera sesión celebrada en la Ciudad de México en 1939*, vol. 1 (1942), pp. 550–556; H. B. NICHOLSON, "The Problem of the Identification of the Central Image of the 'Aztec Calendar Stone,' " in *Current Topics in Aztec Studies: Essays in Honor of Dr. H. B. Nicholson*, edited by Alana Cordy-Collins and Douglas Sharon, San Diego Museum Papers 30 (1993): 3–15.

H. B. NICHOLSON

*See also* **Calendars, Pre-Columbian.**

**AZTECS** (Nahuatl: *Azteca*, "Those of Aztlán"), the term widely employed in the English-speaking world for the people of Mexico TENOCHTITLÁN (modern Mexico City), who dominated an extensive empire in central and southern Mexico at the time of the Spanish conquest. The label is somewhat anachronistic, for the inhabitants of this imperial metropolis were known as Mexica, Colhua Mexica, and/or Tenochca at the time of the Conquest. "Azteca," strictly speaking, applied only to their ancestors, who, according to the traditional histories, had migrated, at the command of their tutelary deity, HUITZILOPOCHTLI, to the Basin of Mexico from a semi-legendary place to the northwest called Aztlán (Place of Cranes or Place of Whiteness). However, since its popularization in the influential writings of Alexander von Humboldt and William H. Prescott during the nineteenth century, the word "Aztec" has achieved such wide currency that it would be impractical to attempt to discard it on the basis of greater technical accuracy. "Aztec" is most usefully employed as a convenient cultural label for the Late Postclassic (ca. 1300–1521) central Mexican peoples in the aggregate rather than as a specific ethnic designation, for Mexica and Tenochca are clearly preferable when referring to the inhabitants of Mexico Tenochtitlán as a sociopolitical entity.

HISTORY

According to their "official" history, the Mexica/Tenochca entered the Basin of Mexico after sojourns in various northern places, including Tollán (present-day Tula), capital of the Toltec Empire, near the close of the twelfth century. After further wandering, they settled at Chapultepec, in the western part of the basin, but were expelled a few years later by a coalition of neighboring communities, headed by Colhuacán. That city had carried on the Toltec dynastic and cultural tradition after the collapse of the Toltec Empire, probably sometime during the thirteenth century. Under the control of Colhuacán, the Mexica/Tenochca endured a "Babylonian captivity" for about a generation, until they eventually escaped to a group of swampy islands in the western portion of the extensive saline lake that covered the center of the Basin of Mexico. There they encountered the oracular sign that indicated the end of their long trek—the eagle perched on the cactus growing from the rock—and founded their city, Mexico Tenochtitlán (Place of the Mexica/Next to the Stone Cactus Fruit). In most accounts this occurred in the year 2 Calli (House): 1324-1325 (a date perhaps more ritual than historical).

This lacustrine zone was controlled by the Tepanecas, whose principal center was the city-state of Azcapotzalco that was rapidly rising to power at the expense of Colhuacán and other city-states in the Basin of Mexico. The Mexica/Tenochca became their tributaries and undertook a series of hydraulic projects that eventually transformed their insular community into an enormous New World Venice, interlaced with innumerable canals and connected to the mainland by four major causeways, with a population perhaps close to a quarter of a

Eagle warrior. One of a pair found within the Precinct of the Eagles at the Templo Mayor. The warrior's suit is decorated with stucco simulating feathers. His face emerges from the eagle's beak. MUSEO TEMPLO MAJOR.

million. Soon after Tenochtitlán's founding, a restive group of Mexica, unhappy over the division of land, moved north to another island and founded an independent community, TLATELOLCO (Place of the Circular Mound), which became a serious political rival of its sister city.

Both Mexica communities expanded rapidly, and by the 1370s each had achieved sufficient importance to consecrate an official Toltec-descended ruler, a TLATOANI. Tenochtitlán crowned Acamapichtli (1376–1396), a part-Mexica scion of the royal dynasty of Colhuacán, which claimed direct descent from the semilegendary Toltec ruler Topiltzín QUETZALCOATL, considered to have been the source of all "legitimate" political power in post-Toltec central Mexico. Tlatelolco crowned Cuacuauhpitzahuac, son of Tezozomoc, ruler of Azcapotzalco. Under these new rulers and their successors, both cities provided Tezozomoc with valuable military assistance as he expanded the Tepanec Empire to include most of the Basin of Mexico and large areas beyond.

About 1426, at the height of his power, the aged Tezozomoc died. After one of his sons, Maxtla, the ruler of Coyoacán, another major Tepanec center, usurped the throne of Azcapotzalco, a general revolt erupted throughout the Tepanec Empire. The rulers of the Mexica twin cities, Chimalpopoca of Tenochtitlán and Tlacateotl of Tlatelolco, were killed during these disturbances. Under a new ruler, ITZCOATL (ca. 1427–1440), Tenochtitlán led the successful attack against Maxtla, who either fled or perished in the flaming ruins of Azcapotzalco.

A new political order was established in the Basin of Mexico in 1433/1434. Itzcoatl's chief ally in the struggle had been his grandnephew, NEZAHUALCOYOTL, heir to the throne of Tetzcoco, a major center of Acolhuacán, the province centered in the eastern Basin of Mexico. His father, Ixtlilxochitl, had been killed on Tezozomoc's orders. Newly installed as the legitimate ruler of Tetzcoco, now capital of Acolhuacán, Nezahualcoyotl, who later achieved fame as the wise and talented "poet king," entered into a firm alliance with Itzcoatl. In a shrewd piece of statecraft designed to nullify the threat of a Tepanec restoration movement, they added, as the junior partner in the coalition, Totoquihuaztli, ruler of Tlacopán—which, although Tepanec in affiliation, had defected from Maxtla.

This new Triple Alliance of Mexico Tenochtitlán, Tetzcoco, and Tlacopán generated great military power and, after subduing most of the former Tepanec tributaries, steadily expanded the sphere of its political and military control. Tenochtitlán steadily gained ascendancy within the alliance, particularly during the reign (1440–1469) of the nephew of Itzcoatl and uncle of Nezahualcoyotl, the greatest of the Tenochca imperialists, MOTECUHZOMA I. Tlatelolco, now separated from its twin city only by a broad canal, cooperated closely in military activities with Tenochtitlán until 1473. In that year, early in the reign of Motecuhzoma I's grandson,

AXAYACATL (1469–1481), a violent rupture occurred between the cities. Tenochtitlán conquered its northern rival and replaced its ruler, who was killed during the conflict, with Tenochca governors. The last surviving founder of the Triple Alliance, the great Nezahualcoyotl, had died the year before this Mexica "civil war." He was succeeded by his son, NEZAHUALPILLI, who became almost as renowned as his father for his wisdom and sagacity.

Two of Axayacatl's brothers, Tizoc (1481–1486) and Ahuitzotl (1486–1502), succeeded him. They continued to expand the imperial frontiers, especially Ahuitzotl, who pushed one boundary to the border of Guatemala. When the son of Axayacatl, MOTECUHZOMA II, succeeded Ahuitzotl in 1502/1503, the power of Mexico Tenochtitlán was near its zenith. Although a fairly large section of western Oaxaca, inhabited by the MIXTECS, remained to be conquered—and Motecuhzoma II succeeded in subduing most of this region during his reign—the period of spectacular Triple Alliance military expansion was almost over. This final phase of the empire of the Triple Alliance was essentially one of consolidation of past gains.

The first vague reports of the operations of the Spaniards in the Caribbean appear to have drifted into Motecuhzoma II's realm, and, according to post-Conquest tales, various signs and portents of impending catastrophe plagued his last years as ruler. Nezahualpilli died in 1516, supposedly prophesying dire events to come, and a favorite of Motecuhzoma II, Cacama, one of Nezahualpilli's sons by a Tenochca wife, succeeded his father on the throne of Tetzcoco.

When the Spanish force landed on the shore of his empire in the spring of 1519, Motecuhzoma II tried to dissuade Hernán CORTÉS from visiting his capital. When all his tactics failed, he received him peaceably—possibly, in part, because he believed him to be a representative of Topiltzín Quetzalcoatl, the Toltec lord who was expected to return to reclaim his royal dignity. Taken prisoner shortly thereafter in his own palace, Motecuhzoma II remained under the control of Cortés until 30 June 1520, when he died as a result of wounds received from missiles hurled by his own people during an attack on the Spaniards quartered in his father's palace—or possibly was put to death on Cortés's orders.

Motecuhzoma II was succeeded by his brother, CUITLAHUAC, who expelled Cortés's army from the city. However, Cuitlahuac perished in the great smallpox epidemic that ravaged the empire in the fall of 1520 and was succeeded by his cousin, CUAUHTEMOC, who conducted the final, desperate defense of the twin cities, ultimately surrendering to Cortés in Tlatelolco on 13 August 1521. Taken along on Cortés's 1524–1525 expedition to Honduras, this last *tlatoani* of Mexico Tenochtitlán was implicated in an alleged conspiracy against the Spaniards and hanged in southern Campeche by his conqueror. The city that had ruled the largest polity in North America in the early sixteenth century had become the headquarters of a foreign colony ruled from a European capital thousands of miles across the sea.

CIVILIZATION

Aztec civilization, defined as the prevailing culture of the Nahuatl-speaking city-states of central Mexico in the two centuries before the Conquest, was the heir to millennia of intensive cultural development in MESOAMERICA. It constituted a final synthesis of the major achievements of the leading pre-Aztec cultural traditions—including OLMEC, Classic VERACRUZ, Tlatilco, CUICUILCO, TEOTIHUACÁN, XOCHICALCO, CACAXTLA, and TOLTEC. Aztec civilization affected millions of persons inhabiting thousands of communities of all sizes, some of which were larger than any contemporary city in Spain. The elaborate religious/ritual system, which emphasized blood sacrifice, played a particularly pervasive role in all aspects of Aztec life. The subsistence base, featuring an extensive array of nutritious food products, most of them previously unknown to the Old World, was highly productive. Large surpluses were produced for commercial purposes and for meeting tribute obligations.

The societies of the many subject city-states that constituted the basic sociopolitical units of the Triple Alliance Empire were highly stratified, and occupational specialization was well developed. The Aztec artistic achievement was quite impressive, particularly in monumental stone sculpture. Although cut off while in full flower and dominated by an alien culture structured on very different lines, Aztec civilization left a profoundly important heritage that has greatly enriched the intricate and colorful cultural mosaic of modern Mexico.

ROBERT H. BARLOW, *The Extent of the Empire of the Culhua Mexica* (1949); MIGUEL LEÓN-PORTILLA, *Aztec Thought and Culture,* translated by Jack Emory Davis (1963); PEDRO CARRASCO, "The Social Organization of Ancient Mexico," in *Handbook of Middle American Indians,* vol. 10, edited by Gordon Ekholm and Ignacio Bernal (1971), pp. 349–375; H. B. NICHOLSON, "Religion in Pre-Hispanic Central Mexico," in *Handbook of Middle American Indians,* vol. 10, edited by Gordon Ekholm and Ignacio Bernal (1971), pp. 395–446; NIGEL DAVIES, *The Aztecs: A History* (1973); FRANCES E. BERDAN, *The Aztecs of Central Mexico: An Imperial Society* (1982); H. B. NICHOLSON and ELOÍSE QUIÑONES KEBER, *Art of Aztec Mexico: Treasures of Tenochtitlan* (1983); MARY G. HODGE, *Aztec City-States* (1984); RUDOLF VAN ZANTWIJK, *The Aztec Arrangement: The Social History of Pre-Spanish Mexico* (1985); NIGEL DAVIES, *The Aztec Empire: The Toltec Resurgence* (1987); ROSS HASSIG, *Aztec Warfare: Imperial Expansion and Political Control* (1988); and EDUARDO MATOS MOCTEZUMA, *The Aztecs* (1989).

H. B. NICHOLSON

AZTLÁN, legendary homeland of the Mexicas (AZTECS). It was from Aztlán that the Mexicas were said to have begun their odyssey to the promised land, TENOCHTITLÁN. Scholars are in disagreement as to the geographical location of Aztlán, placing it anywhere from present New Mexico to California. Some see it as a spiritual rather than a real place. In contemporary times, the term *Aztlán* became an integral part of the political ideology of the CHICANO movement, referring to the U.S. Southwest or other areas of large Chicano population. The usage of *Aztlán* by Mexican-American political activists and writers was particularly significant in the early phase of the Chicano movement (1965–1976).

DAVID MACIEL

**AZUELA, MARIANO** (*b.* 1 January 1873; *d.* 1 March 1952), Mexican writer. Azuela wrote more than twenty novels, numerous short stories, three plays, biographies, and books of essays. He was born in Lagos de Moreno, Jalisco, and studied medicine in Guadalajara. From early on he alternated between practicing that profession and writing. He published his first book, the short novel *María Luiza,* in 1907, but did not receive international or even national recognition until the mid-1920s, when *Los de abajo* (*The Underdogs*) was ''discovered'' and praised as a great novel reflecting the cultural heritage of the MEXICAN REVOLUTION. This book had originally appeared in serial form and then was published in one volume at the end of 1915 in El Paso, Texas, but the definitive edition was published by the author himself in 1920, when he moved to Mexico City. Azuela's narrative work is a vast mural on which appear the changes and critical characters of Mexican society in the first half of the twentieth century, beginning with the years immediately preceding the Revolution.

Honoré de Balzac and Émile Zola were decisive influences on his work. Latin American ''modernista'' literature (not to be confused with European and North American ''modernism'') was clearly imprinted in Azuela's style.

Two qualities distinguish Azuela as a twentieth-century artist: the acuity with which he captures his characters as social actors, and the lucid way in which he insists, throughout all of his work, that Mexico's social and political problems are rooted in the moral decay of society. No one was better than he at portraying the opportunism, social climbing, resentment, and greed that arose during the Mexican Revolution and later spread throughout all of Mexican society.

Azuela's vision, however, was static and prototypical. His characters are not psychologically complex or capable of dramatic change, and his moralistic clarity becomes at times an obsession. This gives his work the air not of a great human comedy, but of a gallery of scenes with vivid, precise, and incisive images that lack perspective and movement. This mixture of strengths and defects explains why critical judgment and history have almost unanimously declared *Los de abajo* Azuela's masterpiece. It is not by chance that the subtitle of the book is *Cuadros y escenas de la Revolución Mexicana* (Sketches and Scenes of the Mexican Revolution) by which the author himself clearly shows that his vision is more episodic than dramatic. With all its defects, *Los de abajo* continues to be the most intense description of the revolutionary masses and all their contradictions.

Azuela's intense and austere realism influenced other major works, such as Martín Luis Guzmán's *El águila y la serpiente* (1928), Nellie Campobello's *Cartucho* (1931), Rafael F. Muñoz's *Vámonos con Pancho Villa* (1931), and Juan Rulfo's *Pedro Páramo* (1955). His works are available in *Obras completas,* edited by Francisco Monterde, 3 volumes (1958–1960).

LUIS LEAL, *Mariano Azuela* (1971), and ''Mariano Azuela,'' in *Latin American Writers,* edited by Carlos A. Solé and Maria Isabel Abreu, vol. 2 (1989), pp. 457–464; STANLEY L. ROBE, *Azuela and the Mexican Underdogs* (1979).

JORGE AGUILAR MORA

# B

**BABYLONIAN CAPTIVITY** (1580–1640), the period when Spain ruled Portugal. Since Portugal first declared her independence in the twelfth century, Spaniards had yearned to regain control of the western kingdom. The successive deaths of SEBASTIAN (1578) and Cardinal Henry (1580) without issue made it possible for Philip II of Spain to claim Portugal and her empire. Thereafter three successive sovereigns, PHILIP II, III, and IV, ruled Portugal from a distance via councils of regency and with the aid of an itinerant advisory body, the Council of Portugal, but proved unable to honor pledges to preserve the integrity of the empire. As the eastern empire began to crumble in response to indigenous pressures and challenges posed by Holland and England, the Portuguese also witnessed the loss of much of their navy and, for a time, of the sugar-producing captaincies of northeastern Brazil as well as the growth of commodities prices and taxes used to defend Spanish but not Portuguese interests. A series of protest revolts in 1637 were indications of widespread discontent within the kingdom. On 1 December 1640 a group of young nobles entered the royal palace in Lisbon, compelled the resignation of Margaret of Mantua, the last Spanish regent, and acclaimed João, duke of Bragança, as the first king of the restored monarchy.

JOEL SERRÃO, ed., *Dicionário de história de Portugal*, 4 vols. (1971); JOAQUIM VERÍSSIMO SERRÃO, *História de Portugal*, vol. 4 (1979).

DAURIL ALDEN

*See also* **Bragança, House of; João IV.**

**BACA FLOR, CARLOS** (*b.* ca. 1865; *d.* 20 February 1941), Peruvian artist. Born in Islay, formerly Peruvian now Chilean territory, Baca Flor moved with his family to Santiago, Chile, in 1871. At age fifteen he entered the School of Fine Arts in Santiago, where he studied with Cosme San Martín and the Italian Giovanni Mochi. Awarded the Prix de Rome in 1887, he declined the prize rather than renounce his Peruvian citizenship. He moved to Lima shortly thereafter, where the government granted him a fellowship to study at the Royal Academy of Fine Arts in Rome. Three years later he went to Paris to study with Benjamin Constant and Jean-Paul Laurens at the Julian Academy. He never returned to Peru.

For many years Baca Flor lived in extreme poverty, but his luck changed when he obtained first prize at the Salon des Artistes in 1907. Soon afterward, banker John Pierpont Morgan commissioned him to do his portrait.

Subsequently, he obtained portrait commissions from major personalities in the financial world. He painted one hundred and fifty portraits, among them that of Cardinal Eugenio Pacelli, later Pope Pius XII. In 1926 he was elected a member of the Academy of Fine Arts in Paris.

Baca Flor died in Neuilly-sur-Seine, considering himself a Peruvian although he had spent only eight years in his native country. His impeccable technique, at times brilliant composition, and the amazing realism of his portraits are recognized even by those who perceive his academic style as anachronistic.

JUAN E. RÍOS, *La pintura contemporánea en el Perú* (1946), pp. 25–27.

MARTA GARSD

**BACHARÉIS,** term employed in nineteenth-century Brazil to designate all those who had graduated from an educational institution. More specifically, it referred to graduates in law from Coimbra University or from one of the Brazilian law schools, São Paulo or Olinda. This educational experience provided them with a common cultural and political outlook that was inherited from the Portuguese Enlightenment. During the reign of PEDRO II (1840–1889), the *bacharéis* occupied all the important positions in the state bureaucracy and distinguished themselves as ministers, senators, representatives, and attorneys. They became the most evident symbol of the political world of the elite.

ALBERTO VENANCIO FILHO, *Das arcadas ao bacharelismo* (1982); RICHARD GRAHAM, "Locating Power," in his *Patronage and Politics in Nineteenth-Century Brazil* (1990).

LÚCIA M. BASTOS P. NEVES

**BACHILLER Y MORALES, ANTONIO** (*b.* 7 June 1812; *d.* 10 January 1889), Cuban writer, historian, and archaeologist. Born in Havana, Bachiller y Morales became a lawyer and a university professor. He was persecuted and exiled by the Spanish authorities when the TEN YEARS' WAR (1868–1878) began because he favored Cuba's autonomy from Spain. He is best known for his extensive and tireless research, the basis of studies in which he brought together information that had not previously attracted attention. Perhaps the most important of these studies is his three-volume history of Cuban letters and education (*Apuntes para la historia de las letras y instrucción publica de la isla de Cuba,* 1859–1860), but he also made significant contributions on the period of the British domination of Havana (*Cuba: Monografía histórica . . . desde la perdida de la Habana hasta la restauración española,* 1883) and on the pre-Columbian inhabitants of Cuba (*Cuba primitiva,* 1880). Although Bachiller y Morales made quite a few mistakes in his haste to gather information, the efforts of modern historians would have been far less fruitful without his dedication and spadework. He died in Havana.

In the absence of English materials see MAX HENRÍQUEZ UREÑA, *Panorama histórico de la literatura cubana* (1963), vol. 1, pp. 361–364. See also JOSÉ MARTÍ's piece on Bachiller y Morales, *Obras completas* (1963), vol. 5, pp. 141–153.

JOSÉ M. HERNÁNDEZ

**BACKUS AND JOHNSTON,** a company started in 1889 by American engineers Jacob Backus and J. Howard Johnston, with the first customized smelter in the copper center of Casapalca, Peru. A few years later the company reduced the cost of transporting copper for export, making use of the arrival in the high Andes in 1893 of the Central Railway. As the company gained control of mineral transport, it lowered the amounts paid for copper to rival producers. This practice soon drove many Peruvian producers out of copper mining and led to a virtual foreign copper monopoly. By the end of World War I the New York–based CERRO DE PASCO CORPORATION had taken over Backus and Johnston, and by 1930 few other locally owned mining smelters remained. A large measure of the profitability of Andean copper can be attributed to the low cost of labor. The cheap labor force of villagers had left the nearby villages, attracted by the cash offered for work in the mines. Bad working conditions, low pay, and company inattention soon led to strikes. After years of struggle miners won the right to an eight-hour day and other concessions. Labor conditions remained poor, and mine workers continued to be organized and militant.

ROSEMARY THORP and GEOFFREY BERTRAM, *Peru, 1890–1977: Growth and Policy in an Open Economy* (1978), esp. pp. 73–83; FLORENCIA MALLON, *The Defense of Community in Peru's Central Highlands: Peasant Struggle and Capitalist Transition, 1860–1940* (1983), esp. pp. 126, 135–136.

VINCENT PELOSO

*See also* **Copper Industry.**

**BÁEZ, BUENAVENTURA** (*b.* 1812; *d.* 1884), five-time president of the Dominican Republic. Báez was born in Azua to a wealthy landowner and his African slave. During the Haitian occupation of Santo Domingo, Báez represented Azua in the Haitian Congress and Constituent Assembly. He distrusted the Dominican independence movement and refused to recognize its authority after the proclamation of independence on 27 February 1844. Throughout his political career, Báez sought to place his country under the protection of a major foreign power, believing that the Dominican Republic did not have the strength to maintain genuine independence. With the aid of his future archrival, General Pedro SANTANA, he assumed the presidency for the first time in 1849.

*First Presidential Term (24 September 1849–15 February 1853)* Báez negotiated with both France and England for their possible acquisition of the Dominican Republic. He became the champion of the interests of the upper and middle classes by promoting the development of industry and furthering the educational system through the opening of national colleges at Santo Domingo and Santiago de los Caballeros. Báez concluded a concordat with the Vatican by which the Roman Catholic church was permitted to provide religious instruction in Dominican public schools. During his first term, the country suffered frequent attacks by Haiti, all of which were repelled. In 1853 Báez was forced into exile by Santana.

*Second Presidential Term (8 October 1856–12 June 1858)* Báez began his second term by unleashing a fierce persecution of Santana and his followers. He issued paper currency, which led to a devaluation of the peso and the ruin of many landowners, particularly the tobacco cultivators of the Cibao. A revolt in that fertile agricultural region toppled Báez, who fled to Spain. While still in exile there, he advocated Spain's annexation of the Dominican Republic.

*Third Presidential Term (8 December 1865–29 May 1866)* During his third term, Báez established a truly despotic regime marked by his effort to crush all opposition. He antagonized Dominican patriots by negotiating a deal with U.S. Secretary of State William H. Seward, by which the Dominican Republic would allow the United States to acquire the Samaná Peninsula in return for economic aid. Once again, a revolt in the Cibao forced Báez to flee the country.

*Fourth Presidential Term (2 May 1868–January 1874)* Báez's fourth term was the bloodiest and the most anarchic of his five terms. It is known in Dominican history as the "Regime of the Six Years." After failing to sell Samaná to the United States for $2 million, Báez offered the entire country to Washington. This plan met with a positive response from U.S. President Ulysses S. Grant, but the determined resistance of Senator Charles Sumner of Massachusetts prevented the annexation. By 1874, revolutionary forces compelled Báez to flee to Curaçao.

*Fifth Presidential Term (27 December 1876–2 March 1878)* Báez began his final term by promising democratic, liberal reforms, but he was soon indulging in familiar repressive measures. He also renewed his efforts to incorporate his country into the United States. His final exile from Santo Domingo began in March 1878. He died in Puerto Rico.

EMILIO RODRÍGUEZ DEMORIZI, *Papeles de Buenaventura Báez* (1969); IAN BELL, *The Dominican Republic* (1981).

KAI P. SCHOENHALS

See also **Dominican Republic.**

**BÁEZ, CECILIO** (*b.* 1 February 1862; *d.* 18 June 1941), politician, intellectual, diplomat, public servant, and provisional president of Paraguay (1905–1906). Cecilio Báez was one of the founders of the Liberal Party in 1887 and later its president. He was a deputy in Congress for several terms, beginning in 1895. He might be remembered most as the party's leading theoretician. Báez was also known for denouncing Francisco Solano LÓPEZ, the controversial leader who led Paraguay into disastrous WAR OF THE TRIPLE ALLIANCE in 1864. He was appointed provisional president on 9 December 1905 for eleven months. Because of his influence, he was often able to keep the Liberals somewhat united in spite of their tendency to splinter into factions. By profession a doctor of law and a historiographer, Báez was instrumental in shaping a national education program. His prolific writings dealt with Paraguayan history as well as literary, legal, and political issues. He was a great advocate of democracy as well as a strong critic of the Catholic church. Báez was the National University's rector throughout the 1920s and 1930s. After the CHACO WAR with Bolivia, Báez, as foreign minister, signed the peace treaty on 28 July 1938.

PAUL H. LEWIS, *Paraguay Under Stroessner* (1980); HARRIS GAYLORD WARREN, *Rebirth of the Paraguayan Republic* (1985); RIORDAN ROETT and RICHARD SCOTT SACKS, *Paraguay: The Personalist Legacy* (1991).

MIGUEL A. GATTI

See also **Paraguay: Political Parties.**

**BAHAMAS, COMMONWEALTH OF THE,** an archipelago of over 700 islands, stretching from less than fifty miles off the coast of Florida south toward Haiti. The total land area is over 5,000 square miles, but only sixteen of the islands are populated to any large extent (1990 population 253,000). The capital, Nassau, is located on the central island of New Providence. Historically, the Bahamas' claim to fame lies in the fact that its easternmost island, San Salvador, formerly called Guanahani and then Watlings Island, was the first land discovered by Christopher COLUMBUS on 12 October 1492. "Bahamas" comes from the Spanish *bajamar*, meaning "shallow water," and refers to the shallow waters that surround the islands, making them ideal harbors. The Spanish made no attempt to colonize the islands, however, because they were settled by an indigenous population, the ARAWAKS, who had no apparent treasures nor developed civilization. Almost all of the Indians died from contact with the Spanish or were dragged off to work in the mines of Hispaniola.

In 1629, the islands were granted to Sir Robert Heath, attorney general of England. In 1647 the crown made another grant to the Company of Eleutherian Adventurers, who colonized the island of Eleuthera. The Eleutherian Adventurers, the first English settlers of the Bahamas, came from Bermuda under the direction of Sir William Sayle, seeking liberty and freedom of religion. In 1670, a third grant was issued by Charles II to six lord proprietors from Carolina.

The eighteenth century brought a flurry of activity to the islands. The first royal governor, Sir Woodes Rodgers, was sent by the crown to Nassau in 1718. By the middle of the century, Nassau had become the hub of activity for pirates because of the island's strategic location. During the AMERICAN REVOLUTION, loyalists fled to the islands along with many freed slaves. In 1782, the Spanish attacked New Providence, which was finally ceded to Great Britian in exchange for East Florida under terms of the Treaty of Paris (1783). The influx of loyalists spurred economic development, but not without competition from the landed elite. Both fared well, however, owing to the profitability of the cotton harvests before the devastation caused by the chenille bug in 1788.

The islands experienced relative peace throughout the nineteenth century. The abolition of slavery in 1838 brought social and economic reconstruction, although a high percentage of the slaves were freed before that date. During the U.S. Civil War, the colony prospered owing to its ideal situation as a depot for vessels running the blockade of the Confederacy.

The House of Assembly, formed in 1729, remains the most important political institution. It was controlled almost exclusively by white merchants and settlers throughout the nineteenth century. In the twentieth century the oligarchy was run by a group of merchants known as the "Bay Street Boys," named after Nassau's main commercial downtown street. Politics changed in 1962 when the House voted for universal suffrage. With the formation of the popularly supported Progressive Liberal Party (PLP), white minority rule ended in 1967.

The PLP began a program of national development and controlled migration, and instituted a highly successful Bahamianization program in 1973. The islands gained their independence on 10 July of that year but retain ties with Great Britain through the Commonwealth. The leader of the PLP, Sir Linden Oscar Pindling, was prime minister from 1967 to 1992. Hubert A. Ingraham of the Free National Movement was elected prime minister in 1992.

The main source of foreign currency for the Bahamas is TOURISM, followed by the well-developed offshore banking system for international investors. Because of the lack of taxes, and the relatively stable political situation, the Bahamas is an attractive tax haven. It is home to hundreds of European, American, and Canadian investors.

The Bahamas had a series of conflicts with the United States in the 1980s over its financial secrecy laws, which have allowed some U.S. investors to avoid taxation in the United States, and also about DRUG trafficking. Consequently, the Bahamas was excluded from the U.S. Caribbean Basin Initiative. Since 1985, however, relations have improved. In 1989 the U.S. Senate voted against a bill proposing to make the Bahamas ineligible for U.S. aid.

ALAN BURNS, *History of the British West Indies* (1965); MICHAEL CRATON, *A History of the Bahamas,* 2d ed. (1968); GORDON K. LEWIS, *The Growth of the Modern West Indies* (1968); PAUL AL-BURY, *Story of the Bahamas* (1975). For more statistical information see *The Caribbean Yearbook 1979/80* (1980) and *The Bahamas Handbook* (annual). See also TONY THORNDIKE, "Bahamas," in *South America, Central America, and the Caribbean 1991* (1990).

DARIÉN DAVIS

**BAHIA,** a state in Northeastern Brazil with an area of 216,612 square miles. The population of 11,808,810 (1991) is 67 percent mulatto, 27 percent white, and 11 percent black. The capital city is SALVADOR.

The Baía de Todos os Santos (All Saints Bay), discovered by Amerigo VESPUCCI in 1501, gave its name to the state. The Portuguese launched a plan to colonize Bahia in 1530. The main product was sugarcane, cultivated in the fertile soil of the RECÔNCAVO, the region surrounding the bay. COTTON and TOBACCO were also grown, the latter a valuable item in the SLAVE TRADE. The expansion of cattle raising led to the occupation of the interior of the state. The educational and cultural life of the colony was organized primarily by the JESUITS, who also worked on the conversion of the Indians to Christianity.

In spite of the Dutch invasion (1623–1624), the seventeenth century was the apogee of colonial life in Bahia, thanks to the expanding production of both sugar and tobacco, which responded to the higher demands in the European and African markets, respectively. The social structure was hierarchical, oligarchic, and repressive. Administrative positions were filled by whites, with the slaves brought from Africa constituting the labor force. Indian labor was used mostly in cattle raising in the interior. Salvador was the most important city of the colony until the second decade of the nineteenth century, when the coffee industry vaulted Rio de Janeiro and São Paulo to paramount importance.

Due to strong resistance by the Portuguese, Bahia did not gain its independence (1823) until one year after the rest of the country did. Even though many *baianos* occupied prominent positions in the national administration, Bahia became a second-class province during the empire (1822–1889), primarily because of the declining importance of its exports. Economic stagnation lasted until 1907, when CACAO, cultivated in the southern part of the state, became the major export.

The coming to power of Governor José Joaquim Seabra (1912), with his politics of "national salvation" aimed at ending the powerful oligarchies in the country, typified the ascension of sectors of the urban middle class to positions of command. The sugar barons, dominant in the earlier period, had lost both the economic power and the political influence that they had previously enjoyed. The administrative decentralization of the empire was replaced by centralized governments in the republic, which aimed to integrate a fragmented country.

Oligarchic and conservative, the government of Bahia opposed the Revolution of 1930. The political movement, however, stirred up popular demonstrations. The depression of the 1930s was extremely severe in the state, due to its heavy dependence on cacao exports, which fell drastically. Social instability and strike attempts were curbed by strong state repression. Bahia was then governed by Juraci Magalhães who, influenced by Franklin D. ROOSEVELT's New Deal, launched a small-scale program of public works and succeeded in enhancing the economic situation of the state.

The ESTADO NOVO (1937–1945) of Getúlio VARGAS installed a dictatorial government under which the states were ruled by intervenors appointed by Vargas. Otávio Mangabeira, who served as governor from 1947 to 1951, is considered the most outstanding political figure in the state after Rui BARBOSA.

Agriculture and commerce still are the main activities of the state. After the creation of the Industrial Park of Aratu during the 1970s, however, Bahia became the industrial leader in the Northeast, although its capital-intensive industries have not created much local employment. Given Bahia's attractive beaches, more attention is being paid to the development of TOURISM.

A. J. R. RUSSELL-WOOD, *Fidalgos and Philanthropists: The Santa Casa da Misericórdia of Bahia, 1550–1755* (1968); THALES DE AZEVEDO, *Povoamento da cidade do Salvador*, 3d ed. (1969); CONSUELO NOVAIS SAMPAIO, "Crisis in the Brazilian Oligarchical System: A Case Study on Bahia, 1889–1937" (Ph.D. diss., Johns Hopkins University, 1979); KATIA M. DE QUEIRÓS MATTOSO, *Bahia, século XIX: Uma provinia no Império* (1992); JOÃO JOSÉ REIS, *Slave Rebellion in Brazil: The Muslim Uprising of 1835 in Bahia* (1993).

CONSUELO NOVAIS SAMPAIO

*See also* **Brazil: Revolutions.**

**BAHÍA,** the name given to one of several prehistoric cultures in coastal Ecuador during the Regional-Developmental Period (500 B.C.–A.D. 500). Bahía is named after the large bay at the mouth of the Chone River, Bahía de Caráquez, but its territory extends 90 miles down the coast to southern Manabí Province. It was formally defined by Ecuadorian Emilio Estrada in the late 1950s, on the basis of his deep excavations in the modern city of Bahía de Caráquez and nearby sites. Other Bahía occupations have been documented at Los Esteros and Tarquí (near modern Manta), Salango, and LA PLATA Island.

Where not destroyed by modern settlement, some sites appear to have been true urban centers with ceremonial precincts and rectangular platform mounds having a formal grid plan. La Plata Island served as an important religious sanctuary where regular pilgrimages were made for ritual events and where votive offerings of figurines and other objects were repeatedly deposited. Ceremonial activity has also been documented at Salango, in southern coastal Manabí, where archaeologists have uncovered the remains of a 120-square-yard, adobe-walled temple structure bordered by deep wall trenches, stone alignments, and linear posthole patterns. Given the large number of Bahía burials uncovered and the richness of their associated grave offerings, the structure has been interpreted as a ceremonial/mortuary one for elite sectors of Bahía society.

Apart from these scientific excavations, much knowledge of this culture comes from the elaborate ceramic artifacts that have been unearthed both by professional archaeologists and by commercially motivated looters. Although some traits show continuity with the earlier Chorrera culture (such as iridescent painting), new vessel forms, decorative techniques, and thematic imagery also appear in Bahía pottery. New types of ceramic artifacts include miniature house models, head rests, and "golf-tee" ear plugs said to represent Asiatic influences, presumably through trans-Pacific contact. Anthropomorphic figurines appear in a wide variety of forms and sizes, including the small, solid, mold-made Esteros type and the larger, hollow La Plata type. The latter are decorated with multicolored postfire pigments similar to those of JAMA-COAQUE figurines. Crudely shaped anthropomorphic figures also appear on tusk-shaped stone pendants. One artifact type unique to the Bahía culture is the carved stone plaque made from volcanic tuff, which is apparently restricted to La Plata Island. Typically these are decorated on one side with carved geometric designs in a quadripartite layout, usually small incised circles inside an X-shaped figure. No contextual information is available, but suggested functions range from gaming pieces to navigational devices.

The urban character, elaborate ceremonialism, and mortuary ritual of the largest Bahía sites indicate considerable sociopolitical complexity, very likely a stratified chiefdom, or *señorío*, with a well-defined regional settlement hierarchy. In spite of the littoral nature of the site thus far studied, the Bahía culture probably had a strong agricultural base supported by a tributary population of inland farmers and craft specialists. External contacts were most intensive with adjacent Regional-Developmental chiefdoms to the north, south, and east, although long-distance voyaging for exotic resources, such as precious stones, may have occurred.

EMILIO ESTRADA, *Arqueología de Manabí central* (1962); MATTHEW STIRLING and MARIAN STIRLING, "Tarquí: An Early Site in Manabí Province, Ecuador," in *Smithsonian Institution, Bureau of American Ethnology, Bulletin* 186 (1963): 1–28; JORGE G. MARCOS and PRESLEY NORTON, "Interpretación sobre la arqueología de la Isla de la Plata," in *Miscellánea antropológica ecuatoriana* 1, no. 1 (1981): 136–154; ROBERT A. FELDMAN and MICHAEL E. MOSELEY, "The Northern Andes," in *Ancient South Americans*, edited by Jesse D. Jennings (1983); PRESLEY NORTON et al.,"Excavaciones en Salango, provincia de Manabí, Ecuador," in *Miscelánea antropológica ecuatoriana* 3 (1983): 9–80.

JAMES A. ZEIDLER

*See also* **Guangala.**

**BAHÍA BLANCA,** city at the southern edge of the Argentine province of Buenos Aires (1991 population of 271,467) located on a natural bay. Founded in 1828 as a military outpost against roaming Pampa Indians, it was used by Juan Manuel de ROSAS as a stronghold against the Indians in 1833. Following the Campaign of the Desert (1879–1883), a concerted effort by the Buenos Aires government to clear the Indians from the PAMPA to make room for agrarian colonists, and the completion of a railway link with Buenos Aires in 1885, it became an important center of colonization and the end station of the General Roca railway. The hinterland was settled predominantly by families of Italian ancestry who managed successful farmsteads and cattle ranches and founded urban enterprises in the city. Nearby Puerto Galván is the site of an oil refinery that processes crude oil brought from Plaza Huincul, at the foot of the Andes. Packing plants, tanneries, transportation workshops, grain-processing mills, and a large chemical plant that uses petroleum derivatives dominate the economic activities of the city, which has also developed into a cultural center of the southern pampa. The Universidad del Sur, founded in 1956, has nearly 15,000 students. Bahía Blanca is connected by major highways with Mar del Plata and Buenos Aires. Puerto Belgrano is an important strategic base for the navy and the air force.

PEDRO GONZÁLEZ P., *Bahía Blanca como capital de una nueva provincia* (Bahía Blanca, 1962); and MARÍA E. REY, *Historia de la industria en Bahía Blanca* (Bahía Blanca, 1980).

CÉSAR N. CAVIEDES

**BAHÍA, ISLAS DE.** The Bay Islands of Honduras, just off the north coast of that country, constitute the smallest and most distinctive of the eighteen departments of the Republic of Honduras. The elongated cluster of eight islands and sixty-five cays has a total land area of just under ninety-two square miles. The major islands (from west to east, Utila, Roatán, Barbaret, and Guanaja) are continental in geological structure and surrounded by reefs in unusually clear water. Perhaps no other part of the Caribbean has experienced more cultural diversity than these islands; they have been occupied by nine distinct groups since aboriginal times. Occupants have included Pech (Paya) Indians, colonial Spaniards, multinational pirates, Englishmen, Garífuna (Black Caribs), Anglo-Antilleans, Afro-Antilleans, North Americans, and Spanish Hondurans.

While the earlier archeological record indicates that aboriginal islanders were influenced by the high cultures of Mesoamerica (primarily MAYA), later pre-Columbian artifacts are similar to those of the adjacent mainland, the home of Indians identified as Pech. Columbus visited these islands in 1502 during his fourth voyage, the first to Central America.

The native islanders, during the first century of uncontested Spanish colonization, were enslaved, Christianized, and used as a labor supply. Bartolomé de LAS CASAS exaggerated the contact population, saying it was "more than 150,000 souls"; it was more likely only several thousand strong when first encountered by the Spaniards. By 1544, documents show that only about 1,000 remained. The census of 1639 counted 400 souls. Shortly afterward, the Spaniards depopulated the islands because the natives were aiding pirate intruders.

Non-Spanish raiders found the islands particularly strategic and attractive because the gold-carrying Honduras Fleet called at nearby Trujillo, and other shipping routes passed nearby. Deep embayments on Roatán's south coast were the best refuges in the region. The largest attack was perhaps that of William Jackson, who with 1,500 men and sixteen vessels took Trujillo in 1642. The buccaneers wintered on Roatán.

The English military continued to disrupt the Spanish influence over the islands, particularly during 1742–1749 and 1779–1782. The ruined English fortifications around Port Royal, dating from these two major occupations, can still be seen. Anthony's Cay, also on Roatán, was another English site of this period.

In 1797, the British-organized importation of some 2,000 Black Caribs (now called Garífuna) from the island of Saint Vincent in the Windward Islands introduced another culture to the islands. This marked the beginning of a permanent settlement pattern that has persisted until today. Most of the Garífuna settled the beachlands around the Bay of Honduras, but their first village was Punta Gorda, on the north coast of Roatán.

English speakers, still dominant in the islands, became firmly established after Cayman Islanders arrived in 1835, a year after the abolition of slavery. For a decade during the mid-nineteenth century, when the English claimed the islands as a crown colony, the traditions and social inclinations of Anglo- and Afro-Antilleans became well embedded.

North Americans visited the islands in the 1860s, as traders in the banana and coconut commerce with New Orleans; since then they have come as tourists who enjoy diving and fishing in the clear waters.

A relict English-speaking enclave on the rimland of the western Caribbean, the Bay Islands are experiencing a modern Hispanicization from the mainland populations. Although the Republic of Honduras has had formal political power in the islands since 1859, only since the 1970s have there been effective attempts to incorporate the islands into the mainland system. Attracted primarily by economic opportunities represented by a developing tourism industry, Spanish-speaking LADINOS from the mainland are increasing their proportion of the population and asserting their culture. According to the national census of May 1988, the islands are home to 22,062, roughly three-fourths of whom live on Roatán, the most developed island. The largest settlements are the capital, Coxen Hole, on Roatán (3,901); Bonacca, the quaint stilt house settlement off Guanaja (2,027); Oak Ridge, on Roatán (1,304); and East Harbour, on Utila (1,261).

WILLIAM V. DAVIDSON, *Historical Geography of the Bay Islands, Honduras: Anglo-Hispanic Conflict in the Western Caribbean* (1974); ELISSA WARANTZ, ''The Bay Islands English of Honduras,'' in *Central American English,* edited by John Holm (1983).

WILLIAM V. DAVIDSON

**BAIÃO,** a popular form of MUSIC, dance, and song in northeastern Brazil, typically played by trios of accordion, triangle, and *zabumba* (bass drum). The *baião,* and related genres such as the *baiano* and *abaianada,* most likely originated in the nineteenth century as a social dance music and musical pattern in rural northeastern Brazil among the mestizo population. The name probably comes from an early association with the state of Bahia. The music and dance elements of *baião* were influenced by, if not derived from, Afro-Brazilian styles. An urban form of the *baião* was created and popularized nationally in the 1940s by Luiz GONZAGA, who mixed a rhythm played on the *viola* (a ten-string folk guitar) by northeastern bards with drum patterns from BANDAS DE PÍFANOS (fife-and-drum bands). In the 1950s and 1960s it became a national symbol of the Northeast when millions of northeasterners migrated to the South (especially to São Paulo) in search of work. Musically, the *baião* is characterized by a syncopated duple rhythm played on the *zabumba* and a melodic scale featuring a flatted seventh. The songs' texts dwell on love and on the natural beauty and chronic problems of the Northeast. They are usually told from a male perspective, often in slang and a heavy northeastern accent.

JOSÉ RAMOS TINHORÃO, *Pequena história da música popular: da modinha ao tropicalismo,* 5th ed. (1986), esp. pp. 219–229; MUNDICARMO MARIA ROCHA FERRETTI, *Baião dos dois: A música de Zédantas e Luiz Gonzaga . . .* (1988); CHRIS MC GOWAN and RICARDO PESSANHA, *The Brazilian Sound: Samba, Bossa Nova, and the Popular Music of Brazil* (1991), esp. pp. 135–136.

LARRY N. CROOK

**BAJA CALIFORNIA,** a peninsula about 850 miles long in the extreme northwestern part of the Republic, extending southward from the boundary with CALIFORNIA and separated from the mainland of Mexico by the Gulf of California. Physiographically, it is formed by a fault-block mountain with a steep escarpment facing east and a gentle slope toward the Pacific. The southern tip of the peninsula and the extreme north have a climate similar to that of the Mexican mainland and receive summer rains totaling 10–25 inches per year, but the rest of the peninsula is extremely arid, with virtually no surface water. Today, it is divided into two states: Baja California, which became a state in 1952, with a population of about 1.6 million in 1990, and Baja California Sur, which became a state in 1974, with a population of approximately 375,000 in 1990.

Occupied since pre-Columbian times by simple hunting and gathering societies, the peninsula was discov-ered by the Spaniards in the early 1530s and explored by Fortún Jiménez de Bertadoña in 1534, Hernán CORTÉS in 1535, and Francisco de Ulloa in 1539. The Jesuits established the mission of Loreto in 1697, and by the time they were expelled in 1767, they operated 19 missions and associated settlements for some 6,000 Indians. Through the nineteenth century, Baja California was characterized by scattered settlements that focused on stock raising and by a limited agriculture based on well irrigation. In 1888, it was divided into two territories.

In the early twentieth century, railway connections to California and irrigation from the Colorado River began to transform northern Baja California, and in 1948 it was connected to the rest of Mexico by railroad. The northern irrigated valleys became centers for producing wine grapes, olives, vegetables (especially tomatoes), wheat, and barley. The region became Mexico's major wine producer after an expansion of vineyard plantings in the 1970s. Tijuana has gained great importance as a tourist center, drawing many North Americans since the Prohibition era and World War II, and still offers a race course, gambling, and a flavor of the exotic to the more than 30 million tourists who cross the border each year.

Baja California Sur has followed a different economic course. After centuries of isolation, it was linked to the mainland by ferry service in 1924, and in 1973 a paved highway from south of Ensenada to La Paz was completed. Resorts have been developed at San José del Cabo, Cabo San Lucas, and outside La Paz.

PABLO MARTÍNEZ, *A History of Lower California* (1960); ROBERT COOPER WEST, ed., *Handbook of Middle American Indians,* vol. 1 (1964), pp. 55–56, 369–370; ADRIÁN VALADÉS, *Historia de la Baja California: 1850–1880* (1974); JORGE L. TAMAYO, *Geografía moderna de Mexico,* 9th ed. (1980), pp. 49–50, 58–59, 378–379; ROBERT COOPER WEST and JOHN P. AUGELLI, *Middle America: Its Lands and Peoples,* 3d ed. (1989), pp. 245, 359–360.

JOHN J. WINBERRY

**BAJÍO,** an area recognized since colonial times as the ''Granary of Mexico'' because of its fertile soils and production of corn, beans, and wheat. Formed by the basins of Guanajuato and Jalisco, it covers parts of the states of Jalisco, Guanajuato, Querétaro, and Michoacán. The Bajío lies at an altitude of about 6,500 feet, and its surface is covered by thick lacustrine sediments enriched with volcanic ash. It receives about 25 inches of rainfall a year, almost all of which falls during the summer months.

During the pre-Columbian era, the Bajío was on the northern frontier of Mesoamerica and was occupied largely by nomadic Chichimecs. Opened to Spanish colonization after the MIXTÓN WAR of 1541, the area drew Otomí and Tarascan farmers from the south and east, followed by Spanish missionaries, who began producing wheat, and by ranchers, who introduced herds of livestock. The discovery of silver at Zacatecas in 1546, at Guanajuato in 1563, and later at sites to the north and east, created markets for agricultural products, and garrison towns such as Celaya (1571) were established to protect the silver route from Zacatecas to Mexico City from hostile Indians.

By the mid-seventeenth century, the Bajío was Mexico's major wheat-producing area. With this success came the expansion of cultivated land, the decline of livestock, the development of large estates, and the rapid growth of population, especially during the eighteenth century. Irrigation also became important; Spanish *hacendados* used springs but also irrigated with water from the LERMA RIVER and its tributaries. The earliest of these works, dating from 1648, was the dam on the Laguna de Yuriria. For the most part, wheat was grown on irrigated land, and maize was raised on nonirrigated plots. During the colonial period a textile industry based on wool, and later cotton, grew up in the cities of the Bajío, especially Querétaro, Celaya, and Salamanca.

The Bajío remained Mexico's most productive agricultural region until the 1950s, when new lands were opened in the irrigated valleys of the northwest. Even though much of the Bajío was broken up into *ejidos* during the 1930s, the region remains important for farming, growing wheat, truck crops (especially strawberries), alfalfa, corn, and beans. New irrigation complexes such as the Solís dam on the Lerma River (1949) have replaced the old systems, whose relict features are still visible in the landscape today.

D. A. BRADING, *Haciendas and Ranchos in the Mexican Bajío: León, 1700–1860* (1978); MICHAEL E. MURPHY, *Irrigation in the Bajío Region of Colonial Mexico* (1986); ROBERT COOPER WEST and JOHN P. AUGELLI, *Middle America: Its Lands and Peoples*, 3d ed. (1989), pp. 258–260, 304–305.

JOHN J. WINBERRY

**BAKER, LORENZO DOW** (*b.* 15 March 1840; *d.* 21 June 1908), native of Wellfleet, Massachusetts, leading Cape Cod shipowner, and a principal founder of the modern banana-exporting industry in the Caribbean. Captain Baker first brought a small cargo of BANANAS from Jamaica to New Jersey in 1870. In subsequent years he greatly expanded this trade, developing it between Jamaica and Boston. In 1884 he led the formation of the Boston Fruit Company, which in 1899 merged with Minor C. Keith's Tropical Trading & Transport Company and other banana interests to become the UNITED FRUIT COMPANY. Baker continued to serve the company as its representative in Jamaica until just before his death in Boston. His development of the banana industry contributed to considerable economic growth in Jamaica.

FREDERICK U. ADAMS, *Conquest of the Tropics: The Story of the Creative Enterprises Conducted by the United Fruit Company* (1914); *National Cyclopædia of American Biography*, vol. 14 (1917), pp. 350–351; PHILIP K. REYNOLDS, *The Banana: Its History, Cultivation and Place Among Staple Foods* (1927); CHARLES M. WILSON, *Empire in Green and Gold* (1947).

SUE DAWN MCGRADY

**BALAGUER, JOAQUÍN** (*b.* 1 September 1907), Dominican author, lawyer, politician, and president of the Dominican Republic (1960–1961, 1966–1978, 1986–). Balaguer, a native of Villa Bisono, studied law at both Santo Domingo and Paris, receiving a doctorate of law from each. In 1930 he became involved in the conspiracy of Rafael Estrella Ureña against president Horacio Vásquez, which brought Rafael-Leónidas TRUJILLO MOLINA to power. Balaguer served the Trujillo regime in important ambassadorial posts abroad and as minister of education, vice president (1957–1960), and president (1960–1961) at home. Whereas most members of Trujillo's government used their positions for personal enrichment, Balaguer continued to lead his modest bachelor existence.

In the wake of Trujillo's assassination in 1961, Balaguer served as an important transitional figure between the end of the era of Trujillo and the presidential elections in 1962. He initiated a number of reforms that were designed to persuade the Organization of American States to lift its sanctions against the Dominican Republic. Balaguer opposed the attempt of Trujillo's brothers José Arismendi and Héctor Bienvenido to resurrect Trujilloism without Trujillo. He presided over the Council of State that ruled the country until the inauguration of the new president in February 1963. As the nation's political situation became volatile in late 1962, Balaguer decided upon exile in New York City. Thus he was absent from the Dominican Republic during Juan

Joaquín Balaguer. UPI / BETTMANN ARCHIVE.

BOSCH's ephemeral presidency (1963); the military coup and subsequent triumvirate headed by Donald Reid Cabral, and the 1965 revolution, civil war, and foreign intervention.

During the presidential elections of 1966, Balaguer was the candidate of the Reformist Party (PR), which he founded during his years in exile. He won 57 percent of the vote. Thus began the twelve-year era of Balaguer, which witnessed his reelection as president in 1970 and 1974. The era was marked by massive aid from the United States, an economic boom triggered by the rise in world sugar prices, and a large building program that included the restoration of the colonial part of Santo Domingo.

After an interlude of presidents belonging to the Dominican Revolutionary Party (PRD) from 1978 to 1986, Balaguer was elected to the presidency twice more (1986, 1990). It was Balaguer's desire to preside over the 1992 celebrations accompanying the five-hundredth anniversary of Christopher Columbus's arrival on Hispaniola. Balaguer will be remembered as the Dominican Republic's outstanding statesman of the twentieth century. His contributions to Dominican literature have also been significant, especially his critical history of Dominican literature, *Historia de la literatura dominicana* (1956), and his other literary criticism, his historical works on the Trujillo era, including *Memorias de un cortesano* (1989), and his work on Dominican relations with Haiti, *La isla revés: Haiti y el destino dominicano* (1983). Balaguer's intense rivalry with Bosch extended to literary as well as political pursuits.

Balaguer's writings also include *La política internacional de Trujillo* (1941), *Semblanzas literarias* (1948), *Entre la sangre del 30 de mayo y la del 24 de abril* (1983), *La voz del capitolio* (1984), and *Memorias de un cortesano de la ''era de Trujillo''* (1988). See also JAMES NELSON GOODSELL, ''Balaguer's Dominican Republic,'' in *Current History* 53, no. 315 (1967): 298–302.

KAI P. SCHOENHALS

*See also* **Dominican Republic.**

**BALAIADA,** a rural uprising of 1838–1841 in the Brazilian provinces of Maranhão and Piauí. A relatively numerous peasantry had developed in connection with the cotton plantations in northern Maranhão. They, along with slaves, and cowboys from the cattle areas of southern Maranhão and Piauí, were the principal supporters of the movement. Arbitrary military recruitment, personal grievances, and resentment against the Portuguese elite, which had managed to remain influential after independence, were the main reasons for the revolt. In the cattle areas of southern Maranhão and in Piauí, the movement was initially supported by FAZENDEIROS (ranchers) as well. In Piauí the particular target was the arbitrary rule of the governor, the viscount of Parnaíba.

The rebels adopted the demands of the former Patriot Party, now the Liberal Party—expulsion of the Portuguese and suspension of the police chiefs responsible for recruitment—and claimed recognition for their officials. The liberal elite refused to join a popular movement led by cowboys like Raimundo Gomes Vieira, peasants like Balaio (Manuel Francisco dos Anjos Ferreira), and maroons like Cosme Bentos das Chagas.

During the uprising, which began in December 1838, the rebels managed to control large parts of the interior and twice occupied the city of Caixas. Government troops proved inefficient because of numerous desertions and lack of experience with guerrilla warfare. The new commander in chief, Luís Alves de LIMA E SILVA, the future duke of Caixas, arrived with reinforcements from Rio de Janeiro in February 1840. He divided the rebels by granting amnesty to those who captured runaway slaves.

Defections led to a radicalization of the remaining *balaios* around Gomes and an alliance with the rebellious slaves led by Cosme, but they could not long resist the numerous and now well-organized government troops. By January 1841, Maranhão and Piauí were considered pacified. Many prisoners were executed.

JOSÉ RIBEIRO DO AMARAL, *Apontamentos para a história da revolução da Balaiada na província do Maranhão*, 3 vols. (1898–1906); MARIA JANUÁRIA VILELA SANTOS, *A Balaiada e a insurreição de escravos no Maranhão* (1983); MARIA AMÉLIA FREITAS MENDES DE OLIVEIRA, *A Balaiada no Piauí* (1985); MATTHIAS RÖHRIG ASSUNÇÃO, *A guerra dos Bem-te-vis: A Balaiada na memória oral* (1988).

MATTHIAS RÖHRIG ASSUNÇÃO

**BALBÁS, JERÓNIMO DE** (d. 22 November 1748), RETABLO master. Balbás was born in Zamora, Spain, and lived in Cádiz in the early eighteenth century; later he worked in Seville and in Marchena. In 1718 he was in New Spain. Reminiscent in design of his principal retablo for the Sagrario of the cathedral of Seville (1706–1709, destroyed 1824), his Retablo de los Reyes for the cathedral of Mexico City (1718–1737), with four large *estípites*, determined the direction that much of the art of New Spain was to take for the rest of the century. The final breakdown of the Renaissance grid scheme in retablo design and the introduction of the *estípite* along with a new vocabulary of motifs are due to Balbás's work in the cathedral of Mexico City. He stayed on in New Spain and executed numerous other retablos, including the altar of Pardon and the central free-standing retablo, or ''ciprés,'' of the cathedral; only the first survives, reconstructed after a fire in 1967.

MANUEL TOUSSAINT, *Colonial Art in Mexico* (1967); CONCEPCIÓN AMERLINCK, ''Jerónimo de Balbás, artista de vanguardia, y el retablo de la Concepción de la Ciudad de México,'' *Monumentos históricos* 2 (1979): 25–34; GUILLERMO TOVAR DE TERESA, *México barroco* (1981), pp. 86–87.

CLARA BARGELLINI

**BALBÍN, RICARDO** (*b.* 29 July 1904; *d.* 9 September 1981), Argentine political leader and one of the principal Radical Party figures in the postwar period. Originally from Buenos Aires, Balbín was elected in 1930 as a Radical congressman from La Plata but was unable to serve because of the military coup of that same year. He was one of the leading *intransigentes* (Intransigent Radicals) who, with Arturo FRONDIZI, was cofounder of the Movimiento de Intransigencia y Renovación (MIR) in 1945. With Frondizi, Balbín (as party whip) led the Radicals in the Argentine Congress under Juan PERÓN until 1949, when the government began a campaign against him, which led to his forced resignation as congressman and imprisonment. In the 1951 election, he was the unsuccessful Radical presidential candidate against Perón.

Balbín broke with Frondizi and the *intransigentes* after Perón's ouster and in 1956 established the Radical Civic Union of the People (UCRP), a more conservative and decidedly anti-Peronist party, which nominated him in the election won by Frondizi in 1958. With the demise of the *intransigentes*, Balbín emerged as the principal leader of the Radical Party and was one of the country's most important political figures until his death. In 1970 he led his party in a broad civilian front, La Hora del Pueblo (The People's Turn), working on behalf of the restoration of civilian rule, and was again defeated in his bid for the presidency in the 1973 elections.

In the wake of the electoral defeat, a left-wing faction within the party, the Movimiento de Renovación y Cambio, led by Raúl ALFONSÍN, emerged to challenge his leadership, critical of both his backroom-style politics and conservative program. Following the 1976 coup, he was an outspoken critic of the military government and twice imprisoned.

GABRIEL DEL MAZZO, *El radicalismo: Notas sobre su historia y su doctrina*, vol. 3 (1959); MARCELO LUIS ACUÑA, *De Frondizi a Alfonsín: La tradición política del radicalismo*, vol. 2 (1984).

JAMES P. BRENNAN

*See also* **Argentina: Political Parties.**

**BALBOA, VASCO NÚÑEZ DE** (*b.* ca. 1475; *d.* January 1519), a Spanish conquistador from Jerez de los Caballeros in Estremadura, and the first known European to see the Pacific Ocean. A poor, illiterate HIDALGO, he sailed for the New World in 1501 with the expedition of Rodrigo de BASTIDAS, exploring the northern coast of modern Colombia. After settling on Hispaniola, he failed as a farmer, and in 1510 he escaped his creditors by stowing away on a vessel bound for the coast of Urabá (Colombia). The expedition, led by Martín Fernández de ENCISO, sailed to relieve the settlement founded near Cartagena by Alonso de OJEDA, and now led by Francisco PIZARRO, which was in desperate straits. Balboa, accepted as a common soldier, advised moving the colony west across the Gulf of Urabá, a region he had visited with Bastidas. The wretched settlers took the advice and found a plentiful supply of food, much gold, and Indians without poisoned arrows.

Seen as the savior of the colony, Balboa quickly gained popularity and respect among the men. The settlement of Santa María de la Antigua del Darién was founded in 1510 in Panama (then called Darién and, later, Castilla del Oro) under the jurisdiction of Diego de NICUESA. Therefore, Balboa noted, Enciso had no authority. When Nicuesa appeared, the colonists of Antigua forced him aboard an unseaworthy ship, and he disappeared at sea. The pompous Enciso was then charged with usurping the authority of Nicuesa and was expelled from the colony. He returned to Spain, where he leveled charges of usurpation against Balboa, who realized that he needed to counter them with a spectacular achievement. In late 1511 the king had named Balboa interim governor of Darién, and in 1513 he was appointed supreme commander of the colony. He also received word of an impending order directing him to return to Spain to face charges. Instead, Balboa moved with some urgency to find the great body of water south of the isthmus, of which a friendly cacique had spoken.

On 1 September 1513, Balboa set out with 190 Spaniards, 1,000 Indian porters, and some bloodhounds. Af-

Vasco Núñez de Balboa. Anonymous engraving from *Retratos de los españoles ilustres con un epítome de sus vidas* (1791). ORGANIZATION OF AMERICAN STATES.

ter extreme hardships—cutting through dense jungle and swamps, crossing rough mountains, and fending off hostile natives—the expedition finally reached its objective. Advancing alone to a peak on 25 (or 27) September, Balboa gazed upon the vast "South Sea," subsequently called the Pacific. Four days later he waded into the surf, claiming for Spain the ocean and the shores washed by it. The enterprise succeeded brilliantly for Balboa because he had subjugated many tribes without the loss of a single Spaniard, and he returned triumphantly to Antigua in January 1514 with a fortune in gold, pearls, and slaves.

Balboa is often portrayed as having treated the Indians humanely, but this is true only in a relative sense. More than most conquistadores, he befriended Indians, enjoying good relations with some thirty caciques. He also kept various mistresses. Yet he did not hesitate to fight those whom he considered obstinate. He was a man of his time and circumstances, sometimes enslaving Indians and punishing them severely. Among other atrocities, he ordered Indian homosexuals burned at the stake, and dogs were set upon recalcitrant caciques.

Meanwhile, the king—ignorant of Balboa's great achievement, and persuaded by Enciso and others of his culpability—appointed a new governor of Darién. He was Pedro Arias de ÁVILA (Pedrarias Dávila), the aging scion of a prominent family. Sailing for Panama with a large fleet in April 1514, Pedrarias carried orders to suspend Balboa's authority and bring him to justice. Initial inquiry acquitted Balboa, and Pedrarias came to resent his popularity, especially after Balboa's deeds became known in Spain. Though still subject to Pedrarias, Balboa was appointed ADELANTADO of the Southern Sea and captain-general of the provinces of Coiba and Panama in 1515. Relations between the two rivals appeared to improve when Pedrarias's daughter María was betrothed to Balboa in 1516. In fact, the rancorous old man nursed a grudge. While the "son-in-law" made plans to explore the Pacific coast of Panama on his own, he was betrayed by a friend, who accused him of ignoring Pedrarias's authority. Balboa was arrested on trumped-up charges of treason. Found guilty, and denied an appeal to Spain, he was decapitated at Acla.

The best biography of Balboa in English is KATHLEEN ROMOLI, *Balboa of Darien: Discoverer of the Pacific Ocean* (1953). In Spanish, the standard work is ANGEL DE ALTOLAGUIRRE Y DUVALE, *Vasco Núñez de Balboa* (1914). Very useful are CARL ORTWIN SAUER, *The Early Spanish Main* (1966), and HUBERT HOWE BANCROFT, *History of Central America*, vol. 1 (1882), both of which have good maps. See also the work of the official chronicler and contemporary of Balboa, GONZALO FERNÁNDEZ DE OVIEDO Y VALDÉS, *Historia general y natural de las Indias,* 5 vols. (1959).

WILLIAM L. SHERMAN

**BALBUENA, BERNARDO DE** (*b.* ca. 1562; *d.* 11 October 1627), a major poet of colonial Spanish America. Balbuena was born in Valdepeñas, La Mancha, but emi-grated to Mexico, possibly with his father, about 1564. He studied first in Guadalajara and then in Mexico City. In 1585 while at the University of Mexico, he won the first of several prizes for poetry. Beginning in 1586, he occupied a series of ecclesiastical posts in the Guadalajara region, where he composed most of the poetry that would bring him fame. Balbuena returned to the capital to oversee publication of his *Grandeza mexicana* (1604), an idealized description and eulogy of Mexico City that presaged and contributed to the development of creole patriotism. Thereafter, however, his career in the church took precedence. He went back to Spain to resume his studies, earning a doctorate in theology from the University of Sigüenza in 1608. Appointment as *abad mayor* (abbott) of Jamaica soon followed, and in 1619 he was named bishop of Puerto Rico, an office he held until his death.

Balbuena also published *Siglo de oro en las selvas de Erífile* (1608), a pastoral romance, and *El Bernardo, o Victoria de Roncesvalles* (1624), an epic poem largely composed before 1600 glorifying Spain's past and present. His poetry displays a baroque mixture of erudition; fertile invention; vigorous, evocative language; and rich (perhaps excessive) ornamentation.

For biographical information see J. ROJAS GARCIDUEÑAS, *Bernardo de Balbuena: La vida y la obra* (1958). A convenient collection of some of Balbuena's best work is in BERNARDO DE BALBUENA, *Grandeza mexicana, y fragmentos del Siglo de oro y El Bernardo,* 3d ed. (1979). Scholarly criticism has focused on the epic *El Bernardo*. The most complete study is JOHN VAN HORNE, *El Bernardo of Bernardo de Balbuena* (1927). For a more recent view see GILBERTO TRIVIÑOS, "Bernardo del Carpio desencantado por Bernardo de Balbuena," in *Cuadernos Americanos* 236 (May–June 1981): 79–102.

R. DOUGLAS COPE

**BALCARCE, MARIANO** (*b.* 8 November 1807; *d.* 20 February 1885), Argentine diplomat. The son of Antonio González Balcarce, a military hero of the struggle for independence, Mariano Balcarce was born in Buenos Aires. He spent most of his life in diplomatic service in Europe. His first assignment, at age twenty-four, was as an assistant to the Argentine minister to Great Britain. He later moved to Paris, where he was living at the time of his death. Balcarce negotiated the treaty by which Spain recognized Argentine independence, and he assiduously publicized the attractions of Argentina for prospective immigrants. He befriended numerous Argentine and other Latin American visitors to France and established a particularly close relationship with José de SAN MARTÍN during the latter's years of exile in France; he married Mercedes de San Martín, the Liberator's daughter, in 1832.

*Diccionario histórico argentino*, vol. 1 (1953), p. 415; and CÉSAR H. GUERRERO, *San Martín y su familia* (1978), pp. 81–89.

DAVID BUSHNELL

269

**BALDOMIR, ALFREDO** (*b.* 1894; *d.* 1948), president of Uruguay (1938–1943). Baldomir was the brother-in-law of President Gabriel TERRA, who chose him as his potential successor. Baldomir had been chief of police in Montevideo at the time of Terra's 1933 coup.

The 1938 election was a family affair for the Colorado-backed president. Terra had the party offer two candidates: his brother-in-law, Baldomir, who received 121,000 votes, and his father-in-law, Eduardo BLANCO ACEVEDO, who received 98,000. The Colorado Party, with a total of 219,000 votes, thus defeated the Herrerist Blancos (National Party), which offered only one candidate, who had 114,000 votes.

With an economic upturn and a resurgence of the Batllist tradition, Baldomir felt that Terra's alliance with the Blancos, led by Luis Alberto de HERRERA, as defined in the 1934 Constitution, had outlived its usefulness. The Blancos were opposed to much of Baldomir's domestic program and were critical of his cooperation with the United States at the start of World War II. Their guaranteed control of half of the seats in the Senate left them with a strong veto power. Consequently, on 21 February 1942 Baldomir postponed the upcoming March elections, dissolved Congress, and called for a constitutional plebiscite to restore the normal functioning of the electoral system. He created a Council of State, to which he submitted his constitutional proposal on 29 May. The new constitution did away with the division of the Senate between the 1933 coup leaders (Terra and Herrera) and restored full constitutional democracy. Baldomir is quoted as having said, "We have the costliest electoral system on the continent, but it is cheaper than revolution."

PHILIP B. TAYLOR, JR., *Government and Politics of Uruguay* (1960).

MARTIN WEINSTEIN

*See also* **Uruguay: Political Parties.**

**BALDORIOTY DE CASTRO, RAMÓN** (*b.* 28 February 1822; *d.* 30 September 1889), a leading member of Puerto Rico's autonomy movement. Of humble roots, Baldorioty received his early education from Padre Rufo Fernández, who recognized the youth's superior intellect. In 1846, Fernández arranged for Baldorioty to study at the University of Madrid. After returning to Puerto Rico, Baldorioty taught at the School of Commerce, Agriculture, and Navigation (1854–1870).

A member of Puerto Rico's Liberal Reformist Party, Baldorioty served in the Constitutional Cortes of 1869 and as a deputy in the Cortes of 1870–1871. After the Spanish monarchy was restored in 1875, Baldorioty went into exile to Santo Domingo for four years.

As a Liberal Reformist, Baldorioty advocated basic civil rights, abolition of slavery, and administrative decentralization. However, the party split into two factions, one favoring assimilation into Spain's political system and the other seeking autonomy. Upon his return from exile in 1878, Baldorioty steered liberals toward the Republican Autonomist wing of the Liberal Reformist Party. He led efforts to reorganize the party along autonomist lines, and at the Assembly of Ponce, in 1887, he presided over the newly created Puerto Rican Autonomist Party. The Autonomists eventually secured Puerto Rican autonomy from Spain in late 1897, eight years after Baldorioty's death.

EDWARD J. BERBUSSE, *The United States in Puerto Rico, 1898–1900* (1966); LIDIO CRUZ MONCLOVA, *Baldorioty de Castro (Su Vida—Sus Ideas)* (1966); PILAR BARBOSA DE ROSARIO, *De Baldorioty a Barbosa: Historia del autonomismo puertorriqueño, 1887–1896* (1974); LUIS GONZÁLEZ VALES, "The Challenge to Colonialism (1866–1897)," in *Puerto Rico: A Political and Cultural History*, edited by Arturo Morales Carrión (1983).

JOHN J. CROCITTI

**BALL GAME, PRE-COLUMBIAN,** a very complex game played with a rubber ball by the ancient civilizations of MESOAMERICA (Mexico, Guatemala, and adjacent territories). The AZTEC word for the game was *ulama*. Rubber, native to the New World, was unknown in Europe until Columbus brought back a solid rubber ball. In 1528 Hernán Cortés brought a team of Aztec players to demonstrate the game before the Spanish court.

The pre-Columbian game was played a bit like soccer, except that the feet were not employed to advance the ball. Players could strike it with hips, legs, or elbows. The fifteen-pound rubber ball was deflected from a U-shaped yoke worn over the hips. Protective padding was worn around the waist and on the arms and knees, and gloves protected the hands. There were probably "training" games. Official games were performed within stone-masonry ball courts with side enclosures and end zones. The ball was deflected back and forth into the narrow court from sloping benches and vertical walls that sometimes held stone rings for scoring. A point was lost if the ball touched the paved court.

This ball game was played in all regions of Mesoamerica, with variations, for 3,000 years (1500 B.C.–A.D. 1500). It still survives in Sinaloa, Mexico. In the Classic Period, prior to Aztec times, the game was more of a religious ritual than a team sport. It also had political and military overtones. However, its fundamental symbolism reflected Mesoamerican philosophy pertaining to the maintenance of agricultural fertility and the cosmos itself. The rubber ball, ideally kept constantly in motion, represented the sun, the moon, or Venus.

At the conclusion of a ritual game the loser (or perhaps the winner) was decapitated. This sacrifice was believed to aid the sun on its journey from day to night and its reappearance at dawn, after having defeated the lords of the underworld. Like the sun, the chosen ball player was metaphorically transformed and reborn. The symbolism of the ball game was characteristically du-

Mayan ball players from the Classic period. Terra-cotta miniatures from Jaina Island, Yucatán, A.D. 600–900. PHOTO BY LEE BOLTIN.

alistic: dry season–rainy season, sky–underworld, day–night, sun–moon, and death–rebirth.

Spanish chroniclers recorded eyewitness accounts of the Aztec game, and archaeology provides us with narrative carved stone sculpture and ceramics depicting the pre-Columbian cult and its meanings. Among the finest surviving portable stone objects from Mesoamerica are the decorated hip yokes and associated paraphernalia. These were probably ceremonial replicas of the wood or leather equipment used in the game.

GERARD VAN BUSSEL, PAUL VON DONGON, and TED J. J. LEYENAAR, eds., *The Mesoamerican Ball Game* (1991); VERNON SCARBOROUGH and DAVID WILCOX, eds., *The Mesoamerican Ball Game* (1991).

LEE ALLEN PARSONS

**BALLAGAS Y CUBEÑAS, EMILIO** (*b.* 7 November 1908; *d.* 11 September 1954), Cuban poet and essayist. Born in Camagüey, Cuba, Ballagas's writing career began with a 1926 essay about Cuban patriot José MARTÍ, which won him a scholarship sponsored by the *Revista Martiniana* to study at the University of Havana. Better known as a poet, he published his first compositions in *Antenas* in 1928 and in the avant-garde *Revisita de Avance* the following year. While a student at the university, Ballagas published his much-acclaimed "Elegía de Mariá Belén Chacón" in *Revista de Avance* (1930). One

year later he published *Júbilo y fuga,* which confirmed Ballagas's importance as a national and international poet and signaled the first of three stages in his poetry.

Ballagas completed his Ph.D. in pedagogy in 1933 and taught at the Normal School for teachers in Santa Clara, becoming its director the following year. His *Cuaderno de poesía negra* (1934) and *Antología de la poesía negra hispanoamericana* (1935) exemplify the tradition of Afro-Cuban poetry. Although many of Ballagas's poems highlight the folkloric aspects of Afro-Cuban traditions, some speak to the economic and social conditions of blacks on the island.

During a trip to Paris in 1937 to research Amerindian languages at the Bibliothèque Nationale, Ballagas met many of the best-known poets of the period. In 1939 he published *Sabor eterno,* a collection of poems about love, written with the intense emotions that characterized the second stage of his poetry. Ballagas completed a second Ph.D. in 1946 and published his dissertation, "Situación de la poesía afroamericana," in the *Revista Cubana* and the anthology *Maps de la poesía negra americana* (1946). He traveled to New York and became associated with the Institute for the Education of the Blind.

Ballagas's religious feelings, which are expressed in the third stage of his poetry, are evident in *Nuestra Señora del Mar* (1943), dedicated to the patron saint of Cuba, the Virgen de la Caridad del Cobre. He continued his religious poems in *Cielo en rehenes,* which won the

National Prize for Poetry in 1951, although it was not published until 1955, and *Décimas por el júbilo martiano en el centenario del apóstol José Martí*, a patriotic as well as spiritual book, which won the Centenario Prize in 1953, commemorating Martí's birth. Ballagas died in Havana.

CINTIO VITIER, *Lo cubano en la poesía* (1958); SAMUEL FEIJÓO et al., *Lunes de Revolución* 26 (1959); ARGYLL PRYOR RICE, *Emilio Ballagas, poeta o poesía* (1966); ROSA PALLAS, *La poesía de Emilio Ballagas* (1973); ROGELIO DE LA TORRE, *La obra poética de Emilio Ballagas* (1977); ARGYLL PRYER RICE, "Emilio Ballagas," in *Latin American Writers*, edited by Carlos A. Solé and Maria Isabel Abreu (1989), pp. 1081–1087; JULIO A. MARTÍNNEZ, ed., *Dictionary of Twentieth-Century Cuban Literature* (1990), pp. 43–50.

WILLIAM LUIS

**BALLET FOLKLÓRICO DE MÉXICO,** form of popular entertainment that emerged in Mexico in the mid-1940s to promote popular cultural nationalism, usually with government support. The best-known company is Amalia Hernández's Ballet Folklórico de México, which performs in the Bellas Artes Palace in Mexico City and sponsors an international touring group. An early concern with folk culture was gradually supplanted by emphasis on spectacular choreography and dramatic costumes. Similar folk-dance groups arose in Cuba and Venezuela, where they focused on the African and other traditional heritages of the people.

The concern for the preservation of authentic folk dance and for regionalism has stimulated the creation of many groups, especially at universities and among ethnomusicologists, in Mexico, Santo Domingo, Puerto Rico, Panama, Colombia, Peru, Argentina, and Brazil. Folkloric material is increasingly available through recordings, brochures, televised festivals, and videotapes. In the southwestern United States, Hispanics have established dance groups in their schools in efforts to maintain their culture and support political and union activities. A major dance competition is held annually in Tucson, Arizona.

"Ballet Folklórico Nacional de México," video released by RTC (1987); and *Ballet Folklórico de México*, performance catalog published yearly by the Instituto Nacional de Bellas Artes.

GUY BENSUSAN

*See also* **Music: Popular Music and Dance.**

**BALLIVIÁN, JOSÉ** (*b.* 30 November 1805; *d.* 16 October 1852), president of Bolivia (1841–1847). Born in La Paz, he is perhaps best known as the victorious general in the 1841 battle of Ingaví, in which the Bolivian army beat the Peruvian invaders under the leadership of General Agustín GAMARRA, forever ending Peruvian plans to annex Bolivia. Ballivián was also a capable administrator and one of the best nineteenth-century Bolivian presidents. Although he joined the military early in life, having fought as a teenager in the Spanish and patriot armies, Ballivián was a self-taught man who fostered science and culture. He was fortunate that during his government the country enjoyed relative prosperity due to revenues from taxes on GUANO from the Pacific coast, quinine from the eastern foothills, and a silver boomlet. Most important was his attempt to consolidate Bolivia's eastern frontier regions. He founded the department of Beni in the Amazon basin of northeastern Bolivia, promoted the exploration of the Otuquis River region in Santa Cruz, and attempted but largely failed the exploration, military conquest, and settlement of the CHACO.

The recent publication in Spanish of JANET GROFF GREEVER's 1957 dissertation *José Ballivián y el oriente boliviano*, translated by José Luis Roca (1987), is one of the few widely available works on the Ballivián administration. HUMBERTO VÁZQUEZ-MACHICADO, "Sobre la vida del General José Ballivián (1804–1852)," in *Obras completas de Humberto Vázquez-Machicado y José Vázquez-Machicado*, vol. 4 (1987), provides important information on Ballivián's life. Though the interpretation is dated, the most inclusive political narration of the Ballivián administration is ALCIDES ARGUEDAS, *Historia de Bolivia: Los caudillos letrados, 1828–1848* (1923).

ERICK D. LANGER

**BALMACEDA FERNÁNDEZ, JOSÉ MANUEL** (*b.* 19 July 1840; *d.* 19 September 1891), diplomat, politician, and president of Chile (1886–1891). The son of politically prominent and wealthy parents, Balmaceda briefly studied at a seminary, an experience that may have contributed to his anticlericalism. Although a large landowner, he also became involved in a variety of tasks: editor of various newspapers, private secretary to a president, and a diplomat. Not surprisingly, he won, at age twenty-four, the first of his many congressional elections. While serving as a deputy he also undertook certain diplomatic missions, arranging a border settlement with Argentina. During the administration of Domingo SANTA MARÍA (1881–1886), he held the posts of minister of foreign relations, minister of war, and the more important position of minister of the interior. Since he was handpicked by Santa María, his election to the presidency was virtually assured, thanks to his mentor's massive intervention in the political process.

Balmaceda took over Chile at a transitional time. Increasingly, the nation's economy, and its revenue base, rested on the mining and exporting of nitrates. The new president had clear ideas of what he wanted to do with these funds: build railroads and public buildings, expand educational facilities, modernize the military, colonize the newly opened southern territories, and reward his political henchmen and their families with lucrative government positions and contracts.

Certain forces, however, stood in the way of Balmaceda's programs. The politicians wanted their place at the public trough. They particularly disliked the fact that the newly created ministry of public works seemed so powerful and that Balmaceda often used his executive powers to create jobs without consulting the legislature. The deputies and senators resented that the president alone seemed to have the power to dispense largess.

The second problem was the nature of the NITRATE trade. Nitrates, while an essential component of fertilizers and explosives, were still a commodity whose value fluctuated with the state of the world economy. When prices fell, the nitrate producers, or *salitreros*, generally responded by limiting production, in hopes of driving up the mineral's value. While such production cutbacks proved beneficial to the mining interests, they hurt the government, which depended upon the export levy on nitrates to sustain the régime and its various public-works projects. Hence, Balmaceda viewed as an enemy anyone who could reduce production. His particular bête noire was John Thomas North, an English financier who owned much of what was worth owning in the nitrate-rich province of Tarapacá: a bank, a supply company, the local source of water, and the railroad that carried the *salitre* from the pampas to the port of Iquique.

The conflict between these two men became quite hostile. North, by keeping prices high for transport, increased the cost of the nitrate and hence limited its sale. Balmaceda, who resented the loss of potential income,

José Manuel Balmaceda Fernández. ORGANIZATION OF AMERICAN STATES.

tried to break North's monopoly on the nitrate-transportation network by offering railroad concessions to other foreign financiers. North deeply resented Balmaceda's efforts and tried to marshal his friends in the Chilean Congress to prevent the president from implementing his policies.

Balmaceda's principal problem was not North or his associates but his own methods of ruling. Although Balmaceda had initially enjoyed the support of a majority of the congress, he began to lose popularity. In part, various politicians, including some in his own party, disliked the way Balmaceda had been elected president. Others resented his seemingly unlimited control over patronage, particularly his willingness to appoint men to positions on the basis of talent, not political connections.

Legislative animus toward the president increased when he ruthlessly intervened in the 1888 congressional elections. Worse, Balmaceda lost his majority in Congress when the legislators concluded that he would select Enrique Salvador Sanfuentes to succeed him. It became obvious that if he wished to rule, Balmaceda would have to consult the legislature.

Balmaceda went on the offensive, demanding a strengthening, not a diminution, of presidential powers. Doubtless, these proposals shocked the Congress, which might have expected compromise. Clearly, the nation had reached an impasse: throughout 1890 the Congress demanded that the president create a cabinet to its liking before the legislature would approve the budget. Balmaceda refused. Since the president and the Congress seemed more intent on insulting each other than on addressing the Country's pressing problems, the nation stagnated.

Thanks to the intervention of Archbishop Mariano Casanova, Balmaceda succeeded in forming a new cabinet acceptable to the legislature. When it collapsed, Balmaceda formed one composed of his friends, further antagonizing the Congress, which still refused to pass a budget.

Increasingly, Balmaceda ruled by decree, which created more uncertainty than it solved problems. Believing that the president might act illegally, his legislative foes created a junta to coordinate their efforts should it be necessary to resist his government. They soon had a reason: in January 1891, Balmaceda, citing the legislature's earlier refusal to approve his request for funding, unilaterally declared that he would use the budget authorized for 1890 for 1891 instead. Considering this act a violation of the 1833 Constitution, the junta rebelled, thereby initiating the Revolution of 1891.

Balmaceda's military efforts seemed as ill-fated as his political programs. Since the rebels controlled the nitrate-rich north, they had more money than the legitimate government. Worse, the rebels, who enjoyed naval supremacy, successfully prevented Balmaceda from taking possession of two cruisers under construction in Europe. All the president could do was mobilize his army, whose morale seemed to have deteriorated as much, if not more than many of their weapons, and await the ultimate invasion.

The attacks came in August. By the end of the month, the rebels controlled Santiago. As the congressionalist mobs looted the homes of his supporters and killed his officers, Balmaceda took refuge in the Argentine embassy. He remained there until 19 September 1891, the day after his term of office expired. Then he shot himself.

It is easier to say what Balmaceda was not than what he was: his willingness to deal with foreign investors other than North indicated that he was not an economic nationalist; his cynical manipulation of elections demonstrated that he was not a democrat; his brutal suppression of strikes showed that he was not a friend of the worker. While he was perhaps a visionary, his political methods seemed more typical of a bygone era than of a nation groping its way toward democracy.

MAURICE H. HERVEY, *Dark Days in Chile: An Account of the Revolution of 1891* (1892); JULIO BAÑADOS ESPINOSA, *Balmaceda: su gobierno y la revolución de 1891* 2 vols. (1894); RICARDO SALAS EDWARDS, *Balmaceda y el parlamentarismo en Chile,* 2 vols. (1925); JOSÉ MIGUEL YRARRÁZAVAL LARRAIN, *El presidente Balmaceda,* 2 vols. (1940); HAROLD BLAKEMORE, "The Chilean Revolution of 1891 and Its Historiography," in *Hispanic American Historical Review* 45, no. 3 (1965): 393–421, and his *British Nitrates and Chilean Politics, 1886–1896: North and Balmaceda* (1974): HERNÁN RAMÍREZ NECOCHEA, *Balmaceda y la contrarevolución de 1891,* 2d ed. (1969); CRISÓSTOMO PIZARRO, *La revolución de 1891* (1971).

WILLIAM F. SATER

**BALSAS RIVER** originates in the southeastern Mesa Central and empties into the Pacific Ocean near the city of Lázaro Cárdenas, Michoacán. Forming one of the largest basins in Middle America (44,828 sq. mi.), it flows from east to west in a low depression bounded on the north by the Cordillera Neovolcánica, on the south by the Sierra Madre del Sur, and on the east by the Sierra de Oaxaca. Cut off by these ranges from moisture-bearing winds off both the Pacific and the Gulf of Mexico, the Balsas basin is hot and dry. Near its origin, the river is called the Mezcala; about halfway through its course to the Pacific, it becomes the Balsas. Approximately 60 miles inland from its mouth, it is joined by the Tepalcatepec, which flows south through the northwestern extension of the Balsas depression; thereafter the Balsas flows through a narrow canyon to the Pacific.

During pre-Columbian times, the Balsas basin was an important source of the gold given as tribute to the Aztecs. Colonial settlement of the region was typified by scattered Indian and mestizo subsistence farmers, and cattle raising was the most important economic activity. In 1907, however, the Italian émigré Dante Cussi established Nueva Italia and Lombardia haciendas under a contract with the federal government to develop the area. He introduced irrigation and limited commercial agriculture, but most of these lands were collectivized in 1938.

In 1947 the Comisión del Tepalcatepec was created for the integrated development of that 7,000-square-mile segment of the Balsas basin. The commission, headed by ex-President Lázaro CÁRDENAS, was given broad powers to construct dams for irrigation and hydroelectricity, to develop lines of communication and transportation, to create and expand settlement centers, and to deal with agricultural and credit matters. In 1960 it was absorbed by the Comisión del Río Balsas, with Cárdenas again as director.

The largest project on the Balsas is El Infiernillo dam, built in 1964 about 35 miles inland from the Pacific. Forming a lake 65 miles long, it provides the lower Balsas with irrigation water and central Mexico with nearly 1 million kilowatts of electricity. In 1971 a smaller dam, La Villita, was built downstream to provide electricity to the iron and steel complex at Lázaro Cárdenas.

ROBERT COOPER WEST, ed., *Handbook of Middle American Indians,* vol. 1 (1964), pp. 106, 381; DAVID BARKIN and TIMOTHY KING, *Regional Economic Development: The River Basin Approach in Mexico* (1970); JORGE L. TAMAYO, *Georgrafía moderna de México,* 9th ed. (1980), pp. 55, 139–140; ROBERT COOPER WEST and JOHN P. AUGELLI, *Middle America: Its Lands and Its Peoples,* 3d ed. (1989), pp. 28–29, 350.

JOHN J. WINBERRY

**BALSEIRO, JOSÉ AGUSTÍN** (*b.* 23 August 1900; *d.* 1992), Puerto Rican writer and professor. Balseiro earned a law degree from the University of Puerto Rico (1921), and an honorary doctorate from the Catholic University of Chile. His writings are varied. His three novels move from the biographical mode of *La ruta eterna* (1923) to the indictment of social ills in *La gratitud humana* (1969). His poetry began emphasizing love and wine (*La copa de Anacreonte,* 1924) and ended with love and transcendence (*El ala y el beso,* 1983). His best-known critical works are *Novelistas españoles modernos* (1933), *Expresión de Hispanoamérica* 2 vols. (1960–1963), and *The Americas Look at Each Other* (1969).

Balseiro's critical essays, his creative works, his teaching (at the University of Illinois–Urbana, Duke University, and elsewhere), and his many lectures throughout Latin America won him wide recognition, including membership in the Spanish Royal Academy, Madrid's Center of Historical Studies, Mexico's Academy of Letters, and Argentina's Sarmiento Institute. He received the Orders of Isabel la Católica (Spain) and Vasco Núñez de Balboa (Panama). Balseiro also served as Puerto Rico's senator-at-large.

JUAN ENRIQUE COLBERG, *Cuatro autores clásicos contemporáneos de Puerto Rico* (1966); *Diccionario de literatura puertorriqueña,* vol. 2, pt. 1 (1974); NICOLÁS KANELLOS, ed., *Biographical Dictionary of Hispanic Literature in the United States* (1989).

MARÍA A. SALGADO

**BALTA, JOSÉ** (*b.* 1814; *d.* 26 July 1872), president of Peru (1868–1872). A soldier of common background and strong convictions, he led troops from Chiclayo on the northern coast against the government when President Mariano Ignacio PRADO issued decrees to curb the political power of Catholic bishops. With army support, Balta remained in power for a full presidential term. Convinced that Peru must escape its financial dependence on local guano consignees, he placed the Ministry of Finance in the hands of Nicolás de PIÉROLA and approved his policy of domestic spending of income earned by contracting for a guano monopoly with the Dreyfus Company of France. Thereafter military salaries and pensions rose, and public facilities improved. Contractors laid hundreds of miles of new rail lines throughout the country, including the famous Central Railway linking Lima with the mining center of La Oroya in the Andean highlands. But expenditures quickly outran income from all sources, and public sentiment soon associated the military with public waste. Balta and Piérola clashed repeatedly until Piérola resigned in 1871. Balta then incurred new debts to the Dreyfus Company. At the end of Balta's term, Peru faced a foreign debt of £49 million, a tenfold increase over what it had been when he took office. By the election of 1872 military leadership was in disrepute. Balta's secretary, Ricardo Palma, and North American entrepreneur Henry MEIGGS, among others, persuaded him not to prevent the inauguration of his successor. In the military uprising that followed this decision, Balta was imprisoned and shot dead in his cell by guards.

FREDRICK B. PIKE, *The Modern History of Peru* (1967), esp. pp. 125–126, 131–132; HENRY F. DOBYNS and PAUL L. DOUGHTY, *Peru: A Cultural History* (1976), esp. pp. 191–194.

VINCENT PELOSO

**BALTIMORE INCIDENT,** an 1891 diplomatic dispute between the United States and Chile. Following the September collapse of the BALMACEDA government, Captain Winfield Schley permitted some of the sailors serving on the cruiser U.S.S. *Baltimore* to have shore leave on 16 October in Valparaíso. Schley failed to realize that the presence of uniformed American sailors might fan latent Chilean hostility into a firestorm of confrontation.

Various brawls between American servicemen and Chileans erupted in Valparaíso's sleazy waterfront saloons and brothels. By the evening's end, the police had jailed seventeen Americans, and two U.S. sailors had died from knife wounds.

The Americans charged that the police not only failed to protect them but had joined the crowds in beating the sailors. The Chilean courts disagreed with the American charges, however, concluding that the U.S. sailors had started the brawl. Benjamin Harrison, the American president, regarded the incident as an insult to the United States and demanded an apology and compen-

sation from the Chilean government. Refusing to apologize, Chile's foreign minister, Manuel Antonio Matta, publicly described Harrison as either stupid or a liar. The irate American president sent an ultimatum to the Chilean government: either apologize for injuring the American servicemen and offer compensation, or the United States would declare war.

Chile, having only recently ended a costly revolution, was ill prepared for a confrontation with the United States. Worse, Santiago feared that Argentina, Bolivia, and Peru would take advantage of a war with the United States to attack Chile. Finally, Chile's allies in Europe—Germany and Great Britain—indicated that they would not attempt to restrain Washington. Friendless and surrounded by potential enemies, Chile acceded to Washington's demands, paying compensation and apologizing for the episode. The *Baltimore* incident remained a sore point in relations with the United States because many Chileans regarded the diplomatic confrontation as yet another example of American imperialism.

JOYCE S. GOLDBERG, *The "Baltimore" Affair* (1986); WILLIAM F. SATER, *Chile and the United States: Empires in Conflict* (1990), 61, 66–68.

WILLIAM F. SATER

*See also* **United States–Latin American Relations.**

**BANANA INDUSTRY.** The rise of oceangoing steamships during the latter third of the nineteenth century stimulated banana exports from the Caribbean region to the United States and Europe, and later from South America and Africa. Bananas, in many varieties, are a tropical grass of the Musaceae family. Of Far Eastern origin, they spread to Africa and in the sixteenth century were brought by Canary Islanders to Latin America, where they became a common local food. Banana exports began in the era of rapid sailing ships after 1850, but did not become important until steamships made the export of perishable fruit more practical after 1860.

A Boston ship captain, Lorenzo Baker, was among the early banana shippers, developing trade between Jamaica and Boston. Baker and Andrew Preston led the formation of the BOSTON FRUIT COMPANY in 1885, which greatly expanded this enterprise. Meanwhile, other shippers developed banana exports along the Caribbean coast of Central America, where banana production and export became closely associated with railroad construction. Minor C. KEITH was especially important with his Tropical Trading and Transport Company in developing Costa Rican banana exports, which amounted to more than a half million stems annually by 1885. Other shippers based on the American Gulf Coast developed banana exports from Colombia, Nicaragua, and Honduras before the turn of the century. Boston Fruit and Tropical Trading and Transport merged in 1899, creating the UNITED FRUIT COMPANY, which came to domi-

Leading Latin American Banana Producers, 1948–1989 (metric tons)

| Country | 1948–52 | 1970 | 1975 | 1980 | 1985 | 1987 | 1989 |
|---|---|---|---|---|---|---|---|
| Brazil | 2,084 | 6,408 | 5,311 | 6,736 | 4,815 | 5,188 | 5,502 |
| Dom. Rep. | 208 | 775 | 799 | 901 | 914 | 1,045 | 1,193 |
| Colombia | 354 | 780 | 1,050 | 1,030 | 1,200 | 1,340 | 3,550 |
| Costa Rica | 434 | 1,146 | 1,121 | 1,092 | 1,008 | 925 | 1,335 |
| Ecuador | 360 | 2,700 | 2,544 | 2,269 | 1,970 | 1,962 | 3,336 |
| Guatemala | 185 | 487 | 520 | 650 | 690 | 709 | 420 |
| Honduras | 802 | 1,200 | 852 | 1,330 | 1,091 | 1,020 | 1,220 |
| Mexico | 412 | 1,136 | 1,194 | 1,515 | 1,151 | 1,489 | 1,185 |
| Panama | 249 | 947 | 989 | 1,050 | 1,067 | 907 | 1,030 |
| Venezuela | 756 | 968 | 860 | 983 | 989 | 1,000 | 1,636 |

nate the industry. Samuel Zemurray's CUYAMEL FRUIT COMPANY and the Vacarro brothers' STANDARD FRUIT AND STEAMSHIP COMPANY were important competitors.

In the early twentieth century these companies were fiercely competitive as they gained land, railroad concessions, and shipping and distribution rights for the production and export of bananas. In 1929 United Fruit purchased Cuyamel; ZEMURRAY soon emerged as the chief executive at United Fruit and led it to an even more dominant position in the industry by 1950. The tendency was for banana production to shift from the Caribbean islands to the Caribbean and Pacific lowlands of Central America and to Panama, Colombia, and Ecuador, although since 1960 there has been renewed development of banana production in the eastern Caribbean.

Large-scale export of bananas required substantial capital investment in production, pest and disease control, and transportation. Bananas were thus an important agroexport for the liberal development schemes of the late nineteenth and early twentieth centuries and provided considerable revenue for modernization in Jamaica, Central America, and Ecuador as close ties developed between the fruit companies and the governments. Costa Rica was the leading exporter in the early twentieth century, but by the 1940s Honduras had taken over that position, to be replaced by Ecuador in 1951.

The major Latin American producers and exporters of bananas in recent years are indicated in the accompanying tables.

Because of heavy damages from storms or disease, especially Sigatoka or Panama disease, the companies required large expanses of land for their plantations and were often criticized for making much of the land unfit for future cultivation because of excessive cultivation and use of pesticides. Yet the banana companies also greatly improved the transportation and communication systems, paid better wages than native-owned firms dealing in agroexports such as coffee, and contributed to educational and health improvements in the countries where they operated.

Growing opposition to the powerful foreign banana interests eventually supported nationalist efforts to curtail their power, so that in the second half of the twentieth century, some of their lands were expropriated, they were taxed more heavily, and incentives for native-owned production resulted in more native ownership and in more competition among the foreign companies. United Fruit was taken over by Eli Black, and then went bankrupt, being succeeded by United Brands in the early 1970s; Castle and Cooke had taken over Standard Fruit by 1968. These companies were joined in production by a rising number of national companies.

Leading Latin American Banana Exporters, 1950–1987 (metric tons)

| Country | 1950 | 1960 | 1970 | 1975 | 1980 | 1985 | 1987 |
|---|---|---|---|---|---|---|---|
| Brazil | 152 | 242 | 204 | 147 | 67 | 105 | 81 |
| Colombia | 144 | 191 | 262 | 486 | 692 | 783 | 962 |
| Costa Rica | 223 | 273 | 867 | 1,077 | 1,027 | 857 | 943 |
| Ecuador | 165 | 1,076 | 1,246 | 1,450 | 1,437 | 1,075 | 1,402 |
| Guatemala | 160 | 198 | 220 | 260 | 336 | 366 | 380 |
| Honduras | 351 | 363 | 812 | 420 | 987 | 872 | 904 |
| Panama | 189 | 263 | 601 | 558 | 505 | 686 | 676 |

SOURCE: James W. Wilkie, ed., *Statistical Abstract of Latin America*, vols. 20–28 (1980–1990); Economic Commission for Latin America and the Caribbean, *Statistical Yearbook for Latin America and the Caribbean* (1990).

FREDERICK UPHAM ADAMS, *Conquest of the Tropics* (1914, repr. 1976); PHILIP KEEP REYNOLDS, *The Banana: Its History, Cultivation and Place Among Staple Foods* (1927); CHARLES DAVID KEPNER, JR., and JAY H. SOOTHILL, *The Banana Empire: A Case Study of Economic Imperialism* (1935, repr. 1967); CHARLES M. WILSON, *Empire in Green and Gold: The Story of the American Banana Trade* (1947); STACY MAY and GALO PLAZA, *The United Fruit Company in Latin America* (1958); HENRY B. ARTHUR, JAMES P. HOUCK, and GEORGE L. BECKFORD, *Tropical Agribusiness Structures and Adjustments— Bananas* (1968); WILHELM BITTER, *Die wirtschaftliche Eroberung Mittelamerikas durch den Bananen-Trust* (1971); ORGANIZATION OF AMERICAN STATES, EXECUTIVE SECRETARIAT FOR ECONOMIC AND SOCIAL AFFAIRS, *Sectoral Study of Transnational Enterprises in Latin America: The Banana Industry* (1975); THOMAS MC CANN, *An American Company: The Tragedy of United Fruit,* edited by Henry Scammell (1976); WILSON RANDOLPH BARTLETT, JR., "Lorenzo Dow Baker and the Development of the Banana Trade between Jamaica and the United States, 1881–1890," (Ph.D. diss., American University, 1977); THOMAS L. KARNES, *Tropical Enterprise: The Standard Fruit and Steamship Company in Latin America* (1978); MAURICE BRUNGARDT, *The United Fruit Company in Colombia* (1987); ROBERT THOMSON, *Green Gold: Bananas and Dependency in the Eastern Caribbean* (1987).

RALPH LEE WOODWARD, JR.

**BANANEROS.** *See* **Great Banana Strike.**

**BANCO COMERCIAL Y AGRÍCOLA (ECUADOR),** a leading financial institution from 1895 to 1926, located in the prosperous port of Guayaquil, the nation's commercial center. The bank handled much of the proceeds from coastal Ecuador's successful cacao export trade. The governing Liberal Party's (1895–1944) heavy borrowing, however, dangerously depleted bank reserves, leaving currency issues improperly backed. Highland critics of the Liberal Party objected to the emerging close relationship between government and the bank. Criticism grew more urgent after the economic collapse of 1922. Following a 1925 coup by young military officers, the government closed the Banco Comercial y Agrícola and created a new central bank. Some historical interpretations depict 1895–1925 as an era of "bank rule" over Ecuador.

The best treatment of fiscal and monetary issues is LINDA ALEXANDER RODRÍGUEZ, *The Search for Public Policy: Regional Politics and Government Finances in Ecuador, 1830–1940* (1985). For the broader political economic context see OSVALDO HURTADO, *Political Power in Ecuador,* translated by Nick D. Mills, Jr. (1985). Detailed discussion of banking can be found in JULIO ESTRADA YCAZA, *Los bancos del siglo XIX* (1976). The socioeconomic context is analyzed in the path-breaking study by LOIS CRAWFORD DE ROBERTS, *El Ecuador en la época cacaotera* (1980).

RONN F. PINEO

*See also* **Urvina Jado, Francisco.**

**BANCO DE AVÍO.** The Banco de Avío para Fomento de la Industria Nacional, the first industrial development bank founded in Latin America, was set up by the Mex-

ican government on 16 October 1830 to provide long-term loans at low rates of interest to the nation's fledgling cotton textile industry. Capitalized by a levy of 20 percent on the duties from cotton textile imports, the bank was to have capital of 1 million pesos. During its twelve years of operation it made loans to twenty-nine industrial enterprises. Most of the bank's loans went to cotton and wool textile firms, but it also extended credit to paper mills, iron foundries, and other enterprises. The capital it provided supplemented the equity capital raised by the industrialists; roughly 6 percent of the capital invested in the textile industry came from the bank. The bank was dissolved on 23 September 1842 by order of General Antonio López de SANTA ANNA, who had already alienated much of its assets in an attempt to obtain cash for a bankrupt fisc.

LINDA IVETTE COLÓN REYES. *Los orígenes de la burguesía y el Banco de Avío* (1982); ROBERT A. POTASH, *The Mexican Government and Industrial Development in the Early Republic: The Banco de Avío* (1983).

STEPHEN H. HABER

*See also* **Banking.**

**BANCO DE LA REPÚBLICA (COLOMBIA),** Colombia's central bank. The second central bank in Latin America (the first was Peru's), it was established in 1923 to serve as a lender to Colombia's commercial banks, to administer its international reserves, to issue its currency, and to serve as the government's BANKING agent. Since 1951 the bank has played an active role in managing Colombia's money supply and in promoting national economic development through credit facilitation. The institution has gone through three stages in its management of the money supply: the first (1923–1931), under the gold standard; the second (1932–1950), when it gradually gained influence over Colombia's money management; and the third (1950 to the present), when it controlled the money supply.

The historical reasons for the creation of the bank in 1923 were several. Major among them was the fact that Colombia (within Latin America) was one of the nations with the least foreign investment. This situation drove the Colombian government to seek better relations with the financial markets in New York and London. By 1922 it had become clear that Colombia's finances needed expert guidance. This was provided by the Edward Kemmerer Mission (1923), which recommended the creation of the Banco de la República. This, in turn, led to substantial increases in foreign investment from the United States and Great Britain.

During the financial crisis of 1929–1931, the bank took over the management of Colombia's salt and emerald mines, as collateral for its stabilization of the currency and finances. Its nonfinancial roles include the promotion and protection of Colombia's cultural heritage, the establishment of modern research facilities, and the sponsorship of many cultural activities. These include the Museo del Oro (Bogotá), organized in 1939, and the Biblioteca Luis Ángel Arango (named for a former director of the bank), formally founded in 1958, with branches in every major Colombian city.

JULIE JONES and WARWICK BRAY, *Preconquest Goldsmiths' Work of Colombia in the Museo del Oro, Bogotá* (1957); ADOLFO MEISEL ROCA ET AL., *El Banco de la República: Antecedentes, evolución y estructura* (1990).

J. LEÓN HELGUERA

**BANCO DE LONDRES Y MÉXICO,** originally (1863) the London Bank of Mexico and South America. It first had two branches, one in Mexico City and one in Lima, but in the late nineteenth century both became domestic banking institutions—the Banco de Londres y México in 1889 and the Banco del Perú y Londres in 1897—with a combination of local and European shareholders. The Banco de Londres y México, as it was known from the 1860s, introduced modern banking practices in various Mexican cities, although it was surpassed in importance by the Banco Nacional de México (1884), against which it struggled for preeminence until the outbreak of the Mexican Revolution in 1910. In the 1930s and 1940s the Banco de Londres regained some of the business it had lost due to the revolution and subsequent civil war. It was absorbed by the SERFIN financial group of Monterrey in 1977 and today continues its activities under that name.

DAVID M. JOSLIN, *A Century of Banking in Latin America* (1963); *100 años de banca en México: Primer centenario del Banco de Londres y México, S.A. (1864–1964)* (1964).

CARLOS MARICHAL

**BANCO DE SAN CARLOS (POTOSÍ),** a mining bank in Potosí (1779–1825) that was the amplification of earlier credit institutions. The first of these was a private company created by leading *azogueros* (refiners) in 1746–1747 to provide loans and supplies. This establishment was taken under partial royal direction in 1752 as a *banco de rescates*, a bank that bought raw silver from the refiners, for cash, at a discount. It had mixed success. In 1779 Jorge Escobedo y Alarcón, governor of Potosí, resolved to take the bank fully into royal control as the Banco de San Carlos. It continued to buy silver at a discount and now also was charged with collecting the 10 percent crown royalty on silver produced. Fed by the discount, the loan fund grew large. Loans, however, were rarely invested productively, since the *azogueros*—the social elite among Potosí refiners, not known for their entrepreneurship—contrived to take most of the funds themselves.

ROSE MARIE BUECHLER, *The Mining Society of Potosí, 1776–1810* (1981); GUILLERMO MIRO DELLI-ZOTTI, *El Real Banco de San Carlos de Potosí y la minería altoperuana colonial, 1779–1825* (Banco de España, 1991).

PETER BAKEWELL

**BANCO DE SAN CARLOS (SPAIN),** the first national bank of Spain, established in 1782 in Madrid during the reign of CHARLES III. Its original purpose was to stabilize the credit of the government, servicing the state bonds called *vales reales* that had been issued to cover the expenses incurred by the monarchy in its European and American wars at the end of the eighteenth century. Although essentially a government bank, the Banco de San Carlos was privately owned. Among its stockholders were Spanish capitalists, French rentiers, and, surprisingly, a large group of Indian community treasuries of Mexico. The bank continued to provide financial services to the Spanish government during the Napoleonic Wars and most of the reign of FERDINAND VII (1814–1833), but in 1828 it was restructured and became the Banco de San Fernando. Today it is known as the Banco de España.

EARL HAMILTON, "Plans for a National Bank in Spain, 1701–1783," in *Journal of Political Economy* 58, no. 3 (1949): 315–336; PEDRO TEDDE, *El Banco de San Carlos (1782–1829)* (1988).

CARLOS MARICHAL

**BANCO DO BRASIL,** Brazil's first formal bank and Latin America's first modern-style bank, founded in 1808 after the Portuguese prince-regent Dom JOÃO VI established his court in Rio de Janeiro. As a mixed institution under state control, the Banco do Brasil served as a commercial bank, the government's fiscal agent, and Brazil's first bank of issue. The bank realized great profits but played an inadequate commercial role because it concentrated on financing government deficits. It greatly expanded its issues of currency, particularly to finance Brazil's war in the Banda Oriental (today Uruguay) between 1825 and 1828. When Dom João left Brazil for Portugal in 1821, he took all of the precious metals that backed the bank's issues. This first Banco do Brasil tottered and finally closed its doors in 1829.

The second Banco do Brasil was founded in Rio in 1851 by the entrepreneur Baron of MAUÁ as a private commercial bank with a capital of 10,000 contos (about £1.2 million or $5 million). Two years later Parliament merged this bank with another private bank and eventually with three provincial banks to form the third Banco do Brasil. A bank of issue, it also served as the country's largest financial institution and the government's banker. Although its stocks were held privately, it often benefited from government contracts and loans and was an important vehicle for enacting public policy.

The Banco do Brasil lost its dominant position during the explosion of new banks created during the ENCILHAMENTO between 1889 and 1891. In 1894 Congress merged the Banco do Brasil with the country's largest bank, the Banco da República dos Estados Unidos do Brasil, to create the Banco da República, capitalized at 200,000 contos (about $40 million). This was again a semipublic bank with a government-appointed president who had veto power. It was the sole government agency for affecting the exchange rate, collecting and depositing tax revenues, servicing the foreign debt, and lending to the federal treasury, while also being the largest commercial bank in the country. Severely weakened by many poor loans granted during the Encilhamento, the Banco da República had to be bailed out by the state in 1900.

In 1905 the institution reformed its charters, reduced its capital to 70,000 contos, and again assumed the name Banco do Brasil. The new bank, now with one-third public ownership, continued its previous public functions but refrained from investment banking. The bank's branches spread throughout the country; by 1930 it had over eighty. Although an attempt in the early 1920s to give the bank many of the powers of a central bank proved short-lived, after 1937 it played an important role in long-term industrial and agricultural loans.

The Banco do Brasil continues as one of the most important semipublic banks in the country, acting as a commercial lender and a government agent. By 1964 it was the twenty-eighth largest bank in the world and the largest in Latin America and the entire third world. But as the state's institutionalized financial presence increased after the 1950s with the creation of a central bank, the Banco Nacional do Desenvolvimento Econômico e Social (BNDES), the Banco Nacional da Habitação (BNH), and public banks in all of the states, the Banco do Brasil's importance as an agent of state policy declined. The growth of private Brazilian and foreign banks has reduced its relative commercial position as well. Even so, it continues to be, as it has been for most of its history, the largest bank in Brazil.

VICTOR VIANA, *O Banco do Brasil: Sua formção, seu engrandecimento, sua missão nacional* (1926); CLAUDIO PACHECO, *História do Banco do Brasil*, 4 vols. (1973); STEVEN TOPIK, ''State Enterprise in a Liberal Regime: The Banco do Brasil, 1905–1930,'' in *Journal of Inter-American Studies and World Affairs* 22, no. 4 (1980): 401–422.

STEVEN TOPIK

*See also* **Banking.**

**BANDA DE PÍFANOS,** a fife-and-drum ensemble—also called *zabumba, banda cabaçal,* and *esquenta mulher*—common among the mestizo populations of northeastern Brazil. Most likely brought to Brazil by Portuguese settlers as early as the sixteenth century, these ensembles are used for the rituals of folk Catholicism (prayer sessions, pilgrimages, processions) and for such secular functions as dramatic and social dances and revelry. The musicians, who are almost always male, learn to play strictly by ear and are typically rural agricultural workers or urban laborers. The bands comprise four to six instruments, including two *pífanos* (cane flutes), a *zabumba* (bass drum), a *tarol* (snare drum), a *surdo* (tenor drum), and *pratos* (hand cymbals). The repertoire consists of devotional music for the veneration of saints as well as music for social dancing and secular festivities. For religious occasions such as a novena (prayer session devoted to a saint), *bandas de pífanos* accompany the singing of hymns and praise songs, and play devotional music in honor of the saint in march and waltz rhythms. Secular dance music, such as BAIÃO, *forró,* and *xote,* is played for community parties, in commercial dance halls, and on radio shows. *Bandas de pífanos* perform frequently during the June festivals honoring Saint Anthony, Saint John, and Saint Peter.

CÉSAR GUERRA-PEIXE, ''Zabumba: Orquestra nordestina,'' in *Revista brasileira de folclore* 10, no. 26 (1970): 15–38.

LARRY N. CROOK

*See also* **Music: Popular Music and Dance.**

**BANDA ORIENTAL,** historical designation of the northeastern region of the RÍO DE LA PLATA estuary used to distinguish it from the southern shores, the traditional core of the Argentine Republic. The name was applied by custom to the relatively well-populated stretch of land between the lower course of the URUGUAY RIVER, south of Fray Bentos, and the city of Rocha, near the Atlantic coast. It became official when the province joined the UNITED PROVINCES OF THE RÍO DE LA PLATA (1812), represented by José G. ARTIGAS (1764–1850).

The regional strife that colored most of the early years of independence in the Río de la Plata region contributed to alienating the inhabitants of the northeastern shores, a feeling that intensified when the Congress of TUCUMÁN (1816) ratified the independence of the United Provinces without mentioning the Banda Oriental, politically controlled at that time by Artigas. In 1817, taking advantage of the isolation and relative weakness of the province, Brazilian troops invaded the territory and exiled Artigas to Paraguay. The Brazilian occupation continued until 1825, when Colonel Juan A. LAVALLEJA and his famous Thirty-Three Companions stormed Montevideo to liberate the Banda Oriental. With the help of Argentine troops, liberation was achieved in Ituzaingó in February of 1827, and in the following year Argentina and Brazil relinquished their claims to the Banda Oriental. Under the name of Uruguay it became an independent country.

LUCÍA SALA DE TOURON, *Evolución económica de la Banda Oriental* (Montevideo, 1967); and JOSÉ C. WILLIMAN, *La Banda Oriental en la lucha de los imperios: 1503–1818* (Montevideo, 1975).

CÉSAR N. CAVIEDES

**BANDEIRA, MANUEL CARNEIRO DE SOUZA** (*b.* 19 April 1886; *d.* 13 October 1968), Brazilian poet. Born in Recife, Pernambuco, Bandeira moved to Rio at the age of ten. He planned to be an architect, but his studies were interrupted by tuberculosis. While ill, he wrote verses that filled his idleness and alleviated his suffer-

279

ing, but eventually he began to write great poetry. His health improved, and in 1917 he published his first volume of poetry, *A cinza das horas* (The Ashes of the Hours).

He lived for thirteen years in a working-class suburb of Rio and later taught literature at the Pedro II School and what is now the Federal University of Rio de Janeiro.

Bandeira's work has been divided into two not very distinct phases. The first comprises his three earliest collections of poems. *A cinza das horas* follows symbolist and Parnassian ideals. *Carnaval* (1919) reveals independent traits that depart from the literary conventions of the time and includes "Os Sapos," later a national anthem of the modernists. *O ritmo dissoluto* (Dissolute Rhythm, 1924) contains unconventional themes and forms.

*Libertinagem* (Libertinage, 1930) is the first volume of Bandeira's second phase. It reveals a transition to the modernistic aesthetic in several ways: the adoption of Portuguese as spoken in Brazil; prosaic themes; popular aspects of Brazilian culture; and humor, varying from fine irony to straight jokes. Additional works by Bandeira include *Estrela da manhã* (Morning Star, 1936), *Lira dos cinqüent'anos* (Lyrics of Fiftieth Birthday, 1940), *Belo, Belo* in his *Poesias Completas* (3d ed., 1948), *Mafuá do malungo* (2d ed., 1954), *De poetas e poesia* (1954), *A Brief History of Brazilian Literature* (1958), *Estrela da tarde* (Evening Star, 1963), *Estrela da vida inteira* (Whole Life Star, 1966), *Andorinha, andorinha* (1966), and *Poesia completa e prosa* (4th ed., 1983). *This Earth, That Sky: Poems by Manuel Bandeira,* translated by Candice Slater, appeared in 1988.

Bandeira continued to be open to new approaches, even having written concretist poems. He always remained, however, an essentially lyric poet. His poetry, often tinged with irony, melancholy, and tragic humor, betrays reminiscences of his own life. He is also recognized as a literary critic, anthologist, essayist, and translator.

GILDA E ANTÔNIO CÂNDIDO, "Introdução," in *Estrela da vida inteira* (1966); CLAUDE L. HULET, "Manuel Bandeira," in *Brazilian Literature,* edited by Claude L. Hulet, vol. 3 (1975), pp. 9–24; JOAQUIM FRANCISCO COELHO, *Biopoética de Manuel Bandeira* (1981), and *Manuel Bandeira, pré-modernista* (1982); EMMANUEL DE MORAIS, "Uma vida cada vez mais cheia de tudo," in Bandeira's *Vou-me embora pra Pasárgata* (1986); GILBERTO MENDONÇA TELES, "Manuel Bandeira," in *Latin American Writers,* edited by Carlos A. Solé and Maria Isabel Abreu, vol. 2 (1989), pp. 629–641.

MARIA ISABEL ABREU

**BANDEIRAS,** large companies of armed colonists and Indian warriors that left the captaincy of SÃO VICENTE and penetrated the vast wilderness to the north, west, and south in search of gold and Indian slaves in the sixteenth, seventeenth, and eighteenth centuries. The *bandeirantes* (participants in the *bandeiras*) are responsible for the exploration of the great Brazilian west, numerous discoveries of gold, and the enslavement of thousands of Indians.

The first *bandeiras* were organized in the late sixteenth century as prospecting expeditions in search of gold and precious minerals, but the failure to find significant lodes shifted the focus to Indian slaving. Outfitted in the town

*Guerrilla.* Conflict between Indians and Bandeiras. Engraving by Rugendas from *Viagem pitoresca atréves do Brasil.* ICONOGRAPHIA.

of São Paulo, *bandeiras* included whites, MAMELUCOS, and Indians. They carried arms, gunpowder, lead, collars, chains, bows, and arrows. Gone for months, even years, at a time, the expeditions subsisted off of manioc flour and food hunted from the forest. These expeditions were financed privately from São Vicente by investors who expected to be rewarded with gold or Indian slaves.

The GUARANI INDIANS living in Jesuit missions became the targets of the slaving *bandeiras*. Manoel Preto led attacks against the missions in the 1610s. In 1628, Antônio Rapôso TAVARES led a *bandeira* of some three thousand men to Guairá, where he attacked and burned several missions, enslaved the Indians, and marched them back to São Vicente. Later *bandeiras* led by André Fernandes and Paulo de Amaral destroyed other missions. Soon thereafter the Jesuits moved their remaining missions to what is today Rio Grande do Sul, Uruguay, Paraguay, Argentina, and Mato Grosso. The *bandeiras* followed them and continued to take slaves.

In response to intense lobbying by the Jesuits, Pope Urban VIII issued a bull (1639) which reiterated the freedom of Indians and excommunicated those who held Indians in servitude. In São Paulo an angry town council responded by expelling the JESUITS from São Vicente. The Jesuits also received permission to arm their Indians in self-defense. The fortified missions then repulsed the *bandeiras*. A *bandeira* led by Pascoal Leite Paes was turned back in 1639, as was another at the Mbororé River in 1641. Thereafter, the *bandeiras* left the missions alone. Slaving continued, however, against tribal Indians.

A new phase of *bandeirante* activity began in the 1690s, when the first substantial discoveries of gold were made in MINAS GERAIS. Large *bandeiras,* led by former Indian slavers, were mounted to search for precious metals. Veteran *bandeirante* Bartolomeo Bueno da Silva, the younger, trekked through Goiás, where he discovered gold in the 1720s. Fernão Dias Pais sought emeralds in a quixotic quest that yielded only tourmalines.

The crown used *bandeiras* for political ends. Some expeditions were outfitted to wage war against Indian enemies or runaway slaves. A *bandeira* led by Domingos Jorge Velho destroyed the QUILOMBO of PALMARES in the 1690s. Antônio Rapôso Tavares led a *bandeira* across South America in 1647 to reconnoiter a possible route to Peru. His expedition logged 7,000 miles through the Chaco, the eastern Andes, and down the Madeira and Amazon rivers to the Atlantic Ocean. *Bandeirantes* explored the far west and claimed it for Portugal. They were soon followed by a wave of prospectors, slaves, farmers, and traders who effectively won the far west for Brazil.

RICHARD M. MORSE, *The Bandeirantes: The Historical Role of the Brazilian Pathfinders* (1965); ALCANTRA MACHADO, *Vida e morte do bandeirante* (1978); JOHN HEMMING, *Red Gold: The Conquest of the Brazilian Indians* (1978).

ALIDA C. METCALF

See also **Entrada; Slavery.**

**BANDITRY** can be defined simply as the act of taking property from another by using force or the threat of force. But Latin American bandits have appeared in varied and complex guises. Some common criminals simply brutalized and abused their fellow men. However, banditry also arose because throughout Latin American history, elite rule restricted access to economic opportunity and political expression. Domination by the wealthy forced the rural masses to defend their interests through various means. Eric J. Hobsbawm coined the term ''social bandits'' to describe Robin Hood–style outlaws who championed the oppressed peasants.

When elites denied them access to land or to a living wage, the rural masses struck back using legal and extralegal tactics, including banditry. In early-twentieth-century southern Bolivia, the peasants used banditry, mass mobilization, or litigation, depending on the strength of their corporate identity and cohesiveness. During the Mexican Revolution, peasants formed regional bandit gangs to combat the encroachment of large haciendas or other forces of change that disrupted traditional Indian village life.

Some outlaws gained reputations as social bandits and were celebrated in folklore and music. The Latin American masses sometimes viewed bandits as heroes striking a blow against their rich oppressors. Argentina's rural poor identified with the persecution suffered by legendary gauchos like Juan Moreira and Martín Fierro. Lampião (Virgolino Ferreira da Silva) and Antônio Silvino in Brazil, Pío Romero in Bolivia, and Manuel García in Cuba became symbols of popular resistance to oppression.

But bandit myth, like most myth, expresses only half-truths. Peasant stories about bandits exhibit what Erick D. Langer has termed ''a selective memory.'' Such tales romanticize bandits and ignore their ignoble deeds, such as robbing, terrorizing, and killing peasants. Few romanticized bandits actually lived the heroic, idealized lives attributed to them in popular culture or in Hobsbawm's social bandit model.

Myth and folklore color some famous bandits so completely that accurate historical depiction is difficult. To compound matters, official government sources often purposely blur the distinction between bandit and revolutionary. Elitist officials typically labeled as bandits any groups that threatened their political monopoly. The U.S. press and government officials of the 1920s termed Augusto Sandino's Nicaraguan forces ''bandits'' to discredit them. The unduly positive images of historical bandits generated in folklore were offset by the negative images from politically motivated government sources.

MOTIVES AND SUPPORT

Why did bandits steal? A desire for profit motivated many gangs. Unlike mythical bandits, however, actual gangs acted more often on the basis of self-interest and opportunism than in the defense of peasant-class inter-

Group of *cangaceiros*, including Lampião (far left) (1928). ICONOGRAPHIA.

ests. As Paul J. Vanderwood has shown, the marginalized rural poor fomented disorder, including bandit attacks, and profited from the resulting conflict. Guerrilla bandits (discussed below) are one example of those who profited from disorder.

Eleodoro Benel (1873–1927), a bandit leader in northern Cajamarca, Peru, was one of many such grasping, rural petty tyrants whose main goal was self-aggrandizement. Such profiteers formed whatever alliances they deemed useful. Bandit leaders cooperated more often with the powerful, not the humble, elements of society.

Economic self-interest also motivated many nineteenth-century bandits, as in Cuba's La Habana Province, where they consciously pursued their own personal gain in an opportunistic fashion. Manuel García's career as a profit-minded bandit antedated his service to the Cuban independence movement.

In addition to a desire for economic gain, personal and familial conflict drove some men to banditry. Family feuds, endemic to the Brazilian backlands, moved Lampião to take up the outlaw life. The Brazilian "good thief," Antônio Silvino, followed the leads of his father and godfather into bandit life. And the GAUCHOS of the Argentine plains often turned into outlaws after killing someone in a knife fight.

Local elites, not the peasant masses, generally provided the support, material assistance (food, arms, clothing), hiding places, and intelligence needed by bandit gangs. In Brazil, Silvino and Lampião cooperated with elites, not the peasant masses. Bandits in Peru, Mexico, and Argentina operated in a similar fashion.

These elite–bandit alliances helped keep local oligarchies in power and gave a degree of legitimacy to the outlaws. A politically powerful family could insulate bandits from police and legal authorities.

### GUERRILLA BANDITS

If officials labeled revolutionaries as bandits, bandits sometimes professed to have political aims, to cover their crimes with a veneer of legitimacy. Christon Archer coined the term "guerrilla bandits" to describe opportunists who used war as an excuse to pillage. Marginal rural people became guerrilla bandits, drawn to war by coercion or by promises of booty. They exhibited little loyalty and switched sides according to their assessment of the best potential profit. Guerrilla banditry became common in Venezuela, Mexico, Cuba, and elsewhere during the wars for independence and civil wars of the nineteenth century.

### POLITICAL BANDITS

Unlike prepolitical social bandits or self-serving guerrilla bandits, political bandits had a consciousness of and loyalty to a larger political movement. They did not switch sides for financial gain but instead labored for a political, partisan, or regional agenda. They exhibited clear partisan rather than class leanings. Political banditry was evident in independence-era Cuba, early-twentieth-century Cajamarca, Peru, and the Colombian VIOLENCIA of 1945–1965, which left between 100,000 and 300,000 people dead. The Cuban independence period illustrates both political banditry and the interpretive debates going on in the study of banditry. Louis A.

Pérez, Jr., sees banditry in western rural Cuba as motivated by peasant resentment of their marginalization by expanding sugar plantations. In contrast, Rosalie Schwartz argues that western Cuba's banditry reflects neither class conflict nor social banditry. First, many bandit gangs emerged before the process of sugar plantation expansion began. Second, the land concentration that Pérez considers a cause of banditry in fact came after many bandit gangs had emerged.

The peasant villages that purportedly supported and sustained social bandits did not exist in the bandit-infested areas of western Cuba. Manuel García put banditry and extortion at the service of the independence movement. His letters and broadsides show a clear political agenda, not typical of Hobsbawm's social bandit.

The Colombian *Violencia* offers another example of banditry, which even Hobsbawm acknowledges to be "in essence more political than social." The *serrano* (mountain region) uprisings during the Mexican Revolution offer another good example of political banditry cutting across class barriers. In both cases, conflict and banditry broke down along partisan or regional, not class, lines. In both cases, there was a political consciousness and agenda at work, a situation not typical of the prepolitical social bandit. Even Gilbert Joseph, who defends to a degree Hobsbawm's views, agrees that the political strategies of the peasants were not archaic "in the sense of being outmoded or prepolitical."

Banditry, then, can be an expression of mass discontent, a means of achieving a political agenda, or a yearning for economic betterment. Banditry could be a tactic of rural elites as well as the rural poor; outlaw networks often cut across class lines. Many bandit gangs developed and profited from close ties to regional and local power brokers: the CAUDILLOS (political bosses) or *coroneis* (planter elite).

What about women bandits? We know that a woman called María Bonita died with Lampião in a hail of gunfire in 1938. And "La Carambada," a female bandit who dressed in male clothing, robbed travelers in Querétaro, Mexico, during the mid-nineteenth century. Women most likely lived with male bandit gangs at their hideouts.

Richard Slatta, Gilbert Joseph, and others have begun placing Latin American banditry in a broader, more comparative perspective. Wider comparisons highlight the similarities and differences among bandits as well as the roles of culture, regionalism, and other variables. Yet more research is needed. Instead of blithely accepting bandit images from folk legends and literature as fact, scholars must use them as lenses for viewing peasant cultures. Even if folk views of heroic bandits do not reflect historical reality, they do reflect much about the yearnings and values of Latin America's rural masses.

In sum, Latin American elites and masses both participated in banditry. The rural poor sometimes used banditry to express political sentiments. At other times banditry represented an economic alternative in a world of opportunity narrowly restricted by the elite. On occasion, economic self-interest and political rebellion came together, as in the case of guerrilla banditry.

Latin American elites long have recognized the dangerous political potential of banditry and have made vigorous efforts to contain it. But although they have been victimized by the elite, the rural poor have not remained passive victims. If denied legitimate means of survival and participation, people will strike back violently at their oppressors.

BILLY JAYNES CHANDLER, *The Bandit King: Lampião of Brazil* (1978); ERIC J. HOBSBAWM, *Bandits*, rev. ed. (1981); PAUL J. VANDERWOOD, *Disorder and Progress: Bandits, Police, and Mexican Development* (1981); CHRISTON I. ARCHER, "Banditry and Revolution in New Spain, 1790–1821," in *Biblioteca Americana* 1, no. 2 (1982): 58–89; GONZÁLO G. SÁNCHEZ and DONNY MEERTENS, *Bandoleros, gamonales y campesinos: El caso de la Violencia en Colombia* (1983); RICHARD W. SLATTA, ed., *Bandidos: The Varieties of Latin American Banditry* (1987); ERICK D. LANGER, *Economic Change and Rural Resistance in Southern Bolivia, 1880–1930* (1989); LOUIS A. PÉREZ, JR., *Lords of the Mountain: Social Banditry and Peasant Protest in Cuba, 1878–1918* (1989); ROSALIE SCHWARTZ, *Lawless Liberators: Political Banditry and Cuban Independence* (1989); RICHARD W. SLATTA, "Banditry as Political Participation in Latin America," in *Criminal Justice History: An International Annual* 11 (1990): 171–187; GILBERT M. JOSEPH, "On the Trail of Latin American Bandits: A Reexamination of Peasant Resistance," in *Latin American Research Review* 25, no. 3 (1990): 7–53.

RICHARD W. SLATTA

**BANKING.** Although several special types of credit institutions emerged in Latin America in the late colonial period, it was not until the third quarter of the nineteenth century that modern banks and banking practices became permanently established in the hemisphere's republics. At that time the expansion of trade and the financial requirements of national governments impelled the creation of new types of credit institutions and the reform of monetary systems throughout the area. By the end of the century there existed a broad variety of banks, both domestic and foreign owned, mostly concentrated in commercial and mortgage banking as opposed to industrial finance.

In the 1920s the trend toward greater specialization in banking accelerated, a process reflected in the creation of central banks in most nations. The establishment of state development (industrial, agricultural, and foreign trade) banks was perhaps the characteristic feature of Latin American banking during the 1930s and 1940s. In subsequent decades private banking was diversified on a local and regional basis, foreign banks multiplied in various financial centers, and new types of banking instruments and institutions linked to burgeoning capital markets were developed.

THE EARLIEST BANKS

Historians have not yet satisfactorily explained the impact of banking on the overall processes of economic development in Latin America, concentrating instead mainly on institutional histories. It is worthwhile emphasizing, however, that the birth of banking was the result of a slow process of expanding and maturing credit markets, during the nineteenth century, that served the needs of agriculture, ranching, mining, manufacturing, and, of course, trade. In addition, the larger banks served the financial needs of governments, always a critical function.

The first banks, which were not destined to survive, were closely tied to government finance. Neither the first BANCO DO BRASIL, established in 1808, nor the Banco de Buenos Aires, founded in 1822, nor the BANCO DE AVÍO of Mexico, created in 1830, was able to weather the financial crises generated by deficit-ridden governments. Only in Brazil did commercial banking begin to flourish with the establishment of banks in Rio de Janeiro (1838), Maranhão (1844), and Bahia (1844). After the 1850s, however, banking institutions began to multiply in other nations, some of which were to prove more durable. Among the more important national banks were the Banco de la Provincia de Buenos Aires (1854), the Banco Nacional de Chile (1865), the Banco del Perú (1863), the Banco Español de la Isla de Cuba (1856), and the Crédito Inmobiliario y Fomento Cubano (1857).

BANKING CRISES

The first regionwide banking crisis occurred as a result of the world recession that began in 1873. Numerous banks in Chile, Peru, Argentina, and Brazil failed, thinning the ranks of the financial institutions in many cities. However, in the 1880s a new banking boom took place, a reflection of the general process of economic modernization in most Latin American nations. This development included the building of railway systems, the introduction of tramways, establishment of telephone and electrical enterprises in the larger cities, and the expansion of the leading export sectors: agriculture, ranching, and mining. To finance these activities it became necessary to create many new banks, not only in the capitals but also regionwide. The leaders in this process were the larger state banks—the Banco Nacional (Argentina), the Banco Nacional de México, and the Banco do Brasil—which began to go heavily into branch banking and to dominate the commercial credit markets through their branches in both the capital and many secondary cities. In the late 1880s, provincial governments began to stimulate the establishment of regional banks, modeled to a large degree on the U.S. free banking system. This new practice, carried out with great speed, combined with the rapid expansion of burgeoning stock markets in Rio de Janeiro, Buenos Aires, and Santiago de Chile to spur a wave of feverish financial speculation.

A second great financial crisis shook many Latin American capitals in the early 1890s. In Argentina virtually all the state-owned banks were forced to close in the midst of a general financial panic that brought the government to its knees. In Brazil, the financial craze (ENCILHAMENTO) that marked the transition from empire to republic in 1889 soon led to financial crisis and banking retrenchment. In Chile the banking boom of the late 1880s was cut short by the civil war that toppled the administration of President José Balmaceda in 1891.

THE GROWTH OF SPECIALIZED BANKING

From 1900 to 1914 there was a new stage in the history of banking in Latin America as specialization became more important. The largest domestic banks concentrated on lending to the government but also participated in commercial banking, providing loans to merchants and landowners. At the same time, there emerged a large number of specialized mortgage banks that helped finance the rapid development of cities like Buenos Aires, Rio de Janeiro, São Paulo, Mexico City, and Havana. The mortgage banks also provided funds to rural property owners, who prospered with the expansion of exports. There simultaneously developed additional and different specialized banking institutions: cooperative banks; a few mining and industrial banks; many private financial companies (mostly involved in real estate speculation); and a large number of foreign banks.

Foreign banks had actually begun playing an important role in the 1860s with the establishment of British-owned commercial banks in Buenos Aires, Rio de Janeiro, Lima, Santiago, and Mexico City. Some of these expanded rapidly—for example, the Bank of London and the Río de la Plata, which quickly established branch offices not only in various cities in Argentina but also in Uruguay and Paraguay. British banks dominated foreign banking in Latin America until the 1890s, when a number of German-owned banks were established in the principal cities of the region. In contrast to the British banks, which tended to be independent companies, the German banking firms were direct subsidiaries of the biggest German commercial banks, the Deutsche, Disconto, and Dresdner banks. In any case, the foreign-owned banks in Latin America tended to specialize principally in the financing of foreign trade, in foreign exchange transactions, and in providing loans to such foreign-owned enterprises as railways, mines, and public utilities.

In 1914 the outbreak of World War I provoked a brief financial crisis in many Latin American countries, but subsequently most banks prospered with the export boom generated by war demand. A new development at the time was the penetration of U.S. banking houses in the region, particularly in the Caribbean but also in several South American capitals. Here the National City Bank took the lead, controlling most of the new branches.

CENTRAL BANKING

During the 1920s, central banks began to be established in various Latin American nations. The first such banks were created largely as a result of financial advisory missions led by Professor Edwin W. KEMMERER of Princeton University to Chile, Peru, Bolivia, Ecuador, and Colombia, all of which established central banks in the 1920s under his direct inspiration. In Mexico the central bank, the BANCO DE MÉXICO, was set up in 1925 under the guidance of local financial and legal experts, such as the lawyer Manuel GÓMEZ MORÍN, who later played an important role in conservative political circles. In Argentina central banking came more slowly; it was not until after the outbreak of the Great Depression, and the mission to Buenos Aires of Bank of England director Sir Otto Niemeyer in 1932, that the government decided in 1935 to establish the Banco Central de la Repúblic Argentina, whose first president was the illustrious economist Raúl PREBISCH. In Brazil the Getúlio VARGAS administration (1930–1945) adopted a different banking strategy, deciding to continue using the services of the Banco Central da Republica do Brasil to manage most government finance. Not until 1965 was the Brazilian central bank established.

The state took an even more direct role in the banking sector in the 1930s and 1940s in most Latin American nations, creating a great array of specialized agricultural, industrial, and mining credit institutions. In Mexico this was the period of the founding of the NACIONAL FINANCIERA (1934), the Banco de Crédito Ejidal (1935), the Banco Nacional de Comercio Exterior (1938), and several other financial agencies. In Peru the Banco Agrícola was set up in 1931, the Banco Industrial in 1937, and the Banco Minero in 1941. In Argentina the Banco de Crédito Industrial, set up in 1941, was transformed into the Banco Nacional de Desarrollo in 1971. In Chile the Corporación de Fomento de la Producción (CORFO) was set up in 1939, and in Brazil the Banco Nacional do Desenvolvimento Econômico e Social was established in 1952; there also were several state-promoted regional development banks, such as the Banco de Crédito da Amazônia, set up in 1942, and the Banco do Nordeste, in 1952. In Venezuela the role of the Corporación Venezolana de Fomento (CVF) must be underscored, since it has been the main agency for promoting public investment in basic infrastructure, as well as in the industrial and agricultural sectors, since the 1950s.

## REGIONAL BANKING

A major innovation in the 1960s was the establishment of regional, multilateral development banks, the most important being the INTER-AMERICAN DEVELOPMENT BANK (IDB), headquartered in Washington, D.C. This bank pooled the resources of many Latin American countries and also tapped the international capital markets for additional funds. Under its first president, Dr. Felipe HERRERA, the IDB established a new financial strategy consisting of providing long-term loans to governments and state agencies to help modernize infrastructure, agriculture, education, and selected industries. As a multilateral institution it has proved as durable and successful as its elder colleague, the World Bank, and has provided the region with a high volume of development financing on reasonable terms. Other regional development banks have been established by governments in Central America and the Caribbean, although they remain relatively small.

While the commercial banks dominated Latin American credit markets until World War II, there have subsequently developed many different specialized companies to provide financing for private enterprise and investment. The growth of private financial institutions other than commercial banks began in the 1950s and 1960s, and has continued since. In the mid-1960s the assets of the private financial companies (financieras) equaled those of the commercial banks and later surpassed them. Nonetheless, it should also be kept in mind that many financieras and insurance firms are owned or controlled by a banking group, a fact that confirms both the trend toward financial specialization and the traditional high level of concentration of banking capital in most of Latin America.

## CURRENT TRENDS

The 1980s were a period of dramatic change in the Latin American banking world. Following an enormous wave of financial speculation fueled by a foreign debt boom in the late 1970s came a series of economic crises that deeply affected the solvency of many Latin American banks, including a major drop in petroleum prices in the early 1980s, a foreign debt crisis that began in 1982, and domestic economic recessions that plagued most Latin American economies during the decade. As a result, several governments took measures to restructure their banking systems.

In August 1982 President José LÓPEZ PORTILLO of Mexico announced the nationalization of virtually the entire commercial banking system and the expropriation of dollar deposits from tens of thousands of depositors. The losses suffered by private citizens were on the order of several billion dollars, but the government absorbed the external debts of the banks, which surpassed $10 billion. The former stockholders of the commercial banks were subsequently compensated with approximately one-third of the stock of the state-owned banks and with facilities for the establishment of many new private financial companies, mostly involved in stock market operations.

In Peru, in 1987 President Alan GARCÍA announced the nationalization of commercial banks, but the uproar and opposition were so great that his action helped spur the political campaign of the writer Mario VARGAS LLOSA against the García administration. Eventually the Peruvian authorities were forced to water down their measures and begin a gradual process of reprivatization. In 1989, Brazilian President Fernando COLLOR DE MELLO announced the nationalization of all commercial bank deposits, which were then valued at more than $100 billion. Despite great opposition, the government maintained this control for eighteen months, after which there began a renewed process of liberalization of the banking system. Meanwhile, in Mexico the government of Carlos SALINAS DE GORTARI began a process of re-privatization of the Mexican commercial banks in 1990, which for some time proved a financial success and a source of considerable income for the government.

INTER-AMERICAN DEVELOPMENT BANK, *Annual Report* (1961–1991); DAVID JOSLIN, *A Century of Banking in Latin America* (1963); CENTRO DE ESTUDIOS MONETARIOS DE LATINOAMÉRICOS (CEMLA), *Annual Report* (1980–1990) and specialized country studies; JOSÉ MANUEL QUIJANO, *La banca: Pasado y presente (problemas financieros mexicanos)* (1983); JAVIER MARQUEZ, *La banca mexicana: Septiembre de 1982–junio de 1985* (1987); BARBARA STALLINGS, *Banker to the Third World: U.S. Portfolio Investment in Latin America, 1900–1986* (1987); PAUL W. DRAKE, *The Money Doctor in the Andes: The Kemmerer Mission, 1923–1933* (1989).

CARLOS MARICHAL

**BANZER SUÁREZ, HUGO** (*b.* 1926), president of Bolivia (1971–1978). Born in the small town of Concepción, Banzer Suárez studied at the Military Colleges in La Paz and Argentina. Following the 1952 revolution led by the Nationalist Revolutionary Movement (MNR), his military career almost ended because the size of the armed forces was severely reduced.

Following the overthrow of the MNR in 1964 by General René BARRIENTOS ORTUÑO, Banzer's career took a decidedly political turn when he began a 22-month term as the military government's minister of education. From 1967 to 1971 he held a number of other posts, including military attaché in Washington.

In 1971, Banzer emerged as the leader of a conservative faction of the armed forces whose goal was the overthrow of the populist government headed by General Juan José TORRES GONZÁLEZ. The group's first attempt failed and Banzer was imprisoned and then exiled to Argentina. On 21 August 1971 a civilian-military alliance launched a second, successful coup that installed Banzer, then only a colonel, as president of Bolivia.

Banzer had a great deal of difficulty in maintaining the fragile coalition—dubbed the Nationalist Popular Front. By 1974, he had opted to eliminate political party support and ruled with the support of prominent members of the private sector and the military. In March 1979 Banzer and several prominent members of the private sector and dissident politicians founded the Nationalist Democratic Action (Acción Democrática y Nacionalista—ADN) mainly to establish a political mechanism to defend the former dictator against charges of wrongdoing. Banzer ran as the ADN's candidate in the 1979 and 1980 elections, in which, surprisingly, his party finished third, demonstrating that he still enjoyed a great deal of popular support.

In the July 1985 election, Banzer received the largest number of votes (28.6 percent), winning the first round by a small margin. Since he did not have the support in the congressional runoff to be named president, he gave his support to the MNR candidate, Victor PAZ ESTENSSORO, a move many have considered a significant act of statesmanship that contributed to the continuity of democratization in Bolivia.

Again the ADN candidate in the 1989 elections, Banzer ran a close second to the MNR candidate. Again the election was to be decided by Congress. When agreement with the MNR proved impossible, Banzer agreed to support the Movement of the Revolutionary Left (MIR) candidate, Jaime PAZ ZAMORA, as president. His health deteriorating, Banzer relinquished leadership of the ADN in the aftermath of its 1993 electoral defeat.

JAMES M. MALLOY and EDUARDO GAMARRA, *Revolution and Reaction: Bolivia, 1964–1985* (1988); FLOREN SANABRIA G., *Banzer: Democracia y nacionalismo* (1989).

EDUARDO A. GAMARRA

*See also* **Bolivia: Political Parties.**

**BAPTISTA, MARIANO** (*b.* 16 July 1832; *d.* 19 March 1907), president of Bolivia (1892–1896). One of the greatest political orators of Bolivia, Baptista is also considered the ideologist of the Conservative (or Constitutionalist) Party, which prevailed from 1884 to 1899. Dedicated to politics all his adult life, Baptista was a supporter of the dictatorship of José María LINARES (1857–1861). As a diplomat, Baptista represented Bolivia well in border negotiations with virtually all neighboring countries. Elected vice president during the Gregorio PACHECO administration (1884–1888), Baptista became one of the most important Conservative politicians. He wrote profusely in various newspapers in favor of the Catholic church, mining interests, and RAILROAD development, and against the anticlerical Liberal Party. When Baptista was elected president in 1892 he had the misfortune of presiding over the collapse of international silver prices and the economic crisis it triggered in Bolivia. During his administration he fostered railroad construction and the exploitation of rubber resources in the Acre region of northeast Bolivia.

There is no biography of Baptista. The best source on his life is his monumental *Obras completas* (1932). References to Baptista are in HERBERT S. KLEIN, *Bolivia: The Evolution of a Multi-Ethnic Society* (1982), pp. 159–161.

ERICK D. LANGER

*See also* **Bolivia: Political Parties.**

**BAQUEDANO, MANUEL** (*b.* 1826; *d.* 1897), Chilean military leader. Born in Santiago, Baquedano ran away at the age of twelve and sailed as a stowaway in the expedition sent to destroy the PERU-BOLIVIA CONFEDERATION. In 1839 he fought in the battles of Portada de Guias and Yungay. During the civil war of 1851 he fought in the battle of Loncomilla against his father. In 1854 he was separated from military service by the government of Manuel MONTT but was reinstated in 1859. Baquedano fought against the Araucanian Indians in 1868 and was a brigadier general when the WAR OF THE PACIFIC (1879–1883) broke out. In February 1880 he commanded 14,800 men during the campaign against Tacna and Arica. Following this series of victories, he commanded 26,500 troops in the attack on Lima. On 13 and 15 January 1881 he won the bloody battles of Chorillos and Miraflores, which led to the capitulation of Lima and drove Peru to accept defeat.

Following the war Baquedano was promoted to generalissimo. In 1881 the Conservative Party proclaimed him their presidential candidate, but he refused to accept. Between 1882 and 1894 he served in the Chilean Senate. In early 1891 the Chilean Congress asked Baquedano to support its position against President José Manuel BALMACEDA, but he declared neutrality and took no part in the revolution of 1891. Following Balmaceda's 1891 suicide, Baquedano took command of the nation until those opposed to Balmaceda could take charge.

JORGE CARMONA YAÑEZ, *Baquedano*, 2d ed. (1978); *Historia militar de Chile*, 2d ed., 3 vols. (1984).

ROBERT SCHEINA

**BAQUERIZO MORENO, ALFREDO** (*b.* 28 September 1859; *d.* 20 March 1951), president of Ecuador (1916–1920). Baquerizo, a native of Guayaquil, first earned distinction as a writer of prose and poetry before embarking on a career in politics. He held various government posts—mayor of Guayaquil (1890–1896); secretary to the minister of the superior court in Guayaquil (1894–1901); minister of foreign relations (1902–1912); vice president of Ecuador (1903–1916); and senator from Guayas province and president of the Senate (1912–1916)—before being elected president. In office he helped resolve Ecuador's lingering boundary dispute with Colombia (the Muñoz–Vernaza–Suarez Treaty, 1916). Baquerizo signed legislation in 1918 that legally ended the institution of forced labor (*concertaje*), although the law was seldom enforced. His adminstration did, however, implement a successful anti–yellow fever campaign in Guayaquil in 1919. During his term the Ecuadorian CACAO export economy began to decline, due to rising competition from British and Portuguese colonies in Africa and to *Monilia*, a plant fungus that destroyed many Ecuadorian plantations. At age seventy-two, Baquerizo briefly served as interim president (September 1931–August 1932) following General Luis Larrea Alba's failed bid to establish a dictatorship. He died in New York City.

FREDRICK B. PIKE, *The United States and the Andean Republics: Peru, Bolivia, and Ecuador* (1977), provides the standard account of twentieth-century Ecuadorian politics. Superb analysis of fiscal and monetary issues in the early twentieth century are in LINDA ALEXANDER RODRÍGUEZ, *The Search for Public Policy: Re-gional Politics and Government Finances in Ecuador, 1830–1940* (1985).

RONN F. PINEO

*See also* **Plaza Gutiérrez, Leonidas.**

**BAQUIANO.** GAUCHOS of the Río de la Plata developed a wide range of equestrian skills. The *baquiano* (or *baqueano*; guide or scout) provided a particularly important service on the seemingly trackless pampa. Skilled gaucho *baquianos* led military expeditions, wagon trains, herds of cattle, and foreign travelers across vast stretches of open plains. They navigated by the stars, landmarks, and even the taste of the grass. Because of the demand for their knowledge of terrain, trails, water holes, and such, scouts earned higher wages than the average ranch hand. Domingo F. SARMIENTO singled out the *baquiano* as one of four special gaucho types that he described in 1845.

DOMINGO F. SARMIENTO, *Life in the Argentine Republic in the Days of the Tyrants,* translated by Mary Mann (1971); RICHARD W. SLATTA, *Gauchos and the Vanishing Frontier* (1983).

RICHARD W. SLATTA

**BAQUÍJANO Y CARRILLO DE CÓRDOBA, JOSÉ DE** (*b.* 13 March 1751; *d.* 24 January 1817), Peruvian intellectual, educator, and high court judge. The precocious and ambitious son of a wealthy, titled family in Lima, Baquíjano obtained a doctorate in canon law from Lima's University of SAN MARCOS at the age of fourteen. After an unsuccessful trip to Spain seeking a high court (*audiencia*) appointment (1773–1776), he returned to Lima and in 1778 joined the faculty at San Marcos.

In 1781 Baquíjano delivered the university's welcoming eulogy for Viceroy Augustín de Jáuregui. Royal censure of the published text, replete with references to prohibited literature, was followed by unsuccessful efforts to win either the rectorship of San Marcos or the senior chair of civil law.

Baquíjano's fortunes improved in the 1790s. He wrote articles for the *Mercurio peruano*, secured the senior chair in canon law at San Marcos, and again set off for Spain to pursue an appointment to Lima's AUDIENCIA.

Persistence paid off. After being named a criminal judge on the Lima court in 1797, an unusual accomplishment for a native son at the time, Baquíjano advanced to the civil chamber in 1806. Although he was named to the Council of State by the Cortes of Cádiz in February 1812, Baquíjano was never seated. By the time he reached Spain, Ferdinand VII had returned and nullified the Cortes' actions. Baquíjano died in Seville, still loyal to the Spanish monarchy.

MARK A. BURKHOLDER, *Politics of a Colonial Career: José Baquíjano and the Audiencia of Lima* (1980).

MARK A. BURKHOLDER

**BARAGUA, PROTEST OF.** *See* **Zanjón, Pact of.**

**BARALT, RAFAEL MARÍA** (*b.* 3 July 1810; *d.* 4 January 1860), Venezuelan writer and historian. After spending his childhood in Santo Domingo, Baralt returned to Venezuela in 1821. His first task as a historian was to accompany Santiago MARIÑO on the western campaign and organize and publish the documents pertaining to it. During the administration of José Antonio PÁEZ, he traveled to Caracas and mingled with the intellectuals of the city. He joined the Economic Society of the Friends of the Country and participated with Agustín CODAZZI in editing the *Resumen de la geografía de Venezuela* (1841) and the *Atlas físico y político de Venezuela* (1840). He also prepared one of his best-known works, the *Resumen de la historia de Venezuela*, published in Paris in 1841. The government placed Baralt in charge of studying the border disputes with British Guiana.

In September 1841 Baralt left for Europe, working in the Spanish archives and making connections in the Spanish literary world. He settled permanently in Spain, where he was intensely active intellectually and published numerous works. In 1853 Baralt was elected a regular member of the Royal Academy of the Spanish Language, and he held important public posts in Spain. He was director of the official periodical, *Gaceta de Madrid*, and administrator of the National Printing House.

AUGUSTÍN MILLARES CARLO, *Rafael María Baralt (1810–1860): Estudio biográfico, crítico y bibliográfico* (1969); and PEDRO GRASES, *Biografía de Rafael María Baralt, 1810–1860* (1973).

INÉS QUINTERO

*See also* **Venezuela: Organizations.**

**BARBADOS,** the most easterly of the Caribbean islands (1990 population 260,000). It has one of the highest population densities in the world (1,542 per square mile). Under the direction of William Courteen, the British settled and colonized Barbados in 1627. There was a lack of agricultural production and a scarce supply of indigenous labor.

Consequently, the British imported ARAWAK Indians from what is today known as Guyana to begin INDIGO and TOBACCO production. With the introduction of SUGAR to the island, the smallholdings economy was transformed into a plantation economy, and thousands of African slaves were imported to work in the fields. The harshness of SLAVERY led to several revolts, the most famous occurring in 1702 and 1816. Slavery, although abolished in 1838, left intact a highly stratified class-based society, organized in part on color. The landed elite, who had established a parliamentary system to represent their interests in 1639, remained in power as politics excluded the majority of the population until the 1930s.

In 1938 the Barbados Progressive League was formed under the direction of Grantley Adams; it was renamed the Barbados Labour Party (BLP) in 1946. In 1944, this popular-based party gained a minority in the House of Assembly. Three years later, after a successful campaign that extended the franchise, the BLP was able to secure a majority in the elections. After the introduction of universal adult suffrage in 1951, the BLP won sixteen of the twenty-four seats. Adams became premier of Barbados, and in January 1958 prime minister of the newly formed WEST INDIES FEDERATION, which sought regional cooperation among the English-speaking Caribbean islands. Meanwhile, the Democratic Labour Party, headed by Errol Barrow, began to call for independence, which was granted by Great Britain in 1961. Barrow became the country's first prime minister in that year and remained in office until his death in 1987.

Today the primary sources of foreign currency for Bajans, as Barbadians are called, are TOURISM and the SUGAR INDUSTRY, to which 80 percent of the agricultural land is dedicated.

RONALD TREE, *A History of Barbados*, 2d ed. (1977); M. S. DANN, *Everyday Life in Barbados: A Sociological Perspective* (1979); INGRID KOWLER, comp., *What You Should Know About the Caribbean* (1980); HILARY BECKLES, *A History of Barbados: From Amerindian Settlement to Nation-State* (1990).

DARIÉN DAVIS

**BARBERO, ANDRÉS** (*b.* 28 July 1877; *d.* 14 February 1949), Paraguayan physician, scientist, and philanthropist. Born into a very wealthy Asunción family, Barbero decided at an early age to pursue a career in the sciences, despite the backwardness of his country's scientific establishment. Accordingly, he studied MEDICINE, graduating in 1904. His practice lasted only a short time, however, and he soon abandoned it to dedicate himself to teaching and scientific research.

In 1921 Barbero founded the Sociedad Científica del Paraguay together with naturalists Guillermo Tell Bertoni and Emilio Hassler. He also established a journal, the *Revista Científica del Paraguay*, which he edited for many years and which he filled with his own erudite pieces on Paraguayan flora and fauna.

Barbero's greatest contribution came in the field of philanthropy. He almost single-handedly created and maintained the Paraguayan Red Cross, the School for Rural Obstetrics, the National Cancer Institute, and a dozen other institutions emphasizing public health. After his death in 1949, his family donated still more funds for a new foundation, La Piedad, which supported efforts in many fields, from investigations into the indigenous languages of the Chaco to the care of retirees in the capital city, to the maintenance of various museums.

WILLIAM BELMONT PARKER, ed., *Paraguayans of To-Day* (repr. 1967), pp. 115–118; CARLOS ZUBIZARRETA, *Cien vidas paraguayas*, 2d ed. (1985), pp. 239–241.

THOMAS L. WHIGHAM

**BARBOSA, DOMINGOS CALDAS** (*b.* 1738; *d.* 9 Nov. 1800), Brazilian poet, singer, and songwriter. The son of a slave woman and a Portuguese merchant, Barbosa studied at Jesuit schools in Rio. His early satires got him into trouble with the authorities and led to a military assignment in a distant province until 1762. He went to Portugal with the hope of entering the university, but his father's death prevented him from doing so. Introduced by family friends to the Lisbon court, he gained favor as a poet and performer of original songs. As a composer, he was a central figure in the emergence and dissemination of the *modinha* and Afro-Brazilian *lundu* song forms. With the aid of his protectors, Barbosa also took holy orders. His case is an example of the symbiosis of religious and secular spheres in his day.

Barbosa was a founding member and first president of the stylish Nova Arcádia literary club. His poems, collected in the two volumes of *Viola de Lereno* (1798, 1826), exemplify both neoclassicism and innovative applications of Afro-Brazilian language. Father Barbosa's work is both transitional, ranging from a strict continental style to a more flexible New World expression, and synthetic, drawing on erudite as well as popular sources.

JANE M. MALINOFF, "Domingos Caldas Barbosa: Afro-Brazilian Poet at the Court of Dona Maria I," in *From Linguistics to Literature: Romance Studies Offered to Francis M. Rogers,* edited by Bernard H. Bichakjian (1981); DAVID BROOKSHAW, *Race and Color in Brazilian Literature* (1986).

CHARLES A. PERRONE

**BARBOSA, FRANCISCO VILLELA** (*b.* 20 November 1769; *d.* 11 September 1846), marqués of Paranaguá and minister of the Empire of Brazil. Born in Rio de Janeiro, where his father dealt in commerce, Barbosa graduated in 1796 with a degree in mathematics from the University of Coimbra, later becoming a professor of geometry at the Royal Navy Academy in Lisbon.

His political role was particularly important during the reign of Pedro I (1822–1831). After serving as Rio de Janeiro's representative to the Lisbon Cortes, he returned to Brazil in 1823 and was appointed minister of the empire and of foreign affairs. He also held, on various occasions, the post of navy minister (1823, 1825, 1826, 1829, 1831, and 1841). He supported the dissolution of the Constituent Assembly and participated in the framing of the Constitution of 1824. He was a state councilor, and in 1825 he took part in the negotiations to recognize Brazil's independence. In 1826, Barbosa was appointed a senator, but his fidelity to PEDRO I forced him to withdraw, temporarily, from public life after Pedro's abdication in 1831. Later, he championed the project that advanced the coming of age of PEDRO II. He wrote several works, chiefly treatises on geometry.

JANUÁRIO DA CUNHA BARBOSA, "Biografia dos brasileiros distintos por letras, armas, virtudes, etc.: Francisco Villela Barbosa," in *Revista do Instituto Histórico e Geográfico Brasileiro* 9 (1847): 398–408; MOACIR WERNECK DE CASTRO and FRANCISCO DE ASSIS BARBOSA, "Marquês de Paranaguá," in *Enciclopédia Mirador Internacional,* vol. 16 (1983), p. 8,598.

LÚCIA M. BASTOS P. NEVES

**BARBOSA DE OLIVEIRA, RUI** (*b.* 5 November 1840; *d.* 1 March 1923), Brazilian statesman, jurist, writer, and diplomat. Barbosa was a leader in many of the great causes that transformed Brazil in the late nineteenth century, leading to the abolition of SLAVERY, the fall of the empire, the creation of the republic, the development of a federal system, and the separation of church and state all within a period of two years. Born in Salvador, Bahia, Barbosa attended law school in Recife and São Paulo, returning to Salvador to practice law. He quickly turned to journalism, becoming a defender of civil rights and a proponent of abolition. Barbosa first served as a representative from Bahia in the imperial parliament, and later as a senator from 1891 to 1923. While he joined the republican cause only shortly before the fall of Dom PEDRO II in 1889, he became one of its greatest leaders, helping to consolidate the new government. Barbosa acted as the first minister of finance for the provisional government of the republic (1889–1891), in which capacity he instituted sweeping banking and monetary reforms, es-

Rui Barbosa de Oliveira. ICONOGRAPHIA.

tablished high tariffs, and abandoned the gold standard. Credited by some historians with being the first minister of finance (and the only one up until the 1930s) to break with liberal economics in order to spur industrial development, Barbosa is characterized by others as doing so simply to curry favor with the elite banking community in order to appease criticism of the new regime. Industrial development and the beginnings of import-substitution were fortuitous by-products.

Barbosa was the principal author of the Constitution of 1891, which he based to an important extent on the United States Constitution, especially in the design of federalism. This naturally gave to U.S.–Brazilian relations "an intimate approximation," in Barbosa's words, though he was not as ready as the great foreign minister, the baron of RIO BRANCO, to follow the lead of the United States in international matters as part of an "unwritten alliance." This reluctance became especially evident at the Second International Peace Conference at The Hague in 1907, which Barbosa attended at the foreign minister's request. Barbosa (and Brazil) gained international renown at the conference for his eloquent arguments in defense of the equality of all nations and, specifically, in favor of the right of small or weak nations to equal representation on an International Court of Justice. This position was at odds with that of the United States and other powers, which sought a smaller court dominated by them. The conference ended without a decision on the court but with Brazilian prestige and Barbosa's popular reputation significantly enhanced.

Barbosa ran for the presidency in 1910 and 1919, touring the provinces and taking issues directly to the voting public for the first time in Brazilian politics. Both bids for higher office were unsuccessful, however, undermined in part by the opposition of influential members of the military, whose involvement in government Barbosa had attacked repeatedly throughout his career. Barbosa was elected to the Brazilian Academy of Letters in 1908 and served as its president until 1919. His published works on finance, civil liberties, education, and the law number more than 150 volumes.

RAYMUNDO MAGALHÃES, JR., *Rui: O Homem e o mito* (1964); E. BRADFORD BURNS, *The Unwritten Alliance: Rio-Branco and Brazilian-American Relations* (1966); PINTO DE AGUIAR, *Rui e a economia brasileira* (1973); JOSÉ DE ARRUDA PENTEADO, *A consciência didática no pensamento pedagógico de Rui Barbosa* (1984); STEVEN TOPIK, *The Political Economy of the Brazilian State, 1889–1930* (1987).

ELIZABETH A. COBBS

See also **Brazil: Constitutions.**

**BARBOSA Y ALCALÁ, JOSÉ CELSO** (*b.* 27 July 1857; *d.* 21 September 1921), Puerto Rican politician and physician. Born in the town of Bayamón to a humble family of African descent, Barbosa rose to a position of prominence in the political life of Puerto Rico. He earned a medical degree at the University of Michigan (1880) and then returned to his homeland to become a fervent advocate of annexation to the United States, which he saw as the only way to free Puerto Rico from the bonds of Spanish colonialism. Barbosa joined the Liberal Reform Party in 1883, and he spent the rest of his life leading the movement for Puerto Rico's incorporation as an autonomous unit within the United States. In 1898 he formed what a year later became known as the Republican Party of Puerto Rico, which he led until his death. From 1900 to 1917, Barbosa served on an executive council arranged by the FORAKER ACT. This post allowed him further participation in Puerto Rico's early attempt to settle its status after independence from Spain.

JOSÉ CELSO BARBOSA, *José Celso Barbosa, pionero en el cooperativismo puertorriqueño, siglo XIX* (1982); RAYMOND CARR, *Puerto Rico, A Colonial Experiment* (1984); ROBERT J. ALEXANDER, ed., *Biographical Dictionary of Latin American and Caribbean Political Leaders* (1988).

TODD LITTLE-SIEBOLD

**BARBUDA,** a 62-square-mile LEEWARD ISLAND in the Caribbean, located about 30 miles north of ANTIGUA. A dependency of Antigua, Barbuda was settled by the British in the mid-1630s shortly after the colonization of Antigua. In 1674, Sir Christopher Codrington established the first major sugar plantation in Antigua and subsequently leased the island of Barbuda to cultivate food for the estate. Blacks brought from Africa to work in Barbuda became unwilling subjects of a breeding experiment to produce physically larger and stronger slaves. Evidence of this experiment can be seen today in their descendants; the people of the island are recognized for their large stature. The current population of some fifteen hundred are predominantly African in descent and live in the island's only village, named after Codrington.

Politically, Barbuda remains linked to Antigua. In 1967, Antigua received full self-government as an associated state of the United Kingdom, and in November 1981, Antigua and Barbuda acquired independence as a single territory. Attempts by Barbuda to obtain independence from Antigua have failed.

CARLEEN O'LOUGHLIN, *Economic and Political Change in the Leeward and Windward Islands* (1968), pp. 30–32; BEN BOX and SARAH CAMERON, eds., *1992 Caribbean Island Handbook* (1991), pp. 318–321, 327.

D. M. SPEARS

**BARCO VARGAS, VIRGILIO** (*b.* 17 September 1921), president of Colombia (1986–1990). From a prominent Cúcuta family, Barco combined study in the United States (including doctoral work in economics at MIT) with politics in his home city. In the 1960s he held several cabinet posts and was highly regarded as mayor of

Bogotá (1966–1969); he later served as ambassador in Washington, D.C. After an aborted candidacy for president in 1982 he won a landslide victory in 1986. The economy performed creditably under his administration, but the Barco years were better known for the upward spiral of violence propagated by guerrillas, right-wing death squads (which acted with suspicious impunity), and drug traffickers. Colombia's drug cartels stepped up their attacks on judges, journalists, and officials, culminating in the murder of Barco's presumptive successor, Luis Carlos GALÁN, in August 1989. Over the next several months hundreds were killed in cartel-ordered bombings, while the government's hard line produced few results. The definitive incorporation of the M-19 guerrilla movement into legal politics, near the end of Barco's term, brightened the scene somewhat.

IGNACIO ARIZMENDI POSADA, *Presidentes de Colombia, 1810–1990* (1990), pp. 301–305.

RICHARD J. STOLLER

*See also* **Drugs and Drug Trade.**

**BAREIRO, CÁNDIDO** (*b.* 1838?; *d.* 4 September 1880), Paraguayan diplomat and president (1878–1880). Bareiro was one of a score of young Paraguayans sent to Europe for advanced study by the Carlos Antonio LÓPEZ government in the late 1850s. Bareiro's field was diplomacy, and within a few years he received an appointment as minister to Paris and London. His stay in the European capitals coincided with the WAR OF THE TRIPLE ALLIANCE (1864–1870), in which Paraguay faced the combined military might of Brazil, Argentina, and Uruguay. Bareiro's loyalty to the López regime and his unceasing efforts to counter Allied propaganda in Europe brought him some acclaim among those few Paraguayans then living abroad.

He finally returned to a wrecked and occupied Asunción in 1869. At once he became the focus of a Lopizta group that included Bernardino CABALLERO and Patricio ESCOBAR, both war heroes. Other conservatives, many with Brazilian connections, came to join this same group, which, after Bareiro's death evolved into the Colorado Party. Bareiro himself manipulated various Paraguayan factions, as well as the Brazilian occupiers, during the 1870s. In this, he worked hard to oppose the liberals who had tried to undercut the influence of the traditional rural elites.

Bareiro was elected president in 1878. Though his administration was short lived and his attempts to resuscitate the economy woefully inadequate, he did make an honest attempt to curb the corruption that had seeped into Paraguayan politics since the war. He also had the satisfaction of seeing Paraguayan claims over the Chaco Boreal upheld in an arbitration award.

Bareiro died suddenly of a stroke while working at his desk in the presidential palace.

HARRIS GAYLORD WARREN, *Paraguay and the Triple Alliance: The Postwar Decade, 1869–1878* (1978), pp. 52–57, 73–74, 180–181, 274–275, and *Rebirth of the Paraguayan Republic: The First Colorado Era, 1878–1904* (1985), pp. 41–50.

THOMAS L. WHIGHAM

**BARILOCHE,** city of 55,000 inhabitants (1980) on the southwestern border of the province of Río Negro in Argentina. San Carlos de Bariloche was founded in 1670 by the Jesuit Nicolás Mascardi on the southern shores of Lake Nahuel Huapí as a mission for the nomadic Mapuche Indians. Veterans of the wars against the MAPUCHES as well as German and Italian homesteaders settled the shores of the lake and the upper reaches of the Limay River in spite of the constant threat from the Indians.

Since the 1920s, Bariloche has been a tourist center for skiers on Cerro Catedral and summer visitors of Nahuel Huapí, Traful, Futalaufquén, Mascardi, and Espejo (the Argentine lake district). It also attracts tourists traveling to Chile across the Andes via the Laguna Frías, Puerto Blest, and Paso Puyehue route. Comfortable, modern hotels accommodate guests from Argentina, Uruguay, and Brazil in the summer and skiers from North America and Europe in the winter. Bariloche is also an administrative and educational center for most of the Andean province of Río Negro. The city is the site of the Museo de la Patagonia, and flights to Buenos Aires are readily available. Railroad connections exist with San Antonio Oeste, on the Atlantic coast, and with Bahía Blanca, in the province of Buenos Aires.

R. LUCIONI, *Así es Bariloche* (Buenos Aires, 1973).

CÉSAR N. CAVIEDES

**BARING BROTHERS,** a London merchant bank founded in 1763 by the Baring family to finance trade with the United States and India. During the Napoleonic Wars it was engaged in substantial operations for the British treasury. The firm soon became one of the major powers in international finance. Between 1820 and 1870 it provided numerous government loans for France, Spain, Portugal, Russia, and Canada, among others. In Latin America it placed a Buenos Aires foreign loan in 1824, a Chilean railway loan in 1858, and a Venezuelan loan in 1862. During the 1880s it became the principal banker to the governments of Argentina and Uruguay, leading international banking syndicates in issuing six Argentine national loans and three Uruguayan loans. However, its excesses led to bankruptcy in November 1890, causing a major financial crisis in London, known as the Baring panic. Upon its reorganization in 1892, the firm reassumed its role as leading banker to Argentina, issuing eight loans for that nation between 1907 and 1914. In later years its importance in Latin American finance declined, although it continued to maintain close ties with the Argentine government until 1946, when Argentine president Juan Domingo PERÓN liquidated the foreign debt of the government. In other fields of international finance, Baring Brothers remained active on the London money market, particularly as investment counselor to British firms operating abroad. In the 1970s Baring Brothers once again began placing international loans for Latin American governments, frequently as a member of the banking syndicates that issued external bonds. Rash speculation in the Far East brought the firm to the brink of collapse in 1995.

RALPH HIDY, *The House of Baring in American Trade and Finance: English Merchant Bankers at Work, 1763–1861* (1949); ARMANDO O. CHIAPELLA, *El destino del empréstito Baring Brothers* (1975); PHILIP ZIEGLER, *The Sixth Great Power: A History of One of the Greatest of All Banking Families, the House of Baring, 1762–1929* (1988).

CARLOS MARICHAL

**BARNET, MIGUEL** (*b.* 28 January 1940), Cuban novelist, poet, essayist, and ethnologist. Born in Havana, educated in a local American primary school, and later a student of the distinguished ethnographer Fernando ORTÍZ, Miguel Barnet came of age during the final years of the Fulgencio BATISTA dictatorship. With the triumph of the CUBAN REVOLUTION, he became an active contributor to the process of literary experimentation and cultural reclamation it set in motion. Barnet first came to national attention as the poet of *La piedra fina y el pavorreal* (1963) and the much-praised *La sagrada familia* (1967), a lyrical autopsy of petit bourgeois domestic life. Publication of *Biografía de un cimarrón* (1966; *The Autobiography of a Runaway Slave*, 1968), the first in an ethnic tetralogy of documentary narratives, brought almost immediate international acclaim and established him as an innovating pioneer of the testimonial genre in contemporary Latin America. *La canción de Rachel* (1969; *Rachel's Song*, 1991), *Gallego* (1981), and *La vida real* (1986) confirmed his reputation as Cuba's premier exponent of the documentary novel.

Barnet explores the common ground between anthropology and literature, blending the methods and procedures of the novelist's and biographer's art—oral history—and the ethnographer's record of popular life and culture. Each work is a vivid textual re-creation of the spoken voice of ordinary, often-disdained or socially slighted Cuban citizens: a runaway black slave; a small-time mestizo female cabaret entertainer of the 1940s; a Spanish immigrant to the island; and a peasant migrant to the United States. The individuals usually absent from conventional history thus become emblematic personifications of Cuba's evolving historical experience and ethnocultural development; those lost to national recollection are reclaimed for the collectivity: "Memory, as a part of the imagination," Barnet notes in the prologue to *La vida real*, ". . . [is] the essential key of all my work of testimony."

Barnet has been a professor of folklore at Havana's School for Art Instructors (1961–1966), a researcher for the Institute of Ethnology and Folklore of the Cuban Academy of Science, and most recently a member of the editorial board of *Unión*, the journal of the Union of Cuban Artists and Writers (UNEAC). His other collections of poetry include *Isla de Guijes* (1964), *Orikis y otros poemas* (1980), and *Carta de noche* (1982).

SEYMOUR MENTON, *Prose Fiction of the Cuban Revolution* (1975), esp. pp. 83–85; ROBERTO GONZÁLEZ ECHEVARRÍA, "*Biografía de un cimarrón* and the Novel of the Cuban Revolution," in *Novel* 13, no. 3 (1980): 249–263; JULIO A. MARTÍNEZ, ed., *Dictionary of Twentieth Century Cuban Literature* (1990), pp. 59–64; EMILIO BEJEL, *Escribir en Cuba: Entrevistas con escritores cubanos, 1979–1989* (1991), pp. 15–29.

ROBERTO MÁRQUEZ

**BARNOLA, PEDRO PABLO** (*b.* 28 August 1908; *d.* 12 January 1986), Venezuelan writer and educator. As a student at the Academy San Ignacio de Loyola in Caracas, Barnola was the first Venezuelan to join the JESUITS after their reestablishment in the country. He completed his studies first in Europe (1925–1932) and later in the United States (1935–1940). Ordained a priest in 1938, he dedicated himself to teaching at the Academy San Ignacio. He was director of the magazine *SIC*, rector of the Andrés Bello Catholic University, editorial director of the *Obras completas de Andrés Bello* (1951), and member of the editorial commission for the *Obras completas de Rafael María Baralt*. He was a regular member of the Royal Academy of the Spanish Language and an outstanding defender of the purity of Castilian Spanish. He collaborated with Professor Ángel Rosenblat on the first volume of the *Diccionario de Venezolanismos* (1983). He is the author of numerous works of literary criticism. The principal ones include: *Altorrelieve de la literatura venezolana* (1970); *Estudios crítico-literarios* (1945, 1953, 1971); and *Raíz y sustancia de la civilización latinoamericana* (1953).

HORACIO JORGE BECCO, *Pedro Pablo Barnola, S.J., Bibliografía (1935–1985)* (1986).

INÉS QUINTERO

**BARRACAS,** old borough of the city of BUENOS AIRES, Argentina, located close to the mouth of the Río de las Matanzas, also known as Riachuelo, flowing into the estuary of RÍO DE LA PLATA. It was named thus for the numerous warehouses for hides and agricultural products located in this area in colonial and early republican times. With the arrival of Italian immigrants in the 1880s and their establishment in this sector of the city there emerged the borough of La Boca, which increased in importance when port facilities for domestic navigation were built on the Riachuelo, communicating with the estuary by means of the Southern Canal. Toward the end of the twentieth century Barracas lost significance as a warehouse and port district and has become mostly a residential area for lower-middle-class families.

CÉSAR N. CAVIEDES

**BARRADAS, RAFAEL** (*b.* ca. 4 January 1890; *d.* 12 February 1929), Uruguayan painter. Born in Montevideo, Barradas had a brief career as an illustrator and journalist for newspapers and magazines such as *El Tiempo*, *Bohemia*, and *La Semana*; in 1913 he founded the periodical *El Monigote* (The Bumpkin). Barradas traveled to Europe that year and settled in Spain, where he worked as an illustrator for the magazines *La Esquella de Torratxa*, in Barcelona, and *Paraninfo*, in Zaragoza. He exhibited at the Galerías Dalmau in Barcelona in 1916 and the following year in the Salón de los Humoristas in Madrid. In his first solo exhibition at the Galerías Layetanas (1918), he introduced an aesthetic conception which he called *vibracionismo*, his interpretation of futurism and cubism.

During the early 1920s Barradas worked in Madrid as scenographer and toy and poster designer. He also illustrated editions of books by Charles Dickens, Alexandre Dumas, and Félix Lope de Vega and was costume designer for Federico García Lorca's *El maleficio de la Mariposa*. He frequented the *Ultraístas*, a group of poets that included Jorge Luis Borges, and collaborated with the latter on the magazine *Tableros*. He worked on *Los Magníficos*, portraits of popular Spanish types, rendered in monumental geometric forms. He devised *clownism*, an expressionistic style in which he painted picturesque

details of busy urban areas. In 1924 he was awarded the Grand Prix at the International Exhibition of Decorative and Industrial Arts in Paris. Back in Barcelona, he painted a series of watercolors called *Estampones de Montevideo* (Prints of Montevideo), humorous views of that city.

In 1928 Barradas returned to Montevideo, where he died a few months later. His last work was a series of madonna and child images rendered in a postcubist style. Barradas, who produced his most significant work in Spain, is considered an innovative personality in the history of Uruguayan art.

ANGEL KALENBERG, *Seis maestros de la pintura uruguaya: Juan Manuel Blanes, Carlos Federico Sáez, Pedro Figari, Joaquín Torres-García, Rafael Barradas, José Cuneo* (1987); DAWN ADES, *Art in Latin America: The Modern Era, 1820–1980* (1989); RAQUEL PEREDA, *Barradas* (1989) and *Rafael Barradas* (1992).

MARTA GARSD

**BARRAGÁN MORFIN, LUIS** (*b.* 9 March 1902; *d.* 22 November 1988), Mexican architect and landscape architect. Barragán trained as a civil engineer at the Escuela Libre de Ingeniera, in his native Guadalajara, Jalisco, and received his diploma 13 December 1923, after which he presented his admission thesis for the architecture program. Upon admission, he left for a year's study and travel in Europe (1924–1925). He returned to a Mexico radically changed by revolution and land reform and found his architecture program disbanded. As the youngest son of a landowning family, he joined his brother's construction firm in the development of urban

*The Lovers' Fountain.* Sculpture by Luis Barragán Morfin. Water originally ran from the horizontal beam. IGNACIO SAN MARTÍN.

Guadalajara. Without formal design training Barragán found the need to overlap architecture with civil engineering and, working with his brother Juan José Barragán, produced a number of projects, including the house for Enfraín González Luna (1929–1931).

At the invitation of architect-engineer José Luis Creixell and the primitive painter Jesús (Chucho) Reyes Ferreira, Barragán began work in Mexico City on several International Style buildings. Barragán's twenty-year design and intellectual collaboration with Reyes and the émigré sculptor Mathias GOERITZ was a major turning point in modern architectural design and theory. They worked separately or in consultation with one another, each taking the lead in their individual discipline. Barragán, the architect, treated a building site like a transparent solid defined by its light, natural configuration, and context. He moved through the site to find indications of forms and connections as a sculptor would explore the volume of a block of stone to find its contained figure. Program requirements and circulation then cut the volume, disciplined the light, and defined enclosures from a plan diagram sketched on the ground for workmen or on a scrap of paper for a client's information. Barragán, Reyes, and Goeritz took the indigenous architectural style of Mexico through the filter of the International Style into the intellectual abstraction and pragmatism of projects like the Towers of Satellite City and Casa Gilardi in Mexico City, then returned to the memory of Barragán's childhood home, Hacienda de Corrales, near Mazamitla, Jalisco, to design projects like the contemporary equestrian hacienda San Cristobal, near Mexico City (1967–1968). In the more than fifty international projects attributed to Barragán, the hacienda form always alludes to Mexico.

One of Mexico's most important architects and architectural design theorists, Barragán was a founding member of the Mexican Society of Landscape Architects and its honorary president for life (1973), a recipient of the Premio Nacional de Artes (first prize for architecture) (1976), and honorary fellow of the American Institute of Architects (1976), the second winner of the Pritzker Prize for Architecture (1980), and an honorary member of the American Academy and Institute of Arts and Letters (1984). His architecture was the subject of exhibitions at the Museum of Modern Art in New York (1976) and the Museo Rufino Tamayo in Mexico City (1985) and a traveling exhibition organized by *Montage Journal* of Boston (1989–1994). Luis Barragán's death in Mexico City was honored by a memorial exhibition at the Palacio de Bellas Artes.

EMILIO AMBASZ, *The Architecture of Luis Barragán* (1976); LUIS BARRAGÁN, *Luis Barragán: The Pritzker Architectural Prize* (acceptance speech, 1980); LUIS BARRAGÁN et al., *Ensayos y apuntes para un bosquejo crítico: Luis Barragán* (1985); "Luis Barragán, arquitecto," in *Arquitectura*, 70 (March 1989): 51–85; JOSÉ CHECA ALVAREZ and MANUEL RAMOS GUERRA, *Obra construida: Luis Barragán Morfin, 1902–1988* (1989); MAX UNDERWOOD, "Architect of the Intangible," in *Americas* 43, no. 4 (1991): 6–15; AR-

MANDO SALAS PORTUGAL, *Photographs of the Architecture of Luis Barragán* (1992); ESTELLE JACKSON et al., *Luis Barragán: The Architecture of Light, Color, and Form* (catalog for *Montage Journal* traveling exhibition, 1995).

ESTELLE JACKSON

**BARRANCA YACO,** site in the Argentine province of Córdoba where the Federalist chieftain Juan Facundo QUIROGA was assassinated on 16 February 1835. Quiroga was returning to Buenos Aires from a mission to the Argentine northwest when an armed band murdered him. An investigation and trial ordered by the Buenos Aires strongman Juan Manuel de ROSAS put the blame on the Reinafé brothers, who controlled the province of Córdoba; they were later executed. Rosas's enemies alleged that he himself was behind the crime, hoping to eliminate a potential rival, but there is no evidence to support the charge. However, Rosas used the crime as proof that internal security was in peril and as justification for his own return to the governorship of Buenos Aires with "the Sum of Public Power."

DOMINGO F. SARMIENTO, *Life in the Argentine Republic in the Days of the Tyrants; or, Civilization and Barbarism* (1974), chap. 13; JOHN LYNCH, *Argentine Dictator: Juan Manuel de Rosas 1829–1853* (1981).

DAVID BUSHNELL

**BARRANCABERMEJA,** a Colombian port and refinery town. This Magdalena River town of 70,000 people in the department of Santander developed in tandem with the Colombian petroleum industry. Commonly referred to as "Barranca" after the red clay banks of the river, the town remained quite small until the discovery of petroleum in the early twentieth century. The 1921 de Mares concession of oil fields to Jersey Standard (later Exxon) authorized refinery construction shortly thereafter. Under the restrictive Petroleum Law of 1919, the concession reverted to national control forty years later. In 1951, Exxon and ECOPETROL jointly expanded the capacity of the refinery. Its present 150,000 barrels per day capacity represents two-thirds of the country's potential. Jersey Standard's concession came in the midst of intense nationalist feeling over the 1903 separation of Panama, which was quite visible in the 1920s. Labor strife has been common in the Barrancabermeja refinery, with major conflicts in 1925, 1936, 1948, 1963, and in the 1980s.

A. EUGENE HAVENS and MICHEL ROMIEUX, *Barrancabermeja: Conflictos sociales en torno a un centro petrolero* (1966); RENÉ DE LA PEDRAJA TOMAN, *Energy Politics in Colombia* (1989).

DAVID SOWELL

**BARRANQUILLA,** a city 12 miles from the mouth of the MAGDALENA RIVER, near the Caribbean coast of Colombia, and capital of the department of Atlántico. In 1985 the city had a population of about 1,121,000, making it the fourth largest in Colombia.

Founded in 1629, the city developed slowly over the next two centuries as a river port. Despite its favorable location, the city's growth was hindered by a shifting sandbar at the mouth of the river, which obstructed the passage of steam-powered vessels. In 1870–1871 a railroad was completed that bypassed the sandbar, linking Barranquilla with satellite ports on nearby Sabanilla Bay. As a consequence, Barranquilla became Colombia's principal Caribbean port, overtaking Cartagena and Santa Marta.

Barranquilla later lost its leadership among Colombian ports, accounting for only 9 percent of the country's total commerce by tonnage in 1987. In the meantime, it had become an important manufacturing center, producing processed foods and beverages, textiles, apparel, and petrochemicals.

THEODORE E. NICHOLS, "The Rise of Barranquilla," *Hispanic American Historical Review* 34 (1954):158–174, and *Tres Puertos de Colombia: Estudio sobre el desarrollo de Cartagena, Santa María y Barranquilla* (1973).

HELEN DELPAR

**BARREDA, GABINO** (*b.* 1818; *d.* 1881), Mexican philosopher and educator. Born in Puebla, Barreda is credited with introducing Comtian POSITIVISM to Mexico. After studies in Mexico at the Colegio de San Ildefonso, he entered law school but later abandoned it to pursue his passion for the natural sciences in the Mining School and School of Medicine. After enlisting as a volunteer in the war against the United States, he left in 1847 for Paris, where he took courses with Auguste Comte. Returning to Mexico in 1851, he completed his degree as a medical doctor and taught in the School of Medicine.

In 1867 President Benito Juárez appointed him to preside over a commission to reorganize Mexican education. The resulting *Leyes orgánicas de la educación pública* in 1867 and 1869 made public schooling lay, free, and obligatory for the Federal District and territories. Professional school programs were reformed to eliminate speculative thinking and emphasize the positive sciences. Attention was focused on the founding of the Escuela Nacional Preparatoria for men in the old Colegio de San Ildefonso, with Barreda its director.

With a uniform curriculum based on Comte's interpretation of the physical and social sciences, the school addressed what Barreda believed were the causes of Mexican backwardness: a disdain for productive labor and entrepreneurialism; a proclivity for clericalism, which had inhibited the development of a scientific attitude; and a liberal preoccupation with abstract principle. Like Comte, Barreda believed in a hierarchical social order in which a team of social engineers would aid captains of industry to ensure orderly economic progress.

Opposition to Barreda's positivst ideas on the part of Liberals and Catholics led to his appointment in 1878 as

ambassador to Germany. However, his intellectual contribution was great. He is credited with the formation of a generation of Mexican positivists, many of whom successfully combined statesmanship and business, among them Francisco BULNES, Francisco G. Cosmes, Joaquín Casasús, José Yves LIMANTOUR, Pablo Macedo, Justo Sierra, Roberto Núñez, Rafael and Emilio Pardo, Porfirio Parra, Rafael Reyes Spíndola, Rafael Hernández Madero, and Miguel Macedo.

WILLIAM DIRK RAAT, "Leopoldo Zea and Mexican Positivism: A Reappraisal," in *Hispanic American Historical Review* 48 (1968): 1–18; LEOPOLDO ZEA, *El positivismo en México* (1968); Mary Kay Vaughan, *The State, Education, and Social Class in Mexico, 1880–1928* (1982); FRANCISCO JAVIER GUERRA, *México, del antiguo regimen a la revolución*, vol. 1 (1988); CHARLES A. HALE, *The Transformation of Mexican Liberalism* (1989).

MARY KAY VAUGHAN

**BARREDA Y LAOS, FELIPE** (*b.* 1888; *d.* 1973), Peruvian historian, lawyer, diplomat, educator. He was educated in a JESUIT school and at the University of San Marcos in Lima, where he became a professor. He was the author of several books, including treatises on intellectual currents in colonial Peru, Hispanic culture, and other diplomatic, educational, and historical subjects. Initially influenced by POSITIVISM, his view of the colonial past was critical of the influence of the scholastic tradition in Peru. In later works, however, he emphasized the unity of the peninsular and American Hispanic tradition and the beneficial effects of Hispanic culture in America. He also assumed a continental view in his diplomatic works.

See his *Dos Américas: Dos mundos* (1952) and *Vida intelectual del virreinato del Perú*, 3d ed. (1964).

ALFONSO W. QUIROZ

**BARREIRO, ANTONIO** (*b.* ca. 1780; *d.* after 1835), *assessor* (legal adviser) of NEW MEXICO during the 1830s. Barreiro was sent by the Mexican government in 1831 to establish a judicial system. After a year in the territory, Barreiro published his report, *Ojeada sobre Nuevo-México*. The work synthesized data collected earlier in the century by Alexander von HUMBOLDT, reports of soldiers of the presidio of Sante Fe, and the reports of the representatives to the first National Congress in Mexico.

Barreiro's *Ojeada* represents a plea for Mexico City to provide a modicum of investment in the rich territory he described. Government support to aid in the building of stone bridges, for example, would ease the difficult conditions for transport and export. Strengthening the powers of the governor and New Mexican courts of first instance could aid in the punishment of petty crime and greater deliberation on matters of import to the citizens. National warehouses, an adequate building in which to house the public treasury, and stronger defenses along the New Mexican frontier would increase and secure tariff revenues, encourage and streamline trade, and dissuade both the raids of "wild Indians" and the grasping Americans interested in extending "the boundary of Louisiana to the left bank of the Bravo or North River" (Rio Grande). Barreiro concluded, "Only the attention of the government toward this country, which is worthy of a better fate, will remove all the obstacles to its welfare. Only an extraordinary effort on the part of the government will develop the valuable elements which lie submerged there and which will some day raise it to the height of prosperity."

Partly due to the publication of his report, Barreiro won election in 1834 and 1835 as New Mexico's deputy to the Mexican Congress. With a printing press imported from Missouri in 1834, Barreiro published the first New Mexican newspaper, *El Crepúsculo de la Libertad.*

PEDRO BAUTISTA PINO, ANTONIO BARREIRO, and JOSÉ AGUSTÍN DE ESCUDERO, *Three New Mexico Chronicles,* translated and edited by H. Bailey Carroll and J. Villasana Haggard (1942); FRANCES LEON SWADESH, *Los Primeros Pobladores: Hispanic Americans of the Ute Frontier* (1974); PEARCE S. GROVE, BECKY J. BARNETT, and SANDRA J. HANSEN, *New Mexico Newspapers: A Comprehensive Guide to Bibliographical Entries and Locations* (1975); DAVID J. WEBER, *The Mexican Frontier, 1821–1846: The American Southwest under Mexico* (1982).

ROSS H. FRANK

**BARRETO PAULO.** *See* **Rio, João do.**

**BARRETO DE MENEZES, TOBIAS, JR.** (*b.* 7 June 1839; *d.* 26 June 1889), Brazilian philosopher and jurist, founder of the Recife School. Born in Campos, in the province of Sergipe, to a family of very modest circumstances, Barreto learned Latin from a priest and, from the age of fifteen, made his living teaching humanities. He studied law in Recife and became known for his poetical disputes with Antônio de CASTRO ALVES. As a member of the Generation of 70 he fought for intellectual renewal in the Brazilian Empire.

Unlike most of his generation, who turned to French POSITIVISM, Barreto found inspiration in German authors. In the areas of religious criticism (Georg von Ewald, Ludwig Feuerbach), political ideas (von Gneist, Frobel), and law (von Ihring), they seemed to him to offer views more suitable to combat the spiritualist and neo-Thomist eclecticism then dominant in Brazil. His "Germanism" produced a model for solving Brazilian problems and enabled him to criticize the French-inspired Brazilian liberals, the francophile elite of the Southeast, and the dominant juridical conceptions.

Although he was married to the daughter of a Liberal *fazendeiro* (rancher), Barreto suffered social and racial discrimination as a result of his mixed heritage. After a brief and not very successful involvement in local and regional politics (he was a Liberal member of the provincial assembly in 1878–1879), he gained influence by becoming a professor at the law faculty of Recife in

1882. In his lectures he defended the view that law is neither divine nor natural, but a product of history. A supporter of philosophical monism, he was responsible for the wide dissemination of Ernst Haeckel's theories in Brazil and became famous for his polemics against ultramontanist and idealist positions.

Although Barreto was widely attacked, his views were supported by his friend, the literary critic Sílvio ROMERO, and by a group of students who played major roles during the Old Republic: Clóvis Beviláqua, Higino Cunha, Benedito Leite, and Artur Orlando.

TOBIAS BARRETO, JR., *Obras completas,* 10 vols. (1925–1926); HERMES LIMA, *Tobias Barreto: A época e o homem* (1939); PAULO MERCADANTE and ANTONIO PAIM, *Tobias Barreto na cultura brasileira: Uma reavaliação* (1972); CENTRO DE DOCUMENTAÇÃO DO PENSAMENTO BRASILEIRO, *Tobias Barreto: Bibliografia e estudos críticos* (1990).

MATTHIAS RÖHRIG ASSUNÇÃO

**BARRETT, RAFAEL** (*b.* 1876; *d.* 17 December 1910), Anglo-Spanish anarchist writer who influenced an entire generation of Paraguayan radical intellectuals. Born in Santander, Spain, in 1876, Barrett moved to Asunción in 1904. Working days in the general statistics office, he devoted his nights to journalistic efforts, churning out article after article of social criticism, focusing especially on the plight of poor workers in the yerba plantations of eastern Paraguay. His principal writings, compiled in a volume entitled *El dolor paraguayo* (1910), have been favorably compared with the works of Peru's Clorinda MATTO DE TURNER, Ecuador's Jorge ICAZA CORONEL, and Bolivia's Alcides ARGÜEDAS. Afflicted with tuberculosis, Barrett left his Paraguayan wife and children behind at San Bernardino and returned to Europe, where he died at Arcachón, France.

RAFAEL BARRETT, *El dolor paraguayo* (1978); CARLOS ZUBIZARRETTA, *Cien vidas paraguayas,* 2d ed. (1985), pp. 248–251.

THOMAS L. WHIGHAM

**BARRIENTOS ORTUÑO, RENÉ** (*b.* 1919; *d.* 27 April 1969), army officer and president of Bolivia (1966–1969). Barrientos, a native of Cochabamba, graduated in 1943 from the military academy from which he had earlier been expelled for supporting the government of President Germán BUSCH (1937–1939). He played an active though very junior role in the 1944 peasant congress sponsored by the regime of President Gualberto VILLARROEL (1943–1946) and the Movimiento Nacionalista Revolucionario (MNR). Although he stayed in the army after the overthrow of Villarroel, he was retired for participating in an MNR insurrection against the conservative government.

He participated in the 1952 MNR revolution that launched the Bolivian National Revolution. While the MNR was in power, he became head of the air force and of the "military cell" of the MNR. In the 1964 election, as a result of military pressure, the civilian selected to run as the MNR candidate for vice president with President Víctor PAZ ESTENSSORO was forced to step down. René Barrientos was put in his place. Even before becoming vice president in August, Barrientos was leading a conspiracy to overthrow Paz Estenssoro, which came to fruition on 4 November 1964. For some time after Paz Estenssoro's overthrow, Barrientos and General Alfredo OVANDO were "copresidents." During that period, there were violent clashes between the regime and organized labor, particularly the miners. The mining camps were occupied by troops and many miners and members of their families were either killed or wounded.

In 1966 General Barrientos was elected president. Although his regime continued to rule in a high-handed fashion and was particularly hostile to organized labor, it did enjoy wide support among the peasantry. Barrientos spoke Quechua, and spent much time traveling in rural areas. He also continued to support the land redistribution that had taken place under the MNR government as well as extensive programs of extending technical help to the Indian peasants. Peasant support was of key importance in helping the Barrientos government to defeat the guerrilla effort launched in 1967 by Ernesto "Che" GUEVARA. Guevara was executed by the Bolivian army unit that captured him. Barrientos died in the mysterious crash of a helicopter he was piloting.

CHRISTOPHER MITCHELL, *The Legacy of Populism in Bolivia: From the MNR to Military Rule* (1977).

ROBERT J. ALEXANDER

**BARRILLAS, MANUEL LISANDRO** (*b.* 1844; *d.* 1907), president of Guatemala (1885–1892). Barrillas was appointed provisional president in 1885 after the death of Justo Rufino BARRIOS and was constitutionally elected the following year. Like Barrios, he was a coffee grower who participated in the Liberal Revolution that swept the Conservatives from power in 1871. His liberal credentials and vast coffee holdings in San Marcos and Retaluleu ensured a smooth rise to power. The Barillas administration rested largely on its ability to induce the nation's Indian majority to labor on large coffee FINCAS. When the Indians resisted, his government, with the aid of the military, resorted to a number of forced-labor schemes that included the MANDAMIENTO, debt bondage, and a vagrancy law.

The Barrillas government coincides with a tremendous expansionary period for Guatemala's COFFEE INDUSTRY. In the late 1880s and early 1890s world prices for Guatemalan coffee reached record high levels. Coffee cultivation was introduced to large new tracts of land to take advantage of the favorable world market. It is in this period that Guatemala gained its reputation as a producer of one of the world's finest mild coffees.

SANFORD A. MOSK, "The Coffee Economy of Guatemala, 1850–1918: Development and Signs of Instability," in *Inter-American Economic Affairs* 9 (1955): 6–20.

WADE A. KIT

**BARRIOS, AGUSTÍN** (*b.* 23 May 1885; *d.* 7 August 1944), Paraguayan musician and composer. Born in San Juan Bautista in the Paraguayan Misiones, Barrios came from an impoverished background. He nonetheless attained fame early on as a local prodigy with the guitar. At the end of the century, he was discovered by Gustavo Sosa Escalada, the country's most famous guitarist, who helped Barrios to develop his skill with the instrument. After studying at the Colegio Nacional in Asunción, Barrios began a concert tour of South America in 1910. The tour lasted fourteen years, and included extended stays in Chile, Argentina, Uruguay, and Brazil.

In his presentations, Barrios often appeared in Indian costume, replete with feathers, and went under the stage name of *Cacique Mangoré*. Throughout this time Barrios also composed pieces for the guitar, a good many of which he attributed to obscure European composers in the belief that they would then be taken more seriously.

After a brief return to Paraguay in the mid-1920s, Barrios again left the country, this time in the company of a diplomat, Tomás Salomini, who served as his patron and who arranged recitals for him in Cuba, Mexico, and, in 1934, in several European capitals. Barrios was the first major Latin American musician to play before European audiences. He has frequently been compared to Andrés Segovia as an interpreter, and to Niccolò Paganini as a virtuoso. He evidently wrote over a hundred works, though many of these are now lost. His extant corpus includes *Danza paraguaya*, *El catedrál*, and *Rapsodia andaluza*. Starting in 1939, Barrios taught at the National Music Conservatory in San Salvador, El Salvador, where he died.

PETER SENSIER, "Augustín Barrios," *Guitar* 2:12 (1974), p. 22; BACÓN DUARTE PRADO, *Agustín Barrios: Un genio insular* (1985).

MARTA FERNÁNDEZ WHIGHAM

**BARRIOS, EDUARDO** (*b.* 25 October 1884; *d.* 13 September 1963), Chilean novelist, short-story writer, and playwright. Known primarily for his psychological novels, Barrios subordinated action to character portrayal in his works. Many of his protagonists are will-less, alienated men destined to failure. His first collection of stories, *Del natural* (1907), reflects the tenets of nineteenth-century realism and Zola's naturalism. The unifying theme is love, which Barrios examines within the context of middle-class mores. The title story of his second collection, *El niño que enloqueció de amor* (1915), is a psychological study of a nine-year-old boy who becomes enamored of an older woman and goes mad when he discovers her with her boyfriend. The story re-creates the imaginary world of a child who is increasingly alienated from adults. Critics have seen precursors of modernism in the extreme delicacy of the boy's portrait. Barrios's novel *Un perdido* (1918) combines a subtle character analysis with a detailed description of the Chilean middle class. *El hermano asno* (1922), which deals with the repressed erotic yearnings of a friar named Lázaro, has been called anticlerical because Lázaro witnesses an apparent crime and Church authorities try to silence him. *Tamarugal* (1944) and *Gran señor y rajadiablos* (1948) are set in rural areas; the former deals with life in the nitrate mines in the north of Chile, while the latter portrays life on a typical Chilean farm around the turn of the century. *Los hombres del hombre* (1950) is a psychological portrait of a man who suspects his wife of infidelity. Barrios also wrote a number of plays, including *Lo que niega la vida* (1913), *Vivir* (1916), and *¡Ante todo la oficina!* (1925).

JAIME PERALTA, "La novelística de Eduardo Barrios," in *Cuadernos Hispanoamericanos* 173 (1964): 357–367; MANUEL E. RAMÍREZ, "Some Notes on the Prose Style of Eduardo Barrios," in *Romance Notes* 9 (1967): 40–48; JERRY L. BENBOW, "Grotesque Elements in Eduardo Barrios," in *Hispania* 51 (1968): 86–91; NED J. DAVIDSON, *Eduardo Barrios* (1970); SILVIA MARTÍNEZ DACOSTA, *Dos ensayos literarios sobre Eduardo Barrios y José Donoso* (1976); JOHN WALKER, *Metaphysics and Aesthetics in the Works of Eduardo Barrios* (1983); LUIS A. MANSILLA, "Eduardo Barrios," in *Araucaria de Chile* 28 (1984): 141–144; SILVIA MARTÍNEZ DACOSTA, *Los personajes en la obra de Eduardo Barrios* (1988).

BARBARA MUJICA

**BARRIOS, GERARDO** (*b*. 3 October 1813; *d*. 29 August 1865), general and president of El Salvador (1859–1863). Born to a wealthy, well-connected family in the department of San Miguel, Barrios remains a popular figure in the history of modern El Salvador. He was the first president in Central America to introduce reforms based on LIBERALISM-POSITIVISM, and set the course for the modernization of Salvadoran society.

Barrios's family had extensive landholdings, on which they grew indigo. Young Gerardo felt a vocation for the military and joined the militia at a young age. By 1840 he had already participated in the overthrow of one president, José María Cornejo, and fought in battles at Mixco, San Miguelito, Espíritu Santo, Perulapía, and in Guatemala. He joined other Central American leaders in the struggle against the American filibuster William WALKER in Nicaragua in the 1850s. In this campaign Barrios earned a reputation as a skillful leader and formed a close relationship with the Guatemalan president Rafael CARRERA. In July 1858, Carrera decorated Barrios with the Cross of Honor. This friendly association was not destined to last long, however, for Barrios was more of an ideologue than Carrera, and friction developed after Barrios succeeded to the presidency of El Salvador when President Miguel de Santín de Castillo's health failed in 1858.

Barrios then embarked on a remarkable new course

Gerardo Barrios. PHOTO COURTESY OF HARVARD COLLEGE LIBRARY.

that revealed his deep admiration for the United States and Europe. In fact, Barrios often spoke of the perfection of the British and French political institutions. He undertook the modernization of the Salvadoran government: an expansion and centralization of the bureaucracy, the restoration of San Salvador as the national capital, and the transfer of the Supreme Court back to San Salvador. Barrios next overhauled the legal system by drafting new civil and penal codes and altering the process of justice. The right to collect taxes was removed from local jurisdiction and decreed a national responsibility. He repatriated the remains of the great Liberal leader of independence Francisco Morazán, who was actually Honduran, and buried them in San Salvador with much ceremony. Barrios extended the term of the presidency from two to six years, increased the role of the executive branch at the expense of the legislative, and upheld the democratic transfer of office. He returned office to Santín upon the latter's recovery late in 1859, but arranged to have himself elected the following year.

In 1860, Barrios began to promote the production of COFFEE on a large scale, by lowering production taxes on the new crop, exempting the coffee labor force from military service, and distributing land to those promising to grow coffee on two-thirds or more of the area. Barrios's government took an unprecedented, active role in the economy of the nation when it purchased a boat and attempted to export coffee to California itself. Furthermore, Barrios followed the French model and transformed the old-style Salvadoran militias into a modern national army; he also created a military academy with a Colombian as its head.

By 1862, Barrios's liberalism had begun to encroach on the privileged position of the Roman Catholic church. Although he was not an enemy of the church, as president Barrios stressed the ultimate authority of secular over religious authorities. He required all priests to declare obedience to the state, thereby provoking conflict with the Vatican and stirring up fears among other Central American leaders. In 1862, Barrios reached a concordat with the Holy See in which priests agreed to swear loyalty to the Constitution but not to the actual government. Barrios's main efforts were concentrated in education and the expansion of transportation and communication. By 1863, he had many enemies both within El Salvador and across Central America. He repelled a Guatemalan invasion in early 1863, but before the end of the year Carrera returned and conquered El Salvador. Barrios was caught in Nicaragua while trying to escape. He languished in jail and was executed in 1865. Thus ended the first liberal-positivist experiment in Central America.

GOVERNMENT OF EL SALVADOR, *Gerardo Barrios: Héroe nacional de El Salvador* (n.d.); EMILIANO CORTÉS, *Biografía del capitán general Gerardo Barrios* (1965); JOSÉ DOLORES GÁMEZ, *Gerardo Barrios ante la posteridad* (1965); ÍTALO LÓPEZ VALLECILLOS, *Gerardo Barrios y su tiempo*, 2 vols. (1967).

KAREN RACINE

**BARRIOS, GONZALO** (*b*. 1902), Venezuelan politician. The son of a well-to-do family from Portuguesa State, Barrios studied law at the Central University of Venezuela, where he was a prominent member of the Generation of 1928. After returning from a European exile in 1936, he became a founder of the Venezuelan Organization (Organización Venezolana—ORVE), the National Democratic Party (Partido Democrático Nacional—PDN), and Democratic Action (Acción Democrática—AD). During the AD *trienio* (1945–1948) he served as a member of the revolutionary junta, secretary of the presidency, and governor of the Federal District. After 1958 he held a series of important positions in AD (including secretary-general) and in government (minister of the interior, senator). After running as AD's unsuccessful presidential candidate in 1968, he continued to play an active role in party and national affairs.

JOHN D. MARTZ, *Acción Democrática: Evolution of a Modern Political Party in Venezuela* (1966); ROBERT J. ALEXANDER, ed., *Biographical Dictionary of Latin American and Caribbean Political Leaders* (1988).

WINFIELD J. BURGGRAAFF

*See also* **Venezuela: Political Parties.**

**BARRIOS, JUSTO RUFINO** (*b*. 19 July 1835; *d*. 2 April 1885), president of Guatemala (1873–1885). Born in San Lorenzo, department of San Marcos, Guatemala, Justo Barrios was the son of Ignacio Barrios, a prominent dealer in horses and cattle and landowner, and Josefa Auyón de Barrios. He led the Liberal Reforma of 1871 and represented the shift in power from the Conservative elite of Guatemala City to the Liberal coffee interests of the western highlands.

Barrios received his elementary and secondary education from tutors and schools in San Marcos, Quetzaltenango, and Guatemala City, where he studied law and earned his certificate as a notary in 1862. In Guatemala City he came under the influence of leading Liberals, Miguel García Granados and Manuel Dardón, but he returned to his family lands in 1862 and especially developed his estate "El Malacate" along the Mexican border.

In 1867 Barrios joined the Liberal insurgency against President Vicente CERNA. When an attack on the barracks at San Marcos failed, Barrios fled into Chiapas, in southern Mexico, where in 1869 he organized a rebel force in collaboration with Field Marshal Serapio CRUZ. After Cruz's death in 1870, García Granados joined the movement and formed a provisional government early in 1871, with Barrios as military commander. They quickly gained control of the western highlands, and in a manifesto issued at Patzicía on 3 June 1871 they stated the goals of their revolution. The crucial battle came at San Lucas Sacatepéquez, on the heights above Guatemala City, where on 29 June, Barrios routed Cerna's army. On the following day he marched into the capital victorious. García Granados served as the first president under the Reforma. Barrios wanted more sweeping reforms, however, and in 1873 he won election as president of Guatemala.

Barrios quickly forged a strong dictatorship, eliminating the Conservative opposition and greatly strengthening the power of the state. He represented the coming to power in Guatemala of the liberal-positivist philosophy that would remain dominant until at least 1944. Barrios promoted strongly anticlerical legislation, suppressed the tithe, abolished the regular orders, expropriated church property, and greatly reduced the number of priests in the country; he also established religious liberty, civil marriage and divorce, and state collection of vital statistics. He launched a public education system at all levels and took the University of

Portrait of Justo Rufino Barrios on five-quetzal note. COURTESY OF CHRISTOPHER LUTZ / CIRMA.

SAN CARLOS out of the control of the church, making it the state university and establishing other secondary and normal schools. His educational reforms, however, benefited primarily the upper and middle classes of Guatemala City and Quetzaltenango. Most rural Guatemalans continued to have little access to education and often now lost their village priests, who formerly had provided some education to parishioners. Barrios's restructuring of the university emphasized professional and technical education at the expense of the humanities and liberal arts, another reflection of positivist thinking.

Barrios put great emphasis on material progress. Coffee exports increased enormously as he encouraged the encroachment of ladino planters on Indian communal lands and made their labor more accessible to planters, began a railroad system, and developed ports and roads. He facilitated formation of banks and other financial institutions to provide credit for economic development and modernization. New ministries of agriculture, development, and education reflected this emphasis on economic growth as well as the increased role of the state. Barrios also attracted immigration and investment from overseas; German and U.S. influence increased notably. His administration codified the laws and promulgated a new constitution in 1879, under which he was reelected in 1880. His policies spurred substantial modernization of both Guatemala City and Quetzaltenango.

In foreign affairs Barrios played an important role in the neighboring states of El Salvador and Honduras, and in 1882 he settled differences with Mexico at the cost of giving up Guatemalan claims to Soconusco and other parts of Chiapas. He renewed the Guatemalan claim to Belize, however, repudiating the WYKE-AYCINENA TREATY of 1859 with Great Britain. He also tried to revive the unionist spirit of Francisco Morazán and sought to reestablish the Central American federation by means of Guatemalan military power. That effort, however, ended abruptly in 1885 when Salvadoran forces defeated the Guatemalan army at Chalchuapa, where Barrios died in battle.

Barrios established a new "coffee elite" centered in the western highlands around Quetzaltenango, reducing the power of the Guatemala City merchant elite that had dominated the country since the late colonial period. At the same time, he greatly accelerated exploitation of the indigenous population and moved Guatemala more rapidly into an export-led economy dependent on foreign markets and investment. Although celebrated in Guatemalan history as the "Reformer" who ended the long Conservative dictatorships of Rafael Carrera and Vicente Cerna (1839–1871), his own dictatorial rule and strengthening of the military established a pattern of repressive government for subsequent Liberal governments even to the present. Barrios's personal wealth increased enormously during his rule, especially in comparison with earlier Guatemalan presidents. In this, too, he set a pattern that many of his successors would emulate.

Although there is an extensive literature on Barrios in Spanish, there is relatively little in English. The standard biography is PAUL BURGESS, *Justo Rufino Barrios: A Biography* (1926, 2d ed. 1946). JIM HANDY, *Gift of the Devil: A History of Guatemala* (1984), has a useful chapter on the Barrios period. Excellent for understanding his economic policy is DAVID J. MC CREERY, *Development and the State in Reforma Guatemala, 1871–1885* (1983). Two helpful doctoral dissertations are available in English, but have been published only in Spanish: HUBERT J. MILLER, *La iglesia y el estado en tiempo de Justo Rufino Barrios* (1976); and THOMAS R. HERRICK, *Desarrollo económico y político de Guatemala durante el período de Justo Rufino Barrios (1871–1885)* (1974). Among the many works by Central American authors, the most useful are PEDRO JOAQUÍN CHAMORRO ZELAYA, *El patrón: Estudio histórico sobre la personalidad del General Justo Rufino Barrios*

(1966); CARLOS WYLD OSPINA, *El autócrata: Ensayo político-social* (1929); VÍCTOR MIGUEL DÍAZ, *Barrios ante la posteridad* (1935); and CASIMIRO D. RUBIO, *Biografía del general Justo Rufino Barrios, reformador de Guatemala: Recopilación histórica y documentada* (1935).

RALPH LEE WOODWARD, JR.

*See also* **Central America; Education.**

**BARRIOS DE CHAMORRO, VIOLETA** (*b.* 18 October 1929), president of Nicaragua (1990–). Elected president as the representative of the fourteen-party National Opposition Union (Unión Nacional Opositora—UNO) coalition, Barrios de Chamorro seemed an unlikely candidate. She was born in the southern Nicaraguan province of Rivas to wealthy, landowning parents and attended Catholic schools. In 1950 she married Pedro Joaquín CHAMORRO CARDENAL, a leader of the middle-class opposition to the dictatorship of the SOMOZA family. Nonetheless, her political participation during the decades of the 1950s, 1960s, and 1970s was confined to that of supportive wife and mother.

In January 1978 Chamorro Cardenal was assassinated, probably by a member of the Somoza family. The assassination set off a wave of strikes and mass insurrection that helped carry the Sandinista Liberation Front (Frente Sandinista de la Liberación Nacional—FSLN) into power. Doña Violeta, as she is called, was named a member of the five-person ruling junta. She resigned from that body less than a year later.

For the remainder of the 1980s, her political participation was confined to criticizing the FSLN and supporting the CONTRA war from her position as owner of

Violeta Barrios de Chamorro campaigning in the general elections of 1990. JASON BLEIBTREU / SYGMA.

the daily newspaper LA PRENSA, which she inherited from her late husband. Other members of her family took more prominent roles in politics.

Barrios de Chamorro reentered formal politics when she ran for president in 1990. Running on the promises to end the Contra war and repair the economy, she portrayed herself as the traditional mother who would reconcile the Nicaraguan family just as she had reconciled her own politically torn family. She won the election with 55 percent of the vote.

Since Barrios de Chamorro's election, the civil war has ended, for the most part. Massive devaluations and cuts in real wages (now among the lowest in the hemisphere) have eliminated hyperinflation. Her relative independence from the United States, whose support was essential in putting her into power, has come as something of a surprise to both her supporters and detractors. Her administration has often chosen to govern in coalition with moderates in the FSLN rather than with the far-right members of the UNO. This choice has hastened the disintegration of the inherently unstable fourteen-party UNO coalition.

SALMAN RUSHDIE, "Doña Violeta's Version," in *The Jaguar Smile: A Nicaraguan Journey* (1987), pp. 145–153; DENIS LYNN DALY HEYCK, "Violeta Chamorro," in *Life Stories of the Nicaraguan Revolution* (1990), pp. 37–52; KAREN KAMPWIRTH, "The Mother of the Nicaraguans: Doña Violeta and the UNO's Gender Agenda" in *Latin American Perspectives* (1995).

KAREN KAMPWIRTH

*See also* **Nicaragua: Political Parties.**

**BARROS, ADHEMAR DE** (*b.* 22 April 1901; *d.* 12 March 1969), three-time governor of São Paulo (1957–1961), and frequent populist candidate for president (1955, 1960, 1965).

The Barros family lived on its extensive coffee lands and owned businesses in the interior of São Paulo. Adhemar attended high school in the capital, completed his medical training in Rio, and interned in Europe. His political career began with Getúlio VARGAS's surprise appointment as state interventor in 1938. Adhemar seized the opportunity to build hospitals, roads, clinics, and schools, making a name for himself as a vigorous administrator.

In 1945 Adhemar formed the populist-style Social Progressive Party (PSP) and ran for governor in 1947. Finding his upper-class background a hindrance, he adopted the image of a rough-and-tumble provincial. Spending both his own and illicitly raised money, he hired publicity experts, conducted polls, purchased media exposure, and flew his own airplane to expand his following. In office he stressed building programs— schools, hospitals, highways, and dams—that glorified his image as "the manager." Tempted by the presidency in 1950, he withdrew in favor of Vargas with the understanding that the latter would support him in 1955.

Adhemar's flamboyant career was blocked by the meteoric rise of Jânio QUADROS, who defeated him in the 1954 gubernatorial election. An indictment for corruption stalled his campaign for president the following year. Absolved of the charges and vindicated by his mayoral victory in 1957 and his gubernatorial defeat of Quadros in 1963, Adhemar hoped to win the presidency in 1965. The military revoked his political rights because of graft, however, and he died three years later in self-imposed exile.

THOMAS E. SKIDMORE, *Politics in Brazil, 1930–1964* (1967); GUITA GRIN DEBERT, *Idelogia e populismo* (1979); REGINA SAMPAIO, *Adhemar de Barros e o PSP* (1982); ISRAEL BELOCH and ALZIRA ALVES DE ABREU, comps., *Dicionário histórico-biográfico brasileiro, 1930–1983* (1984).

MICHAEL L. CONNIFF

**BARROS, JOÃO DE** (*b.* ca. 1496; *d.* 21 October 1570), bureaucrat, humanist, lord-proprietor (*donatario*) in Brazil, historian. The son of a member of the lower nobility, João de Barros served as a page to Prince João, future king of Portugal. From 1525 to 1528 he was treasurer of the Casa da India, Mina, e Ceuta. In 1532 Barros became factor (*feitor*) of the Casa da India e Guiné (also called the Casa da India e Mina), a post he held until 1567. He was the author of *Clarimundo* (1522), a romance of chivalry, and *Ropica Pnefma* (1532), an allegory greatly influenced by Erasmus.

In 1535 Barros became the seventh of the twelve lords-proprietor to be awarded hereditary captaincies in Brazil between 1534 and 1536. He received several grants of land on the northern coast of Brazil along with two other lords-proprietor, Aires da Cunha and Fernão Álvares de Andrade. In 1535 the three lords-proprietor financed an expedition to explore and settle their lands, but most of the fleet was shipwrecked and little came of the effort. In 1555 or 1556, Barros sent another expedition that included his sons, Jerónimo and João, but this effort, too, was unsuccessful, leaving Barros in very serious financial straits. Many historians, unaware of the second expedition, have combined the two into one and have asserted, without evidence, that Barros's sons were on the 1535 voyage. After suffering a stroke in 1567, Barros retired to his country estate, São Lourenço do Ribeiro de Alitem, near Pombal, where he died.

Published between 1552 and 1615, Barros's most important literary work was the four-volume *Décadas de Asia*, modeled on Livy's *History*. Covering Portugal's overseas activity to 1538, the work is of great value to historians because of Barros's access to materials as factor of the Casa da India e Guiné, his incorporation of Portuguese translations of Asian chronicles and other documents that have since disappeared, and his use of eyewitness accounts of those Portuguese returning from overseas.

A very good biography in English is CHARLES R. BOXER, *João de Barros: Portuguese Humanist and Historian of Asia* (1981). A number of documents regarding the career of Barros were published by ANTÓNIO BAIÃO, "Documents inéditos sôbre João de Barros," in *Boletim da segunda classe*, vol 11, edited by Academia das Sciências de Lisboa (1916–1917), pp. 202–355. The major documents for the grant of his captaincy in Brazil, and not included in the preceding work, are transcribed by ANTÓNIO BAIÃO in his introduction to the fourth edition of *Asia de Joam de Barros* (1932), the first of the *Décadas*. Also useful in assessing Barros's role as a humanist strongly influenced by Erasmus is JOSÉ V. DE PINA MARTINS, *Humanismo e Erasmismo na cultura portuguesa do século XVI: Estudo e textos* (1973).

FRANCIS A. DUTRA

*See also* **Explorers and Exploration.**

**BARROS ARANA, DIEGO** (*b.* 16 August 1830; *d.* 14 November 1906), Chilean historian and diplomat. One of Chile's premier scholars, Barros Arana graduated from the Instituto Nacional, Chile's finest secular high school. As a liberal historian he tended to equate conservative ideology with backwardness; consequently, his works tended to flay both the Roman Catholic church and the authoritarian regime of Manuel MONTT. He was a professor at the University of Chile and later was the director of the Instituto Nacional. He enjoyed an active political life, serving as a deputy for the Liberal Party. Barros Arana's articles in various newspapers so incensed Montt that Barros Arana fled his homeland.

Upon his return, he took up once again a life of scholarship and public service. An extremely prolific historian, Barros Arana published a variety of biographies as well as a multivolume history of Chile. He also acted as Chile's minister to Argentina, where he negotiated a treaty resolving the question of the ownership of PATAGONIA. Rather than follow his instructions, Barros Arana gave up Chile's claim to the disputed territory, permitting the Argentines to occupy TIERRA DEL FUEGO. This act not only compromised Chile's claims to vast territory but also threatened Santiago's vital trade routes to Europe. Recalled in disgrace to Chile, he became an object of public scorn, although he continued in public life, serving as a deputy. Barros Arana's scholarship had a lasting impact on Chilean intellectual life, influencing subsequent generations.

GERTRUDE YEAGER, *Barros Arana's Historia jeneral de Chile: Politics, History, and National Identity* (1981); ALLEN WOLL, *A Functional Past: The Uses of History in Nineteenth-Century Chile* (1982).

WILLIAM F. SATER

**BARROSO, ARY** (*b.* 7 November 1903; *d.* 9 February 1964), Brazilian songwriter. Barroso was one of his country's most influential composers of samba music; his songs were renowned for their beautiful melodies and picturesque language, and often celebrated Brazil, its people, and culture. Barroso's "Aquarela do Brasil" (known elsewhere simply as "Brazil") ranks among the world's best-known popular tunes of the twentieth century.

Born in Ubá, Minas Gerais, Barroso moved in 1920 to Rio, where he played for dance-hall orchestras and later became a successful writer of hit songs for Carnaval. He helped develop the genre called *samba-canção*, a softer, more sophisticated SAMBA that emphasized melody more than rhythm and featured more complex harmonies. With "Aquarela do Brasil" (Watercolor of Brazil), Barroso created another style, *samba-exaltação*, so-called for its characteristic grand, epic songs with soaring melodies that "exalted" a particular subject. Among his other standards are "Na batucada da vida" (a strong indictment of poverty), "No tabuleiro da baiana" (On the Baiana's Tray), "Na baixa do sapateiro" (also called "Bahia"), "Rio de Janeiro," and "Inquietação" (Disquiet).

For the last fifty years, Barroso has been one of the most recorded Brazilian composers both inside and outside his country, and his songs have reached the world through the animated films of Walt Disney (such as *The Three Caballeros*), movies such as Terry Gilliam's *Brazil* (1985), and countless interpretations by world pop and jazz artists. "Aquarela do Brasil" rivals "The Girl From Ipanema" as the most internationally famous Brazilian tune of all time.

VASCO MARIZ, *A canção brasileira*, 5th ed. (1985); CHRIS MC GOWAN and RICARDO PESSANHA, *The Brazilian Sound: Samba, Bossa Nova, and the Popular Music of Brazil* (1991).

CHRIS MCGOWAN

**BARROSO, GUSTAVO DODT** (*b.* 29 December 1888; *d.* 3 December 1959), Brazilian writer, journalist, and politician. Barroso was a pioneer of the Brazilian folklore movement known as Northeastern Regionalism. Under the pen name "João do Norte" he wrote *Terra de sol* (1912), in which he praised the backlands peasantry for hard work, devotion to family, religious zeal, and closeness to nature. In *Heróes e bandidos: Os cangaceiros de Nordeste* (1917), he adopted the view that backlands bandits such as Antonio Silvino were predisposed to crime because of their race, lack of education, and the "savagery" of their environment. In the 1930s he became a supporter and one of the most influential propagandists of *integralismo*, the Brazilian variant of FASCISM.

Born in Fortaleza, Ceará, Barroso studied in Ceará, attended the Law School of Fortaleza from 1907 to 1909, and graduated in 1911 from the Law School of Rio de Janeiro. In 1914 he was appointed secretary of justice and interior for the state of Ceará and later directed *Diário Oficial*. A prolific writer, he published 128 books, including folklore, short stories, history, biography, criticism, plays, poetry, essays, a dictionary, memoirs, translations, and children's readers. He founded and directed the National Historic Museum, edited the Rio magazines *Fon-Fon* and *Selecta,* and served on the 1919 Brazilian delegation to the Versailles Peace Congress. In March 1923 he was elected a member of the BRAZILIAN ACADEMY OF LETTERS. Other writings include *O integralismo em marcha* (1933) and *O que o integralista deve saber* (1935).

RAIMUNDO DE MENEZES, *Dicionário literário brasileiro, ilustrado* (1969); RALPH DELLA CAVA, *Miracle at Joaseiro* (1970).

TERESA MEADE

**BARRUNDIA, JOSÉ FRANCISCO** (*b.* 12 May 1787; *d.* 4 August 1854), proponent of Central American independence, ideological leader of the radical liberals during the early national period. The son of prominent Guatemalan CREOLES Martín Barrundia and Teresa Cepeda y Coronado, Barrundia was a brilliant lawyer, orator, and writer. Educated in Guatemala, he was among the intellectual elite of the late colonial period. In 1811 he translated John Milton's *Paradise Lost* and several classical Italian works into Spanish.

As a *regidor* (alderman) on the Guatemala City Coun-

José Francisco Barrundia. Anonymous engraving. BENSON LATIN AMERICAN COLLECTION, UNIVERSITY OF TEXAS AT AUSTIN.

cil, Barrundia revealed his liberal political views. He participated in the ill-fated BELÉN CONSPIRACY of 1813 but escaped capture and a death sentence by hiding from the police of Captain General José BUSTAMANTE Y GUERRA for the next five years. As a member of the Tertulia Patriótica, along with José María Castilla, Pedro MOLINA, Manuel Montúfar, Marcial Zebadúa, and José Beteta, he plotted Guatemalan independence. He also joined with Molina in editing the pro-independence newspapers *El Editor Constitucional* and *El Genio de la Libertad.* When Barrundia opposed annexation to Mexico, Captain General Vicente FILÍSOLA branded him a terrorist and "dangerous subject." Upon the separation of Central America from Mexico in 1823, Barrundia served on the Council of Government (1823–1825) and was a co-author of the Constitution of 1824. In 1825 he was elected as the first vice president of the UNITED PROVINCES OF CENTRAL AMERICA but refused the office.

Barrundia's erudite writings in periodicals, several of which he edited, made him one of the most influential liberals of his era. His strident, uncompromising liberalism made him appear arrogant to some, but he was foremost among the so-called *exaltados,* or *fiebres,* of the early national period. He served briefly as president of the United Provinces (26 June 1829–16 September 1830), but it was in the legislatures of both Central America and Guatemala that his leadership was most prominent. In the election of 1830, Francisco MORAZÁN defeated him for the presidency of Central America, but the speech Barrundia delivered in turning over the office of president to Morazán was eloquent and gracious. He was elected governor of Guatemala in the same year, but he refused that office, preferring to remain in the legislature. His essays and other political writings formed a major part of the liberal polemic in Guatemala for the first thirty years of independence.

Under Governor Mariano GÁLVEZ (1831–1838) Barrundia served as minister of education, and he was also the major advocate for Guatemala's 1836 adoption of Louisiana's LIVINGSTON CODES of penal law, which he translated from English. Division among the liberals led him to oppose Gálvez in 1837 and collaborate briefly with Rafael CARRERA, the peasant guerrilla leader, to bring down Gálvez's government in 1838. He was unable to control the rebel caudillo, however, and spent much of the remainder of his life in exile, actively conspiring to overthrow the Conservative Carrera. He played a prominent part in the brief Liberal Revolution of 1848 in Guatemala but was once more forced into exile.

Barrundia spent his last years in Washington, where he served from 1852 until his death (in New York) as the Honduran minister to the United States. He was the leading ideologue and champion of the liberal cause in Central America and a strong supporter of Francisco Morazán and Central American union.

DAVID VELA, *Barrundia ante el espejo de su tiempo,* 2 vols. (1956–1957), is the standard work on Barrundia. In English, MARIO RODRÍGUEZ, *The Cádiz Experiment in Central America, 1808 to*

1826 (1978), and *A Palmerstonian Diplomat in Central America* (1964), both contain insight on Barrundia's career, as does RALPH LEE WOODWARD, JR., *Rafael Carrera and the Emergence of the Republic of Guatemala, 1821–1871* (1993).

RALPH LEE WOODWARD, JR.

**BARRUNDIA, JUAN** (*b*. 8 October 1788; *d*. ca. 1843), first governor of the state of Guatemala (12 October 1824–6 September 1826) following its organization within the UNITED PROVINCES OF CENTRAL AMERICA in 1824. Like his better-known brother, José Francisco BARRUNDIA, he was among the radical liberals (*fiebres*) who supported the independence movement. In 1826 federal president Manuel José ARCE deposed and imprisoned him. After his release, Barrundia hid out in Suchitepéquez until Francisco Morazán's military triumph of 1829. MORAZÁN restored Barrundia as governor of Guatemala, and Barrundia served from 30 April 1829 until 30 August 1829, when the legislature elected Pedro MOLINA to succeed him. Doctor Mariano GÁLVEZ defeated Barrundia for the governorship in the election of 1831. In 1836 Barrundia presided over the federal congress in San Salvador. With a conservative change in government, he went into exile at San Cristóbal de las Casas, Chiapas, Mexico, where he died.

DAVID VELA, *Barrundia ante el espejo de su tiempo*, 2 vols. (1956–1957).

RALPH LEE WOODWARD, JR.

**BASADRE, JORGE** (*b*. 12 February 1903; *d*. 24 June 1980), Peru's most prolific twentieth-century historian. He was trained in the schools of Lima and the National University of San Marcos, where he earned the Litt.D. and LL.D. degrees. In 1928 he joined the Faculty of Letters at San Marcos as a professor of history and then, in 1931, the Faculty of Law. In addition to teaching, he administered the university library for two terms in the 1930s and 1940s, and during World War II he directed the National Library. There he launched a drive to make the library's treasures more accessible to scholars. At the end of the war he served as minister of public education in the national government (1945). Historians throughout the world recognized his work. He received honors from many academies and visiting appointments to the Carnegie Foundation (1931–1932), the Ibero-American Institution of Berlin (1932), the Universidad de Sevilla (1933), and the Universidad de Buenos Aires (1942). He wrote a prodigious number of historical studies, which began to appear in the 1920s and did not stop until after his death. Among the more widely known are *La iniciación de la república* (2 vols., 1929–1930), *La multitud, la ciudad y el campo en la historia del Perú* (1929), *Perú: Problema y posibilidad* (1931), and the renowned *Historia de la república del Perú, 1822–1933*. Begun in 1939 as a three-volume survey, a sixth edition

(1968–1970) expanded the encyclopedic history of the republic to a monumental 17 volumes.

To complement this great work, Basadre compiled a two-volume *Introducción a las bases documentales para la historia de la república del Perú, con algunas reflexiones* (1971), an erudite evaluation of the sources used in the expanded history. With illustrations and introductory essays to each section, it stands as a major work in its own right. His numerous articles appeared in newspapers and historical journals in several languages. Many were collected in a single posthumous volume, *La vida y la historia* (1975).

HOWARD CLINE, *Latin American History: Essays on Its Study and Teaching, 1898–1965*, 2 vols. (1967), pp. 413–460; *Historia; problema y promesa: Homenaje a Jorge Basadre*, 2 vols. (1978).

VINCENT PELOSO

**BASALDÚA, HECTOR** (*b*. 29 September 1895; *d*. 21 February 1976), Argentine painter, printmaker, stage designer, and illustrator. Basaldúa was born in Pergamino, Buenos Aires Province. In 1914 he studied in the capital city at the private academy of the Italian artist Bolognini, and later at the National Academy of Fine Arts under Pío Collivadino. Between 1923 and 1930 he studied in Paris under Charles Guérin, André Lothe, and Othon Friesz. Basaldúa received a gold medal for stage design at the Paris International Exhibition, in 1937, and first prize for painting at the Argentine National Salon of Plastic Arts. He visited the United States to study theater techniques in 1946, and was the designer of opera and ballet sets at the Teatro Colón, Buenos Aires. In 1980 the National Museum of Fine Arts, in Buenos Aires, held a retrospective of his works. A quick perception of reality and an unerring feeling for decorative effect are basic to Basaldúa's work. His activity as a stage designer and book illustrator gave to his work an artificial tone related to rapidly captured images.

*Museum of Modern Art in Latin America* (1985); VICENTE GESUALDO, ALDO VIGLIONE, and RODOLFO SANTOS, *Diccionario de artistas plásticos en la Argentina* (1988).

AMALIA CORTINA ARAVENA

**BASEBALL.** *See* **Sports.**

**BASEL, TREATY OF (1795),** an agreement between France and Spain that restored to Spain peninsular territory lost during the Franco-Spanish War (1793–1795) and gave France Santo Domingo. Spain was ill prepared for war, and when defeat appeared inevitable, Manuel de GODOY led the way out, an effort which earned him the title "Prince of Peace." His justifications for making peace were economic difficulties, a shortage of troops, and lack of money—hardly novel conditions in eighteenth-century Spain. The treaty angered the British, who subsequently renewed a vigorous and damaging attack on Spanish shipping; in October 1796, Spain declared war on Great Britain. In 1797 the British navy imposed a total blockade on Cádiz and reduced the number of ships that arrived from 171 in 1796 to 9 in 1797.

ANDRÉS MURIEL, *Historia de Carlos IV* (1959): JOHN FISHER, *Commercial Relations Between Spain and Spanish America in the Era of Free Trade, 1778–1796* (1985).

SUZANNE HILES BURKHOLDER

**BASES ORGÁNICAS,** Mexican constitutional charter. In October 1841, General Antonio López de SANTA ANNA took control of Mexico following a successful revolt against the incumbent president, Anastasio BUSTA-MANTE. To the surprise of many observers, Santa Anna permitted the election of a congress that was charged with drawing up a new constitution for the country. The congress met in 1842, but dominated by liberals and federalists, it proposed a constitution that Santa Anna did not like. Hence, as he had done in 1834, he used the army to force the closure of the congress. To replace it, he nominated an assembly of prominent citizens who were likewise charged with producing a new charter. They duly obliged with what was known as the Bases Orgánicas, promulgated on 14 June 1843. These comprised 202 articles that were to form the constitution of the nation. They stipulated a highly centralized government with political power firmly vested in the center and in the dominant social and financial elite. The Bases Orgánicas were replaced in 1846 when Mexico reverted to a federal form of government with the mercurial Santa Anna once again at its head.

For the text of the Bases Orgánicas, see FELIPE TENA RAMÍREZ, *Leyes fundamentales de Mexico, 1808–1971* (1971), pp. 405–436.

MICHAEL P. COSTELOE

*See also* **Mexico: Constitutions.**

**BASSO MAGLIO, VICENTE** (*b.* 22 December 1889; *d.* 15 September 1961), Uruguayan poet, writer, journalist, and editor. His career in journalism began when he was an editor for *La Reforma, El Día,* and *La Razón,* all in Montevideo. Subsequently he was director of *El espectador* and its subsidiary broadcasting system, Difusoras del Uruguay. Basso Maglio's most acclaimed poetry collection, *Canción de los pequeños círculos y de los grandes horizontes* (1927), features the poet's transcendental, mystical comprehension of the relationship between man and God. His dense, hermetic expression sometimes reveals an excessive confidence in abstract symbols to communicate the complex web of relationships linking inner and outer reality. Other works by Basso Maglio include the acclaimed *La expresión heróica* (1928) and *Tragedia de la imagen* (1930), a work on modern art.

SARAH BOLLO, *Literatura uruguaya, 1807–1965,* vol. 2 (1965); FRANCISCO AGUILERA and GEORGETTE MAGASSY DORN, *The Archive of Hispanic Literature on Tape: A Descriptive Guide* (1974).

WILLIAM H. KATRA

**BASSOLS, NARCISO** (*b.* 22 October 1897; *d.* 24 July 1959), Mexican intellectual and public official, a member of the intellectual generation of 1915, whose leaders, the "Seven Wise Men," included Alfonso CASO Y ANDRADE, Manuel GÓMEZ MORÍN, and Vicente LOMBARDO TOLEDANO.

Born in Tenango del Valle, Bassols was the greatnephew of President Sebastián Lerdo de Tejada and the son of a humble judge, Narciso Bassols. He attended the National Preparatory School in Mexico City (1911–1915), and graduated from the National School of Law on 29 May 1920, after which he taught at both institutions. At the law school he made his mark as a brilliant professor, and scores of his students went on to become leading public officials. As dean of the law school from 1928 to 1929, he attempted to introduce academic reforms, including a trimester system, which provoked a student rebellion. Meanwhile, in addition to his academic duties, he wrote the agrarian law of 1927. He continued teaching law, becoming professor of constitutional law and of writs and guarantees, but left teaching in 1931 to pursue a career in public life.

Bassols employed his multiple talents in reconstructing Mexico's modern banking system in 1930 and 1931. He also became a key cabinet member in the six-year interregnum between the presidencies of Plutarco ELÍAS CALLES and Lázaro CÁRDENAS, serving as secretary of public education (1931–1934) and secretary of government (1934). He served as secretary of the treasury in the first cabinet of Cárdenas, but believing loyalty and integrity to be more important than political expediency, he resigned in 1935, when Cárdenas broke with Calles. Bassols later served as ambassador to London, Paris, and Moscow. Disenchanted with the direction of public policy, in 1941 he founded the League of Political Action with Vicente Lombardo Toledano, and in 1947 he was one of the founders of the Popular Party, the forerunner of the Popular Socialist Party, which for many years was the only leftist opposition party in Mexico.

*Narciso Bassols: En memoria* (1960); JOHN W. F. DULLES, *Yesterday in Mexico: A Chronicle of the Revolution, 1919–1936* (1961); NARCISO BASSOLS, *Obras* (1964); and RODERIC AI CAMP, *Mexican Political Biographies, 1884–1935* (1991).

RODERIC AI CAMP

*See also* **Mexico: Political Parties.**

**BASTIDAS, RODRIGO DE** (*b.* ca. 1460; *d.* 1526), early Spanish explorer. With a royal commission to explore and trade, Bastidas sailed from Cádiz in 1500 or 1501 with three ships carrying more than fifty people, including some women. He was neither a pilot, an adventurer, nor a man of arms; rather, he was a successful and respected notary in Triana (Seville). He was also unusual among leaders of early expeditions because of his relatively humane treatment of the Indians. Exploring regions not previously seen by Europeans, he discovered the Magdalena River, the Gulf of Urabá, and eastern Panama. By contrast with most later expeditions in the area, his was remarkable for its comparatively good relations with the local inhabitants, whose wealth of gold and pearls was willingly traded for Spanish trinkets. Though his ships were wrecked, Bastidas salvaged seventy-five pounds of gold and pearls, returning to Spain a rich man. He moved his family to Hispaniola, where he prospered as a cattleman. Made governor of Santa Marta in 1520, Bastidas was assassinated in Cuba by an ambitious lieutenant.

Bastidas is discussed at some length in HUBERT HOWE BANCROFT, *History of Central America,* vol. 1 (1882). See also KATHLEEN ROMOLI, *Balboa of Darien, Discoverer of the Pacific* (1953), and CARL ORTWIN SAUER, *The Early Spanish Main* (1966).

WILLIAM L. SHERMAN

**BASURTO, LUIS** (*b.* 11 March 1920; *d.* 9 July 1990), Mexican playwright, actor, director, producer, and critic. A native of Mexico City, Basurto studied law, philosophy, and literature at the National Autonomous University of Mexico and began his career as a journalist. For many years he wrote film and theater reviews and a regular Thursday column in the *Crónica de México.* He was a tireless performer known throughout the Hispanic world. When he was awarded the Juan Ruiz de Alarcón Prize for literature shortly before his death, it was fitting tribute to a man who brought enormous talent and energy to the Mexican theater for more than fifty years.

Several of Basurto's twenty-six plays, some of which date from the 1940s, have become classics of the Mexican repertory. In more than 7,000 performances *Cada quien su vida* (1955) has shown with compassion and understanding the realities of Mexico's marginal classes during a New Year's Eve celebration. Other major works include *Los reyes del mundo* (1959), *Con la frente en el polvo* (1967), and *El candidato de Dios* (1986). At the time of his death Basurto was directing *Corona de sangre* (1990), the history of Padre Pro, who was executed for treason without trial in 1927 but had recently been beatified by the Vatican. Many of his plays have strongly Catholic themes. Basurto was adept at mixing sensational and often degenerate aspects of society with a strong social message.

FRANK DAUSTER, *Historia del teatro hispanoamericano (siglos XIX y XX),* 2d ed., (1973).

GEORGE WOODYARD

**BATÁN GRANDE,** region in the mid-La Leche Valley at the northern end of the north coast of Peru. Much of the area comprises the *yunga* life zone, which is characterized by year-round humidity and intense sun. From the early twentieth century until 1969, Batán Grande was owned by the Juan Aurich hacienda, which produced cacao, citrus and other fruits, and rice. Since the 1969 AGRARIAN REFORM, intensive commercial cultivation of sugarcane has predominated.

The extensive forest of algaroba (*Prosopis pallida*) situated in the western portion of Batán Grande is the largest (at least 25 square miles) of its kind remaining on the Peruvian coast today. Protected as the Poma National Archaeological and Ecological Reserve, it provides a refuge area for diverse fauna that has largely disappeared elsewhere on the coast, such as iguana, squirrels, anteaters, parrots and numerous other bird species, and even boa constrictors. The reserve also protects at least thirty major archaeological sites (spanning ca. 2000 B.C. to A.D. 1532), including the site of SICÁN, the capital of the Middle Sicán religious state that controlled or influenced much of the Peruvian coast from circa A.D. 900 to 1100. Cemeteries around these mounds contain numerous shaft tombs endowed with impressive quantities of precious and base metal objects. Organized grave looting, beginning in the 1930s—some of the worst ever seen in the New World—has brought infamy to the region.

Batán Grande was a major pre-Hispanic metallurgical center from circa A.D. 900 up to the time of the Spanish Conquest. In fact, the name Batán Grande derives from the numerous metal-working tools in its vicinity. The *batán* is a large anvil stone with a shallow central concavity used in conjunction with a rocking stone, called a *chungo,* to crush ore for and slag from arsenical copper (a type of bronze) smelting.

At the time of the Conquest, local inhabitants spoke the now extinct Muchik language and belonged to the ethnic polities of Jayanca and Túcume, according to Sebastián de la Gama's *Visita de Jayanca* (1540).

PAUL KOSOK, *Life, Land, and Water in Ancient Peru* (1965), pp. 115–180; IZUMI SHIMADA, "Temples of Time: The Ancient Burial and Religious Center of Batán Grande, Peru," in *Archaeology* 34, no. 5 (1981): 37–45; SUSAN RAMÍREZ, "Social Frontiers and the Territorial Base of Curacazgos," in *Andean Civilization and Ecology,* edited by Shozo Masuda, Izumi Shimada, and Craig Morris (1985), pp. 423–442; IZUMI SHIMADA, "Cultural Continuities and Discontinuities on the Northern North Coast, Middle-Late Horizons," in *The Northern Dynasties: Kingship and Statecraft in Chimor,* edited by Michael E. Moseley and Alana Cordy-Collins (1990), pp. 297–392.

IZUMI SHIMADA

**BATISTA, CÍCERO ROMÃO** (Padre Cícero) (*b.* 24 March 1844; *d.* 20 July 1934), Brazilian priest and political leader of Ceará. Born at Crato in Juàzeiro, in 1865 Cícero entered the seminary at Fortaleza and was one of its first graduates. Ordained in 1870, he began his clerical career as a teacher in Crato. Two years later he was

Padre Cícero. ICONOGRAPHIA.

appointed to the chaplaincy in Juàzeiro. In 1889, a communion wafer Cícero administered reportedly turned to blood in the mouth of one of his parishioners. This "miracle" gave him religious power, which he later converted into political strength; he became one of the most influential political bosses in the Northeast, and the village of Juàzeiro became a site for religious pilgrimages. Although the church disavowed the "miracle" and restricted his religious activities, it made no attempt to remove him, for the peasants of the interior regarded him as a saint. Although he clashed with both ecclesiastical and governmental authority, his movement did not seek to destroy political or religious order, but rather attempted to improve the social and economic conditions of his followers. Juàzeiro do Norte became the economic and industrial center of the backlands under his leadership. His followers marched on Fortaleza, bringing about the downfall of its state government. Padre Cícero continues to be regarded as an unofficial saint in the Northeast, and each year large numbers of pilgrims gather at his grave in Juàzeiro.

RALPH DELLA CAVA, *Miracle at Joaseiro* (1970); RONALD M. SCHNEIDER, *"Order and Progress": A Political History of Brazil* (1991).

MICHAEL L. JAMES

**BATISTA Y ZALDÍVAR, FULGENCIO** (*b.* 16 January 1901; *d.* 6 August 1973), the Cuban army's strongman in the 1930s, elected president in the 1940s, and dictator in the 1950s. The son of a farm and railroad laborer, Batista was born in Banes, Oriente Province. He spent his early years in poverty and attended a Quaker missionary school. At twenty he joined the Cuban army because it offered an opportunity for upward mobility. He attended evening classes at the National School of Journalism, from which he graduated. In 1928 he was promoted to sergeant and assigned as stenographer at Camp Columbia in Havana.

The deepening economic depression and the overthrow of Gerardo MACHADO's dictatorship in 1933 had released a wave of uncontrolled anger and anxiety. Unhappy with a proposed reduction in pay and an order restricting their promotions, the lower echelons of the army began to conspire. On 4 September 1933, Batista, together with anti-Machado student leaders, assumed the leadership of the movement, arrested army officers, and overthrew the provisional government of Carlos Manuel de CÉSPEDES. They appointed a five-man junta (the Pentarchy) to rule Cuba and, on 10 September, named Ramón GRAU SAN MARTÍN as provisional president. Grau's nationalistic and revolutionary regime was opposed by the United States, which refused to recognize it. Batista soon became a colonel and chief of staff of the army.

On 14 January 1934, the alliance between students and the military collapsed. Batista forced Grau to resign, thus frustrating the revolutionary process that had begun with Machado's overthrow. Batista ruled through puppet presidents until 1940, when he was elected president. Desiring to win popular support, he sponsored an impressive body of welfare legislation. Public administration, health, education, and public works improved. He legalized the Cuban Communist Party and in 1943 established diplomatic relations with the Soviet Union. Immediately following the Pearl Harbor attack, Batista brought Cuba into World War II on the Allied side. Air and naval bases were made available to the United States, which purchased all of Cuba's sugar production and provided generous loans and grants. In 1944 Batista allowed the election of his former rival, Grau San Martín.

Batista settled in Daytona Beach, Florida, where he wrote *Sombras de América* (published in Mexico in 1946). In 1948, while still in Florida, he was elected to the Cuban Senate from Santa Clara province. He returned to Cuba that same year, organized his own party, and announced his presidential candidacy for the June 1952 elections. On 10 March 1952, however, Batista, joined by a group of army officers, overthrew the constitutionally elected regime of President Carlos Prío Socarrás. Batista suspended Congress and the 1940 constitution, canceled the elections, and dissolved all political parties. University students soon began to show their opposition by rioting and demonstrating. On 26 July 1953, young revolutionaries led by Fidel CASTRO unsuccessfully attacked the Moncada military barracks in Oriente Province. Some of the attackers were killed and others, including Castro, were jailed.

In a rigged election in November 1954, Batista was reelected for a four-year term. Corruption in his administration reached unprecedented proportions, leading students to increase their protests. After his release from prison in 1956, the revolutionary leader Fidel Castro went to Mexico to prepare an expedition that landed in Cuba in December of that year and began guerrilla operations. On 13 March 1957, an attack on the Presidential Palace by students and followers of deposed President Prío nearly succeeded in killing Batista. The Batista government met terrorism with counterterrorism. By 1958 national revulsion against Batista had developed. Finally, defections from the army precipitated the fall of the regime on 1 January 1959. Batista escaped to the Dominican Republic and later to Madeira. He died at Guadalmina, near Marbella, Spain.

HUGH THOMAS, *Cuba: The Pursuit of Freedom* (1971); JAIME SUCHLICKI, *Historical Dictionary of Cuba* (1988) and *Cuba: From Columbus to Castro,* 3d ed. (1990).

JAIME SUCHLICKI

**BATLLE, LORENZO** (*b.* 10 August 1810; *d.* 8 May 1887), general and president of Uruguay (1868–1872). When the Great War (GUERRA GRANDE) began in 1839, Batlle became a captain on the side of the Colorado Party (Unitario) and played an active role in the circle associated with the *Defensa* of Montevideo. From 1847 to 1851, he was minister of war and the navy in the cabinet of Joaquín Suárez and became a central figure in the postwar period, which was characterized by political experimentation, efforts toward a stable peace, and the ongoing debate concerning political parties. First he joined the ranks of the so-called Conservative Party, a Colorado group with an oligarchic slant and strong support from the military and financial sectors. He subsequently became a member of the Liberal Union and then returned to the Colorados. He became minister of finance in the government of Gabriel Antonio Pereira (1856–1857) and minister of war and the navy again during the dictatorship of Venancio FLORES (1865–1868).

Batlle was elected president in 1868, introducing a "politics of partisanship" with a decided elitist bent. During his administration, he faced a grave economic crisis, permanent conflict with his party's regional caudillos, and the outbreak of the so-called Revolution of the Lances led by the Blanco caudillo Timoteo Aparicio. After his presidency, he went into a long period of retirement from public life, interrupted only in 1886 when he became a leader of the Quebracho Revolution against the dictatorship of General Máximo Santos. Batlle died in poverty a year later.

JUAN E. PIVEL DEVOTO, *Historia de los partidos políticos en el Uruguay,* 2 vols. (1942); JOSÉ P. BARRÁN and BENJAMÍN NAHUM, *Historia rural del Uruguay moderno,* vol. 1 (1967); LUCÍA SALA DE TOURÓN and ROSA ALONSO ELOY, *El Uruguay comercial, pastoril y caudillesco,* vol. 2 (1990).

GERARDO CAETANO

*See also* **Uruguay: Political Parties.**

**BATLLE BERRES, LUIS CONRADO** (*b.* 1897; *d.* July 1964), president of Uruguay (1947–1951). Luis Batlle Berres was the nephew of the great leader of the Colorado Party and founder of modern Uruguay, José BATLLE Y ORDÓÑEZ. He began his political career in the 1920s as a deputy in Congress for Montevideo. Elected vice president in 1946, he succeeded to the presidency upon the death of Tomás BERRETA. Smart and ambitious, "Lusito," as he was known, found himself constrained by the Batllist faithful, the adoring but increasingly conservative followers of José Batlle led by his sons Lorenzo and César. In 1948 Batlle Berres had signaled his independence by starting his own newspaper, *Acción,* as a voice separate from EL DÍA, the Colorado newspaper founded by José Batlle and run by his sons. He thus distanced his own political movement, List 15, from his cousins' List 14. His faction proved to be dominant within the party in the 1950 elections.

Batlle Berres favored the continuation of a presidential system, even in the face of an almost religious demand by the Batllist faithful to create a COLEGIADO (collegial executive system). Batlle Berres's urban populist coalition had swept his faction to such a convincing victory in 1950 that the Blanco (National Party) leader, Luis Alberto de HERRERA, was willing to join with Lorenzo and César in support of a collegial executive in order to prevent a new political dynasty. Unable to withstand the List 14 and Herrerist calls for constitutional reform, Batlle Berres supported the 1951 plebiscite that gave Uruguay a collegial executive system under the new 1952 Constitution. Nevertheless, Batlle Berres's List 15 continued to dominate Colorado voting, giving him the most powerful voice in Uruguayan politics through the mid-1950s. Following his death, the leadership of List 15 passed to his son Jorge Batlle, and this sector of the party became known as Radical Batllism.

PHILIP R. TAYLOR, JR., *Government and Politics of Uruguay* (1960); SANTIAGO ROMPANI, ed., *Luis Batlle: Pensamiento y acción,* 2 vols. (1965); MARTIN WEINSTEIN, *Uruguay: The Politics of Failure* (1975).

MARTIN WEINSTEIN

*See also* **Batllismo; Uruguay: Political Parties.**

**BATLLE Y ORDÓÑEZ, JOSÉ** (*b.* 21 May 1856; *d.* 20 October 1929), journalist and president of Uruguay (1903–1907, 1911–1915). One of the most important and influential personalities in Uruguayan history, José Batlle y Ordóñez's first avocation was philosophy rather than politics. With an initial Catholic education, he was influenced as a youth by the ideas of Karl Christian Friedrich Kraus. His transition to a rationalist, spiritualist philosophy would mark his later public career. Also early in his life, he began a lifelong journalism career, writing for such periodicals as *La Razón, La Lucha,* and *El Espíritu Nuevo.*

FROM ANTIMILITARISM TO SOCIAL REFORM

Batlle y Ordóñez began his political life between 1876 and 1886, confronting the military dictatorships of Lorenzo LATORRE and Máximo Santos. He participated in the 1886 Quebracho Revolution against Santos, which, despite military defeat, marked the beginning of a political transition toward civilian rule. In this same year he founded the newspaper *El Día,* which served as a mouthpiece for the Colorado Party. From its pages, he led the opposition to the Santos regime. After its early financial problems and government repression, *El Día*'s low price and street distribution caused it to become the foremost newspaper in Uruguayan history.

With Santos out of power, Batlle y Ordóñez—part of the group of allies of then Minister Julio HERRERA Y OBES—was appointed as political chief of the department of Minas by President Máximo TAJES. This was his first position as a public servant, and it lasted only six months. Already deeply involved in the political militancy of the Colorado Party, he was elected to the Chamber of Deputies in 1893 and the Senate in 1896. He opposed the oligarchic practices of President Herrera y Obes (1890–1894) and worked intensely on the organization of a popular faction within the Colorado Party. He adamantly opposed the presidency of Juan Idiarte Borda, who, assassinated in 1897, never finished his term.

Batlle y Ordóñez supported the rise to power of Juan L. CUESTAS, which began a dramatic political ascent that would win him the presidency of the Senate. He supported the 10 February 1898 coup led by Cuestas and formed part of the interim state council. He was considered a favorite to succeed to the presidency in 1903, but in 1901 he seemed to lose all chances when he strongly rejected the Blancos (Nationalists) and was displaced from the presidency of the Senate. Cuestas withdrew his support for Batlle y Ordóñez due to the latter's proven independence of character. Conservative Uruguayans also began to oppose Batlle. They saw him as a "war candidate," due to his growing ill-will toward the Nationalists and his doctrinaire defense of the "politics of partisanship," which threatened the system of COPARTICIPACIÓN. They also mistrusted some of the reformist ideas he outlined in his critiques of the gold-supporting

oligarchy in 1891 and in his editorials supporting workers' movements in 1895.

GOVERNMENT AND CIVIL WAR

With arduous effort, Batlle y Ordóñez won over the internal factions of the Colorados along with a group of dissident Blancos. This assured him a majority among the legislators. He was elected president by the General Assembly on 1 March 1903. His first presidency was marked by the Blanco uprisings of 1903 and 1904 led by the caudillo Aparicio SARAVIA. Batlle y Ordóñez was also confronted by two antagonistic visions of the political future of the country: the continuance and deepening of *coparticipación* versus the "politics of partisanship." Saravia's death in 1904 marked the end of the revolution and the consolidation of "partisanship."

Reformist measures adopted during the first administration of Batlle y Ordóñez included the abolition of the death penalty, legalization of divorce by mutual consent, a law of labor regulation, expansion of public education, creation of the Colleges of Commerce and of Agronomy

José Batlle y Ordóñez. ORGANIZATION OF AMERICAN STATES.

and Veterinary Science, and a plan for public works and roads. At the end of his presidential term in 1907, Batlle y Ordóñez left almost immediately on a trip to Europe and the Near East that lasted almost four years. In 1907 he participated in the Second International Peace Conference in The Hague. While visiting many European countries, he studied their social conflicts and joined in ideological debates, thereby polishing many of the ideas and proposals that constituted the reformist plan he would implement during his second presidential term. He returned to Uruguay in February 1911 and on 1 March was again elected president by an overwhelming majority of legislators in the General Assembly. (The Blanco Party had abstained from the legislative elections in 1910 after another attempt at revolution failed.)

THE RISE AND FALL OF REFORM

The second presidency of Batlle y Ordóñez constituted the decisive period during which his reformist plan was implemented. The debate over a broad range of initiatives dominated the public stage. These reforms generated strong resistance from the Blanco Party (which abandoned its abstentionist posture in 1913), from management guilds, from foreign capital (especially British), and from the army.

The Batllist plan was organized around six major reforms. First, economic reform was based on the nationalization of strategic sectors and industrialization through protectionist legislation. Second, social reform centered on "critical support" for unions, "protective" social legislation for workers and other philanthropic measures. Third, rural reform was aimed at the gradual elimination of large ranches, the promotion of a more balanced and automated livestock industry, and the transformation of rural poverty. Fourth, fiscal reform sought tax increases for the wealthy, a decrease in taxes on consumption, the use of economic pressure as an instrument of social justice, and the stimulation of economic development. Fifth, moral reform promoted the concept of a cosmopolitan nation, secular politics, and various feminist principles. Finally, political reform promoted public debate and supported proposals that the executive branch be organized in a collegiate system.

Not all of these reforms came to fruition, due in some cases to strong opposition and in others to ambiguity among the Batllists themselves. Also, proposals for political reform did not include essential democratic changes that the opposition demanded, such as the secret ballot, proportional representation, and guarantees against electoral fraud. The essence of the reform plan was implemented before the democratization of the political system, which occurred with the second constitution in 1919. Batllism suffered a defeat in the decisive elections of 30 July 1916 for members of the National Constituent Assembly. Batlle's successor to the presidency, Feliciano VIERA, adopted the so-called "halt politics," which drastically decreased proposals for reform.

From 1916 to the end of the 1920s, the predominant atmosphere in public policy favored putting the brakes on reform. Batllism gradually lost its political initiative and strength.

THE LAST YEARS

Although with less power than earlier, Batlle y Ordóñez continued to be politically active throughout the last years of his life. He was one of the fundamental backers of the political accord from which sprang the new constitution. In 1921 and 1927 he served briefly as president of the National Council of Administration, the central component of the new collegiate executive branch. He was a major force behind the effort to attain electoral unity among distinct Colorado Party factions. He made exhausting tours of the country, seeking grassroots support for his reforms, and until his death he led the often acerbic debates in the inner recesses of the Colorado Party. Even in the midst of political uproar, he constantly promoted political debate from the pages of *El Día*.

Batlle y Ordóñez died just a few days before the great stock market crash on Wall Street. The Great Depression had its effects on Uruguay, among them putting a halt to a good part of the reformist projects of Batllism. Most of the first three decades of the twentieth century in Uruguay are referred to by historians as the Batllist Era. Whether in a spirit of polemic or agreement, the ideas and symbols associated with Batlle y Ordóñez remain present in the Uruguayan public debate.

MILTON VANGER, *José Batlle y Ordóñez of Uruguay, the Creator of His Times, 1902–1907* (1963) and *El país modelo* (1983); CARLOS REAL DE AZÚA, *El impulso y su freno* (1964); GÖRAN LINDAHL, *Batlle, fundador de la democracia en el Uruguay* (1971); JOSÉ P. BARRÁN and BENJAMÍN NAHUM, *Historia rural del Uruguay moderno*, vols. 5–7 (1977–1978), and *Batlle, los estancieros y el Imperio Británico*, 8 vols. (1979–1987); CARLOS ZUBILLAGA, *El reto financiero: Deuda externa y desarrollo en el Uruguay, 1903–1933* (1982); *El primer batllismo: Cinco enfoques polémicos* (1985); RAÚL JACOB, *Modelo batllista: ¿Variación sobre un viejo tema?* (1988); GERARDO CAETANO, *La República Conservadora, 1916–1929*, 2 vols. (1992–1993).

GERARDO CAETANO

*See also* **Uruguay: Political Parties.**

**BATLLISMO,** the political philosophy and social program of José BATLLE Y ORDÓÑEZ (1856–1929), president of Uruguay (1903–1907, 1911–1915). It was a philosophy that emphasized nationalism and social, political, and economic development. While recognizing the economic inequalities among men, Batlle did not subscribe to Marxist interpretations of class struggle. For him, the best way to solve the differences in society was by creating an interventionist state to regulate the imbalances of society and work for a more equitable distribution of wealth. *Batllismo* held that a modern state could operate only with a politically active population aware of its rights and obligations. Therefore, elections and mechanisms for political participation were considered to be very important. While in office, Batlle enacted an extensive social program and nationalized industries.

ROBERTO B. GIUDICI, *Batlle y el batllismo* (1928), and *Los fundamentos del batllismo*, 2d ed. (1947); MARTIN WEINSTEIN, *Uruguay: The Politics of Failure* (1975).

JUAN MANUEL PÉREZ

*See also* **Uruguay: Political Parties.**

**BATON ROUGE, BATTLE OF,** a conflict between British and Spanish troops on 21 September 1779. Baton Rouge, Louisiana, which had formerly been French, became part of British West Florida in the 1763 Treaty of Paris. Spain decided to take the frontier post when it declared war on Britain during the American Revolution. General Bernardo de GÁLVEZ led a force of over 1,000 men from New Orleans in an attack on the British fort commanded by Lieutenant Alexander Dickson. Gálvez laid siege to the main redoubt with ten heavy cannons during the night of 20 September and began a devastating bombardment the following morning. With the fort damaged beyond repair, the British surrendered that afternoon with little loss of life on either side. Dickson also surrendered British claims to Natchez, thereby giving Spain the entire Mississippi River valley.

JOHN W. CAUGHEY, *Bernardo de Gálvez in Louisiana, 1776–1783* (1934); JACK D. L. HOLMES, *The 1779 "Marcha de Gálvez": Louisiana's Giant Step Forward in the American Revolution* (1974); J. BARTON STARR, *The American Revolution in West Florida* (1976).

LIGHT TOWNSEND CUMMINS

**BATRES JUARROS, LUIS** (*b.* 7 May 1802; *d.* 17 June 1862), Guatemalan politician and businessman. Born in Guatemala City, Batres Juarros received a law degree from San Carlos University in 1823. He fought against Francisco MORAZÁN in the civil war and then emigrated to the United States for a time. After 1839 he became a very important figure among supporters of the Guatemalan conservative regime. He served several terms as a representative in Congress and was a minister of war, of finance, and of the interior. He also held the positions of mayor of Guatemala City (1845), state advisor, and attaché to the consulate of commerce. He played a key role in the drafting of the Constitution of the Republic in 1851, reorganized the mint, and defended the reestablishment of the Jesuits in 1851.

*Noticia biográfica del Señor Don Luis Batres* (1862); LORENZO MONTÚFAR Y RIVERA MAESTRE, *Reseña histórica de Centro América*, 7 vols. (1878–1888); MIGUEL GARCÍA GRANADOS, *Memorias del General García Granados* (1952); MARIO RODRÍGUEZ, *A Palmerstonian Diplomat in Central America: Frederick Chatfield, Esq.* (1964); LUIS BELTRANENA SINIBALDI, *Fundación de la República de Guatemala* (1971); PEDRO TOBAR CRUZ, *Los montañeses* (1971);

AGUSTÍN ESTRADA MONROY, ed., *Hombres, fechas y documentos de la patria* (1977).

ARTURO TARACENA ARRIOLA

**BATRES MONTÚFAR, JOSÉ** (*b.* 18 March 1809; *d.* 9 July 1844), Guatemalan writer, soldier, and politician. Born in San Salvador, in 1824 he entered the Cadet School, and with the rank of second lieutenant of artillery, he participated in the FEDERAL WAR at the side of President Arce. He was taken prisoner in the battle of Mexicanos in 1828. While in prison he learned English and began to read Byron, who inspired his later literary work. In 1829 he returned to Guatemala and began his career as a writer. Of primary note are his lyrical compositions in the romantic style, especially *Tradiciones de Guatemala*, which consists of three satirical pieces—the last unfinished—in which he describes the life-style and mentality of the dominant class in Guatemala at the beginning of the nineteenth century. These are written along the lines of the *Novelle galanti* of Giovanni Casti.

In 1836, Batres Montúfar graduated from the Academía de Estudios, and as a surveyor he participated in the 1837 engineering commission that, under the direction of John Baily, explored the San Juan River of Nicaragua for the possible development of an interoceanic canal. His younger brother Juan died during this endeavor. He was named political head of Amatitlán in 1839, and in 1840 fought as captain of artillery, defending Guatemala City against Francisco MORAZÁN. In 1842 he was elected as a representative to Congress from the department of San Marcos.

JOSÉ BATRES MONTÚFAR, *Poesías de José Batres y Montúfar* (1845); FERNANDO CRUZ, "El poeta D. José Batres," in *Biografías de literatos nacionales*, vol. 1 (1889), pp. 153–260; ANTONIO BATRES JÁUREGUI, *José Batres Montúfar* (1910); JOSÉ ARZÚ, *Pepe Batres íntimo. Su familia, su correspondencia, sus papeles* (1940); ADRIÁN RECINOS, "Introducción," in *Poesías de José Batres Montúfar* (1940); THOMAS IRVING, "Pepe Batres, poeta de Guatemala," in *Revista Iberoamericana* 23, no. 45 (1958): 93–111.

ARTURO TARACENA ARRIOLA

**BAUXITE INDUSTRY.** Bauxite, the commercial source of aluminum and its compounds, has been mined in and exported from Latin America since World War I. Surinam, Guyana, Jamaica, Venezuela, Brazil, and on a much lesser scale Argentina, Haiti, Mexico, and the Dominican Republic have been or are involved in the bauxite-aluminum industry.

Early known South American deposits of bauxite were located in northern South America. British Guiana (now Guyana) and Netherlands Guiana (now Surinam) were producing two-thirds of the world's bauxite by the end of World War II. During that war, the bauxite reserves in Jamaica were seriously assessed, and Alcan aluminum, a Canadian company, began large-scale mining development, including the construction of Port Esquivel, during the 1950s. Two U.S.-based companies, Kaiser Bauxite and Alcoa (Aluminum Company of America), began Jamaican bauxite operations in the early 1960s. Haiti and the Dominican Republic were also mining bauxite on a much smaller scale.

By the 1960s, Latin American leaders were becoming alarmed because the mining of bauxite, a nonrenewable resource, was not proving beneficial to the countries of origin. Bauxite is strip-mined, and the work is not labor intensive. The ore was being shipped overseas for processing, and aluminum prices and production were controlled by multinational corporations. Regional authorities began to negotiate for a larger share of the profit, local construction of alumina refineries and smelters, and more local control over the decision-making process. Guyana's bauxite gave rise to political maneuvers that became volatile. In 1964 the victorious political faction guaranteed Alcoa the right to the peaceful removal of bauxite at constant 1938 prices, but the People's National Congress Party won a majority in 1973 and assumed control of all foreign trade in 1974, in part to meet the government policy of gaining a larger share of bauxite profits. Jamaica, with a growing sense of nationalism, demanded—and got—a 600 percent increase in its share of the profits and the right to purchase 51 percent of the Kaiser and Reynolds operations.

Venezuela's bauxite industry was developed during the 1960s and 1970s, using power from the government-built Guri Dam on the Caroni River to process Caribbean bauxite. Venalum, a subsidiary of Corporación Venezolana de Guyana (CVG), runs the largest alumina smelter in the world, and Interalumina, another CVG unit, operates a billion-dollar alumina-processing plant built in 1983 to handle bauxite discovered at Los Pijiguaos. Thus, CVG created the first fully integrated aluminum industry in the developing world, with all three stages (bauxite mining, alumina smelting, and aluminum production) under its control. At least half of the final product is contracted to a Japanese syndicate.

Bauxite was mined in Minas Gerais, in southeastern Brazil, before 1967, but until that year, when aerial side-looking radar surveys became possible, little was known about the huge bauxite deposits in Brazil's Amazon region. Brazil's mining and aluminum-processing facilities have expanded greatly since the original Trobetas project was completed in 1979, some 540 miles west of Belém, by the Mineração Rio do Norte (MRN). Throughout the 1980s, using a variety of financial and ownership arrangements with Alcan, Billiton Metais (a Shell subsidiary), Norsk Hydro (Norway), Reynolds Alumino (a Reynolds Aluminum subsidiary), and Nippon Amazon Aluminum (Japan), several Brazilian companies began bauxite, alumina, and aluminum production in the states of Pará, São Paulo, and Rio de Janeiro for domestic use and export primarily to Japan, Norway, and the United States.

Competition in the world's bauxite-aluminum industry is intense. Guinea and Australia have developed their huge bauxite deposits, and multinational companies remain dominant. Aluminum prices are strongly affected by recessionary times. (For example, in October 1990 the price of aluminum was 88 cents per pound; by September 1991 it had fallen to 56 cents per pound.) A continuing emphasis on using recycled aluminum has also reduced world demand. Venezuela and Brazil have managed to maintain competitive prices, but Jamaican production dropped 40 percent after 1980, and Surinam, which has been plagued by recurring civil disorder since gaining independence in 1975, has been unable to guarantee delivery of the only known abrasive-grade bauxite in the Western Hemisphere. Industries that utilize this substance for precise grinding and metal finishing have thus turned to sources outside Latin America.

EDUARDO GALEANO, *Open Veins of Latin America: Five Centuries of the Pillage of a Continent* (1973); ROSEMARY D. F. BROMLEY and RAY BROMLEY, *South American Development: A Geographical Introduction* (1982); UNITED NATIONS, *Latin American Development in the 1980s* (1982); ROBERT N. GWYNNE, *Industrialization and Urbanization in Latin America* (1986); U.S. DEPARTMENT OF THE INTERIOR, BUREAU OF MINES, *Minerals and Materials* (1987, 1988, 1989); HENRY R. ENSIMINGER, *The Mineral Industry of Brazil* (1988); CLIVE Y. THOMAS, *The Poor and the Powerless: Economic Policy and Change in the Caribbean* (1988); ERROL D. SEHNK and PATRICIA A. PLUNKER, *Bauxite, Alumina, and Aluminum* (1989); U.S. DEPARTMENT OF THE INTERIOR, BUREAU OF MINES, *Minerals Yearbook Area Reports* (1990).

LESLEY R. LUSTER

**BAY OF PIGS INVASION,** the U.S.-sponsored military venture into revolutionary Cuba on 17 April 1961. The invasion by U.S.-backed Cuban exiles was a major watershed in both the CUBAN REVOLUTION and the relations between Cuba and the United States. The invasion was the result of escalating Cold War fears within the Eisenhower administration about the revolutionary processes at work in Cuba. Although the exact point at which the United States decided to use Cuban exiles to militarily overthrow the Castro regime is uncertain, by the fall of 1960 the CENTRAL INTELLIGENCE AGENCY was actively training about 1,500 troops in Guatemala for that purpose.

Escalating tension over expropriations of U.S. assets and property in Cuba drove the planning until January 1961, when incoming President John F. Kennedy gave his approval to Eisenhower's plan for the invasion, with the single condition that U.S. forces not be directly involved. Just three months later an invading force of approximately 1,300 men landed at the Bay of Pigs, on the island's south coast, and were quickly defeated by well-armed Cuban forces under the personal command of President Fidel CASTRO. Twelve hundred men were captured, but they were released after the United States agreed to send $53 million worth of medicine, food, and supplies.

The invasion failed for several reasons. An initial air strike on Cuban planes left several intact, and Kennedy would not allow U.S. forces to destroy them. These planes gave the defending Cubans a decisive advantage. The U.S. also overestimated the level of discontent within the country. Having counted on simultaneous uprisings within Cuba, U.S. planners were dismayed by the lack of support for the invasion and shocked by the effectiveness of the Cuban military response.

Within Cuba, the images of Fidel Castro personally directing the defeat of the U.S.'s proxy army provided the revolutionary leader with a massive boost in popularity and proved a crucial factor in the consolidation of his domestic political support. With the prestige afforded by the victory at the Bay of Pigs, Castro officially declared Cuba a socialist nation.

PETER WYDEN, *Bay of Pigs: The Untold Story* (1979); TRUMBULL HIGGINS, *The Perfect Failure: Kennedy, Eisenhower, and the CIA at the Bay of Pigs* (1987).

TODD LITTLE-SIEBOLD

**BAZAINE, FRANÇOIS ACHILLE** (*b.* 13 February 1811; *d.* 23 September 1888), French military commander in Mexico (1863–1867). Born near Metz, Bazaine joined the French Foreign Legion in 1832, serving in Algeria and Spain. He served with General Élie-Frédéric Forey in the Crimea (1854–1856) and in the Italian campaign (1859). Bazaine took North African troops with him to Mexico in 1863, and NAPOLEON III appointed him on 16 July 1863 as supreme commander of FRENCH INTERVENTION forces, replacing Forey.

In Mexico, Bazaine's aim was to reconcile the various factions and win over moderate opinion to the empire. He disliked the Mexican Conservatives and followed Napoleon's policy of blocking any reversal of the Reform Laws. He became critical of Emperor MAXIMILIAN's indecision. The peak of Bazaine's career was the Oaxaca campaign of 1865. With 8,000 men he took the city on 9 February and captured Porfirio DÍAZ, Liberal military commander. He put into effect Napoleon's evacuation policy during 1866 and left Mexico on the last convoy on 12 March 1867, returning to France without military honors, since Mexico had already become an embarrassment to Napoleon.

At the outbreak of the Franco-Prussian War in 1870, Bazaine commanded the 103,000 men of the Third Army Corps, with headquarters at Metz. Although he held down a Prussian army in Lorraine, he was unjustly accused of treason for surrendering Metz in October 1870 after a seventy-day siege. After returning from captivity in Germany and seventeen months of house arrest, he was courtmartialed on 6 October 1873 and sentenced to twenty years on the prison island of Sainte Marguerite, from which he escaped on 10 August 1874. He spent the last years of his life in Spain.

JACK AUTREY DABBS, *The French Army in Mexico, 1861–1867* (1963); ALFRED. J. HANNA and KATHRYN A. HANNA, *Napoleon III and Mexico: American Triumph over Monarchy* (1971).

BRIAN HAMNETT

*See also* **Miramón, Miguel.**

**BAZÁN, JUAN GREGORIO** (*d.* 1570), conquistador of Tucumán province and lieutenant governor. Begun in 1549, the permanent occupation of Tucumán was characterized by jurisdictional conflicts between Spaniards. Bazán, born in Talavera de la Reina, Spain, was present at the founding of Santiago del Estero (1553) and of San Miguel de Tucumán (1565), and became governor of the town of Esteco in 1567. He unsuccessfully combed the countryside for Indians to serve as laborers for newly founded towns. The Lules Indians attacked him and his party on their return from Peru, where he had gone to meet his newly arrived family. Bazán was killed, as was his son-in-law, Diego Gómez de Pedraza, who uttered a phrase during the battle that has remained part of Argentine folklore: "Caballero soy y no voy huyendo" ("I am a gentleman, and I do not flee").

ROBERTO LEVILLIER, *Descubrimiento y población del norte argentino* (1943); RICARDO LEVENE, *A History of Argentina* (1963).

NICHOLAS P. CUSHNER

**BEAGLE CHANNEL DISPUTE,** the territorial conflict between Argentina and Chile that brought the two countries to the brink of war in 1978. The Beagle Channel (named after Charles Darwin's ship) lies at the tip of South America, just south of TIERRA DEL FUEGO. An 1881 treaty between Argentina and Chile established the Beagle Channel as their international border for part of the Tierra del Fuego area, but the treaty did not specify the exact location of the channel. Of particular interest was whether the Beagle Channel—and thus the border—ran north of the three key islands of Picton, Lennox, and Nueva (which would make them Chilean), or south of the islands (which would make them Argentine). The issue was not the islands themselves, which are cold and barren, but rather that ownership of them might allow Chile to claim sovereignty or establish an exclusive economic zone 200 miles into the South Atlantic, inhibiting Argentina's ability to project its influence into that region, its key islands (including the FALKLAND ISLANDS), and ANTARCTICA.

In July 1971 Argentina and Chile agreed to accept Great Britain as arbitrator in an arrangement under which the crown would either accept or reject the recommendation of an expert panel of international jurists. The panel decided in favor of Chilean sovereignty of the three islands, and in May 1977 the British government accepted their recommendation. Argentina rejected the award on narrow technical grounds, and both countries began to prepare for possible conflict. At what seemed to be the last minute before hostilities broke out, the two nations agreed to Vatican mediation in December 1978. This mediation led to the 1984 Treaty of Peace and Friendship, which awarded the islands to Chile, but prohibited Chile from claiming sovereignty or establishing an economic zone in the South Atlantic.

JACK CHILD, *Geopolitics and Conflict in South America: Quarrels Among the Neighbors* (1985), esp. pp. 77–85; MICHAEL A. MORRIS, "Southern Cone Maritime Security After the 1984 Argentine-Chilean Treaty of Peace and Friendship," in *Ocean Development and International Law* 18, no. 2 (1987): 235–254; PHILIP KELLY and JACK CHILD, eds., *Geopolitics of the Southern Cone and Antarctica* (1988), esp. pp. 36–39 and 75–77.

JACK CHILD

**BEALS, CARLETON** (*b*. 13 November 1893; *d*. 26 June 1979), leftist journalist from the United States who specialized in Latin America. Born in Kansas and educated at the University of California, Berkeley, Beals covered political unrest and social change from Mexico in the latter years of Venustiano Carranza (1914–1920) to the Cuba of Fidel Castro. An outspoken opponent of U.S. threats against the Mexican government's ostensibly radical policies in the mid-1920s, he was also one of the few observers to criticize President Plutarco Elías Calles's abandonment of these plans and movement toward authoritarianism.

Beals's most dramatic feat was his interview with Nicaraguan rebel Augusto SANDINO in the war-torn jungles of Nicaragua in February 1928. While not entirely uncritical, his series of articles in *The Nation* conveyed the strengths of the Sandino movement at a crucial point in the debate concerning the U.S. military intervention.

A member of the cosmopolitan intellectual community of Mexico City in the 1920s, Beals met and wrote about many of Latin America's political and cultural leaders of the era, including the Mexican muralist Diego Rivera and the Peruvian politician-intellectual Víctor Raúl Haya de la Torre. He was one of the few reporters to deplore the 1954 overthrow of Guatemala's leftist government by the United States. The final chapter in his Latin American career was his coverage of Fidel Castro's revolution in Cuba in the 1950s. Later Beals wrote popular fiction and local U.S. history.

Two of Beals's many books are *Mexican Maze* (1931) and *Banana Gold* (1932). See also JOHN A. BRITTON, *Carleton Beals: A Radical Journalist in Latin America* (1987).

JOHN A. BRITTON

**BEANS,** widely cultivated legumes that have nourished the people of Latin America for millennia. Throughout the region, few meals lack beans. In Mexico, people typically eat mashed beans with corn tortillas, whereas in

Brazil, since colonial times, a ladle of soupy beans poured over rice is the core component of many daily diets. In this way, the majority of Latin Americans survive on the near complete protein provided by a mixture of beans and rice or maize.

While hundreds of species exist, many of them indigenous to the American tropics, the multiple varieties of the common bean (*phaseolus vulgaris*), including dried black, pinto, and red beans, are the most widespread in Latin America. Another species, commonly known as lima or butter beans (*phaseolus lunatus*), is also widely grown in the region. Both were among the earliest domesticated plants of the Western Hemisphere, with evidence of their cultivation dating from 7000–5000 B.C.

Archaeologists differ over the locations in which bean agriculture first developed in America, but it is now believed that it occurred independently in Mexico's Tamaulipas desert and Peru's highland Callejon de Hayulas valley. The culture gradually spread throughout North and South America well before 1492. After Columbus, Europeans eventually recognized the utility of dried beans on long ocean voyages, and their journeys helped introduce American beans throughout the world.

The production of beans has generally been taken for granted in Latin America. Their low cost and high nutritional value assured that they were always being cultivated by someone. Indians grew them with maize, weaving the vines between stalks of corn. On sugarcane plantations, captive Africans commonly received small plots of land in order to grow beans to feed themselves. Peasants invariably mixed beans with other subsistence crops. Coffee growers frequently left extra space between the rows of trees in order to intercrop beans and other vegetables.

Competing export crops and livestock land uses have caused problems for bean farming in Latin America. The expansion of soybean agriculture in the last decades of the twentieth century reduced the land devoted to growing common beans, and in Brazil the once ubiquitous black bean nearly disappeared from the market. At the same time, the population explosion caused increased demand, and bean prices skyrocketed. To keep underpaid workers fed, some governments subsidized bean farmers, while many others artificially manipulated prices. All the same, as late as 1980, small family farmers produced more than three-quarters of the beans grown in Latin America, revealing the continued decentralization of bean cultivation.

Bean supply shortages and price hikes worsened as Latin American governments tried to liberalize their economies. Strapped by heavy foreign debt burdens, officials simultaneously encouraged foreign-exchange–earning export crops while cutting back on subsidies for staple crops like beans. In the inflation-plagued 1980s and 1990s, fluctuations in the availability of beans and other basic foodstuffs contributed to social and political unrest in Peru, Argentina, and Venezuela. In Brazil, the looting of supermarkets in cities such as Rio de Janeiro became commonplace in 1992.

ALVIN SILVERSTEIN and VIRGINIA SILVERSTEIN, *Beans: All About Them* (1975); LUIS LÓPEZ CORDOVEZ, "Trends and Recent Changes in the Latin American Food and Agriculture Situation," in *CEPAL Review* (April 1982): 7–41; CHARLES B. HEISER, JR., *Seed to Civilization: The Story of Food,* new ed. (1990).

CLIFF WELCH

**BEAR FLAG REVOLT,** an 1846 uprising by Anglo-American settlers against Mexico. On 14 June 1846 a group of thirty-three Anglo-American California settlers led by a trapper named Ezekiel Merritt took control of the plaza in the town of Sonoma north of San Francisco and proclaimed a California Republic. When the Mexican garrison in Sonoma capitulated without a fight, the Bear Flaggers took Colonel Mariano G. VALLEJO, commander of the garrison, and his brother Salvador to Captain John C. Frémont's camp near the confluence of the Sacramento and San Joaquin rivers. FRÉMONT, on a topographical mission for the U.S. government, covertly encouraged the proclamation of the California republic but remained officially aloof.

The Bear Flaggers controlled Sonoma until July 1846, when U.S. forces began the occupation of Alta California. Although rumors of war between Mexico and the United States had been circulating through the U.S. naval force off the California coast, the Bear Flag proclamation was the immediate catalyst for the U.S. conquest of the province. Commodore John D. Sloat, commander of the U.S. Pacific squadron, assuming that Frémont had already received news of the MEXICAN-AMERICAN WAR, calculated that blame could be shifted to Frémont if the occupation of California proved premature. Thus, on 7 July 1846, Sloat landed a force of marines at Monterey, initiating the conquest of CALIFORNIA.

ROBERT S. SMILIE, *The Sonoma Mission* (1975); DAVID J. WEBER, *The Mexican Frontier, 1821–1846: The American Southwest Under Mexico* (1982).

ROBERT H. JACKSON

**BECAN,** an ancient city-state located in the Mexican state of Campeche, near the geographical center of the Yucatán Peninsula. Occupation dates from about 600 B.C. to A.D. 900. The fortress of Becan, built probably by a classic MAYA group about A.D. 350, consists of a dry moat nearly 1.5 miles in circumference. The moat originally measured about 52 feet across and 16 feet deep with an earthen parapet on the interior lip of the moat, giving a total height from the bottom of about 45 feet. The seven narrow causeways that led into the fortress were all cut in the fourth century A.D., indicating that the city was threatened at that time. This was a general period of warfare among the aristocratic rulers of vari-

ous city and regional states as they attempted to expand their boundaries and power.

Becan appears to have fallen into a period of disuse after circa 500, another time of general disruption in the Maya lowlands. Between about 650 and 840 the city was revitalized, the moat cleaned out, and many large structures built. These buildings are in the Río Bec and Chenes architectural styles, with large "earth monster" mouth doorways and much serpent symbolism. Corner towers and the famed "false temple towers" of the Río Bec style are typical at Becan as well as at the site of Río Bec itself. Storage rooms, multi-apartment palaces, and reservoirs made the fortified zone highly functional.

The nearby sites of Río Bec, Xpuhil, and Chicanna were contemporary, and in the eighth century the surrounding countryside was packed with people and gridded with stone walls. Over 4,000 square miles of terraced hillsides and nearby wetland gardens in swamps attest to intensive food-production systems. The aristocrats of the Late Classic period in this region appear to have lived mainly on their country estates in small and large palaces.

A generalized feudal system characterized Late Classic social structure here. Warfare must have been a threat, however, considering that Becan was reactivated in the Late Classic period. Raids from Maya states farther to the north occurred at other sites and may have been feared here. In any event, the great collapse of southern Maya civilization was only slightly delayed in the Río Bec region, perhaps for a hundred years. By 1000 even the rural zone was deserted.

R. E. W. ADAMS, "Río Bec Archaeology and the Rise of Maya Civilization," in *The Origins of Maya Civilization,* edited by R. E. W. Adams (1977), and "Settlement Patterns of the Central Yucatan and Southern Campeche Regions," in *Lowland Maya Settlement Patterns,* edited by Wendy Ashmore (1981); SYLVANUS GRISWOLD MORLEY and GEORGE W. BRAINERD, *The Ancient Maya,* 4th ed., revised by Robert J. Sharer (1983), pp. 302–304.

R. E. W. ADAMS

**BECERRA-SCHMIDT, GUSTAVO** (*b.* 26 August 1925), Chilean composer. Becerra was born in Temuco and studied at the National Conservatory and at the Faculty of Musical Arts, University of Chile, under the guidance of Pedro Humberto ALLENDE and Domingo Santa Cruz. He taught composition and musical theory from 1953 to 1956. From 1958 to 1961 he was the director of the renowned Institute of Musical Extension and its research publication, *La revista musical chilena.* In 1969 he was elected to the Fine Arts Academy of Chile and two years later received the Premio Nacional de Arte. For a number of years he resided in Europe, serving as the cultural attaché at the Chilean embassy in Bonn. In 1974 he became a professor of composition at the University of Oldenburg (Germany).

At the beginning of his career Becerra cultivated a

neoclassical style, but soon started using more contemporary techniques, including dodecaphonism. The pointillism he practiced during the late 1950s and the 1960s gave way to a more romantic *Klangfarbenmelodie* (tone-color melody) and the use of what Becerra called a "complementary polychordal system." His String Quartets nos. 4, 5, and 6 (1958, 1959, 1960) and his Symphony no. 2 (1955–1958) are good examples of those techniques. Becerra also tried to combine more accessible musical elements into his works, like Chilean folk music and Javanese music, which he used with very modern devices.

During the 1960s Becerra experimented with aleatoric techniques, as in his Symphony no. 3 (1960), the Guitar Concertos nos. 1 and 2 (1964, 1968), and his oratorio *Macchu Picchu* (1966), with words by Chilean poet Pablo Neruda. Becerra composed works of pure experimental theater, such as *Juegos* (Games) for piano, Ping-Pong balls, and live recording (1966). Other important works by Becerra include String Quartet no. 7 (1961); Quintet for piano and string quartet (1962); a leftist political composition *Chile 1973,* for voice and small orchestra (1973–1974); Trio for flute, violin, and piano (1958); *Saxophone Quartet* (1959); *Llanto por el hermano solo* for choir (1966); *Responso para José Miguel Carrera* for voice, wind quintet, piano, and percussion (1967); *Morula, gastrulay blastula* (1969), for piano and tape (1969); *Provocation* (1972), a minidrama; *Parsifae* (1973), an opera; and *Diez trozos para ocho solistas* (1977).

*Primer festival de música de América y España* (1964), pp. 59, 63; LUIS MERINO MONTERO, "Los cuartetos de Gustavo Becerra," in *Revista musical chilena* 19 (1965): 44–78; JOHN VINTON, ed., *Dictionary of Contemporary Music* (1974), p. 61; GÉRARD BÉHAGUE, *Music in Latin America: An Introduction* (1979), pp. 320–321; *New Grove Dictionary of Music and Musicians* (1980).

ALCIDES LANZA

**BECKMAN REVOLT** (1684), a rebellion that resulted in the expulsion of the Jesuits from the captaincy of Maranhão and the removal of its governor. Both were responses to the actions of the Portuguese crown in 1680 prohibiting enslavement of the Brazilian Indians in the state of Maranhão, assigning their welfare to the JESUITS, and establishing a Lisbon-based company of merchants who pledged to furnish the state with 600 African slaves annually in return for a monopoly on its exports. Manoel Beckman, the wealthy planter who led the uprising, and many other rebels were hanged; five others received lesser sentences.

MURRAY GRAEME MAC NICOLL, "Seventeenth-Century Maranhão: Beckman's Revolt," in *Estudios Ibero-Americanos,* 4 (1978):129–140; JOHN HEMMING, *Red Gold: The Conquest of the Brazilian Indians* (1978).

DAURIL ALDEN

*See also* **Slavery: Brazil.**

**BEDOYA DE MOLINA, DOLORES** (Bedoya González, María Dolores; *b.* 20 September 1783; *d.* 9 July 1853), Guatemalan politician. Like most of her brothers, she was from early on an advocate of Central American independence. She married the statesman Pedro MOLINA in 1804 and moved to Granada, Nicaragua, where he served as doctor for the fixed battalion until 1811. On returning to Guatemala in 1814, she lent her support to her brother Mariano, imprisoned as a result of the BELÉN CONSPIRACY against Captain General José de BUSTAMENTE in 1813. She supported Molina's campaign for independence in the pages of *El Editor Constitucional,* and during the proclamation of independence from Spain on 15 September 1821, she led a crowd of advocates for independence outside the Palace of Government. Emancipation brought with it the conflict between republicans and those who favored annexation with the Mexican Empire of ITURBIDE. This conflict resulted in the assassination of Mariano Bedoya by the government's annexationist forces on 29 November 1821 and the exile of the Molina-Bedoya family to Verapaz. Bedoya always supported the political career of her husband, whether it was as leader of the Liberal Party, chief of state, or political exile.

CARLOS GÁNDARA DURÁN, *Pedro Molina* (1936); RUBÉN LEYTON RODRÍGUEZ, *Doctor Pedro Molina* (1958); JOSÉ ANTONIO MOBIL, *100 personajes históricos de Guatemala* (1979).

ARTURO TARACENA ARRIOLA

**BEDOYA REYES, LUIS** (*b.* 1919), Peruvian politician and lawyer, charismatic mayor of Lima for two terms (1964–1969), and a contender for the presidency of Peru in the elections of 1980 and 1985. His political activities started with his support of the civilian president José Luis BUSTAMANTE Y RIVERO (1945–1948). In 1956 he contributed to the formation of the centrist Christian Democratic Party (PDC) and became its first general secretary. His close links with Popular Action, headed by his friend Fernando BELAÚNDE TERRY, led to his nomination as minister of justice when Belaúnde was elected president in 1963. He renounced this ministerial post to run for mayor of Lima in 1964.

Clearly at odds with the PDC's leader, Héctor Cornejo Chávez, Bedoya formed the Christian Popular Party in 1966. Extremely popular in Lima, Bedoya headed the Right's feeble opposition to the military dictatorship between 1974 and 1980. In 1978, Bedoya received the second most votes as representative to the Constituent Assembly. He has since been associated with the political right, which suffered sound defeats in the presidential elections of 1985 and 1990.

PEDRO PABLO KUCZYNSKI, *Peruvian Democracy Under Economic Stress: An Account of the Belaúnde Administration, 1963–1968* (1977); JOHN CRABTREE, *Peru Under García: An Opportunity Lost* (1992).

ALFONSO W. QUIROZ

*See also* **Peru: Political Parties.**

**BEDREGAL DE CONITZER, YOLANDA** (*b.* 21 September 1918), Bolivian poet, novelist, and artist. Probably the best-known Bolivian female poet, Bedregal is called simply "Yolanda of Bolivia." She has received the most prestigious literary awards of Bolivia, among them, the Erich Guttentag National Prize for her novel *Bajo el oscuro sol* (1971). Her poetry covers a variety of themes and styles, but its most prominent characteristic is a special sensibility for childhood—she has written several books of poetry for children. Another very important subject in her writing is the land and native people of Bolivia. Although at times Bedregal casts the Indian in a romantic light, she grasps the spirit of Indian culture (especially AYMARA culture). In her latest poetry, such as the collection *Nadir* (1950), strongly religious (even mystical) motifs are evident.

Despite her importance to Bolivian literature, very few critical works have been published about Bedregal. For a general survey see MAJORIE AGOSIN, "Para un retrato de Yolanda Bedregal," *Revista iberoamericana* 52, no. 134 (1986): 267–270.

LEONARDO GARCÍA PABÓN

**BÉJAR, HÉCTOR,** Peruvian author, journalist, and Castroist guerrilla leader in the 1960s. Involved in radical politics since his years as an art and law student, he formed and led the Army of National Liberation (ELN), which launched a guerrilla campaign in 1965. In prison after 1966, he contributed to the understanding of the character, limitations, and rigidities of the Peruvian GUERRILLA MOVEMENT by writing a treatise prized and first published in Cuba. The guerrilla movement, he explained, developed out of the climate of rebellion and oppression after the end of General Manuel ODRÍA's dictatorship. Freed by the military government after the amnesty of 1970, Béjar accepted a government post to conduct official propaganda among peasants.

HÉCTOR BÉJAR, *Peru 1965: Notes on a Guerrilla Experience* (1970).

ALFONSO W. QUIROZ

*See also* **Peru: Revolutionary Movements.**

**BELALCÁZAR, SEBASTIÁN DE** (also Benalcázar: *b.* 1490?; *d.* 30 April 1551), Spanish conquistador. Born probably as Sebastián Moyano, like many illiterate and humble folk, Belalcázar changed his name to that of his home town: Belalcázar, province of Córdoba. His later fame and success demonstrated the possibilities for social mobility in the New World. Belalcázar came to Santo Domingo in 1507, joined Vasco Núñez de BALBOA in Darién in 1513, received an *encomienda* in Panama in 1519, and became first *alcalde* of León, Nicaragua, in 1523. Participating as captain in the capture of the Inca Emperor ATAHUALPA at Cajamarca, Peru, in 1532, he received 2.25 of the 217 shares of the booty amassed from Atahualpa's treasure and became rich.

Investing in new expeditions and freeing himself from the authority of Francisco PIZARRO, Belalcázar moved north and conquered southern Colombia. He helped found the cities of Quito in 1534, Guayaquil in 1535, and Cali and Popayán in 1536. In 1538 he pushed even farther north toward the gold and dense population of the Chibcha (MUISCA) Indians, but Gonzalo JIMÉNEZ DE QUESADA and Nicolás FÉDERMAN and their expeditions from Santa Marta and Coro, respectively, had already arrived. They each claimed the Chibcha territory but agreed in 1539 to journey to Spain together to resolve the dispute there.

Although unsuccessful in his Chibcha claim, Belalcázar received many honors in Spain. He was made governor of Popayán for life, had his three mestizo children legitimized, and married his son to a Spanish noblewoman. Back in Cali in 1542, he found himself reluctantly drawn into the Peruvian civil wars; he survived even when on the losing side, as in Viceroy Blasco NÚÑEZ VELA's defeat at Iñaquito in 1546. While others lost their heads, as Núñez Vela did, or were shunted aside, as Jiménez and Féderman were, Belalcázar successfully defended his governorship in southern Colombia against all comers from 1536 until his 1550 *residencia* (impeachment) and death sentence. That sentence, based on his 1546 execution of Jorge Robledo for encroaching on the Popayán territory, was being carried by Belalcázar to Spain for appeal when he died in Cartagena.

A comprehensive biography is DIEGO GARCÉS GIRALDO, *Sebastián de Belalcázar: Fundador de ciudades, 1490–1551* (1986). An older and never finished work detailing Belalcázar's day-by-day activities is JACINTO JIJÓN Y CAAMAÑO, *Sebastián de Belalcázar*, 3 vols. (1936–1949). For documents on Belalcázar, see JORGE A. GARCÉS G., ed., *Colección de documentos ineditos relativos al adelantado capitán don Sebastián de Belalcázar, 1535–1565* (1936). In English a succinct account can be found in JAMES MARVIN LOCKHART, *The Men of Cajamarca* (1972), pp. 122–129. A lively read is JOHN HEMMING, *The Search for El Dorado* (1978).

MAURICE P. BRUNGARDT

**BÉLANCE, RENÉ** (*b.* 28 September 1915), Haitian poet. After graduating from the École Normale (Port-au-Prince), Bélance entered government service (departments of justice and commerce). He wrote for *Le nouvelliste, Conjonction,* and *Optique,* among other journals. In an interview in *Callaloo,* he says he was mistakenly labeled a surrealist because his *Luminaires* (1943) was published at the same time as the "hermetic" work of Magloire Saint-Aude. After spending several years in Puerto Rico, Bélance settled in the United States and taught at Brown University. Although he wrote some metrical verse, he favors free verse and poetic prose, with deep roots in African rhythms and dance. He writes with a deceptive simplicity—"Je sais des musiques sereines / au charme délicieux." L.-S. Senghor saw him as "the most gifted of the young Haitian poets" (*Anthologie de la nouvelle poésie nègre et malgache,* 2d ed., 1969). Other poetical works by René Bélance include *Rythme de mon coeur* (1940), *Pour célébrer l'absence* (1943), *Survivances* (1944), *Épaule d'ombre* (1945), and *Nul ailleurs* (1983).

NAOMI M. GARRET, *The Renaissance of Haitian Poetry* (1963), pp. 175–184; F. RAPHAËL BERROU and PRADEL POMPILUS, *Histoire de la littérature haïtienne illustrée par les textes,* vol. 3 (1977), pp. 389–393; RENÉ BÉLANCE, "Poems and Interview," in *Callaloo* 15, no. 3 (1992): 601–610.

CARROL F. COATES

**BELAÚNDE, VÍCTOR ANDRÉS** (*b.* 15 December 1883; *d.* 14 December 1966), Peruvian intellectual, educator, publisher, and diplomat. Born in Arequipa and educated as a lawyer at the universities of Arequipa and San Marcos in Lima, Belaúnde taught history at San Marcos and the Catholic University. In addition to his academic activities, he headed the Boundaries Section of the Ministry of Foreign Affairs during the crucial period of international disputes with Ecuador, Colombia, and Chile between 1907 and 1911. His main intellectual contributions address the issues of Peruvian nationality and its role in solving national problems. Belaúnde was initially influenced by POSITIVISM before embracing French idealist and Catholic philosophies. He believed in the need to integrate Peruvians of disparate historical backgrounds within a Peruvian national ideal. He named this ideal *peruanidad* ("Peruvianness"). Peruvian social problems should not lead to revolutionary changes, as proposed by José Carlos MARIÁTEGUI and Víctor Raúl HAYA DE LA TORRE, but to social and cultural conciliation. Only through a strong feeling of national unity and a deep understanding of the genuine contributions of Peruvian history would Peru be able to form part of the community of modern nations.

Belaúnde publicized Peruvian cultural contributions as the editor of a new and third version of the landmark *Mercurio Peruano,* first published in 1791–1795. The new *Mercurio Peruano,* which appeared with brief interruptions between 1918 and 1978, published articles on a wide variety of national and international subjects. It became the longest-lasting cultural journal in Peru.

Exiled for his political opposition to President Augusto LEGUÍA (1919–1930), Belaúnde taught in several U.S. universities, including Columbia, Virginia, Miami, and Chicago. On his return to Peru in the early 1930s, he helped successfully mediate the border dispute between Colombia and Peru. As president of the Catholic University and minister of foreign affairs in 1957, he achieved national stature as an intellectual eminence. In his later years Belaúnde held a high diplomatic post at the United Nations in New York City, where he died.

See his *La realidad nacional* (1931), *Peruanidad* (1957), and *Meditaciones peruanas* (1963); and FREDERICK PIKE, *The Modern History of Peru* (1967).

ALFONSO W. QUIROZ

**BELAÚNDE TERRY, FERNANDO** (*b.* 7 October 1912), Peruvian politician, twice president of Peru (1963–1968, 1980–1985). Representing civilian centrist political forces opposed to militarism and the Peruvian Aprista Party's established influence, Belaúnde received enthusiastic initial support of his populist modernizing ideology. He was born in Lima to a family of intellectuals and politicians from Arequipa. His father, Rafael, brother of the distinguished nationalist intellectual Víctor Andrés BELAÚNDE, went into exile in France during Augusto B. LEGUÍA's regime in the early 1920s. Thus, Fernando was able to study mechanical and electrical engineering in Paris between 1924 and 1930 and later architecture at the universities of Miami and Texas, from which he graduated in 1935.

Upon his return to Lima, Belaúnde established in 1937 the professional journal *El Arquitecto Peruano,* which became an influential means of spreading modern ideas on urbanization. Belaúnde also became professor of urban studies and founder of the Institute of Urban Studies. In 1944, Belaúnde supported the successful bid for the presidency by José Luis BUSTAMANTE Y RIVERO's National Democratic Front. He consequently was elected congressional deputy for Lima. After Bustamante's ouster by a military coup in 1948, Belaúnde resumed his professional and teaching activities. With the return of

Fernando Belaúnde Terry, ca. 1980. RENÉ PINEDO / ARCHIVO CARETAS, LIMA.

democracy in 1956, Belaúnde's presidential candidacy was supported by the Front of Democratic Youth. Although he was not elected, Belaúnde was soon able to establish a new political party, Popular Action, which, together with the support of the Christian Democratic Party, would be the base for his second and successful candidacy for the presidency in 1962.

During his first presidency Belaúnde had to face the powerful opposition coalition of the Aprista Party and the Odriista National Union. He tried to carry out a program of extensive public works financed by foreign and domestic credit. However, between 1965 and 1968 inflation increased and political scandals (corruption, contraband, and unpopular agreements with a foreign oil company) were uncovered. Military pressure mounted as a consequence of the substantial authority ceded to the army to fight the guerrilla movement of 1965. The military ousted Belaúnde in 1968 and continued to govern until 1980. Reelected as president in 1980, Belaúnde again confronted daunting economic problems and the growth of a new rural and urban armed struggle led by Shining Path (Sendero Luminoso). His popularity, and that of his party, fell as a consequence of an overall inefficient government between 1980 and 1985.

FERNANDO BELAÚNDE TERRY, *Peru's Own Conquest* (1965); PEDRO PABLO KUCZYNSKI, *Peruvian Democracy Under Economic Stress: An Account of the Belaúnde Administration, 1963–1968* (1977).

ALFONSO W. QUIROZ

See also **Peru: Political Parties.**

**BELÉM,** city in Brazil near the mouth of the AMAZON RIVER. Belém is located on the south bank of the Pará River, about 60 miles from the Atlantic Ocean. Long the capital of the state of PARÁ, it had more than a million inhabitants in 1990. The region was densely settled by native peoples when the Europeans first reconnoitered it in 1500.

Within a hundred years, several British and Dutch agricultural colonies sprang up in the vicinity. In 1616 Francisco Caldeira Castelo Branco (CAPITÃO MOR of Rio Grande do Norte) founded the modern city, called Santa María de â Belém. He and a lieutenant, Pedro Teixeira, used Belém as a base from which to drive out the foreigners. In addition to its location, Belém offered maritime passage and anchorages protected from the awesome tidal bore that swept up the Amazon River.

Belém served the Portuguese as a strategic gateway to the entire Amazon basin. In the 1660s it became the economic emporium of the AMAZON REGION, and governors often resided there instead of in the capital at São Luís. By the eighteenth century, Belém merchants had organized shipyards, trade, and Indian slaving expeditions throughout the region.

At the height of the RUBBER boom in the early 1900s,

U.S. entrepreneur Percival FARQUHAR built modern docks to accommodate oceangoing ships. The collapse of the boom only temporarily deflated Belém's economy, and today the city provides governmental, political, economic, financial, educational, and defense services for the local population and the country as a whole.

JOHN URE, *Trespassers on the Amazon* (1986).

MICHAEL L. CONNIFF

**BELÉN,** small town on the URUGUAY RIVER, south of the Yacuy River, in the department of El Salto. It was founded in 1801 and is famous for having been the first populated place in the BANDA ORIENTAL to rebel against Spanish rule in 1810.

ELZEAR GIUFFRA, *La república del Uruguay* (Montevideo, 1955).

CÉSAR N. CAVIEDES

**BELÉN CONSPIRACY,** an attempt made in December 1813 to secure Guatemala's independence from Spain. Alienated by the political repression imposed by Captain General José de BUSTAMANTE, a group of Guatemalan creoles seeking independence met in the cells of the Convent of Belén in Guatemala City near the end of 1813. There they planned to seize Bustamante, Guatemala's Archbishop Ramon Casaus y Torres, and principal military officers. Bustamante had originally seemed sympathetic to the creoles' concerns but soon acted against their interests. A number of rebellions occurred throughout the region in 1813, illustrating disgruntlement with and rejection of Bustamante's control, and by extension that of the CORTES OF CÁDIZ as well. In March, creoles revolted in El Salvador, and in December of that year, creoles in León and Granada rebelled. The revolts were put down and the participants imprisoned by Bustamante.

The Belén conspirators sought to free the soldiers of the patriot army of Granada held prisoner by Bustamante and, more important, ultimately to declare independence. Their plans fell apart when they were discovered and arrested by local soldiers. Among those captured were Joaquín Yudice, Tomás Ruiz, and Fray Víctor Castrillo. The ringleaders and ten lesser participants were sentenced to hang but were later pardoned on 2 May 1818. Others were sent to Africa for ten years hard labor. José Francisco BARRUNDIA escaped capture but was sentenced in absentia. He spent six years in hiding in Guatemala.

MARIO RODRÍGUEZ, *La conspiración de Belén en nueva perspectiva* (1965); RICHARD E. MOORE, *A Historical Dictionary of Guatemala* (rev. ed. 1973); RALPH LEE WOODWARD, JR., *Central America: A Nation Divided* (1976); MARIO RODRÍGUEZ, *The Cádiz Experiment in Central America, 1808 to 1826* (1978); J. DANIEL CONTRERAS R., *Breve historia de Guatemala* (1983).

HEATHER K. THIESSEN

**BELGIAN COLONIZATION COMPANY.** Encouraged by King Léopold I of Belgium, a small group of investors in 1841 organized the Belgian Colonization Company to take advantage of economic opportunities in Guatemala. In 1842 the limited-liability company purchased 8,000 *caballerías* (264,000 acres) of undeveloped lands and assumed concessions and obligations for immigration, construction of a deep-water port, and other economic development in the department of Santo Tomás on Guatemala's north coast. In return the company received monopolies and exemptions favoring its commerce over all competitors. It could collect tolls for ten years on the planned road between the port and the Motagua River, and it would hold a ten-year monopoly on steam navigation on the river. Foreign immigrants to the Santo Tomás colony automatically became Guatemalan citizens and enjoyed a twenty-year exemption from most taxes. They were exempt from all commodity monopolies (*estancos*) but were prohibited from introducing goods under *estanco* from the colony into the interior. Although obligated to serve in the municipal militia, the colonists were exempt from service to Guatemala.

Conceptually the enterprise promised public and private rewards, but in fact it experienced problems on both sides of the Atlantic. In Belgium the organizers and directors—speculators and close friends of Léopold I—tried, against the wishes of his anticolonialist legislature, to acquire overseas territories using the private sector. The company enjoyed royal and ministerial subsidies and favors, and it reported regularly, though confidentially, to Léopold and his cabinet. In Guatemala the political scene was reversed. The Liberal government of the 1830s, which favored foreign investment, had been succeeded by Rafael CARRERA's xenophobic Conservative ministers, although members of the Constituent Assembly with business and commercial interests championed the Belgian proposals. The company bribed prominent advocates for the enterprise, paying through a Guatemalan firm (PULLIEIRO, BALCÁRZEL, and Associates) in Izabal and Santo Tomás whose public-works concessions and constructions the company promised to buy. Two Conservative members of the Assembly argued that Guatemala would suffer as badly from a future Belgian commercial monopoly at Santo Tomás as from the present British monopoly exercised from Belize. They predicted that a Belgian enclave would threaten Guatemalan sovereignty over its Caribbean coastline and the adjacent littoral province. The Assembly nevertheless approved the contract on 4 May 1842.

In May 1843 a communitarian settlement began at Santo Tomás. In the first year the company sent fewer than 200 temporary settlers and workers, with inadequate provisions. The landless residents fell prey to disease, dissension, and intrigue. The colonial administration changed personnel four times. In March 1844, Major Augustin Scévola Guillaumot arrived as the new colonial director, with extraordinary powers to institute a "military regime" for order and work. He also held covert instructions to lay the foundation for a future action to separate the District of Santo Tomás from Guatemalan jurisdiction. He raised the immigrant population to 800 civilians and 48 Belgian soldiers, like himself, who were officially on leave but posted to service with the company.

Guillaumot began surveying and clearing lands. Sealing off Santo Tomás as an ethnic enclave, he fired the Indian workers, drove the native-born residents from the colony, and rejected proposals from Guatemalan and Belize merchants to establish branch outlets at Santo Tomás. He violated the company's customs exemptions by importing luxury goods duty free for sale in the interior. The commandant of Izabal, Gerónimo Paiz, entered Santo Tomás in May 1844 with a detachment of soldiers and reestablished a national presence. He installed a port authority and customs director subordinate to his authority. In November, Carrera created a Permanent Commission on Santo Tomás Affairs and appointed General Manuel José ARCE as *corregidor*. Guillaumot resigned. The settlement faltered. Many of the colonists moved inland to the capital or relocated in Belize or Honduras. The colonial population plunged to 280.

Both the company in Brussels and its settlement at Santo Tomás struggled unsuccessfully through the next decade. Léopold tried to save the enterprise in 1846. Through his minister of foreign affairs he ordered the Belgian minister to Mexico, Édouard Blondeel van Cuelebrouck, to negotiate the transfer of Santo Tomás in full sovereignty to Belgium. The Guatemalan government rejected any proposal that ceded sovereignty or conveyed rights of extraterritoriality, insisting that a Guatemalan commission be assigned to Santo Tomás with full authority to intervene in all operations of the colony. Meanwhile a change of government in Brussels in March 1846 brought to power a cabinet unsympathetic to Léopold's overseas adventurism. The new cabinet withdrew support. The company attempted to reorganize in order to prevent bankruptcy. Guatemala permitted the Belgian Colonization Company to struggle on until no hope remained that it could meet its contractual obligations. Carrera finally implemented the Decree of Forfeiture in 1854.

For the early years of the colony, see JOSEPH FABRI, *Les belges au Guatemala (1840–1845)* (1955). The origins of the Belgian interest in Guatemala may be found in WILLIAM J. GRIFFITH, *Empires in the Wilderness: Foreign Colonization and Development in Guatemala, 1834–1844* (1965), esp. pp. 217–250. Company documents and correspondence are printed in NICOLAS LEYSBETH, *Historique de la colonisation belge à Santo-Tomas, Guatemala* (1938). A comprehensive history is ORA-WESTLEY SCHWEMMER, "The Belgian Colonization Company, 1840–1858" (Ph.D diss., Tulane University, 1966).

WES SCHWEMMER CADY

**BELGRANO, MANUEL** (*b.* 3 June 1770; *d.* 20 June 1820), Argentine independence leader. Born into a wealthy merchant family, Belgrano was educated in his native

Buenos Aires and at the University of Salamanca in Spain. He was admitted to the practice of law and in the last years of the colonial regime also belonged to a circle of creole professional men, all influenced by ENLIGHTENMENT thought, who were eager to promote economic development and practical improvements in infrastructure. Becoming secretary of the Buenos Aires Consulado, or merchant guild, he worked to encourage new productive activities and to improve the system of education. He also served in the local militia forces opposing the British invasions of 1806–1807.

Belgrano's initial response to the Spanish imperial crisis of 1808 was to support a project for constitutional monarchy in the American colonies under Princess CARLOTA JOAQUINA, sister of King FERDINAND VII, a captive of Napoleon. She was currently in Rio de Janeiro as wife of the Portuguese prince regent. This scheme came to nothing, and following the May Revolution of 1810 Belgrano threw in his lot frankly with the patriot cause. He served on the Buenos Aires junta itself, but in early 1811 set off for Paraguay as commander of an expedition sent to bring that province under control of the new authorities. He was defeated militarily, but soon afterward Paraguayans carried out their own revolution against Spain, for which Belgrano's proselytizing efforts in Paraguay had helped prepare the ground.

In 1811 Belgrano assumed command of patriot forces in the Argentine northwest, facing the royalists in Upper Peru (later Bolivia). He won some victories, but his own invasion of the Bolivian Andes in 1814 ended in defeat. Having yielded his command to José de SAN MARTÍN, Belgrano traveled to Europe in 1815 as part of a diplomatic mission that hoped to negotiate an agreement with Spain for an independent Argentine monarchy under a prince of the Spanish royal family. The idea was flatly rejected by Spain. On his return to Argentina, Belgrano worked both to obtain a formal declaration of independence (as finally effected on 9 July 1816) and to create a constitutional monarchy under a descendant of the Incas. In his final years, he again served militarily on the northern front while trying to mediate in political quarrels among various bands of patriots.

Among the leaders of Argentine independence, Belgrano is second only to San Martín in the esteem of later generations, although no great military or political triumphs are associated with his name. None of the forms of constitutional monarchy that he backed ever took hold. However, he served his country steadily and disinterestedly, enjoying the respect if not always winning the agreement of his fellow revolutionaries.

The classic study is BARTOLOMÉ MITRE, *Historia de Belgrano y de la Independencia Argentina* (1857; many later editions). A good modern study, by one of his descendants, is MARIO BELGRANO, *Historia de Belgrano*, 2d ed. (1944). In English the highlights of his career are covered in both JOHN LYNCH, *The Spanish American Revolutions, 1808–1826*, 2d ed. (1986), chaps. 2 and 3, and TULIO HALPERÍN-DONGHI, *Politics, Economics, and Society in*

*Argentina in the Revolutionary Period*, translated by Richard Southern (1975).

DAVID BUSHNELL

## BELIZE

### THE MAYA

Projectile points discovered near Ladyville tend to confirm the presence of early humans in Belize around 9000 B.C. Settled farming communities began to appear between 2500 and 1250 B.C. There is evidence of maize cultivation, pottery production, and trade in jade and obsidian at several pre-Classic sites (1250 B.C.–A.D. 250). There are indications of terracing and canal building at Pulltrouser Swamp and Cerros, in northern Belize, and at Nohmul, near Orange Walk Town. A manufacturing industry produced oval axes, hoes, and adzes at Colha, near Cerros. Pyramids typical of the Classic period of Maya architecture were constructed at Nohmul.

Excavation of Maya sites in Belize is ongoing and has accelerated over the last two decades. The major sites include: Santa Rita, Cerros, Nohmul, Cuello, Lamanai, ALTÚN HA, Xunantunich, and CARACOL. The latter is perhaps the largest site in Belize. An enormous ceremonial center covering 5 square miles, it includes a temple towering 136 feet, the tallest structure in Belize.

Most Maya centers in the lowlands of Belize experienced political and economic decline in the tenth century A.D. for reasons still not well known. Some populations dispersed along lakeshores and rivers. However, the arrival of the Spanish in the sixteenth century found many communities still flourishing and engaging in an extensive trading network.

### THE SPANISH

Hernán Cortés (1485–1547) may have passed through Belize en route to Honduras in 1524–1525. However, it was not until 1544 that the province of Chetumal, which included portions of Belize, was successfully conquered. Belize was incorporated into the two newly created provinces of Chetumal (north) and Dzuluinicob (south). A contributing factor in the ease of conquest may have been pre-Conquest population decline. Population in the region declined between 1517 and 1542 from about 800,000 to about 250,000.

For almost a century, from 1544 to 1638, the Spanish dominated communities at Tipu in the west and Lamanai in the northwest. Indians in these areas were granted in ENCOMIENDA to Spaniards and were forced to supply labor and cacao beans. Anti-Spanish rebellions occurred during 1567 and 1568. In 1638 Lamanai and Tipu joined in a widespread rebellion that expelled the Spaniards from most of Belize until after 1695.

### THE BAY SETTLEMENT

The date of the first British settlement in the Bay of Honduras has not been documented. Legends tell of a settlement along the Cockscomb coast in the 1630s, while others argue that a Scottish-born privateer, Peter WALLACE, founded a settlement in 1638. Sustained settlement by British settlers owed its origin to the logwood tree, which was used to produce dyes (blacks, blues, and purples) for woolen, linen, cotton, and hat manufacturing in the European textile industry. While the Treaty of Madrid (1670) between England and Spain marked the first acknowledgment that England had some rights in the West Indies, these were never clearly defined. If logwood cutters viewed this treaty as supporting their territorial claims along the Central American coast, neither the British or Spanish governments ever supported their claims.

This illegal settlement in the heart of the Spanish Empire was under frequent attack from Spanish authorities in Yucatán and was abandoned and resettled several times. Article 17 of the Anglo-Spanish Treaty of 1763 gave the settlement some legitimacy by legalizing the cutting, loading, and carrying away of logwood.

By the time logwood cutting was legalized, the baymen had turned to the more profitable logging of mahogany. Mahogany, used in shipbuilding and in the English furniture industry, remained the principal export of the settlement until the mid-twentieth century. Since the baymen were said to prefer hard liquor to hard labor, they began importing African slaves after 1724 to cut timber. Several slave revolts between 1765 and 1773 plus the large number of runaways who sought asylum in Yucatán suggest that while slavery in Belize may have differed from sugar plantations in the Caribbean, it was probably no less onerous.

The earliest form of government in the settlement was public or town meetings. From these, magistrates were elected to administer a code based on common law and ancient usage called "Burnaby's Code," written by Admiral Sir William Burnaby, commander in chief at Jamaica.

By 1779 the bay settlement consisted of plantations along the banks of several rivers, with settlers numbering about 500 and slaves totaling about 3,000. Saint George's Cay, a small island just off the coast, was the nominal capital. The Spaniards successfully attacked Saint George's Cay in 1779, forcing the settlers and their slaves to march overland to Mérida. Four years later, in compliance with the Treaty of Versailles (3 September 1783), the Spanish granted the British logwood concessions between the Hondo and Belize rivers. Three years later, the treaty was extended by the Convention of London (1786) to permit the extraction of both logwood and mahogany as far south as the Sibún River. The treaty also forced the British to abandon settlements at Roatán and along the MOSQUITO COAST. Some 2,214 settlers and their slaves from these settlements moved to Belize.

In 1798 the Spanish, under the command of the captain-general of Yucatán, Arturo O'Neil, launched an unsuccessful attack on the bay settlement, known since as the Battle of Saint George's Cay. The settlers' success in this battle is commemorated on 10 September. Well-prepared and armed with advance information from spies in Havana, the British repelled a much larger Spanish force, although one weakened by yellow fever. This represented the last serious attempt by the Spanish to dislodge the Baymen from their settlement.

BELIZE AND THE CENTRAL AMERICAN REPUBLICS

With the onset of the independence of CENTRAL AMERICA in 1821, the British threat had been reduced to the single settlement of Belize. The thirty years after independence saw the reestablishment of the settlement of the Bay Islands, the reassumption of the British protectorate over the Mosquito Coast, the expansion of the boundaries of Belize, and a tremendous expansion of commercial relations between Great Britain and Central America, with most of the trade passing through Belize. The absence of any deep-water port along the Caribbean coast dictated that British goods be shipped to Belize and then transshipped in coastal vessels to Central American ports. The British entrance into the Central American retail trade coincided with the appearance of commission houses and branches of British commercial companies in Belize. By 1831, considering the British Caribbean as a whole, Belize ranked second only to Jamaica as an importer of British manufactures. However, unable to induce the British to relinquish their position in Belize and unable to develop a satisfactory alternate commercial route, the Central Americans became increasingly hostile regarding the status of Belize.

In 1828 Great Britain claimed the territory of Belize on the basis of conquest, long use, and custom and in 1835 asked Spain to cede the territory. When no response was forthcoming, the British began to exercise more formal jurisdiction over the territory. By the time the CLAYTON–BULWER TREATY (1850) between Great Britain and the United States was negotiated, the British position was that they had acquired rights of possession.

To legitimize her jurisdiction, Britain signed a treaty with Guatemala on 30 April 1859. The first six articles of this treaty defined the boundaries of Belize. Article 7 provided for the construction of a road from Guatemala City to the Caribbean coast. Guatemala viewed this as compensation for the loss of territory. When Guatemala failed to ratify a supplementary convention to this treaty in 1863, during the stipulated period, the British felt that they were now released from the obligation under article 7. This was disputed by Guatemala. This dispute has festered for more than a century. Guatemala continues to question whether Britain legitimately occupied the territory of Belize.

The bay settlement formally became the Crown Colony of British Honduras in 1862. It was administered by a lieutenant governor who was under the nominal supervision of the governor of Jamaica. When these ties with Jamaica were severed in 1884, the position of lieutenant governor was elevated to governor.

A DEPRESSED ECONOMY

After 1850 Belize's lucrative reexport trade to Central America declined severely and the economy became dependent on the country's own natural resources. The mahogany trade dominated the economy until well into the twentieth century. The peak year in the nineteenth century was 1846, when exports totaled 13.7 million feet. Thereafter, the wholesale cutting of young trees and the exhaustion of almost all accessible trees seriously depleted the country's timber resources. The increased costs of extracting less accessible reserves combined with declining prices in Europe led to declining profits. By 1870 exports totaled only 2.75 million feet. Levels of exports equal to those of 1846 were not reached again until 1906, when 11 million feet were exported.

Landownership was increasingly monopolized by a small number of families who developed partnerships with metropolitan companies. Four companies—Young, Toledo, and Company; Sheldon Byass and Company; John Carmichael; and the British Honduras Company—owned most of the land by 1870. In 1875 the British Honduras Company became the Belize Estate and Produce Company. Five years after it acquired property from Young, Toledo, and Company, it became the largest landholder in the colony.

The emancipation of the slaves in the 1830s brought little economic improvement in their lives. Using a "company store" approach, these freedmen were kept permanently in debt to the lumber companies. Advances on wages were paid to mahogany workers just prior to the Christmas season. Quickly expended, supplies for the cutting season had to be purchased on credit from the employer at exorbitant markups.

A limited trade in CHICLE, the coagulated latex of the sapodilla tree, began in the late nineteenth century. This tree extract, used in the manufacture of chewing gum, was shipped to the United States. Wrigley's was the predominant purchaser. Exports reached a peak in 1930 with more than 4 million pounds. Thereafter, the industry went into a decline brought on by overtapping of the trees, the world depression, and a switch to synthetics.

Bananas were first exported in 1890. Between 1896 and 1912 annual exports averaged 500,000 bunches. Prospects appeared bright until 1913, when Panama disease struck the area and exports began a rapid decline. In the same area of the Stann Creek Valley where bananas had previously been grown, a grapefruit industry was established in the 1920s. By 1933 more than 13,000 cases were being exported. Although several attempts were made to develop the sugar industry prior to World War II, none proved very successful.

By 1890 Belize had a population of about thirty thousand. Twelve thousand people (largely CREOLES of African and Caucasian descent) lived in Belize City.

Another ten thousand Spanish-speaking MESTIZOS, refugees from the CASTE WAR in Yucatán, were living in the Corazal district. Four thousand Kekchi and Maya were living in the southern and western regions. Three thousand Garifuna (Black Caribs), who had arrived in the colony in the early 1800s from Honduras, lived in Stann Creek and Punta Gorda and surrounding villages. Small numbers of East Indians, imported to work on sugar estates, lived in the south.

However, for most of the period, the capital, Belize City, was the colony. The creoles dominated the political and social life of the colony and, together with a small group of Europeans, they also controlled the economy.

FROM COLONY TO INDEPENDENCE, 1862–1981

In 1871 the Crown Colony system of government was introduced. The Legislative Assembly was replaced by a Legislative Council composed of five official and five unofficial members, all appointed by the lieutenant governor. This council remained in force until 1936, when elections were again resumed. By 1945 six members of the council were elected and four were appointed by the governor. New constitutions in 1954 and 1960 increased the role of elected officials vis-à-vis the governor. Membership in the Legislative Assembly, which also included six ministries, was expanded to eighteen, eleven of whom were elected. The governor's powers were curbed and he was required to act with the advice of the ministers.

The 1964 Constitution granted internal independence. However, the continuing dispute with Guatemala delayed the event until 1981. In preparation, a new capital, BELMOPAN, was constructed some 50 miles west of Belize City. Disastrous hurricanes in 1931, 1955, and 1961 had made this a necessity. On 21 September 1981 Belize achieved full independence with a parliamentary democracy based on the Westminster system.

A prime minister and cabinet make up the executive branch, while a twenty-eight-member elected House of Representatives and eight-member appointed Senate form a bicameral legislature. The British monarch is the titular head of state and is represented in Belize by a governor general who must be a Belizean.

POLITICAL DEVELOPMENTS SINCE 1945

The rapid decline in the mahogany industry in the 1920s, the Great Depression of the 1930s, and the hurricane of 10 September 1931, which killed a thousand people, prompted considerable labor agitation in the 1930s. Antonio Soberanis Gómez (1897–1975) lobbied for improved wages and work for the unemployed. The General Workers Union merged interests with a growing nationalist movement to form Belize's first political party, the People's United Party (PUP), in 1950. Shortly thereafter, George PRICE, one of its founders, was elected party leader. Prince won an unbroken series of local and national elections until 1984. Over a thirty-year period the PUP obtained continuous mandate from the electorate first to launch a final attack against colonialism and then to lead the new nation into economic prosperity.

The principal opposition party, the United Demo-

Albert Street, Belize City, on the eve of Belize's independence from Great Britain. UPI / BETTMANN ARCHIVE.

cratic Party, was founded in 1973 from three smaller parties. Manuel ESQUIVEL served as party chairman from 1976 to 1982 and since 1982 has been party leader. In 1984 he led the UDP to a stunning victory (twenty-one of twenty-eight seats) and became Belize's second prime minister. During a five-year term, his sound fiscal management and encouragement of foreign investment in tourism and manufacturing have helped invigorate the country's economy. However, party wrangling, charges of corruption, and a series of contested party caucuses led to a surprising electoral defeat in 1989. By winning fifteen of the twenty-eight seats, the PUP was restored to power and George Price once again became prime minister.

Following the return to power, the PUP government led by Price steered a course similar to his predecessor's by encouraging agricultural exports and expanding textile manufacturing. Belize took a leadership role in the new ecotourist movement, which seeks to promote preservation of flora and fauna while providing expanded opportunities for the ecologically minded traveler. Several major new hotels were completed in Belize City and a new deep water port completed at Big River. Improvements were also made in the country's infrastructure, although construction of a much-needed hospital in Belize City suffered repeated delays. By 1992, Belize's economy was suffering from the worldwide recession.

Buoyed by 1993 elections Price decided to call a general election before the end of his term. Soon after this fateful decision a series of events developed in rapid

succession which contributed to his government's defeat on 30 June. These included Britain's announcement that it would withdraw all of its defense forces from Belize by January 1994 and a 25 May coup in Guatemala. The opposition UDP had attacked the Price government for failing to satisfactorily address the security implications for Belize of these two events. The UDP won sixteen of twenty-nine seats in the new parliament and on 3 July, Manuel Esquivel was sworn in again as prime minister. He quickly made good on several of his campaign promises by introducing free education at all levels and announced structural reforms to depoliticize the public service.

BELIZE IN THE 1990s
Since 1945 the economy has diversified and sugar has replaced mahogany as the principal export. Other major exports include garments, citrus fruit (oranges and grapefruits), bananas, and fish (principally lobster). Tourism has become a major source of revenue. In 1989 the number of tourists visiting Belize reached 229,000, up 400 percent from a decade earlier. While most of the tourists have been attracted to the offshore islands for skin and scuba diving, the present government encourages ecotourism on the mainland and is improving access to archaeological sites. Belize cooperates with Mexico, Guatemala, and Honduras to promote Mundo Maya, tourist ventures in the former Maya areas.

Despite this diversification, the economy faces major problems, including high unemployment, inadequate roads, depressed sugar prices, a constant "brain drain" of Belizean creoles to the United States, and a growing drug-trade problem, which has brought with it increased domestic violence in Belize City.

Two useful general histories of the colonial period to 1970 are NARDA DOBSON, *A History of Belize* (1973), and CEDRIC H. GRANT, *The Making of Modern Belize: Politics, Society, and British Colonialism in Central America* (1976). Diplomacy in the region prior to 1900 is covered in R. A. HUMPHREYS, *The Diplomatic History of British Honduras, 1638–1901* (1961). Recent archaeological work on the Maya is discussed in NORMAN HAMMOND, "The Emergence of Maya Civilization," in *Scientific American* 255, no. 2 (August 1986): 106–115. The Spanish conquest of Belize is reviewed by ELIZABETH GRAHAM, DAVID M. PENDERGAST, and GRANT D. JONES, "On the Fringes of Conquest: Maya-Spanish Contact in Colonial Belize," in *Science* 246 (8 December 1989): 1254–1259. Britain's informal empire in Central America is the subject of ROBERT A. NAYLOR's *Penny Ante Imperialism: The Mosquito Shore and the Bay of Honduras, 1600–1914* (1989).

Useful studies of the eighteenth and nineteenth centuries include: O. NIGEL BOLLAND, *Colonialism and Resistance in Belize: Essays in Historical Sociology* (1988), PETER ASHDOWN, "The Belize Elite and Its Power Base: Land, Labour, and Commerce Circa 1890," in *Belizean Studies* 9, no. 5/6 (1981): 30–43; and WAYNE M. CLEGERN, *British Honduras: Colonial Dead End, 1859–1900* (1967). The labor struggles of the 1930s are described by PETER ASHDOWN, "Antonio Soberanis and the Disturbances in Belize 1934–1937," in *Caribbean Quarterly* 24, no. 112 (1978): 61–74. The recent impact of the Anglo-Guatemalan boundary dispute is reviewed by ALMA H. YOUNG and DENNIS H. YOUNG, "The Impact of the Anglo-Guatemalan Dispute on the Internal Politics of Belize," in *Belizean Studies* 18, no. 1 (1990): 11–35. The history of Belize since independence is the subject of JULIO A. FERNÁNDEZ, *Belize: Case Study for Democracy in Central America* (1989).

BRIAN E. COUTTS

*See also* **British–Latin American Relations.**

**BELLEGARDE, LUIS DANTÈS** (*b.* 18 May 1877; *d.* 14 June 1966), Haitian educator, politician, diplomat, and author. A native of Port-au-Prince, Bellegarde taught at the secondary and university levels before entering politics. He joined the Ministry of Foreign Affairs around 1905 and was minister of public instruction and agriculture in 1918–1921. In 1950 he was president of the Constituent Assembly. Bellegarde's diplomatic activity included service as ambassador to France and the Vatican (appointed 1921) and as ambassador to the United States (appointed 1931) and to the United Nations.

Bellegarde was coauthor of almost twenty books on Haitian history, politics, and sociology. Among them are *La nation haïtienne* (1938), written with Sténio Vincent, and *Haïti et son peuple* (1953), written with Mercer Cook.

Bellegarde remains controversial for his pro-French, Christian, and Western views. Nevertheless, his contributions to Haitian social thought; foreign, financial, and economic policy; and education are clear. He died in Port-au-Prince.

PAUL BLANCHET, "Sur la tombe de Dantès Bellegarde," in *La Nouvelliste*, 17 June 1966; PATRICK BELLEGARDE-SMITH, *In the Shadow of Powers: Dantès Bellegarde in Haitian Social Thought* (1985).

ANNE GREENE

**BELLI, GIOCONDA** (*b.* 9 December 1948), Nicaraguan poet and novelist. Best known for her autobiographical, erotic, and feminist celebration of sexuality and the female body, Belli has published four books of poetry: *Sobre la grama* (1974); *Línea de fuego* (1978), winner of the Cuban Casa de las Américas Prize; *Truenos y arcoiris* (1982); and *De la costilla de Eva* (1987; *From Eve's Rib*, 1993). In testimony to her rising reputation in Central America, all four books were republished together as *Poesía reunida* (1989). An ardent supporter of the Sandinista revolution, Belli wrote eloquently of the loss of friends and comrades in the fighting. Her first novel, *La mujer habitada* (1988; *The Inhabited Woman*, 1994), recounts the struggle of a Latin American woman to transcend the politics of individualistic bourgeois feminism and join the broader historical struggle of all oppressed peoples. Her second novel, *Sofía de los presagios* (1990), depicts the feminist struggles of a woman in contemporary Nicaragua. In addition to English, much of Belli's work has been translated into German.

For studies of Belli's narrative, see MARÍA SALGADO, "Gioconda Belli, novelista revolucionaria," and VICENTE CABRERA, "La intertextualidad subversiva en *La mujer habitada*," in *Monographic Review/Revista Monográfica* 8 (1992): 229–242 and 243–251; LUIS T. GONZÁLEZ DEL VALLE, ed., *Critical Essays on the Literatures of Spain and Spanish America* (1991); and LADY ROJAS TREMPE, "La alteridad indígena y mágica en la narrativa de Elena Garro, Manuel Scorza y Gioconda Belli," in *Alba de América: Revista Literaria* 9 (1991): 141–152. For studies of her poetry, see KATHLEEN MARCH, "Gioconda Belli: The Erotic Politics of the Great Mother," in *Monographic Review/Revista Monográfica* 6 (1990): 245–257; and ELECTRA ARENAL, "Two Poets of the Sandinista Struggle," in *Feminist Studies* 7, no. 1 (1981): 19–27.

ANN GONZÁLEZ

**BELLO, ANDRÉS** (*b.* 29 November 1781; *d.* 15 October 1865), Venezuelan polymath and public servant, the most distinguished Latin American intellectual of his (and perhaps any other) century. Born and educated in Caracas, Bello accompanied Simón BOLÍVAR (1783–1830), whom he had briefly taught, as a member of the first Venezuelan diplomatic mission to Britain (1810). The collapse of the Venezuelan Republic stranded him in London, where he lived, often penuriously, for more than eighteen years. In the 1820s he coedited the influential Spanish-American journals *La Biblioteca Americana* (1823) and *El Repertorio Americano* (1826–1827), and worked as an official of the Chilean and Colombian legations. At the invitation of the Chilean government, he moved to Santiago in 1829. He was employed thereafter as senior official in the foreign ministry, as editor of the government gazette *El Araucano*, and as first rector of the newly founded University of Chile (1843–1865)—still colloquially known in Chile as *la casa de Bello* (Bello's house). He was a senator from 1837 to his death.

The extraordinary range of Bello's genius was reflected in prolific writings on international and Roman law, philosophy, literature, drama, grammar, and science. His poems, especially the two great "London poems," "Alocución a la poesía" (Allocution to Poetry,

Andrés Bello. BENSON LATIN AMERICAN COLLECTION, UNIVERSITY OF TEXAS AT AUSTIN.

1823), and "A la agricultura de la zona tórrida" (Agriculture in the Torrid Zone, 1826), have often been seen as the true starting point of all postcolonial Latin American literature. Bello's work as a jurist was crowned by his single-handed authorship of the classic Civil Code of the Republic of Chile (1855). His numerous writings on language culminated in the *Gramática de la lengua castellana destinada al uso de los americanos* (Grammar of the Spanish Language for the Use of Americans, 1847), which won him honorary membership in the Real Academia in Spain. He made radical proposals to modify the orthography of Spanish; several features of his scheme remained in use in Chile until around 1910. His guidance also shaped a school of Chilean historians.

Bello's influence on the intellectual life of nineteenth-century Chile is incalculable. At the heart of all Bello's work lay the belief that Latin America, now politically free, needed to create its own cultural and intellectual traditions, traditions that would be authentically Latin American, without repudiating the achievements of European civilization. At his funeral in 1865 the scientist Ignacio Domeyko (1801–1889) doubted "that one man, in one lifetime, could know so much, could do so much, could love so much." Bello's bicentennial in 1981 was extensively commemorated throughout Spanish America.

RAFAEL CALDERA, *Andrés Bello*, translated by John Street (1977); JOHN LYNCH, ed., *Andrés Bello: The London Years* (1982).

SIMON COLLIER

**BELLY, FÉLIX** (*b.* October 1816; *d.* 3 November 1886), French journalist and promoter of a Nicaraguan trans-isthmian canal. Belly visited Nicaragua and received a canal concession in 1858 from the government of General Tomás MARTÍNEZ. Belly's settlement of a boundary dispute between Nicaragua and Costa Rica cleared the way for work to begin. Yet Belly faced other problems. The U.S. government disapproved of Belly's work, fearing that he was an agent of French imperialism. More serious still was a shortage of investment capital. Belly surveyed a canal route, but financial problems and renewed border disputes terminated the project.

CYRIL ALLEN, *France in Central America: Félix Belly and the Nicaraguan Canal* (1986); DAVID I. FOLKMAN, JR., *The Nicaragua Route* (1972).

STEVEN S. GILLICK

**BELMOPAN,** capital of Belize. Discussion of the need for a new capital for the British colony of British Honduras took place for years before it was actually built. Four reasons were advanced: first, the old capital, Belize City, lying a scant eighteen inches above sea level, had been devastated by major hurricanes in 1931 and 1955. Second, planners hoped to reduce the overwhelming centralization of educational, economic, political, and cultural functions in Belize City. Third, some people believed that Belize City, with its squalid slums, inadequate sanitation, and severe overcrowding, had reached the limits of urbanization. Finally, the government hoped to focus attention on the neglected interior of the country.

Planning began in earnest following Hurricane Hattie, which struck Belize City on 31 October 1961 and killed 262 people and destroyed or damaged 75 percent of the city's structures. A site near Roaring Creek Village, some 50 miles southwest of Belize City, was selected. Safe from the onslaught of hurricanes, it had an abundant supply of potable water from the Belize River and was located at the intersection of two of the country's major highways.

Designed to be built in five stages over a twenty-year period, only $12 million was initially available in the form of loans and grants from the British government. Of 8,100 acres purchased for the site, 450 acres were cleared. Construction began in 1966, and the new capital opened officially in 1970. By then buildings to house the national government, civil servants, and essential public services had been completed. The central area for public buildings includes three plazas, government, civic administration, and commercial, which are connected by pedestrian walkways. The government complex, in the shape of a MAYAN temple, includes a series of gray concrete-block buildings that house the principal ministries and is crowned by the National Assembly.

Twenty years after the first offices were occupied, the buildings, with their cell-like offices, were severely overcrowded, and in 1991 construction began on two massive new office structures. Other buildings completed since 1970 include the government printery, the public works department, a police training complex, the national archives, and Belize House, the residence of the governor general. Municipal buildings housing police, fire officials, a post office, and a civic center have also been completed. The commercial sector has grown more slowly. More than eight hundred residences have been constructed and occupied since 1970.

While some early planners envisioned a busy city of thirty thousand people with tree-lined avenues by the 1980s, population growth has been modest. In 1990 the population was estimated at 5,256. On the positive side, the new capital has spurred agricultural and commercial development in the center of the country and now is an important transportation hub for the country. On the negative side, only two embassies and few industries have relocated to Belmopan. With scarcely a green lawn or a shade tree to be found in the dry season and few social and cultural amenities, many civil servants continue to commute from Belize City.

*Belmopan, Belize C. A.*, Miscellaneous Collection #97 (ca. 1970), National Archives (26-28 Unity Blvd., Belmopan, Belize); PETER FURLEY, "A Capital Waits for Its Country," in *Geographical Magazine* 43, no. 10 (1971): 713–716; KEVIN C. KEARNS, "Belmopan: Perspective on a New Capital," in *Geographical Review* 63, no. 2 (1973): 147–169; M. DAY, G. GRUSZCZYNSKI, and

K. SCHUPARRA, "Belmopan, The Hummingbird Highway, and Other Regional Influences," in *Environment and Resources in the Hummingbird Karst of Central Belize*, University of Wisconsin–Milwaukee, Department of Geography, Occasional Papers Series, no. 2 (1987): 42–49, and figs. 9 and 10, pp. 15–16.

BRIAN E. COUTTS

**BELO HORIZONTE**, a major industrial center, and the capital of MINAS GERAIS, the second most populous state in Brazil. Located on a plateau in the mountains of southeastern Brazil at an elevation of approximately 2,500 feet, greater Belo Horizonte has a population of more than three million. It is the third largest city and industrial center in Brazil.

State politicians and planners created the city in the 1890s to replace the small, isolated state capital at Ouro Prêto. They hoped to create a new and dynamic political and economic center for the state. After a contentious debate, the state government decided to build the new capital on the site of Curral del Rei, a small hamlet with some 8,000 inhabitants, located in the center of the state. Inspired by the examples of Washington, D.C., and Paris, planners designed the central area of the city using a geometric grid plan.

From its inauguration in 1897 until World War II, Belo Horizonte served mainly as a bureaucratic and administrative center, with a growing population, but little heavy industry. By the early 1940s the city had a population approaching a quarter million.

Over the next four decades, Belo Horizonte rapidly industrialized, becoming a major center for the production of iron and steel, automobiles, and cement. Located in the heart of a region rich in iron ore, bauxite, manganese, and gold, the city has also developed into a major center for mining and construction companies.

Belo Horizonte has become a more dominant economic and political capital for Minas Gerais than its planners ever envisioned. State planners and politicians now search for ways to decrease the concentration of nearly one-third of the state's industrial production in a single city.

JOHN D. WIRTH, *Minas Gerais in the Brazilian Federation, 1889–1937* (1977); MARSHALL C. EAKIN, "Creating a Growth Pole: The Industrialization of Belo Horizonte, Brazil, 1897–1987," *Americas* 47 (1991): 383–410.

MARSHALL C. EAKIN

*See also* individual industries.

**BELTRÁN, LUIS** (*b.* 7 September 1784; *d.* 8 December 1827), Franciscan friar and chaplain of several Platine armies during the struggle against Spain. Born near Mendoza, Argentina, Fray Beltrán entered the Franciscan order when barely sixteen years old and soon moved to the convent in Santiago, Chile. His military career started after he joined José Miguel CARRERA's army as chaplain and took part in the battle of Hierbas Buenas in 1812. Although this battle was disastrous for the rebels, it allowed Beltrán to demonstrate his skills at military engineering. He later held, for example, the post of director of ordnance (1820–1824) for the Chileans and worked in that same capacity under Simón BOLÍVAR in Peru in 1824. An argument with Bolívar, however, led to a suicide attempt by Beltrán and dimmed his lifework and health thereafter. Lieutenant Colonel Beltrán left the army in 1827 and retired to Buenos Aires, where he renewed his interest in the religious life he had never formally abandoned. He was named "heroic defender of the nation" by Buenos Aires. He died in Buenos Aires.

ALFREDO GARGARO, *Pedro Regalado de la Plaza, director de la maestranza del ejército de los Andes* (1950); RICARDO PICCIRILLI ET AL., *Diccionario histórico argentino*, vol. 1 (1953), pp. 520–521.

FIDEL IGLESIAS

**BELTRÁN, LUIS (SAINT)** (*b.* 1 January 1526; *d.* 10 October 1581), Spanish Dominican missionary and patron saint of Colombia. Born in Valencia and ordained in 1547, Beltrán arrived in Cartagena in 1562. After proselytizing among the Indians of the northern coast, he served for three years as *doctrinero* of Turbará, near present-day Barranquilla. A letter from Bartolomé de LAS CASAS warning him to be careful of how he confessed and absolved *encomenderos* of their sins may have led him to a more determined defense of the Indians. Appearing before one banquet table of *encomenderos*, Beltrán dramatically squeezed the corn *arepas* (pancakes), the fruit of Indian labor, so hard that blood supposedly trickled onto the white tablecloth. His conflicts with *encomenderos* and his fame as a holy man grew. Brought back to Cartagena as a preacher and fundraiser, Beltrán addressed audiences all along the Caribbean coast from Nombre de Dios to Santa Marta. On his way to serve as prior of the Dominican friary in Bogotá, he was ordered back to Spain, where he arrived in 1569. Chosen to head several Spanish religious houses, he died in Valencia. He was beatified by Paul V in 1608 and canonized by Clement X in 1671.

See JUAN MANUEL PACHECO, S.J., *Historia extensa de Colombia*, vol. 13, *Historia eclesiástica*, tomo 1, *La evangelización del Nuevo Reino, siglo xvi* (1971), esp. pp. 485–488.

MAURICE P. BRUNGARDT

**BELTRÁN, MANUELA** (*b.* 1724; *d.* ?), Comunero insurgent. A heroine of the COMUNERO REVOLT that swept through the uplands of NEW GRANADA in 1781, Manuela Beltrán remains an obscure figure. Born of Spanish ancestry in Socorro, province of Tunja, she appears to have been a woman of modest means. Her home, a prosperous agricultural, commercial, and textile manufacturing town, was hit hard by the ambitious, intemperately applied revenue measures of Regent Visitor Gutiérrez de

Piñeres. Riots erupted in Socorro on 16 March 1781 following the promulgation of the decree separating the collection of the ALCABALA and the Armada de Barlovento taxes, which people mistakenly believed to be a new tax. Emerging from the angry crowd, Manuela Beltrán, in the midst of riotous applause, dramatically tore down the Armada de Barlovento ordinance, an act that at least symbolically marked the beginning of the Comunero revolt. Thereafter, Beltrán disappeared from history, but she is representative of the prominent role that women so often played in the popular protests of the eighteenth century.

PABLO E. CÁRDENAS ACOSTA, *El movimiento comunal de 1781 en el Nuevo Reino de Granada (reivindicaciones históricas)*, vol. 1 (1960), esp. p. 101; JOHN LEDDY PHELAN, *The People and the King: The Comunero Revolution in Columbia, 1781* (1978), esp. pp. 46–60.

ALLAN J. KUETHE

**BELTRÁN, PEDRO** (*b.* 17 February 1897; *d.* 16 February 1979), Peruvian landowner, economist, publisher, and politician. Born in Cañete, he became a distinguished representative of liberal interests among the economic elite of coastal Peru. He studied at San Marcos University and in London at Kings College and the London School of Economics, from which he received a master's degree in economics in 1918. On his return to Peru, he promoted agricultural modernization and organized COTTON and SUGAR producers. By 1929, Beltrán had become the president of the influential National Agrarian Society and a member of the board of directors of the Peruvian Reserve Bank.

After the fall of President Augusto B. LEGUÍA in 1930, Beltrán continued to exercise his influence as a leading exporter of agricultural goods through the daily newspaper *La Prensa*, which he bought in 1934. Between 1944 and 1946, Beltrán was the Peruvian ambassador to the United States and presided over the Peruvian delegation at the Bretton Woods conference. He vigorously opposed state controls over imports and foreign currency exchange under president José Luis BUSTAMANTE Y RIVERO (1945–1948). In 1956, Beltrán was imprisoned by Manuel ODRÍA for his opposition as head of the National Coalition, a civilian political group. In 1959–1960, during the second Prado administration, he served as minister of finance. In 1974 the military government expropriated his newspaper. He lived thereafter in exile in New York City, where he died.

ROSEMARY THORP and GEOFFREY BERTRAM, *Peru, 1890–1977: Growth and Policy in an Open Economy* (1978); GONZALO PORTOCARRERO MAISCH, *De Bustamante a Odría* (1983).

ALFONSO W. QUIROZ

**BELTRÁN, WASHINGTON** (*b.* 7 February 1885; *d.* 2 April 1920), Uruguayan lawyer, journalist, and politician. While earning very high grades in Montevideo's

National University, School of Law and Social Sciences, Beltrán published several articles of note in scientific and literary journals. Later, he extended his expertise into philosophical and legal terrains, with the publication of articles such as "Los filósofos del siglo XVIII," "El contrato social," and "Fallos de la Alta Corte de Justicia en materia civil, penal, comercial, administrativa y de lo contencioso administrativo" in Buenos Aires's *Revista de Derecho* between 1908 and 1909. With Carlos Roxlo he directed the newspaper *El Civismo* and later wrote on political issues for *La Democracia* and other newspapers. He also served in the Justice Department. As codirector and principal writer of *El País*, he consistently opposed the socialist and populist program of Colorado Party leader José BATLLE Y ORDÓÑEZ, during Batlle's second term as president from 1911 to 1915. In 1914 Beltrán was elected deputy to the National Congress. Between 1916 and 1917 he served as a member of the National Constituent Assembly, which approved a two-party governing council, the COLEGIADO, to replace the presidency. Beltrán was killed in 1920 during a pistol duel with Batlle.

WILLIAM H. KATRA

*See also* **Uruguay: Constitutions; Uruguay: Political Parties.**

**BELZU, MANUEL ISIDORO** (*b.* 4 April 1808; *d.* 27 March 1865), president of Bolivia (1848–1855). Born into a poor artisan family in La Paz, Belzu was educated at the Franciscan monastery. At thirteen he ran away from the monks and joined an army fighting Spanish forces. He fought for various generals, including Agustín Gamarra of Peru and Andrés Santa Cruz, José Ballivián, and José Miguel de Velasco of Bolivia. He became minister of war in the Velasco government in February 1848.

Belzu seized control of the government in December 1848. Employing populist rhetoric, he was the first general to base his regime on the urban artisans and CHOLOS (people of mixed Indian and European heritage). Although he remained in power until 1855, when he "constitutionally" handed the presidency to his son-in-law, General Jorge Córdova, Belzu failed to consolidate control. He survived one assassination attempt in 1850 and forty-two revolutions against his authority. From 1855 to 1857, he represented Bolivia in Europe, where he remained until 1865. That same year he returned to Bolivia in order to prevent the assumption of power by Mariano MELGAREJO, who had him assassinated.

OFICINA NACIONAL DE ESTADÍSTICA DE BOLIVIA, *De siglo a siglo, hombres celebres de Bolivia* (1920), pp. 85–89; JULIA DÍAZ ARGUEDAS, *Los generales de Bolivia (rasgos biográficos) 1825–1925* (1929), pp. 431–439; FAUSTO REINAGA, *Belzu: Precursor de la revolución nacional* (1953); HERBERT S. KLEIN, *Bolivia: The Evolution of a Multi-Ethnic Society* (1982), pp. 128–131, 133–135.

ERWIN P. GRIESHABER
ERICK D. LANGER

**BEMBERG, OTTO** (*b.* 1827; *d.* 1895), German-born businessman in Argentina. Bemberg arrived in Buenos Aires in the 1850s and established a prosperous import-export business. He married the daughter of the influential Senator Mariano Ocampo and served as Argentine consul in Paris during the WAR OF THE TRIPLE ALLIANCE (1865–1870). He became involved in the arms trade with Argentina, and following his return to Buenos Aires, he became an agent for many important French industrial companies, especially the Schneider firm, which exported railway and other heavy equipment to the Río de la Plata.

With offices in Buenos Aires and Paris, Bemberg began to specialize in financial dealings, and he was the agent for a large number of Argentine provincial loans issued on the Paris Stock Exchange in the 1880s. He was an agent to various French banks and helped arrange financing for a French-owned railway in Argentina and for the construction of the port works in Rosario.

In 1888 Bemberg established the Quilmes Beer Company, long the largest brewery in Argentina, which remains owned by the Bemberg family. The brewery expanded production spectacularly between 1900 and 1925 and also bought competing breweries to establish its dominance. The company was nationalized by the government of Juan D. PERÓN in 1947 and was returned to the Bemberg family in 1955.

JOSÉ LUIS TORRES, *Algunas maneras de vender patria* (Buenos Aires, 1973).

CARLOS MARICHAL

**BENALCÁZAR, SEBASTIÁN DE.** *See* **Belalcázar, Sebastian de.**

**BENAVENTE, TORIBIO DE.** *See* **Motolinía, Toribio de.**

**BENAVIDES, ALONSO DE** (*b.* before 1579; *d.* ca. 1636), Franciscan missionary and propagandist in New Mexico. The personification of Christian spiritual conquest, Benavides acted in New Mexico in the seventeenth century with a zeal reminiscent of his sixteenth-century brethren. He was born at San Miguel, in the Azores, and entered the FRANCISCAN order in Mexico City, serving subsequently in various capacities. Appointed superior of the New Mexico missions and agent of the INQUISITION, Benavides presented his credentials to Governor Felipe de Sotelo Osorio at Santa Fe early in 1626. During his three-year term, Benavides labored actively not only among PUEBLO INDIANS, but also among APACHES. When the ardent friar returned to Mexico City in early 1630, Franciscan authorities sent him to Spain to lobby at court. His sanguine report of missionary progress and potential in New Mexico, published the same year, and a revised version prepared for the pope in 1634 remain valuable ethnohistorical sources.

FREDERICK WEBB HODGE et al., eds., *Fray Alonso de Benavides' Revised Memorial of 1634* (1945); PETER P. FORRESTAL, trans., and CYPRIAN J. LYNCH, ed., *Benavides' Memorial of 1630* (1954).

JOHN L. KESSELL

*See also* **Missions.**

**BENAVIDES, OSCAR RAIMUNDO** (*b.* 1876; *d.* 1945), Peruvian general and twice de facto president of Peru (1914–1915, 1933–1939). Born in Lima, he was one of the first professional officers to graduate from the Peruvian Military School in the 1890s. He completed studies in science at the San Marcos University in 1905 and his military training in France in 1907. In 1911 he became nationally known for his swift mobilization of an army he led to Iquitos during the military actions arising from a dispute between Peru and Colombia over a jungle area.

As chief of staff of the Peruvian army in 1913, he did not endorse President Guillermo BILLINGHURST's bid to enhance his executive power. Consequently, Benavides was temporarily ousted from the army. Soon, however, he led the first institutional military coup in Peruvian history against Billinghurst in 1914. In 1915 constitutional order was restored. Benavides continued his military service into the 1920s, when his opposition to President Augusto B. LEGUÍA resulted in his exile to Guayaquil, where he continued to conspire. When Colonel Luis M. SÁNCHEZ CERRO overthrew Leguía in 1930, he appointed Benavides ambassador to Spain and Great Britain and then called him back to Peru during the brief war with Colombia in 1932.

After Sánchez Cerro was assassinated in 1933, the Peruvian Congress designated Benavides president of the republic. During his administration he proscribed the APRA movement and in 1936 held elections which were nullified because of the electoral victory of the candidate supported by the APRA. He established the social security system and carried out a program of public works in the midst of a slow economic recovery after 1933. In 1939, Benavides handed over power to his relative, civilian Manuel PRADO.

DAVID WERLICH, *Peru: A Short History* (1978), pp. 201–337; ALFONSO W. QUIROZ, ''Financial Development in Peru Under Agrarian Export Influence, 1884–1950,'' in *The Americas* 47 (1991): 447–476.

ALFONSO W. QUIROZ

*See also* **Peru: Political Parties.**

**BENEDETTI, MARIO** (*b.* 14 September 1920), Uruguayan writer. Along with Juan Carlos ONETTI, Benedetti is the most highly regarded member of the literary generation of 1945. In his most important works of fiction, the novels *La tregua* (1960), *Gracias por el fuego* (1965), and *El cumpleaños de Juan Angel* (1971), and a set of short stories titled *Montevideanos* (1959), he portrays Uruguay's mundane, hedonistic urban middle class. His characters are consumed by anguish without the means for self-realization. Many are frustrated public employees, incapable of taking important initiatives or expressing great passions, who listlessly await easy solutions to their economic and sexual problems. Benedetti treats with empathetic tenderness, and sometimes with irony, his countrymen's dissatisfactions with and resentment toward life, and their vague nostalgia for an unrecoverable past.

Benedetti has also published several important collections of essays. *Literatura uruguaya siglo XX* (1963; rev. ed. 1969), *Letras del continente mestizo* (1967), and *Sobre artes y oficios* (1968) qualify him as one of Uruguay's most authoritative cultural and literary critics. Notable works concerning politics and the national situation are the witty and penetrating *El país de la cola de paja* (1960) and *Terremoto y después* (1973), which analyzes the urban guerrilla war of the Tupamaros and the military's severe response; *El escritor latinoamericano y la revolución posible* (1974), which considers the role of culture in promoting radical social change across the continent; and *Primavera con una esquina rota* (1982), chronicle of the writer's years of exile during the military dictatorship from 1972 to 1986.

Among his works for the theater, the acclaimed *Pedro y el capitán* (1979) is about Uruguay's experience under military rule; it explores the existential situation of an incarcerated political activist and the self-justifications of his military torturer. Benedetti's considerable output of lyrical poetry—sixteen collections since 1945—received widespread recognition when the famed Catalán singer Joan Manuel Serrat featured his verse in the recording *El sur también existe.* In another recording, *Las dos voces,* Benedetti's poems are juxtaposed with short songs by Uruguayan protest singer Daniel Viglietti. The songs address issues such as exile, the Chilean coup of 1971, and the suffering resulting from military violence. Since 1980, Benedetti has emerged as perhaps Uruguay's most visible and respected intellectual.

ROSA BOLDORI et al., *Mario Benedetti: Variaciones críticas,* edited by Jorge Rufinelli (1973); CORINA S. MATHIEU, *Recopilación de textos sobre Mario Benedetti* (1976), and *Los cuentos de Mario Benedetti* (1983).

WILLIAM H. KATRA

**BENEDICTINES,** a religious order of the Roman Catholic church consisting of both monks and nuns. Members of the Benedictine Order, known for their formative influence in the Christianization of Europe, were relegated to a secondary status in the European settlement of Latin America. Unlike the other major religious orders of Europe (the JESUITS, FRANCISCANS, and DOMINICANS), the Benedictines played a minor role in the colonizing and evangelization of Latin America. This was due in part to the control exercised by Spanish and Portuguese monarchs under the Royal Patronage of the Indies promulgated by Pope Julius II in 1508. Philip II of Spain, while encouraging missionary ventures of the mendicant orders from Spain and Portugal, was reluctant to give approval to petitions of the monastic orders to establish foundations in the New World. Many of the monastic communities were themselves reluctant to undertake large-scale missionary activity in the sixteenth and seventeenth centuries. The principal reason for this reluctance was due to Benedictine efforts to reestablish a contemplative way of life, a process that was at odds with the call to evangelize Latin America.

## BRAZIL

Nonetheless, there was a Benedictine presence in Latin America from the sixteenth century—primarily in Brazil. From 1582–1598, monks of the Portuguese Benedictine Congregation established monasteries at Bahia (1581), Rio de Janeiro (1586), Olinda (1586) and São Paulo (1598). These communities exerted a considerable influence on the pastoral and liturgical life of the Brazilian Catholic church. After Brazil obtained its independence from Portugal in 1822, all Benedictines in Brazil were united into the Benedictine Brazilian Congregation (1827). Repressive laws of the Brazilian government reduced the numbers and influence of the congregation to the point where, in 1894, there were only ten monks remaining. At this juncture, the German Beuron Congregation of Benedictines committed themselves to revivify monastic life in Brazil. Within fifteen years, they restored six abbeys, several priories and smaller houses, and sent monks to do missionary work among the Indians of the Amazon River Basin. The twentieth century was marked by a renewed growth in the numbers and influence of the Benedictine Brazilian Congregation, which by 1985 had grown to seven abbeys and 170 monks.

## OTHER PARTS OF LATIN AMERICA

Outside Brazil, the period from 1500 to 1900 was practically devoid of organized Benedictine activity. Individual missionary monks, a number of Benedictine bishops, and a few communities of Benedictine women appeared throughout these centuries, but it was only at the end of the nineteenth century that an aggregate presence began with the foundation of a number of new houses.

In 1899 monks of Belloc Abbey in France founded the Abbey of Niño Dios in Argentina. Like the first Brazilian abbey three centuries earlier, this monastery grew rapidly and exerted much influence. In 1903 monks of Silos Abbey in Spain started the first of what were intended to be several foundations in Mexico. Successive persecutions by the Mexican government forced the monks to flee that country in 1915, and to settle in Buenos Aires, where they started the Abbey of San Benito. At the same time, Silos established the first Benedictine foundation in Chile (Nuestra Señora de las Nieves del

Puente). Two more foundations in Chile followed in 1920 and 1977. Another Chilean house was the monastery of Las Condes (1938), eventually taken over by the Beuronese Congregation. German-speaking monks from Einsiedeln, Switzerland, were also responsible for the establishment of the Abbey of Los Toldes in Argentina (1948). Noteworthy in the wave of new houses after World War II were seven monasteries of Benedictine sisters. By 1985, Benedictine women had thirty monasteries and over 500 members throughout Latin America.

## NEW FOUNDATIONS AND REFORMS

In March 1960 Pope John XXIII urged the superiors of North American religious communities to intensify their missionary efforts in Latin America. A wave of new foundations followed in both Central and South America as a result of this appeal, including several of the Cistercian Order of Strict Observance (Trappist) in Argentina and Chile. This thrust toward a more contemplative religious life was affirmed by the Latin American bishops in their historic meeting in Medellín, Colombia, in 1968.

One of the fruits of the reform of religious life in the Roman Catholic church brought about by Vatican Council II (1962–1965) was the organization of all Benedictine monasteries in Latin America into the Congregation of Cono-Sur in 1970. This congregation then divided itself into three geographic areas: CUMBRA (Brazil), ABECA (Caribbean, Central America), and Cono-Sur (the remaining South American nations). The congregation's members have held triennial reunions since 1972 and have become a vital component of the Latin American church, staffing schools, serving as centers for prayer and scholarship, and providing pastoral care. By 1985 the congregation numbered over 270 monks, with twice that number of Benedictine women.

ANTONIO LINAGE CONDE, *El monacato en España e Hispanoamérica* (1977), esp. pp. 619–660; OLIVER KAPSNER, "The Benedictines in Brazil," in *American Benedictine Review* 28 (1977):113–132; JEAN LECLERCQ, "Espasione monastica fuori dell'Europa: America Latina," in *Dizionario degli Istituti di Perfezione* 5 (1978):1734–1735; MAURO MATTHEI, "Implantación del Monacato Benedictino Cisterciense en el Cono Sur," in *Cuadernos Monásticos* 52 (1980):21–128; LEANDER HOGG, "Philip II of Spain and the Benedictines in the New World," in *American Benedictine Review* 35 (1984):364–377.

JOEL RIPPINGER, O.S.B.

*See also* **Catholic Church.**

**BENÍTEZ, GREGORIO** (*b.* 1834; *d.* 1910), Paraguayan diplomat and author. Born in the interior town of Villarrica, Benítez received his education there and at Asunción. In the early 1850s, he was noticed by officials of the Carlos Antonio LÓPEZ government, who decided to groom him for a career in the state bureaucracy. In 1856, he received an assignment to act as secretary to the president's son, General Francisco Solano LÓPEZ, who was at that time war minister. Benítez later accompanied the younger López to Buenos Aires on a mission to mediate a dispute between that province and the Argentine Confederation.

His position as a diplomat established, Benítez was designated secretary of legation at London in 1860. After the beginning of the WAR OF THE TRIPLE ALLIANCE in 1864, he went to the continent to solicit European support for the Paraguayan cause. He became his country's chief diplomatic representative in Prussia, France, and Britain before journeying to the United States in 1868. In Washington and other cities, Benítez tried to gain North American help in arranging peace negotiations with Argentina and Brazil, but these efforts were rebuffed by the two nations, who went on to defeat the Paraguayans in 1870.

Benítez reemerged on the diplomatic scene more than twenty years later when he negotiated an 1894 boundary agreement with the Bolivians that set limits on expansion in the Gran Chaco territory. Though this treaty, jointly issued with Bolivian diplomat Telmo Ichazo, was tragically short-lived, it nonetheless permitted some respite from the escalation of tensions between the two countries.

Benítez wrote several informative memoirs, including *La triple alianza de 1865: Escapada de un desastre en la guerra de invasión al Paraguay* (1904) and *Anales diplomático y militar de la guerra del Paraguay* (1906).

LUIS G. BENÍTEZ, *Historia de la cultura en el Paraguay* (1976); HARRIS GAYLORD WARREN, *Rebirth of the Paraguayan Republic: The First Colorado Era, 1878–1904* (1985).

MARTA FERNÁNDEZ WHIGHAM

**BENÍTEZ, JAIME** (*b.* 29 October 1908), Puerto Rican intellectual, politician, and member of the United States Congress (1973–1977), and one of the architects of modern Puerto Rico, especially its system of higher education. He was born in Vieques and educated in public schools in Puerto Rico; he received a master's degree in law from Georgetown University in 1931 and a master of arts from the University of Chicago in 1938. From 1931 to 1942, Benítez taught political science at the University of Puerto Rico and served as chancellor and then president of the university—and the entire university system—from 1942 until 1971. As president, he directed a complete reorganization of the university, publishing his plan in *La reforma universitaria* (1943). He established a university museum and a research library in the university's main campus at Río Piedras. Benítez attracted major intellectuals to teach at the university, among them the Spanish poets Pedro Salinas and Juan Ramón Jiménez, and founded and contributed to the literary review *La Torre*.

Benítez wrote influential books on education, including *Education for Democracy on a Cultural Frontier* (1955), *Ética y estilo de la universidad* (1964), *Junto a la Torre:*

*Jornadas de un programa universitario* (1963), and *La universidad del futuro* (1964). He wrote for SUR and *Cuadernos Americanos*, the most prestigious cultural journals of Latin America, was a member of the United States National Commission for UNESCO (1948–1954), and lectured at many universities around the world. Benítez worked closely with Puerto Rican statesman Luis MUÑOZ MARÍN to establish the Commonwealth of Puerto Rico. He was a member of the Constitutional Convention of Puerto Rico and served as chairman of the Committee on Bill of Rights (1951–1952). He was a delegate to the Democratic National Convention in 1976 and was elected as a Popular Democrat to the U.S. House of Representatives in 1972 for a four-year term. From 1980 to 1986 he was a professor of government at the Inter-American University in Puerto Rico, and in 1984 he became a professor of government at the American College in Bayamón, Puerto Rico.

CESÁREO ROSA-NIEVES, *Biografías puertorriqueñas: Pérfil histórico de un pueblo* (1970); *Hispanic Members of Congress, 1822–1994* (1996).

GEORGETTE MAGASSY DORN

**BENÍTEZ-ROJO, ANTONIO** (*b.* 14 March 1931), Cuban novelist, essayist, and short-story writer. Benítez Rojo was born in Havana, received bachelor's degrees from the University of Havana in literature and accounting, and studied statistics at American University in Washington, D.C. He has served as director of statistics for the Ministry of Labor and for the Theater Group of the National Council of Culture. He was editor in chief of the magazine *Cuba* and contributed articles to the magazines *El Caimán Barbudo*, *Bohemia*, *Casa de las Américas*, and others. He also published articles in foreign publications such as *Les Lettres Nouvelles* (France) and *Cuadernos del Ruedo Ibérico* and *Insula* (Spain). In 1967 he won the Casa de las Américas prize for a collection of short stories, *Tute de reyes* (1967). In 1968, Cuba's Union of Writers and Artists (UNEAC) gave him its short-story prize for *El escudo de hojas secas*. Prior to his leaving Cuba, he was a researcher at the Center of Literary Research at the Casa de las Américas.

Although Benítez-Rojo never came into direct conflict with the Cuban government, in 1980 he opted not to return to Cuba during a stay in Europe. A professor of literature at Amherst College in Amherst, Massachusetts, he has published many books of essays and novels, among them *El mar de las lentejas* (*The Sea of Lentils*, 1990), and *La isla que se repite* (*The Repeating Island*, 1992). His literary style is crisp and straightforward, his essays characterized by sharp insight. In general he has a historical approach to fiction. His work has been translated into several languages.

JULIO A. MARTÍNEZ, ed., *Dictionary of Twentieth-Century Cuban Literature* (1990), pp. 65–71. See also SYDNEY LEA, "Introduction," in *The Sea of Lentils*, translation of *El mar de las lentejas*, translated by James Maraniss (1990), and SEYMOUR MENTON, *Prose Fiction of the Cuban Revolution* (1975).

ROBERTO VALERO

**BENNETT, MARSHALL** (*b.* before 1775; *d.* 1839) Belize entrepreneur. Bennett was involved with every major enterprise in the Bay of Honduras. His foresight, enterprise, and success were unique for the time. A commanding figure in the oligarchy that ruled Belize, he was first elected magistrate in 1789 and served consecutively from 1813 to 1829. Besides being chief magistrate and the wealthiest merchant, Bennett was the senior judge of the Supreme Court, colonel commander in the militia, agent for Lloyds of London, a major shipowner, and the only Belize merchant to open a branch in Guatemala, where he spent most of his time after 1828.

The mahogany trade was Bennett's prime concern, and he had separate arrangements with Guatemalan chief of state Mariano GÁLVEZ and Central American Federation President Francisco MORAZÁN to control mahogany lumbering on the Caribbean coast. Although apparently trusted and respected by his many associates, he was accused of breaking up Gregor MAC GREGOR's settlement at Black River, reneging on a colonization contract with Gálvez, and manipulating the Eastern Coast of Central America Company for his own purposes.

MARIO RODRÍGUEZ, *A Palmerstonian Diplomat in Central America: Frederick Chatfield, Esq.* (1964); WILLIAM JAY GRIFFITH, *Empires in the Wilderness: Foreign Colonization and Development in Guatemala, 1834–1844* (1965); O. NIGEL BOLLAND, *The Formation of a Colonial Society: Belize from Conquest to Crown Colony* (1977); ROBERT A. NAYLOR, *Penny Ante Imperialism: The Mosquito Shore and the Bay of Honduras, 1600–1914* (1989).

ROBERT A. NAYLOR

**BENT'S FORT,** largest of the trading posts located outside of Mexican territory to capitalize on the potential offered by the Santa Fe trade. Originally known as Fort William, it was built in 1833 near the confluence of the Arkansas and Purgatoire rivers in what is now Colorado. Owners Charles Bent and Ceran St. Vrain profited not only from the fur trade and the sale of merchandise to surrounding Indians, Mexicans, and Anglos, but also from the traffic in arms and ammunition to NAVAJOS, APACHES, and other native groups who used these weapons to raid northern Mexican settlements. The booty taken in livestock was often sold to Bent's Fort or similar trading emporiums. In this way, U.S. traders influenced shifts in the traditional balance of power and trading relationships among Indians and Mexicans, which further weakened Mexico's tenuous hold on its far northern territory.

DAVID LAVENDER, *Bent's Fort* (1954); DAVID J. WEBER, *The Mexican Frontier, 1821–1846: The American Southwest Under Mexico* (1982).

SUSAN M. DEEDS

**BERBEO, JUAN FRANCISCO** (*b.* 17 June 1729; *d.* 28 June 1795), a leader (*capitán*) of the COMUNERO REVOLT in New Granada (1781). Berbeo was a member of the second-tier elite of his native SOCORRO, politically well connected but economically in modest circumstances. In April 1781, after a month of popular protests against new taxes, he led the Socorro *cabildo* into an alliance with the protesters, thus confirming Socorro's leading role in the rebellion. With Archbishop Antonio CABALLERO Y GÓNGORA Berbeo negotiated the June 1781 agreement that led to the demobilization of the *comuneros'* army of several thousand—an agreement that Caballero soon nullified—and in 1782 Berbeo and almost all of the other participants were pardoned. Berbeo claimed that he joined the rebellion in order to moderate its course and to preserve Socorro's ultimate obedience to the crown, but the Socorro elite doubtless sympathized with many of the plebeians' complaints against the fiscal and administrative effects of recent BOURBON REFORMS.

JOHN LEDDY PHELAN, *The People and the King: The Comunero Revolution in Colombia, 1781* (1978).

RICHARD STOLLER

**BERENGUER, AMANDA** (*b.* 1921), Uruguayan poet. Born in Montevideo, she began her literary career in earnest with the publication of her third book of poems, *Elegía por la muerte de Paul Valéry* (1945). Her first two publications, *A través de los tiempos que llevan a la gran calma* (Through the Times That Lead to the Great Calm, 1940) and *Canto hermético* (1941), had very limited circulation. With *El río* (1952) and *La invitación* (1957), Berenguer begins to develop a personal and original poetic voice; *Contracanto* (1961) is a collection of brief poems. With *Quehaceres e invenciones* (Chores and Inventions, 1963), Berenguer reaches linguistic and lyrical precision in poems of oneiric and enigmatic landscapes.

She is considered a representative of a new and daring voice in Uruguayan poetry. In *Declaración conjunta* (Joint Statement, 1964), *Materia prima* (Raw Material, 1966), and *Composición de lugar* (To Lay One's Plans, 1976), the lyric voice searches for a vision of the world that rejects tradition through the creation of new poetic structures. Her *Poesía 1949–1979* (1980) includes her complete works up to that time, except for the first three books of poems. *Identidad de ciertas frutas* (The Identity of Certain Fruits, 1983) continues to construct peculiar and innovative imagery. In 1986 Berenguer received the Reencuentro de Poesía Award granted by the University of the Republic in Montevideo. She is considered one of the main poets of contemporary Uruguay by Angel Rama, Mario Benedetti, and others.

EMIR RODRÍGUEZ MONEGAL, *Literatura uruguaya de medio siglo* (1966); ALEJANDRO PATERNAIN, *Treinta y seis años de poesía uruguaya* (1967).

MAGDALENA GARCÍA PINTO

**BERESFORD, WILLIAM CARR** (*b.* 2 October 1768; *d.* 8 January 1854), British general who led the troops that accompanied Sir Home Popham in his invasion of Buenos Aires in 1806. Having begun his service in the British army at the age of seventeen, Beresford enjoyed great success as an officer in Egypt and South Africa between 1799 and 1805. It was after victory at Capetown, South Africa, in 1806 that Beresford and his troops were assigned to join Popham in his expedition to the Río de la Plata. In June 1806, Beresford's troops captured Buenos Aires and placed the area under British rule. In believing the Spanish-Americans to be on the verge of rebellion, Popham and Beresford misjudged the citizens' loyalty to Spain and encountered some opposition among the people of Buenos Aires before Santiago de Liniers's reconquest of the city less than two months later.

After escaping from imprisonment by the conquering Spaniards, Beresford returned to England, where he served as one of Wellington's lieutenants in numerous battles with the French.

ALEXANDER I. SHAND. *Wellington's Lieutenants* (1902); ENRIQUE WILLIAMS ALZAGA, *Fuga del General Beresford, 1807* (1965).

JOHN DUDLEY

**BERGAÑO Y VILLEGAS, SIMÓN** (*b.* 1784; *d.* 1828), Guatemalan journalist. Bergaño y Villegas was born in Escuintla, Guatemala. Biographers think that, due to his limited economic resources, he was self-educated. Owing to an accident in his youth, he had to use crutches throughout his life and to spend much time in a wheelchair.

Bergaño y Villegas was both an excellent journalist and a poet. From 1804 to 1807 he edited the *Gazeta de Guatemala*, which, at the time, was a sixteen-page weekly containing the writings of various intellectuals. Bergaño y Villegas's encyclopedic knowledge made his writings a threat to the conservative ideas of the time. Some of his writings in the *Gazeta de Guatemala* appeared under the pseudonym Bergoñer de Segiliú. Nevertheless he was tried for his writings by the INQUISITION in 1808 and sentenced to exile in Spain. He was taken to Havana, where he fell ill and spent several months in a hospital, thus evading transport to Spain. In Cuba he founded the periodical *Correo de las Damas* (1811), which was shut down by the bishop of Havana. In 1812 he founded the *Diario Cívico*. He died in Havana.

SALOMÓN CARRILLO RAMÍREZ, *El poeta Villegas, precursor de la independencia de Centro América*, 2d ed. (1960); CARLOS C. HAEUSSLER YELA, *Diccionario general de Guatemala* (1983), vol. 1, pp. 235–236; JOSÉ A. MOBIL, *100 personajes históricos de Guatemala* (1991), pp. 142–144.

OSCAR G. PELÁEZ ALMENGOR

*See also* **Journalism.**

**BERGES, JOSÉ** (*b.* late 1820s; *d.* 21 December 1868), Paraguayan diplomat and jurist. Berges was a charming, quick-witted man whose social skills and intelligence were early recognized by President Carlos Antonio LÓPEZ, who appointed him to the office of district judge in the mid-1840s. His success in this position was such that López soon transferred him to the diplomatic service, where he distinguished himself on several key occasions. In 1851 he negotiated an agreement in Montevideo whereby Paraguay agreed to support a military alliance against the Argentine dictator Juan Manuel de ROSAS. Five years later he went to Rio de Janeiro to work with Brazilian diplomats on a mutual trade and boundary treaty.

Berges's finest moment as a diplomat, however, came in 1860, when he journeyed to Washington, D.C., to argue Paraguay's case before an arbitration commission called to decide culpability in the WATER WITCH dispute with the United States. The decision of the chief arbitrator favored the Paraguayans, and when Berges returned to Asunción, his fame had grown so much that some even spoke of his succeeding the aging López.

When López died in 1862, he was instead succeeded by his eldest son, General Francisco Solano LÓPEZ. The new president, though in many ways an egomaniac, saw no reason to hold Berges's popularity against him and soon appointed him foreign minister. In this capacity, he sent notes of protest to Brazil when that country intervened in Uruguay in 1864. These protests were only a prelude to the six-year WAR OF THE TRIPLE ALLIANCE, which commenced shortly thereafter. During the course of the fighting, the Paraguayan army invaded northeastern Argentina, and Berges was named to organize a short-lived puppet regime at Corrientes.

After López abandoned his Argentine campaign in late 1865, Berges returned to Asunción, where he headed up virtually all public administration in the Paraguayan capital. Three years later he was accused of conspiring against the Solano López regime. After being subjected to merciless torture, he confessed and was then summarily shot along with other supposed plotters.

ARTURO BRAY, *Hombres y épocas del Paraguay* (1957), vol. 2, pp. 69–98; CHARLES J. KOLINSKI, *Historical Dictionary of Paraguay* (1973), p. 25; CARLOS ZUBIZARRETA, *Cien vidas paraguayas*, 2d ed. (1985), pp. 142–145.

THOMAS L. WHIGHAM

**BERMAN, SABINA** (*b.* 21 August 1952), Mexican dramatist, scriptwriter and short story writer. She studied psychology and, later, directing and play writing under the guidance of Héctor AZAR, at the Centro de Arte Dramático (CADAC), and with Abraham Oceransky and Hugo Argüelles. Three of her plays received the national prize for drama: *Bill* or *Yankee* (1979), about a psychotic Vietnam veteran in Mexico, *Rompecabezas* (1981), about Trotsky's assassination, and *Herejía* (1982), a well-structured play about Judaism in colonial Mexico. One of her best works is the children's play *La maravillosa historia del Chiquito Pingüica* (1982), a modern interpretation of the Mayan legend of the founder of Uxmal.

MALKAH RABELL, *Decenio de teatro 1975–1985* (1986); GUILLERMO SCHMIDHUBER DE LA MORA, "*Los viejos* y la dramaturgia mexicana," *Cahiers du C.R.I.A.R.*, no. 7 (1987): 127–133; RONALD D. BURGESS, *The New Dramatists of Mexico, 1967–1985* (1991).

GUILLERMO SCHMIDHUBER

**BERMEJO, ILDEFONSO** (*b.* 1820; *d.* 1892), Spanish publicist and writer active in Paraguay. A budding journalist with experience in Madrid, Bermejo first came to Asunción in 1855 at the behest of the Carlos Antonio LÓPEZ government, which had hired him to help launch several projects of a cultural nature. Over the next few years, Bermejo was the main force behind such state-sponsored newspapers as *El Semanario de Avisos y Conocimientos Útiles*, *El Eco del Paraguay*, and *La Época*. More important, he trained a team of young Paraguayans in the field of journalism, and his flair and erudition appeared in much of their subsequent work. In 1860, for instance, they produced *La Aurora*, an ambitious literary and scientific review, the first publication of its kind in the still very isolated Paraguay.

Aside from his journalistic work, Bermejo founded several secondary-level educational institutions, including the Aula de Filosofía. He also wrote plays for the newly constructed Teatro Nacional.

Bermejo had an irascible character that all too often conflicted with the rather conservative members of the Asunción elite. After disagreements with officials of the Francisco Solano LÓPEZ regime in 1863, he returned to Europe, where he published a scathing account of his Paraguayan experiences, *Repúblicas americanas: Episodios de la vida privada, política, y social de la República del Paraguay* (1873), in which he lampooned the López family and the country he had left behind.

RAFAEL ELADIO VELÁZQUEZ, *Breve historia de la cultura en el Paraguay* (1980), pp. 156–157, 169–171; EFRAÍM CARDOZO, *Apuntes de historia cultural del Paraguay* (1985), pp. 248–274 passim.

THOMAS L. WHIGHAM

**BERMEJO RIVER,** waterway that arises in southern Bolivia, crosses the Chaco, and flows 650 miles through shifting channels to join the PARAGUAY RIVER south of the Paraguayan port of Pilar, in Argentine territory. Along with the Pilcomayo, it is one of the two main tributaries of the Paraguay River. First explored in 1778, the river is navigable by small craft for 158 miles at all times and for 399 miles during high waters. The river, which carries large amounts of sediment, is difficult to navigate and serves few colonists. As a result of the Machaín–Irigoyen arbitration treaty signed by Paraguay and Argentina on 3 February 1876, the PILCOMAYO RIVER, rather than the Bermejo, became the western boundary separating Argentina and Paraguay.

Although THOMAS J. PAGE, *La Plata, the Argentine Confederation, and Paraguay* (1859), is a major primary source on Carlos Antonio López, it also provides an excellent description of Paraguayan rivers. EMILIO CASTRO BOEDO, *Estudios sobre navegación del Bermejo y colonización del Choco* (1873), focuses on the historical significance of the Bermejo. UNITED STATES ARMY CORPS OF ENGINEERS, *The Paraguayan River System* (1954), esp. pp. 18–19, evaluates the degree of navigability of Paraguayan rivers in the 1950s, with suggestions for development. HARRIS GAYLORD WARREN, *Paraguay and the Triple Alliance: The Postwar Decade, 1869–1878* (1978), esp. pp. 258–261 and 280–283, includes some economic, geographic, and social information.

VERA BLINN REBER

**BERMÚDEZ, JOSÉ FRANCISCO** (*b.* 23 January 1782; *d.* 15 December 1831), officer in the Venezuelan Emancipating Army. Bermúdez was involved with the cause of independence from 1810. In 1812 he participated in the Barcelona campaign, and with the fall of the First Republic that year, he left for Trinidad. With Santiago MARIÑO, he invaded Venezuelan territory in 1813 and participated in the liberation of eastern Venezuela. When the Second Republic fell in 1815, he went to Cartagena and the Antilles and joined the troops of Mariño to participate in the Guiana campaign (1816–1817). Simón BOLÍVAR appointed him commander in chief of the province of CUMANÁ in 1817 and later commander in chief of the Army of the East. He participated in the Battle of CARABOBO in 1821 and in the battles which finally consolidated the liberation of Venezuelan territory. With the creation of GRAN COLOMBIA, he was appointed intendant and commander of the department of Orinoco. Between 1828 and 1830, he put down various insurrections in eastern Venezuela. The following year he retired from public life.

SANTOS ERMINY ARISMENDI, *De la vida del General José Francisco Bermúdez* (1931); MINISTERIO DE LA DEFENSA, *Próceres del ejército (biografías): Generales José Francisco Bermúdez, Francisco Mejía* (1980); JOSÉ FRANCISCO BERMÚDEZ, *General en jefe José Francisco Bermúdez: Bicentenario de su nacimiento* (1982).

INÉS QUINTERO

**BERMÚDEZ VARELA, ENRIQUE** (*b.* 11 December 1932; *d.* 16 February 1991), former colonel in the Nicaraguan National Guard and military commander of the Nicaraguan Democratic Forces (Fuerzas Democráticas Nicaragüenses—FDN), an anti-Sandinista counterrevolutionary organization. Educated primarily at the Military Academy of Nicaragua, Bermúdez entered the National Guard in 1952. As a military engineer, he occupied various positions within the Department of Transit and the Department of Roads. In 1965, Bermúdez served with the Inter-American Peace Force in the Dominican Republic and later obtained appointment as military attaché to the Nicaraguan embassy in Washington, D.C. In 1981, Bermúdez helped establish the

FDN, a radical group devoted to the overthrow of the Sandinista government.

CHRISTOPHER DICKEY, *With the Contras: A Reporter in the Wilds of Nicaragua* (1985); ROY GUTMAN, *Banana Diplomacy: The Making of American Policy in Nicaragua, 1981–1987* (1988).

D. M. SPEARS

*See also* **Nicaragua: Political Parties.**

**BERNAL JIMÉNEZ, MIGUEL** (*b.* 16 February 1910; *d.* 12 July 1956), Mexican composer and musicologist. Born in Morelia, Michoacán, Bernal Jiménez started his musical career as a choirboy at the Morelia cathedral and began musical studies at the Colegio de Infantes with Mier y Arriaga and Aguilera Ruiz. Later he entered the Escuela Superior de Música Sagrada in Morelia. After his graduation in 1928 he went to Rome to study organ, composition, Gregorian chant, and musicology at the Pontificio Istituto di Musica Sacra, graduating in 1933. He returned to Morelia, where he began teaching at the Escuela Superior de Música Sagrada, where in 1936 he became director. While there, he started the magazine *Schola Cantorum.* During this period he toured Mexico and the United States, performing organ concerts, conducting choirs, and giving lectures. From 1954 to 1956 he was dean of music at Loyola University in New Orleans, where he taught until his death in León, Guanajuato, Mexico.

Bernal wrote several works for the stage, among them *Tata Vasco* (1941), an opera commemorating the fourth centenary of the arrival of Vasco de QUIROGA, first bishop of Michoacán, and two ballets: *Tingambato* (1943), based on a Tarascan legend, and *Los tres galanes de Juana* (1952). He also wrote the *Suite michoacana* (1940), and *Noche en Morelia* (1941), as well as a considerable number of major compositions and sacred vocal music. He has also written a number of important musicological essays based on his researches.

B. I. HARRISON, "Old Mexican Organs," in *Diapason* 56 (June 1955): 35; M. QUEROL GAVALDÁ, "Bernal Jiménez, Miguel: La técnica de los compositores," in *Anuario Musical* 10 (1955): 224ff.; *New Grove Dictionary of Music and Musicians*, vol. 2 (1980).

SUSANA SALGADO

**BERNAL Y GARCÍA PIMENTEL, IGNACIO** (*b.* 13 February 1910; *d.* 24 January 1992), Mexican archaeologist. Born in Paris, Bernal came from a family of illustrious Mexican historians: he was the grandson of Luis García Pimentel and the great-grandson of Joaquín GARCÍA ICAZBALCETA. In 1943 he joined Alfonso CASO in the MONTE ALBÁN excavations and began his lifelong interest in the ARCHAEOLOGY of Oaxaca. Bernal received a doctorate from the Universidad Nacional Autónoma de México in 1949. His books *Urnas de Oaxaca* (1952,

with Caso) and *La cerámica de Monte Albán* (1967, with Caso and Jorge Acosta) established the foundations of Oaxaca archaeology. From 1949 to the 1960s he directed excavations at seven sites in Oaxaca, including YAGUL and DAINZÚ. In 1962 he was chosen the first director of the Museo Nacional de Antropología e Historia; he retired in 1976. Despite a heavy schedule of teaching and administration, Bernal produced 270 publications.

Among Bernal's most important publications are *Bibliografía de arqueología y etnografía: Mesoamérica y el norte de México 1514–1960* (1962); *Mexico Before Cortez,* translated by Willis Barnstone (1963); "Archaeological Synthesis of Oaxaca," in *Handbook of Middle American Indians*, vol. 3, edited by G. R. Willey (1965), pp. 788–813; "The Mixtecs in the Archaeology of the Valley of Oaxaca," in *Ancient Oaxaca*, edited by John Paddock (1966), pp. 345–366; *The Olmec World,* translated by Doris Heyden and Fernando Horcasitas (1969); *The Ballplayers of Dainzú,* with ANDY SEUFFERT, translated by Carolyn B. Czitrom (1979). See also WIGBERTO JIMÉNEZ MORENO, "Ignacio Bernal," in *Notas mesoamericanas*, no. 10 (1987); KENT V. FLANNERY, "Ignacio Bernal," in *American Antiquity* 59, no. 1 (1994): 72–76.

MICHAEL D. LIND

**BERNARDES, ARTUR DA SILVA** (*b.* 8 August 1875; *d.* 23 March 1955), president of Brazil (1922–1926). Bernardes was born in Viçosa, Minas Gerais, the son of a Portuguese solicitor. He attended the Lazarist school in Caracas and studied law in Ouro Prêto, where he was a leader in the *Bucha*, a secret student society inspired by the German *Burchenschaft*. After completing his studies, he returned to Viçosa to work as a lawyer, and in 1903 he married Clélia Vaz de Melo.

Bernardes began his political career in the early 1900s, holding various posts in Minas Gerais, including president of the municipal chamber, chief executive of Viçosa, and state deputy. Between 1909 and 1915, he served as a federal deputy. As his political career advanced, Bernardes became the secretary of finances for the state of Minas Gerais in 1910, serving until 1914. Four years later, he was elected governor of Minas Gerais.

Elected president of Brazil in 1922, Bernardes, however, ruled the country under a state of siege during most of his presidency, with challenges coming from both the Right and the Left. The most celebrated opposition faction was led by the Communist revolutionary leader Luís Carlos PRESTES.

President Bernardes implemented constitutional reforms that strengthened executive powers and sought reductions in public expenditures. He withdrew Brazil from the League of Nations in 1926 because it refused to admit Germany as a member nation.

After his presidential term ended, Bernardes (a senator from 1929 to 1932) helped organize the unsuccessful Constitutionalist Revolution against Getúlio VARGAS in 1930. He was exiled to Portugal in 1932 for five years. Elected federal deputy upon his return to Brazil, Bernardes continued his nationalistic campaign in which he advocated exploitation of the country's natural resources solely by Brazilians. He lost reelection in 1937 but returned to politics in 1945, when he organized the political party União Democrática Nacional (UDN). Soon after, however, he broke with this party and founded the Partido Republicano (PR), of which he was president until his death in 1955.

NEVES FONTOURA, *A Aliança Liberal e a Revolução de 1930* (1963); *Almanaque Abril* (1994).

IÊDA SIQUEIRA WIARDA

**BERNI, ANTONIO** (*b.* 14 March 1905; *d.* 13 October 1981), Argentine painter. Berni was born in Rosario, where in 1916 he studied at the Centre Catalá under Eugenio Fornels and Enrique Munné. In 1925 he went to Madrid, and then to Paris, where he studied at the Académie de la Grande Chaumière under André Lothe and Othon Friesz. The influence of the surrealists Salvador Dali and Giorgio de Chirico is evident in his early works. Berni met the Mexican David Alfaro SIQUEIROS in Buenos Aires in 1933, after which he favored representation in his work. In the following decades Berni developed his style in neorealistic, narrative compositions. His creation of two folk figures, "Juanito Laguna" and "Ramona Montiel," constitutes the visual and conceptual synthesis of his attempts to incorporate decorative elements in his art. Berni's creative imagination and enthusiasm were manifest until his last days, when he created three-dimensional animals in assemblages with mannequins, a curious return to the surrealistic output of his early years. Berni received the first prize for painting at the National Salon of Buenos Aires (1937) and the Grand Acquisition Prize, also at the National Salon (1940).

JOSÉ VIÑALS, interviewer, *Berni, palabra e imagen* (1976); VICENTE GESUALDO, ALDO VIGLIONE, and RODOLFO SANTOS, *Diccionario de artistas plásticos en la Argentina* (1988).

AMALIA CORTINA ARAVENA

**BERRETA, TOMÁS** (*b.* 22 November 1875; *d.* 1 August 1947), president of Uruguay (1947). Berreta was from the department of Canelones, where he was a farmhand, cattle driver, policeman, chief of police (1911–1916), and quartermaster general (1917). He was elected to Parliament in 1923 and served as minister of public works (1943–1946) during the presidency of Juan José de AMÉZAGA before being elected president. He died five months into his term.

A man of humble background and a descendant of Italian immigrants, Berreta exemplified through his career the changing nature of Uruguayan society in his day. At age seventeen he met José BATLLE Y ORDÓÑEZ while delivering a report to the newspaper *El Día*. Their friendship helped launch Berreta's political career from a department that was still rural and in which the ideas of BATLLISMO were just beginning to blossom.

DANIEL VIDART, *Tomás Berreta: Apología de la acción* (1946); JUAN CARLOS PEDEMONTE, *Los presidentes del Uruguay* (1984); MARTIN WEINSTEIN, *Uruguay: Democracy at the Crossroads* (1988).

JOSÉ DE TORRES WILSON

**BERRÍO, PEDRO JUSTO** (*b.* 28 May 1827; *d.* 14 February 1875), Antioquian (Colombian) statesman. A leader in the department of ANTIOQUIA's struggle for self-determination, Berrío, a native of Santa Rosa de Osos, received his doctorate in law at Bogotá in 1851. He subsequently served in the Antioquian Assembly (1852–1853), as a magistrate (1854), and in the national Congress (1856–1857). A Conservative, he led the partisan forces that in December 1863 overthrew the Liberal regime of Antioquia. Berrío's nearly universal support in the department won his government formal recognition from the national Liberal president, Manuel MURILLO TORO, on 18 April 1864. As governor (10 January 1864–7 August 1873), he actively promoted internal improvements such as the Antioquia Railroad. Berrío's importance derives from his success in keeping Antioquia out of the Colombian economic and social turmoil of the 1860s and early 1870s. Antioquia's economy and prosperity expanded considerably during his tenure. Berrío died in Medellín.

JOAQUÍN EMILIO JARAMILLO, *Vida de Pedro Justo Berrío* (1927); and ESTANISLAO GÓMEZ BARRIENTOS, *Del Dr. Pedro Justo Berrío y del escenario en que hubo de actuar* (1928); JAVIER GUTIÉRREZ VILLEGAS, *Pedro Justo Berrío* (1975).

J. LEÓN HELGUERA

**BERRO, CARLOS** (*b.* 17 January 1853; *d.* 15 October 1930), Uruguayan politician. Berro was born in Montevideo, but his family, exiled for belonging to the Blanco (National) Party, resettled in Santiago, Chile, where he received with honors his doctorate in jurisprudence. He returned to his homeland in 1873 and was named counseling judge of the department of Colonia. In 1885 he was elected national representative for the department of Lavalleja. In 1890 he was appointed Minister of justice, culture, and public education by President Julio HERRERA Y OBES. Between 1891 and 1896 he represented the department of Treinta y Tres in the Senate. In the uprisings of 1894 and 1897, Berro joined with the revolutionary forces of Aparicio SARAVIA, the military leader of the Partido Nacionalista. In 1898 he was elected national representative for the department of Montevideo and in 1907 he was elected first vice president of the Directorate. An active militant in the Blanco Party, he participated in the constituent assembly, which in 1917 enacted the first constitutional reform in the history of Uruguay.

Berro's career illustrates the evolution of the Blanco Party at the turn of the century. A student in exile, graduate of a foreign school, and noted lawyer, judge, legislator, revolutionary, and party boss, he later returned to civil activities and participated in the transformation of the Blanco Party into a force that disputed power at the ballot box rather than through revolution. In the elections for the constituent assembly of 30 June 1916 (the first elections in Uruguay to use the secret ballot and proportional representation), Berro was elected, and he helped to write the Constitution of 1917.

JOSÉ M. FERNÁNDEZ SALDAÑA, *Diccionario Uruguayo de biografías, 1810–1940* (Montevideo, 1945); BROTHER DAMASCENO, *Ensayo de historia patria*, vol. 2 (1950).

JOSÉ DE TORRES WILSON

*See also* **Uruguay: Constitutions; Political Parties.**

**BERTONI, MOISÉS** (*b.* 1858; *d.* 19 September 1929), Swiss-born naturalist active in Paraguay. A native of the Alpine cantor of Tessin, Bertoni left an indelible mark on scientific investigation in Paraguay. He attended the universities at Geneva and Zurich where he studied SCIENCE before arriving in South America in 1884. Advised by the French geographer Elisée Reclus that the Misiones region of northeastern Argentina boasted flora and fauna found nowhere else, Bertoni relocated across the Paraná River to Paraguay in 1887. On the edge of the river, he built a fine home and laboratory at an isolated camp from which he conducted all manner of biological research. He published scores of articles and papers on such topics as yerba mate, ethnobotany, and the habits of aquatic mammals.

President Juan Gualberto González brought Bertoni to Asunción in the early 1890s to head the Jardín Zoológico and the newly established agricultural school. In 1893, while serving in that latter post, he recruited a number of Swiss colonists to settle at Colonia Guillermo Tell (later called Puerto Bertoni) in southeastern Paraguay. He acted as patron to these immigrants, a good many of whom stayed on in the country despite the fact that the colony did not prosper. For his part, Bertoni continued to edit scientific journals and write works on natural history, many of which were printed on a primitive press at Guillermo Tell. His magnum opus, *Descripción física y económica del Paraguay*, filled seventeen volumes, but Bertoni was only able to print four before his death.

CARLOS ZUBIZARRETA, *Cien vidas paraguayas*, 2d ed. (1985), pp. 257–261; HARRIS GAYLORD WARREN, *Rebirth of the Paraguayan Republic: The First Colorado Era, 1878–1904* (1985), pp. 292–293.

THOMAS L. WHIGHAM

**BERTRAND, FRANCISCO** (*b.* 1866; *d.* 1926), president of Honduras. Francisco Bertrand served as president of Honduras three times between 1911 and 1919. Through a policy of reconciliation and control, he imposed order on Honduras's traditionally unstable political system.

His first term, 28 March 1911 to 31 January 1912, arose out of an agreement between the government of General Miguel DÁVILA and rebels led by General Manuel BONILLA. Under the Tacoma Pact of 1911, these parties agreed to end hostilities. Bertrand was appointed provisional president and oversaw elections that Bonilla won without opposition. In the succeeding administration, Bertrand became secretary of government and justice, and later vice president. Following Bonilla's death in 1913, Bertrand served as interim president from 20 March 1913 to 28 July 1915. Six months before the end of his presidency, he resigned to campaign for a third term. His third term, from 1 February 1916 to 9 September 1919, was one of relative stability. Bertrand's attempt to impose his own successor, however, led to a rebellion and a return to political chaos. On 9 September 1919, Bertrand resigned from office and left the country.

LUCAS PAREDES, *Drama político de Honduras* (1958), esp. pp. 241–268; RAÚL ARTURO PAGOAGA, *Honduras y sus gobernantes* (1979), esp. pp. 46–49.

PETER A. SZOK

**BERUTI, ANTONIO LUIS** (*b.* 2 September 1772; *d.* 3 October 1841), military officer in the struggle for Argentine independence. Born in Buenos Aires, Beruti studied in Spain but even before the 1810 revolution was involved with other creole patriots in conspiracy against the colonial regime. He became a strong supporter of the May Revolution of 1810 and of Mariano MORENO against rival revolutionary factions. Beruti held military positions in both Buenos Aires and the interior and accompanied José de SAN MARTÍN in his crossing of the Andes in 1817. After independence he was an active UNITARIST and opponent of the dictatorship of Juan Manuel de ROSAS. As such he took part in the civil wars against Rosas, and following the Unitarists' defeat at Rodeo del Medio, Mendoza, in September 1841, he suffered an attack of delirium from which he soon died.

JACINTO R. YABEN, *Biografías argentinas y sudamericanas*, vol. 1 (1938), pp. 578–579.

DAVID BUSHNELL

**BERUTTI, ARTURO** (*b.* 27 March 1862; *d.* 3 January 1938), Argentine composer. Born in San Juan, Argentina, Berutti studied composition with his father, a composer and pianist, and with Ignacio Álvarez. Later, in Buenos Aires, he was a student of Nicolás Bassi's. At twenty he published his fantasia *Ecos patrióticos* and began writing a series of articles in the *Revista Mefistófeles* to promote musical nationalism. After winning an official scholarship, Berutti traveled to Germany and enrolled at the Leipzig Conservatory (1884), where he studied with Carl Reinecke and Salomon Jadassohn. In 1887 the Stuttgart Orchestra premiered his *Obertura Andes*. He composed two symphonies on Latin American subjects; *Rivadavia* and *Colombiana* (both in 1888). After traveling to Paris, he settled in Milan, where he wrote the *Sinfonía Argentina* (1890) and *Vendetta,* his first opera, which premiered at the Teatro Lirico in Vercelli. In 1893 his *Evangelina* was performed at Milan's Teatro Alhambra.

Berutti, like the Brazilian Antônio Carlos GOMES, was one of the few South American composers whose operas met with success in Italy. He composed *Pampa* (1897), the first Argentine opera based on the native drama of Juan Moreira. It was followed by *Taras Bulba* (1895), which premiered at the Teatro Regio in Turin, *Yupanki* (1899), *Khrysé* (1903), and *Los héroes* (1909), based on an incident of the de Rosas period. He also composed *Facundo Quiroga* and *El espectro,* both unpublished, and *Horrida Nox,* the first Argentine opera with a Spanish libretto. Although based on Latin American subjects, all of Berutti's operas—as was true of other Latin American operas of the time—were European and classical in style and musical structure. While he was a passionate promoter of nationalism, as a composer Berutti is aesthetically linked to the romantic tradition. With short trips to Argentina, he resided in Europe until 1903, when he returned to Buenos Aires, where he continued to compose until his death. In addition to operas and symphonies, he composed orchestral works and vocal and piano pieces.

RODOLFO ARIZAGA, *Enciclopedia de la música argentina* (1971); GÉRARD BÉHAGUE, *Music in Latin America* (1979); *New Grove Dictionary of Music and Musicians,* vol. 2 (1980).

SUSANA SALGADO

**BETANCES, RAMÓN EMETERIO** (*b.* 8 April 1827; *d.* 18 September 1898), Puerto Rican abolitionist and revolutionary. A physician, graduate of the University of Paris, Betances lived in exile most of his adult life due to his activism against the Spanish colonial government. During his last residence in Puerto Rico (1853 to 1867), he founded a secret abolitionist society to emancipate slave children in Mayagüez. Exiled again in 1867, he organized an armed expedition that resulted in the failed uprising against Spanish rule of 23 September 1868, known as the GRITO DE LARES.

A good biographical sketch of Betances appears in ADOLFO DE HOSTOS, *Diccionario histórico bibliográfico comentado de Puerto Rico* (1976), pp. 161–171. Also see JAY NELSON TUCK and NORMA COOLEN VERGARA, *Heroes of Puerto Rico* (1969).

OLGA JIMÉNEZ DE WAGENHEIM

*See also* **Slavery.**

**BETANCOURT, RÓMULO** (*b.* 22 February 1908; *d.* 28 September 1981), president of Venezuela (1945–1948, 1959–1964). The founder of contemporary Venezuelan democracy, Betancourt was also a hemispheric leader and symbol of democratic values and practices. A strong critic and opponent of both Marxist and right-wing authoritarianism, he personified enlightened democratic reformism in the Americas. He was also the founder and organizational genius of Venezuela's political party Democratic Action (Acción Democratica—AD), which he regarded as among his most important achievements. Betancourt's AD has remained a dominant force in Venezuelan politics for a full half-century and has survived his death.

Born to a modest family in Guatire, a town east of Caracas, Betancourt became absorbed by politics during his student days. Emerging as a leader of the "Generation of '28," he was a major participant in the uprising which protested the government of long-time dictator Juan Vicente GÓMEZ. The February 1928 uprising led to the exile of Betancourt and other young Venezuelans until Gómez's death in 1935. It also nourished their intellectual and political hunger for democracy in Venezuela, and led to a search for new political and doctrinal solutions to national problems, especially those related

Rómulo Betancourt. MIR, COLECCIÓN CATALA, INSTITUTO AUTÓNOMO BIBLIOTECA NACIONAL, CARACAS.

to the overwhelming influence of petroleum on society and national life.

Betancourt assumed a major role in building a reformist political organization following his 1936 return to Caracas. (He returned again in 1941.) He built the nucleus for what later became AD, formally established in September 1941. Having purged Marxist elements from the organization, Betancourt stressed the need for open debate and discussion of petroleum policy and other major issues. When the AD and lesser opposition parties were effectively barred from meaningful participation in elections set for 1945, Betancourt and his colleagues joined with junior military officers to overthrow the existing regime. This so-called October Revolution (1945) introduced a three-year period, the *trienio*, which was marked by dramatic and far-reaching reforms.

For more than two years a seven-person junta headed by Betancourt led Venezuela toward an institutionalized open political system. The Constituent Assembly wrote a new constitution (signed into law 5 July 1947) and national elections held 14 December 1947 brought to office a government headed by the AD's Rómulo GALLEGOS early in 1948. Betancourt and other members of the junta had pledged not to seek office in the next administration. When the government of Gallegos, an eminent writer but inexperienced politician, was overthrown less than a year after being inaugurated, Venezuela entered a decade of military authoritarianism dominated by Marcos PÉREZ JIMÉNEZ.

Betancourt spent a decade of exile in Cuba, Costa Rica, and Puerto Rico. Other prominent party leaders had similar experiences, and those in the underground were persecuted and killed. When a massive civic protest finally led to the collapse of the Pérez Jiménez government in January 1958, Betancourt and other democratic leaders returned home. They created a new arrangement of power sharing, and Betancourt won election to the presidency in December 1958. Although he took office with the support of other democratic parties, he experienced an extraordinarily difficult incumbency.

Remnants of rightist militarism instigated two substantial uprisings. An assassination attempt planned by the Dominican strongman Rafael Leónidas TRUJILLO killed a member of Betancourt's party; Betancourt's hands were burned and his equilibrium was affected. Meanwhile, young admirers of Fidel CASTRO and the Cuban revolution mounted an armed insurgency that brought violence and terrorism in the cities of Venezuela at a time when Betancourt was grappling with a depressed economy left by the corrupt military dictatorship.

Betancourt courted the private sectors, encouraged properly controlled foreign investment, and moved toward a meaningful program of agrarian reform. Labor was supported, education received special attention, and other measures sought to correct social injustices. Betancourt also established warm relations with the Kennedy administration in Washington. The personal friendship of the two presidents grew strong as Venezuela emerged as the model of democratic reformism in Latin America.

As required by the 1961 Constitution, Betancourt left office after his five-year term (1959–1964). Once power had been transferred to Raúl LEONI, another member of the AD's founding generation, Betancourt went into exile for nearly five years, during which time he recuperated from the serious injuries suffered during the attempted assassination. After returning, he declined to run for the presidency in 1973, instead backing Carlos Andrés PÉREZ.

In his final years Betancourt was still a powerful force in AD. A tenacious defender of democratic values, he brooked no opposition to his vision of representative government throughout the hemisphere. He died after suffering a stroke during a visit to New York City and was buried in Caracas.

ROBERT J. ALEXANDER, *The Venezuelan Democratic Revolution* (1964) and *Rómulo Betancourt and the Transformation of Venezuela* (1982); CHARLES J. AMERINGER, *The Democratic Left in Exile: The Anti-Dictatorial Struggle in the Caribbean, 1945–1959* (1974); RÓMULO BETANCOURT, *Venezuela: Politics and Oil*, trans. Everett Baumann (1979); JUAN LISCANO and CARLOS GOTTBERG, *Multimagen de Rómulo: Vida y acción de Rómulo Betancourt en gráficas*, 5th ed. (1978); JOHN D. MARTZ, *Acción Democrática: Evolution of a Modern Political Party in Venezuela* (1964); JOHN D. MARTZ and DAVID J. MYERS, eds., *Venezuela: The Democratic Experience*, rev. ed. (1986); FRANKLIN TUGWELL, *The Politics of Oil in Venezuela* (1975); RAMÓN J. VELÁSQUEZ, J. F. SUCRE FIGARELLA, and BLAS BRUNI CELLI, *Betancourt en la historia de Venezuela del siglo XX* (1980).

JOHN D. MARTZ

*See also* **Venezuela: Political Parties.**

**BETANCOURT CISNEROS, GASPAR** (*b.* 28 April 1803; *d.* 20 December 1866), Cuban advocate of annexation to the United States. Born in Camagüey, Betancourt Cisneros, also known by his pen name El Lugareño, was a progressive businessman who sponsored the establishment of schools, built bridges, and promoted the construction of the first railroad in his native province of Camagüey. A firm believer in constitutionalism and deeply influenced by physiocratic ideas, he distributed a large portion of his estate to peasants at a minimal cost. He also rejected slavery as the worst evil. Always concerned with Cuba's future, in 1823 Betancourt Cisneros went in search of Simón BOLÍVAR in order to request his support for overthrowing the Spanish yoke. Later he advocated Cuba's annexation to the United States, although, in his view, "Annexation is not a sentiment but a calculation . . . it is the sacred right of self-preservation." Toward the end of his life, however, he returned to his advocacy of independence as he came to distrust U.S. intentions. Betancourt Cisneros died in Havana.

For a discussion of some of Betancourt Cisneros's ideas, see GERALDO E. POYO, *"With All, and for the Good of All"* (1989); also, RAMIRO GUERRA, *Manual de historia de Cuba* (1975).

JOSÉ M. HERNÁNDEZ

**BETANCUR CUARTAS, BELISARIO** (*b.* 4 February 1923), president of Colombia (1982–1986). The second of twenty-two children of a poor family from Amagá, Antioquia, Betancur received a law degree in Medellín in 1947 and worked in Conservative journalism there. In the 1960s he served in the congress and as minister of labor. In 1979 he was appointed ambassador to Spain. After two unsuccessful runs for the presidency, Betancur finally won in 1982. He inherited a banking crisis and a developing recession, which he handled with relative success. His major domestic initiative was an opening to Colombia's guerrilla groups, culminating in truce agreements with three of the four largest in May–August 1984. But by late 1985 these truces collapsed, as dramatically illustrated by M-19's seizure of the Palace of Justice in Bogotá in 1985. Increased pressure against cocaine traffickers, after years of official nonfeasance, led to the assassination of Betancur's minister of justice in April 1984. On the international front, Betancur's advocacy for developing countries at the United Nations in October 1983 won wide applause, as did his role in the Contadora peace process for Central America.

IGNACIO ARIZMENDI POSADA, *Presidentes de Colombia, 1810–1990* (1990), pp. 295–300; OLGA BEHAR, *Las guerras de la paz* (1985); ANA CARRIGAN, *The Palace of Justice* (1993).

RICHARD J. STOLLER

*See also* **Colombia: Revolutionary Movements.**

**BETHANCOURT, PEDRO DE SAN JOSÉ DE** (also Betancur; *b.* 21 March 1626; *d.* 25 April 1667), founder of charitable institutions in Guatemala. Born in Villaflor, Canary Islands, Hermano Pedro (as he is known today) traveled to Guatemala in 1650–1651 by way of Cuba. He studied for the priesthood in Santiago de Guatemala but gave up after three years. While he was in nearby Petapa, a vision of the Virgin came to him. Newly encouraged, he returned to Santiago, where, upon relating his experience to his confessor, he was admitted to the Third Order of the Franciscans. Inspired to help the poor and sick, he established a primary school and hospital in a straw hut, becoming known as the "Servant of God." Through charity he raised funds to build a hospital and formed a group of followers whom he called BETHLEHEMITES, in recognition of the importance he placed on the Nativity as a period of Christian devotion each year. When he died, leadership for his work passed to Rodrigo de Arias MALDONADO, known as Rodrigo de la Cruz. Hermano Pedro was buried in the Chapel of the Third Order in the San Francisco church in Santiago (now Antigua), where his tomb continues to be a much-visited shrine. Many miraculous healings have been attributed to him. The request for his beatification was considered from 1712 to 1771, when Pope Clement XIV granted him the status of "Servant of God." Beatification waited until 22 June 1980.

DAVID VELA, *El Hermano Pedro* (1935); MAXIMO SOTO HALL, *Pedro de San José Bethencourt: El San Francisco de Asís americano* (1949).

DAVID L. JICKLING

**BETHLEHEMITES,** a religious order founded in Guatemala to extend health care and education to the poor. Pedro de San José de BETHANCOURT received great popular support for his work with the poor as a Franciscan lay worker in the last half of the seventeenth century in Santiago de Guatemala. In 1658 he founded a convalescent hospital in Santiago, which received royal approval in 1660. His followers and fellow workers became known as Bethlehemites, in recognition of the importance he attached to the Nativity as a period of Christian devotion each year. When Hermano Pedro died in 1667, leadership of the movement passed to his assistant, Rodrigo de Arias MALDONADO, known as Rodrigo de la Cruz. The local bishop, Payo Enríquez de Ribera, was another enthusiastic supporter of the hospital and educational work of the Bethlehemites. When he was transferred to Mexico in 1668, he called for the Bethlehemites to establish a hospital in Mexico City and later in Veracruz.

The formal creation of the order, with branches for both men and women, was approved by Pope Clement X in 1674. Two provinces were established: one in Peru with twenty-two centers and the second in Mexico, Guatemala, and Cuba with eleven centers. Many men and women from Spain joined the order through the Convent of Belem in Havana.

The early history of the order and of its founders was written in 1723 by a Spanish theologian, Joseph García de la Concepción. During the smallpox epidemic of 1736 the order was acclaimed for its outstanding services to the stricken in the countries where its members worked. Today the Bethlehemites continue their activities in Guatemala and Spain.

JOSEPH GARCÍA DE LA CONCEPCIÓN, *Historia Belemitica*, 2d ed. (1956).

DAVID L. JICKLING

**BIANCO, JOSÉ** (*b.* 21 November 1908; *d.* 24 April 1986), Argentine writer, editor, and literary critic. Born in Buenos Aires, Bianco served from 1938 to 1961 as editorial director of Victoria OCAMPO's influential literary and intellectual review SUR. After he broke with Ocampo over a visit he made to Cuba (the Cuban Revolution occasioned many partings in Argentine cultural life in the 1960s), Bianco played a major role in the development of the University of Buenos Aires Press, one of the significant axes of cultural development in Argentina until the university was taken over by the military regime in 1966. Throughout his life, Bianco published his critical essays in an impressively diverse array of forums, from the oligarchic daily *La Nación* to the Cuban revolutionary journal *Casa de las Américas*. *Ficción y reflexión* (1988) is an anthology of Bianco's literary criticism.

Bianco's creative literature is most identified with early texts: *Sombras suele vestir* (1941), a novel that anticipates the formal experimentation of works twenty years later in its utilization of a fragmented point of view and the counterpoint between narrative shifts and the cruel human drama it chronicles; and *Las ratas* (1943), where a plot turning on murder-suicide displaces the traditional omniscience of the mystery story with the relativization of narrative knowledge. *Las ratas* was enthusiastically acclaimed by Jorge Luis BORGES at a time when the latter was particularly interested in detective fiction, a genre with a long record of influence in Argentine literature.

ANTONIO PRIETO TABOADA, "El poder y la ambigüedad en *Sombras suele vestir*, de José Bianco," in *Revista Iberoamericana* 49, no. 125 (1983): 717–730; "Ficción y realidad de José Bianco, 1908–1986," in *Revista Iberoamericana* 52, no. 137 (1986): 957–962; "Entrevista: José Bianco," in *Hispamérica* 17, no. 50 (1988): 73–86; HUGO BECCACECE, "Estudio preliminar," in José Bianco, *Páginas de José Bianco* (1984), pp. 11–31.

DAVID WILLIAM FOSTER

**BICALHO OSWALD, HENRIQUE CARLOS** (b. 1918; d. 1965), Brazilian engraver and painter. The son of the painter Carlos Oswald, Bicalho Oswald enrolled in the mid-1940s in the National School of Fine Arts in Rio de Janeiro. While in Paris in 1958, he became acquainted with the printmaker Johnny Friedlaender. Upon his return from Europe in 1959, Henrique settled in Salvador and accepted a position as head of the printmaking department at the University of Bahia. Alongside Hansen-Bahia (Karl Heinz Hansen) and Mario Cravo, Bicalho Oswald helped popularize engraving in Bahia. Although he executed religious canvases and decorative and abstract works, Henrique is best known for figurative works documenting the landscape and daily life of Bahia, including *Inflation, Alone,* and *Northeastern Migrants.*

DAWN ADES, *Art in Latin America* (1989), p. 339.

CAREN A. MEGHREBLIAN

**BIDLACK TREATY (TREATY OF NEW GRANADA, 1846),** an agreement between the United States and New Granada recognizing New Granada's sovereignty over the Isthmus of Panama. U.S. Minister Benjamin Alden Bidlack negotiated the pact without specific instructions, except to supply information on isthmian transit and to prevent other powers from obtaining transit rights. New Granada viewed the Moskito Indian king, who had claim to land from Panama up to Nicaragua, and the General Juan José Flores expedition being organized in London as elements in a concerted British plan to dominate all the isthmian routes. The United States was also concerned with a French transit company that had commissioned an excellent study and map of a canal route. Under the agreement the United States assured the "perfect neutrality" of, and New Granada's sovereignty over, the isthmus. In return New Granada, in clause XXXV of the treaty, gave the United States exclusive rights of transit "upon any mode of communication that now exists, or that may be, hereafter, constructed." Simultaneously with the transit treaty, Bidlack and New Granada's commissioner Manuel María Mallarino negotiated a commercial treaty, which was signed on 12 December 1846 and proclaimed 12 June 1848.

The Bidlack Treaty was the only pact in the nineteenth century in which the U.S. government agreed to defend a Latin American state's sovereignty at the request of that state. Clause XXXV served as the basis for protecting the Panama Railroad, completed in 1855. It also was used in the 1880s to justify maintaining U.S. vessels at Panama during the Ferdinand de LESSEPS canal venture. International law specialist John Basset Moore used clause XXXV in 1903 to argue that the United States had the "right of way" necessary to build a canal without Colombia's consent.

DAVID HUNTER MILLER, ed., *Treaties and Other International Acts of the United States of America*, vol. 5 (1937), pp. 115–160; E. TAYLOR PARKS, *Colombia and the United States, 1765–1934* (1935); CHARLES I. BEVANS, ed., *Treaties and Other International Agreements of the United States of America*, vol. 6 (1971), pp. 865–881; DAVID MC CULLOUGH, *The Path Between the Seas: The Creation of the Panama Canal, 1870–1914* (1977); JOHN E. FINDLING, *Dictionary of American Diplomatic History*, 2d ed. (1989).

THOMAS SCHOONOVER

*See also* **Panama Canal.**

**BIENAL DE SÃO PAULO,** an international art exhibition held in São Paulo every two years. Inaugurated in 1951, the first Bienal de São Paulo was organized by Laurival Gomes Machado, the director of the São Paulo Museum of Modern Art, and Sérgio Milliet, art critic. The model they envisioned for São Paulo resembled that established for the Venice Biennale: to stimulate artistic production and creativity, provide international exposure for young artists, and enable artists to compete internationally and be judged by an international committee. Locally, it contributed to ending Brazil's artistic and cultural isolation while exposing Brazilians, and specifically Brazilian artists, to the major international artistic movements of the twentieth century.

In the first São Paulo Bienal, artists from nineteen countries exhibited 1,800 works of art. Little-known Brazilian artists such as Lasar SEGALL, Cândido PORTINARI, DI CAVALCANTI, and Vítor BRECHERET had the opportunity to exhibit alongside such internationally established artists as Picasso and Léger. By the second Bienal in 1953, artists from forty countries participated. Di Cavalcanti received a best-painter prize, while Eliseu Visconti was allocated a special room to exhibit his works. Over the years, critics claim, however, that rather than opening the door to new aesthetic experimentation, the bienals have become institutionalized and have restricted creativity.

MARIO PEDROSA, "A bienal de ca' para lá," in *Arte Brasileira Hoje*, edited by Ferreira Gullar (1973); *Arte no Brasil*, vol. 2 (1979), pp. 897–899.

CAREN A. MEGHREBLIAN

**BIG STICK POLICY,** a descriptive phrase attributed to President Theodore ROOSEVELT, who described his guiding philosophy in dealing with Latin America as "Speak softly and carry a big stick." More than any U.S. leader, Roosevelt argued that forceful diplomatic policies and occasional landings of U.S. troops were necessary to preserve U.S. strategic interests in the Caribbean and to safeguard foreign lives and property when national governments were unable (or unwilling) to carry out their obligations. Latin American critics charged that the professed reasons for employing the Big Stick were guises to conceal U.S. efforts to create an "informal empire" in Latin America, especially in the Caribbean, so as to advance the interests of U.S. business.

LESTER D. LANGLEY, *The Banana Wars: United States Intervention in the Caribbean, 1900–1934* (1983); DAVID HEALY, *Drive to Hegemony: The United States in the Caribbean, 1898–1917* (1988); RICHARD H. COLLIN, *Theodore Roosevelt's Caribbean* (1990).

LESTER D. LANGLEY

*See also* **Clark Memorandum; Roosevelt Corollary; United States–Latin American Relations.**

**BIGAUD, WILSON** (*b.* 1933), Haitian painter who has been an integral part of the renaissance of Haitian ART. He is hailed as an innovator of the *vraiment naïf* genre with his paintings of pop-eyed rural folk and people with disproportionate bodies. The renowned artist Hector Hyppolite took Bigaud as an apprentice when the latter was only fifteen years old. Bigaud joined the Centre d'Art in Port-au-Prince in 1946 and shortly thereafter painted his masterpiece, *Miracle at Cana* (1950–1951), for the Holy Trinity Cathedral. In this work, all Bigaud's trademark elements are present: a jungle murder, a cemetery, drums, and voodoo images, all bathed in a rich yellow light. His *Adam and Eve* is considered the best of all Haitian primitive paintings. In the late 1950s Bigaud

suffered a series of nervous breakdowns that interrupted and changed his style, after which he became a recluse.

SELDEN RODMAN, *The Miracle of Haitian Art* (1974); ELEANOR INGALLS CHRISTENSEN, *The Art of Haiti* (1975); MADAME SHISHI, *"Les Naïfs Haitiens": An Introduction to Haitian Art and History* (1982).

KAREN RACINE

**BIGNONE, REYNALDO** (*b.* 21 January 1928), Argentine military leader and president (1982–1983). Born in Morón, province of Buenos Aires, he graduated from the Military Academy (COLEGIO MILITAR) in 1947. After attending senior military schools in Argentina and Spain, he became the director of the Military Academy in 1975. Throughout his career, Bignone led numerous missions to Europe. Between 5 December 1980 and 4 December 1981 he was the commander of the Campo de Mayo military base, Argentina's most important military installation and detention site for those suspected of being guerrillas. General Bignone retired on 4 January 1982. Following the disastrous FALKLANDS/MALVINAS WAR, Bignone was named provisional president by the outgoing military junta and given the task of overseeing the transition to civilian rule. The Bignone junta passed an amnesty law absolving military figures who had participated in the DIRTY WAR, but it was voided by the new civilian government that took office on 10 December 1983.

OSCAR R. CARDOSO et al., *Falklands—The Secret Plot* (1987); MARTIN EDWIN ANDERSEN, *Dossier Secreto* (1993).

ROBERT SCHEINA

**BILAC, OLAVO** (*b.* 16 December 1865; *d.* 18 December 1918), Brazilian poet. Declared in 1907 "the prince of Brazilian poets," Bilac was one of the greatest figures in Parnassianism. This movement in poetry, like naturalism in the novel, displayed the same antiromantic revolt that dominated the literary scene at the end of the nineteenth century. Bilac was born in Rio de Janeiro. His first book of poems, *Poesias* (1888), was warmly received, and the author was lauded by the leaders of Parnassianism. In the first poem of the collection, "Profissão de fé" (Profession of Faith), the author insists on the Parnassian ideal of language perfection. He viewed the poet's task as similar to that of a goldsmith fashioning delicate jewels: "When I write, I envy the goldsmith/I imitate the love/With which he, in golden relief/Creates his flowers." He expressed his love for the Portuguese language in "Língua Portuguesa": "I love your agrestic lushness and your aroma/Of virgin forests and large oceans!/I love your rude and dolorous idiom." He conserved this spirit throughout his life.

Bilac worked with a great variety of themes—personal and historical—the latter ranging from classical

Rome to Brazilian history. His lyrical production diverges from exaggerated sentimentalism to sensualism. In "Ouvir estrelas" he converses with the stars, explaining, "Love and you will understand them./Only one in love is/Able to listen to and understand the stars." His love poems, the best of his work, are still very much alive. Part of the contemporaneous force of Bilac's lyrics lies in the plasticity of the universe created by his verse: forms, colors, textures, sounds, and movements breathe life into his imagined world.

Bilac had illustrious careers in government and literature. He was a founding member of the Brazilian Academy of Letters, and he was above all a revered poet whose verse resounds in the voice and heart of his people. Additional works by Bilac include *Poesias* (2d ed., 1902), *Conferências literárias* (1906), *Ironia e piedade* (1916), and *Últimas conferências e discursos* (1924).

ELOI PONTES, *A vida exuberante de Olavo Bilac* (1944); MANUEL BANDEIRA, in *Apresentação da poesia brasileira* (1946), pp. 108–118; EUGÊNIO GOMES, in *Visões e Revisões* (1958), pp. 126–133, 134–141, 215–295; FERNANDO JORGE, *Vida e poesia de Olavo Bilac* (1963); CLAUDE L. HULET, "Olavo Bilac," in *Brazilian Literature*, vol. 2 (1974), pp. 78–94; and MARISA LAJOLO, *Os melhores poemas de Olavo Bilac* (1985).

MARIA ISABEL ABREU

**BILBAO BARQUÍN, FRANCISCO** (*b.* 9 January 1823; *d.* 19 February 1865), Chilean radical. Born in Santiago and educated at the Instituto Nacional, Bilbao quickly revealed radical tendencies. His controversial article "La sociabilidad chilena" (The Nature of Chilean Society), published in the journal *El Crepúsculo* (June 1844), was immediately condemned by the authorities as blasphemous and immoral, though not subversive. In October 1844 Bilbao left for Europe, staying in Paris and making the acquaintance of the French thinkers Hugh-Félicité-Robert Lamennais (1782–1854), Jules Michelet (1798–1874), and Edgar Quinet (1803–1875). From autumn 1847 to summer 1848 he traveled in Germany, Austria, and Italy: he was in Paris in time to witness revolutionary activity there.

In February 1850 Bilbao returned to Chile where, with Santiago ARCOS and others, he formed the SOCIEDAD DE LA IGUALDAD (Society for Equality) in April 1850. The society's leaders took nicknames from figures of the French Revolution: Bilbao's was Vergniaud, a testimony to his considerable talent for oratory. He went into hiding when the society was suppressed in November 1850. He fought in the Santiago insurrection of 20 April 1851 and later went into hiding and then into exile in Peru; he never returned to Chile. In 1855 he moved to Europe and in 1857 he made his final move to Argentina.

Bilbao's writings, liberal and democratic in content, are high-flown and often very lyrical. His works *La América en peligro* (America in Danger, 1862) and *El evangelio americano* (The American Gospel, 1864) high-light the contrast between the free and prosperous United States and the "disunited states" of Spanish America.

ALBERTO J. VARONA, *Francisco Bilbao, revolucionario de América* (1973); SOLOMON LIPP, *Three Chilean Thinkers* (1975), chap. 1.

SIMON COLLIER

**BILLINGHURST, GUILLERMO ENRIQUE** (*b.* 1851; *d.* 1915), Peruvian populist president (1912–1914), heir to the dictatorial tradition of civilian CAUDILLO Nicolás de PIÉROLA. Born in Arica to a family whose wealth originated in the NITRATE business, Billinghurst supported, financially and politically, Piérola's forceful actions to become president.

In 1894–1895 Billinghurst financed Piérola's forces fighting a civil war against General Andrés CÁCERES. Following Piérola's success in 1895, Billinghurst became first vice president and president of the Chamber of Senators. In 1898 he was in charge of negotiating a settlement over the Chilean-occupied territories of Tacna and Arica, which was turned down by the Chilean legislature. Failing to obtain official support due to Piérola's pact with the Civilista Party, Billinghurst lost the presidential elections of 1899. However, after reorganizing Piérola's former Democratic Party in 1908, Billinghurst became mayor of Lima (1908) and in 1912 was finally elected president of the republic. Attempting to establish stronger executive and protectionist changes, he faced a strong opposition by the Civilistas. When he tried to close the legislature in 1914, Billinghurst was ousted by a military coup led by General Oscar Benavides. Billinghurst died in Iquique.

JORGE BASADRE, *Historia de la República del Perú*, vol. 8 (1964); STEVE STEIN, *Populism in Peru* (1980).

ALFONSO W. QUIROZ

**BIMINI** (Biminis), a large cay and two small islands running southward approximately fifty miles from the east coast of Florida. It is a popular tourist site, especially for sailing and fishing. Local legends suggest that the mythological Atlantis lies submerged beyond North Bimini, while others state that it is the site of Ponce de León's Fountain of Youth. With a total land area of only nine square miles, Bimini is home to about 1,700 inhabitants. It is part of the Bahama archipelago and has two main settlements: Alice Town and Bailey Town. Alice Town is the site of the Lerner Marine Laboratory, operated by the American Museum of Natural History and is the place where Ernest Hemingway wrote his novel *Islands in the Stream*.

One of the best general surveys is *Bahamas Handbook* (annual). See also JAMES E. MOORE, *Pelican Guide to the Bahamas* (1980).

DARIÉN DAVIS

**BINGHAM, HIRAM** (*b.* 19 November 1875; *d.* 6 June 1956), U.S. explorer, scholar, author, and politician who sought the fabled Incan "lost city" of VILCABAMBA and instead encountered (1911) and later popularized the ceremonial site of MACHU PICCHU in the Urubamba canyon of Cuzco, Peru. Born to a distinguished family of Protestant missionaries in Honolulu, Bingham studied at Yale to become a pastor and later at Berkeley and Harvard, where he specialized in Latin American history. Married to an heir of a wealthy Connecticut family, Bingham was able to finish his graduate studies and embark on several expeditions to South America. These included field trips to Colombia, Venezuela, and Peru between 1909 and 1915, when he was an assistant professor at Yale. Finding academic life too stifling, Bingham joined the U.S. military as an aviator during World War I. Later he entered politics in Connecticut, where he was elected lieutenant governor in 1922, governor in 1924, and U.S. senator in 1924, serving until 1933. He died in Washington, D.C. He wrote several books, including *Inca Land* (1922), *Elihu Yale* (1939), and *The Lost City of the Incas* (1948).

ALFRED M. BINGHAM, *Portrait of an Explorer* (1989).

ALFONSO W. QUIROZ

*See also* **Archaeology.**

**BÍO-BÍO,** region of central Chile, with 1,569,431 inhabitants (1984), comprising the provinces of Concepción, Ñuble, Bío-bío, and Arauco. The region is dominated by the Bío-bío River, which arises at Lakes Icalma and Galletué near the Argentine border. After 238 miles the river empties into the Pacific Ocean not far from the cities of Concepción and Talcahuano. It is navigable only for small barges owing to numerous narrows and treacherous rapids. The valley of the Bío-bío has traditionally held great historical significance: the upper course, known as Lonquimay Valley, was used by the MAPUCHE Indians in their incursions into the Pacific side of the Andes. The conqueror Pedro de Valdivia, arriving in 1541, found the river a formidable barrier to overcome before entering into Mapuche (Araucanian) territory.

In 1550, the city of CONCEPCIÓN was built to serve as a regional center, and numerous fortified outposts, such as Los Ángeles, Mulchén, and Angol, were erected to keep the Mapuches at bay. Several times these outposts were destroyed by Indian uprisings. At the height of colonial rule, Concepión had grown into one of the most significant centers of colonization and military power in Chile, and after independence from Spain, its elite competed with that of SANTIAGO for primacy in the country. Wheat, wine, and cattle were the economic mainstays until coal was discovered in Lota in 1848 and the region embarked on the path to industrialization. Today the iron mill of Huachipato and the fisheries of San Vicente (both near Talcahuano), the paper mills of Laja, and the textile works of Concepción are the foundations of the industrial economy of this region.

INSTITUTO GEOGRÁFICO MILITAR, "La región de BioBio," in *Geografía de Chile,* vol. 30 (Santiago, 1985); and CARLOS CASTRO, *Carbón del BioBio* (1988).

CÉSAR N. CAVIEDES

**BIOY CASARES, ADOLFO** (*b.* 15 September 1914), Argentine novelist, essayist, and short-story writer. Born in Buenos Aires, he studied law and philosophy and letters, but chose instead to run his family's ESTANCIA. In 1932 he became a close friend of Jorge Luis BORGES, with whom, under the pseudonyms of H. Bustos Domecq, B. Suárez Lynch, and B. Lynch Davis, he wrote several detective stories. He is chiefly identified as a writer of fantastic literature due to his novel *La invención de Morel* (1940; *The Invention of Morel and other Stories,* 1964), which was awarded the Municipal Prize for Literature in 1941. This book marks the beginning of the modern science-fiction narrative in Argentine literature. In the same year, he wrote and published, together with his wife, the writer Silvina Ocampo, and Borges, the now classic *Antología de la literatura fantástica.*

Bioy demonstrated a wide range of narrative interests, from thrillers to love stories, with existentialist, Gothic, and pseudoscientific themes, and displayed his ability for light humor as well as dark irony and hallucinatory fantasies. He has written about thirty books, many of which have been made into movies and television productions in Argentina and Italy, and he has received the Cervantes Prize (Spain, 1991), the Mondello Award (Italy, 1984), and the National Literary Award (Argentina, 1962 and 1967). In 1973 he was awarded the major literary prize of his country, the Grand Prize of the Argentina Society of Writers.

DAVID P. GALLAGHER, "The Novels and Short Stories of Adolfo Bioy Casares," in *Bulletin of Hispanic Studies* 52 (1975); 247–266; SUZANNE J. LEVINE, *Guía de Adolfo Bioy Casares* (1982); THOMAS C. MEEHAN, "Temporal Simultaneity and the Theme of Time Travel in a Fantastic Story by Adolfo Bioy Casares," in *Kentucky Romance Quarterly* 30, no. 2 (1983): 167–185.

ANGELA B. DELLEPIANE

**BLACK CARIBS.** *See* **Caribs.**

**BLACK LEGEND, THE,** a body of traditional literature hostile to Spain, its people, and its culture. The national stereotype derived from this literature portrays the Spanish as uniquely cruel, bigoted, lazy, and ignorant.

The term was apparently coined by Julián Juderías in his book *La Leyenda negra y la verdad histórica* (1914). The author of revisionist works on a variety of topics, Juderías was convinced that Spain and its culture had been systematically vilified by foreign authors who were inspired by PROTESTANTISM or the ENLIGHTENMENT. His

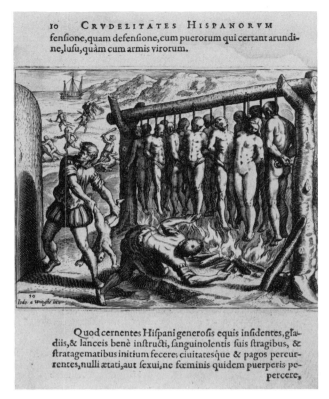

Engraving by DeBry illustrating the Black Legend.
HENRY E. HUNTINGTON LIBRARY.

book, which was extremely popular in Spain, is basically a defense of Spanish accomplishments. In 1944 the Argentine scholar Rómulo Carbia applied the concept to the historical treatment of the Spanish conquest of America and linked the Black Legend specifically to the work of Bartolomé de LAS CASAS, whose *Brevísima Relación de la destrucción de las Indias* had been widely circulated in translation since the sixteenth century. In Carbia's view, Las Casas had exaggerated the brutality of the Conquest in an effort to secure improved treatment for the Indians, and in so doing he had provided Spain's political and religious enemies with a rich source of propaganda. Like Juderías, Carbia was primarily interested in defending the Spanish record.

The publication of Lewis Hanke's *The Spanish Struggle for Justice in the Conquest of America* (1949) opened a North American debate over the Black Legend and placed Las Casas squarely at its center. Hanke contended that the efforts of Las Casas and the legislation that resulted from them were unique in the history of colonizing powers. Only Spain had attempted to place its conquests on a moral footing. Though the works of Las Casas were misused by Spain's enemies, his career in itself was a partial refutation of the Black Legend. This position was hailed by Ramón Menéndez Pidal in his *El Padre Las Casas, su doble personalidad* (1963), a curious work that went on, somewhat inconsistently, to

accuse Las Casas of paranoia. Opposition to Hanke's views came primarily from Benjamin Keen (1969), who noted that neither the bishop nor his reforms had done the Indians much good, and that the Spanish conquest was as brutal and unprincipled as Las Casas had claimed. The Black Legend, in other words, was not legend but fact. Francisco López de Gómara, Girolamo Benzoni, and other chroniclers of the Conquest provided independent support for the accusations of Las Casas, and their works, too, had been widely circulated throughout Europe. Keen warned against the promulgation of a White Legend by those sympathetic to Spanish culture.

The Keen–Hanke debates narrowed the Black Legend to the single issue of the Conquest, but the broader accusations of Juderías had not been forgotten. The work of Sverker Arnoldsson (1960), William Maltby (1971), and others showed that anti-Spanish attitudes predated the publication of Las Casas and had multiple roots. Italy, Germany, England, and the Netherlands developed "Black Legends" of their own, in most cases as a reaction to the development of Spain as a world power in the sixteenth century. In a collection of documents published in 1971, Charles Gibson recognized this fact and provided examples of anti-Spanish writing from the sixteenth century to the twentieth that reflect a wide spectrum of political and intellectual hostility. Though generally balanced in his approach, Gibson was more sympathetic to Hanke than to Keen.

These disputes were clouded from the beginning by problems of definition. With few exceptions, contributors to the debate failed to distinguish the Black Legend as a body of anti-Spanish literature from the Black Legend as a component of popular mentality. The process by which propaganda, much of it ephemeral, was absorbed and converted into broadly held stereotypes therefore remained unclear, and the usefulness of the Black Legend as a case history in the development of national consciousness went largely unexplored. Additional confusion arose from Keen's refusal to compare Spanish behavior with that of other nations. As Gibson pointed out, if the term "Black Legend" is to have meaning, it must refer to the assumption that Spanish actions were *uniquely* evil. This crucial point has not always been acknowledged. No one has claimed that the Spanish were without guilt, but were they in fact worse than their imperial rivals? If they were not, then the Black Legend was by definition false.

Whatever its intellectual limitations, the controversy over the Black Legend eventually resulted in a rough consensus. Most scholars came to agree that there is in fact a body of literature which portrays Spain, its history, and its people in a consistently unfavorable light. This literature achieved a measure of acceptance in the non-Hispanic world and resulted in a widespread perception that the Spanish people were uniquely cruel, lazy, bigoted, and ignorant, and that their culture had contributed little of value to Western civilization.

The origins of this literature and of the perceptions embedded within it were recognized as multiple. Propaganda aimed at resisting Spanish imperial policies in the sixteenth and seventeenth centuries was common to virtually every western European nation. The revolt of the Netherlands alone produced hundreds of pamphlets that were reprinted and translated into other languages until the end of the Thirty Years' War. The work of Las Casas was often appropriated by these propagandists, but given the bishop's polemic intent, his writings would in any case have created a negative impression. Other accounts of the Conquest, though not necessarily intended as polemics, tended to corroborate Las Casas, for Spanish behavior in the Conquest was appalling. It was not, however, unparalleled; and there is merit in Hanke's claim that no other imperial power made equivalent efforts, even in theory, to protect indigenous populations.

The Black Legend was further reinforced by Spain's historic role as a champion of Catholicism. The implacable hostility of Protestant authors, most of them Dutch or English, was echoed during the Enlightenment when Voltaire and others found in Spanish culture a symbol of the superstition and ignorance they sought to combat. The INQUISITION, itself the subject of a vast and often sensational literature, was seen as an expression of the Spanish character. The result of these efforts was cumulative because writers tended to repeat the stories of their predecessors, creating episodes in Spanish history that were in the truest sense legendary.

More recently, anti-Spanish propaganda was disseminated in the United States to justify the SPANISH-AMERICAN WAR, and negative interpretations of Spanish colonial rule were revived in parts of Latin America by the movement known as INDIGENISMO. The *indigenistas* sought to promote Indian cultural values as a fundamental component of nationalism, but their effort was in one respect self-defeating. Those outside the Hispanic world have rarely made distinctions among the Spanish-speaking peoples. In North America, where anti-Spanish characterizations were at one time common in popular literature, films, and school textbooks, the traditional image of the cruel and lazy Spaniard was easily transferred to Latin Americans and Hispanic Americans. By the end of the twentieth century increased sensitivity to racial and ethnic stereotypes had modified the textbooks, but unsympathetic portrayals of Hispanic characters remained common in the movies and on television. Fictional Mexicans, Cubans, and Colombians had come to display the negative traits formerly attributed to Spaniards.

Meanwhile, in scholarship the Black Legend had lost some of its virulence. Since the publication of *España defendida* (1604) by Francisco Gómez de Quevedo y Villegas, Spanish writers and publicists had attacked the Black Legend with varying degrees of skill. Their efforts were often little known outside the Iberian Peninsula, but Keen was right to point out that some Yan-

kees, too, were "more sympathetic than is generally supposed." At least three generations of scholarship have produced a more balanced appreciation of Spanish conduct in both the Old World and the New, while the dismal records of other imperial powers have received a more objective appraisal. If few scholars would now argue that Spain's reputation was beyond reproach, fewer still would claim that it was uniquely reprehensible. Remaining echoes of the Black Legend were heard primarily in the acrimonious debate over the Columbus Quincentenary and in works that deplored the integration of non-European peoples into the world economy. The targets were pervasive Eurocentrism and the mythology of development capitalism rather than Spanish culture, but the parallel with earlier uses of anti-Spanish material was troubling. In the Anglo-Saxon world, where true appreciation of either Spanish or Latin American culture is rare, the death of the Black Legend cannot be taken for granted.

JULIÁN JUDERÍAS Y LOYOT, *La Leyenda negra y la verdad histórica* (1914); RÓMULO D. CARBIA, *Historia de la leyenda negra hispano-americana* (1944); LEWIS HANKE, *The Spanish Struggle for Justice in the Conquest of America* (1949) and *Bartolomé de Las Casas: Bookman, Scholar and Propagandist* (1952); SVERKER ARNOLDSSON, *La Conquista española de América según el juicio de la posteridad: Vestigios de la leyenda negra* (1960) and *La Leyenda negra: Estudios sobre sus orígenes*, translated by Mateo Pastor-López and others, in *Acta Universitatis Gothoburgensis* 66, no. 3 (1960); BENJAMIN KEEN, "The Black Legend Revisited: Assumptions and Realities," *Hispanic American Historical Review* 49, no. 4 (1969): 703–719; CHARLES GIBSON, *The Black Legend: Anti-Spanish Attitudes in the Old World and the New* (1971); WILLIAM S. MALTBY, *The Black Legend in England: The Development of Anti-Spanish Sentiment, 1558–1660* (1971).

WILLIAM S. MALTBY

**BLACK PEOPLES.** *See* **African Brazilians: Color Terminology; Africans in Hispanic America.**

**BLAINE, JAMES GILLESPIE** (*b*. 31 January 1830; *d*. 27 January 1893), American politician and secretary of state. Blaine attempted to mediate the WAR OF THE PACIFIC. Fearful that Chile's demands that Peru cede territory would only prolong ill feelings and thus perhaps precipitate another war, Blaine encouraged Chile to accept a monetary indemnity rather than annex Peru's territory. Chile, however, resented Blaine's heavy-handed policies, which it considered hypocritical, and threatened to use force if Washington persisted in its efforts to force Santiago to relinquish its claims to Tarapacá. Facing a strong Chilean navy, Blaine retreated. The assassination of President James Garfield in 1881 led to a change of administrations and Washington's foreign policy. Frederick Frelinghuysen replaced Blaine as secretary of state. Blaine's ill-fated policies angered Chile, which considered his support of the Pan-American movement to be yet another example of

American imperialism and a desire to force Chile to give up the territory it had won.

HERBERT MILLINGTON, *American Diplomacy and the War of the Pacific* (1948); WILLIAM F. SATER, *Chile and the United States: Empires in Conflict* (1990), pp. 38–39, 77.

WILLIAM F. SATER

**BLANCO, ANDRÉS ELOY** (*b*. 6 August 1897; *d*. 21 May 1955), Venezuelan poet, journalist, and statesman. A prolific author of poetry, theater, stories and anecdotes, innumerable articles in periodicals, and political speeches, Blanco is chiefly remembered today for his very popular poems in a folkloric vein and for his humorous writings. He was also, however, a lifelong (and frequently imprisoned or exiled) opponent of successive dictatorships and an important figure in the evolution of what came to be the Acción Democrática party. He is credited with important contributions in the drafting of the 1947 Constitution, and he served as minister of foreign affairs during the brief presidency of Rómulo GALLEGOS (February–November 1948). In his poetry he was among the earliest in this century to reabsorb traditional Hispanic popular forms and themes into contemporary poetic practice; many of his works in this mode are charming, some are memorable. Juan Liscano and Efraín Subero note an underlying Christian attitude in his hopeful celebrations of common people and his vision of the nation. Subsequent generations of poets have turned away from Blanco's regionalist or nativist manner. Some of his verses have entered oral tradition, and he remains widely read by the general public, for whom he stands alone among modern Venezuelan poets as a national icon.

ANDRÉS ELOY BLANCO, *Obras completas* (1973), is the best available presentation of the texts and contains excellent essays by various specialists. EFRAÍN SUBERO has edited *Apreciaciones críticas sobre la vida y la obra de Andrés Eloy Blanco*, 2d ed. (1974), a valuable compendium of studies and essays, many of them by Blanco's contemporaries. For detailed discussion of his place in Venezuelan literary history, see JOSÉ RAMÓN MEDINA, *Ochenta años de literatura venezolana* (1981), and JUAN LISCANO, *Panorama de la literatura venezolana actual* (1984).

MICHAEL J. DOUDOROFF

**BLANCO, JOSÉ FÉLIX** (*b*. 24 September 1782; *d*. 18 March 1872), officer in the Venezuelan Emancipating Army, politician, and historian. Blanco studied in the seminary of Caracas and was ordained a priest in 1809. At the beginning of the movement for independence in 1810, he joined the patriotic forces as an army chaplain. He participated in numerous campaigns from 1812 to 1817, when Simón BOLÍVAR assigned him to the administration of the missions of Caroní. Blanco attended the Congress of CÚCUTA in 1821. Political and military activities distanced him from his priestly duties and, in 1833, he requested (of Rome) and was granted secular-

ization. Over the next two decades, Blanco was commandant of Maracaibo, secretary of war and the navy, a candidate for vice president and president of the Republic, and secretary of finance and foreign affairs.

After leaving public life in 1854, Blanco repeatedly sought reordination, which was finally granted in 1863. From 1855 until his death, he dedicated himself to the compilation and organization, with Ramón Azpurua, of the documents and testimonies relative to the history of the emancipation. The voluminous collection was published after his death under the title *Documentos para la historia de la vida pública del Libertador* (1875–1877). Its fourteen volumes constitute, even today, one of the most important collections of documents on Latin American emancipation.

LINO IRIBARREN CELIS, *El padre Blanco, ilustre prócer de la independencia* (1961); and CAROLE LEAL CURIEL, *Convicciones y conversiones de un republicano: El expediente de José Félix Blanco* (1985).

INÉS QUINTERO

**BLANCO, JUAN** (*b*. 29 June 1920), Cuban composer. Born in Havana, Blanco began his traditional composition studies at the Municipal Conservatory in Havana and then studied at the University of Havana under the guidance of Harold Gramatges and José ARDÉVOL. During the mid-1950s he taught himself the techniques of *musique concrète*, electronic music, recording, as well as the use of sound for films. In 1969 he became the main musical adviser for the House of the Americas in Havana. Blanco is a prolific writer and critic who has published many articles and written criticism for several Cuban magazines and newspapers. Almost all his compositions since 1965 involve the use of electronic techniques and mixed media. Blanco has done extensive research with "spatial techniques," in some cases utilizing multiple loudspeaker networks. *Poema espacial*, no. 3 ("Viet-Nam," 1968), combines sound and light and requires the use of four tape tracks distributed among thirty-seven loudspeakers.

Other important compositions are *Canto a la paz* for soloists, mixed choir, and orchestra (1952); Elegy for orchestra (1956), a memorial to the fighters who died during the Cuban Revolution; *Divertimento* for string orchestra (1954); Quintet for winds, timpani, and piano (1972); *Música para danza* (1961); Études, nos. 1 and 2 for tape (1962–1963); *Texturas* for orchestra and tape (1963–1964); *Pirofonías* (1976); Episodes for orchestra (1964); *Contrapunto espacial*, no. 1 (1965–1966); *Erotofonías* for orchestra and tape (1968); and *Erotofonías*, no. 2 (1974) for tape. Blanco composed tape music for the Cuban Pavilion at Expo '67 and Expo '70 and for the São Paulo Biennial in 1988. For several years he has produced and directed the International Festival of Electroacoustic Music in Varadero, Cuba.

JOHN VINTON, ed. *Dictionary of Contemporary Music* (1974), pp. 84–85; *Primer festival latinoamericano de música contemporá-*

*nea* (1977), p. 34; GÉRARD BÉHAGUE, *Music in Latin America: An Introduction* (1979), p. 301.

ALCIDES LANZA

**BLANCO ACEVEDO, EDUARDO** (*b.* 19 March 1894; *d.* 1971), Uruguayan politician. Born in Montevideo, Blanco Acevedo received his medical degree in 1908 from the Facultad de Medicina de Montevideo. After joining the diplomatic corps, he served as attaché to the Uruguayan embassy in France in 1909, undersecretary at the Uruguayan embassy in Belgium in 1912. From 1914 to 1919 he worked as a surgeon in various French hospitals; he was appointed chief surgeon of the Rothschild Hospital in 1915. The French government conferred on him the title of chevalier in the Legion of Honor. His family was historically associated with the Colorado Party and related to president and later dictator Gabriel TERRA, in whose regime, which began 31 March 1933, Blanco Acevedo participated. When Terra's mandate ended, according to the stipulations of the Constitution of 1934, Blanco Acevedo was one of the candidates who hoped to succeed him in the 1938 elections. Also running in the election was General Alfredo BALDOMIR, who won, it is said, due to the women's vote, which was exercised for the first time in Uruguay. Nevertheless, Blanco Acevedo's politics (Blanco Acevedismo) remained a conservative force within the Colorado Party, and Blanco Acevedo held the post of national adviser to the government from 1952 to 1955.

ARTURO SCARONE, *Uruguayos contemporáneos* (1937); JOSÉ M. PEÑA, *Eduardo Blanco Acevedo* (1950); BENJAMIN NAHUM et al., *Crisis política y recuperación económica, 1930–1950* (1984).

JOSÉ DE TORRES WILSON

*See also* **Uruguay: Political Parties.**

**BLANCO ENCALADA, MANUEL** (*b.* 21 April 1790; *d.* 5 September 1876), first president of Chile, first commander of the Chilean navy, and longest-surviving hero of Chile's WARS OF INDEPENDENCE. Born in Buenos Aires, he served in the Spanish navy before returning to South America to play his part in the struggle for independence, during which he fought in numerous actions in Chile. In June 1818 he was named commander of the newly formed Chilean navy, handing it over to Lord Thomas Alexander COCHRANE at the end of that year; but when Cochrane left Chile in January 1823, Blanco Encalada resumed command.

As president of Chile from July to September 1826, he was the first Chilean head of state to be called President rather than Supreme Director. In 1837 he was given command of the first Chilean offensive against the PERU–BOLIVIA CONFEDERATION. His assent to the Treaty of Paucarpata (17 November 1837), entailing Chilean withdrawal from Peru, was repudiated by the govern-

ment and led to his court-martial, but he was acquitted. He was later intendant of Valparaíso (1847–1852) and minister to France (1852–1858).

BENJAMIN V. MAC KENNA, *El teniente general don Manuel Blanco Encalada* (1917).

SIMON COLLIER

**BLANCO FOMBONA, RUFINO** (*b.* 17 June 1874; *d.* 17 October 1944), Venezuelan writer. One of the most widely read Latin American authors of his generation, Blanco Fombona began his career as a politician at the age of eighteen when he participated in a movement against President Raimundo ANDUEZA PALACIO. At twenty, he went to Philadelphia as Venezuelan consul. Two years later he moved to The Hague in the same capacity. Between 1900 and 1905 he served the government of Cipriano CASTRO as secretary general of the state of Zulia (1900), consul to the Netherlands (1901–1904), and governor of the Amazon Territory (1905). His political career ended in 1910, when Juan Vicente GÓMEZ forced him into exile in France and Spain until 1936. In exile, Blanco Fombona carried on an ardent campaign against Gómez, and fought despotism in his writings and through participation in a number of abortive anti-Gómez revolts.

Both before and during his exile, Blanco Fombona wrote a number of important essays and novels. His works reflected his life, often in an autobiographical manner, and his commitment to expressions of Spanish Americanism. Like Leopoldo LUGONES in Argentina and José VASCONCELOS in Mexico, he relied on creole themes that dealt with political corruption, anti-imperialism, and celebration of the best aspects of Spanish-American society. Several times nominated for the Nobel Prize in literature, he produced works that included a wide range of subjects and genres, from poetry to history, from literary criticism to political commentary.

ANGEL RAMA, *Rufino Blanco Fombona y el egotismo latinoamericano* (1975); GUILLERMO SERVANDO PÉREZ, ''Rufino Blanco Fombona,'' in *Latin American Writers*, edited by Carlos A. Solé, vol. 2 (1989), pp. 503–511. Works by Rufino Blanco Fombona: Poetry—*Trovadores y trovas* (1899); *Pequeña ópera lírica* (1904); *Cantos de la prisión y del destierro* (1911). Novels—*El hombre de hierro* (1907); *El hombre de oro* (1916); *La mitra en la mano* (1927); *La Bella y la Fiera* (1931); *El secreto de la felicidad* (1933). Literary criticism—*Grandes escritores de América* (1917); *El modernismo y los poetas modernistas* (1929). History—*La evolución política y social de Hispanoamérica* (1911); *El conquistador español del siglo XVI* (1921); *Bolívar y la guerra a muerte: Época de Boves, 1813–1814* (1942); *Mocedades de Bolívar: El héroe antes del heroismo* (1942); *El espíritu de Bolívar* (1943).

WINTHROP R. WRIGHT

**BLANCO GALDÓS, HUGO** (*b.* 1934), Quechua-speaking agronomist, Trotskyist, and former student leader. Born in Cuzco, in 1958 Blanco organized the small tenant farmers of the coffee-growing valleys of La Convención in the high jungle north of Cuzco into a peasant federation that challenged the traditional landlord class. After a series of strikes, land invasions, and armed clashes with the police as well as the spread of such tactics into the southern and central sierra, the government of Manuel PRADO was compelled to establish a commission to study the possibility of agrarian reform. Imprisoned in 1963, Blanco was later released, served as an adviser to the government of Juan VELASCO on agrarian reform, and continues to be active in leftist politics.

HUGO BLANCO, *Land or Death: The Peasant Struggle in Peru* (1972).

PETER F. KLARÉN

**BLANCO GALINDO, CARLOS** (*b.* 12 March 1882; *d.* 3 October 1953), president of Bolivia (June 1930–March 1931). Born in Cochabamba to a patrician family with roots going back to the time of Bolívar. Blanco Galindo was an urbane scholar and army officer with a long history of public and international service. Upon the dissolution of the Hernando Siles Reyes government in May 1930, a military junta chaired by Blanco Galindo assumed power. As the new acting president, he was determined not to stay in power, however, and prepared the way for an elected civilian government, that of Daniel SALAMANCA, who was inaugurated on 5 March 1931. Blanco Galindo's short term was one of the most productive in Bolivia's history. Among its achievements was an educational reform that included university autonomy. After 1931 Blanco Galindo continued to serve the nation and Cochabamba but stayed aloof from the squabbles of the military during the tragic CHACO WAR. He died in Cochabamba.

*Quien es quien en Bolivia* (1942), pp. 45–46; PORFIRIO DÍAZ MACHICAO, *Historia de Bolivia*, vol. 2, *Guzmán, Siles, Blanco Galindo* (1955), pp. 139–165.

CHARLES W. ARNADE

**BLANDENGUES,** a special MILITIA created in 1797 by Spanish authorities in the RÍO DE LA PLATA region to protect frontier settlements from Indian attack and to combat banditry. In some areas the troops also fought smuggling and the illegal slaughter of wild cattle by traders of dried hides. An early decree authorizing the creation of the force called for eight companies of 100 men each, but these numbers were never reached. Manuel BELGRANO, Ernesto QUESADA, José RONDEAU, José

Blandengues, ca. 1890. COLLECTION OF VICENTE GESUALDO.

Gervasio ARTIGAS, and other future leaders of the independence movement acquired valuable military experience in their ranks. The Blandengues were particularly important in the pre-independence period of the BANDA ORIENTAL (present-day Uruguay). Artigas, joining in 1797, fought with this group against the British invasions of 1806 and 1807, rising to the position of *capitán*. After declaring his commitment to the independence movement in 1811, he commanded his former Blandengue soldiers in important early victories against Spanish royalist forces.

WILLIAM H. KATRA

See also **Wars of Independence.**

**BLANES, JUAN MANUEL** (*b.* ca. 1 June 1830; *d.* 15 April 1901), Uruguayan artist, regarded as the founder of Uruguayan art. Born in Montevideo, Blanes abandoned school at age eleven to work and help his humble family. Around 1843 he moved with his mother and brothers to El Cerrito, returning to Montevideo in 1853, where he made his living as a typographer. In 1855 Blanes moved to the town of Salto, where he taught painting at the School of Humanities and painted commissioned portraits. In 1856 he painted eight pictures of Justo José de URQUIZA's military victories for the general's San José Palace. He returned to Montevideo at the outbreak of a yellow fever epidemic, which he documented in a now lost painting (1857). At Urquiza's request he painted the general's family as well as religious themes for the chapel at San José Palace. In 1860, on a grant from the Uruguayan government, he moved to Paris, then to Florence, where he studied at the Florentine Academy with Antonio Ciseri. From then on academic neoclassicism marked his artistic production.

In 1865 Blanes returned to Uruguay and for the next fifteen years received commissions to paint the portraits of famous Latin American personalities, including Paraguayan President Francisco SOLANO LÓPEZ. His historical paintings earned him prestige in Argentina and Chile. Blanes revealed a naturalistic approach to painting when dealing with subjects of contemporary significance (*Yellow Fever in Buenos Aires*, 1871) and in his series of gauchos (*Dawn*). From 1879 to 1883 he was living once again in Florence, where he painted *Paraguay: Image of Your Desolate Country* (ca. 1880), an allegorical image of Paraguay after the devastating WAR OF THE TRIPLE ALLIANCE. After returning to Montevideo in 1883, he worked on a portrait of Uruguayan general José ARTIGAS. The Argentine government commissioned his renowned *Review of Río Negro by General Roca and His Army*. Blanes moved to Pisa in 1898, where he died. He was buried at the Pantéon Nacional in Montevideo.

ANGEL KALENBERG et al., *Seis maestros de la pintura uruguaya* (1987); DAWN ADES, *Art in Latin America: The Modern Era, 1820–1980* (1989), pp. 28–30, 68.

MARTA GARSD

**BLEST GANA, ALBERTO** (*b.* 4 May 1830; *d.* 9 November 1920), Chilean novelist and diplomat. One of the most important Latin American novelists of his period, Blest Gana studied engineering in France and taught mathematics in Chile before embarking on his first series of novels, the best known of which are *Martín Rivas* (1862) and *El ideal de una calavera* (A foolish ideal, 1863). The first of these, his most popular novel, depicts the fortunes of a provincial youth in the Santiago of 1850, with a wealth of precise social observation: it is as good a fictional account of mid-nineteenth-century Santiago as can be found. He greatly admired Honoré de Balzac (1799–1850) and regarded him as something of a model. In 1866 Blest Gana joined the staff of the Chilean embassy in Washington, D.C., and spent most of the rest of his life abroad as a diplomat, serving successfully as ambassador to both France and Britain.

A long hiatus in his creative work ended with the publication of *Durante la reconquista* (During the reconquest, 1897), a lengthy and somewhat ponderous historical novel portraying the years 1814 to 1817 in Chile. *Los transplantados* (The uprooted, 1904) scrutinizes rich South Americans in high-society Europe. In 1909 Blest Gana reverted to the theme of the Santiago of his youth in the charming *El loco Estero* (The madman Estero), whose opening pages evoke in superb fashion the victory parade at the end of Chile's war against the Peru-Bolivia Confederation. At its best, Blest Gana's style is lively, but his work is uneven in quality. His older brother Guillermo Blest Gana (1829–1905) was among the better-known poets of nineteenth-century Chile.

RAÚL SILVA CASTRO, *Alberto Blest Gana*, 2d ed. (1955).

SIMON COLLIER

**BLOQUEO DE 1902, EL,** blockade of the Venezuelan coast by the German and British navies to demand payment of the public foreign debt. From the start of the twentieth century, Venezuela, under President Cipriano CASTRO, had suspended payments on the debt because of the grave fiscal and political crises throughout the country. On 9 December 1902, German and British warships took the principal ports of Venezuela, landing troops and capturing ships as a means of pressing for payment on debts that Venezuela owed those countries. The blockade was also supported by Italian forces and received the backing of France, Belgium, Holland, and other European powers. The debt was 165 million bolívars, which reached 186 million bolívars when war claims and other damages suffered by nationals of those countries were added. The situation was critical, since Venezuelan revenues were less than 30 million bolívars annually, and the Venezuelan government did not acknowledge the elevated amount of the claims.

Through the mediation of the United States, the conflict was resolved on 13 February 1903 with the signing of the Washington Protocols, through which Venezuela agreed to reinitiate payment on the debt, once the sum of the claims was dropped from 186 million to 39 million bolívars. Venezuela agreed to use 30 percent of its customs receipts to pay off its debts.

HOLGER H. HERWIG and J. LEÓN HELGUERA, *Alemania y el bloqueo internacional de Venezuela, 1902–1903* (1977); and MANUEL RODRÍGUEZ CAMPOS, *Venezuela, 1902: La crisis fiscal y el bloqueo, perfil de una soberanía vulnerada,* 2d ed. (1983).

INÉS QUINTERO

**BLUE BOOK,** U.S. State Department publication with the full title *Consultation Among the American Republics with Respect to the Argentine Situation* (1946). Compiled at the direction of Spruille BRADEN, who had been ambassador in Buenos Aires before returning to Washington late in 1945 as under secretary of state for American Republic affairs, the *Blue Book* documented Argentina's wartime relations with the Axis powers. Braden's intention was to discredit Juan PERÓN, the leading candidate in the Argentine presidential election of February 1946. Using captured German archives and decoded Axis telecommunications, State Department investigators produced the *Blue Book* in time for the election. Its data are generally accurate but pertain chiefly to the period prior to Perón's political rise in 1944; its interpretations are heavily biased against Argentina. The *Blue Book* boomeranged: Argentine voters saw it as U.S. interference in their internal affairs. Urged on by the slogan that the United States had handed the Peronists, ''¿Braden o Perón?,'' they elected Perón president.

SPRUILLE BRADEN, *Diplomats and Demagogues: The Memoirs of Spruille Braden* (1971).

RONALD C. NEWTON

**BLUEFIELDS,** a Nicaraguan town at the mouth of the Escondido River on the Bay of Bluefields on the Caribbean Sea. Protected by a series of islands, it has the best harbor in eastern Central America, through which bananas, mahogany, and cedar passed in the nineteenth and early twentieth centuries. More recently, the chief exports included palm and coconut oil and alligator skins. The town was founded by the British and was claimed by them as part of their protectorate over the MISKITO INDIANS during the nineteenth century. Jamaican blacks and their descendants dominate the town's population, followed by Miskito Indians, Nicaraguans, and North Americans. After 1865, the town took on the ambience of an antebellum southern city of the United States as many southerners fled there to escape Reconstruction. Their presence increased tension with the British and Nicaraguans, which climaxed in 1894 when José Santos ZELAYA claimed sovereignty over the community. The U.S. government sided with Zelaya to drive the British from Bluefields, but the conflict between the North American residents and the Nicaraguan president remained. Bluefields became a center of revolutionary activity when the Americans there allied themselves with the Nicaraguan factions that succeeded in ousting Zelaya in 1909. From then until the U.S. withdrawal from Nicaragua in 1933, Bluefields served as a port of entry for U.S. marines sent to the country to maintain order. Until the Sandinista revolution in 1979, the fiercely independent Miskito Indians governed the region with little allegiance to the central government in Managua. The Miskitos resisted the Sandinistas—at times violently—and some of them joined the contra war to overthrow the FSLN regime. The Miskito resistance, the contra war, and concomitant economic hardships forced the Sandinistas to abandon their efforts to control Bluefields.

LESTER B. LANGLEY, *The Banana Wars: An Inner History of American Empire, 1900–1934* (1983); CRAIG L. DOZIER, *Nicaragua's Mosquito Shore: The Years of British and American Presence* (1985); ROY GUTMAN, *Banana Diplomacy: The Making of American Policy in Nicaragua, 1981–1987* (1988).

THOMAS M. LEONARD

**BOBADILLA, FRANCISCO DE** (*d.* ca. 1502), governor and judge of the island of Hispaniola. Bobadilla was probably from an Aragonese family, although the date and place of his birth are uncertain. Appointed on 21 May 1499, he was given authority superseding that of Christopher COLUMBUS. The purpose of the royal appointment was to end instability and strife in the colony. Arriving in Santo Domingo on 23 August 1500, Bobadilla might have seen the executed enemies of Columbus while disembarking. He had Columbus jailed upon his return from an expedition into the interior in September 1500. It was Bobadilla's intention to send him to the Spanish court for trial, where a powerful group rejecting the pretensions of the Italian explorer was active.

As planned, both Columbus and his brother Bartolomé were returned under arrest to Spain. The crown, however, convinced that Bobadilla had exceeded the authority of his instructions, freed the Columbus brothers soon after their arrival in Spain. Bobadilla, disgraced for acting too strongly against Columbus, embarked for Spain in 1502. Unfortunately, that June his fleet was caught in a powerful hurricane in which almost all the ships were lost and much of the documentation involving the early administration of the island destroyed. The historian Oviedo characterized Bobadilla as ''honest and religious.''

J. MARINO INCHAUSTEQUI, *Francisco de Bobadilla: Tres homónimos y un enigma colombino decifrado* (1964).

NOBLE DAVID COOK

**BOBO, ROSALVO** (*d.* 1929), Haitian populist leader of the CACOS rebellion of 1915. On 28 July 1915, U.S. Marines landed at Port-au-Prince in response to the orders of Admiral William B. Caperton to restore civil order following the death of President Jean Vilbrun Guillaume SAM. They were also to prevent Rosalvo Bobo, Sam's political opponent and critic of U.S. IMPERIALISM in Haiti, from assuming the presidency.

Bobo opposed the McDonald contract, an attempt by a U.S. company to build a railroad through northern Haiti that would have involved the seizure of Haitians' property through eminent domain. He was also against U.S. receivership of Haitian customs. Thus the United States blocked his election to the Haitian presidency in 1915, instead ensuring that of Philippe-Sudré DARTIGUENAVE, a puppet ruler. Bobo fled to Cuba, then to Jamaica and finally France, where he died.

JAMES LEYBURN, *The Haitian People* (1941); HANS SCHMIDT, *The United States Occupation of Haiti* (1971); DAVID NICHOLLS, *From Dessalines to Duvalier: Race, Colour and National Independence in Haiti* (1979).

THOMAS O. OTT

**BOCAIÚVA, QUINTINO** (*b.* 4 December 1836; *d.* 11 July 1912), journalist and a founding father of the Brazilian Republic. Born Quintino Ferreira de Souza, Bocaiúva was the main author of the Republican Manifesto of 1870, in which he defended the idea of a Liberal and federalist republic to be engendered through pacific means, by "evolution" rather than "revolution." He also criticized the isolation of Brazil as a monarchy among the neighboring republics. "We belong to America and want to be Americans" is one of the most quoted phrases of the manifesto. Elected president of the Republican Party in May 1889, Bocaiúva was prominent among those who instigated the MILITARY QUESTION and, through it, promoted the alliance of the Republicans with the army, the "yellow button" as they termed it. For this reason he was called a militarist and even an opportunist by his fellow Republicans.

When the Republic was proclaimed, on 15 November 1889, Bocaiúva was the only civilian leader to head the military parade alongside Marshal Deodoro da FONSECA and Lieutenant Colonel Benjamin CONSTANT BOTELHO DE MAGALHÃES. A prominent figure of the new regime, he was Minister of Foreign Affairs until the collective resignation of the first Republican ministry on 20 January 1891 and senator for Rio de Janeiro, elected in 1890 and reelected several times until his death. From 1901 until 1903, he served as governor of the state of Rio de Janeiro.

GEORGE C. A. BOEHRER, *Da Monarquia à República: História do Partido Republicano no Brasil, 1870–1889*, translated by Berenice Xavier (1954), is still the main source for the study of the Republican Party during the Monarchy. For the life and political ideas of Bocaiúva, see EDUARDO SILVA, ed., *Idéias políticas de Quintino Bocaiúva*, 2 vols. (1986).

EDUARDO SILVA

See also **Brazil: Political Parties**

**BODEGA Y QUADRA, JUAN FRANCISCO DE LA** (*b.* 22 August 1737; *d.* 26 March 1794), Spanish naval officer, explorer of the Pacific Northwest. Born in Lima, Peru, Bodega became a Spanish naval officer and was posted to the department of San Blas in 1774. The following year he had command of the *Sonora* on its voyage to southern Alaska. Bodega was promoted to ship's lieutenant in 1776 and commanded *La Favorita*, which sailed to Alaska, in 1779. He remained in San Blas in 1780–1781, then went to Peru to obtain artillery in 1782. After serving in Spain from 1783 to 1789, Bodega returned to San Blas as its commandant in 1790. He was at Nootka in 1792 as the Spanish commissioner under the 1790 convention with Great Britain. With his British counterpart, George Vancouver, Bodega circumnavigated the island later named for both men. After returning to San Blas in 1793, he retired because of poor health. Bodega died in Mexico City.

MICHAEL E. THURMAN, *The Naval Department of San Blas, 1767–1798* (1967); WARREN L. COOK, *Flood Tide of Empire: Spain in the Pacific Northwest, 1543–1819* (1973).

W. MICHAEL MATHES

See also **Explorers and Exploration.**

**BOERO, FELIPE** (*b.* 1 May 1884; *d.* 9 August 1958), Argentine composer and teacher. Born in Buenos Aires, Boero studied with the composer Pablo Berutti until 1912, when, as a winner of the *Premio Europa* (Europe Prize) established by the Argentine Ministry of Culture, he traveled to France to study at the National Conservatory in Paris under Paul Vidal and Gabriel Fauré (1912–1914). Upon his return to Argentina he founded the National Music Society—later known as the Argentine Association of Composers—which was dedicated to the promotion of Argentine works. A high point in his pedagogic career came in 1934, when the National Council of Education commissioned Boero to create and direct a choral group of two thousand voices. In 1935 he became a member of the National Fine Arts Committee and was appointed music professor and choir director at both the Mariano Acosta Normal School for Teachers and the Manuel Belgrano Institute.

Boero's first opera, *Tucumán,* which premiered in 1918 at the TEATRO COLÓN in Buenos Aires, was the first opera on a Spanish libretto to be composed in the nationalist style; it won the Municipal Prize. Boero wrote seven more works for the stage: the opera-ballet *Ariana y Dionysos* (1916) and the operas *Raquela* (1918), *Siripo* (1924), *El Matrero* (1925), *Zincalí* (1933), plus two incidental works: *Las bacantes* (1925) and *El inglés de los "güesos"* (1938). *El Matrero,* premiered at the Colón in 1929 under the baton of Ettore Panizza, became the most performed, most popular Argentine opera of the first half of the twentieth century, and was recorded by RCA Victor. Boero composed several orchestral works, among them *Suite de danzas argentinas* (1920–1930), *Madrugada en la pampa* (1930), *Suite argentina* (1940), a Mass (1918) on Latin text, as well as works for vocal soloist and orchestra, for orchestra with choir, choral works, songs, many works for piano, and a collection of children's songs.

RODOLFO ARIZAGA, *Enciclopedia de la música argentina* (1971); GÉRARD BÉHAGUE, *Music in Latin America* (1979); *Composers of the Americas*, vol. 15 (1969), pp. 29ff.; *New Grove Dictionary of Music and Musicians*, vol. 2 (1980).

SUSANA SALGADO

**BOFF, LEONARDO** (*b.* 14 December 1938), Brazilian theologian. A Franciscan priest born in Concordia, Brazil, Boff is arguably Brazil's best-known theologian and is one of the world's foremost liberation theologians. He studied theology in Brazil and Germany, where he did his doctoral work, and was ordained in 1964. His book *Jesus Christ, Liberator*, which portrayed Christ as a liberator of the poor, brought him international visibility and acclaim after its publication in 1972 (English trans. 1978). Since then, Boff has published scores of books that deal with a wide range of themes. In 1972 he was named editor of Brazil's foremost theological journal, the *Revista eclesiástica brasileira*.

In the late 1970s, as Brazil's military regime began to show signs of unraveling and as the opposition conquered new spaces for contestation, Boff became more involved in writing about explicitly political themes. He expressed his support for the leftist Workers' Party and, in the mid-1980s, declared his admiration for the Soviet Union.

In the mid-1970s, the Vatican began investigating Boff's work on the grounds that it strayed too far from Catholic orthodoxy. Boff's life after the publication of *Church: Charisma and Power* (1981; English trans. 1985) was marked by increasing controversy as his work came under attack by conservative theologians and clerics. Calling for a church born from the faith of the poor, Boff's book criticized the Catholic church for being authoritarian and excessively concerned with power. Conservatives counterargued that Boff was unduly critical of the institution, and that the pope and bishops must assume responsibility for leadership in the church. In this view, popular religion therefore holds no special claim to truth in the church.

In September 1984, Boff went to Rome to defend his writings. After several months of deliberation, the Vatican formally criticized Boff's work in May 1985, imposing a silence that was lifted the following year. Because Boff was so prominent, this sanction was broadly perceived as an attack upon the LIBERATION THEOLOGY movement. In May 1991, Boff was again sanctioned by the Vatican, which required him to resign as editor of the *Revista Eclesiástica Brasileira* and ordered him not to publish any works for a year.

LUIS MARCOS SANDER, *Jesus, o Libertador: A Cristologia da libertação de Leonardo Boff* (1986); HARVEY COX, *The Silencing of Leonardo Boff: The Vatican and the Future of World Christianity* (1988).

SCOTT MAINWARING

*See also* **Catholic Church.**

**BOGOTÁ CONFERENCE (1948).** *See* **See Pan-American Conferences.**

**BOGOTÁ, SANTA FE DE**

### *The City*

The capital and largest city of Colombia, Santa Fe de Bogotá is also the capital of the department of Cundinamarca. In 1985 the city had a population of nearly four million. It is located in the Eastern Cordillera of the Andes on the eastern edge of a basin known as the *sabana* of Bogotá at an elevation of about 8,600 feet. Rising sharply above the city to the east are two peaks, Monserrate and Guadalupe. Because of its altitude, Bogotá has a cool climate with an average temperature of 57°F.

Although Bogotá has been an important administrative, cultural, and economic center since the sixteenth century, its growth was long impeded by its inland location and high altitude. Before the advent of modern modes of transportation, access to the MAGDALENA RIVER and the Caribbean Sea required a long and arduous journey. Communication with the Pacific Ocean and other regions of Colombia was equally difficult.

In the 1530s the area around modern Bogotá was part of the domain of the powerful Chibcha chieftain, or *zipa*, called Tisquesusa. Spaniards under Gonzalo JIMÉNEZ DE QUESADA (*d.* 1579) reached the *sabana* in 1537 and proceeded to subjugate the region despite Chibcha resistance. There is some confusion about the circumstances of the founding of Bogotá. The traditional date for the city's foundation is 6 August 1538. According to historian Juan Friede, Jiménez laid claim to the *zipa's* territories in the latter's capital, called Bogotá (Bacatá), on 6 August 1537. However, the formal establishment of the Spanish city of Santa Fe took place on 27 April 1539, at a nearby site called Teusaquillo.

Santa Fe (Santafé) quickly became the principal city of the Kingdom of New Granada, which embraced most of modern Colombia. An AUDIENCIA, or high court, was installed in Santa Fe in 1550; a bishopric was established in 1553 and elevated to the rank of archbishopric in 1564. In the eighteenth century, the Spanish government selected Santa Fe as the capital of the new Viceroyalty of NEW GRANADA.

Despite its status as a colonial capital, Santa Fe de Bogotá grew slowly; its population was only about 28,000 in 1761. In the late eighteenth and early nineteenth centuries, the city's intellectual life was stimulated by the scientific teachings and projects of José

View of Planetarium Museum and Plaza de Torres, Santa Fe de Bogotá, 1983. ORGANIZATION OF AMERICAN STATES.

Celestino MUTIS (1732–1808), a Spanish botanist who lived in Santa Fe from 1761 to 1808. This period also saw the establishment of the city's first newspapers and journals, notably the *Papel Periódico* (1791–1797) and the *Semanario . . . del Nuevo Reino de Granada* (1808–1810).

The city played a major role in Colombia's independence movement from Spain. A dispute in Santa Fe between a Creole and a Spaniard on 20 July 1810 helped to trigger the deposition of the viceroy, an event commemorated as Colombia's national holiday. After independence, Santa Fe, now renamed Bogotá, became the capital of Gran Colombia and later (1831) of New Granada or Colombia.

Colombia's political instability and sluggish economy during the first decades after independence inhibited change in Bogotá, which had a population of only about 30,000 in 1851. The heart of the city was still the square on which the eighteenth-century cathedral was located. The square was given its present name of Plaza de Bolívar after a statue of Simon BOLÍVAR was erected there in 1846. In 1848 President Tomás Cipriano de MOSQUERA laid the cornerstone of the national capitol on the south-

ern side of the square, but work on the project soon halted (1851).

After 1870, the expansion of commercial agriculture, especially the development of coffee exports, brought modest economic growth to Colombia, which was reflected in Bogotá. The population grew from about 41,000 in 1870 to 121,000 in 1912. Colombia's first successful bank, the Banco de Bogotá, opened its doors in 1871, followed by the Banco de Colombia in 1875 and others. Although Bogotá lagged behind Medellín in textile manufacturing, numerous industries were established during this period, among them the brewery Bavaria (1891) and Cementos Samper (1909). Work was resumed on the capitol (though it remained incomplete until the mid 1920s), and on other public buildings, such as the Teatro Colón, which was modeled on the Paris Opéra. Efforts were also made to improve the quality of urban life through improved paving and the construction of sewers, aqueducts, parks, and bridges. Gas lighting was introduced in 1876 and illumination by electricity in the early 1890s.

During these years affluent bogotanos began moving north to the nearby hamlet of Chapinero, which was annexed to the city in 1885. By this time a trolley line extended from the Plaza de Bolívar along the Carrera Séptima, the city's main thoroughfare, to Chapinero. Between the 1880s and 1909, Bogotá was gradually connected by rail to the Magdalena as well.

Throughout the nineteenth century, Bogotá's elites enjoyed a reputation for sardonic wit and literary distinction and boasted of the city's claim to be the "Athens of South America." They were also noted for their conservative political views and, like the city's population as a whole, for their devotion to Catholicism. William L. Scruggs (1836–1912), who served as U.S. minister in the 1870s and 1880s, observed that "there is probably no city on the continent where the external forms of religion are more rigidly observed."

Scruggs was also impressed by the "insubordination" of the lower classes, who were mainly MESTIZOS. The economic quickening of the late nineteenth century brought dislocation to many workers, and government monetary policy contributed to an inflationary trend in the 1890s. In 1893 the publication of a series of articles in a leading newspaper accusing the lower classes of drunkenness and immorality produced a riot that left from forty to forty-five persons dead. During the disorders the rioters attacked police stations as well as the homes of public officials.

Bogotá's growth accelerated after 1930 for several reasons. With the expansion of commercial agriculture and import-substitution industrialization, Colombia's economy was growing at a more rapid rate than before. Bogotá became more important as a manufacturing center, accounting for 29 percent of the nation's industrial employment by 1975. The enlarged socioeconomic role of the state increased the size of the bureaucracy and gave birth to numerous public agencies headquartered in the capital. Agricultural modernization and endemic rural violence displaced many peasants who migrated to Bogotá. As a result, by 1973 Bogotá contained 13.6 percent of Colombia's population as compared to 4.1 percent in 1938. In 1964 more than 50 percent of the city's population had been born in other parts of the country.

The aspirations and tensions fueled by these changes contributed to the rise of the charismatic Liberal leader Jorge ELIÉCER GAITÁN (*b.* 1898), who served as mayor of Bogotá in 1936–1937. During the violence that followed his assassination in 1948 (referred to as the BOGOTAZO), hundreds of buildings and shops in the central business district were damaged or destroyed, including the departmental headquarters of Cundinamarca, the ministries of justice and interior, and two buildings of the archdiocese. (In 1985 a government assault against guerrillas who had taken possession of the Palace of Justice severely damaged the building and cost nearly one hundred lives.)

Since 1930 the northward drift of the upper and upper-middle classes has continued, accompanied by a similar movement of offices and commercial establishments. Lower-income residential areas have become concentrated in the central, southern, and western sectors, with much self-built irregular housing in the latter two. In 1983 municipal authorities created the Corporación Candelaria to restore and preserve fifty-four blocks in the city's central district, mainly in the historical quarter called the Candelaria.

In 1954 the national government incorporated Bogotá into a Special District (Distrito Especial) that also included six nearby municipalities: Bosa, Engativá, Fontibón, Suba, Usaquén, and Usme. The chief executive officer, or ALCALDE MAYOR, of the Special District was appointed by the president until 1986, when the position was made elective. In the constitution of 1991 the Special District was renamed the Capital District (Distrito Capital). It was to be governed by an elective mayor and district council, along with neighborhood officials. The constitution also restored to the city its colonial name of Santa Fe de Bogotá.

PEDRO M. IBÁÑEZ, *Crónicas de Bogotá*, 4 vols., 2d ed. (1913–1923); JUAN FRIEDE, *Invasión del país de los Chibchas: Conquista del Nuevo Reino de Granada y fundación de Santafé de Bogotá* (1966); ALAN GILBERT, "Bogotá: Politics, Planning, and the Crisis of Lost Opportunities," in *Latin American Urban Research,* vol. 6: *Metropolitan Latin America: The Challenge and the Response,* edited by Wayne A. Cornelius and Robert V. Kemper (1978), pp. 87–126; ENRIQUE DURAND, "Bogotá: Echoes of the Past," in *Américas* 39 (November–December 1987):24–30; DAVID SOWELL, "The 1893 *bogotazo*: Artisans and Public Violence in Late Nineteenth-Century Bogotá," in *Journal of Latin American Studies* 21 (1989): 267–282.

HELEN DELPAR

### The Audiencia

The AUDIENCIA of Santa Fe de Bogotá was first installed in 1550, with jurisdiction over the area that today con-stitutes most of the modern republics of Colombia and Venezuela. Spanish settlements on the Caribbean coasts were previously under the jurisdiction of the audiencias of Panama and Santo Domingo, but after Spaniards had penetrated into the Andean interior (where they established the Kingdom of New Granada in 1539), CHARLES I decided to create the new Audiencia of Santa Fe in order to impose royal control over New Granada's unruly conquerors and ENCOMENDEROS, and to enforce the NEW LAWS of 1542. By 1563 the audiencia's territorial jurisdiction had taken the shape that it was to retain for most of the colonial period. This extended over much of modern Colombia, apart from the great southern territory of the province of Popayán, which became part of the Audiencia of Quito (established in 1563), and most of modern Venezuela, except Caracas which remained within the jurisdiction of the Audiencia of Santo Domingo.

The first audiencia tribunal consisted of four OIDORES (judges), all lawyers, one of whom was appointed as president. The first president died en route to Bogotá, however, and the presidency was not subsequently exercised until 1563, by Andrés Venero de Leiva (1563–1574). Government then returned to the audiencia as a collegiate body until the presidency was revived under Antonio González (1590–1597) and Francisco de Sande (1597–1602). The first half-century of the audiencia's life was one of considerable turbulence, characterized by conflicts with *encomenderos*, clergy, and among the *oidores* themselves.

In 1605, the crown sought to strengthen the audiencia's authority and efficiency by altering its presidency. Juan de Borja became governor and CAPTAIN-GENERAL of New Granada and *presidente de capa y espada*, with military duties and powers. From 1630, the crown tried further to consolidate the audiencia's authority by appointing Spanish nobles as presidents, in a largely ineffective effort to counter the power of local elites.

During the eighteenth century, the audiencia underwent fresh alterations to its jurisdiction, power, and composition. Reform began in 1717, following a crisis within the audiencia in 1715 when the *oidores* deposed and imprisoned President Francisco de Meneses. The Audiencia of Santa Fe was enlarged to include Panama in its jurisdiction, and in 1719 the first viceroy of New Granada replaced the audiencia's president as the crown's leading official. Suppressed in 1723, the Viceroyalty of New Granada was reestablished in 1739, and Santa Fe again became an audiencia, with the viceroy as governor and captain-general of New Granada and ex officio president of the audiencia.

The second Bourbon reform of the audiencia stemmed from CHARLES III's program of colonial reform and was implemented in New Granada during the *visita general* of 1778–1783. The audiencia was expanded in 1776 to include a regent and a *fiscal del crimen* (crown criminal prosecutor). Also, another *oidor* was added. Furthermore, it was "Europeanized" by the appointment of peninsular lawyers who were free of local ties. To further reduce their susceptibility to local interests, they now served for shorter periods and were discouraged by the Madrid government from marrying into local CREOLE society. Subordinated to the viceroys in Santa Fe, the eighteenth-century audiencia reflected the general shift from the consensual government of the Hapsburg monarchy to the centralized, absolutist model favored by the Bourbons.

The audiencia judges were forced to leave Bogotá when viceregal government was overthrown in 1810, and the audiencia moved to Panama until New Granada was reconquered by Spain in 1815. When Spanish rule ended in 1819, the Viceroyalty and Audiencia of Santa Fe were supplanted by republican government.

R. B. CUNNINGHAM GRAHAM, *The Conquest of New Granada, Being the Life of Gonzalo Jiménez de Quesada* (1922); MANUEL LUCENA SALMORAL, *Nuevo Reino de Granada, Real Audiencia y Presidentes: Presidentes de Capa y Espada (1605–1628)* (1965) and *Nuevo Reino de Granada, Real Audiencia y Presidentes: Presidentes de Capa y Espada (1628–1654)* (1967); SERGIO ELÍAS ORTÍZ, *Nuevo Reino de Granada, Real Audiencia y Presidentes: Presidentes de Capa y Espada (1654–1719)* (1966); ANTHONY MC FARLANE, *Colombia Before Independence: Economy, Society, and Politics Under Bourbon Rule* (1993).

ANTHONY MCFARLANE

**BOGOTAZO,** a riot in Bogotá, Colombia, after the fatal shooting of Jorge E. GAITÁN on 9 April 1948. Gaitán, head of the Liberal Party, was a popular hero whose death enraged his lower- and middle-class followers. A mob soon murdered the assassin, Juan Roa Sierra. The rioters then turned their fury on institutions associated with the ruling Conservative Party and the existing social order, such as government buildings, churches, the Jockey Club, and *El Siglo*, a Conservative newspaper. Many shops were looted, and thousands may have been killed or wounded before order was restored on 11 April. Disturbances also took place in other cities. The Conservative president, Mariano OSPINA PÉREZ, blamed the riot on a communist plot and added Liberals to his cabinet, but the Bogotazo exacerbated partisan tensions and contributed to the deepening *violencia*.

ARTURO ALAPE, *El Bogotazo: Memorias del olvido*, 3d ed. (1984); HERBERT BRAUN, *The Assassination of Gaitán: Public Life and Urban Violence in Colombia* (1985).

HELEN DELPAR

**BÓIA-FRIA,** a Brazilian rural manual laborer who is hired temporarily and has no relationship to the place of employment. The name *bóia-fria* literally means the cold food included as part of a worker's wages. Alternate names for these migrant workers include: *avulso* (separate), *contínuo* (messenger), *clandestino* (clandestine [in the northwest]), *volante* (from *voar*—to fly), *safrista* (from *safra*—sugar harvest), *eventual* (for the event),

*diarista* (daily), and *temporário* (temporary). The practice originated in industries that required a large number of seasonal manual laborers, such as those engaged in the harvest of coffee beans, and was adopted by others that required a reduced labor force on a full-time basis but employed temporary workers to improve commercial yield. The practice provoked a rural exodus. *Bóia-frias* typically live in the urban periphery and at harvest time move to the fields, where they live in extreme poverty. Their level of education is low, and illiteracy predominates. Their basic diet consists of plain rice or rice and beans.

MARIA DA CONCEIÇÃO DE MELLO LUCAS, *O bóia-Fria: Acumulação e miséria*, 2d ed. (1975); AURÉLIO BUARQUE HOLANDA FERREIRA, *Novo dicionário da língua portuguesa*, 2d ed. (1986).

DALISIA MARTINS DOLES

**BOISO–LANZA PACT (1973),** an agreement guaranteeing the Uruguayan military an advisory role and participation in political decision making. The military and, at that time constitutional, President Juan María BORDABERRY were the principal parties to the February 1973 agreement, which was openly recognized by the military through such institutions as the National Security Counsel (Cosena) and the Joint Chiefs of Staff (Esmaco). On 9 February of that year, the military had published communiqués outlining a confusing program that contained some hints of populism. A few days later, in a meeting at the Boiso-Lanza military base in the department of Montevideo, the military presented its demands to President Bordaberry, who was seeking a corporate-style reorganization of the state without precedent in the political tradition of the country. On 27 June 1973, Bordaberry dissolved the Parliament and severely limited civil liberties, beginning the military regime that would last until 1 March 1985.

ANGEL COCCHI, *Nuestros partidos*, vol. 2 (1984); GERARDO CAETANO and JOSÉ RILLA, *Breve historia de la dictadura* (1991).

JOSÉ DE TORRES WILSON

**BOLAÑOS, CÉSAR** (*b.* 4 June 1931), Peruvian composer. He was born in Lima and began his musical studies with Andrés Sas at the National Conservatory in Lima and then studied electronic music at the RCA Institute of Electronic Technology in New York City (1958–1963). His postgraduate studies took place at the Latin American Center for Advanced Musical Studies at the Torcuato di Tella Institute in Buenos Aires, where his mentors were composers Alberto GINASTERA and Gerardo GANDINI. Bolaños collaborated with the electronic music laboratory, founded in Buenos Aires in 1964. He taught the seminar on electroacoustic composition and gave classes on audiovisual theory. His main compositional efforts since 1970 have utilized computers, and many of his works were created at the facilities of Honeywell Bull Argentina. To refer to some of these works generically Bolaños used the acronym ESEPCO, for *estructuras sonora-expresivas por computación* (digital sonic-expressive structures). At the Di Tella Laboratories in 1964 he created his first electronic tape composition, *Intensidad y altura,* based on a poem by César VALLEJO. Other important compositions by Bolaños include *Ñacahuasu* for chamber orchestra and narrator (1970); *Ensayo* for string orchestra (1956); *Cantata solar* for orchestra, choirs, solo voices, and tape (1963); *Variaciones* for alto, flute, clarinet, bass clarinet, double bass, and percussion (1963), with text by César Vallejo; *Divertimento,* no. 1 for flute, clarinet, bass clarinet, trumpet, harpsichord, piano, double bass, and percussion (1966); and *Divertimento,* no. 3 for flute, clarinet, bass clarinet, piano, and percussion (1967). Among his most theatrical works are *I-10-AIFG/Mn1-1* for flute, violin, accordion, two percussionists, and three narrators (1969); *Alfa-Omega* for two narrators, theatrical mixed choir, electric guitar, double bass, two percussionists, two dancers, tape, slide projections, and lights (1967), which utilizes biblical texts; and the celebrated *I-10-AIFG/Rbt-1* for three narrators, horn, trombone, electric guitar, two percussionists, two operators for keyboard controlled lights and six radios, nine slide projectors with automatic synchronization, tape, and instrumental amplification, with black lights for the reading of scores and "programmed conducting" using synchronized light signals (1968).

*Anuario/Yearbook: Inter-American Institute for Musical Research* (Tulane University), vol. 3 (1967), pp. 140–141; *Compositores de América,* vol. 17 (1971), pp. 39–46; GÉRARD BÉHAGUE, *Music in Latin America: An Introduction* (1979), pp. 312–313.

ALCIDES LANZA

**BOLAÑOS, LUIS DE** (*b.* 1549; *d.* 11 October 1629), Franciscan missionary. Called the Apostle of Paraguay, Bolaños was born in Marchena, Spain, in Andalusia. He joined the FRANCISCAN order as a youth and was ordained a deacon. In 1572 he volunteered to serve as a missionary in the Río de la Plata and left Spain with his mentor and friend Fray Alonso de Buenaventura. After arriving in Paraguay in 1575, the two friars preached to GUARANIS near Asunción and then in the northern area of the Jejui Guazú River, where the followers of Cacique Overá were resisting Spanish pressure. There in 1580, the missionaries founded Altos, the first enduring reduction of Paraguay. Later, Bolaños and Buenaventura founded Ypané, Atyrá, Tobatí, Itá, Yaguarón, Yuty, and Caazapá, which all survive. Bolaños attempted to work in the part of Guairá that is now the state of Paraná in Brazil, but the Spanish colonists there expelled him for blocking their exploitation of Native American labor. After mastering the Guarani language, Bolaños wrote a Guarani grammar and vocabulary and became the primary translator into Guarani of the catechism of the Council of Lima of 1583, the basis for instruction in the Franciscan reductions and the later JESUIT missions of Paraguay.

In 1585 Bolaños was ordained a priest, and after 1600 he cooperated with Governor Hernando ARIAS DE SAAVEDRA, Bishop Martín Ignacio de Loyola, and colonizer Juan de GARAY to extend Spanish secular and religious authority. The more famous Jesuit reductions of Paraguay founded after 1610 were partly the fruition of the methods of Franciscans like Bolaños, who advised Father Manuel de Lorenzana and other members of the Society of Jesus. Though famous as a missionary, Bolaños was also an able administrator. At the end of his life, he retired to the Franciscan house in Buenos Aires, where he died. In 1979 his body was returned to Asunción, Paraguay, where he is a national hero.

BUENAVENTURA ORO, *Fray Luis Bolaños, apóstol del Paraguay y Río de la Plata* (1934); ANDRÉS MILLÉ, *Crónica de la Orden Franciscana en la conquista del Perú, Paraguay y el Tucumán y su convento del antiguo Buenos Aires, 1612–1800* (1961); MARGARITA DURÁN ESTRAGO, *Presencia franciscana en el Paraguay,* vol. 1 (1987).

JAMES SCHOFIELD SAEGER

**BOLEADORAS,** a leather and stone weapon of the PAMPAS. Indigenous civilizations strongly influenced the material culture and language of the Río de la Plata. Indians developed the *boleadoras* and the GAUCHO adopted it. The dangerous weapon consists of two or three rawhide thongs, each tipped with leather-covered rocks or metal balls that are bound together at one end. After whirling the *boleadoras* around his head, the Indian or gaucho would fling it at the feet of a fleeing rhea, horse, or bull. Entangled in the thongs, the animal crashed to the ground. In addition to its utility in hunting, the weapon proved effective in cavalry warfare. Indians of the pampas reputedly trained their horses to run and escape even when entangled in *boleadoras.*

RICHARD W. SLATTA, *Gauchos and the Vanishing Frontier* (1983), esp. pp. 8, 87.

RICHARD W. SLATTA

**BOLERO,** a form of Latin American music that originated in southern Spain. It was rhythmically modified in late colonial Cuba and made more lyrical in the Yucatán. During the 1930s the powerful radio station XEW helped to popularize the form in Mexico City, where by 1940 it had acquired a sophisticated smoothness that suited it to the dance floor.

Many regional Mexican songs were recast in the slightly syncopated 2/4 bolero rhythm (eight beats, with the third left out). Well-known guitar trios such as the widely traveled Los Panchos, Las Calaveras, and Los Diamantes helped make the romantic bolero international and gave it a similar sound in Mexico, Spain, Puerto Rico, Peru, and Argentina. Some of the most famous boleros are "Solamente una vez" by Agustín Lara, "Muñequita linda" (also called "Te quiero dijiste") by María Grever, "Perfidia" by Alberto Domínguez, and the best-selling recording of all, "Bésame mucho" by Consuelo Velásquez.

See *New Grove Dictionary of Music* (1980); CLAES AF GEIJERSTAM, *Popular Music in Mexico* (1976); IRIS ZAVALA, *El bolero* (1991).

GUY BENSUSAN

**BOLÍVAR, SIMÓN** (*b.* 24 July 1783; *d.* 17 December 1830), foremost leader of Spanish American independence. Born in Caracas to a wealthy landed family with slave-worked cacao plantations, Simón Bolívar received little formal education, although his private tutor, Simón Rodríguez, helped instill in him an admiration for the thinkers of the European Enlightenment. Bolívar traveled to Europe in 1799, and in Madrid in 1802 he married María Teresa Rodríguez de Toro, the daughter of a Caracas-born aristocrat. Upon her death soon after they returned to Venezuela, he made a second trip to Europe, during which he vowed to work for the liberation of Spanish America.

When the Napoleonic invasion of Spain triggered the crisis of the Spanish monarchy in 1808–1810, Bolívar played a minor role in the various attempts to set up a governing junta in Caracas. However, once a junta was created, in April 1810, he became an active participant in the revolutionary movement. After heading a diplomatic mission sent to London, he pressed for an outright declaration of independence, which was issued on 5 July 1811.

Having served as a colonial militia officer, though without formal military training, Bolívar was eventually given military command of the key coastal fortress of Puerto Cabello, whose loss in July 1812 served to hasten (though it hardly caused) the collapse of Venezuela's First Republic. When the Venezuelan dictator Francisco de MIRANDA accepted the inevitable and signed a capitulation to the royalists, Bolívar was one of those who angrily arrested him and by preventing his escape in effect turned Miranda over to the Spanish. Bolívar himself soon escaped to Curaçao and from there to Cartagena in New Granada, where he issued the CARTAGENA MANIFESTO (the first of his major political documents) and sought assistance for a new attempt to liberate Venezuela. With help from the United Provinces of New Granada, he invaded his homeland in 1813, and in less than three months swept into Caracas. This *campaña admirable* (admirable campaign), as it has been called, first earned Bolívar the title of "Liberator" and made him the acknowledged political as well as military leader of Venezuela.

Bolívar chose not to restore the federal constitution adopted in 1811 by the First Republic, believing that federalism was a dangerously weak form of government. The Second Republic that he then created, a frank military dictatorship, was no more successful than its predecessor, for it was soon being worn down by the

Portrait of Simón Bolívar by José Gil de Castro, 1825. ORGANIZATION OF AMERICAN STATES.

assault of royalist guerrilla bands. Appealing to the Venezuelan masses to reject an independence movement whose principal figures (like Bolívar) were drawn from the creole elite, the royalists found a favorable response especially among the rough cowboy population (*llaaneros*) of the Orinoco plains. Before the end of 1814, Bolívar was again a fugitive in New Granada.

Despite his distaste for federalism, Bolívar repaid the New Granadan federalists grouped in the United Provinces for the aid they had given him by helping them subdue Bogotá, whose leaders favored a strong central authority. But he had little desire to take part in this or other internecine conflicts of the New Granadan patriots, especially when the defeat of Napoleon in Europe and restoration of FERDINAND VII to his throne now permitted Spain to redouble its efforts to suppress colonial rebellion. In mid-1815 Bolívar left New Granada, shortly before the arrival of the Spanish expeditionary force that would reconquer most of it for the king. Bolívar went first to Jamaica, where in his "Jamaica Letter" he offered a keen analysis of the present and future state of Spanish America. He next moved to Haiti, where he obtained help from the Haitian government for a new attempt to liberate Venezuela—and for a second attempt when the first ended in failure. By the end of 1816, he had regained a foothold and made contact with revolutionary bands still active in northeastern Venezuela.

In July 1817, Bolívar's forces seized Angostura (today Ciudad Bolívar), on the lower Orinoco River. The port of Angostura gave Bolívar a link to the outside world, while the Orinoco River system facilitated contact with pockets of patriot resistance in other parts of the Orinoco Basin, including the Apure region, where José Antonio PÁEZ had won increasing numbers of llaneros over to the patriot cause. When Páez accepted Bolívar's leadership, the Liberator gained a critically important ally. As a llanero himself, Páez helped to give the independence struggle a more popular image. So did Bolívar's declaration (issued soon after his return to Venezuela in 1816) making abolition of slavery one of the patriot war aims. The mostly llanero cavalry of Bolívar and Páez could not dislodge the veteran Spanish troops occupying Andean Venezuela; but neither could the royalists make much headway on the Orinoco plains.

Bolívar sought to institutionalize the revolutionary movement by calling elections for a congress, which assembled at Angostura in February 1819 and ratified his leadership. Yet Bolívar's long-term objectives were not limited to Venezuela. In May 1819 he embarked on the campaign that took him westward across the llanos and over the Andes to central New Granada, where on 7 August he won the decisive battle of Boyacá. The victory opened the way to Bogotá, occupied three days later, and gave Bolívar control of an area with important reserves of recruits and supplies. It also gave him a victorious momentum that he never entirely lost.

Bolívar placed the New Granadan officer Francisco de Paula SANTANDER in charge of the recently liberated provinces and then returned to Angostura, where, at his urging, in December 1819, the congress proclaimed the union of Venezuela, New Granada, and Quito (Ecuador) a single Republic of Colombia (usually referred to as GRAN COLOMBIA). The following year Bolívar turned his attention to the part of Venezuela still under royalist control. Military operations were suspended tempo-

rarily by an armistice of November 1820, but the victory at Carabobo, in June 1821, brought the war in Venezuela to a close except for royalist coastal enclaves that held out for another two years.

Meanwhile Gran Colombia was given a constitution by the CONGRESS OF CÚCUTA, meeting in 1821 on the border between Venezuela and New Granada. The document was not entirely to Bolívar's liking, but he agreed to serve under it when the Congress named him first constitutional president, with Santander as vice president. Since Bolívar intended to continue leading the military struggle against Spain, Santander became acting chief executive in the Colombian capital of Bogotá, charged with organizing the home front and mobilizing resources.

After a local uprising in Guayaquil threw off royalist control of that port city, Bolívar sent his trusted lieutenant Antonio José de SUCRE to Ecuador with a Colombian auxiliary force. While Bolívar fought his way through southern New Granada, Sucre penetrated the Ecuadoran highlands. After Sucre defeated the royalists at the battle of PICHINCHA (May 1822), on the outskirts of Quito, Bolívar entered Quito as well. Continuing to Guayaquil, he obtained its semivoluntary incorporation into Gran Colombia just before he met there with the Argentine liberator José de SAN MARTÍN. The exact substance of their discussions was never revealed, but it would seem that one thing they disagreed on was how to complete the liberation of Peru, where San Martín controlled the coastal cities but not the highlands. Soon afterward, San Martín abandoned Peru, and Bolívar accepted a call to take his place.

Once he reached Peru, in September 1823, Bolívar found Peruvian collaboration to be somewhat fickle, but by mid-1824 he was ready for his last great campaign. On 6 August he scored an important victory at Junín, in the central Peruvian Andes, and on 9 December, in the battle of AYACUCHO, his army (commanded by Sucre) obtained the surrender of the main royalist army. In the following weeks Sucre mopped up remnants of royalist resistance in Upper Peru (modern Bolivia).

A few days before Ayacucho, Bolívar, from Lima, issued a call to the Spanish American nations to meet at Panama and create a permanent alliance. He did not have a Pan-American gathering in mind, for he failed to invite the United States, Brazil, and Haiti—even while hoping that Great Britain would send an observer. The United States and Brazil were invited by the administration of Vice President Santander in Bogotá, though in the end they did not take part; and neither did the Panama Congress of 1826 produce the hoped-for league of Spanish American states. Bolívar's design for the congress, however, revealed his ambivalence toward the United States, whose institutions he admired in principle but considered unsuited to Latin American conditions and whose growing power he foresaw as a long-term threat. His interest in having British representation clearly reflected both his belief that British friendship was essential for the security and economic development of the new republics as well as his deep admiration for Great Britain and its system of constitutional monarchy.

Bolívar soon followed Sucre to Upper Peru, where he assumed provisional direction of the newly independent nation that was to name itself Bolivia in his honor. Bolívar did not stay there long, but when the Bolivians invited him to draft their first constitution, he gladly accepted. The proposal that he later submitted (in May 1826) had some progressive features, yet its centerpiece—a president serving for life with power to name his successor—aroused wide criticism as a disguised form of monarchy. Bolívar was gratified that both Bolivia and Peru adopted, at least briefly, the main lines of his scheme. However, his hope that Gran Colombia, too, would adopt some form of it was never realized.

Bolívar's interest in reforming Colombian institutions was heightened by the rebellion of Páez in April 1826 against the government of Santander. The Liberator returned home before the end of the year, settled Páez's rebellion with a sweeping pardon, and added his support to demands for an immediate reform of the constitution. These actions led to a conflict with Santander, who became a leader of the opposition to Bolívar at the constitutional reform convention that met at Ocaña from April to June 1828. When the sessions ended in deadlock, Bolívar's supporters called on him to assume dictatorial powers to "save the republic," and he agreed to do so.

As dictator, Bolívar rolled back many of the liberal reforms previously enacted in Gran Colombia, including a reduction in the number of monasteries and abolition of Indian tribute. He did not necessarily oppose the reforms in question; he merely decided they were premature. And he did not touch the free-birth law that Gran Colombia had adopted for gradual elimination of slavery.

Bolívar's dictatorship was bitterly opposed by the adherents of Santander, some of whom joined in the abortive September 1828 attempt to assassinate Bolívar. After that, political repression became harsher, and Santander was sent into exile, but scattered uprisings still broke out. Also, serious disaffection arose in Venezuela, which was ideologically the most liberal part of the country as well as generally resentful of being ruled from Bogotá. The last straw was an intrigue by Bolívar's cabinet to recruit a European prince to succeed him as constitutional monarch when the Liberator died or retired. Páez again rose in rebellion in late 1829, and this time Venezuela became a separate nation.

Another convention that met in Bogotá in January 1830 did produce a new constitution, but it could not stem dissolution of the union. Ailing and disheartened, Bolívar stepped down from the presidency in March 1830 and set off for self-imposed exile. He died at Santa Marta before he could board ship, though not before Ecuador seceded from the union and newly autonomous Venezuela prohibited its most famous son from setting foot on its soil.

Though at the end it seemed to Bolívar that his work had been in vain, he is revered today as the one person who made the greatest contribution to Spanish American independence. His contribution was not just military but also political, in the articulation of patriot objectives and the establishment of new states. Moreover, he has been claimed as a precursor by every ideological current, from the revolutionary Left (which admires him for his opposition to slavery and distrust of the United States) to the extreme Right (which approves his authoritarian tendencies): there is something about Bolívar to appeal to every taste and every age.

The best English-language biographies are GERHARD MASUR, *Simón Bolívar* (1948; rev. ed 1969); the highly critical SALVADOR DE MADARIAGA, *Bolívar*, (1952; repr. 1979); and AUGUSTO MIJARES, *The Liberator*, translated by John Fisher (1983). Bolívar can be studied in his own words in *Selected Writings of Bolívar*, compiled by Vicente Lecuna, edited by Harold A. Bierck, Jr., translated by Lewis Bertrand, 2 vols. (1951), and in those of his Irish aide in DANIEL F. O'LEARY, *Bolívar and the War of Independence*, translated and edited by Robert F. McNerney, Jr. (1970). His campaigns are exhaustively covered in VICENTE LECUNA, *Crónica razonada de las guerras de Bolívar*, 3 vols. (1950); and on his political ideas, VÍCTOR ANDRÉS BELAÚNDE, *Bolívar and the Political Thought of the Spanish American Revolution* (1938) is still useful. His relations with Europe and European perceptions of Bolívar are the subject of ALBERTO FILIPPI, ed., *Bolívar y Europa en las crónicas, el pensamiento político y la historiografía*, 2d ed. (1988). A special issue of the *Hispanic American Historical Review* 63, no. 1 (1983), contains essays by a group of specialists on particular aspects of his career. The subsequent image of Bolívar is brilliantly analyzed in GERMÁN CARRERA DAMAS, *El culto a Bolívar* (1969).

DAVID BUSHNELL

*See also* **Wars of Independence.**

**BOLIVIA.** [Coverage begins with a two-part survey of Bolivian political history. There follow a variety of entries on specialized topics: **Agrarian Reform; Constitutions; Organizations** (civic, cultural, labor, etc.); and **Political Parties**.]

### *The Colonial Period*

CONQUEST AND SETTLEMENT

The first substantial Spanish incursion into the lands now called Bolivia took place in 1535, the year Diego de ALMAGRO led his great expedition south from Peru toward Chile. On its way, the expedition passed over the high Bolivian plateau now known as the altiplano.

A little south of Cuzco, Almagro moved from Quechua-dominated territory into AYMARA lands. Over the previous several centuries, the Aymara speakers had organized themselves into more than a dozen substantial polities. Prominent among these were the Colla, around the northern and western shores of Lake Titicaca, and the Lupaqa, great raisers of llamas on the southwest fringes of the lake. Two hundred and fifty miles southeast of Titicaca were the less rich and powerful Charca, whose name became attached to the Spanish highland region that developed around and south of the lake and embraced most of the Aymara peoples. The province of CHARCAS was the direct ancestor of modern Bolivia. (The highland region was also known up to about 1700 as the Provincias de Arriba, or "Upper Provinces," and after that as Alto Perú, or "Upper Peru".)

The Aymara polities had been incorporated into the INCA Empire about 1460, becoming the province named Collasuyo. But loss of independence brought surprisingly little change in politics, economy, and society. Extraction of tribute and the implantation of Quechua-speaking colonies (*mitmaq*)—for example, in the valleys of Cochabamba—were the main exceptions.

Permanent Spanish occupation of Aymara lands did not begin until 1538, and was facilitated by native conflicts. In that year, the Lupaqa, probably prompted by the anti-Spanish rebel leader MANCO INCA, attacked the Colla. The Colla had been stubbornly pro-Spanish since the Inca war of succession, in which they had supported HUASCAR in his struggle against his brother ATAHUALPA. (Huascar had been assassinated by Atahualpa; the newly arrived Spaniards then propitiously executed the latter.) At the Lupaqa attack, the Colla called for Spanish help. The ranking Spanish leader in Cuzco, Hernando PIZARRO, decided to oblige. A quick Spanish victory at the Desaguadero River, at the southern tip of Titacaca, opened the way into the remaining Aymara lands. Many Aymara yielded peacefully, but not all. In the eastern Andean ranges (now known as the Cordillera Real), the Chicha polity, encouraged by Manco's agents, led other Aymara in opposition. Late in 1538, a fierce battle ensued in the Cochabamba Valley, in which the Spanish, now under Gonzalo PIZARRO, and a number of Incas loyal to them prevailed, though barely. By 19 March 1539, Gonzalo Pizarro was back in Cuzco, bringing with him Aymara leaders who had surrendered.

At about the same time, the Spaniards accomplished two other objectives in Aymara territory that had enduring effects. The first, the work of Pedro Anzures de Campo Redondo, a subordinate of the Pizarros, was the foundation, possibly in mid-1538, of Villa de Plata in a temperate valley 140 miles south of Cochabamba. This town, which soon became the city of La Plata (renamed SUCRE in 1839), was the political and administrative capital of the colonial province of Charcas from 1559 until independence and then, to 1898, of the sovereign state of Bolivia. Its name, "Silver," reputedly commemorates a 1538 event of still greater moment for Bolivian history: the Spanish location, 70 miles southwest of the town's site, of the silver deposits of Porco, worked by the Incas and doubtless by the Aymara and others before them. The Pizarros immediately seized a major interest in Porco. Henceforth, "Charcas" became synonymous with silver.

That association was vastly strengthened in 1545 with the discovery of the Cerro Rico (Rich Hill) at POTOSÍ, between Porco and La Plata. The mines of Rich Hill and of the area around Potosí yielded about half the silver produced by Spanish America from 1550 to 1650 and continued yielding abundantly until the 1890s (see also MINING). Potosí itself soon attracted tens of thousands of inhabitants, becoming before 1600, despite its altitude of over 13,000 feet, one of the three largest cities of Spanish America—matched only by Lima and Mexico City in size and wealth. Its growth conjured into existence, or at least stimulated the rise of, many smaller towns in the Bolivian highlands. One such town was LA PAZ, founded in 1548 some 40 miles southeast of the lower end of Titicaca. The aim here was to safeguard from native attack the increasingly important road linking Spanish Peru with Potosí, Porco, and La Plata. In due course La Paz became a large trading and agricultural center in its own right, the main Spanish city in northern Charcas, and, from the 1890s on, the de facto capital of Bolivia.

Among the areas that sold goods to Potosí were the eastern interior lowlands. Here, in conquest and settlement, there was a great contrast with the highlands, since the impetus had come from the southeast in a series of expeditions across the Gran Chaco from Paraguay between 1537 and 1547. The result, in 1561, was the foundation of the city of Santa Cruz de la Sierra, 160 miles northeast of La Plata, by Ñuflo de Chávez. The city lay at the foot of the Andes' easternmost salient into the interior and was from the start the key Spanish center in lowland Charcas. It has grown in recent decades to rival La Paz in wealth and political influence.

While the native people of the plains posed little threat to Spanish settlement, those of the *montaña* region, the wide foothill zone east and southeast of La Plata, were a different matter. The Spaniards called them, generically, CHIRIQUANOS. This expansive and bellicose culture, reportedly of GUARANÍ origin, proved as resistant to Spanish incursions as it had been to the Incas'. The threat it posed to the main Spanish centers in Charcas was contained by the founding of defensive frontier towns such as Tarija (1574) and Tomina (1575). But from mountain retreats the Chiriguanos continued to threaten until the end of the colonial period.

EARLY COLONIAL GOVERNMENT AND ECONOMY
The Chiriguanos were, however, only a small worm in the opulent apple of Charcas. Once the richness of Potosí became apparent, Spaniards flooded in, closely pursued by the Spanish state in the form of the Audiencia of Charcas. This blend of high court and governing council was formally created in 1558–1559, with its seat in La Plata. There it remained, the main administrative body of Charcas, until independence. Its jurisdiction embraced what is now Bolivia and large parts of present-day Chile, Peru, Paraguay, and Argentina. Within this vast territory arose several regional governorships, each to some degree independent of the au-

diencia. The only substantial one falling inside what is now Bolivia was that of Santa Cruz de la Sierra, created in the 1590s.

State influence in Charcas grew by another quantum leap in the 1570s with the arrival of Don Francisco de TOLEDO, fifth viceroy of Peru. Toledo is renowned for the five-year *Visita General* (general inspection) he made of the central part of his viceroyalty; half of the time (late 1572–mid-1575) was spent in Charcas. There, as in Peru itself, he directed the relocation (*reducción*) of native people to new communities, fewer and larger than their traditional ones. The aim here was multiple; to separate the people from their familiar surroundings, so that they could be more easily Hispanicized (in, for example, religion and civil government); to simplify organization of their labor; and to facilitate tribute collection. Many of the displaced people abandoned the new towns; but Toledo certainly achieved permanent disruption of old patterns. He reassessed tributes and generally redefined them as cash rather than kind for convenience of collection. This change forced Indians to participate in the money economy of the Spanish world by selling either their goods or their labor for cash. Toledo also extended the reach of the state by introducing

*corregidores* (district officers) to administer Indian affairs in rural areas. He organized the founding of COCHABAMBA in 1570 or 1571, partly as a barrier against the Chiriguanos. The city then grew rapidly as the focus of a large and fertile farming region closely tied to the Potosí market.

It was in Potosí that Toledo wrought his best-remembered reforms. First he organized the notorious MITA, the system of forced labor that brought to Potosí each year, at least initially, more than 13,000 native men to work in mines and refineries. Forced Indian labor had been sent to Potosí before Toledo's time; but he systematized and enlarged the practice (see also SLAVERY). Many *mita* workers, with their families, stayed in Potosí after their year of service was over, adding to its population. Others left but did not return home. For various reasons they preferred to join the swelling number of displaced people that was one notable outcome of Spanish colonial practices throughout the central Andes in the sixteenth century.

Toledo's other major effort at Potosí was to promote the refining of ores by amalgamation with mercury. The technique, developed in Mexico about 1555, had been slow to reach the Andes, though it was poised for ad-

Potosí, Bolivia. Reproduced from John Ogilby, *America, Being an Accurate Description of the New World* (London, 1670). BY PERMISSION OF THE HOUGHTON LIBRARY, HARVARD UNIVERSITY.

vance there when Toledo decided to push it forward. He first stimulated mercury production at HUANCAVELICA, southeast of Lima. Then he encouraged experts to demonstrate the method in Potosí. The outcome of this innovation, allied with cheap and plentiful *mita* labor, was a phenomenal boom that reached its peak in 1592. But the gain was at great cost to the native people. Not only were they uprooted and forced into dangerous work at low pay but they were driven from the central role they had played in silver production. Expensive refining mills were needed to make amalgamation profitable, and such investment was beyond the Indians' capacity.

By 1600, the best ores at Potosí had been mined, though vast quantities of lesser material remained. This depletion led to a search for new silver deposits all over highland Charcas. The richest discovery was at a site on the altiplano 120 miles southeast of La Paz. The ores proved so good and plentiful that in 1607 a new town, Oruro, was created nearby. Production there never equaled Potosí at its peak, but it remained important. Other and lesser deposits were briefly exploited around Potosí throughout the seventeenth century. Their effect was only briefly to interrupt the downward trend of the district's output. By the early 1700s, production had returned to the levels of the 1560s (pre-*mita* and pre-amalgamation). It stayed there until the 1740s, when a 1736 reduction from a fifth to a tenth in the royalty taken by the crown on silver production and a later increase in the labor impositions on the *mita* workers spurned a modest recovery, which lasted the rest of the century.

Whatever the fluctuations in silver output, the mining towns (above all Potosí) needed food and multitudinous other goods. This led, from about 1550 on, to the articulation of a vast economic zone to supply their requirements. The valleys around Cochabamba, and Mizque to the southeast of it, were early and lasting examples of these backward linkages from mining. Their livelihood depended on sales of maize, wheat, sugar, and livestock in Potosí. The YUNGAS (steep valleys) east of La Paz on the inland Andean slopes became a prime source of coca for the mines; though coca also came to Potosí from far more distant areas near Cuzco. On the lands around Lake Titicaca the ancient tradition of llama breeding continued, now directed particularly to the freighting of ores and the raw materials of silver production. What is now northwest Argentina grew in settlement before 1600 in response to the demand for its products—cotton cloth, mules, sugar, wine—in the mining zone. Possibly half or more of the silver drawn from the mines went to buying supplies through a far-flung network of interregional trade.

EARLY COLONIAL SOCIETY

Most of the supplies that went to mining towns were produced on land owned by colonists, not on Indian holdings. By the 1560s, *chacras* (small farms) had appeared, for example, in the deep valleys around Potosí. And over the next century haciendas (larger estates) developed in the more fertile regions of Charcas, especially in the eastern middle-altitude valleys. Some of the lands taken for *chacras* and haciendas had fallen free because of native population losses, caused by newly introduced diseases and the general disruption of the Conquest and its aftermath of settlement. The population decline in some parts of highland Charcas between the 1570s and the 1680s reached almost 60 percent and had probably been severe before 1570 as well.

Some of the record loss, it is true, was the result of movement of people rather than of deaths or lack of births. Migrants (*mitayos*) were hard, sometimes even impossible, to count. Many left their original villages to escape tribute and *mita*, going to cities and towns (such as Potosí), to estates and farms owned by colonists, or to other native communities (where they would be classed as FORASTEROS, or outsiders, and as such, under Spanish law, exempted from forced labor and tribute). Migrants provided much of the labor needed by Spanish landowners and by miners outside Potosí, since hardly any *mitayos* were sent to the district mines.

Native community life survived despite all the pressures applied to it, as a visitor to highland Bolivia can see today. Nine-tenths of Charcas's people remained rural, and nearly all of them were Indian peasants who spoke only their own language. Viceroy Toledo had ordered that the *reducciones* into which he tried to congregate these people in the 1570s should have a Spanish style of town government, with aldermen, magistrates, constables, and the like. But these positions generally went to the same sort of men who had held authority before the Conquest: the responsible and conservative elders of the communities. Similarly, the *curacas* (regional nobles) of pre-Spanish times continued to exist and to exercise authority. They generally had power over several villages, with rights to use community labor and lands. From the start they were crucial to Spanish control of native society, acting as links between colonial officials and Indian village leaders. Their position was often hard. They might be obliged, for example, to produce a constant yield of tribute or draft laborers from a shrinking population; they would have to make up any shortfall themselves. Under such pressures, *curacas* might maltreat their own people or partially Hispanicize themselves by engaging in profit-oriented trade or market agriculture to gain the cash they needed to meet Spanish demands. Thus, in the long term, old social and political relationships tended to change and weaken. But native institutions were resilient; and, suitably adapted to new demands, a distinct Indian culture was still in place when the colonial era ended.

Long before then, however, Charcas had taken on a clear identity of its own in several respects besides the native. The wealth and urban growth associated with mining gave it high status in Spanish America. In 1609, for instance, the see of La Plata was raised to an archbishopric, becoming junior in South America only to

Lima. (No other archdiocese was created anywhere else in the Indies before 1700). Four years before, bishoprics had been created in La Paz and Santa Cruz de la Sierra, which now became suffragan, along with Tucumán and Asunción, to La Plata. In 1624 the city of La Plata added to its cathedral and audiencia the University of San Francisco Xavier, where Jesuits trained priests and, after 1681, lawyers, for much of southern South America.

Despite the decline of mining, there was much building and decoration of churches in Charcas in the seventeenth century. A growing number of Indian and mestizo craftsmen participated in this work, and distinctive styles took shape. For instance, in 1592 an Indian sculptor named Tito Yupanqui made the famous image of the Virgin that has remained the object of such devotion at Copacabana, at the southern end of Titicaca. By 1700, clear schools of native and mestizo painting were emerging in La Plata, Potosí, and the La Paz–Titicana region (the Colla school). The painters' subjects were mainly devotional.

THE EIGHTEENTH CENTURY

Broadly speaking, the eighteenth century in Upper Peru saw the reversal of trends established after 1600. Silver production at Potosí stopped falling about 1725 and began to rise again at mid-century. (Oruro's low point had in fact come in 1660–1680; after that its output gently rose for a century.) Native population stabilized, probably after a devastating epidemic of influenza or pneumonic plague that spread from Buenos Aires up into the central Andes in 1719–1720. Generally, thereafter, rural peasant populations grew, though the population of the Spanish-dominated towns languished for much of the century, reflecting the weakness of mining and hence of the demand for supplies in the mining centers. The exception was La Paz, which, thanks to its governmental and marketing role amid a relatively dense native population, continued to grow, though slowly. By 1750 it was, with 40,000 people, the largest town in Upper Peru.

Among the most notable reversals in the eighteenth century was the reimposition of state power. Charcas, like most of Spanish America, had since about 1600, been under ever less effective Spanish control. Like most of the empire, it felt a revived presence of the state once the Bourbons came to power in 1700. The first serious sign came in the late 1720s with the *revisita* (recount) of the population ordered by the viceroy, the marqués de Castelfuerte (1724–1736). Castelfuerte's aim was, first, to find out how much of the central Andean population had died in the epidemic of 1719–1720; and, second, with this new count, to improve the collection of Indian tribute, which, he rightly thought, had become slack and corrupt.

The full weight of reform did not fall on Upper Peru until much later in the century. The greatest change of all came in 1776, when the province was shifted from the Viceroyalty of Peru into the newly formed Viceroyalty of Río de la Plata. Now its exports and imports passed largely through Buenos Aires; and internal trade patterns also changed, reorienting southward. In 1784 the centralizing system of local government by intendants was installed, replacing the rule by *corregidores* put in place by Toledo. Now Upper Peru was divided into four intendancies: La Paz, Cochabamba, Potosí, and Chuquisaca (La Plata). The Spanish government also tried to stimulate mining by, for example, taking over the mining bank, the BANCO DE SAN CARLOS, in Potosí, improving the supply of mercury, and sending in foreign experts to demonstrate (unsuccessfully, in the event) new refining methods.

A rash of revolts throughout the central Andes was one outcome of this growing state presence after 1700. In Upper Peru the first outbreak occurred at Cochabamba in November 1730, when mestizos, who were exempt from tribute, took exception to Castelfuerte's attempt to increase tribute income by reclassifying them as Indians. The mestizos were encouraged by creoles (American-born white settlers), who had their own grievances against Spaniards. The anti-Spanish alliance of different classes and ethnic groups was even more striking in the Oruro plot of 1739, a creole and mestizo reaction to increasing taxation. The leader, Juan Vélez de Córdoba, claimed descent from the Incas. The plotters' manifesto promised a restoration of the Inca monarchy, with equality for creoles, mestizos, and Indians, and abolition of tributes, *mita* (draft) labor, and *reparto* (the forced sale) of goods to Indians by *corregidores*. The Oruro plot, like the earlier disturbance at Cochabamba, was easily put down. But the Oruro manifesto, a true rebel program, may have been an inspiration for the far more widespread rebellion led by TÚPAC AMARU in Peru in 1780–1781.

That great and menacing movement—a reaction in the short term to a recent increase in sales tax, the creation of internal customshouses that imposed taxes and restrictions on interregional trade, and the abuses of *reparto*, which had been legalized in 1756—was centered just south of Cuzco. This rebellion was followed by a derivative revolt in Upper Peru, led by a native trader named Julián Apasa, who took the Indian pseudonym TÚPAC CATARI. Apasa laid siege to La Paz in 1781 before he was captured by Spanish forces late in that year. In the same year a creole movement, with strong links to Túpac Amaru and allied with local Indians and mestizos, took Oruro out of Spanish control. This insurrection, too, was put down before 1781 was out.

INDEPENDENCE

The risings of 1781 in Upper Peru, like that of Túpac Amaru farther north, were not bids for independence. However, they did demonstrate the strong aversion to the state's increasing exactions that became the fundamental motive for the pursuit of independence three and four decades later. Bolivia's advance to independence was set in motion, like the other Spanish American movements, by Napoleon's invasion of Spain in

1808. The Bourbon monarchy was unseated; political disarray descended on Spain and the empire. In the confusion, a group of radical creoles in La Paz, led by Pedro Domingo Murillo, decided to make a bid for autonomy. In July 1809, the group declared itself to be a governing junta ruling in the name of Ferdinand VII. The movement never had time to prove the authenticity of this allegiance; it was suppressed by the end of January 1810 by troops sent in from Peru. Still, this had been the first declaration of independence in Spanish America, and Bolivians remember Murillo proudly.

After this defeat, events proceeded much more slowly. Bolivia was the last Spanish mainland territory to become independent. The problem was twofold. First, the proximity of Peru, which was the Spanish stronghold in South America, made for easy suppression of dissidence in Upper Peru, as the Murillo episode had shown. Second, the government of the Río de la Plata (the incipient Argentina), where home rule was permanently achieved in 1810, had long sought to bring Upper Peru under its control. Buenos Aires therefore sent no fewer than four expeditionary forces into Upper Peru between 1810 and 1817. Although these found many local allies against Spanish forces from Peru, the Upper Peruvians had little enthusiasm for rule from Buenos Aires, so no lasting anti-Spanish alliance developed. The result was much fighting in and over Upper Peru for several years, and much loss of life and property, without conclusive change. Matters were not advanced by the activities of several dozen *caudillos* (pro-independence local leaders) who between 1810 and 1816 fought guerrilla style outside the towns.

After 1816, destruction and exhaustion greatly hindered further internal bids for freedom; and Buenos Aires finally realized that Chile would be a better assault route on Peru. Resistance to Spain therefore dwindled in the province until 1823, when a mestizo from near La Paz, Andrés de SANTA CRUZ, once a royalist officer and now an independence leader under Antonio José de SUCRE, BOLÍVAR's chief lieutenant, inflicted defeats on the Spanish at Zepita and elsewhere in the north. The Spanish were able to dislodge Santa Cruz, but by this time Bolívar's Venezuelan and Colombian forces were assembling in Peru, and the writing was on the wall. In 1824 Bolívar and Sucre defeated the Spanish twice in Peru, at Junín and at Ayacucho. After these victories there remained only a shadow of royalist resistance in Upper Peru. Royalist troops in fact deserted to Sucre as he entered the region in January 1825. Thus freedom came quietly and anticlimactically to the country that in August 1825 would call itself Bolivia after the man responsible for its final liberation.

ARTHUR F. ZIMMERMAN, *Francisco de Toledo, Fifth Victory of Peru, 1569–1581* (1938, repr. 1968); CHARLES ARNADE, *The Emergence of the Republic of Bolivia* (1957); EDUARDO ARZE QUIROGA, *Historia de Bolivia. Fases del proceso hispanoamericano: Orígenes de la sociedad boliviana en el siglo XVI* (1969); JOHN HEMMING, *The Conquest of the Incas* (1970); JOSEP M. BARNADAS, *Charcas. Orí-genes históricos de una sociedad colonial, 1535–1565* (1973); BARTOLOMÉ ARZÁNS DE ORSÚA Y VELA, *Tales of Potosí*, edited by R. C. Padden (1975); ORLANDO CAPRILES VILLAZÓN, *Historia de la minería boliviana* (1977); NICOLÁS SÁNCHEZ-ALBORNOZ, *Indios y tributos en el Alto Perú* (1978); HERBERT S. KLEIN, *Bolivia: The Evolution of a Multi-Ethnic Society* (1982); SCARLETT O'PHELAN GODOY, *Rebellions and Revolts in Eighteenth-Century Peru and Upper Peru* (1985); THÉRÈSE BOYUSSE CASSAGNE, *La identidad aymara: Aproximación histórica (siglo XV, XVI)* (1987); OLIVIA HARRIS, BROOKE LARSON, and ENRIQUE TANDETER, comp., *La Participación indígena en los mercados surandinos: Estrategías y reproducción social, siglos XVI a XX* (1987); BROOKE LARSON, *Colonialism and Agrarian Transformation in Bolivia: Cochabamba, 1150–1900* (1988); ROGER N. RASNAKE, *Domination and Cultural Resistance. Authority and Power Among an Andean People* (1988).

PETER BAKEWELL

### Since 1825

Bolivian history after independence can be characterized as primarily a struggle to integrate the extremely diverse country into a cohesive whole. Three basic issues defined this struggle: first, the way in which indigenous peoples participated in the political and economic life of the country; second, export-oriented trade versus internal economic development; and third, the extension of the CREOLE-led state into the sparsely inhabited frontier areas.

Bolivia was in many ways an artificial creation, as were virtually all other states in Spanish America. Antonio José de SUCRE, the Venezuelan-born patriot general who favored an independent upper Peruvian state, effectively appealed to Simón BOLÍVAR's vanity by naming the new polity after the Liberator. Bolivian leaders could only point to the rather flexible jurisdiction of the colonial high court, the Audiencia of Charcas, as the basis for the new state. Indeed, the events that spawned the Bolivians' sense of separateness took place only a few decades before independence. First, the Spanish crown's decision in 1776 to split Upper Peru from the Viceroyalty of Lima and to integrate the territory into the new Viceroyalty of Buenos Aires severed ties with the rest of Peru. Then, despite the early efforts of Bolivian patriot forces during the WARS OF INDEPENDENCE, the Audiencia of Charcas remained a bastion of royalism and so became separated from independence-minded Argentina.

BOLIVARIAN DREAMS
When patriot forces under Sucre's command finally liberated Upper Peru, the region had been wracked by almost sixteen years of civil war. Despite the flooded silver mines, the periodic looting of the royal mint by patriot and royalist forces, and the devastated countryside, Bolivia was one of the most powerful and prosperous countries in South America. It had large numbers of tribute-paying Andean peasants, access to silver (albeit on a reduced scale in comparison with that of the colonial period), and a relatively stable centralized government during the first few decades after in-

dependence. Sucre's presidency (1825–1828), though brief, brought about administrative reforms and ANTI-CLERICAL legislation, wresting away much of the power of the Catholic church.

Andrés de SANTA CRUZ, another warrior from the independence wars, ruled Bolivia for ten years (1829–1839). He felt powerful enough to re-create the Bolivarian dream of a union of Spanish American republics by annexing Jujuy, the northern-most province of Argentina, and by creating the PERU-BOLIVIAN CON-FEDERATION (1836–1839). Under the confederation, Peru was divided into a northern and a southern section, with Bolivia remaining whole. Internal opposition forces, both Peruvian and Bolivian, and the invasion by Chile destroyed these plans and led to Santa Cruz's downfall.

Unlike the decades-long attempts to reconstitute larger political units, the social and economic reality of Bolivia quickly set limits to the liberal idealism of the patriot generals who took over the new country's government. Despite a number of economic missions by British agents, the London stock market crash of 1825 eliminated the promised large investments slated to revitalize the mining industry. Local elites and southern import-export merchants financed most mining activity but were unable to come up with the huge sums required to reactivate on any large scale the colonial silver mines. Indeed, without the effective state subsidies of the colonial MITA (forced Indian mine labor), abolished at independence, mining activity only sporadically paid off.

The most vibrant part of the economy rested upon the shoulders of the Andean peasants, who in many ways controlled the economic pulse of the nation. As urban centers lost population, the rural economy took on greater importance, and trade, often crossing national boundaries, depended largely on the participation of the indigenous population. Even export activities, such as silver mining and wool, depended heavily on Indians for transport and the provision of foodstuffs and other goods, including most of the wool itself.

The Bolivian state treasury also depended largely upon the Indians. Although Bolívar had abolished tribute payments in 1824 and again in 1825 and had decreed that Indian community lands should be distributed among the peasants and the surplus land sold, these laws were never implemented. The communities continued to control between one-third and three-quarters of all lands in the highlands, the most densely populated regions of the country. Already under the Sucre administration a uniform tax on all citizens had to be abandoned and Indian tribute reinstituted under a different name, the *contribucíon indígenal*. Santa Cruz formalized this arrangement, for tribute was one of the few constant sources of income that, unlike taxes on mining and trade, did not fluctuate substantially. Tribute payments thus provided the resources for Santa Cruz to project Bolivian power beyond its own borders and help create temporarily his version of the Bolivarian pan–Spanish American union.

During this period, governments were also concerned with securing the far-flung Bolivian frontiers. On the eastern frontiers, toward the densely forested slopes and plains of the Amazon and Chaco basins, Santa Cruz fostered the growth of small-scale cattle ranching through liberal land grants. To the west, in the bone-dry Atacama Desert, the Sucre and Santa Cruz administrations invested heavily in developing ports, particularly Cobija, that would provide access to world markets and goods from European countries. The lack of water and later, under the Peru-Bolivian Confederation, the natural advantages of the Peruvian port of Arica condemned these efforts to eventual failure.

Thus, on balance, the first two decades of Bolivian independence were positive. Bolivia remained a militarily powerful force and had a relatively stable and efficient government. However, an economy based largely on internal trade, the relatively low productivity of silver mines, and the predominance of Indian communities made for relatively slow growth.

POLITICAL STRIFE: 1841–1880

The battle of Ingaví (1841), in which Bolivian forces led by José BALLIVIÁN vanquished the invading Peruvian army under Agustín GAMARRA, was a turning point in Bolivian history, showing the futility of the Bolivarian goal of establishing supranational political units. Ballivián, who proceeded to rule Bolivia from 1841 to 1847, was more concerned with domestic matters. He attended to expanding control of the eastern lowland regions, creating the Beni Department out of the northeastern section of the country. Ballivián also financed expeditions into the Chaco region and construction of a series of fortresses against the Chiriguano and Chaco tribes, the most serious military threat of the southeastern frontier. Later regimes continued many of these policies and extended the eastern frontier significantly through the use of Franciscan missions, fortresses, and land grants to military veterans.

Ballivián's fall in 1847 brought about increasing political strife. Even those presidents who were able to hold on to power were constantly threatened by new uprisings. The most important political figures of the period, Manuel Isidoro BELZÚ (1848–1855), José María LINARES (1857–1861), and Mariano MELGAREJO (1864–1870), constantly had to suppress uprisings to remain in power. Belzú's regime fostered internal production, and his power resided in the urban artisans and, to a lesser extent, the Indian community. Despite Belzú's political support among protectionist artisans and Indians, this period is marked by the rise of the export-oriented silver-mining economy and, closely related, the triumph of liberal and free-trade policies.

During the 1850s new entrepreneurs took over the ailing silver mines of central and southern Bolivia. Most were merchants connected to Chilean interests, which provided some capital. These new owners modernized the machinery and MINING methods, improved production, and brought about steady export growth. In the 1870s silver and NITRATE production grew rapidly on the Pacific coast, but this activity from the start was dominated by Chileans, both as mine owners and workers. The growth of export activities strengthened the hand of liberals, who saw free trade as a way to compete effectively on world markets. This was especially true of the new freedom to export silver ore, which previously had to be sold to the state mint.

The growing strength of liberal ideologues can be seen even during the notorious Melgarejo regime, when the government used liberal ideology to justify many abusive policies. Both Brazil and Chile were beneficiaries of new treaties that gave away Bolivian territory for little or no compensation. More important, legislation in 1866 and 1868 authorized the first systematic attacks on Indian community lands. Community members were to purchase their own fields within a ninety-day period, otherwise the land would be sold to the highest bidder. Melgarejo's army brutally crushed Indian resistance and, in the south at least, creoles permanently wrested away many community lands. In the more heavily Indian north, Melgarejo's cronies and relatives usurped even more land, but during the massive Indian rebellion of 1869–1870 that helped topple the caudillo's regime, the communities repossessed most of their fields by force.

As a result of the political turmoil in the country, the Pacific coast region had been virtually ignored. The substantial economic growth of the region remained poorly controlled by the Bolivian governments. Instead, Chilean interests dominated the region. Finally, in the 1870s

Bolivia attempted to counteract Chilean power by allying itself closely with Peru. A dispute over taxing the riches of the Atacama Desert precipitated a Chilean invasion in 1879. Even with the aid of Peruvian forces the allies lost quickly and decisively. After only a few months of combat Bolivia had lost its coastal region and thereafter remained essentially sidelined from the war while the Chileans concentrated on destroying the Peruvian military and occupying that country. Thus, the period of internal strife and caudillo rule after the battle of Ingaví had disastrous consequences. Bolivia lost much of its territory and, with the application of liberal policies to promote corrupt practices, also much of its economic and military power.

REIGN OF THE SILVER OLIGARCHY: 1880–1899

The WAR OF THE PACIFIC completely discredited the military and its caudillos, permitting the silver-mining interests to take power directly. This period also marks the beginning of a two-party system, in which ideologies became more important than the personal charisma of party leaders. The Liberal Party followed liberal precepts such as restricting the power of the CATHOLIC CHURCH; it also was in favor of continuing the war with Chile. However, from 1880 to the end of the century the Conservative (or Constitutionalist) Party, representing the Sucre-based silver-mining oligarchy, ruled the country. The Conservatives elected the most important silver miners as their presidential candidates and they imposed an essentially liberal model of economic development on the country. Their program consisted of four planks: the encouragement of free trade; the creation of a RAILROAD network facilitating the export of minerals; the creation of a rural land market through the abolition of Indian communities; and, in an effort to prevent a reoccurrence of the War of the Pacific fiasco, the development of frontier regions by promoting missions and the sale of land grants.

The Conservatives' program was generally successful, though it did not benefit all sectors of the population equally. For example, the war with Chile and the advent of free trade turned the elites of the southernmost department, Tarija, from contrabandists into important merchants who supplied imports to the silver mines of southern Potosí as well as to the rapidly expanding Chaco frontier. The mine owners also gained as a result of a vigorous railroad building program, financed largely by Chile, which connected the silver mines with the Pacific coast and so drove down transportation costs. On the other hand, the combination of cheap transport to the coast with no improvements in internal communications hurt Bolivian agrarian interests, since the fertile valleys were not connected to the highland mining areas. The railroads harmed regions such as the fertile Cochabamba Valley, which could not compete with the import of cheap foodstuffs over the railroads.

Efforts to populate the frontiers also met with only limited success. The state put frontier territory up for sale in large units but at low prices per hectare. Despite the obligation of grantees to live on the land or bring in families to live on the grants, few actually followed the letter of the law. Instead, huge tracts came under the control of largely absentee landowners. As a result, frontier development took place in a limited manner; only extensive agriculture such as cattle ranching took up vast extents of fertile land.

This period also marks the subjection of tribal peoples who had remained largely outside the state's jurisdiction. The most important group, the CHIRIGUANOS, over 100,000 strong, finally submitted to the frontier colonists after numerous engagements in the southeastern Andean foothills. The wars of 1874–1877 and the messianic uprising of 1892 led to the defeat of the Chiriguano forces, the killing of many warriors, the enslavement of women and children, and the distribution of Chiriguano land among the victors. Only the FRANCISCAN missions of the region provided some refuge, but even they over the long run changed indigenous culture substantially.

The situation of indigenous peoples in the highlands also degenerated. The abolition of Indian communities, legislated in 1874 but not implemented until 1880, adversely affected the indigenous population in the highlands. After the plots of each individual community member were measured, the land became available for sale. Most commonly, purchasers used methods such as getting the Indians into debt (by advancing money to pay for their land titles), outright fraud, or coercion to acquire parcels of community land. In the south, Indians sold only small portions of their total holdings at any one time, but which also significantly weakened the communities over the long term. In northern Potosí, Oruro, and elsewhere, communities remained virtually intact. As earlier, the attack on Indian lands was strongest in the north, around La Paz and Lake Titicaca. There, whole communities lost their lands, and the purchasers, mainly elites from La Paz and the surrounding towns, turned the Indians into peons of the newly formed HACIENDAS.

The animosity of the highland Indians towards government land-sale policies helped tip the balance against the Conservatives in the FEDERALIST WAR (1898–1899). When the deputies from Sucre rammed through legislation in 1898 that would keep the capital permanently in that city, the deputies from La Paz walked out and conspired with the opposition Liberal Party to overthrow the Conservative regime. The Conservatives, tied so closely to the silver-mine owners, were already weakened, for the declining price of silver had precipitated a severe financial crisis for the government.

That same year the city of La Paz rose in revolt under the aegis of the Federalist and Liberal parties. The Liberals also urged the Indian communities of the ALTIPLANO, under the leadership of ZÁRATE WILLKA, to rebel. In turn, the Liberals promised relief from the land usurpations. With the altiplano under the control of the In-

Plaza Murillo, La Paz, Bolivia. COURTESY OF PETER MC FARREN, B.P.A.

dians, the Conservative army was unable to advance much past Oruro. In the final battle, the Indians and the *paceño* (La Paz residents) forces under Liberal General José Manuel PANDO beat the Conservatives. Willka, however, massacred a detachment of Liberal troops and declared war on all whites. The creoles united and beat Willka's forces. In turn, Pando and the Liberals did not honor their agreement with the Federalists other than to make La Paz the de facto capital. Thus, the Federalist War marked the end of Conservative Party dominance, the transfer of the capital from Sucre to La Paz, and a shift away from silver as the principal export.

## THE TIN BOOM: 1900–1932

Fortuitously for Bolivia a new product, TIN, rapidly took the place of silver as the principal export. Using the railroad system built for silver export as well as Chilean, British, and North American capital, tin production expanded quickly throughout the first decades of the twentieth century. Like the silver-mining oligarchy, the three most important tin miners were Bolivian nationals. Indeed, the Aramayo family was able to make the transition from silver to tin. The other major tin miners

were Mauricio Hochschild and Simón Patiño. Patiño clearly dominated, controlling about 50 percent of the total exports from the early twentieth century to the nationalization of mines in 1952. The mining of tin required much larger infusions of capital than silver, however, and the most important tin miners closely allied themselves with U.S., British, or French companies. Patiño's main backer was National Lead, headquartered in the United States. In conjunction with this company, Patiño by the 1920s had extended his holdings to British smelting works and Malaysian tin mines. His Bolivian holdings became only a small portion of his business empire.

The tin boom brought unheard-of prosperity to the northern part of Bolivia. La Paz replaced Sucre as Bolivia's financial center, and many of the city's elite participated in the tin boom. The continued sale of Indian community land helped foster this boom atmosphere, for many elite *paceños* purchased large extents of community lands to use as collateral for shares in mining ventures. Thus, notwithstanding Liberal promises to stop the usurpation of community lands and the altiplano Indians' decisive participation in the Liberal victory during the Federalist War, the sale of community lands increased during the two decades of Liberal Party dominance.

As during the Conservative epoch, the north was more affected than the southern regions of the Bolivian highlands. Only the Indian rebellions of Jesús de Machaca (1921) and CHAYANTA (1927), although brutally repressed by the army, convinced the government to make the acquisition of Indian lands much more difficult. By the 1920s, however, the haciendas had expanded to encompass two-thirds of the highlands; only one-third remained in the hands of the Indians. This almost exactly reversed the land-holding patterns of forty years earlier. The expansion of the haciendas at the expense of the Indian communities marginalized the highland Indian from mainstream society and the national economy, a process that was reversed only in the middle of the twentieth century. Also, the integration of large numbers of previously free Bolivian peasants into haciendas caused much resentment. The relatively recent usurpation of their land helped create a climate of resistance that would combine with other factors to bring about widespread rebellion in the 1940s and 1950s.

The indigenous peoples of the eastern Bolivian frontiers did not fare much better than those in the highlands. The Amazonian RUBBER boom (1871–1912) greatly affected those living in the northeastern quarter of the country. There, virtual slaving expeditions provided the rubber barons with laborers to work in the jungle. In 1905 a Brazilian-aided rebellion in the northeastern jungles of the Acre region brought about the loss of that rubber-rich territory to Brazil despite General José M. Pando's personal efforts to suppress the uprising. As a result, the Liberal administration eased requirements for the purchase of frontier lands, thereby alienating vast amounts of tribal lands. The ANTICLERICAL government also restricted frontier missions and began to secularize many, preventing many indigenous peoples from doing anything but becoming hacienda peons on the frontier because colonists almost immediately displaced the mission Indians from their land. In addition, the Liberals reorganized frontier territories which they began to militarize. Relations between the army and the indigenous peoples on the frontier were never good; the poorly disciplined soldiers in the tiny frontier forts usually enforced the rule of the large frontier landholders and in so doing did not endear themselves to the Indians. Frontier economic development projects by foreign companies, such as the vast land grant to a German merchant firm around the secularized Franciscan missions of Villa Montes, only brought about the alienation of lands with little actual development.

Serious opposition to the Liberal regime developed only after 1914, when a dissident group of Liberals formed the Republican Union. This was also a reaction to Ismael MONTES, undisputed leader of the Liberals and twice president of Bolivia (1904–1909, 1913–1917), whose autocratic style antagonized fellow politicians during the brief but severe downturn in the Bolivian economy at the beginning of World War I.

Convinced that the Liberals would not give up power through peaceful means, the Republicans revolted successfully in 1920, remaining in power until 1934. Republican leaders generally carried out policies similar to those of the Liberals but were also more responsive to lower-class demands. This resulted in some contradictory behavior. Republicans were as beholden to the tin interests as the Liberals. While Juan Bautista SAAVEDRA (president, 1921–1925) created the first rudimentary labor and social legislation, he also permitted the 1923 massacre of mine workers and their families in Uncía. Likewise, although the sale of Indian community lands virtually ended when the Republicans took over, the army under the Hernando Siles government (1926–1930) killed hundreds of Indians during the Chayanta uprising of 1927.

The militarization of the Chaco frontier also became problematic when, after 1927, armed clashes between the small frontier garrisons of Bolivian and Paraguayan soldiers became increasingly frequent. Indeed, Republican president Daniel SALAMANCA's decision to launch an offensive against Paraguayan positions in 1932 started the CHACO WAR (1932–1935), which led to a costly defeat and initiated a process that would result in the 1952 revolution, the second twentieth-century social revolution (after Mexico) in Latin America.

THE CHACO WAR AND ITS AFTERMATH: 1932–1952
In the beginning of the Chaco War, it appeared that the German-trained Bolivian army would easily beat the poorly outfitted Paraguayan forces. This was almost certainly Salamanca's calculation. He was an intense nationalist who was coming under increasing domestic pressure when the Great Depression wiped out large parts of the Bolivian economy. But the Bolivians faced severe supply problems, poor military leadership, a heavy reliance on mobilized highland Indians who were unaccustomed to the lowland heat and dense underbrush, and the hostility of the poorly treated indigenous peoples in the Chaco. Consequently, they suffered defeat after defeat at the hands of the much better adapted Paraguayan forces. Only in 1935 was the Bolivian military able to reverse the tide of war and win back at least the oil-bearing Andean foothills around Villa Montes.

By the end of the war the Bolivian army had lost a quarter (sixty-five thousand) of its soldiers, a huge number out of a total population of about 2 million inhabitants. The military began to meddle in national politics, helping to overthrow Salamanca in 1934. The home front had also fallen apart, with widespread resistance to military recruitment in the countryside. Banditry flourished behind the front, often fueled by armed deserters. The Indians who had been sent to the front, from the communities and the haciendas, learned about military organization and how to use weapons, and they came into greater contact with the highly politicized urban working classes. The ignominious defeat of Bolivian forces led to the radicalization of workers, the small but important middle sectors, and even significant elements of the Bolivian army. As after the War of the Pacific, revulsion towards the political and social systems that had brought about defeat led to significant change. However, by now a much larger segment of the population participated in one way or another in politics, and more radical options were discussed.

The military ruled Bolivia from 1936 to 1939, and under the presidencies of General David TORO (1936–1938) and Germán BUSCH (1938–1939) the "military socialist" governments tried to institute populist and reformist measures. Toro created a Ministry of Labor and in 1937 nationalized the Bolivian holdings of Standard Oil of Bolivia, which controlled virtually all oil production in the country. In the new Constitution of 1938 the state took on a much more active role in the country's economy, reversing the laissez-faire Liberal Constitution of 1880. In 1939, however, Busch suspended the constitution and became dictator. After his suicide the same year and the brief rule of General Carlos Quintanilla (1939–1940), elections placed General Enrique PEÑARANDA, another Chaco War veteran but with a more traditional political vision, in the presidency (1940–1943).

During the political ferment in the aftermath of the Chaco War, political parties became more class based, and a number of important radical and moderate leftist parties arose. On the basis of José Antonio Arze's extremely strong showing in the 1939 elections, in which he garnered 10,000 votes out of a total of 58,000 despite having no organized party, the leftists formed the Party of the Revolutionary Left (PIR). Another important revolutionary leftist party was the Revolutionary Workers

Party (POR), which was Trotskyist in orientation. In turn, the more moderate and middle-class Left in 1940 formed the National Revolutionary Movement (MNR), heavily influenced by the success of fascist ideology in Europe because of its nationalistic emphasis. All of these parties called for the nationalization of the tin mines, and a struggle ensued to attract the tin-mine workers to their cause. Only the POR and the PIR addressed rural problems in any coherent way, advocating the abolition of personal servitude on the haciendas and expropriation of the LATIFUNDIA, or the very largest estates.

In 1943, Major Gualberto VILLARROEL, with the help of the MNR, overthrew the Peñaranda government. An alliance of the MNR and the POR permitted the formation of the first national miners' union under the leadership of POR leader Juan LECHÍN OQUENDO. In turn, Villarroel, styling himself a new Inca, in 1945 called for an Indigenous Congress, which attracted over a thousand Indian CACIQUES from throughout highland Bolivia. Villarroel decreed the abolition of the hated unpaid labor services on the haciendas and promised to provide the Indian communities with schools. These laws were never put into effect, for in 1946 a civilian mob overthrew the increasingly repressive Villarroel regime and hung the president from a lamppost in the main plaza of La Paz.

Nevertheless, contacts between radicalized mine workers and hacienda peons, especially in the Cochabamba area and near the mines, became increasingly common and led to the subversion of the hacienda regime from within. The most important rebellion, which occurred in 1947 in Ayopaya, Cochabamba, involved hundreds of hacienda workers. Elsewhere, as in the Cinti district of southern Bolivia, revolts also flared on the haciendas. The rule of haciendas, previously based on paternalistic ties between landowners and peons, was increasingly undermined by this activity and owners resorted to brutal repression.

The Conservative governments that followed Villarroel, in alliance with the PIR, had increasing difficulty ruling the country. The miners, backed by the POR, and the middle-class MNR adopted more radical positions as the PIR ministers were forced to deal with the unrest. Thus, in 1947 the PIR minister of labor sent troops into the Catavi mines and massacred striking workers. These actions destroyed the PIR's popular base and made the POR and MNR more revolutionary than ever. In 1949 the MNR attempted to take over the country in a civilian coup, but their efforts failed after two months of intense fighting in all major Bolivian cities. The MNR became more popular and won the 1951 presidential elections with Víctor PAZ ESTENSSORO as their candidate, but he was prevented from taking power by military intervention.

Denied political power through legitimate means, the MNR rose in revolt again in 1952. After three days of warfare, in which the miners came down from the mountains and the conquered armories were opened to the public, the army was finally beaten.

## THE BOLIVIAN SOCIAL REVOLUTION: 1952–1986

The 1952 revolution marks a watershed in Bolivian history. The traditional parties had been discredited, and the army destroyed. The miners had helped with the brief civil war and were the only ones who had weapons. The new regime, with Víctor Paz Estenssoro at the head, decreed the nationalization of the tin mines, creating Comibol, the state-run mining company. MNR leaders dropped literacy requirements for voting, suddenly enfranchising the Indian masses.

These events created momentum for change in the countryside as well. With the help of mine workers, the peons of the highlands mounted attacks on the hacienda system. Landowners fled the countryside and the largely Indian masses took over the haciendas, burning some to the ground. Under pressure from these developments, the Paz government decreed a land reform package in 1953 that led to the expropriation of most medium-sized and large estates in the highlands. These reforms legalized the de facto takeover of the haciendas, but they also created a long, drawn-out process that soon sapped the rural movement of its strength and tied the peasants to the MNR regime. The government created *sindicatos* (unions) of peasants, which were beholden to the MNR. The Indian communities, in turn, received very little and even lost lands where they had rented them out to outsiders.

These reforms meant that the peasants, once they had their land, became a conservative political force, since they had no reason to wish for other radical change in the country. During its twelve-year reign (1952–1964), the MNR used the peasants to counterbalance the much more radical mine workers. Their conservatism persisted even after the overthrow of the MNR by the revitalized army in 1964, when charismatic General René BARRIENTOS ORTUÑO fashioned the so-called ''military-peasant pact.'' This arrangement, recalled numerous times when the military gained power, essentially meant that peasant leaders promised to remain quiescent if the military did not attack their interests. The arrangement apparently worked even in 1966 when the Argentine revolutionary Ernesto (''Che'') GUEVARA established a guerrilla campaign in the southeastern Andean foothills. The guerrillas received no significant peasant support, and after a year they were captured and some, including Guevara, were executed after a massive army campaign.

The effects in the eastern lowlands were quite different from those in the highlands. Rather than bringing about much social change, most large landowners maintained control over their estates. Moreover, in an effort to stimulate the lowland economy as a way of attracting peasants from the overcrowded highlands, the MNR regime and the United States sent vast amounts of capital into the region. Most of the capital went to the large landlords, who established sugar and, briefly in the 1970s, cotton plantations. As a result, the economy of Santa Cruz boomed, bringing about rapid population growth in the city of Santa Cruz and increasing political and economic clout for Santa Cruz landlords.

After Barrientos's death in an accident in 1969, the army continued to rule but was unable to remain united. In 1970, General Juan José TORRES GONZÁLEZ took over the government, leading the country sharply to the left. Before he could effect major changes, however, he was overthrown in 1971 in a bloody coup led by General Hugo BANZER SUÁREZ, who established a right-wing military dictatorship. During the Banzer years, true economic growth took place. Utilizing many of the infrastructural developments begun under the MNR government, such as those in the Santa Cruz area, the Banzer regime diversified exports and expanded the production of foodstuffs. Road building, new airports, and other infrastructional improvements continued as well.

Economic growth began to slow in the late 1970s, however, and Banzer also came under pressure from the Carter administration in the United States to hold free elections. After hunger strikes by the opposition, elections were finally held in 1979. A period of political confusion resulted. For two years military and civilian regimes alternated, with the MNR splitting into two major factions, one center-right led by former president Víctor Paz Estenssoro and the other led by left-leaning former president (1956–1960) Hernán SILES ZUAZO. In addition, a more radical leftist party, the Movement of the Revolutionary Left (MIR), and a new right-wing party, the Nationalist Democratic Action (ADN), with former General Hugo Banzer at the helm, also became significant political forces. In 1980, General Luis GARCÍA MEZA took over in what became known as the "cocaine coup," since many members of the military government had close ties to cocaine trafficking, which had been growing in Bolivia since the 1970s. However, internal resistance and the regime's inability to receive international recognition forced García Meza to resign in 1982. After a brief transition, Hernán Siles Zuazo and his leftist alliance, the Democratic and Popular Union (UDP), assumed the presidency they had won in elections just prior to the 1981 coup. However, Siles proved unable to unite his diverse supporters. With tin prices falling and an overblown bureaucracy, the state experienced a severe fiscal crisis, making it impossible to fulfill the long-repressed demands of labor and other groups. As a result, government and the economy spun out of control, with inflation reaching 40,000 percent in 1985. Exhausted, Siles called elections early. The 1952 revolutionary model, with heavy participation by the state, had clearly failed in this multiparty environment.

NEW PATTERNS: SINCE 1986

In the 1985 elections three parties, the MNR, the MIR, and the ADN, won almost equal shares of the votes. After intense negotiation, the MNR's Víctor Paz Estenssoro became president with the support of the leftist MIR. However, Paz forged an alliance with the ADN and proceeded to dismantle virtually all of the old revolutionary institutions he himself had built thirty years earlier. He dismantled the state mining company (Comibol), opened up the country to almost unrestricted free trade, and emasculated the mine workers and their unions by "relocating" many mine workers and their families in the subtropical jungle. Significantly, he attempted to impose a new unitary rural land tax that encompassed both peasant lands and commercial estates, but peasant resistance brought about its repeal.

Many "relocated" miners migrated to urban centers, others went into the subtropical jungles of the Chaparé to grow coca. Indeed, to a large extent the money brought in by the cocaine trade helped support the Bolivian economy. Moreover, Bolivian drug dealers increasingly began producing more refined products in an effort to cut out the largely Colombian middlemen.

The 1989 elections again resulted in a deadlock, with no party receiving a plurality. This time, in a surprise move, the leftist MIR allied itself with the right-wing ADN, and MIR leader Jaime PAZ ZAMORA became president. In fact, the neoliberal course that the Paz government had embarked upon could not be changed given the demise of state-centered models of economic growth. As a result, the MIR moved to the center and also used its power to break even further the strength of the once-powerful unions. Among the members of the revolutionary alliance, only the peasantry remains a powerful force within Bolivian politics and, because they still represent the largest voting block, will likely continue to do so for some time to come.

By far the best history of Bolivia in any language is HERBERT S. KLEIN, *Bolivia: The Evolution of a Multi-Ethnic Society* (1982). Many overviews, almost exclusively emphasizing politics, exist as well, such as ENRIQUE FINOT, *Nueva historia de Bolivia: Ensayo de interpretación sociológica de Tiwanaku a 1930* (1946); AUGUSTO GUZMÁN, *Breve historia de Bolivia* (1969); HERBERT S. KLEIN, *Parties and Political Change in Bolivia: 1880–1952* (1969); MARIANO BAPTISTA GUMUCIO, *Historia contemporanea de Bolivia*, 2d ed. (1978); JORGE FELLMANN VELARDE, *Historia de Bolivia*, 2d ed., 3 vols. (1978–1981).

ERICK D. LANGER

**BOLIVIA: AGRARIAN REFORM.** Agrarian reform in Bolivia consisted of legal measures enacted in 1953 as a result of the 1952 social revolution. Land tenure has been a divisive issue in Bolivian history. The census of 1950 was the last one before the 1953 land reform and it was used as the basis for the land reform law. The data has been interpreted by authors in different ways. It is agreed that 90 percent of the land was under semifeudal cultivation and was owned by just 6 percent of the proprietors, who held from 1,000 to 10,000 hectares (1 hectare equals 2.47 acres). Also all but 9.3 percent of the land was owned by absentee landowners. Of the land not owned by absentees, just 2.8 percent still belonged to Indian communities, who at the time of the creation of an independent Bolivia in 1825 had held most of the land. Furthermore, the rural workers on the estates, nearly all of whom were classified as Indians, had to provide legally sanctioned personal services.

The agrarian reform's key purpose was to disperse land ownership, promote the breakup of large holdings, and abolish servitude. Besides mandating the redistribution of land and the end of unpaid services, the law encouraged the restoration of Indian communities with modern means of cultivation. This did not happen, but strong peasant unions emerged as a unit of rural organization and production. The strength and number of these *sindicatos* varied from region to region. The law strongly encouraged an increase in agricultural production, protection of natural resources, and internal migration to the less populated eastern regions.

The 1953 law defined six types of land tenure systems, each with different reform requirements. Twenty years later, more than 250,000 new titles, some for expropriated land totaling about 16.25 million acres, had been issued. With the breakup of many large estates, a decline in production occurred. The new freeholders were mostly subsistence farmers. But in the 1990s the positive effects of the reform are generally cited, those effects being a relatively peaceful countryside with a rural population that enjoys full political and economic rights.

HERBERT S. KLEIN, *Parties and Political Change in Bolivia, 1880–1952* (1969); WALTRAUD QUEISER MORALES, *Bolivia: Land of Struggle* (1992).

CHARLES W. ARNADE

## BOLIVIA: CONSTITUTIONS

### Constitución Vitalicia

Simón BOLÍVAR, who in 1825 guided the creation of Bolivia, presented the new nation with its first constitution. Composed by Bolívar, it was approved by the Bolivian assembly in November 1826 but never used.

This 132-article constitution, which represented Bolívar's personal political philosophy, combined various constitutional models, beginning with Athenian democracy. Powers were divided among the electors and the legislative, executive, and judicial branches. The legislature was tricameral: tribune, senate, and censors. Suffrage was broader than was usual for the early nineteenth century. Every ten citizens selected one elector who served for four years. Electors presented candidates for the legislature and local offices and chose censors, who held office for life and were the ultimate guardians of the constitution and individual liberties. The judiciary was independent and selected by the senate from a list prepared by the electors. The executive department was headed by a life-term president who selected his successor. The president, who could appoint only treasury officials, was commander of the army and

could not be impeached or held responsible by the other branches. The constitution was officially abrogated with the Treaty of Piquiza with Peru on 6 July 1828.

MANUEL ORDOÑEZ, ed., *Constitución política de la república de Bolivia, leyes y disposiciones más usuales*, vol. 2 (1917); VICTOR ANDRÉS BELAUNDE, *Bolívar and the Political Thought of the Spanish American Revolution* (1938); PLÁCIDO MOLINA MOSTAJO, *El libertador en Bolivia* (1975).

CHARLES W. ARNADE

### Constitutions

Since its declaration of independence on 6 August 1825, Bolivia has had sixteen constitutions, all providing for a representative government, a strong and centralized executive power, the protection of human rights, independent legislative and judicial branches, and a semirigid constitutional amendment process. The constitutions can be broadly classified into three groups, according to their ideological orientation: liberal–republican, socialist, and nationalist.

The Liberal–Republican phase began in 1826 with the constitution drafted specifically for Bolivia by Simón BOLÍVAR. It established a popular representative form of government divided into four branches (electoral, legislative, executive, and judicial) and expressly guaranteed civil liberties, property rights, and equality of all before the law. It also set the precedent for a strong executive. One of its most controversial clauses provided that the president serve for life. In addition, the president had the power to name local government officials (such as mayors and prefects) and was exempted from any responsibility for his administration's actions.

In the Bolivarian constitution, the legislative, judicial, and electoral branches were independent of the executive. The tricameral legislative branch was divided into two houses with fixed terms—the tribunes (4 years) and senators (8 years)—and one with a life term—the censors. The judicial branch was made up of a Supreme Court and lower district courts in each department, as well as justices of the peace for each town or village. The electoral branch was composed of representatives popularly elected in each province (one representative per 100 citizens). Although this Constitution claimed to establish "popular-representative" government, voting rights were restricted by age, literacy, and job/occupation requirements.

The 1826 constitution remained in effect for only two years and was modified by the 1831 constitution, which eliminated the censors and substituted a four-year presidential term for the lifetime term. In addition, the 1831 constitution stated that if no candidate managed to win an absolute majority of the vote (50 percent plus one), the Congress would have to choose among the top three candidates. This provision, which remains in force, has become crucial to the political process due to the inability of any party to obtain an absolute majority. Despite its short lifespan, the Bolivarian constitution, together with the 1831 amendments, laid the foundation for all future constitutions, and in subsequent versions very few substantive changes have been made.

The nine constitutions ratified between 1834 and 1880 reflect the intense political instability that plagued Bolivia. During this period constitutions were used to reflect the personal political whims of the current president rather than to introduce real changes in the political system. Among the most significant changes were the introduction of the responsibility of the president (1834); the elimination of the president's power to sign federation or alliance treaties, following the disastrous PERU–BOLIVIAN CONFEDERATION (1836–1839); the establishment of a one-term waiting period before the president could seek reelection (1839); and the direct election of the president by secret ballot (1839). In addition, although the 1843, 1851, 1861, 1868, and 1871 constitutions sought to increase the power of the executive, the 1878 constitution gave the legislative branch more extensive powers. The 1878 constitution, which was ratified in the 1880 constitution and modified in 1931, remained in effect until 1938.

The 1938 constitution, of which the 1945 and 1947 constitutions were expansions, was the first one based upon socialist doctrine. It incorporated the principle of social justice and gave the state more responsibility for guaranteeing human rights such as health and education. Workers were given the right to organize, conduct collective bargaining, and strike.

The National Revolution of 1952 ushered in the nationalist phase of Bolivia's constitutional history. The 1961 constitution, drafted by the Nationalist Revolutionary Movement (MNR) regime, incorporated the reforms instituted by the 1952 National Revolution: universal suffrage, agrarian reform, nationalization of the mines, popular militias, and a larger role of the state in the economy. It also instituted the requirement of party affiliation for deputies to seek election, and it gave more power to the legislature by removing the president's veto power over its resolutions.

The constitution of 1967, which remained in effect until August 1994, was very similar to that of 1961. The main difference is that it established a one-term waiting period between reelections and provided basic guidelines for the electoral bodies and political parties. The constitution can be amended by a two-thirds vote of the legislature, and the reforms cannot be vetoed by the executive. Despite the seemingly large number of constitutions, scholars such as Ciro Trigo, Tomás Elío, and Floren Sanabria G. have argued that there has in fact been only one constitution since 1826 that, although modified repeatedly, has remained in effect until the present day. With the reestablishment of democracy in 1982, however, there has been growing consensus in favor of further constitutional reform, designed to reflect more accurately the altered political circumstances of the country. This consensus finally materialized in reforms adopted in August 1994 when Congress approved a sweeping law that amended thirty-five articles of the constitution through the Constitutional Amendments Law. The 1994 reforms include direct election of half of the members of the lower house of Congress from single-member districts; an increase of the terms for presidents, members of parliament, mayors, and municipal council members to five years, with general and municipal elections alternating every two and a half years; clear procedures favoring the direct election of the president and all mayors; voting age lowered to eighteen; increased powers for departmental prefects; and departmental assemblies composed of national representatives doing double duty as the assembly members in the departments from which they had been elected; the establishment of an independent human rights ombudsman; and the establishment of a constitutional tribunal.

CIRO FÉLIX TRIGO, *Las constituciones de Bolivia* (1958); TOMÁS MANUEL ELÍO, "Discurso del Dr. Tomás Manuel Elío, presidente honorario del Colegio de Abogados de La Paz, sobre la unidad de la constitución política," in Ramón Salinas Mariaca, *Las constituciones de Bolivia* (1989); FLOREN SANABRIA G., *La constitución política de Bolivia: 1967* (1990).

ANNABELLE CONROY

## BOLIVIA: ORGANIZATIONS

### Bolivian State Petroleum Corporation
### Yacimientos Petroliferos Fiscales
### Bolivianos—YPFB

The government-owned YPFB was established in 1937 when the Bolivian government of Colonel David TORO expropriated the holdings of the Standard Oil Company of New Jersey. It was given the monopoly to explore and exploit the petroleum resources of Bolivia.

Until the Bolivian National Revolution in 1952, the YPFB was unable to keep up with the country's demand for petroleum and its derivatives. A marked increase in output between 1952 and 1956, however, fulfilled the national demand and provided a small amount for export. The revolutionary government, hoping that petroleum could take the place of the declining tin-mining industry as the country's major source of foreign exchange, ended the monopoly of the YPFB. A new petroleum code allowed foreign oil companies to enter the petroleum business, and the Gulf Oil Corporation began to exploit deposits, and built a pipeline to the Chilean port of Arica. The Gulf concession was expropriated by the government of General Alfredo OVANDO in 1969.

Under President Hugo BANZER in the 1970s, foreign oil firms were again authorized, but those which obtained concessions were more interested in natural gas than in petroleum. YPFB continued to be the country's largest oil company and to refine all the oil processed in the country. It also exported natural gas to Argentina and Brazil. Popular pressure against attempts by the governments of Presidents Jaime PAZ ZAMORA and

Gonzalo Sanchez de Lozada in the early 1990s to privatize government firms, including the YPFB, successfully thwarted such efforts.

ROBERT J. ALEXANDER, *The Bolivian National Revolution* (1957); GUILLERMO LORA, *A History of the Bolivian Labour Movement* (1977); CHRISTOPHER MITCHELL, *The Legacy of Populism in Bolivia: From the MNR to Military Rule* (1977).

ROBERT J. ALEXANDER

### Bolivian Workers Central
### Central Obrera Boliviana—COB

Established immediately following the Bolivian National Revolution in April 1952, the Bolivian Workers Central quickly came to include most of the country's trade unions. It was headed from the beginning by Juan LECHÍN, who was also executive secretary of the Mine Workers Federation (FSTMB).

In its first few months, the COB was controlled by the Trotskyist Partido Obrero Revolucionario (POR), because Lechín and other union leaders belonging to the National Revolutionary Movement (MNR), which had come to power with the Revolution, were principally occupied as members of the new government. However, in October 1952, when the Trotskyists put the COB on record against major parts of the proposed government decree nationalizing the big mining companies, the MNR unionists moved immediately to remove the Trotskyists and to assure their own party's control of the COB.

During the first administration of President Victor PAZ ESTENSSORO (1952–1956), the COB officially "cogoverned" with the MNR, its leaders naming and holding the ministries of mines, labor and peasant affairs. However, that situation ended in 1957, when the COB leaders came into conflict with the price stabilization policies of President Hernán SILES.

The COB leadership finally broke with the revolutionary government of the MNR in 1964, when Juan Lechín was denied the party's presidential nomination. They supported the overthrow of President Paz Estenssoro in November 1964, but soon were in conflict with the new military regime. During much of the period 1965–1969, the COB was outlawed.

When General Alfredo OVANDO seized power in mid-1969, he formed an alliance with the COB. When he was overthrown by a military coup the following year, the COB was successful in imposing General Juan José TORRES as his successor. Under Torres the COB took the lead in establishing the Popular Assembly, which the Trotskyists and others looked upon as an embryonic "soviet," à la Russia in 1917. However, with the overthrow of General Torres by General Hugo BANZER in 1971, there began an eleven-year period of military rule in which the COB was clandestine much of the time.

With the inauguration late in 1982 of President Hernán Siles, with COB backing, the COB rebounded, reaching the height of its political influence. During the three years of Siles's second government, the COB successfully fought by demonstrations and general strikes any effort to impose an economic stabilization policy.

Siles finally called elections in 1985, one year early, and Paz Estenssoro returned to power. This time, however, he was determined not only to enforce a stabilization policy but to close down much of the unprofitable tin-mining sector and to privatize some other government-owned parts of the economy. When the COB sought to carry out a general strike against these policies, the Paz Estenssoro government broke the strike.

This showdown with Paz Estenssoro, and particularly the closing of a large part of the mining industry, greatly reduced the power of the Central Obrera Boliviana, the mine workers having been for forty years the backbone of the COB. It was no longer, along with the armed forces, one of the major power centers of the country's politics. One casualty of this change was Juan Lechín, who for the first time since 1952 ceased to be the president of the COB.

ROBERT J. ALEXANDER, *Organized Labor in Latin America* (1965); GUILLERMO LORA, *A History of the Bolivian Labour Movement* (1977).

ROBERT J. ALEXANDER

### Federation of Bolivian University Students
### Federación Universitaria Boliviana

The Federation was a student organization founded in 1928 by radical intellectuals at Cochabamba with the support of the government of Hernán SILES. Its manifesto was influenced by the university reform movement in Argentina and by Marxism, INDIGENISMO, and nationalism. The Federation's primary concerns were the socialization of natural resources, agrarian reform, the integration of Indians, strong support for the nascent labor movement, and the complete reintegration of the Pacific littoral.

The Federation lost momentum during the 1930s but was rejuvenated in 1939, when it declared itself the intellectual workers' vanguard and called for social revolution. In 1940 the Federation signed a pact of unity with various regional leftist groups and supported the candidacy of Marxist José Antonio ARZE in the presidential elections. It continued to support Arze, who had been the key leader of its 1928 convention, and the radical Revolutionary Party of the Left (PIR), which he founded in mid-1940.

The Federation opposed the fascist leanings of the Gualberto VILLARROEL government. It ceased to play a role in politics after 1946 because of its support for the discredited PIR, and was dissolved in 1952.

HERBERT KLEIN, *Parties and Political Change in Bolivia, 1880–1952* (1971), esp. pp. 99–101, 298–302, 329–331.

MARIA LUISE WAGNER

*See also* **Bolivia: Political Parties.**

### Syndical Federation of Bolivian Mineworkers
### Federación Sindical de
### Trabajadores Mineros de Bolivia—FSTMB

The FSTMB, a national union of mineworkers, was established in 1944 under the government of Colonel Gualberto VILLARROEL, a coalition of young military men and the National Revolutionary Movement (MNR) that came to power in December 1943. The first "permanent secretary" was Juan LECHÍN, a white-collar employee of Patiño Mines, who was also a local soccer hero and former subprefect in the Catavi area. In 1945 Lechín was elected to the new post of executive secretary, which he was to hold for almost half a century.

During the Villarroel regime, the FSTMB became the largest and most powerful labor organization in Bolivia. However, in the six years following the overthrow and murder of Villarroel in 1946, there was continuing conflict between the federation and succeeding governments. During this period the MNR and the Trotskyist Revolutionary Workers Party (POR) were the principal groups within the union. With the Bolivian National Revolution in April 1952, which brought the MNR to power, Lechín became minister of mines, and the FSTMB became the most important part of the new Bolivian Workers Central (COB). The miners federation was given "workers' control" in the newly nationalized mining industry, with union officials having virtual veto power over the mine managers. This power virtually ended in the administration of Hernán SILES (1956–1960), and with the overthrow of the MNR regime in November 1964, the FSTMB opposed the government's efforts to raise efficiency and productivity in the mines.

During the administrations of General Alfredo OVANDO (1969–1970) and General Juan José TORRES (1970–1971), the FSTMB enjoyed a rapprochement with the government, but it was forced underground during most of the 1971–1982 period, when military regimes ruled Bolivia. By contrast, during the second administration of President Siles (1982–1985), the FSTMB was a major factor in preventing the enactment of an economic stabilization program. When Siles was succeeded by President Victor PAZ ESTENSSORO (1985–1989), the power of the miners federation was largely destroyed. In 1986 Juan Lechín was defeated for reelection as executive secretary of the FSTMB. He also resigned as head of the COB.

ROBERT J. ALEXANDER, *The Bolivian National Revolution* (1958); GUILLERMO LORA, *A History of the Bolivian Labour Movement* (1977).

ROBERT J. ALEXANDER

## BOLIVIA: POLITICAL PARTIES

### Overview

Political parties in Bolivia have rarely been strong organizations with coherent ideological programs and stable followings; typically, they have served as instruments of access to state patronage, their rise and fall being a function of the fate of their leader. The personal nature of political parties, together with their purely instrumental function, accounts both for the lack of a stable party system and for the strange alliances that are sometimes formed between parties with seemingly opposing ideologies.

Political parties emerged in Bolivia only toward the second half of the nineteenth century. Until then, the most common means of accessing power was through military force, and the followers of a particular leader or caudillo were referred to by his name. Thus, the followers of Andrés de SANTA CRUZ were referred to as *crucistas,* those of José BALLIVIÁN as *ballivianistas,* and so on.

The end of the WAR OF THE PACIFIC (1879–1883) brought in the Liberal–Conservative period (1884–1935), in which party lines were drawn according to economic interests. The Conservative Party, a fusion of the Constitutional and Democratic parties, represented the interests of the traditional large landowners and the silver-mining entrepreneurs of the south; the Liberal Party, on the other hand, became associated with the term La Rosca, a derogatory term referring to the tin-mining oligarchy and the personnel it used to influence policy making.

The 1930s and 1940s saw the rise of three types of political parties, each with a different notion of how to resolve the nation's problems. The nationalist revolutionary type, represented by the Nationalist Revolutionary Movement (Movimiento Nacionalista Revolucionario—MNR), believed that economic and social development could come about only through the creation of a strong centralized state directed by middle-class technocrats and supported by a multiclass alliance. Marxist-style parties originated among the working class, particularly the mine workers, and in the universities. They were broadly divided into Trotskyists, represented by the Revolutionary Workers Party (Partido Obrero Revolucionario—POR) and Stalinists, represented by the Leftist Revolutionary Party (Partido de la Izquierda Revolucionaria—PIR). Finally, nationalist authoritarian parties, represented by the Bolivian Socialist Falange (Falange Socialista Boliviana—FSB), advocated a corporatist national economic order and a federal political system.

The MNR, which came to power with the 1952 Bolivian Revolution, had a significant impact on the development of party politics, and formed the point of departure for many of today's political parties. By forming a multiclass support base, the MNR enjoyed single-party dominance from 1952 to 1964. However, the increasingly conflicting agendas housed under the MNR umbrella soon led a number of factions to break away from the party. Scholars have identified no fewer than thirty-one splinter parties that emerged from the MNR, including the Historical National Revolutionary Movement (MNR Histórico—MNRH), the National Revolutionary Movement of the Left (Movimiento Nacionalista Revolucionario de la Izquierda—MNRI), the Nationalist Leftist Revolutionary Party (Partido Revolucionario de la Izquierdia Nacional—PRIN), and the Authentic Revolutionary Party (Partido Revolucionario Auténtico—PRA).

The transition to democracy, which began in 1978, brought several changes to the political system, but the personalized and instrumental nature of political parties remained intact. As a result of a complex system of proportional representation, one of the most important changes was the proliferation of *taxi partidos*, parties so small that as the popular saying goes, they could hold their conventions inside taxicabs. This trend contributed to the inability of any one party to obtain an absolute majority in national elections.

These developments produced a significant trend toward the formation of political pacts/coalitions. Two examples stand out. The winning party of the 1982 elections, the Democratic Popular Unity (Unidad Democrática Popular—UDP), was composed of a broad coalition of leftist parties: the MNRI, the Movement of the Revolutionary Left (Movimiento de la Izquierda Revolucionaria—MIR), the Bolivian Communist Party (Partido Comunista Boliviano—PCB), and the Social Democratic Party (Partido Social Demócrata—PSD), among others. In the 1989 elections, the MIR joined its longtime enemy—General Hugo BANZER SUÁREZ and his Nationalist Democratic Action (Acción Democrática Nacionalista—ADN)—to form the Patriotic Accord (Acuerdo Patriótico—AP). This coalition placed the presidency in the hands of the MIR, which finished third in the elections.

Another significant change has been the emergence of parties headed by popular leaders who draw their support mainly from the marginalized urban poor. Such is the case with the Conscience of the Fatherland (Conciencia de la Patria—CONDEPA), led by a popular media personality, and with the Civic Solidarity Union (Unión Cívica de la Solidaridad—UCS), led by a successful beer entrepreneur.

In the 1993 elections the major parties/coalitions were MNR, AP, UCS, and CONDEPA. Despite winning the elections with a plurality of the votes, the MNR formed a coalition with UCS, the Free Bolivia Movement (Movimiento Bolivia Libre—MBL), and the Tupac Katari Revolutionary Movement (Movimiento Revolucionario Tupac Katari—MRTK) to insure not only the presidency but also a two-thirds majority in the national Congress.

JAMES M. MALLOY, *Bolivia: The Uncompleted Revolution* (1970); JAMES M. MALLOY and RICHARD THORN, eds., *Beyond the Revolution: Bolivia Since 1952* (1971); CHRISTOPHER MITCHELL, *The Legacy of Populism in Bolivia: From the MNR to Military Rule* (1977); RAÚL RIVADANEIRA, "Partidos políticos, partidos taxi y partidos fantasmas: La atomización de los partidos de Bolivia," in *Nueva sociedad* 74 (September–October 1984): 75–90; EDUARDO GAMARRA, "Political Stability, Democratization and the Bolivian National Congress" (Ph.D. diss., University of Pitts-

burgh, 1987); MARIO ROLÓN ANAYA, *Política y partidos en Bolivia*, 2d ed. (1987); JAMES M. MALLOY and EDUARDO GAMARRA, *Revolution and Reaction: Bolivia 1964–1985* (1988); FERNANDO CALDERÓN, "Cuestiones por la sociedad: Los partidos en Bolivia," in *Los sistemas políticos de América Latina*, edited by Lorenzo Meyer and José Luis Reyna (1989); JORGE LAZARTE, "Partidos políticos e informalización de la política," in *Democracia y gobernabilidad: América Latina*, edited by René Antonio Mayorga (1992).

ANNABELLE CONROY

*See also* **Caudillismo.**

### Bolivian Communist Party
### Partido Comunista Boliviano—PCB

The first Communist Party in Bolivia was established in the late 1920s under the guidance and patronage of the Communist International. Although it was underground, it gained considerable influence in the nascent organized labor movement, and was represented in 1929 at the Congress of Latin American Communist Parties in Buenos Aires. The party was obliterated during the CHACO WAR between Bolivia and Paraguay (1932–1935). In 1940 a new Communist-controlled party was established. The Party of the Revolutionary Left (PIR) was headed by José Antonio ARZE, who ran for president in the election of that year and did surprisingly well in the country's principal cities, although he was badly defeated by the government nominee, General Enrique PEÑARANDA.

In the following years, the PIR emerged as a major element in the labor movement, coming to control the Confederación Sindical de Trabajadores de Bolivia. During the government of President Gualberto VILLARROEL, which encouraged the organization of the mineworkers union (FSTMB) under the leadership of the Movimiento Nacionalista Revolucionario (MNR), the PIR was in strong opposition, and Arze spent most of the period in the United States, where he taught at the Communist Party's training school in New York City.

In the six years following the overthrow of the Villarroel regime in July 1946, the PIR cooperated closely with the reactionary government of the period. As a consequence, the youth of the party withdrew to form the Partido Comunista (PCB) in 1950, and the PIR was dissolved.

The PCB strongly opposed the MNR regime (1952–1964) and began to gain some influence in organized labor, particularly among the mineworkers. It supported the 1964 overthrow of the MNR government by Generals René BARRIENTOS and Alfredo OVANDO. In 1964 a pro-Maoist faction split from the PCB to form the Partido Comunista de Bolivia (Marxista-Leninista). Both parties refused to join the guerrilla operation of Ernesto "Che" GUEVARA in eastern Bolivia in 1966–1967, and both participated in the so-called Popular Assembly during the government of President Juan José TORRES (1970–1971).

The pro-Maoist faction declined in the 1970s and 1980s, while the pro-Soviet party continued to be a major force in organized labor. In 1985 and again in 1987, the PCB's former secretary-general, Simón Reyes, was elected executive secretary of the FSTMB, which had been headed since its establishment almost half a century before by Juan LECHÍN OQUENDO. Neither Communist faction, however, became a major factor in national politics.

HOOVER INSTITUTION, *Yearbook of International Communist Affairs* (1970s, 1980s).

ROBERT J. ALEXANDER

### Bolivian Socialist Falange
### Falange Socialista Boliviana—FSB

Founded in Santiago, Chile, in 1937 by Oscar Unzaga de la Vega, Hugo Arias, and Germán Aguilar Zenteño, the Bolivian Socialist Falange was once considered the second largest party in Bolivia. Inspired by the nationalist rhetoric of the Spanish Falange and right-wing Catholic movements in Spain, the FSB was once at the forefront of calls for the nationalization of the Bolivian tin mines. Following the 1952 revolution, however, the FSB led all opposition efforts against the ruling Nationalist Revolutionary Movement (MNR). As a result, prominent members of the FSB were imprisoned and systematically persecuted.

In 1964, the FSB was one of the principal civilian forces that helped the military bring down the MNR. In an ironic twist, seven years later, the MNR and FSB leadership joined forces with then Colonel Hugo BANZER SUÁREZ to overthrow a populist faction of the armed forces. The FSB did not survive the military period mainly because the space it once occupied was filled by the Nationalist Democratic Action (ADN), a party founded by General Banzer Suárez in 1979. By the mid-1980s the FSB had become just another of Bolivia's numerous minuscule political parties. Under David Añez Pedraza, who became the FSB's leader in 1982, the party attempted to move toward the left, precipitating an internal battle that led to the formation of the Socialist Movement (MAS).

ALBERTO CORNEJO, *Programas políticos de Bolivia* (1949); and JAMES DUNKERLEY, *Rebellion in the Veins: Political Struggle in Bolivia, 1952–1982* (1984).

EDUARDO A. GAMARRA

### Conservative Party
### Partido Conservador

Formally known as the Constitutional Party, the Conservative Party was formed in the aftermath of the Chilean defeat of Bolivian forces during the WAR OF THE PACIFIC (1879–1884). The Conservatives and Liberals were the first formal political parties in Bolivia based on ideology rather than personalistic leadership. The Conservatives ruled Bolivia from 1884 to 1899 and were the principal political force during the last two decades of the nineteenth century, which is frequently called the period of the Conservative oligarchy. Led primarily by wealthy silver miners from the southern part of the country with close ties to Chilean capitalists, the Conservatives favored a peace treaty and closer ties with Chile. Their vision of the country's economic development rested upon the building of railroads to foster silver exports, the creation of a dynamic land market (at the expense of Indian communities), and the settlement of Bolivia's eastern frontiers. Under the influence of party leader and chief ideologue Mariano BAPTISTA (president of Bolivia, 1892–1896), the Conservative Party also favored the Catholic church. Although they differed over religious issues, the Conservatives favored the same economic liberalism as their principal political opponents, the Liberal Party.

The best analysis in English of the formation of the Conservative Party is HERBERT S. KLEIN, *Parties and Political Change in Bolivia: 1880–1952* (1969), chap. 1. See also MARIANO BAPTISTA, *Obras completas* (1932–1934). On the Conservatives' Indian land policies, see TRISTAN PLATT, *Estado boliviano y ayllu andino* (1982).

ERICK D. LANGER

### Constitutionalist Party
### Partido Constitucional

The Constitutionalist Party, whose program was based on the writings of its founder, Mariano BAPTISTA, and on the Bolivian constitution of 1878, represented the interests of the landowning and mining elite. After Bolivia's defeat in the WAR OF THE PACIFIC (1880), the party favored a quick peace settlement with Chile that would include indemnification for lost territory and enable Bolivia to construct a railroad for mining exports.

In the presidential elections of 1884 the Constitutionalists supported Gregorio PACHECO of the Democratic Party, which had proclaimed itself the party of national reconciliation. During Pacheco's presidency, the Constitutionalist Party became known as the Conservative Party and played an important role under the leadership of Baptista. Its primary concerns were the creation of a powerful parliamentary regime, the promotion of economic growth based on massive railroad construction, and the defense of the interests of the Roman Catholic church.

Following its defeat by the Liberals in 1899, the Constitutionalist Party began to decline.

HERBERT KLEIN, *Parties and Political Change in Bolivia, 1880–1952* (1971); GUILLERMO LORA, *Historia de las partidos políticos de Bolivia* (1987); MARIO ROLON ANAYA, *Política y partidos en Bolivia*, 2d ed. (1987).

MARIA LUISE WAGNER

## Democratic Popular Unity
### Unidad Democrática Popular—UDP

The Democratic Popular Unity was founded on 13 April 1978 as a "popular, nationalist, anti-imperialist and revolutionary" opposition political front. It grouped the Nationalist Revolutionary Movement of the Left (Movimiento Nacionalista Revolucionario de la Izquierda—MNRI), the Movement of the Revolutionary Left (Movimiento de la Izquierda Revolucionaria—MIR), the Bolivian Communist Party (Partido Comunista Boliviano—PCB), and other, minor parties under a single banner.

The UDP participated in the 1978, 1979, and 1980 elections but was unable to achieve a majority until 1982, when the Congress voted the UDP into office. Under the leadership of Hernán SILES ZUAZO, the party governed the country between 1982 and 1985. Faced with the most severe economic crisis in Bolivian history and plagued by debilitating internal divisions stemming from the conflicting agendas of the coalition's parties, the UDP was forced to call early elections in 1985. By 1986, the MIR, the PCB, and the Christian Democrats had abandoned the UDP, which then ceased to exist as a party.

ANNABELLE CONROY

## Liberal Party
### Partido Liberal

The Liberal Party came to power in 1899 after defeating the Conservative Party in the FEDERALIST WAR (1898–1899) and remained in power until 1920. The Liberals continued many of the programs of the Conservatives, such as encouraging the sale of Indian community lands and developing the infrastructure for the export economy, especially the RAILROAD network that carried minerals to the Pacific coast. This era coincided with the TIN-mining boom, which utilized the rail network first developed by the Conservatives for SILVER exports. After unsuccessful attempts to put down Brazilian FILIBUSTERING expeditions, the Liberal administration was forced to sell the Acre region in the northeastern part of the country to Brazil in 1903. The party then began to promote a liberal land-grant policy in 1905 to settle frontier lands. Only when it became clear that wealthy absentee landowners had purchased vast extents without populating the frontiers was this policy stopped in 1915. Although the party had been founded by Eliodoro Camacho in 1883 as a force advocating the continuation of the WAR OF THE PACIFIC (1879–1884), it was the most important Liberal president, Ismael MONTES, who signed the definitive peace treaty with Chile. The Liberal Party era was one of political peace and prosperity, during which Bolivia modernized rapidly.

The best description of the Liberal Party era is HERBERT S. KLEIN, *Parties and Political Change in Bolivia: 1880–1952* (1969),

pp. 31–63. See also JUAN ALBARRACÍN MILLÁN, *El poder minero en la administracíon liberal* (1972).

ERICK D. LANGER

## Movement of the Revolutionary Left
### Movimiento de la Izquierda Revolucionaria—MIR

Founded in 1971 by Jaime PAZ ZAMORA, Oscar Eid, Antonio Araníbar, and Jorge Ríos Dalenz, the MIR evolved from a university student organization to one of the three most significant political parties in Bolivia. This young party gained quickly after experiencing severe repression in the 1970s under a military government. Between 1982 and 1985, the MIR formed the Popular Democratic Union (Unidad Democrática y Popular—UDP), a coalition that governed Bolivia in which Paz Zamora served as vice president. In 1989 Paz Zamora was elected president of Bolivia by Congress.

Initially a conglomeration of different Marxist groups, the MIR underwent several major splits in the 1980s. In 1983 a labor faction, headed by Walter Delgadillo, founded a so-called MIR-Masas. In 1985 the original founders of the party went their separate ways. Antonio Araníbar left the party and founded the MIR–Bolivia Libre (MIR–BL). Owing to a National Electoral Court decision favoring Jaime Paz Zamora's faction, the MIR–BL became the Movimiento Bolivia Libre in 1986. Between 1986 and 1989 Paz Zamora's faction grew in size as middle-class professionals and factions of the Nationalist Revolutionary Movement (MNR) and leftist parties joined it. To contest the 1989 elections, Paz Zamora adopted a more fashionable social democratic orientation as the party's new allies became part of the "New Majority" (NM) alliance. This alliance served Paz Zamora well in his quest to become president of Bolivia in 1989.

With Paz Zamora as president of Bolivia, a number of additional splits rent the MIR–NM as several leftist members resigned when the party's leadership formed an alliance—the so-called Acuerdo Patriótico (AP)—with former dictator Hugo BANZER SUÁREZ. In 1991 generational splits also became evident as a group of young lawyers demanded a larger role in the party's leadership and in the distribution of patronage. This group, derogatorily referred to as the "abogansters," exerted enough pressure to secure governmental posts.

In 1993, the MIR suffered a serious blow when General Banzer, the AP's candidate, lost the general elections. Paz Zamora distanced himself from the party and the MIR experienced a scramble for leadership among potential successors. While the MIR lost much of the support it enjoyed in 1989, the municipal elections in December 1993 revealed that the party still had a following in a few districts around the country.

JAMES M. MALLOY and EDUARDO GAMARRA, *Revolution and Reaction: Bolivia, 1964–1985* (1988); CARLOS MONTAÑO DAZA, *De*

*Paz a Paz: Historia del MIR* (1990); SUSANA PEÑARANDA DE DEL GRANADO and OMAR CHÁVEZ ZAMORANO, *El MIR: Entre el pasado y el presente* (1992).

EDUARDO A. GAMARRA

### Nationalist Democratic Action
### *Acción Democrática Nacionalista—ADN*

General Hugo BANZER SUÁREZ founded the ADN as a civilian political group that could defend him and his colleagues against charges of corruption and human rights violations during his seven-year period (1971–1978) as president of Bolivia. The party, organized in 1979, placed third in both 1979 and 1980. It won in 1985 and came in second in 1989 and again in 1993. To its members, the ADN and Banzer were instrumental in the consolidation of democracy in Bolivia. In 1985 Banzer supported the Nationalist Revolutionary Movement (MNR) government by entering into a "pact for democracy." Then in 1989 the ADN entered into a coalition dubbed the Acuerdo Patriótico (AP) with the Movement of the Revolutionary Left (MIR) to govern Bolivia.

In the early 1990s Banzer's health deteriorated considerably, a factor that may have contributed to his November 1993 decision to step down as party chief. With Banzer gone, internal divisions surfaced, forcing a scramble for leadership. Splits appeared along generational and regional lines. A younger, modernizing faction confronted others in the party that were linked to Bolivia's traditional political class. In mid-1991 a new group led by Jorge Landívar, a former president of the Santa Cruz Civic Committee, asserted some influence within the party. Without Banzer's leadership, however, the party's survival in the long run is questionable.

JAMES M. MALLOY and EDUARDO GAMARRA, *Revolution and Reaction: Bolivia, 1964–1985* (1988); HORACIO TRUJILLO, *Los partidos políticos en América Latina: Partidos políticos y sistema de partidos en Bolivia* (1991).

EDUARDO A. GAMARRA

### Nationalist Revolutionary Movement
### *Movimiento Nacionalista*
### *Revolucionario—MNR*

Founded in 1941 by Víctor PAZ ESTENSSORO, Hernán SILES ZUAZO, Walter GUEVARA ARZE, and Augusto Céspedes among others, the MNR is Bolivia's most important political party. Responsible for launching the 1952 revolution, pushing through universal suffrage and land reform, and nationalizing Bolivia's MINING INDUSTRY, the MNR governed until 1964, when it was overthrown by a military coup headed by General René BARRIENTOS ORTUÑO.

One of the principal reasons for the party's downfall was a permanent state of internal factionalism. By the late 1950s, Guevara, Paz, and Siles had formally split. During the military period these factional disputes had become so intense that by the time the military formally

retired from politics in the late 1970s, there were at least thirty factions of the original MNR.

The 1980s were essentially a period of realignment as a number of MNR factions joined Paz's Historic MNR (MNR-H). By the mid-1980s the MNR-H dropped the H and reclaimed the MNR. In 1985 factional disputes again arose as the MNR launched the New Economic Policy and joined General Hugo BANZER SUÁREZ in the Nationalist Democratic Action (ADN) *Pacto por la democracia.* Senior party members formed a variety of so-called *comités de defensa del MNR,* groups that lacked any real power but generated a significant amount of internal turmoil. The naming of Gonzalo SÁNCHEZ DE LOZADA as the party's presidential candidate in 1989 produced great internal turmoil. Sánchez came in first but failed to win a majority of the vote. This threw the election into Congress, which did not elect him. This prompted the *comités de defensa del MNR* to challenge his grip on the party. These groups remained active and often announced the formation of a "true" MNR.

The most significant faction of the MNR other than the branch headed by Víctor Paz Estenssoro was founded in 1971 by Hernán Siles Zuazo as the MNR de Izquierda (MNRI). In the late 1970s it became the principal party in the Popular Democratic Union (Unidad Democrática y Popular—UDP). But even these factions were not immune to internal splits. By 1982, when Siles Zuazo became president, splits in the MNRI were already very visible. At least three factions were identifiable, including a group calling itself "Palaciego," which surrounded Siles Zuazo. Another faction, the so-called MNRI–Legalista, split with Siles Zuazo in 1983 and joined the opposition in Congress. A group of technocrats in the MNRI formed another faction called the MNRI–Siglo XX. In the long run the Palaciego and Siglo XX factions prevailed. For the 1985 elections, the MNRI ran a hapless campaign as it resorted to two technocrats who had served in several cabinet posts to run as the principal candidates. The appeal of these candidates did not transcend the groups surrounding Siles Zuazo. A peasant sector labeling itself the MNRI-1 contested the elections and disappeared shortly thereafter.

After 1985 the MNRI maintained a very minimal presence in Congress, having won less than 5 percent of the vote. Owing to Siles Zuazo's deteriorating health, the MNRI gradually disappeared.

JAMES DUNKERLEY, *Rebellion in the Veins: Political Struggle in Bolivia, 1952–1982* (1984); and HORACIO TRUJILLO, *Los partidos políticos en América Latina: Partidos políticos y sistema de partidos en Bolivia* (1991).

EDUARDO A. GAMARRA

### Party of the Revolutionary Left
### *Partido de la Izquierda Revolucionaria—PIR*

As is true of other mid-twentieth-century Bolivian parties, the roots of the PIR lie in the disappointment of the young members of the middle class over Bolivia's backwardness and defeat in the CHACO WAR. The PIR was organized in Oruro in July 1940 and the next year issued a detailed program marking it as a socialist party. Its leaders were the charismatic José Antonio ARZE and Ricardo Anaya, both law professors from Cochabamba. For about three decades the PIR was an important party but never achieved a national electoral victory. It disbanded in 1952 following the victory of the Nationalist Revolutionary Movement (Movimiento Nacionalista Revolucionario—MNR) but regrouped in 1956. Eventually it faded into oblivion. The PIR's program, genuinely Marxist but unaffiliated with world communism, was closer to the prevalent Latin American socialist-indigenist thinking. It was strongly anti-imperialist, which its members interpreted as opposition to the pervasive influence of the United States.

ALBERTO S. CORNEYO, *Programas políticos de Bolivia* (1949), pp. 180–294; HERBERT S. KLEIN, *Parties and Political Change in Bolivia, 1880–1952* (1969).

CHARLES W. ARNADE

## Patriotic Agreement
## Acuerdo Patriótico (AP)

In August 1989 General Hugo BANZER SUÁREZ's Nationalist Democratic Action (ADN) and Jaime PAZ ZAMORA's Movement of the Revolutionary Left (MIR) established the Acuerdo Patriótico (AP). Essentially a gentleman's agreement between both men, the pact served both to end an impasse in the Congress between the three top vote getters in the May 1989 elections and to elect Paz Zamora as president of Bolivia. Paz Zamora and Banzer signed no documents, arguing that they would prove that their word could be trusted. Despite the rather unholy nature of the alliance between two erstwhile enemies—Paz Zamora was imprisoned during Banzer's seven-year dictatorship in the 1970s—the AP held office for four years. A bipartisan council (Consejo Político del Acuerdo Patriótico) headed by General Banzer was established to sort out relations between the ADN and the MIR. As part of the original agreement, Luis Ossio Sanjinés, the ADN's vice-presidential candidate in May 1989, was named vice president of the country. In December 1989 and December 1991, the AP, now a political party, ran a single slate of candidates for municipal elections; General Banzer ran as the party's candidate for the 1993 general elections. Following Banzer's defeat at the polls, the AP ended rather unceremoniously in August 1993.

EDUARDO A. GAMARRA, "Crafting Political Support for Stabilization: Political Pacts and the New Economic Policy in Brazil," in *Democracy, Markets, and Structural Reform in Latin America*, edited by William C. Smith, Carlos H. Acuña, and Eduardo A. Gamarra (1994), and "Market-Oriented Reforms and Democratization in Bolivia," in *A Precarious Balance*, edited by Joan M. Nelson, vol. 2 (1994).

EDUARDO A. GAMARRA

## Republican Party
## Partido Republicano

The Republican party, formally called the Republican Union, was formed in 1914 by an offshoot of the Liberal Party and other opposition groups and ruled Bolivia from 1921 to 1934. Marred by continual infighting, the Republicans espoused a traditional liberal ideology like their predecessors, the Liberals. Juan Bautista SAAVEDRA, the first Republican president (1921–1925), passed some social legislation but also permitted the massacre of miners at Uncía in 1923. Hernán SILES ZUAZO, president from 1926 to 1930, supported university reform, but had to deal with the beginnings of the Great Depression. Siles tried to remain in office past his term, but a military junta overthrew his government and in 1931 gave the reins of power to Daniel SALAMANCA, one of the founders of the party. As the economic and social situation worsened, Salamanca dragged Bolivia into the disastrous CHACO WAR, bringing about his own downfall in 1934 and the demise of the Republican Party as a political force.

The best analysis of the Republican period is in HERBERT S. KLEIN, *Parties and Political Change in Bolivia: 1880–1952* (1969), pp. 64–159. See also DAVID ALVÉSTEGUI, *Salamanca, su gravitación sobre el destino de Bolivia*, 4 vols. (1957–1970); and PORFIRIO DÍAZ MACHICADO, *Historia de Bolivia*, vols. 1–3 (1954–1955).

ERICK D. LANGER

**BOLOGNESI, FRANCISCO** (*d.* 1880), Peruvian national hero and military commander in charge of the defense of the Peruvian garrison in Arica during the WAR OF THE PACIFIC (1879–1883). Together with Alfonso Ugarte, Bolognesi is considered the premier military hero. Both died in the battle of ARICA (1880) and are credited with heroic self-sacrifice in defense of Peru. However, the battle and the war resulted in sound defeats for the Peruvian army. This legacy is a cornerstone of official Peruvian nationalism.

Bolognesi was typical of those military officers who were trained during the struggles among military chieftains during the mid-nineteenth century in Peru, as opposed to the professional military cadre that appeared in the 1890s. Bolognesi supported General Ramón CASTILLA against Generals José Rufino ECHENIQUE and Manuel Ignacio VIVANCO in 1853–1858. He studied artillery in Europe and became commander general of artillery in 1862. During the War of the Pacific he led the Third Division in the battles of San Francisco, Tarapacá, and Arica. Outnumbered by Chilean forces in Arica he refused to surrender and rallied his soldiers to "fight until firing the last bullet."

JORGE BASADRE, *Historia de la República del Perú*, vol. 5 (1963).

ALFONSO W. QUIROZ

**BOLTON, HERBERT EUGENE** (*b.* 20 July 1870; *d.* 30 January 1963), U.S. historian of the Spanish BORDER-LANDS. Born in Wisconsin, Bolton earned a bachelor's degree from the University of Wisconsin and a Ph.D. from the University of Pennsylvania in 1899. He then taught at the University of Texas and at Stanford University. At the University of California at Berkeley, from 1911 to 1950, Bolton popularized Spain in the Americas, advocated archival and trail research, published documentary and narrative history, trained hundreds of graduate students, and earned a national reputation. For his presidential address to the American Historical Association in 1932, he summarized his popular undergraduate course, "History of the Americas," in a single lecture, "The Epic of Greater America." He devoted most of his attention, however, to the narrower region he had defined in *The Spanish Borderlands: A Chronicle of Old Florida and the Southwest* (1921). His student and biographer, John Francis Bannon, considers *Rim of Christendom: A Biography of Eusebio Francisco Kino, Pacific Coast Pioneer* (1936) his most impressive piece of scholarship.

Bolton has been criticized for his anecdotal style and alleged blindness to the tragedies of conquest; his fascination with the lives of notable white men, at the apparent expense of others; and his lack of interest in the region's people after the eighteenth century. Whatever his faults, Bolton stimulated an outpouring of Borderlands studies that each generation since seems bent on surpassing.

JOHN F. BANNON, *Herbert Eugene Bolton, The Historian and the Man, 1870–1953* (1978); HERBERT E. BOLTON, *Coronado, Knight of Pueblos and Plains* (1949, repr. 1990); JOHN L. KESSELL, "Bolton and *Coronado,*" *Journal of the Southwest* 32, no. 1 (1990): 83–96.

JOHN L. KESSELL

**BOMBAL, MARÍA LUISA** (b. 8 June 1910; d. 6 May 1980), Chilean novelist, born in Viña del Mar. Two highly original novels, *La última niebla* (1935) and *La amortajada* (1938), translated into English by the author herself as *The House of Mist* (1947) and *The Shrouded Woman* (1948), attest to María Luisa Bombal's outstanding position among Latin American writers. Educated in France, she lived most of her life away from her country.

An innovative novelist, Bombal was very influential in the development of contemporary narrative in Latin America, and she has had a profound effect on the development of a feminine perspective among Latin American women writers because of her treatment of the feminine characters in her work. Her novels are perfect narratives of fantasy and feminine sensitivity. She is a good representative of the feminist will to surpass the limitations imposed on women by society, and her works are an example of the stylistic experimentation of the period.

After having accomplished both an expression of women's views and the development of a new style, Bombal ceased to publish new works. In her old age she returned to her native country and enjoyed a brief recognition of her influence on younger writers, particularly women. Today, a literary prize for novels is given in her name.

HERNÁN VIDAL, *María Luisa Bombal: La feminidad enajenada* (1976); MERCEDES VALDIVIESO, "Social Denunciation in the Language of 'The Tree' by María Luisa Bombal," in *Latin American Literary Review* 9 (1976): 70–76; LUCÍA GUERRA-CUNNINGHAM, *La narrativa de María Luisa Bombal: Una visión de la existencia femenina* (1980), and "María Luisa Bombal," in *Spanish American Women Writers* (1990): 41–52.

S. DAYDÍ-TOLSON

**BONAMPAK,** a small pre-Hispanic MAYA site in the southern Maya lowlands of Chiapas, Mexico. Bonampak is known for its stunning full-color fresco murals. The murals occupy the interior wall and ceiling surfaces of a small masonry building with three corbel-vaulted rooms. The long wall of the building, facing into a large plaza, has a separate entrance for each room.

The murals, preserved by a thin coating of limestone caused by roof seepage, are famed for the richness of information they provide about elite Maya society in the Late Classic Period (A.D. 790). The (probably historical) narrative scene depicts preparations for a raiding party, its successful return with captives, their torture, and finally the celebration of the event.

The mural of the first room includes preparations notable for the presence of a Maya band with trumpets, rattles, tortoise shells struck with deer antlers, and large drums and for conferences between the ruling chief and his nobles. The second room shows the raiding party and the torture of the captives (their fingernails drip blood). In the third room, the celebration includes dancing on the steps (those in front of the building?) and ritual bloodletting rites by the ruler and his family.

The detail in the murals shows several changes of fine clothing, especially woven cloth and featherwork, loincloths of captives, footwear, weaponry, musical instruments, ceremonial rituals, paraphernalia, and sacrifices. They include hieroglyphic inscriptions with names of the participants, dates of the events, and descriptions of the ceremonies.

The site is 19 miles south of YAXCHILÁN, on the Usumacinta River, and has Yaxchilán emblem glyphs, but none of its own. The earliest and latest Maya long counts are 9.8.9.0.0. (A.D. 602) and 9.18.0.0.0. (A.D. 790).

See CARNEGIE INSTITUTION OF WASHINGTON, *Ancient Maya Paintings of Bonampak, Mexico,* suppl. publication 46, (1955), for full color reproductions of the Tejeda paintings and two Healy photographs. See also SYLVANUS G. MORLEY and GEORGE W. BRAINERD, *The Ancient Maya,* 4th ed. (1983), esp. pp. 315, 416–421.

WALTER R. T. WITSCHEY

**BONAPARTE, JOSEPH** (b. 7 January 1768; d. 19 July 1844), king of Spain. The oldest brother of NAPOLEON Bonaparte, Joseph was born into a family of the minor nobility in Corte, Corsica. He became a lawyer in 1788 and held a series of posts in Corsica and, after 1793, in

France, where he and his family found refuge after the British seized the island. As Napoleon rapidly rose through the French military ranks (he was proclaimed emperor in 1804), Joseph's career gradually became entwined with the military successes of his ambitious brother. Napoleon's dream of a French empire extending across all Europe led him to invade Portugal in 1807 and Spain in 1808, forcing the abdication of the ruling Spanish Bourbon family (first Charles IV and then Ferdinand VII). With the monarchs now absent, Napoleon proclaimed the reluctant Joseph king of Spain in June 1898. These unpopular actions sparked the Peninsular War, a fierce Spanish guerrilla resistance to French incursions that was aided militarily and financially by Great Britain. As king, Joseph's actions were dictated by Napoleon's interests. His tremendous unpopularity led Spaniards to nickname him Pepe Botella (Pepe the Tippler), a vice he was not known to possess.

The rupture of legitimate monarchial power created a crisis of political legitimacy and a power vacuum in Spain's American colonies. French usurpation of the Spanish crown set in motion the Spanish American movements for independence, the causes of which had been developing for several decades. Influential criollo leaders, long discontented with the contradictions and restrictions of Spanish colonial administration, aware that their interests and those of Spain were different, and disillusioned by the rapid decline of the once powerful Spanish metropolis, saw in this turn of events an opportune moment to assert their independence. Joseph died in Florence, Italy.

WILLIAM SPENCE ROBERTSON, *France and Latin American Independence* (1939; repr. 1967); GABRIEL H. LOVETT, *Napoleon and the Birth of Modern Spain,* 2 vols. (1965); OWEN CONNELLY, *The Gentle Bonaparte: A Biography of Joseph, Napoleon's Elder Brother* (1968); MICHAEL ROSS, *The Reluctant King* (1976).

J. DAVID DRESSING

**BONFIM, NOSSO SENHOR DO** (Our Lord of the Good Ending), a term that refers to the patron saint of Bahia, also identified as Jesus Christ, and to the church of the same name in Salvador, Bahia. African Brazilians identify Jesus with the West African YORUBA deity Oxalá. The Festa do Nosso Senhor do Bonfim, one of Brazil's most traditional celebrations, is held in January on the second Sunday after Epiphany (Day of Kings). Its origins and practices are both Portuguese and Yoruban. In the traditional style of Portuguese pilgrimages, visitors and devotees engage in a near-riotous carnival-like atmosphere of feasting, drinking, singing, and dancing in the church's neighborhood. Located on a hill and outlined in electric lights at night during the celebration, the church can be seen 7.5 miles away. On Thursday preceding the Sunday celebration, the faithful march from the center of Salvador to the church accompanied by musical groups as a preview of CARNIVAL. The governor of Bahia and the mayor of Salvador appear at the church. Priestesses in

the CANDOMBLÉ religion participate in the ritual washing of the gleaming white steps of the church. Some claim that the church steps are the sacred stones of Oxalá. The water used is drawn from the well of Oxalá. Sweeping and washing churches for "promises"—pledges to God to do something special if God grants a request—is a Portuguese tradition. A Miracle Room in the church contains innumerable ex-votos, including wood, plaster, and wax reproductions of human body parts and photographs, letters, and paintings. These objects are hung on the walls and from the ceiling in gratitude for cures and other special favors performed by Nosso Senhor do Bonfim.

RUTH LANDES, *The City of Women* (1947), esp. pp. 232–244; LUÍS DA CÂMARA CASCUDO, *Dicionário do folclore brasileiro,* 2d ed. (1962), pp. 128–129.

ESTHER J. PRESSEL

*See also* **African–Latin American Religions.**

**BONIFAZ ASCASUBI, NEPTALÍ** (also Ascazubi; *b.* 29 December 1870; *d.* 1960?), was elected president of Ecuador in 1931 but did not serve. A wealthy sierra landowner, in 1925 he became president of Ecuador's newly created Central Bank. His successful election bid brought together an unlikely coalition of small businessmen, artisans, campesinos, and workers—conservatives, liberals, and socialists—all adversely affected by the Great Depression. His platform, the Compactación Obrera Nacional (National Workers' Compact, 1932), called for mildly progressive reform. Bonifaz defeated his Liberal opponent, Modesto Larrea Jijón, in Ecuador's first free election in nearly forty years. However, Liberals still controlled Congress, and they distrusted Bonifaz, believing that he would favor banking and landowning interests. Congress voted to disqualify president-elect Bonifaz in 1932 on the grounds that he was not born in Ecuador. The charge was true: the son of a diplomat, Bonifaz had been born at the Peruvian embassy in Quito—technically not Ecuadorian soil. More seriously, Bonifaz had listed his citizenship as Peruvian until he was forty-six years old. Following Congress's action, Bonifaz lost an ensuing military struggle over the presidency, the WAR OF FOUR DAYS. Hundreds died in bitter house-to-house combat in Quito.

Brief treatment of Bonifaz and the War of Four Days can be found in DAVID W. SCHODT, *Ecuador: An Andean Enigma* (1987), and in OSVALDO HURTADO, *Political Power in Ecuador,* translated by Nick D. Mills, Jr. (1985). FREDRICK B. PIKE, *The United States and the Andean Republics* (1977), provides the standard account of twentieth-century Ecuadorian politics. RAFAEL QUINTERO LÓPEZ, *El mito del populismo en el Ecuador* (1980), offers an extended reinterpretive discussion.

RONN F. PINEO

*See also* **Velasco Ibarra, José María.**

**BONIFAZ NUÑO, RUBÉN** (*b.* 12 November 1923), Mexican writer. Born in Córdoba, Veracruz, Bonifaz Nuño received a law degree from the National University but has devoted himself primarily to literature, mostly poetry, since the publication of *La muerte del ángel* (The Death of the Angel) in 1945. He won a scholarship from the Centro Mexicano de Escritores for the 1951–1952 academic year. In 1953 he published *Imágenes* (Images), a collection of poems that combined classical Greek and Latin influences with Nahuatl. He turned even more fully to the indigenous world in *Siete de espadas* (Seven of Spades), published in 1966, followed by *El ala del tigre* (The Wing of the Tiger) in 1969. In 1974 he was awarded the National Literature Prize. He is also known for his translations of the *Georgics* by Virgil (1963) and the *Eclogues* by Dante (1965), as well as for his essays.

Critics have placed Bonifaz Nuño in the "generation of the 1950s" with Jaime Sabines, Rosario CASTELLANOS, and Jaime García Terres. Whether he is addressing the themes of solitude, disillusionment, misery, immortality, or hopelessness, Bonifaz's poetry is defined by a preference for urban spaces, experimental innovations with traditional poetic forms, a unique mixture of high and popular cultures, and a profound belief in the power of language and poetry to unmask enigmas and reinvent the world. A member of El Colegio Nacional and the Mexican Language Academy, he currently directs the Instituto de Investigaciones Filológicas at the National University.

MARCO ANTONIO CAMPOS, "La poesía de Rubén Bonifaz Nuño," in Klahn and Jesse Fernández, eds., *Lugar de encuentro: Ensayos críticos sobre poesía mexicana actual* (1987), pp. 59–65; FRANK DAUSTER, "Rubén Bonifaz Nuño: The Shadow of the Goddess," in his *The Double Strand: Five Contemporary Mexican Poets* (1987), pp. 103–133.

NORMA KLAHN

**BONILLA, POLICARPO** (*b.* 17 March 1858; *d.* 11 September 1926), president of Honduras, 1894–1899. Bonilla emerged as the Liberal Party's heir apparent during Céleo Arias's failed bid for the presidency in 1887. Upon Arias's death in 1890, the Liberals chose Bonilla to be their candidate against the Progressive Party's nominee, Ponciano Leiva, in the 1891 elections. The Progressives stole the election, then harried the opposition Liberals into exile. From his Nicaraguan asylum, don Policarpo invaded Honduras, unleashing that country's bloodiest civil war. Bonilla's forces, amply supported by Nicaraguan strongman José Santos ZELAYA, managed to overthrow the government after more than two years' struggle.

As diligent in office as he had been intransigent in the field, Bonilla rewrote the nation's constitution in 1894 to reflect his brand of doctrinaire liberalism, established in it the preeminence of the executive branch, and revamped public administration at every level. He firmly believed that disciplined political parties competing in honest electoral contests would cure much of what ailed Honduras, but he made little headway in persuading his fellow Hondurans to accept this Anglo panacea. Although mildly xenophobic (his legal practice exposed him to the seamy side of international capitalism), Bonilla continued his predecessors' efforts to foster development through mining and banana export, and he tried unsuccessfully to refund his country's enormous foreign debt.

A lifelong "Unionist," Bonilla took the lead in a misguided attempt to revive the Republic of Central America shortly before leaving office in 1899. Hoping to return to law or retail trade after his term in office, he instead spent much of his remaining years in jail, in exile, or abroad on diplomatic missions. He represented Honduras at Versailles after World War I, courageously speaking against trying German leaders as war criminals and challenging Woodrow WILSON to redefine the Monroe Doctrine to fit League of Nations principles. He ran for president in 1923 but lost. Three years later he died in New Orleans.

ARO SANSO (pseud., Ismael Mejía Deras), *Policarpo Bonilla: Algunos apuntes biográficos* (1936); WILLIAM S. STOKES, *Honduras: An Area Study in Government* (1950); LUCAS PAREDES, *Drama político de Honduras* (1958), chaps. 13–20; CHARLES ABBEY BRAND, *The Background of Capitalistic Underdevelopment: Honduras to 1913* (Ph.D. diss., University of Pittsburgh, 1972); RICHARD L. MILLETT, "Historical Setting," in *Honduras: A Country Study*, edited by James D. Rudolph (2d ed., 1984). KENNETH V. FINNEY, *In Quest of El Dorado: Precious Metal Mining and the Modernization of Honduras, 1880–1900* (1987), pp. 70–75.

KENNETH V. FINNEY

*See also* **Central America.**

**BONILLA CHIRINOS, MANUEL** (*d.* 21 March 1913), president of Honduras (1903–1907 and 1912–1913). The offspring of poor, country folk, Manuel Bonilla began his career as a soldier and Liberal partisan. He rose to brigadier general during Marco Aurelio Soto's regime (1876–1883) and served his party as commander during the 1892–1894 Liberal Insurgency. After serving part of a term as vice president and minister of war, General Bonilla broke with the Liberal Party and went into exile.

In 1902 he formed the National Party to run for president in 1903. Although he received more votes than the other candidates, he did not receive a majority, and Congress gave the presidency to Juan Ángel Arias. General Bonilla responded by ousting Arias and installing himself as president. When dissident Liberal legislators, led by Dr. Policarpo BONILLA, challenged the régime, General Manuel Bonilla sent his chief of police, Lee CHRISTMAS, to arrest the congressmen and close the Congress. During his first administration, he rewrote the constitution, gave a decided push to education and the North Coast banana companies, submitted the Nicaraguan border dispute to international arbitration, and tried to form peaceful alliances with his Central American neighbors.

In late 1906, dissident Hondurans invaded Honduras from Nicaragua to topple President Bonilla. The rebels occupied Tegucigalpa in March, 1907, sending Bonilla into exile. Four years later, General Bonilla, backed by Samuel ZEMURRAY, unleashed a counterrevolution on the North Coast. After U.S. diplomatic negotiation with the belligerents, an election was held, which Bonilla won (1912). He died the next year.

ARO SANSO (pseud., Ismael Mejía Deras), *Policarpo Bonilla: Algunos apuntes biográficos* (1936); WILLIAM S. STOKES, *Honduras: An Area Study in Government* (1950); LUCAS PAREDES, *Drama político de Honduras* (1958), chaps. 21–30, 32; CHARLES ABBEY BRAND, "The Background of Capitalistic Underdevelopment: Honduras to 1913" (Ph.D. diss., University of Pittsburgh, 1972); RICHARD L. MILLETT, "Historical Setting," in *Honduras: A Country Study*, edited by James D. Rudolph (2d ed., 1984).

KENNETH V. FINNEY

**BONNET, STEDE** (*d.* 1718), British pirate. A retired officer and successful Barbados planter, Major Bonnet was an unlikely, latecoming pirate. His decision to turn to piracy has been attributed both to the desire to flee a nagging wife and to Bonnet's own mental instability. Captaining the *Revenge* (later the *Royal James*), he plundered several ships along the Atlantic seaboard before briefly joining the infamous Blackbeard (Edward Teach) in August 1717. At Blackbeard's suggestion, he surrendered to the King's Pardon (offered by Britain's King George I) in September, only to find that Blackbeard had used the occasion of his capitulation to steal his loot. Abandoning plans to privateer in the war against Spain, he unsuccessfully pursued Blackbeard, then recommenced pirating off the Carolina coast. Captured twice (he escaped the first time) by Colonel William Rhet, he was brought to trial, sentenced, and hanged in Charleston.

CAPTAIN CHARLES JOHNSON [Daniel Defoe?], *A General History of the Robberies and Murders of the Most Notorious Pirates*, edited by Arthur L. Layward (1926), pp. 67–84; ROBERT E. LEE, *Blackbeard the Pirate: A Reappraisal of His Life and Times*, 2d ed. (1976), pp. 30–33, 37–39, 52–53.

PHILIPPE L. SEILER

*See also* **Piracy.**

**BONNY, ANNE,** an early-eighteenth-century pirate. Born near Cork, Ireland, Anne Bonny was the illegitimate daughter of an adulterous lawyer and his maid. At first, her father attempted to disguise her as a young male relative. When this ruse failed, he openly took up residence with Anne and her mother. His law practice suffered as a result of this affair, and he decided to emigrate to South Carolina along with Anne and her mother. He became a successful merchant in Charleston and later purchased a sizable plantation.

Anne's potential inheritance attracted many suitors, yet she eloped with James Bonny, a sailor of questionable integrity. The couple moved to New Providence in the Bahamas, a well-known pirate's haven. As part of his campaign to impose royal authority on the island, Captain Woodes Rogers offered to pardon James Bonny for whatever past crimes he had committed. Bonny not only accepted the pardon, but also spied on his former shipmates.

In the meantime, Anne had fallen in love with Captain "Calico Jack" Rackam and sought a divorce by sale from her husband. When he refused, Rackam and Anne, who posed as a seaman, hijacked a ship and fled the island. Together they raided coastal areas from Jamaica to Cuba. Her continuing masquerade did not prohibit intimate contact with Rackam and at one point she remained ashore in Cuba to bear their child. She had rejoined Rackam when they accepted the royal decree of amnesty for pirates in 1717. They later enlisted on the *Griffin*, a privateering ship, on which they mutinied and returned to PIRACY. Still disguised as a man, Anne became infatuated with another sailor. The object of her affections turned out to be Mary READ, another woman impersonating a seaman. The triangle formed by the two women and Rackam naturally led to a complex set of accusations, relationships, and clandestine rendezvous.

Anne fought courageously as a pirate and vehemently resisted capture by authorities. At her trial on 28 November 1720, Anne suprised the court with the revelation that she was an expectant mother. Anne's condition saved her from the gallows and she even mocked Rackam on the day of his execution. Anne spent time in prison for her crimes, although she occasionally was granted leaves. Her life after prison passed without notoriety.

CHARLES JOHNSON, *A General History of the Robberies and Murders of the Most Notorious Pirates from Their First Rise and Settlement in the Island of Providence to the Present Year*, edited by Arthur L. Hayward (1926); GEORGE WOODBURY, *The Great Days of Piracy in the West Indies* (1951); RAFAEL ABELLA, *Los piratas del Nuevo Mundo* (1989).

JOHN J. CROCITTI

**BONPLAND, AIMÉ JACQUES** (*b.* 29 August 1773; *d.* 11 May 1858), naturalist. Bonpland was born in La Rochelle, France, and studied medicine at the University of Paris. However, his real interest was in natural science. From 1799 to 1804 he accompanied Alexander von HUMBOLDT on his travels to South America, where he collected 60,000 plants. Bernardino RIVADAVIA invited Bonpland to visit Buenos Aires. In 1817, with his wife and two assistants, he did so, and stayed. In 1818 he was named naturalist of the Río de la Plata, and became deeply interested in the possibility of cultivating YERBA MATÉ in the former Jesuit REDUCCIÓNES. Bonpland practiced medicine in Buenos Aires, and in 1821 was named to the chair of medicine of the Instituto Médico Militar. While traveling to the old Jesuit missions, he ran afoul of the dictator of Paraguay, José Gaspar Rodríguez de FRANCIA, who kept him in Paraguay from 1822 to 1831.

Bonpland spoke out against the ROSAS dictatorship and became involved in anti-Rosas activity. He remained in the provinces of Misiones and Corrientes, and in 1854 was named director of the Museo de la Provincia in Corrientes. Bonpland conducted numerous scientific expeditions, sending back to France and Germany flora and fauna of the Río de la Plata. He died in São Borja, Brazil.

ADOLPHE BRUNEL, *Biographie d'Aimé Bonpland: Compagnon de voyage et collaborateur d'Al* (1871); GUILLERMO FURLONG CARDIFF, "En el centenario de Aimé Bonpland, 1858–1859," in *Anales de la Academia argentina de geografía*, no. 2 (1958).

NICHOLAS P. CUSHNER

**BORBA GATO, MANUEL DE** (*b.* ca. 1628; *d.* 1718), explorer and administrator in Brazil's mining region. One of the most famous *bandeirantes* (São Paulo explorers who sought wealth and slaves in frontier regions), Borba Gato participated in expeditions, in search of gold and jewels, that crossed the frontier region between his native São Paulo and Bahia. From 1674 to 1681 he accompanied his father-in-law, Fernão Dias Pais, on one of the largest and best organized of these missions. Although it failed in its quest for emeralds, the expedition opened up new areas for other mining and for eventual settlement. Then, implicated in the 1682 murder of the general administrator of mines, Dom Rodrigo de Castelo Branco, near Sumidouro, Borba Gato fled to the Rio Doce region. Never ceasing to look for mineral wealth, he remained in voluntary exile for nearly twenty years.

Borba Gato's exoneration of the murder charge came through the intervention of political allies in 1700. In that same year Borba Gato revealed that he had found gold in the Rio das Velhas area, a discovery that would make him one of the mining zone's richest men. With wealth came power, and he moved quickly into administrative posts. Beginning as the chief customs officer of Rio das Velhas, he rose in 1702 to general administrator of mines for the region.

When civil war flared up in 1708 between those who had come to the mines from São Paulo and the EMBOABAS (outsiders), people from other areas, Borba Gato at first showed sympathy for his Paulista compatriots. Siding with two of his kinsmen in a dispute with the *emboabas'* leader, Borba Gato called the latter a thief and ordered his banishment from the area. He never carried out this order, however, and in fact tried to effect a reconciliation. Throughout the war he maintained a position of neutrality. After hostilities ended in 1709, Borba Gato received royal grants of land and the position of superintendent of mines as a reward for his loyal service.

MANOEL S. CARDOZO, "The *Guerra dos Emboabas:* Civil War in Minas Gerais, 1708–1709," in *Hispanic American Historical Review* 22, no. 3 (1942): 470–492; CHARLES R. BOXER, "The Gold Rush in Minas Gerais" and "Paulistas and Emboabas," chaps. 2 and 3 in his *The Golden Age of Brazil, 1695–1750* (1962).

ROGER A. KITTLESON

**BORDABERRY, JUAN MARÍA** (*b.* 1928), president of Uruguay (1972–1976). The constitutional period of his presidency ended in June 1973 with his dissolution of Congress. From then, until his deposition in 1976 for refusing to negotiate a return to constitutional government, he headed a military regime (1973–1985).

Bordaberry started his political career as a member of Benito NARDONE's populist *ruralista* movement, which played a major role in the National (Blanco) party's election victory of 1958. He later joined the Colorado party of Jorge PACHECO ARECO, was elected a senator (1969–1971), and was nominated for president by Pacheco Areco. In the 1971 elections Bordaberry's slate of candidates received only 22 percent of the total vote. The narrow Colorado victory over the Blanco candidate, Wilson FERREIRA ALDUNATE, is widely believed to have been the result of fraud.

Bordaberry's government was characterized by vigorous repression of all popular protest movements and the persecution of the Tupamaro urban guerrilla movement, which, according to military sources, was defeated in 1972. Following passage of the State Security Bill of 1972, arbitrary detentions, torture, and attacks by paramilitary groups became endemic. In 1973/1974 all opposition media were shut down, and all political and trade union activity was proscribed. In an essay titled "Las opciones" (1980) and during a speech at the National University in Santiago de Chile (1987), Bordaberry maintained that due to divine right, rulers are not obliged to seek legitimation by democratic vote. He has not held public office since 1976.

JUAN MARÍA BORDABERRY, *Hacia una doctrina política nacional* (1974); OSCAR H. BRUSCHERA, *Las décadas infames: Análisis político, 1967–1985* (1986); MARTIN WEINSTEIN, *Uruguay: Democracy at the Crossroads* (1988).

DIETER SCHONEBOHM

**BORDERLANDS, THE,** a term popularized by historian Herbert Eugene BOLTON (1870–1953) for those parts of the United States once occupied by Spain, mostly south of an imaginary sagging line from Chesapeake Bay west to San Francisco Bay, and sometimes including the north Mexican states. Thanks to explorations undertaken by Hernando de SOTO, Francisco Vázquez de CORONADO, and Juan RODRÍGUEZ CABRILLO between 1539 and 1543, Spaniards had a remarkably accurate early idea of the vastness and variety of the region. Spanish occupation flowed from the Caribbean and central New Spain, driven piecemeal by the search for exploitable resources,

Christian missionary zeal, defense of more central provinces, and advantage in the imperial contest for North America. Through almost three centuries, the Caribbean rim and the northern frontier of New Spain remained a thinly peopled fringe of civil outposts, MISSIONS, and PRESIDIOS. From the humid Gulf coast of greater Florida, Louisiana, and Texas, through the arid, basin-and-range high desert of New Mexico, and on up California's foggy shore; from hunting-fishing-gathering Karankawas, Seris, and CHUMASH, through Plains APACHES, COMANCHES, NAVAJOS, and Pimas, to the PUEBLO-dwellers of New Mexico and Arizona; from St. Augustine (1565) and Santa Fe (1610), through El Paso (1683), Pensacola (1698), and San Antonio (1718), to Tuscon and San Francisco (1776), the only thing that binds the Borderlands together is the history and heritage of the colonial encounter between Spaniards and Native Americans.

Although many scholars have abandoned the term Borderlands, and indeed the concept of the region, no one has come up with an acceptable alternative. Studies of the western Borderlands (from Texas and Tamaulipas to both Californias) have proceeded with little attention to the eastern Borderlands (the coastal Carolinas, Georgia, Florida, Alabama, Mississippi, and Louisiana) and vice versa. Recently, however, a reunification seems to be taking place. Indicative of the trend are David J. Weber's *The Spanish Frontier in North America, 1513–1821* (1992); the three-volume *Columbian Consequences*, edited by David Hurst Thomas and subtitled, respectively, *Archaeological and Historical Perspectives on the Spanish Borderlands West* (1989), *Archaeological and Historical Perspectives on the Spanish Borderlands East* (1990), and *The Spanish Borderlands in Pan-American Perspective* (1991); and the *SMRC-Newsletter*, published since 1967 by the Southwestern Mission Research Center in Tucson, which includes studies about the Borderlands from the Atlantic to the Pacific.

HERBERT E. BOLTON, *The Spanish Borderlands: A Chronicle of Old Florida and the Southwest* (1921); JOHN F. BANNON, *Bolton and the Spanish Borderlands* (1964) and *The Spanish Borderlands Frontier, 1513–1821* (1970); ELLWYN R. STODDARD ET AL., eds., *Borderlands Sourcebook: A Guide to the Literature on Northern Mexico and the American Southwest* (1983); R. REID BADGER and LAWRENCE A. CLAYTON, *Alabama and the Borderlands: From Prehistory to Statehood* (1985), and *The Spanish Borderlands Sourcebooks*, a 27-volume set of mostly reprinted articles and documents under the general editorship of DAVID H. THOMAS (1991–1992).

JOHN L. KESSELL

**BORGE, TOMÁS** (*b.* 13 August 1930), Nicaraguan leader and cofounder of the Sandinista National Liberation Front. Tomás Borge was born into the family of a drugstore owner in Matagalpa. His political experience began in 1946 with the Independent Liberal Party's student arm, the Democratic Youth Front. He mobilized high school and university students in traditional Liberal areas against the SOMOZA family. He met Carlos FONSECA and Silvio MAYORGA in 1954, upon entering law school at the National Autonomous University in León. Two years later he was arrested in connection with the assassination of Anastasio Somoza García and convicted on the basis of false testimony. After being severely tortured, he escaped to Costa Rica in 1959. In 1960 he sought support from Fidel CASTRO for the nascent revolutionary movement in Nicaragua. He helped found the Sandinista National Liberation Front in July 1961.

In 1963 Borge led combatants in the attack on the National Guard post in Río Coco. Two years later he became an organizer of the short-lived Republican Mobilization movement. This venture failed in 1966, so he returned to guerrilla warfare, participating in the ill-conceived battle at Pancasán in 1967. Borge fled to Costa Rica, then spent time in Peru and Cuba before returning to Nicaragua in 1971. The National Guard captured him in 1976 and again subjected him to torture. The Sandinista takeover of the National Palace in August 1978 led to Borge's release from prison. He subsequently assumed the leadership of the Prolonged Popular War faction with Henry RUÍZ and Bayardo ARCE.

After the July 1979 Sandinista victory and Somoza's exile, Borge became minister of the interior, in charge of the police and security forces. He also managed the government's relations with the indigenous peoples on the Atlantic coast. In the 1980s he wrote on many subjects, including human rights, national sovereignty, and revolutionary ideology. While in power, Borge was considered the principal representative of the intransigent, Marxist-Leninist wing of the Sandinista regime. He was replaced as minister of the interior by the Chamorro government in April 1990. As of 1993 he was writing articles for Latin American, North American and European journals.

TOMÁS BORGE, "Tomás Borge Speaks on Human Rights in Nicaragua," in *International Press*, 16 March 1981, pp. 245–250; DAVID NOLAN, *The Ideology of the Sandinistas and the Nicaraguan Revolution* (1984); JOHN BOOTH, *The End and the Beginning: The Nicaraguan Revolution*, 2d ed. (1985).

MARK EVERINGHAM

*See also* **Nicaragua: Political Parties.**

**BORGES, JACOBO** (*b.* 28 November 1931), Venezuelan artist. Born in a rural area near Caracas, Borges attended only primary school. In 1949–1951 he studied painting at the Cristóbal Rojas School of Fine and Applied Arts in Caracas while simultaneously working for an advertising agency and drawing comic strips. In 1952 he won a scholarship from Metro-Goldwyn-Mayer as part of a promotion of its film *An American in Paris* to study in Paris, where he joined the Young Painters' group and developed an expressionist style with social and political implications. Upon his return to Caracas in 1956, he became a very active artist and soon held his first solo exhibition. Selected as one of the Venezuelan entries to the São Paulo Bienal in 1957, he won an honorable mention. From 1957 until 1965 he was a member of the Round Table Group and Whale Group cooperative. From 1965 until 1971, Borges stopped painting and devoted himself to theater and film design. He returned to painting in 1971, and five years later an exhibition of forty-eight of his canvasses, Magic of a Realist Critic, was presented in Caracas and Mexico City. He wrote and illustrated *The Mountain and Its Era* (1979). In 1988 he represented Venezuela at the Venice Biennale and was included in the Latin American Spirit show at the Bronx Museum, New York, and the Guggenheim Museum exhibit, Fifty Years: Anniversary Collection. Major retrospectives of his work have been held in the Staatliche Kunsthalle (Berlin, 1987) and the Museo de Arte Contemporáneo (Caracas, 1988).

ROLDÁN ESTEVA GRILLET, *Siete artistas venezolanos siglo XX: Rafael Monasterios, Armando Reverón, Héctor Poleo, Alejandro Otero, Carlos Cruz Diez, Jesús Soto y Jacobo Borges* (1984); JACOBO BORGES (CDS Gallery, New York, 1990), with introductory essays by Carlos Fuentes and Dore Ashton.

BÉLGICA RODRÍGUEZ

**BORGES, JORGE LUIS** (*b.* 24 August 1899; *d.* 14 June 1986), Argentine writer. Born in Buenos Aires, Borges attended the Collège de Calvin in Geneva during World War I. In the period immediately after the war, he became involved with ultrism, an avant-garde movement in Madrid, and on his return to Argentina helped start an Argentine ultraist group. His earliest surviving poems are iconoclastic, showing concern with the trench warfare of the Great War and sympathy for the Bolshevik Revolution. In the 1920s Borges published three books of poetry (*Fervor de Buenos Aires, Luna de enfrente,* and *Cuaderno San Martín*) and three books of essays (*Inquisiciones, El tamaño de mi esperanza,* and *El idioma de los argentinos*); his writings of the period are imbued with cultural nationalism, in keeping with his support for the populist leader Hipólito YRIGOYEN.

In the early 1930s Borges worked for a time on the literary supplement of Natalio Botana's innovative daily *Crítica*; it was there that he first published the sketches of the lives of various gangsters, pirates, imposters, and murderers that became his first book of fiction, *Historia universal de la infamia* (1935). In 1937 he became an employee at the Miguel Cané Municipal Library in Buenos Aires, a job that afforded him abundant time for reading and writing. From 1939 to 1953 he produced his most famous stories, collected as *Ficciones* (1944) and *El Aleph* (1949). These years also saw the publication of the essays in *Otras inquisiciones* (1952), most of which were first delivered as lectures in Argentina and Uruguay after Borges was fired from his job in the municipal library for signing a petition against the alliance of the Argentine military with the Nazis. His lectures and es-

says were no doubt celebrated in part because he was viewed as a symbol of opposition to Juan Domingo PERÓN. When Perón fell in 1955, Borges was named director of the National Library, a job he held until the return of peronism.

The final years of Borges's life were marked, or perhaps marred, by celebrity. Beginning in 1961 when he was awarded the Formentor Prize (an international publishers' prize, which he shared with Samuel Beckett), Borges's work was translated into many languages and became the subject of an ever more vast critical bibliography. Borges was also pursued by students of literature and by journalists; even one of Woody Allen's characters in *Manhattan* boasts of her intentions to interview him. As a result, we know Borges's opinions on soccer, politics, Richard M. Nixon, Argentina, blacks, the English language, Federico García Lorca, and so forth, and for a time these (often misinformed or bigoted) opinions seemed to eclipse Borges's own work. Even years after his death, the details of his life seem to have the power to fascinate or titillate the public, particularly the Argentine public; revelations on his love life, brushes with psychoanalysis, proxy marriage, and death in Geneva have all, rather improbably, been major news in Argentina and elsewhere.

Of greater interest in the long run, perhaps, are Borges's complex relations to Argentine culture, history, and politics. His initial populist nationalism (and en-

Jorge Luis Borges speaking in Washington, D.C., 1976. ORGANIZATION OF AMERICAN STATES.

thusiasm for Yrigoyen) included a measure of intolerance for "low-brow" Argentine culture: he condemned the poet Alfonsina STORNI for what he termed her shrill sentimentality, and he made similar attacks on Carlos GARDEL's tangos in the 1920s and 1930s. The national tradition to which he was to prove most faithful was liberal and cosmopolitan, as defined in his lecture "The Argentine Writer and Tradition" in 1951 (later included in the second edition of *Discusión* in 1957); his version of the Argentine national tradition necessarily competed with a number of others, and one of them, that of Perón, was to prove rather more decisive.

Two stories written in the late 1940s illustrate Borges's complex relations to the time in which he lived. "La fiesta del monstruo," written (in collaboration with Adolfo BIOY CASARES) in 1947 but not published until after the fall of Perón, is a ferocious satire on the Peronist mass meetings in the Plaza de Mayo in the first years of the new regime; the "Monster" of the story is Perón himself, who inspires his followers from afar in their torture and killing of a Jewish passerby. The story is narrated by a brash young Peronist and is an obvious recasting of two crucial liberal texts of the nineteenth century by opponents of the government of Juan Manuel de Rosas: Esteban ECHEVARRÍA's short story "El matadero" and Hilario ASCASUBI's gauchesque poem "La refalosa."

In 1948 Borges's sister and mother were arrested for taking part in a demonstration against the new Peronist constitution (which among other things, of course, gave women the right to vote). A few months later, Borges wrote a curious story, "Historia del guerrero y de la cautiva," which (when compared to "La fiesta del monstruo") is a rather more nuanced reflection on the need for political action. The character Droctulft, the Germanic invader of Italy who changes sides to join the inhabitants of Ravenna in the defense of their city, is an unequivocal convert to "civilization" but is offset in the story by an English captive woman who chooses to remain with her Indian husband. The captive's story is retold later by Borges's English grandmother, Fanny Haslam de Borges, in a way that barely alludes to the two events that consolidate her feelings of solidarity with the captive woman she saw so many years before on the pampas: her husband, Colonel Francisco Borges, was killed in the civil war in 1874 when he chose to follow Bartolomé MITRE against Adolfo ALSINA; the English captive's husband was no doubt to be captured or killed in the "Conquest of the Desert" in 1879. Who is to know, Borges seems to be saying, whether one ultimately is taking the part of civilization or of savagery?

For details of Borges's life, see EMIR RODRÍGUEZ MONEGAL, *Jorge Luis Borges: A Literary Biography* (1978), though the text is sometimes rather untrustworthy; of great interest also is ESTELA CANTO, *Borges a contraluz* (1989). SYLVIA MOLLOY, *Las letras de Borges* (1979), translated as *Signs of Borges* (1994), is the best critical book on the author; see also BEATRIZ SARLO, *Jorge Luis Borges* (1993) and DANIEL BALDERSTON, *Out of Context* (1993). A good article on Borges's cultural nationalism is GRACIELA MONTALDO, "Borges: Una vanguardia criolla," in *Yrigoyen, entre Borges y Arlt (1916–1930)*, edited by David Viñas (1989), pp. 213–232. Reference works include DANIEL BALDERSTON, *The Literary Universe of Jorge Luis Borges* (1986), which indexes most of Borges's works; EVELYN FISHBURN and PSICHE HUGHES, *A Dictionary of Borges* (1990), which focuses on the stories; and ION AGHEANA, *Reasoned Thematic Dictionary of the Prose of Jorge Luis Borges* (1990).

DANIEL BALDERSTON

*See also* **Literature.**

**BORGES DE MEDEIROS, ANTÔNIO AUGUSTO** (*b.* 19 November 1863; *d.* 25 April 1961), Brazilian statesman and political boss of RIO GRANDE DO SUL (1903–1930). Born the son of an imperial judge in Capavaca, Rio Grande do Sul, Borges graduated from the Recife Law School in 1885 and agitated for the republic in his native province. A member of the federal Constituent Assembly, he supported Júlio de CASTILHOS's coup in 1892 and fought the rebels in the FEDERALIST REVOLT of 1893–1895. Picked by Castilhos as governor in 1898, Borges served the Riograndense Republican Party boss until Castilhos's death in 1903. Borges then became party leader and ruled the state until 1930, serving as governor a total of twenty-five years.

Like Castilhos, a Comtian positivist, Borges used the former's autocratic constitution to promote public education and rural property taxes; he also balanced the budget and practiced labor paternalism. With Senator Pinheiro MACHADO, Borges made the Riograndense Republicans contenders in national politics against counterparts in Minas and São Paulo. The gauchos opposed the Paulistas successfully in 1910, played arbiter in 1919, lost in 1922 and 1930, but then incited a revolt, overthrowing the regime. Riograndense economic interests, which were tied to the domestic foodstuffs market, often collided with those of the export-oriented Paulistas.

In 1928 Borges made Getúlio VARGAS governor, and he backed Vargas's revolution in 1930. He soon broke with Vargas, supporting São Paulo's CONSTITUTIONALIST REVOLT (1932). Following the defeat of that movement and his imprisonment in Pernambuco, Borges de Medeiros received the second largest number of votes for the presidency in the Constituent Assembly of 1933–1934, losing to his protégé Vargas. Elected to Congress in October 1934 on the opposition ticket, Borges advocated a parliamentary regime to preclude a presidential dictatorship. His fears were realized three years later, when Vargas declared the authoritarian ESTADO NÔVO regime and closed Congress, effectively terminating Borges's political career.

JOÃO NEVES DA FONTOURA, *Memorias.* Vol. 1, *Borges de Medeiros e Seu Tempo* (1958); JOSEPH L. LOVE, *Rio Grande do Sul and Brazilian Regionalism, 1882–1930* (1971); CARLOS E. CORTÉS, *Gaúcho Politics in Brazil* (1974), pp. 1–88; ISRAEL BELOCH and ALZIRA

ALVES DE ABREU, eds., *Dicionário histórico-biográfico brasileiro, 1930–1983* (1984), pp. 2142–2151; LUIZ CARLOS BARBOSA LESSA, *Borges de Medeiros* (1985).

JOSEPH L. LOVE

**BORJA CEVALLOS, RODRIGO** (*b.* 19 June 1935), president of Ecuador (1988–1992). Born in Quito of a family descended from early Spanish settlers, Borja graduated with distinction from the law school of the Universidad Central in 1960. Already a member of the Liberal Party, he soon entered politics and was first elected to Congress in 1962. Borja was later a central figure among the young Liberals who broke with the traditional leadership to found a new political party, the Izquierda Democrática (Democratic Left—ID) in 1977. Borja was elected congressman from the province of Pichincha in 1970. When constitutional rule was suspended by military *golpe* (1972), he turned to building and developing the ID as Ecuador's first national, mass-based political party.

When military rule came to an end, Borja ran for the presidency in 1978, finishing fourth but establishing himself and his party as a major political contender. Subsequently seated in Congress in honorary office, Borja became a leading spokesman of Ecuador's center Left, and in 1984 he was narrowly defeated in the presidential race. Continuing as the leading opposition congressman, Borja was again the ID candidate in 1988 and won by a comfortable margin. Inaugurated in August 1988, he faced high inflation, economic recession, a huge foreign debt, and declining oil prices. Despite his prestige as a leader of Latin American social democracy, he was forced to adopt basically neoliberal policies, such as cutting subsidies and using free-market practices. Continuing austerity and economic hardship cost his party popular support, and the ID lost its majority in the 1990 congressional elections. Constitutionally prohibited from a second consecutive term as president, Borja continued to grapple with economic pressures as his administration drew to a close.

OSVALDO HURTADO, *Political Power in Ecuador*, translated by Nick D. Mills, Jr. (1980); JOHN D. MARTZ, *Politics and Petroleum in Ecuador* (1987).

JOHN D. MARTZ

*See also* **Ecuador: Political Parties.**

**BORJA Y ARAGÓN, FRANCISCO DE** (Príncipe de Esquilache; *b.* 1583; *d.* 26 September 1658), twelfth viceroy of Peru. The prince of Esquilache, scion of a distinguished Spanish family related to Pope Alexander VI and Saint Francis Borja, was one of the most cultured of royal bureaucrats, an accomplished poet, patron of the arts, and administrator. Esquilache was appointed VICEROY in 1614, when he was only thirty-two years old. His rule was marked by its concern with the practice of

idolatry among the Indians and with the security of the empire in the face of continuing Dutch threats. His correspondence with the crown was copious and became a model for other viceroys. Nevertheless, there is debate over Esquilache's personal involvement in governing Peru, since it is possible that he left many details to his well-trained staff. Anxious to hurry back to the court to greet the new monarch, PHILIP IV, he left the viceroyalty in 1621, before his successor arrived. He spent the last thirty years of his life writing poetry.

JUAN WYSKOTA Z., *El virrey poeta: Seis años de administración de don Francisco de Borja y Aragón en el Perú (1615–1621)* (1970).

JOHN F. SCHWALLER

**BORNO, JOSEPH LOUIS E. ANTOINE FRANÇOIS** (*b.* 1865; *d.* 19 July 1942), president of Haiti (1922–1930). Before becoming president, Borno served as minister of foreign affairs and ambassador to the Dominican Republic. He was an advocate of the U.S. intervention in Haiti, inducing the Haitian government to sign the 1915 treaty by which it pledged total cooperation with the United States.

On 12 April 1922, Borno was elected to his first term as president of Haiti. He was reelected in 1926. His first term was relatively stable, but the second ended in crisis with the United States. The combination of the poor economic conditions and the tensions arising from the U.S. occupation led to an uprising against the U.S. Marines in 1929. In 1930, he accepted President Herbert Hoover's investigating committee's recommendations that U.S. Marines be gradually withdrawn and that popular elections be held. He agreed to step down and supported the U.S. selection of Eugene Roy as provisional president until elections could be held. Roy was replaced by Stenio Vincent.

Two works that relate to the U.S. occupation of and involvement in Haiti, 1915–1934, are HANS SCHMIDT, *The United States Occupation of Haiti, 1915–1934* (1971); and ARTHUR C. MILLSPAUGH, *Haiti Under American Control, 1915–1930* (1970); ROBERT D. HEINL, JR., and NANCY G. HEINL, *Written in Blood: The Story of the Haitian People* (1978).

DARIÉN DAVIS

**BORRERO Y CORTÁZAR, ANTONIO** (*b.* 28 October 1827; *d.* 9 October 1911), president of Ecuador (1875–1876). A moderate politician, Borrero was selected by Conservative president Gabriel GARCÍA MORENO (1861–1865, 1869–1875) to run for the vice presidency in 1863. Borrero won in a landslide despite the fact that he did not want the job. He immediately resigned, disgusted by García Moreno's rigging of the election. When García Moreno was assassinated in 1875, Borrero won the subsequent election for president. He hoped to be a healer, peacemaker, and reconciler for a nation so often bloodied by regional and ideological battles. However, in seeking to find a middle road between Liberals and Conservatives, he managed only to antagonize both.

General Ignacio de VEINTIMILLA overthrew Borrero in 1876. After seven years in exile in Peru, Borrero returned to serve as governor of Azuay province (1888–1892). A man of laws, a well-read—if not well-traveled—intellectual, Borrero was known by contemporaries as the "Cato of Cuenca," or the "Washington of Azuay." Borrero is sometimes viewed by historians as the first Progresita, the grouping of pragmatic political moderates that governed Ecuador from 1883 to 1895. He died in CUENCA, his birthplace.

On Ecuadorian politics, see OSVALDO HURTADO's interpretive history, *Political Power in Ecuador*, translated by Nick D. Mills, Jr. (1895); and FRANK MAC DONALD SPINDLER's descriptive *Nineteenth Century Ecuador: An Historical Introduction* (1987). For summary treatment of nineteenth-century Ecuadorian political economy, consult DAVID W. SCHODT, *Ecuador: An Andean Enigma* (1987).

RONN F. PINEO

*See also* **Alfaro Delgado, José Eloy.**

**BOSCH GAVIÑO, JUAN** (*b.* 30 June 1909), Dominican novelist, sociologist, historian, politician, and president of the Dominican Republic (1963). Bosch, a native of La Vega, published his first collection of short stories, *Camino Real*, in 1933. One year later, Rafael Leónidas TRUJILLO MOLINA arrested Bosch for conspiracy against his regime. Released in 1935, Bosch became literary editor of the Dominican Republic's most prestigious newspaper, *Listín Diario*. In 1936 he published one of his most popular novels, *La Mañosa*. Unable to live under the Trujillo dictatorship, he fled his country in 1938. During the next twenty-three years of exile, Bosch resided in Cuba, Costa Rica, Bolivia, Chile, and Venezuela. He was one of the organizers of the DOMINICAN REVOLUTIONARY PARTY (PRD), which was founded in 1939 at Havana. Later, he served as secretary to Cuban President Carlos Prío Socarrás (1948–1952) and helped to organize the abortive attempt to overthrow Trujillo, known as Cayo Confite.

After Trujillo's assassination in 1961, Bosch returned to his native land in order to organize the PRD on Dominican soil. In December 1962, he won the first presidential elections held in the Dominican Republic since 1930. Inaugurated in February 1963, he was deposed after only seven months by a military coup backed by elements of the military (under General Elías Wessín y Wessín), the landowning and business elites, the hierarchy of the Roman Catholic church, and the military attachés of the United States. Bosch was once again forced into exile, from which he did not return until 1966.

The regime installed by the military coup in September 1963 proved to be most unpopular and was removed by a revolution that occurred on 24 April 1965. The chief aim of the revolutionaries, who called themselves Con-

stitutionalists, was to return Bosch to the presidency of the nation. In order to prevent this possibility, U.S. President Lyndon Johnson dispatched U.S. Marines to Santo Domingo on 28 April. Some historians have claimed that Bosch was a coward for not returning to his country to lead the Constitutionalists in their battle against the Loyalists of Wessin y Wessin and the interventionist forces of the United States. Bosch has responded to this criticism by stating that agents of the Federal Bureau of Investigation surrounded his residence in Puerto Rico in order to prevent his return to Santo Domingo.

Both Bosch and his rival, Joaquín BALAGUER, returned from exile for the presidential elections of 1966, in which they were the candidates for the Dominican Revolutionary Party, and the Reformist Party, respectively. Balaguer possessed decisive advantages during the electoral campaign and won the election. In 1973 Bosch broke with the Dominican Revolutionary Party, which he had helped to found, and formed his own political movement, the Party of Dominican Liberation (PLD). When the PLD ran for the first time in 1978, it obtained only an insignificant number of votes, but by the elections of 1982, it was represented in the Dominican Congress by six deputies. In 1986 the PLD obtained 18.3 percent of the vote as well as sixteen deputies and two senators in the Congress. With the disintegration of the Dominican Revolutionary Party into various factions, the PLD emerged as the main challenger of Balaguer's Reformist Party.

During the presidential elections of 1990, Bosch and Balaguer faced each other once again, the latter winning by a narrow margin. Bosch accused his opponent of electoral fraud and threatened to take the dispute to the streets, a move from which he was dissuaded by former U.S. President Jimmy Carter, who mediated between the octogenarian rivals. Although deeply involved in Dominican politics for over five decades, Bosch will probably be remembered more for his literary achievements than for his accomplishments in the political realm.

Bosch's writings include *Cuentos escritos en el exilio* (1962), *The Unfinished Experiment* (1966), *Composición social dominicana* (1970), *El oro y la paz* (1976), and *33 artículos de temas políticos* (1988). See also JOHN BARTLOW MARTIN, *Overtaken by Events: The Dominican Crisis from the Fall of Trujillo to the Civil War* (1966); and COMITÉ PRO HOMENAJE A JUAN BOSCH, *Juan Bosch: Un hombre de siempre* (1989).

KAI P. SCHOENHALS

*See also* **Dominican Republic.**

**BOSSA NOVA,** Brazilian music genre that emerged in Rio de Janeiro in the late 1950s. It became highly popular around the world in the 1960s due to its casual sophistication, light breeziness, and infectious swing. Bossa has been characterized by rhythmic elements of SAMBA, a highly syncopated style of playing guitar, a generally subdued vocal style when sung, and harmonic influences from both American cool jazz and classical music. Guitarist-vocalist João GILBERTO developed the characteristic bossa rhythmic style on guitar. Antônio Carlos ("Tom") JOBIM was the genre's most influential composer, and pianists João Donato and Luis Eça, guitarists Luiz Bonfá and Baden Powell, vocalist Nara Leão, singer-songwriters Carlos Lyra, Roberto Menescal, and Ronaldo Bôscoli, and poet-lyricist Vinícius de Moraes were other key figures.

"Chega de saudade" (1958), performed by Gilberto and written by Jobim and de Moraes, is considered the first bossa single; Gilberto's 1959 LP of the same name was the style's first album. The 1959 French-Brazilian movie *Orfeu Negro* (*Black Orpheus*), which included songs by Bonfá, Jobim, and de Moraes, popularized the bossa tunes "Manhã de Carnaval" and "A felicidade" around the world. Charlie Byrd and Stan Getz's 1962 album "Jazz Samba," with songs by Jobim, de Moraes, Bonfá, and Powell, was a smash hit and launched bossa in North America. A boom ensued, and dozens of jazz musicians recorded bossa compositions. In 1964, the style had reached the peak of its popularity with the release of "Getz-Gilberto," an album that teamed saxophonist Getz with Gilberto and Jobim. The LP earned four Grammys, spent ninety-six weeks on the pop charts, and included the now-famous tune "The Girl From Ipanema" (sung by Gilberto and his wife Astrud). Bossa nova had an enormous musical influence on American jazz and international pop in general in the 1960s, and since then has continued to be one of Brazil's most popular styles.

RUY CASTRO, *Chega de saudade* (1991); CHRIS MC GOWAN and RICARDO PESSANHA, *The Brazilian Sound: Samba, Bossa Nova, and the Popular Music of Brazil* (1991).

CHRIS MCGOWAN

*See also* **Music: Popular Music and Dance.**

**BOSTON FRUIT COMPANY,** a banana import firm in the United States. In 1885, when twelve New Englanders under the leadership of Captain Lorenzo D. BAKER and Andrew W. Preston invested $15,000 to establish the Boston Fruit Company, the enterprise joined at least sixty other banana companies founded late in the nineteenth century to transport bananas from Central America and the West Indies to the United States. By 1890, when the company was incorporated in Massachusetts, Boston Fruit had become the most successful banana company in the United States. The initial investment had grown to $531,000. There were several reasons for the company's success in transporting and marketing one of the world's most perishable fruits. Replacing sailing vessels with steamships, the company soon purchased two of the fastest cargo ships operating in the Caribbean. Because Boston Fruit established extensive banana plantations in Jamaica, the company was as-

sured a steady supply of the golden fruit—upward of 250,000 stems a year by 1892. In order to expand the distribution and sales of its bananas, Boston Fruit formed the Fruit Dispatch Company, which allowed it to reach U.S. inland markets. In 1899 Boston Fruit merged with Minor C. KEITH's three banana companies, with extensive holdings in Costa Rica, Panama, and Colombia, to form the UNITED FRUIT COMPANY.

CHARLES M. WILSON, *Empire in Green and Gold: The Story of the American Banana Trade* (1947), pp. 69–97; STACY MAY and GALO PLAZA, *The United Fruit Company in Latin America* (1958), pp. 5–7; WILSON RANDOLPH BARTLETT, JR., "Lorenzo Dow Baker and the Development of the Banana Trade Between Jamaica and the United States, 1881–1890" (Ph.D. diss., American University, 1977).

DIANE STANLEY

*See also* **Banana Industry; Fruit Industry.**

**BOTA DE POTRO.** GAUCHOS made much of their clothing and equipment from leather, plentiful on the livestock-rich pampa. To fashion supple, open-toed riding boots, gauchos killed a colt and stripped the hide from its back legs. The soft skin covered the gaucho's foot, calf, and thigh. As with other elements of gaucho dress, these boots were likely first developed by Indians of the pampa. The fragile boots wore out after a few months, so another colt would have to be killed. Ranchers called for outlawing the boots because they believed that gauchos stole colts just to fashion them. As wild horses became less plentiful on the plains during the late nineteenth century, imported machine-made boots replaced the homemade variety.

MADALINE WALLIS NICHOLS, *The Gaucho* (1968), p. 13; RICHARD W. SLATTA, *Gauchos and the Vanishing Frontier* (1983), pp. 74–75.

RICHARD W. SLATTA

**BOTERO, FERNANDO** (*b.* 19 April 1932), Colombian artist. Born in Medellín, Botero began his career as a writer and illustrator for the Sunday literary supplement of *El Colombiano,* a Medellín newspaper, where his articles on Picasso and Dalí resulted in his expulsion from Jesuit secondary school. He moved to Bogotá in 1951, when he had had his first one-man show. The following year he went to Madrid, where he enrolled in the Real Academia de San Fernando and studied the works of Goya and Velazquez in the Prado. He then went to study art history and fresco painting at the Academia San Marco in Florence. In 1955 he returned to Bogotá, and exhibited at the Biblioteca Nacional. His work was not well received, however, and he moved to Mexico City the following year. From 1958 to 1960 he taught at the Escuela de Bellas Artes at the National

*Military Junta.* Oil on canvas by Fernando Botero, 1973. PRIVATE COLLECTION, COURTESY OF MARLBOROUGH GALLERY.

University in Bogotá. Botero received the award for the Colombian section of the Guggenheim international exhibition in 1960. That same year he moved to New York, where he lived until 1973. In 1961 the Museum of Modern Art of New York acquired his painting *Mona Lisa at Age 12.* This period reflects his fascination with the Renaissance masters.

In 1973 Botero moved to Paris. Although his subject matter continued to center on small-town Colombia, as evidenced by satirical images of clerics, military men, politicians, and marginals, Botero soon turned to sculpting the images and figures that appeared in his paintings. He had retrospective exhibitions in Germany (1970), Colombia (1973), the Netherlands (1975), the United States (1979–1980), and Germany (1979–1980). After his retrospective at the Museum of Contemporary Art in Caracas in 1976, the Venezuelan government awarded him the Order Andrés Bello, reserved for outstanding figures in Latin American culture. The department of Antioquia honored him with the Cruz de Boyaca for services to his nation. Botero's work has appeared at exhibitions at the Bronx Museum (New York, 1988) and at the Indianapolis Museum, the Hayward Gallery (London), and Centro de Arte Reina Sofia (Madrid), all in 1989.

EDUARDO SERRANO, *Cien años de arte colombiano* (1985); EDWARD J. SULLIVAN, *Ferdinand Botero* (1993).

BÉLGICA RODRÍGUEZ

**BOUCHARD, HIPÓLITO** (*b.* 13 August 1783; *d.* 5 January 1837), naval hero of Argentine independence. Born in France, Bouchard had been active in his country's merchant marine and in privateering by the time he reached Buenos Aires in 1809. There he stayed, and after the May Revolution of 1810 he was one of the cadre of foreign sailors who gave the Argentine patriots a respectable naval force, especially for corsair operations. Bouchard was naturalized as an Argentine citizen in 1813. He sailed with Admiral Guillermo BROWN to the Pacific in 1815 and starting in 1817 commanded the frigate *Argentina* on a privateering voyage that took it around the world. He was a member of the expedition in 1820 that carried José de SAN MARTÍN to Peru. Thereafter he continued serving Peru, where he acquired a sugar estate and spent the last part of his life as *hacendado.*

LEWIS WINKLER BEELER, *Los corsarios de Buenos Aires, sus actividades en las guerras hispano-americanas de la independencia, 1815–1821* (1937); HÉCTOR RAÚL RATTO, *Capitán de navío Hipólito Bouchard,* 2d ed. (1961).

DAVID BUSHNELL

## BOUNDARY DISPUTES

### *Overview*

Latin American countries have a long tradition of settling boundary disputes peacefully. Approximately seventeen border conflicts have been effectively resolved, more than in any other region of the world, since the Independence era. These were concluded through arbitration and mediation by European nations, the United States, Latin American countries, and tribunals of jurists. Generally these conflicts have been adjudicated as a response to immediate crises. In addition, the INTER-AMERICAN SYSTEM since the turn of the century and the ORGANIZATION OF AMERICAN STATES (OAS), founded in 1948, created mechanisms for the peaceful conclusion of border controversies. Several pending boundary disputes in the late twentieth century are still based on the diverse claims of a colonial legacy. However, they have taken on new dimensions because the territories with rival claims contain energy and economic resources of great value. Strategic areas, too, are sources of future conflict, as are tensions arising between states from the migration and dislocation of people.

THE COLONIAL LEGACY

Boundaries in Latin America have been shaped by the colonial heritage of the Spanish and Portuguese empires in the New World. Independent states inherited demarcation lines that were once administered by Portuguese and Spanish ecclesiastical, civil, and legal bodies, each of which influenced the establishment of independent countries. Boundaries were confirmed by the principle of *uti possidetis juris,* which holds that new nations adopt the same boundaries as the colonial entity they replace. Since Independence in the early nineteenth century, there have emerged numerous boundary conflicts which reflect confusion over the jurisdiction of colonial viceroyalties and their subdivisions, such as captaincies-general, presidencies, and *audiencia*s. The boundaries of these smaller administrative units were frequently as vague as the larger entities of which they were once a part. Today, at least twelve countries from Mexico to the Antarctic have unsettled boundary issues and territorial claims against one or more of their neighbors. Each of them can be traced back through three hundred or more years of history, beginning with the competing imperial interests of Spain, Portugal, and their European rivals for domination of the American continent.

SOUTH AMERICA: THE NORTHERN TIER

At the northern tier of South America, boundary issues occupy a major portion of the diplomatic activity of the region's nations. For most of the nineteenth century and on into the twentieth, Colombia and Venezuela struggled to establish an acceptable boundary. An agreement in 1881 gave Colombia the entire Guajira Peninsula, which juts out into the Caribbean Sea. In 1894 Bogotá agreed to cede the eastern portion of this territory, but Venezuela rejected the compromise and demanded that the matter be submitted to arbitration. Since the 1920s partial boundary markings have been agreed on, but a definitive demarcation line including the Guajira Peninsula has yet to be established. In the late twentieth century, sea rights in the Gulf of Venezuela, the entry-way from the Caribbean to Venezuela's petroleum fields in Lake Maracaibo, with possible oil resources of its own, have been a major issue in a boundary dispute between these nations. A 1980 accord gave 75 percent of the Gulf and an archipelago at its mouth to Venezuela and set up provisions for sharing equally any oil that might be found there.

Since the mid-nineteenth century, Venezuela has had a border dispute with Guyana (formerly British Guiana) in which it claims a 53,000-square-mile area west of the Essequibo River—well over half of Guyana's territory. The area contains BAUXITE, aluminum, timber, potentially vast hydroelectric power, and possible oil deposits off the northern coast. Since 1966 several attempts have been made to establish a boundary. Both countries have agreed to use diplomatic means to resolve the conflict, namely the good offices of a mediator. Venezuela has suggested the secretary general of the UNITED NATIONS, and Guyana had proposed that the International Court of Justice rule in the matter. Like Venezuela, Guyana has an unsettled boundary with its eastern neighbor, Suriname. The dispute originates from a late-eighteenth-century conflict between British and Dutch settlers. The issue centers on the validity of a boundary formed by the Courantyne-Kutari rivers and the New River.

SOUTH AMERICA: THE ANDEAN STATES

Most of South America's Andean countries have as yet been unable to establish definitively accepted boundary lines. Disagreement has arisen over vast unsettled lands of earlier colonial powers and newfound mineral and sea resources in the region.

The WAR OF THE PACIFIC (1879–1882), one of the great conflicts in South American history, arose from vague boundaries. Chile, Bolivia, and Peru vied for the vast NITRATE and GUANO resources in the ATACAMA DESERT. The conflict also had roots in a disputed boundary between Bolivia and Chile that stemmed from their imperial colonial legacy. Territory belonging to the Bolivian department of Atacama on the Pacific Ocean had been designated as part of the Viceroyalty of the Río de la Plata (with its capital Buenos Aires) in 1776. When Bolivia became independent, the area in question joined the new nation.

In the 1840s Peru issued licenses to companies exploiting resources in its territory of Tacna, Arica, and Tarapacá. Chile meanwhile claimed territory up to twenty-three degrees south latitude, a claim Bolivia rejected outright, saying it was an encroachment into its domain. In 1874 Chile and Bolivia established their boundary of 24° south latitude while agreeing to share resources between the twenty-third and twenty-fifth parallels through a condominium arrangement. When Peru nationalized all private mines in its nitrate-producing area of Tarapacá in 1875 to create a national monopoly, Chilean mine owners in the territory resisted the action. Bolivia in turn proposed a new tax on nitrates exported from its Atacama region in 1878. The Anglo Chilean Nitrate and Railroad Company, which had been granted a concession by Bolivia, refused to pay an export tax on its nitrate exports.

The intense rivalry among the Andean states for the vast resources in the Atacama along with a Bolivian-Peruvian treaty alliance resulted in war. When Chile ended Peru's control of the sea and defeated its army, Bolivia could no longer remain in the conflict and lost its Atacama territory. The Treaty of ANCÓN (1883), which ended the conflict, stipulated that Chile could hold Tacna and Arica for ten years. A plebiscite would decide the future disposition of the two areas. In 1929 Arica was ceded to Chile and Tacna to Peru. Bolivia lost its outlet to the sea.

In the 1990s Bolivia continues to look for access to the Pacific Ocean through territory it lost to Chile. It wants a free port on the Pacific Ocean and unimpeded access to it without paying compensation to Chile. Bolivia has presented its case for resolution before the OAS as a "hemisphere problem." This conflict is further complicated by the fact that the only corridor that Chile feels would be feasible is located along its northern border with Peru and consists of territory taken from the latter in the War of the Pacific. Peru has a treaty right, dating from 1929, to approve any arrangement involving its former territory should Chile decide to cede it to a third party.

Peru and Colombia had conflicting claims to LETICIA, a 4,000-square-mile area near the Putumayo River in the northeastern Peru–southeastern Colombia region. The dispute emerged from the confusion of boundaries between the colonial viceroyalties of Peru and New Granada and the existence of rubber in the region. The borders agreed upon in 1924 gave Colombia much of the disputed area between the Putumayo and Amazon rivers, including the town of Leticia. Although both sides ratified the treaty, Peru—resenting the loss of land—invaded Leticia in 1932. The LEAGUE OF NATIONS created a Commission of States (Spain, Cuba, the United States, and Brazil) to regulate the disputed region. In 1934 both nations accepted the boundaries set by the 1924 agreement, and the disputed area was then ceded to Colombia.

Vague colonial jurisdiction in a 100,000-square-mile jungle, bounded by the eastern slopes of the Andes, the Ecuadorian-Colombian border, and the Marañon River, brought Peru and Ecuador to war in 1941. Oil and RUBBER resources made land claims in this area valuable. The Rio Protocol of 1942, drawn up by mediators (the United States, Argentina, Brazil, and Chile as "guarantor powers") and signed by both countries, gave most of the disputed territory to Peru. In 1960 Ecuador, smarting under the 1942 accord, formally declared the Rio Protocol null and void. That same year, fighting broke out in a still-unmarked area between the two states that was believed to have oil resources. Again in 1981, armed conflict erupted in the same region, known as the Cordillera del Condor. Ecuador called for the OAS to convene a meeting of its foreign ministers to deal with the issue. The four "guarantor states" of 1942 again arranged a cease fire in 1981. In the mid-1990s, Ecuador still demanded that the 1942 Rio Protocol be renegotiated. Peru asked that only the remaining unmarked border of 125 miles be established.

Paraguay and Bolivia lost substantial territory in two nineteenth-century conflicts: Paraguay in the Paraguayan War (1864–1870), or WAR OF THE TRIPLE ALLIANCE, and Bolivia in the War of the Pacific. They had conflicting territorial claims in the CHACO, an area of 150,000 square miles believed to have oil deposits. Boundaries were not established in the area either during the colonial era or after independence. Although both nations lay claim to the Chaco under the principle of *uti possidetis juris*, Paraguay began colonization projects in the 1930s to assert effective occupation, or *uti possidetis actual*. The three-year CHACO WAR (1932–1935) ended with that nation occupying a substantial part of the Chaco. In 1938 a peace treaty establishing boundary lines did not give Bolivia the access to the Atlantic by way of the Río de la Plata waterway system that it wanted. However, the mediating powers did give some of the territory under Paraguayan military occupation to Bolivia. A buffer zone of approximately 60 miles was established to separate Paraguay from Bolivia's oil deposits in the Camiri region in the Chaco.

Boundaries between Argentina and Chile were settled rather easily in the late nineteenth and early twentieth centuries. The Great Andean Range, stretching 2,900 miles and separating the two states, was considered an easily recognizable divide. Between 1881 and 1905 the boundary along the northern portion of the Andes was set at a point "that divided the waters." Later erosion by rivers flowing eastward toward Argentina pushed the watershed west of the Andes to Chile. Consequently, Argentina pressed for the water divide, while Chile favored the crest. By 1905 arbitration had set a boundary line agreeable to both countries.

Further south, a more contentious boundary dispute erupted between Argentina and Chile over the ownership of three islands, Lennox, Picton, and Nueva, in the Atlantic mouth of the BEAGLE CHANNEL, north of Cape Horn. The key issues were whether the channel entered the Atlantic north or south of the islands and where the channel ended and the Atlantic Ocean began. The dispute also included jurisdiction over surrounding waters, which involved potential offshore rights to rich FISHING areas and undersea oil as well as strategic access to the Antarctic.

Both states agreed to submit the issue for arbitration by the British crown. A special tribunal selected by Argentina and Chile from the World Court assisted England in six years of study that resulted in awarding the three islands to Chile in 1977. Argentina rejected the decision. Three years later, under the good offices of the Vatican, Chile would receive all the disputed islands but only limited offshore rights in the Atlantic meridian passing through Cape Horn. Both countries would share scientific and economic ventures in the archipelago as well. Chile, which owned 12 miles of territorial waters east of the islands, would have to share resource development in the outer 6 miles of that strip. Argentina, sovereign in a 200-mile area into the Atlantic, would have to allow Chile to take part in resource development there, too. In 1984, with still no resolution to the issues, Pope John Paul II drafted a "friendship pact," signed by both countries, which provided for continued mediation of this boundary and territorial issue. Later in the year, both countries accepted a treaty that was essentially the same as the 1980 proposal.

Brazil concluded boundary settlements with all of its neighbors (mostly Spanish American states) in the first decade of the twentieth century. Since the colonial era, Brazil had been expanding in all directions either through treaty agreements with Spain or later through occupation in the vast unchartered lands of the southern continent. In the so-called Age of Territorial Diplomacy (1880–1900), Brazil fixed its borders with countries contiguous to it mostly through the latter method.

In 1903 boundary settlements with Bolivia concerning the rubber-producing ACRE region gave the territory to Brazil. In return Brazil paid about $10 million to Bolivia for the construction of a railroad to the sea by way of the Amazon River. Other boundaries were fixed in a treaty agreement with French Guiana (1900), in a convention with Argentina (1910) ratifying a treaty concluded in 1898, and in treaties with Peru (1904), Colombia (1928), Venezuela (1929), and Dutch Guiana (1931).

### CENTRAL AMERICA, MEXICO, AND THE UNITED STATES

Boundary disputes in Central America have been similar in origin to those in the Southern Hemisphere. Conflicting territorial claims and the existence of valuable economic resources have been prominent among the sources of these disputes. When the Central American Federation broke up in 1838, disputes over boundaries occurred throughout the region. Yet in the twentieth century, demarcation lines have generally been established peacefully. There have been exceptions to this trend, most notably the El Salvador–Honduras War (SOCCER WAR) in 1969. Honduras claimed territory corresponding to the colonial bishopric of Honduras. El Salvador asserted its sovereignty based on administrative areas established during Spanish rule. When Honduras expelled Salvadoran migrants from the disputed area, war broke out. The OAS was called upon to step in and mediate the issue. It took ten years for it to do so, but the result was a peace treaty signed in 1980. The agreement established a boundary for 135 miles. A commission of representatives from both nations was formed to determine the remaining areas for demarcation, mainly in the Chalatenango, La Unión, and the Goascoran River delta.

A Guatemala-Belize (formerly British Honduras) dispute as well as a Nicaragua-Colombia conflict over several Atlantic islands reflect more than border issues. They involve territorial claims of each state. As has been common in all of Latin America, conflicting colonial jurisdictions have been the main cause of the dispute between Nicaragua and Colombia over nine islands off the former's eastern coast. Nicaragua claims sovereignty over five of them. The dispute began when Spain gave the viceroyalty in New Granada (Colombia) responsibility for defending SAN ANDRÉS and PROVIDENCIA islands in 1803. This order was rescinded in 1806, and similar authority was given to the captaincy-general of Guatemala, of which Nicaragua was a part. During the U.S. military intervention in Nicaragua, Managua was persuaded in 1928 to recognize Colombian sovereignty over San Andrés, Providencia, and Santa Catalina islands. Nicaragua abrogated the treaty in 1980. The dispute continues unresolved.

The Guatemala-Belize controversy originated with Great Britain's effective occupation of Spain's eastern Central American territory in the seventeenth century. Guatemala claims the area on the principle of *uti possi-*

*detis juris,* asserting sovereignty based on colonial jurisdiction. When British Honduras (now Belize) declared its independence in September 1981, it became a member of the British Commonwealth and the United Nations over Guatemala's protest. In a Heads of Agreement (Britain, Belize, and Guatemala) document drawn up the same year, Guatemala yielded on the territorial claim and Belize granted it permanent and unimpeded access to its isolated port of PUERTO BARRIOS on the Gulf of Honduras. However, negotiations have not yet resolved this dispute definitively.

The Treaty of GUADALUPE–HIDALGO (1848), ending the MEXICAN–AMERICAN WAR (1846–1848), established the middle portion of the Rio Grande as the boundary between Mexico and the United States. Floods and torrential rains in 1864 forced the river southward around an area in the El Paso–Ciudad Juárez vicinity called the Chamizal. This left Mexican territory on the north bank. The United States assumed the boundary had changed by erosion. Mexico in turn claimed the course of the Rio Grande had altered suddenly, leaving its land on the north bank of the river. A subsequent boundary dispute in 1884 over the Morteritos Island at the Texas-Tamaulipas border concluded that the demarcation line would move if the river shifted gradually. An International Border Commission was created in 1889 to implement the new guideline and deal with future disputes of this kind.

The commission was unable to resolve the disputed Chamizal area, as both states recognized that its proximity to the expanding urban centers of El Paso and Ciudad Juárez made the area valuable. Yet Mexico and the United States agreed to arbitrate the issue in 1910. The appointed commission concluded that the Rio Grande had changed course in a sudden and violent shift in 1864. Therefore, the boundary was to be reestablished as it existed in 1864. Although Washington rejected the decision, various governments attempted to resolve the controversy.

Finally, in 1963 the Kennedy administration concluded that Washington's rejection of the commission's decision had been a mistake. The dispute was resolved so that Mexico received 630 acres of the Chamizal area, including Córdova Island, an area that juts into United States territory. The latter, in turn, received 193 acres. A final agreement was signed by Presidents Lyndon B. Johnson and Gustavo Díaz Ordaz in October 1967. The resolution of this protracted controversy was cited as a model for the peaceful settlement of border disputes by American states. Washington, therefore, created the Chamizal National Memorial and Mexico built a park in Ciudad Juárez commemorating the settlement.

### CONTEMPORARY BOUNDARY AND TERRITORIAL DISPUTES

Causes of the Argentine-British FALKLANDS-MALVINAS WAR (1982) over a group of disputed islands go back to the sixteenth century, when both Spain and England made claims of discovery. England, France, and Spain established settlements there in the seventeenth and eighteenth centuries. After independence Buenos Aires claimed the islands, located some 300 miles east of the Patagonian city of Río Gallegos. However, Britain took effective control of them in 1833. Argentina seized the islands in April 1982, but Britain recaptured them two and a half months later after a brief war. Although diplomatic relations were restored between the two countries in 1990, as of 1994 there was no final settlement.

Several Latin American countries, namely Argentina, Brazil, Chile, Ecuador, and Peru, have laid claim to territory in ANTARCTICA. They have done so because of the area's geological and political continuity with the South American mainland. These states have asserted interest in a quadrant between longitude 0° and 90° west in which they have overlapping claims. But issues such as sovereignty, resources, and the presence of non–Western Hemisphere countries pose a threat to their claims there.

Chile, Argentina, and Brazil have also viewed their interests in the Antarctic as part of a wider strategic role in the South Atlantic. The Antarctic Treaty of 1959, ratified by mid-1961 by the twelve states named in the preamble (thirty-nine states by 1994) might prevent a Latin American power struggle there, but a confrontation is a possibility.

GORDON IRELAND, *Boundaries, Possessions, and Conflicts in South America* (1938); WILLIAM J. DENNIS, *Tacna and Arica: An Account of the Chile-Peru Boundary Dispute and of the Arbitrations by the United States* (1967); PETER CALVERT, *Boundary Disputes in Latin America* (1983); JACK CHILD, ed., *Maintenance of Peace and Security in the Caribbean and Central America* (1984); JACK CHILD, *Geopolitics and Politics in South America: Quarrels Among Neighbors* (1985); WILLIAM I. KRIEG, *Ecuadorian-Peruvian Rivalry in the Upper Amazon*, 2d ed. (1986); J. R. V. PRESCOTT, *Political Frontiers and Boundaries* (1987); JORGE GUMUCIO GRANIER, *The United States and the Bolivian Seacoast* (1988); ALAN C. LAMBORN and STEPHEN P. MUMME, *Statecraft, Domestic Politics, and Foreign Policy Making: The El Chamizal Dispute* (1988); STEPHEN P. MUMME, *The United States-Mexico Boundary* (1991); MARSHALL BERTRAM, *The Birth of Anglo-American Friendship: The Prime Facet of the Venezuelan Boundary Dispute* (1992); PAUL GANSTER and EUGENIO O. VALENCIANO, eds., *Mexican-U.S. Border Region and the Free Trade Agreement* (1992); and Ronald B. St. John, *Boundaries, Trade, and Seaports: Power Politics in the Atacama Desert* (1992).

THOMAS DODD

### Brazil

At independence, Brazil, the largest Latin American country and fifth largest country in the world, shared ill-defined boundaries with every South American country and territory except Chile. Between 1895 and 1909, under the leadership of diplomat Barão do RIO BRANCO and utilizing the principle of *uti possidetis* (ownership by occupation rather than claim), the Brazilian government succeeded in delineating approximately 9,000 miles of frontier, adding nearly 342,000 square

miles to its national territory in the process. Aided by his diplomatic training abroad, and employing skilled Brazilian geographers and cartographers to illustrate Brazil's claims, Rio Branco sought international arbitration to resolve Brazil's boundaries. In 1895 U.S. president Grover Cleveland arbitrated the settlement of the boundary of Misiones, between Argentina and Brazil, in Brazil's favor. In 1900, in an agreement arbitrated by the president of the Swiss Confederation, France relinquished the entire territory of Amapá to Brazil, resolving the Brazil-French Guiana border. In 1904 the king of Italy arbitrated settlement of the boundary shared by Brazil and British Guiana; Brazil and Peru reached an amicable agreement along the lines proposed by Brazil in 1909.

The desire to secure the potentially rubber-rich Amazon Basin during the RUBBER boom (ca. 1875–1912) was a driving force behind Brazil's diplomatic offensive and was central in the volatile controversy over the Bolivian territory of Acre, which lay along Brazil's central-eastern boundary. By 1900 nearly 60,000 rubber gatherers had migrated from northeast Brazil into the nominally Bolivian territory. In 1899 and again in 1902 the Brazilian migrants rebelled against Bolivian attempts to assert authority in the region and attempted to force the Bolivian government to relinquish the territory to Brazil. The dispute was settled by the Treaty of PETRÓPOLIS (17 November 1903), in which Bolivia ceded the territory of Acre (73,000 square miles) to Brazil in exchange for lands bordering the Madeira River, a Brazilian commitment to construct the Madeira-Mamoré railroad to provide an Atlantic outlet for Bolivian goods, and an indemnity of $10 million.

In 1906 Brazil reached agreement with the Netherlands on the Brazil–Dutch Guiana boundary, and in 1907 negotiated successfully with Colombia to confirm Brazilian title to lands involving approximately one-third of the state of Amazonas. An agreement with Venezuela in 1905 settled the northern frontier.

GORDON IRELAND, *Boundaries, Possessions, and Conflicts in South America* (1938); E. BRADFORD BURNS, *Nationalism in Brazil* (1968); ROLLIE E. POPPINO, *Brazil: The Land and People* (1968); HAROLD EUGENE DAVIS et al., *Latin American Diplomatic History* (1977).

FRANCESCA MILLER

**BOURBON REFORMS,** commonly defined as the reorganization of the military, commercial, and administrative structures that the Bourbon dynasty inherited in 1700 from its Hapsburg predecessors. Accomplished by ambitious innovations in the collection and generation of royal revenues, this reorganization aimed to modernize the mercantile system, strengthen the royal government administratively and financially, and improve the military position of the Spanish Empire in the face of fierce international competition. The reforms began in the reigns of PHILIP V (1700–1724, 1724–1746) and FER-

DINAND VI (1746–1759), but the colonial reorganization reached its fullest expression through the ambitious measures advanced under CHARLES III (1759–1788) and sustained by CHARLES IV (1788–1808). Although introduced piecemeal and unevenly in the several colonies, these reforms altered profoundly the character of colonial governance and, by the final decade of the eighteenth century, approximated a unified program.

Innovations in each category of reform occurred under the early Bourbons. For the administration, Philip in 1721 definitively transferred the primary responsibility for governing the empire from the COUNCIL OF THE INDIES to the newly created Ministry of the Navy and the Indies, which in 1754 was divided into separate units. In America, he reestablished the Viceroyalty of NEW GRANADA in 1739. At mid-century, Ferdinand halted the sale of AUDIENCIA offices. And overall, in a multitude of minor steps, the reforms increasingly extended royal authority through centralization.

In the sphere of commercial policy, a series of actions dating from the late 1730s and extending into the early 1750s—highlighted by the work of ministers José del Campillo y Cossío and the Marqués de la ENSENADA—curbed the vast privileges of the powerful Consulado (Merchant Guild) of Cádiz, which held a legal monopoly over the American trade. To break the lingering power of Seville, from which the *consulado* had been transferred in 1717, the crown reformed the method of electing officers and liberalized the regulations governing membership. It also developed plans to deregulate radically the colonial trade, opening America to all the ports of Spain. Although this step was thwarted during the reaction following the fall of Ensenada in 1754, the FLEET SYSTEM to South America was nevertheless abolished in favor of register ships. Other measures designed to broaden commercial access to the American marketplace entailed the establishment of privileged TRADING COMPANIES, including those of Caracas (1728), Havana (1740), and Barcelona (1755).

Additional innovations also pointed toward the future. In the regular army, fixed battalions with modernized command structures replaced garrisons comprised of separate companies, beginning with Havana (1719), continuing with Cartagena (1736), Santo Domingo (1738), New Spain (1740), and Panama (1741), and eventually including the other strongpoints of America.

The crown also experimented with new royal monopolies to enhance its income. In 1717 it established a TOBACCO monopoly in Cuba, primarily to supply the royal factory in Seville. Tobacco monopolies were also organized in Peru (1745), Chile (1753), and Upper Peru (1755). In New Granada the crown installed an *aguardiente* (brandy) monopoly in 1736 and a decade later extended it to the presidency of Quito.

Soon after Charles III became king, the 1762 British capture of Havana exposed the vulnerability of imperial defense, imposing urgency on the reformist agenda and elevating military concerns to unparalleled primacy. In 1763, when he regained Havana at the price of Florida in the Treaty of Paris, Charles dispatched to Cuba a reform commission led by the Conde de Ricla as governor and Alejandro O'REILLY as sub-inspector general of the army, and at court he established an interministerial commission, the Junta de Ministros, to coordinate the colonial reorganization. O'Reilly expanded Havana's regular army, but more importantly he involved Cubans directly in the task of defense through the establishment of a disciplined militia. This system provided for the systematic arming and training of the colonial population and granted militiamen the *fuero militar* (military privilege).

Minister of War and Finance Marqués de Esquilache, who dominated the Junta de Ministros at court, worked closely with Ricla to find the means to help support the expanded military. The *alcabala* was increased from 2 to 6 percent, and excise taxes were placed on the sale of colonial liquors. A military intendant was installed with supreme authority over the treasury. Finally, the royal decree of 1765 conceded to Cuba and the other Caribbean islands free trade with the major ports of Spain, thus encouraging legal commerce, stimulating economic growth, and enhancing royal revenues. Meanwhile, a modernization of the royal mail service improved communications with the colonies.

In 1764 the crown extended the military reform to NEW SPAIN through the mission of Lieutenant General Juan de Villalba, which both reorganized the regular army and established a disciplined militia, and in 1765, O'Reilly also reformed the Puerto Rican military. Royal orders to raise disciplined militias were sent to the governors of Caracas and Buenos Aires and the viceroy of Peru. To improve royal finance, Esquilache established a program to make the tobacco monopoly virtually universal in the colonies. In 1765 he commissioned José de GÁLVEZ as visitor-general to New Spain, which was financially responsible for both its own military costs and enormous subsidies to the Caribbean islands. Gálvez improved the collection and administration of royal revenues and placed the new tobacco monopoly on a workable footing. In naming officials, Gálvez angered colonists through his blatant favoritism of Spaniards over what he believed were less reliable Americans. Although the pace of reform slowed following the fall of Esquilache in 1766, Alejandro O'Reilly, now inspector-general of the American army, brought Santo Domingo, Cartagena, and Panama into the new defense system immediately following the FALKLAND ISLANDS crisis of 1770–1771.

The colonial reorganization resumed its vigor when Gálvez became minister of the Indies in January 1776, on the eve of the AMERICAN REVOLUTION. Gálvez commissioned José Antonio de Areche and Juan Francisco GUTIÉRREZ DE PIÑERES to lead reform missions—similar to his own in New Spain—to Peru and New Granada as well as subvisits to Chile and Quito by Tomas Álvarez de Acevedo and José García-Pizarro. Massive resistance led by TÚPAC AMARU of Peru and the COMUNEROS of New Granada swept the upland interiors, blunting the successes of these undertakings and leaving enduring scars. Meanwhile, military reform continued to progress. Miners' guilds with broad powers to promote production were installed in New Spain (1777) and Peru (1787), and to improve MINING practices, the crown sent technical missions to both of these viceroyalties and to New Granada during the 1780s.

The INTENDANCY SYSTEM of provincial governance provided the administrative underpinning for fiscal reform. In 1776 an intendancy was established in Caracas on the same basis as that in Cuba. Six years later, when Gálvez introduced this institution into Río de la Plata, the office was broadened to include government and justice, thereby effecting a rationalization and centralization of the instruments of provincial administration. On this basis, the intendant system was extended to Peru in 1784 and New Spain, Guatemala, and Chile in 1786, but not to volatile New Granada. Other innovations included the establishment in 1776 of the Viceroyalty of the Río de la Plata and the Commandancy General of the Interior Province of New Spain, and, in 1777, the CAPTAINCY General of Caracas.

Commercial deregulation constituted the capstone of the colonial reorganization. Following the concession of imperial free trade to the Caribbean islands in 1765, the crown cautiously pursued liberalization, a process highlighted by the incorporation of Yucatán into the Caribbean system in 1770 and, four years later, the legalization of intercolonial trade on the Pacific coast. As minister, Gálvez quickened the tempo of deregulation through a series of measures culminating in the Regulation of Free Trade of October 1778, which definitively broke the Cádiz monopoly, although certain restrictions lingered on the commerce of New Spain and Caracas.

Charles IV sustained this reformist agenda, although his government set a moderate tone in the enforcement of revenue regulations and attempted to limit conflicts with the colonial elites. Caracas and New Spain were incorporated fully into the system of free trade during 1788–1789; the SLAVE TRADE of Cuba, Santo Domingo, Puerto Rico, and Caracas was opened to all Spanish subjects; and, beginning with Havana in 1794, a host of new colonial merchant guilds were organized, breaking the grip of Lima and Mexico City on the colonial marketplaces. Following the death of Gálvez in 1787, the Ministry of the Indies was split into two portfolios, and in 1790 their functions were assigned to the corresponding Spanish ministries, a step toward standardizing metropolitan and colonial governance.

The Bourbon Reforms produced mixed results. Spain reconquered Florida during the American Revolution and the empire stood well defended as the century advanced, but by arming Americans effectively and granting them military privileges, the crown risked losing political control, a danger destined to become reality during the independence movement of the early nine-

teenth century. Commercial deregulation undoubtedly stimulated legal commerce. The tariffs collected on this trade, when combined with record royal income from other sources—especially from mining taxes, the *alcabala,* and the tobacco monopoly—brought unparalleled wealth to the royal treasury, but much of this revenue was squandered on the military, while, on another level, tensions between Spain and its colonies lingered. Although the intendancies made provincial governance more efficient, their powers produced stress within the administrative hierarchy, and their subdelegates, operating at the local level, came to resemble the CORREGIDORES they had replaced.

The wars of the French Revolution and NAPOLEON I interrupted the reformist process, placing burdens on the imperial system that could not have been anticipated. The program of Charles III never had a long-term opportunity to be fully tested.

JOHN LYNCH, *Spanish Colonial Administration, 1782–1810: The Intendant System in the Viceroyalty of the Río de la Plata* (1958); JOHN R. FISHER, *Government and Society in Colonial Peru: The Intendant System, 1784–1814* (1970); D. A. BRADING, *Miners and Merchants in Bourbon Mexico, 1763–1810* (1971); CHRISTON I. ARCHER, *The Army in Bourbon Mexico, 1760–1810* (1977); JACQUES A. BARBIER, "The Culmination of the Bourbon Reforms," in *Hispanic American Historical Review* 57 (1977): 51–68; MARK A. BURKHOLDER and D. S. CHANDLER, *From Impotence to Authority: The Spanish Crown and the American Audiencias, 1687–1808* (1977); JOHN R. FISHER, *Commercial Relations Between Spain and Spanish America in the Era of Free Trade, 1778–1796* (1985); ALLAN J. KUETHE, "Towards a Periodization of the Reforms of Charles III," in *Iberian Colonies, New World Societies: Essays in Memory of Charles Gibson,* edited by Richard L. Garner and William B. Taylor (1985), and *Cuba, 1753–1815: Crown, Military, and Society* (1986); ALLAN J. KUETHE and LOWELL BLAISDELL, "French Influence and the Origins of the Bourbon Colonial Reorganization," in *Hispanic American Historical Review* 71 (1991): 579–607.

ALLAN J. KUETHE

**BOVES, JOSÉ TOMÁS** (*b.* 18 September 1782; *d.* 5 December 1814), officer in the Spanish army. A native of Spain, Boves received his nautical education in Asturias, obtained his pilot's license in 1803, and joined a mercantile business with interests in Venezuela. He was accused of smuggling, imprisoned in Puerto Cabello, and later confined in the town of Calabozo. When the War of Independence broke out, Boves declared himself to be on the side of emancipation. But he then became suspect when he supported the royalist leader, Domingo Monteverde, and was imprisoned in 1812 at Calabozo. That same year he joined the royalist ranks under the command of Eusebio Antoñanzas, who released him from prison, and was appointed commander in chief of Calabozo.

Boves rapidly attained great popularity among the inhabitants of the plains for his favorable attitude toward sacking and looting. His detailed knowledge of the plains territory brought him numerous victories over republican troops. In testimonies of the time and in the collected writings on Venezuelan independence, Boves stands out for his fierceness and cruelty to those he defeated. He rebelled against his immediate superior and ignored the authority of the royal *audiencia.* After his death at the battle of Urica, the royalist cause lost popularity among the people of the plains.

JUAN USLAR PIETRI, *Historia de la Rebelión de 1814* (1954); ACISCLO VALDIVIESO MONTAÑO, *José Tomás Boves, caudillo hispano* (1955); and GERMÁN CARRERA DAMAS, *Boves: Aspectos socioeconómicos de la independencia,* 3d ed. (1972).

INÉS QUINTERO

**BOX, PELHAM HORTON** (*b.* 29 March 1898; *d.* 23 May 1937), British historian who applied modern research methods to the study of Paraguay in the 1930s. The University of Illinois awarded him the Ph.D. in 1927 and in 1930 published his dissertation, *Origins of the Paraguayan War,* which was translated into Spanish in 1936. This revisionist work viewed José Gaspar Rodríguez de FRANCIA (1766–1840) as a revolutionary dictator who ruled with the consent of the peasantry and blamed the WAR OF THE TRIPLE ALLLIANCE on Francisco Solano LÓPEZ. Now dated, the book remains a starting point for researchers. Box taught for several years at Birkbeck College and two years at King's College, London.

PELHAM HORTON BOX, *The Origins of the Paraguayan War* (1930, repr. 1967); *Times* (London), 28 May 1937, p. 18b.

VERA BLINN REBER

**BOYACÁ, BATTLE OF,** the most decisive engagement of Colombian independence. The culmination of a campaign begun by Simón BOLÍVAR in late May on the Venezuelan llanos, the clash took place on 7 August 1819 at Boyacá, about 9 miles southwest of Tunja on the road to Bogotá. With an army of Venezuelans, New Granadans, and British legionnaires, Bolívar crossed the eastern plains, scaled the Andes, and emerged in the series of upland valleys leading to the capital of the Viceroyalty of New Granada. After several inconclusive engagements, Bolívar consolidated his foothold and on 5 August occupied Tunja, placing himself between the main royalist army under Colonel José María Barreiro and Bogotá. When Barreiro tried to outflank Bolívar and secure the road to the capital, fighting broke out at a small bridge over the Boyacá River. Numerically, forces were evenly matched—about 2,850 patriots against 2,700 royalists—but the patriots were in better fighting condition. Combat lasted two hours, and neither side suffered major casualties. However, the patriots claimed the field and took most of the enemy prisoner, including Barreiro. Three days later Bolívar entered Bogotá, and with the momentum gained in this victory, the patriots fanned out through most of the rest of central New Granada.

JUAN FRIEDE, ed., *La batalla de Boyacá, 7 de agosto de 1819, a través de los archivos españoles* (1969); CAMILO RIAÑO, *La campaña libertadora de 1819* (1969); DANIEL FLORENCIO O'LEARY, *Bolívar and the War of Independence,* translated and edited by Robert F. McNerney, Jr. (1970), pp. 162–165.

DAVID BUSHNELL

*See also* **Wars of Independence.**

**BOYER, JEAN-PIERRE** (*b.* 1776; *d.* 9 July 1850), ruler of Haiti (1818–1843). The regime of Jean-Pierre Boyer marked a vital watershed in the development of Haitian government and society in the nineteenth century. Born in Port-au-Prince, Boyer began his career when he joined the revolutionary forces led by Pierre Dominique Toussaint L'OUVERTURE that abolished slavery and freed Haiti from French colonial domination. In the power struggles dividing Haitians after independence, Boyer, himself a mulatto, sided with mulatto leader Alexandre Sabès PÉTION and, in March 1818, succeeded Pétion as head of the Republic of the South. In 1821, after the death of his major rival in the North, Henri CHRISTOPHE, Boyer unified the country. Under his auspices, Haiti began to consolidate its status as an independent nation. In 1822, out of fear of French plans for reprisal, Boyer sent his troops to the vulnerable eastern half of Hispaniola, which, with Boyer's encouragement, had recently declared its independence from Spain. He remained in control of the region for the remainder of his twenty-five-year reign. In 1825, Boyer obtained France's diplomatic recognition (by paying an indemnity of 150 million francs), an achievement that had eluded earlier leaders of the young nation and that marked the end of Haiti's status as an international pariah. Recognition from the British came in 1826, after which other countries followed suit.

Despite these successes on the international front, Boyer faced serious challenges at home. The most significant problem was trying to reconcile the needs and interests of two major sectors of the population: the mulatto elite and the black peasantry. During his early years in power, Boyer tried to win the loyalty of the peasantry through land distribution. This popular policy was started by Pétion and contributed to the predominance of small-scale, subsistence agriculture, especially in the South. Yet, Boyer also responded to the demands of mulatto landowners for a restoration of plantation agriculture. In May 1826, he implemented the Code Rural in an attempt to force peasants to work for the large estates. The code stipulated that all peasants were to contract themselves to an estate owner or be considered "vagabonds" liable to arrest and forced labor on public-works projects. It also provided for a rural police force to inspect plantations and keep order in the countryside. Yet, because of government laxness as well as lack of cooperation from some estate owners, it was impossible to enforce the code. Thus, Boyer witnessed the decline of Haiti's once-productive plantation system and the rise of subsistence farming as a way of life for most Haitians.

Boyer's regime also saw a hardening of social and class divisions based on skin color as well as property ownership. In general, government fell into the hands of the more educated, Westernized mulattoes while blacks dominated the military. This split helped undermine the success of Boyer's effort to entice free blacks from the United States to settle in Haiti. During the Boyer period, about 13,000 blacks arrived on the island with the hope of becoming property owners and living in a more egalitarian society; yet, due to problems created by language and cultural differences as well as mulatto social prejudice against blacks, little more than half that number stayed. The revolt of 27 January 1843 led to his exile on 13 March, first in Jamaica and later in Paris. In sum, Boyer not only brought about Haitian unity and consolidated his nation's claim to sovereignty but also oversaw the emergence of a society with color and class divisions that have continued to shape Haitian society and politics to this day.

JAMES GRAHAM LEYBURN, *The Haitian People* (1968); DAVID NICHOLLS, *From Dessalines to Duvalier: Race, Colour and National Independence in Haiti* (1979); FRANK MOYA PONS, "Haiti and Santo Domingo, 1790–ca. 1870," in *The Cambridge History of Latin America*, vol. 3, edited by Leslie Bethell (1985), pp. 237–275; MICHEL-ROLPH TROUILLOT, *Haiti: State Against Nation* (1990).

PAMELA MURRAY

**BRACERO,** the program developed through a series of agreements by the governments of Mexico and the United States (1942–1964) to import temporary Mexican farm workers into the United States. The term *bracero* comes from the Spanish word *brazo* (arm). A bracero, thus, was also the worker who participated in the bracero program.

The United States experienced a shortage of labor during World War II that led to the formal agreement with Mexico in 1942 for temporary admittance into the United States of mainly agricultural workers. By the terms of the initial accord, the U.S. Department of Agriculture administered the program, recruiting workers, placing them with private employers, and guaranteeing acceptable wages and working conditions. The Mexican government established regional recruiting centers where individuals applied for contracts to work in the United States. Once chosen, workers were transported to a U.S. reception center to sign government-standardized work contracts with employers. The contracts provided wage rates equivalent to those of U.S. workers for comparable work, adequate housing at no cost, low-priced meals, a guarantee of work for 75 percent of the contract term, insurance, and return transportation to Mexico at the end

of the contract. Some 300,000 braceros participated in the program during World War II, and by the end of the program in 1964 more than 4 million Mexican nationals had worked in the United States under the program.

This labor agreement was at times a source of conflict. When renegotiating the agreement in 1953, Mexico took a firm position for control of bracero wage rates. The United States responded to the impasse in negotiations with an "open border policy," that is, not impeding the flow of illegal immigrants to the United States. When thousands of workers flocked to the northern border, Mexican officials, and even the army, attempted to prevent them from crossing into the United States. This Border Incident of 1954 came to a head when the braceros marched in protest and the Mexican government ended its attempt to prevent immigration. A new accord was reached in March 1954, and in June U.S.

Bracero reaping a harvest of gladiolus buds from a coastal San Diego, California, ranch. © DON BARTLETTI / LOS ANGELES TIMES.

authorities initiated "Operation Wetback" to deport Mexican workers who were illegally in the United States in order to discourage further illegal entry and to force U.S. employers to hire contract labor under the bracero program.

Despite the problems, the program had benefited both countries. The United States obtained low-cost labor for work where it was difficult to attract Americans. Mexico was able temporarily to export surplus labor, and the remittances of the braceros were a significant source of foreign exchange and income to the impoverished sending communities. Since termination of the bracero program, the labor flows have continued through migration of undocumented workers. Uncontrolled labor migration from Mexico to the United States remains a major issue between the two countries.

ERNESTO GALARZA, *Merchants of Labor: The Mexican Bracero Story* (1964); RICHARD B. CRAIG, *The Bracero Program* (1971); PETER KIRSTEIN, *Anglo over Bracero: A History of the Mexican Worker in the United States from Roosevelt to Nixon* (1977); MANUEL GARCÍA Y GRIEGA, *The Importation of Mexican Contract Laborers to the United States, 1942–1964: Antecedents, Operation, and Legacy* (1981); KITTY CALAVITA, *Inside the State: The Bracero Program, Immigration, and the I.N.S.* (1992).

PAUL GANSTER

*See also* **United States–Mexican Border.**

**BRADEN, SPRUILLE** (*b.* 13 March 1894; *d.* 10 January 1978), U.S. mining entrepreneur and diplomat. Born in Elkhorn, Montana, and educated at Yale, Braden managed numerous copper-mining and business ventures in South America, particularly in Chile. By the early 1930s, he was owner or director of power and light companies in South America and of diverse North American firms. He served intermittently as a diplomat in the 1920s and turned to full-time public service in 1935, when President Franklin D. ROOSEVELT named him ambassador-delegate to the Chaco Peace Conference. Braden was among the first to sound the alarm over Axis incursions into the Western Hemisphere. As ambassador to Colombia (1938–1941), he struggled against German-controlled airlines in that country (and against the Germans' partner, Pan-American World Airways). He gained further fame for his anti-Axis operations as ambassador to Cuba (1941–1944).

The apogee and collapse of Braden's career came in 1945–1947. In 1945 he was named ambassador to Argentina, with which the State Department had been feuding since Argentina's refusal to join the hemispheric anti-Axis front in 1942. He clashed with Colonel Juan PERÓN, Argentina's emerging strongman, as well as with the Rockefeller (that is, Latin Americanist or liberal) faction of the State Department and with the British, both of whom urged conciliation with Argentina. Braden rallied the Argentine opposition to Perón and later attempted to use Argentina's flirtation with the Axis (documented in

the BLUE BOOK) to influence the election of 1946. These acts were considered violations of diplomatic norms and were also failures: Argentina was admitted to the United Nations at the San Francisco Conference (1945) and Perón was elected president (1946). Confirmed as under secretary of state for American Republic affairs late in 1945, Braden imposed his anti-Peronism on U.S. foreign policy; however, this policy became irrelevant in the cold war. The ensuing stalemate between Braden and Ambassador George Messersmith in Buenos Aires was resolved in June 1947 when Secretary of State Dean Acheson dismissed the ambassador and allowed Braden to resign. In retirement, Braden became a vocal cold warrior.

SPRUILLE BRADEN, *Diplomats and Demagogues: The Memoirs of Spruille Braden* (1971); ROGER R. TRASK, "Spruille Braden Versus George Messersmith: World War II, the Cold War, and Argentine Policy, 1945–1947," in *Journal of Interamerican Studies* 26, no. 1 (February 1984): 69–95.

RONALD C. NEWTON

**BRADEN COPPER COMPANY.** *See* **Gran Minería.**

**BRAGANÇA, HOUSE OF,** noble house of Portugal whose members founded the Bragança dynasty that ruled Portugal from 1640 to 1910 and Brazil from 1822 to 1889. Descended from Dom Afonso (natural son of Dom JOÃO I of Portugal) and Dona Beatriz Pereira Alvim (daughter of Condestável Nuno Alves Pereira), who married in 1401; the family takes its name from the city of Bragança, in the northeastern extremity of Portugal. Land donations by Dom João and Condestável Pereira formed the nucleus of the dukedom, which later included extensive holdings in a large number of villages, manors, and fortresses. The dukes appointed ecclesiastical, administrative, judicial, and fiscal authorities throughout their lands and they enjoyed the prerogatives of royal princes outside the line of succession: they granted titles of nobility, and attended meetings of the Council of State, presiding in the king's absence. Despite such privileges, the House of Bragança entered into conflict with Dom JOÃO II, of Aviz, who at the beginning of his reign (1481–1495) sought to strengthen his royal power by demanding from the nobility a pledge of allegiance according to a new formula that linked and subordinated the nobles to royal power far more than the previous pledge. The duke of Bragança, Dom Fernando II, protested the wording of the new formula as too rigorous and demeaning to his dignity. Although the duke eventually swore allegiance, when Dom João II ordered a new survey of all the land in the kingdom, without exception, Dom Fernando and other other nobles conspired against the king. Dom Fernando was brought to trial, decapitated, his family exiled, and all the holdings of the House of Bragança confiscated and distributed among the favorites of Dom João II. In 1497 all rights were restored to the house.

In 1580 the Aviz dynasty ended with the death of Dom Henrique I. PHILIP II of Spain assumed the Portuguese crown, and Portugal remained united to Spain until 1640. In 1637 the idea of restoration began to take root, and the natural choice for a sovereign was Dom João II, eighth duke of Bragança. The duke and his followers used the outbreak of the Catalunian rebellion in Spain to proclaim the separation of Portugal from Spain, and in 1640 the duke became JOÃO IV, king of Portugal. The Braganças governed Portugal during some of its most challenging periods: the recovery from the economic and fiscal devastation left by its former union with Spain, the threat of Spanish military intervention, the animosity of the pope who supported Spain, and the Dutch conquest of Brazil. During the eighteenth century the dynasty experienced a golden age under JOÃO V, impelled by his administrative and political acumen and the wealth from the Brazilian gold mines. The nineteenth century brought the Napoleonic invasion, the escape of the Bragança in 1809 to Brazil (where they remained until 1821), and finally the loss of Brazil.

In 1822 Dom Pedro, prince regent of Brazil and heir to the Portuguese throne, proclaimed Brazilian independence and became PEDRO I of Brazil. The Brazilian branch of the Bragança dynasty came to govern Brazil and Portugal under constitutional monarchies. Pedro I became PEDRO IV of Portugal upon his father's death in 1826, but in the same year he abdicated the throne of Portugal in favor of his daughter, MARIA II, and 1831 he abdicated the throne of Brazil in favor of his son, PEDRO II. The last Bragança monarchs tried, without success, to forestall the republic but the Republic of Brazil was proclaimed in 1889, and Pedro II exiled. Portugal was proclaimed a republic in 1910, causing Dom Manuel II to leave the country.

JOÃO AMEAL, *História de Portugal* (1968); NEILL MACAULAY, *Dom Pedro* (1986).

LYDIA M. GARNER

## BRAMUGLIA, JUAN ATILIO

**BRAMUGLIA, JUAN ATILIO** (*b*. 19 January 1903; *d*. 4 September 1962), Argentine labor lawyer, foreign minister, and supporter of Juan PERÓN. As legal counsel for the railroad workers' union, Bramuglia's strong initial support of Perón earned him appointments in the government. In 1944 he was named general director of social welfare, and from 1944 to 1945 he served as federal intervenor in the province of Buenos Aires. When Perón was elected president in 1946, Bramuglia became foreign minister. Bramuglia sought recognition of Argentine claims in ANTARCTICA and the FALKLAND ISLANDS (MALVINAS) and achieved some success in presenting Perón's "third position" in international affairs. In 1948 he was provisional president of the Third Assembly of the United Nations in Paris, and in 1949 he was elected chairman of the United Nations Security Council. After incurring the displeasure of Evita PERÓN, Bramuglia resigned from government and pursued scholarly activi-

ties. His published works include *Jubilaciones ferroviarias* (1941) and *La previsión social Argentina* (1942).

SAMUEL L. BAILY describes Bramuglia's importance in Perón's first administration in *Labor, Nationalism, and Politics in Argentina* (1967). JOSEPH A. PAGE, *Perón, A Biography* (1983), discusses his role in Perón's nationalization of the labor movement. Evita's dislike of Bramuglia is covered in EDUARDO CRAWLEY, *A Nation Divided: Argentina, 1880–1980* (1984), esp. pp. 116–117.

JAMES A. BAER

**BRAÑAS GUERRA, CÉSAR** (*b*. 13 December 1899; *d*. 22 February 1976), Guatemalan poet, journalist, and writer, and one of the founders of the influential Guatemalan daily *El Imparcial* (1922–1985). Born in Antigua, Brañas was the best-known of a family of important literary figures. His father was an immigrant from Galicia and his mother a schoolteacher in Antigua. His prolific output of poetry, novels, historical works, and critical essays was highly influential in mid-twentieth-century Guatemala. Like Miguel Ángel ASTURIAS, he contributed to a social consciousness among the Guatemalan intelligentsia. His large library, a part of the University of San Carlos, is especially useful for study of the nineteenth and early twentieth centuries.

FRANCISCO ALBIZÚREZ PALMA and CATALINA BARRIOS Y BARRIOS, *Historia de la literatura guatemalteca*, 3 vols. (1981–1987), vol. 2, pp. 167–203; CARLOS C. HAEUSSLER YELA, *Diccionario general de Guatemala* (1983), vol. 1, p. 260.

RALPH LEE WOODWARD, JR.

**BRANCO, MANUEL ALVES** (Caravelas, Visconde de; *b*. 7 June 1797; *d*. 13 July 1855), Brazilian politician. Born in Bahia, he attended the University of Coimbra in Portugal, where he studied law. He returned to Brazil in 1824 and began a distinguished career in politics. Branco was elected a deputy from Bahia in 1830. In 1835 he was named minister of justice in the triumvirate regency (1831–1835). During his tenure as minister he was responsible for Lei no. 57 (6 October 1835), which abolished the civil and religious entailment (*morgados* and *capelas*), and Lei no. 4 (10 June 1835), which imposed a death penalty on slaves who physically hurt their owners. The latter law became one of the principal juridical foundations for imperial slavery legislation. In 1837 Branco was elected senator from Bahia. In 1842 PEDRO II named Branco as one of his first councilers of state. He became the first Brazilian to hold the post of president of the Council of Ministers, created in 1847. As the first prime minister of the Empire, Branco was a militant politician in the Liberal Party. Noted for his skills as an orator and his deep knowledge of the law, Branco was one of the most significant politicians during the period of the Brazilian monarchy.

SACRAMENTO AUGUSTO VICTORINO ALVES BLAKE, *Diccionario bibliographico brasileiro*, 7 vols. (1897); JOACHIM NABUCO, *Um estadista do imperio: Nabuco de Araujo: Sua via, suas opinões, e sua época*, 3 vols. (1897); EUL-SOO PANG, *In Pursuit of Honor and Power: Noblemen of the Southern Cross in Nineteenth-Century Brazil* (1988).

EUL-SOO PANG

*See also* **Brazil: Second Empire.**

**BRANDÃO, IGNÁCIO DE LOYOLA** (*b.* 31 July 1936), Brazilian author. Brandão's writing career began at the age of sixteen, when he was a movie reviewer for a newspaper in Araraquara, his hometown, in the hinterland of the state of São Paulo. Soon after his twenty-first birthday, he moved to the state capital, where he became a journalist. The peculiarities and problems of urban life made a profound impression on him, and for the next eight years he witnessed the people's increasing mistrust in the government, and the resulting turmoil that led to a military coup in 1964. Being a reporter, Brandão had firsthand knowledge of the turbulence of the metropolis, intensified by a period of extreme violence between police and militants following the coup. This environment pervades his fiction. His first book, *Depois do sol* (1965, After the Sun), a collection of short stories, was followed by *Bebel que a cidade comeu* (1968, Bebel, Swallowed Up by the City). Both books portray the social and psychological crises of 1960s Brazil, resulting from political oppression and economic unrest. Brandão eventually abandoned his career as a journalist and devoted himself to his fiction, though his novels and short stories retain a journalistic feel, revealing the author's analytical mind and stylistic irreverence, which often extends to graphic layouts emulating newspapers. His criticism of the government led to censorship of his novel *Zero,* which was banned from publication in Brazil for six years (1969–1975). He became, then, the first Brazilian writer to resort to publication abroad; *Zero* was printed in Italy (1974) before its publication in Portuguese. The first English-language translation was published in the U.S. in 1984. Brandão also wrote travel logs, including *Cuba de Fidel: viagem à ilha proibida* (1978, Fidel's Cuba: Voyage to a Forbidden Island) and *O verde violentou o muro: visões e alucinações alemãs* (1984, The Greenery that Shook the Wall: German Visions and Hallucinations). Brandão is a prolific writer whose work has evolved with the times; he remains faithful to his primary vision of a world unredeemable in its unfairness and cruelty.

ERILDE MELILLO REALE, *Il Doppio Segno di Zero* (1976) and *Raccontes in un Romanzo* (1979); EMILIO RODRÍGUES MONEGAL, "Writing Fiction Under the Censor's Eyes," in *World Literature Today* (1979); UTE HERMANNS, *Mithos and Realität im Roman Zero* (1984); LARRY ROTHER, "Life Under the Mili-tech," review of *Não Verás País Nenhum, New York Times,* 29 September 1985; CANDACE SLATER, "Brazilian Literature: Zero," *Review* 32 (January–May 1994).

REGINA IGEL

*See also* **Brazil: Revolution of 1964; Literature: Brazil.**

**BRANNON DE SAMAYOA CHINCHILLA, CARMEN** (pseud. Claudia Lars; *b.* 1899; *d.* 1974), Salvadoran modernist writer. The daughter of an Irish-American father and Salvadoran mother, Lars grew up on a *finca* (farm) in Sonsonate. She was educated by nuns in Santa Ana and exhibited a literary inclination from a very early age. In her youth she fell in love with the Nicaraguan poet Salomón de la Selva, who introduced her to the world of European romantic literature and served as her mentor. However, her father disapproved of the match and sent her to live with relatives in New York. Upon her return to El Salvador, Lars fell in with a group of modernist and humanist writers known as the Generation of the 1930s, which had assembled around Alberto MASFERRER's newspaper *La Patria* and included Serafín Quiteño and SALARRUÉ. Lars emigrated to San Francisco in 1944, where she experienced the drudgery of working in a biscuit factory. In 1974 she returned to El Salvador. The theme of the mysteries of life and the cosmos dominates her major novels and poems. Lars is considered one of the first great modern female literary figures of Hispanic America.

CLAUDIA LARS, *Estrellas en el pozo* (1934); *Canción redonda* (1937); *Donde llegan los pasos* (1953); *Tierra de infancia* (1958); and *Obras Escogidas* (1973).

JUAN FELIPE TORUÑO, *Desarrollo literario de El Salvador* (1958), pp. 325–328; MATILDE ELENA LÓPEZ, "Prólogo" to *Obras Escogidas* (1973); LUIS GALLEGOS VALDÉS, *Panorama de la literatura salvadoreña* (1981), pp. 225–238.

KAREN RACINE

**BRÁS PEREIRA GOMES, WENCESLAU** (*b.* 26 February 1868; *d.* 15 May 1966), president of Brazil (1914–1918). After serving as governor of the state of Minas Gerais (1908–1910) and vice president under Hermes da Fonseca (1910–1914), Brás was elected president of Brazil in 1914. The Brás presidency marked the end of the extreme federalism of Brazil's early republican years, as the federal government took an increasingly active role in directing state politics and the national economy. Under Brás, force and intimidation were used in several federal interventions into the internal affairs of politically weak states, as well as for the suppression of the Contestado Rebellion along the Santa Catarina-Paraná border. Brás's presidential policies favored the most powerful states. São Paulo and Minas Gerais, which were allied in a power-sharing arrangement known as the politics of *café-com-leite* (an allusion to the prominent coffee-growing and ranching economies of São Paulo and Minas Gerais, respectively).

Aside from declaring war on the Central Powers in 1917, thus making Brazil the only South American republic to join the Allies, Brás is best known for signing the Civil Code of 1917. The Brás presidency is also notable for a rise in domestic industrial production stimulated by the disruptions of international trade and credit brought on by World War I. In November 1918

Brás left office amid a Spanish flu epidemic that ravaged Rio de Janeiro. He subsequently returned to Minas Gerais to lead a private life out of the public spotlight.

RAÚL ALVES DA SOUZA, *História política dos governos da república* (1927), pp. 195–216; JOHN D. WIRTH, *Minas Gerais in the Brazilian Federation, 1889–1937* (1977); E. BRADFORD BURNS, *A History of Brazil* (1980).

DARYLE WILLIAMS

**BRASÍLIA,** the capital of Brazil since 1960 (1992 estimated population 1.6 million). Like many seats of national government, Brasília was a deliberate creation rather than a city that arose spontaneously and organically. The idea of relocating the capital of Brazil from Rio de Janeiro to the backward, sparsely inhabited interior to encourage settlement and development was talked about as early as 1761. In 1891, 5,500 square miles of the Planalto Central were set aside for the site of the future Federal District, but the project did not begin in earnest until 1955, when five possible sites were evaluated in detail by Belcher Associates of Ithaca, New York. The final choice, made in 1956, was located 35 miles southeast of the small town of Planaltina.

The city would probably never have been built had it not been for the efforts of the remarkably dynamic Juscelino KUBITSCHEK, who had risen from humble origins in the state of Minas Gerais to become the president of Brazil in 1956. Kubitschek promised in his campaign to bring Brasília to reality. Presidents were allowed to serve only one term, and Kubitschek, realizing he had to present his successor with a fait accompli, knew he only had five years to get the city built. To design the city he commissioned the architect Oscar NIEMEYER, who had designed the barrio of Pampulha in Belo Horizonte, the capital of Minas Gerais, when Kubitschek was governor. Niemeyer was a disciple of Le Corbusier, the father of the modern glass tower, which was beginning to dominate the skylines of many Latin American cities, symbolizing their yearning for progress. Niemeyer devoted himself to Brasília's public buildings. He drew a central square as monumental and majestic as Mexico's prehistoric TEOTIHUACÁN, with two rows of green-glass ministries leading down to the Congress, whose two chambers, offset by white towers, resemble two bowls, one face up, the other down; to the president's delicately arched white-marble Planalto Palace; and to the serenely lyrical Itamariti Palace, headquarters of the Ministry of Foreign Affairs, a low-slung structure sitting in water and accessible only by ramps, with an outer sheath of tall, slender arches that were, like the Planalto Palace's, a stylization of colonial architecture. The Costa e Silva Bridge, another of the city's architectural wonders, whose 500-foot free span was the great-

View of Congress from the Presidential Palace, Brasília. CHIP AND ROSA MARIA PETERSON.

407

est of any suspension bridge in Latin America, took six years to finish.

An open competition for the city plan was won by Niemeyer's Rio de Janeiro colleague, Lúcio COSTA. Niemeyer and Costa shared a vision of an egalitarian utopia where all classes would live together and the slums that marred Brazil's other cities would be avoided. Costa's Pilot Plan was shaped like an airplane whose fuselage was devoted to Niemeyer's design for the public buildings, and whose wings were the residential areas, each with sixty "superquadras," which were minicommunities patterned after a medieval town and serviced by their own schools, churches, and shopping areas. Each six-story block of apartments was separated by green space and was raised on pilings so children could play under it.

Many criticized the city for its sterile modernity. At the time of its inauguration on 21 April 1960, Brasília seemed to some visitors too rational, too programmed. If one wanted to have a night on the town, for instance, one did this in the Sector of Diversions. To minimize the number of intersections, street corners, and stoplights and thus ensure the unimpeded circulation of traffic, Costa had created a "speedway city" with a convoluted system of ramps, cloverleafs, and pedestrian overpasses. The problem with this was that it increased the distance to everything and discouraged pedestrian travel. Brasília became the hub of a vast highway system, with interstates shooting off to distant cities like Belém, Cuiabá, Belo Horizonte, and Salvador. The dream of national integration was achieved, but at a cost of several billion dollars, which sent inflation spiraling, created social unrest, and led to the 1964 military coup.

Brasília made aesthetic waves, but the hoped-for social revolution did not take place. After 1960 the apartments in the blocks were placed on the open real-estate market, and the construction workers who had built the city and been affectionately dubbed *candangos* by Kubitschek (most were dark-skinned poor from the Northeast) were bought out and forced to live in unplanned satellite cities 20 miles away. Today the federal district's population is about 3 million. Less than a million live in the Pilot Plan itself; the rest live in the satellite cities. The rich live in mansions along two artificial V-shaped lakes below the Pilot Plan created by Paranoá dam, an area that Niemeyer and Costa planned as a park for everybody but, Niemeyer complained, was "usurped by the bourgeoisie." The surrounding *cerrado*, or savanna, studded with small, warped trees, is spectacularly open. With the concrete slabs of many buildings cracked and coated with black mildew, the city's modernity is no longer so shocking. André Malraux, on a 1959 visit, called Brasília the Capital of Hope, but five years later it became the headquarters of twenty-five years of brutal military dictatorship. With the return to civilian rule in 1985, Brasília has become a symbol of appalling political corruption.

NORMA EVENSON, *Two Brazilian Capitals* (1973); JUSCELINO KUBITSCHEK, *Por que construi Brasília* (1975); ALEX SHOUMATOFF, *The Capital of Hope* (1980).

ALEX SHOUMATOFF

*See also* **Architecture.**

## BRASSEUR DE BOURBOURG, CHARLES ÉTIENNE

(*b.* 8 September 1814; *d.* January 1874), French prelate, antiquarian, and pioneer ethnohistorian. Ordained in 1845, Brasseur enjoyed a variety of postings in the Americas, where he was able to make most of his lasting contributions. Among the countries he visited were Canada (1845–1846), the United States (on at least two occasions, in 1848 and 1854), Mexico (1848–1851, 1863–1866, and 1871), Nicaragua and El Salvador (1854), Guatemala (1855–1857 and 1863), and Honduras (1863).

Brasseur is significant today primarily for his discovery, translation, and publication of several important colonial sources concerning Mesoamerican Indians, principally the Maya. These include Diego de LANDA's *Relación de las cosas de Yucatán*, the POPOL VUH, the *Título de los señores de Totonicapán*, the Troano Codex, and the *Memorial de Tecpán Atitlán*, or *Annals of Cakchiquels*. He also compiled and published linguistic materials for both highland Maya (primarily Quiché, including the *Rabinal Achí* drama) and lowland Maya (Yucatecan) peoples that continue to be useful to scholars. Unfortunately, Brasseur's historical interpretations of the documents he worked so tirelessly to discover were judged even by his contemporaries to be seriously flawed. Of little use to present-day scholars on the region, his pronouncements retain only a documentary interest.

To his credit Brasseur did much to promote American studies in his native France, through cofounding the Société Américaine de France (1857) and participating in the subsequent Société d'Ethnographie and the Société de Géographie of Paris. He also raised popular consciousness concerning the indigenous peoples and civilizations of Mesoamerica through his publication of many episodes and discoveries made during his travels.

ADRIÁN RECINOS, "Cien años de la llegada del Abate Brasseur de Bourbourg a Guatemala," in *Anales de la Sociedad de Geografía e Historia*, 29 (January–December 1956): 12–17; CARROLL EDWARD MACE, "Charles Étienne Brasseur de Bourbourg, 1814–1874, in *Handbook of Middle American Indians*, vol. 13, *Guide to Ethnohistorical Sources*, part 2, edited by Robert Wauchope, Howard F. Cline, and John B. Glass (1973), pp. 298–325.

ROBERT M. HILL II

## BRATHWAITE, EDWARD KAMAU

(*b.* 11 May 1930), Caribbean historian, poet, and critic. Born in Bridgetown, Barbados, Brathwaite attended high school at Harrison College in Barbados, and college at Cambridge University. He was a professor of history at the University of the West Indies and later became a professor of comparative literature at New York University. As a historian, Brathwaite's scholarly publications include the important works *The Folk Culture of the Slaves in Jamaica* (1969; rev. ed. 1981) and *The Development of Creole Society in Jamaica, 1770–1820* (1971). He is the author of ten collections of poetry and several plays. *The Arrivants: A New World Trilogy* (1973) secured his reputation as a major poet of the Caribbean. In *Roots* (1993), a collection of literary scholarship and criticism, and in other critical writings, Brathwaite shows himself to be foremost among the theorists of Caribbean literature and culture.

Major themes of Brathwaite's poetry are Caribbean history and identity; SLAVERY and colonization are integrally connected to the themes of fragmentation and alienation. Brathwaite's poetry attempts to provide a "whole, living tradition" out of which can be derived a new consciousness.

GORDON ROHLEHR, "The Historian as Poet," in *The Literary Half-Yearly* 11 (July 1970): 171–178, and "Islands," in *Caribbean Studies* 10 (January 1971): 173–202; KENNETH RAMCHAND, "Edward Brathwaite," in *An Introduction to the Study of West Indian Literature* (1976), pp. 127–142; MAUREEN WARNER-LEWIS, *Notes to Masks* (1977); MERVYN MORRIS, "This Broken Ground: Edward Brathwaite's Trilogy of Poems," in *New World Quarterly* 23 (June–September 1977): 91–103; LLOYD BROWN, "The Cyclical Vision of Edward Brathwaite," in *West Indian Poetry* (1978), pp. 139–158; N. MACKEY, "Edward Brathwaite's New World Trilogy," in *Caliban* 3 (Spring–Summer 1979): 58–88; VELMA POLLARD, "The Dust—A Tribute to the Folk," in *Caribbean Quarterly* 26 (March–June 1980): 41–48.

EVELYN J. HAWTHORNE

**BRAVO, CLAUDIO** (*b.* 8 November 1936), Chilean artist. A virtuoso of realism in painting, drawing, and lithography, Bravo was born in Valparaíso into a wealthy family. He attended Miguel Venegas Cienfuentes's art school from 1947 to 1948. In 1961, he moved to Spain, where he earned his living painting realistic portraits of the Spanish aristocracy. In the mid-1960s, he turned to trompe l'oeil paintings of isolated objects, such as motorcycle paraphernalia, clothing, folded and crumpled pieces of papers, wrapped canvases (*Homage to St. Teresa*, 1969; oil on canvas), and packages (*Blue Package*, 1971). His emphasis on texture, angled lighting, and narrow foreground planes derived from his studies of Francisco de Zurbarán's *bodegones*. Bravo replaced the Spanish master's empty backgrounds with skyscapes and white walls. The realism of Bravo's painting contrasts with his avoidance of all contextual references. His rendering of commonplace objects, biblical themes, and kneeling figures in undefined places or empty space has been interpreted as a surrealist trait. In 1972 Bravo moved to Tangier, Morocco.

WILLIAM DYCKES, "The New Spanish Realists," in *Art International: The Lugano Review* 17 (September 1973): 29–33, 45; EDWARD J. SULLIVAN, *Claudio Bravo* (1985).

MARTA GARSD

**BRAVO, LEONARDO** (*b.* 1764; *d.* 14 September 1812), Mexican insurgent leader. The Chilpancingo-born patriarch of a large family, Bravo joined the insurgent movement in May 1811, along with his son Nicolás and his brothers Miguel, Víctor, and Máximo, when Hermenegildo GALEANA came to his hacienda of Chichihualco. Bravo became one of José María MORELOS's most distinguished officers. He played a major role, first in the fortification, and later in the defense, of CUAUTLA, where the insurgents, besieged by the royalists, held out for seventy-two days despite a lack of supplies. When the siege was lifted at the beginning of May 1812, Bravo traveled to the hacienda of San Gabriel, where he was captured by partisans of the colonial regime. He was taken to Mexico City, where he was tried and executed despite the efforts of his relatives, and even of Morelos, to obtain a pardon in return for the exchange of a sizable group of royalist prisoners.

JOSÉ MARÍA MIQUEL I VERGÉS, *Diccionario de insurgentes* (1969), 85–86; VIRGINIA GUEDEA, *José María Morelos y Pavón: Cronología* (1981); and ERNESTO LEMOINE, *Morelos y la revolución de 1810* (1984).

VIRGINIA GUEDEA

**BRAVO, MARIO** (*b.* 27 July 1882; *d.* 17 March 1944), Argentine Socialist congressman and senator. Bravo, who was elected a national deputy from the city of Buenos Aires four times (1913–1914, 1914–1918, 1918–1922, and 1942–1946) and a senator twice (1923–1931 and 1932–1938), was one of the leading Argentine Socialist Party politicians of the early twentieth century. Born in the city of Tucumán, Argentina, he received his law degree from the University of Buenos Aires and joined the Socialist Party soon thereafter. He rose rapidly through the party's ranks, becoming its general secretary in 1910, the same year in which he embarked on his career in public office. As a legislator, he was best known for initiating measures to democratize the selection process of the city council (*consejo deliberante* ) of the federal capital, a change that took effect in 1918, as well as for bringing attention to the conditions of sugar-plantation workers in his home province of Tucumán. A well-regarded poet, his literary efforts focused primarily on social issues and themes. Collections of his poems include *Poemas del campo y de la montaña* (1909); *La huelga de Mayo* (1909) and *Canciones y poemas* (1918).

RICHARD J. WALTER

*See also* **Argentina: Political Parties.**

**BRAVO, NICOLÁS** (*b.* ca. 1784–1792; *d.* 22 April 1854) Mexican independence leader and politician. Born in Chilpancingo, Bravo and his family joined the insurgency, in which he distinguished himself in a series of campaigns against the royalists. Captured in 1817, he was imprisoned until October 1820. He supported the Plan of IGUALA in 1821, emerging as one of the major political figures of the new order.

Although Bravo served in the regency in 1822, he later opposed Emperor Agustín de ITURBIDE, eventually becoming part of the government that replaced the emperor. Elected vice president in 1824, he became the Grand Master of the "aristocratic" ESCOCESES (Scottish rite Masons), and in January 1828 joined a conservative revolt against the growing power of the radical YORKINOS (York rite Masons), which failed and led to his exile to South America.

Upon his return, Bravo served as commander of the Army of the North, deputy to Congress, and interim president in 1839, 1842–1843, and 1846–1847. During the U.S. invasion in 1847, Bravo commanded troops in battles in PUEBLA, the defense of the capital, and the last stand in Chapultepec Castle, where he was captured. Although invited to join the revolution of Ayutla, he declined because of illness.

LEONARD PARRISH, "The Life of Nicolás Bravo, Mexican Patriot" (Ph.D. diss., University of Texas, 1951); JAIME E. RODRÍGUEZ O., "The Struggle for the Nation: The First Federalist-Centralist Conflict in Mexico," in *The Americas* 49 (July 1992): 1–22.

JAIME E. RODRÍGUEZ O.

**BRAY, ARTURO** (*b.* 1 April 1898; *d.* 2 July 1974), Paraguayan military figure and writer. Born in Asunción to an English father and a Paraguayan mother, Arturo Bray was educated in Asunción and departed for England in 1914 to study medicine. The next year he enlisted in Lord Kitchener's New Armies as a private. He served for two years on the Western Front during World War I, rising to the rank of lieutenant in the infantry. After the war, he returned to Paraguay and quickly received a commission.

During the 1922 military rebellion, Bray remained loyal to the government and held a number of posts in the 1920s. In 1930 he was named director of the Escuela Militar; the following year he was appointed interim chief of police of Asunción. At the outbreak of the CHACO WAR, Bray was promoted to lieutenant colonel, becoming a divisional commander in 1933. He commanded a unit of infantry at the battle of Boquerón that year. A failed military operation in late 1933 led to his detention until 1935 and left him permanently embittered against many Liberal colleagues within and without the army. Eventually he was cleared of charges and in 1936 participated as chief of the Paraguayan military delegation to the Chaco Peace Conference.

The *Febrista* coup of 1936 resulted in his dismissal from the army and his arrest. With the Liberal restoration in the late 1930s Bray again became chief of police of Asunción; he was promoted to colonel and in 1938 served as minister of the interior. Differences (dating back to the Chaco War) with José Félix ESTIGARRIBIA

and other Liberals led to Bray's diplomatic "exile" as minister to Spain and Portugal (1939–1940) and minister to Chile (1940–1941). The 1941 seizure of power by Higinio MORÍNIGO after the death of President Estigarribia spelled the end of Bray's public career.

During his military career, Bray had published professional articles in Paraguayan and foreign newspapers and periodicals. As a private citizen after 1941, he devoted himself to writing. *Hombres y épocas del Paraguay* (1943) and *Solano López, soldado de la gloria y infortunio* (1946) are his best-known works. Later he added another volume to *Hombres y épocas*. He also translated several historical works from English to Spanish. He died in Asunción in 1974.

CARLOS R. CENTURIÓN, *Historia de la cultura paraguaya*, vol. 2 (1961), pp. 435–438; ARTURO BRAY, *Armas y letras*, 3 vols. (1981).

JERRY W. COONEY

**BRAZ, WENCESLAU.** *See* **Brás Pereira Gomes, Wenceslau.**

**BRAZIL** [Coverage begins with a three-part survey of Brazilian political history. There follow a variety of entries on specialized topics: **Amnesty Act; Civil Code; Constitutions; Council of State; Economic Miracle; Electoral Reform; the Empire; Geography; Independence Movements; Liberal Movements; National Security; the New Republic; Organizations** (cultural, economic, labor, regulatory, etc.); **Political Parties; the Regency; Revolutions;** and **Viceroys.**]

### The Colonial Era, 1500–1808

FIRST CONTACTS

The first European presence in what was initially called the Land of the True Cross (Terra da Vera Cruz) and later Brazil (in recognition of red dyewood [*pau brasil*]) was the arrival in April 1500 of the fleet commanded by the Portuguese Pedro Alvares CABRAL. After notifying the king, the fleet continued around Africa to India. As follow-up fleet to that of Vasco da GAMA, which had inaugurated the sea route from Lisbon to India (1498), Cabral's ships had been destined for India. By sweeping out into the Atlantic to avoid the doldrums, Cabral sailed so far off course to the west as to encounter, by chance, the South American continent. In accordance with the Treaty of TORDESILLAS (1494), he claimed the new land for Portugal. Although the Spaniard Vicente Yáñez PINZÓN had preempted Cabral by a few months, this claim was not challenged. Other early travelers included the Florentine pilot Amerigo VESPUCCI, who sailed the coastline of Brazil to the Río de la Plata naming topographical features (1501–1502). The following quarter of a century was to witness landfalls on the coast, or residence, by other Europeans.

In a 1 May 1500 letter to King MANUEL I, professional scribe Pero Vaz de Caminha reported on the coastal

TUPINAMBÁ. He described well-built men, physically attractive and modest women, as well as their good health, nakedness, and bodily decoration. The Portuguese pursued a policy of pacification, and relations were cordial. The Indians offered bows, arrows, cloths and hats made of feathers, parrots, and special beads, and received from the Portuguese red caps, linen bonnets, bracelets, and rosaries. Masses were said on shore. Vaz de Caminha extolled the beauties of the land, its agricultural promise, the innocence of the people, and their rich potential for conversion to Christianity.

## PEOPLING BRAZIL

Native American populations were the first victims of the European arrival. Friendly encounters gave way to hostilities, barter to slavery. Indian campaigns were initiated by Mem de SÁ in Bahia in the 1570s. Indian-European relations were to be characterized by tension. To survive, Indians accommodated to European pressures, retreated beyond European spheres of influence, or resisted. By the end of the sixteenth century, they had been ousted from most coastal regions. But they could not escape European diseases (smallpox, measles, and common cold) to which they had no immunity, European mores (alcohol consumption and use of clothing), forced relocations, long migrations, and destruction of

their beliefs. They were victims of *paulista* slaving BANDEIRAS, official and unofficial slaving expeditions in the Amazon, forced labor, unjustified attacks, and systematic genocide. In the sixteenth century, Indian peoples were enmeshed in Gallo-Portuguese hostilities, and the struggle against the Dutch in the seventeenth century found Indian peoples divided in their loyalties, even within the same family. Gold rushes to Goiás and Mato Grosso took Europeans farther into Indian territories. European intrusions into Amazonia also had fatal results. An Indian population guesstimated at 2.4 million in 1500 had probably declined by half by 1808.

This drastic decline was in sharp contrast to the population increases of persons of Portuguese and African birth or descent. The number of Portuguese grew through immigration in the sixteenth and seventeenth centuries and, more slowly, through natural reproduction as more white women became available. Push and pull factors stimulated migration from Portugal and the Atlantic islands. Crown-sponsored migration occurred in the eighteenth century. The typical migrant was male, in his twenties or early thirties, from north of the Tagus, and of limited financial means. The absence of adequate regulatory procedures meant the virtual absence of immigration data. A greater crown presence, suppression of hostile Indians, and economic upturns spurred mi-

*Recovery of Bahia from the Dutch*. Oil on canvas by Fray Juan Bautista Maino, 1625. BRADLEY SMITH / LAURIE WINFREY.

gration in the seventeenth and eighteenth centuries. This was accelerated by news of gold strikes in Brazil, which drained Portugal of three thousand to four thousand emigrants annually.

The third major component of Brazil's population was of African origin. Brazil was the major importer of slaves to the Americas. Estimates put this forced migration at between 4 and 5 million by 1810. The trade was dictated by supply and demand, internal conditions in Africa, and changing fads in Brazil. Its composition was characterized by a number of males double that of females, some young adults, and few children. Slaves in Brazil had low rates of natural reproduction and high mortality. In regions of greatest economic intensity, sugar and mining, there was a slave majority. By 1808, slaves made up about 38 percent and whites, free blacks, and mulattoes each about 28 percent of Brazil's population.

Excluding Indians, Brazil's population was about 30,000 in 1600, 300,000 by 1700, 2 million by 1776, and about 3 million by 1808. At the end of the colonial period, Indians in settled areas numbered only 6 percent of the population.

SETTLEMENT

The two centuries following Cabral's landfall was characterized by reticence in going beyond coastal regions to the interior of the territory claimed by Portugal. Even along the coast, settlement was irregular. Only in the late sixteenth century were there tentative, and individual, moves away from the coast. In the seventeenth century, there was movement inland from coastal enclaves of Salvador and Recife to the *agreste* and *sertão* and northward to Belém and into the lower Amazon. People traveled from Rio de Janeiro and São Paulo to the west and south. Increasing immigration from Portugal, Madeira, and the Azores, and internal migration fueled such moves. There was a variety of actors: slaves accompanied by owners; missionaries were pioneers to the far north, Amazonia, and far south; cattle ranchers went to Ceará, Piauí, Maranhão, and Minas Gerais; clerics and friars, authorized and unauthorized, roamed the colony; there were few white women or families. *Bandeirantes,* or pioneers, commonly associated with São Paulo but also from Bahia and Pernambuco, came closest to the stereotype of frontiersmen. They splayed out across Brazil as far as the Andes, the Platine region, and the far west.

In the mid-seventeenth century the *bandeira* of Antônio Rapôso TAVARES traversed Brazil from São Paulo to Belém using interlocking river systems, and Fernão Dias Pais died searching for silver and emeralds in São Paulo and Minas Gerais (1681). Such treks, which lasted years, pioneered fluvial and terrestrial routes, and were undertaken strictly for profit in the form of Indian slaves, gold, and precious stones. Their predations on the periphery of Portuguese territories bordering on Upper Peru and New Granada, and to the south, with attacks into Spanish Guairá and Tape, disturbed Luso-Spanish relations.

Sparked by gold-rush fever, the first sustained moves to the west came in the eighteenth century. The São Francisco River and the river systems of Amazon-Madeira-Mamoré-Guaporé and Tieté-Paraná-Paraguay made the interior accessible. Portugal faced boundary disputes with Spain, notably in the Río de la Plata region. Through the treaties of Madrid (1750), Pardo (1761), and SAN ILDEFONSO (1777), and surveys of questionable accuracy, Portugal sought resolution of such disputes. By 1808, much of Brazil—not only on the peripheries but in the vast expanses between settlement nuclei—still was unsurveyed, and unknown and unsettled by Europeans. Settlements were isolated, huddled together around a major town. The frontier was a mathematical conundrum and geopolitical concept rather than a known quantity.

A yardstick for measuring such settlement is the establishment of townships. With the exception of São Paulo, before the eighteenth century urban development was predominantly on the coast. Urbanization was synonymous with port towns and cities—Belém, São Luís, Recife, Salvador, Rio de Janeiro, Santos—which played multiple roles as commercial emporia, administrative centers, and defensive barriers. In the eighteenth century, the crown attempted to stabilize and regulate this moving population by elevating mining encampments to town status in Minas Gerais, Goiás, and Mato Grosso. By 1808, the greatest concentration of urban population was in the northeast. Salvador counted about 51,000; Recife, 25,000; and Rio de Janeiro, 50,000. São Paulo numbered about 24,000 in 1803 and Vila Rica 7,000 inhabitants in 1804. The population of Brazil was predominantly rural.

CROWN AND LOCAL GOVERNMENT

The Portuguese crown was slow to establish a royal presence in Brazil. It declared the dyewood trade a royal monopoly, and farmed it out to contractors. Spurred by French interlopers and threats of foreign occupation, JOÃO III (1521–1557) granted hereditary captaincies to twelve donataries. Each comprised 50 leagues of coast and had no western limit. Each donatary had jurisdiction in civil and criminal cases, made appointments, granted land allocations, and was responsible for defense, colonization, and conversion of Indians. In return, he received revenues and certain privileges and prerogatives.

Only ten captaincies were settled. Lack of capital, initiative, and leadership doomed some; disaffected colonists and Indian attacks undermined others. The only successes were Pernambuco under Duarte Coelho Pereira and São Vicente under Martim Afonso de SOUSA. Flemish capital underwrote the latter, but the shared prosperity was founded on cultivation of sugarcane.

Disenchantment led the crown to induce some donataries to forfeit their rights, a precondition to appointment of a captain-general. In 1549 Tomé de SOUSA took up his post and established a capital at Salvador on the Bay of All Saints. Crown government was consolidated under Governor-General Mem de Sá (1558–1572), who ousted the French from the Bay of Guanabara, founded Rio de Janeiro, defeated coastal Indians, encouraged Jesuit missionaries, and brought order to administration.

Until 1808, the senior crown representative in the colony was a governor-general or, after 1720, a viceroy, who reported to the Casa da India, founded in Lisbon in 1503 in recognition of the importance of Asia to Portugal. The shift in power in Asia from Portugal to the United Provinces in the seventeenth century led to the establishment in 1642 of an OVERSEAS COUNCIL in Lisbon with umbrella responsibility for the administration of the Portuguese empire. The council, along with viceroys and governors-general, acted in consultation with the sovereign, whose decisions were final. No Casa do Brasil was created to administer Portuguese America nor was a special bureaucracy assembled. Colonial policy was formulated in Lisbon, senior civil servants were mostly Portuguese-born and Portuguese-trained, and institutions were modeled on—or extensions of—metropolitan counterparts.

The Estado do Brasil underwent administrative restructurings, usually of short-lived duration. From 1621 to 1652 and from 1654 to 1772 the captaincies of Maranhão, Pará, and some smaller captaincies formed the Estado do Maranhão e Grão-Pará. The southern captaincies were detached from the authority of the governor-general in Bahia, united as the Repartição do Sul, and placed under Governor-General Salvador Correia de SÁ E BENEVIDES in 1658. This was in recognition of his service to king and country. After his death, they reverted to the jurisdiction of the governor-general in Salvador. New captaincies were created to meet new needs for administrative control stemming from demographic growth, changing commercial emphases, and strategic concerns. Gold strikes and immigration to the west led to the creation of the captaincies-general of São Paulo (1720), Minas Gerais (1720), Goiás, and Mato Grosso (1748). By 1800, there were ten captaincies-general and seven subordinate captaincies.

The centralized government of the state of Brazil was in the hands of a governor-general or viceroy, resident in Salvador from 1549 to 1763 and, with the transfer of the capital, thereafter in Rio de Janeiro. He exercised far-reaching jurisdiction over administrative, military, commercial, and fiscal matters; presided over the High Court; assumed responsibility for pacification and protection of Indians; distributed land grants; and made appointments subject to royal approval. He received instructions from the Overseas Council or from the king and reported to Lisbon. Beginning in the latter seventeenth and continuing into the eighteenth century, however, the governors of the captaincies gradually usurped his authority. Although they were subordinate to governors-general or viceroys according to the chain of command, governors often acted without consultation or bypassed the king's senior representative in the colony and dealt directly with the council or king in Lisbon. Gomes Freire de ANDRADE, governor of Rio de Janeiro (1733–1763), saw his jurisdiction expanded so that by 1748 captaincies subordinate to him were more strategically sensitive, commercially important, and extensive than those under the jurisdiction of the viceroy.

During the eighteenth century there were some superb administrators: Pedro de Noronha and Vasco Fernandes Cezar de Menezes were viceroys in Portuguese India and later in Brazil; André de Mello de Castro was governor of Minas Gerais and later viceroy. Among governors, Lourenço de Almeida saw service in India and as governor of Pernambuco and Minas Gerais.

Fiscal matters fell under the jurisdiction of the treasurer-general in the capital, who acted in consultation with a treasury council that included four High Court judges. Each captaincy had a crown-appointed treasurer and staff of whom only the most senior was dispatched from Portugal. The treasury was responsible for overseeing royal financial interests and leasing crown monopolies on such a variety of commodities and services as brazilwood, salt, whale fishery, tobacco sales, or river crossings. Some were leased in Lisbon, as was the case of the lucrative diamond contract. The treasury did not itself collect taxes. This was farmed out in a competitive bidding system and included collection of tithes—an ecclesiastical tax (*dízimos*) inappropriately used as general funds—of 10 percent on all agricultural production, customs dues, and import and export dues on all commodities, including slaves. Such contracts and proprietary offices spurred self-interest, extortionary practices, corruption, and mismanagement, and defaults were frequent.

The Desembargo do Paço in Lisbon appointed magistrates and undertook judicial reviews. Only in 1609 was a high court (*relação*) established in Salvador. This was suppressed in 1626 and reestablished in 1652. A second high court was created in Rio de Janeiro in 1751. These were the supreme courts, from which there was appeal to the CASA DA SUPLICAÇÃO in Lisbon. The chancellor was the chief officer of the High Court, which was manned by ten judges who were well paid, enjoyed privileges and exemptions, and, like all crown appointees, were trained at the University of Coimbra.

Captaincies in Brazil counted one or more judicial COMARCAS, whose chief officer was an *ouvidor geral*. The crown also appointed *juízes de fora*. Career magistrates, including those who were Brazilian born, were rotated. Constraints against engaging in commerce or contracting marriages locally were intended to preserve judicial impartiality but were of limited success. Judges administered Portuguese laws. No codification was made specifically for Brazil, nor was there a counterpart to the Spanish *Código Negro*.

The administration of law was cumbersome; the appeals process was protracted; self-interest and venality in the bureaucracy and among the judiciary made it nigh impossible for all but the very rich and very poor to obtain a fair hearing. Judicial tours of inspection by district judges were too irregular to be effective. The magistracy exercised jurisdiction over areas not strictly judicial and reported to the king on the political, economic, and social state of their regions. As such, they formed part of the checks-and-balances of colonial administration and contributed indirectly to royal decision making for Brazil.

Forts were built and irregular marine patrols were mounted to defend the 4,603 miles of coast against foreign attacks. Professional officers commanded troops of the line, but defense of the colony depended on militia regiments under honorary masters-of-the-field or colonels. The quality of military personnel was low. They were ill equipped, underpaid, often without formal training, and wore ragged uniforms. The exceptions were two troops of dragoons posted to the Diamond District in the 1720s to impose stability and curb contraband in diamonds. Regular and militia troops escorted bullion shipments, attacked Indians, suppressed groups of runaway slaves, and crushed revolts. Free blacks and mulattoes had their own regiments and distinguished themselves fighting against the DUTCH. They won a hard-fought and protracted battle to have officers of their own color, the same privileges and exemptions granted to their white counterparts, and eligibility for promotion.

Crown government in Brazil was undermined by difficulties of communication to and from Lisbon and within the colony. Rugged terrain and vast distances made law enforcement difficult, military campaigns logistic nightmares, and tax collection partial. Effectiveness of crown government declined in proportion to increased distance from administrative centers. Viceroys, governors-general, and governors were forced to react to local crises, often without adequate consultation. They were exposed to charges of *lèse-majesté*, to detractors maligning them at court, and to formal administrative reviews during (*devassas*) and concluding (*residências*) their terms. Renewals of triennial terms made crown officials vulnerable to local pressures. Many invested financially, politically, socially, and emotionally in Brazil. Although the most senior crown officials were often well trained, effective, impartial, and honest administrators, the standard deteriorated rapidly in subordinate positions. Disputes over jurisdiction and ill-defined mandates led to turf wars between different branches of government as well as individuals. Ecclesiastics did not hold high public offices. Nor, with rare exceptions, did persons of African or Jewish descent.

## MUNICIPAL GOVERNMENT

The SENADO DA CÂMARA was the local town council. Elections occurred annually. Eligibility requirements included age, property ownership, financial and social standing, and civil status. Clerics were excluded, as were, for the most part, persons of African descent. Two "ordinary judges" presided over a council of three, and there was a procurator. Paid appointees included a scribe, attorney, doctor, and in some cases a surgeon and public health and law enforcement officers. Responsibilities included price regulation, setting professional standards, overseeing guild exams, licensing, public health, marketing regulations, taxation, all public services, public works, maintaining public order, and celebrating religious and civil holidays. The "judges," who usually lacked legal training, had limited jurisdiction in civil cases of the first instance.

Municipal councils had a high degree of autonomy and enough political and economic clout to influence legislation and policies by bringing pressure to bear on a viceroy or governor and at court. The crown attempted to bring councils to heel by appointment of a *juiz de fôra* in an oversight capacity, but with limited effect. Councillors enjoyed privileges and exemptions and pressed for privileges granted to councillors in Lisbon and Oporto. Passions and tensions ran high at election time and rigging was not unknown. Councils were not self-perpetuating oligarchies, but membership represented powerful family and other corporate groups. Policies reflected self-interest as well as the public good.

## CHURCH AND RELIGION

By virtue of PADROADO REAL conceded by papal bulls predating establishment of royal government in Brazil, the crown could create archbishoprics and bishoprics, make appointments, and set ecclesiastical and missionary policy. By 1808, Brazil counted one archbishopric in Salvador (established in 1676) and six bishoprics: Pernambuco, Rio de Janeiro, Maranhão, Mariana, São Paulo, and Pará. There were ecclesiastical courts. Although ecclesiastical dignitaries were of high caliber, priests were often poorly educated, poorly paid, and vulnerable to venality, self-interest, and profit. Many depended on their congregations for financial support, levied outrageous fees for services, and engaged in contraband and commerce. The church never formally opposed the institution of SLAVERY and had a mixed record in evangelization and religious education of slaves but, although there were examples aplenty of backsliding and syncretism, Roman Catholicism was generally the accepted norm. The church owned landed estates, urban properties, and slaves, and often clashed with the religious orders, the Society of Jesus in particular.

The Holy Office, or INQUISITION, had no separate tribunal in Brazil. Clerics resident in the colony were designated to represent it in enquiries. Agents of the Inquisition from Portugal made special visits to Bahia (1591–1593 and 1618), Pernambuco (1593–1595) and Belém (1763–1769), but the most intensive period of enquiries throughout Brazil was the first half of the eighteenth century. Expulsion of JEWS from Portugal led many to come to Brazil in the sixteenth century. Emigration was particularly heavy between 1587 and 1601, when Jews were permitted to sell their goods before leaving Portugal. Jewish emigrés established congregations in Pernambuco in the seventeenth century. The rumor that many Catholic priests were Judaizers (secret Jews) called into question the sincerity of forced conversions. Crypto-Jews could not escape the charge of being ''of tainted blood'' (*de sangue infecta*). Denunciations against them were made in secret. There were few charges of heresy; most crypto-Jews were accused of sexual deviance, bigamy, adultery, blasphemy, and practice of Jewish rites. Seventeen Judaizers were extradited from Brazil to Portugal in the first half of the seventeenth century and eight in the second. Most were from Bahia. In the eighteenth century most were from Rio de Janeiro. There was intensive persecution of Judaizers who were extradited. Between 1644 and 1748, eighteen Brazilian Jews were executed by the Inquisition in Lisbon. Other punishments included flogging, the galleys, jail, and property confiscation.

Religious orders in the colony included JESUITS, FRANCISCANS, DOMINICANS, BENEDICTINES, AUGUSTINIANS, and CARMELITES. The fact that half of the bishops in Brazil came from their ranks indicates their strength. The orders played roles of varying importance in evangelization and missionary activities. They provided social services such as hospitals, apothecaries, prison assistance, and alms. The religious orders became wealthy as owners of estates and urban properties and engaged in commerce as well. In the absence of a banking system, they played a major role in the colonial economy as the only sources for credit and loans. All maintained monasteries. Because of their wealth and large numbers, they were charged as drains on colonial resources; although many were Brazilian-born, few became provincials, posts most often held by Portuguese.

The first of many convents for women was established in Salvador in 1677. Such institutions owed their genesis less to religious than secular factors: first, to obviate the practice of predominantly elite families sending daughters to convents in Portugal rather than having them marry in Brazil; second, to curb the currency drain from the colony in the form of dowries. Convents in Brazil were places of seclusion or retreat for young women, for the divorced or separated, or for wives whose husbands were absent. After a probationary period, supplicants took vows and were admitted as nuns in one of two categories, namely of the black or the white veil, a distinction which reflected the social background of the supplicants, with nuns of the black veil enjoying higher status. The majority of women were in temporary vows. Convents owned properties, engaged in commercial activities, and made interest-generating loans. Visitors to Brazil lauded the musical and culinary skills of such conventuals and speculated on sexual activities, but could not undermine the religious devotion of such nuns.

The Society of Jesus, unchallenged as the most influential, wealthiest, and most commercially active religious entity in the colony, also numbered the best-trained and educated religious and most dedicated missionaries. Manuel da NÓBREGA, José de ANCHIETA, and Antônio VIEIRA, whose missionary zeal carried him to the Amazon, spearheaded evangelization, especially among Indians. The Jesuits operated the only post-secondary schools, which did not exclude persons of African descent; their colleges made a unique contribution to education in the colony.

The Jesuits protected the Indians from labor-hungry colonists by collecting them in ALDEIAS. The *aldeias*, with regular work days, organization, and prohibitions of nudity and polygamy, however, eroded Indian authority and cultural traditions and isolated rather than prepared the Indians for integration into mainstream colonial society. The control of the *aldeias* as well as the Jesuit activity on the peripheries, in Maranhão and Pará, and in the disputed borderlands to the south, created suspicion that resulted in temporary and regional expulsions of the Jesuits, culminating in the expulsion of the society from Brazil in 1759.

THE ECONOMY

The Portuguese crown regarded Brazil as a ''milch cow'' to be exploited for the benefit of the metropolis as a source of raw materials where production was heavily regulated and imports and exports (including slaves) were taxed repeatedly. The economy, in which the crown held monopolies, was export-oriented. Colonists were also expected to contribute to the costs of royal marriages, the rebuilding of Lisbon after the 1755 earthquake, the upkeep of garrisons, and the ''extraordinary'' expenditures of the crown. Tithes (*dízimos*) on agricultural products, a 20 percent tax on extractive industries, and prohibition of manufacture that might compete with Portuguese industry heavily discouraged colonial economic and commercial initiatives.

The mainstay of the Brazilian economy was agriculture, and SUGAR was preeminent. Colonists built on experience gained in Madeira and São Tomé. Sugarcane was introduced into Brazil during the captaincy period. Bahia and Pernambuco retained their preeminence, but there was also production in Rio de Janeiro and elsewhere. By 1570, Brazilian production rivaled that of Madeira and São Tomé. The industry thrived until 1610, when production flagged, but it recovered during the seventeenth century despite Dutch destruction of mills. The industry was vulnerable to inflation, rising costs, prices on European markets, global demand, competition from the Caribbean, and changing labor-supply conditions in Africa. In Brazil, transportation inadequacies, crop disease, ants, and weather affected productivity and distribution. But sugar was the most consistent generator of revenue throughout the colonial period.

Production demanded heavy capital investment in labor, land, and machinery. Smaller plantations with thirty to forty slaves predominated, although some had two hundred or more. Cane was crushed in oxen- or water-driven mills, and the juice boiled, scummed, and purged before the syrup was collected in earthernware jars where it crystallized. The only technological innovation was in the early seventeenth century when the three-roller vertical mill replaced the two-roller vertical mill. There were two basic grades: white and *muscavado*. An important derivative was rum.

Tobacco from Bahia, dipped in molasses after curing, was exported to West Africa in exchange for slaves. For smoking, or when taken as snuff, it found markets in Europe and even Asia. Other regional export economies included cacao and, later, rice, cotton, and coffee. Brazil produced a wide range of tropical crops. In the subsistence sector manioc, maize, beans, and wheat were important. Urban demands led to manipulation of supply to force up prices. Livestock-raising was important in the interior of the northeast, the north, Minas Gerais, and Rio Grande do Sul. There was a domestic market for meat, tallow, and salted meat. Hides were used in-country as well as exported.

The extractive industries came to importance in the eighteenth century. Gold production in Minas Gerais peaked in the 1730s but strikes in Goiás (1725), Mato Grosso (1734), and elsewhere led to overall production increases into the early 1750s. Alluvial panning was predominant. There was some gallery mining, but the industry was characterized by labor intensity. Inefficient modes of production and absence of technological innovation contributed to its decline as much as overregulation. A variety of expedients to tax production, including capitation taxes, quotas, and smelting houses, did not stem endemic contraband. Gold production provided an important incentive to subsistence agriculture and stimulated commerce and merchant communities in port cities, notably Rio de Janeiro.

Diamonds were officially discovered in the 1720s near Vila do Príncipe. After flooding the European market, the crown controlled production through demarcating a closely supervised Diamond District and accepting bids for the diamond contract. In 1771, however, the contract was abolished and operation reverted to the crown.

Brazil was part of a global trade network that included Europe, Africa, India, and East Asia. There was a thriving but illegal trade from Spanish America through Río de la Plata and the Portuguese Colônia do Sacramento (founded 1680). Brazil was superbly endowed with deep-water ports which became commercial emporia. Imports from Portugal and Europe included farm animals, flour, salt, olive oil, cod, cheese, wine, textiles, manufactured goods, and machinery, which were exchanged for agricultural products, gold, and diamonds. Slaves from Africa were paid for in tobacco and even bullion, and homeward-bound East Indiamen unloaded silks, china, and oriental exotica. From Africa came bananas, plantains, certain gourds, okra, squashes, and oils, in return for sweet potatoes, peanuts, manioc, maize corn, squashes, pumpkins, and capsicums. In the sixteenth and seventeenth centuries much of the carrying was in Dutch bottoms. There was a thriving domestic trade along the coast and inland by land and navigable rivers; there were also local and regional networks for distribution.

FOREIGN INTERLOPERS

Brazil's prosperity, coupled with changing alliances in Europe, made it vulnerable. At the forefront of the BRAZILWOOD trade through the 1540s, the French seized the Portuguese factory at Itamaracá in 1531. In 1555 Nicolas Durand de VILLEGAGNON established a settlement in the Bay of Guanabara until dreams of "La France Antarctique" were ended by Mem de Sá in 1565. The French also established São Luis but were expelled from Maranhão in 1615. They briefly occupied Rio de Janeiro in 1711. The ascension of Spain's PHILIP II to the Portuguese throne led to the union of Portugal with Spain (1580–1640).

Brazil bore the brunt of the predations of the Dutch West India Company: the seizure of Brazilian vessels, the invasion and occupation of Bahia (1624–1625), and the occupation of Pernambuco (1630–1654). The Dutch period in Pernambuco was at its height during the governorship (1637–1644) of Count Johan MAURITS of Nassau-Siegen. Artists, botanists, and zoologists recorded in words and pictures the flora and fauna of Brazil. Religious toleration made Dutch Brazil a haven for Jews and Judaizers. But wars of attrition devastated the northeast and revenues from sugar failed to reach Dutch expectations. Beginning with a 1645 revolt led by João Fernandes Vieira, the Dutch were ousted in 1654.

The British did not invade or occupy Brazil but were influential in commerce from the seventeenth century when Charles II took a Portuguese bride (1662). England enjoyed commercial concessions and provided a market for Brazilian sugar in exchange for British manufactured goods, notably textiles and, in the eighteenth century, grain. British exports to Portugal were reexported to Brazilian markets. Portuguese wines and then Brazilian gold paid for such purchases. The British provided credit for Luso-Brazilian merchants in the eighteenth century and were a constant presence in colonial commerce. After 1776 U.S. vessels regularly put into Brazilian ports.

LABOR

Indian labor was coopted for collection of brazilwood. Indians worked on sugar plantations of the northeast, often alongside African slaves, until their phasing out in favor of Africans by the 1630s. Despite prohibitions on enslavement except in special circumstances, Indian labor continued legally and illegally, especially in São Paulo, Rio de Janeiro, and the north. Demands for more labor led the Portuguese to extend to Brazil a trade structure already institutionalized between West Africa and the Atlantic Islands and Portugal in the mid-fifteenth century.

African slaves were the field hands of plantations and cattle ranches and worked in diamond and gold placer mining as well as in domestic service. Some had skills as artisans, porters, or boatmen. In the fields and mines, especially, they had terrible conditions, long hours, physically demanding labor, and suffered harsh punishments. They lived in crowded quarters, were exposed to diseases, suffered dietary deficiencies, and had a low average life expectancy. Domestic slaves may have had less arduous working conditions but were also subject to physical and mental abuse. Some negotiated agreements with owners whereby they could practice a trade or other occupation without direct supervision on condition that a portion of their income be given to the owner. While encouraging illegal activities such as prostitution and contraband, and spurring some to run away, this system enabled slaves to acquire money enough to buy their freedom.

There was a free wage-labor sector which included Indians and persons of African descent. The former were employed in regional industries such as making rope out of fibers, gathering fruits, logging, and sail-making, and in expeditions as scouts. The latter worked as overseers, drovers, ferrymen, and tradespeople. But the majority of skilled jobs were held by whites who dominated the guilds, owned taverns and shops, and held supervisory positions.

SOCIETY

Colonial Brazil was paradoxical in that it bore the European legacy of a society of estates, yet permitted increasing (especially in the eighteenth century) social and financial mobility and blurring of lines of social or racial demarcation. Place of birth, pedigree, religious orthodoxy, occupation, wealth, civil status, and legal status as free or slave were less subject to interpretation than were skin hues and attributes based on perception. Among persons of European descent, there were tensions between Portuguese born and Brazilian born; among persons of African descent, between those of different African "nations," between mulattoes and blacks, between free and slave, and even between those who had been born free or had bought their own freedom, or had been given their freedom by an owner. In a society characterized by miscegenation and subjective racial classifications for persons of mixed blood (*caboclo, mameluco, mestiço* for Indian-Caucasian; *mulato, pardo* for African-Caucasian; *cafuzo* for Indian-African), division by racial phenotypes is inappropriate. Although eligibility for public office was denied to persons of African descent and New Christians, there were exceptions. Prominent persons with African blood included Henrique DIAS, the black veteran guerrilla leader who distinguished himself in the War of Divine Liberty against the Dutch; João Fernandes Vieira, commander of a force of blacks and mulattoes who was described in an official document as the "prime cause" of the Portuguese capture of Pernambuco from the Dutch; and Antônio VIEIRA, the Jesuit who championed the cause of black slaves and Amerindians. Fluidity and not rigidity increasingly characterized social and racial relations in colonial Brazil.

The ruling class was usually white, of Portuguese descent, and landowning. Families such as the Albuquerque Coelho in Pernambuco, Correia de Sá in Rio de Janeiro, or Dias d'Avila in Bahia were all-powerful. Sugar planters and mill owners (*senhores de engenhos*) and cattle ranchers, often characterized as "poderosos do sertão" (powerful men of the backlands), exerted strong control over the social, commercial, and political life of the colony. In the eighteenth century they were joined by an emerging merchant and business community, especially in Salvador and Rio de Janeiro. Mining entrepreneurs dominated Minas Gerais, Mato Grosso, and Goiás. Dignitaries of church and state also belonged to the ruling class.

An urban middle class was composed of lawyers, doctors, surgeons, businessmen and merchants, priests and friars, and low-ranking civil servants at the upper end and, at the lower, artisans, store and tavern owners, and free-wage laborers. In the eighteenth century, increasing manumissions created an African community of freepersons engaged in commerce. The underclass included "tame" Indians, slaves, and a large number of poor and destitute who were stricken by disease and malnutrition, and reduced to begging.

The basic social unit was the family, either nuclear or extended, with linkages through marriage or godparenthood. Usually marriages were between persons of equal social or economic standing and civil status. For the white elite and upper classes, marriage was an instrument to consolidate and extend a family's reputation and fortune. The female partner was often younger than the male, sometimes disproportionately so. DOWRIES were important and took the form of currency or land, property, or cattle.

There was a double standard governing female and male behavior: white females were expected to be chaste, faithful, and secluded; for the male, no shame or sanctions were attached to sexual promiscuity, extramarital relations, and the taking of a concubine. There was a double standard (among whites) also regarding white and nonwhite women: the latter were expected to be sexually available and have lower moral standards. Recent studies, however, undermine the stereotype of the patriarchal family as the norm for the colony. While accurate for the upper classes, many middle- and lower-class families were headed by women. Desertion and widowhood, not infrequent, threw responsibilities onto women. Among whites, widows administered ranches, estates, and mines; women of African descent—both slave and free—played a crucial role in marketing. Exorbitant fees led to a low incidence of legal marriages. Marriages between free persons of African descent and slaves were less common. The civil status of offspring followed that of the mother. Some slaves would find a free or freed woman of color or Indian woman to bear their children. Indian-black or Indian-white unions were less frequent than white-black unions.

URBAN CULTURE

Only Salvador, Rio de Janeiro, and, fleetingly, Vila Rica do Ouro Preto developed an urban culture. Urban planning was not absent, but topography dictated city configurations after the initial phase. The central area had (where appropriate) governor's and bishop's palaces; city chambers; main church; Jesuit college; monasteries; and the Santa Casa da Misericórdia, a charitable organization. Portugal maintained a cultural hegemony over colonial Brazil. Despite requests, no university was authorized, nor was there a legal printing press, and the book trade was closely supervised. Brazilian students attended the University of Coimbra or other European universities. Institutions of higher education were limited to Jesuit colleges.

In the eighteenth century, literary academies came into being but were usually of short duration and little lasting impact. Theater was a form of recreation. Religious music showed mainly European antecedents, while secular music bore both Portuguese and African imprints. Religious art and architecture also derived from Europe, but Brazilian baroque, which found its greatest expression in Minas Gerais, was unique. There were few examples of secular art of any quality and the fine arts were not prominent. A number of persons of African descent were sculptors, painters, instrumentalists, and composers. The lay brotherhoods were major promoters of architecture and decorative arts in the building of churches and chapels, but there was no tradition of artistic patronage among the elites or merchant classes. The colonial literary scene included clerically penned treatises, histories, and poetry, ranging from the satirical Gregório de MATOS to the epic *O Uruguai*, written by José Basílio da GAMA.

LATE COLONIAL PERIOD

The reign of JOÃO V (1706–1750) was a watershed in terms of absolutist rule. JOSÉ I (1750–1777) appointed Sebastião José de Carvalho e Mello, later marqués of POMBAL, secretary of state for foreign affairs and war. José continued the centralization of power: the authority of the Overseas Council was eroded by ministerial appointments; new administrative captaincies were created; and the capital was moved from Salvador to Rio de Janeiro in 1763. A new Royal Treasury was created in Lisbon and treasury boards were established in each captaincy. Boards of inspection were established in major port cities.

In an attempt to nationalize the Luso-Brazilian economy, monopoly trading companies, such as Company of Grão-Pará e Maranhão (1755) and Company of Pernambuco e Paraíba (1759), were created to offer more regular shipping, promote exports, and provide labor. The fleet system was abolished and prohibitions lifted on coastal trade. The economic center of Brazil moved from the northeast to the center-southern region.

Pombal's measures could not rectify the mid-century economic downturn prompted by the decline in gold production, but his measures did stimulate Brazilian agriculture. Toward the end of the century sugar exports increased, tobacco was flourishing, exports of hides were up, and newer crops of cotton, cacao, and coffee found European markets. New regions—Pará (cacao) and Maranhão (cotton and rice)—became major producers. There was diversification in the agricultural economy. Cotton moved into second place behind sugar as the major export crop. Pombal's attempts to shore up merchants and make them less dependent on foreign capital and thence more competitive led to a decrease in British imports and a downturn in Britain as a market for Brazilian exports while stimulating commerce between captaincies. Some of Pombal's reforms and initiatives were rejected by his successors, but he had set in motion an inexorable momentum for change.

During this period the Jesuits were expelled from Brazil (1759) and the remaining religious orders weakened. Indian *aldeias* were placed under secular control. Pombal abolished the distinction between Old and New Christians (1773). But he did not remove the double standard applied to persons of African descent and Indians or products of Indian-white liaisons; laws to benefit Indians in terms of personal freedoms, ownership, and right to trade were not matched by legislation favoring Africans.

Earlier Luso-Spanish rivalries in the Río de la Plata region escalated into warfare, which cost both parties a great deal of money and manpower. Spanish attacks on Colônia do Sacramento culminated in its conquest in 1762 and subsequent Spanish invasion of Rio Grande do Sul. Colônia was returned, but a Spanish expeditionary force under Pedro Antônio de CEVALLOS took Colônia and Santa Catarina in 1777. The Treaty of San Ildefonso (1777) returned Santa Catarina and Rio Grande do Sul to Portugal, but the Portuguese ceded Colônia. In 1801 Portugal made incursions into Siete Missiones and held the conquered lands.

Brazil had not been devoid of collective uprisings, born of social tensions within the colony or reflecting resentment toward decisions taken in Lisbon which favored metropolitan interests over those of the colonists of Portuguese America. Such were short-lived and of local impact: the BECKMAN REVOLT in Maranhão (1684); Guerra dos Emboabas (1708–1709) in Minas Gerais; Guerra dos Mascates in Pernambuco (1710–1711); and the uprising over proposed foundry houses in Vila Rica (1720). The Enlightenment spurred colonial self-assessment vis-à-vis the metropolis and fanned aspirations if not of separation from Portugal at least of more control over colonial affairs. Two such movements were aborted. The 1789 INCONFIDÊNCIA MINEIRA in Minas Gerais was made up of a good measure of elite self-interest, reaction against proposed supplementary tax-

**Brazil at the End of the Colonial Era**

ation, and a corrupt governor. Its hero and front man, and the only one to be hanged, was Joaquim José da SILVA XAVIER, better known as Tiradentes. The CONSPIR- ACY OF THE TAILORS in Bahia (1798) involved a group of mulattoes espousing ideals of liberty, equality, and fra- ternity, as well as a Bahian church.

At the end of the colonial era Brazil was prosperous: exports and domestic commerce were growing; popu- lation had increased; cities were growing. When Napo- leon invaded Portugal in 1807, the prince regent Dom João, with British assistance, evacuated his court from Lisbon in November 1807. After touching at Salvador, he disembarked in Rio on 7 March 1808. Dom João opened the ports of Brazil to trade with all friendly nations and rescinded prohibitions on colonial manu- facturing, unknowingly paving the way toward Brazil- ian independence. While still a colony of Portugal,

Brazil was the residence of a European monarch and his court and the seat of metropolitan government—a dis- tinction unique in Latin America.

CHARLES R. BOXER, *Salvador de Sá and the Struggle for Brazil and Angola, 1602–1686* (1952), *The Dutch in Brazil, 1624–1654* (1957), and *The Golden Age of Brazil, 1695–1750* (1962); GILBERTO FREYRE, *The Masters and the Slaves: A Study in the Development of Brazilian Civilization,* translated by SAMUEL PUTNAM, rev. ed., (1963); CAIO PRADO, JR., *The Colonial Background of Modern Bra- zil,* translated by SUZETTE MACEDO (1967); DAURIL ALDEN, *Royal Government in Colonial Brazil with Special Reference to the Admin- istration of the Marquis of Lavradio, Viceroy 1769–1779* (1968); A. J. R. RUSSELL-WOOD, *Fidalgos and Philanthropists: The Santa Casa da Misericórdia of Bahia, 1550–1755* (1968); KENNETH R. MAXWELL, *Conflicts and Conspiracies: Brazil and Portugal, 1750– 1808* (1973); STUART B. SCHWARTZ, *Sovereignty and Society in Colonial Brazil: The High Court of Bahia and Its Judges, 1609–1751* (1973); A. J. R. RUSSELL-WOOD, ed., *From Colony to Nation: Essays* on the Independence of Brazil (1975); JOHN HEMMING, Red Gold: The Conquest of the Brazilian Indians (1978); JAMES LANG, Portuguese Brazil: The King's Plantation (1979); A. J. R. RUSSELL-WOOD, The Black Man in Slavery and Freedom in Colonial Brazil (1982); STUART B. SCHWARTZ, Sugar Plantations in the Formation of Brazilian Society: Bahia, 1550–1835 (1985); LESLIE BETHELL, ed., Colonial Brazil (1987); JOHN HEMMING, Amazon Frontier: The Defeat of the Brazilian Indians (1987); ALIDA C. METCALF, Family and Frontier in Colonial Brazil: Santana de Parnaíba, 1580–1822 (1991); MURIEL NAZZARI, Disappearance of the Dowry: Women, Families, and Social Change in São Paulo, Brazil (1600–1900) (1991); A. J. R. RUSSELL-WOOD, Society and Government in Colonial Brazil, 1500–1822 (1992); STUART B. SCHWARTZ, Slaves, Peasants, and Rebels: Reconsidering Brazilian Slavery (1992).

A. J. R. RUSSELL-WOOD

See also **Mining; Slave Trade.**

### Brazil 1808–1889

#### FROM COLONY TO INDEPENDENCE

Brazil's nineteenth-century political trajectory was unique in the Western Hemisphere in that it became and remained a monarchy for eighty-one years. This was largely due to a single peculiar event: when Napoleon's armies invaded the Iberian Peninsula in 1807, ostensibly to punish the Portuguese for violations of his continental policy, the prince regent, João, the future JOÃO VI, decided to retreat to his dominions in South America. Escorted by the British navy, he arrived in Rio de Janeiro with all his court and the royal treasury to begin what became a fourteen-year sojourn. His arrival represented the first step toward independence, since the king immediately opened the ports of Brazil to foreign shipping and turned the colonial capital into the seat of government.

To this end, João installed novelties that until then had been forbidden to the colonials: among them printing presses, schools of higher learning, iron mills, and a gunpowder factory. He established a botanical garden to acclimatize plants that might diversify the economy and contracted numerous foreign scientists and technicians to stimulate mining, metallurgy, and the fine arts. Unfortunately, his reign also intensified most of the policies that had made the colony a hellish place for most of its inhabitants: he permitted the renewal of attacks on native tribal peoples, he condoned the continuation of the SLAVE TRADE even while signing a treaty to restrict it, he accelerated the bestowal of vast land grants upon courtiers and local notables, he persisted in expansionism in the Río de la Plata, where patriots were seeking to establish republics independent of Spain, and he resisted forcefully the spread among his subjects of the liberal and democratic ideals of the North American and French Revolutions. Dependent on the British for help in regaining his kingdom, João agreed in 1810 to reduce tariffs on British goods and granted British merchants extraterritoriality, a humiliating concession.

João remained in Rio de Janeiro even after the fall of Napoleon. In 1815, Brazil was declared a kingdom, co-equal with Portugal, partly to cast a larger shadow among the diplomats assembled at the Congress of Vienna. João's tropical idyll was finally brought to an end by liberal revolutionaries in Lisbon, who in 1820 called together a parliament and demanded his return. Fearing the loss of his European throne, he complied, leaving his son PEDRO behind as regent. Soon after, Brazilian delegates to the Portuguese parliament withdrew, incensed at mercantilist proposals that would have returned them to a colonial status.

#### INDEPENDENCE

The drift toward separation accelerated as Pedro gave evidence of his willingness to lead such a movement. For the rich, monarchy offered the prospect of legitimacy and, therefore, stability, qualities frighteningly lacking among the new Spanish American republics but essential in a state that would contain a majority of slaves and their descendants. Independence was declared, by the prince regent himself, on 7 September 1822. The Portuguese garrisons were cut off by sea and nearly all were persuaded to evacuate peacefully, so that the costs of war were small. Brazil was declared an empire, to emphasize again to the Europeans the vast potential of a territory grander than any of theirs, even the czar of Russia's. Pedro's marriage to an Austrian princess, LEOPOLDINA, had already established an impressive dynastic linkage.

Great Britain, which saw an advantage in the establishment of a strong monarchical, liberal state in South America, acted as broker in the delicate issue of recognition. Although the United States quickly recognized Brazil, none of the European monarchies would do so until Portugal had been reconciled to its loss. This was at last accomplished when Brazil accepted responsibility for a part of the Portuguese national debt—even though João had taken the whole of the treasury from Rio de Janeiro when he returned to Lisbon. Brazil, under duress, also renewed the trade treaty with Britain, including its disastrous provisions of low tariffs and extraterritoriality.

#### THE EMPIRE

Pedro convened an assembly to frame a constitution but, displeased with the result, sent soldiers to close the assembly down and wrote one of his own that reserved the crown's right not only to executive but also to so-called moderative powers, including those of dismissing cabinets and legislatures and of naming a council of state and the senate. Participation in political life was limited by indirect elections and income qualifications for office holding and voting. The abolition of slavery was proposed by the savant José Bonifácio de ANDRADA E SILVA, Pedro's closest adviser, but it was not given serious consideration, nor did Brazil honor renewed commitments to the British to restrict the slave trade. The legislature abolished royal land grants but could not agree on an alternate means of alienating frontier land; consequently, land began to be usurped on a vast scale, in a contest that excluded prospective farmers of modest means.

Pedro soon wore away his popularity among the Brazilian elite. His "bestowed" constitution caused a sizable rebellion in the Northeast. He leaned too much on emigré Portuguese cronies of questionable repute. His public affair with a married woman, D. Domitila de Castro, whom he ennobled, scandalized them, and when his wife died, as it was said of a broken heart, he had to settle for a much less advantageous second marriage to Princess AMÉLIA, a niece of the king of Bavaria. Pedro's foreign adventures were even more damaging. He persisted in the campaign to incorporate Uruguay into his realm, but, faced with military defeats, rising deficits, and inflationary pressures, he was forced to recognize its independence, again with the good offices of the British. Finally, after the death of his father João, Pedro used state resources to try to put his daughter Maria on the throne of Portugal, an ambition that looked toward eventual reunification. In 1831, angered by bottle-throwing anti-Portuguese rioters in the capital and seething disloyalty in the army, Pedro abdicated and departed for Portugal.

THE REGENCY

Left behind was his son, PEDRO II, who was too young to take the throne. A regency was formed, at first a triumvirate. Its agenda was decidedly liberal and decentralizing, a reaction to the authoritarian emperor. New laws were passed or old ones newly enforced to create provincial assemblies, to turn much of the administration of justice to locally elected or nominated judges, and to guarantee jury trials and habeas corpus. The COUNCIL OF STATE, considered too much an arbitrary instrument of monarchical power, was abolished. Entailed estates (of which there had been few) were abolished. None of these measures could have any effect, however, upon the informal institutions of elite power, the ties of kinship, loyalties, and connections that underlay party membership and penetrated the bureaucracy. Arranged marriages, dowries, godparenthood, nepotism, and clientelism all stood as respected social bulwarks against the penetration of individualism, competition, and social mobility.

The regency carried out similarly ineffectual forays against the institution of slavery. Indian slavery was abolished and the African slave trade declared illegal. Unfortunately, many of the semisedentary tribes that might have served the purpose of steady labor had already disappeared. Along the frontier settlers thereafter followed their own policy of extermination of tribal peoples who chose resistance over retreat. The regency took no effective measures to enforce its ban on the African trade, which only intensified under the threat of the new law.

The interim government's greatest threat, however, was that of regionalism, unacknowledged during the first reign. Support for the throne waned the greater the distance from Rio de Janeiro. Despite the ADDITIONAL ACT OF 1834, the central government appointed the provincial presidents and judges and controlled most sources of tax revenue. In the southernmost province of Rio Grande do Sul, the policy of low tariffs ruined beef jerky producers, who could not compete in the domestic market with those of Buenos Aires. This conflict, and

Rio de Janeiro. Reproduced from Johann Moritz Rugendas, *Malerische Reise in Brasilian* (Paris, 1835). BY PERMISSION OF THE HOUGHTON LIBRARY, HARVARD UNIVERSITY.

continued cross-border involvement in the affairs of Uruguay, led to the FARROUPILHA REVOLT (1835–1845). In the north, the bloodiest rebellion, the Cabanagem revolt (1834–1840), broke out in Pará province, where struggles between political factions led finally to an uprising by the enslaved Indian and African masses. Indeed, the threat of social revolution everywhere forced the liberal regency to reimpose central authority, accompanied by ferocious reprisals against lower-class participants.

THE SECOND REIGN

These troubles were a mirror of those of the former Spanish viceroyalties, which fragmented further during this period. It is remarkable that Brazil weathered this storm and remained intact. At court, the more conservative faction sought to put a stop to the decentralization and liberalizing tendencies of the regency—policies which it supposed would eventuate in a republican revolution—by bringing Pedro II to the throne before the age of constitutional majority. The precocious Pedro himself agreed to this measure, a veiled sort of coup d'état, and took the throne in 1840.

Pedro II turned out to be an ideal monarch for balancing his country's political and economic forces. He favored the most gradual of reforms, so that, until the end of his reign, he appeared to their proponents, including the slaves, to favor them, and to those opposed to reform, including the slave owners, to protect them from the reformers. Two law schools, founded in 1831 in Recife and São Paulo, provided the empire a class of loyal bureaucrats who staffed the state administration. The factions of the regency evolved into Liberal and Conservative parties, which Pedro balanced against each other through the use of the moderating power. The army's senior general, the duke of Caxias, Luís Alves de LIMA E SILVA, was a close friend of the emperor, and the leading officers associated themselves with one party or another, which guaranteed their advancement as ministries succeeded each other. The emperor used his power to appoint councillors and senators and to bestow honors and lifetime peerages to reward service and loyalty within the established order. The ministry came to be directed by a prime minister, responsible to his party, so that for all the world the second empire resembled Westminster.

The empire interfered very little in the rights of citizens: freedom of speech, the press, and association were openly exercised. But the legislature did not end income requirements on the right to vote, and indirect elections and the lifetime senate were preserved. Unhappily, elections were an entire fraud, engineered by whichever ministry had been called to power. Local party leaders, furthermore, frequently resorted to election-time violence.

The reign of Pedro II, given these arrangements, could not be entirely tranquil. Regional rebellions, however, did come to an end. Liberals rose up in 1842 and 1848, briefly and unsuccessfully. The mass of the population, however, remained entirely alienated from government and its decisions. The squatters' rights of frontier dwellers were continually ignored, those among the poor who had not sworn fealty to an elite family risked impressment into the army—the equivalent of a death sentence—and everywhere intermittent unrest and flight among the slaves demanded much of the attention of the police and militia. On occasions these outrages caused open rebellion.

The government nevertheless was much fortified by the appearance of a profitable export to replace the decadent gold mines—COFFEE. Conveniently for taxation purposes, coffee was produced in the region surrounding the capital of Rio de Janeiro. Coffee was well suited to local soils and climate and in demand by the rapidly growing urban markets of the industrialized countries, especially Germany and the United States. Coffee was the salvation of a moribund plantation system. SUGAR had gone into decline as more fertile areas came into production and Europeans began growing beet sugar.

It is remarkable that this vast subcontinent was unable to produce any significant amount of any other commodity for world trade. For a brief period during and after civil war in the United States, COTTON became an important export, fostered by British agents. In the final years of the empire, RUBBER, gathered from wild trees in the Amazon basin under conditions differing only superficially from slavery, grew rapidly in value and volume. Unfortunately, it was destined to be cultivated as an exotic in southeast Asia, just as coffee had been transferred to Brazil. Coffee profits made possible the replacement of mule trails, which had been the nearly exclusive means of transport, with railways, at least in the southeast, beginning in 1867. The first steamboat braved the currents of the Amazon in 1853, and Brazil was connected with Europe by telegraph cable in 1874.

The second reign increased the empire's range of economic independence when, upon the lapse of its commercial treaty with Great Britain, it refused to renew on the same terms. Brazil soon began to increase its tariffs, achieving protection for a number of locally manufactured products, including Rio Grande do Sul's jerky. In retaliation, the British began to press much harder for the abolition of the slave trade, a business that now was entirely in the hands of local or emigré merchants, well connected at court. When the British squadron went so far as to sail into Brazilian harbors to capture slavers, however, the government decided in 1850 to enforce the law of 7 November 1831 that abolished the African slave trade rather than admit its inability to defend its waters against superior forces.

REFORMS

At mid-century a reform ministry undertook a number of measures designed to overcome the country's more and more evident backwardness relative to the industrializing countries. A commercial code based on the

British model was implemented to foster foreign trade. Increased banking activities were authorized, as well as guarantees of interest on railroad bonds. The anomalous lack of a law on the alienation of public lands was at last resolved with passage of the LAND LAW OF 1850: in the future they were to be sold in lots, the better to stimulate smallholding. Unfortunately, the law also permitted the legalization of past usurpations of crown lands, which, because surveyors were not contracted to demarcate remaining crown lands, stimulated continued usurpations. The government failed to recognize Indian rights to tribal lands excepting those bestowed upon them by its own acts. These were limited to missionary villages—the empire turned over to Italian CAPUCHIN FRIARS the task of acculturating tribal peoples on the frontier. Even these grants were nearly always encroached upon and extinguished.

Also during this period slaves on a few plantations were experimentally replaced with wage workers. Since native-born Brazilian country people were accustomed to squat on free frontier land or to receive customary rights of tenure on the lands of estate owners in return for minor responsibilities, they were not expected to take up wage work, nor were slaves expected to remain on the plantations once freed. Planters, therefore, desired European immigrants, who were preferred because they were white. Unfortunately, a group of Swiss and German plantation laborers imported in the mid-1850s proved intractable, principally because the immigrants were saddled with the cost of passage and because the landowners were unable to deal with workers who insisted on equal social treatment. There were, however, a few colonization projects that offered European immigrants smallholdings on frontier lands. Although abandoned to their own devices, these pioneers managed to survive and multiply in Rio Grande do Sul, Santa Catarina, and Espírito Santo provinces.

The empire resolved several border disputes, but at considerable cost in blood. In 1852, having invaded Uruguay and put a puppet in charge, the empire, then in league with Argentine rebels, gained a major victory over the dictator Juan Manuel de ROSAS. In 1864, it again invaded Uruguay, provoking the Paraguayan dictator, Francisco Solano LÓPEZ, who feared for the survival of his own country, to invade both Argentine and Brazilian territory. The ensuing WAR OF THE TRIPLE ALLIANCE (Uruguay, again under Brazilian control, joined the allies) lasted five years, killing off much of the male population of Paraguay. The slices of territory gained from Uruguay and Paraguay also cost the empire its stability. The war had been fought largely by troops of mixed race, some of them slaves recruited with the promise of freedom, who, in Argentina and Paraguay, had encountered societies free of the taint of slavery; it had been extremely expensive, making necessary a large increase in the foreign debt; and the officer class had grown and become a formidable and potentially challenging political force.

A postwar Conservative cabinet undertook to carry out further structural reforms in response to the weaknesses revealed by the wartime crisis. A census was carried out for the first time: 10 million inhabitants were counted, an increase of 7 million over the estimates of the turn of the century. The budgets of scientific and educational institutions were much increased. Obstacles to the organization of corporations were partially removed. Most important, the government at last sought to transform the aging slave labor force, which had declined to 1.5 million in 1872. (Some slaves had children, but most were single African males.) Pressed by foreign opinion, the threat of slave rebellion, and the realization that wage labor had to be gradually introduced, the legislature passed a law in 1871 (the FREE BIRTH LAW), freeing the children of slave mothers. This was a very gradual measure, since the children were obliged to work for their keep until age twenty-one. Coffee plantation owners, meanwhile, had been trying to stave off inevitable collapse by importing young male slaves from the economically stagnant Northeast.

DECLINE AND FALL

In 1868, the emperor expelled the Liberals from power. Although this action was constitutional, some Liberals interpreted it as a coup d'état, and they reacted by forming, in 1870, the Republican Party. In its principles it was decidedly ideological, a clear alternative to liberalism, and most of its leading members were inspired by Comtian POSITIVISM, secularism, and social Darwinism. Unlike that of other Liberals, their position on slavery was muted, but they were greatly concerned with the question of decentralization, or federalism. Their insistence on devolution of powers and revenues to the provinces (to be called states when the republic was at last formed) was an expression of the annoyance of the southeastern and southern provinces at the overrepresentation of the economically decadent and traditional Northeast, a circumstance that caused them a net loss of tax revenues. Republicanism also appealed to opportunism, as the more prosperous and politically ambitious foresaw a decline of a dynasty that lacked a male heir. Even so, it won few local or provincial elections during the 1870s and 1880s, and only in São Paulo, Minas Gerais, and Rio Grande do Sul did its candidates gain enough votes to represent a margin of victory in its coalitions with the major parliamentary parties.

One of the more contradictory aspects of the monarchy was its relation to the Catholic church. Catholicism remained the official religion, and the empire retained powers over it that the Portuguese crown had gained centuries before. Close church-state ties proved to be a hindrance to the residence and immigration of Protestants and Jews. Only tardily did the legislature act to reduce the disabilities that non-Catholic citizens suffered. In 1874, Pedro exercised his constitutional power to forbid the application of the pope's condemnation of the Masons. He then jailed two bishops who refused to obey this order. Curiously, his intent was to defend the right of free association of influential members of the elite, some of whom were priests, but he employed an archaic prerogative to do so. The case embarrassed the throne, while failing to gain the sympathy of Liberals and Republicans who favored the separation of church and state.

The movement toward abolition of slavery was only briefly turned aside by the 1871 Free Birth Law. Adherents multiplied among middle-class townspeople and especially among the free working class, which consisted largely of persons of color, many of them former slaves. Brazilian slavery had permitted manumission, and freedom through flight was becoming easier to achieve. In São Paulo, coffee planters contemplated final abolition as they observed that their slaves were willing to accept labor contracts and as the evident truth finally struck them that European immigration could be achieved only after slavery had been done away with. In 1885, sexagenarian slaves were freed, and finally, in 1888, Brazil became the last country in the Western world to abolish slavery entirely.

Had the franchise been in the meantime extended, and its free exercise guaranteed, this act would have granted the empire many more years of existence. It was signed by Princess Isabela, daughter of the emperor, acting as regent while her father was ill. She immediately became the idol of the freedmen and freedwomen. The empire, furthermore, while far from colorblind, had permitted the rise of many persons of color in the ranks of the bureaucracy. As it happened, the franchise had been further restricted by "reform" in 1881 and the empire was doomed. The instrument of its overthrow was the army. The inevitable cuts in its budget after the war had caused great anguish, which was exacerbated by Pedro's inability to deal tactfully with an officer class that prided itself on its pridefulness. Unfortunately, the duke of Caxias, upon whom the emperor had depended for this chore, had died in 1880. The Republican Party used every opportunity to heighten these tensions, and some of its leaders called openly for an army coup to bring about the downfall of the empire.

Many among the ruling elite did not expect the empire to deal effectively with the very rapid social and economic changes of the 1880s: urban growth (the city of Rio de Janeiro reached half a million by 1890), the beginning of mass immigration, the enlargement of the free population of color, and the increase in factory production. While these underlying forces may have been influential, it was an army general of limited political and economic awareness who, on 15 November 1889, packed the imperial family off into exile. The republican era had begun.

ALAN K. MANCHESTER, *British Preeminence in Brazil: Its Rise and Decline* (1933); STANLEY STEIN, *Vassouras: A Brazilian Coffee Country, 1850–1900* (1957); CLARENCE H. HARING, *Empire in Brazil: A New World Experiment with Monarchy* (1958); ANYDA MARCHANT, *Viscount Mauá and the Empire of Brazil* (1965); RICH-ARD GRAHAM, *Britain and the Onset of Modernization in Brazil, 1850–1914* (1968); LESLIE BETHELL, *The Abolition of the Brazilian Slave Trade* (1970); ROBERT BRENT TOPLIN, *The Abolition of Slavery in Brazil* (1972); PETER L. EISENBERG, *The Sugar Industry in Pernambuco: Modernization Without Change, 1840–1910* (1974); VICTOR NUNES LEAL, *Coronelismo: The Municipality and Representative Government in Brazil*, translated by June Henfrey (1977); THOMAS FLORY, *Judge and Jury in Imperial Brazil, 1808–1871* (1981); NATHANIEL H. LEFF, *Underdevelopment and Development in Brazil*, 2 vols. (1982); ROBERT CONRAD, *Children of God's Fire: A Documentary History of Black Slavery in Brazil* (1983); BARBARA WEINSTEIN, *The Amazon Rubber Boom, 1850–1920* (1983); RON SECKINGER, *The Brazilian Monarchy and the South American Republics, 1822–1831: Diplomacy and State Building* (1984); EMILIA VIOTTI DA COSTA, *The Brazilian Empire: Myths and Histories* (1985); WARREN DEAN, *Brazil and the Struggle for Rubber* (1987); NEILL MACAULAY, *Dom Pedro: The Struggle for Liberty in Brazil and Portugal* (1986); MARY C. KARASCH, *Slave Life in Rio de Janeiro, 1808–1850* (1987); JOSEPH SWEIGART, *Coffee Factorage and the Emergence of a Brazilian Capital Market* (1987); RODERICK BARMAN, *Brazil: The Forging of a Nation, 1798–1852* (1988); LESLIE BETHELL, *Brazil: Empire and Republic, 1822–1930* (1989); RICHARD GRAHAM, *Patronage and Politics in Nineteenth-Century Brazil* (1990).

WARREN DEAN

## Brazil Since 1889

PROCLAMATION OF THE REPUBLIC

The year 1889 is traditionally considered a turning point in Brazilian history. The abolition of SLAVERY in 1888 resulted in an increase in immigration and in-migration from the countryside to urban centers, the weakening of the old Rio de Janeiro coffee planters' oligarchy, and the emergence of a military in alliance with the middle sectors—the preconditions for the proclamation of the republic in 1889. Abolition was not solely responsible for the downfall of the empire, however. Most historians also view military discontent, church-state conflicts, and the alienation of the people as contributing factors.

On 15 November 1889 a military coup, supported by small groups of civilian conspirators, resulted in the establishment of the Republic. The army officers had lost political power after the WAR OF THE TRIPLE ALLIANCE against Paraguay and were influenced by POSITIVISM, while the bishops were disaffected because of the refusal of the state to accept the authority of the Catholic church regarding FREEMASONRY. Royal patronage of the church also caused friction, stemming mainly from its reduction in size, the closing of monastic orders, and the limiting of resources available to clerical institutions.

Other historians favor different interpretations. Edgard Carone ascribes the fall of the empire to a betrayal of the aristocracy, which was not hereditary and traditional and thus had no organic link to the monarchy. Leoncio Basbaum concludes that the republic was poor in men and ideas and was established for lack of a better alternative. Another author, João Cruz Costa, sees an important role for the middle class in the proclamation of the republic, although he attributes more significance to the antagonism of the military and clergy toward the empire. José Murilo de Carvalho denies that the people were indifferent and apathetic to the proclamation of the republic, as claimed by Aristides Lobo. In Murilo de Carvalho's opinion, people were active in religious brotherhoods, popular festivities, and mutual help organizations. This activity involved communal behavior and was devoid of individualistic attitudes inspired by bourgeois values, which were weak in Brazilian cities, where administrative and political functions prevailed. He also emphasizes the distance between formal and real life due in part to the pervading influence of slavery. In his view, people were not apathetic but cynical about the proclamation of the republic. José Luiz Werneck da Silva calls attention to the fact, generally unacknowledged, that people demonstrated in the streets on the day of the proclamation of the republic and invaded the capital's municipal chamber, thus deposing the monarchy before Marshal Manuel Deodoro da FONSECA led a parade elsewhere and officially proclaimed the republic.

At the time there were several currents of republican thought. Silva Jardim developed a concept of a republic based on the social contract of Jean Jacques Rousseau, while a significant segment of the officers supported Auguste Comte's positivism. The military also aspired to vote and claimed a full citizen's status, with the right to be elected, hold free meetings, publicly express their opinions, and have greater weight in the decision-making process of the state. Raul Pompéia argued that the army was indeed made up of the common man. Republicans excluded labor from the political system mainly because of illiteracy, the presence of many immigrants in its ranks, and fear of anarchist ideology.

CONSOLIDATION OF THE REPUBLIC: 1889–1894
An elected constituent assembly met in 1890 to draft the first republican constitution. It was based on a committee proposal subsequently revised by Rui BARBOSA DE OLIVEIRA, who tried to conciliate the authoritarian state defended by positivists against the federalism favored by political leaders.

The Constitution of 1891 reflected the ideal of restricted democracy supported by liberals. The constitution embodied the principle that political rights are granted by society to those deemed deserving of them. And so the vote was to be direct but not to include the illiterate (some 83 percent of the population), minors (under twenty-one years), common soldiers, clergy, and women. (In the first direct election for president in 1894, only about 2 percent of the total population voted.) Deleted from an early version of the Constitution was the obligation of the state to provide education, which had figured in the empire's charter. The republic maintained the prohibition against the foundation of new monastic orders, the exclusion of the JESUITS, and the ban on religious teaching in public schools.

Additional features of the Brazilian charter were the establishment of three separate and independent powers: judicial, legislative (Chamber of Deputies and Senate), and executive; a presidential regime; federalism; separation of church and state; and the rights to freedom of thought, assembly, profession, and property. During the operation of this constitution (1894–1930), the executive was supported by the wealthiest states—São Paulo and Minas Gerais—which formed a coalition with Rio Grande do Sul, Rio de Janeiro, and Pernambuco; this regionalism hampered the formation of national parties. In São Paulo, politics were controlled by coffee plantation owners and export-import commercial concerns.

The Constituent Assembly elected the first president and vice president, Deodoro da Fonseca and Floriano PEIXOTO, respectively. Fonseca, who had been ruling since the fall of the empire, was supported by part of the army. Peixoto was backed by a substantial part of the army and by urban industrial and service sectors. During Fonseca's rule (1889–1891), the country was disturbed by economic and political crises. The old coffee plantations of the state of Rio de Janeiro declined due to the abolition of slavery, soil exhaustion, and plant disease. To fight the depression, Finance Minister Rui Barbosa launched a policy of economic recovery based upon an increase of currency emissions and credit. He attempted to redirect the economy toward activities other than agriculture for export. The policies of Rui Barbosa that led to the ENCILHAMENTO, a period of feverish, speculative economic activity, are a matter of controversy. Public credit that had been restricted to coffee production and export was thenceforth extended to industry and other activities. The devaluation of currency and the imposition of tariffs to be paid in gold produced an increase in custom duties and deterred the importation of competitive manufactured goods. At the same time, special measures ensured the entry of capital goods and raw materials. Industrial expansion was further favored by declines in energy prices. Labor costs also fell due to a surplus of labor; this, however, sparked workers' strikes and conflict between labor and the federal government. Negative aspects of the Encilhamento included a high rate of inflation, increased speculation, formation of fictitious enterprises to gain favorable credits, corruption, and bankruptcies.

Bankruptcies were frequent but mostly related to fake or small, weak enterprises, whereas the major industrial concerns acquired capital in spite of inflation and increased production. Nevertheless, popular discontent exploded as food prices and rent rose, salaries and wages remained low, and unemployment became extensive. The executive, which lost the support of Congress, was closed by President Deodoro, who decreed a state of siege and announced new elections. Opponents sought support from the navy, which revolted under the command of Admiral Custódio de MELO. To avoid civil war, Deodoro resigned in 1891 and Vice President Peixoto took over (1891–1894). He reversed the policy of enlarging the currency, suspended the state of siege, and deposed state governors who had supported the former president. In 1892 an unsuccessful uprising at two fortresses in Rio de Janeiro sought immediate presidential elections.

In 1893, with the support of Admiral Luís Filipe SALDANHA DA GAMA, a monarchist who claimed that Floriano Peixoto's government was unconstitutional, the navy, under the leadership of Custódio de Melo revolted once again. In the same year, federalists in Rio Grande do Sul rebelled against the authoritarian local government and, after joining forces, dominated the south of the country. The decisive victory of federal forces in 1894 ended a period of troubled consolidation of the republic, although the hopeless resistance of Saldanha da Gama lasted until August 1895. The main urban centers were also disturbed by conflicts between the National Guard, police, and army and between Brazilians and Portuguese.

DEVELOPMENT OF THE REPUBLIC: 1894–1930

The recovery and expansion of COFFEE plantations, employing free, mostly immigrant labor in São Paulo, was responsible for the victory of Prudente José de MORAIS (1894–1898) as presidential candidate and the return to power of the coffee oligarchy. Morais pacified Rio Grande do Sul, but during his rule a rural movement sprang up in the interior of Bahia, where in 1893 Antônio Vicente MENDES MACIEL, a messianic religious leader called the Counselor by his followers, settled the village of CANUDOS. An economically self-sufficient peasant community, it served as a refuge for the poor and unemployed, refused to pay taxes, and led a revolt that lasted until 1897.

Despite the fact that the Morais government made no attempt to promote it, industry, with the help of exports and the inflow of foreign capital and immigrants, developed. Nevertheless, in the early decades after the founding of the republic, the country's economy remained massively agricultural, essentially dominated by coffee produced for export. The pattern of land ownership varied widely. Prosperous coffee plantations prevailed in São Paulo, declining coffee plantations prevailed in Rio, and deteriorating SUGAR plantations characterized the Northeast. Sharecroppers and salaried field hands replaced slaves. Blacks and people of color were dominant, but great numbers of European immigrants were brought in to work on São Paulo plantations. In declining gold-mining areas (Minas Gerais, Goiás, Mato Grosso) and in the Northeast backlands, extensive cattle raising and agriculture developed. The Indian population was still important in the central plateau. The Amazon basin—typified by communal and tribal subsistence agriculture and gathering, fishing, and hunting—was largely unexploited and sparsely populated. RUBBER was the only important export from the area.

The main urban industrial centers were Rio de Janeiro (the capital), São Paulo, Recife, Salvador, Belo Horizonte, and Pôrto Alegre. The pattern of urban development did not center around one primary city, as was the case in some Latin American countries.

After the efforts of Rui Barbosa, the federal government had no industrialization policy. From 1895 to 1904, investments in import machinery for textile mills diminished because of the fall of coffee prices beginning in 1896, a policy of deflation, reduction of tariffs, and a bank panic in 1900 at a time of intensive gold speculation. The government negotiated a funding loan with the Rothschild group to stabilize currency. In 1903 a general strike occurred in Rio de Janeiro to protest low salaries, unemployment, and poor health and housing conditions. In the early twentieth century, competition in the international coffee market caused prices to fall further. In 1906 valorization agreement among the main coffee-producing states to limit exports led to an increase in prices from 1909 to 1912 and helped to stabilize currency and expand the importation of capital goods. In the period from 1915 to 1919, imports of equipment dwindled due to World War I, while industrial production increased at different rates in various regions due to full employment of industries to attend the increased market.

In 1912 strikes reached a peak. A general strike in São Paulo during World War I marked the height of anarchist influence and the beginning of its decline. From 1920 onward the unions won recognition, several laws protecting labor were enacted, and security for laborers injured in work-related accidents began to be developed. Founded in 1922, the Communist Party tended to supersede anarchism.

In 1922, MODERN ART WEEK, organized by São Paulo intellectuals, questioned Brazil's traditional European-inspired elite culture. The movement encompassed all forms of art, sought the Brazilian popular roots of national culture, and had strong political overtones. The 1920s also witnessed protests against the old republican order—the manipulation of votes, the absence of electoral fairness, the coalition among the larger states, and the exclusion of the majority from the political process through the literacy requirement for voting. Also criticized were the distorted structure of land ownership, in which inefficiently exploited large estates stood alongside landholdings too small to support a family, the abuses against sharecroppers, the absence of labor laws to protect field hands, and the dominance of foreign capital in the economy.

The *tenente* (lieutenant) revolts of 1922 and 1924–1925 voiced some of these qualms as well as aspirations for the reform of federalism, restoration of balance between the three branches of government, the secret ballot, individual rights, and nationalism. The *tenente* movement is variously interpreted as military intervention to uphold legitimacy or as an expression of middle-class discontent with the corrupt democratic system of the 1920s. The military body known as the PRESTES COLUMN wandered through the interior for several years without fighting a decisive battle with the regular military forces. Its leader, Captain Luís Carlos PRESTES, became a mythic figure called the Cavalier of Hope. The degree of popular support for the *tenentes* column is a matter of debate.

The states' policy of supporting coffee prices could not cope with the plummeting prices resulting from the Great Depression of 1929. The problem was reinforced by the credit restriction imposed by the last president of the Old Republic period, Washington Luís, who aimed at restoring convertibility of the currency through a funding loan.

THE 1930 REVOLUTION AND ITS AFTERMATH

The REVOLUTION OF 1930 that brought Getúlio VARGAS to power has been regarded as a movement of the industrial bourgeoisie seeking to overthrow a state dominated by the coffee landlords and the commercial complexes linked to them. Nevertheless, the associations of entrepreneurs in São Paulo, Brazil's main industrial center, supported President Washington Luís, and two years after the victory of Vargas, they revolted against his rule. Furthermore, the industrial bourgeoisie was too weak to form a national movement of its own, depending as it did upon foreign capital and state support. Also, industry stood to benefit from a policy aimed at avoiding the collapse of the coffee economy.

Another interpretation of the period views the revolution as a result of conflict that pitted the middle classes (public and commercial employees; liberal professionals; and small commerical, industrial, and financial entrepreneurs) with low political consciousness against the oligarchies. The weak middle classes might have found political expression in the *tenentes* movements, but the latter were unable to establish common ground with the civilian middle classes, whose goals were different. When the *tenentes* reached power in 1930, they did not represent middle-class interests. The Depression and cancellation of coffee price supports led to a diversification of production (coffee represented 70 percent of total exports), which in turn weakened the coffee oligarchy.

The Aliança Liberal (Liberal Alliance), organized in 1930, was a coalition of dissident oligarchies from Minas Gerais, Rio Grande do Sul, and Paraíba that supported Vargas in his 1930 bid for the presidency against Júlio PRESTES, the candidate favored by Washington Luís. Vargas lost the possibly fraudulent election. Revolt broke out after João Pessoa, Vargas's vice-presidential candidate, was assassinated in Recife. A joint civilian-military movement quickly swept Vargas into power as provisional president in October 1930.

Francisco Weffort observed a political void in 1930 stemming from the weakness of the industrial bourgeoisie; the crisis of hegemony of the coffee bourgeoisie (plantation owners, export-import concerns); the lack of cohesion and limited consciousness of the middle sectors; and the diffuse thinking of the popular masses, who favored the formation of a state of compromise above

class interests. Into this void stepped the coalition that brought Vargas to power. It included regional interest groups harmed by São Paulo's dominance, *tenentes* discontented with the republic's lack of authenticity, and urban middle sectors negatively affected by the Depression. The senior officers in the army were divided. At the heart of the coalition were elements of the bourgeoisie (commercial, industrial, financial) and part of the middle classes, with the latter in a subordinate position. Labor was excluded from power.

Vargas's rule reflected this coalition when in 1931 he established the Conselho Nacional do Café (renamed Departamento Nacional do Café in 1933), which from 1931 to 1944 was in charge of buying coffee and burning it, thus forcing coffee planters to restrict their fields and crops. Further encouraging this process, the government transferred resources from coffee plantations to industries and to other types of agriculture. In 1933 the planters' debts to banks had reduced by 50 percent. The coffee policy diminished unemployment, ensured a certain level of income for the growers, maintained the internal market, and resulted in an effective antidepression policy. Brazil showed signs of economic recovery in 1932, much earlier than other nations. Yet in spite of these measures, a 1932 revolt in São Paulo called for the return to constitutional rule. Afterward, the *tenentes* were excluded from the governments of some states.

The Ministry of Labor, Industry, and Commerce, founded in 1930, was in charge of implementing the new regime's philosophy of cooperation between capital and labor. Labor laws, later codified, aimed at forcing workers into government-regulated unions. Entrepreneurs were also pressed to join unions. Conflicts between labor and capital were to be decided by labor courts. The government collected a mandatory tax on unions to whom it later dispensed these resources. Unions were discouraged from delving into politics. Their role was to promote culture. The right to strike was restricted. Nevertheless, workers formed FACTORY COMMISSIONS to resist government control.

Vargas's rule (1930–1945) was characterized by nationalism, economic self-sufficiency, restriction of immigration and foreign capital, and state regulation and direct participation in the economy. Vargas returned Brazil to democratic rule, reestablishing in 1933 the National Constituent Assembly, comprising representatives of employee and employer unions. The Constitution of 1934, Brazil's third, was based on the corporatist ideas of Germany's Weimar Republic. It incorporated Vargas's labor and electoral laws (women's suffrage, the right to vote at age eighteen). The state regulated the ownership and exploitation of underground resources and water, established free and mandatory primary education, and created the regional minimum wage.

In 1933 the Brazilian Integralist Action Party (Ação Integralista Brasileira—AIB) was founded. With fascist leanings, the party supported a centralized and strong federal state, powerful municipal chambers, indirect elections, and representatives from employer and employee unions. The patriarchical Catholic family would be the cell of society. Plinio SALGADO, its leader and founder, had belonged to the Modern Art Week movement. Most of the supporters of this party were professionals and members of the navy.

Opposed to the AIB was the National Liberating Alliance (Aliança Nacional Libertadora—ANL), a loose coalition of liberals and Communists. In 1935 it acquired a stronger Communist overtone when Luís Carlos Prestes became its honorary leader. Its program was land reform, nationalization of foreign enterprises, suspension of foreign debt payments, and establishment of a democratic bourgeois government as a step toward larger popular participation. In November 1935 the ANL, supported by some military sectors, attempted to take power in Rio de Janeiro, Recife, and Natal but failed for lack of popular support. The government then "found" the COHEN PLAN, a forgery that contained a blueprint for Communist terrorism. It was used as a justification for launching a coup d'état in 1937 that established the lengthy dictatorship of Vargas, known as the ESTADO NÔVO. From that time both followers of the AIB and the Communists were repressed.

### THE ESTADO NÔVO (NEW STATE): 1937–1945

It is almost impossible to summarize the many interpretations of the Estado Nôvo and their views as to whether it was authoritarian or totalitarian and fascist in nature. The army was not monolithic, giving Vargas room to play one faction against the other and remain somewhat independent. Corporatism had some impact, but it was mostly a matter of rhetoric. For some the Estado Nôvo was a decisive moment in state building for its creation of a rational-legal bureaucracy that promoted industrialization.

Ruling without parties under the new Constitution of 1937, Vargas's government favored national integration, import substitution, industrialization, and urban over rural interests, policies that profoundly transformed Brazil in the war years. His government also realigned Brazil from neutrality to an anti-Axis stance in January 1942, thereby enabling the country to obtain U.S. credit for the construction of the VOLTA REDONDA steel mill. The sinking of Brazilian ships in March 1942 led to a declaration of war on the Axis powers five months later and Brazilian participation in the Italian campaign. Returning from Europe, officers in the BRAZILIAN EXPEDITIONARY FORCE would play a key role in the downfall of Vargas in October 1945. The removal of Vargas was linked to the defeat of the Axis powers, the quelling of political discontent through repressive labor practices, and the refusal to adopt rural labor laws. In 1945 workers, through urban labor strikes organized by factory commissions, supported a return to democracy. Pressure for the end of the dictatorship also came from political parties such as the National Democratic Union (União Democrática Nacional—UDN), representing ur-

ban bourgeois liberalism; the Social Democratic Party (Partido Social Democrático—PSD), the party of traditional landed interests; and the Brazilian Labor Party (Partido Trabalhista Brasileiro—PTB), based on the official bureaucracy of the unions and organized by Vargas himself. Finally democracy was restored, and General Eurico DUTRA won the presidential election with the support of Vargas, the PTB, and the PSD.

### DEMOCRACY: 1945 TO 1964

From an economic standpoint, the 1945–1964 period was one of installing and developing the import-substitution industrialization model to its limits. This model implied the need for direct state intervention in the economy. The Dutra government (1946–1951) tried briefly to reestablish free trade, but the quick loss of foreign money reserves earned by Brazil during World War II led to a policy of selected noncompetitive imports. In spite of democracy's return, labor unions suspected of Communist leanings were closed and the Communist Party itself was outlawed.

The return of Vargas as president (1951–1954) meant continuation of state enterprises in strategic sectors (water, power, electricity, steel, petroleum), economic planning, and co-option of urban labor, which had been repressed under Dutra's conservative rule. Opposition to these policies as well as nationalism, eventually led the army to try to overthrow the president. After an attempt on the life of journalist Carlos LACERDA that killed an air force major, the generals demanded Vargas's resignation. Instead, he committed suicide in 1954. In November 1955 the vice president who had taken over, João Café FILHO (1954–1955), was replaced by the president of the Chamber of Deputies, Carlos Luz, allegedly because of an illness of the former. But during the same year, Luz and leading supporters fled for fear of an army takeover. Also in 1955, Juscelino KUBITSCHEK was elected president, and War Minister Henrique LOTT ensured his taking office despite maneuvers to keep him out. A transitional government headed by Nereu Ramos (speaker of the Senate), chosen by the Chamber of Deputies, ruled from November 1955 to the end of January 1956, when Kubitschek assumed power.

The Kubitschek government (1956–1961) adopted an economic planning policy inspired by U.S. economist Walt W. Rostow's theory of takeoff. It concentrated investments in an area (Minas Gerais, São Paulo, and Rio de Janeiro) where the preconditions for self-sustained growth existed. The plan of targets (1958) provided for government investment in that area to unclog bottlenecks for industrial growth—for example, power, transportation (mainly shipyards and cars), roads, and chemical industries. The government also sought private and foreign investments for the region. Planners assumed that as the area developed, it would carry in its wake the growth of the other regions so that industry would bring change to the backward rural areas. Kubitschek diverged from Vargas by fostering foreign in-

# Brazil

1 ALAGOAS
2 ESPÍRITO SANTO
3 FEDERAL DISTRICT
4 PARAÍBA
5 RIO DE JANEIRO
6 RIO GRANDE DO NORTE
7 SANTA CATARINA
8 SERGIPE

vestment. The march to the west and the establishment of the capital in BRASÍLIA (1960) would, he believed, redistribute the population, which was concentrated along the coast, and integrate the country. Between 1955 and 1961, industrial production grew 80 percent in constant prices. From 1957 to 1961, the real rate of growth was 7 percent per year and nearly 4 percent per capita. Brazil had achieved virtual self-sufficiency in light consumer goods by the mid-1950s.

Kubitschek has been criticized, however, for reinforcing regional differences, neglecting backward states, depressing the standard of living of urban workers, and promoting inflation through the construction of Brasília at a time of declining export earnings. Furthermore, some have asserted that the option for roads and an automobile industry instead of trains was a mistake in a

country that imported petroleum. Finally, education and agriculture were the forgotten goals. Foreign indebtedness reached higher levels that were difficult to reduce.

In the 1945–1964 period, the Social Democratic Party and the Brazilian Labor Party formed a dominant political alliance that implied the exclusion of rural workers and cooptive populist policies toward urban workers. The economic policies of the alliance broadened the gap between rural and urban areas and caused heavy migration from countryside to cities (mainly from the Northeast to São Paulo), which resulted in the growth of tenements and shacks and mass unemployment. The 1946 constitution (Brazil's fifth), adopted the Vargas labor code.

The government of Jânio QUADROS, who succeeded

429

Kubitschek in 1961, made a frustrated attempt to reestablish a market economy, follow an independent foreign policy, and impose an authoritarian regime combating corruption and administrative inefficiency. After eight months, Quadros suddenly resigned, hoping to return with increased authority, but the interference of the military prevented that maneuver from succeeding.

Popular and labor mobilization and division within the military made it possible for Vice President João GOULART to complete the term (beginning in September 1961) but within a parliamentary system. Goulart, former labor minister of Vargas and PTB leader, fought for the return of presidential government in 1962 and won a January 1963 plebiscite on that issue. To gain labor support, Goulart departed from the traditional PSD–PTB policy of demobilizing workers, which helped to break the power of the bureaucracy in the government-controlled unions. The plan of basic structural reforms sponsored by Goulart, including land and tax reforms, antagonized landowners. Educational and housing reforms were less controversial, but industrialists felt aggrieved by the revived workers' movement and increases in wages.

From the beginning of Goulart's term until his overthrow by the military in April 1964, inflation worsened while the split between leftist-nationalists and anti-Communists within labor became wider. A general radicalization of mass movements took place, and leftist unions became more powerful, independent, and better coordinated on the national level, particularly in the General Command of Workers (Comando Geral do Trabalho). Unions pressed for higher wages and joined the movement for basic reforms. Rural workers were organized both locally and nationally, and literacy campaigns, involving an effort to promote political awareness, were launched. The students' movement, led by the National Students Union (UNE), coordinated its activities with workers' protests. A segment of the Catholic clergy supported reform, while some members were outright revolutionary. Several popular fronts were formed, while the PSD, UDN, PTB, and PCB suffered splits. In the last case, dissidents formed the Labor Policy (Política Operária—POLOP), which revised the Marxist analysis and strategies of the PCB.

The discontent with structural inequalities was reinforced by the declining growth rate of industrial production due to international market conditions and exhaustion of the import-substitution model. Through domestic production, the country had replaced a large number of imported goods until most imports (e.g., petroleum), could not be substituted for. Also, regional differences of income, as well as class differences, had deepened.

The 1964 military coup against Goulart had the support of the great majority of the military and part of the industrial and the landed elites. It could count on the immediate recognition of the new regime by the United States. The supposed threat of the so-called unions' re-public, the basic reforms of Goulart, a law restricting the repatriation of profits by foreign enterprises, and the high rate of inflation were factors behind the coup, particularly since some of the army leaders no longer supported civilian rule and had a nationalistic ideology.

## THE MILITARY REGIME AND THE RETURN TO DEMOCRACY: 1964–1994

After the 1964 coup Congress lost its power, becoming a mere rubber stamp. Opponents of the new regime lost their political rights. Under the regime's First Institutional Act, Marshal Humberto CASTELO BRANCO, the coup's leader, was selected as president by the military leaders and given automatic approval by Congress. The CGT, Peasant Leagues, and UNE and its affiliates were dissolved. Labor unions were purged, and some state governors were removed. Strict censorship was established, and the secret police gained new power. In 1969 university professors were dismissed, the number of social science classes was reduced, and a mandatory course on moral and civic education was imposed. The Second Institutional Act established indirect elections for the presidency; denied illiterates the vote; extinguished old political parties; and organized two new ones, the Brazilian Democratic Movement (Movimento Democrático Brasileiro—MDB), as the opposition and the National Renovating Alliance (Aliança Renovadora Nacional—ARENA), as the pro-government organization. The same act gave the president the right to suspend Congress, to expel members of parliament, to suspend political rights for ten years, and to decree a state of siege. In 1966 the federal legislature was suspended; subsequently it was this demoralized Congress that elected General Artur da COSTA E SILVA president and approved Brazil's sixth constitution in 1967 (drafted by a committee of jurists close to the regime), which incorporated the institutional acts. Under this charter the executive could enact laws by decree, suspend political rights of members of Congress, and extend the jurisdiction of the military courts to civilians committing political crimes. In 1969 extensive amendments to the Constitution further centralized power in the federal government and further weakened Congress in relation to the president.

During the rule of Castelo Branco (1964–1967), Costa e Silva (1967–1969), and the military junta that briefly replaced the latter when he became ill, the economic depression deepened partly because of deflationary austerity measures. Opposition was forced underground, assuming the form of urban and rural guerrilla activity. Part of the Catholic clergy remained the last open resistance to the military regime; some clerics supported rural unionism and other organizations of the poor as they worked for a humanized capitalism preached by Father Bastos d'Ávila. Anti-Communist organizations were supported by a segment of the industrial bourgeoisie. The Superior War College defended an all-encompassing concept of national security including government repression of dissidents by imprisonment without due process, torture, murder, and secret burial under a false or no name.

Whereas the Left deemed that the national economic crisis could be resolved only by a radical redistribution of wealth, the Right believed that growth and modernization could be achieved through a pattern of income concentration. The military government emphasized the expansion of manufactured and agricultural exports and a process of modernization. During the rule of Emílio Garrastazú MÉDICI (1969–1974), important sectors of business and finance were restructured, inflation was reduced to 20 percent in 1971 (it had been 80 percent in 1963), exports grew from $2.7 billion in 1968 to $6.2 billion in 1973, exchange reserves reached $1 billion, and foreign capital once again entered the country. Before 1964 the country had achieved self-sufficiency in most durable goods. The goals of the plan of 1970–1973 were the development of capital goods production and nuclear power and the massive absorption of technology.

For many the so-called BRAZILIAN MIRACLE legitimized the military regime. By the same token, the decline of the economy after 1974, resulting in part from higher petroleum prices, promoted a democratization process. President Ernesto GEISEL (1974–1979), under the pressure of large strikes and public opinion, started a gradual return to democracy with the constitutional amendment of 1978 that revoked the institutional acts, restored local elections, and allowed the formation of new political parties. João Baptista FIGUEIREDO (1979–1985) granted political amnesty in 1979 and made it easier to organize parties. Remodeled and new parties, the Catholic church, and class organizations participated in a huge campaign for direct and immediate presidential elections in which the masses would participate. Instead, indirect elections were held on 15 January 1985, with Tancredo NEVES and José SARNEY chosen as president and vice president, respectively. The latter assumed office in 1985 due to the illness and death of the former. Two years after the drafting of Brazil's seventh constitution in 1988, Fernando COLLOR DE MELLO became the first president elected by direct popular vote since 1961. In 1992 he became the first ever to be removed from office in an impeachment process, which was completed with his resignation in December 1992. His vice president, Itamar FRANCO, completed his term of office in 1994.

Between 1950 and 1980, the country underwent deep changes. In 1950, 64 percent of the total population was rural and 36 percent urban. In 1980 the figures were,

Metalworkers demonstrating in São Paulo, 1980. SEBASTIÃO SALGADO / MAGNUM.

431

respectively, 33 percent and 67 percent. In 1980, Greater São Paulo reached over 12.5 million inhabitants—more than 10 percent of the total population. The number of workers grew 500 percent between 1950 and 1980, when they represented 32.7 percent of the population, and 52.1 percent of labor was concentrated in the production of capital goods. In 1980 the primary sector of the economy incorporated 29.9 percent, the secondary 24.4 percent, and the tertiary 45.7 percent. The participation in elections broadened from 15 percent of the population in 1945 to 48 percent in 1982.

During the military regime, the malnourished increased from 27 million in 1961–1963 (38 percent of the population) to 72 million in 1974–1975 (67 percent); the percentage dropped slightly in 1984 to 65 percent. In the 1980s, the richest 1 percent of the population increased its share of the national income from 13 percent to 17.3 percent, whereas the poorer 50 percent suffered a decline from 13.4 percent to 10.4 percent. In 1989, 18.9 percent of the population age fifteen or more (17.2 million people, concentrated mainly in the Northeast) were illiterate. Over 44 percent of all families earned less than twice the minimum wage, and only 3.5 percent of the members of these families went to college (1989).

Poverty and lack of proper sanitary conditions were responsible for the persistence of epidemic diseases such as malaria, and for the reappearance of cholera in 1989, with 1.1 million cases.

The relationship between the volume of foreign debt and the internal gross production deteriorated from 18.9 in 1980 to 46.3 in 1984. Conspicuous consumption by the government, extensive investments in nuclear programs, and military expenditures represented a drawback. The breakdown of democracy weakened parties and reinforced populist, authoritarian, and clientele practices. The problem of maldistribution of infrastructure, income, and land remained; the number of landless rural workers increased while the number of sharecroppers dwindled and that of migrant salaried field hands grew.

Both the internal gross production and employment fell 4 percent in 1990, and in January 1991 inflation reached 20.21 percent per month. Collor's government adopted a stabilization plan in January 1991 to balance the budget, contain inflation, and free the economy. To reduce public expenditures, the bureaucracy was limited and public enterprises were sold at auction. Steps taken to reduce inflation were an increase in interest rates, control of monetary circulation, and the opening of the internal market. Inflation, however, moved to ever-higher levels, reaching about 40 percent per month early in 1994.

JOSÉ MARIA BELLO, *História da República* (1940); HÉLIO SILVA, *O ciclo de Vargas*, 12 vols. (1964–1974); THOMAS E. SKIDMORE, *Politics in Brazil, 1930–1964: An Experiment in Democracy* (1967); LEONCIO BASBAUM, *Historia sincera da República*, 4 vols. (1968–1976); EDGARD CARONE, *A Primeira República, 1889–1930* (1969); ROBERT M. LEVINE, *The Vargas Regime: The Critical Years, 1934–1938* (1970); RONALD M. SCHNEIDER, *The Political System of Brazil: Emergence of a "Modernizing" Authoritarian Regime, 1964–1970* (1971); HÉLIO SILVA, *1889: A República não esperou o amanhecer* (1972); EDGARD CARONE, *A Segunda República, 1930–1937* (1973), and *A Terceira República, 1937–1945* (1976); FLAVIO RABELO VERSIANI and JOSÉ ROBERTO MENDOÇA DE BARROS, eds., *Formação econômica do Brasil* (1978); MANOEL MAURICIO DE ALBUQUERQUE, *Pequena história da formação social brasileira* (1981); JOSÉ MURILO DE CARVALHO, *Os Bestializados: O Rio de Janeiro e a república que não foi* (1987); JOÃO CRUZ COSTA, *Pequena historia da república*, 3d ed. (1989); LINCOLN DE ABREU PENA, *Uma história da República* (1989); RONALD M. SCHNEIDER, *"Order and Progress": A Political History of Brazil* (1991); JOSÉ LUIZ WERNECK DA SILVA, ed., *O feixe e o prisma: O autoritarismo como questão teórica e historiográfica* (1991); and E. BRADFORD BURNS, *A History of Brazil*, 3d ed. (1993).

EULALIA MARIA LAHMEYER LOBO

*See also* **Agriculture; Cities and Urbanization; Economic Development; Military Dictatorships; Slavery; Tenentismo.**

**BRAZIL: AMNESTY ACT** (1979), a bill passed by the Brazilian Congress on 22 August 1979 to provide amnesty to most Brazilian political prisoners and exiles. While benefiting approximately 4,500 people, the act excluded any persons found guilty of murder, kidnapping, or terrorist activities and classified them as common criminals. Sixty-nine amendments were added to the bill, including one that allowed families of missing people to petition for a certificate of presumed death and another that guaranteed normal benefits to families of those political prisoners who had died while in custody. The amendments also allowed exonerated former government employees to petition for reinstatement at their previous grade. By allowing the return of opposition leaders from exile, the Amnesty Act was an important step toward the return of free elections in Brazil.

MARTI HARDEN, ed., *Latin American Index* (1979), pp. 44, 48, 60, 62; MARIA HELENA MOREIRA ALVES, *State and Opposition in Military Brazil* (1985), pp. 211–212; THOMAS E. SKIDMORE, *The Politics of Military Rule in Brazil, 1964–85* (1988), pp. 218–219.

MICHAEL J. BROYLES

**BRAZIL: CIVIL CODE** (1916). Following four unsuccessful attempts during the nineteenth century to codify Brazilian civil law, the Brazilian Civil Code (Codigo Civil Brasileiro), drafted by Clóvis Bevilaqua, was approved by Congress (Law 3,071 of 1 January 1916) and took effect on 1 January 1917. Corrections ordered by Law 3,725 of 15 January 1919 were promulgated on 13 July 1919. The Civil Code superseded the Ordinações Filipinas, compiled in Portugal in 1603, and remains in effect, although it has been altered significantly by subsequent laws.

Widely praised at the time for its "scientific" and practical nature, the Civil Code is divided into two parts. The "general" part deals with persons, property, and legal acts; the "special" part treats the rights of family, rights of things, laws of obligations, and rights of succession. The Civil Code is a conservative document that reinforces capitalist and patriarchal social relations. Especially concerned with relations within the family, it declares the husband the legal head of household and leaves married women legally incapacitated. A wife can assume *patria poder* only in the case of the legal absence of her husband. The husband has the right to administer the wife's property, and she has to secure his authorization to pursue a profession as well as to accept or relinquish an inheritance. The Civil Code originally permitted annulment of marriage (under restrictive circumstances) and legal separation (*desquite*) only; divorce was legalized in 1977 (Law 6,515 of 26 December 1977), but only once in any person's lifetime.

A useful early edition of the Civil Code, which includes a historical and descriptive introduction and an index, is *Código civil brasileira,* edited by Paulo de Lacerda (1916). A recent compilation of modifications of the Civil Code is *Código civil e legislação complementar,* edited by Geraldo Magela Alves (1989). An English translation is *The Civil Code of Brazil,* translated by Joseph Wheless (1920).

SUSAN K. BESSE

*See also* **Ordenações do Reino.**

**BRAZIL: CONSTITUTIONS.** Since proclaiming independence in 1822, Brazil has had eight constitutions, well below the Latin American average of 12.75 constitutions per country. None has worked very well. It is not clear, however, to what extent the causes should be attributed to the constitutional rules or to the individuals governing under and around these rules. Until Brazil can resolve some of its most pressing economic, social, and political problems, it is doubtful that any constitution will work well.

THE 1824 CONSTITUTION
Brazil's first constitution was its most enduring, lasting sixty-five years with only one amendment. Modeled upon the French Constitution of 1814, it established a hereditary Catholic monarchy headed by Dom PEDRO I. This lengthy document, containing 172 articles, inaugurated Brazil's tradition of complex and lengthy constitutions. It established a centralized, unitary system of government. Although it divided the country into provinces and counties (*municípios*), these territorial units had little independent authority. The central government was divided into four powers: legislative, executive, judicial, and moderating.

Legislative power was exercised by a bicameral General Assembly with a Chamber of Deputies, whose members were chosen for a four-year term, and a Senate, whose members were chosen for life. The number of deputies per province depended upon population,

and each province had half as many senators as deputies. Both houses were selected indirectly by provincial electors chosen by parish assemblies, but the emperor selected senators from lists of three nominated by provincial electors. The government's manipulation of the electoral process, however, destroyed even the limited representative nature of the assembly. The assembly both enacted and interpreted the laws. It had the power to choose a new dynasty if the royal family became extinct and to elect a regent if the emperor was a minor. The deputies could impeach all officials except the emperor, who was legally inviolable.

The emperor exercised both the executive and moderating powers. The moderating power was designed to resolve conflicts among the other powers of government. The executive had extensive powers, including appointments, foreign relations, security, execution of the laws, appropriations, and veto of ecclesiastical decrees. The moderating power included selecting senators, calling extraordinary legislative sessions, approving or vetoing legislation, dissolving the Chamber of Deputies and calling new elections, nominating or dismissing ministers of state, suspending judges, and granting pardons and amnesties. The emperor also appointed for life a Council of State that advised him and resolved administrative law disputes.

The judiciary consisted of a Supreme Tribunal of Justice, Provincial Tribunals (*Relações*), law-trained judges, and elected justices of the peace. Lay jurors determined the facts in both civil and criminal cases. Judges had life tenure, but they could be transferred or suspended by the emperor.

This was in many ways a progressive constitution. It guaranteed many individual rights, protected freedom of thought and expression, and abolished many cruel penalties inherited from Portugal. Equal protection of the laws was guaranteed to citizens. Even though Catholicism was the state religion and only Catholics could become deputies, it provided for religious tolerance. On the other hand, it permitted SLAVERY and failed to create procedural devices to protect basic rights.

THE 1891 CONSTITUTION
In 1889 the monarchy was overthrown by the military, whose first act, drafted by Rui BARBOSA, abolished the Constitution of 1824 and proclaimed the Republic of the United States of Brazil. Heavily influenced by the U.S. Constitution, the 1891 Constitution was Brazil's shortest, containing only ninety-one articles and eight transitional provisions. It changed Brazil into a republican federation and converted the former provinces into twenty sovereign states. It also extended the franchise to all adult males.

The government was reduced to three branches: executive, legislative, and judicial. The bicameral legislature consisted of a Chamber of Deputies and a Senate. Each state and the federal district elected three senators; deputies were apportioned by population, each state having at least four. Senators were elected for nine years; deputies for three years. In contradistinction to the United States, the legislature was authorized to enact national codes of civil, commercial, and criminal law.

The executive was headed by a president elected by direct vote for a four-year term and ineligible for immediate reelection. His powers included administration of the armed forces, conducting foreign affairs, vetoing or approving legislation, granting pardons, and calling extraordinary congressional sessions. With Senate approval, the president could appoint members of the Supreme Court and the diplomatic corps. He appointed inferior federal judges from lists submitted by the Supreme Court.

As in the United States, the Constitution created the highest court, the Supreme Federal Tribunal, and authorized the legislature to establish the inferior federal courts. Unlike the United States, Brazil's Constitution expressly conferred the power to determine the constitutionality of legislation upon the judiciary. The jury system was retained. Guarantees of judicial independence were taken directly from Article III of the U.S. Constitution: life tenure and nondiminution of salaries.

Basic constitutional rights, such as liberty and property, which previously had been assured only to Brazilian citizens, were extended to foreign residents. Habeas corpus, which had merely a statutory basis under the empire, was made a constitutional right. The penalties of death, banishment, and galley service were abolished.

This U.S.-inspired Constitution worked poorly. The period during which it was in force, known as the Old Republic, was marked by continual political instability and widespread electoral fraud. In 1926 a constitutional amendment greatly expanded the power of the federal government to intervene in the states, limited state autonomy, cut back habeas corpus, and modified congressional powers.

THE 1934 CONSTITUTION

Even as amended, the 1891 Constitution never conformed to Brazilian political reality. It perished in 1930, a casualty of a military revolt that brought to power Getúlio VARGAS, whose provisional government promptly modified the 1891 Constitution to assume dictatorial powers. An unsuccessful São Paulo revolt against the dictatorship eventually led to restoration of constitutional government. In 1934 a new constitution, modeled upon the Weimar Constitution of 1919 and the Spanish Constitution of 1931, was adopted. This was even longer than prior constitutions, containing 187 articles and 26 transitional provisions.

Federalism and the tripartite division of powers were retained, but the powers of the federal government were enhanced at the expense of the states. Legislative power was actually controlled by the Chamber of Deputies, with the Senate assuming the role of a fourth power, similar to the moderating power of the emperor. The deputies, apportioned by population, were elected for four-year terms. Five-sixths were chosen by universal direct vote of the people in each state, while one-sixth were chosen by indirect vote of professional associations, divided between employers and employees. The executive power was exercised by the president and his cabinet. There was no vice president.

The Constitution created two new courts, the electoral and labor courts. The former represented a reaction to the electoral fraud that had characterized the Old Republic, while the latter reflected Vargas's concern with protection of the working class.

The 1934 Constitution made several other important innovations. It was the first to extend the franchise to all Brazilians over the age of eighteen, regardless of sex. Voting, which had been optional during the Old Republic, was made obligatory for all males and for female civil servants. It created the writ of security (*mandado de segurança*), a summary procedure to protect liquid and certain constitutional rights unprotected by habeas corpus. It also began the process of nationalization of certain sectors of the economy, such as navigation, newspapers, advertising agencies, mining, and insurance.

THE 1937 CONSTITUTION

In 1937, the year before his presidential term was to expire, Getúlio Vargas staged a coup d'état and proclaimed the ESTADO NÔVO. Vargas replaced the 1934 Constitution with a shadow constitution that enabled him to exercise dictatorial powers. Constitutional provisions for democratic institutions and representative elections were never carried out. Vargas dissolved all political parties and held no elections. Even the plebiscite that Article 187 required to legitimize the Constitution was never held. Article 180 authorized the president to legislate by decree-law until Congress met. Congress never met, and Vargas issued more than 8,000 decree-laws between 1937 and 1945.

During the entire period of the 1937 Constitution, individual rights were suspended by a continual state of emergency. A number of rights protected in prior constitutions remained unprotected in the 1937 Constitution. The state of emergency lasted until 30 November 1945, a month after Vargas was overthrown by the military.

THE 1946 CONSTITUTION

The Constitution of 1946 was even longer than its predecessors, containing 218 articles and 36 transitional provisions. Like the 1891 Constitution, it reflected the influence of the U.S. Constitution, particularly with respect to federalism. In structure and in protection of socioeconomic rights, it reflected the Weimar Constitution. As a reaction to the Vargas dictatorship, it denied the executive the power to issue decree-laws. The legislative resembled that of prior constitutions but functioned very inefficiently, resulting in the growth of administrative decrees as a substitute for legislation. The judiciary recovered its autonomy as well as the power of judicial review. Article 125 provided for creation of the Public Ministry, a civil-law institution that performs prosecutorial functions and defends the interests of law and society before the courts. Individual rights were generously protected, and exclusion from judicial consideration of any injury to an individual right was expressly prohibited.

The demise of the 1946 Constitution began in 1961, when President Jânio QUADROS resigned, claiming that Brazil was ungovernable under the existing constitutional regime. Vice President João GOULART was permitted to assume the presidency only after a constitutional amendment created a parliamentary regime. Thus restructured, the new government functioned poorly, and a 1963 constitutional amendment restored presidential powers. Miscalculating the depth of his political support, Goulart tried moving the country to the left and was overthrown by the military in 1964.

The 1946 Constitution remained in force, as modified by a series of INSTITUTIONAL ACTS issued by the military high command, functioning as a self-designated ambulatory constituent assembly. The military quickly selected General HUMBERTO CASTELLO BRANCO as the new president, removed opposition legislators, and deprived opponents of political and civil rights for ten years. The president packed the Supreme Court, increasing its size from eleven to sixteen ministers. The president was empowered to issue decree-laws in matters involving national security, finances, and administration.

THE 1967 CONSTITUTION

The 1967 Constitution, formally ratified by a Congress from which most political opposition had been purged, centralized power in the executive and in the federal government. The president was elected by an electoral college, but in practice only a military leader could be a candidate. The legislative provisions resembled those of the 1946 Constitution except for authorization of the president to enact decree-laws even when the legislature was in session. The Constitution guaranteed an impressive array of individual rights, but they were seldom in force.

A period of constant crisis followed promulgation of the Constitution, due to widespread opposition to military government. The military responded by issuing an additional dozen institutional acts. Act 5 (13 December 1968) removed virtually all restraints on presidential power. The president suspended all legislative bodies and exercised total legislative power himself. The president compulsorily retired three unduly independent Supreme Court members and many lower-court judges, as well as suspending habeas corpus for crimes against national security.

In August 1969 President Artur da COSTA E SILVA suffered a stroke. Rather than permit the civilian vice president to replace him, a military junta assumed the presidency. The junta also issued Constitutional Amendment 1, rewriting the entire text of the 1967 Constitution.

THE 1969 CONSTITUTION

Whether the 1969 Constitution should be regarded as a new constitution or merely an amendment is an unsettled issue. This Constitution further strengthened executive powers, expanding the presidential term to five years and authorizing the president to issue decree-laws not only with respect to national security, but also taxation, creation of public employment, and public salaries. The greatest expansion resulted from giving the president power to submit short-fused bills on any subject. Each house had forty-five days to consider such bills; if labeled urgent, both houses had only forty days for joint consideration. Bills not considered during these periods were deemed automatically approved.

The protection previously accorded to individual rights was badly diluted. Moreover, such rights were suspended until 1 January 1979, when Institutional Act 5 finally expired. In January 1985 Brazil elected, albeit indirectly, its first civilian president since 1960. Restoration of democracy led to the adoption of a new constitution in 1988.

THE 1988 CONSTITUTION

The 1988 Constitution is a lengthy, detailed, and convoluted document, containing 245 articles and 70 transitory provisions. Heavily influenced by the 1976 Portuguese Constitution, the text contains a plethora of detailed rules normally found in ordinary legislation. Paradoxically, despite the great detail with which many subjects have been regulated, some 285 ordinary statutes and 41 complementary laws are required to effectuate its provisions. Thus far, Congress has failed to enact much of the necessary implementing legislation.

The Constitution is a hodgepodge of progressive, conservative, liberal, radical, and moderate provisions. This is partly because it was drafted from scratch by the entire 559 members of Congress and partly because the initial drafts contemplated a parliamentary system. At the last minute, Congress switched to presidentialism but left numerous parliamentary provisions in the text.

The 1988 Constitution weakens the executive and strengthens the legislature. It makes the president accountable to Congress, which can impeach, as it did Fernando COLLOR DE MELLO, Brazil's first popularly elected president since Quadros. Congress has exclusive power to control rule making by administrative agencies. All acts of the executive, including acts of indirect administration, are theoretically subject to control by one or both houses of Congress.

The president has no power to issue decree-laws. He can, however, issue delegated laws and provisional measures. Except for a few reserved subjects, Congress may delegate to the president the power to enact legislation, a power that has been relatively unimportant. In cases of relevance and urgency, the president may also issue provisional measures, which have the force of law, but if they are not converted into law within thirty days, they lose their efficacy *ab initio*. The provisional measure, designed as an extraordinary device, has been used routinely. In June 1990 the Supreme Federal Tribunal declared unconstitutional an attempt by then President Collor de Mello to repromulgate a provisional measure after Congress had specifically disapproved it, but repromulgation of provisional measures upon which Congress has failed to act has become routine.

The 1988 Constitution considerably strengthens the powers of the judiciary. Courts have much greater financial independence and substantially greater power to declare statutes unconstitutional. Among the most impressive achievements of the new Constitution are its procedural innovations in the protection of constitutional and legal rights. Substantive guarantees of individual rights are also impressive, protecting virtually every human right. Unfortunately, this is an area where the gap between the Constitution on paper and the Constitution in practice looms largest. Torture and maltreatment of common criminals is a fact of life in many Brazilian police stations and jails despite the constitutional guarantee of "respect for physical and moral integrity" of all prisoners. The Constitution also protects a vast array of socioeconomic rights. Education, health, labor, leisure, security, social security, protection of maternity and infancy, and assistance of the unprotected are declared to be social rights. Article 7 contains thirty-four subsections that read like a miniature progressive labor code.

A number of provisions make little or no sense and may, if enforced, seriously handicap the development and modernization of Brazil. For example, the framers included a provision that makes charging an annual real rate of interest in excess of 12 percent the crime of usury. Had it been enforced, this provision would have destroyed the Brazilian financial system. A major obstacle to reducing the bloated bureaucracy is a provision that grants tenure to all civil servants with five years of public service, regardless of the legality of their status. Several nationalistic provisions discouraging or discriminating against foreign investment have been seriously criticized. Provisions mandating allocation of fixed percentages of federal tax revenues to certain sectors have made controlling inflation more difficult.

The 1988 Constitution was intended to endure for only five years. It mandated that a plebiscite be held in 1993 to determine whether Brazil should remain a republic or become a constitutional monarchy, and whether it should retain a presidential system or adopt a parliamentary system. In the plebiscite, a majority voted to retain both republicanism and presidentialism. Another provision mandates that the constitutional text be revised by a vote of an absolute majority of the members of the National Congress in 1993. A scandal involving corruption in the congressional budget process delayed this revision until March 1994. More than 17,000 amendments to the Constitution were proposed, but only six were ultimately adopted. The only significant constitutional amendment passed by Congress was Amendment of Revision 1 of 1 March 1994, which creates the Emergency Social Fund. This amendment changes the revenue-sharing rules of the 1988 Constitution, but only for fiscal years 1994–1995. The result is to transfer an estimated $9 billion from the state and local governments to the federal government, a measure invaluable to the success of the current stabilization program (Plano Real), which has lowered the monthly inflation rate from roughly 50 percent to about 3 percent. This leaves major constitutional reforms as a key item on the agenda of Brazil's newly elected president, Fernando Henrique Cardoso.

The complete Portuguese texts of the first seven constitutions plus an index are published in *Constituições do Brasil* (1986). The most recent Portuguese text of the 1988 Constitution with amendments is *Constituição da República Federativa do Brasil*, edited by Juarez de Oliveira, 9th ed. (1994). An annotated English translation of the Constitution without the amendments by KEITH S. ROSENN is in JACOB DOLINGER and KEITH S. ROSENN, eds., *A Panorama of Brazilian Law* (1992), pp. 383–518; with amendments in ALBERT BLAUSTEIN and GILBERT FLANZ, eds., *Constitutions of the Countries of the World*, vol. 3 (1993), pp. 1–136, plus supplement (May 1994), pp. 1–19. Helpful sources placing Brazilian constitutions in historical perspective are LUIZ F. D'ÁVILA, ed., *As Constituicões Brasileiras* (1993); FRANCISCO DE ASSIS ALVES, "Constituições do Brasil," *Revista de Direito Constitucional e Ciência Política* (Special number, 1987): 1–72; RODRIGO M. CARNEIRO DE OLIVEIRA, "As Constituições Brasileiras: Uma análise histórica para a revisão constitucional de 1993," pamphlet published by Pinheiro Neto-Advogados, São Paulo, Brasil, 23 August 1993; and MANOEL OCTAVIANO JUNQUEIRA FILHO, "Constituições do Brasil (Evolução histórica)," in *Enciclopédia Saraiva do Direito*, vol. 18 (1977), pp. 354–380.

An early discussion in English of Brazil's first two constitutions can be found in HERMAN G. JAMES, *The Constitutional System of Brazil* (1923). Two helpful articles providing an overview of the 1988 Constitution are MANOEL CONÇALVES FERREIRA FILHO, "Fundamental Aspects of the 1988 Constitution," in Jacob Dolinger and Keith S. Rosenn, eds., *A Panorama of Brazilian Law* (1992), pp. 11–25; and KEITH S. ROSENN, "Brazil's New Constitution: An Exercise in Transient Constitutionalism for a Transitional Society," in *American Journal of Comparative Law* 38 (1990): 773–802. An interesting historical perspective on the use and misuse of the decree-law and the provisional measure is TIMOTHY POWER, "The Pen Is Mightier Than the Congress: Presidential Decree Power in Brazil" (paper presented at the Eighteenth International Congress of the Latin American Studies Association, Atlanta, Georgia, 10–12 March 1994).

KEITH S. ROSENN

**BRAZIL: COUNCIL OF STATE,** an institution that advised the Brazilian crown on the use of the MODERATIVE POWER, matters of state, general measures of public administration, declarations of war, and treaties with foreign nations. Formed in 1824, its members were party leaders who were appointed for life and who frequently were appointed to cabinet posts. During the First Empire the constitution required the crown to consult the council, whose perception as a tool of PEDRO I made it increasingly unpopular.

The council was abolished during the Regency and reinstated in 1841 with modifications: imperial consultation became optional except on the exercise of the moderative power, its membership was increased from ten to twelve permanent members, and it became a court of appeals for administrative justice. It was divided into a plenary council and four sections: empire, finances, foreign relations and justice, and war and navy. The plenary council advised the emperor, and the four sections advised the respective ministries on administrative matters. Although consultation was now optional, there developed a de facto system of decision making in which its advice was required, making the council an unofficial legislative body that influenced all areas of administration. In 1889 it was abolished by the republic.

JOSÉ HONÓRIO RODRIGUES, *O Conselho de estado, o quinto poder?* (1978).

LYDIA M. GARNER

**BRAZIL: ECONOMIC MIRACLE (1968–1974),** a period of prosperity that was marked by high annual rates of economic growth, an expanded number of public and private development projects, and an increase in the volume and the diversity of exports. The miracle resulted from the economic policies adopted by military leaders following the 1964 coup against João GOULART. These policies were designed to favor business and encourage foreign and domestic investment. The economy stagnated in the first few years after the coup, but beginning in 1968 improved dramatically, and continued to grow for the next six years. Between 1968 and 1974 the annual real gross domestic product rose by an average of 11 percent, compared to the average 3.7 percent in the preceding five years.

The industrial sector expanded at an annual average rate of 12.6 percent as basic industries substantially increased production. Steel output rose from 2.8 million tons in 1964 to 9.2 million tons in 1976, and passenger car production soared from 184,000 vehicles in 1964 to 986,000 in 1976. Increased manufacturing capacity helped diversify exports. Coffee accounted for 42 percent of exports in the mid-1960s, but only 12.6 percent in 1974; manufacturing jumped from 7.2 percent of exports to 27.7 percent. To create and maintain this growth, the military regimes sharply augmented spending for development projects and improved conditions for business. When President Artur da COSTA E SILVA closed the National Congress in December 1968, he revised tax policy to reduce the constitutionally mandated amount of tax revenue the national government shared with the states, from 20 percent to 12 percent. This shift allowed the government to undertake massive economic development projects, such as the TRANSAMAZON HIGHWAY. Besides shifting resources to development projects, the military maintained relatively low tax rates

and checked labor costs by cracking down on strikes and labor turmoil. As a result, foreign investors infused large amounts of capital.

The economic boom helped generate public support for military rule and justify that rule to critics abroad. Although federal spending and foreign capital further developed the industrial infrastructure of Brazil, the "economic miracle" failed to address some basic problems. Wealth was unevenly distributed, with only 20 percent of the population owning 63 percent of the country's wealth. By increasing federal spending and manipulating the financial system, the military regimes created the conditions for the inflation that followed. Moreover, the overreliance on foreign capital led to the massive external debt of the 1980s.

THOMAS SKIDMORE, *The Politics of Military Rule in Brazil* (1988); WERNER BAER, *The Brazilian Economy* (1989).

ROSS WILKINSON

*See also* **Economic Development.**

**BRAZIL: ELECTORAL REFORM LEGISLATION.** Brazil's Electoral Code, Law 4.737 (15 July 1965), and Organic Law on Political Parties, Law 5.682 (21 July 1971), date back to the period of the military dictatorship. While some of their provisions have been revoked or modified by constitutional reforms or subsequent legislation, they remain in force as basic legislation on the electoral rules.

The restoration of democracy in 1985 produced basic changes in the electoral rules. These changes were mandated by Constitutional Amendment 25 (15 May 1985), which reinstituted direct elections for the president and vice president and for municipal offices, permitted reorganization of banned political parties, enfranchised illiterates, and eliminated a constitutional provision that required loss of mandate for a senator or deputy who failed to follow his or her political party.

The right to vote was further expanded by the 1988 Constitution. Article 14 provides that "popular sovereignty shall be exercised by universal suffrage through direct and secret vote, with equal value for all." Illiterates and juveniles as young as sixteen may vote in all elections, but literacy is required in order to be eligible to run for public office. Voting is mandatory for all literate persons between the ages of eighteen and seventy. Suffrage is, however, not universal, for conscripts are disfranchised during their period of obligatory military service.

Supervision of elections and political parties, as well as the resolution of election disputes, is committed to the Electoral Courts, which are staffed by regular members of the judiciary. The Electoral Code sets out in great detail the rules for the operation of the Electoral Tribunals, whose jurisdiction is defined by the 1988 Constitution. It also sets out in great detail rules for the registration of voters and the conduct of elections, including measures such as secret ballots, transportation to the polls, and processing of returns. Candidates must be registered by parties. The Code provides methods for supervision of the balloting process and for nullifying contested ballots. It also defines a series of electoral crimes, triable before the Electoral Tribunals. Finally, the Code regulates electoral propaganda. Supervision of this propaganda by the Electoral Courts was eliminated by Law 7.332 (1 July 1985).

The Electoral Code and the Organic Law of Political Parties with subsequent amendments are published in JUAREZ DE OLIVEIRA, ed., *Código Eleitoral: Lei orgânica dos partidos políticos; Legislação correlata e Súmulas do Tribunal Superior Eleitoral*, 10th ed. (1993). A useful historical perspective on Brazilian electoral reform can be found in TOSHIO MUKAI, "Sistemas eleitorais no Brasil," *Revista de Direito Constitucional e Ciência Política* (Special number, 1987): 307–348.

KEITH S. ROSENN

*See also* **Brazil: Constitutions; Judicial Systems: Brazil.**

**BRAZIL: FIRST EMPIRE.** The first Empire (1822–1831) was a period of consolidation of Brazilian independence and of struggle between the crown and the elites. Territorial unification of the empire, foreign recognition of its independence, and the enactment of a constitution were the major achievements of the period. The convergence of the conflicting ideologies of centralism and federalism, an opposition to monarchical absolutism and centralized power, and the fear of reunification with Portugal led to continual conflict between the crown and the General Assembly for control of political power, and eventually paralyzed the government. A number of royal actions irrevocably alienated the Chamber of Deputies; among them PEDRO I's dissolution of the constituent assembly and his subsequent granting of a centralizing constitution, the disclosure of secret conventions in the treaty with Portugal, and the Anglo-Brazilian treaty to end the SLAVE TRADE, which was signed and ratified by the emperor without the General Assembly's knowledge. Pedro's inheritance of the Portuguese throne in 1827 fueled anti-Portuguese tendencies and reawakened fears of reunification and the suspicion that Pedro's interests were with Portugal.

Despite the adversarial climate of the First Empire, a supreme court of justice, a postal service, and a criminal code were established. During this period several separatist insurrections were suppressed with various degrees of success. In 1824 the CONFEDERATION OF THE EQUATOR was defeated, but the revolt in the Cisplatine province led to a protracted war and ultimately to the creation of Uruguay. Economic progress was scant: measures to promote immigration failed, coffee exports tripled but the prices for other exports fell due to international competition, inflation was high, public and foreign debt rose, the exchange rate declined, the equalization of duties did not allow for increases of revenues, and the Bank of Brazil was liquidated. The continual political and institutional crises led to the abdication of Pedro I in 1831.

JOHN ARMITAGE, *A History of Brazil*, 2 vols., (repr. 1970); EMILIA VIOTTI DA COSTA, *The Brazilian Empire: Myths and Histories* (1985), pp. 1–77; NEILL MACAULAY, *Dom Pedro: The Struggle for Liberty in Brazil and Portugal, 1798–1834* (1986), pp. 87–253; LESLIE BETHELL, ed., *Brazil Empire and Republic, 1822–1930* (1989).

LYDIA M. GARNER

**BRAZIL: SECOND EMPIRE.** The reign of PEDRO II (1840–1889) was a period of recentralization, restoration of order and legitimate authority, state building, and economic development, especially in the years 1845–1870. Consensus among parties and the elite on fundamental issues promoted political unity and a liberal and stable regime. Federalism receded, and the cycle of revolts ended. Institutionalized control over the provinces was established as was crown authority over the executive and legislative branches. The Council of State was reinstated, and reform of the Criminal Procedures Code gave the executive control over the police and judiciary.

Empiricism and gradualism guided the government on legislation. Freedom of the press, a two-party system, and parliamentarism were institutionalized and electoral reforms were implemented. The banking, diplomatic, and administrative systems were organized, civil laws were consolidated, and a commercial code was compiled. The economy grew as Brazil became the leading exporter of coffee, as imports and exports increased, and as the tariff reform of 1844 strengthened finances. The quickening of the economy fostered railway building, introduction of steam navigation, construction of public works, incorporation of joint-stock companies, development of public utilities, increasing urbanization, and some industrial growth. Under British pressure the SLAVE TRADE had ended, and in 1867 the government began to plan the gradual abolition of SLAVERY. Beyond Brazil's borders progressive involvement in the Plata region helped to defeat Juan Manuel de ROSAS of Argentina, but the WAR OF THE TRIPLE ALLIANCE (1865–1870) proved a costly victory for the empire. The last two decades of the monarchy brought impressive growth in population, immigration, wage labor, capital accumulation, and economic prosperity, as well as measures for administrative decentralization. It was also a time of ferment. The centralization that had provided stability was seen now as an impediment to progress. Divergent views and interests among elite groups broke the unity of the social and political pact. POSITIVISM influenced the younger generation, especially that in the army, which developed a messianic view and contempt for civilian politicians. Old issues resurfaced. In the early 1870s, state control of the church on temporal matters led to the Religious Question, which only reinforced the perception of a powerful and unbending state. The law of the Free Womb (FREE BIRTH LAW) and the concept of gradual abolition of slavery were attacked as inadequate, and the abolitionist movement increasingly gained strength. Republican propaganda grew in its advocacy of federalism and changes in the MODERATIVE POWER and the Council of State.

The increasing unrest was only slightly checked by a complacent political elite, which was certain of the strength and solid foundations of the political system. In reality, the lack of mechanisms to handle and accommodate the compounding political and social changes occurring in society paralyzed the system, ensuring its demise. In 1888 Princess ISABEL abolished slavery by bypassing the traditional system of decision making. Unrest in the army, manipulated by a small group of civilians, led to the easy overthrow of the monarchy in 1889.

RICHARD GRAHAM, *Britain and the Onset of Modernization in Brazil, 1850–1914* (1968); ROBERT CONRAD, *The Destruction of Brazilian Slavery, 1850–1888*, 2d ed. (1972); EMILIA VIOTTI DA COSTA, *The Brazilian Empire: Myths and Histories* (1985); LESLIE BETHELL, ed., *Brazil Empire and Republic, 1822–1930* (1989).

LYDIA M. GARNER

**BRAZIL: GEOGRAPHY.** Brazil is characterized by diversity and marked regional contrasts. This variety reflects its size (3.3 million square miles), making it the world's fifth largest country. It occupies almost half of South America and is more than 2,700 miles in extent from north to south and from east to west. It is also essentially tropical, extending from 5° N to 33° S, with only 6 percent of its territory south of the Tropic of Capricorn. Bounded on the east by the Atlantic Ocean, it has frontiers with all the countries of South America except Chile and Ecuador. The lack of a Pacific seaboard may have inhibited notions of "manifest destiny," but the political boundaries, empty lands, and resource potential foster an active interest in Amazonia. The population is a mélange of Amerindians, Portuguese, Africans, south and east Europeans, and Asians, with a profound contrast in distribution between the coastlands and the still empty interior.

PHYSICAL ENVIRONMENT

Lowland areas (below 650 feet) are limited to the Amazon basin, the far south, the Pantanal of Mato Grosso, and a narrow coastal plain. Much of the country consists of upland, the Brazilian highlands south of the Amazon and the Guyana highlands to the north. These are formed by geologically ancient crystalline rocks, partially overlain by limestone and sandstone sediments, and in the south by basaltic lavas. The terrain is generally of gently rounded hills, with occasional resistant residuals on the crystalline areas and more angular tablelands in the sediments and basalts. Highest points are the Pico da Neblina (9,885 feet) on the Venezuelan border and the Pico de Bandeira (9,479 feet) in the southeast. The uplands closely abut the shore from Salvador to Pôrto Alegre as complex ranges or a single escarpment in excess of 2,500 feet.

This barrier is cut by few rivers, posing a major obstacle to colonial and contemporary access to the interior. The rivers are generally broken by falls and rapids, limiting their navigability. Those of the center form tributaries of the Amazon; the Paraná-Paraguay-Uruguay system debouches into the Río de la Plata, and the São Francisco parallels the coast for 750 miles before tumbling over the 275-foot Paulo Afonso falls to reach the sea.

A humid tropical climate gives average temperatures above 68° F and rainfall above 47 inches, both of which vary with increasing altitude and latitude. Rainfall seasonality and temperature range increase away from the equator, and the interior SERTÃO (hinterland) of the northeast experiences low and markedly seasonal rainfall and occasional drought. Southern Brazil has a temperate climate, subject to frost hazard, which fosters a different agriculture.

The climax vegetation is mainly woodland, though varying from evergreen equatorial forest in Amazonia to tropical forest on the coastal uplands and the Araucária pine forest in the south. There are patches of grassland savanna in northern Amazonia, and the central highlands are covered by shrub grassland called *cerrado*. The semiarid Sertão sustains only poor *caatinga* thorn scrub, and southern Rio Grande do Sul has an extension of the pampas grassland.

The thick forests engendered notions of fertility, but most soils are fragile, leached, and of low productivity. Significant exceptions are the *massapé* soils of coastal Pernambuco and Bahia and *terra roxa* of the basalt plateaus.

Brazil is, however, evidently rich in other natural resources and these have exerted considerable influence on the pattern of occupation. Between 1500 and 1930 the development process can be described as the assembling of a loose jigsaw, as various resources were identified and exploited, prompting the settlement of different areas. These include dyewood along the coast before 1550, sugar on the *massapé* soils in the sixteenth and seventeenth centuries, gold in Minas Gerais, Goiás, and Mato Grosso (1690–1750), and coffee in Rio de Janeiro and São Paulo (1830–1930). Gathering of spices and later rubber fostered slight and largely ephemeral exploitation of Amazonia before 1910, and the *caatinga* and pampas supported pastoralism, which provided meat, hides, and draft animals for other regions. More recently base metals such as iron, manganese, and bauxite; abundant hydroelectricity; and, since 1970, offshore oil, have provided major resources for industrialization.

## POPULATION

There has been rapid demographic growth in the twentieth century. From an estimated 3.8 million inhabitants at the end of the colonial period, Brazil's population rose to 17.4 million in 1900 and 51.9 million in 1950. Estimated population in 1990 was 150 million, and the projection for 2000 is 179.5 million. Since 1950 the annual rate of increase has exceeded 2.2 percent, and consequently almost two-thirds of Brazilians are below twenty-five years of age.

The precolonial population has been calculated at about 2 million, but this was diminished by disease, warfare, miscegenation, and acculturation, and surviving Amerindians are mainly confined to Amazonia. Colonial immigration from Portugal was limited, possibly to around 1 million people, and an estimated 2.5 to 3 million African slaves imported between 1538 and 1850 provided much of the labor force. Following emancipation in 1888, there was substantial IMMIGRATION from Iberia, Italy, Germany, and eastern Europe, and between 1908 and 1935 from Japan, to São Paulo and the south. Total foreign immigration between 1884 and 1933 was almost 4 million people. As a result of miscegenation Brazil's population is ethnically heterogeneous, but with significant regional variations in the admixture.

Overall population density is low, less than six persons per square mile, but there is a distinct contrast between the coastal states from Ceará to Rio Grande do Sul, with densities generally above twelve per square mile, and the interior of Amazonia and the center-west, where it is below two. Since 1950 the population has become increasingly urbanized, and two-thirds are now defined as urban dwellers. This urbanization has been fueled by migration from the countryside to the larger cities. Some 36 million people live in ten metropolitan regions, of which São Paulo, Rio de Janeiro, Belo Horizonte, Recife, and Pôrto Alegre are the largest.

## ECONOMY

Urban-based manufacturing and services dominate the gross domestic product and provide two-thirds of employment. The Brazilian economy ranks as the world's eleventh largest, and recent investments by the government and multinational corporations have given it the status of Newly Industrializing Country, with significant metal, engineering, and vehicle industries. The agricultural sector encompasses small-scale subsistence, traditional plantation crops such as sugar and coffee, pastoralism, and innovative production of soybeans, citrus, and vegetables.

As a consequence of economic development, profound spatial inequities exist, within the cities between skyscrapers and *favelas*, between the towns and the countryside, and regionally. Most of the stimuli of modernization have concentrated in the southeast and south and their principal cities. The northeast, particularly the *sertão*, remains impoverished, while the interior is still undeveloped, despite the construction of Brasília and major penetrative highways and the exploitation of minerals, timber, and land.

PRESTON E. JAMES, *Latin America*, 4th ed. (1969), pp. 683–897; JOHN DICKENSON, *Brazil* (1982); INSTITUTO BRASILEIRO DE GEOGRAFIA E ESTATÍSTICA, *Geografia do Brasil*, 5 vols. (1989); INSTITUTO BRASILEIRO DE GEOGRAFIA E ESTATÍSTICA, *Anuário estatístico do Brasil, 1990* (1990); NEIL MAC DONALD, *Brazil: A Mask Called Progress* (1991).

JOHN P. DICKENSON

**BRAZIL: INDEPENDENCE MOVEMENTS.** Unlike Spanish America, which experienced a long and at times bloody struggle for independence from Spain, Portuguese America was emancipated from European domination in three distinct steps: (1) in 1808 the prince regent and his court were established in Rio de Janeiro, and the ports of Brazil were formally opened to international commerce, ending the old mercantilist system; (2) in 1815 the United Kingdom of Portugal and Brazil was proclaimed; and (3) in 1822 the heir to the Portuguese throne, Dom PEDRO I, declared Brazil's independence and became the first emperor of a new world monarchy. Much institutional and dynastic continuity was thus preserved in Brazil, and while there were separatist revolts (most significantly in Pernambuco in 1817), the transition from colonial to national status was considerably less traumatic than it was elsewhere in the hemisphere.

This outcome was partly the result of international circumstances and the particular relationship that the PORTUGUESE EMPIRE had with respect to the great naval power of the period, Great Britain. Yet the failure of a series of nationalist plots in Brazil in the last two decades of the eighteenth century also played a significant role. The most important of these conspiracies were in Minas (1788–1789) and Bahia (1798). Each was very different in composition, objectives, and consequences. The Minas conspiracy was republican in inspiration and looked to the newly established United States as a model. Involved in this plot were leading members of the regional oligarchy, including magistrates, priests, landowners, and businessmen, as well as the commanding officer of the local professional military and members of the officer corps, including the Alferes Joaquim José da SILVA XAVIER (Tiradentes). The Minas plotters wanted independence for Brazil but they equivocated over changes in Brazilian society and were divided in their attitudes toward slavery. The Bahian plot involved shopkeepers, soldiers, and even slaves, who, unlike the white elite members of the Minas group, were in the main African Brazilians and *pardos* (in colonial terminology, persons of mixed racial origins, originally applied to the offspring of African women and European men, but by the late eighteenth century this group encompassed almost a quarter of the population in many areas). The Bahian conspirators wished to see a revolution in social relationships and the elimination of discrimination based on skin color. They were more concerned with social reform than with independence and took as their model the revolution in France. But like the Minas plotters they were uncovered and imprisoned before they were able to act. The Portuguese authorities dealt with both plots harshly. Tiradentes was hanged and quartered and his co-conspirators exiled. The Bahian plotters were executed or abandoned along the African coast.

Enlightened members of the Portuguese government, however, used the failure of the two plots to co-opt leading younger Brazilian intellectuals by granting them access to government patronage and exploiting Brazilian elite fears of racial upheaval (something well demonstrated by the slave revolt in Haiti). Thus, young Brazilians like José Bonifácio de Andrada e Silva received a government scholarship for study and travel in Europe, high positions in the administration in Portugal, and membership in the Lisbon Academy of Sciences. Men like Andrada e Silva would later play key roles in the emergence of an independent Brazil, ruled by monarchical institutions and led by the BRAGANÇA dynasty.

KENNETH R. MAXWELL, *Conflicts and Conspiracies: Brazil and Portugal, 1750–1808* (1973); A. J. R. RUSSELL-WOOD, *From Colony to Nation: Essays on the Independence of Brazil* (1975); NEILL MACAULAY, *Dom Pedro: The Struggle for Liberty in Brazil and Portugal, 1798–1834* (1986).

KENNETH MAXWELL

*See also* **Inconfidência dos Alfaites; Inconfidência Mineira.**

**BRAZIL: LIBERAL MOVEMENTS.** Liberal movements during the monarchy (1822–1889) varied considerably between partisan developments and inchoate reform mobilizations. Responding to the absolutism and Portuguese interests associated with PEDRO I, political and socioeconomic elite members and (often urban, middle-sector) radical ideologues joined in opposition. Although repressed in the Constituent Assembly of 1823 and the secessionist CONFEDERATION OF THE EQUATOR (1824), they were successful in parliamentary obstruction after 1826. That, and the associated street violence and military insubordination, unexpectedly led the emperor to abdicate (1831).

Though colored by lusophobia, this movement emphasized the native elite's control of the state and their aspiration to more decentralized rule and revenue sharing at the local and provincial levels. These issues drove elite members to spurn the radicals (EXALTADOS) and form the Moderado Party, which dominated Parliament, elected the regents, nearly rewrote the Constitution of 1824, and did, in fact, reform it in the ADDITIONAL ACT OF 1834. The Moderados hoped ideally to create a progressive nation; more pragmatically, they hoped to eliminate the possibilities of absolutist restoration and to secure political support in the face of rightist and leftist pressure. By 1835, certain elite groups held the decentralizing reforms responsible for uprisings that threatened social revolution and national dismemberment. Representatives of these groups left the Moderados, joined the reactionaries in parliament, and formed the Conservative Party, which soon dominated the state and began the legislative reversal of the reforms (1836–1841). The more liberal minority joined the *exaltados* to form the Liberal Party, and broke the Conservatives' control of the state by successfully conspiring to bring PEDRO II to power in 1840. They correctly anticipated that he would call them to form his first cabinet. Their excesses, however, led the emperor's advisers to bring a more conservative cabinet to power (1841), which completed the legislative reaction and drove the Liberals of São Paulo and Minas Gerais to revolt (1842). Their military defeat crowned the success of the reactionaries and the creation of a highly centralized, authoritarian regime.

Ephemeral Liberal administrations and one failed revolt in the 1840s confirmed the subsequent era (1842–1862) as one in which reactionary triumph abruptly shifted to a kind of halting, conservative reformism in 1853. That year the emperor tapped the Conservative chieftain, the marquês de PARANÁ, to bring about partisan conciliation and electoral reform. After Paraná, the Conservatives' moderate wing reached out to the Liberals and led them toward the gradualist reformism of the Progressive League (ca. 1862–1868) and its cabinets (1862, 1864–1868).

The last such cabinet, beset by the purists of both parties, was undermined by the emperor, who then called in the reactionary cabinet of 1868. The Liberal response (ranging from the dramatic reforms of the Liberal Manifesto of 1869 to the 1870 formation of the Republican Party) reflected the florescence of 1860s criticism associated with such figures as Teofilo OTTONI and Aureliano Cándido TAVARES BASTOS. Critics called for the ABOLITION OF SLAVERY, direct elections, separation of church and state, the reform or eradication of the crown's role, and decentralization. However, they lacked organizational or ideological unity. The Liberals, occasionally in power after 1878, divided over the choice and extent of reforms; the Republicans did not officially endorse abolition; and abolition had adherents in the two traditional parties.

However divided, such liberal reformism, often associated with the Generation of 1870 or the Recife School, suggests vague coherence and a general movement in opposition to the status quo (although POSITIVISM's increasing influence complicates the use of "liberal"). As such, it retains importance in understanding the milieu and mobilization that informed both the abolitionist movement (1879–1888) and the monarchy's political crisis, culminating in the Republic of 1889.

JOAQUIM NABUCO, *Um estadista do império*, 3 vols. (1898–1899); EMILIA VIOTTI DA COSTA, *The Brazilian Empire* (1985); ILMAR ROHLOFF DE MATTOS, *O tempo saquarema* (1987); RODER-

ICK J. BARMAN, *Brazil: The Forging of a Nation* (1988); LESLIE BETHELL, ed., *Brazil: Empire and Republic* (1989); RICHARD GRAHAM, *Patronage and Politics in Nineteenth-Century Brazil* (1990).

JEFFREY D. NEEDELL

*See also* **Brazil: Political Parties.**

**BRAZIL: NATIONAL SECURITY DOCTRINE,** a set of principles and beliefs that evolved out of the Brazilian officer corps' participation in the dismantling of the empire in 1889. Out of that experience came the belief that the military was directly responsible for the well-being of the nation.

In the first quarter of the twentieth century, the officer corps, especially the army, considered the military as the only force capable of both building a national consciousness that superseded regional differences and solving the problems of the country. This view colored the military's vision of its mission and its role in society, and influenced its actions. Though the doctrine of national security grew out of early experiences, it was refined from 1949 to 1964 at the Escola Superior de Guerra (ESG, or Higher War School) and the Escola de Comando e Estado Maior do Exército (ECEME, or Army Command and General Staff School). The doctrine offered the rationale for the 1964 military coup that overthrew President João GOULART and provided the justification for repressive actions of the subsequent military governments. According to the doctrine, national security and economic development were possible only if Brazil's economic, political, and social structures were altered, and civilian elites lacked both the will and ability to make changes. Inherent in national security ideology was adherence to the capitalist development model, with government intervention, and anticommunism as espoused by the United States.

Courses studied at the ESG and ECEME, which included classes on INFLATION, banking reform, LAND TENURE, voting systems, transportation, EDUCATION, and conventional and guerrilla warfare, gave Brazilian officers the confidence that they had the ideology, trained personnel, and institutional will to maintain internal order while developing the country. That belief led the officer corps, many of whom helped formulate the national security doctrine as instructors or students at the ESG and ECEME, to overthrow the Goulart government and install a series of military presidents who attempted to implement the doctrine's precepts.

The economic policies of the various military governments attacked inflation and promoted rapid growth, which led to the so-called economic miracle. Rapid development allowed the military governments to claim legitimacy on the basis of seemingly successful economic policies. Ironically, the "miracle" coincided with the period of the greatest political repression. Using the national security doctrine as justification, the military governments imposed CENSORSHIP, eliminated popular participation in politics, controlled labor unions and political organizations, and curtailed civil and HUMAN RIGHTS. Political rights were denied opponents of the regimes, and arbitrary arrests, exile, torture, and murder with methods used in the name of national security through statutes such as the SNI Law, the National Security Law, AI-5, and the 1969 Constitution.

Use of the doctrine to justify government actions began to lose force with the relaxation of the system in the late 1970s and early 1980s, and seemed to disappear with the return to civilian rule in 1985. The officer corps now concentrates on preparation for external threats, and the development of technical expertise and institutional discipline; it generally takes a nonpolitical stance. Still, underlying military thinking is the concept that economic and social progress occurs when internal order is maintained.

Numerous works speak of the national security doctrine but the most comprehensive is ANTÔNIO ARRUDA, *ESG História de sua doutrina* (1980). ALFRED STEPAN, ed., *Authoritarian Brazil: Origins, Policies, and Future* (1973), provides an excellent analysis in the chapter "Professionalism of Internal Order and Military Role Expansion." Formulation and implementation of the doctrine is sprinkled throughout THOMAS E. SKIDMORE, *The Politics of Military Rule in Brazil, 1964–1985* (1988), and RONALD SCHNEIDER, *Order and Progress: A Political History of Brazil* (1991).

SONNY B. DAVIS

*See also* **Brazil: National Security Law.**

**BRAZIL: NATIONAL SECURITY LAW,** a legal justification for the Brazilian military junta's crackdown on political opposition. Established on 29 September 1969, the law gave the government vast discretion in defining crimes against national security and allowed detention for up to twenty days without charge. Prohibited conduct included fomenting class struggle, distributing subversive propaganda, engaging in public strikes, and inciting collective disobedience. Criminal sanctions prevented journalists and editors from reporting events or opinions that violated the national security law. The numerous arrests under this law, frequently accompanied by torture, created a climate of fear that sustained the power of Brazil's authoritarian regime for over a decade.

PETER FLYNN, *Brazil: A Political Analysis* (1972); MARIA HELENA MOREIA ALVES, *State and Opposition in Military Brazil* (1985); THOMAS E. SKIDMORE, *The Politics of Military Rule in Brazil, 1964–85* (1988).

MICHAEL A. POLL

**BRAZIL: NEW REPUBLIC,** a term denoting both the period in Brazilian politics and the governmental system that began on 15 March 1985, when civilians regained control of the federal government after twenty-one years of authoritarian military rule. The transition to democratic civilian rule was the culmination of ABERTURA, a lengthy process of political liberalization that began in the late 1970s under military president João Baptista FIGUEIREDO. Initially, Brazilians hoped that the New Republic would restore political freedoms and achieve economic growth under democratic procedures. The widespread social and political mobilization against military rule seemed to promise a period of more inclusive politics, incorporating grass-roots organizations, church-based social movements, and unionized labor into the more traditional political establishment. This optimism, however, has been marred by incessant political gridlock, economic stagnation, high inflation, scandal, and deteriorating social conditions, which have plagued Brazil during the 1980s and 1990s.

The New Republic began under unexpectedly tense circumstances when illness prevented President-elect Tancredo NEVES from assuming the presidency and Vice President–elect José SARNEY was sworn in as "acting president." Sarney assumed full presidential powers the week before Neves's death in April 1985. Sarney's coalition government was an immediate victim of the widespread grief and disappointment surrounding Neves's death, as well as its own numerous political missteps. During his five-year presidency, Sarney was generally unsuccessful at effective leadership of the executive branch. The executive was unable to form a lasting coalition with the legislative branch to overhaul Brazil's political system. The Constituent Assembly, convened in late 1986 to write a new federal constitution, also proved ineffective in implementing most major reforms of the national political system. Although democratic procedures, most notably open elections and the lack of direct military intervention in politics, were consolidated and expanded during Sarney's presidency, a party system weakened by extreme factionalism and corruption undermined much of the program of political reform. Economic reform packages such as the Cruzado Plan (1986) and the Verão Plan (1989), which included currency devaluation, price controls, wage freezes, and debt renegotiations, provided only temporary respites from high inflation and economic instability.

Hopes for true change in national political and economic life were renewed during the 1990 presidential race, the first direct presidential elections in Brazil since 1960. In the November runoff election, former metalworker Luiz Ignácio (Lula) da SILVA, a candidate of the Workers Party (PT), faced the conservative governor of the state of Alagoas, Fernando COLLOR DE MELLO. Collor defeated Silva and immediately after assuming the presidency enacted a radical economic reform package that included strict price controls, the seizure of private assets, and the aggressive downsizing of the federal bureaucracy and state-owned enterprises. Like its predecessors, this economic stabilization package functioned briefly and drastically reduced inflation. The Collor administration crumbled when a 1992 congressional committee uncovered massive corruption within the executive branch. Collor was impeached and resigned in December 1992, and Vice President Itamar FRANCO became president. The Brazilian republican system continues to strain under the weight of a bloated federal bureaucracy, recurring economic recessions, and abysmal social disparities. The New Republic consolidated the end to active military presence in national politics, but not to the socioeconomic distortions of the authoritarian period. The economic stabilization package and political reforms introduced during the early months of Fernando Henrique CARDOSO's presidency, which began in January 1995, may prove to correct some of these distortions.

JOHN WIRTH et al., eds., *State and Society in Brazil: Continuity and Change* (1987); THOMAS SKIDMORE, *The Politics of Military Rule in Brazil, 1964–85* (1988), pp. 256–310; ALFRED STEPAN, ed., *Democratizing Brazil: Problems of Transition and Consolidation* (1989); SONIA ALVAREZ, *Engendering Democracy in Brazil: Women's Movements in Transition Politics* (1990); MIGUEL REALE, *De Tancredo a Collor* (1992); PEDRO COLLOR, *Passando a limpo: A trajetória de um farsante* (1993).

DARYLE WILLIAMS

## BRAZIL: ORGANIZATIONS

### Advanced Institute of Brazilian Studies
### Instituto Superior de Estudos Brasileiros—ISEB

Created by Decree 37608 on 14 July 1955, the ISEB was devoted to the study of Brazilian development problems. Part of the Ministry of Education and Culture, ISEB's roots were in the private Brazilian Institute of Economics, Sociology, and Politics (IBESP). The ISEB was designed as a vehicle through which leading academics could address issues of development and industrialization by pursuing research and providing training courses to Brazilian government officials. From its beginning at the start of the Juscelino KUBITSCHEK presidency, the ISEB supported the "nationalist-developmentalist" policies of the administration. The ISEB included among its scholars Hélio JAGUARIBE, Cândido Mendes de Almeida, Roberto CAMPOS, Nélson Werneck SODRÉ, and Roland Corbisier. Plagued by internal divisions and political disputes, the ISEB was reorganized in 1959 and many of its members resigned. The institute became increasingly nationalistic in its views on development and foreign investment, and broadened the political scope of its activities to establish ties to student groups, syndicalists, the Communist Party (PCB), and various nationalist groups. The military government that seized power in 1964 closed the ISEB and opened an investigation into the activities of its members and the political leaders who had supported it.

THOMAS E. SKIDMORE, *Politics in Brazil* (1967); ISRAEL BELOCH and ALZIRA ALVES DE ABREU, eds., *Dicionário histórico-biográfico brasileiro, 1930–1983* (1984).

WILLIAM SUMMERHILL

### Frente Agrária

In 1962, the Brazilian Catholic church established the Frente Agrária to promote the interests of rural workers through the formation of labor unions. Begun in the South, the Frente was preceded in the Northeast by the church's Rural Assistance Service (SAR; founded 1949) and Rural Orientation Service of Pernambuco (SORPE: founded 1961). New church teachings promulgated by the peasant-born Pope John XXIII inspired the young priests who led the organization. Although the church wanted them to combat communism and Peasant League influences in the countryside, some of the Frente's radical clergy eventually worked together with Communists in the Superintendency of Agrarian Reform (SUPRA). The 1964 military coup d'état suppressed the front and jailed its leaders.

EMANUEL DE KADT, *Catholic Radicals in Brazil* (1970); THOMAS C. BRUNEAU, *The Political Transformation of the Brazilian Catholic Church* (1974).

CLIFF WELCH

### Brazilian Bar Association
### Ordem dos Avogados do Brasil—OAB

The Brazilian Bar Association is authorized by the Brazilian government to regulate entry to the bar and to uphold professional conduct among lawyers. Its predecessor was the Instituto da Ordem dos Advogados Brasileiros, founded in 1843, when statutes were approved by the emperor, Dom PEDRO II. The OAB was effectively organized in 1931, with government approval of the statutes coming in December of that year. At present the OAB's organization stems from 1963 legislation that recognizes it as an organ working in the public interest and that mandates a federated structure. In each state capital there is a section of the OAB, with councilors who serve as members of the Federal Council of Lawyers. Also serving as members of the council are all its former presidents. The presidencies of the Federal Council and of the OAB are coextensive and are customarily occupied by well-known and highly reputable lawyers. The OAB has regularly published a law journal and a newsletter. During the recent period of redemocratization and at earlier turbulent periods of Brazilian history, the OAB was often at the forefront in defending human and civil rights and in upholding democratic institutions.

THOMAS E. SKIDMORE, *Politics in Brazil, 1930–1964: An Experiment in Democracy* (1967), *The Politics of Military Rule in Brazil, 1964–1985* (1988); ALFRED STEPAN, ed., *Democratizing Brazil: Problems of Transition and Consolidation* (1989).

OLAVO BRASIL DE LIMA JÚNIOR
DOUGLAS COLE LIBBY

### Brazilian Institute of the Environment and Renewable Natural Resources
### Instituto Brasileiro do Meio Ambiente e dos Recursos Naturais Renováveis—Ibama

The Brazilian Institute of the Environment and Renewable Natural Resources enforces federal environmental laws and international treaties with environmental content to which Brazil is a signatory. Created in 1988 under President José SARNEY, the institute initially suffered a severe lack of human and financial resources. Sarney's successor, Fernando Collor de MELLO, accorded the environment a higher priority in his administration and elevated Ibama to the status of an autonomous ministry. Resource allocation to Ibama then improved, but chronic insufficiencies remained the norm.

In Brazil's decentralized postmilitary political system, a significant amount of environmental protection is being implemented by state agencies, not Ibama. Its most visible activities tend to be in the Amazon, where, with all nine states that comprise "Legal Amazonia," Ibama has made accords to interact with their law enforcement agencies in the protection of flora and fauna. Endeavors to reduce deforestation are utilizing satellite technology to identify sites of illegal burning, with mixed results; a decrease in deforestation in one year has been followed by an increase the next, perhaps due as much to climatic factors ("wet" versus "dry" years) as to Ibama's enforcement efforts.

Government agencies are rarely the topic of book-length works and only occasionally of articles. More often, agencies are discussed in the context of a larger theme. The following are some of the works in which Ibama receives attention: MARIANNE SCHMINK and CHARLES H. WOOD, *Contested Frontiers in Amazonia* (1992); "International Network Formed to Map Tropical Deforestation by Satellite," in *International Environment Reporter: Current Report* 13, no. 2 (14 February 1990): 65–66; and "Brazil Beefs Up Efforts Aimed at Slowing Amazon Deforestation," in *International Environment Reporter: Current Report* 13, no. 14 (21 November 1990): 485–486. For the federal legislation over which Ibama has jurisdiction see PRESIDÊNCIA DA REPÚBLICA, SECRETARIA DO MEIO AMBIENTE, INSTITUTO BRASILEIRO DO MEIO AMBIENTE E DOS RECURSOS NATURAIS RENOVÁVEIS—IBAMA, *Coletânea da legislação federal de meio ambiente* (1992).

LAURA JARNAGIN

*See also* **Environmental Movements, Latin America.**

### Brazilian Labor Confederation
### Confederação Operária Brasileira—COB

As an increasing number of artisans and tradesmen organized mutual aid societies and unions in the first years of the twentieth century, anarchist and socialist leaders in Rio and São Paulo saw the need for a central labor organization. Rio labor leaders formed a regional labor federation in 1903, and in 1906 they sponsored Brazil's first national labor congress. These labor leaders formed the Confederação Operária Brasileira (COB) in 1908 to help coordinate national labor policies.

The COB represented some fifty unions throughout Brazil, but more than half of them were located in the cities of Rio and São Paulo. The Confederação published a national labor newspaper, the pro-anarchist *A Voz do Trabalhador,* which sought to coordinate union and leftist politics. As an umbrella organization, the COB was only as effective as the unions it represented. COB activists sponsored the Second National Labor Congress in 1913 to establish a set of national policies for Brazilian workers. The participants protested the federal government's antilabor practices, especially its use of a 1907 deportation law to expel foreign-born anarchists.

The COB not only had to contend with government repression, it also presided over a weak and divided labor movement. Divisions by ethnicity, race, and gender plagued Brazil's nascent labor movement in the first two decades of the twentieth century. Union and leftist groups also conducted ideological debates. Many anarchists concentrated on cultural and educational programs for the working class and did little to organize among the rank and file. With the advent of World War I, many of them articulated antiwar positions while ignoring such issues as the increasing cost of living and the intensification of work regimes on the shop floor. The persistent weakness of local unions undermined the effectiveness of the COB. The Confederação faded during the 1910s, but many of its leaders went on to participate in the Third National Labor Congress in 1920 and continued to coordinate anarchist activities throughout Brazil in the 1920s and early 1930s.

One of the most complete studies of the early labor movement is JOHN W. F. DULLES, *Anarchists and Communists in Brazil, 1900–1935* (1973). The most complete single volume on workers and labor in these years is BORIS FAUSTO, *Trabalho urbano e conflito social* (1976). For an analysis of the rise and fall of the anarchist movement, see SHELDON L. MARAM, "Labor and the Left in Brazil, 1890–1921: A Movement Aborted," in *Hispanic American Historical Review* 57 (1977): 254–272. For analyses of the divisions within the labor movement in São Paulo, see GEORGE REID ANDREWS, "Black and White Workers: São Paulo, Brazil, 1888–1928," in *Hispanic American Historical Review* 68 (1988): 491–524, and JOEL WOLFE, "Anarchist Ideology, Worker Practice: The 1917 General Strike and the Formation of São Paulo's Working Class," in *Hispanic American Historical Review* 71 (1991): 809–846.

JOEL WOLFE

### Indigenist Missionary Council
### Conselho Indigenista Missionário—CIMI

CIMI was founded in 1972 by the Catholic bishops of Brazil to defend the rights of Brazilian Indians. In a reversal of the former view of how missionary effort should be directed, CIMI has seen as its primary duty not the conversion of Indians to Christianity but the conversion of the wider society to a recognition of the Indians' right to self-determination. The council has worked in support of the Indians' cultural distinctiveness, and has aided their efforts to regain and secure traditional lands. CIMI has denounced acts of violence against and economic exploitation of Indians, and has assisted Indian leaders in setting up their own organizations and in defining common problems and strategies.

THOMAS C. BRUNEAU AND W. E. HEWETT, "Catholicism and Political Action in Brazil: Limitations and Prospects," in *Conflict and Competition: The Latin American Church in a Changing Society*, edited by Edward R. Cleary and Hannah Stewart-Gambino (1992), pp. 45–62; JUDITH R. SHAPIRO, "Ideologies and Catholic Missionary Practice in a Post-Colonial Era," in *Comparative Studies in Society and History*, vol. 23, no. 1 (1981), pp. 130–149, and "From Tupã to the Land Without Evil: The Christianization of Tupi-Guarani Cosmology," in *American Ethnologist* 14 (1987): 125–133.

NANCY M. FLOWERS

*See also* **Catholic Church; Indian Policy; Missions.**

### Democratic Rural Union
### União Democrática Ruralista—UDR

The UDR was formed in Brazil in 1985 to represent the interests of large landowners and cattle ranchers in the debate over AGRARIAN REFORM that accompanied the transition from military to civilian rule. Started in the prairie lands of central Brazil, the UDR soon became a national presence, due in part to its provocative founding president, the Goiás-based physician and rancher Ronaldo Ramos Caiado.

The UDR developed a reputation as the most reactionary of landowner groups, the shock troop at the front of the battle against land reform. Raising money through widely publicized cattle auctions, the UDR organized mass rallies in the nation's capital and enhanced its political power through campaign contributions and running its own candidates. The UDR took credit for the absence of land distribution measures in the October 1985 agrarian reform law and tried, unsuccessfully, to exclude the issue from the 1988 national constitution.

In 1989, Caiado ran for president as the UDR candidate, receiving a small percentage of votes. Thereafter, the UDR pursued two characteristic strategies: it continued to lobby government to slow the agrarian reform process and it threatened violence to prevent landless peasants from occupying disputed lands. In various cases, UDR members were implicated as the alleged sponsors of gunmen who killed peasant and rural labor activists.

While the UDR could take credit for frustrating agrarian reform, the very existence of the organization raised questions about the strength of Brazil's rural elite and showed how far the country had come from the days when the rural oligarchy could take its influence for granted.

CHICO MENDES, *Fight for the Forest* (1989); BIORN MAYBURY-LEWIS, *The Debate Over Agrarian Reform in Brazil* (Papers on

Latin America, no. 14, Columbia University, 1990); and "UDR cria milícia armada contra sem-terra," in *Folha de São Paulo* (30 June 1994): p. 9.

CLIFF WELCH

### Development Superintendency of the Northeast
### Superintendência do Desenvolvimento do Nordeste—SUDENE

SUDENE is a special government agency concerned with the economic development of the Brazilian Northeast's coastal and *sertão* regions. Established in 1959 under President Juscelino KUBITSCHEK, it was designed to address the growing unrest in the impoverished Northeast. Congress allocated the necessary funds and gave SUDENE the authority to control and coordinate the activities of other federal agencies in the Northeast. Led by the noted economist Celso FURTADO, SUDENE drafted ambitious programs for attracting industry to the Northeast, marketing food, and moving poor families out of the *sertão*. An interesting feature of Furtado's program was a tax credit that allowed corporations to reduce their income tax liabilities by investing the tax savings in SUDENE projects. Initially, tax evasion created problems with this plan, but eventually it became vital to the program. Funding from the Brazilian and U.S. governments was considerable, but many projects were hampered by both state and national politics. During the 1960s and 1970s, SUDENE fell short of many of its goals. There were few changes in the region's agrarian structure, and attempts to combat unemployment through industrialization generated few jobs because most firms were located in the cities of Recife and Salvador. To address such shortcomings, the government created the Ministry of the Interior, which made SUDENE subject to its control, and centralized federal decision making. Although later downgraded somewhat as a result of its ineffectiveness during the drought of 1970, SUDENE nevertheless brought about many changes in the Northeast that continue to be felt. Recent emphasis has been placed upon the encouragement of private investment by local and foreign investors to promote regional development.

RIORDAN ROETT, *The Politics of Foreign Aid in the Brazilian Northeast* (1972); WERNER BAER, *The Brazilian Economy: Growth and Development*, 3d ed. (1989).

MICHAEL L. JAMES

### Escola Superior da Guerra (ESG),

Brazil's Superior War College. Following the failure of two short-lived military institutions in the 1890s and 1930s, the ESG was founded in 1949 on the recommendation of a commission of the General Staff (now the General Staff of the Combined Armed Forces), which, after surveying the post–World War II political and strategic scene, concluded that Brazil possessed all the geopolitical prerequisites to become a world power but lacked a political elite prepared to lead the nation to prosperity and international prestige. The commission thus favored the founding of an institution to prepare promising civilian and military personnel with the potential to rise to the highest levels of political, economic, social, and strategic leadership.

The ESG was initially commanded by General Oswaldo Cordeiro de Farias, a veteran of the Revolution of 1930 and of the BRAZILIAN EXPEDITIONARY FORCE (FEB) of 1944–1945. From this early association with the military reformers (*Tenentes*) and the World War II veterans (*Febianos*), who had been trained by the French Military Mission of 1919–1940, these military intellectuals and civilian technocrats came to prominence after the coup of 1964 and were referred to as the SORBONNE GROUP.

The curriculum of the ESG centers on the *curso superior*, a study of development, strategy, and internal and international policies. It is open to officers of all three services above the rank of lieutenant colonel or its equivalent, as well as selected civilians—academics, government functionaries, and businessmen—who are generally in the majority. The final phase of the program consists of teams engaged in simulated strategic planning on various issues.

The ESG also offers courses on the General Staff of the Combined Armed Forces as well as on national mobilization. Seminars on current topics are scheduled all year. The motto of the ESG, "Security and Development" (a modern version of Comtian "Order and Progress"), is disseminated by the ESG's Alumni Association, which is active throughout Brazil.

THOMAS E. SKIDMORE, *Politics in Brazil: 1930–1964* (1967); RAYMOND ESTEP, *The Military in Brazilian Politics, 1821–1970* (1971); HENRY H. KEITH and ROBERT A. HAYES, eds., *Perspectives on Armed Politics in Brazil* (1976); JOSÉ OSVALDO DE MEIRA PENNA, *O Dinossauro* (1988).

LEWIS A. TAMBS

### General Labor Command
### Comando Geral dos Trabalhadores—CGT

As Brazil's first functioning national trade union confederation, the CGT spoke for an insurgent labor movement that demonstrated organizational sophistication and an unprecedented capacity for mass mobilization during the early 1960s. The creation of a unified national labor organization, banned by law, had been heatedly debated in 1960 at the Third National Union Congress in Rio de Janeiro. After ousting conservatives from the National Confederation of Industrial Workers (CNTI) the next year, the proponents of a more aggressive and independent union movement formed a coordinating body during an August 1961 strike in support of João "Jango" GOULART's accession to the presidency following the resignation of Jânio QUADROS. This General Strike Command was renamed the General Labor

446

Command during the Fourth National Union Congress held in São Paulo in August 1962. The CGT was to be an "organ of orientation, coordination, and direction" linking legally recognized unions, federations, and confederations throughout Brazil.

Although never legally recognized, the CGT nonetheless played a prominent role in political and economic affairs in the last years of the Populist Republic. Led by a new generation of Communist, nationalist, and *trabalhista* (laborite) trade unionists, the CGT experimented with the use of general strikes that involved hundreds of thousands of workers. In 1962 the CGT organized Brazil's first politically motivated strikes that could credibly claim to be national in scope.

With the CGT's top leaders increasingly elected to local, state, and national legislative bodies, organized labor fought boldly for a program of change inspired by the *reformas de base* (basic reforms) of Goulart and his Brazilian Labor Party (PTB). Although the CGT's power was exaggerated, it won a number of important victories including the "thirteenth salary" (a legally mandated Christmas bonus) and the legalization of rural trade unionism. In March 1964, however, Goulart and his supporters proved too weak to prevent the right-wing military coup that outlawed the CGT and persecuted its leaders and supporters.

On the CGT, see LUCÍLIA DE ALMEIDA NEVES DELGADO, *O Comando Geral dos Trabalhadores no Brasil 1961–1964* (1981) and SÉRGIO AMAD COSTA, *O C.G.T. e as lutas sindicais Brasileiras (1960–1964)* (1981). For more general treatments, see KENNETH P. ERICKSON, *The Brazilian Corporative State and Working-Class Politics* (1977); and JOVER TELLES, *O movimento sindical no Brasil* (1962; repr. 1981). On two key CGT leaders and their base inR io de Janeiro, see HÉRCULES CORRÊA, *A Classe Operária e seu Partido* (1980); and issue #3 of *Memoria e Historia* (1987) on Roberto Morena.

JOHN D. FRENCH

*See also* **Communism; Labor.**

### *Getúlio Vargas Foundation*
### *Fundação Getúlio Vargas—FGV*

A quasi-governmental but politically independent research and education center, the FGV was created in 1944 by Luís Simões Lopes, the head of the Departamento Administrativo do Serviço Público (DASP), during the ESTADO NÔVO as part of an effort to make the bureaucracy more efficient and professional. The FGV studies administrative problems and trains future administrators.

Today, FGV is a vast complex of institutes, schools, centers, and a press that provides scholarly impetus in economics, public administration, accounting, education, human resources, political science, contemporary history, and documentation. FGV economists established the Instituto Brasileiro de Economia (IBRE) and the publications *Revista Brasileira de Economia* and *Conjuntura Econômica*, as well as a graduate school in eco-

nomics. They have provided three finance ministers, a minister of planning, a president of the Central Bank, and a president of the National Development Bank (BNDE). In public administration, the FGV created two graduate schools and a research center (Rio de Janeiro and São Paulo) and two journals, *Revista de Administração Pública* and *Revista de Administração de Empresas*. Similar leadership has been exercised in political science with the Instituto de Direito Público e Ciência Política (INDIPO), which offers graduate courses and publishes the *Revista de Ciência Política*. Linked to INDIPO is perhaps the best-organized archive in Latin America, the Centro de Pesquisa e Documentação de História Contemporanea (CPDOC). CPDOC focuses on post-1930 Brazilian political history and has the personal papers of most of the men who shaped the 1930–1964 period.

ROBERT T. DALAND, ed., *Perspectives of Brazilian Public Administration* (1963); ISRAEL BELOCH and ALZIRA ALVES DE ABREU, eds., *Dicionário histórico-biográfico brasileiro, 1930–1983*, vol. 2 (1984), 1407–1408; W. MICHAEL WEIS, "The Fundação Getúlio Vargas and the New Getúlio," in *Luso-Brazilian Review*, 24, no. 2 (1987): 49–60.

W. MICHAEL WEIS

*See also* **Brazil: National Bank for Economic Development.**

### *Indian Protection Service*
### *Serviço de Proteção ao Indio—SPI*

Originally known as the Service for the Protection of Indians and the Settlement of National Workers (SPILTN), the SPI was the first Brazilian federal agency charged with protecting Indian peoples against acts of frontier violence, persecution, and extermination. In the wake of the first public international accusations of indigenous genocide (XVI Congress of Americanists in Vienna, 1908) and in the midst of a period of intense national debate concerning the rights of indigenous peoples, President Nilo Peçanha, on 20 June 1910, signed Decree no. 8.072, the legislation mandating the formation of the SPI under the directorship of General Cândido Mariano da Silva RONDON. Reflecting the positivist ideals of Rondon and his supporters, this legislation recognized the rights of indigenous peoples to the lands they traditionally inhabited, as well as to their traditional customs, and provided for the demarcation of lands for which indigenous peoples would have exclusive usufructory rights. The SPI was charged with ensuring implementation of this legislation and also for facilitating the establishment of new settlements in areas previously unoccupied by peoples of European descent.

To mediate against the possibility of violent interethnic conflicts, Rondon adopted a strategy, known as PACIFICATION, for establishing friendly relations with previously uncontacted indigenous peoples. In a country as vast as Brazil and with a consistently small oper-

447

ating budget, the SPI had difficulty carrying out its responsibilities. From the 1920s until its dissolution, the SPI was fraught with scandal and corruption. It was replaced by the NATIONAL INDIAN FOUNDATION (FUNAI) in 1967.

SHELTON H. DAVIS, *Victims of the Miracle: Development and the Indians of Brazil* (1977), pp. 1–18; MANUELA CARNEIRO DA CUNHA, *Os direitos do índio: Ensaios e documentos,* (1987), pp. 78–82; GREG URBAN and JOEL SHERZER, eds., *Nation-States and Indians in Latin America* (1991), esp. pp. 218–222, 236–258.

LAURA GRAHAM

*See also* **Indians.**

### National Bank for Economic Development
### Banco Nacional de Desenvolvimento
### Econômico e Social—BNDE, BNDES

Created in 1952 by the Joint Brazil–United States Economic Commission (1951–1953), the BNDES (originally the BNDE) has been the major source of long-term financing of capital investment in Brazil since its creation. The scope of its operations was somewhat limited in the 1950s. The Bank Reform Act (Law 4595 of 1964), however, expanded its functions and programs by creating a group of special funds designed to serve different sectors of the economy, the most important of which was the Special Agency of Industrial Financing (FINAME). The BNDES's funds stem from two forced savings funds: the Program of Social Integration (PIS) and the Public Employees Financial Reserve Fund (PASEP, originally at the Bank of Brazil). The BNDE carried out a selective credit policy according to the norms determined by the National Monetary Council (CMN) through the network of public and private development banks set up with the 1964–1966 reforms.

The main publicly owned development banks subordinate to the BNDES are the Bank of the Northeast (BNB, 1952), the Bank of Amazonia (BASA, 1966), the National Bank of Cooperative Credit (BNCC, 1966), the Regional Development Bank of the Extreme South (BRDE, 1962), and the state development banks, which are owned and operated by the various states. The BNDES also owns its own participation corporation, BNDES Participações (BNDESPAR), to spur equity financing in addition to the BNDES system's role as a minority shareholder.

The divestiture ("privatization") of enterprises held by the BNDES, started in late 1991, should decrease the BNDES's role in direct ownership of the Brazilian corporate structure. However, the BNDES should still have an important role in financing basic infrastructure investment.

JOHN H. WELCH, *Capital Markets in the Development Process: The Case of Brazil* (1993).

JOHN H. WELCH

*See also* **Banking; Economic Development.**

### National Conference of Brazilian Bishops
### Conferência Nacional dos Bispos do
### Brasil—CNBB

Created in 1952, the National Conference of Brazilian Bishops (CNBB) has become the most important organization within the Brazilian Catholic church. It was one of the first national episcopal conferences in the world and the first one in Latin America. Although the CNBB and other national episcopal conferences have circumscribed authority according to canon law, the CNBB has been of fundamental importance, for it has given the Brazilian church a centralized structure and a voice on behalf of the country's bishops.

Between 1952 and 1964, the CNBB supported ecclesiastical innovation and many reformist measures promoted by Brazil's governments. During this period, Bishop Hélder CÂMARA, the prime mover behind the CNBB's creation, served as secretary-general. In 1964, however, support grew within the Brazilian hierarchy for more conservative positions, and shortly after the military coup, the CNBB issued a statement that praised the armed forces for their intervention. Known for their progressive orientations, Câmara and his supporters were defeated by a conservative slate in CNBB elections in October 1964.

In 1968, Bishop Aloísio Lorscheider was elected secretary-general and began a new period of CNBB activism. During the 1970s, the CNBB became known for its criticisms of human rights violations, its calls for more attention to the plight of the poor, and its support for ecclesiastical innovations, especially CHRISTIAN BASE COMMUNITIES. It also became a more organized institution that presented official church reactions to major public issues; by 1968 it was the only legitimate national voice for the Brazilian Catholic church. In the 1980s, reflecting worldwide trends in the Roman Catholic church as well as a period of democratization in Brazil, the CNBB retreated from the more visible political role it had assumed in the 1970s. Representing about 370 bishops, it is one of the three largest national bishops' conferences in the world.

THOMAS BRUNEAU, *The Political Transformation of the Brazilian Catholic Church* (1974), esp. pp. 107–126; GERVÁSIO FERNANDES DE QUEIROGA, *Conferência Nacional dos Bispos do Brasil: Comunhão e corresponsabilidade* (1977).

SCOTT MAINWARING

*See also* **Catholic Church; Liberation Theology.**

### National Guard

The part-time civilian militia in Brazil that was established on 18 August 1831 during the politically tumultuous period following Brazilian independence from Portugal. In its founding charter the militia was pledged to defend the Constitution of 1824 and to maintain internal order. The new government hoped that the force would counterbalance the army, which still harbored

Portuguese officers whose loyalties were suspect. Though it persisted into the twentieth century, when it became a mere reserve force of the army (as determined by the Constitution of 1934), the National Guard played its most significant role during the forty years following its formation.

Participation in the National Guard was mandatory for free men between the ages of eighteen and sixty who were not already serving in another military force and who possessed the minimum annual income required for voting. Guard units were organized by county, and most members were artisans, modest farmers, or petty businessmen—in short, a group which stood several notches above the poorest men, who were often forcibly recruited into the army. Although men of color were admitted from the beginning, their chance to become officers narrowed in the 1830s, when reform measures in many provinces deprived the rank and file of the right to elect local officers and placed provincial governments in charge of the appointments. This change precipitated the Guard's slide into the mire of electoral fraud, as officer positions were bestowed on those who could swing the vote in the right direction. The process was accelerated between 1850 and 1871, during which time local units often became the personal armies of the rural colonels who commanded them.

Although the National Guard drew praise for its performance in the WAR OF THE TRIPLE ALLIANCE (1864–1870), its past could not be erased, and the state finally curtailed its functions in 1873. From that point on, the Guard lost its policing powers and would be called into action only during times of extreme crisis.

Sources in English are limited, though a good discussion is found in FERNANDO URICOECHEA, *The Patrimonial Foundations of the Brazilian Bureaucratic State* (1980). See also JEANNE BERRANCE DE CASTRO, *A milícia cidadã: A Guarda Nacional de 1831 a 1850* (1977).

JUDITH L. ALLEN

### National Housing Bank
### Banco Nacional de Habitação—BNH

Created as part of the financial market reforms of Humberto Castelo BRANCO's administration by Law 4380 of 1964, the BNH served as the center of the Housing Finance System (Sistema Financeira de Habitação—SFH). The reformers designed the system to create a supply of mortgage funds for lower-income groups, to be financed through the creation of inflation-indexed passbook savings deposits. The BNH supervised the activities of three sets of institutions: the state and federal savings banks (*caixas econômicas estaduais e federais*), the housing credit societies (*sociedades de crédito imobiliário*), and savings and loan associations (*associações de poupança e emprestimo*). Like many thrift systems throughout the world, the Brazilian thrift system has suffered from significant nonperforming loans and difficulties competing

with other parts of the financial system. Any improvement in the Brazilian government's fiscal situation and the efficiency of the financial system will depend upon the improvement in financial status of these institutions. As a first step to this adjustment, the government dissolved the BNH in the reforms of 1987–1989.

JOHN H. WELCH, *Capital Markets in the Development Process: The Case of Brazil* (1993).

JOHN H. WELCH

*See also* **Banking; Economic Development.**

### National Indian Foundation
### Fundação Nacional ao Índio—FUNAI

Successor to the Indian Protection Service (or SPI), FUNAI is the governmental agency charged with the protection of the rights of indigenous peoples and the demarcation of their lands. The agency was established in 1967 at the urging of the minister of the interior, General Albuquerque Lima, in response to allegations of administrative corruption among officials of the SPI and findings of an investigative commission led by Attorney General Jader Figueiredo (Figueiredo Report [1968]). Although founded to rectify the corruption and misdeeds of the SPI, FUNAI itself has had a checkered history, with instances of corruption, neglect of its responsibility to demarcate indigenous lands, failure to protect the interests of those whom the agency is purported to defend, and economic exploitation. For example, since its establishment, the agency has been involved in numerous scandals invoking illegal mineral and timber extraction. One reason for these problems is that, prior to the Constitution of 1988, FUNAI was subordinate to the Ministry of the Interior, an administrative status that often conflicted with the agency's legal objectives. To repair the agency's ambiguous structural position, the new constitution transferred its supervision to the Ministry of Justice.

In 1986, following a period of administrative chaos during which FUNAI had five different presidents in a one-year period, the agency underwent reorganization. Its form as a centrally administered agency with headquarters in Brasília and multiple regional *delegacias*, was decentralized such that greater regional administrative power was localized in five *superintendencias* (Curitiba, Cuiabá, Recife, Belém, Manaus)—a change that enabled regional political and economic interests to have greater sway in questions related to indigenous peoples. Moreover, because it provided a space for local economic interests to reassert themselves in decisions related to indigenous peoples, such as use of land, decentralization effectively offset the benefits of FUNAI's changed administrative status within the Ministry of Justice under the new constitution. In addition FUNAI was made responsible for coordinating services provided by other ministries (for example, Education, Health, and Welfare) rather than for offering these services itself, as previously.

SHELTON H. DAVIS, *Victims of the Miracle: Development and the Indians of Brazil* (1977); CENTRO DE DOCUMENTAÇÃO E INFORMAÇÃO, *Povos indígenas no Brasil—85/86. Aconteceu Especial 17.*

LAURA GRAHAM

*See also* **Indians.**

## National Institute of Colonization and Agrarian Reform
### Instituto Nacional de Colonização e Reforma Agrária—Incra

Incra was founded in 1970 during General Emílio Garrastazu MÉDICI's presidency. It was one of several agencies created under the 1964–1985 military-technocratic authoritarian regime to develop the AMAZON REGION. Its four main tasks were: to alleviate conflict over land tenure; to resettle thousands of landless peasants, especially from the northeast of Brazil; to establish cooperatives for the peasants' economic support; and to standardize and modernize existing legal forms of large-scale ownership so as to increase production and hence government revenues.

Incra's dual role of simultaneously supporting both colonization projects and large land sales to various capitalist enterprises was inherently too contradictory for the agency to do both well. By the mid-1970s, Incra was acquiescing to political and economic pressures from business groups, usually to the detriment of colonization projects, which were expensive undertakings under the best of conditions. As a result, original settlement goals never came close to being met, and many settlements were later abandoned.

After the establishment of Brazil's new democracy in the mid-1980s, Incra's mandate emphasized agrarian reform, support to settlements, and clarification of property titles for lands held in abeyance since José SARNEY's administration. Incra reported to the minister of agriculture and agrarian reform and, like most government agencies, suffered from a lack of funds.

Scholarly treatments of Incra are usually subsumed in broader works treating agrarian reform or development of the Amazon in general, or have been the subject of doctoral dissertations. One of the best and most comprehensive studies of Incra in English is found in STEPHEN G. BUNKER, *Underdeveloping the Amazon: Extraction, Unequal Exchange, and the Failure of the Modern State* (1985). See also OTÁVIO GUILHERME VELHO, *Capitalismo autoritário e campesinato: Um estudo comparativo a partir da fronteira em movimento* (1976); PETER FLYNN, *Brazil: A Political Analysis* (1978); esp. pp. 451–454; and THOMAS E. SKIDMORE, *The Politics of Military Rule in Brazil, 1964–1985* (1988), esp. pp. 298–302.

LAURA JARNAGIN

*See also* **Land Tenure: Brazil.**

## National Students Union
### União Nacional dos Estudantes—UNE

The UNE emerged from the Second National Students Conference, held in Rio de Janeiro in 1938. Formally recognized by presidential decree in 1942 as the representative entity of Brazil's university students, the UNE initially devoted itself to creating branches throughout the states. The UNE's organization inspired similar efforts at the level of Brazilian secondary schools, giving rise to the Secondary Students Union of Brazil (UBES). The UNE soon devoted itself to political issues beyond the universities, working during 1940–1941 to secure Brazil's entry into World War II on the side of the Allies. It also participated in campaigns against the "fifth column" and provided domestic support to the BRAZILIAN EXPEDITIONARY FORCE. Later in the 1940s and 1950s the UNE led political campaigns in defense of the state petroleum monopoly, in opposition to the rising cost of living, and in support of an independent foreign policy. In the early 1960s the UNE pursued university reforms, leading a strike in 1962 that shut down almost all of Brazilian higher education for three months. In 1967–1968 the UNE staged protests against the dictatorship in major Brazilian cities. Government repression and imprisonment of student leaders in the late 1960s made it difficult for the organization to maintain its bases of support and level of activity. The UNE returned to the public arena only with the lessening of repression in the second half of the 1970s.

THOMAS E. SKIDMORE, *Politics in Brazil, 1930–1964* (1967); ISRAEL BELOCH and ALZIRA ALVES DE ABREU, eds., *Dicionário histórico-biográfico brasileiro, 1930–1983* (1984).

WILLIAM SUMMERHILL

## Pastoral Land Commission
### Comissão Pastoral da Terra—CPT

The Pastoral Land Commission (CPT) is an organ of the Brazilian Catholic church that deals with the problems of the poor in rural areas. Linked to the progressive sectors of the church, it was officially created in its present form in 1975; its precursor dates back to 1972. The CPT was created in response to a need felt by radical pastoral agents, who sought an end to the widespread violence of landowners and the state against the rural poor during the period of military rule (1964–1985), especially in the Amazon region. It offers legal services, encourages the creation of rural unions, denounces the use of violence against the rural poor, and offers courses in faith and politics.

Since its creation, the CPT has been highly controversial. It regularly clashed with the military government and large landowners, which saw the CPT as obstructionist and even subversive. It has also come under fire from conservative bishops, who believe that the CPT is excessively involved in politics, that it has at times incited peasants to seize land, that it is too close to the

Workers' Party, and that it reduces the Bible's message to a political one.

COMMISSÃO PASTORAL DA TERRA, *CPT: Pastoral e compromisso* (1983); VANILDA PAIVA, ed., *Igreja e questão agrária* (1985), esp. pp. 129–136, 248–273.

SCOTT MAINWARING

*See also* **Catholic Church; Liberation Theology.**

### Peasant Leagues

Various *ligas camponensas* were formed after World War II to defend the interests of tenant and small farmers and rural laborers. There were two distinct phases of league activity, one (1945–1947) led by the Brazilian Communist Party (PCB), and the other (1955–1964) led by peasants, students, and politicians from the Northeast. By the time they were suppressed, the Peasant Leagues had attained both national and international notoriety.

With political liberalization in 1945, the PCB established leagues throughout Brazil and used them to register new voters. By enfranchising thousands of peasants, many Communists won electoral office. In 1947, the government suppressed the PCB and its leagues were disbanded. In 1955, a former PCB militant organized the Agricultural Society of Farmers and Ranchers (SAPP) at the Galiléia plantation in Pernambuco State. To red-bait SAPP, landowners called it a "peasant league," but their plan backfired and dozens of Peasant Leagues formed throughout the state and region.

The leagues, headed by Francisco Julião, achieved national recognition in 1960, when they forced the state government to divide Galiléia lands among peasants. Dedicated to a policy of confiscating land without compensating owners in cash, the Peasant Leagues' call for agrarian reform "by law or by force" became predominant in the rural labor movement. In 1962, the leagues expanded into thirteen of Brazil's twenty-two states and started a weekly newspaper, *Liga*. Numerous groups of students, women, and soldiers imitated the peasants by naming their organizations "*ligas.*"

The leagues' growth peaked in 1963 when internal squabbles fractured the organization. A decentralized structure enabled some local leaders to emphasize land seizures, others union organizing, and still others armed rebellion. When news of league guerrilla bands reached the United States, the Kennedy administration made the Northeast a test case for Alliance for Progress programs designed to thwart revolution. The PCB and Catholic church also challenged the leagues. Isolated, they were repressed by the military in 1964.

SHEPARD FORMAN, *The Brazilian Peasantry* (1975); FLORENCIA MALLON, "Peasants and Rural Laborers in Pernambuco, 1955–

Francisco Julião and Luis Carlos Prestes at Radical Agrarian Reform campaign meeting. Rio de Janeiro, September 1961. ICONOGRAPHIA.

1964," in *Latin American Perspectives* 5, no. 4 (1978):49–70; ELIDE RUGAI BASTOS, *As ligas camponesas* (1984).

CLIFF WELCH

### Superintendency for the Development of Amazonia Superintendencia do Desenvolvimento da Amazonia—SUDAM

SUDAM is a Brazilian government agency that administers developmental projects in Amazonia—a vast 2-million-square-mile area of northern Brazil, with a 1990 population of 8 million. Created in 1966, SUDAM is headquartered in Belém, Pará. The agency's main function is the supervision of the Fiscal Incentive Law of October 1966, which grants tax exemptions and deductions for certain investments within the region. The agency emphasizes projects that call for territorial occupation for the extraction of regional resources by regional labor.

In 1970 disputes over land ownership between SUDAM-supported ranchers and indigenous Indians and rural peasants led to violence. By 1973 the upheaval caused a shift in government policy from supporting homesteads to promoting large agribusiness interests, whose purpose was to lay the groundwork for the expansion of large domestic and multinational agribusinesses into the Amazon Basin and to increase the export agricultural capacity of the Brazilian economy. These new goals threatened the territorial integrity of the Indians and increased the disparities between land-poor and land-rich inhabitants, while creating a class of exploited agricultural workers. This decreased the food supply in the domestic market, which worsened the severe pattern of hunger and malnourishment already present.

Today SUDAM's primary purpose is still the development of the Amazon Basin. To this end, SUDAM intends to use one-fifth of the total Amazon Basin as "sustained yield" forest reserves, that is, forests that are replanted after the original trees are cut down. However, since more than 90 percent of the nutrients in a rain forest ecosystem are contained in the trees, the assumption that a rain forest can be used as a sustained-yield forest is a controversial one.

STEFAN H. ROBOCK, *Brazil: A Study in Development Progress* (1975); SHELTON H. DAVIS, *Victims of the Miracle* (1977); LAWRENCE S. GRAHAM and ROBERT H. WILSON, *The Political Economy of Brazil: Public Policies in an Era of Transition* (1990).

MICHAEL J. BROYLES

### Superintendency of Agrarian Reform—SUPRA

SUPRA, established in October 1962, was an executive-branch agency charged with implementing the rural policies of President João Goulart, including land and labor reforms. SUPRA distributed some land to landless peasants and started a campaign to form 2,000 unions, establish 500 labor courts, and register 3 million new

voters by 1965. To do this, SUPRA opened dozens of regional offices and contracted experienced Communist and Catholic labor organizers. The effort was to regiment the fractious rural labor movement and thereby weaken the rural oligarchy. Hundreds of new unions had been established by April 1964, when the military coup d'état outlawed SUPRA and persecuted its agents for subversion.

JOHN W. F. DULLES, *Unrest in Brazil: Political and Military Crises, 1955–1964* (1970), pp. 220–275; ASPÁSIA DE ALCÂNTARA CAMARGO, "A questão agrária: Crise de poder e reforma de base," in *História de civilização brasileira*, no. 10, tomo 3, *O Brasil republicano*, vol. 3, *Sociedade e política* (1930–1964), edited by Boris Fausto, 3d ed. (1986), pp. 121–224.

CLIFF WELCH

### Superior Military Tribunal

Brazil's military supreme court. This judicial body came to prominence in national life after the 1964 military coup. Under a variety of institutional acts and the Constitution of 1967, civilians charged with crimes relating to national security were removed from the jurisdiction of the civilian courts and put under the jurisdiction of this military court. The power of the Superior Military Tribunal even extended to the governors of Brazil's constituent states, who no longer had special forums in which to be tried. This judicial body also was empowered to silence and punish military officers who were critical of the regime.

The use of the military tribunal for trying individuals charged with political crimes was the result of pressure from conservative hardliners angered over the ability of individuals to appeal to civilian courts after being tried by Military Police Investigation panels. Extending the jurisdiction of the Superior Military Tribunal enabled the military regime to toss aside a variety of legal guarantees, especially the right of habeas corpus, and made it much easier for the regime to ignore the rights of political prisoners. A wide variety of regime critics were tried by the Superior Military Tribunal, including intellectuals, labor leaders, politicians, and military officers. The jurisdiction of the tribunal effectively ended in 1978 with a reform package that restored some individual legal safeguards and independence to the nation's judicial system.

RONALD M. SCHNEIDER, *The Political System of Brazil: Emergence of a "Modernizing" Authoritarian Regime, 1964–1970* (1971); PETER FLYNN, *Brazil: A Political Analysis* (1978); MARIA HELENA MOREIRA ALVES, *State and Opposition in Military Brazil* (1985).

SONNY B. DAVIS

### Union of Farmers and Agricultural Laborers of Brazil—ULTAB

Founded in 1954, ULTAB helped the Brazilian Communist Party (PCB) coordinate and control the national rural labor movement. Although non-Communists participated in ULTAB, the party paid the salaries of top directors such as Lindolfo SILVA and Heros Trench and financed ULTAB's monthly journal, *Terra Livre.* Active in nearly every state, ULTAB enabled the PCB to overwhelm rivals like the Peasant Leagues and Frente Agrária.

With headquarters in São Paulo's state capital, ULTAB sought to weaken the influence of the state's powerful coffee- and sugar-growers' lobby by unionizing sugarcane and coffee harvesters. While providing a welcome challenge to growers, ULTAB has been criticized for neglecting the immediate needs of workers by favoring political over economic solutions to their problems. On numerous occasions, ULTAB squelched labor protests in order to demonstrate the PCB's authority over rural workers to enhance its image among bureaucrats and politicians with whom the party hoped to ally in backing agrarian reform laws.

When the government-sanctioned National Confederation of Agricultural Laborers (CONTAG) formed in November 1963, the semiclandestine ULTAB disbanded and its militants joined the new organization. A third of CONTAG's elected officers, including its president, responded to party discipline.

ROBERT E. PRICE, "Rural Unionization in Brazil," the Land Tenure Center, University of Wisconsin, Madison (1964); VERENA STOLCKE, *Coffee Planters, Workers, and Wives: Class Conflict and Gender Relations on São Paulo Plantations, 1850–1980* (1988), pp. 100–108.

CLIFF WELCH

### Union of Indigenous Nations
### União das Nações Indígenas—UNI

UNI, founded in June 1980, was the first independent organization of Brazilian indigenous peoples. Although never formally recognized by the government, it had immense symbolic significance for the development of political consciousness during the 1980s. Created and led by indigenous peoples, UNI's objectives were to give voice to the concerns of the people; to assist them in their struggles to secure rights to land, self-determination, and autonomy; and to help them develop cultural and community projects. From the time of its founding until the beginning of the 1990s, UNI representatives were involved in drafting the sections of Brazil's new constitution that deal with indigenous peoples, establishing alliances between members of Brazil's approximately 180 indigenous groups, and promoting recognition of strategies common to indigenous peoples and other oppressed sectors of the Brazilian population. For example, UNI was active in the formation of the Alliance of the Peoples of the Forest (March 1989), an organization comprised of indigenous peoples, rubber tappers, and river dwellers who recognized their common struggles, renounced old animosities, and pledged to promote their common interests. It also founded, in 1987, the Center for Indigenous Research (Centro de Pesquisa Indígena) in

Goiânia. The Terena leader Domingos Verissimo Marcos (Marcos Terena) served briefly as UNI's first president; he was succeeded by Ailton Krenak.

In the early 1990s indigenous peoples started to become more organized at community and regional levels, and independent indigenous organizations began to proliferate throughout Brazil. As a result, UNI eventually disbanded as a national organization and the political configuration of indigenous organizations entered into a process of redefinition. By the mid-1990s, approximately 100 independent indigenous organizations were active in Brazil. Among these was the Center for Indigenous Culture in São Paulo (Nucleo de Cultura Indígena—NCI), founded by Krenak. No single entity had yet developed that claimed to represent the interests of all of Brazil's diverse indigenous peoples.

ISMAELILLO WRIGHT and ROBIN WRIGHT, *Native Peoples in Struggle: Cases from the Fourth Russell Tribunal and Other International Forums* (1982), p. 66.

LAURA GRAHAM

*See also* **Indians.**

## BRAZIL: POLITICAL PARTIES

### Brazilian Democratic Movement
### Movimento Democrático Brasileiro—MDB

The Brazilian Democratic Movement (MDB) was founded in 1966, after the two-year-old military regime decreed that Brazilian politics be restructured as a two-party system. Under the new two-party system, the MDB was the official opposition party and the more conservative National Renovating Alliance (ARENA) was the official pro-regime party. Following the relegalization of a multiparty system in 1979, the MDB was dissolved. The bulk of the MDB party structure and leadership subsequently formed the Brazilian Democratic Movement Party (PMDB).

The MDB initially drew its membership from parties such as the Brazilian Labor Party (PTB) and Social Democratic Party (PSD), which had formerly occupied the center-left end of the political spectrum before the military government purged the Congress and executive of leftist party members. As the only legal opposition party, the MDB maintained a critical stance towards the military regime's authoritarian policies, which stimulated rapid economic expansion while clamping down on political dissent and social unrest. However, the legal restrictions placed on individual and party activism circumscribed the MDB's abilities to challenge authoritarian rule.

Throughout its existence, the MDB maintained minority representation in federal and state legislatures, with the greatest party representation found in the urban, industrialized states of the Southeast and South. Although the party rarely exercised political supremacy at the federal or state levels, several of the party's most prominent members, including Ulysses GUIMARÃES and Tancredo NEVES, played crucial roles in the political re-democratization process known as *abertura* (1979–1985).

''Movimento Democrático Brasileiro,'' in *Dicionário histórico-biográfico brasileiro, 1930–1983*, vol. 3, edited by Israel Beloch and Alzira Alves de Abreu (1984), pp. 2,322–2,324; MARIA HELENA MOREIRA ALVES, *State and Opposition in Military Brazil* (1985); and MARIA D'ALVA GIL KINZO, *Legal Opposition Politics Under Authoritarian Rule in Brazil* (1988).

DARYLE WILLIAMS

### Brazilian Democratic Movement Party
### Partido do Movimento Democrático
### Brasileiro—PMDB

The Brazilian Democratic Movement Party is one of the few Brazilian parties to have maintained a political profile consistent with that which it had at the time of its founding in the 1970s. When, in 1965, the military regime banned existing parties, a diversified group of opposition forces formed the Brazilian Democratic Movement (MDB). The Brazilian Democratic Movement Party formally came into being when the 1979 reform reinstated the multiparty system, and it has remained the country's largest party, albeit in a context of extreme and continuing political fragmentation. During the process of DISTENSÃO (gradual liberalization) carried out by the military government in the 1970s, PMDB's widest support generally came from the urban and industrialized centers of south central Brazil, but it became a progressively national party owing to local municipal organizational efforts throughout the country. Largely because of its organizational power and its identification with resistance to military government, the PMDB was well prepared to garner popular support once redemocratization began in earnest.

The party's historical trajectory can be outlined as follows: First, in the context of the restrictions imposed by the authoritarian regime, it firmly established itself as the party of resistance and won widespread popular support in elections held in the late 1970s. Second, during the 1980s it continued its strategy as a catchall party, but given the multiplication of parties and the resulting dispersion of the federal and state parliaments into numerous factions, its dimensions were substantially reduced. Finally, it continues as a party linked to popular interests.

The PMDB's greatest victory came in the general elections of 1986 and can be attributed to the momentary, preelection success of President José SARNEY's economic plan, which included wage and price freezes. Since then, two events have contributed to the party's loss of electoral support: a 1988 internal rift in which the left wing abandoned ship to form its own party—the Brazilian Social Democratic Party—and the first post-

authoritarian presidential elections, in 1989, when none of the larger parties, PMDB included, were able to capture the votes of the electorate.

OLAVO BRASIL DE LIMA JÚNIOR, ''Electoral Participation in Brazil (1945–1978): The Legislation, the Party System, and Electoral Turnouts,'' *Luso-Brazilian Review* 20, no. 1 (1983): 65–92; MARIA D'ALVA GIL KINZO, *Oposição e autoritarianismo: Gênese e trajetória do MDB* (1988); THOMAS E. SKIDMORE, *The Politics of Military Rule in Brazil, 1964–1985* (1988); ALFRED STEPAN, ed., *Democratizing Brazil: Problems of Transition and Consolidation* (1989); OLAVO BRASIL DE LIMA JÚNIOR, *Democracia e instituições políticas no Brasil dos anos 80* (1993).

OLAVO BRASIL DE LIMA JÚNIOR
DOUGLAS COLE LIBBY

### Brazilian Communist Party
### Partido Comunista Brasileiro—PCB

In March 1922 a group of former anarchist activists met in Rio de Janeiro to found Brazil's Communist Party. Led by journalist Astrogildo Pereira, this group of male artisans were breaking ranks with Brazil's anarchists. Their main goals were to create a national proletarian movement that could coordinate its activities throughout Brazil and to tie this movement to the Soviet Union's new Third International. The party sought to establish centralized control of all labor and left-wing movements. In turn the PCB became a component of the international structure of Communist parties (the Comintern) centered in Moscow.

Unlike the anarchists, who had eschewed participation in the political system, the Communists relied on a two-track program to gain power. At Moscow's behest, they both participated in elections and planned military coups. In 1930 the party leadership even relinquished power to a military man, the former TENENTE Luís Carlos PRESTES, in accordance with the Comintern's directives. Rather than organizing among the nation's urban and rural laborers, Prestes and his followers launched a revolt in Brazil's Northeast (far from the industrial centers of São Paulo and Rio) in November 1935. The coup's failure ushered in almost a decade of intense government repression of the PCB as well as labor and leftist groups that had had little contact with the Communists.

During the period of nominally open politics from 1945 to 1964, the PCB reemerged. With Prestes still controlling the party, it again followed policies prescribed by the Soviet Union. By participating in elections, Prestes and other party members gained seats in both national and state legislatures in the mid-1940s, only to lose their positions when the federal government of Eurico Gaspar DUTRA (1946–1951) followed the lead of the United States by declaring the PCB an illegal political party.

An important generational and ideological division

developed within the PCB at this time. Younger members who worked in factories and on large plantations began to organize among the rank and file. Although formally Communists, many of these younger members openly defied the PCB's national politics, which often called for making alliances with industrialists and other elites. These young activists managed, for the first time, to spread the PCB's influence within the urban and rural trade union movements from the mid-1940s through the mid-1960s.

By 1962 there had emerged within the party a pro-Chinese splinter group, which in that year formed the Communist Party of Brazil (Partido Comunista do Brasil—PC do B). Prestes and other Communists clandestinely maintained the party during the 1964–1985 military dictatorship and emerged as participants in the broad-based opposition Brazilian Democratic Movement Party (PMDB) coalition. At first the PCB openly opposed many programs of the newly formed Workers Party (PT). But in the late 1980s, the PCB leadership formally admitted it did not have the allegiance of Brazil's working people and ceded that responsibility to the PT.

Two volumes by JOHN W. F. DULLES, *Anarchists and Communists in Brazil, 1900–1935* (1973), and *Brazilian Communism, 1935–1945: Repression during World Upheaval* (1983), detail the founding and operation of the PCB. An excellent institutional history of the party is provided in RONALD H. CHILCOTE, *The Brazilian Communist Party: Conflict and Integration, 1922–1972* (1974). On the often conflict-laden relationship between the PCB and rank-and-file workers, see JOEL WOLFE, *Working Women, Working Men: São Paulo and the Rise of Brazil's Industrial Working Class, 1900–1955* (1993).

JOEL WOLFE

*See also* **Brazil: Revolutions.**

### Conservative Party

The Conservative Party was the most important of the Brazilian monarchy. Founded in 1837 by reactionaries among the liberal MODERADOS, the party dominated the last years of the Regency (1831–1840) and the seminal beginnings of the Second Reign (1840–1889). Indeed, its leaders figured in the most important initiatives of the period, for example, the *conciliação* (1853–1857), which ended the initial partisan struggles between Conservatives and Liberals; foreign policy in the Río de la Plata area (1848–1870); far-reaching reformism in the early 1870s; and the final abolition of slavery in 1888. From 1837 to the monarchy's fall in 1889, there were forty cabinets; Conservatives controlled more than half of the cabinets over more than thirty-two years in power. Moreover, nine of the ten longest administrations had Conservative leadership, including the three longest and most decisive: that of the Marquês de Olinda and

Viscount de MONTE ALEGRE (1848–1852), that of Marquês de PARANÁ (1853–1857), and that of Viscount do RIO BRANCO (1871–1875).

The party was born of the reaction against Regency decentralization and democratization, which were perceived to be the cause of the secessionist popular revolts of the era. The most dynamic party element, called the Saquaremas, dominated the party during the period when these issues remained unresolved, ca. 1837–1852. Generally trained magistrates, Saquaremas were identified with the slaveholding planter and merchant interests of Rio de Janeiro, allied to similar elements of Bahia and Pernambuco, and emphasized an authoritarian, constitutional state as the only secure guarantor of social order and national integrity. Eusébio de QUEIRÓS, Paulino José Soares de Sousa (later Viscount do URUGUAI), and Joaquim José Rodrigues Tôrres (later Viscount de ITABORAÍ), the Saquarema "trinity," organized the Conservative majority in the Chamber and, working closely with Bernardo Pereira de VASCONCELOS and Honório Hermeto Carneiro Leão (later Marquês de Paraná), led the parliamentary *Regresso*, or reaction, which, by 1841, reversed the liberal reforms of 1831–1834. As ministers, senators, and councilors of state, they later figured in the repression of the last Liberal revolts of 1842 and 1848 and oversaw the ministry of 1848–1853, which consolidated the Monarchy as the preeminent force in national politics and in the international relations of the Río de la Plata.

With the maturity of Pedro II by the 1850s, a movement against Saquarema hegemony and partisan strife triumphed, associated with the Marquês de Paraná's opening to Liberals and electoral reforms. By the 1860s, key moderate Conservatives, such as José Tomás NABUCO DE ARAÚJO, shifted over to the Liberals, and the Conservative Party itself was increasingly dominated by Paraná's protege, the one-time Liberal, José Maria Paranhos de Silva (later Viscount do Rio Branco). The latter was able to defeat the Saquaremas' heirs in the struggle over gradual abolition of slavery in 1871, thus fatally dividing the party. By 1888, the party's reformist wing successfully presided over slavery's complete abolition. The ideological incoherence this suggests points to the party's increasing demoralization and disarray, central to the context for the military's republican coup of 1889.

JOAQUIM NABUCO, *Um estadista do império* (1898–1899); JOSÉ ANTONIO SOARES DE SOUSA, *A vida do visconde do Uruguai* (1944); ILMAR ROHLOFF DE MATTOS, *O tempo saquarema* (1987); RODERICK BARMAN, *Brazil: The Forging of a Nation, 1798–1852* (1988); JOSÉ MURILO DE CARVALHO, *Teatro de sombras* (1988); EMÍLIA VIOTTI DA COSTA, *The Brazilian Empire* (1988); RICHARD GRAHAM, *Patronage and Politics in Nineteenth-Century Brazil* (1990); JEFFREY D. NEEDELL, "Brasilien 1830–1889," in Raymond Buve and John Fisher, eds., *Handbuch der Geschichte Lateinamericas*, vol. 2 (1992).

JEFFREY D. NEEDELL

### Integralist Action
### Ação Integralista Brasileira—AIB

The AIB (commonly known as Integralismo) was the first Brazilian fascist movement to gain national prominence. Formed in 1932 and headed by Plínio Salgado, the AIB was primarily modeled after the Italian and Portuguese fascist movements, although it did use Nazi-influenced trappings such as green shirts to distinguish its members and the swastika-like Greek sigma as a party sign. Its nationalistic goal was an "integral" state with a single authoritarian leader.

The AIB, whose motto was "God, Country, and Family," took the nationalism, Catholicism, and antiforeign nature of the Revolution of 1930 to an extreme. As Brazil's urban middle class became increasingly poorer during the worldwide Great Depression, the AIB attacked liberals, Communists, foreigners, and Masons, but never clearly articulated a positive political platform. Gustavo BARROSO, president of Brazil's Academy of Letters and the AIB's chief ideologue, was a rabid anti-Semite whose Jew-baiting dominated the AIB's public discourse even though the Jewish population of Brazil was small.

In 1937 Salgado was one of three candidates in the presidential election and may have been strong enough to play power broker in a close election. When Getúlio VARGAS declared the ESTADO NOVO dictatorship in 1937, the presidential election was canceled and all political parties, including the AIB, were banned. When a group of Integralists attacked the Presidential Palace in 1938, most AIB leaders were arrested and Salgado was exiled to Portugal. Many important members of Estado Novo, however, including Justice Minister Francisco Campos and Federal Chief of Police Fillinto Müller, remained tied to both Salgado and the Integralist platform. More recently the Integralist party has been legally reconstituted in a number of Brazilian states, although its membership is tiny.

ROBERT LEVINE, *The Vargas Regime: The Critical Years, 1934–1938* (1970), esp. pp. 81–99, 159–175; HELGIO TRINDADE, *Integralismo: O fascismo brasileiro na década de 30* (1979); STANLEY HILTON, *Hitler's Secret War in South America, 1939–1945* (1981), esp. pp. 82–93; RENÉ GERTZ, *O fascismo no sul do Brasil: Germanismo, nazismo, integralismo* (1987).

JEFFREY LESSER

See also **Fascism.**

### Brazilian Labor Party
### Partido Trabalhista Brasileiro—PTB

Getúlio VARGAS created the PTB along with the Social Democratic Party (Partido Social Democrático—PSD) in early 1945. The two political parties sought to represent Vargas's constituencies in the electoral politics that followed the ESTADO NÔVO dictatorship. The PTB was to be a non-Communist alternative for the country's recently enfranchised industrial workers. Vargas hoped that the PTB would mirror the British Labour Party by marshaling union support. The PTB never achieved such status. Rather than becoming the institutional representative of Brazilian workers, the party served as the home base for a series of populist politicians, beginning with Vargas himself.

Vargas and his allies closely controlled the PTB's affairs, and by doing so failed to build ties to either unionized or nonunionized workers. The party was particularly weak in the state of São Paulo, Brazil's industrial heartland. From its founding in 1945 to Vargas's suicide in 1954, the PTB served as an electoral vehicle for the former dictator, who refashioned himself as a pro-worker populist. Vargas was elected president in 1950 running as a PTB candidate.

With Vargas's passing, control of the party fell to his former minister of labor and fellow GAÚCHO, João (Jângo) GOULART. From the mid-1950s through the early 1960s, government labor bureaucrats and left-wing populists fought for control of the PTB. Jângo's elevation to the presidency in 1961 intensified this conflict. In the early 1960s, Goulart's brother-in-law, Leonel BRIZOLA, controlled the radical wing of the PTB that effectively pushed Jângo to adopt policies favoring urban and rural labor. This turn to the left hastened the military coup of 1964.

During the late 1970s and early 1980s, Brizola sought to lead a reconstituted PTB that would continue in the spirit of Vargas and Goulart. Brizola lost access to the party's name and so formed the Democratic Labor Party (Partido Democrático Trabalhista—PDT). The reconstituted PTB became a home base for conservative unionists who opposed the "new unionism" of the Workers Party (Partido dos Trabalhadores—PT).

For a detailed analysis of the PTB's role in national politics, see THOMAS E. SKIDMORE, *Politics in Brazil, 1930–1964: An Experiment in Democracy* (1967). Case studies of the PTB are provided in MARIA ANDRÉA LOYOLA, *Os sindicatos e o PTB; Estudo de um caso em Minas Gerais* (1980), and MARIA VICTORIA BENEVIDES, *O PTB e o trabalhismo em São Paulo, 1945–1964* (1989). On the origins of the PTB, see ANGELA CASTRO GOMES, *A invenção do trabalhismo* (1988).

JOEL WOLFE

### Liberal Alliance
### Aliança Liberal—AL

Founded in August 1929 by political leaders in Minas Gerais and Rio Grande do Sul, this opposition party supported Getúlio VARGAS as president and João PESSOA as vice president in the 1930 elections. The Liberal Alliance was formed when President Washington Luiz, a representative of São Paulo's large landowners, announced that he had decided to break the tradition of alternating politicians from São Paulo and Minas Gerais in the presidency and intended to support São Paulo state president Júlio PRESTES as his successor.

The AL was composed of a number of groups whose

power was not based on coffee wealth and who looked to modernize Brazil's economy. It represented an emerging middle class increasingly disenfranchised by the central government's policy of favoring the interests of the major plantation owners. The AL platform was based on national political reform, including a secret vote and popular representation, freedom of the press, educational reform, and the adoption of protectionist policies for export products other than coffee.

After a campaign marked by violence, the Vargas-Pessoa ticket was defeated amid accusations of widespread fraud. After Pessoa's assassination in July, some members of the AL called for an armed rebellion. In October the Revolution of 1930 began, putting Vargas in power for the next fifteen years.

JOHN W. F. DULLES, *Vargas of Brazil: A Political Biography* (1967), esp. pp. 49–67; BORIS FAUSTO, *A revolução de 1930: Historiografia e história* (1986).

JEFFREY LESSER

### Liberal Party
### Partido Liberal

The Liberal Party, one of the two great parties of the monarchy (1822–1889), formed (ca. 1837) in opposition to the Conservative Party's reactionary, authoritarian regime. A minority party, the Liberals circumvented Conservative hegemony by an 1840 coup (the *Majoridade*, bringing the adolescent emperor to power early in return for cabinet control). When the emperor's advisers engineered their fall (1841), the Liberals revolted (1842) in São Paulo and Minas Gerais and were pitilessly repressed. This failure, and that of Pernambuco's PRAIEIRA REVOLT (1848), confirmed the Conservatives' goal: state power was to be preeminent and exercised indirectly by the crown through cabinet control of patronage, elections, and legislation.

In order to defend and increase their partisans, the Liberal cabinets of the mid-1840s refused to reverse such control. This pragmatism caused a rift between purists and the party's leadership. Indeed, pragmatists from both parties joined to form the Conciliation cabinets (1853–1857) and some successors, culminating in the Progressive League (1862).

This league was a parliamentary coalition in which moderate Conservative dissidents led the Liberals against the Conservative Party (despite divisions over reforms and marked internal suspicion) and presided over cabinets in 1862 and 1864–1868. The league's gradual reformism and crown support were undermined in parliament, where the purists of both parties attacked them as either going too far or attempting too little.

In 1868, the emperor brought the Conservatives to power (partly to support the Conservative general leading imperial forces in the WAR OF THE TRIPLE ALLIANCE); they held it exclusively until 1878. This monopoly led to Liberal radicalization. The Progressive League leaders and the old Liberal purists united to refound the Liberal Party and called for dramatic reforms in the Liberal Manifesto of 1869. A radical faction called for even more dramatic reform, and others went still further, deciding to form the Republican Party (1870).

The Liberals used reformism to critique the Conservative cabinets until 1879; afterward several Liberal cabinets, increasingly divided, failed to effect such programs themselves: abolition of SLAVERY, reform of the emperor's prerogatives, decentralization, separation of church and state. By 1889, the last prime minister, a Liberal, led a party so badly splintered that his refurbished radical proposals (designed to save the monarchy) failed to secure support in the Chamber of Deputies, thereby adding to the postabolitionist milieu of political crisis.

JOAQUIM NABUCO, *Um estadista do império*, 3 vols. (1898–1899); EMILIA VIOTTI DA COSTA, *The Brazilian Empire* (1985); ILMAR ROHLOFF DE MATTOS, *O tempo saquarema* (1987); RODERICK J. BARMAN, *Brazil: The Forging of a Nation* (1988); LESLIE BETHELL, ed., *Brazil: Empire and Republic* (1989), chaps. 2–4; RICHARD GRAHAM, *Patronage and Politics in Nineteenth-Century Brazil* (1990).

JEFFREY D. NEEDELL

*See also* **Brazil: Liberal Movements; Concilição.**

### Moderados

This Brazilian political party that initially dominated the Regency (1831–1840), imposing decentralization and a limited monarchy. Liberal monarchists had joined more radical elements to oppose Pedro I's pretensions and Portuguese interests during the First Reign (1822–1831). They sought to force Pedro I to accept greater parliamentary participation and more freedom for men of property to direct affairs in their provinces. When Pedro's abdication brought them to power, they elected the three regents who governed for the emperor's child heir, PEDRO II. Class prejudice, monarchism, and provincial revolts soon forced them to break with the radicals (1831–1832) and elect Diogo Antônio FEIJÓ (1784–1843) as sole regent in 1835. Simultaneously, they reformed the Constitution of 1824 with the ADDITIONAL ACT (1834), which curbed the crown and devolved power to parliament and provincial electors.

Personal resentment of Feijó and unchecked threats of provincial secession and social revolt soon disenchanted the *moderados'* right wing. They made a reactionary parliamentary alliance with former supporters of Pedro I, and they founded the Conservative Party in 1837. Feijó resigned, and the Conservative majority elected Pedro de Araújo LIMA, later Marqués de Olinda, sole regent in 1837. The minority *moderado* left wing, known as the *progressistas*, joined the old radicals in support of the 1834 reforms and Feijó, thus forming the Liberal Party.

OCTÁVIO TARQÜINIO DE SOUSA, *Bernardo Pereira de Vasconcellos e seu tempo* (1937), *Historia de dois golpes de estado* (1939), and *Diogo Antônio Feijó* (1942); RODERICK BARMAN, *Brazil: The Forging of a Nation, 1798–1852* (1988).

JEFFREY D. NEEDELL

*See also* **Brazil: Political Parties** and **Regency.**

### National Democratic Union of Brazil
### União Democrática Nacional—UDN

Founded in April 1945 as a coalition of groups opposed to the ESTADO NOVO, an authoritarian regime headed by Getúlio VARGAS, the UDN maintained a prominent role in Brazilian politics until the party was disbanded in 1965. During its existence, party membership and party platforms were in constant tension between moderates and hard-liners. In general the party tended to represent moderate-to-conservative, middle-class interests, supporting basic democratic processes, morality in public life, and state nonintervention in the economy. The UDN sharply opposed the populist, nationalist elements of the presidencies of Getúlio Vargas (1951–1954), Juscelino KUBITSCHEK (1956–1961), and João GOULART (1961–1964). In 1964 the UDN supported military intervention to restore economic stability and combat alleged communist infiltration of Brazilian politics and society. After disbandment in 1965, most party members joined the pro-government National Renovating Alliance (Aliança de Renovação Nacional—ARENA).

The party fielded four presidential candidates: Eduardo Gomes (defeated in 1945 and 1950), Juarez Távora (defeated in 1955), and Jânio Quadros (victorious in 1960). The UDN enjoyed greater electoral success in national legislative races, winning enough seats to become the principal opposition party from 1945 to 1960, and in state elections, particularly in the Northeast, Minas Gerais, and Rio de Janeiro. The UDN consistently experienced difficulties in reconciling its heterogeneous bases of support, which ranged from staunch anticommunists who often called for military intervention to moderates who advocated stable political and economic development through democratic measures.

THOMAS SKIDMORE, *Politics in Brazil, 1930–1964: An Experiment in Democracy* (1967); MARIA VITÓRIA BENEVIDES, *A UDN e o udenismo* (1981); MARIA VITÓRIA BENEVIDES, "União Democrático Nacional," in *Dicionário históricobiográfico brasileiro* (1984), pp. 3,396–3,403; OTÁVIO SOARES DULCI, *A UDN e o antipopulismo no Brasil* (1986).

DARYLE WILLIAMS

### National Renovating Alliance
### Aliança Renovardora Nacional—ARENA

In an effort to reduce the number of political parties, considered a root cause of Brazil's problems, and to instill discipline in the political system, the military re-

gime of Humberto CASTELLO BRANCO issued the Second INSTITUTIONAL ACT on 27 October 1965 and the Complementary Act No. 4 on 30 November 1965. The former act dissolved all existing political parties in Brazil, while the latter act allowed the formation of political organizations only if such bodies were endorsed by at least 120 congressmen and 20 senators. The result was the formation of two parties: ARENA and the Brazilian Democratic Movement (Movimento Democratico Brasileiro—MDB), an opposition party.

Despite appearances, the various military administrations in Brazil maintained tight control of ARENA and the political system. The president of the republic was head of the party and selected all its candidates. ARENA politicians were in the majority in both houses of congress and in all the state assemblies, and they also held most of the governorships and mayoral offices. However, the 1974 congressional and state assembly elections, held during the period of political relaxation, indicated the growing strength of the MDB opponents. As opposition to the military government grew, ARENA politicians gradually attempted to distance themselves from identification with the military regime.

In an effort to strengthen the weakened government party by splitting the opposition or by forming coalitions with more conservative elements of the opposition, the government of João Baptista de FIGUEIREDO dissolved the two-party system and allowed the creation of multiple parties. By the end of 1979 ARENA had re-formed as the Social Democratic Party (Partido Democrático Social—PDS). The PDS was defeated soundly in the 1985 presidential election that returned Brazil to civilian rule.

PETER FLYNN, *Brazil: A Political Analysis* (1978); RONALD M. SCHNEIDER, *The Political System of Brazil: Emergence of a "Modernizing" Authoritarian Regime, 1964–1970* (1971); RIORDON ROETT, *Brazil: Politics in a Patrimonial Society* (1978); MARIA HELENA MOREIRA ALVES, *State and Opposition in Military Brazil* (1985); THOMAS E. SKIDMORE, *The Politics of Military Rule in Brazil, 1964–1985* (1988).

SONNY B. DAVIS

### Party of Brazilian Social Democracy
### Partido da Social Democracia Brasileira—PSDB
### Tucanos

The PSDB is an offshoot of the Brazilian Democratic Movement Party (PMDB). Founded on 24 June 1988, the PSDB included such national leaders as Mário Covas, Fernando Henrique CARDOSO, Franco Montoro, José Richa, José Serra, and Pimenta da Veiga. The PSDB program defends the principles of social democracy and the parliamentary system. In the presidential campaign of 1989, the PSDB nominated Mário Covas, who placed fourth in the election with 10.8 percent of the vote. In the elections of October 1990, the party elected only one governor, Ciro Gomes, of Ceará. Mário Covas was defeated in the elections for the governorship of the state of São Paulo in 1990.

The party's nickname, Tucanos, refers to a family of tropical New World birds (*Ramphastidae*), notable for their large, colorful beaks, and also to a training plane manufactured by Embraer for the Brazilian air force and used by the British and Egyptian air forces.

*Brazil A/Z: Enciclopédia alfabética em un único volume* (1988).

SHEILA L. HOOKER

### Popular Action
### Ação Popular—AP

Created in 1962 by a contingent of young Brazilian radicals, Popular Action was a small (no more than 3,000 members) yet influential movement that sought to transform Brazilian society. Its members engaged in grass-roots political work with the poor, encouraging popular organization and mobilization, with the ultimate objective of realizing socialism. AP was an important part of the burgeoning Left in Brazilian politics between 1962 and 1964. Most of the founding members had previously been active in progressive Catholic circles, and this religious genesis strongly marked the movement until after the 1964 military coup. Nevertheless, AP was independent of the church.

After the 1964 coup, AP underwent a rapid process of radicalization, embracing Marxism, Maoism, and eventually armed struggle. Like the other small guerrilla groups that stippled the Brazilian political scene after 1964, AP had a tragic postcoup fate; many activists were imprisoned and tortured. By 1973, the military government had vanquished the guerrilla left. Reduced to a small Maoist party with several dozen members, AP decided in 1973 to join forces with the Communist Party of Brazil.

LUÍZ GONZAGA DE SOUZA LIMA, *Evolução política dos católicos e da igreja no Brasil* (1979), esp. pp. 43–51; HAROLDO LIMA and ALDO ARANTES, *História da Ação Popular* (1984).

SCOTT MAINWARING

### Republican Party
### Partido Republicano—PR

The Republican Party emerged in Brazil with the founding of the first Republican Club in Rio de Janeiro on 3 November 1870. One month later, the Republican Manifesto enunciated the party's principles, calling for an end to the monarchy and the creation of a federal republic. Republican sentiment had surfaced as early as 1789 in Brazil with the INCONFIDÊNCIA MINEIRA, and had been important in separatist movements during the 1810s, 1820s, and 1830s. The turmoil of the 1830s, however, when Brazilians experimented with federalism, caused republican sentiment to subside, and by mid-century politically active Brazilians had come to appreciate the stability of their monarchy. The potential for political

discontent, nonetheless, had been retained in the divisions between the Liberal and Conservative parties. The fall of the Liberal cabinet in 1868 caused disgruntled members to seek radical redress by supporting the republican cause. Other political and economic forces also contributed to the appeal of republicanism in 1870. The WAR OF THE TRIPLE ALLIANCE (1865–1870), which cast Brazilian soldiers into closer contact with their Argentine and Uruguayan allies, heightened the appreciation for republican government elsewhere. The growth of cities brought with it the increased importance of educated, professional groups sympathetic to republican ideals. Furthermore, after 1850 economic power transferred from the Paraíba Valley to the rich coffee lands of São Paulo province. Since political influence did not immediately follow, Paulista planters tended to support republicanism. In 1884, São Paulo elected three Republican representatives to the national Chamber of Deputies, the first Republicans to sit in Parliament. With the return of the Liberals to national power in 1878, however, many Republicans had deserted their new party and returned to the Liberal fold. In 1886–1887 the Republican Party re-emerged under a leadership more heavily influenced by the positivist vision of a dictatorial republic and supported by important sectors of the military. On 15 November 1889 the military deposed Emperor PEDRO II and ushered in a republican form of government.

FRANCISCO JOSÉ DE OLIVEIRA VIANA, *O ocaso do império*, 3d ed. (1959); HEITOR LYRA, *História da queda do império*, 2 vols. (1964); E. BRADFORD BURNS, *A History of Brazil*, 2d ed. (1980), esp. pp. 224–225; EMILIA VIOTTI DA COSTA, *The Brazilian Empire* (1985), esp. pp. 202–233.

JOAN MEZNAR

### Brazilian Workers Party
### Partido dos Trabalhadores—PT

During the late 1970s, while Brazil was still under military rule, workers in the metallurgical industries (especially in automobile factories) located in São Paulo's industrial suburb of São Bernardo do Campo organized through factory commissions to push for increased wages and improved working conditions. The strike waves that these workers launched in 1978 and 1979 (in 1979 alone, more than 3 million workers were involved in 113 strikes in fifteen states) ushered in a form of organizing known as the "new unionism" and eventually led to the founding of the Brazilian Workers Party (PT) in 1979 and 1980.

These workers founded their own party—under new political guidelines set out in 1979 by the dictatorship— because they saw the main opposition party (the Brazilian Democratic Movement [MDB], later the Brazilian Democratic Movement Party [PMDB]), the reconstituted Brazilian Labor Party (PTB), and the Brazilian Communist Party (PCB) as too alienated from the concerns of rank-and-file workers. Thus, on May Day 1979, a group of labor leaders from the metalworkers' unions (who referred to themselves as labor's "authentic" leaders) issued a set of goals. They sought: (1) direct negotiations between workers and employers and, therefore, an end to the state-run industrial-relations system; (2) the formal acceptance by employers and the state of FACTORY COMMISSIONS and the recognition of union delegates on the shop floors as the primary bargaining agents for workers; (3) complete autonomy from the federal government's Ministry of Labor; and (4) the unrestricted right to strike.

The "authentics," led by Luís Inácio da SILVA (popularly known as Lula), formed the Central Workers' Union (CUT) in 1983 to coordinate national labor practices for the unions associated with the PT. The CUT opposed the more conservative unions associated with the PMDB and PCB that organized into the General Confederation of Workers (CGT), which modeled itself on the AFL-CIO of the United States.

The PT is really Brazil's first national political party. It is not simply a vehicle for a single politician, and it has a well-defined structure that is rooted not only in the factory commissions, but also in CHRISTIAN BASE COMMUNITIES and rural workers' movements. Indeed, the PT has organized throughout Brazil to push for improved conditions not only for industrial workers, but also for rural proletarians and the poor, who do not have access to steady employment. The PT has been successful in electing big-city mayors, state governors, and state and federal representatives and senators. The party's leader, Lula, finished second in the 1989 presidential election.

The single best study of the PT is MARGARET E. KECK, *The Workers Party and Democratization in Brazil* (1992). A good work on the party's origins is ISABEL RIBEIRO DE OLIVEIRA GÓMEZ DE SOUZA, *Trabalho e política: As origens do Partido dos Trabalhadores* (1988). An informative study that provides a good analysis of the PT's organizing in the rural sector as well as a detailed description of the 1989 presidential campaign is EMIR SADER and KEN SILVERSTEIN, *Without Fear of Being Happy: Lula, the Workers Party, and Brazil* (1991). For an analysis of the relationship of the PT to Brazil's increasingly important feminist groups, see SONIA E. ÁLVAREZ, *Engendering Democracy in Brazil: Women's Movements in Transition Politics* (1990).

JOEL WOLFE

*See also* **Liberation Theology.**

**BRAZIL: THE REGENCY (1831–1840).** The period in Brazilian history following the 1831 abdication of Pedro I was a time of sweeping reform and chaos. In the absence of a ruling monarch, the General Assembly appointed a three-man regency to govern until Dom Pedro's son reached the age of eighteen. Its tenure was characterized by a political and constitutional vacuum, unstable governments, subordination of the executive to the legislative, transference of central power to provincial assemblies, and Liberal measures to create a federalist form of government. Reforms enacted in 1834 curtailed the power of the executive and of the emperor,

and decentralized the government. The regents lost some prerogatives of the executive and of the moderative powers, including the ability to dissolve the Chamber of Deputies and to confer titles of nobility, and became subordinate to the legislative. The ADDITIONAL ACT (1834) transferred to the provinces powers heretofore belonging to the central government, abolished the Council of State and entailed estates, and created elected provincial assemblies. The National Guard was created to counterbalance the army.

The reforms rendered the central government a shadow, eliminated the center of authority and legitimacy, and encouraged regionalist centrifugal forces. A number of revolts and uprisings ensued, among them: Cabanos—Pernambuco and Alagoas (1835–1836); Cabanagem—Pará (1831–1833, 1835–1837); Balaiada (1838–1840); SABINADA—Bahia (1838–1840); and FARROUPILHA—Rio Grande do Sul (1835–1845).

The threat of anarchy resulting from Liberal policies caused a realignment of political forces bent on restoring order and the authority of the central government. The retrogression began in 1837, during the regency of the conservative leader Pedro de Araújo LIMA, viscount of Olinda, with passage in May 1840 of the Law of Interpretation, which took away some prerogatives of provincial governments, and of a project to amend the Criminal Procedure Code to return to central control the police and judicial appointments. The crisis of political legitimacy continued, however, and in 1839 the country was near chaos and in danger of political dissolution. Luís Alves de LIMA E SILVA, duke of Caxias, utilized a core of loyal officers (the Sacred Battalion) at the head of the newly created National Guard to put down the rebellions. The success of the guard notwithstanding, the early accession of Pedro II was seen as the only solution to restore order and legitimacy. Although the Liberals initiated the movement for his majority for their own reasons, public support ultimately swayed the conservatives. In 1841, Pedro II assumed the throne at age 15, thereby ending the Regency.

THOMAS W. PALMER, JR., "A Momentous Decade in Brazilian Administrative History, 1831–1840," in *Hispanic American Historical Review* 30, no. 2 (May 1950): 209–217; JOÃO PANDIÁ CALOGERAS, *A History of Brazil*, translated and edited by Percy Alvin Martin (1939; repr. 1963), pp. 119–140; SÉRGIO BUARQUE DE HOLLANDA, *Historia geral da civilização brasileira*, vol. 6, no. 2 (1964), pp. 9–60; E. BRADFORD BURNS, *A History of Brazil*, 2d ed. (1980), pp. 170–176; RODERICK J. BARMAN, *Brazil: The Forging of a Nation, 1798–1852* (1988), pp. 189–209.

LYDIA M. GARNER
ROBERT A. HAYES

## BRAZIL: REVOLUTIONS

### Communist Revolts of 1935

In 1934 and 1935, the Brazilian Communist Party (PCB) initiated a two-track policy in its attempt to gain power.

On the one hand, it participated in a popular-front–inspired strategy of making alliances with progressive political groups for an eventual electoral movement. This policy led to the creation in March 1935 of the National Liberation Alliance (ANL). On the other hand, Luís Carlos PRESTES and other party leaders planned to stage a coup d'état with disaffected military men. The Comintern in Moscow initiated both strategies, in keeping with its own foreign-policy objectives. The popular front sought to limit the growing influence of FASCISM, and the coup was an attempt to undermine the smooth functioning of the U.S. and British colonial networks, formal and informal. Moreover, Comintern planners, including Brazilian exiles, looked to the experience of China—another large agrarian country—as their guide for formulating policies for Brazil.

Conceived in Moscow as part of the Soviet Union's offensive against Brazil as a U.S. client, the November 1935 putsch attempt (also known as the *intentona*) was a complete failure that adversely affected any group that had had ties to the ANL but had played no role in the uprising. A group of noncommissioned army men initiated the revolt on the evening of 23 November 1935 in the city of Natal, Rio Grande do Norte. Another group of men rebelled in Recife, Pernambuco. As the federal and state governments moved to crush this small-scale military uprising, Prestes and other PCB leaders initiated a similar uprising in Rio de Janeiro. Loyal troops quickly beat back the rebels.

In just four days, the PCB's quixotic putsch attempt not only failed but also ushered in a decade of state-sponsored repression of all left-wing and labor groups, even though they had not participated in the failed uprising. Getúlio VARGAS's police arrested politicians of various leanings associated with the ANL, and the federal government purged labor union leaders throughout Brazil. The failed coup gave Vargas and his allies the political pretext for instituting a state of siege and eventually establishing the ESTADO NÔVO dictatorship in 1937.

The standard work on politics in the mid-1930s, which includes analyses of the ANL and the *intentona*, is ROBERT M. LEVINE, *The Vargas Regime: The Critical Years, 1934–1938* (1970). Specific studies of the 1935 uprising include THOMAS E. SKIDMORE, "Failure in Brazil: From Popular Front to Armed Revolt," in *Journal of Contemporary History* 5 (1970): 137–157, and STANLEY E. HILTON, *Brazil and the Soviet Challenge, 1917–1947* (1991).

JOEL WOLFE

### Constitutionalist Revolt (São Paulo)

In 1932 the Brazilian state of São Paulo rebelled against the central government. The seeds of this uprising were sown right after the Revolution of 1930, when the Democratic Party (PD) expected to run the state by replacing the São Paulo Republican Party (PRP). President Getúlio VARGAS, however, put *tenentes* (army lieutenants) in control of the state and agreed with their objections to a speedy reconstitutionalization of Brazil. Leaders of São Paulo, a state accustomed to a dominant national role, became so alienated by Vargas that the PD and PRP formed the anti-Vargas, pro-constitution Frente Única Paulista (FUP), which plotted with the Rio Grande do Sul Frente Única Riograndense (FUR) to overthrow Vargas. In May 1932 Vargas promised a constitutional assembly election in 1933, and São Paulo achieved its cherished FUP state government. But in July, General Bertoldo Klinger, chosen by the plotters in April to lead the revolt, was dismissed by Vargas from his troop command in Mato Grosso, a development that, according to a FUP–FUR agreement, called for revolt. Paulistas, incited by pro-constitution, anti-Vargas oratory, were determined to overthrow Vargas and thus regain their state's dominant nationale role. So they sent troops to battle and were disappointed when the other states, especially Rio Grande do Sul and Minas Gerais, did not join the rebellion. In September, after the Paulistas retreated before superior federal forces, their state troops surrendered, to the surprise of their politicians. Vargas exiled São Paulo's leaders to Portugal, but he treated the people of São Paulo generously and implemented his plans for a constitution.

EUCLYDES FIGUEIREDO, *Contribuição para a história da Revolução Constitucionalista de 1932* (1954); PAULO NOGUEIRA FILHO, *A guerra cívica, 1932*, 4 vols. (1965–1967, 1981); JOHN W. F. DULLES, *Vargas of Brazil* (1967).

JOHN W. F. DULLES

### Federalist Revolt of 1893

In the state of Rio Grande do Sul, a challenge to Governor Júlio de CASTILHOS arose in 1893. Rebels joined forces with the naval rebellion of Admiral Custódio de MELO to oppose the republican regime of Floriano Vieira PEIXOTO, convulsing Rio Grande do Sul in a civil war that took 10,000 casualties before its end in August 1895. Led by Gaspar Silveira Martins, Federalists ranged from monarchists to dissident Republicans, united by hatred of Castilhos and resentment of his Republican Party's monopoly on power. They called for his ouster, abrogation of his authoritarian, positivist 1891 state constitution, and Brazil's conversion to a parliamentary regime. Support from Peixoto and the army gave Castilhos military superiority. Rebels raided north into Santa Catarina in November 1893, linking up with naval rebels who had taken that state's capital, and into Paraná, to take Curitiba on 20 January 1894, before turning back. The death of leading rebel general Gumercindo Saraiva, assumption of the presidency by Prudente de Morais, and defeat of Admiral Luís Felipe SALDANHA DA GAMA's invasion of Rio Grande in April 1895, led to the revolt's demise.

Two and a half years of fighting, with mass atrocities on both sides, bred hatreds that deeply divided Rio

Grande for three decades. These years also confirmed the Castilhista machine's control of the state and laid the foundations for future Riograndense strength in national politics.

JOSEPH L. LOVE, *Rio Grande do Sul and Brazilian Regionalism, 1882–1930* (1971); SILVIO DO DUNCAN BARETTA, "Political Violence and Regime Change: A Study of the 1893 Civil War in Southern Brazil" (Ph.D. diss., Univ. of Pittsburgh, 1985).

JOAN BAK

### Liberal Revolution of 1842

In 1841 there was a revolt in the Brazilian provinces of Minas Gerais and São Paulo against the measures taken by the Conservative cabinet. The dismissal of several Liberal provincial presidents, the dissolution of the Chamber of Deputies, the reform of the Criminal Procedure Code, and the reinstatement of the Council of State were acts strongly opposed by Liberals since they weakened provincial authority and strengthened the central government. The conspirators aimed at bringing down the Conservative cabinet and reversing the changes, but the revolt was poorly planned and miscalculated. The national uprising, which was expected to follow events in São Paulo and Minas Gerais, never materialized, and the rebellious military forces were few, disorganized, and plagued by desertion. The central government, in turn, acted swiftly with a military campaign led by Luís Alves de LIMA E SILVA, the baron of Caxias, which brought the revolt to an end in August 1842.

As the first major challenge to the reign of PEDRO II, the revolt was especially threatening to the central government because of the political and social status of its leaders and the geographical location of the provinces involved. Its defeat accelerated the pace of political and administrative centralization. In 1844 amnesty was granted to all participants.

RODERICK J. BARMAN, *Brazil: The Forging of a Nation, 1798–1852* (1988), pp. 212–216.

LYDIA M. GARNER

### Revolts of 1923–1924

Political and economic unrest sparked revolts in Rio Grande do Sul and São Paulo in 1923 and 1924. When the governor of Rio Grande do Sul, Antônio Augusto Borges de Medeiros, ran for a fifth consecutive term, his opponents united in the Liberation Alliance to support the candidacy of Joaquim Francisco de Assis Brasil. Borges apparently garnered the requisite three-quarters of the popular vote, but the Libertadores claimed fraud, and on inauguration day (25 January 1923), uprisings erupted throughout the state. The unrest was resolved in December 1923 with the Pact of Pedras Altas, a compromise that maintained Borges's right to the governorship while granting some concessions to the opposition.

Discontent continued to simmer, nonetheless, especially in the state's outlying areas.

On 5 July 1924, the second anniversary of the Tenentes' Revolt (see TENENTISMO), military officers who remained unhappy with the political preeminence of Brazil's coffee elite represented by President Artur da Silva BERNARDES rebelled in several states. They were most successful in São Paulo, where they captured and held the state capital for almost three weeks before fleeing into the interior. By late 1924 the rebel forces, under the leadership of Isidoro Dias Lopes, had moved into the state of Paraná, where they controlled the towns of Guaíra, Foz do Iguaçu, and Catanduvas. Meanwhile, rebellion erupted once again in Rio Grande do Sul, this time in army garrisons of the Missões district. The Paulistas found support for their movement in Luis Carlos PRESTES, a young captain at the time, who linked Rio Grande's revolt to that of São Paulo. Many gaucho rebels, when forced into flight by government forces, joined Isidoro Dias Lopes's troops in Paraná. Following the fall of Catanduvas, the center of the rebellion, on 27 March 1925, leaders agreed to carry the struggle to overthrow Bernardes to the more remote interior. Thus began the three-year march of the PRESTES COLUMN through the backlands of Brazil.

E. BRADFORD BURNS, *A History of Brazil* (1970); JOSEPH L. LOVE, *Rio Grande do Sul and Brazilian Regionalism, 1882–1930* (1971); EDGARD CARONE, *Revoluções do Brasil contemporâneo, 1922–1938* (1975); RONALD M. SCHNEIDER, *"Order and Progress": A Political History of Brazil* (1991).

JOAN E. MEZNAR

### Revolution of 1930

Unsuccessful in the presidential race of 1930, Getúlio VARGAS, governor of Rio Grande do Sul, led a military uprising that overturned the government of Brazil. The revolt began in Porto Alegre, capital of Rio Grande do Sul, the southernmost state of Brazil. There was little bloodshed.

The "revolution" stemmed in part from the domination of Brazil by the state of SÃO PAULO since the fall of the monarchy in 1889, and in part from the fact that the incumbent president, Washington LUÍS PEREIRA DE SOUSA of São Paulo misjudged the mood of the nation when he imposed another paulista as the official candidate for the presidential election of March 1930 after an earlier promise that the new chief executive would come from MINAS GERAIS. Minas Gerais politicians felt betrayed by this action and broke the traditional alliance of the two states. Led by Antônio Carlos de Andrada, they threw their support to a reluctant presidential opposition candidate, Getúlio Vargas, in the 1930 presidential race. Minas Gerais and Rio Grande do Sul formed a political alliance with the tiny northeastern state of Paraíba to oppose the official paulista candidate, Júlio PRESTES. This new political group, called the Liberal Alliance, opposed the traditional Republican Party of Brazil, which controlled the seventeen other states. Vargas, an astute political realist, doubted the voting power of the three-state Liberal Alliance.

The presidential campaign was traditional, and though Brazil was in an economic crisis, Vargas did not mount a populist crusade. He campaigned in a low-keyed manner against political corruption, favored amnesty for the 1922 and 1924 military rebels, and pushed for a reorganization of the federal Justice and Education departments. He privately assured President Luís that if he, Vargas, lost the race he would support the victor unconditionally.

During the campaign the world market price of coffee dropped to less than five cents a pound (from its high of twenty-three cents in 1928). This change profoundly affected the financial structure of the nation, as the president spent great sums of federal funds to support the coffee export price and prevent the collapse of the paulista coffee economy.

The election, held 1 March 1930, came out as predicted by Vargas. Although he was very popular, the franchise was extremely limited, and Prestes won with just over 1 million votes to Vargas's 750,000. In Rio Grande do Sul, one of Vargas's closest advisers, Oswaldo ARANHA, claimed that Prestes's victory had been obtained fraudulently and declared that the time had come for an armed rebellion.

Active revolutionary plotting began in Rio Grande do Sul and soon spread through the rest of Brazil as economic conditions continued to deteriorate. Military dissidents—most notably the group of *tenentes* who had led rebellions against political corruption in 1922 and 1924—were contacted. The revolution broke on 3 October, and by 24 October the country was securely in the rebels' hands. Luís and Prestes went into exile, and the Vargas forces took over.

In the fifteen years the Vargas forces remained in control of the nation, they temporarily shifted economic and political power away from São Paulo and Minas Gerais. The new wave of politicians also increased the role of the government in the nation's economic life.

THOMAS E. SKIDMORE, *Politics in Brazil, 1930–1964* (1967); JORDAN M. YOUNG, *The Brazilian Revolution of 1930 and the Aftermath* (1967); BORIS FAUSTO, *A revolução de 1930* (1970); PETER FLYNN, *Brazil: A Political Analysis* (1978).

JORDAN M. YOUNG

### Revolution of 1964

In a military coup (31 March–2 April 1964) the Brazilian armed forces overthrew the democratically elected government of President João GOULART and went on to rule Brazil for the next twenty-one years. Believing Goulart to be a radical leftist, the military high command and the political Right had long opposed him. The candidate of the Brazilian Labor Party (PTB), Goulart was elected vice president in 1960. When President Jânio QUADROS

resigned in August 1961, the military vehemently opposed Goulart's inauguration. Only after the congress created a quasi-parliamentary system, stripping the president of many of his powers, was he allowed to be sworn in. In January 1963, a national plebiscite abolished the compromise solution and reinstated Goulart's full presidential powers.

Goulart inherited major economic problems from previous administrations. His mishandling of the economy aggravated these problems and along with a move to the left, contributed to the crisis leading to the coup. After drawn-out negotiations with the International Monetary Fund, the government abandoned any effort to formulate an economic austerity plan and to resolve a balance of payments and external debt crisis. By early 1964 the annual inflation rate approached 100 percent. When Goulart staged a series of mass rallies calling for such basic reforms as nationalization of foreign corporations, the franchise for illiterates, and agrarian reform, the military high command made plans for a coup d'état.

As peasants organized unions in the countryside and leftist labor leaders mobilized workers in the cities, many Brazilians believed the country was moving toward a leftist revolution. Opponents on the Right increasingly called for a military coup and mobilized resources to check the government. The U.S. government, also fearing a leftist revolution, supported the conspirators and the coup. By 1964, the political Center was rapidly disappearing as both the Right and the Left promoted political polarization.

Goulart's intervention into the military chain of command provided the spark for the coup. His mishandling of a naval mutiny infuriated the high command. In a nationally televised speech to a group of sergeants on 30 March, he essentially called for them to disobey their superiors should they feel their orders were not in the best interest of the nation. Incensed by the speech, the commander of the First Army in Minas Gerais, General Olímpio Mourão Filho, ordered his troops to move on Rio de Janeiro on the morning of 31 March, thus setting the coup into action. Within hours other army commanders joined the coup led by General Humberto CASTELLO BRANCO. Goulart fled into exile in Uruguay, and the military took control in a virtually bloodless coup d'état.

THOMAS E. SKIDMORE, *Politics in Brazil, 1930–1964* (1967); ALFRED STEPAN, "The Breakdown of Democratic Regimes: Brazil," in *The Breakdown of Democratic Regimes: Latin America*, edited by Juan J. Linz and Alfred Stepan (1978); RENÉ ARMAND DREIFUSS, *1964: A conquista do estado* (1981); WANDERLEY GUILHERME DOS SANTOS, *Sessenta e quatro: Anatomia da crise* (1986).

MARSHALL C. EAKIN

*See also* **Military Dictatorships.**

**BRAZIL: VICEROYS OF,** highest royal official in Brazil. Usually military men of noble birth, viceroys in Brazil occupied the office of governor-general of Bahia from 1549 to 1720. They were the highest appointed royal officials in colonial Brazil. Like the other governors, the viceroys represented the king and embodied royal authority. Called the "shadows of the King," they were similar to but not as powerful as the Spanish American viceroys. They were royal commissioners who enforced the king's justice in his domain in colonial Brazil. In theory the captains-general or governors were subordinate to the viceroy, but in practice the viceroy's authority was limited to his own captaincy. As the supreme commander of all the armed forces in his district, he was responsible primarily for defending his captaincy from Indian attacks and foreign interlopers.

After 1720 the governors-general of Brazil used the title of viceroy. The early governors-general centralized governmental administration and consolidated royal control over Brazil. They dispensed royal justice, collected taxes, founded towns, oversaw the work of the church, and appointed judges. The viceroys of Brazil sat on the High Court (*Relação*) and presided over the meetings of the town councils in Salvador da Bahia and Rio de Janeiro. Colonial Brazilians complained that the viceroys and governors-general interfered in local affairs. In the eighteenth century their power increased to the point where the viceroys could recall a disobedient governor and recommend a successor, but they had no coercive powers to remove a stubborn captain-general. The eighteenth-century captain-general Gomes Freire de ANDRADE (1685–1763) exercised more power and governed a larger domain in Rio de Janeiro, Minas Gerais, and São Paulo than did the viceroys. By the eighteenth century the captains-general reported directly to the king rather than to the viceroy. The viceroys of the eighteenth century were stronger than their predecessors and more effective administrators.

The viceroy in Brazil ordinarily served a term of six and one-half years in the sixteenth century, three and one-half years in the seventeenth century, and six years in the eighteenth century. As appointed royal representatives, the viceroys tried to be independent of local interests. Their authority increased in times of war and foreign attacks, since their military powers were great. Among the outstanding viceroys were the count of Sabugosa (1720–1735), the marquis of Lavradio (1769–1779), and Luís de Vasconcelos e Sousa (1778–1790). Under close local and royal scrutiny, the viceroys were subject to an inspection at the end of their term (*residencia*). As chiefs of state and official royal representatives, the viceroys tried to keep Brazil unified and loyal to the crown while defending the domain from foreign interlopers.

GOVERNORS-GENERAL AND VICEROYS OF BRAZIL
(1549–1769)

Tomé de Sousa (1549–1553)
Duarte da Costa (1553–1556)
Mem de Sá (1556–1570)
D. Luís de Brito e Almeida—North (1570–1572)

D. Antônio de Salema—South (1570–1572)
D. Luís de Brito e Almeida—North (1572–1577)
Lourenço da Veiga (1577–1581)
Cosme Rangel (1581–1583)
Manuel Teles Barreto (1583–1587)
Junta do Governo: D. Antônio de Barreiros and Cristóvão de Barros (1587–1591)
D. Francisco de Sousa (1591–1602)
D. Diogo Botelho (1602–1608)
D. Diogo de Meneses e Siqueira—North and South (1608–1612)
D. Gaspar de Sousa (1612–1617)
D. Luís de Sousa (1617–1621)
D. Diogo de Mendonça Furtado (1621–1624)
Matias de Albuquerque (1624)
D. Francisco Nunes Marinho d'Eça (1624–1626)
D. Francisco de Moura Rolim (1624–1626)
Diogo Luís de Oliveira (1626–1635)
D. Pedro da Silva (1635–1639)
D. Fernando Mascarenhas, count of Torre (1639)
D. Vasco Mascarenhas, count of Óbidos (1639–1640)
D. Jorge Mascarenhas, marquis of Montalvão, considered the first viceroy of Brazil (1640–1641)
Junta do Governo: Bishop D. Pedro, Luís Barbalho, and Provedor-Mor Lourenço Brito Correia, who assumed office upon the death of his predecessor (1641–1642)
Antônio Teles da Silva (1642–1647)
Antônio Teles de Meneses, count of Vila Pouca de Aguiar (1647–1650)
João Rodrigues de Vasconcelos e Sousa, count of Castelo Melhor (1650–1654)
D. Jerônimo de Ataíde, count of Atouguia (1654–1657)
Francisco Barreto (1657–1663)
D. Vasco de Mascarenhas, count of Óbidos, considered the second viceroy of Brazil (1663–1667)
Alexandre e Sousa Freire (1667–1671)
Francisco Correia da Silva (declined the appointment)
Afonso Furtado de Castro do Rio de Mendonça, viscount of Barbacena (1671–1675)
Junta do Governo: Desembargador Agostinho de Azevedo Monteiro, Álvaro de Azevedo, and Antônio Guedes de Brito, who assumed office on the death of his predecessor (1675–1678)
Roque da Costa Barreto (1678–1682)
Antônio de Sousa de Meneses, the Braço de Prata (1682–1684)
Antônio Luís de Sousa, marquis of Minas (1684–1687)
Matias da Cunha (1687–1688)
D. Frei Manuel da Ressurreição (1688–1690)
Antônio Luís Gonçalves da Câmara Coutinho (1690–1694)
D. João de Lencastre (1694–1702)
D. Rodrigo da Costa (1702–1708)
D. Luís César de Meneses (1708–1710)
D. Lourenço de Almada (1710–1711)
D. Pedro de Vasconcelos e Sousa (1711–1714)

D. Pedro de Noronha, count of Vila Verde and marquis of Angeja, third viceroy of Brazil (1714–1718)

D. Sancho de Faro e Sousa, count of Vimieiro (1718–1719)

Interim government of the Archbishop: Dom Sebastião Monteiro da Vide, chancellor of the High Court, Caetano de Brito de Figueredo, and Master of the Field João de Araujo e Azevedo (1719–1720)

Vasco Fernandes César de Meneses, count of Sabugosa, fourth viceroy of Brazil (1720–1735)

André de Mello e Castro, count of Galveas, fifth viceroy of Brazil (1735–1749)

D. Luís Pedro Peregrino de Carvalho Meneses e Ataíde, tenth count of Atouquia (1749–1754)

Interim government of the Archbishop: Dom José Botelho de Mattos, chancellor of the High Court, Manuel Antônio da Cunha Sotto Maior, and Colonel Lourenço Monteiro (1755)

D. Marcos de Noronha e Brito, sixth count of Arcos (1755–1760)

D. Antônio de Almeida Soares e Portugal, first marquis of Lavradio, third count of Arintes (1760)

Interim government of the Archbishop: Tomás Rubi de Barros Barreto, José Carvalho de Andrade, and Barrose Alvim (1760–1763)

D. Antônio Alvares da Cunha, count of Cunha (1763–1767)

D. Antônio Rolim de Moura, count of Azambuja (1767–1769)

### GOVERNORS-GENERAL OF RIO DE JANEIRO
(1769–1808)

D. Luis de Almeida, Portugal Soares d'Eça Alarcao e Melo Silva e Mascarenhas, second marquis of Lavradio (1769–1779)

D. Luís de Vasconcelos e Sousa, count of Figueiro (1778–1790)

D. José Luís de Castro, second count of Rezende (1790–1801)

Fernando José de Portugal e Castro, count of Resende (1801–1806)

Marcos de Noronha e Brito, eighth count of Arcos (1806–1808)

DAURIL ALDEN, *Royal Government in Colonial Brazil with Special Reference to the Administration of the Marquis of Lavradio, Viceroy 1769–1779* (1968); HELIO VIANNA, *Dicionário da história do Brasil: Moral e civismo* 4th ed. (1976), pp. 265, 266, 552, 553.

PATRICIA MULVEY

**BRAZILIAN ACADEMY OF LETTERS,** a Brazilian equivalent of the French Academy, founded in 1897. The academy's rules and rites reflected the centrality of French models for almost all formal cultural expression in nineteenth-century Brazil after the FRENCH ARTISTIC MISSION (1816). Its purpose was to celebrate earlier Brazilian literature and to promote present literary effort

and literati as respectable and necessary constituents of society at a time when Brazil was perceived to be undergoing national regeneration. Founders of the academy included leading figures in the abolition movement (1888) and militants of the Republic (1889). Many were veterans of the era's new, mass-circulation periodicals; many, like other members of the social and political elites, were liberal professionals who cultivated belles lettres in their youth and leisure.

Unlike Joaquim NABUCO, better known as a celebrated abolitionist, most founders were contemporary literati who have since fallen into relative obscurity: like Coelho Neto, Olavo BILAC, José Veríssimo, Silvio ROMERO, and the Viscount de TAUNAY. However, there is one significant exception. The Forty Immortals were presided over by MACHADO DE ASSIS, Brazil's preeminent novelist, who devoted his last years to the academy's survival. Early on, the ideal of literary integrity was challenged by the desire to cultivate public support through the inclusion of key public figures, a tendency that triumphed in that first generation. The goal of securing a place in the nation's establishment was thus satisfied, although many continue to despair at the cost.

JOSUÉ MONTELLO, *O presidente Machado de Assis* (1961); JOÃO ALEXANDRE BARBOSA, *A tradição do impasse* (1974); NICOLAU SEVCENKO, *Literatura como missão* (1983); JEFFREY D. NEEDELL, *A Tropical Belle Époque*, chap. 6 (1987).

JEFFREY D. NEEDELL

**BRAZILIAN EXPEDITIONARY FORCE (FEB),** a unit that served in Italy with U.S. General Mark Clark's Fifth Army from August 1944 to May 1945 in the Allied campaign against the German Nazis and Italian Fascists. Led by General João Batista Mascarenhas de Morais, the Força Expedicionária Brasileira, as the unit was known in its home country, was comprised of 25,334 officers and men, of whom some fifteen hundred were casualties. On 15 September 1944, the Sixth Regimental Combat Team (São Paulo) entered the line north of Pisa near the Serchio Valley and advanced northward as the Germans withdrew to the Gothic Line. By October only the First Division remained after two others were canceled by President Getúlio VARGAS. The First Infantry, Sampaio (Rio de Janeiro), Eleventh Infantry (Minas Gerais), Divisional Artillery (Rio and São Paulo), Ninth Engineering Battalion (Mato Grosso), Second Motorized Reconnaissance Squadron (Rio), and First Medical Battalion (Rio and São Paulo) were deployed south of Bologna, in the Reno Valley, ahead of which lay Monte Castelo, a key position in the Gothic Line. The FEB launched four unsuccessful assaults on Monte Castelo between 24 November and 12 December 1944. After ten more cold, grueling weeks a fifth attack, on 21 February 1945, succeeded. The FEB pushed forward with the U.S. Tenth Mountain Division and by April received the surrender of three Italian divisions and the 148th German Grenadier Division. The Brazilians then pushed into the Po Valley and on to the French frontier.

Distrustful of this truly national, combat-tested force, Vargas disbanded it upon its return to Brazil in July 1945 and ignored General Mascarenhas. Chief of Staff Colonel Floriano de Lima Brayner was shipped back to Italy to care for the Brazilian cemetery at Pistóia, and the junior officers were posted to isolated interior garrisons. Nevertheless, many of the staff and line officers (henceforth called *Febianos*) later achieved prominence, especially during the 1964 revolution against President João GOULART, after which Chief of Operations Humberto CASTELLO BRANCO served as president (1964–1967). Supporters of the uprising included Chief of Intelligence Amaury Kruel, who commanded the powerful Second Army (São Paulo), and Staff Liaison Officer Carlos de Meira Matos, who led the Minas Gerais column against Brasília. Brazilian-based FEB interior officer Henrique Batista Duffles Teixeira LOTT served as minister of war (1954–1960) and was a presidential candidate (1960), and coconspirator Artur da COSTA E SILVA actually served as president (1967–1969).

Line officers João Segadas Vianna and Jurandir Mamede founded the Anti-Communist Crusade. Legalist infantry colonel Nélson de Melo served as minister of war (1961–1962) but later broke with Goulart and joined the conspiracy. Raimundo Ferreira de Souza led his Sampaio regiment against the Goulart government. Ernesto GEISEL became president (1974–1979). On 29 October 1945 FEB Artillery Commander Oswaldo Cordeiro de Farias delivered the military's ultimatum to Vargas, provoking his resignation. The Febianos Cordeiro de Farias and César Obino were also instrumental in founding the ESCOLA SUPERIOR DA GUERRA (Superior War College), in 1949. Many Febianos made fast friends with U.S. liaison officer Vernon A. Walters, later the U.S. defense attaché to Brazil (1962–1967). Thus, the friendships forged on World War II Italian battlefields affected Brazil from 1945 on.

JOÃO BATISTA MASCARENHAS DE MORAIS, *A FEB pelo seu comandante* (1947); JOEL SILVEIRA, *As duas guerras da FEB* (1965); FLORIANO DE LIMA BRAYNER, *A verdade sobre a FEB* (1968); RAYMOND ESTEP, *The Military in Brazilian Politics, 1821–1970* (1971); LEWIS A. TAMBS, "Five Times Against the System," in *Perspectives on Armed Politics in Brazil,* edited by Henry H. Keith and Robert A. Hayes (1976), pp. 177–206; VERNON A. WALTERS, *Silent Missions* (1978).

LEWIS A. TAMBS

**BRAZILIAN HIGHLANDS** (also, *Planalto central* or, less frequently, *Planalto Brasileiro*), a plateau region of southeastern Brazil located chiefly in the states of Minas Gerais and São Paulo. The climate is temperate. Elevations of the low mountains, hilly uplands, and tabular plateaus characteristic of the highlands average 1,970–2,950 feet above sea level and are generally highest near the Atlantic coast. The highlands meet the Atlantic coast in a steep slope called "the Great Escarpment," which stretches from the city of Salvador, Bahia, to Pôrto Alegre, Rio Grande do Sul. Three major river systems—the Amazon, the Paraná and the São Francisco—drain the region.

CARA SHELLY

**BRAZILNUT INDUSTRY.** The *castanha do Pará* (Pará chestnut) grows on black, Amazonian rain-forest giants (*castanheiras*) that tower 150 feet in the air and have a girth of 20 feet. Gatherers wait until the grapefruit-sized *ouriço* (outer casing) falls to the ground before collecting the fifteen to twenty nutritious nuts (17 percent protein) found inside the hard casing. One tree produces between 250 and 500 pounds of nuts in a good season. The nuts are so important to the Amazonian economy that the Brazilian government passed a law in 1965 making it illegal to cut down *castanheiras*.

In January, gatherers, who often double as SERINGUEIROS (rubber gatherers), begin harvesting the nuts. They break open the shells with machete-type knives (*terçados*), leaving the heavy, bulky *ouriços* on the forest floor. Some *seringueiros* collect more than three tons of Brazilnuts in one rainy season. They take their harvest to the trading center (*barracão*), where in 1989 they were paid three or four cents a pound for unshelled Brazilnuts. Shelling plants process the nuts, which are soaked for twenty-four hours, placed in boiling water for a few minutes, then shelled with a hand-operated machine. The majority of shelling plants are located in Pará and Bélem.

Before World War II, most Brazilnuts were exported to Europe; afterwards, the United States received most of them; and by 1990, the United States imported $16 million worth of Pará chestnuts annually. The nuts became such an important part of the extractive reserve program begun in the 1980s that manufacturers soon produced and marketed other Brazilnut products, such as hair conditioners, based on its oil, to appeal to environmentally conscious consumers.

BENJAMIN H. HUNNICUTT, *Brazil: World Frontier* (1969); ANDREW REVKIN, *The Burning Season* (1990).

CAROLYN JOSTOCK

**BRAZILWOOD,** a dyewood from various tropical trees (especially genus *Caesalpinia*) whose extracts yield shades of red and purple. *Caesalpinia enchinata,* Brazil's first important export, lured French and Portuguese traders to the coast in the early 1500s; its similarity to *Caesalpinia brasiliensis,* a species indigenous to the Near East and long familiar to Europeans, gave Brazil its name.

Although Brazil's earliest permanent settlements sprang from brazilwood trading forts and factories, participants in the trade did not intend to settle the region. In the 1530s, however, Portugal's increased interest in colonization stemmed in part from the crown's desire to establish control of the dyewood trade in the face of French competition.

European traders depended on indigenous peoples to fell the dyewood trees and transport the wood to collection points. The Portuguese employed a factory system: the Indians brought the wood to forts on the coast, where ships later called for it. The French, on the other hand, collected cargoes by anchoring offshore and sending crewmen to arrange an exchange with local tribes.

Initially, the brazilwood trade was based on peaceful barter between Europeans and Indians, but these arrangements soon degenerated into coercion of indigenous peoples.

ALEXANDER MARCHANT, *From Barter to Slavery: The Economic Relations of Portuguese and Indians in the Settlement of Brazil, 1500–1580* (1942); JOHN HEMMING, *Red Gold: The Conquest of the Brazilian Indians* (1978).

CARA SHELLY

**BRECHERET, VÍTOR** (*b.* 22 February 1894; *d.* 17 December 1955), Brazilian sculptor. Born in Italy, Brecheret moved to Brazil with his sister in 1913 and began his formal artistic education at the Liceu de Artes e Ofícios de São Paulo in 1912. For the next six years he studied art in Europe, where he came to greatly appreciate the work of the French sculptor Auguste Rodin. While in Rome, he won first place in Rome's International Exhibition of Fine Arts for his *Despertar*.

When Brecheret returned to São Paulo in 1919, he set up a studio, and by January 1920 he had met fellow artists DI CAVALCANTI, Hélios Seelinger, Menotti des Picchia, and Oswald de ANDRADE, who recognized his importance for modernism. That same year he was selected to submit plans for a monument commemorating the participation of the BANDEIRA in Brazil's early history. In 1921, after his *Eva* was acquired by the prefecture of São Paulo, Brecheret obtained a government stipend to finance a second trip to Europe. Before leaving for France, however, he selected twelve of his sculptures for exhibition during São Paulo's MODERN ART WEEK in 1922.

Between his return to Brazil in 1930 and his death in 1955, Brecheret realized numerous exhibitions and founded the Sociedade Pró-Arte Moderna (1932). He received the French Legion of Honor and won the National Prize for Sculpture in the 1951 São Paulo Biennial. He also did several commemorative public monuments.

MÁRIO DA SILVA BRITO, *História do modernismo brasileiro* (1978), esp. pp. 104–134; ARACY AMARAL, *Artes plásticas na Semana de 22: Subsídios para uma história da renovação das artes no Brasil,* 4th ed. (1979), esp. pp. 240–242.

CAREN A. MEGHREBLIAN

**BRENNER, ANITA** (*b.* 13 August 1905; *d.* 1 December 1974), journalist, author, and editor who lived in Mex-ico. Born of American Jewish parents in Aguascalientes, Mexico, Brenner matured in Mexican, Jewish, and North American cultures. She was a member of the cosmopolitan intellectual community in Mexico City in the 1920s and did key archival research for Ernest Gruening's *Mexico and Its Heritage* (1928). Her first book, *Idols Behind Altars* (1929), emphasized the Indian component of Mexican art and culture. In the 1930s Brenner worked as a journalist and completed a doctorate in anthropology at Columbia University. She wrote the text to accompany George Leighton's photographs for *The Wind That Swept Mexico* (1943), an overview of the Mexican Revolution. From 1955 to 1971 she was editor of *Mexico This Month,* an English-language magazine based in Mexico.

ANITA BRENNER, *Idols Behind Altars* (1929) and *The Wind That Swept Mexico* (1943). See also ERNEST GRUENING, *Mexico and Its Heritage* (1928), esp. pp. 393–493, in which Brenner's research appeared.

JOHN A. BRITTON

**BRESSER PEREIRA, LUIZ CARLOS** (*b.* 30 June 1934), Brazilian economist. Born in São Paulo, Bresser Pereira received a law degree from the University of São Paulo (USP) in 1957. After joining the faculty of the Getúlio Vargas Foundation in São Paulo (FGV-SP) in 1959, he went to Michigan State University, where he earned an M.B.A. in 1961. Returning to Brazil, he continued his academic career at FGV-SP, becoming a full professor in 1972, the same year in which he earned a Ph.D. in economics from USP. A prolific writer, he has written more than fifteen books and hundreds of articles covering a broad array of subjects. Sometimes characterized as a neo-structuralist, he took the role of the state in the process of economic development as a major theme of research. In the early 1980s, together with Yoshiaki Nakano, he wrote seminal contributions to the formulation of the theory of inertial inflation. He also had a successful career in the private sector (as administrative director of a major Brazilian supermarket chain) and was politically active (as one of the leading economists of PMDB—the main opposition party to the military regime).

In 1983, Bresser Pereira was appointed president of the state-owned bank of São Paulo (BANESPA), and from March 1985 to April 1987 he served both the Montoro and the Quércia administrations as state secretary. Appointed by President José SARNEY, Bresser Pereira replaced Dilson Funaro on 29 April 1987 as Brazil's finance minister after the collapse of the Cruzado Plan. His stabilization program (the Bresser Plan) relied on a temporary price freeze and on measures of fiscal austerity. When the resistance of President Sarney to fiscal austerity became evident, Bresser Pereira resigned on 18 December 1987. He is also known for his attempts to persuade foreign creditors of the necessity for debt relief in developing countries.

CARLOS ALBERTO PRIMO BRAGA

**BRIERRE, JEAN-FERNAND** (pseud. Jean-François; *b.* 28 September 1909; *d.* 24 December 1992). Haitian writer and government official in Haiti and Senegal. In 1932, after serving as secretary to the Haitian Embassy in Paris (1929–1930), Brierre founded the opposition newspaper *La Bataille*. The paper was suspended and Brierre was imprisoned. After an appointment as inspector of schools in Jérémie, Brierre finally became ambassador to Argentina under President Paul MAGLOIRE. Imprisoned again by President François DUVALIER in 1961, Brierre left for Jamaica. He settled in Dakar when Senegalese President Léopold Sédar Senghor offered him a position in the ministry of culture.

Brierre's writing has been characterized by a celebration of the suffering and the triumphs of black people, especially Haitians. Addressing both slaves and his contemporaries in "Black Soul," Brierre wrote that "the black serpent of pain ripples through the contortions of your body." A current of Christian ideology informs even his more erotic poetry. Brierre published copiously from his early twenties into his seventies in Haiti, Argentina, Paris, and Dakar. His name has been associated variously with the Haitian Indigenist poets as well as with the negritude poets.

Works by Jean-Fernand Brierre include: *Le drapeau de demain* (play, 1931); *Chansons secrètes* (poetry, 1933); *Nous garderons le dieu* (poetry, 1945); *Les aïeules* (drama, 1945); *Black Soul* (poetry, 1947); *Belle* (drama, 1948); *Dessalines nous parle* (poetry, 1953); *Au milieu des flammes* (drama, 1953); *Les horizons sans ciel* (novel, 1953); *Pétion et Bolívar, avec Adieu à la Marseillaise* (poetry, 1955); *La Source* (poetry, 1956); *La Nuit* (poetry, 1957); *Hommage au Maître Occilius Jeanty* (poetry, 1960); *Cantique à trois voix pour une poupée d'ébène* (poetry, 1960); *Or, uranium, cuivre, radium* (poetry, 1961); *Découvertes* (poetry, 1966); *Un autre monde* (essay, 1973); *Images d'argile et d'or* (poetry, 1977); *Un Noël pour Gorée* (poetry, 1980); and *Sculptures de proue* (poetry, 1983).

NAOMI M. GARRET, *The Renaissance of Haitian Poetry* (1963), pp. 148–158; MAURICE A. LUBIN, "Jean-F. Brierre and His Work," in *Black World* 22, no. 3 (1973): 36–48; F. RAPHAËL BERROU and PRADEL POMPILUS, *Histoire de la littérature haitïenne illustrée par les textes*, vol. 3 (1977), pp. 190–237; Max Dominique, *L'Arme de la critique littéraire: Littérature et idéologie en Haïti (1988)*, pp. 173–203.

CARROL F. COATES

**BRIÓN, LUIS** (*b.* 1782; *d.* 27 September 1821), Venezuelan naval commander. The son of a successful Flemish Jewish merchant of Curaçao, Brión became commander of Simón BOLÍVAR's Venezuela squadron in 1813 and his most trusted naval adviser. He played a major role in the assault on Spanish maritime interests in the Caribbean during the WARS OF INDEPENDENCE, bringing British arms to Bolívar's support and thwarting the reconquest campaign of General Pablo MORILLO. His commercial connections in the Caribbean, especially with Maxwell Hyslop at Jamaica, also helped secure credit for Bolívar's forces. Brión's bitter rivalry with French privateer Louis-Michael AURY undermined the patriot naval effort when Aury refused to serve under Brión's command in 1816, but Brión's fleet, operating out of Margarita Island, continued to harass the Spaniards. In 1820 Brión took charge of the transition from a privateer fleet to a more formal Venezuelan navy, but when he became ill in the spring of 1821, his command was transferred to Lino de Clemente.

STANLEY FAYE, "Commodore Aury," in *Louisiana Historical Quarterly* 24, no. 3 (1941): 611–697; ENRIQUE ORTEGA RICAURTE, *Luis Brión de la Orden de Libertadores: Primer Almirante de la República de Colombia y General en jefe de sus ejércitos 1782–1828* (1953); JANE LUCAS DE GRUMMOND, *Renato Beluche: Smuggler, Privateer, and Patriot, 1780–1860* (1983); JAIME DUARTE FRENCH, *Los tres Luises del Caribe: ¿Corsarios o libertadores?* (1988).

RALPH LEE WOODWARD, JR.

**BRITISH HONDURAS.** *See* **Belize.**

**BRITISH IN ARGENTINA.** Just before the advent of Juan D. PERÓN in 1943, the British in Argentina numbered about 40,000. Compared with Italians, Spaniards, or even Jews, this figure appears small. Nevertheless, the British community in Argentina was the largest outside the empire and commanded formidable assets in Argentina. British railways there were not far short of the network in Britain, while port installations, MEAT-PACKING plants, grain elevators, banking, and even retailing exhibited remarkably high British participation. However, with the substantial dismantling of the Anglo-Argentine connection between 1946 and 1955, numbers dwindled to 16,000 British residents, becoming a community less distinct within the country's population at large.

The Anglo-Argentine connection began with the British penetration of the South Atlantic in the seventeenth century and intensified with the commercial association of London and Buenos Aires in the 1820s. The restricted market in Britain for Argentine products, however, prevented Argentina from keeping up debt service on British capital investment. On the other hand, British export trade to Argentina remained the weakest element of the economic trilogy—foodstuffs, manufactures, and capital. By 1914, British exports were worth only half of Argentina's exports to the United Kingdom. Henceforward, the British persistently sought opportunities to compel the Argentines to reject foreign manufactures even though Britain was a proponent of free trade. Although World War I afforded Britain the opportunity to uproot German business through the use of blacklisting and shipping controls, the United States took advantage of the opening. By the 1920s the Anglo–United States trade rivalry in Argentina was so great that war seemed imminent.

The D'Abernon trade mission in 1929 would have diverted enough Argentine purchases to Britain to enforce a balance of trade, but the agreement remained unsigned when Hipólito YRIGOYEN's government was overthrown by General José Evaristo URIBURU. The ROCA–RUNCIMAN PACT (1933), however, turned the tide in Britain's favor. It harnessed the Argentines to obsolete British manufacturing by threatening Argentina's meat industry with the diversion of British import trade to her colonies.

In reality, the treaty led directly to the dissolution of the very Anglo-Argentine connection it was intended to shore up. It was a political gift to incipient Peronism, which made it a byword for the collaboration of the ruling oligarchy with British imperialism. In June 1943 Peronists overthrew the "vendepatria" elite. Three years later Perón became president and ordered the buying up of British assets and the diversification of Argentina's commerce and industry.

HENRY S. FERNS, *Britain and Argentina in the Nineteenth Century* (1960); ANDREW GRAHAM-YOOLL, *The Forgotten Colony: A History of the English-Speaking Communities in Argentina* (1981); ROGER GRAVIL, *The Anglo-Argentine Connection, 1900–1939* (1985).

ROGER GRAVIL

## BRITISH INVASIONS, RÍO DE LA PLATA,

efforts of a British expeditionary force (1806–1807) to take Buenos Aires from Spain. In 1804 Spain aligned with Napoleonic France, only to have its navy devastated at Trafalgar in 1805. British trade with the Río de la Plata had been flourishing since the 1780s, and fueled by the Venezuelan patriot Francisco de MIRANDA's promises of Spanish American sympathy for direct relations with Britain, some British sectors advocated open support for independence struggles. Commodore Sir Home POPHAM, a seasoned veteran of the Napoleonic Wars, attracted by commercial possibilities in South America, ordered 1,600 troops to invade Buenos Aires, which they did in June 1806. Faced with an invasion led by General William Carr BERESFORD, the viceroy, Fernando Rafael de SOBREMONTE, fled with the Spanish garrison and the treasury, leaving the city to civilians. The British were welcomed at first, but the civilians soon turned on them. After two months a ragtag militia led by a French officer in the imperial employ, Captain Santiago de LINIERS, captured Beresford and his troops. A coalition emerged of Spanish merchants, led by Martín de ÁLZAGA, creole merchants (led by Juan Martín de PEUYRREDÓN), and lesser imperial officers. Popham ordered General John Whitelocke to lead a second expedition to retake the viceregal capital. After seizing Montevideo in May 1807, Whitelocke fought his way to Buenos Aires with 7,000 soldiers but was mowed down by civilians and militia armed with cannon and muskets captured from Beresford. Whitelocke proved himself profoundly incompetent, leading his forces down narrow streets, where bullets rained down from the rooftops. He surrendered unconditionally on 7 July 1807.

The British invasions shattered the legitimacy of the viceroy, who had left his capital with threadbare defenses. Liniers became the interim viceroy but was much more attuned to the interests of creoles than of peninsular concerns, thereby opening a power struggle between pro-Spanish (led by Álzaga) and patriotic factions. Each side squared off in armed confrontation between various factions of the militia. The creole majority of the militia soon defeated Álzaga's followers. The municipal CABILDO also had become a battlefield for internecine bickering. Peninsular sympathizers eventually convinced Charles IV to replace Liniers with Balthasar de CISNEROS. He proved to be as incompetent as Sobremonte; therefore the creoles, supported by the militia, declared open defiance on 25 May 1810. The British invasions instigated a sequence of events leading to independence in the Río de la Plata and to the militarization of local politics.

HENRY STANLEY FERNS, *Britain and Argentina in the Nineteenth Century* (1960), esp. pp. 18–47; TULIO HALPERÍN DONGHI, *Politics, Economics, and Society in Argentina in the Revolutionary Period* (1975), esp. pp. 133–139.

JEREMY ADELMAN

## BRITISH–LATIN AMERICAN RELATIONS.

Commercial interaction has been the mainspring of British–Latin American relations, with the English goal being commercial ascendancy and the means varying with historical circumstances. England began a continuous and expanding role in Latin America by challenging Spain's efforts to monopolize the wealth of the new lands discovered by COLUMBUS. An assortment of corsairs based in the Old World, among them Francis DRAKE and John Hawkins, preyed on Spanish shipping and plundered the American coasts during the Elizabethan Age. In the seventeenth century, England established enclaves in several small islands in the Lesser Antilles, in neighboring Guiana, in the Bahamas and Bermuda, in what is now Belize and along the Mosquito Coast of Central America, and gained strategic advantage by seizing Jamaica in 1655. Privateering and PIRACY now blended with contraband trade, dyewood and mahogany lumbering, and colonizing ventures as the English expanded their efforts to breach the Spanish monopoly. An era of plunder left a trail of carnage and wreckage over a wide expanse of the Caribbean.

As Spanish power waned in the eighteenth century, England was able to wring commercial concessions from Spain in the Americas. By mid-century England had become the major market for the raw materials of Spanish America and the principal source for its manufactured goods, with Spanish merchants in Cádiz and Seville serving more as intermediaries in this trade. During the prolonged wars of the French Revolution, Spain's interaction with her colonies was often interrupted, enabling England to make further commercial inroads. The long Napoleonic struggle disrupted traditional trading patterns, and England compensated by expanding commercial ties with Spain's overseas colonies.

Spanish resistance to Napoleon's occupation of the Iberian Peninsula in 1808 prompted CREOLE leaders overseas to vie with royal officials to resist French pretensions by governing in the name of the deposed Spanish king, FERDINAND VII. The ambiguous situation allowed England, now an ally of Spain, to further her commercial penetration of the Spanish Empire. The defeat of Napoleon and the restoration of Ferdinand VII were followed at first by a hesitant and later by a mushrooming independence movement in Spain's colonies. England was in a quandary. An independent Latin America would provide England with commercial access on an unprecedented scale, but as the ally of Spain, England could not officially support Spanish American independence. By insisting that the independence movement was a domestic uprising involving only Spain and her colonies, England dissuaded the other European monarchs from assisting Ferdinand VII.

The English correctly concluded that without outside assistance Ferdinand would be unable to recover his mainland colonies, and one by one, they won their independence. Brazilians were further indebted to the English for their evacuation of the Portuguese court to Rio de Janeiro to escape capture by Napoleon. Brazilian independence, being more a family matter, did not necessitate any juggling of British policy. The United States also supported Latin American independence and, well aware of England's position, used the MONROE DOCTRINE to warn the European powers not to interfere in New World affairs. The new Latin American nations viewed England not only as the major supporter of their independence but also as their principal partner for achieving anticipated prosperity.

In the post-Napoleonic world England emerged as the international hub of commerce. To expand global commerce England led the way in replacing the restrictive policies of mercantilism with freer trade, and preached the comparative advantage of international specialization. Competing for the lion's share of global trade became the focus of the British government during the relatively peaceful nineteenth century, and the tenets of economic liberalism provided the cutting edge. England was confident that in the long run she could not be overtaken by other nations because of the natural advantages she derived from an unrivaled superiority in industry, commerce, and finance. Latin America was a prime target for British commercial expansion, and for the next century England enjoyed an overwhelming preeminence in Latin America that was not seriously challenged until the twentieth century.

Initially, opportunities in independent Latin America were greeted enthusiastically in England, but after the speculative investment bubble of 1824–1826 burst, investors became more wary. Political instability and internecine wars in Latin America during the age of the CAUDILLOS (1825–1870) had a sobering effect and dimmed the vision of Latin America as a new EL DORADO for quick wealth. Absorbing whatever trade existed, the British were unwilling to incur risks by trying to expand it, given the political climate.

As political order and stability were imposed by a new generation of authoritarian leaders after 1870, prospects for commercial expansion in Latin America brightened. The British responded with mounting investment to develop the export sectors of the more promising countries, especially in Argentina, Brazil, and Mexico. Brazil was an early target because the constitutional monarchy was seen as providing a continuity and stability lacking in Spanish America. Later, British commercial interests revolutionized the MEAT INDUSTRY in Argentina, developed the MINING economies in Chile and Mexico, expanded the PETROLEUM INDUSTRY in Venezuela and Mexico, and made similar incursions into most other Latin American countries. RAILROAD construction was launched on a major scale, with the heaviest British commitment in Argentina. Enjoying a dramatic advantage in capital and credit, the British established commanding control in railroads, communications, utilities, port installations, banking, technology, shipping, insurance, government bonds, and trade.

Latin America experienced a degree of prosperity and growth, but its economy tended to become an appendage to that of Great Britain; any benefits that accrued to Latin America were the by-product of prosperity overseas. Latin America emerged as part of the peripheral world serving the major industrial powers, principally England. The heavy British imprint in Latin America eventually generated a reaction against what was perceived as economic IMPERIALISM in the twentieth century, especially in Argentina, which was viewed as almost a British dominion. The first major challenge to British preeminence appeared in the Caribbean with the sudden emergence of the United States as a global industrial power after 1900. New interpretations of the Monroe Doctrine encouraged American business and banking interests to supersede their British counterparts in areas essential to American security.

British ascendancy continued unabated up to World War I and carried into the 1920s, but it encountered more competition from the United States and more resistance within various Latin American nations, a trend that became more apparent between the wars. The Great Depression undercut British–Latin American economic ties. Relations were further strained by anti-imperialist nationalism demanding more autonomy, a trend most evident with Getúlio VARGAS in Brazil, Lázaro, CARDENAS in Mexico, and later Juan PERÓN in Argentina.

World War II marked the end of an era in British–Latin American relations. The postwar realignment witnessed a serious eclipse of British influence both in the world in general and in Latin America in particular. Faced with diminishing assets, Great Britain had to rearrange priorities in an increasingly polarized world. Independence was granted to her tiny Caribbean colonies as the empire was dismantled. Investment and trade with Latin America slowly eroded and passed overwhelmingly to the United States. Military collaboration and economic aid underwrote the new American preeminence. The United States rapidly displaced Great Britain in Latin America as Britain had once displaced Spain.

ALAN K. MANCHESTER, *British Preëminence in Brazil: Its Rise and Decline* (1933); PHILIP A. MEANS, *The Spanish Main: Focus of Envy, 1492–1700* (1935); RICHARD PARES, *War and Trade in the West Indies, 1739–1763* (1936); SIMON G. HANSON, *Argentine Meat and the British Market* (1938); CHARLES W. CENTNER, *Great Britain and Chile, 1810–1914* (1944); WILLIAM W. KAUFMANN, *British Policy and the Independence of Latin America 1804–1828* (1951); J. FRED RIPPY, *British Investments in Latin America, 1822–1949* (1959); HENRY S. FERNS, *Britain and Argentina in the Nineteenth Century* (1960, repr. 1977); ROBERT A. NAYLOR, "The British Role in Central America Prior to the Clayton-Bulwer Treaty of 1850," in *Hispanic American Historical Review* 40 (1960): 361–382; ALFRED TISCHENDORF, *Great Britain and Mexico in the Era of Porfirio Díaz* (1961); ALEC G. FORD, *The Gold Standard, 1880–1914: Britain and Argentina* (1962); RICHARD GRAHAM, *Britain and the Onset of Modernization in Brazil, 1850–1914* (1968); ROBERT A. NAYLOR, *Influencia británica en el comercio centroamericano durante las primeras décadas de la independencia: 1821–1851* (1988).

ROBERT A. NAYLOR

See also **Buccaneers and Freebooters; Falklands/Malvinas War.**

**BRITTO GARCÍA, LUIS** (*b.* 9 October 1940), Venezuelan writer. Twice awarded the Casa de las Américas literary prize (*Rajatabla* [short stories], 1970; *Abrapalabra* [novel], 1979), Britto García engages in linguistic experimentation, in both prose and drama, that ranges from the poetic to the entropic (serving as his point of departure for the deconstruction of contemporary Venezuelan cultural and social phenomena).

Venezuelan culture is also the subject of Britto García's more recent nonfiction works, such as *La máscara del poder* (1988), a systematic investigation of the cultural aspects of populism in Venezuelan politics, and *El imperio contracultural* (1991).

JULIO E. MIRANDA, *Proceso a la narrativa venezolana* (1975), esp. pp. 23–25, 162–165, 219–220. For a detailed discussion of *Abrapalabra,* see Agustín Martínez A., "Discurso político novelesco en *Abrapalabra,* de Luis Britto García," in *Escritura* 8, no. 15 (1983):87–101.

SHELLY JARRETT BROMBERG

**BRIZOLA, LEONEL** (*b.* 22 January 1922), governor of Rio Grande do Sul (1959–1963) and Rio de Janeiro, Brazil (1983–1987, 1991–1995). Born into a poor family in rural Rio Grande do Sul, Leonel Brizola was raised by his mother. He worked hard to complete his education, moving to Pôrto Alegre at age fourteen. By taking different jobs, he managed to complete his engineering degree.

In 1945, as a recruiter for the Brazilian Labor Party (PTB), Brizola cultivated the working-class and socialist identity that helped him win election to the state legislature. His association with João GOULART led to his marriage to the latter's sister and to closer ties to Getúlio VARGAS. After several state posts, Brizola won election as federal deputy in 1954.

In 1955 Brizola's promises to improve the lives of the workers won him the mayoralty of Porto Alegre. For three years he developed his reputation as an engineer with a social conscience, speaking on the radio, writing newspaper columns, meeting with civic groups, and overseeing projects.

His success as mayor led to his victory in the 1958 gubernatorial election. Two controversial nationalizations—the American-owned electric power and telephone companies—projected Brizola onto the national scene. Moreover, he mobilized civilian and military forces in Rio Grande to compel the succession of Goulart to the presidency in 1961. A year later Brizola heightened his national prominence when he was elected Guanabara's federal deputy by the most votes ever cast. From his new political base he pressured Goulart and Congress to carry out major reforms, such as land distribution, rent control, and nationalization of utilities. Although popular among workers, Brizola's campaign alienated businessmen, the upper middle class, the U.S. government, and the military. His tendency to polarize issues contributed to the crisis of 1964.

After the 1964 coup, Brizola fled in exile to Uruguay, where he organized guerrilla resistance and participated in various conspiracies; eventually he settled down and conducted business there. Deported in 1977, he traveled in the United States and Europe, making contacts and developing a democratic socialist image.

In 1979 he returned to Brazil under the amnesty and founded the Democratic Labor Party (PDT), with which he won election as governor of Rio in 1982. He was notable for founding integrated school centers for children, curbing police abuses, and pressuring Congress to hold direct elections for president in 1984–1985. Having run unsuccessfully for president in 1989, he was elected governor of Rio the following year. After a successful term as governor, he again ran an unsuccessful race for president in 1994.

JOHN W. F. DULLES, *Unrest in Brazil* (1970); GUITA GRIN DEBERT, *Ideologia e populismo* (1979); LUÍS ALBERTO MONIZ BANDEIRA, *Brizola e o trabalhismo* (1979); ISRAEL BELOCH and ALZIRA ALVES DE ABREU, comps., *Dicionário histórico-biográfico brasileiro, 1930–1983* (1984).

MICHAEL L. CONNIFF

**BRIZUELA, FRANCISCO** (*b.* 17 February 1879; *d.* 14 August 1947), Paraguayan soldier in the CHACO WAR and civil war of 1947. Born in Carapeguá, Brizuela entered the armed forces at an early age and participated in several of Paraguay's minor civil wars of the 1900–1920 period. Having advanced to the rank of major, he acted as chief of police for Asunción between June 1918 and September 1919.

Brizuela made little secret of his own political ambitions and therefore spent most of the 1920s out of uniform. At the end of the decade, however, he was called out of retirement to command a Paraguayan infantry division in the early stages of the Chaco War. The energetic defense he prepared at Fort Nanawa in 1933 prevented the Bolivians from advancing southward toward Asunción. Soon afterward, they began their long retreat to the Altiplano.

Brizuela later participated in the 1947 civil war. While attempting to fly munitions to rebel forces in Paraguay, he was killed in an airplane accident outside Montevideo.

CARLOS ZUBIZARRETA, *Cien vidas paraguayas* (1985), pp. 311–313; R. ANDREW NICKSON, *Historical Dictionary of Paraguay* (1993), p. 82.

THOMAS L. WHIGHAM

**BROQUA, ALFONSO** (*b.* 11 September 1876; *d.* 24 November 1946), Uruguayan composer. Broqua was born in Montevideo, where he began his music studies. In 1894 he went to Paris and entered the Schola Cantorum, where he studied composition under Vincent d'Indy for six years. After spending some time in Brussels with Eduardo FABINI, he returned to Montevideo in 1904. His first nationalist work, *Tabaré,* based on a poem by Juan ZORRILLA DE SAN MARTÍN, premiered in 1910. Broqua set out to create a new musical aesthetic based on the use of vocal themes and dance forms and rhythms from Uruguayan folk music. *Tabaré,* a lyric poem for soprano, female chorus, and orchestra, was considered a major event at Montevideo. It was performed at the TEATRO SOLÍS on 30 June 1910 and conducted by the composer. That same year the National Orchestra presented his version of *El poema de las lomas,* originally a major piano triptych premiered by Ernest Drangosh in 1909. Two other works from this period are *Quinteto en sol menor* and *La cruz del Sud,* a never performed opera.

In terms of musical form and aesthetics, the Piano Quintet in G minor is the best written of his works; its last movement, *Variaciones sobre temas regionales,* shows a clear influence of the new nationalist style, which he, Fabini, and Luis CLUZEAU-MORTET helped to inaugurate. In 1922 Broqua settled in Paris, where he continued composing. His other major works include *Impresiones sinfónicas* (1912) for orchestra, *Preludios pampeanos* (1938) for guitar, *Evocaciones criollas, Estudios criollos,* and *Preludios* (1929), as well as three suites for guitar and numerous pieces for solo piano and for voice, piano, and guitar. He died in Paris.

*Composers of the Americas,* vol. 16 (1970), p. 59; *New Grove Dictionary of Music and Musicians,* vol. 3 (1980); S. SALGADO, *Breve historia de la música culta en el Uruguay,* 2d ed. (1980).

SUSANA SALGADO

**BROTHERHOODS.** Originating in the Iberian Middle Ages when they were usually formed by the memberships of individual guilds, lay brotherhoods (*confrarias* and *irmandades*) were organized throughout colonial Brazil on the basis of noncraft-oriented social groupings within the local community. Brotherhoods were dedicated to more than fifty patron saints, whose life histories represented an ideal shared by the various social groupings associated with a particular one. These lay sodalities contributed to social cohesion by providing social services, alms, dowries, and burials, according to members' needs, as well as by by promoting religious observances. The diversity of brotherhoods reflected the relative complexity of colonial society. Thus, the elite almost invariably belonged to the Order of Saint Francis of Assisi; slaves and free blacks normally were members of the Brotherhood of Our Lady of the Rosary; while intermediate social and racial groupings formed the dozens of other lay associations.

Historians have tended to emphasize the mutual assistance that characterized the brotherhoods, their role

Members of a Brotherhood. SOLOMON CYTRYNOWICZ / PULSAR IMAGENS E EDITORA.

in upholding practices of the Catholic faith, as well as their contribution to the construction and maintenance of churches. Recent studies, however, have pointed to the associative spirit of brotherhoods as presenting a potential challenge to overbearing colonial authority.

Lay brotherhoods are highlighted in STUART B. SCHWARTZ, "Plantation and Peripheries, c. 1580–c. 1750," in *Colonial Brazil*, edited by Leslie Bethell (1987), esp. pp. 133–139. An important study of the racial demarcations of orders is found in A. J. R. RUSSELL-WOOD, "Black and Mulatto Brotherhoods in Colonial Brazil: A Study in Collective Behavior," in *The Hispanic American Historical Review* 54, no. 4 (1974). A recent major analysis of the role of brotherhoods is contained in CAIO CÉSAR BOSCHI, *Os leigos e o poder* (1986).

DOUGLAS COLE LIBBY

**BROUWER, LEO** (*b.* 1 March 1939), Cuban composer and guitarist. A student of Stefan Wolpe and Vincent Persichetti at the Julliard School of Music, Brouwer also studied at the Hartt College of Music under Isadore Freed. He was a music assistant with Radio Havana (1960–1961) and director of the music department at the Institute of the Film Industry and Art (IAIC) in 1960–1962. He taught theory and composition at the National Conservatory in Havana (1961–1967) and in 1969 he became director of the experimental branch of the IAIC. A guitarist of international recognition, he has made many recordings of classical and contemporary music. He has achieved similar success as a composer of orchestral and chamber music and has written music for film and for the theater. Brouwer used conventional styles at the beginning of his career. For example, in the more than fifty compositions he wrote from 1956 to 1962 he used mostly folkloric elements within a nationalistic and rather conventional style. Having had contacts in the 1960s with contemporary composers like Bogustaw Schäffer and Henyrk Górecki and also with Luigi Nono and Hans Werner Henze, Brouwer turned toward the avant-garde, chance, and experimental music. He has explored contemporary techniques and is probably among the first Cuban composers to successfully utilize the open forms and aleatoric techniques, frequently including graphic and proportional notation in his scores. He has also collaborated with pop artists and mass-media productions.

Among his more important works are *Danzas concertantes* for guitar and string orchestra (1958); *Variantes* for percussion (1962); *Sonograma I* for prepared piano (1963); *Sonograma II* for orchestra (1964); *2 Conceptos del tiempo* for ten players (1965); *Homage to Mingus* for jazz combo and orchestra (1965); *Tropos* for orchestra (1967); *Sonograma III* for two pianos (1968); *5 Epigrams* for cello and piano (1968); *Conmutaciones* for prepared piano and two percussionists (1966); *El reino de esto mundo* for woodwind quintet (1968); *Rem tene verba sequentur* for string quartet (1969); *Cantigas del tiempo nuevo* for actors, children's choir, piano, harp, and percussion (1969); *Exa-*

*edros*, for six players or multiples of six (1969–1970); *Anima Latina* (Madrigali guerrieri ed amorosi) for orchestra (1977); and *Es el amor quién ve*, for voice and chamber ensemble (1972). He has written for guitar *Canticum* (1972); *La espiral eterna* (1970); *Tarantos* (1977); *Per sonare a due* (1973); and *El decamerón negro* (1981).

JOHN VINTON, ed. *Dictionary of Contemporary Music* (1974); *Primero Festival Latinoamericano de Música Contemporánea "Ciudad de Maracaibo"* (1977), p. 34; GÉRARD BÉHAGUE, *Music in Latin America: An Introduction* (1979); *New Grove Dictionary of Music and Musicians* (1980).

ALCIDES LANZA

**BROWN, WILLIAM** (Guillermo Brown; *b.* 22 June 1777; *d.* 3 March 1857), Irish privateer in the service of Buenos Aires during the Wars for Independence. Born in Foxford, Ireland, Brown came to Philadelphia at age nine. He soon signed on a merchant ship and had become a captain before reaching age twenty. In 1809 he arrived in the Río de la Plata, where he played a major role in the Buenos Aires campaign against Montevideo and became one of the principal captains in the Buenos Aires privateering fleet. In 1815 Brown led a privateering expedition into the Pacific in support of Chilean independence, and was joined by the squadron of another notable Buenos Aires privateer, Hipólito BOUCHARD. This expedition harassed Spanish commerce along the Peruvian and Chilean coasts. Following independence, Admiral Brown was a leading officer in the Buenos Aires navy and led Argentine naval forces in the war against Uruguay (1825–1828) and, later, during the administration of Juan Manuel de Rosas, against the French and British blockades.

LEWIS BEALER, *Los corsarios de Buenos Aires, sus actividades en las guerras hispano-americanas de la independencia, 1815–1821* (1937). *Documentos del almirante Brown*, 2 vols. (1958–1959); FELIPE BOSCH, *Historia naval argentina* (1962); DONALD E. WORCESTER, *Sea Power and Chilean Independence* (1962), pp. 11–16.

RALPH LEE WOODWARD, JR.

*See also* **Piracy.**

**BRULL, MARIANO** (*b.* 24 February 1891; *d.* 6 August 1956), Cuban poet. Brull was born in Camagüey Province but spent his childhood in Spain. He returned to Cuba as an adolescent and began publishing his early poems. In 1913 he received a law degree from the University of Havana and worked as a lawyer until 1917, when he obtained a diplomatic post in Washington, D.C. He later served in Cuba's embassies in Peru, Belgium, Spain, Switzerland, France, Italy, Canada, and Uruguay. Brull was published in several key literary magazines, including *Clavileño* and the legendary *Orígenes*, founded by José LEZAMA LIMA. One of the most influential poets of the first decades of this century, he is well known for his *jitanjáforas*, poems constructed with words invented for the beauty of their sound and their rhythm, as the term *jitanjáfora* itself, the title of one of those poems. Well-known poets and critics of his time acclaimed Brull's poetry, among them Paul Valéry, Alfonso REYES, Gastón Baquero, Pedro HENRÍQUEZ UREÑA, and Cintio VITIER, and he exerted great influence upon the following generation of Cuban poets. Among his works are *La casa del silencio: Antología de su obra, 1916–1954* (1976) and *Una antología de poesía cubana* (1984).

ROBERTO VALERO

**BRUM, BALTASAR** (*b.* 18 June 1883; *d.* 31 March 1933), president of Uruguay (1919–1923). Brum was one of the most prominent politicians in the country from 1913 to 1933. As well as president of Uruguay, he was president of the National Council of Administration from 1929 to 1931 and served as minister of public education (1913–1915) and of foreign affairs (1914–1915).

The son of landowners of Brazilian origin, he subscribed to the beliefs of BATLLISM, specifically to its reformist tendencies. He began his political career young and by the age of thirty was minister of education. He was the first president to govern under the system of a collegial executive branch consisting of the president and the National Council of Administration, which had been approved in 1917. During his administration legislation for the benefit of the working class was promoted on issues such as a minimum wage for rural laborers, social security, workplace safety, weekly time off, and an attempt at regulating labor practices regarding women and children.

Brum's administration was followed by Riverista leaders who represented the conservative wing of the Colorado Party. Batllism regained the presidency in 1931 with the election of Gabriel TERRA, although he was more conservative than the original Batllistas. Brum belonged to the National Council of Administration, which confronted the president on more than one occasion. When Terra assumed dictatorial powers in 1933, Brum committed suicide in public as a symbolic gesture, even though his personal liberty was not at stake.

JUAN CARLOS WELKER, *Baltasar Brum: Verbo y acción* (1945); GERARDO CAETANO and RAÚL JACOB, *El nacimiento del terrismo*, vol. 3 (1991).

FERNANDO FILGUEIRA

**BRUNET, MARTA** (*b.* 9 August 1897; *d.* 10 August 1967), Chilean feminist writer. Brunet was born in Chillán and raised in southern Chile but spent most of her life in other countries, living first in Europe (1911–1914) and later working as cultural attaché to the Chilean Embassy in Argentina (1939–1952), Brazil (1962–1963), and Uruguay (1963–1967). She wrote nine novels and ten collections of short stories. Her most important fictional

works are *Montaña adentro* (1923; Deep into the Mountains), "Soledad de la sangre" (1943; "The Solitude of the Blood"), *Humo hacia el sur* (1946; Smoke Towards the South), *María Nadie* (1957; Maria Nobody), and *Amasijo* (1962; Dough for Baking). Her *Obras completas* were published in Chile in 1963.

Although Brunet initially followed the "criollista" tendency in fiction that was prevalent in Chile through the 1930s, she soon went beyond its nativist parameters to present universal concerns through the psychological and existential conflicts of her characters. Based primarily on the world of women, her work characterizes female desire for self-actualization. By means of the opposition between reality and dream, Brunet focuses at once on a woman's submission to the patriarchal forces of family and community and her possibility for spiritual empowerment through the realm of fantasy. In 1961 she became the second woman to receive the National Prize for literature. She died in Montevideo.

ESTHER MELÓN DE DÍAZ, *La narrativa de Marta Brunet* (1975); GABRIELA MORA, "Una lectura de *Soledad de la sangre* de Marta Brunet," *Estudios Filológicos* 19 (1984): 81–90; MARY BERG, "The Short Stories of Marta Brunet," in *Monographic Review/Revista Monográfica* 4 (1988): 195–206.

J. A. EPPLE

*See also* **Literature: Spanish America.**

**BRYAN–CHAMORRO TREATY (1914),** a treaty between the United States and Nicaragua providing for the construction of a canal across Nicaragua. The proposed route followed the nineteenth-century proposal for a waterway using the San Juan River (which forms a part of the Costa Rican–Nicaraguan boundary), Lake Nicaragua, and Lake Managua, and with a possible outlet at the Gulf of Fonseca, which borders on El Salvador, Honduras, and Nicaragua on the Pacific coast of Central America.

The treaty came about because of the breakdown in President William Howard Taft's plan to create a financial protectorate in Nicaragua. In 1907, the Theodore ROOSEVELT administration had lent its support to Central American treaties providing for the peaceful settlement of isthmian disputes. But two years later, despite its professions that U.S. policy would be conducted with "dollars and not bullets," Taft began an intervention in Nicaragua that overthrew President José Santos ZELAYA and culminated in a large-scale military intervention in 1912. General Emiliano CHAMORRO aided the U.S. military in this intervention; and when the country was pacified, President Adolfo DÍAZ seemed secure.

In the aftermath, however, Nicaragua's efforts to secure a badly needed loan to create a national bank and reform the currency were frustrated when the U.S. Senate rejected the loan convention. Nicaragua proposed the canal concession, which ceded (for $3 million) construction rights for a canal across Nicaraguan territory and naval bases on Great and Little Corn islands (on the Caribbean side) and in the Gulf of Fonseca (on the Pacific side). Incoming President Woodrow WILSON and Secretary of State William Jennings Bryan tried to use the proposal to create a protectorate over Nicaragua, but the Senate again balked, and the treaty was not ratified until 1916. Nonetheless, Costa Rica and El Salvador protested that the concession violated existing treaties, and took their case to the Central American Court of Justice. The Court declared in their favor but said that it was unable to enforce the decision against Nicaragua. The Court dissolved shortly afterward.

DANA G. MUNRO, *Intervention and Dollar Diplomacy in the Caribbean, 1900–1921* (1964); WALTER LA FEBER, *Inevitable Revolutions: The United States in Central America* (1984); RALPH LEE WOODWARD, *Central America: A Nation Divided,* 2d ed. (1985); LESTER D. LANGLEY, *The United States and the Caribbean in the Twentieth Century,* 4th ed. (1989).

LESTER D. LANGLEY

*See also* **United States–Latin American Relations.**

**BRYCE ECHENIQUE, ALFREDO** (*b.* 19 February 1939), Peruvian novelist, short-story writer, and journalist. Bryce Echenique was born in Lima to an aristocratic family. He studied literature and law at the University of San Marcos in Lima, receiving a Ph.D. in 1964. He then studied at the Sorbonne in Paris. Beginning in 1968 he taught at the universities of Nanterre, Sorbonne, and Vincennes. In 1980 he relocated to Montpellier and taught literature at Paul Valéry University. In 1986 he moved to Spain.

An original combination of the oral tradition, memory, and humor is the basic feature of Bryce Echenique's entire body of literary work. *Un mundo para Julius* (1970; *A World for Julius,* 1992) was his first novel and one of his most successful ones. It depicts a sector of the Lima oligarchy with authenticity, humor, and irony.

In his novels *Tantas veces Pedro* (1977), *La vida exagerada de Martín Romaña* (1981), *El hombre que hablaba de Octavia de Cádiz* (1985), and *La última mudanza de Felipe Carrillo* (1988), Bryce Echenique narrates the cycle of apprenticeship and maturity in the erotic experience of one Latin American character, of oligarchic origin, in Europe in the 1960s and 1970s. He has also published several short-story collections: *Huerto cerrado* (1968), *La felicidad ja, ja* (1974), *Cuentos completos* (1981), and *Crónicas personales* (1988). His journalistic work is equally extensive in magazines and newspapers.

JESÚS DÍAZ CABALLERO

**BUARQUE, CHICO** (Francisco Buarque de Holanda; *b.* 19 July 1944), Brazilian singer, songwriter, and writer. The son of historian Sérgio Buarque de Holanda, Buarque has distinguished himself as an insightful artist in the field of entertainment. He studied in Rio and São Paulo but abandoned architecture to dedicate himself to music in the mid-1960s. His involvement in drama began in 1966 with the musical settings for a stage version of João Cabral de Melo Neto's verse play *Morte e vida severina* (Death and Life of Severina). Through the historic songwriters' festivals of the late 1960s, Buarque gained national attention as an incomparable songsmith of both traditional vocal samba and BOSSA NOVA. Also known for the social criticism in his lyrics, he went into voluntary exile in Italy in 1969 to escape the military regime, which censored an appreciable portion of his work in the 1970s.

The composer's battles with government censors comprise a major chapter of the history of institutional intervention in the arts during that decade. His most controversial play, *Calabar,* a musical collaboration with Ruy Guerra, reexamined a Brazilian figure accused of treason during the Dutch occupation in the early seventeenth century. In 1974, Buarque published a novel, *Fazenda modelo: Novela pecuária* (Model Farm: A Bovine Novel), an allegorical sociohistorical critique inspired by George Orwell. He also wrote some children's literature. On a cultural mission in 1978, Buarque made his first of several visits to Cuba and introduced some new Cuban music to the Brazilian public. In the 1970s and 1980s, in addition to crafted sentimental songs and numerous masterpiece sambas of social observation, Buarque wrote many songs for films (e.g., *Bye Bye Brazil*) and for his own stage productions, including *Ópera do malandro* (Hustler's Opera), which later was adapted for film. Buarque is respected as one of the leading performing songwriters in the history of the nation and as one of her most perspicacious artists.

CHARLES A. PERRONE, "Dissonance and Dissent: The Musical Dramatics of Chico Buarque," in *Latin American Theatre Review* 22, no. 2 (1989): 81–94; *Masters of Contemporary Brazilian Song: MPB, 1965–1985* (1989).

CHARLES A. PERRONE

**BUCARAM ELMHALIN, ASAAD** (*b.* 24 December 1916; *d.* 5 November 1981), leader of the populist Concentración de Fuerzas Populares (1962–1981) in Ecuador. Born in Ambato to Lebanese parents and self-taught, Bucaram assumed leadership of the Concentration of Popular Forces (Concentración de Fuerzas Populares—CFP) after the resignation of Carlos Guevara Moreno. Elected mayor of Guayaquil (1962–1963) during a period of economic prosperity, he earned a reputation for personal honesty and administrative ability. He was deposed, jailed, and deported by the military government in 1963, when he attempted to mobilize the CFP to defend the government of Carlos Julio AROSEMENA MONROY (1963).

After returning to Ecuador, Bucaram headed the CFP delegation to the 1966 constituent assembly and was elected vice president of the assembly. Reelected as mayor of Guayaquil in 1967, he brought his party into the Front of the Democratic Left (Frente de la Izquierda Democrática—FID), which supported the candidacy of Andrés F. Córdova Nieto in the 1968 presidential election. Elected prefect of Guayas Province in 1970, he was subsequently exiled, a second time, by VELASCO IBARRA.

Bucaram was the leading candidate for president in 1972, but the military coup of 15 February 1972 prevented his election and exiled him a third time. Prior to the restoration of constitutional government in 1979, the military government disqualified his candidacy. Bucaram then selected Guayaquil lawyer Jaime ROLDÓS AGUILERA to run as the candidate of the CFP. Prior to the election of Roldós, however, relations between the two CFP leaders began to deteriorate, and the party subsequently divided into two factions. The conflict was ideological as well as personal. Bucaram was a populist whose power base was primarily regional. Thus, he favored government expenditures that provided patronage for his supporters and coastal public works projects at the expense of fiscal responsibility and projects selected on the basis of national criteria. Bucaram was unsuccessful in his bid to prevent Roldós from taking office but cemented an agreement with the conservatives that allowed him to become president of the Chamber of Deputies, a position he used to obstruct presidential initiatives until his death.

MARCO PROAÑO MAYA, *Bucaram: Historia de una lucha* (1981); JOHN D. MARTZ, "Populist Leadership and the Party Caudillo: Ecuador and the CFP, 1962–1981," in *Studies in Comparative International Development* 18 (1983): 22–49; and *Politics and Petroleum in Ecuador* (1987), esp. pp. 84–90, 247–269.

LINDA ALEXANDER RODRÍGUEZ

*See also* **Ecuador: Political Parties.**

**BUCARELI Y URSÚA, ANTONIO MARÍA** (*b.* 24 January 1717; *d.* 9 April 1779), captain-general of Cuba (1766–1771) and viceroy of New Spain (1771–1779). Born in Seville, Spain, to a noble family, Bucareli joined the Spanish army as a cadet and served in campaigns in Italy and Portugal. He achieved the rank of lieutenant general and was inspector general of cavalry and inspector of coastal fortifications of the Kingdom of Granada. In 1766, he was named governor and CAPTAIN-GENERAL of Cuba, a difficult post which he occupied with distinction. Although Bucareli wished to return to Spain following his Cuban assignment, the crown wanted an experienced administrator in the Mexican viceregency who could deal with the reforms proposed by Visitor General José de GÁLVEZ.

Bucareli was conservative in his approach to change and, where possible, tended to support traditional solutions. He reorganized the militia units, rebuilt coastal fortifications, and oversaw the construction of the fortress of Perote, which was designed to prevent an enemy invasion inland. In the north of New Spain, Bucareli dealt with growing Indian depredations against

frontier presidios and problems related to the exploration and settlement of Alta California. To verify the possibility of Russian penetration on the North American coast, Bucareli dispatched the maritime expedition of Juan PÉREZ, the first in a series of voyages that carried Spanish exploration into Alaskan waters.

As a colonial administrator, Bucareli rejected many of the reforms proposed by Gálvez. He criticized schemes for territorial reorganization and doubted the possible benefits of introducing a system of powerful provincial INTENDANTS. A zealous and capable bureaucrat, Bucareli was able to get the best results out of the cumbersome colonial regime. He is recognized as one of the best eighteenth-century VICEROYS of New Spain. Bucareli died in office, and his remains were interred at the shrine of the Virgin of Guadalupe.

RÓMULO VELASCO CEBALLOS, *La administración de D. Frey Antonio María de Bucareli y Ursúa, cuadragésimo sexto virrey de México*, 2 vols. (1936); BERNARD E. BOBB, *The Viceregency of Antonio María Bucareli in New Spain, 1771–1779* (1962); DAVID A. BRADING, *Miners and Merchants in Bourbon Mexico, 1763–1810* (1971).

CHRISTON I. ARCHER

**BUCARELI Y URSÚA, FRANCISCO DE PAULA** (*d.* after 1770), governor of Buenos Aires (1766–1770), brother of Antonio María Bucareli, viceroy of New Spain. Bucareli, probably born in Seville, Spain, was a career army officer imbued with the ideas of the Spanish version of the Enlightenment. In 1776 he assumed the post of governor of Buenos Aires, where he immediately became involved in expelling the Portuguese from Rio Grande do Sul in May of 1767. In the same year he directed the expulsion of 345 Jesuits from the twelve colleges, residences, and missions of the Río de la Plata. As a result, over fifty estates with thousands of head of cattle, slaves, and real estate were auctioned and sold. In 1770 Bucareli ousted English settlers from Port Egmond in the Falkland Islands, reclaiming the islands for Spain. Soon afterward he returned to Spain, where he died.

NICHOLAS P. CUSHNER

**BUCARELI CONFERENCES,** a series of meetings between representatives of Mexico and the United States in 1923 that reduced tensions between the two nations through largely tentative agreements. Named for the street in Mexico City where they took place, these conferences addressed the impact of Article 27 of the Mexican Constitution of 1917 on property ownership. U.S. owners of Mexican agricultural and petroleum lands feared their loss. The meetings also had an urgency for Mexican President Álvaro OBREGÓN. The United States had not extended diplomatic recognition to his three-year-old regime, which undercut its legitimacy internationally and limited its ability to handle domestic opposition.

The results of these meetings were ambiguous. Obregón reaffirmed the basic intent of Article 27, but the United States extracted two concessions in return for the opening of diplomatic relations: Mexico could take large estates for the purpose of land reform only if the owners received immediate compensation at market value, and oil concessions would not be affected by Article 27 if the owner had taken positive acts to develop this resource before 1917. Most important, these arrangements were not formal treaties. Enforcement depended on the goodwill of both nations.

The meetings also produced two official treaties. One involved claims against the Mexican government as a result of disruptions of the revolution from 1910 to 1920. The other concerned civil disputes between nationals of the two countries since 1868. The treaties set up two claims commissions to settle these cases.

ROBERT FREEMAN SMITH, *The United States and Revolutionary Nationalism in Mexico, 1916–1932* (1972), esp. pp. 213–223; JOSEFINA ZORAIDA VÁZQUEZ and LORENZO MEYER, *The United States and Mexico* (1985), esp. pp. 126–132.

JOHN A. BRITTON

**BUCCANEERS AND FREEBOOTERS.** Although the term *buccaneer* is sometimes used to refer generally to maritime freebooters, in Latin American history it refers specifically to a group that arose in the Caribbean between about 1630 and 1670 to attack Spanish commerce and settlements. The buccaneers of the seventeenth century were in many ways the debased successors of the French corsairs, English sea dogs, and Dutch sea beggars. Unlike these earlier privateers, however, they had New World bases from which to operate. They also differ from later pirates in two important respects: they generally were allowed to use the ports of Spain's rivals in the region and they often operated with either the overt or tacit approval of government authorities. The buccaneers ventured all over the world, but the Caribbean remained their favorite haunt until 1674, when the British enlisted the greatest buccaneer of all, Henry MORGAN, to help curtail their activities.

Buccaneering communities emerged in Jamaica and western Hispaniola, especially at Old Providence, Tortuga Island, and the Bay Islands of the Gulf of Honduras, as well as the islands of the eastern Caribbean. Many of the early buccaneers were unsuccessful French, British, and Dutch colonists who tended to get squeezed out as SUGAR production replaced tobacco in the non-Spanish islands. By 1640 tobacco production exceeded demand, causing a "tobacco depression" that contributed to a historic shift in land and labor to large-scale sugar plantations. In the Caribbean this transition was characterized by fewer but larger landholdings and the replacement of European farm labor with African slaves.

Some of the displaced turned to a life outside the law or moved into regions abandoned by the Spanish, especially the north coast of Hispaniola, where they lived by hunting and killing wild cattle the Spaniards left behind. The term *buccaneer* originated with Frenchmen in that area who roasted meat over open fires on grills called *boucans* and thus were called *boucaniers.* They often sold their meat and hides to passing ships. These wild men—felons, runaway indentured servants, displaced tobacco farmers, sailors, and others—threatened the security and wealth of Spain's colonies, and the Spanish governors responded by driving away their herds in hopes of starving them. In Hispaniola, mobile squadrons called *cinquantaines* were used against the buccaneers after 1640. This action against the buccaneers turned many of them to seafaring robbery and aroused their hatred of the Spanish. Religious prejudices against Spanish Catholicism intensified their sentiments, for most of the buccaneers came from English Puritan or French Huguenot backgrounds and often had strongly rooted Protestant values. By 1650 they had formed well-armed outlaw bands with bold, skillful leaders. These "Brethren of the Main" developed a code of conduct, often formalized in contracts for each voyage, that adhered to customs reflecting their religious and cultural origins. They had little political allegiance, but their presence represented a constant temptation to French and English governors hostile to Spain, as well as an impediment to peaceful settlement and trade.

The idea of employing these desperadoes, most of whom were English or French, as commercial raiders in time of war probably occurred first to the French governor of Saint Christopher, L. de Poincy, in the 1630s. Tortuga Island became the primary base for French buccaneers, whereas English buccaneering centered around Port Royal, Jamaica. The legitimacy of the buccaneers' activities depended on the current relations and policies between the governments of England and France and the government of Spain. When at war, the French and English periodically employed buccaneers to raid Spanish shipping and shore settlements. Yet these governments could not always control or stop the buccaneers once peace was restored. Even when they did not openly encourage the buccaneers, the marauders found friendly ports in the non-Spanish Caribbean and along the North American coast as far north as Boston. Their tactics were violent; calculated terror became one of their most important weapons as they created a climate of fear among the Spanish colonists. Promising to spare the lives of those who did not resist, they tortured and murdered those who did.

THE ENGLISH BUCCANEERS
The Port Royal, Jamaica, buccaneers reached their peak between 1650 and 1680. Between 1655 and 1661 alone, Henry Morgan's buccaneers caused a reign of terror by raiding eighteen cities, four towns, and nearly forty villages. Following major raids on Cuba in 1665–1666, the leadership of the Port Royal buccaneers fell to Morgan, a brilliant tactician who launched several successful but

**Buccaneers**
ca. 1630–1697

*Gulf of Mexico*

*Atlantic Ocean*

BAHAMAS

Havana

*Cuba*

San Juan de Ulúa (Veracruz)

Tortuga
Saint-Domingue

**Santo Domingo**

*Gulf of Honduras*

*Jamaica*

*Puerto Rico*

**Port Royal**

*Hispaniola*

St. Christopher

Bay Islands

*Caribbean Sea*

*Pacific Ocean*

Old Providence

Río Hacha

*Trinidad*

Santa Marta

Maracaibo

Porto Bello

Panamá

250 mi
400 km

brutal enterprises against strategic transit routes in Panama and Nicaragua. His fame reached its height when he led an expedition in 1668 against PORTO BELLO, Panama, surprising the garrison there by entering from a swampy, forested area at night. He pillaged the town and killed most of its inhabitants. After going to Maracaibo, Venezuela, but discovering little booty there, Morgan took three Spanish ships loaded with silver. His final and largest expedition, in 1670, was an assault on Santa Marta, Río Hacha, Portobelo, and Panama City.

When the Treaty of MADRID (1670) established peace between Spain and England, England no longer needed the buccaneers. Governor Sir Thomas Lynch of Jamaica therefore attempted to stifle the buccaneering enterprise. When his lack of sufficient armed forces made this difficult, two of his successors, Lord John Vaughan and the Earl of Carlisle, employed Morgan as lieutenant governor of Jamaica and specifically charged him with suppressing buccaneering. Although his efforts were initially only slightly successful, as demonstrated by major buccaneer raids on Santa Marta in 1677 and on the Honduran coast in 1678, after 1685 the rise of public opposition and arrival of a new frigate squadron led to the decline of buccaneering as many buccaneers dispersed beyond the Caribbean and their activities degenerated into piracy.

THE FRENCH BUCCANEERS
Throughout this period, Tortuga remained wide open. The French, not having signed a treaty with Spain, continued to allow buccaneers to use their Caribbean ports. With the encouragement of Governor d'Ogéron of Tortuga, beginning in 1665, the great buccaneers François

L'OLONNAIS (Jean-David Nau) and Michel le Basque carried out extensive plundering of Caribbean areas even as d'Ogéron attempted to establish a more respectable colony on the coast of Haiti.

The Tortuga buccaneers played a large part in the Caribbean theater of the third Anglo-Dutch War (1672–1678). Still, like the English, the French buccaneers preferred to attack Spanish ships and settlements, a more lucrative activity than participating in the war. The Tortuga buccaneers achieved great success between 1678 and 1685 as they gained a savage reputation. The names of Van Horn, de Graaf, de Grammont, and the Marquis de Maintenor stand out among the raiders of Venezuela, Trinidad, San Juan de Ulúa (Veracruz), and the Yucatán coast. Eventually, however, the French government, too, felt compelled to act against the atrocities of the buccaneers.

As had the Dutch in the Treaty of the Hague (1673) and the English in the treaties of Windsor and Madrid, France promised Spain in the Truce of Ratison (1684) to stop supporting the raiding of the buccaneers. The actual end to buccaneering took longer to achieve, of course. Some buccaneers were bribed into royal service, as in the case of Governor du Casse of Saint Domingue (now the Dominican Republic), who was finally able to pay off and disband most of the buccaneers. His forces helped halt further serious raids, and after Saint Domingue was ceded to France in 1697 by the Treaty of Ryswyck, du Casse persuaded the remaining buccaneers on Tortuga to abandon their activities and settle on the newly recognized French territory to the south. Thus the age of buccaneering ended, although some continued their activities as pirates.

ALEXANDER D. EXQUEMELIN, *The Buccaneers of America* (1864, repr. 1972); PÈRE P-F-X. CHARLEVOIX, *Histoire de l'Isle Espagnole ou de S. Domingue,* 2 vols. (1731, repr. 1943); JAMES BURNEY, *History of the Buccaneers of America* (1816, repr. 1902); C. H. HARING, *The Buccaneers in the West Indies in the XVII Century* (1910); ARTHUR PERCIVAL NEWTON, *Colonising Activities of the English Puritans* (1914); J. H. PARRY, *A Short History of the West Indies,* 4th ed. (1987).

BLAKE D. PATTRIDGE

*See also* **Piracy.**

**BUDDHISM.** Most Latin American Buddhists are of Japanese ancestry and live in Brazil, which has about 175,000 Buddhists. (Brazil has 491,000 persons of Japanese ancestry, Peru has 45,000, and Bolivia has 10,000.) From 1900 until the 1970s approximately 250,000 Japanese immigrants entered Brazil, mostly as agricultural laborers on coffee plantations. After several years they often were able to save enough money to purchase their own farms. Over the years Japanese immigrants and their descendants increasingly adopted Catholicism. By the 1958 census 42.8 percent of Japanese Brazilians had converted to Catholicism, while 44.5 percent remained Buddhists.

Suzuki, who analyzed census data from the 1950s on Japanese Brazilians, determined that adherents of Buddhism and other "Japanese religions" comprised 76.6 percent of the immigrant issei, 32.5 percent of the second-generation nisei, and 21.4 percent of third- and fourth-generation sansei and yonsei. Among both immigrants and their descendants, older people were approximately twice as likely as younger people to follow Japanese religions. Individuals with more schooling in Japan practiced a Japanese religion more often than those with more schooling in Brazil. In rural areas more Japanese Brazilians followed Japanese religions (54.8 percent) than in urban areas (41.7 percent). There was no significant difference between men and women in their commitment to Japanese religions.

Mizuki offers a variety of reasons for the declining numbers of Buddhists. Japanese Brazilians had their children baptized as Catholics to help their children get ahead through the COMPADRESCO (godparent) relationship. Catholic teachers suggested that their Japanese students be baptized to avoid teasing by their peers about being sinners. Also, during World War II, Japanese-language schools and newspapers were shut down and speaking Japanese in public was forbidden. Japanese Brazilians had to learn more Portuguese, consequently developing a broader knowledge about Brazilian culture, including Catholicism.

In recent years Japanese-language newspapers, magazines, radio stations, and schools have emerged, especially in São Paulo, where 75 percent of Japanese Brazilians live. While there are few Japanese immigrants today, there is a large contingent of overseas Japanese businessmen and their families in São Paulo.

TEIITI SUZUKI, *The Japanese Immigrant in Brazil,* vol. 2 (1969), esp. pp. 121–131; THOMAS E. WEIL et al., *Area Handbook for Brazil,* 3d ed. (1975); JOHN MIZUKI, *The Growth of Japanese Churches in Brazil* (1978), esp. pp. 16–19; HIROKI KANAZAWA and LEO LOVEDAY, "The Japanese Immigrant Community in Brazil: Language Contact and Shift," in *Journal of Multilingual and Multicultural Development* 9 (1988): 423–435.

ESTHER J. PRESSEL

*See also* **Japanese–Latin American Relations.**

**BUENA VISTA, BATTLE OF,** also known as the battle of La Angostura, an indecisive engagement between the Mexican and U.S. armies that took place on 22–23 February 1847 southwest of Monterrey, with both sides claiming victory. Following the conquest of northern old Mexico, Upper California, and New Mexico, the United States sought to bring the MEXICAN-AMERICAN WAR to an end by invading the central valley and capturing Mexico City. Antonio López de SANTA ANNA, at that time rebuilding the Mexican Army at San Luis Potosí, intercepted a message between generals Winfield SCOTT and Zachary TAYLOR outlining a plan whereby all of Taylor's regulars (the better half of his army) were to be transferred to Scott for the assault on Veracruz. Santa Anna decided to strike at Taylor's weakened army. In the dead of winter, Santa Anna marched his poorly equipped 18,000-man army north across 200 miles of inhospitable desert. Some 4,000 died or deserted.

Although President James Polk had ordered Taylor to remain on the defensive, Taylor had disobeyed and captured Saltillo on 11 November 1846. It was here that Taylor learned of Santa Anna's advance, so he fell back to a narrow ravine through which the road passed near a ranch named Buena Vista. Mexican scouts came upon American supplies which had not been burned due to the haste of the retreat. Santa Anna apparently concluded that the American army was in flight and ordered his exhausted army to make a forced march over the remaining distances separating the two armies.

By now Taylor held a strong defensive position. The Mexicans attacked on 22 February and pushed back the American left. The Mexican troops held their position throughout the night without camp fires or food. The next day the Mexicans renewed the attack. The fighting became so intense that Taylor was forced to commit his reserves to prevent his left from collapsing. The Mexicans sustained heavy casualties, particularly from the American horse-drawn "flying artillery" and the rifle-armed First Mississippi volunteers led by Colonel Jefferson Davis.

Unexpectedly, Santa Anna ordered his army to fall back, abandoning hundreds of wounded. He ordered his exhausted army on a disastrous march back across the desert to San Luis Potosí, arriving on 9 March. The Mexican Army sustained more than 10,000 casualties, and throughout the campaign, including the long marches across the desert in the winter, the United States suffered 290 dead and missing, plus 500 wounded.

NATHANIEL W. STEPHENSON, *Texas and the Mexican War* (1921); WILFRID HARDY CALLCOTT, *Santa Anna: The Story of an Enigma Who Once Was Mexico* (1936); CARLOS MARÍA DE BUSTAMANTE, *El nuevo Bernal Díaz del Castillo; o sea, Historia de la invasión de los anglo-americanos en México*, 2 vols. (1949).

ROBERT SCHEINA

**BUENAVENTURA,** Columbia's most important port. Buenaventura (1985 population of nearly 200,000) serves as the outlet to the Pacific Ocean for the agricultural and industrial produce of the CAUCA VALLEY region. Established in 1539 amid hostility from the Noanamaes, the port's only passage through the western cordillera to the fertile Cauca Valley was provided by the treacherous Dagua River. It remained isolated and impoverished until the second half of the nineteenth century, when it began to grow as a point of export for sugar and coffee, which helped stimulate demands for the construction of the Pacific railroad to Cali. The completion of the railroad in 1915, along with the construction of the Panama Canal, defined the town's twentieth-century economic function. Although Buenaventura has a poorly developed infrastructure, it has the best port facilities in the country, through which one-half of Colombia's exports and most of its coffee travel.

HERNÁN HORNA, *Transport Modernization and Entrepreneurship in Nineteenth Century Colombia: Cisneros and Friends* (1992); DAVID BUSHNELL, *The Making of Modern Colombia: A Nation in Spite of Itself* (1993).

DAVID SOWELL

## BUENOS AIRES

### THE CITY

The city of Buenos Aires was first settled in 1536 by explorer Pedro de MENDOZA, whose attempt to establish a permanent outpost of the Spanish colonial empire on the banks of the Río de la Plata estuary failed after five difficult years. It was not until 1580 that an expedition from Asunción, Paraguay, led by Juan de GARAY, succeeded in permanently settling the city of Buenos Aires (whose name means "good airs" or "winds," after a popular patron saint of navigators, Nuestra Señora Santa María del Buen Aire). From humble beginnings the city grew to become one of the most important urban centers in the world. Moreover, it came to dominate the rest of the Argentine republic in a manner that has few parallels.

During the Spanish colonial period (1580–1810), the city of Buenos Aires served primarily as an administrative and commercial center. Despite crown restrictions that limited trading activities, the city's strategic location as the principal outlet to the Atlantic for the growing agricultural production of its immensely fertile hinterland led inevitably to its increasing importance within the Spanish realm. In 1618, it became the seat of an imperial governorship and in 1776 was named the fourth viceregal capital of the Americas. At that time, its administrative authority extended through most of southern South America. The population of this city dominated by bureaucrats and merchants increased from some 14,000 people in 1750 to 40,000 by 1800.

The movement for Argentine independence from Spanish control began in the city of Buenos Aires on 25 May 1810 with the convoking of a *cabildo abierto* (open town meeting) and the replacement of the peninsular viceroy with a creole-dominated junta. Over the next decade the city served as the main center of revolutionary activity as a variety of governing bodies, or triumvirates, sought to lead the break from Spain while retaining the territorial integrity of the viceroyalty. During this period a major split occurred among the creole leadership between *Unitarios*, those who favored a strong centralized government located in Buenos Aires, and *Federales*, who championed provincial autonomy. Independence was officially declared in 1816 and confirmed with military victories in the early 1820s.

Independence ended the administrative control the city had once enjoyed over its viceregal dominions, but at the same time it set in motion forces and events that assured Buenos Aires's dominance over the emerging nation it was destined to lead. The elimination of restrictions on trade that came with independence allowed the city to flourish economically. At the same time, the disappearance of the crown protection that had favored certain cities in the interior produced in them a corresponding decline, which led to their subordination to the nation's main port, whose inhabitants became known as *porteños*. Serving as both the capital of the province of Buenos Aires and of the nation, except for minor interruptions, the city developed a predominance in the nineteenth century that resulted in frequent wars and antagonisms with the rest of the republic. These clashes were resolved to some degree in 1880 by the establishment of a separate federal district making Buenos Aires the national capital.

The population growth of Buenos Aires paralleled the city's economic and political expansion. By 1860, the number of *porteños* had more than doubled since the turn of the century, reaching almost 100,000 in that year. This expansion paled, however, in comparison with that which followed. Between 1869 and 1914, the city's numbers exploded from 177,000 to 1,577,000, making Buenos Aires one of the world's ten largest cities. By 1914, one in five of all Argentines lived in the city of Buenos Aires, and when the surrounding provincial cities of what was called Greater Buenos Aires were included, the proportion reached one in four. In 1914, the capital contained seven times as many people as the second-ranking city in the nation, Rosario, in the province of Santa Fe, with its 223,000 inhabitants.

Massive foreign immigration fueled this demographic

explosion. Beginning slowly in the mid-nineteenth century and gaining increasing momentum until the outbreak of World War I, waves of immigration brought hundreds of thousands of foreigners to settle in Argentina. The federal capital absorbed many of these: by 1914 one of every two *porteños* was of foreign birth. About 80 percent of these new arrivals were from Italy and Spain. Also significant within the city was a sizable Jewish community, mostly from Russia, and smaller but important groups from England, France, Germany, and the Ottoman Empire.

Rapid economic growth in the country as a whole, which was based primarily on agricultural exports and foreign investment, accompanied the immigration and demographic expansion. This economic growth in turn spurred the modernization of the city of Buenos Aires. Between 1870 and 1910, Buenos Aires was transformed from an overgrown riverside village to an imposing cosmopolitan metropolis. During this period, there were extensive public improvements in transportation, sanitation, street paving, and services such as gas, water, and electricity. The capital was also the main terminus for Latin America's most extensive railroad system and the construction site of major new facilities for the nation's key port. Widespread civic beautification programs led some to call Buenos Aires the Paris of the Pampas. Even with its growth and change, however, the capital retained the bureaucratic-commercial character that had marked it since the colonial period.

By the early twentieth century, Buenos Aires had emerged as the major capital city of Latin America, increasingly a mecca for visitors from around the world. In 1910 the capital celebrated the nation's centennial in grand style and hosted a major Pan-American Conference. In 1936, another PAN-AMERICAN CONFERENCE in Buenos Aires was capped by the presence of U.S. president Franklin D. ROOSEVELT, who received a tumultuous welcome. For most of these decades, the city was also considered the principal publishing and cultural center of Latin America.

The modernization and beautification of Buenos Aires continued throughout the twentieth century. By the 1940s, the city boasted a public transportation system that ranged from South America's first major subways to taxis, buses, and streetcars. To accommodate these new conveyances, the colonial grid pattern of narrow, congested streets was broken by the construction of broad new avenues to open up the capital's downtown and link it with the rapidly growing suburban districts. At the same time, imposing multistory residential and commercial buildings appeared in the center and near north side, complementing the horizontal growth of the capital.

Another factor in the growth of Buenos Aires in the twentieth century was industrialization. Between 1914 and 1964, for example, the number of industrial establishments in the metropolitan area grew from 17,000 to 73,000 and the number of personnel employed in them

Plaza de Mayo, Buenos Aires, ca. 1930. COLLECTION OF THE MUSEO DE LA CIUDAD DE BUENOS AIRES. GASTON BOURQUIN.

increased from 308,000 to 726,000. Throughout the twentieth century, Buenos Aires and its surrounding suburbs have contained 40 percent of all Argentine industry and better than 50 percent of those who toil in industrial occupations.

This growth of industry has had important demographic consequences. Opportunities for employment in the expanding manufacturing sector of Buenos Aires encouraged native-born Argentines from the interior to relocate to the capital and its environs. Beginning in earnest in the 1930s, hundreds of thousands of *provincianos* undertook the trek to the capital, largely compensating for the decline in foreign-born immigration following the Great Depression. Settling primarily in the suburban areas surrounding the capital, they contributed significantly to the rapid growth of Greater Buenos Aires, which by the 1970s contained almost twice as many inhabitants as the capital itself. By the 1970s, too, native-born Argentines in the metropolitan area outnumbered the foreign born by a ratio of roughly eight to one. Finally, a continuing flow of Argentines to the capital maintained the metropolitan area's demographic predominance. By the 1980s, roughly one in three of Argentina's 30 million inhabitants resided in the capital and Greater Buenos Aires.

The pattern of growth and settlement in Buenos Aires has been from the central core outward. Foreign-born immigrants and native-born migrants alike have gravitated toward the more open and accessible outlying districts of the city and its suburbs, which have grown at phenomenal rates. Even though the downtown districts have remained relatively stable in terms of population, the central core has remained the vital heart of the city and, in many respects, of the country as the principal location of the nation's main governmental, commercial, and residential buildings, and as the site of its most important social and cultural institutions.

A coalition of national and local leaders has directed the growth of Buenos Aires. As the seat of the national administration, the city is officially under the jurisdiction of federal authorities who retain ultimate control over its governance and provide such essential services as fire and police protection and education. Local management is provided by a mayor, the *intendente,* who is selected by the nation's president and confirmed by the national Senate. The *intendente,* in turn, governs in conjunction with a city council, *consejo deliberante,* which since 1918 has usually been elected by popular vote. Although there are restrictions on the operations of municipal government, it has been largely responsible for most of the modernization that has taken place in the capital over the past century, especially in street and highway construction and improvement, public transportation, and the development of parks and plazas.

Containing between 15 and 20 percent of the nation's total population, Buenos Aires has been a valued prize for political parties competing in national elections. The capital has also been the main locale for most of the principal political developments in the nation's history. These events have ranged from the street rallies and demonstrations of democratic election campaigns to the frequent military takeovers that have marked Argentina since 1930. Whatever the occasion, politics and political activity have long been important features of the capital's life.

THE PROVINCE

The city of Buenos Aires has historically had a close and significant relationship with the surrounding province of the same name. During the Spanish colonial period, the city served as the main entrepôt for the exchange of goods from the immediate hinterland as well as, for most of those years, its administrative center. It was from the city, too, that the gradual settlement of provincial frontier towns emanated. After independence, the city served as the capital of the province until 1880. Shortly thereafter, the provincial authorities constructed their own capital at La Plata, about forty miles southeast of the national capital.

Since independence, Buenos Aires has been the nation's largest, wealthiest, and most influential province. Much of its influence has derived from the fact that it contains the heart of the grassy plain known as the PAMPA, the principal location and source of Argentina's agricultural wealth. In the twentieth century, for example, about 40 percent of all the republic's sheep and cattle have been raised in the province. Buenos Aires also generally has been the nation's leading producer of wheat, corn, oats, and barley. Much of the land and the resultant wealth of the province have been controlled by a small group of landowners called *estancieros*, whose family-owned estates (ESTANCIAS) have been passed down from generation to generation. For much of the period after independence, it was the *estancieros,* led by Juan Manuel de ROSAS who dominated both provincial and national political life.

The province of Buenos Aires has experienced many of the same socioeconomic changes as has the federal capital. Foreign immigration had a great impact on the province, dramatically changing its social and demographic composition. Overall, between 1857 and 1941 the province received the greatest number of immigrants of any area in the country, slightly more than 2 million people. As was true of the federal capital, most of these immigrants came from Italy and Spain. By 1914, foreigners represented one in three of the province's inhabitants. Beginning in the 1930s, moreover, the province witnessed a massive internal migration, which continues to the present day. Within the province, the greatest beneficiary of this migration has been Greater Buenos Aires, which grew from a combined population of 458,000 (22 percent of the provincial total) in 1914 to 5,380,000 (60 percent of the provincial total) in 1970. Population growth from both external and internal sources also contributed to the significant urbanization of the province as a whole (about 70 percent of the province's inhabitants lived in urban centers by the mid-1940s) as well as to the marked development of cities such as Bahía Blanca, La Plata, Mar del Plata, and Tandil, outside of Greater Buenos Aires. Much of the major industrial growth of the post-1930 era has also taken place within the province, again especially in Greater Buenos Aires and along the coastal area in general.

Throughout the twentieth century, the province of Buenos Aires has consistently contained some 30 percent of the nation's total population. This demographic preponderance has also meant great political influence, as the province has the single greatest concentration of the country's voters. This rich electoral bounty has made the province the scene of some of the country's fiercest—and occasionally most violent—political struggles. Underscoring the electoral importance of the province of Buenos Aires is that in only one instance in the twentieth century (1916) has an Argentine captured the presidency without also carrying the province. Ironically, no governor or other major political figure of the province has yet been able to win the presidency, despite the enormous electoral advantages that control of the provincial administration provides.

JAMES R. SCOBIE, *Buenos Aires: Plaza to Suburb, 1870–1910* (1974); STANLEY R. ROSS and THOMAS F. MC GANN eds., *Buenos Aires, 400 Years* (1982); JOSÉ LUIS ROMERO and LUIS ALBERTO ROMERO, *Buenos Aires: Historia de cuatro siglos*, 2 vols. (1983); RICHARD J. WALTER, *The Province of Buenos Aires and Argentine Politics, 1912–1943* (1985).

RICHARD J. WALTER

## BUENOS AIRES CONFERENCES. *See* Pan-American Conferences.

## BULAS CUADRAGESIMALES,

new ecclesiastical indulgences introduced into the Spanish Indies in 1794. Because these *bulas cuadragesimales* allowed the grantee to eat meat up to four days a week during Lent, except for the first four days and Holy Week, they took on the label "meat bulls" (*bulas de carne*). Calculated to raise crown revenues during the severe fiscal crisis of the 1790s, income from these indulgences never approached revenues produced from the long-standing BULAS DE SANTA CRUZADA. In 1800 in the Viceroyalty of Peru, net revenues from *bulas cuadragesimales* amounted to 5,000 pesos, whereas income from bulls of the Holy Crusade approached 80,000 pesos.

JOHN JAY TEPASKE

## BULAS DE SANTA CRUZADA,

ecclesiastical indulgences or remissions of temporal or purgatorial punishment dispensed for payment of a fee or donation. In 1509 Pope Julius II awarded the Spanish crown the right to collect fees for the *bulas de santa cruzada* (Bulls of the Holy Crusade) in Spain, which, on 5 September 1578,

Pope Gregory XIII extended to the Spanish Indies. By agreement with the pope, royal income generated by indulgences was reserved exclusively for fighting the heathens, heretics, schismatics, and enemies of the Catholic faith and for building religious edifices such as Saint Peter's in Rome and San Lorenzo del Escorial in Spain. Spanish monarchs, however, used the steady revenues from the *bulas* for their own purposes and in the late eighteenth century to meet financial exigencies throughout the Indies. In 1800 net income from these indulgences amounted to approximately 250,000 pesos annually in Mexico and 80,000 pesos in Peru.

*Recipilación de leyes de los reynos de las Indias*, 4 vols. (1681; repr. 1973), libro I, título XX; GABRIEL MARTÍNEZ REYES, *Finanzas de las 44 diócesis de Indias, 1515–1816* (1980).

JOHN JAY TEPASKE

## BULLFIGHTING,

a colorful spectacle, combining ritualized drama, big business, and life-and-death ballet, that is considered the national fiesta of Spain. Along with Catholicism and the Spanish language, the conquistadores brought to the New World the age-old Iberian custom of playing with the bull and evading its charges. Spain has always been the center of the bullfighting world, but parts of Latin America have an extensive and passionate bullfighting history. Mexico and Venezuela have produced important matadors who have played a key role in the history of the spectacle.

Professional bullfighting on foot dates from the 1770s. Long before that, however, New World Spaniards, especially noblemen on horseback, enjoyed challenging charging bulls. The forces of Hernán Cortés conquered the Aztecs of Tenochtitlán (Mexico City) in 1521, and by 1529 the town council officially mandated bullfights for every 13 August to honor Saint Hipólito and celebrate the conquest of the city.

The first ranch in the New World to raise fighting bulls was established by the conquistador Juan Gutiérrez Altamirano, a cousin of Cortés, who in 1527 received the town of Calimaya from the crown. He subsequently acquired other lands in the Toluca Valley and formed the Atenco hacienda, importing twelve pairs of fighting bulls and one hundred cows from Navarre (the cradle of bullfighting in Spain). Thus was established the renowned Atenco Bull Ranch, which has survived to the present day as the Mexicapán Ranch.

Mexico's first major matador was Rodolfo Gaona (1888–1975). He became a full matador in Spain in May 1908, and he performed successfully there and in Latin America from 1908 to 1920 and in Mexico from 1921 to his retirement in 1925.

Another notable Mexican contribution to world tauromachy was Carlos Arruza (1920–1966). He took the *alternativa* (ceremony to become a full matador) in Mexico City in 1940 and began performing in Spain in 1944, where he was an immediate success. He had extraordinary courage and good technique and was excellent at

*The Best Matador.* Watercolor by Pancho Fierro, 1830. LATIN AMERICAN LIBRARY, TULANE UNIVERSITY.

placing the *banderillas* (barbed, decorated sticks) into the bull. At the top of his form in 1945, he appeared in 108 bullfights in Spain and France (more than any other matador). Retiring in 1953, he returned as a *rejoneador* (bullfighter on horseback) in 1956.

Although Peru has a longer history of bullfights (dating back to 1540) and the oldest permanent bullring still in use in Latin America (the Plaza de Acho, from 1768), Venezuelan matadors have played a much more significant role in the international bullfighting world in the twentieth century. On four occasions Venezuelan matadors have placed at the top of the list of the number of *corridas* fought during the year in Spain: César Girón in 1954 and 1956, and Curro Girón, his younger brother, in 1959 and 1961. Mexican matadors have accomplished this only twice.

César Girón (1933–1971) was the oldest of six brothers, all of whom became professional bullfighters. He took the *alternativa* in Barcelona, Spain, in 1952 with Carlos Arruza as his godfather. (Ironically, Arruza and Girón, after extensive and illustrious careers facing death at the horns of a bull, both died in auto accidents.) He met with great success from then until the end of 1958 (his first "retirement"). Girón was respected for his strong will to succeed, technical facility, expertise in placing the *banderillas,* and aplomb before the bulls.

The ritualized procedures of the bullfight have a uni-

versal sameness. Latin American bullfights and bullfighters, however, share some superficial differences from those of Spain. New World matadors tend to exhibit more variety, utilizing an extensive repertoire of passes. Almost all are skilled in the placing of the *banderillas.* The fighting bull is usually somewhat smaller and lighter than the Spanish animal, giving it more mobility and speed.

For many years no Latin American matador was at the top of the bullfighting world. At the 1991 Fair of San Isidro in Madrid, however, César Rincón, a Colombian, was declared the "absolute best," and he set a record by being carried out of the bullring on his admirers' shoulders on two consecutive days.

ANTONIO GARLAND, *Lima y el toreo* (1948); ANN D. MILLER, *Matadors of Mexico* (1961); PEPE CASTOREÑO, *Historia de los toros en Cali: Segunda época, 1940–1964* (1965); MANUEL LANDAETA ROSALES, *Los toros en Caracas desde 1560 hasta . . .* (1971); JOSÉ LUIS ACQUARONI, "Three Notes on the Genesis of Bullfighting in Latin America," in *Los toros: Bullfighting* (1974); JOSÉ MARÍA DE COSSÍO, "Toros en Méjico," and "Toros en el Perú," in *Los toros: Tratado técnico e histórico,* vols. 4 (1961) and 6 (1981); TIMOTHY MITCHELL, *Blood Sport: A Social History of Spanish Bullfighting* (1991).

ROSARIO CAMBRIA

*See also* **Sports.**

**BULNES, FRANCISCO** (*b.* 4 October 1847; *d.* 22 September 1924), Mexican political writer. Bulnes, a native of Mexico City, received a civil and mining engineering degree from the National School of Mines. After 1874 he turned to politics, journalism, and economic affairs. He was periodically a national deputy and senator for thirty years, and in 1893 and 1903 led in the effort of the CIENTÍFICO group to limit presidential power. He served on numerous committees devoted to banking, mining, and financial legislation, and in 1885 he wrote on the British debt.

Bulnes won notoriety for his polemical works attacking Benito JUÁREZ and the doctrinaire liberal (Jacobin) tradition in Mexican politics, including *El verdadero Juárez* (1904) and *Juárez y las revoluciones de Ayutla y de reforma* (1905). He later defended the regime of Porfirio DÍAZ in *El verdadero Díaz y la revolución* (1920). His intellectual orientation was POSITIVIST, and as a writer he was influenced by Hippolyte Taine. His critical insights have attracted many modern scholars to his work.

GEORGE LEMUS, *Francisco Bulnes: Su vida y sus obras* (1965).

CHARLES A. HALE

**BULNES PRIETO, MANUEL** (*b.* 25 December 1799; *d.* 19 October 1866), president of Chile (1841–1851). Born in Concepción, Bulnes became a soldier at the age of twelve. He distinguished himself in the WARS OF INDEPENDENCE and he fought at the battle of Maipú (5 April 1818). Promoted to general in 1831, he was placed in command of the second Chilean expedition to Peru during the war against the PERU-BOLIVIAN CONFEDERATION, and won the decisive battle of YUNGAY (20 January 1839). On the strength of his popularity as a war hero, he was chosen to succeed Joaquín PRIETO (1831–1841) as Chile's president.

A bluff, amiable man with an enormous appetite, Bulnes served two consecutive terms; he displayed great tolerance in tranquil periods but used a firm hand at times of political agitation (1845–1846 and 1850–1851). He was the first Chilean president to use the late-colonial Casa de la Moneda as the presidential palace.

When he finished his second term in September 1851, Bulnes took charge of an army to quell a major revolt in the southern provinces, which was led by his cousin, General José María de la Cruz (1799–1875). Bulnes defeated Cruz in the bloody battle of Loncomilla (8 December 1851). In 1866, opponents of the reelection of President José Joaquín PÉREZ (1851–1871) proclaimed Bulnes a presidential candidate; had he won, he would have served only one month.

DIEGO BARROS ARANA, *Un decenio de la historia de Chile: 1841–1851*, 2 vols. (1905).

SIMON COLLIER

**BUMBA-MEU-BOI,** Brazil's richest, best-loved folk pageant, depicting the death and resurrection of an ox, its central figure. A slave, named Pai Francisco or Mateus, kills his owner's prize ox, in most versions at the request of his pregnant wife, Mãe Catarina, who craves ox tongue. Pai Francisco is captured, but because the bull is resuscitated he escapes punishment. The pageant includes drama, dance, pantomime, music, and song, the lyrics of which are composed annually and feature commentary on current events. Although the first performance was recorded in 1840 near Recife, Pernambuco, the pageant probably originated in the seventeenth and eighteenth centuries on northeastern coastal plantations as a satirical adaptation of an Iberian folk tradition by African slaves. In the Northeast, where it is most expressive, it is known as *bumba-meu-boi* (Maranhão, Piauí), *bumba* or *boi calemba* (Pernambuco), *três pedaços* (Alagoas), *boi, boi-surubi,* or *boi de careta* (Ceará), and *boizinho* (Bahia). Variants include *boi-bumbá* (Pará, Amazonas), *boi de mamão* or *melão* (Santa Catarina), *boi de chita* (Minas Gerais), and *reis de boi* (Rio de Janeiro).

The pageant is presented in most of Brazil from mid-November through Epiphany (January 6). In Maranhão and Pará, however, it appears during the June festivals (which honor Saints John, Anthony, Peter, and Marsalius), often as a personal religious obligation. *Bumba-meu-boi* in Maranhão reaches heights unmatched elsewhere. African, indigenous, and, more recently, European styles of performance have evolved, each with its distinctive choreography, music, instruments, story-line variations, and apparel. The velvet, hand-beaded ox costumes and massive beaded, feathered, and ribboned hats worn by the performers rival those of CARNIVAL in Rio.

LUÍS DA CÂMARA CASCUDO, *Dicionário do folclore Brasileiro*, 3d ed. (1972); AMÉRICO AZEVEDO NETO, *Bumba-meu-boi no Maranhão* (1983); JOMAR DA SILVA MORAES, "Feasts and Festivals: Maranhão's Bumba-Meu-Bullfest!" in *Companhia do Vale do Rio Doce Annual Report 1990* (1991).

GAYLE WAGGONER LOPES

*See also* **Música Popular Brasileira.**

**BUNAU-VARILLA, PHILIPPE JEAN** (*b.* 26 July 1859; *d.* 20 May 1940), French engineer and promoter of the Panama Canal. Philippe Bunau-Varilla was apparently an illegitimate child from a modest Protestant background whose mother managed to send him to the École Polytechnique on a scholarship. He attended the École des Ponts et Chaussés, where he was spellbound by a lecture of Ferdinand Márie de LESSEPS. After graduation in 1884, he headed for Panama, fortunately on the same ship as Charles Dingler, the head engineer of the French PANAMA CANAL project. When Bunau-Varilla arrived in Panama, he was assigned to head the engineering section of the Culebra and Pacific division. After the Panama Canal Company went bankrupt in 1889, he helped organize and manage the New Interoceanic Canal Company from 1894 to 1902.

Philippe Jean Bunau-Varilla, ca. 1903. LIBRARY OF CONGRESS.

Bunau-Varilla arranged the sale of the company to the U.S. government in 1902 for $40 million and then lobbied and schemed to have the Panamanians revolt so that the U.S. government could acquire a canal treaty from an independent Panamanian government. He reportedly earned several million dollars from the sale of his canal company stock when the United States acquired the rights. He maintained an intermediary role between a Panamanian revolutionary group formed around Dr. Manuel AMADOR GUERRERO and the U.S. government. Bunau-Varilla met frequently with U.S. Assistant Secretary of State Francis Loomis and occasionally with Professor John Bassett Moore, Secretary of State John Hay, and President Theodore ROOSEVELT. During a meeting with Roosevelt on 29 October 1903, Bunau-Varilla was given the signal that the U.S. government would intervene to prevent Colombian soldiers from landing to combat the revolutionary forces. This signal prompted him to leave the meeting hastily and telegraph Amador that the planned revolt could proceed. While serving as Panama's minister, he quickly negotiated a canal treaty with the U.S. government in November 1903—the HAY–BUNAU-VARILLA TREATY—which conceded the United States all the terms it wished for in a canal government.

After the de Lesseps canal company failed, Bunau-Varilla returned to France to enter the publishing business. He acquired a share of *Le Matin*, which he managed for several decades. He was personally involved in exposing as forgeries the documents of the Austrian major C. F. Walsin-Esterhazy, which had suggested that the Jewish officer Alfred Dreyfus was guilty of treason. *Le Matin* also served as a vehicle to combat

Nicaraguan postage stamp showing Mount Momotombo. The image was used to support Bunau-Varilla's claim that Nicaragua was too volcanic for a trans-isthmian canal. © SMITHSONIAN INSTITUTION

opposition to the New Interoceanic Canal Company and to promote Bunau-Varilla's views of the New World and transit affairs.

Bunau-Varilla volunteered for military service in World War I. During the war, he lobbied for chlorination of water as a means of reducing disease and illness among the French troops and after the war continued to urge the chlorination of city water supplies. He died during the German invasion of France in World War II.

PHILIPPE BUNAU-VARILLA, *Panama: The Creation, Destruction, and Resurrection* (1913), and *From Panama to Verdun: My Fight for France* (1940); CHARLES D. AMERINGER, "The Panama Canal Lobby of Philippe Bunau-Varilla and William Nelson Cromwell," in *American Historical Review* 68 (January 1963): 346–363, and "Philippe Bunau-Varilla: New Light on the Panama Canal Treaty," in *Hispanic American Historical Review* 46, no. 1 (1966): 28–52; WILLIAM SPENCE ROBERTSON, "Hay–Bunau-Varilla Treaty," in *Dictionary of American History*, rev. ed. (1976), p. 265; DAVID MC CULLOUGH, *The Path Between the Seas: The Creation of the Panama Canal 1870–1914* (1977); GUSTAVE ANGUIZOLA, *Philippe Bunau-Varilla: The Man Behind the Panama Canal* (1980).

THOMAS SCHOONOVER

**BUNGE, ALEJANDRO** (*b.* 8 January 1880; *d.* 24 May 1943), Argentine economist. Educated in his native Buenos Aires and in Germany, Bunge was the foremost intellectual representative of the 1920s and 1930s reaction against the open, agrarian, exports-led model of economic development that had spurred Argentina's expansion from the late nineteenth century on; he favored a more active role for the state in the promotion of local industries. A leader of the Social Catholic movement, he directed the Círculos de Obreros Católicos between 1912 and 1916, confronting both liberals and socialists in numerous debates about labor policies.

Bunge began his career in public administration as director of statistics of the National Department of Labor between 1913 and 1915, later becoming director of the Office of Statistics between 1915 and 1920 and 1923 and 1925. In 1918 he founded the influential *Revista de Economía Argentina*, a forum for the new economic ideas, which he directed for more than two decades. Bunge also taught economics at the universities of Buenos Aires and La Plata and wrote several books, among which *La economía argentina* (4 vols., 1928–1930) and *Una nueva Argentina* (1940) were the most significant.

CARLOS DÍAZ ALEJANDRO, *Essays on the Economic History of the Argentine Republic* (1970); JOSÉ LUIS DE IMAZ, "Alejandro E. Bunge, economista y sociólogo (1880–1943)," in *Desarrollo económico* 55 (1974): 545–567; JUAN J. LLACH, ed., *La Argentina que no fué* (1985).

EDUARDO A. ZIMMERMANN

**BUNGE, AUGUSTO** (*b.* 25 April 1877; *d.* 1 August 1948), Argentine hygienist and politician. After graduating with honors from the Medical School of the University of Buenos Aires in 1900, Bunge specialized in PUBLIC HEALTH and in 1906 was sent to Europe by the national government to study the organization of public health and safety measures in factories and workshops. He was put in charge of the Industrial and Public Health Section of the National Department of Public Health, where he launched a campaign for the improvement of working conditions in local industries, as can be seen in his *Las conquistas de la higiene social* (1910–1911). He was a founder and member of the Independent Socialist Party (PSI) and was elected to Congress for five consecutive terms in 1916, 1920, 1924, 1928, and 1932. In Congress, he actively promoted social and labor legislation, drafting in 1917 a detailed system of social insurance based on the German and British models.

Bunge's thought was representative of the fusion of biological and social ideas with a strong racialist component that characterized much of the intellectual life of turn-of-the-century Latin America. In several works he argued for a biological foundation of human ethics, and he was a firm believer in the anthropological and moral inferiority of nonwhite races to Caucasians, as stated in his book *El culto de la vida* (1915).

On Bunge's activities as a socialist leader, see RICHARD J. WALTER, *The Socialist Party of Argentina, 1890–1930* (1977) and HORACIO SANGUINETTI, *Los Socialistas Independientes* (1981). On Bunge's work in public health, see HÉCTOR RECALDE, *La higiene y el trabajo*, 2 vols. (1988); on the intellectual background, see EDUARDO A. ZIMMERMANN, "Racial Ideas and Social Reform: Argentina, 1890–1916," in *Hispanic American Historical Review* 72, no. 1 (February 1992): 23–46.

EDUARDO A. ZIMMERMANN

**BUNGE, CARLOS OCTAVIO** (*b.* 1875; *d.* 22 May 1918), Argentine author, educator, and positivist social critic. Born in Buenos Aires, Bunge studied law at the University of Buenos Aires. He later joined the faculty there. Author of numerous works, his most important include: *El espíritu de la educación* (1901), *Nuestra América* (1903), and a biography of Domingo Faustino SARMIENTO. In his work, he criticized the Spanish, American, and African elements of Latin American culture and society. While critical of tyrants, such as Juan Manuel de ROSAS (ruled 1829–1852), he appreciated such modernizing states as the Porfiriato (1876–1910) in México, which promoted order and progress. Reflecting on his own country in *Nuestra América*, he believed that European immigration would facilitate Argentina's efforts to become one of the world's leading nations. In these respects, he was typical of many Latin American intellectuals of his generation who echoed the Eurocentric ideals of Social Darwinism and POSITIVISM.

CARLOS O. BUNGE, *Nuestra América: Ensayo de psicología social*, 6th ed. (1918); JOSÉ LUIS ROMERO, *El desarrollo de las ideas en la sociedad argentina del siglo XX* (1965).

DANIEL LEWIS

**BUÑUEL, LUIS** (*b.* 22 February 1900; *d.* 29 July 1983), surrealist film director and naturalized Mexican citizen. Born in Calanda, Spain, Buñuel studied at the University of Madrid, where his friends included Salvador Dalí and Federico García Lorca. Interested in film from a very young age, Buñuel moved to Paris in 1923 and worked as assistant to the film director Jean Epstein. Buñuel's first film, *Un chien andalou* (1928), a collaborative effort with Dalí, created a scandal and made both of them famous. Their second film, *L'âge d'or* (1930), attracted praise from literary figures, but the "respectable" press was deeply shocked. Fascist thugs took their criticism to the streets, viciously attacking theaters and moviegoers. The Paris prefect of police, believing surrealism to be more dangerous than fascism, banned the film. Buñuel returned to Spain for his third film, *Las hurdes—tierra sin pan* (1932), a documentary about rural misery.

Working for the Republican government of Spain during the Civil War, he produced documentaries and was sent on a diplomatic mission to Hollywood in 1938. After Franco's victory, Buñuel remained in the United States, working on anti-Nazi projects for the Museum of Modern Art in New York, and the U.S. Army during World War II. After the war, Buñuel worked in Hollywood (1944–1946) before moving to Mexico, where he began his most prolific period, directing twenty-one films (including nineteen in Mexico) between 1947 and 1962. His *Los olvidados* (1950) won the prize for the best direction and the International Critics' Prize at the Cannes Festival in 1951, reestablishing Buñuel's international reputation. The film combined elements of a neorealist study of juvenile delinquency and social protest with dream sequences and surrealistic violence that linked *Los olvidados* to his earlier work. Among the outstanding films Buñuel directed in this period are *Subida al cielo* (1951); *El bruto* (1952); *Él* (1952); *La ilusión viaja en tranvía* (1953); *Ensayo de un crimen* (1955); *Nazarín* (1958); *La fièvre monte à El Pao* (1959); *Viridiana* (1961); and *El ángel exterminador* (1962).

Making his first three films outside the film industry afforded Buñuel greater control over his work than he had while working as director for less imaginative producers during this middle period. Nevertheless, Buñuel was able to infuse these projects with his own style while appealing simultaneously to the uneducated audiences and the aesthetically sophisticated. In the words of Raymond Durgnat, Buñuel's films "have thrills galore at a lowbrow level, and a subtler meaning on a highbrow level, and a great deal of human meaning on all levels. But their sorts of aesthetic refinement, philosophical interest, and particularly, moral issues, tend to puzzle the bourgeois middlebrow, to leave him dissatisfied and perhaps a little contemptuous" (p. 13).

Commercial success permitted Buñuel greater artistic control over his French-made films in the late 1960s and early 1970s, including *La voie lactée* (1969), *Le charme discret de la bourgeoisie* (1972), and *Le fantôme de la liberté* (1974). Buñuel sought to portray social reality while undermining conventional ideas and destroying the illusion of the inevitability of the bourgeois world. He died in Mexico City.

ADO KYROU, *Luis Buñuel: An Introduction*, translated by Adrienne Foulke (1963); J. FRANCISCO ARANDA, *Luis Buñuel: A Critical Biography*, translated and edited by David Robinson (1976); RAYMOND DURGNAT, *Luis Buñuel*, new and enl. ed. (1977); LUIS BUÑUEL, *My Last Sigh*, translated by Abigail Israel (1983); PAUL SANDRO, *Diversions of Pleasure: Luis Buñuel and the Crises of Desire* (1987).

D. F. STEVENS

*See also* **Cinema.**

**BURGOS, JULIA DE** (*b.* 17 February 1914?; *d.* 6 July 1953), Puerto Rican poet. Born to a poor family in Carolina, Puerto Rico, Julia Constanza Burgos García studied at the University of Puerto Rico's High School and Normal School. She taught at a small rural school while continuing her university studies. Her first work, a small, typewritten edition of *Poemas exactos a mí misma* (Poems exactly like myself, 1937), was followed by *Poemas en veinte surcos* (Poems in twenty furrows, 1938) and *Canción de la verdad sencilla* (Songs of simple truth, 1939), honored by the Institute of Puerto Rican Literature. In 1940 Burgos left Puerto Rico for New York, where she lived a bohemian life. Later that year she moved to Cuba, where she remained until 1942. A failed love affair brought her back to New York, where she suffered from ill health and the alcoholism that eventually caused her death. Two poems, "Welfare Island," written in English, and "Dadme mi número" (Give me my number) foreshadowed her death, alone and anonymous, in New York. Her body was later brought to Puerto Rico and buried near the Río Grande de Loíza, which she had glorified in one of her most famous poems.

Burgos's poems are about love, death, the passing of time, Puerto Rico, freedom, and justice. Images of rivers and the sea permeate her poetry, especially in *El mar y tú* (The sea and you), published posthumously in 1954.

IVETTE JIMÉNEZ DE BÁEZ, *Julia de Burgos, vida y poesía* (1966); SHEREZADA VICIOSO, *Julia de Burgos, la nuestra* (1987).

ESTELLE IRIZARRY

**BURGOS, LAWS OF,** early Spanish response to reports of abuse of the native Caribbean population. The Laws of Burgos were the response to growing complaints, especially by Dominican Friars, that the colonists on Hispaniola were treating the rapidly declining native population cruelly and inhumanely. The Dominican Antonio de MONTESINOS stated in a sermon delivered in Hispaniola in 1511, "For with the excessive work you demand of them they fall ill and die, or rather you kill them with your desire to extract and acquire gold every day."

The Laws of Burgos, promulgated 27 December 1512, constituted the first comprehensive legislation devoted to regulating the relationship between the Spaniards and the native population. They outlined *encomenderos'* responsibilities toward the natives they held in EN-COMIENDA: bringing the natives together in new villages built near the Spaniards, ensuring that the natives received religious instruction, and providing them with food and clothing. Although at least a third of the natives would continue to labor in the gold mines, their working conditions were carefully specified and numerous abuses, such as beating natives with whips or calling a native a "dog," were explicitly prohibited. While the laws allowed natives to be exploited, their intention was to make the exploitation "just." Despite good intentions, in practice the laws led to no improvement in the natives' living and working conditions.

LEWIS HANKE, *The Spanish Struggle for Justice in the Conquest of America* (1949), pp. 17, 23–24; CHARLES GIBSON, ed., *The Spanish Tradition in America* (1968), pp. 61–82.

MARK A. BURKHOLDER

**BURLE MARX, ROBERTO** (*b.* 1909; *d.* 4 June 1994), foremost landscape architect in Brazil. Roberto Burle Marx was born to a German businessman and his wife, a Brazilian pianist. Although he shared his mother's interest in gardening, Burle Marx originally intended to become a painter. It was while studying art in Berlin in 1928 that he discovered the beauty of Brazil's native plants, which were often neglected in the gardens of his own country.

Returning to Brazil, Burle Marx took up painting as his career and gardening as a hobby. One of his gardens attracted the attention of Lucio COSTA, an architect and longtime friend, who asked Burle Marx to design a garden for a private residence. This garden, containing a variety of Brazilian plants, as opposed to the formal, European-style gardens that had been the custom, was an immediate success and the first of many commissions. Among his many award-winning projects are Flamengo Park and the plant-lined mosaic sidewalks that run along Copacabana Beach in Rio. Not limiting himself to Brazil, he designed gardens for the UNESCO headquarters in Paris, public parks in Venezuela, a waterfront renovation project in Key Biscayne, Florida, and private gardens on three continents and numerous islands.

Burle Marx planned his gardens with a painter's eye. Sharp contrasts in color and shape characterize his style. "The garden must be linked to nature," appears to be his prevailing philosophy. Other Burle Marx hallmarks are his use of stone and water plants, which grace many of his gardens.

Working so intimately with plants, Burle Marx became an advocate for the preservation of Brazil's natural environment and frequently spoke out against the threat that development poses to his beloved plants. He, himself, discovered several of the country's native plants, some of which are named after him.

GERI SMITH, "Thumbs Up," in *Americas* 40 (September–October 1988): 26–31; MICHAEL PARFIT, "A Brazilian Master Who Finds the Art in Nature's Bounty, in *Smithsonian* 21 (July 1990): 96–107.

SHEILA L. HOOKER

**BUSCH BECERRA, GERMÁN** (*b.* 23 March 1903; *d.* 23 August 1939), president of Bolivia (July 1937–August 1939). Busch was born in Trinidad, in the eastern department of El Beni. His father was an eccentric German medical doctor, and his mother, Raquel Becerra, was a native of Trinidad. In his early youth Busch joined the army as a cadet. He became noted for his daring, physical fitness, and hot temper—characteristics that served him well in the CHACO WAR.

After participating in the overthrow of presidents Daniel SALAMANCA, José Luis TEJADA SORZANO, and David TORO, in July 1937 he assumed the presidency in the belief that all three previous presidents had been inept in their handling of the war. On 27 May 1938 Busch was elected constitutional president for the period 1938 to 1942. On 24 April 1939 he declared himself a dictator, proclaiming "military socialism" and undertaking radical reforms that included the nationalization of the Standard Oil holdings. He condemned the German-born tin magnate Mauricio HOCHSCHILD to death and nationalized the tin mines. Prevented by his cabinet from executing the sentence, in a fit of rage, Busch committed suicide in front of his aides, saying it "is best to terminate my life" to convince the Bolivian nation of the righteousness of his action. Although the suicide is an accepted historical fact, there has been some talk of assassination. Just before Busch's death a permanent peace treaty with Paraguay went into effect, although hostilities had long since ended. Busch, considered a forerunner of Bolivia's great reforms of the next three decades, has become virtually a legendary figure in Bolivian history.

MOÏSÉS ALCÁZAR, *Sangre en la historia* (1956); AUGUSTO CÉSPEDES, *El dictator suicida* (1956); PORFIRIO DÍAZ MACHICAO, *Historia de Bolivia*. Vol. 4, *Toro, Busch, Quintanilla* (1957), pp. 59–119.

CHARLES W. ARNADE

**BUSTAMANTE, ANASTASIO** (*b.* 17 July 1780; *d.* 1853), Mexican military man and politician. Born in Jiquilpán, Michoacán, Bustamante studied medicine in Mexico City. During the struggle for independence, he joined the royal army, distinguishing himself in combat. Nevertheless, he supported Agustín de ITURBIDE (later emperor) in 1821. After the fall of the empire, he allied himself with the ESCOCESES (Scottish rite Masons), was elected vice president in 1829, and overthrew the government in January 1830. His administration (1830–1832) was noted for its conservatism, political repression, and the execution of President Vicente GUERRERO. Subsequently ousted and exiled, Bustamante returned to office as president in 1837–1839, 1840, and 1841, becoming one of the most important politicians of the early republic. He also served as senator and participated in various military campaigns, the last of which was the pacification of the Sierra Gorda insurrection in 1848.

CARLOS MARÍA DE BUSTAMANTE, *Continuación del cuadro histórico*, 4 vols. (1953–1963); MICHAEL P. COSTELOE, "The Triangular Revolt in Mexico and the Fall of Anastasio Bustamante," in *Journal of Latin American Studies* 20, pt. 2 (November 1988): 337–360; MICHAEL COSTELOE, "A Pronunciamiento in Nineteenth-Century Mexico, '15 de julio de 1840,' " in *Mexican Studies/Estudios Mexicanos* 4, pt. 2 (Summer 1988): 245–264; JAIME E. RODRÍGUEZ O., "The Origins of the 1832 Revolt," in his *Patterns of Contention in Mexican History* (1992).

JAIME E. RODRÍGUEZ O.

**BUSTAMANTE, CARLOS MARÍA DE** (*b.* 4 November 1774; *d.* 21 September 1848), Mexican patriot, politician, and writer. Born in Oaxaca, Bustamante studied theology and law. He distinguished himself early as a champion of the poor, and during the WARS OF INDEPENDENCE became defense counsel for various conspirators. One of the founders of the *Diario de Méjico* in 1805, he became famous in 1812 as the editor of the antigovernment *El Jugetillo* (The Small Toy) and was chosen "elector" of the city of Mexico that year. Later he became an adviser to José María MORELOS and was instrumental in convincing the insurgents to hold a congress in Apatzingán and in writing the Constitution of APATZINGÁN (1814). After independence he served in nearly every congress from 1822 until his death.

A strong centralist, Bustamante grew increasingly conservative as the country he loved fell into anarchy. He was extremely influential as a journalist and a pamphleteer; over his lifetime he published many newspapers and hundreds of pamphlets. Following his intellectual mentor, Father MIER NORIEGA Y GUERRA, in recovering pre-Columbian and colonial manuscripts and in creating the political myth of the ancient "Mexican Empire," Bustamante also helped to create the "official history" of independence that persists to the present day. In addition, he was one of the principal chroniclers of the period, having written Mexico's history from independence until the U.S. invasion, an event that left him "sick of soul and body" and coincided with his death.

Bustamante's most important historical works are *Cuadro histórico de la revolución de la América mexicana* 3 (1823–1832), and *Continuación del cuadro histórico de la revolución mexicana* 4 (1953–1963). Perhaps the most significant of all his contributions was his personal diary, "Diario histórico de México," forty-eight volumes, which records the events of the period 1822–1848.

JUAN ORTEGA Y MEDINA, *El historiador D. C. M. de Bustamante ante la conciencia histórica mexicana* (1963); EDMUNDO O'GORMAN, ed., *Guía bibliográfica de Carlos María de Bustamante* (1967); VIRGINIA GUEDEA, "Las primeras elecciones populares en la ciudad de México, 1812–1813," in *Mexican Studies/Estudios Mexicanos* 7, pt. 1 (Winter 1991): 1–28, and her "Los procesos electorales insurgentes," in *Estudios de historia novohispana* 11 (1992); JAIME E. RODRÍGUEZ O., "The Struggle for the Nation: The First Centralist-Federalist Conflict in Mexico," in *The Americas* 49 (July 1992): 1–22.

JAIME E. RODRÍGUEZ O.

**BUSTAMANTE Y GUERRA, JOSÉ** (*b.* 1759; *d.* 1825), Spanish naval officer who served as captain-general and governor of Uruguay (1795–1810) and Guatemala (1811–1818). Bustamante distinguished himself in Spain's North African campaign in 1774 and was a member of the Malespina expedition that circumnavigated the globe between 1784 and 1791. He became governor of Uruguay in 1795 and later commanded Spanish naval forces in the Río de la Plata. He was transferred to Guatemala in 1811, where he served as captain-general until 1818. Unsympathetic to the Cádiz Constitution of 1812, Bustamante delayed implementing its reforms in Guatemala and concentrated instead on insulating Central America from the revolutionary events occurring in Mexico. He became notorious in Central American history for authoritarian rule, especially after the restoration of Ferdinand VII of Spain in 1814.

Although Bustamante subdued several revolts and maintained the loyalty of Central America when much of the rest of the Spanish Empire was in rebellion, his draconian policies stimulated animosities among the creoles and sentiment for independence, which erupted soon after his departure. He became director-general of the Spanish Navy in 1819 and died six years later in a shipwreck en route to Buenos Aires.

EDUARDO CÁRDENAS, *20,000 biografías breves* (1963); MARIO RODRÍGUEZ, *The Cádiz Experiment in Central America, 1808 to 1826* (1978).

SUE DAWN MCGRADY

**BUSTAMANTE Y RIVERO, JOSÉ LUIS** (*b.* 1894; *d.* 1990), democratically elected president of Peru (1945) who was ousted in 1948 by a military coup led by General Manuel ODRÍA. Bustamante y Rivero, born in Arequipa, was educated as a lawyer at the universities of Arequipa and Cuzco. During his early political activities he expressed southern regionalist interests influenced by the local version of *pierolismo* (after the civilian CAUDILLO Nicolás de PIÉROLA). He opposed President Augusto B. LEGUÍA's failed policies toward the provinces. In 1930, as political secretary of the Revolutionary Junta in Arequipa, Bustamante supported the military coup led by Colonel Luis M. SÁNCHEZ CERRO. Between 1934 and 1945 he held diplomatic posts in Bolivia, Paraguay, and Uruguay.

In 1945, a group of middle-class leaders of moderate populist ideology, supported by the illegal Aprista movement and the Communist Party, formed the National Democratic Front (FDN) in Arequipa. With the consent of the army, the FDN announced Bustamante's candidacy in the 1945 elections, in which he successfully defeated the right.

In several ways the Bustamante administration continued and enhanced protectionist measures introduced by the previous president, Manuel PRADO. These measures included exchange and price control and import quotas. As a result, the moderate inflation that had begun to rise under the Prado administration increased substantially under Bustamante. The floating internal debt also increased, contributing to inflation. President Bustamante was under the political pressure of the well-organized Aprista Party, which was strongly represented in the parliament. A failed Aprista armed uprising in 1948 precipitated the coup by Odría, who, with the help of U.S. financial advisers, reintroduced liberal economic measures. He died in Lima.

See his *Tres años de lucha por la democracia en el Perú* (1949); GONZALO PORTOCARRERO MAISCH, *De Bustamante a Odría* (1983).

ALFONSO W. QUIROZ

*See also* **Peru: Political Parties.**

**BUSTOS, HERMENEGILDO** (*b*. 1832; *d*. 1907), Mexican painter. Bustos lived his entire life in the town of Purísima del Rincón, Guanajuato. The diverse types of jobs he held—ice vendor, sacristan, carpenter, maguey planter, and musician—allowed him to bring to his canvases a variety of themes, which were combined with the freshness of a small-town painter who worked by assignment.

The great majority of his work consists of ex-votos, a form of religious expression popularized in the eighteenth and nineteenth centuries. These small works, painted in lamina, depict tragic scenes from which the subjects felt they had been saved by the miraculous intercession of a saint, to whom the ex-voto was dedicated. The ex-votos of Bustos are distinguished by the individuality he gave to his subjects. His talent as a portraitist enabled him to capture with a rural flavor the features of his subjects—whom we know by name, thanks to an inscription on the ex-voto.

Bustos did more than paint models; he instilled his subjects with a character that went beyond physical features. Two of his dining-room paintings are outstanding

for their iconography and extraordinary pictorial quality, recalling the botanical illustrations of the eighteenth century. The paintings must have been highly prized by Bustos, since they remained in his home until his death.

PASCUAL ACEVES BARAJAS, *Hermenegildo Bustos; su vida y su obra* (1956); RAQUEL TIBOL, *Hermenegildo Bustos; Pintor del Pueblo*, 2d ed. (1992).

ESTHER ACEVEDO

**BUTANTÃ INSTITUTE,** a center for the study and development of snakebite serum. Founded by Dr. Vital Brazil in 1888, the institute was established not only to prevent deaths by snakebite, but also to find a vaccine for bubonic plague. Butantã functions today in the distribution of antivenom throughout Brazil. The institute is attached to Butantã Snake Farm, the largest in Latin America. Along with the farm and the institute is a museum that houses poisonous snakes and spiders. The museum, which is a popular tourist attraction, has displays that explain the functions of the institute and describe the correct treatment for snakebite. Butantã is located in Pinheiros, a suburb of São Paulo, on the grounds of the Cidade Universitária, under the control of the Ministry of Health. The university itself was built on the former Fazenda Butantã (Butantã Farm).

SHEILA L. HOOKER

*See also* **Medicine.**

**BUTLER, SMEDLEY DARLINGTON** (*b*. 30 July 1881; *d*. 21 June 1940), an American marine officer popularly known as "Old Gimlet Eye." Following his commission in 1898, Butler served during the SPANISH-AMERICAN WAR and in China during the Boxer rebellion of 1900. In 1912, Butler led marine battalions in Nicaragua that helped suppress its civil war and in 1914 at Veracruz, where U.S. forces prevented armaments from reaching Mexico's warring factions. His dominant role during the Haitian intervention in 1915 earned Butler the Congressional Medal of Honor. He was awarded the Distinguished Service Medal for his service in World War I. Butler retired as major general in 1931.

LOWELL THOMAS, *Old Gimlet Eye* (1933); ROBERT E. QUIRK, *An Affair of Honor: Woodrow Wilson and the Occupation of Vera Cruz* (1962); LESTER D. LANGLEY, *The Banana Wars: An Inner History of American Empire, 1900–1934* (1983).

THOMAS M. LEONARD

**CAAGUAZÚ** department in east-central Paraguay with an area of 8,345 square miles and a 1990 population of 462,000. The capital city is Coronel Oviedo (population 21,782). The main physical feature of the department is the Cordillera de Caaguazú, a steplike massif at the southern edge of the Amambay plateau. The forests of the area are timbered, and YERBA MATÉ is grown. Some iron and copper veins add mining resources to the chiefly forestal and agricultural bases of the economy.

GERD KOHLHEPP, "Problems of Dependent Regional Development in Eastern Paraguay," in *Applied Geography and Development* 22 (1983): 7–45.

CÉSAR N. CAVIEDES

**CAAGUAZÚ, BATTLE OF** (28 November 1841), a major victory of Unitarist general José María PAZ in the Argentine civil wars. It was fought on the bank of the Corrientes River in the province of the same name, which was maintaining a precarious independence vis-à-vis the dictatorship of Juan Manuel de ROSAS. Corrientes had placed its forces under the command of Paz, who faced a large invading force led by Rosas's ally General Pascual Echagüe, governor of neighboring Entre Ríos. Having worn down the invaders by delay, Paz employed a masterful combination of battlefield tactics to virtually annihilate the enemy force. The victory gave Corrientes a breathing spell but did not break the power of Rosas, whose armies had meanwhile crushed Unitarist forces elsewhere in the country. Moreover, disunity among Paz, the governor of Corrientes, and their ally Uruguayan president Fructuoso RIVERA precluded taking full advantage of the military success.

JOSÉ MARÍA PAZ, *Memorias*, vol. 4 (1968), chaps. 30–31; PABLO SANTOS MUÑOZ, *Años de lucha (1841–1845): Urquiza y la política del litoral rioplatense* (1973), chaps. 1–2.

DAVID BUSHNELL

**CAAMAÑO DEÑÓ, FRANCISCO** (*b.* 11 June 1932; *d.* 16 February 1973), leader of the 1965 constitutionalist revolt in the Dominican Republic and president of the Dominican Republic (1965). Born in Santo Domingo, Caamaño began a career in the military in 1949, following in the footsteps of his father, Fausto Caamaño Medina, one of Rafael Leonidas TRUJILLO's most notorious generals. His father's influence enabled Caamaño to advance rapidly through the military ranks. When the April 1965 revolt split the military, Colonel Caamaño sided with the rebels in their efforts to reinstate the constitutional government of Juan BOSCH (elected December 1962; overthrown September 1963). Caamaño became the leader of the revolutionary troops, and in an emergency session on 4 May 1965, the Dominican National Assembly elected him constitutional president, a position lasting until 31 August. The United States intervened, installing Héctor GARCÍA-GODOY as interim president of the republic in September. In 1966, following the renewal of hostilities between the rebels and the conservatives, Caamaño was sent to London, effectively exiled, to assume a diplomatic post. A year later he abandoned the position and fled to Cuba, where he spent the next six years planning a campaign to overthrow the government of Joaquín BALAGUER (elected 1966). On 3 February 1973, Caamaño landed with a guerrilla band on Dominican soil. Less than two weeks later, he was captured and executed.

GREGORIO ORTEGA, *Santo Domingo, 1965* (1965); RICHARD W. MANSBACH, *Dominican Crisis, 1965* (1971); PIERO GLEIJESES, *The Dominican Crisis: The 1965 Constitutionalist Revolt and American Intervention*, translated by Lawrence Lipson (1978); HAMLET HERMANN, *Francis Caamaño* (1983); TONY RAFUL, *La revolución de abril de 1965* (1985).

SARA FLEMING

*See also* **Dominican Revolt (1965).**

**CAAMAÑO Y GÓMEZ CORNEJO, JOSÉ MARÍA PLÁCIDO** (*b.* 5 October 1838; *d.* 31 December 1901), president of Ecuador (1884–1888). Caamaño, a wealthy coastal CACAO grower from Guayaquil, was selected to follow President Gabriel GARCÍA MORENO (1861–1865, 1869–1875) in office in 1865. However, he refused. He also opposed the dictatorship of Ignacio de VEINTIMILLA (1876–1883), which led to his arrest and exile in Peru. In 1883 he returned and helped organize the overthrow of Veintimilla. Caamaño joined the provisional government; the subsequent National Convention elected him president. The first of three Progresista (1883–1895) presidents, Caamaño sought to remain independent of both Liberals and Conservatives; his family ties in both the sierra and the coast afforded a further measure of neutrality.

Caamaño had hoped to implement a program of public works but instead spent his term fighting efforts to throw him out of office, employing particular brutality in quelling the revolts of coastal guerrillas (*montoneras*). After his presidency he served as governor of Guayas province (1888–1895). Critics saw Caamaño as leader of a corrupt clique, "the ring" (*la argolla*), thought to be a conspiracy of coastal financial interests who secretly controlled the nation. Caamaño was implicated in the Esmeraldas affair (1894–1895), a scandal that involved the use of the Ecuadorian flag to cover the sale of a Chilean warship to Japan. Accused of taking a bribe (a charge he denied), the former president fled Ecuador when angry citizens laid siege to his home. Caamaño traveled to Spain, where he spent the rest of his life in poverty. He died in Seville.

On nineteenth-century Ecuadorian politics, see OSVALDO HURTADO's interpretive *Political Power in Ecuador*, translated by NICK D. MILLS, JR. (1985); and FRANK MAC DONALD SPINDLER's descriptive *Nineteenth Century Ecuador: An Historical Introduction* (1987). For a brief analysis of Ecuadorian political economy in the nineteenth century, consult DAVID. W. SCHODT, *Ecuador: An Andean Enigma* (1987).

RONN F. PINEO

**CAATINGA** denotes the spiny, stunted, predominantly xerophytic vegetation of the most arid zones of northeastern Brazil's SERTÃO, a region extending from the interior of Minas Gerais and Bahia to the interior of Piauí and Maranhão. Caatinga, literally "the white forest" in Tupi, also refers to areas featuring such vegetation. Characteristics of the driest regions of the *sertão*, *catingueras* (a general term for the hardy plants of the *caatinga*) can withstand droughts lasting as long as three years.

The expansion of cattle ranching in the 1700s prompted European settlement of the inhospitable *caatinga*. During the 1800s cotton strains suited to the harsh climate were developed and cultivated. The population in the *caatinga* remained small, impoverished, and vulnerable to drought and disease.

EDGAR AUBERT DE LA RÜE, *Brésil Aride: La vie dans la Caatinga* (1957); LAURE EMPERAIRE, *La Caatinga du Sud-est du Piauí: Étude ethnobotanique* (1983).

CARA SHELLY

**CABALLERÍA,** a unit of land beyond the perimeter of a city (usually in Mexico) granted by the crown or its officials for the sole purpose of farming (as opposed to stock raising). Theoretically, the *caballería* was calculated to be large enough to provide subsistence for a *caballero*, a gentleman or cavalry man, and his family, in contrast to the *peonía*, a smaller grant of farmland deemed sufficient for a footman and his descendants. Although Viceroy Antonio de Mendoza established a standard size in 1536, in fact the *caballería* varied in expanse according to climate and soil quality. Some reports describe the *caballería* as about twice the size of the *peonía*. In central Mexico, an average-sized *caballería*, according to scholar Charles Gibson, measured 1,104 by 552 *varas de castilla*, or 0.024 square leagues (0.17 square miles or 105 acres).

CHARLES GIBSON, *The Aztecs Under Spanish Rule: A History of the Indians of the Valley of Mexico, 1519–1810* (1964); VICTOR WESTPHALL, *Mercedes Reales: Hispanic Land Grants of the Upper Rio Grande Region* (1983).

SUSAN E. RAMÍREZ

**CABALLERO, BERNARDINO** (*b.* 20 May 1839; *d.* 26 February 1912), Paraguayan military leader and president (1880–1886). Born in the interior town of Ybycuí, Caballero spent his early career in the cavalry and by the beginning of the WAR OF THE TRIPLE ALLIANCE in 1864, had risen to the rank of sergeant. He participated in almost every engagement of the war, from the Mato Grosso campaign to those of Humaitá and the Cordilleras. His success in harassing the advancing Brazilians, as well as his exceptional loyalty, drew the attention of President Francisco Solano LÓPEZ. Advancements for Caballero came rapidly, until 1869, when he achieved the rank of general and with it command over what was left of López's army. Even after the fall of Asunción, he continued the fight, until, in March 1870, the Brazilians cornered and killed López at CERRO CORÁ. Caballero was taken prisoner shortly thereafter.

Caballero's star rose much higher in the postwar period. As one of the only Paraguayan generals to survive the war, he naturally caught the eye of various contending factions, who sought to use him as a figurehead. A Conservative movement led by Cándido BAREIRO secured his appointment as war minister in 1878, but he proved to be his own man.

Caballero assumed the presidency in 1880 after the death of Bareiro. His administration made only limited contributions to the public welfare. It disposed of thousands of hectares of state land by selling them to foreign buyers. Caballero also founded the National Bank and the National Law School. The most important innovation of his tenure, however, was in the political realm. In 1887, with the help of José Segundo DECOUD, he founded one of the country's traditional parties, the Asociación Nacional Republicana, or Partido Colorado. He continued to direct this organization long after he left the presidency in the hands of his colleague Patricio Escobar. Caballero died in Asunción.

HARRIS G. WARREN, *Rebirth of the Paraguayan Republic: The First Colorado Era* (1985), esp. pp. 51–61; CARLOS ZUBIZARRETA, *Cien vidas paraguayas*, 2d ed. (1985), pp. 184–188; *The Cambridge History of Latin America*, vol. 5 (1986), pp. 475–496.

THOMAS L. WHIGHAM

**CABALLERO, PEDRO JUAN** (*b.* 1786; *d.* 13 July 1821), Paraguayan soldier and politician of the independence era. Born in Tobatí, Caballero spent his early youth in the Paraguayan countryside, where he learned to ride and, like many men of his class, to command small bands of troops in the colonial militia. He evidently participated in the Indian campaigns of the first years of the nineteenth century and, by 1810, had attained the rank of captain.

The following year Caballero was catapulted into prominence. The revolutionary junta in Buenos Aires, seeking to gain Paraguay's adherence to the patriot struggle against Spain, had sent an expeditionary force to the province. Commanded by Manuel BELGRANO, this small army anticipated little resistance. The Paraguayans, however, had no desire to be controlled from Buenos Aires, and their militia proceeded to defeat Belgrano in two separate engagements.

In the aftermath of these battles, some Paraguayan officers, Caballero included, actively fraternized with the defeated *porteños*, who convinced them that some form of independence was desirable. Together with colonels Fulgencio Yegros and Manuel Atanasio Cavañas, Caballero organized a conspiracy against the royal government in Asunción. When the plot was discovered in May 1811, Caballero acted in the absence of his associates, seizing the *cabildo* offices and arresting the governor at dawn on the fifteenth of the month.

The rebellion brought Paraguay independence but not political stability. Over the next three years a provisional junta composed of Caballero, Yegros, and three other notables ruled the country, though often in an erratic fashion. Their inability to govern effectively made possible the ascendancy of José Gaspar Rodríguez de FRANCIA, the one outstanding political figure in Paraguay, and a man whom Caballero detested. In 1814, when Francia became dictator, Caballero wisely retired to Tobatí, but six years later he was implicated in a major plot against the dictator. Jailed by Francia's police, he committed suicide in his cell.

LOUIS G. BENÍTEZ, *Historia de la cultura en el Paraguay* (1976), p. 99; JOHN H. WILLIAMS, *The Rise and Fall of the Paraguayan Republic, 1800–1870* (1979), pp. 27–53; CARLOS ZUBIZARRETA, *Cien vidas paraguayas*, 2d ed. (1985), pp. 93–98.

THOMAS L. WHIGHAM

**CABALLERO Y GÓNGORA, ANTONIO** (*b.* May 1723; *d.* March 1796), viceroy of New Granada (1782–1789). A native of Córdoba Province, Spain, Caballero y Góngora became bishop of Yucatán in 1776 and archbishop of Santa Fe de Bogotá in 1779. He later entered the secular realm when, after defusing the COMUNERO REVOLT of 1781, he became VICEROY on 15 June 1782. The archbishop-viceroy championed enlightened education and science, and secured the creation of a mining reform mission. He also imposed centralized control on the colonial army and, to sustain royal authority, gained approval to establish in Santa Fe a veteran regiment reinforced by a disciplined militia.

During much of his administration, Caballero y Góngora resided at Turbaco, near Cartagena, directing ambitious military operations to pacify the aboriginals of Darién. He enhanced treasury receipts impressively but spent huge sums on the military and the bureaucracy. In the name of economy, his successors would dismantle much of his program. Replaced by Francisco GIL DE TABOADA Y LEMOS in January 1789, Caballero y Góngora returned to Córdoba, serving as archbishop until his death.

JOSÉ MANUEL PÉREZ AYALA, *Antonio Caballero y Góngora, virrey y arzobispo de Santa Fe, 1723–1796* (1951); ALLAN J. KUETHE, *Military Reform and Society in New Granada, 1773–1808* (1978); JOHN LEDDY PHELAN, *The People and the King: The Comunero Revolution in Colombia, 1781* (1978).

ALLAN J. KUETHE

**CABALLERO Y RODRÍGUEZ, JOSÉ AUGUSTÍN** (*b.* 28 August 1762; *d.* 7 April 1835), Cuban priest, philosopher, and educator. Along with Francisco ARANGO Y PARREÑO, Caballero was a pioneer of reformism in Cuba. Born in Havana, he was ordained as a priest in 1785. He became professor of philosophy (1785) and later director at San Carlos Seminary, where he was able to influence the intellectual formation of Father Félix VARELA Y MORALES, doubtless the most famous of his disciples. An eloquent orator and a gifted writer and critic, Caballero put his exceptional abilities at the disposal of Cuba's Patriotic Society, a respectable colonial institution where he pleaded constantly for a more flexible approach to human problems. Along with his newspaper articles and his speeches (some of which are magnificent rhetorical pieces), he left us a treatise on logic written in Latin, *Lecciones de filosofía electiva* (1796), the first text for the teaching of philosophy ever produced in Cuba by a Cuban.

Although he mentions in his work empiricist thinkers such as John Locke, Francis Bacon, and Étienne Bonnot de Condillac, Caballero was by no means a radical innovator. Basically he was a follower of the Spanish thinker Benito Jerónimo FEIJÓO, whose chief concern was to free philosophy from its submission to Aristotle and scholasticism, maintaining that all authorities were acceptable provided they taught the truth. Caballero's contribution to modernity, therefore, never went beyond trying to reconcile Cartesian rationalism with Aristotelianism. Faithful to the church, he never hesitated to place faith above reason, although he did favor the teaching of experimental physics and advocated greater freedom for university teachers and broader and deeper techniques of inquiry.

Caballero was also a believer in self-government, and in 1811 he put forward a proposal for the establishment of quasi-autonomist rule in Cuba. Never favoring the separation of Cuba from Spain, he was a moderate, politically and socially. Moreover, he thought that, given the prevailing conditions, slavery was an inevitable crime, although he wrote numerous articles urging slave owners to treat their slaves better. Despite his moderation, Caballero must be credited with laying the groundwork upon which later Cubans built their more radical thoughts.

There are few studies on Caballero's life and work; see ISABEL MONAL, "Tres filósofos del centenario," in *Universidad de La Habana* 192 (1968): 116–122; also, EMILIO ROIG DE LEUCHSENRING, ed., *Homenaje al ilustre habanero pbro. dr. José Agustín Caballero y Rodríguez en el centenario de su muerte, 1835–1935* (1935).

JOSÉ M. HERNÁNDEZ

See also **Cuba: Political Movements; Slavery: Abolition of.**

**CABALLERO CALDERÓN, EDUARDO** (*b.* 6 March 1910; *d.* 1993), Colombian novelist and essayist. Author of more than two dozen books, Caballero Calderón is one of Colombia's major novelists of the twentieth century. He has also published numerous essays on literary, cultural, political, and historical topics. Caballero Calderón began writing in the 1940s and rose to prominence in the 1950s and 1960s. His major novel, *El buen salvaje* (The Good Savage) appeared in 1966, receiving international acclaim in Spain and throughout the Hispanic world. His ten novels, four volumes of short stories, and eleven books of essays have placed him at the forefront of Colombian writers.

Caballero Calderón's earliest publications were essays. The first, a volume titled *Tipacoque* (1941), is a set of nostalgic portraits of rural, provincial life in Colombia. In his book of essays, *Breviario del Quijote* (1947), the author demonstrates the importance of Spanish literary tradition for him and for Latin American writers in general: he writes about his admiration for the *Poema del Cid, Don Quijote,* writings of the Spanish Golden Age, and other classic Spanish texts. For the remainder of his career, he remained closely aligned to the culture of Spain.

Caballero Calderón's early novels dealt with the Colombian civil war commonly known as La VIOLENCIA, a conflict that took place primarily from 1948 to 1958. Many interests were represented in this conflict, but the primary antagonists were the traditional Conservative Party and the Liberal Party. In his novel *El Cristo de espaldas* (1952; Christ on His Back) a son in the Liberal Party is accused of killing his father of the Conservative Party, and the town priest becomes the sacrificial victim when he attempts to justify the son's act. The protagonist of *Siervo sin tierra* (1954) is also a victim of *La Violencia.* The basic thesis of the novel *Manuel Pacho* (1962) is that each person has one opportunity in life to be a hero. In *El buen salvaje,* Caballero Calderón rises above local stories of violence and constructs a self-conscious fiction about a young Latin American intellectual in Paris.

LEON LYDAY and LUIS CARLOS HERRERA et al., "Trayectoria de un novelista: Eduardo Caballero Calderón," in *Boletín Cultural y Bibliográfico* 12, no. 2 (1969): 13–103; JOHN S. BRUSHWOOD, *The Spanish American Novel: A Twentieth-Century Survey* (1975); SEYMOUR MENTON, *La novela colombiana: Planetas y satélites* (1977).

RAYMOND LESLIE WILLIAMS

**CABALLEROS ORIENTALES,** the name of a Masonic lodge that existed in Montevideo, Uruguay, in 1823. The territory was occupied by the Portuguese, who in 1820 had finalized their invasion with the rout of José ARTIGAS. The 1822 Grito de Ypiranga declaring Brazilian independence from Portugal divided Portuguese and Brazilians and created an atmosphere of reaction in which residents of the BANDA ORIENTAL sought to return to the sanctuary of the UNITED PROVINCES OF THE RÍO DE LA PLATA—the principal objective of the Caballeros Orientales. Their attempts failed, however, because of lack of support from the rural caudillos and fear of Brazilian reprisals in the provinces that are now part of Argentina. Members of the group included Manuel and Ignacio ORIBE, Santiago Vázquez, Antonio Díaz, and Juan Francisco Giró, all of whom became outstanding figures in the following years. The secret society produced various underground publications in Montevideo and practically dominated the town council in 1823. On withdrawal of the Portuguese and the beginning of Brazilian domination, the Caballeros Orientales ceased their activities, many of them going into exile in Buenos Aires.

JOHN STREET, *Artigas and the Emancipation of Uruguay* (1959); ALFREDO CASTELLANOS, *La Cisplatina: La independencia y la república caudillesca, 1820–1838* (1974).

JOSÉ DE TORRES WILSON

*See also* **Brazil: Independence Movements; Freemasonry; Orientales.**

**CABALLEROS RACIONALES, SOCIEDAD DE,** one of the first secret societies established in New Spain. (The other was Los GUADALUPES.) The Caballeros Racionales, with Masonic affiliations, was originally founded in Cádiz in 1811 by American Spaniards interested in furthering home rule in their native countries. Several lodges were then established in London and various parts of Spanish America such as Caracas and Buenos Aires. The lodge in New Spain was founded in Jalapa at the beginning of 1812. Its aim was to promote the establishment of an American government in New Spain, and its members supported the insurgent movement against the colonial regime. Besides an organized directorate, the society developed initiation rites, in which the members swore to maintain secrecy, as well as signs by means of which associates recognized one another. The membership of the society exceeded seventy when the colonial authorities discovered its existence in May 1812. They imprisoned many of its members. Others managed to flee, and some, like Mariano Rincón, who later became one of the outstanding insurgent leaders in the Veracruz region, were members of the Governing Junta of Naolingo.

"Logia de los 'Caballeros Racionales' en Jalapa. Fragmentos del proceso del canónigo Cardeña," in *Boletín del Archivo general de la Nación* 3, no. 3 (1932): 390–407; and VIRGINIA GUEDEA, "Las sociedades secretas durante el movimiento de independencia," in *The Independence of Mexico and the Creation of the New Nation,* edited by Jaime E. Rodríguez O. (1989), pp. 45–62.

VIRGINIA GUEDEA

**CABALLO MUERTO,** a complex of early sites located near the modern city of Trujillo in the Moche Valley on the north coast of Peru. The complex, probably the center of a larger multivalley polity, consists of eight U-shaped mound structures that are made of stone set in mud mortar and were sequentially constructed between 1700 B.C. and 400 B.C.

The structure called Huaca de los Reyes (shrine of the kings) is the most elaborate architecturally. Built around 1500 B.C., this site contains several platform mounds, colonnades, stairways, and over fifty rooms, all precisely arranged along three sides of two large plazas and two small plazas. Access to the site is gained from the east, where one enters the largest plaza, which could hold several hundred people. Access to the three remaining smaller plazas could only be gained through very narrow, restricted passageways and staircases.

Niches and column faces within the various plazas are decorated with impressive mud sculptures that probably depicted various aspects of the builders' mythology. The largest plaza is lined with repetitive heads of creator deities as well as full-figure depictions of a main ancestral cultural hero. Just to the west, the smaller of the two main plazas contains more varied depictions of the ancestral cultural hero, possibly reflecting different myths involving this hero. Immediately north and south of this plaza are two small plazas, each containing a mound frontally decorated with paired profile jaguar sculptures. The restricted access to three of the plazas, their small size, and the special nature of their associated mud sculptures suggest these plazas were the scenes of special ceremonial activities by privileged groups within the society that built the structure.

THOMAS POZORSKI, "The Early Horizon Site of Huaca de los Reyes: Societal Implications," in *American Antiquity* 45 (1980): 100–110, "Early Social Stratification and Subsistence Systems: The Caballo Muerto Complex," in *Chan Chan: Andean Desert City,* edited by Michael Moseley and Kent Day (1982), pp. 225–253, and "The Caballo Muerto Complex and Its Place in the Andean Chronological Sequence," in *Annals of Carnegie Museum of Natural History* 52 (1983): 1–40.

SHELIA POZORSKI
THOMAS POZORSKI

**CABANAGEM,** a popular insurrection in the Brazilian Amazon (1835–1840). Detribalized Indians (*tapuios*) and the rest of the formerly free population essentially constituted by people of color were subject to coercive labor arrangements, to army and navy recruitment, and to personal indignities.

In contrast with other parts of Brazil, whites constituted a very small minority in Pará. With the declaration of Brazilian independence, the metropolitan Portuguese sought to maintain the colonial status quo in the province. Although they were forced to concede in 1823, they managed to retain control of the region and to maintain the labor system. Popular uprisings in 1823, 1824, and 1831, supported by the nationalist portion of the elite, sought to end the power of the Portuguese. They were put down with the help of the national army and navy. Massacres like that of 256 prisoners on the prison ship *Palhaço* (1823) contributed to the hostility of the lower classes (*cabanos*) against the white, Portuguese upper class.

In 1834 the authoritarian governor, Lobo de Souza, increased army and navy recruitment to strengthen authority in the province. Conflict within the elite was increased by the suppression of an anti-Masonic pastoral letter of the bishop. The governor, who was a Mason, took action against the popular bishop, Batista Campos, who had published the letter in the diocesan newspaper. The burning of the *fazenda* (ranch) of Campos's protector, Félix Antônio Clemente Malcher, in October 1834 and the subsequent death of the bishop made armed resistance appear to be the only solution for the *cabanos*.

The festival of São Tomé, during which people traveled to Belém, was a propitious time to prepare for the insurrection, which erupted on 6 January 1835. The rebels were led by Antônio Vinagre, a *fazendeiro* whose brother Manuel had been shot by government troops during the expedition against Bishop Campos. *Cabanos* soon took Belém, and most of the government troops joined them. The governor was executed, the Masonic temple was destroyed, and Malcher was freed from jail and proclaimed governor. The rebels sent a message to the imperial court in Rio de Janeiro, telling the government to send no more governors to Pará.

Malcher, a member of the dominant class, was not disposed to support fundamental changes and adopted a conciliatory attitude, seeking to stop acts of vengeance and appealing for a return to work. A month after his installation as governor, he was overthrown and the more popular Francisco Vinagre was proclaimed the new governor. Once in power, however, Vinagre also came into conflict with the *cabanos,* and in June finally agreed to hand power over to the designated governor, Manuel Jorge Rodrigues, a naturalized Portuguese. *Cabano* troops then left Belém but did not lay down their weapons. Persecution of *cabanos* by the new government led to new confrontations.

In the third and most crucial phase of the Cabanagem, Eduardo Angelim Nogueira, a tenant farmer on one of Malcher's properties, assumed leadership of the *cabanos.* Belém was again seized by *cabano* troops in August 1835. Black slaves joined the movement, which clearly envisaged the abolition of coerced labor and of slavery. Angelim Nogueira, seeking to establish government in the traditional way, opposed acts of vengeance and "excesses." Dissension within the *cabano* ranks, the outbreak of disease, and the arrival of government troops led the rebels to abandon Belém in May 1836.

The following years saw brutal repression of *cabanos,* many of whom were executed. The last groups surrendered in Amazonia in 1840. Some found shelter among Indian groups, such as the Mura, who had supported the movement. About one-fifth of the population of Amazonia is said to have perished.

The Cabanagem is distinguished from most other insurrections of the regency by its popular character and leadership, especially in the last phase, and its power over an entire province.

DOMINGOS ANTÔNIO RAIOL, *Motins políticos ou história dos principais acontecimentos políticos de província do Pará desde o ano 1821 até 1835,* 2d ed., 3 vols. (1970); RENATO GUIMARÃES, "Cabanagem: A revolução no Brasil," in *Cadernos do CEAS 71* (January–February 1981); JULIO JOSÉ CHIAVENATO, *Cabanagem: O povo no poder* (1984); CARLOS DE ARAÚJO MOREIRA NETO, *Índios de Amazônia, de maioria a minoria (1750–1850)* (1988).

MATTHIAS RÖHRIG ASSUNÇÃO

**CABAÑAS, JOSÉ TRINIDAD** (*b.* 9 June 1805; *d.* 8 January 1871), military figure and president of Honduras (1852, 1853–1855). Born a creole, the son of José María Cabañas and Juana María Faillos, Cabañas was a Liberal politician whose role in Honduran history dates from his participation in the civil war of 1826–1829 as a follower of Francisco MORAZÁN. In 1844 he defended León, Nicaragua, against Francisco MALESPÍN's forces. In 1845 he led Salvadoran forces against the same Malespín. He served as constitutional president from 1 March 1852 to 28 October 1852 but was deposed by Conservatives in Guatemala (and within Honduras). When war resumed between Honduras and Guatemala, he led Honduran forces to triumph at Chiquimula and Zacapa, in southeast Guatemala, in July 1853 but was unable to hold these positions. Guatemala's capture of the castle of Omoa on 24 August 1853 removed Honduras from the conflict.

Cabañas returned to power as constitutional president from 31 December 1853 to 6 October 1855. Among the important accomplishments of his second presidency were the ratification of a railroad contract with Ephraim George Squier and the formation of the Ferrocarril Interoceánico de Honduras (Interoceanic Railway Company) on 28 April 1854. Interference in Guatemalan affairs led to his overthrow once again, and this time he fled to El Salvador.

A prominent general as well as a politician, Cabañas took to the battlefield again. He was defeated by Guatemalan forces under Rafael CARRERA (1814–1865) at the Battle of Masagua on 6 October 1855. Although his successor, Santos Guardiola, was a Conservative, Cabañas remained active in Central American affairs and participated in a Salvadoran uprising in 1865. (In 1860 he had been connected with an abortive attempt by William WALKER to return to Central America.) His presidencies faced not only Guatemalan opposition but other challenges, such as British efforts to colonize the Bay Islands and frustrated attempts to reunite the Central American federal government. A unionist movement failed when a constituent assembly dissolved shortly after his first presidential term on 10 November 1852.

MEDARDO MEJÍA, *Trinidad Cabañas, soldado de la república federal* (1971); LUIS MARIÑAS OTERO, *Honduras,* 2d ed. (1983); JOSÉ REINA VALENZUELA, *José Trinidad Cabañas: Estudio biográfico* (1984).

JEFFREY D. SAMUELS

**CABEZA DE VACA, ALVAR NÚÑEZ** (*b.* ca. 1490; *d.* 1564), Spanish explorer, conquistador, and author. Cabeza de Vaca was most likely born in Jerez de la Frontera, Andalusia. He was treasurer and marshal of Pánfilo de NARVÁEZ's expedition to Florida (1527–1537) and was appointed governor of the Río de la Plata, in present-day Paraguay (1540–1545). For different reasons, both enterprises proved disastrous for Cabeza de Vaca, the first beginning in shipwreck, the latter ending in political failure.

After accidentally landing south of Tampa Bay in the spring of 1528, the ill-fated expedition of Narváez progressively deteriorated. It was not until eight years later that Cabeza de Vaca, Andrés Dorantes de Carranza, Alonso del Castillo Maldonado, and an African slave named Estevanico, the only four survivors, encountered a party of Spaniards on the west coast of Mexico. Cabeza de Vaca's account, known in Spanish as the *Naufragios* (Shipwrecks), tells the story of his travails and coexistence with the Mariame, Avavare, and Opata peoples. He became a merchant and, with the three other survivors practiced shamanism with such success that hundreds of Indians formed a cult about them and traveled with them across the continent. The *Naufragios* is at once an account of an officer of the crown and the story of a European who penetrated and was penetrated by Native American cultures. On his return to Spain, he was given the governorship of Río de la Plata. The *Comentarios,* written by his amanuensis Pedro Hernández, tells of Cabeza de Vaca's journey from the island of Santa Catalina (Brazil) to Asunción (Paraguay), and the subsequent rebellion of Domingo Martínez de IRALA that ended with Cabeza de Vaca's return to Spain in chains in 1545. He died in Seville.

Although a pirated edition of *Naufragios* appeared in 1542, while Cabeza de Vaca was in Paraguay, the authorized version was published with the *Comentarios* in 1555. The *Naufragios* is the more compelling of the two in its narration of a complete loss of material civilization and total dependence on the Indians. In this regard the *Naufragios* manifests the dubious nature of Western civilization's claims to superiority, since it is the Spaniards who are naked and unable to feed themselves or build boats, who fall into anomie and resort to cannibalism.

Cabeza de Vaca's story is the antithesis to *Robinson Crusoe* as it testifies that the Western individual does not embody the knowledge of European civilizations and must learn from Native Americans to survive. His account of cannibalism among the Spaniards includes a condemnation of the act by the Indians and a description of a highly ritualized consumption of the ashes of dead shamans. Thus, Europeans come to embody the savagery conventionally attributed to Indians.

The most complete edition of Cabeza de Vaca's writing is ALVAR NÚÑEZ CABEZA DE VACA, *Relación de los naufragios y comentarios,* edited by Manuel Serrano y Sanz, *Colección de libros y documentos referentes a la historia de América,* vol. 5 (1906); volume 6 of this collection contains other documents by and on Cabeza de Vaca. For a more recent critical edition, see ALVAR NÚÑEZ CABEZA DE VACA, *Relación,* edited by Enrique Pupo-Walker (1992). For an English version of the *Naufragios,* see ALVAR NÚÑEZ CABEZA DE VACA, *Castaways,* edited by Enrique Pupo-Walker and translated by Frances M. López-Morillas (1993). The standard biography still is MORRIS BISHOP, *The Odyssey of Cabeza de Vaca* (1933). More recent studies are ROLENA ADORNO, ''The Negotiation of Fear in Cabeza de Vaca's *Naufragios,*'' in *Representations,* no. 33 (1991):163–199; MAUREEN AHERN, ''The Cross and the Gourd: The Appropriation of Ritual Signs in the *Relaciones* of Alvar Núñez and Fray Marcos de Niza,'' in *Early Images of the Americas: Transfer and Invention,* edited by Jerry M. Williams and Robert E. Lewis (1993); and JOSÉ RABASA, ''Allegory and Ethnography in Cabeza de Vaca's *Naufragios* and *Comentarios,*'' in *Violence, Resistance, and Survival in the Americas: Native Americans and the Legacy of Conquest,* edited by William B. Taylor and Franklin Pease G.Y. (1994).

JOSÉ RABASA

*See also* **Conquistadores.**

**CABILDO, CABILDO ABIERTO,** town or city council and its ''open'' meeting. The *cabildo* or *ayuntamiento* was created at the founding of a municipality. Each *cabildo* had four or more aldermen (*regidores*) and one or two magistrates (*alcaldes ordinarios*). Other municipal officials, such as the standard-bearer (*alférez real*), chief constable (*alguacil mayor*), and inspector of weights and measures (*fiel ejecutor*), were subordinate to the council.

The cornerstone of Spanish rule and settlement, the *cabildo* distributed town lots and nearby garden plots, supervised the construction and maintenance of roads and public works, provided protection against fraud in the markets and against criminal activities in general, regulated holidays and processions, and performed a variety of other duties essential to a settled, civilized existence. For revenue, the *cabildos* relied on the rent or lease of town property, judicial fines, and other modest sources.

The authority and responsibility of the *cabildo* gave its members power, prestige, and (in some cases) income. As a result, particularly in the sixteenth century, there was substantial interest in securing *cabildo* positions. The crown responded by selling many of those posts of life and, in 1606, confirming that they could be bequeathed upon payment of specified taxes. The result was the solid entrenchment of local families in local offices for generations.

The substantial authority *cabildos* enjoyed in the sixteenth century declined in the seventeenth and eighteenth centuries. In the late eighteenth century, intendants reinvigorated many councils and increased their ability to meet their responsibilities. As representatives of local interests, the *cabildos* were well positioned to take the initiative in response to the abdications of CHARLES IV and FERDINAND VII in 1808, and many advocated greater local and regional autonomy.

In times of local crisis, eminent citizens were convoked to meet and deliberate with the *cabildo* in a *cabildo abierto*. In Buenos Aires, for example, a *cabildo abierto* convoked in 1810 set the course that ultimately led to independence.

CLARENCE H. HARING, *The Spanish Empire in America* (1947); JOHN PRESTON MOORE, *The Cabildo in Peru Under the Hapsburgs* (1954), and *The Cabildo in Peru Under the Bourbons* (1966); PETER MARZAHL, *Town in the Empire: Government, Politics, and Society in Seventeenth-Century Popayán* (1978).

MARK A. BURKHOLDER

**CABOCLO,** a Brazilian term originally applied to Amerindians. It was later expanded to refer to people of mixed Amerindian and European origin, and now commonly refers to the non-Indian people and culture of the Amazon region. The term is often used to distinguish the *caboclos* as "traditional" rural Amazonian inhabitants, as opposed to migrants and other newcomers—although the forebears of present-day Amazonian *caboclos* were also migrants, many of whom came during the rubber booms of the late nineteenth and early twentieth centuries.

The *caboclo* way of life and adaptation to the Amazon forest are similar to those of the Amerindian population. Scientists now study *caboclo* communities to learn more about the complex ecology of the rain forest. The present-day rubber tappers, Brazil nut gatherers, and other riverine populations involved in newly established Amazonian extractive reserves can all be considered *caboclos*.

The term *caboclo* is often used pejoratively and, depending on the context, can means someone of a lower class, an Indian, a "hick," or a bumpkin. Similar southern Brazilian terms include *jeca* and *caipira*. In Afro-Brazilian religions such as CANDOMBLÉ and UMBANDA, the *caboclo* is a deity in the pantheon, represented as an Indian.

EMILIO F. MORAN, "The Adaptive System of the Amazonian Caboclo," in *Man in the Amazon,* edited by Charles Wagley (1974); CHARLES WAGLEY, *Amazon Town* (1976); EUGENE PHILIP PARKER, ed., *The Amazon Caboclo: Historical and Contemporary Perspectives* (1985).

JUDITH LISANSKY

**CABOT, SEBASTIAN** (*b.* ca. 1474, *d.* 1557), Venetian or English navigator. Cabot was born in Bristol or Venice, the son of the explorer John Cabot. He served as cartographer to Henry VIII, accompanied an English force to Spain, and was appointed in 1518 by Holy Roman Emperor Charles V to the Spanish Council of the New Indies. He was named pilot major and in 1525 entrusted with an expedition to develop commercial ties with the Orient. Upon reaching South America and hearing tales from native inhabitants of enormous riches to be found upriver, Cabot chose to explore the Río de la Plata instead of continuing on to the Pacific. He also explored

the Paraguay and Paraná rivers, but returned empty-handed to Spain in 1530. As punishment for the failure of his expedition, he was banished to Africa for two years, but he was then pardoned and regained his title of pilot major. In later life, he returned to England, where he organized an association of merchants to sponsor future expeditions. He died in London.

HENRY HARRISSE, *John Cabot, the Discoverer of North America and Sebastian His Son* (1896); JUAN GIL, *Mitos y utopías del descubrimiento,* vols. 2–3 (1989).

HILARY BURGER

*See also* **Explorers.**

**CABRA.** *See* **African Brazilians: Color Termionology.**

**CABRAL, MANUEL DEL** (*b.* 7 March 1907), Dominican poet and writer. Cabral is considered the greatest poet of his country and one of the best of Latin America. He is admired for the variety of his themes, which range from the African roots of Dominican culture to eroticism. His writings include short stories, novels, essays, plays, poems, autobiographies, epistolary confessions, and parables. Cabral has received prizes and awards from many hispanic countries, including the Premio de la Fundación Argentina para la Poesía. His published works include *Trópico negro* (1941), *Manuel cuando no es tiempo, Compadre Mon* (1942), *Sangre mayor* (1945), *De este lado del mar* (1949), *Los huéspedes secretos* (1951), *La isla ofendida* (1965), *Los relámpagos lentos* (1966), *Los antitiempos* (1967), *Egloga de 2,000* (1970), and *Obra poetica* (1987).

KAI P. SCHOENHALS

**CABRAL, PEDRO ÁLVARES** (*b.* 1467 or 1468; *d.* ca. 1520), Portuguese explorer, leader of the follow-up fleet to Vasco da GAMA's first voyage to India. His expedition made the first recorded sighting of Brazil by the Portuguese on 22 April 1500.

On 15 February 1500, King Manuel I of Portugal chose Cabral, a *fidalgo* of the royal household, to command a fleet of thirteen ships and 1,200–1,500 men to sail for India. The purpose of the voyage was to establish trade and diplomatic relations with the *samorim* of Calicut and other rulers in India.

Cabral left Lisbon on 9 March 1500. On 22 April, Monte Pascoal, a mountain in what is now Brazil, was sighted. Cabral thought he had discovered an island, which he called Ilha de Vera Cruz. Sailing northward, he reached a harbor that he called Porto Seguro (now known as Baía Cabrália). He remained there for eight days and was on friendly terms with the region's inhabitants. The first Catholic Mass in Portuguese America was officiated by Frei Henrique Soares de Coimbra, one of eight Franciscans accompanying Cabral. He also celebrated the second Mass, which was attended by fifty or sixty Amerindians.

On 2 May, Cabral continued on to India. To announce to King Manuel I the discovery of the new land, soon to be called Santa Cruz and then Brazil, he sent one of his supply ships carrying reports by Cabral and by his captains, pilots, and other members of the fleet. Only two of the documents survived: the reports of Pero Vaz de Caminha and Mestre João Faras. Both are addressed to King Manuel and dated 1 May 1500. These two documents are the original manuscripts and seem to have been unknown to all the great chroniclers of the sixteenth century.

After sailing around the Cape of Good Hope and then reaching Calicut on 13 September 1500, Cabral battled Muslim traders and bombed Calicut. However, he established friendly relations with the Hindu ruler of Cochin before beginning his return voyage to Portugal. The *Anunciada*, one of the ships in the Cabral expedition, arrived in Lisbon on 23 June 1501. Cabral himself did not arrive in Lisbon until the end of July.

Despite the importance of Cabral's visit to Brazil and India, relatively little is known about the man, the expedition, and the motives behind the sighting of Brazil and Cabral's brief stay there. In the past, there has been considerable debate over whether Cabral's visit to Brazil was intentional or accidental and whether the Portuguese were aware of its existence before 1500. Although the issue continues to be debated, most scholars now believe that Cabral was unaware of Brazil's existence until winds and currents brought him within sight of land.

The only serious biography of Cabral in English is a short one by JAMES ROXBURGH MC CLYMONT, *Pedraluarez Cabral (Pedro Alluarez de Gouveia): His Progenitors, His Life, and His Voyage to America and India* (1914). The most important documents about Cabral's voyage (with an excellent introduction) have been compiled and translated by WILLIAM BROOKS GREENLEE in *The Voyage of Pedro Álvares Cabral to Brazil and India, from Contemporary Documents and Narratives* (1938). Included are the letters of Pero Vaz de Caminha and Mestre João Faras. The major documents in Portuguese have been collected in ABEL FONTOURA DA COSTA and ANTÓNIO BAIÃO, eds., *Os sete únicos documentos de 1500, conservados em Lisboa/Referentes à viagem de Pedro Álvares Cabral*, 2d ed. (1968). For the most recent analyses of Cabral's voyage, see HAROLD JOHNSON and MARIA BEATRIZ NIZZA DA SILVA, *Nova História da Expansão Portuguesa*. Vol. VI, *O império luso-brasileiro, 1500–1620* (1992), and FRANCIS A. DUTRA, "The Discovery of Brazil and Its Immediate Aftermath," in *Portugal, the Pathfinder*, edited by GEORGE D. WINUS (1994). Other useful discussions are found in LUIS DE ALBUQUERQUE, *Os descobrimentos portugueses* (1983); DAMIÃO PERES, *História dos descobrimentos portugueses*, 3d ed. (1983); and MAX JUSTO GUEDES, "O descobrimento do Brasil," in *História Naval Brasileira*, vol. 1, pt. 1 (1975), pp. 139–174.

FRANCIS A. DUTRA

*See also* **Explorers.**

**CABRAL DE MELO NETO, JOÃO.** *See* **Melo Neto, João Cabral de.**

**CABRERA, LYDIA** (*b.* 20 May 1900; *d.* 19 September 1991), Cuban writer and anthropologist. Daughter of a well-known lawyer and historian, she was tutored at home, where she also became entranced by the tales of the black servants. After her father's death, she studied painting and Oriental art at L'École du Louvre in Paris (1927–1930). Her stay in France coincided with European interest in primitive cultures, a trend that reawakened her childhood fascination with African Cuban culture. She began her new studies at the Sorbonne and did her research in Cuba in 1930. In Paris again, she wrote *Cuentos negros de Cuba* (1934), published in French (1936) to great acclaim. In 1938 she moved back to Cuba, intent on continuing her studies in African Cuban folklore and conducting interviews among the black population. A second collection of short stories (*¿Por qué? . . . Cuentos negros de Cuba*), written in the same direct and colorful style, appeared in 1948. In 1954 she published her first anthropological work, *El monte: Notas sobre las religiones, la magia, las supersticiones y el folklore de los negros criollos y del pueblo de Cuba*, considered by some to be her most important contribution to African Cuban culture. In the 1950s Cabrera became a consultant to the National Institute of Culture and published three major works: *Refranes de negros viejos* (1955), *Anagó: vocabulario Lucumí* (1957), and *La sociedad secreta Abakuá* (1958).

The Cuban Revolution burst upon her whirlwind of activity, and Cabrera moved to Miami, losing most of her research. Slowly, she reestablished her career and in 1970 published *Otán Iyebiyé: Las piedras preciosas* and the fictional tales of *Ayapá: Cuentos de Jicotea* (1971). After a stay in Spain to research some of her lost sources, Cabrera returned to Miami. She received two honorary degrees—from Denison (1977) and the University of Redlands (1981)—and continued her anthropological research: *La laguna sagrada de San Joaquín* (1973), *Yemayá y Ochún* (1974), *Anaforuana: ritual y símbolos de la iniciación en la sociedad secreta Abakuá* (1975), *La Regla Kimbisa del Santo Cristo del Buen Viaje* (1977), *Trinidad de Cuba* (1977), *Reglas de Congo, Palomonte Mayombe* (1979), *Los animales en el folklore y la magia de Cuba* (1988), *La lengua sagrada de los Ñáñigos* (1988), and *Supersticiones y buenos consejos* (1988). She also published two collections of short stories: *Francisco y Francisca: Chascarrillos de negros viejos* (1976) and *Cuentos para grandes, chicos y retrasados mentales* (1983).

JOSÉ ANTONIO MADRIGAL and REYNALDO SÁNCHEZ, eds. *Homenaje a Lydia Cabrera* (1978); NICOLÁS KANELLOS, ed., *Biographical Dictionary of Hispanic Literature in the United States: The Literature of Puerto Ricans, Cuban Americans, and other Hispanic Writers* (1989); JULIO A. MARTÍNEZ, ed., *Dictionary of Twentieth-Century Cuban Literature* (1990).

MARÍA A. SALGADO

**CABRERA, MIGUEL** (*b.* 1695; *d.* 16 May 1768), Mexican painter. Although doubts exist about the authenticity of the document that gives his birth date and nothing is known about his training, Cabrera's will makes it clear that he was a native of Oaxaca. It is believed that by 1719 Cabrera was in Mexico City, where he became the most important painter of his day. With other artists he attempted to found an academy in Mexico City in 1753, and in 1756 he published *Maravilla americana,* an account of his examination of the original image of the Virgin of GUADALUPE. Among his many works, those for the Jesuits are outstanding in number and quality; but he had numerous other important patrons, including the archbishop of Mexico City and the miner José de la Borda in Taxco. His paintings display a sense of ample space and often brilliant, light coloring. Sweetness of expression is a hallmark of his religious figures, whose repetitive portrayal was much appreciated in his time and in the nineteenth century, but has occasioned twentieth-century criticism. Cabrere's reputation has also suffered because of the disparate quality of many paintings signed by or attributed to him, a number of them executed in what must have been a large workshop. He is also known for his portraits and for an extraordinary series of *casta* paintings, depictions of the mixed races that peopled New Spain.

ABELARDO CARRILLO Y GARIEL, *El pintor Miguel Cabrera* (1966); MARÍA CONCEPCIÓN GARCÍA SAIZ, *La pintura colonial en el Museo de América,* vol. 1 (1980).

CLARA BARGELLINI

**CABRERA INFANTE, GUILLERMO** (*b.* 22 April 1929), Cuban novelist and essayist. Cabrera Infante was born in Gibara in Oriente Province. In 1947 he moved to Havana with his parents and began studying medicine at the University of Havana. After quickly deciding to take up writing, he abandoned medicine for journalism. In 1952 he was arrested and fined for publishing a short story that contained English profanities. In the late 1950s he began to earn prizes with his short stories.

Meanwhile, his passion for the cinema led him to film reviewing. With the pseudonym G. Caín [*Cabrera Infante*] he wrote film reviews and articles on the cinema for the weekly *Carteles,* becoming its editor in chief in 1957. He was the founder of Cinemateca de Cuba, the Cuban Film Society, over which he presided from 1951 to 1956. In 1959 he became director of the Cuban Film Institute and of the literary magazine *Lunes de revolución.* In 1962 he served the Cuban government as cultural attaché in Belgium. In 1964 he received the prestigious Biblioteca Breve prize for his novel *Tres tristes tigres* (1971). In 1965 he decided to break with the Cuban government, leaving his diplomatic post and permanently settling in London.

As of the mid-1990s, Cabrera Infante was the best-known living Cuban author. *Tres tristes tigres,* translated into English as *Three Trapped Tigers,* won him world-wide recognition. In this novel, as has been pointed out by such eminent critics as Emir Rodríguez Monegal, language itself is the main preoccupation. Here, too, as in all of Cabrera Infante's work, there is a great deal of humor, especially word games and puns. Because of this aspect of his work, he has been compared to Russian emigré writer Vladimir Nabokov. His mastery of the English language—one of his later novels, *Holy Smoke* (1985), was written in English—has also begged comparison with Joseph Conrad. Cabrera Infante, who became a British citizen, has said ironically that he is as English as muffins and is a happy subject of the queen. Besides *Tres tristes tigres,* some of his best-known works are *La Habana para un infante difunto* (1984) and *Vista del amanecer en el trópico* (1974). His novels have been widely translated.

ROSA MARÍA PEREDA, *Guillermo Cabrera Infante* (1979); STEPHANIE MERRIM, *Logos and the Word: The Novel of Language and Linguistic Motivation in* Grande sertao, veredas *and* Tres tristes tigres (1983); ROSEMARY GEISDORFER FEAL, *Novel Lives: The Fictional Autobiographies of Guillermo Cabrera Infante and Mario Vargas Llosa* (1986); DINORAH HERNÁNDEZ LIMA, *Versiones y re-versiones históricas en la obra de Cabrera Infante* (1990).

ROBERTO VALERO

**CABRERA LOBATO, LUIS** (*b.* 17 July 1876; *d.* 1954), leading Mexican intellectual remembered for a brilliant speech before the Chamber of Deputies advocating an agrarian reform law in 1912, for hundreds of political essays written under the pen name of Blas Urrea, and for his complete intellectual independence from successive post-revolutionary governments.

Cabrera, the son of a humble baker, Gertrudis Lobato, attended the National Preparatory School (1889–1893). He went on to complete his law degree from the National School of Law in 1901, after which he practiced law and taught. A cofounder of the Anti-Reelectionist Party in 1909, he became dean of the National School of Law and a federal deputy in 1912, later serving as an agent of the Constitutionalists in the United States and as Venustiano CARRANZA's treasury secretary. He retired from politics in 1920, and though he was twice offered the presidential candidacy by opposition parties—in 1933 and 1946—he declined to run.

LUIS CABRERA, *Obras Completas,* 4 vols. (1972–1975); RAMÓN EDUARDO RUIZ, "Review of *Obras Completas,* vols. 1–4, by Luis Cabrera," in *Hispanic American Historical Review* (February 1978): 127–130; and FERNANDO ZERTUCHE MUÑOZ, *Luis Cabrera: Una visión de México* (1988).

RODERIC AI CAMP

*See also* **Mexico: Political Parties.**

**CACAO INDUSTRY.** The cacao bean (*theobroma cacao*) comes from the large fleshy pod of a tropical bush or small tree. The plant is American, probably Amazonian in origin, and by the time of the European conquest had long ago diffused by unknown means to other parts of tropical America.

The bean yields chocolate, a nutritious fatty food or drink. In MESOAMERICA cacao was domesticated many centuries before the Europeans arrived, and although tended groves grew on various parts of the Caribbean coast, such as the Gulf of Honduras and Tabasco, it was on the Pacific coastal plain, stretching all the way from Colima to the Gulf of Fonseca, that most production concentrated. Cacao beans were used for coinage, even into the Spanish colonial period, but it was as a drink that it found most favor, and the areas where it was cultivated were coveted by merchants and military states. Large quantities were collected as tribute and traded, and the drink enjoyed considerable prestige, so much so that in at least some areas only the aristocracy was permitted to drink it.

Whatever limits that were placed on its production and consumption disappeared after the European conquest, and cacao became a drink of mass consumption among the Mesoamerican native peoples, especially those of Central Mexico. Spaniards at first found the various chocolate concoctions, most of which contained maize gruel, CHILES, and anatto for coloring, to be unpalatable, but they quickly seized the business opportunities involved, and merchants and *encomenderos* dominated cacao plantations and sales.

SOCONUSCO, a satellite of the Aztec Empire, was the first area of extensive growth and export in the sixteenth century, but as it declined Izalcos, in present-day El Salvador, became the main producer. It, in its turn, was challenged and surpassed by the area around Guayaquil in Ecuador and then by the tropical valleys of Venezuela, and these two regions remained the main rivals for and suppliers of the Mexican market throughout the colonial centuries.

Europeans found that the addition of sugar and vanilla made chocolate tasty, and its consumption spread from Spain all over western Europe. Although eventually surpassed by coffee and tea, it remained entrenched in Catholic countries because although nutritious and filling, it was not prohibited during fasts.

As its use increased, the Dutch, who had captured the offshore island of Curaçao in 1634, began to trade illegally for Venezuelan cacao. Plantations then sprouted in Trinidad, Jamaica, Santo Domingo, and in the French colony of Saint-Domingue. In spite of these rivalries Guayaquil supplied most of Mexico's needs, and Venezuelan cacao dominated the European market throughout the eighteenth century.

Venezuelan production began to decline around 1800, and the destruction caused by the wars of independence further weakened the industry. Amazonian Brazil, long a producer of wild Marañón cacao, filled some of the gap, but Guayaquil, where production quadrupled in the second decade of the nineteenth century, was the main beneficiary.

In the 1820s, with Guayaquil still dominant, important changes in chocolate manufacturing and consumption pushed demand to new heights. In Holland, Conrad Van Houten developed a process for extracting cacao butter, and for manufacturing oil- and fat-free cocoa, a more digestible drink for children. About half a century later the Swiss pioneered the production of milk chocolate and, by the end of the century, hard chocolates, with cut flowers, had become the gifts associated with courtship.

Chocolate soon passed from being a luxury product for women and children to being an item of mass consumption. The emergence of giant firms such as Hershey in the United States; Fry, Cadbury, and Rowntree in Great Britain; Lindt and Tobler in Switzerland transformed marketing and consumption and created massive demand and new areas of production. The growth of the chocolate industry in the twentieth century has been spectacular. Concentrated in New York and London, the cacao market is now worldwide and highly competitive.

Ecuador, the leader in the 1820s, was the first producer for the world market, and the Guayaquil basin, supplied with labor from the depressed *sierra*, produced about 7,000 tons per year by the early 1840s. There it stagnated. Yellow fever and political turbulence hampered Ecuadorian growth until the 1870s, when a new spurt sent annual export to twenty thousand tons by 1900, a trade which supplied almost two-thirds of state revenues.

Venezuelan cacao, while it never regained the prosperity of 1800, remained in second place among Latin American producers until it was passed by Brazil and Trinidad around 1870. Coffee had become Venezuela's leading export.

Competition among Latin American states was not the main problem, however. From early intensive plantations on the islands of São Tomé and Principe, the leading suppliers of cacao in the world in the first decade of the twentieth century, intensive cultivation spread to the African mainland, where Cameroon, Nigeria, Ghana, and, more recently, the Ivory Coast became the world leaders.

Ecuador more or less kept its place until the end of World War I, although competition was affecting prices. Then the groves were hit by witch broom disease. Ecuador converted gradually to bananas, as Venezuela had to coffee, although Ecuador still exports large quantities of cacao. Brazil's cacao, most of which went to the United States, had ceased to be of the "wild" variety, and was now produced in southern Bahia. The Hershey company grew its own cacao in Cuba until its plantations were confiscated by the Cuban revolutionary government in the late 1950s. The Dominican Republic and Venezuela also export considerable quantities.

The great days of American cacao seem to have gone, however, and this American cultigen, which moved through so many Latin American tropical regions and which supplied Latin America with a major trade and export commodity for about four centuries, has now retreated to a minor role. Nigeria and Ghana supply about two-thirds of current world needs.

DORA BORJA LEÓN and ADÁM SZÁSZDI, "El comercio de cacao de Guayaquil," in *Revista de Historia de América* 57–58 (1964): 1–50; JAMES F. BERGMAN, "The Distribution of Cacao Cultivation in Pre-Columbian America," in *Annals of the Association of American Geographers* 59 (March 1969): 85–96; DAURIL ALDEN, *The Significance of Cacao Production in the Amazon Region During the Late Colonial Period: An Essay in Comparative Economic History* (1976); JEAN ASSOMOU, *L'économie du cacao* (1977); MANUEL CHIRIBOGA, *Jornaleros y gran propietarios en 135 años de exportación: Cacaotera, 1790–1925* (1980); NIKITA HARWICH, *Histoire du Chocolat* (1992); EUGENIO PIÑERO, *Veracruz and the Caracas Cacao Trade* (1994).

MURDO J. MACLEOD

**CACAXTLA,** one of many sites in highland Mexico that flourished between the seventh and tenth centuries. Located approximately 80 miles east of Mexico City in the state of Tlaxcala, it contains some of the best-preserved pre-Columbian murals ever discovered in MESOAMERICA. The main mound (*el gran basamento*), stretching over an area approximately 1,200 feet long and rising more than 80 feet, was first excavated in 1975. In its heyday, this great structure rose in giant horizontal terraces interrupted by massive vertical buttresses of masonry. Stairways and columned buildings had shaded portals facing outward from all sides and at all levels. The buildings show at least eight major stages of construction, each with its own pattern of stucco-covered adobe walls, indicating that the *gran basamento* was a combination palace and administrative center.

*Cacaxtla* means "the place of the merchant's back-pack" in NAHUATL, and its murals show warrior-traders carrying weapons and standard consumer goods like obsidian, textiles, and pumice stones for grinding corn as they traveled to other pre-Columbian groups. It is not definitively known which people built and inhabited this site, but currently scholars are leaning toward the Olmeca-Xicalanca, an obscure group with possible origins in the Gulf coast area. Its location in the so-called Teotihuacán Corridor enabled its residents to dominate the traffic between the Gulf coast and the cities of the Central Valley of Mexico.

The justly famous murals show in impressive detail a victory or staged postwar sacrificial ceremony in which jaguar warriors spear unarmed soldiers dressed as birds who writhe hideously at their feet, spreading blood everywhere. Also dominating all the murals are Venus symbols, representing the dreaded "wasp star," which, some argue, celestially determined the occurrence of battles. In their totality, the murals depict a vision of the cycle of life.

Archaeologists date the latest paintings at Cacaxtla at approximately A.D. 790. With the decline of TEOTIHUA-

CÁN, a chain reaction of collapse occurred throughout Mesoamerica, causing residents to abandon the site.

SONIA LOMBARDO DE RUIZ et al., *Cacaxtla: El lugar donde muere la lluvia en la tierra* (1986); GEORGE STUART, "Cacaxtla," in *National Geographic*, 182 (September 1992): 120–136.

GEORGE STUART

**CÁCERES, ANDRÉS AVELINO** (*b.* 1833; *d.* 1923), Peruvian military hero and president (1886–1890, 1894–1895), commander of the highland guerrilla resistance to the Chilean occupation of coastal Peru during the WAR OF THE PACIFIC (1879–1883). Like Francisco Bolognesi, Cáceres was drawn to military life in the 1850s in support of General Ramón CASTILLA against Generals José Rufino ECHENIQUE and Manuel Ignacio VIVANCO. During Castilla's second term in office, Cáceres served as military attaché to the Peruvian legation in France. Upon his return to Peru he supported Colonel Mariano Ignacio PRADO's 1865 revolution against General Juan Antonio PEZET's unpopular though legitimate government. When Manuel Pardo was elected as the first civilian president in 1872, Cáceres served as a faithful military officer. At this time he began to express political differences with his life-long foe Nicolás de PIÉROLA, who conspired against Pardo.

Born in Ayacucho, Cáceres had extensive family and landowning interests in the south-central and central highlands of Peru, which provided him with the power base necessary to conduct his military campaigns against the Chilean army and to advance his own political ambitions. During the War of the Pacific, Cáceres fought in the battles of San Francisco and TARAPACÁ and in the 1881 defense of Lima in San Juan and Miraflores. Wounded in the latter battle, he hid in Lima and later went to the strategic central highland town of Jauja to initiate and lead his military and political resistance, the La Breña campaign. His guerrilla tactics earned him the name "Wizard of the Andes." The support his forces received from peasant communities fighting for their livelihood constituted the key factor of this protracted resistance.

However, Peruvian military and political leaders during the Chilean occupation were divided into several factions. Some, like Francisco García Calderón, had been imprisoned and exiled by the Chilean army. One such faction, led by General Miguel IGLESIAS, signed the Treaty of ANCÓN (1883), which allowed the Chilean army to withdraw from Lima. Cáceres opposed and fought Iglesias and assumed the presidency in 1886. During his term of office the GRACE contract (1889), a costly settlement with foreign creditors, was signed to establish the bases for the economic recovery of Peru in the 1890s. In 1890, Cáceres handed power to General Remigio MORALES BERMÚDEZ, who died in office in 1894. Cáceres's subsequent attempts to regain power faced a popular insurrection led by Piérola, who succeeded in forcing Cáceres to resign and leave the country. After a long exile Cáceres returned to Peru and was awarded the honorific title of marshal in 1919. He died in Lima.

RORY MILLER, "The Making of the Grace Contract: British Bondholders and the Peruvian Government, 1885–1890," in *Journal of Latin American Studies* 8 (1978): 73–100; FLORENCIA E. MALLON, *The Defense of Community in Peru's Central Highlands: Peasant Struggle and Capitalist Transition, 1860–1940* (1983).

ALFONSO W. QUIROZ

**CÁCERES, ESTHER DE** (*b.* 1903; *d.* 1971), Uruguayan poet and educator. After earning a degree in medicine (1929), Cáceres taught humanities at the Teacher Training Institute and the Institute of Advanced Studies, both in Montevideo. She belonged to a cohort of leading women intellectuals and literary figures. Her first book of poetry was *Las ínsulas extrañas* (1929), followed in rapid succession by *Canción* (1931), *Libro de la soledad* (1935), *Los cielos* (1935), and many others. Especially noteworthy is "*Concierto de amor*" *y otros poemas,* with a prologue by Gabriela MISTRAL (1951). In Cáceres's early poetry, the mood alternates between melancholy and joy, as felt through mystical communion with God and other religious experiences. Later works—*Los cantos del destierro* (1963), *Tiempo y abismo* (1965), and *Canto desierto* (1969)—focus more on the subjective anguish caused by metaphysical displacement and the poet's immersion in the turbulent social and political circumstances of the time.

SARAH BOLLO, *Literatura uruguaya, 1807–1965,* vol. 2 (1965); FRANCISCO AGUILERA and GEORGETTE MAGASSY DORN, *The Archive of Hispanic Literature on Tape: A Descriptive Guide* (1974).

WILLIAM H. KATRA

**CÁCERES, RAMÓN** (*b.* 15 December 1866; *d.* 19 November 1911), president of the Dominican Republic (1906–1911). Born in Moca, in the north-central part of the country, to a distinguished and prosperous family, Cáceres, a landowner, was in the forefront of the opposition to president Ulises HEUREAUX (1882–1899). Cáceres earned national recognition when, on 26 July 1899, he assassinated the dictator during a public appearance in Moca. The ensuing political chaos resulted in several years of unstable regimes. Cáceres was forced into exile in 1903 but returned in 1904 to become vice president under Carlos Morales. When the latter abandoned his post in 1906, Cáceres assumed the office.

Cáceres's presidency was one of the most peaceful and prosperous periods in Dominican history. He expanded federal power without debilitating local government, reformed the constitution, began an ambitious public works program, and transferred many privately owned utilities to the public realm. The shifts in economic power engendered by his reform earned him powerful enemies, and there were several unsuccessful

plots against his government. In 1905, a United States customs receivership was established. Cáceres welcomed the prosperity it brought but remained concerned about financial dependence on the United States. Then in 1911, as he took his evening ride, Cáceres was assassinated. His death was followed by a resurgence of political and economic disorder and, ultimately, by the U.S. occupation of the Dominican Republic in 1916.

SELDEN RODMAN, *Quisqueya: A History of the Dominican Republic* (1964), pp. 102–127; PEDRO TRONCOSO SÁNCHEZ, *Ramón Cáceres* (1964).

SARA FLEMING

**CACIQUE, CACIQUISMO.** When the Columbian expeditions reached the Greater Antilles, they found most of the land dominated by chiefdoms. Hispaniola had probably reached a more consolidated level, with fewer, larger, and more powerful entities, some of them perhaps monarchies. The rulers called themselves, at least to the Spanish ear, "caciques," and those who did not immediately oppose the Spaniards found themselves in the tenuous position of brokers or administrators for the Spanish regime. Nearly all finally revolted and were killed in battle or executed.

Spaniards carried the word *caciques* to their conquests of the mainland and took to using the term to describe Indian leaders at the town or village level. There is considerable academic debate as to the roles and fate of this indigenous lower aristocracy. Some have emphasized their importance as brokers, tax collectors, and petty administrators for the local Spanish officials or the *encomenderos*, and discuss how caciques in many areas were squeezed between increasing demands from a growing Spanish population and a declining number of Indian subjects. Evidence for this position consists of data on the number of caciques killed or demoted, and of instances of usurpers placed in theoretically hereditary positions, often, after the early years, by Spanish manipulation of elections. These scholars also show that the imposition of Spanish systems of town government—*cabildos*, or town councils, headed by *alcaldes, regidores*, and sometimes *gobernadores*—was sometimes an attempt to shunt aside traditional cacique kinships.

Others have debated these conclusions, arguing that the native aristocracy survived in some areas for the entire colonial period. These caciques became true brokers and fended off some Spanish intrusions as well as provided for community needs. They became the repositories for native traditions and cultural resistance. This view also points to instances where *cabildos* were skillfully taken over by members of old ruling lineages, so that these caciques became the *alcaldes* and *regidores*. In a few areas there is also evidence that where the office of *gobernador* existed, it was sometimes reserved for a member of a hereditary ruling group. In other cases the

A Carib cacique and his wife. © BODLEIAN LIBRARY, OXFORD.

position was clearly a direct Spanish imposition, and dominated the elected *cabildo*.

It would be safe to say only that the activities, cultural attitudes, and ultimate fates of the colonial cacique class varied widely over time and place between the extremes of rapid extinction and relatively prosperous independence and continuity.

The nineteenth-century history of the term *cacique*, and of its extension, *caciquismo*, is unclear, but they came to be used to describe various kinds of rural *patrones* (bosses, or strongmen) and their systems of wielding power, both in Spanish-speaking America and in Spain. (The Brazilian institution of CORONELISMO has many similarities.)

Some have found the origins of caciquismo in the authoritarian regime of the colonial period, and in the regionalism and disarticulation of that era. Others consider the outbreak of independence, the disappearance of the colonial system, and the resultant legitimacy vacuum as the situation that led to the emergence of local bosses. Some reject explanations based on the colonial or independence periods and have emphasized such factors as: the weakness of the infant nation states which fostered anarchy or virtual autonomy on the peripheries; the lack of political institutions or parties which led people to pledge their allegiances to persons rather than movements; the necessity for a network of patron-client relationships in a hierarchically structured society with chronic insecurity and a tradition of paternalism and LATIFUNDIA; and, in some cases, the desire of undemocratic elites to retain power by using strongmen puppets to do their work of social control.

All of these propositions have been contradicted by yet other scholars. National rulers in the capital, for example, have used coalitions of regional caciques to maintain and even increase their power. Elites have been humbled by local populists, especially when these rural bosses make their bids for the presidency and national power.

The connection between the rural cacique and the national CAUDILLO has also caused debate. Some see them as different generically. Others argue that the caudillo was often an insurgent regional cacique who had seized power in the capital; that is, functionally and systemically the two institutions were linked.

Either the terms require further scrutiny or, perhaps, they have become so stretched by the diversity of explanations and processes packed into them that they have become somewhat empty generalizations.

ROGER M. HAIGH, *Martín Güemes: Tyrant or Tool? A Study of the Sources of Power of an Argentine Caudillo* (1968); FERNANDO DÍAZ DÍAZ, *Caudillos y caciques: Antonio López de Santa Anna y Juan Álvarez* (1972); ROBERT KERN, *The Caciques, Oligarchical Politics, and the System of Caciquismo in the Luso-Hispanic World* (1973); SUSAN RAMÍREZ, "The 'Dueño de Indios': Thoughts on the Consequences of the Shifting Bases of Power of the '*Curaca de los Viejos Antiguos*' Under the Spanish in Sixteenth-Century Peru," in *Hispanic American Historical Review* 67, no. 4 (1987): 575–610; LUIS RONIGER, "Caciquismo and Coronelismo: Contextual Dimensions of Patron Brokerage in Mexico and Brazil," in *Latin American Research Review* 22, no. 2 (1987): 71–99; SAMUEL M. WILSON, *Hispaniola: Caribbean Chiefdoms in the Age of Columbus* (1990); ROBERT S. HASKETT, *Indigenous Rulers: An Ethnohistory of Town Government in Colonial Cuernavaca* (1991); JOHN LYNCH, *Caudillos in Spanish America, 1800–1850* (1992).

MURDO J. MACLEOD

*See also* **Encomienda; Patronage.**

**CACOS,** rebel peasants from the north and west of Haiti in the nineteenth century and during the U.S. occupation (especially 1918 to 1920). Similar in origins to the *piquets* of southern Haiti, many were from the middle or "better-off" levels of the peasantry. Cacos first became of political importance during the so-called Cacos War. Allied with elements of the army, they opposed President Sylvain SALNAVE (1867–1870) and were instrumental in his overthrow. Thereafter they were used by insurgent politicians to achieve power but seldom had influence on central government policy.

From 1915 to 1 October 1918, the U.S. army of occupation in Haiti imposed a *corvée* (compulsory road repair service) against which the Cacos rebelled, first under Charlemagne PÉRALTE (1917–1919) and when he was killed (1919), under Benoît Batraville. The defeat of the Cacos by the U.S. forces took a large and expensive campaign with widespread death and destruction.

MURDO J. MACLEOD

**CAFÉ FILHO, JOÃO** (*b.* 3 February 1889; *d.* 20 February 1970), president of Brazil (1954–1955). Lawyer, strike leader, and popular opposition figure in his native state of Rio Grande do Norte, Café Filho helped the 1930 revolution that brought Getúlio VARGAS to the Brazilian presidency. Without completing the required course work for a degree, he passed an examination that admitted him to the bar. Elected to Congress in 1934, he opposed repression by Vargas. In 1937–1938 he spent six months in exile in Argentina to avoid arrest. He did not return to politics until 1945, near the end of the Vargas dictatorship, and, together with São Paulo's Ademar de BARROS, founded what became the Partido Social Progressista (PRP), which returned him to Congress.

Following Barros's 1950 alliance with Vargas, Café Filho became Vargas's running mate and was narrowly elected vice president despite Catholic objections to his leftist past. When Vargas committed suicide on 24 August 1954, Café Filho assumed the presidency. Members of his cabinet, regarded as conservative and anti-Vargas, opposed the inauguration of Juscelino KUBITSCHEK, elected in 1955, but war minister Henrique LOTT favored the inauguration and carried out a coup on 11 November 1955, while Café Filho was hospitalized for a heart ailment. When Café Filho was released from the hospital later in November, Lott's troops prevented him from resuming the presidency. Congress, favoring Kubitschek's inauguration, declared Café Filho unable to govern, a judgment upheld by the Supreme Court. Before his death, Café Filho served (1961–1969) on the accounts tribunal responsible for ruling on the legality of financial steps taken by the Guanabara State government.

JOÃO CAFÉ FILHO, *Do sindicato ao Catete* (1966); JOHN W. F. DULLES, *Unrest in Brazil: Political-Military Crises, 1955–1964* (1970).

JOHN W. F. DULLES

**CAFUSO/CAFUS.** *See* **African Brazilians: Color Terminology.**

**CAIRÚ, VISCONDE DE.** *See* **Silva Lisboa, José da.**

**CAJAMARCA,** a Quechua word meaning "place or town of cold" that is the name of an important city, province, and department (created in 1855) in northern Peru. Because the department encompasses semitropical valleys and Andean highlands, agricultural and mining production is varied and rich. Its most important commercial crops are sugar, tobacco, and rice. Dairy farming is also important. Miners extract copper, lead, silver, zinc, and iron, especially from the mines of Hualgayoc and Chilete.

Cajamarca has long been important in the history of Peru. It was the indigenous population center where in 1532 Francisco PIZARRO first made contact with the Inca ATAHUALPA, eventually imprisoning and executing him there, despite the payment of a large ransom. Soon thereafter, the native inhabitants of Cajamarca were given in *encomienda* to Melchor Verdugo, their first and perhaps most famous trustee. It was Verdugo who began Spanish silver mining at Chilete as early as 1540, using the Cajamarquinos as laborers.

For most of the colonial era, Cajamarca was known for its abundant crops of wheat, barley, and corn; its deer and smaller game; and its good pastures for cattle grazing. The systematic exploitation of Hualgayoc's silver deposits begun in the late eighteenth century brought a new round of prosperity to the region. The inhabitants had, by this time, also earned fame for their weaving skills.

In the nineteenth century, Cajamarca was the home base of Miguel IGLESIAS's efforts to influence Peruvian politics. During the WAR OF THE PACIFIC (1879–1883), the department was invaded by the Chileans. The city served as the site of a congress of delegates from Peru's northern provinces who elected Iglesias president. In late 1882, this meeting of congress resulted in negotiations leading to the Treaty of Ancón and the end of the war.

CARLOS BURGA LARREA, *Diccionario geográfico e histórico de Cajamarca* (1983); FERNANDO SILVA SANTISTEBAN, WALDEMAR ESPINOZA SORIANO, ROGGER RAVINES, et al., comps., *Historia de Cajamarca: Siglos XVI–XVIII*, vol. 3 (1986).

SUSAN E. RAMÍREZ

**CAJAMARCA, PRE-COLUMBIAN.** Cajamarca is famous as the location of the capture and execution in 1533 of Inca ATAHUALPA by Francisco PIZARRO, leading to the collapse of the INCA Empire. At an elevation of 9,022 feet, Cajamarca is in a large intermontane valley in the north-central Peruvian Andes. The region's prehistory dates to at least 1500 B.C.

Excavations at the site of Huacaloma produced a chronological sequence based on pottery types and radiocarbon dates. The earliest evidence for permanent settlements dates to Early Huacaloma (1500–1000 B.C.), a period when inhabitants of Cajamarca subsisted by deer hunting, gathering, and incipient agriculture (guinea pigs, possibly plant foods), and constructed relatively small ceremonial structures. The brown, often coarse pottery was shaped into neckless jars and other forms and decorated with incisions and appliqué. Late Huacaloma (1000–500 B.C.) communities continued to pursue a mixed economy, but experienced population growth and greater interaction with other regions in the northern Andes. Late Huacaloma pottery displayed new forms, including stirrup spout vessels, variously burnished, painted, and incised.

The Layzón period (500–200 B.C.) represents a sharp break with previous patterns, marked by the replacement of deer hunting with llama herding, the construction of large public buildings, the disappearance of neckless jars and stirrup spout bottles, and the introduction of pottery styles possibly from outside the Cajamarca Basin.

The Cajamarca ceramic tradition developed around 200 B.C. It consists of a cluster of pottery styles distinguished by white or light-colored kaolin pastes. Variations in Cajamarca-tradition ceramics mark different phases in Cajamarca history prior to the Spanish Conquest.

The hilltop locations of Initial Cajamarca (200 B.C.–A.D. 100) sites suggest an increase in population and conflict. Changes in settlement patterns indicate that the small, competitive Initial Cajamarca chiefdoms were integrated into larger political units during the Early Cajamarca (A.D. 100–500) and Middle Cajamarca (A.D. 500–850) periods. By 850 Coyor dominated the Cajamarca region and east to the Marañón River drainage. Middle Cajamarca ceramics were traded throughout the central Andes. Late Cajamarca (A.D. 850–1250) was a period of economic and political decline, indicated by a decrease in the number and complexity of settlements. The Final Cajamarca phase (A.D. 1200–1550) experienced renewed economic and political integration, as a confederation of independent chiefdoms emerged, partially represented by the large sites of Guzmango Viejo, Tantarica, and Santa Delia.

Inca conquest of the Cajamarca region occurred around 1460. The Inca probably founded the city of Cajamarca, creating a provincial center from which to rule much of northern Peru. The seat of a province with 60,000 inhabitants, Inca Cajamarca had a population of 2,000, a royal palace, temples, storehouses, and a central plaza that the chronicler Estete described as larger than any in Spain.

Pizarro and his force entered Cajamarca on 15 November 1532; Atahualpa and an army of 30,000 were camped on the outskirts of the city. Pizarro concealed his forces in the streets and buildings surrounding the plaza. Atahualpa was carried into the plaza on a litter, accompanied by courtiers and servants. The Spanish attacked and Pizarro captured Atahualpa. As ransom, Atahualpa ordered that a room be filled with gold and silver, the famous Cuarto del Rescate, but nonetheless Atahualpa was tied to a post and garroted in the plaza of Cajamarca. Spaniards subsequently destroyed Inca Cajamarca. Only the Cuarto del Rescate remains.

HENRI REICHLEN and PAULE REICHLEN, "Recherches archéologiques dans les Andes de Cajamarca: Premier rapport de la Mission Ethnologique Française au Pérou Septentrional," in *Journal de la Société des Américanistes* 38 (1949): 137–174; AUGUSTÍN DE ZARATE, *The Discovery and Conquest of Peru*, translated by J. M. Cohen (1981); JAPANESE SCIENTIFIC EXPEDITION TO NUCLEAR AMERICA, *Excavations at Huacaloma in the Cajamarca Valley, Peru, 1979* (1982); DANIEL JULIEN, "Late Pre-Inkaic Ethnic Groups in Highland Peru: An Archaeological-Ethnohistorical Model of the Political Geography of the Cajamarca Region," in *Latin American Antiquity* 4 (1993): 246–273.

JERRY D. MOORE

**CAJEME** (José María Leyva; *b.* 1837; *d.* 21 April 1887), YAQUI INDIAN leader. After leaving the Yaqui valley in southern Sonora in his youth, he became a dependable volunteer member of the state forces backing the liberal CAUDILLO Governor Ignacio Pesqueira whenever there was a crisis, including campaigns against his own people in the late 1860s. Rewarding Cajeme with the post of district administrator of the Yaqui valley (1874), the Pesqueira government assumed he would help obtain the Yaquis' total and permanent submission. Instead, he mobilized them (and neighboring Mayos) to achieve the status of separate nations which the two tribes had long claimed was rightfully theirs. Cajeme restructured and disciplined Yaqui society toward greater economic security and military preparedness: instituting a tax system; controlling external trade; reviving the mission practice of community plots and institutionalizing the tribal tradition of popular assemblies as decision making bodies; amassing war material. But by the early 1880s, the advantage of political instability from Pesqueira's fall had given way to national and state governments united in their zeal to colonize the rich lands of the YAQUI and Mayo valleys, employing a large, unrelenting, military force to do so. Though Cajeme was defeated and captured by Ángel Martínez at San José de Guaymas, and executed, Yaqui guerrilla resistance continued through 1910.

RAMÓN CORRAL, "Biografía de José María Leyva Cajeme," *Obras históricas*, vol. 1 (1886), pp. 147–192; CLAUDIO DABDOUB, *Historia de El Valle del Yaqui* (1964), pp. 115–138; EVELYN HUDEHART, *Yaqui Resistance and Survival: The Struggle for Land and Autonomy, 1821–1910* (1984), pp. 93–117.

STUART F. VOSS

**CAKCHIQUELS.** *See* **Kaqchikels.**

**CALAKMUL** is a large MAYA ruin of the Classic period (A.D. 514–990), located in the central Petén in the state of Campeche, Mexico. Huge (over 1.2 miles in diameter), Calakmul has yet to be fully mapped. Most of its 113 stelae—a record for any Maya site—have been recovered. Seventy-nine of these stelae are sculptured and forty are plain. Most are large and flat—more or less in the TIKAL style—but a few are unique in having a male figure on one side and a female on the other, as well as male and female figures facing each other on the same stelae—perhaps representing a royal marriage or a period of joint rule. Recently attempts have been made to decipher some of these stelae, and there are indications of long periods of rule by local dynasties. In fact, Calakmul may have been one of the four initial empires of the Maya lowlands starting as early as A.D. 731, for the city has its own distinctive emblem glyph. Although its pyramids lack the elaborate roof combs of Tikal, the architecture, city planning, and other artistic features of Calakmul show that it fell within the Tikal sphere of influence. There are also indications of conflict with Tikal.

A distinctive feature of Calakmul, unlike other Maya sites, is a limestone ledge sculpture, 21 feet long and 17 feet wide, showing a line of captive figures with their hands tied behind their backs and connected to a huge captive figure standing 9 feet tall. Future explorations will undoubtedly reveal other distinctive features, and full deciphering of Calakmul's many stelae and sculptures may well write another unique history for the Maya region.

JOYCE MARCUS, *The Inscriptions of Calakmul* (1987).

RICHARD S. MacNEISH

**CALCAÑO, JOSÉ ANTONIO** (*b.* 23 March 1900), Venezuelan composer. Calcaño was born and educated in Caracas. After studying for a year at the Academy of Music in Bern, Switzerland, he returned to Caracas, where he had an outstanding career as a music teacher, music historian, and choir director. His compositions contributed greatly to giving Venezuelan music its particular character. His best-known work is the ballet *Miranda en Rusia.* Also well-known is his cantata "Desolación y gloria," written in honor of Simón Bolívar. Calcaño's book *La ciudad y su música* (1958) presents an overview of the musical life of Caracas from colonial times to the 1950s.

OSCAR G. PELÁEZ ALMENGOR

**CALCHAQUÍ, JUAN** (*d.* ca. 1600), Indian chief. In the middle of the sixteenth century, Juan Calchaquí was the principal chief of the region of Tolombón, in the territory which today bears his name, the Calchaquí Valley. In the latter half of the sixteenth century he led the rebellion that spread across almost all of northwest Argentina and part of the southern high plateau of Bolivia. He gained control over the various indigenous groups in the area of the Calchaquí Valley as well as the Omaguaca of the Quebrada de Humahuaca; the Casabindo, the Apatama, and Chicha of La Puna; and the Jurí of Santiago del Estero.

The founding of the Spanish settlements at Córdoba of Calchaquí, Londres in the Hualfín Valley, and Cañete in Tucumán pushed the Indians to the point of war. In 1561, with Juan Calchaquí in the lead, they attacked these new European centers, causing their evacuation. The prestige of Chief Juan Calchaquí was such that his authority extended across all of the northwest of Argentina as well as the eastern plains and the south of La Puna in Bolivia. His reputation gained an almost sacred air. In 1563 the Audiencia of Charcas reported to the king that "they honor him as if he were a burial mound."

HERNANDO DE TORREBLANCA, *Relación histórica de Calchaquí* (1984).

JOSÉ ANTONIO PÉREZ GOLLÁN

**CALDAS, FRANCISCO JOSÉ DE** (*b.* 4 October 1768; *d.* October 1816), astronomer, cartographer, mathematician, and engineer in NEW GRANADA's pro-Independence army. Born in Popayán, Caldas was urged by his family to practice law. Instead he became one of the most prominent creole scientists of the early 1800s, participating in the Royal Botanical Expedition of José Celestino MUTIS (1805) and later becoming director of the Royal Astronomy Observatory of Bogotá. His journal, *El Semanario del Nuevo Reino de Granada,* was one of the first scientific periodicals to be published in Latin America. As professor of mathematics at the progressive Colegio del Rosario in Bogotá, Caldas encouraged the dissemination of modern science, including Newtonian experimental physics and Copernican cosmography.

Although he benefited from his contacts with the influential German investigator Alexander von HUMBOLDT, Caldas called on American scientists to end their dependence on Europeans. He discovered independently that the temperature of boiling water was proportional to atmospheric pressure and devised a formula to measure altitude with a thermometer. He also studied the properties and value of CINCHONA (quinine) bark and of COCHINEAL.

Caldas personified the late colonial Latin American striving for scientific, economic, and, eventually, political independence. After 1810, he served the independence cause as coeditor of the official *Diario Político* and as captain of the newly created Corps of Engineers. Captured by the Spanish royalists in 1816, he was executed as a rebel. His death, and that of other creole insurgent scientists, dealt a near fatal blow to the continuity of scientific inquiry from the colony to the republic.

509

The *Obras completas* (Bogotá, 1966) includes a biographical note by Alfredo D. Bateman. See also THOMAS GLICK, ''Science and Independence in Latin America (with Special Reference to New Granada),'' in *Hispanic American Historical Review* 71, no. 2 (1991): 307–334; and JOHN WILTON APPEL, *Francisco José de Caldas: A Scientist at Work in New Granada* (1994).

IRIS H. W. ENGSTRAND
LOUISA S. HOBERMAN

*See also* **Science.**

**CALDERA RODRÍGUEZ, RAFAEL** (*b.* 24 January 1916), president of Venezuela (1969–1974; reelected 5 December 1993). In 1936, Caldera helped found the National Student Union (Unión Nacional Estudiantil), an anti-Marxist Catholic student organization. He served as attorney general of the republic in 1946, and between 1959 and 1961 as president of the Chamber of Deputies. In 1946, he organized the Independent Political Electoral Organization Committee (Comité de Organización Política Electoral Independiente, COPEI), which became the Social Christian Party (Partido Social Cristiano, COPEI). Elected president in 1968 on a ''democratic progressive'' platform, Caldera formed a government that addressed popular issues such as distribution of wealth, housing, and education. He also established an accord with leftist guerrillas that ended a decade of internal warfare. His foreign policy broke with his predecessors' anticommunism, accepted international social justice, and reflected a growing anxiety over the expansion of Brazil's power. Caldera also negotiated an agreement with Guayana in which both nations agreed not to claim each other's territory for twelve years.

RAFAEL CALDERA, *Idearia: La democracia cristiana en América Latina* (1970); DANIEL H. LEVINE, *Conflict and Political Change in Venezuela* (1973); DAVID J. MYERS, *Democratic Campaigning in Venezuela: Caldera's Victory* (1973); JOHN D. MARTZ and DAVID J. MYERS, *Venezuela: The Democratic Experience* (1977); JESÚS ARAÚJO, *Política y realidad* (1979); DONALD L. HERMAN, *Christian Democracy in Venezuela* (1980); JOSÉ ANTONIO GIL YEPES, *The Challenge of Venezuelan Democracy*, translated by Evelyn Harrison, Lolo Gil de Yanes, and Danielle Salti (1981).

WINTHROP R. WRIGHT

*See also* **Venezuela: Political Parties.**

**CALDERÓN DE LA BARCA, FANNY** (*b.* 23 December 1804; *d.* 6 February 1882), writer and educator. Born Frances Inglis in Edinburgh she, with her family, immigrated to the United States in 1831, after her father's bankruptcy and death. Her mother established schools in Boston and then Staten Island, where in 1838 Frances married Spain's minister to the United States, Ángel Calderón de la Barca. From 1839 to 1842, as wife of Spain's first ambassador to Mexico, she wrote journals and letters from which she gathered the two-volume *Life in Mexico* (1843), a richly detailed portrait of postin-

dependence society. Particularly noteworthy are her observations on politics and daily life in the national capital and surrounding central valley, and in the neighboring regions of Michoacán, Morelos, and Puebla. Upon her husband's death in 1861, she became governess and companion to the Spanish royal family. In 1876, she was accorded the title of *marquesa*.

CHARLES DUMAS, *L'Europe et les Européens au Mexique vers 1840: Selon l'oeuvre de Mme. Calderón de la Barca* (1962); HOWARD T. FISHER and MARION HALL FISHER, *Life in Mexico: The Letters of Fanny Calderón de la Barca* (1966); GUADALUPE APPENDINI, *La vida en México en 1840* (1974).

STUART F. VOSS

**CALDERÓN FOURNIER, RAFAEL ÁNGEL** (*b.* 14 March 1949), president of Costa Rica (1990–1994) and founder of the Social Christian Party. Rafael Ángel Calderón Fournier has spent virtually his whole life involved in Costa Rican partisan politics. He served as a leading member of the national legislature while still a law student at the University of Costa Rica—he received his law degree in 1977—and he has been deeply involved in public life ever since.

He shared with his father, Rafael Ángel CALDERÓN GUARDIA (1940–1944), the distinction of being the youngest presidents in Costa Rican history. They were both only forty years old when elected. (Since then, thirty-nine-year-old José María Figueres Olsen was elected in 1994.) From birth, Calderón Fournier's destiny has been politics, his life intertwined with that of his famous father. He was born in Managua, Nicaragua, while his father was in exile after the defeat of the progovernment forces in the 1948 civil conflict and later was reunited with his exiled father in Mexico, where he spent much of his early youth. When the family returned to Costa Rica, his father's many followers passed their loyalty to his son and namesake.

Following a term in the national legislature (1974–1978), he led the Calderónists into the Unidad coalition that elected Rodrigo CARAZO ODIO president in 1978. He then served as foreign minister from 1978 to 1982 and as a member of the board of the social security system.

After running unsuccessful presidential campaigns in 1982 and 1986, Calderón Fournier was elected for a four-year term in 1990 on a platform that emphasized privatization of the economy while maintaining intact the extensive national social welfare program, much of which his father initiated during his presidency.

RODRIGO CARAZO ODIO, *Acción para la historia* (1982), covers his administration's foreign policy initiatives while Calderón served as foreign minister; see also MARC EDELMAN and JOANNE KENEN, *The Costa Rica Reader* (1989).

JOHN PATRICK BELL

**CALDERÓN GUARDIA, RAFAEL ÁNGEL** (*b.* 10 March 1900; *d.* 9 June 1970), president of Costa Rica (1940–

1944). Calderón Guardia was born in San José, Costa Rica, to a bourgeois, Catholic family. After completing secondary school, he went to Belgium to pursue his medical career. He studied at the Catholic University of Lovain, where he was influenced by Christian-socialist ideas. He then went to the Free University of Brussels, from which he graduated as a surgeon in 1927. In Belgium he married Ivonne Clays before returning to Costa Rica. He later married Rosario Fournier, with whom he had three children, including Rafael Ángel CALDERÓN FOURNIER (president of Costa Rica, 1990–1994). In Costa Rica he practiced medicine, dedicating himself to the poor, an experience that influenced his populist ideas.

Calderón Guardia began his political career in 1930, when he was elected councilman and president of the municipality of San José. In 1934 he was elected to Congress, and in 1936 he became third alternate (vice president) of the Republic. In 1938 he was reelected to Congress and was chosen as its president due to his gift as a political leader. In 1939 he was the presidential candidate of the National Republican Party, and with little opposition he was elected. Even though Calderón Guardia had the support of the oligarchy and the liberal politicians of the time, once in power, he decided to implement a series of social reforms. He recognized the urgency of making changes in society in order to attend to the needs of the working class and avoid serious future conflicts.

His vision and success were shaped by his Christian-socialist ideals, his medical profession, and the Costa Rican economic crisis brought on by World War II and a dependent economy. Domestically, a series of conditions made the country ripe for reformism. The Catholic Church, led by Monsignor Víctor Manuel SANABRIA and following papal encyclicals, supported laws in favor of the working class. The Communist Party under Manuel MORA was advocating state intervention on behalf of the proletariat and the peasants. The union movement had been growing since the beginning of the twentieth century. And several new reformist and revolutionary political parties were demanding reforms in the country. These factors allowed the government of Calderón Guardia to create the University of Costa Rica in 1941, establish a social-security system in 1942, and institutionalize a labor code in 1943. The reforms were made possible by an alliance between the government, the Catholic Church, and the Communist Party. For these reasons, Calderón Guardia is remembered as a statesman, a willful leader, and a social reformer. However, he also displayed a lack of fiscal planning and a tendency toward political favoritism, and he failed to confront Costa Rica's economic problems.

After his term as president, Calderón Guardia continued to exercise a strong influence in the administration of Teodoro PICADO (1944–1948). In 1948 he was again a presidential candidate but lost to the opposition, led by the journalist Otilio ULATE. Not accepting the defeat, Calderón Guardia demanded that Congress nullify the election, which it did. With a strong political opposition and an armed movement under the leadership of José FIGUERES, the country was thrown into civil war in April 1948. After the military triumph of Figueres, Calderón Guardia, Picado, and other leaders went to Nicaragua. Backed by Anastasio SOMOZA, Calderón Guardia invaded Costa Rica in 1948, but the mission failed. In 1955, again backed by Somoza, he undertook another invasion and failed. He lived in Mexico until 1958, when he returned to Costa Rica upon being elected to Congress. In 1962 he ran again for the presidency, but lost. From 1966 to 1970 he served as ambassador to Mexico, then returned to Costa Rica. He died in San José. In 1973 the Congress declared him a national hero in honor of his political legacy and work as a social reformer.

CARLOS ARAYA POCHET, *Historia de los partidos políticos: Liberación nacional* (1968); RALPH LEE WOODWARD, JR., *Central America: A Nation Divided,* 2d ed. (1985).

JORGE MARIO SALAZAR

**CALEDONIA,** a Scottish colony at DARIÉN (in present-day Panama), 1698–1700. Also known as Fort Saint Andrew, New Edinburgh, and New Saint Andrew. Under the leadership of William PATERSON and with backing from London merchants, the Company of Scotland Trading to Africa and the Indies was established in June 1695. In hopes of developing lucrative trade with the Spanish Indies as well as expanding agricultural and mining operations on the isthmus, this company planted a colony of settlers on the Caribbean coast near the Gulf of Darién in 1698. They named the colony Caledonia and established a town called New Edinburgh. Fort Saint Andrew (sometimes called New Saint Andrew) was built on a platform overlooking the site. This first attempt at colonization failed, however, in the face of short supplies and Spanish raiding. Leaving more than four hundred graves at Caledonia, Paterson and all but a dozen of the remaining colonists abandoned the site on 18 June 1699 and left for Scotland via Jamaica and New York. A few weeks later, a Spanish force under Juan Delgado arrived and destroyed the fort, burned New Edinburgh, and captured one of the survivors.

A second expedition reestablished the colony and fort in November 1699, but internal dissension, disease, Spanish threats, and the inability of the company to sustain its own support led to its final abandonment. Fort Saint Andrew surrendered to the Spanish on 30 March 1700 with the understanding that the settlement would be vacated within two weeks. More than a thousand Scots had died in the venture before the remainder left Caledonia on 12 April 1700.

This disaster contributed to ill feeling between England and Scotland as well as between Britain and Spain. A flurry of publications immediately following the disaster reflected the intensity of feeling and interest in the matter.

Among the contemporary publications, see especially *A full and exact collection of all the considerable addresses, memorials, petitions . . . relating to the Company of Scotland Trading to Africa and the Indies. . . .* (1700); WALTER HARRIS, *A Short Vindication of Phil. Scot's Defence of the Scots abdicating Darién* (1700); [GEORGE RIDPATH], *An Enquiry into the causes of the miscarriage of the Scots Colony at Darién* (1700); and [ROBERT FERGUSON], *A just and modest vindication of the Scots design. . . .* (1699). Several rather full treatments of the Darién colonization effort were published early in this century, notably J. S. BARBOUR, *A History of William Paterson and the Darién Company* (1907); FRANK CUNDALL, *The Darién Venture* (1926); GEORGE P. INSH, *The Company of Scotland Trading to Africa and the Indies* (1932); and FRANCIS RUSSELL HART, *The Disaster of Darién: The Story of the Scots Settlement and the Causes of Its Failure, 1699–1701* (1929), the latter containing a large documentary appendix. The most complete account is JOHN PREBBLE, *The Darién Disaster: A Scots Colony in the New World* (1968).

SUE DAWN MCGRADY

**CALENDARS, PRE-COLUMBIAN** In variant forms, a single calendar was shared by the peoples of pre-Conquest Mesoamerica from Nayarit and Tamaulipas in the north of Mexico to Costa Rica in the south. Sometimes called the native "century," it was a cycle of fifty-two years (English: Calendar Round; Nahuatl: *xiuhmolpilli*; Maya: *hunab*). This interval is produced by the simultaneous counting of two subcycles, one of 260 days (English: day count; Nahuatl: *tonalpohualli*; Maya: *tzol kin*), and the other of 365 days (English: vague year; Nahuatl: *ilhuitl*; Maya: *haab*). The numerology of their interaction dictates that the count repeats itself after fifty-two years.

The day count is itself a combination of two cycles, one of thirteen numbers (Spanish: *trecena*) and the other of twenty named days (Spanish: *veintena*). They are counted concurrently, therefore summing to 260 days before repeating. The vague year (approximating the solar year but lacking leap years) was counted by nineteen named "months." The first eighteen had twenty days each, and the nineteenth had five, and was considered unlucky. Within the "months" the days were numbered sequentially, beginning with the start of each "month." The cycle results in 365 days before repeating. The day count was universally synchronized. The names of the numbers and of the days varied by language, but the mathematical correspondence never varied. (In the calendars of Teotihuacán Tlapanec, the days were counted from two to fourteen, which introduces a trivial discrepancy.)

The count of the vague year was more complex because (1) the beginning of the year differed from one group to another by occasional advances of one day (to a total of three) or by retreats of one twenty-day "month" (to a total of thirteen); (2) the count of the days of the "month" could be either from zero to nineteen (Maya) or from one to twenty (Nahuatl); and (3)

the naming of the year could be either from its first day (Maya) or from its 360th (Nahuatl), in other words either initial or terminal. Nonetheless, a date in any Mesoamerican calendar can be converted into the corresponding date in any other, and the pre-Conquest priests not only knew this but carved it in stone. Many events are recorded in two or more calendars.

There was a second major calendar in Mesoamerica, commonly known as the Long Count. It was used by the Olmec (Zoquean speakers) of the area of Tabasco and vicinity and by the Cholan and Yucatecan Maya. Its base was a cycle of 360 days—a *tun* (stone). The much debated date of the founding of Spanish Merida in 1541 has now been reasonably established at 11.16.0.0.0. Reading from right to left, this means 0 *kins* (days), 0 *uinals* (twenty-day "months"), 0 *tuns* (eighteen "month" stones), 16 *katuns* (twenty *tun* periods), and 11 *baktuns* (twenty *katun* periods). The implication is that the Maya era began on a date of 0.0.0.0.4 Ahau 8 Cumku on 11 August 3113 B.C. (Gregorian), Julian day number 584283.

The Long Count calendar was used largely to date the reigns of kings or to record astronomical and mythical events (and sometimes conflating all three). It is preserved on carved stone monuments of the Classic period (third to tenth centuries A.D.) and in unrelated later codices. Recent successes in the reading of the Mayan hieroglyphic writing system have tied much of the dynastic history of the Mayan city states to the Long Count calendar and thus to ecumenical history.

Relating the two major calendrical traditions of Mesoamerica to one another is only possible through secondary inference, since the calendar round is limited to dating events within a fifty-two-year cycle, while the Long Count runs for about 5,025 years. The logic of events themselves is the only clue. The genealogically governed annals of the Mixtec codices, for example, push history back nearly 600 years in the Mixteca. Pre-Conquest Aztec history is genealogical and hence historically more obscure.

While deciphering the calendrical structure of Mesoamerica was not easy, that of the pre-Columbian Inca Empire has been virtually impossible, given that it left no written records. However, R. Tom Zuidema has determined that the Inca created two separate systems through a careful reading of pre-Conquest chronicles whereby a 328-day year was divided into forty-one "time-units." In the regular arrangement, the Inca counted forty-one "weeks" of eight days each; in the second or irregular arrangement, time was calculated according to the days that had elapsed between two astronomical observations in the calendar, taking into account the hierarchical ranking of each strata in a complicated social universe. These systems acted to define space on both land and sky and register in calendrical time the observation of astronomical phenomena and not necessarily to maintain a direct correspondence between the two, except in certain specific times such as at the solstices, the zenith sun, and the antizenith (nadir) sun.

R. TOM ZUIDEMA, "The Inca Calendar," in Anthony F. Aveni, ed., *Native American Astronomy* (1977), pp. 219–259, and *Inca Civilization in Cuzco,* trans. by Jean-Jacques Decoster (1990); GARY URTON, *At the Crossroads of the Earth and the Sky: An Andean Cosmology* (1981).

MUNRO S. EDMONSON

See also **Astronomy; Aztec Calendar Stone.**

**CALFUCURÁ** (*b.* late 1770s; *d.* 1873), Araucanian leader. Calfucurá headed the rise of an important intertribal confederation in the Argentinian pampas that flourished in the last half of the nineteenth century until subjugation by the Argentine army in the 1880s.

In 1835 a group of ARAUCANIANS (also called MAPUCHES) headed by Calfucurá moved east from Chilean homelands near Llaima, in the southern cordillera (in the region of the Imperial River and Cautín), to establish a permanent encampment near a large salt deposit called the Salinas Grandes. Following a struggle for power over control of the Salinas Grandes with the Voroganos—a loosely organized group of Pampas and Araucanian followers of Mariano Rondeau—Calfucurá emerged victorious, and Rondeau's followers joined Calfucurá's Araucanian settlement.

Calfucurá's leadership was derived primarily from personal charisma as well as from military knowledge and status within the Araucanian world. Under his leadership, this Araucanian confederation in the pampas expanded to enjoy relative prosperity and autonomy and to become a large, well-organized threat to Argentine lives and property. Between 1834 and 1856, Calfucurá negotiated temporary alliances between neighboring PAMPAS, TEHUELCHES, RANQUELES, and other Araucanian bands or tribes, and also entered into a structured alliance with the government of Juan Manuel de ROSAS in exchange for annuity payments in goods. Because of their control of the salt mines in the Salinas Grandes, Calfucurá's people escaped dependency on the payments and thrived on intratribal trade in salt—necessary for making CHARQUI (salted meat)—and livestock (mostly cattle and horses).

When the annuity program ended after the fall of Rosas in the 1850s, the Araucanian followers of Calfucurá responded with raids called MALONES (also called *malocas*). In the next two decades in a series of highly organized raids against creole ranching interests in the southern Argentina frontier, Calfucurá's Voroganos acquired hundreds of thousands of head of cattle and horses and hundreds of *cautivos* (captives) to tend to these herds. When Calfucurá died of natural causes in 1873, he left a confederation of Araucanians that included over 224 tribes. This confederation, under the leadership of Manuel Namuncurá, Calfucurá's son, continued to resist Argentine subjugation until 1879.

ESTANISLAO S. ZEBALLOS, *Callvucurá y la dinastía de los Piedra,* (1961); JUDITH EWELL and WILLIAM BEEZELEY, eds. *The Human Tradition in Latin America: The Twentieth Century* (1989), pp. 175–187.

KRISTINE L. JONES

**CALI,** the third largest city in Colombia, located at the southwestern end of the Cauca Valley. The city was founded in 1536 by Sebastián de Belalcázar, a lieutenant of Pizarro. Despite its early foundation, its landlocked position long retarded its economic growth.

During colonial times, Cali was the economic center of slave-owning haciendas that provided supplies for the mining areas of Popayán, Antioquia, and Chocó. In the nineteenth century, the breakdown of mining and the lack of an adequate outlet to the Pacific Ocean kept the area isolated from world markets. One of the main battlegrounds during the slave-owners' rebellion of 1851 and the religious civil war of 1876, Cali remained a small town of 11,000 people, bypassed by the dynamic effects of the tobacco boom and even, at first, by the coffee economy.

The Panama Canal, which opened in 1914, provided an important stimulus to both Cali and the Pacific port of Buenaventura from the 1920s to the 1960s, ultimately establishing Cali as the main commercial center of the Cauca Valley. The importance of this outlet, as compared to the outlet of the Magdalena Valley, was greatly increased not only by the opening of the canal but also by the completion of the railroad (begun in 1878) connecting Cali with Buenaventura. In 1912 Cali had a population of 27,000; by 1918 it had grown to 45,000.

The transformation of the old haciendas into large-scale agribusinesses provided another stimulus to growth in the 1940s and 1950s. The influx of foreign capital into the manufacturing and the intermediate goods sectors made Cali one of the important industrial centers of the country. Industrialization in the region made Cali one of the fastest growing urban centers in a very short time.

Industry did not continue to expand after the 1960s, however. Whatever economic expansion there was came from commerce (including textiles, construction materials, tobacco products, and clothing) and public investment. By the 1990s, moreover, the city showed a prosperity that seemed to come from dubious sources, such as narcotics and related illicit ventures.

GUSTAVO ARBOLEDA, *Historia de Cali: Desde los orígenes de la ciudad hasta la expiración del período colonial,* 3 vols. (1956); JOSÉ ANTONIO OCAMPO, "El desarrollo económico de Cali en el Siglo XX," in *Santiago de Cali, 45 años de historia* (1981), pp. 127–148; GERMÁN COLMENARES, *Cali: Terratenientes, mineros, y comerciantes. Vol. I, Sociedad y economía en el Valle del Cauca* (1983); JOSÉ ESCORCIA, *Desarrollo político, social y económico, 1800–1854. Vol. III, Sociedad y economía en el Valle del Cauca* (1983).

JOSÉ ESCORCIA

**CALIFORNIA.** During the eighteenth century, California consisted of two mission frontiers—BAJA CALIFORNIA, developed after 1697 by the JESUITS; and Alta California, controlled by the FRANCISCANS from 1769. Until 1804, both areas were included in the same administrative jurisdiction.

With the exception of a small region in the southern part of the peninsula where small-scale commercial farming and marginal silver mining developed after 1750, Baja California held little attraction for colonists. On this frontier the Jesuits did not establish the first missions until after 1697 and without government financial support. Between 1697 and 1840 twenty-seven missions were established, by the Jesuits (1697–1768), the Franciscans (1769–1773), and the DOMINICANS (1774–1840). The Indians who were resettled in the mission communities experienced high rates of mortality from disease and other factors and declined in total numbers from an estimated 50,000–60,000 in the 1690s to a mere 2,000 by the mid-1840s. Following the secularization of the missions in the 1830s, Baja California remained an isolated territory until a French MINING company began to exploit its copper deposits in the 1870s.

In response to reports of Russian activities in Alaska and Captain James Cook's exploration of the Pacific islands, the Spanish began their occupation of Alta California, the modern state of California, in 1769 under the direction of Visitor-General José de GÁLVEZ. The Spanish government encountered such considerable difficulty in populating the region with settlers that Alta California remained a mission frontier until the early years of the nineteenth century. Between 1769 and 1823 the Franciscans established twenty-one missions in the region, and the viceregal government founded four PRESIDIOS (military garrisons) and three pueblos (civilian communities). The death rates among the Indians gathered into the missions were high, but until the 1820s the Franciscans, backed by the military, were able to resettle thousands of Indians in the missions. Between 1769 and 1832 the Franciscans baptized nearly 88,000 Indians in the missions, but during those years almost 64,000 of them died.

After about 1800 a vibrant but illegal trade in hides and tallow developed. Foreign merchants bartered manufactured goods for cattle hides and tallow from mission herds in a trade legalized by the newly independent Mexican government in 1823. The outbreak of the war for independence in central Mexico in 1810 placed increased pressure on the Franciscans to produce surplus goods to supply military garrisons cut off from their traditional sources of supplies there and intensified illegal trade with foreign merchants. Growing production levels in turn forced the Franciscans to recruit additional workers to replace the Indian converts, who died at alarming rates in the missions.

In 1833 a short-lived liberal congress in Mexico legislated the secularization of the Alta California missions.

Theoretically, the missions were to be converted to formal autonomous Indian pueblos, with their land, livestock, and other communal goods distributed among the Indians. However, local politicians were able to establish de facto independence from Mexico City and to administer the secularized missions for their own benefit. Under the colonization laws passed by the Mexican government in the 1820s, different governors of California made more than 800 grants of large tracts of land in the province to prominent politicians and settlers. The recipients of such grants stocked their ranches with livestock from the mission herds and increased their exports of hides and tallow.

In the 1830s and 1840s a growing number of Anglo-Americans and Europeans settled in Alta California. A small minority married into local families and became Mexican citizens, but the majority remained hostile to Mexicans and the Mexican government. In 1846 in Sonoma they declared an independent California republic. Within a month of this so-called BEAR FLAG REVOLT, U.S. forces began the conquest of the province. (As early as the 1820s, the U.S. government had tried to buy California from Mexico.) U.S. forces also occupied Baja California in 1846 and 1847, but they returned the province to Mexico under the terms of the 2 February 1848 Treaty of GUADALUPE HIDALGO.

ZEPHYRIN ENGELHARDT, O.F.M., *Missions and Missionaries of California*, 4 vols. (1929–1930); PEVERIL MEIGS, *The Dominican Mission Frontier of Lower California* (1935); SHERBURNE F. COOK, *The Conflict Between the California Indians and White Civilization* (1976); DAVID J. WEBER, *The Mexican Frontier 1821–1846: The American Southwest Under Mexico* (1982); ROBERT H. JACKSON, "Demographic Change in Northwestern New Spain," in *The Americas* 41, 4 (April 1985): 462–479, and "Population and the Economic Dimension of Colonization of Alta California: A Study of Four Mission Communities," in *Journal of the Southwest* 33, no. 3 (1991): 387–439.

ROBERT H. JACKSON

*See also* **Copper Industry; Slavery: Indian Slavery and Forced Labor; Missions.**

**CALIFORNIOS,** technically, the Spanish-speaking residents of Alta California during the Spanish and Mexican era (1769–1848). More commonly the term referred to the property-holding elite, the 500 families who were given land grants during this period, including the most politically prominent families: the Bandinis, Carrillos, Picos, de la Guerras, Vallejos, Coronels, Castros, Alvarados, and others. Together they enjoyed economic and political dominance during the Mexican era (1821–1848). Among their numbers were a few Americans who had married into Californio families, such as Abel Stearns and John Warner.

Prominent Californios served as members of the State Constitutional Convention that met at Monterey in 1849. Others served as officials of town and county governments during the first few decades after the American takeover. After 1848, however, the economic and political fortunes of the Californios generally declined because of the immigration of more than 100,000 people to California during the gold rush. The newcomers' demand for land prompted squatter violence and the passage of several discriminatory laws that led to the loss of Californios' land. The Land Act, passed by Congress in 1851, established a lengthy process, lasting an average of twenty years, of legitimizing Californio land claims, leading to increased squatterism and speculation. In order to pay new, higher land taxes (Americans based land value on future productivity rather than actual usage) and lawyers' fees, the Californios mortgaged their grants; many ultimately lost them to banks, lawyers, and moneylenders. Some of the sons of the Californios became bandits, such as Nicolás Sepúlveda, Chico Lugo, Pedro Vallejo, and Ramón Amador; others continued to be active in politics; and many Californio families intermarried with Anglo immigrants.

LEONARD PITT, *The Decline of the Californios: A Social History of the Spanish-Speaking Californians, 1846–1890* (1966); RICHARD GRISWOLD DEL CASTILLO, *The Los Angeles Barrio, 1850–1890: A Social History* (1979); DOUGLAS MONROY, *Thrown Among Strangers: The Making of Mexican Culture in Frontier California* (1990).

RICHARD GRISWOLD DEL CASTILLO

**CALIMA,** archaeological region located in the western highlands and the middle Cauca Valley, Colombia. Human occupation dates from the eighth millennium B.C. to the sixteenth century. The first inhabitants were hunters and gatherers who made use of the abundant plants available in the region. Evidence of this early occupation has been found at several open sites, notably El Pital. Dates for these locations range from about 7500 to 2200 B.C. Pollen diagrams suggest maize was present in the region about 5000 to 3000 B.C., but it is not clear yet if it played an important role in the economy of these early settlers.

Later periods include Ilama (*ca.* 1000 to 0 B.C.), Yotoco (A.D. 0 to 1200) and Sonso (A.D. 1200 to 1600). The Ilama period marks the introduction of pottery richly decorated with incisions. There is evidence that Ilama people cultivated maize and developed metallurgy. Burials suggest there were some differences between the elite and the commoner in terms of access to exotic goods. Elite items generally copied designs from afar; gold objects sometimes imitated statuary from the Upper Magdalena region to the west.

Pottery was painted during the Yotoco period. Agriculture consisting of beans, maize, and gourds is associated with this development stage, as is the elaboration of some impressive large adornments of gold. Agricultural intensification is suggested by evidence of ridges and drainage systems in the valleys associated with the Yotoco period. Some Yotoco burials were extremely lavish, with gold objects and adornments elaborated in exotic raw materials such as seashells. Other burials, in contrast, contained only pottery vessels. This evidence suggests some degree of social inequality. Also, as Yotoco sites are more abundant than Ilama sites, it has been suggested that the Yotoco population was larger.

The Sonso period is described as one of dramatic change in social organization in the Calima region. Pottery was more simple, lacking the well-crafted designs of the Yotoco ceramics. Gold objects were not as impressive as those of the Yotoco period, generally consisting of small earrings. Agricultural practices also changed. Instead of in the valleys, the Sonso people cultivated on the slopes of the mountains.

Sonso is frequently described as a period of decadence. Nonetheless, evidence of social complexity continues to be found from this period, and some burials evidence an impressive number of pots. Also, the large number of Sonso sites reported suggests continuation of population growth. At the time of the Spanish Conquest, the native populations in the area were dominated and few traces of the pre-Columbian inheritance remain in the region.

The basic source for archaeological studies in the Calima region is *Pro Calima* (1980–1988), published in English in Basel, Switzerland. See also LEONOR HERRERA, MARIANNE CARDALE, and WARWICK BRAY, "El Hombre y su medio ambiente en Calima," in *Revista Colombiana de Antropología* (1983), and "Costa del Pacífico y vertiente oeste de la Cordillera Occidental," in *Colombia Prehispánica-Regiones Arqueológicas* (1989). For a general discussion on social complexity in the area, see CARL HENRIK LANGEBAEK, "Estilos y culturas en Colombia prehispánica," in *Gran Enciclopedia de Colombia* (1991). A recent overview of Colombian archaeology is CARL HENRIK LANGEBAEK, *Noticias de Caciques muy Mayores: Orígen y desarrollo de sociedades complejas en el nororiente de Colombia y norte de Venezuela* (1992).

CARL HENRIK LANGEBAEK R.

*See also* **Archaeology.**

**CALLADO, ANTÔNIO** (*b.* 26 January 1917), Brazilian journalist, playwright, and novelist. Born in Niterói, Rio de Janeiro, Callado worked in London for the BBC from 1941 to 1947. He is best known for his novels dealing with religious and political themes. Perhaps his most famous work, *Quarup* (1967) describes the transformation of a missionary priest into a revolutionary who discovers his own sexuality in the process. *Bar Don Juan* (1971) relates the points of view of six would-be revolutionaries who plot to overthrow the military government. Callado has received literary prizes that include the Golfinho de Ouro, the Prêmio Brasília, and the Goethe Prize for Fiction for *Sempreviva* (1981). He has also written nonfiction.

WILSON MARTINS, "Le Roman politique d'Antônio Callado," in *Europe: Revue littéraire mensuelle* no. 640–641 (1982): 43–47; MALCOLM SILVERMAN, "A ficção em prosa de Antônio Callado," in *Moderna ficção brasileira,* 2d ed. (1982), pp. 19–33; CRISTINA FERREIRA PINTO, *A viagem do herói no romance de An-*

*tônio Callado* (1985); NAOMI HOKI MONIZ, ''Antônio Callado,'' in *Dictionary of Brazilian Literature*, edited by Irwin Stern (1988), pp. 69–71.

GARY M. VESSELS

### CALLADO JUNIOR, JOAQUIM ANTÔNIO DA SILVA

(*b.* 11 July 1848; *d.* 20 March 1880), Brazilian flute virtuoso, teacher, prolific composer of popular instrumental dance pieces, and key figure in the history of Brazilian music. Son of a bandmaster in Rio de Janeiro, Callado received an appointment to teach flute at the Imperial Conservatory of Music in 1870, during which time he organized a popular musical ensemble called ''Choro carioca.'' The first of many CHORO ensembles in Rio, the traditional group included a solo flute or other woodwind instrument, with various guitar-type and occasional percussion instruments. Repertoire consisted of polkas, quadrilles, schottisches, waltzes, *lundus* (Afro-Brazilian dance), and polka-*lundus*. With the addition of a singer, the performance was called a *seresta*. Callado became famous as the composer of *Querida por todos*, a polka dedicated to a well-known woman composer, Chiquinha GONZAGA.

One of Callado's principal contributions was to establish the *choro* as a form of popular music and to develop an individualized style of popular composition that served as a model for later composers. The *choro* became the favored form of Heitor VILLA-LOBOS to express musical elements that were distinctively Brazilian.

GÉRARD BÉHAGUE, *Music in Latin America* (1979); DAVID P. APPLEBY, *The Music of Brazil* (1983).

DAVID P. APPLEBY

### CALLAMPAS

(literally, ''mushrooms''), a Chilean expression used to describe the shantytowns that have developed in urban centers. The dwellers in these centers often illegally occupy marginal land on which they erect homes consisting of wood and discarded materials. Without running water, gas, or power, unless they illegally tap into an electrical grid, these homes provide housing for those seeking work in the city. They became known as *callampas* because they appear so quickly and spread so rapidly. During the Allende years (1970–1973), *callampas* were often organized politically by members of the Movement of the Revolutionary Left (MIR), who converted them into centers of support for the Unidad Popular government.

GARY MAC EOIN, *No Peaceful Way: Chile's Struggle for Dignity* (1974); CÉSAR L. CAVIEDES, *The Politics of Chile: A Sociogeographical Assessment* (1979).

WILLIAM F. SATER

*See also* **Favela.**

### CALLAO,

city of Peru (1994 population 588,600) and the port for the capital city of Lima, located about 10 miles from the heart of Lima. Although Callao was separated from the capital throughout most of its history, today the two cities merge into one megalopolis. But Callao has retained its uniqueness, and *chalacos*, as its citizens call themselves, still like to distinguish themselves from the residents of Lima.

Callao was founded in 1537 and served as a small way station along the Rímac River and a port of entry for Lima, which was founded by Francisco Pizarro in 1535. Its harbor, protected by San Lorenzo Island, is one of the best along Peru's generally open desert coastline, and by the end of the colonial period Callao had taken on a naval and commercial importance of its own.

It has witnessed many earthquakes, coups, and sieges, beginning as long ago as 1624, when Dutch raiders bombarded the port. A terrifying earthquake and tidal wave destroyed the entire city in 1746. The fortress of Real Felipe, which emerged in the rebuilt city of the late eighteenth century, played an important role in the independence of Peru, its control often being key to the control of the capital.

On 2 May 1866 Callao withstood a bombardment by a Spanish fleet bent on reducing the port to ashes, and that day is remembered as one of the grandest in the history of Peruvian arms. The action also persuaded the Spanish to give up their amorphous pretensions to reestablish their empire in that part of the world.

Facing the sea, Callao played an important role in the commercial history of Peru. In the nineteenth century a series of export-based booms focused attention on the port. GUANO exports triggered the first modernization of the country from the 1840s through the 1870s, and Callao prospered from the hundreds of ships employed in that trade that visited annually to refit and revictual after loading guano at the CHINCHA ISLANDS south of Callao. Later in the century the railroad boom in Peru spurred further economic growth of the city, and when the great copper and silver mines of the interior were once again tapped by modern technology and foreign capital in the early twentieth century, much of the prosperity flowed through Callao.

Callao emerged in the twentieth century as an industrial leader and the first fishing port of Peru. From cement factories to beer breweries, Callao grew as industry located there to take advantage of its proximity to the sea and to the capital. And when Peru became the world's leading fish-exporting nation in the 1950s, based on the rich catches in the waters of the HUMBOLDT CURRENT, Callao was the leading seaport for this booming industry, servicing the fleets and building the boats and ships in its shipyards.

Streetcars, modern sanitation, and constantly improving port facilities kept Callao as the nation's major port. When Lima relocated its principal airport to Callao with the opening of the modern Jorge Chávez International

Airport in 1962, Callao also became the principal port of entry for air travelers to Peru.

JORGE BASADRE's *Historia de la república del Perú* 7th ed. 11 vols. (1983) contains numerous references to the history of Callao.

LAWRENCE A. CLAYTON

**CALLEJA DEL REY, FÉLIX MARÍA, CONDE DE CAL-DERÓN** (*b.* 1757; *d.* 24 July 1828), commander of royalist forces in the War of MEXICAN INDEPENDENCE and VICEROY of New Spain (1813–1816). Born in Medina del Campo, Castilla la Vieja, Spain, Calleja entered the infantry regiment of Savoy as a cadet in 1772. He saw wartime service in the abortive 1775 expedition to Algiers, served aboard the floating artillery platforms during the 1782 siege of Gibraltar, and was present at the siege of Menorca. Promoted to the rank of captain in 1789, Calleja accompanied his patron, Viceroy Conde de Revillagigedo, to Mexico. From 1790 to 1797 he held important commissions to inspect frontier districts, to raise militia units, and to conduct detailed geographical and resource studies. After promotion to colonel in 1798, he took command of the Tenth Militia Brigade, based at San Luis Potosí, in 1799. Calleja further strengthened his position in the Mexican north through marriage in 1807 to María Francisca de la Gándara, daughter of a wealthy landowner. He was promoted to brigadier in 1810 and to field marshal in 1811.

Although surprised by the HIDALGO revolt of September 1810, Calleja acted quickly to mobilize the militia brigade at San Luis Potosí, which formed the core of the effective royalist Army of the Center, and successfully dispersed the rebels at Aculco (7 November 1810), Guanajuato (25 November 1810), and Puente de Calderón (17 January 1811). In 1812, following the defeat of Hidalgo, Calleja led his army out of the Bajío provinces to raze the insurgent town of Zitácuaro and south to Cuautla, where his army besieged the defensive positions of José María MORELOS. Both sides suffered terrible hardships during the seventy-two-day siege, and starvation forced the insurgents to flee Cuautla.

Calleja introduced a controversial counterinsurgency system designed to mobilize the urban and rural populations and to free army units to chase major insurgent forces. On 4 March 1813, he was named viceroy of New Spain. By 1815 his forces had eliminated Morelos and fragmented if not defeated the insurgency. By the time he transferred command to Viceroy Juan RUÍZ DE APO-DACA on 19 September 1816, Calleja had come to believe his own propaganda that the royalists had won the war.

Calleja returned to Madrid, where he received the title of Conde de Calderón. In 1819, King FERDINAND VII named him CAPTAIN-GENERAL of Andalusia, governor of Cádiz, and general in chief of the Spanish army that was being assembled to reconquer the Americas. In the military campaign of 1820 and the restoration of the constitution, Calleja was arrested and experienced political difficulties that continued until the return of absolutism in 1823. In 1825, he went to Valencia, where he remained until his death.

Material on Calleja's campaigns during the War of Mexican Independence can be found in LUCAS ALAMÁN, *Historia de México desde los primeros movimientos que prepararon su independencia en el año de 1808 hasta la época presente,* 5 vols. (1849–1852; repr. 1942); WILBERT H. TIMMONS, *Morelos: Priest Soldier Statesman of Mexico* (1963); HUGH M. HAMILL, *The Hidalgo Revolt: Prelude to Mexican Independence* (1966); CHRISTON I. ARCHER, "La Causa Buena: The Counterinsurgency Army of New Spain and the Ten Years' War," in Jaime E. Rodríguez O., ed., *The Independence of Mexico and the Creation of the New Nation* (1989); and BRIAN R. HAMNETT, *Roots of Insurgency: Mexican Regions, 1750–1824* (1986). For biographical data, see JOSÉ DE JESÚS NÚÑEZ Y DOMÍNGUEZ, *La virreina mexicana: Doña María Francisca de la Gándara de Calleja* (1950); and CHRISTON I. ARCHER, *The Army in Bourbon Mexico, 1760–1810* (1977).

CHRISTON I. ARCHER

**CALLEJAS ROMERO, RAFAEL LEONARDO** (*b.* 14 November 1943), president of Honduras (1990–1994) who promoted economic development along neoliberal lines. The son of a landowning family, Callejas earned B.S. (1965) and M.S. (1966) degrees in agricultural economics at Mississippi State University. Beginning in 1967 he was an economic planner in the Honduran government and a board member of several Honduran public and private corporations.

Callejas was an unsuccessful National Party presidential candidate in 1981 and 1985 before winning in 1989 as head of the MONARCA (Rafael Callejas National Renovation Movement) faction of the National Party. He favored development under U.S. president Ronald Reagan's CARIBBEAN BASIN INITIATIVE and enjoyed strong U.S. support in his campaign. His popularity with conservative leaders in the industrial nations helped him gain favorable international financial agreements that contributed to economic gains early in his administration as he devalued the currency, privatized government enterprises, and pursued other structural adjustments favored by the U.S. AGENCY FOR INTERNATIONAL DEVELOPMENT (AID). By 1993, however, Honduras was in serious financial difficulty and suffered severe shortages of foodstuffs, problems that contributed to a Liberal victory in the November 1993 presidential election. Although Callejas was the third elected civilian president to rule Honduras in succession since 1980, the armed forces, which remained autonomous under Callejas, continued to be a strong force in Honduran politics.

For a more detailed biographical sketch of Callejas, see the entry by RALPH LEE WOODWARD, JR., in the *Encyclopedia of World Biography,* vol. 18, edited by David Eggenberger (1994). For a detailed overview of recent Honduran political history, see ALISON ACKER, *Honduras: The Making of a Banana Republic* (1988); JAMES DUNKERLEY, *Power in the Isthmus, A Political History of Modern Central America* (1988); and TOM BARRY and KENT

NORSWORTHY, *Honduras: A Country Guide* (1990). More detail on Callejas's presidential administration may be found in HOWARD H. LENTER, *State Formation in Central America: The Struggle for Autonomy, Development, and Democracy* (1993).

RALPH LEE WOODWARD, JR.

**CALLEJÓN DE HUAYLAS,** a well-watered, mostly temperate, and healthy valley between the Cordillera Blanca and the Cordillera Negra in the Department of Ancash, Peru. The Callejón de Huaylas has attracted attention several times during its history. In the 1540s it was the site of an uprising by Alonso de Cabrera against Diego de ALMAGRO and his son after Francisco PIZARRO's murder. Toward the end of the sixteenth century, the Spanish discovered silver at Cerro Colqueporco (Quechua for "well of silver"). The ore proved low yielding and the site never prospered. Both the liberators José SAN MARTÍN and Simón BOLÍVAR used the valley as a base during the WARS OF INDEPENDENCE because of its strategic value and its easy communications with the coast on the west, Trujillo on the north, and Huanuco to the southeast. In 1885, the valley was the staging ground for a serious uprising, led by Pedro Pablo Atusparia, against the abuses of peasant authorities, increased taxes, and the growing use of forced labor. The valley was and still is famous for its fertile soil and agricultural abundance.

RUBEN VARGAS UGARTE, *Historia general del Perú*, 10 vols. (1971); DAVID P. WERLICH, *Peru: A Short History* (1978); WILLIAM W. STEIN, *El levantamiento de Atusparia* (1988).

SUSAN E. RAMÍREZ

**CALLES, PLUTARCO ELÍAS** (*b.* 25 September 1877; *d.* 19 October 1945), president of Mexico (1924–1928). The poor relation of a notable family in the northwestern state of Sonora, Calles was an aspiring young professional and entrepreneur who had met with only limited success before the MEXICAN REVOLUTION. Initially on the periphery of Francisco MADERO's movement against the Porfirio DÍAZ regime, from a minor appointment in the new state government he rose steadily in the ranks of what became the constitutionalist army, becoming Alvaro OBREGÓN's principal political associate. As president, and then as *jefe máximo* (supreme chief) in the wake of the assassination of president-elect Obregón (1928), Calles dominated the national government for more than a decade and initiated the institutionalization of the Revolution.

Until the Revolution, Calles's life had been punctuated with misfortune and disappointments. He was the illegitimate son of Plutarco Elías, scion of one of the most prominent families in northeast Sonora in the nineteenth century. Following the death of his mother when he was four, he was raised by his stepfather, Juan B. Calles, who owned a small cantina in Hermosillo (and from whom he took his second family name). After be-

ing educated in Hermosillo, Calles became a schoolteacher. The death of his first wife, Francisca Bernal, in 1899 prompted him to move to the port of Guaymas, where he began a decade-long search for economic success and social mobility. To do so, he relied on his connections with, and the support of, his father's family, the Elíases. First a school inspector and newspaper editor in the port, Calles next was appointed municipal treasurer (he lost the post when funds were discovered missing), followed by a stint as manager of his half brother's hotel until it burned. He moved in 1906 to Fronteras, where he managed his father's modest hacienda, was bookkeeper for and shareholder in a small flour mill, and served as municipal secretary—at last achieving modest success and some local prominence. But he then became embroiled in the Elíases' conflict with the local cacique (boss) and in a dispute with farmers over water rights. As a result he returned to Guaymas in 1910 to manage a hotel and open a commission business in partnership.

Though not an active participant in the local Maderista movement, Calles lent it some support—his store

Plutarco Elías Calles, ca. 1924. BENSON LATIN AMERICAN COLLECTION, UNIVERSITY OF TEXAS AT AUSTIN.

as a meeting place. He used this connection to run unsuccessfully for the state legislature in 1911. Again he returned to northeast Sonora, opening a general store (in partnership) in the border town of Agua Prieta, a most fortunate choice. The railroad running through the town connected Arizona with important mining districts in the interior of Sonora; and the new governor, José M. Maytorena, was looking for a loyal follower who, as the town's police chief, would secure customs revenues, quiet disgruntled former insurgents, and forestall a rumored invasion from Arizona by the radical Magonista revolutionaries. His choice of Calles proved to be the turning point of the latter's life. Calles proved to be a capable, diligent local official, against the Orozquista rebels (1912) and the Huerta coup a year later (being among the first to proclaim armed resistance in the state).

Calles soon developed a working relationship with Obregón, who was emerging as the leader of the revolutionary jefes in the northwest. While Obregón carried the constitutionalist movement beyond the state, Calles remained to manage the military and political affairs of Sonora. As governor of Sonora (1915–1916, 1917–1919) and working with Obregón's other principal Sonoran associate, Adolfo DE LA HUERTA (governor, 1917, 1919–1920), Calles set forth a radical program to promote education on a broad scale; break up monopolies (including the cancellation of all prior government concessions which had tax exemptions) and support small entrepreneurs; extend secularization (including the legalization of divorce and the expulsion of all priests); establish an agrarian commission to distribute the expropriated land of those deemed enemies of the Revolution; foster government patronage of workers, assisting in their organization and legislating rights and benefits; and limit foreign influence (principally, severe economic and social restrictions on Chinese immigrants, and cancelling contracts with some large foreign investors). This radical program put Calles at loggerheads with President Venustiano CARRANZA. Obregón sought to moderate these concepts, but failed in his efforts to establish singular control over the state. He was forced to work with Calles and de la Huerta, forming a triumvirate.

When Obregón announced his presidential candidacy, Calles resigned as secretary of industry, commerce, and labor (1919–1920). Soon after, he led the military forces and proclaimed the Plan of Agua Prieta against Carranza's attempt to impose his successor, and then served as Obregón's interior secretary (1920–1923). When Obregón chose to support Calles over de la Huerta as his successor, and de la Huerta led a revolt, Calles commanded the troops in the northwest. As president, Calles pressed his radical anticlericalism in the face of the CATHOLIC CHURCH's challenge to the restrictions of the 1917 Constitution and then of the CRISTERO REBELLION (1926–1929). But his support of agrarian reform and the workers' movement ebbed as he moder-

ated his policies and concentrated on the development of the nation's infrastructure (especially irrigation, roads, air and postal service, a telephone network, national banking and investment institutions) and on the promotion of enterprise, even to the point of supporting large-scale domestic and foreign investors.

To retain control over the national government in the wake of the assassination of president-elect Obregón, Calles and his followers pursued a limited and expedient institutionalization of the hierarchical, personalist system that had bound the ruling coalition of revolutionary jefes together: the National Revolutionary Party. However, the Maximato (the oligarchic rule of the Callista political machine) increasingly lost a popular base, as it turned away from the Revolution's promises of reform and as the Great Depression deepened. Reformers in the party used its structure to institute a radical program and mobilize popular support, coalescing around Lázaro CÁRDENAS. Again employing expediency, Calles responded by acceding to some of the reformist demands and settling on Cárdenas for the 1934 presidential elections, as the best option to contain growing party dissidence and rising popular alienation. This time, however, his expedient adjustments set in motion forces he could not control. Cárdenas mobilized popular support and employed the institutional prerogatives of the party and the presidency to the fullest. When Calles resisted, he was deported (April 1936). He remained in California until Cárdenas's successor, Manuel ÁVILA CAMACHO, permitted his return in 1941 and accorded him full honors at his funeral four years later.

JUAN DE DIOS BOJÓRQUEZ, Calles (1923); RAMÓN PUENTE, Calles (1933); FRANCISCO R. ALMADA, La Revolución en el Estado de Sonora (1971); HECTOR AGUILAR CAMÍN, La frontera nómada: Sonora y la Revolución Mexicana (1977); ALEJANDRA LAJOUS, Los orígenes del partido único en México (1981); LUIS JAVIER GARRIDO, El partido de la Revolución institucionalizada (medio siglo de poder político en México) (1982).

STUART F. VOSS

**CALÓGERAS, JOÃO PANDIÁ** (b. 19 June 1870; d. 21 April 1934), Brazilian statesman, minister, and author. Educated as an engineer, Calógeras served as a federal deputy (1897–1899 and 1903–1914). He sponsored a law giving the government control over subsoil resources, and was active in boundary and military questions. Close to reformist army officers, who backed his appointment as minister of agriculture, industry, and commerce in 1914, he rose to minister of economy (Fazenda) in 1915–1917. He reorganized government finances and foreign loans, thereby preventing foreign creditors from gaining control over customs receipts.

At the Versailles Conference, he served as delegation chief after Epitácio PESSOA was elected president. In 1919, Pessoa named him the first and only civilian to serve as the republic's minister of war (1919–1922). He oversaw the reorganization of the army, the establishment of army aviation and the French Military Mission, the creation of new training schools, a re-armament program, the massive building of new barracks, and the development of a national defense policy. Military professionalization contributed to the revolt of July 1922 that began the cycle of rebellion leading to the Revolution of 1930. Calógeras backed Getúlio VARGAS in the 1930 election and was participating in the constituent assembly when he died in 1934. A convert to Catholicism, in 1932 he was president of the Liga Eleitoral Católica. His books and articles ranged from history and government to engineering and religion.

EGYDIO MOREIRA DE CASTRO E SILVA, *À margem do ministério Calógeras* (1961); LAWRENCE H. HALL, "João Pandiá Calógeras, Minister of War, 1919–1922: The Role of a Civilian in the Development of the Brazilian Army," Ph.D. diss., New York University (1983); JOÃO PANDIÁ CALÓGERAS, *A History of Brazil*, translated and edited by Percy A. Martin (1939).

FRANK D. McCANN, JR.

**CALPULLI** (from *calpolli*, "big house"), a Nahuatl term for a subdivision of an ALTEPETL, sometimes used synonymously with or replaced by TLAXILACALLI. There have been several definitions for *calpulli*, ranging from "kin group" to "temple" to the better-known "territorial district" (such differences arising from regional variation). There is greater agreement on the functional nature of the *calpulli*, often combined in groups of four, six, or eight within a single *altepetl*. The *calpulli* was the basic holder and distributor of usufruct on land to citizens, and the unit responsible for tribute collection and delivery. Each had its own leader and nobility, as well as a temple and market area. *Calpulli* were ranked in importance and proportionally represented in rotation at the level of *altepetl* administration. They were often divided into even smaller units, sometimes called *calpulli* or *tlaxilacalli* themselves. After the Spanish invasion, the *calpulli* persisted, retaining much of its pre-Hispanic organization.

Among the many scholars who have addressed the nature of the *calpulli* are EDWARD CALNEK, "The Internal Structure of Tenochtitlán," in *Ancient Mesoamerica, Selected Readings*, edited by John Allen Graham (1981), pp. 337–338; FRANCES BERDAN, *The Aztecs of Central Mexico: An Imperial Society* (1982), pp. 56–59; RUDOLF VAN ZANTWIJK, *The Aztec Arrangement: The Social History of Pre-Spanish Mexico* (1985); S. L. CLINE, *Colonial Culhuacán, 1580–1600: A Social History of an Aztec Town* (1986); SUSAN SCHROEDER, *Chimalpahin and the Kingdoms of Chalco* (1991); JAMES LOCKHART, *The Nahuas After the Conquest: A Social and Cultural History of the Indians of Central Mexico, Sixteenth through Eighteenth Centuries* (1992), esp. pp. 16–19.

ROBERT HASKETT

**CALUSA,** a native group in southwest Florida during the colonial period. The Calusa and their pre-Columbian ancestors inhabited the Gulf coast from Charlotte Harbor south to the Ten Thousand Islands (Florida Keys). They developed a powerful chiefdom based on the collection of marine foods rather than farming.

On his initial voyage to La Florida in 1513, Juan PONCE DE LEÓN tried to introduce a settlement among the Calusa but was driven away. In 1566 Pedro MENÉNDEZ DE AVILÉS established a Spanish garrison staffed with soldiers and Jesuit priests in the village of Calos; it was withdrawn in 1569. Spanish contact remained sporadic until 1697, when a Franciscan attempt to missionize the Calusa also failed. Diseases and raids by other native groups soon devastated the Calusa. Only remnants were still surviving in 1743, when Jesuits established the short-lived mission of Santa María de Loreto on the Miami River.

JOHN M. GOGGIN and WILLIAM C. STURTEVANT, "The Calusa: A Stratified Nonagricultural Society (with Notes on Sibling Marriage)," in *Explorations in Cultural Anthropology: Essays in Honor of George Peter Murdock*, edited by Ward H. Goodenough (1964); CLIFFORD M. LEWIS, "The Calusa," in *Tacachale: Essays on the Indians of Florida and Southeast Georgia during the Historic Period*, edited by Jerald Milanich and Samuel Proctor (1978); RANDOLPH J. WIDMER, *The Evolution of the Calusa: A Nonagricultural Chiefdom on the Southwest Florida Coast* (1988); JOHN H. HANN, ed. and trans., *Missions to the Calusa* (1991).

JERALD T. MILANICH

*See also* **Missions: Spanish America.**

**CALVO, CARLOS** (*b.* 26 February 1822; *d.* 3 May 1906), Argentine diplomat and jurist. Born in Montevideo and educated in Buenos Aires, Calvo lived in the tumultuous early years after independence in the Río de la Plata region. In 1859, the president of Paraguay, Carlos Antonio LÓPEZ, appointed him Paraguay's representative to mediate a conflict between Great Britain and Paraguay. His mission was a success. Thereafter he retired from public life to write. In 1868, he published a book that gave him international recognition, *Derecho internacional teórico y práctico de Europa y América*, which contained the essence of what has come to be known as the CALVO DOCTRINE.

He argued that America as well as Europe consisted of free and independent nations and that their sovereignty not be ignored. He declared that sovereign states enjoyed the right to freedom from intervention by other states. Moreover, foreigners were not entitled to rights not accorded to nationals. Thus, the essence of Calvo's ideas were nonintervention and the absolute equality of foreigners with nationals. According to Calvo, European interventions in Latin America were a violation of the equality of sovereign nations, and no nation had the right to employ force against another for the enforcement of contracts or agreements between its citizens and those of the other. Many Latin American countries have incorporated this clause into contracts with international corporations.

Calvo enjoyed a long diplomatic career. In 1878, he served as a delegate to the International Congress of Geography that met in Paris. He was minister plenipotentiary to the postal congress of Paris (1878) and Vienna (1891). In 1883 he became special envoy and minister plenipotentiary to Berlin and to the Russian and Austrian emperors in 1889 and 1890, respectively. In 1899, Calvo was appointed minister to France and the Holy See. He died in Paris.

PERCY BORDWELL, "Calvo and the 'Calvo Doctrine,' " *Green Bag* 18 (July 1906): 377–382; JOSÉ YVES LIMANTOUR, *Memoria sobre la vida y obra de D. Carlos Calvo* (1909); A. S. DE BUSTAMANTE, "Carlos Calvo" in *Encyclopaedia of the Social Sciences*, vol. 3 (1930).

JUAN MANUEL PÉREZ

**CALVO DOCTRINE,** a concept stressing absolute state sovereignty and equality, developed by Carlos CALVO, an Argentine diplomat and jurist. The Calvo doctrine was first presented in Calvo's treatise *El derecho internacional teórico y práctico* (1868). His stress on sovereignty and equality was prompted by a number of European interventions—armed, diplomatic, and financial—on behalf of their citizens to recover damages resulting from debt default, civil war, and revolution. These states claimed special protection for their nations. Calvo rejected these claims for special treatment. He laid down rules that all foreign claims had to be submitted to the national courts in the first instance and later go through the proper diplomatic channels. His approach was strongly supported by the Latin American states and resulted in a convention on the rights of aliens being considered at the PAN-AMERICAN CONFERENCES.

Calvo's doctrine gave birth to the Calvo Clause, which a number of American states, such as Mexico, required to be inserted in contracts with foreign companies: all disputes had to be settled in the country of origin, and the company could not appeal to its government for help.

DONALD RICHARD SHEA, *The Calvo Clause: A Problem of Inter-American and International Law and Diplomacy* (1955); ANN VAN WYNEN THOMAS and A. J. THOMAS, JR., *Non-Intervention: The Law and Its Import in the Americas* (1956); and HAROLD E. DAVIS, JOHN J. FINAN, and F. TAYLOR PECK, *Latin American Diplomatic History: An Introduction* (1977).

LARMAN C. WILSON

*See also* **Drago, Luis María.**

**CAMACHO ROLDÁN, SALVADOR** (*b.* 1 January 1827; *d.* 19 June 1900), Colombian Liberal politician, publicist, and businessman. Born in Nunchía, Casanare, Camacho received his doctorate in law and became a judge in 1848. His prominence brought him increasingly higher appointments during the 1850s, including the governorship of Panama (1852–1853). Camacho was elected to the House of Representatives in 1854 and served both there and in the Senate for the next thirty years. A fiscal expert, he served successively as minister of finance and development (1870–1872) and of foreign affairs (1878). He had been president designate (1868–1869) and acting president (December 1869) but never became president, except for one day in July 1871. Camacho's decades of public service left him poor until 1887, when he established the Librería Colombiana and the dry goods firm of Camacho Roldán y Tamayo, in Bogotá. He edited numerous important newspapers from 1849 to 1881. Camacho advocated a technologically oriented educational system as the means to economic growth. His *Escritos varios* (3 vols., 1892–1895, repr. 1983) were culled from his extensive corpus of economic and political works. His travels are recorded in *Notas de viaje* (1898). Camacho is best known for his *Memorias* (2 vols., 1894, 1924, repr. 1946). He died at "El Ocaso," his country house, at Zipacón, Cundinamarca, about thirty miles from Bogotá.

ANTONIO JOSÉ IREGUI, *Ensayo biográfico: Salvador Camacho Roldán* (1919).

J. LEÓN HELGUERA

**CÂMARA, HÉLDER** (Dom Hélder; *b.* 7 February 1909), Brazilian Catholic archbishop. Born in the poor northeastern state of Ceará, Câmara was ordained as a priest at age twenty-two. As a young cleric, he joined Ação Integralista Brasileira, a movement that sympathized with fascism. In 1936, he went to Rio de Janeiro to work with archbishop Sebastião Leme. In the 1940s, when he served as national assistant to Brazilian Catholic Action, Câmara moved toward liberal theological and political positions.

In 1952, Câmara was named auxiliary bishop of Rio. That same year, he helped create the National Conference of Brazilian Bishops (CNBB), which became the most important organization within the Brazilian Catholic church. From 1952 until 1964, he served as secretary-general of the CNBB. In 1955, Câmara created the São Sebastião Crusade, a liberal organization whose objective was to improve the living conditions in Rio's *favelas* (slums).

On 12 March 1964, three weeks before the military coup, Câmara was named archbishop of Recife and Olinda. The new archbishop repeatedly denounced the military regime for human rights abuses, for neglecting the poor, and for imposing an economic model that concentrated wealth. His courageous statements in the face of constant intimidation made the diminutive cleric the most famous church leader in Brazil. At first relatively isolated in his criticisms of the military government, by the late 1960s Câmara had the support of a substantial part of the church hierarchy. He and many of his close associates in the archdiocese were frequently harassed by the military government; some were expelled from Brazil, tortured, and even killed. Câmara was a leading figure in the turn of the Brazilian church toward more progressive ecclesiastical and political positions in the 1960s and 1970s.

After retiring as archbishop in 1985, Câmara continued to work in Recife, mostly among the urban poor. His successor, José Cardoso Sobrinho, dismantled many of the programs Câmara had established and clashed with many who had worked with the retired archbishop.

José de Broucker, *Dom Hélder Câmara* (1970).

Scott Mainwaring

*See also* **Brazil: Organizations; Catholic Church.**

**CAMARENA, ENRIQUE** (*b.* 26 July 1947; *d.* February 1985), a U.S. Drug Enforcement Administration (DEA) agent who was abducted on 7 February 1985, and then tortured and murdered, while on assignment in Mexico. Camarena's body was discovered one month later on a ranch in Guadalajara. Mexican officials placed blame for the murder on a Guadalajara drug kingpin, Rafael Caro Quintero. The DEA, however, conducted a lengthy and controversial investigation that linked high-ranking Mexican officials to the murder, including Rubén Zuno Arce, a prominent Mexican businessman and brother-in-law of former Mexican President Luis echeverría. The controversy heightened when Mexican officials refused to allow DEA agents to participate in the investigation or view evidence as it was uncovered. Eventually, the U.S. government claimed that the Camarena case was intimately linked to members of Mexico's political elite, and the DEA charged that some Mexican officials were involved in a cover-up.

The Camarena case strained relations between the United States and Mexico. Frustrated by the slow pace of the case, in February 1985 the U.S. government brought pressure to bear on the Mexican government by ordering detailed inspections of all vehicles entering the United States from Mexico, virtually closing the border and threatening the economies of Mexican border cities and states. The difficulties intensified when DEA agents masterminded the April 1990 kidnapping and forcible extradition of a Guadalajara physician, Humberto Alvarez Machain, who was implicated in the torture of Camarena. The U.S. Supreme Court ruled, in 1993, that Alvarez Machain's forcible abduction from a foreign country did not prohibit his trial in the United States. The court's decision, while hailed as a victory against terrorism and drug trafficking, was seen as a major threat to national sovereignty by Mexico and other Latin American countries.

At the end of numerous trials in the United States and Mexico, nineteen Mexican citizens, ranging from civilians to police officers and high-ranking persons, were indicted in the kidnapping, torture, and/or murder of DEA agent Camarena. The case produced great resentment in Mexico because of the overbearing attitude of the U.S. officials and violations of Mexican sovereignty; it reinforced images in the United States of corruption and noncooperative attitudes on the part of Mexican officials.

Andreas Lowenfeld, "Mexico and the United States, an Undiplomatic Murder," in *The Economist,* 30 March 1985; u.s. house of representatives, committee on the judiciary, *Drug Enforcement Administration Reauthorization for Fiscal Year 1986: Hearing Before the Subcommittee on Crime . . . May 1, 1985* (1986); Andreas Lowenfeld, "Kidnapping by Government Order: A Follow-up," in *The American Journal of International Law* 84 (July 1990): 712–716; William Dirk Raat, *Mexico and the United States: Ambivalent Vistas* (1992).

Paul Ganster

*See also* **Drugs and Drug Trade.**

**CAMARGO, SERGIO DE** (*b.* 1930), Brazilian sculptor. A native of Rio de Janeiro, Camargo left Brazil in the 1940s. In 1946 he entered the Academia d'Altimira art school in Buenos Aires, where he studied with the artist Emilio pettoruti and one of the school's founders, the painter Lucio fontana. He went to Europe for the first time in 1948, and studied philosophy at the Sorbonne in Paris. Influenced by Constantin Brancuşi, Jean Arp, and Georges Vantongerloo, he began to sculpt. From 1948 to 1974, Camargo lived in Paris. In 1953, he traveled to Rio de Janeiro, where he exhibited several of his sculptural works in Rio's National Salon of Modern Art. He also made a brief trip to China.

Although figural sculpture predominated in his early years, Camargo experimented with wood reliefs, geometric abstractionism, and constructivism. Along with contemporaries Julio Le Parc and Carlos cruz diez, Camargo is also one of the pioneers of kinetic art. Using a cylinder or cube, he arranges forms and explores the "madness of order." He received the International Sculpture Prize at the 1963 Paris Biennale. In 1965, he began sculptural pieces for Oscar niemeyer's Foreign Ministry Building in Brasília. In the same year, he was named best national sculptor in the São Paulo Bienal. He returned to Rio de Janeiro in 1974, and in 1977 he won the sculpture award given by the São Paulo Association of Art Critics. In the 1980s Camargo had solo exhibitions in both the Rio and São Paulo museums of modern art, and he participated in the 1982 Venice Biennale.

*Arte no Brasil,* vol. 2 (1979), esp. p. 933; dawn ades, *Art in Latin America* (1989), esp. pp. 270–275.

Caren A. Meghreblian

**CAMARILLA,** popular term to describe a political network in Mexico. Throughout much of the nineteenth and twentieth centuries, Mexican political leaders have relied on personal networks or contacts to achieve successful careers in public life. These groups, which are frequently known as *camarillas,* have been described as the cement of Mexican politics. Since the 1940s, the most important locus of *camarilla* formation has been at the universities, especially the National University, and within the federal bureaucracy. Generally, politicians use their influence as professors and public officials to promote the careers of their disciples and to expand personal ties vertically and horizontally throughout the public arena.

PETER H. SMITH, *Labyrinths of Power* (1979); and RODERIC A. CAMP, "Camarillas in Mexican Politics," in *Mexican Studies* 6 (1990): 85–107.

RODERIC AI CAMP

**CAMBACERES, EUGENIO** (*b.* 24 February 1843; *d.* 14 June 1889), Argentine novelist. Cambaceres was born in Buenos Aires into a wealthy landholding Argentine family of French heritage. Like other young Argentines of fortune, he frequently traveled to Europe, making his headquarters in Paris. There and in his native city he was known as a man-about-town, very fond of the ladies; he married an opera diva shortly before his death. During the 1870s, Cambaceres engaged unsuccessfully in politics, and only during middle age, in the 1880s, did he start writing novels. In six short years, he produced four volumes—*Sin rumbo* (1885) is his masterpiece. This promising literary career was cut short when he died of tuberculosis.

All of his novels—*Potpourri* (1882), *Música sentimental* (1884), *Sin rumbo*, and *En la sangre* (1887)—are cast in the naturalist mold, influenced by the French writer Émile Zola. Cambaceres bitterly attacks society, but unlike Zola fails to give moral guidance. In most of his work, we find a typical naturalistic stress on the sordid; the romantic love of earlier nineteenth-century Spanish American novels has given way to an obsession with sex. In its best moments, however, *Sin rumbo* transcends its naturalist theme and trappings and becomes a powerfully dramatic novel, written with intensity and great narrative art. It has become a classic, one of the most dynamic and significant works of nineteenth-century Spanish American literature.

MYRON I. LICHTBLAU, "Naturalism in the Argentine Novel," in his *The Argentine Novel in the Nineteenth Century* (1959), pp. 163–184; R. ANTHONY CASTAGNARO, *The Early Spanish American Novel* (1971), pp. 119–129; MARÍA LUISA BASTOS, introduction to *Sin rumbo* (1971), pp. 7–29.

GEORGE SCHADE

**CAMILLE, ROUSSAN** (*b.* 27 August 1912; *d.* 7 December 1961), Haitian poet and journalist. Camille first wrote for *Le temps*, often publishing poems along with his regular columns. He was named editor in chief of *Haïti Journal* (1935) and director (1936), after the death of Charles Moravia. From 1947 to his death, he held several official positions: division head in the ministry of public instruc-

tion (during World War II), vice-consul of Haiti in New York City (1947–1948), secretary to President Dumarsais Estimé (1948–1950), and director of cultural affairs. Camille was imprisoned briefly after serving President Estimé. At the news of Camille's death, Franck Fouché published a poem to "celebrate the multiple presence of a great poet" (*Symphonie en noir majeur*, 1962).

Camille moved away from French poets toward the inspiration of Langston Hughes and Nicolás Guillén. He wrote with empathy for the victim—whether slave, prostitute, or child—and a sense of fraternity with his fellow poets. He was awarded the Dumarsais Estimé Prize for his collected poetry when he submitted the manuscript of *La multiple présence* in 1961. Among his other works are *Assaut à la nuit* (1940), and *La multiple présence, derniers poèmes* (1978).

NAOMI M. GARRET, *The Renaissance of Haitian Poetry* (1963), pp. 167–175; F. RAPHAËL BERROU and PRADEL POMPILUS, *Histoire de la littérature haïtienne illustrée par les textes*, vol. 3 (1977), 237–252.

CARROL F. COATES

**CAMNITZER, LUIS** (*b.* 1937), Uruguayan artist. German born, Camnitzer emigrated with his family to Uruguay in 1939. He studied sculpture and architecture at the Universidad de la República Oriental del Uruguay in Montevideo in the 1950s, and at the Akademie der Bildenden Künste in Munich (1957). He received a John Simon Guggenheim Memorial Fellowship in 1964 and moved to New York City, where he was also granted a Memorial Foundation for Jewish Culture Fellowship (1965–1966). He was a founding member of the New York Graphic Workshop (1967). During this period he used text without images to describe spaces and objects in installations. He has taught at the Pratt Institute, Fairleigh Dickinson University, and the State University of New York (Old Westbury).

Using text, a site plan, and schematic representations, Camnitzer acknowledged the 1969 massacre in Puerto Montt, Chile. In an installation consisting of a wall of boxes, each wrapped in bloodstained gauze to symbolize anonymous political victims, Camnitzer presented the theme of political repression in Latin America (*Leftovers*, 1970). In the 1980s he addressed themes related to human rights and environmental decay in Latin America. An outsider to the art market system, Camnitzer has devoted a great deal of his time to writing about art and organizing noncommercial exhibitions.

ANGEL KALENBERG, *Luis Camnitzer* (1987); CARLA STELLWEG, " 'Magnet–New York': Conceptual, Performance, Environmental, and Installation Art by Latin American Artists in New York," in Luis R. Cancel et al., *The Latin American Spirit: Art and Artists in the United States, 1920–1970* (1988), pp. 299–301; LUIS CAMNITZER, GERARDO MOSQUERA, and MARÍA DEL CARMEN RAMÍREZ, *Luis Camnitzer: A Retrospective Exhibition 1966–1990* (1991).

MARTA GARSD

**CAMÕES, LUÍS VAZ DE** (*b.* 1525?; *d.* 10 June 1580), Portuguese poet. One of the most renowned figures of Portuguese letters, Luís de Camões authored a substantial corpus that includes the epic poem *Os Lusíadas* (*The Lusiads,* 1572), a cornerstone of his fame in world literature, lyric poetry (principal editions published in 1595 and 1598), plays, and familiar epistles. Little biographical information is known about Camões, although it's certain that he spent many of his adult years as a soldier in the Portuguese Empire. His poetry, written in both Portuguese and Spanish, was composed in the traditional style (the *medida velha,* as it was known in the poet's time) as well as in the *dolce stil nuovo,* introduced into Portugal by Francisco de Sá de MIRANDA. *Os Lusíadas* consists of 1,102 stanzas in ottava rima divided into ten cantos and reflects the epic imagination of the sixteenth-century Portuguese. The theme is nothing less than the history of Portugal—and it is the nation that emerges as the collective hero—articulated around the voyage of Vasco da GAMA to India in 1497. *Os Lusíadas* was the model for Bento Teixeira's *Prosopopéia* (1601), an encomiastic poem about Jorge de Albuquerque COELHO, governor of Pernambuco.

JORGE DE SENA, *Trinta anos de Camões, 1948–1978: Estudos camonianos e correlatos* (1980); MARIA DE LOURDES BELCHIOR and ENRIQUE MARTÍNEZ-LÓPEZ, eds., *Camoniana Californiana: Commemorating the Quadricentennial of the Death of Luís Vaz de Camões; Proceedings of the Colloquium Held at the University of California, Santa Barbara, April 25 and 26, 1980* (1985); DAVID QUINT, "Voices of Resistance: The Epic Curse and Camões's Adamastor," in *New World Encounters,* edited by Stephen Greenblatt (1993).

JOSIAH BLACKMORE

*See also* **Portuguese Empire.**

**CAMPA SALAZAR, VALENTÍN** (*b.* 14 February 1904), Mexican labor union leader and presidential candidate, a controversial figure in the railroad workers' union and a longtime activist of the Mexican Communist Party while it was underground. Born in Monterrey, Nuevo León, Campa completed only his first year of secondary education before he began working for La Corona, a subsidiary of the Royal Dutch Company, in 1920. He was a labor activist and organizer, cofounding the Sindicato Unitario Mexicano. Imprisoned thirteen times for his labor organizing, first in 1927, Campa spent ten years in Lecumberri Prison after a 1958–1959 railroad strike. Campa ran for president on the legalized Mexican Communist Party (PCM) ticket in 1976 and served as a federal deputy for the PCM in the 1979–1982 legislature.

VALENTÍN CAMPA SALAZAR, *Mi testimonio* (1978).

RODERIC AI CAMP

**CAMPERO, NARCISO** (*b.* 29 October 1813; *d.* 12 August 1896), president of Bolivia (1880–1884). Campero was born in Tojo in the department of Tarija. Near the beginning of his military career, he fought in the battle of Ingavi in November 1841. He attended military school in Paris in 1845. From 1859 to 1879 Campero served in military, diplomatic, and administrative posts, usually under Liberal presidents. When the WAR OF THE PACIFIC began in 1879, he was appointed general of the Fifth Division. Because of their confidence in Campero, the Bolivian directors of the Huanchaca Silver Company sent provisions to the Fifth Division. When the inhabitants of La Paz overthrew President Hilarión DAZA on 27 December 1879, they named Campero as their new leader. Following the advice of the silver barons, Campero gradually removed Bolivia from the war by 1884. Meanwhile, to legitimize his new government, Campero called a constituent assembly, which met in 1880. The delegates not only confirmed Campero as president but also approved a new constitution for Bolivia that remained in force until 1938. By cooperating with the mining oligarchy, Campero brought an end to unstable caudillo rule and, through the Constitution of 1880, allowed a small elite of mine owners to open Bolivia to the industrial world.

JULIO DÍAZ ARGUEDAS, *Los generales de Bolivia (rasgos biográficos) 1825–1925* (1929), pp. 247–261; HERBERT S. KLEIN, *Parties and Political Change in Bolivia, 1880–1952* (1969), pp. 14, 18.

ERWIN P. GRIESHABER

*See also* **Mining.**

**CAMPESINO,** the Spanish word for "peasant." In modern times the term has taken on a broader meaning in Spanish America. Now *campesino* is used to refer to all members of the Latin American rural working class. This includes agricultural wage laborers (*jornaleros*) and small landholders (*minifundistas*). The term also still refers to peasants (*mozos colonos*) who peform labor for the right to farm a small plot of land or in exchange for agricultural produce. *Campesino* is a very general term which encompasses all rural people of the lower economic strata, including men, women, and children.

RACHEL A. MAY

*See also* **Colono.**

**CAMPISTEGUY, JUAN** (*b.* 7 September 1859; *d.* 1937), president of Uruguay (1927–1931). Campisteguy, born in Montevideo, entered politics when he joined the revolutionary movement against the autocratic regime of Máximo Santos in 1886. His career within the ruling Colorado party was closely linked to José BATLLE Y ORDÓÑEZ, of whose newspaper *El Día* he was one of the founding editors.

After two terms as member of the House of Representatives (1891–1897), Campisteguy was minister of finance (1897–1898) during Juan Lindolfo CUESTAS's constitutional presidency as well as during his autocratic period following the 1898 coup. In 1903/1904, as minister of government under Batlle y Ordóñez, Campisteguy was one of the architects of the government victory over the Blanco rebellion led by Aparicio SARAVIA. He was subsequently a senator (1905–1911); a member of the Constituent Assembly for the Colorado party's Riverista faction, which opposed Batlle's plans for the introduction of a *colegiado* system (1917); a deputy (1920–1923); and a member of the National Council of Administration (1921–1927).

Important achievements of Campisteguy's presidency were the creation of the state-owned Frigorífico Nacional (National Meat Packing Plant, 1928) and the Comité de Vigilancia Económica (Committee of Economic Vigilance, 1929).

PHILIP BATES TAYLOR, *Government and Politics of Uruguay* (1960); GÖRAN E. LINDAHL, *Uruguay's New Path: A Study in Politics During the First Colegiado, 1919–33* (1962).

DIETER SCHONEBOHM

**CAMPO, ESTANISLAO DEL** (*b.* 7 February 1834; *d.* 6 November 1880), Argentine poet, legislator, journalist, civil servant, and officer of the Civic Guard. His admiration for Hilario ASCASUBI and the GAUCHESCA LITERATURE prompted him to write poetry in this style. He even adopted the pseudonym of Anastasio el Pollo (Anastasio the Chicken) as a sign of respect for Ascasubi's *Aniceto el Gallo* (Aniceto the Rooster). In 1866 del Campo wrote the gauchesca poem *Fausto,* in which one GAUCHO, chatting with another, tells the plot of the Gounod opera that he happened to see in Buenos Aires's Teatro Colón. The novelty of this text is that del Campo injected an urban, highly cultured subject into gauchesca literature. He erased the disparity between the popular language and the cult subject of the Faustian legend by reducing it to the concrete reality and perceptions of the gaucho. In spite of the hilarity of the text, the gaucho-narrator and his friend are never ridiculed. On the contrary, their deep friendship is emphasized. The poem is also famous for its romantic descriptions, without parallel in gauchesca literature.

Committed to the party of General Bartolmé MITRE, del Campo fought at the battles of CEPEDA (1859) and PAVÓN (1861) for a Buenos Aires state separate from the ARGENTINE CONFEDERATION. In the late 1860s del Campo was elected to the House of Representatives of the province of Buenos Aires as a member of the Liberal Party. In 1874 he was made lieutenant colonel of the Civil Guard. Del Campo took part in the Mitre revolution against Nicolás AVELLANEDA. He retired from public life in April 1880 and died six months later in Buenos Aires.

MANUEL MÚJICA LÁINEZ, *Vidas del Gallo y el Pollo* (1966); ENRIQUE ANDERSON IMBERT, *Análisis de "Fausto"* (1968); TERESA SALAS and HENRY RICHARDS, "La función del marco y la armonía simétrica en el *Fausto* de Estanislao del Campo," in *Kentucky Romance Quarterly* 17 (1970): 55–66; OLLIE OLYMPO OVIEDO, "The Reception of the Faust Motif in Latin American Literature: Archetypal Transformations in Works by Estanislao del Campo, Alberto Gerchunoff, João Guimaraes Rosa, Carlos Fuentes, and Jaime Torres Bodet" (Ph.D. diss., New York University, 1978).

ANGELA B. DELLEPIANE

**CAMPO, RAFAEL** (*b.* 24 October 1813; *d.* 1 March 1890), president of El Salvador (1856–1858). Educated at the University of San Carlos de Guatemala, Campo continued his father's successful agricultural and commercial enterprises in El Salvador and was among the first coffee planters in the country. He became politically active in the Conservative Party and was elected president on 30 January 1856, taking office on 12 February. He turned over power to his vice president, Francisco Dueñas, on 12 May of the same year, but resumed the presidency on 19 July. Regarded by many as a puppet of Guatemalan caudillo Rafael CARRERA, the conservative Campo allowed greater political freedom than in other Central American states of the period.

In July 1856 Campo joined the other Central American states in the NATIONAL WAR against William WALKER, sending Salvadoran troops to Nicaragua under Ramón Belloso and Gerardo BARRIOS. Upon returning from the war in Nicaragua, Barrios failed in an effort to overthrow Campo in June 1857. Barrios gained power in 1858, however, when Campo stepped down on 1 February of that year, after the serious cholera epidemic of 1857 had exhausted the country. Campo later served as foreign minister under Francisco Dueñas, and was president of the Constitutional Convention of 1871. A critic of the Liberal governments that followed, Campo was in exile in Nicaragua for most of the decade following, but in 1882 he returned to Sonsonate, his birthplace, where he worked for the establishment of the hospital there. He died in Acajutla.

PHILIP F. FLEMION, *Historical Dictionary of El Salvador* (1972), pp. 29–30; MARÍA LEISTENSCHNEIDER and FREDDY LEISTENSCHNEIDER, *Gobernantes de El Salvador: Biografías* (1980), pp. 103–105.

RALPH LEE WOODWARD, JR.

**CAMPO GRANDE,** capital of Mato Grosso do Sul State in central-west Brazil. This city first obtained its economic importance in 1914 when Brazil's railroad pushed through southern Mato Grosso, making Campo Grande an economic hub of the region. Prior to this, the majority of transportation through southern Mato Grosso was dependent upon water routes. In 1979 Campo Grande became the capital upon the division of Mato Grosso into Mato Grosso and Mato Grosso do Sul. As of 1989 the population of Campo Grande was about 435,448. The principal agricultural products include rice, soybeans, and wheat.

CAROLYN E. VIEIRA

## CAMPOMANES, PEDRO RODRÍGUEZ, CONDE DE

(*b.* 1 July 1723; *d.* 3 February 1802), president of the Council of Castile (1783–1791). The son of a poor Asturian hidalgo, Campomanes, an attorney, became a *fiscal* (crown attorney) of the Council of Castile in 1762. Committed to royal absolutism yet open to Enlightenment ideas, Campomanes was essentially a utilitarian who believed that the interests of special groups like the MESTA (sheepowners' corporation), clergy, and guilds were detrimental to the welfare of the state. In his capacity as policymaker and royal adviser to CHARLES III, Campomanes embarked upon a program of agrarian reform that advocated free grain trade within Spain, limits on ecclesiastical entailment of land, crown incorporation or *señorios* (noble or aristocratic estates), and elimination of guild restrictions. He was instrumental in the movement to repopulate deserted regions of Spain (1767), founded the Royal Economic Society of Madrid (1775), and used his position as president of the *Mesta* (1779) to weaken that institution and its agricultural privileges. His policy toward America included promoting colonial trade and prohibiting American manufacture.

LAURA RODRÍGUEZ DÍAZ, *Reforma e ilustración en la España del siglo XVIII: Pedro Rodríguez de Campomanes* (1975); MANUEL BUSTOS RODRÍGUEZ, *El pensamiento socio-económico de Campomanes* (1982).

SUZANNE HILES BURKHOLDER

## CÁMPORA, HÉCTOR JOSÉ

(*b.* 1909; *d.* 1980), president of Argentina (1973). Although Alejandro LANUSSE allowed Juan D. PERÓN to return from exile in Spain to Argentina, a 9 July 1972 rule required that candidates be in residence by 25 August 1972. Whatever the reason, Perón did not return until November, thereby forfeiting his eligibility to run for president and enabling someone else, namely Héctor Cámpora, to risk defeat. Lanusse also ruled that the Peronists had to capture 50 percent of the vote to take office. Lanusse's rule notwithstanding, Cámpora was sworn in with 49 percent on 25 May 1973 but remained president only until 13 July 1973.

Born in 1909 in Mercedes, Buenos Aires Province, Cámpora trained in odontology and practiced as a dentist during his periodic political eclipses. He was national deputy for his province from 1946 to 1952 and served as president of the national Chamber of Deputies (1948–1952). He advised on Argentina's constitutional reform of 1949 and in 1951 assisted Brazil with the same issues of the presidential mandate and term in office. The following year he was returned for another six years as deputy. After the military coup of September 1955 Cámpora fled to Chile, where he remained until 1963, when the amnesty allowed him to return.

Though usually viewed as a puppet of Perón, Cámpora did not lack ideas of his own. His presidency showed conciliation to guerrillas, labor militants, and students. Such policies cost him Perón's support, so that

he fell on 13 July 1973. Raúl Lastiri bridged the rest of the gap until Perón himself assumed the presidency on 12 October 1973. Following Perón's death on 1 July 1974, Cámpora opposed Perón's wife, Isabel. He ran for president on the Authentic Peronist Party ticket with Oscar Alende. After the military coup of 24 March 1976, Cámpora sought asylum in Mexico's embassy in Buenos Aires. He died of throat cancer, for which the military had denied him treatment, at the end of 1980.

JOSÉ LUÍS BERNETTI, *El peronismo de la victoria* (1983); DONALD C. HODGES, *Argentina, 1943–1987: The National Revolution and Resistance* (1988).

ROGER GRAVIL

## CAMPOS, FRANCISCO LUIZ DA SILVA

(*b.* 18 November 1891; *d.* 1 November 1968), Brazilian presidential adviser. The son of Jacinto Alves da Silva Campos and Azejúlia de Souza e Silva, Campos was born in Dores de Indaiá, Minas Gerais. A lawyer, politician, and educator, he married Lavinia Ferreira da Silva, with whom he had two children. The couple eventually separated; later he lived with Margarita Leite.

As an educator, Campos was a professor at the Faculty of Law in his home state and a tenured professor at the Federal University of Rio de Janeiro. As a politician, he held various posts, including state legislator, federal legislator, secretary of the interior for the state of Minas Gerais, and mayor of Belo Horizonte. He was also a leader in the Liberal Alliance, which supported the presidential candidacy of Getúlio VARGAS, a movement that culminated in the Constitutionalist Revolution of 1930.

As the country's first minister of health and education (1930–1932), Campos reformed the training procedures for primary school teachers and established a federal university educational system. He wrote a number of works on education, including *Educação e cultura* (1940). As a jurist, Campos authored case studies and opinions that still appear in constitutional, administrative, and civil law texts.

In 1932, as Vargas's interim minister of justice, Campos had a great impact on the implantation of the ESTADO NOVO (New State) program and authored the 1937 *Estado Novo* charter, in which many corporatist features were outlined. In addition, he was the main author of the Institutional Act No. 1, which juridically incorporated the revolution in the spring of 1964. He died in Belo Horizonte in 1968.

MICHAEL L. CONNIF and FRANK D. MC CANN, eds., *Modern Brazil* (1989); ALFRED STEPAN, ed., *Democratizing Brazil* (1989).

IÊDA SIQUEIRA WIARDA

## CAMPOS, JULIETA

(*b.* 8 May 1932), Mexican novelist, essayist, and translator. Born in Cuba, Campos has resided in Mexico since 1960 and is a naturalized Mexican. As writer-in-residence at the Centro Mexicano de

Escritores (1966–1967) and on staff at the Instituto de Investigaciones Estéticas at the National University of Mexico (1969–1970), Campos has been active in the cultural politics of the country. She began as an essayist and translator in Mexican journals and cultural supplements in the 1950s and became a collaborator and member of the editorial board of *Vuelta* in 1977. She served as director of the *Revista de la Universidad de México* from 1981 to 1984. Campos won the Xavier Villaurrutia Prize for her novel *Tiene los cabellos rojizos y se llama Sabina* (1974), and in 1993 her novel *El miedo de perder a Eurídice* (1979) was translated into English. Rejecting traditional narrative forms of plot, linearity, and spatial and temporal specificity, she elaborates in her writing a self-reflexive and imaginative perspective on identity, nostalgia, love, time, and death. Her critical work includes assessments of literary authors and periods, discussions of the nature and function of literature, and the study of Nahuatl stories within the problematics of oralism and literacy.

JUAN BRUCE-NOVOA, "Julieta Campos' *Sabina*: In the Labyrinth of Intertextuality," in *Third Woman* 2, no. 2 (1984): 43–63; EVELYN PICON GARFIELD, "Julieta Campos," in her *Women's Voices from Latin America* (1985), pp. 73–96; FABIENNE BRADU, "Julieta Campos: La cartografía del deseo y la muerte," in her *Señas particulares: Escritora* (1987), pp. 71–85; MARÍA INÉS LAGOS-POPE, "Cat/Logos: The Narrator's Confession in Julieta Campos' *Celina o los gatos*," in *Splintering Darkness: Latin American Women Writers in Search of Themselves*, edited by Lucia Guerra-Cunningham (1990), pp. 31–42.

NORMA KLAHN

**CAMPOS, LUIS MARÍA** (*b.* 1838; *d.* 1907), Argentine military leader. Born in Buenos Aires, Campos entered the army in 1859 as a sublieutenant in the national guard regiment. He fought in the battles of CEPEDA and PAVÓN, which ended the long struggle among the provinces, earning the rank of sergeant major. Campos served throughout the WAR OF THE TRIPLE ALLIANCE (1864–1870), perhaps the bloodiest in Latin American history. He fought at Paso de la Patría, Estero Bellaco, and CURUPAYTY. Seriously wounded at San Ignacio, Campos was sent to the province of San Juan to recover. Returning to the war, he fought at most major engagements, including Lomas Valentinas and Angostura. Late in the war he was decorated by the commander in chief of Allied Forces, CONDE D'EU, for his bravery.

Between 1870 and 1873 Campos fought against Ricardo LÓPEZ JORDÁN, the rebellious caudillo of Entre Ríos. In 1875 he was named inspector general of arms, and in 1892 he was appointed chief of staff of the army and then minister of war and navy until 1896. In March 1896 he mobilized the national guard for a possible international conflict, and in 1898 he again became minister of war. At this time the Army War College was established under his supervision. He was promoted to lieutenant general in 1899 and retired in January 1906.

*Ejército argentino: Cronología militar argentina, 1806–1980* (1982); FELIX BEST, *Historia de las guerras argentinas*, 2 vols. (1983).

ROBERT SCHEINA

**CAMPOS, MANUEL JORGE** (*b.* 22 April 1847; *d.* 15 December 1908), Argentine general who led troops in support of the Radical Party rebellion against President Miguel JUÁREZ CELMAN in July 1890. Born in Buenos Aires, Campos was a career military officer who saw service in the WAR OF THE TRIPLE ALLIANCE, fought to support the national government against regional caudillos, and served with General Julio ROCA in campaigns to conquer the Indians of Argentina's southern plains.

In 1890 the leader of the Radical Party, Leandro ALEM, sought assistance from expresident Bartolomé MITRE and General Campos in a revolt against the Conservative president. Campos led his troops in a desultory fashion while Mitre negotiated the resignation of the president and the assumption of Vice President Carlos PELLEGRINI, a compromise that angered Alem. In 1892 Campos became the chief of police in the federal capital, and he later served as a senator, then a national deputy, in Congress.

DAVID ROCK, *Argentina, 1516–1987: From Spanish Colonization to Alfonsín* (1987), provides a good description of the revolt of 1890 within the framework of the development of middle-class politics. For more on Campos's participation in the revolt, see DOUGLAS W. RICHMOND, *Carlos Pellegrini and the Crisis of the Argentine Elites, 1880–1916* (1989), esp. pp. 42–44.

JAMES A. BAER

**CAMPOS, ROBERTO (DE OLIVEIRA)** (*b.* 17 April 1917), Brazilian minister of planning and economic coordination (1964–1967). Diplomat, economist, professor, public official, and legislator, Campos has been a central participant in Brazilian economic affairs since joining the foreign service in 1939. He is known for his neoliberal (conservative) economic positions, including less state intervention and fewer restrictions on foreign capital investment. He attended many of the international economic conferences held in the 1940s, including the Bretton Woods Conference. As a government economic adviser in the 1950s, Campos helped found the National Economic Development Bank (Banco Nacional de Desenvolvimento Econômico—BNDE) to finance infrastructure and served as its director-superintendent (1955–1958) and president (1958–1959). He has held many posts in government, acting as ambassador to the United States (1961–1963) and to London (1975–1982), federal senator (1983–1991), and federal deputy (1991–).

As minister of planning and economic coordination (1964–1967), Campos was the principal architect of the Economic Action Plan of the Government (Plano de Ação Econômica do Governo—PAEG), which included budget-balancing and restrictions on money-supply growth to fight inflation and institutional reforms to provide the foundation for further economic expansion. Among the reforms enacted were indexed government bonds, called Readjustable Obligations of the National Treasury (Obrigações Reajustáveis do Tesoro Nacional—ORTN), and a general indexation system, termed *correção monetária* (monetary correction); a noninflationary and regressive wage policy; a weakening of job security; a housing finance system; limited, proproduction land reform; and a central bank. PAEG brought down inflation, but at the cost of an unpopular recession. The reforms established the basic institutional framework for subsequent Brazilian economic life and provided the foundations for the subsequent high-growth period called the ECONOMIC MIRACLE (1968–1974).

ISRAEL BELOCH and ALZIRA ALVES DE ABREU, eds., *Dicionário histórico-biográfico brasileiro, 1930–1983* vol. 1 (1984); LEÔNCIO MARTINS RODRIGUES, *Quem é quem na constituinte: Uma análise sócio-política dos partidos e deputados* (1987); WERNER BAER, *The Brazilian Economy: Growth and Development,* 3d ed. (1989).

RUSSELL E. SMITH

*See also* **Delfim Neto, Antônio; Economic Development; Furtada, Celso; Simonsen, Mário Henrique.**

**CAMPOS CERVERA, HÉRIB** (*b.* 1905; *d.* 28 August 1953), Paraguayan poet. Widely considered to be Paraguay's finest poet of the post–Chaco War (post-1935) generation, Campos Cervera has left an indelible mark on the literature of his country. Descended from a well-known family of artists and writers, he began his life's work in poetry while teaching engineering at the Colegio Nacional and at the Escuela Normal de Profesores. Initially, his poems appeared only in student newspapers, but he soon gained a literary following in intellectual circles in Asunción.

Campos Cervera's earliest works were heavily influenced by the modernism of Rubén DARÍO and other turn-of-the-century writers. After a time, however, he became attracted to the *vanguardista* school and soon became its principal exponent in Paraguay. During the 1930s Campos Cervera was forced into exile because of his political associations. This stay outside of the country was actually helpful in developing his talent: in Buenos Aires, he discovered the writings of Federico García Lorca (who became his personal friend), and he helped found the literary group *Vy'araity,* which counted among its members his aunt Josefina PLÁ, the novelist Augusto ROA BASTOS, and such figures as Hugo RODRÍGUEZ ALCALÁ and Oscar Ferreiro.

Campos Cervera's finest work can be found in his poetic compilation *Ceniza redimida.* He also was among the first to popularize poetry in the GUARANÍ language. He died in Buenos Aires.

RAÚL AMARAL, *Escritos paraguayos* (1984), pp. 217–227; CARLOS ZUBIZARRETA, *Cien vidas paraguayas,* 2d ed. (1985), pp. 322–325.

MARTA FERNÁNDEZ WHIGHAM

**CAMPOS-PARSI, HÉCTOR** (*b.* 10 October 1922), Puerto Rican composer, music critic, teacher, and concert manager. Campos-Parsi completed his early education in Ponce and then went on to study biology and psychology at the University of Puerto Rico. In 1945 he entered the school of medicine at the National University of Mexico, but ill health forced him to abandon this pursuit. He received a fellowship to the New England Conservatory from 1947 to 1950 and, while in New England, also studied with Aaron Copland who arranged for him to work in Paris under Nadia Boulanger from 1950 to 1953. He was named director of the music division of the Institute of Puerto Rican Culture in 1958 and in 1970 to the Academy of Arts and Sciences. A prolific composer in various styles, he is best known for his *Sonatina para piano y violín* for which he won the Maurice Ravel Prize in 1953, *Tres fantasías para piano* (1950), and *Juan Bobo y las fiestas* (1957). Copland's influence is most evident in Campos-Parsi's folkloric works such as *Yerba bruja* (1962) and *Arawak* (1970).

General overviews of his life and work can be found in FERNANDO CALLEJO Y FERRER, *Música y músicos puertorriqueños* (1971) and FERNANDO H. CASO, *Héctor Campos-Parsi en la historia de la música puertorriqueña del siglo XX* (1980).

JACQUELYN BRIGGS KENT

**CAMPOS SALES, MANUEL FERRAZ DE** (*b.* 13 February 1841; *d.* 28 June 1913), president of Brazil (1898–1902). Born in Campinas, São Paulo, Campos Sales studied and practiced law before being elected a provincial deputy by the Liberal Party in 1867. He became an organizing member of the Republican Party of São Paulo in 1871, and was elected to the provincial chamber in 1881 and the national legislature in 1885 as a Republican and doctrinaire federalist. He was voluble, principled, and politically astute.

With the establishment of the Republic, Campos Sales served as minister of justice in General Manoel Deodoro da FONSECA's governments and built the administrative and judicial basis of the new republic. Weathering the political conflicts of the 1890s, he was elected president in 1898. His administration is best known for the reconstruction of the nation's finances and the creation of the political process that characterized the Republic until 1930.

In the economic crisis characterized by rampant inflation and speculation, known as the ENCILHAMENTO, Campos Sales made financial reconstruction the priority of the administration. Bolstered by the "funding loan" he negotiated with the Rothschilds, the government carried out deflationary currency policies, cut spending, abandoned public works, increased taxes and tariffs, and emphasized agriculture over industry. Notwithstanding considerable unpopularity for his policies, by 1902 Campos Sales had rehabilitated the national finances and international credit.

Elected in an atmosphere of regional revolts and fractious party politics, Campos Sales proclaimed himself above partisan politics. He articulated the POLÍTICA DOS GOVERNADORES, in which incumbent state governments supplied loyal federal congressional delegations in exchange for nonintervention in state affairs. Relying heavily on the larger states' economic and demographic strengths, the political system revolved around São Paulo and Minas Gerais. This reciprocity created a hierarchy of interlocking interests and loyalties down to the *coroneis*, the local bosses who delivered the votes for patronage and financial favors.

Sales died in Santos, São Paulo.

MANUEL FERRAZ DE CAMPOS SALES, *Da propaganda a presidencia* (1908; repr. 1983); CELIO DEBES, *Campos Sales: Perfil de um estadista*, 2 vols. (1978).

WALTER BREM

*See also* **Coronel, Coronelismo.**

**CANALES, NEMESIO ROSARIO** (*b.* 18 December 1878; *d.* 14 September 1923), Puerto Rican writer and statesman. Nemesio R. Canales interrupted his studies of medicine in Saragossa, Spain, in 1898, when Puerto Rico came under United States sovereignty. He left the island two years later to study at the Baltimore School of Law. After graduating in 1903, he returned to Puerto Rico to practice law and began a career in politics. He wrote articles for the *Revista de las Antillas* and *La Semana*, and a column for the Ponce newspaper *El Día*; he also co-founded *Juan Bobo*, a weekly, and edited *Cuasimodo*, an inter-American journal on culture. Concerned with politics and the economy as well as social, labor, and cultural issues, he served in the Puerto Rican Congress and in the Department of Justice. His most famous work is a collection of humorously ironic articles entitled *Paliques* (Chit-chat, 1913). Canales also published a novel, *Mi voluntad se ha muerto* (My will has died), in 1921, and a drama, *El héroe galopante* (The galloping hero), in 1923, the year of his death in New York.

JOSÉ GELPÍ, ed., *Nuevos Paliques y otras páginas de Nemesio R. Canales* (1965); MARÍA TERESA BABÍN, *Genio y figura de Nemesio R. Canales* (1978).

ESTELLE IRIZARRY

**CANANEA,** a copper MINING center in the northwestern state of Sonora that became for the Mexican Revolution a symbol of North American control over the economy, of the Porfirio DÍAZ regime's compliance in it, and of the rise of the labor movement to correct abuses and resist that alliance.

Though mines in the locality had been worked since the 1760s by a series of owners, they had remained

William Greene speaking in the commissariat at Cananea. ARCHIVO GENERAL DE LA NACIÓN, MEXICO.

small operations due to limited capital and Apache raiding (1820s–1860s). The North American adventurer-entrepreneur William Greene—through the application of large-scale corporate finance and organization beginning in 1896—transformed Cananea into one of the leading mining centers in Mexico. In addition to the mining of copper, Greene formed land, cattle, lumber, and railroad companies which, along with government concessions to supply basic services, enabled him to attain hegemony over the area's economy. Close ties with the political circle of Luis TORRES that controlled the state government ensured cooperative local authorities.

Syndicalist ideas among workers from the United States and a cell of followers of the opposition Mexican Liberal Party helped foster unionist sentiment among the nearly 5,400 Mexican workers. The strike of 1–3 June 1906 involved a large proportion of the latter. Alarmed North American employees initiated the subsequent widespread violence, which brought in federal troops and "volunteers" from Arizona, whose presence sparked a formal national inquiry. Strike leaders Manuel M. Dieguez and Esteban Baca Calderón figured prominently in the Revolution.

ESTEBAN BACA CALDERÓN, *Juicio sobre la guerra del Yaqui y génesis de la huelga de Cananea* (1956); DAVID M. PLETCHER, *Rails, Mines, and Progress: Seven American Promoters in Mexico, 1867–1911* (1958); MANUEL J. AGUIRRE, *Cananea: Las garras del imperialismo en las entrañas de México* (1958); RAMÓN EDUARDO RUIZ, *The People of Sonora and Yankee Capitalists* (1988).

STUART F. VOSS

**CAÑARI,** Indians of the southern Ecuadorian Andean provinces of Canar and Azuay. In the pre-Inca period the Cañari were one of the major groups of advanced sedentary peoples in Ecuador. The Cañari were especially noted for their fine gold working. During the mid-1400s INCA conquest, the Cañari organized a powerful resistance, but they were defeated by the 1470s. The Inca forceably relocated many Cañari to other parts of the empire. Some Cañari served in the elite Inca imperial guard. Inca Emperor Tupac Yupanqui (r. ca. 1471–1493) married a Cañari princess who bore him a child, HUAYNA CAPAC, (r. ca. 1493–1527). The Inca valued the region, creating a new imperial center at Tomebamba. Inca Quechua language replaced Cañari and closely related Puruha. The Cañari sided with HUASCAR (r. ca. 1527–1532) in the war against his half-brother ATAHUALPA (r. ca. 1532–1533). Victorious Atahualpa cruelly punished the Cañari. The Cañari assisted the conquering Spaniard Sebastián de BELALCÁZAR, beginning in 1534.

The standard reference on the Andean Indians is still JULIAN H. STEWARD, ed., *Handbook of South American Indians*, vol. 2, *The Andean Civilizations* (1946). Information can also be found in GARCILASO DE LA VEGA, *Royal Commentaries of the Incas and General History of Peru*, translated by HAROLD V. LIVERMORE (1966).

RONN F. PINEO

**CANARY ISLANDS,** a group of ten small islands (Tenerife, La Palma, Gomera, Hierro, Grand Canary, Fuerteventura, Lanzarote, Alegranza, Graciosa, and Isla de Lobos) lying 50 miles west of the coast of Morocco that comprise two provinces of Spain. Known to the ancient world as the Fortunate Islands, they received their current name from Pliny the Elder in reference to the large dogs (*canes*) found there by King Juba II of Mauretania when he explored the islands around 40 B.C. Along with the dogs, Juba found the islands inhabited by Guanches, a people of obscure origin, who successfully defended their domain against the king.

Europeans first visited the Canaries in 1330, when a French ship landed on the islands. This was followed fourteen years later by an expedition led by Luis de la Cerda, a grandson of Alfonso X of Castile, with the objective of converting the Guanches under a papal grant. This and similar attempts by the Spanish failed, both in their religious intent and in establishing a European colony there, Finally, in 1402, two Frenchmen, Jean de Bethencourt and Gadifer de la Salle, successfully conquered most of the Canaries. Henry III of Castile gave Bethencourt money and the title of king of the islands in return for recognition of Castile's legal claim to possession. By 1491 the islands were completely under the Spanish flag when Alonzo de Lugo invaded Tenerife. The British often challenged the Spanish for possession of the Canaries. It was on Santa Cruz on one of these forays that Lord Nelson lost his arm in 1797.

The Canary Islands had long had a thriving SUGAR INDUSTRY until competition from the West Indies proved overwhelming. The Canaries did, however, become a prime producer of COCHINEAL dye, striking a blow at the dye industry of Central America. In turn the Canary dye industry was destroyed by the introduction of chemical dyes. Since the voyage of Columbus, the islands have served as a stopping point for ships to replenish their supplies before continuing on to the Americas.

JOHN MERCER, *Canary Islands: Fuerteventura* (1973); ALFRED W. CROSBY, *Ecological Imperialism: The Biological Expansion of Europe, 900–1900* (1986).

SHEILA L. HOOKER

**CAÑAS, JOSÉ MARÍA** (*b.* 1809; *d.* 30 September 1860), commander of the Central American army in the NATIONAL WAR against William WALKER in Nicaragua. Born in El Salvador, Cañas was an officer in Francisco MORAZÁN's army and later rose to prominence in Costa Rica as an ally of his brother-in-law, President Juan Rafael MORA PORRÁS. After General Cañas distinguished himself at the battle of Rivas (11 April 1856), Mora named him inspector general of the Central American allied army in January 1857 and later commander in chief of the Central American forces. When Mora was ousted from the presidency of Costa Rica in 1859, Gerardo BARRIOS put Cañas in command of the Salvadoran army. In 1860, after supporting Mora's unsuccessful attempt to return to power in Costa Rica, Cañas and Mora were executed at Puntarenas. Cañas also represented Costa Rica in the intrigues relating to U.S. and British efforts to gain canal rights through Guanacaste in the border area between Nicaragua and Costa Rica during Mora's administration.

RAFAEL OBREGÓN, *Costa Rica y la guerra contra los filibusteros* (1991), has a detailed biographical sketch of Cañas on pages 291–293. Also useful are ALEJANDRO BOLAÑOS-GEYER, *William Walker, the Gray-Eyed Man of Destiny*, vol. 4 (1990), and A. PAUL WOODBRIDGE, *Los contratos Webster-Mora y las implicaciones sobre Costa Rica y Nicaragua* (1967).

RALPH LEE WOODWARD, JR.

**CAÑAS, JOSÉ SIMEÓN** (*b.* 18 February 1767; *d.* 4 March 1838), Salvadoran intellectual and politician. Born in Santa Lucía Zacatecoluca, El Salvador, to a wealthy family, Cañas was educated as a priest in Guatemala, where he received his doctorate in theology. He became rector of the University of SAN CARLOS in 1802. He joined with José Matías DELGADO and Manuel José ARCE in supporting Central American independence in 1821. As a member of the Central American Congress, on 31 December 1823 Cañas made the motion to abolish slavery in Central America, enacted the following year. He subsequently supported the cause of Central American unity. He died, and is buried, in San Vicente, El Salvador.

MIGUEL ÁNGEL ESPINO, *La vida de José Simeón Cañas, padre de los esclavos* (1955), originally published in ADOLFO PÉREZ MENÉNDEZ and JOSÉ LUIS ANDREU, eds., *Colección patria grande. Época de la independencia. Biografías populares de los hombres símbolos de Centro América* (1938). RAMÓN LÓPEZ JIMÉNEZ, *José Simeón Cañas: Su obra, su verdadera personalidad y su destino* (1970); MANUEL VIDA, *Nociones de historia de Centro América (especial para El Salvador)*, 5th ed. (1957), pp. 143–147; RAMÓN LÓPEZ JIMÉNEZ and RAFAEL DÍAZ, *Biografía de José Simeón Cañas* (1968).

RALPH LEE WOODWARD, JR.

*See also* **Central America; Slavery, Abolition of.**

**CANCHA RAYADA, BATTLE OF,** a clash between the patriot army and Royalist forces on 19 March 1818, during Chile's war for independence. The Argentine general José de SAN MARTÍN had been pursuing the Spanish forces near Talca when he decided to stop for the night. Fearing an assault, San Martín was repositioning his troops when the Royalists suddenly attacked under cover of darkness. Surprised, some of the patriot units panicked. While San Martín's men were mauled, the Chileans had to absorb heavier losses, and their commander, Bernardo O'HIGGINS, who had his horse shot out from under him, suffered an arm wound. Given the high casualty rate, rumors spread that both O'Higgins and San Martín had perished. These tales proved false: the independence army, though badly battered, regrouped. Fortunately for the patriot cause, although

O'Higgins's units had suffered heavy losses, the elements under the command of the other patriot officer, Juan Gregorio de LAS HERAS, emerged unscathed and hence able to actively pursue the war.

STEPHEN CLISSOLD, *Bernardo O'Higgins and the Independence of Chile* (1968), 62, 159–169, 171; SIMON COLLIER, *Ideas and Politics of Chilean Independence, 1808–1833* (1968), p. 231.

WILLIAM F. SATER

**CANCIÓN RANCHERA,** a Mexican variation of the Spanish *canción* (song) brought to America during the sixteenth to nineteenth centuries and popularized in the 1940s and 1950s by such Mexican matinee idols as Jorge NEGRETE and Pedro INFANTE. It is commonly sung by MARIACHI groups, the *conjunto*, the *dueto*, the *trío*, and the country singer. It is a genre associated with the rural, agricultural worker—*ranchera* means "from the ranches," or "from the countryside." A rural working-class dialect of Spanish commonly characterizes the lyrics. Frequent themes include unrequited love, abandonment by a lover, and unfaithful women. The brokenhearted lover, mostly male but not always, narrates a tale of woe regarding a love affair gone awry and the subsequent drinking sprees the spurned lover undertakes to ease the pain. Well-known *canción ranchera* composers include Tomás Méndez, José Alfredo Jiménez, and Cuco Sánchez.

VICENTE T. MENDOZA, *La canción mexicana: Ensayo de clasificación y antropología* (1982); MARÍA HERRERA-SOBEK, *Northward Bound: The Mexican Immigrant Experience in Ballad and Song* (1993).

MARÍA HERRERA-SOBEK

*See also* **Music: Popular Music and Dance.**

**CANDAMO, MANUEL** (*b.* 1842; *d.* 7 May 1904), the son of one of the wealthiest merchants of mid-nineteenth-century Peru, whose fortune rested on shipping (especially the trade in indentured Asians), guano, and railroad construction. The family was typical of that group of merchants and entrepreneurs who replaced the aristocracy as the ruling elite of the country. The aristocracy had banned political parties as tasteless and dangerous. But Candamo was active in the Civilista Party and won election as the mayor of Lima. In 1902 he gained further public attention as an activist president of the Lima Chamber of Commerce. He became a candidate for president of Peru in 1903 as a moderate conciliator between two intransigent factions of the Democratic and Civilista parties. The Civilista Party disappeared briefly when leading members joined former Democrats in the Liberal Party. This action prompted another faction of Civilistas to form a surprise alliance with the Constitutionalist Party, the party of the military. Candamo remained the single Civilista trusted by and popular with all factions. Inaugurated in November after he won the election, he fell ill and died the following July. Thereafter mutual distrust sowed discord once again among party factions.

FREDRIK B. PIKE, *The Modern History of Peru* (1967), esp. pp. 190–191; DAVID P. WERLICH, *Peru: A Short History* (1978), pp. 131–132.

VINCENT PELOSO

*See also* **Peru: Political Parties.**

**CANDANEDO, CÉSAR** (*b.* 12 May 1906), Panamanian writer. Candanedo was born in David, Panama. Self-taught, he was awarded a scholarship by the World Health Organization to pursue studies in the School of Public Health of the University of Chile. After completing his studies, he worked as a public health inspector for the Department of Public Health in Panama. This position gave him the opportunity to travel and to become familiar with the diverse regions of the country and, in particular, to become aware of the hopelessness that permeates every aspect of the daily existence of Panama's rural population.

In his first book, *Los clandestinos* (1957; The Clandestine Ones), he depicted the impact of the United Fruit Company and the Canal Zone on the living conditions of Panama's rural population. His later works, *La otra frontera* (1967; The Other Frontier), *El cerquero y otros relatos* (1967; The Encloser and Other Stories), *Memorias de un caminante* (1970; Memories of a Traveler), *Palo duro* (1973; Hard Truncheon), and *El perseguido* (1991; The Fugitive) reaffirm his reputation as both a writer of vigorous works of social protest and a writer of regional literature. *El perseguido* received first prize in the 1986 Ricardo Mirõ competition.

ELSIE ALVARADO DE RICROD, "Reseña de *Los clandestinos* de César Candanedo," in *El Panamá América* (1958); CARLOS GUILLERMO WILSON, *Aspectos de la prosa narrativa panameña contemporánea* (Ph.D. thesis, 1987), pp. 108–110; DAVID FOSTER, comp., *Handbook of Latin American Literature,* 2d ed. (1992), pp. 463–464.

ELBA D. BIRMINGHAM-POKORNY

**CANDIOTI, FRANCISCO ANTONIO** (*b.* 1743; *d.* 25 August 1815), Argentine landowner and supporter of the independence movement. With large landholdings in the present-day provinces of Santa Fe and Entre Ríos, Candioti, "prince of the gauchos," generously provided arms and provisions for his friend Manuel BELGRANO at the outbreak of the independence movement in 1810. Responding to widespread provincial sentiment against the centralist ambitions of *porteño* (Buenos Aires) leaders, he sought out the support of José Gervasio ARTIGAS, whose federalist sympathies he largely shared. In 1815 Artigas loyalists led by José Eusebio Hereñú dislodged the *porteño* army under José Miguel Díaz Vélez, dis-

solved the provincial junta, and constituted the newly autonomous province of Santa Fe, with Candioti as its first governor. Aged and sickly, however, Candioti could contribute little to the province's defense against destructive Indian raids after the rapid departure of federalist forces. He died shortly after *porteño* troops reoccupied the city and put a temporary end to the newly won autonomy.

JORGE NEWTON, *El príncipe de los gauchos* (1941).

WILLIAM H. KATRA

**CANDOMBLÉ,** an Afro-Brazilian religion of YORUBA origin developed primarily in the Northeast by African slaves from Nigeria and their descendants. Candomblé may have been introduced as early as the eighteenth century, but it became firmly entrenched in Afro-Brazilian culture in the early nineteenth century, when enslaved members of the Oyo and Dahomey empires flowed into Brazil. The Candomblé community of Engenho Velho in Bahia, perhaps the oldest in Brazil, was founded around 1830. Oral tradition also dates the Casa das Minas of Maranhão to the mid-nineteenth century. "Candomblé" is the term specifically given to the religious traditions developed by Africans from the Gulf of Guinea, but it is often broadly applied to any Afro-Brazilian religion incorporating divination and possession ritual. In the Americas, it is most closely related to SANTERÍA, developed in Cuba by slaves from the same regions of West Africa.

Candomblé is based on the principles of harmony and balance between human beings and the forces of nature. All living beings and natural phenomena are considered creations of one supreme god, called Olodumare, and each is made of *axe*, divine energy. Different complexes of *axe* make up individual people, as well as phenomena such as rainbows, thunder, and wind. *Axe* may also take the specialized form of ORIXÁS, deities who personify specific aspects of Olodumare.

In Brazil, *orixás* are the principal intermediaries between humans and God; ancestor worship was not equally cultivated, although it is an integral part of the religion's African tradition. Through divination and possession rituals, priests communicate with *orixás* to determine the causes of specific problems, and to find out the steps necessary to correct them. Devotees of Candomblé undergo extensive initiation, during which time they learn the various means of communicating with spiritual forces in order to maintain a harmonious balance of sacred energies.

In the Oyo and Dahomey empires each town worshipped a patron *orixá*. Some, like Xangô, the royal *orixá* of the Oyo kings, became popular throughout the entire empire. During the SLAVE TRADE African towns such as Kêtu and Abeokuta lost large numbers of inhabitants to Brazil. These people brought with them the cults of their *orixá*, and eventually Afro-Brazilians incorporated the worship of all the major *orixás* in each community of

Candomblé ceremony in Bahia, Brazil. CYNTHIA BRITO / PULSAR IMAGENS E EDITORA.

devotees. Candomblé represents an adaptation of many traditions to the conditions of the New World. Because African slaves were forcibly baptized and converted to Catholicism, they were unable to practice Candomblé openly. They continued to secretly worship African deities by outwardly equating them with CATHOLIC saints in a process of SYNCRETISM.

In Brazil, Candomblé has an important social aspect. Each community is divided into houses (iles), which create new familial relationships among devotees. The senior initiate, traditionally a woman, is considered a spiritual mother (mãe de santo). As head of the household, she is responsible for the spiritual well-being of all the initiates, including the observance of obligations and annual celebrations for the orixás, as well as for the household's material needs. Seniority is based upon the number of years an individual has been initiated, regardless of chronological age. Respect for elders is rigidly observed, as are other values imparted through the social aspect of Candomblé. The distribution of responsibilities, hierarchies, and specific cultural and ritual traditions varies, based on the size and ethnic origins of the house. Many houses identify themselves with the names of African "nations," such as Kêtu, Gege, or Mina. These communities are also known as terreiros or roças, references to the land they occupy. In Brazil, portions of the terreiro are devoted to a specific orixá, where its sacred objects are kept.

Candomblé worship has been traditionally discouraged by supporters of the Catholic church and other Christian sects. In the 1920s and 1930s police regularly raided terreiros in major cities such as Salvador and Recife, confiscating ritual objects and imprisoning worshippers. Candomblé began to gain broader acceptance in the 1930s, as international scholars convened in two Afro-Brazilian congresses. These academics pressed for the acceptance and appreciation of Candomblé as part of Brazil's African cultural heritage. Simultaneously, Candomblé principles were gaining wider acceptance through the related syncretic religions of UMBANDA, and to a lesser extent, Macumba, CABOCLO, and Quimbanda. In each of these religions, devotees consult deities or spirits for answers to their problems through divination or possession ritual. Some of these traditions, such as Candomblé Caboclo, originated during SLAVERY through the intermingling of African and indigenous religious rituals.

Candomblé is now practiced openly, although it remains concentrated in its area of origin, the northeastern region. Although traditionalism is a hallmark of most terreiros, innovation can also be seen as Candomblé continues to evolve. Some Candomblé houses maintain ongoing relationships with their counterparts in West Africa and in other communities in the Caribbean and North America where Yoruba-based religion is practiced.

RAYMUNDO NINA RODRIGUES, *O Animismo Fetichista dos Negros Bahianos* (1935); DONALD PIERSON, *Negroes in Brazil: A Study of Race Contact at Bahia* (1942); EDISON CARNEIRO, *Candomblés da Bahia*, 3d ed. (1961); ROGER BASTIDE, *The African Religions of Brazil: Toward a Sociology of the Interpenetration of Civilizations*, translated by Helen Sebba (1978), and *O Candomblé da Bahia*, 2d ed. (1978); GARY EDWARDS and JOHN MASON, *Black Gods: Orisa Studies in the New World* (1985); MANUEL QUERINO, *Costumes africanos no Brasil*, 2d ed. (1988).

KIM D. BUTLER

*See also* **African–Latin American Religions.**

**CANÉ, MIGUEL** (*b.* 27 January 1851; *d.* 5 September 1905), Argentine writer and statesman. Cané's most enduring achievement remains *Juvenilia* (1884), a memoir of student days at the Colegio Nacional in Buenos Aires. He never abandoned literature and produced many essays and miscellaneous writings as a member of the generation of '80. His commentaries on national affairs in the newspapers *La Tribuna* and *El Nacional* earned Cané the appellation of chronicler of his generation.

Cané entered politics in 1874 and supported Adolfo ALSINA, who suppressed a revolution headed by Bartolomé MITRE. He held various positions, including congressman (1875), director of the postal and telegraph service (1880), municipal intendent of Buenos Aires (1892), minister of foreign affairs (1893), and the first dean of the School of Philosophy and Letters at the University of Buenos Aires (1900). He was also minister plenipotentiary to Colombia and Venezuela in 1881 and to Spain in 1886.

Although Cané professed liberalism, he had reservations about Argentine democracy. He distrusted the United States and its use of the MONROE DOCTRINE and supported protectionist economic legislation. He favored the residence law, which curtailed the growing influence of foreign labor by banning undesirable foreigners, and approved of other legislation upholding oligarchic interests and policies. Cané became more and more conservative in the last years of his life as a national senator (1902–1905).

RAÚL H. CASTAGNINO, *Miguel Cané: Cronista del ochenta porteño* (1952); RICARDO SÁENZ HAYES, *Miguel Cané y su tiempo, 1851–1905* (1955); ROBERTO F. GIUSTI, "Miguel Cané: El escritor y el político," in *Comentario*, Buenos Aires (April–June 1956): 25–37.

MYRON I. LICHTBLAU

*See also* **Literature: Spanish America.**

**CANECA, FREI JOAQUÍM DO AMOR DIVINO** (*b.* 20 August 1779; *d.* 13 January 1825), Brazilian Carmelite friar, priest, journalist, and revolutionary. Born in Recife, Pernambuco, Caneca joined the Carmelite order in his native province and achieved prominence as a teacher of geometry and rhetoric. In 1817 he joined the Pernambucan republican revolt, for which he forfeited a nomination to be bishop of Maranhão and spent four years in prison in Salvador da Bahia. Freed after the 1821 liberal coup in Bahia, Frei Caneca returned to Pernambuco, where he became a member of the provincial junta. In 1822 he disavowed the regional republicanism of 1817 and advocated Pernambuco's adherence to the independent Brazilian monarchy proclaimed by Emperor PEDRO I in Rio de Janeiro. He founded a newspaper, *Typhis Pernambucano*, to propagate his liberal-federalist-constitutionalist ideology.

Frei Caneca denounced the emperor's closing of the national Constitutional Convention of 1823 and led the fight in Pernambuco against the ratification of Pedro's centralist Constitution of 1824. After Pedro declared the constitution ratified, despite its rejection by the municipal councils of Recife and other northeastern cities, Frei Caneca declared it void in Pernambuco and called for the formation of an autonomous government for the Northeast. The result was the separatist CONFEDERATION OF THE EQUATOR, which was crushed by imperial troops in 1824. Frei Caneca and fifteen other confederation leaders were condemned for insurrection; he died before a firing squad in Recife.

JOAQUÍM DO AMOR DIVINO CANECA, *Ensaius políticos de Frei Caneca* (1976); JOÃO AFREDO DE SOUZA MONTENEGRO, *O liberalismo radical de Frei Caneca* (1978).

NEILL MACAULAY

**CAÑEDO, FRANCISCO** (*b.* 1839; *d.* 5 June 1909), governor of the state of Sinaloa. One of many migrants from neighboring Tepic, Cañedo began work as an errand boy and then clerk in large merchant houses, first in Mazatlán and then in Culiacán. Aided by marriage into the notable Batiz family, by the patronage of Culiacán's leading political family (the Vegas), and by his cultivation of close ties with Porfirio DÍAZ, Cañedo rose to preeminence in Sinaloan politics through the 1870s. Serving as governor (1877–1880, 1884–1888, 1892–1909), he assumed sole control of the state government thereafter until his death. He incorporated Mazatlán's notables into his political circle, ending the bitter and destructive rivalry between the state's two cities. Cañedo followed Porfirista policies faithfully. He consolidated control by eliminating all *municípios* (municipalities) but the district seats, which were firmly controlled by the prefects he appointed.

EUSTAQUIO BUELNA, *Apuntes para la historia de Sinaloa, 1821–1882* (1924; 2d ed., 1966); AMADO GONZÁLEZ DÁVILA, *Diccionario geográfico, histórico, y estadístico del Estado de Sinaloa* (1959), pp. 82–86; STUART F. VOSS, "Towns and Enterprise in Northwestern Mexico: A History of Urban Elites in Sonora and Sinaloa, 1830–1910," (Ph.D. diss., Harvard University, 1972), pp. 126–154, 343–444.

STUART F. VOSS

**CAÑEDO, JUAN DE DIOS** (*b.* 18 January 1786; *d.* 28 March 1850), Mexican politician and diplomat. A scion of one of the great families of Jalisco, Cañedo studied law in Guadalajara. He was active in politics from 1811 until his death, distinguishing himself as a champion of legislative power and of federalism. Cañedo served in various elected positions: the *ayuntamiento* (city council) of Guadalajara (1811); the Cortes in Spain (1813; 1820–1821); the Mexican Constituent Congress (1823–1824); senator from Jalisco (1825–1828); deputy from Jalisco (1830–1831; 1849); and president of the *ayuntamiento* of Mexico City (1844). He also served as minister of foreign affairs from 1828 to 1829 and again from 1839 to 1840. He was Mexico's minister to South America (1831–1839); England (1846); and France (1847). A leader of the political opposition, Cañedo was brutally murdered in March 1850. Those responsible were never brought to justice.

ROBERT JOSEPH WARD HENRY, "Juan de Dios Cañedo: Político y diplomático" (licentiate thesis, Universidad Iberoamericana, Mexico, 1968); JAIME E. RODRÍGUEZ O., "Intellectuals and the Mexican Constitution of 1824," in *Los intelectuales y el poder en México,* edited by Roderic Ai Camp, Charles A. Hale, and Josefina Zoraida Vázquez (1991); "The Origins of the 1832 Revolt," in *Patterns of Contention in Mexican History,* edited by Jaime E. Rodríguez O. (1992); "The Constitution of 1824 and the Formation of the Mexican State," in *The Evolution of the Mexican Political System,* edited by Jaime E. Rodríguez O. (1993).

JAIME E. RODRÍGUEZ O.

**CANEK, JACINTO** (*b.* ca. 1731; *d.* 14 December 1761), a Maya who led an Indian uprising in Yucatán. Born Jacinto Uc de los Santos, this Indian from Campeche led a Maya cultural revitalization movement that ultimately challenged Spanish rule in colonial Yucatán. In 1761 in the village of Cisteíl he proclaimed himself to be King Canek (the legendary name of Maya kings), whose coming had been foretold in Maya prophecy. Thousands of Indians joined his movement, which combined traditional Maya and Christian elements and sought both cultural and political autonomy. The Spanish colonial authorities, using their military might, finally defeated Canek's forces in battle, thus crushing the movement. Canek was captured, tried, and executed by being torn limb-from-limb.

MARÍA TERESA HUERTA and PATRICIA PALACIOS, eds., *Rebeliones indígenas de la época colonial* (1976); NANCY M. FARRISS, *Maya Society Under Colonial Rule: The Collective Enterprise of Survival* (1984).

ROBERT W. PATCH

**CANELONES,** second-largest department of Uruguay in terms of population (359,700 in 1985) and part of Greater MONTEVIDEO. Originally this department was the main supplier of vegetables and fruits for the capital city, but urban sprawl has engulfed most of the valuable agricultural land. Food-processing plants, factories for manufacturing durable goods, a paper mill, and granite/mica schist quarries are among the main supporters of the department's economy. Its major center is the town of Canelones (17,316 inhabitants in 1985), 27 miles north of Montevideo. Founded in 1774, it was for a short time the capital of Uruguay (in 1828). Canelones caters to the needs of the vegetable growers and small industries of the department.

BEATRIZ TORRENDELL, *Geografía histórica de Canelones* (Montevideo, 1986).

CÉSAR N. CAVIEDES

**CANGACEIRO,** bandit of northeastern Brazil. *Cangaceiros* operated in the SERTÃO (backlands) during the nineteenth and early twentieth centuries. Feared and sometimes revered by rural tenants and small landholders, they represented a challenge to authorities and unscrupulous *coronéis* (local political bosses). Many began their careers by exercising private vengeance on family enemies, but most became bandits for personal gain and notoriety. *Cangaceiros* reflected the breakdown of traditional authority in the *sertão* and often operated with the protection of competing *coronéis*. Increased political centralization and more efficient policing led to their demise by the 1930s. *Cangaceiros* are a popular subject of regional literature, music, and art.

JOÃO GUIMARÃES ROSA, *The Devil to Pay in the Backlands,* translated by James L. Taylor and Harriet De Onís (1963); BILLY JAYNES CHANDLER, *The Bandit King: Lampião of Brazil* (1978); LINDA LEWIN, "The Oligarchical Limitations of Social Banditry in Brazil: The Case of the 'Good' Thief Antônio Silvino," and BILLY JAYNES CHANDLER, "Brazilian *Cangaceiros* as Social Bandits: A Critical Appraisal," in *Bandidos: The Varieties of Latin American Banditry,* edited by Richard W. Slatta (1987), pp. 67–112.

ROBERT WILCOX

*See also* **Banditry; Coronel; Jagunço; Lampião; Sertão; Silvino, Antônio.**

**CANNIBALISM,** the practice of eating the flesh or other parts of the human body. There is no doubt that some Indian tribes of Latin America practiced cannibalism in one form or another well into the twentieth century. Because it was abhorrent to Europeans, cannibalism became a pretext for attacks on Indians, who soon became wary of talking about it, and the custom has been virtually abandoned. It was reported most frequently in the tropical lowlands of South America and in the circum-Caribbean region, but was not confined to these areas. Human sacrifice and cannibalism were widely practiced in Colombia before the Conquest. The word "cannibal" has a Latin American origin. It comes indirectly from COLUMBUS, who heard the CARIB Indians

Cannibalism, as depicted in DeBry's *Grandes voyages*. COURTESY OF THE JOHN CARTER BROWN LIBRARY AT BROWN UNIVERSITY.

called *Caniba*. The Caribs were feared cannibalistic warriors of the Antilles in his time. The use of "cannibal" in literature may have been heightened by its similarity to *can*, which means dog in Spanish.

There were two types of cannibalism in Latin America, exocannibalism, eating members of an enemy group, and endocannibalism, eating members of one's own group. The former was a celebration of victory over an enemy. The symbolic treatment of the enemy as a game animal was an extreme form of racism that served to heighten enthusiasm for warfare. In the times just after Brazil was colonized, the TUPINAMBÁ would go on raids against other Indian villages. If they were successful in killing the enemy, they would butcher the bodies and feast on them in the jungle before returning home. If they captured live male prisoners, they took them back to the Tupinambá village, where they allowed the prisoners to live for a time, sometimes for many years. After a ritual "escape," they would sacrifice, roast, and eat a prisoner. Many cannibalistic people have expressed a taste for human flesh. From this, some observers have drawn the conclusion that human flesh was an important part of the diet; however, these gustatory expressions were highly symbolic. Desiring to eat the enemy was an expression of fierceness that elevated the status of the warrior and struck fear into his enemies.

Endocannibalism symbolized very different things: reverence for the dead, an incorporation of the spirit of the dead into living descendants, or the separation of the soul from the body. A Mayorúna man once expressed a wish to remain in his village and be eaten by his children after his death rather than be consumed by worms in the white man's cemetery. In recent times, the Panoan, YANOMAMI, and other lowland groups have consumed the ground-up bones and ashes of cremated kinsmen in an act of mourning. This still is classified as endocannibalism, although, strictly speaking, "flesh" is not eaten. The Yanomami mix the bones and ashes with plantain soup before consuming the mixture.

Theories proposing that a lack of protein in the South American tropical forest environment stimulated cannibalism have not received support from recent studies, which show that tropical forest tribes have a more-than-adequate protein intake and are successful hunters despite environmental limitations. The theory that the AZTECS depended on the consumption of sacrificial victims for food lacks convincing data on the extent of this consumption. Some Aztecs consumed parts of some victims; however, most estimates of the number of victims eaten represent figures lower than what would have provided a critical amount of protein. Evidence points to Latin American exocannibalism as a symbolic expression of the domination of an enemy in warfare rather than as a significant source of protein.

ALFRED MÉTRAUX, "Warfare, Cannibalism, and Human Trophies," in *Handbook of South American Indians* (1949), vol. 5, pp. 383–409; GERTRUDE E. DOLE, "Endocannibalism among the

Amahuaca Indians," *Transactions of the New York Academy of Sciences* 24, no. 2 (1962): 567–573; MICHAEL HARNER, "The Ecological Basis for Aztec Sacrifice," *American Ethnologist* 4 (1977): 117–135; NAPOLEON A. CHAGNON and RAYMOND B. HAMES, "Protein Deficiency and Tribal Warfare in Amazonia: New Data," *Science* 203 (1979): 910–913; BERNARD R. ORTIZ DE MONTELLANO, "Counting Skulls: Comment on the Aztec Cannibalism Theory of Harner-Harris," *American Anthropologist* 85, no. 2 (1983): 403–406.

JAMES DOW

**CANNING, GEORGE** (*b.* 11 April 1770; *d.* 8 August 1827), British statesman. Despite a long career in public service, George Canning distinguished himself primarily during his term as Great Britain's foreign secretary between 1822 and 1827. He had, in fact, previously served as foreign secretary, from 1807 to 1809, before resigning amid controversy following British military losses to Spain.

In his second term as foreign secretary, Canning broke new ground in recognizing the legitimacy of several newly independent nations in Latin America. After separating Great Britain from the so-called Holy Alliance in 1823, Canning helped prevent other European nations from aiding Ferdinand VII of Spain in his bid to recapture his former colonies. Canning sent the first British consul to Buenos Aires and served as mediator in the Argentine-Brazilian territorial dispute which led to the establishment of the state of Uruguay.

Canning's diplomatic successes in Latin America and elsewhere led to his ascendancy to prime minister in 1827, an office he held for only a few months before his death.

LESLIE BETHELL, *George Canning and the Independence of Latin America* (1970); WENDY HINDE, *George Canning* (1989).

JOHN DUDLEY

**CANO, MARÍA DE LOS ÁNGELES** (*b.* 12 August 1887; *d.* 26 April 1967), Colombian labor leader and feminist. An icon of the Colombian Left, Cano was born into a prominent family in Medellín. Small in stature, she had great energy combined with a deeply felt social conscience. Reared in a liberal-minded home, she absorbed secular literature, encouraged by her educator father. She became a journalist in Medellín, thereby gaining access to international wire services, which from 1922 on, reported on the Soviet Union. Cano came to admire that nation greatly and also began to meet with artisans and workers, who as part of May Day festivities proclaimed her the "Flower of Medellín Labor" in 1925. Over the next several months, Cano made seven nationwide tours in which she spoke out for socialism and workers' rights. Despite official persecution, workers' groups proclaimed her the "National Flower of Labor," in November 1926. She was among the founders of the Partido Social Revolucionario in September 1927. Although she was not a participant in the banana workers' strike against UNITED FRUIT COMPANY (November–December 1928) at Santa Marta, her oratory on behalf of labor did help to create a climate favorable for such action. Cano was imprisoned and harassed, yet she continued her activities. After the mid-1930s, her health deteriorated, however, and her political activities ceased. Cano died in Medellín.

IGNACIO TORRES GIRALDO, *María Cano, mujer rebelde* (1972); MARÍA CANO, *Escritos* (1985); GILBERTO MEJÍA V., *Memorias: El comunismo en Antioquia (María Cano)* (1986); LEÓN ZULETA RUIZ, comp., *Flor del trabajo y semilla de esperanza: Memorias de su centenario* (1988); ROBERT H. DAVIS, *Historical Dictionary of Colombia* (1993).

J. LEÓN HELGUERA

*See also* **Communism; Feminism.**

**CANTILO, JOSÉ LUIS** (*b.* 6 February 1871; *d.* 11 October 1944), Argentine politician and journalist. First elected a provincial deputy for Buenos Aires in 1896, Cantilo rose through the ranks of the Unión Cívica Radical, participating in the Radicals' last armed protest in 1905. Cantilo was a close associate of Hipólito YRIGOYEN and joined the national Congress in the wake of the reform of the suffrage law in 1912. President Yrigoyen named him intervenor in the province of Buenos Aires in 1917, in an effort to defuse the opposition of conservatives. Soon afterward, Cantilo returned to the capital as intendant (1917–1922); there he dealt with the social upheaval of 1917 to 1921. He did not stand out as either a great conciliator or an effective administrator, but he was a loyal follower of the Radical faction led by Yrigoyen. From 1922 to 1926, Cantilo served as governor of the province of Buenos Aires, where he was charged repeatedly by Conservatives and dissident Radicals with undiluted partisanship but nevertheless succeeded in displacing the Conservatives and consolidating a Radical hold. He was again intendant of the capital from 1926 to 1930. Had Yrigoyen not stood for reelection in 1928, Cantilo would have been the logical Radical candidate. With the coup d'état in September 1930, Cantilo was forced to leave politics. A decade later, with signs that the country would return to unobstructed democratic rule, he was elected to Congress in 1940. He served very briefly as a foreign minister until March 1941, when he was replaced by a Conservative Hispanophile. From 1941 until his resignation in June 1943, he was president of the Cámara (lower House of Representatives). As the country polarized between archconservatives and rising trade unions, and faced military rumblings, the political room for a liberal like Cantilo quickly contracted.

RICHARD J. WALTER, *The Province of Buenos Aires and Argentine Politics, 1912–1943* (1985), esp. pp. 44–74, and *Politics and Urban Growth in Buenos Aires: 1910–1942* (1993).

JEREMY ADELMAN

**CANTINFLAS** (Mario Moreno; *b.* 12 August 1911; *d.* 20 April 1993), Mexican comedian and film star. Cantinflas began studies in medicine at the National Autonomous University of Mexico (UNAM), but dropped out for a career as a popular stage comedian in *carpas* (traveling stage shows). From the onset, Cantinflas created a unique comic persona, dressing in ragged clothes, his pants close to falling off, and using a rapid, nonsensical manner of speech. He debuted in cinema with a small part in *No te engañes corazón* (1936). The two films that followed, *Asi es mi tierra* (1937) and *Águila o Sol* (1937), marked Cantinflas as a rising star. His role in *Ahí está el detalle* (1940) assured his popularity and success. Cantinflas went on to star in over forty features. Among his best-known and praised films are *El gendarme desconocido* (1941), *El 7 machos* (1951), *El bombero atómico* (1952), *Ni sangre ni arena* (1941), *El señor fotógrafo* (1952), and *Abajo el telón* (1954). He also starred in two Hollywood productions, *Around the World in 80 Days* (1956) and *Pepe* (1960). Cantinflas, whose career spanned over fifty years, is Mexico's best-known film celebrity, both nationally and internationally.

LUIS REYES DE LA MAZA, *El cine sonoro en México* (1973); E. BRADFORD BURNS, *Latin American Cinema: Film and History* (1975); CARL J. MORA, *Mexican Cinema: Reflections of a Society: 1896–1980* (1982); and JOHN KING, *Magical Reels: A History of Cinema in Latin America* (1990).

DAVID MACIEL

**CANTÓN, WILBERTO** (*b.* 15 July 1925; *d.* 5 March 1979), Mexican dramatist. Cantón was a prominent, popular playwright who wrote more than two dozen plays. He also was a director, translator, critic, and journalist, holding such posts as head of the theater department of Mexico's National Institute of Fine Arts. He wrote two basic types of plays: those employing historical Mexican settings for dramatic action and those treating contemporary Mexican social problems. Outstanding works include *El nocturno a Rosario* (1956), *Malditos* (1958), and *Nosotros somos Dios* (1963). The theater at the General Society of Mexican Writers in Mexico City is named for him.

SAMUEL TRIFILO, "The Theater of Wilberto Cantón," in *Hispania* 54, no. 4 (1971): 869–875; CARL R. SHIRLEY, "A *Curriculum Operum* of Mexico's Wilberto Cantón," in *Latin American Theatre Review* 13, no. 2 (1980): 47–56, and "The Metatheatrical World of Wilberto Cantón," in *Latin American Theatre Review* 23, no. 2 (1990): 43–53.

CARL R. SHIRLEY

**CANTORIA,** a tradition of improvised, sung popular poetry practiced in Northeastern Brazil. It consists of two poets, or *cantadores,* singing alternate strophes in a given style while accompanying themselves on musical instruments: *repentistas* on the guitarlike *viola, emboladores* on tambourines or shakers. Because of its improvised nature the poetry is referred to as the *repente,* from the Portuguese word for "sudden." Sometimes the singing takes on the character of a *desafio* (challenge) between contestants. The tunes are repetitive and melodically simple; the focus is on the content and beauty of the poetry and on adherence to a given metric pattern and rhyme scheme. These patterns derive from traditional European poetics, reflecting the historical roots of *cantoria* in the troubadour tradition of southern Europe. Historically *cantoria* belonged to the rural interior of the Northeast. Currently it is finding its way into urban centers.

F. COUTINHO FILHO, *Violas e repentes* (1953); LEONARDO MOTA, *Violeiros do Norte,* 4th ed. (1976), and *Cantadores,* 5th ed. (1978); LUÍS DA CAMARA CASCUDO, *Coleção reconquista do Brasil.* Vol. 81, *Vaqueiros e cantadores* (1984), pp. 126–226.

JENNIFER FOX

Cantinflas in a scene from *El siete machos* (1951).
ORGANIZATION OF AMERICAN STATES.

**CANTÚ, FEDERICO** (*b.* 3 March 1908; *d.* 1989), Mexican painter. Born in Cadereyta, Nuevo León, Cantú studied at the San Carlos Academy of Fine Arts in Mexico City and later lived and worked in France between the world wars. While in Europe, he was exposed to the works of

Botticelli, El Greco, and the English Pre-Raphaelites. Back in Mexico, Cantú became one of a group of painters who rejected the politics of muralism and returned to easel painting with an intimate and classicizing sensibility. As a devout Christian, Cantú made the central theme of his art a contemporary representation of Christian subjects, such as annunciations and crucifixions. A virtuoso engraver, he produced prints depicting the Passion and other devotional themes. He also executed many frescoes in churches, among them a monumental crucifixion in the Santísima Trinidad in Mexico City. For many years, Cantú was an instructor of drawing and painting at the Esmeralda School of Fine Arts. He died in Mexico City.

MC KINLEY HELM, *Modern Mexican Painters* (1948); AUGUSTÍN ARTEAGA, *Federico Cantú, una nueva visión* (1989).

ALEJANDRO ANREUS

**CANUDOS CAMPAIGN,** military action of 1896–1897, aimed at dispersing the backlands, religiously based community of Canudos in Bahia, Brazil. Republican authorities mistakenly thought that the messianic community headed by Antônio CONSELHEIRO was a base for monarchist restoration, and a series of misunderstandings made it the object of a bloody campaign. In November 1896 and January 1897, two successively larger units of federal and state troops marched on Canudos. Both units were routed decisively.

Oddly, senior commanders ignored the after-action reports of the defeated officers and so planned their responses based on rumor and conjecture. As Canudos took on the press image of a monarchist hotbed, frustrated Republican extremists, called Florianistas after deceased acting president Marshal Floriáno Vieira PEIXOTO (d. June 1895), hoped that victory in Bahia would bring them back to power.

Ardent Florianista colonel Antônio Moreira César, leading 1,300 soldiers and state police and exuding overconfidence, refused a briefing from his unfortunate predecessor and attacked the now reinforced and well-entrenched townspeople on 2 March 1897. Moreira César had a reputation for violence and a willingness to shoot civilians. His impulsiveness and the lack of an army supply service led him to march through a hot, arid region without adequate water supplies. He was mortally wounded in an ill-considered attack made without an attempt to parley. Although well armed and occupying the high ground, the troops fled in panic after the colonel's death, abandoning their equipment and wounded to the townspeople.

The defeat coincided with President Prudente José de MORAIS's return from sick leave, a subsequent shake-up in army administration, and suppression of a revolt at the Rio de Janeiro military school. The extreme turbulence of 1897 saw four ministers of war and five adjutants-general. Forced recruitment filled the battalions ordered to advance on Canudos in two columns from Salvador and Aracajú under Generals Arthur Oscar de Andrada Guimarães, João da Silva Barbosa, and Cláudio do Amaral Savaget. The planned pincer attack failed and, in late June 1897, the troops were trapped on Favela Hill before the town. Soldiers' wives did a lively business selling hoarded food to the hungry. Women played roles on both sides in this disaster. On 14 July, the encircled units broke out, taking about 1,700 casualties in the process, but finally able to send requests for reinforcements. Engaged in daily combat, the soldiers slit the throats of over 2,000 prisoners.

Minister of War Carlos Machado de Bittencourt took charge of the reinforcements, but General Arthur Oscar's mismanagement was so unnerving that officers excused themselves from joining the expedition. The only general who would command the new battalions was Carlos Eugênio de Andrada Guimarães, Arthur Oscar's brother. State police from São Paulo, Pará, and Amazonas eagerly joined the fray. By the end of September, siege lines surrounded the town, where hundreds of dead lay unburied, as fifteen cannon fired at point-blank range. An assault on 1 October left 587 army dead or wounded, with perhaps as many as 5,500 townsfolk either dead or missing. The next day the first parley between the combatants produced the surrender of several hundred, mostly women and children. On 4 October dynamite bombs and kerosene eliminated the last resistance.

The fighting cost the army heavily; of the 9,542 officers and men sent to Canudos, 4,193 were wounded between July and October 1897, while the townsfolk dead were estimated in the thousands. The campaign showed the army to be ill-organized, ill-equipped, ill-trained, and ill-led, with deficient recruitment and supply systems, and a willingness to fire on those defined as "bad Brazilians." The dreary experience would be used in coming decades to justify military reforms.

HENRIQUE DUQUE-ESTRADA DE MACEDO SOARES, *A Guerra de Canudos* (1902); EUCLYDES DA CUNHA, *Canudos (diario de uma expedição)* (1939), and *Rebellion in the Backlands*, translated by Samuel Putnam (1944); TRISTÃO DE ALENCAR ARARIPE, *Expedições militares contra Canudos: Seu aspecto marcial*, 2d ed. (1985); MARCOS EVANGELISTA DA COSTA VILLEJA, JR., *Canudos: Memórias de um combatente* (1988); E. BRADFORD BURNS, "The Destruction of a Folk Past: Euclides da Cunha and Cataclysmic Cultural Clash," in *Review of Latin American Studies* 3, no. 1 (1990): 17–36; ROBERT M. LEVINE, *Vale of Tears: Revisiting the Canudos Massacre in Northeastern Brazil, 1893–1897* (1992).

FRANK D. MCCANN JR.

**CAPABLANCA, JOSÉ RAÚL** (*b.* 19 November 1888; *d.* 8 March 1942), Cuba's foremost chess player and world champion. Ever since 1894, when a world chess championship began to be recognized by most nations, only three non-Europeans have held the title—two Americans, Paul Morphy and Bobby Fischer, and the Cuban

539

Capablanca. Having learned to play when he was not quite five years old, he soon amazed his father and the members of the prestigious Chess Club in Havana. In 1906 he made a name for himself when he participated in a lightning (speed chess) tournament at the Manhattan Chess Club in New York. Three years later he defeated the United States champion, Frank J. Marshall, and from then onward he achieved a series of brilliant successes that culminated when he ended Emanuel Lasker's long reign over the world of chess in March 1921. Capablanca held most of the world's chess records during his lifetime, and has been regarded by some experts as the greatest chess player of all time. He lost his crown in 1927 to the Russian Alexander Alekhine, who later always found pretexts to avoid Capablanca's repeated challenges for a rematch.

See WILLIAM WINTER, *Kings of Chess: Chess Champions of the Twentieth Century* (1966); DAVID HOOPER and DALE BRANDETH, *The Unknown Capablanca* (1975); IRVING CHERNEV, *The Golden Dozen: The Twelve Greatest Chess Players of All Times* (1976). A short biography of Capablanca may be found in JOSÉ I. LASAGA, *Cuban Lives: Pages of Cuban History,* vol. 2, translated by Nelson Durán (1988), pp. 373–383.

JOSÉ M. HERNÁNDEZ

*See also* **Sports.**

**CAPE VERDE ISLANDS,** a group of volcanic islands with a population (1990 estimate) of 339,000 in the Atlantic Ocean, 400 miles west of Senegal. Uninhabited when they were first visited by Portuguese sailors in 1456, the Cape Verde Islands became the first Portuguese colony in Africa in 1462. Because of an arid climate, they had relatively little agricultural potential, although the Portuguese tried to make plantation crops viable. Some Europeans settled there, including exiles of various sorts and Flemish colonists, but the majority of the people were Africans, most brought as slaves from the mainland. They created a cotton-cloth industry whose unique products were much valued in the African trade. Some free Africans and political refugees of noble rank also came to the island, and the island's political elite and its major landowners were primarily of mixed race (mestizos).

Cape Verde's primary value was as a way station for Europeans trading in Africa and sailing to American and Asian locations, thanks to its prevailing winds and currents. Its location and arid climate made its inhabitants often turn to maritime pursuits, as crews on merchant ships and whalers, and to immigration, especially to Portugal, Brazil, and North America.

In the 1950s local inhabitants who resented the privileges given to metropolitan Portuguese in the government and economy developed an independence party linked to Portuguese Guinea. The Portuguese revolution of 1974 resulted in the freedom of all its African colonies. Cape Verde became an independent republic on 5 July 1975.

JOHN THORNTON

*See also* **Portuguese Empire.**

**CAPELLANÍA,** an ecclesiastical endowment. The *capellanía,* or chantry, was one of several pious works commonly founded during the colonial period. The purpose of the chantry was to say masses in perpetuity for the spiritual benefit of the founder and his family. The chantry consisted of a capital endowment invested in real estate as a mortgage or lien at a standard rate of interest (7 percent until 1622, 5 percent thereafter). Other forms of endowment were also accepted, including real estate and voluntary encumbrances on previously unencumbered property.

In general the chantry served as a means of maintaining capital within one extended family, as a hedge against Spanish inheritance laws, which tended to fragment wealth. The founder of the chantry might indicate that one son would serve as the chaplain, another the patron or administrator, and a third, perhaps, the borrower of the capital endowment who would pay the interest. Although an ecclesiastical institution, the church intervened only in instances of legal disputes over the administration of the chantry. The chantry was one of several forms of permanent income recognized by the CATHOLIC CHURCH as sufficient for the purpose of ordination. Consequently the chantry was a means of providing family members with an income upon entering the clergy.

ARNOLD J. BAUER, "The Church in the Economy of Spanish America: *Censos* and *Depósitos* in the Eighteenth and Nineteenth Centuries," in *Hispanic American Historical Review* 63 (1983): 707–733; JOHN F. SCHWALLER, *Origins of Church Wealth in Mexico: Ecclesiastical Revenues and Church Finances, 1523–1600* (1985), esp. pp. 111–127.

JOHN F. SCHWALLER

**CAPELO, JOAQUÍN** (*b.* 1852; *d.* 1928), Peruvian sociologist and engineer who was author of the three-volume *Sociología de Lima* (1895–1902). In it he employed an organic metaphor to suggest the institutional structure of society in Lima. Elected to the Senate to represent highland Junín in 1900, he later wrote *Los menguados* (1912), a novel that deplored the corrupt practices common in Peruvian elections. A reformer, he sought legal protection for exploited workers in the lead mines. Yet he believed that ultimately society must rely on the individual to improve his own conditions. Although he sought legislation to enforce basic fair treatment of plantation workers by the owners, he argued that the worker must be left to advance his own cause. If he did not, the government should no longer interfere. His favorite public works project was the construction of a trans-Andean roadway from the coast to the eastern town of Pichis near the Amazon lowlands, and he made several reports to various ministries of government on the subject. The best of his ideas appeared in a two-volume study, *La vía central del Perú* (1895–1896). Capelo later became a leader of the *indigenista* movement in Peru. Along with Pedro ZULEN and Dora Mayer de Zulen, he helped publish the *indigenista* organ, *El deber pro-indígena*. In the pamphlet *La despoblación* (1912), he argued that the slow rate of population growth in Peru was the measure of the country's loss of its "potential." He died in Paris.

LEOPOLDO ZEA, *The Latin-American Mind,* translated by JAMES H. ABBOTT and LOWELL DUNHAM (1963), pp. 194–195; THOMAS M. DAVIES, JR., *Indian Integration in Peru: A Half Century of Experience, 1900–1948* (1974), esp. pp. 50–52.

VINCENT PELOSO

*See also* **Indigenismo.**

**CAPISTRANO DE ABREU, JOÃO** (*b.* 23 October 1853; *d.* 13 August 1927), Brazilian historian, scholar, and journalist. A landowner's son born in Maranguape, Ceará, Capistrano's formal education stopped at the *colégio* (secondary school). Widely read in French, English, and German, he was profoundly influenced by Auguste Comte and Herbert Spencer. In 1875, Capistrano moved to Rio de Janeiro, where he lived until his death, and worked as a school teacher, journalist, and bureaucrat. His historical writings drew on a formidable talent for archival research and displayed an original, penetrating mind. However, this work was largely restricted to short articles and reviews that did not sustain the promise of his first book, *O descobrimento do Brasil e seu desenvolvimento no século XVI* (1883). A distrust of worldly success, deep pessimism about life, the premature death of his wife, and time spent on scholarly translations and ethnographic research explain Capistrano's failure to write what contemporaries expected of him: a definitive study of colonial Brazil. *Capítulos de história colonial, 1500–1800* (1907), a commissioned work, is no more than suggestive of such a study. Nonetheless, his writings remain invaluable for their insights and analytical power, and Capistrano stands at the forefront of Brazilian historians.

JOSÉ AURÉLIO SARAVIA CÂMARA, *Capistrano de Abreu tentativa biobibliográfico* (Rio de Janeiro, 1965); JOSÉ HONÓRIO RODRIGUES, *História e historiadores do Brasil* (São Paulo, 1965), pp. 34–53.

RODERICK J. BARMAN

*See also* **Positivism.**

**CAPITANÍA.** *See* **Captaincy System.**

**CAPITÃO DO MATO,** literally, bush captain. During SLAVERY in Brazil, bush captains were recruited from among the free population, usually MULATTOES. Their job was similar to that of "patrollers" in the U.S. South: bush captains were contracted by plantation owners to hunt down and return escaped slaves. In the sugar areas of the North and Northeast they were used to locate QUILOMBOS, maroon communities of fugitives. Bush captains became infamous for their brutal tactics.

MARY C. KARASCH, *Slave Life in Rio de Janeiro, 1808–1850* (1987).

KIM D. BUTLER

**CAPITÃO MOR,** regimental colonel who was a military assistant to the governors of the captaincies. In the early colonial period, a *capitão mor* was a military commander of a front-line regiment. Each DONATÁRIO (lord proprietor) had a *capitão mor* of his territory. The early *capitão mor* was the person who governed new colonies for a period of three years. Since such a vast distance separated the colony from the kingdom, the *capitães mor* increased their power and became the political bosses of their districts. Often despotic in their application of local rule, they were in charge of enforcing royal laws, recruiting the militias, and serving as provincial governors. After 1764 they could impress men into the army, act as judges of final authority, and imprison deserters and vagrants. They could intervene in court trials or ecclesiastical affairs and even prevent couples from getting married. Usually they were local landowners of prominent families, who frequently abused their powers.

After their military power was curtailed, the *capitães mor* remained political bosses of their districts, exercising local autonomy in the sparsely populated rural areas where they were the real power. By the eighteenth century the title *capitão mor* was held by a governor of an unincorporated territory or by the commandant of a military company.

BAILEY W. DIFFIE, *Latin American Civilization: Colonial Period* (1945).

PATRICIA MULVEY

**CAPITULATIONS OF SANTA FE,** the April 1492 agreements between the Catholic monarchs, Ferdinand II and Isabella I, and Christopher COLUMBUS detailing the terms of royal support for Columbus's voyage to the New World. The capitulation is similar to a royal patent, in this case authorizing and regulating the relationship between the crown and an agent. By these agreements at the military encampment of Santa Fe on the edge of Granada, Isabella and Ferdinand bestowed on Columbus the offices of viceroy, admiral, and governor in any newly found lands. Further, Columbus received the right to one-tenth the value of the sale of "pearls, precious stones, gold, silver, spices," and other commodities. He was given the title of "don," and the capitulation was transferable to his heirs in perpetuity. In return, Columbus was to undertake the expedition, providing leadership and part of the funding. Many have questioned why the monarchs were so generous in their bestowal of privileges to the Italian; perhaps it was due to the recent fall of Granada, the prospect of converting pagan peoples, or the belief that if Columbus was successful, the crown could recover its investment.

SAMUEL ELIOT MORISON, *Journals and Other Documents on the Life and Voyages of Christopher Columbus* (1963); WILLIAM D. PHILLIPS, JR., and CARLA RAHN PHILLIPS, *The Worlds of Christopher Columbus* (1992).

NOBLE DAVID COOK

**CAPOEIRA,** a stylized martial art of Afro-Brazilian origin, rhythmically performed to the music of percussion and the berimbau, a bow-shaped instrument using a gourd as a resonating chamber to amplify low tones produced by tapping its single string. With graceful and powerful movements resembling gymnastic floor exercise, the *capoeirista* strikes simulated blows primarily with the feet and head, which the partner/opponent parries, evades, and returns. This dance/fight and the accompanying music, developed in organized clubs and training schools presided over by master teachers, emerged in the twentieth century from an earlier form of deadly foot-fighting. Often assisted by daggers, razors, stones, and clubs, it was practiced by individual slaves and free men of the urban lower class and by groups organized into gangs known as *maltas*. Although the modern form is now known and practiced to some degree in most parts of Brazil, the main historical centers have been Rio de Janeiro and Salvador, Bahia. In the latter city *capoeira* is often associated with the Afro-Brazilian religious tradition known as CANDOMBLÉ.

Several hypotheses exist on the etymology of the terms. *Capoeira,* which in standard Brazilian Portuguese also refers to second-growth brushland, was derived from the TUPI linguistic elements *caá* (vegetation, forest) and *puêra* (that which has disappeared). Also called *capoeira* is a partridgelike bird native to Brazil. Typically inhabiting scrubland, the male of the species aggressively resists intrusions into its territory by attacking and clawing rivals. *Malta* may be related to old Lisbon slang for itinerant laborers and street rowdies who stereotypically were migrants from the island of Malta, or it may denote the clannishness of members who stuck together like the wax-and-tar sealing mixture of the same name. While most studies of *capoeira* suggest it is a uniquely Brazilian phenomenon, some modern sources, particularly those focusing on the Afro-Brazilian culture of Salvador, Bahia, surmise it may have remote Angolan origins.

WALDOLOIR REGO, *Capoeira Angola* (1968); BIRA ALMEIDA, *Capoeira, a Brazilian Art Form* (1982); THOMAS H. HOLLOWAY, " 'A Healthy Terror': Police Repression of *Capoeiras* in Nineteenth-Century Rio de Janeiro," *Hispanic American Historical Review* 69, no. 4 (1989); 637–676.

THOMAS H. HOLLOWAY

## CAPTAIN-GENERAL

### Brazil

The captain-general was a military man who acted as head of the captaincy. He was a provincial governor whose duties were primarily military and defensive in nature as the supreme commander of all the armed forces in his captaincy. He was also the chief administrative officer responsible for exercising absolute power and administering the king's justice in his domain. As a colonial governor, the captain-general embodied the king and royal authority. After 1720 the captain-general of Bahia was elevated to the office of viceroy, and after 1763 so, too, was the captain-general of Rio de Janeiro. Although the captain-general could be a dictator by local standards, his power was curtailed by royal authorities overseas and the local town councils. The geographic vastness of Brazil also limited the governor's power. The governors meddled in municipal affairs by controlling nominations to governmental office and extending the terms of office of local officials. The captains-general could also initiate public works. The earliest captains-general had to subjugate and pacify the Indians, Christianize them, build forts and towns, introduce agriculture and commerce, and make the new colonies self-sufficient. Soldiers of fortune and daring military men like Tomé de SOUSA and Martim Afonso de SOUSA made effective captains-general, because they were able administrators and courageous commanders.

BAILEY W. DIFFIE, *A History of Colonial Brazil, 1500–1792* (1987).

PATRICIA MULVEY

### Spanish America

A captain-general was the chief executive of an AUDIENCIA district whose location made it susceptible to internal or external military threats. The title was combined with that of viceroy for the chief executives of the viceroyalties, and commonly with those of president and governor in non-viceregal districts. A captain-general has less prestige and authority then a viceroy, but because of his assignment to oversee the *audiencia*'s defense, he had more responsibility than an executive who bore only the titles of president or president/governor of an *audiencia*. In his combined roles, the captain-general was a powerful official with administrative, judicial, military, and legislative responsibilities.

The crown's decision to employ the title of captain-general was explicit recognition that some portions of the empire were militarily vulnerable. Since the vast viceroyalties of New Spain and Peru each had vulnerable areas, the viceroys were also titled captains-general and charged with overseeing their defense. By the late sixteenth century, however, the incursions of foreign interlopers in the Caribbean region and the continued conflict between Spanish settlers and the Araucanians in Chile led the crown to start using the title in conjunction with those of president and governor for the chief executive of several *audiencias*. Specifically, it named captains-general for Chile in 1567, for Santo Domingo in 1577, for Tierra Firme in 1596, and for Guatemala in 1609. When an *audiencia* was created in Manila in 1583, its chief executive was also named a captain-general.

As part of their increased reliance upon military administrators, the Bourbon monarchs converted the presidencies of Guadalajara (1708) and Quito (1767) into captaincies-general, created the captaincy-general of Venezuela (1777), and reestablished captaincies-general in Chile (1778) and Manila (1783).

A captain-general was responsible for the defense of the captaincy-general and specifically charged with maintaining fortifications, arms, and equipment in good condition. As commander in chief, a captain-general was also responsible for military justice and served as the court of appeal for any cases that involved persons entitled to the military FUERO or judicial privileges.

The crown selected captains-general from among experienced army or navy officers and appointed them for a specific term, normally eight years. At the conclusion of their term, they were subject to a judicial review (*residencia*).

CLARENCE H. HARING, *The Spanish Empire in America* (1947).

MARK A. BURKHOLDER

**CAPTAINCY SYSTEM,** the first governmental framework for the settlement and colonization of Brazil (1534–1549). In the 1530s King JOÃO III decided to transfer the captaincy system from Portugal to Brazil to secure the land more firmly for Portugal by encouraging permanent settlements to replace the trading stations (*feitorias*) originally established there. This system had been pioneered in the Atlantic islands, where land grants had been given to the Portuguese nobility and their younger sons to produce sugarcane. Brazil was, therefore, divided into fifteen captaincies granted to twelve noblemen who would be responsible for settlement and entrusted with vast civil and economic powers. Similar to the proprietary colonies of English North America, these huge land grants were semifeudal, in that vast powers were granted to private individuals, but also capitalistic, since their objective was to create profitable enterprises in South America. The captaincies stretched from the Amazon River to south of São Vicente. Each captaincy occupied 30 to 100 leagues of coastline stretching inland to the vague line of the Treaty of TORDESILLAS. Only two of the original captaincies were a success. Martim Afonso de SOUSA's settlement of São Vicente and Duarte COELHO PEREIRA's territory of Pernambuco flourished with sugarcane plantations. Most of the original *donatários* (lord proprietors) of the captaincies were absentee landowners, who were able to sell deeds of land (*sesmarías*) with full title to settlers.

The general failure of the early captaincies and foreign threats to Portuguese control of Brazil led to the demise of the system in 1549, when the first governor-general, Tomé de SOUSA, was sent to take power away from the original *donatários*. Private capital was unable to bear the expenses of settlement. The land was vast, the Indians were hostile to the incursions of settlers, and the country was too profitable to be left to private individuals. Despite its failure, the captaincy system set up a decentralized system of local government and gave future states of Brazil their territorial limits. Some of the hereditary captaincies lasted until the seventeenth and eighteenth centuries, when they reverted to the crown.

CAPTAINCIES OF COLONIAL BRAZIL

| | |
|---|---|
| Rio Grande | São Tomé |
| Paraíba | Rio de Janeiro |
| Itamaracá | Santo Amaro |
| Pernambuco | São Vincente |
| Bahia | Santa Ana |
| Ilhéus | Itaparicá |
| Pôrto Seguro | Paraguaçu |
| Espírito Santo | |

JAMES LOCKHART and STUART B. SCHWARTZ, *Early Latin America* (1983), p. 185.

PATRICIA MULVEY

543

**CAPUCHIN FRIARS,** an autonomous branch of the Franciscan order of priests and brothers of the Roman CATHOLIC CHURCH. In early–sixteenth-century Italy a group of Franciscans sought to reform the order and return to a more pure observance of the rule established by Saint Francis. The result was the formation of the Capuchin branch, which became a separate order in 1528. The name "Capuchin" derives from the long, pointed hood of the order's habit, a distinctive mode of dress adopted when the order was founded. The friars became known as some of the most effective preachers and missionaries of the sixteenth and seventeenth centuries.

Beginning in 1578, the Capuchins established themselves in Spain, and from there joined other religious orders in sending missionaries to the New World. The first Capuchin community in the Americas was founded in Darién (on the Caribbean coast of Panama) in 1648, but was abandoned soon thereafter. In 1650, the Capuchins established a successful mission at Cumaná in Venezuela. Within a short period of time Capuchins staffed MISSIONS in Caracas, Trinidad, Guayana, Santa Marta, and Maracaibo. In the eighteenth century, in particular, they founded numerous settlements in northern South America. Based on a system of both common responsibility and private ownership, Indians at the missions were expected to work for the community a total of twelve hours per week. The Capuchins directed classes in catechism, reading, writing, and crafts.

As a result of the struggle for independence, the friars were imprisoned or forced out of New Granada beginning in 1812. The missions were restaffed in 1835, however, when friars fled the suppression of religious communities in Spain. In 1849, expelled from the missions once again, the Capuchins dispersed and founded communities in Guatemala, El Salvador, and Ecuador.

In Brazil, French Capuchins made advances into the Amazon region in the first decades of the seventeenth century, but they were almost immediately replaced by Portuguese. These friars, with varying degrees of success, established missions throughout the seventeenth and eighteenth centuries, as they had in northern South America. In the process they began valuable ethnographic and linguistic studies of the native peoples. In the nineteenth century the influence of freemasonry led the government to undertake the dissolution of the monasteries, and the Capuchins suffered loss of property and personnel. Direct persecution, however, ended with the establishment of laws separating church and state at the end of the nineteenth century.

Today the Capuchin friars work in nearly every country of Latin America. They are active in ministries, in such areas as preaching, hospital work, and education.

ANTONIO DE EGAÑA, *Historia de la Iglesia en la América Española,* vol. 2 (1966).

BRIAN C. BELANGER

See also **Anticlericalism.**

**CARA SUCIA,** a large Late Preclassic (400 B.C.–A.D. 250) site located on the Pacific Coastal plain, in the southwest corner of the Department of Ahuachapán in western El Salvador. Very little archaeological research has been done at Cara Sucia, but a general chronology of historical and cultural development has been determined. The site is composed of low clusters of temple mounds, whose architecture and arrangement are characteristic of the Pacific coastal plain centers of the Late Preclassic period. This architectural organizational pattern contrasts with that of the nearby Salvadoran piedmont and highland basins. Piedmont sites typically have wide, artificial terraces that support potbelly monuments and jaguar heads, while highland sites have larger and more complex ceremonial centers.

In addition to its large size, Cara Sucia's impressive inventory of sculpture also emphasizes that this was an important ceremonial center. Cara Sucia is notable for its numerous Late Preclassic "jaguar head" sculptures. These jaguar heads are squarish, stylized stone faces. The dominant decorative motifs that form the face are rectangles and scrolls.

During the Middle Classic (A.D. 400–700), the massive Valley of Mexico center of TEOTIHUACÁN influenced much of the southern Pacific coastal plain. Cara Sucia is strongly linked by style of ceramics, architecture, and sculpture to the site of Bilbao, Guatemala in the Late Classic period (A.D. 700–900). Bilbao, in turn, appears to have strong connections to Teotihuacán. Thus, Cara Sucia was probably indirectly influenced by Teotihuacán.

Trade of CACAO (*Theobroma cacao*) and obsidian (volcanic glass), both ritually important and utilitarian goods, appears to have been the basis of long distance interactions with Teotihuacán. Excavations have shown that cacao was present at Cara Sucia. A deposit of carbonized tree seeds included some tentatively identified as *Theobroma cacao.* A fragment of a life-sized cacao pod effigy found at Cara Sucia also indicates the ritual importance of cacao cultivation there. An l-shaped ball court, Balsam Coast–style sculpture, and ceramics indicate that the Postclassic-period (A.D. 900–1500) Cara Sucia settlement prospered, probably largely due to trading cacao.

STANLEY H. BOGGS, "Las esculturas espigadas y otros datos sobre las ruinas de Cara Sucia, Departamento de Ahuachapán," in *Anales del Museo Nacional "David J. Guzmán"* nos. 42–48 (1968–1975): 37–56; PAUL E. AMAROLI, "Cara Sucia: Nueva luz sobre el pasado de la costa occidental de El Salvador," in *Universitas* 1 (1984): 15–19; ARTHUR A. DEMAREST, *The Archaeology of Santa Leticia and the Rise of Maya Civilization,* in publication 52 of the Middle American Research Institute, Tulane University (1986); *Informe preliminar de las excavaciones arqueológicas en Cara Sucia, Departamento de Ahuachapán, El Salvador,* manuscript on file, Patrimonio Cultural, El Salvador, and the Department of Anthropology, Vanderbilt University (1987).

KATHRYN SAMPECK

See also **Archaeology.**

**CARABOBO, BATTLE OF,** the last major military engagement of the WAR OF INDEPENDENCE in Venezuela, named after the savanna southwest of Valencia on which it took place. On the morning of 24 June 1821 the patriots, under the command of Simón BOLÍVAR, faced royalist troops under the leadership of General Miguel de la TORRE. The latter had taken command of the Spanish forces after the departure of General Pablo MORILLO the previous year. Bolívar's forces consisted of the Colombian troops that had marched with him over the Andes. These troops were joined at Carabobo by the *llaneros* ("plainsmen") of José Antonio PÁEZ. The patriot force of approximately six thousand outnumbered the royalists by perhaps a thousand. The battle lasted less than an hour, with light casualties on both sides. Losses were reportedly heaviest on the patriot side, with approximately two hundred killed and wounded, including nearly all of the British legion. Half of the royalist force was captured, the rest fleeing to the fort at Puerto Cabello. The patriots also gained important munitions, including artillery pieces and a large amount of ammunition.

The battle was important as a symbol of the strength of the patriot forces fighting on their territory, and their victory in effect freed Venezuela and New Granada from the Spanish. Bolívar entered Caracas less than a week later. In addition, with patriots now in charge of northern South America, Bolívar was able to focus his efforts on the south. In 1821 the Liberator organized a government at Cúcuta on the border of New Granada and Venezuela, marking the beginning of the construction of the Venezuelan nation.

LINO DUARTE LEVEL, *Cuadros de historia militar y civil de Venezuela* (1917); DANIEL FLORENCIO O'LEARY, *Bolívar and the War of Independence* (1970); JOHN V. LOMBARDI, *Venezuela: The Search for Order, the Dream of Progress* (1982).

GARY MILLER

*See also* **Cúcuta, Congress of.**

**CARACAS,** the capital of Venezuela as well as that of the municipality of Libertador and the Federal District. The city lies in a narrow valley some 15 miles from east to west. Its northern boundary is a spur of the Coastal Range, whose most famous peak, El Ávila (7,100 feet), dominates the center of the metropolitan area, and whose tallest peak, Naiguaitá (9,000 feet), stands at the eastern end of the valley. The name Caracas honors one of the indigenous tribes of the area.

The Federal District, created in 1909, included the municipalities of Libertador (Caracas) and Vargas (La Guaira). About 12 miles by road from Caracas, La Guaira was until recently the major port of the country. The Metropolitan Area of Caracas was created in 1950 and includes five municipalities (Libertador, Sucre, Baruta, El Hatillo, and Chacao). The city, at an average altitude of 3,400 feet, has a balmy climate. The valley is subject to seismic activity, and Caracas has suffered a number of earthquakes, notably in 1641, 1812, and 1967.

FOUNDATION AND COLONIAL PERIOD

The forbidding coastline of central Venezuela and the resistance of local tribes, particularly under the leadership of Guaicaipuro, delayed the process of Spanish conquest and colonization of the valley. Diego de LOSADA founded Santiago de León de Caracas in mid-1567. The site, at the western end of the valley, consisted of a central plaza and twenty-four blocks. The first CABILDO (municipal council) to which there is written reference was held in 1568, and the lands and Indians of the valley were divided among the Spaniards who accompanied Losada.

Caracas became the capital of the province of Venezuela in 1578, with a Spanish population of 60 *vecinos* (entitled residents), corresponding to some 300 persons, and some 7,000 Indians among the *encomiendas* of the valley. The town received a royal patent as a city in 1591.

By the early 1600s, the economy was based on the production of cacao, corn, and wheat as well as cattle and mules, all of which were traded through the port of La Guaira; the valley also produced sugar, beans, fruit, and other agricultural items for local consumption. In 1636 the bishopric was officially transferred from Coro to Caracas, where the bishops had been resident since 1613. The seventeenth century was one of slow growth, retarded severely by the earthquake of 1641. Estimated population by the end of the century was only some 350 *vecinos*, or about 1,750 people who could claim to be of Spanish origin.

In the eighteenth century there were important changes in the activities of the city. The Royal and Pontifical University of Caracas was founded in 1725, and in 1728 the Caracas Company (COMPAÑÍA GUIPUZCOANA) began its monopoly of the commerce between Spain and Venezuela. In the last quarter of the century, Caracas became the seat for fiscal matters with the creation of the intendancy (1776); for military and political matters with the creation of the captaincy-general of Venezuela (1777), which included the provinces of Cumaná, Guayana, Maracaibo, Margarita, and Trinidad; for judicial and administrative matters with the creation of the AUDIENCIA Real (1786); and for commercial and agricultural affairs with the creation of the CONSULADO Real (1793). In 1804 an archbishopric was established in Caracas and the city became the official religious administrative center. In 1808 it received the first printing press in the colony.

By the end of the colonial period Caracas had an estimated population of 42,000 inhabitants, and a very prosperous economic base, and had become the administrative center of the colony, but the city itself did not reflect this importance. Its most distinguished public building was the recently constructed San Carlos military barracks. The cathedral, while the biggest church, was neither architecturally significant nor well appointed. The Plaza Mayor was used as an open-air market. Water flowed down the center of the streets, and sidewalks were unknown, in part because there was no wheeled transport. Although foreigners praised the city for its climate and magnificent geographical setting, its clean streets and pleasant inhabitants, a fellow colonial from Mérida, Antonio Ignacio Rodríguez Picón, said of Caracas in 1803 that it was not much different from Mérida in terms of architecture; that only the central streets, where the rich and aristocratic lived, were well paved and pleasing of aspect; that the city was full of blacks, mulattoes, and Canary Islanders; and that it had little more than cockfights as public entertainment. There was no public lighting, and the city retired for the night at nine.

### THE NINETEENTH AND EARLY TWENTIETH CENTURIES

Independence was declared in Caracas on 5 July 1811, and between the long years of warfare and the devastating earthquake of 1812, the city suffered damages that were not fully repaired for more than fifty years. The travel accounts of these years are unanimous in remarking on the desolation and poverty of Caracas, in sharp contrast with its beautiful setting.

Between 1870 and 1888, Antonio GUZMÁN BLANCO held effective power in Venezuela and made a concerted effort to beautify and dignify the capital city. The center of the city received particular attention: the Plaza Bolívar (Mayor) was redesigned, the Capitol was built, and El Calvario became an elegant park. Churches, theaters, aqueducts, boulevards, and the new cemetery "General del Sur," which became a monument to mortuarial art, were all constructed. The streets were lighted by gas, a telephone system was installed, and the Caracas–La Guaira railroad was opened in 1883. Railroad connections were extended to Puerto Cabello and Valencia by 1895. This was the last face-lift Caracas would receive for sixty years.

### CONTEMPORARY CARACAS

After 1936, improved public-health measures and the development of the PETROLEUM INDUSTRY combined to increase the population of Caracas at a rapid rate. As can be seen in the accompanying table, the metropolitan

TABLE 1    Caracas: Population, 1881–1990

| Census Year | Caracas | Metropolitan Area |
| --- | --- | --- |
| 1881 | 55,638 | 77,911 |
| 1936 | 203,342 | 258,513 |
| 1950 | 495,064 | 693,896 |
| 1971 | 1,658,500 | 2,183,935 |
| 1990 | 1,824,892 | 2,784,042 |

area is growing faster than Caracas itself, but attempts to design an overall plan for urban growth have not had much success. The military government of the 1950s built, extended, and improved streets and highways, facilitating the city's expansion and improving connec-

Downtown Caracas, 1990. PHOTO BY GORKA DORRONSORO.

tions with the port and airport on the coast. It also continued the urban renewal in the center of the city that was begun by the government of Isais MEDINA ANGARITA in the 1940s.

Caracas remains the administrative, commercial, and cultural center of Venezuela. The petroleum revenues that are distributed by the national government tend to stay close at hand, and many companies locate in Caracas because of the ease of communications. Caracas has a number of public and private universities, numerous publishers and newspapers, various theater and ballet groups (both public and private), and several orchestras and ensembles. Cultural life tends to coalesce in the environs of the recently built Teresa Carreño Cultural Complex in the sector of Los Caobos. Nearby are the Ateneo, the National Gallery of Art, the Museum of Fine Arts, the Museum of Contemporary Art "Sofia Imber," and the Children's Museum.

In the last few decades new buildings have sprung up to such an extent that the valley is completely urbanized; Caracas has passed from being an overgrown town characterized by one- and two-story buildings with red-tiled roofs to a city more defined by skyscrapers. Although the Sierra del Ávila was declared a park, most of the other hillsides have been built up, and the two extremes of the valley are characterized by *ranchos* (slum housing). The Caracas metropolitan area now suffers greatly from inadequate public services, particularly with regard to water and sewage systems. The complex terrain, the rate of growth, and the complications of various local jurisdictions in the metropolitan area are having a devastating effect on the city. Caracas is no longer described as "la sucursal del cielo" (a branch of heaven) but rather as "Caracas la horrible" and "la ingobernable" (the ungovernable).

The most comprehensive study of Caracas is the multivolume collection produced by the UNIVERSIDAD CENTRAL DE VENEZUELA, *Estudio de Caracas*, 8 vols. in 15 pts. (1967–1973). Two classic studies of the city, also published in commemoration of its 400th anniversary, are JOSÉ ANTONIO DE ARMAS CHITTY, *Caracas: Origen y trayectoria de una ciudad*, 2 vols. (1967); and ANTONIO ARELLANO MORENO, *Caracas: Su evolución y su régimen legal*, 2d ed. (1972). Two specialized books of interest are MARCO AURELIO VILA, *Área Metropolitana de Caracas* (1965); and IRMA DE SOLA RICARDO, *Contribución al estudio de los planos de Caracas: La ciudad y la provincia, 1567–1967* (1967). Among the hundreds of books describing the city and its customs, the most frequently cited are ARÍSTIDES ROJAS, *Crónicas de Caracas: Antología* (1962); and ENRIQUE BERNARDO NÚÑEZ, *La ciudad de los techos rojos: Calles y esquinas de Caracas*, 4th ed. (1973).

SUSAN BERGLUND

**CARACAS, AUDIENCIA OF,** the juridical and administrative tribunal established by the Spanish crown in the province of Caracas. Created by a royal *cédula* of 31 July 1786 as part of the Bourbon dynasty's politics of centralization of control over its American dominions, it

had jurisdiction over all the territory of the captaincy general of Venezuela.

From the beginning of the eighteenth century, there was a special commitment to reorganize the Spanish Empire in hopes of guaranteeing royal authority, centralizing colonial administration, and obtaining more wealth in order to maintain Spain's internal economy and recover its imperial status in Europe. During the first few decades of that century, the COMPAÑÍA GUIPUZCOANA was established (1728); the posts of lieutenant governor and judge advocate were created; the power of the town magistrates was eliminated; and the Viceroyalty of NEW GRANADA was formed.

In the latter part of the eighteenth century, during the reign of CHARLES III, the politics of centralization and control was pushed even further through the creation of the intendancy of the army and royal finances (1776), the captaincy general of Venezuela (1777), the Royal Council of Caracas (1793), and the Royal Audiencia of Caracas (1786). Altogether these reforms tended to consolidate Bourbon absolutism, enhance the economic prosperity of the colonial territories, and raise the efficiency of their administrations.

The object of the Spanish system of *audiencias* was to restore royal authority in the American dominions and to regulate the activities of colonial authorities and society in general. They were organs of enormous relevance not only from a judicial standpoint, but in terms of government and administration of the most diverse affairs. Before the creation of the Audiencia of Caracas, judicial affairs of the provinces belonging to the captaincy general of Venezuela were handled by the *audiencias* of Santo Domingo and Santa Fé de Bogotá. In 1673 the ministers of the tribunal of Santo Domingo solicited the king to establish a tribunal in Caracas. A similar solicitation was made in 1753 by the governor of the province of Venezuela, and another in 1769 by the Cabildo of Caracas. In this last petition, the officials stressed the high costs of administration of justice due to the great distances involved and the increase in the number of cases as a result of population increase. They also denounced the corruption and delays which plagued the system of *audiencias*. Nevertheless, the petition was denied in 1770. Not until the separation of the provinces of Maracaibo and Barinas from the Viceroyalty of New Granada and their incorporation into the captaincy general of Venezuela would the creation of the Audiencia of Caracas take place.

The creation of the Audiencia of Caracas meant the centralization of all the judicial, political, and administrative functions within the territory known today as Venezuela, which before had been handled by the *audiencias* of Santo Domingo and Santa Fé de Bogotá. Its first members were the commander in chief of Venezuela, Juan Guillelmi, who presided; the regent, Antonio López de Quintana; the judges, Francisco Ignacio Cortínes, Juan Nepomuceno de Pedrosa, and José Patricio de Ribera; and the civil and criminal prosecutor, Julián

Díaz de Saravia. Administrative personnel included a chief warrant officer, a court clerk, a court reporter, a recording chancellor, an attorney for the poor, litigating attorneys, four solicitors, an appraiser, a distributor, two ordinary receivers, a receiver of court punishments, and assistants.

The *audiencia*, or tribunal, had various functions: It saw to the maintenance of royal authority, controlled the functionaries of the crown, advised the governor, resolved ecclesiastical affairs, saw to the supervision of the royal finances, intervened in military statutes, ensured fair treatment of the Indians, and maintained constant communication with the king and the COUNCIL OF THE INDIES to keep them up to date on provincial affairs.

The fact that the *audiencia* possessed the highest judicial authority also meant that its actions were determining factors regarding political control of the territories within its jurisdiction. This helped integrate judicial and political forces throughout the disjointed and dispersed provinces which made up the Venezuela of the day. This integration was a basic contributing factor toward the development of legal studies in Venezuela, aiding the founding of the Caracas Academy of Attorneys in 1788 and the creation of the Academy of Spanish and Public Law in 1790, both initiatives sponsored by the regent Antonio López de Quintana.

Nevertheless, the administration of justice was irregular and arbitrary, which resulted in the arrival of Joaquín Mosquera y Figueroa, who was sent to investigate accusations against the Audiencia of Caracas which had been brought before the crown. Moreover, the predominance of Spanish ministers occupying high positions, the large amount of power with which the *audiencia* was invested, and its fierce reaction against any move to alter the colonial order resulted in numerous confrontations between the creole elite and the predominantly Spanish authorities of the *audiencia*. The Caracas city council made known its reservations regarding the authority of the tribunal. The prerogatives invested in the *audiencia* resulted in a loss of municipal autonomy and affected the political interests of the prominent citizens of Caracas. The Royal Council of Caracas, again under the control of the powerful creoles, also had reservations. As a result of this attitude, when the emancipation movement broke out, one of the first measures taken by the JUNTA SUPREMA OF CARACAS was the dismissal and expulsion of the ministers of the *audiencia*. It was reestablished in 1812, but because of the war it functioned irregularly. In 1813 it was dissolved, then reinstated for a short time in 1814, and dissolved once again in 1816 by order of Fernando VIII. With the final defeat of Spanish forces in 1821, the Royal Audiencia was permanently dissolved.

HECTOR PARRA MÁRQUEZ, *Historia del Colegio de Abogados de Caracas*, 2 vols. (1952–1971); ALÍ ENRIQUE LÓPEZ BOHORQUEZ, *La Real Audiencia de Caracas: Su origen y organización 1786–1805* (1976); GUILLERMO MORÓN, *Proceso de integración de Venezuela, 1776–1793* (1977); MARIO BRICEÑO IRAGORRY, *El Regente Here-*

*dia, o, la piedad heróica* (1980); TERESA ALBORNOZ DE LÓPEZ, *Una visita a la Real Audiencia de Caracas entre 1804–1809* (1981); ALÍ ENRIQUE LÓPEZ BOHORQUEZ, *Los ministros de la Real Audiencia de Caracas, 1786–1810* (1984); and JOSÉ FRANCISCO HEREDIA, *Memorias del Regente heredia*, 3d ed. (1986).

INÉS QUINTERO

*See also* **Bourbon Reforms.**

**CARACAS COMPANY,** a mercantile enterprise chartered to control trade between Venezuela and Spain from 1728 to 1784.

The Caracas Company, or Real Compañía Guipuzcoana de Caracas, was formed in Spain in 1728 by José de PATIÑO. The company was given the exclusive right to control the CACAO trade between Venezuela and Spain. In return for this monopoly, the Caracas Company agreed to suppress the contraband trade, defend the Venezuelan coast, stimulate regional production of cacao, and provide slaves to the colony.

The Caracas Company was a mixed success. The first four decades of its existence were marked by expansion and profit. The production and legal exportation of cacao increased significantly, from 2.5 million pounds per year in the 1720s to over 6 million pounds annually in the early 1760s. This expansion, however, did little to enhance the overall condition of the colony. The planters elected to increase production in order to counteract the lower prices paid by the Caracas Company for cacao. This pushed the expansion of the plantation system—a classic case of growth without development. The efforts to halt contraband activities were not totally successful. Finally, the Caracas Company was unable to supply the colony with sufficient numbers of black slaves or European goods. These problems, the BOURBON REFORMS, and the wars that disrupted trading patterns caused the company's fortunes to decline; the crown terminated the company's charter in 1784.

The Caracas Company's most enduring legacy was that it ensured the primacy of Caracas over the remainder of the captaincy-general. By expanding the economic sphere of the capital, in terms of both area and power, the activities of the Caracas Company preceded the political centralization of the colony later in the eighteenth century.

ROLAND DENIS HUSSEY, *The Caracas Company, 1728–84: A Study in the History of Spanish Monopolistic Trade* (1934); FRANCISCO MORALES PADRÓN, *Rebelión contra la Compañía de Caracas* (1955); ROBERT J. FERRY, *The Colonial Elite of Early Caracas: Formation and Crisis, 1567–1767* (1989).

GARY M. MILLER

*See also* **Commercial Policy: Colonial Spanish America.**

**CARACAS CONFERENCE (1954).** *See* **Pan-American Conferences.**

**CARACOL,** the largest MAYA archaeological site in the modern country of Belize. It is centrally located near the resource-rich Maya Mountains about 2.5 miles from the Guatemalan border. Caracol played a prominent role in Classic Maya history, and its archaeological remains document the existence of a sizable middle level of Classic Maya society.

Around A.D. 650, Caracol occupied over 35 square miles and contained appoximately 36,000 structures and 150,000 people. The site maintained over 28 miles of internal roads that linked outlying architecture to epicentral groups; intervening areas contained households and terraced field systems, making Caracol a true "garden city." The earliest remains known from Caracol date to approximately 300 B.C.; the latest are dated to just before A.D. 1100. A hieroglyphic text records Caracol's defeat of Tikal, Guatemala, in A.D. 562. Following this and other war events, the site prospered and controlled much of the southern Maya lowlands until A.D. 700. The site also records a period of prosperity following A.D. 800. At this time Caana, a massive building complex rising some 139 feet, was completely refurbished and new monuments erected. Even though Caracol carved no new monuments following A.D. 850, archaeological remains indicate that the site was occupied for another 200 years.

Besides its extensive hieroglyphic record and size, Caracol is also noted for its burial practices and for evidence pertaining to the existence of a middle level of Classic Maya society. Of 176 burials investigated, 74 were in formal tombs; 8 tombs contained painted Maya dates. Together with caches and incense burners, the contents and distribution of these chambers throughout the site have aided in the identification of a sizable middle level of Classic Maya society, which arose following Caracol's successful warfare activities.

Despite Caracol's earlier size and prosperity, pottery and other remains left on building floors suggest that warfare may have led to an abrupt and nearly total abandonment of epicentral Caracol shortly before A.D. 900. However, portions of the site continued to be occupied sporadically for another 200 years.

DIANE CHASE and ARLEN CHASE, *Investigations at the Classic Maya City of Caracol, Belize, 1985–1987* (1987), *Mesoamerican Elites: An Archaeological Assessment* (1992), pp. 30–49; *Studies in the Archaeology of Caracol, Belize* (1994).

ARLEN F. CHASE
DIANE Z. CHASE

**CARAMURÚ** (Diogo Álvares Correia; *d.* 5 April 1557). Born in Viana do Castelo, northern Portugal, Caramurú arrived in Bahia de Todos os Santos, Brazil, sometime between 1509 and 1511 under uncertain circumstances: he may have been a *degredado* (criminal), a shipwrecked sailor, or a deserter. Because of his skills with firearms, he was befriended by the local TUPINAMBÁ Indians, one of whom he married.

With his knowledge of TUPI and of the lands and waters around All Saints Bay, Caramurú, the "Man of Fire," as the Amerindians dubbed him, proved extremely useful to a succession of Europeans who came to Bahia, among them ship captains; a lord proprietor, Francisco Pereira Coutinho; Brazil's first two governors-general, TOMÉ DE SOUSA and Duarte da Costa; and the first members of the Society of Jesus. He became an adviser to the proprietor, though it remains unknown whether he ignited or defused an indigenous uprising against him. He also aided Tomé de Sousa in the selection of a site for the city of Salvador, Brazil's first capital. He left part of his estate to the Jesuits and became the first civilian to be interred in their church in Salvador, where he died.

JOEL SERRÃO, ed., *Dicionário de história de Portugal* (1971), vol. 1, pp. 479–480, which includes an extensive bibliography.

DAURIL ALDEN

**CARAMURUS,** a Brazilian political movement that called for the return of Brazil's first emperor after his abdication in 1831. The departure of Dom PEDRO I, the first monarch of independent Brazil, ushered in a period of political confusion in the country. Moderate and radical liberals, many of whom had been instrumental in forcing Pedro I to give up his throne, struggled to enact a series of reforms, many of which promised to decentralize the young nation's political system. In reaction to this wave of liberalism and also to the anti-Portuguese sentiment the liberals often exhibited, a range of highly placed political and military figures, most of them born in Portugal, came together in a conservative political coalition. Centered on a simple restorationist program—a call for the return of Dom Pedro I either as monarch or as regent for his six-year-old son—the Caramurus managed to gain some popular support in both urban and rural areas and became a serious threat to the moderate liberal-controlled government of the early regency (1831–1840).

During the short life of their movement, the Caramurus acted as a provocative conservative opposition. They were active in the press; in fact, the movement took its name from the title of its leading newspaper, *O Caramuru*. They also organized their own association, the Sociedade Conservadora da Constituição Jurada do Império (Society for Conserving the Constitution as Sworn), which later became the Sociedade Militar (Military Society). The attacks that the Caramurus launched through these various organs came to a head in a conspiracy against the liberal government in 1832. Though suppressed easily, this plot demonstrated the seriousness of the conflict between these largely Portuguese conservatives and the state. The simplicity of the Caramuru program ultimately proved to be a fatal weakness. With the death of Pedro I in Portugal in 1834, the movement lost its definition and its members drifted into coalitions with other political factions.

THOMAS FLORY, ''Race and Social Control in Independent Brazil,'' in *Journal of Latin American Studies* 9, no. 2 (1977): 199–224; RODERICK J. BARMAN, *Brazil: The Forging of a Nation, 1798–1852* (1988); LESLIE BETHELL and JOSÉ MURILO DE CARVALHO, ''1822–1850,'' in *Brazil: Empire and Republic, 1822–1930*, edited by Leslie Bethell (1989).

ROGER A. KITTLESON

**CARAZO ODIO, RODRIGO** (*b.* 27 December 1926), president of Costa Rica (1978–1982), founder of the University for Peace (1980). Born in Cartago, Rodrigo Carazo began his distinguished career in public service in the aftermath of the 1948 revolution, when he was named a city councilman in Puntarenas. Shortly after receiving his degree in economics and administration from the University of Costa Rica (1951), he served at the national level during the first elected presidency of José FIGUERES FERRER (1953–1958).

Carazo began his political career as a follower of Figueres and held high positions in his administration and in that of Francisco ORLICH BOLMARCICH (1962–1966). He broke with the National Liberation Party (PLN) and formed the Democratic Renovation Party, a group that later joined with other parties to form the Unity Party, which supported his successful candidacy in 1978.

Although he came to the presidency on a ground swell of popular support for reform, his administration became embroiled in logistical support for the Sandinista revolution in Nicaragua. Because of charges of arms trafficking against members of his administration and oil crisis–induced inflation, his administration came to be popularly identified with high inflation and declining living standards after a generation of sustained economic growth. Despite many positive programs and high initial popularity, Carazo could not overcome the twin blows of rising oil prices and falling coffee prices.

Carazo has since become a private businessman, although in 1983–1984 he did briefly attempt to create a new political party, Partido Radical Democrático (Radical Democratic Party).

RODRIGO CARAZO ODIO, *Acción para la historia* (1982); RICHARD BIESANZ, KAREN ZUBRIS BIESANZ, and MAVIS HILTUNEN BIESANZ, *The Costa Ricans* (1982; rev. ed. 1988).

JOHN PATRICK BELL

*See also* **Costa Rica: Political Parties.**

**CARBALLIDO, EMILIO** (*b.* 22 May 1925), Mexican playwright. Carballido, a native of Córdoba, Veracruz, has been at the center of the Mexican theater since the 1950s. A prolific playwright with nearly 100 plays published and performed, he has set the standard of quality and originality in the contemporary theater while championing a younger generation of writers. Imbued with boundless energy, enthusiasm, and a superb sense of humor, Carballido is identified primarily with the theater, although he also has written several stories, novels, and movie scripts. His creative spirit has led him to experiment with virtually all forms of theater, including farce, children's theater, allegory, opera, and monologue, as he plays constantly with elements of tragedy, comedy, folklore, classical myth, satire, and politics.

Beginning with his earliest play in 1948, Carballido has mixed realism and fantasy in innovative ways, building a pattern of experimentation in his search for ways to express a Mexican reality deeply rooted in tradition. His provincial plays, such as *Rosalba y los Llaveros* (1950) and *La danza que sueña la tortuga* (1955), were surpassed by daring experiments with magic and symbolic figures such as those in *La hebra de oro* (1956). His farces, such as *¡Silencio, pollos pelones, ya les van a echar su maíz!* (1963), are entertaining and provocative. In 1966 *Yo también hablo de la rosa*, a dramatization of the creative process built around the metaphor of the rose and the infinite ways of perceiving reality, became a classic of the Mexican theater. In recent years Carballido has continued to be experimental. *Tiempo de ladrones: La historia de Chucho el Roto* (1984) glorifies a Mexican-style Robin Hood in a complex play written for two settings (*dos tandas*). His *Rosa de dos aromas* (1987) has been particularly popular for its portrayal of two women ''married'' to the same man. Carballido has set the standards, then broken them, throughout his long and productive career.

MARGARET S. PEDEN, *Emilio Carballido* (1980); JACQUELINE EYRING BIXLER, ''A Theatre of Contradictions: The Recent Works of Emilio Carballido,'' *Latin American Theatre Review* 18, no. 2 (1985): 57–65; JUDITH ISHMAEL BISSETT, ''Visualizing Carballido's *Orinoco*: The Play in Two Imagined Performances,'' *Gestos* 5, no. 9 (April 1990): 65–74; DIANA TAYLOR, ''Theatre and Transculturation: Emilio Carballido,'' in *Theatre of Crisis: Drama and Politics in Latin America* (1991).

GEORGE WOODYARD

**CARBALLO, AIDA** (*b.* 1916; *d.* 19 April 1985), Argentine printmaker, illustrator, and ceramist. Carballo studied in Buenos Aires at the Prilidiano PUEYRREDÓN School of Fine Arts, at the Ceramics National School, and at the De la Cárcova School of Fine Arts. In 1959 the French government awarded her a grant to study in Paris. She also studied engraving and drawing in Madrid and Barcelona. Her engravings describe Buenos Aires life in its rich local color. She produced work of marked linear accent, which has a haunting, overwhelming effect, presenting a complex, ironic vision of the contemporary world.

LILY SOSA DE NEWTON, *Diccionario biográfico de mujeres argentinas*, 3d ed. (1986); VICENTE GESUALDO, ALDO BIGLIONE, and RODOLFO SANTOS, *Diccionario de artistas plásticos en la Argentina* (1988).

AMALIA CORTINA ARAVENA

**CARBO Y NOBOA, PEDRO JOSÉ** (*b.* 19 March 1813; *d.* 24 December 1895), leading proponent of LIBERALISM in nineteenth-century Ecuador. A persistent voice for coastal interests, Carbo, a native of Guayaquil, served in Congress and as a diplomat in the early decades of the republic. His fierce ideological battles against archconservative dictator Gabriel GARCÍA MORENO (1861–1865, 1869–1875) proved to be the defining struggles of Carbo's career. He led the opposition to García Moreno's concordat with the Holy See of 1862. Named president of the Senate in 1867, Carbo used his position to battle the figurehead presidents named by García Moreno. In 1869 Liberals supported Carbo in his bid for the presidency, but he was defeated and exiled to Panama.

During the dictatorship of Ignacio de VEINTIMILLA (1876–1883), Carbo accepted appointments as minister of the Treasury (1876) and supreme chief of Guayaquil province (1883). His anticlerical policies, including steps toward the secularization of education, greatly angered the CATHOLIC hierarchy and led to armed revolts against the government. As Veintimilla grew increasingly corrupt and violent, Carbo left the government, ultimately joining the Liberal opposition. After Veintimilla's defeat in 1883, Carbo served as head of the provisional government. In the last years of his life Carbo wrote *Páginas de la historia del Ecuador* (1898), a work that brought together his liberal perspectives on nineteenth-century Ecuadorian politics.

On nineteenth-century Ecuadorian politics, see OSVALDO HURTADO's interpretive *Political Power in Ecuador,* translated by Nick D. Mills, Jr. (1985); and FRANK MAC DONALD SPINDLER's descriptive *Nineteenth Century Ecuador: An Historical Introduction* (1987). For a brief analysis of Ecuadorian political economy in the nineteenth century, consult DAVID W. SCHODT, *Ecuador: An Andean Enigma* (1987).

RONN F. PINEO

**CÁRCANO, MIGUEL ÁNGEL** (*b.* 18 July 1889; *d.* 1978), Argentine author and statesman. Born in Buenos Aires, Cárcano trained as a lawyer at the University of Buenos Aires. Beginning in 1913, with his thesis *Las Leyes agrarias argentinas,* Cárcano gained prominence as a historian. As a law professor at the University of Buenos Aires, he won his first national literary prize for the classic *Evolución histórica del régimen de la tierra pública, 1810–1916,* which describes the inequities of land alienation in Argentina.

Cárcano moved from academics to politics. He represented Córdoba province in the national Chamber of Deputies beginning in 1929. He remained active after the Revolution of 1930 and the formation of the Concordancia, and was reelected in 1931 and 1934. He served as a member of the diplomatic mission that negotiated the controversial ROCA–RUNCIMAN PACT of 1933. Later, President José Agustín JUSTO named him minister of agriculture in 1935. While remaining active in national affairs, he completed his public service as ambassador to Great Britain from 1942 to 1946.

MIGUEL A. CÁRCANO, *Evolución histórica del régimen de la tierra pública, 1810–1916* (1925), and *Realidad de una política* (1938).

DANIEL LEWIS

**CÁRCANO, RAMÓN JOSÉ** (*b.* 18 April 1860; *d.* 2 June 1946), Argentine politician and historian. Born and raised in, and long-time political chieftain of, the province of Córdoba, Cárcano was a remarkably successful conservative politician. Educated at the University of Córdoba, he affiliated with governors Antonio del Viso and Miguel Juàrez CELMAN (the latter was elected president in 1886). Cárcano was elected to the national Congress in 1884 and two years later returned to Córdoba, where he occupied several key ministerial posts, including justice and education. Between 1890 and 1910 he devoted himself to teaching law and writing. Elected again to Congress in 1910, he returned to public life as one of the most respected politicians of the interior provinces. Cárcano was passed over repeatedly, though always in the running, as candidate for president. He was instrumental in the rise of President Roque SÁENZ PEÑA, who promulgated the suffrage law of 1912. In 1913 he returned to Córdoba as governor and dominated the province for the next several decades. During his terms, he earned the reputation for sponsoring transportation and public works development. He also served as ambassador to Brazil (1933–1938). Cárcano wrote several classic accounts of mid-nineteenth-century Argentine politics and was twice president of the National Academy of History.

RAMÓN JOSÉ CÁRCANO, *Del sitio de Buenos Aires al campo de Cepeda (1852–1859)* (1921); *Guerra del Paraguay, acción y reacción de la Triple Alianza* (1941); and *Mis primeros ochenta años* (1945); NATALIO BOTANA, *El orden conservador: La política argentina entre 1880 y 1916* (1977).

JEREMY ADELMAN

**CARDENAL, ERNESTO** (*b.* 20 January 1925), Nicaraguan writer and minister of culture (1979–1988). Born into a wealthy family in Granada, Cardenal received his early education from the Christian Brothers and the Jesuits. A precocious writer, he allied himself with Carlos Martínez Rivas and others of the Generation of 1940. As a student of philosophy at the Universidad Nacional Autónoma de México (1942–1947), Cardenal joined other Nicaraguan exiles opposed to the dictatorship of Anastasio SOMOZA GARCÍA. Reading T. S. Eliot and the Imagists (Ezra Pound and Amy Lowell, among others) during two subsequent years of study at Columbia University (1947–1949) shaped his emerging *exteriorista* poetics, which emphasized nonmetaphoric language and concrete (frequently historical) detail.

Cardenal's political, poetic, and critical abilities were evident in *La ciudad deshabitada* (1946), *Proclama del conquistador* (1947), and his introduction to *Nueva poesía nicaragüense* (1949; translated as *New Nicaraguan Poetry*).

Following a year of study in Spain (1949–1950), he returned to Managua for seven years, where he operated a bookstore and formed a small publishing company (both called El Hilo Azul) with ex-*vanguardista* José CORONEL URTECHO. He continued to write poetry on romantic and, increasingly, political themes.

Influenced by the Chilean poet Pablo NERUDA and others, Cardenal explored Latin American indigenous culture and native resistance to domination, concerns that are prominent in *Con Walker en Nicaragua* (1952). His participation in the anti-Somoza April Rebellion of 1954 supplied themes for *La hora cero* or *Hora O* (1957–1959), especially that of the renewal of life through revolutionary activity. A religious conversion in 1956 led him to two years (1957–1959) of study with Thomas Merton at a Trappist monastery in Gethsemane, Kentucky, and two more years at a Benedictine monastery in Cuernavaca, Mexico; ultimately he went to Colombia to study for the priesthood (1961–1965). Cardenal's evolving political and religious views issued in the lyrical poems of *Gethsemani, Kentucky* (1960), *Epigramas* (1961), *Salmos* (1964; a recasting of the Psalms in terms of present-day political realities and language), and *Oración por Marilyn Monroe y otras poemas* (1965).

In 1966 Cardenal established on the island of Solentiname in Lake Nicaragua an experimental Christian contemplative colony oriented to agricultural, social, political (anti-Somoza), and cultural work among the largely illiterate rural population. During the Solentiname years, Cardenal published the political poems of *El estrecho dudoso* (1966), *Homenaje a los indios americanos* (1969), and *Canto nacional* (1972) and the Christian-Marxist exegetical dialogues of *El evangelio en Solentiname* (1975). The Solentiname community was destroyed by Somoza's National Guard in 1977. Increasingly Marxist in orientation during the 1970s, Cardenal became a cultural ambassador for the anti-Somoza FSLN (Sandinista National Liberation Front) in 1976. Appointed minister of culture by the new Sandinista government in 1979, he projected a "revolutionary, popular, national, and anti-imperialist" cultural policy modeled substantially upon the earlier Solentiname experiments (especially the controversial *exteriorista* poetry workshops and primitivist painting). Ambitious plans for film production and a national system of centers for popular culture, libraries, museums, and theater and dance companies were frustrated by the post-1982 budget crisis, exacerbated by the Contra war financed by the United States. The Ministry of Culture ceased to exist as a separate entity in 1988.

The best single source on Cardenal is PAUL W. BORGESON, JR., *Hacia el hombre nuevo: Poesía y pensamiento de Ernesto Cardenal* (1984). On the Ministry of Culture see DAVID E. WHISNANT, "Sandinista Cultural Policy: Notes Toward an Analysis in Historical Context," in *Central America: Historical Perspectives on the Contemporary Crises*, edited by Ralph Lee Woodward, Jr. (1988), and *The Politics of Culture in Nicaragua* (1995). Cardenal's own major statements on culture, together with those of other members of the FSLN's national directorate, appear in NICARAGUA, MINISTRY OF CULTURE, *Hacia una política cultural de la Revolución Popular Sandinista* (1982), esp. pp. 162–273. An illuminating set of interviews (including one with Cardenal) is in STEVEN WHITE, ed., *Culture and Politics in Nicaragua: Testimonies of Poets and Writers* (1986). Also useful is JOHN BEVERLEY and MARC ZIMMERMAN, *Literature and Politics in the Central American Revolutions* (1990).

DAVID E. WHISNANT

*See also* **Liberation Theology; Nicaragua: Political Parties.**

**CÁRDENAS, BERNARDINO DE** (*b.* 1579; *d.* 20 October 1668), bishop of Paraguay (1642–1651) and opponent of the JESUITS. Born in La Paz, Upper Peru, Cárdenas joined the FRANCISCAN order at the age of fifteen. After ordination, he preached for twenty years in native languages to the Quechua and AYMARA peoples of Peru and Upper Peru, who reputedly revered him. His reputation caused King Philip IV in 1638 to nominate, and Pope Urban VIII in 1640 to appoint, Cárdenas bishop of Paraguay. Consecrated in Santiago del Estero in 1641, Cárdenas then left for Asunción, where the bulls of his investiture were read in 1642.

Cárdenas allied himself with labor-hungry Paraguayan settlers who coveted the Guaranis in Jesuit missions as workers. He also insisted on visiting all curacies and parishes of his bishopric, including the Jesuit missions, a policy that Jesuits opposed. These disputes intensified friction between colonial Franciscans and Jesuits. The Jesuits challenged the validity of the bishop's consecration, hoping to remove him from the province. Cárdenas also fought with Governor Gregorio de Hinestrosa, a Jesuit ally, who brought Guaraní forces from the Jesuit missions to Asunción to shield the Jesuits from the Paraguayans, an action that the Paraguayans resented.

Cárdenas criticized Jesuit economic practices and accused the fathers of teaching false doctrine. In 1644 the governor expelled Cárdenas from Paraguay. Supported by Franciscans throughout South America, the exiled bishop spoke against his adversaries and persuaded the Audiencia of Charcas to order his reinstatement. He returned to Asunción in 1647 to face a new governor, Diego de Escobar Osorio, whose death in 1649 allowed the Paraguayans to name Cárdenas to the post. This right, they claimed, they had possessed since the Conquest. Applauded by the Asunción *cabildo*, the bishop-governor expelled the Jesuits from the capital, and a mob vandalized their property. Jesuit interests, however, finally prevailed; a mission army defeated the Paraguayan militia near San Lorenzo in 1650 and occupied and sacked Asunción. Although Cárdenas was then exiled from Paraguay, the king in 1660 ordered him reinstated as bishop. Old and feeble, he rejected further Paraguayan conflicts and instead accepted the bishopric of Santa Cruz de la Sierra, Upper Peru, where he served until his death. His legacy in Paraguay was an intensified anti-Jesuit feeling, and later rebellions in the 1720s (*see* ANTEQUERA Y CASTRO) and 1730s (*see* COMUNERO REVOLT) recalled his anti-Jesuit efforts.

*Colección general de documentos tocantes á la persecución que los regulares de la Compañía suscitaron y siguieron tenazmente por medio de sus jueces conservadores desde 1644 hasta 1660 contra el Ilmo. Rmo. Sr. Fr. D. Bernardino de Cárdenas, Obispo del Paraguay,* 2 vols. (1768); HARRIS GAYLORD WARREN, *Paraguay: An Informal History* (1949); ADALBERTO LOPEZ, *The Revolt of the Comuneros, 1721–1735* (1976).

JAMES SCHOFIELD SAEGER

**CÁRDENAS ARROYO, SANTIAGO** (*b.* 4 December 1937), Colombian painter. Born in Bogotá, Cárdenas studied painting at the Rhode Island School of Design (B.F.A. in 1960). After traveling in Europe, he returned to the United States and enrolled in the School of Fine Arts at Yale University, where he studied with Alex Katz, Jack Tworkov, and Neil Welliver, receiving his M.F.A. in 1964. Even before graduation, his work had appeared in his native Colombia at the Asociación de Arquitectos Javerianos, Bogotá (1963). He won first prize for painting at the Art Festival of New Haven, Connecticut (1964). In 1965 he returned to Bogotá and began teaching painting and drawing at the National University, the University of the Andes, and the University of Bogotá. He continued exhibiting his work and won national first prize and regional first prize in painting, III Croydon Salon, Bogotá (1966). In 1967 he had solo exhibitions at the Museum La Tertulia, Cali, and the Belarca Gallery. In 1972 he won first prize at the III Biennale of Art Coltejer, Medellín, Colombia, and was named director of the School of Fine Arts of the National University of Colombia, Bogotá. The following year he had a solo show at the Center for Inter-American Relations, New York, followed by another at the Museum of Modern Art, Bogotá (1976), and the Art Museum, National University, and the Garcés Valásquez Gallery, Bogotá, in 1980.

GLORIA PEÑA DE KAHN, comp., *Panorama artístico colombiano* (1981); EDUARDO SERRANO, *Cien años de arte colombiano, 1886–1986* (1986).

BÉLGICA RODRÍGUEZ

**CÁRDENAS DEL RÍO, LÁZARO** (*b.* 21 May 1895; *d.* 19 October 1970), President of Mexico, 1934–1940. Born in the small provincial town of Jiquilpán, in the western state of Michoacán, Mexico, Cárdenas was the oldest son of a shopkeeper. He left school after the fourth grade and worked as a clerk in the local tax office. Following his father's death in 1911, Cárdenas, a quiet, serious, conscientious youth, became a surrogate parent for his many siblings; several of his brothers emulated him by pursuing careers in the military and pol-

itics. A fierce patriotism nurtured by the liberal school curriculum and a hungry though unfocused ambition lurked behind Cárdenas's stolid mien, and in 1913, three years after the MEXICAN REVOLUTION broke out, the eighteen-year-old enlisted with rebels resisting the military regime of Victoriano HUERTA. After initial setbacks (he was captured in 1923, escaped, and had to lie low in Guadalajara for some months), Cárdenas began a rapid rise through the ranks, helped by the friendship and patronage of his commanding general, Plutarco ELÍAS CALLES. After campaigns against the YAQUIS in Sonora, the Villistas in Chihuahua, and the rebel-bandit forces of Chávez García in his home state, Cárdenas became interim governor of Michoacán (1920) and military commander on the isthmus (1921) and in the oil country of the Huasteca (1925–1928), where he condemned the corruption and arrogance of the foreign oil companies. During these years he developed close political alliances with President Elías Calles (1924–1928), with his fellow Michoacano, the radical Francisco MÚGICA, and with his own chief of staff, Manuel ÁVILA CAMACHO, member of a powerful revolutionary clan in the state of Puebla. As a military leader Cárdenas was bold to a fault, his impetuosity leading to defeats in 1918 and 1923, on which occasion he was severely wounded.

In 1928 Cárdenas was elected governor of his home state, where he undertook to accelerate agrarian reforms, develop education, and foster labor and peasant organizations, which he did through the radical anticlerical Confederación Revolucionaria Michoacana de Trabajo. His creation of a solid political base, however, was compromised by several leaves of absence, which he took in order to serve as president of the nascent National Revolutionary Party (PNR) (1930–1931), as minister of government (1932), and as minister of war (1933). Politically shrewd beneath a sphinxlike exterior, Cárdenas grasped—as some rival revolutionary caudillos, such as Adalberto Tejeda of Veracruz, failed to do—that the federal government, considerably strengthened and consolidated by the presidency and *maximato* of Calles, was the surest ladder of political advancement. Loyalty paid off, and in 1933 Cárdenas was chosen—in effect by Calles—as the PNR presidential candidate. Calles, who had governed through the medium of three relatively pliant presidents, no doubt expected that he could control his old protégé, in which respect, political opinion concurred. However, the onset of the Depression had undermined the broadly export-oriented economic project of the 1920s, and those who favored both a more interventionist state and a greater commitment to social legislation saw Cárdenas, known as a reformist governor of Michoacán, as the best hope within the party.

Cárdenas's radicalism—a practical, populist desire for social betterment rather than any bookish Marxism—was further stimulated by his extensive presidential campaign of 1934, which set the style for a peripatetic presidency: a quarter of his six years in office were spent on the road, touring Mexico, reaching remote villages, listening to local complaints, distributing patronage and public works, often by executive fiat. The rapport Cárdenas thus achieved with popular groups, which endured long after his presidency, served him in good stead when, in 1935–1936, he challenged Calles's authority, marshaling trade unions and peasant groups, generals and politicos, in order to force the dismayed *jefe máximo* (highest chief) into exile. By mid-1936, Cárdenas was emphatically master in his own house; the authority of the presidency had been reinforced, an assertion of presidential power that had been unusually bloodless.

During the middle years of his *sexenio,* Cárdenas enacted a raft of reforms that changed the political face of Mexico. Most important, he confiscated some 45 million acres of private land and distributed it in the form of *ejidos*—peasant communities in which the land was individually worked or, as on the big Laguna cotton estates, collectively farmed. With the *ejidos* came a rapid expansion of rural schools, now commited to a form of socialist education which sought to instill nationalism, class consciousness, and anticlericalism. Welcomed by some, this ambitious program of social engineering offended many, especially devout Catholics. In the face of protests, parental boycotts, and a good deal of local violence, Cárdenas, who had never shared Calles's dogmatic anticlericalism, reined in revolutionary anticlericalism, declaring that material betterment was the greater priority. Meanwhile, the president encouraged the political organization of the peasantry under the aegis of a national confederation which, in 1938, formally incorporated itself into the offical party as the National Campesino Federation (CNC).

A similar process of mobilization and incorporation affected the considerably smaller working class. During the *maximato,* the hegemony of the once-dominant Regional Confederation of Mexican Workers (CROM) was splintered, and the ravages of the Depression, though less severe and prolonged in Mexico than in some other Latin American countries, encouraged a new working-class militancy, upon which Cárdenas could capitalize, especially as the economy revived after 1933. Major industrial unions were formed in the leading sectors of industry—oil, mining, railways—and they began to press, strenuously and effectively, for national collective contracts. Meanwhile, the Mexican Federation of Labor (CTM), led by the flamboyant Marxist Vicente LOMBARDO TOLEDANO, arose from the ashes of the CROM; and, by virtue of a politically close alliance with the president, Lombardo and the CTM came to play a role in the 1930s similar to that of Luis N. MORONES and the CROM in the 1920s. The CTM benefited from sympathetic official arbitration in strikes and, in return, it backed the government, as did the Mexican Communist Party (PCM), which, pledged to a collaborationist popular-front strategy, now enjoyed a brief heyday as a political, ideological, and cultural force. In 1938 the CTM joined the CNC as corporate pillars of the new

official party, the Party of Mexican Revolution (PRM).

The radical thrust of the Cárdenas administration was evident in a series of nationalizations. Several mines and factories that threatened closure became workers' cooperatives. In 1937–1938 the railways were nationalized and placed under a workers' administration (conservative critics pointed to the inefficiency of the operation; radicals contended that the workers—seeking to run a decrepit system at low cost—made the best of a bad job). Most dramatic of all was the petroleum nationalization of March 1938, the first major seizure of oil assets by a developing country. Confronted by a long-runnning labor dispute, intransigent managers, and a perceived threat to Mexico's economic well-being and national sovereignty, Cárdenas expropriated the Anglo-American companies and established a state oil company, PETRÓLEOS MEXICANOS (PEMEX). Two consequences followed. Relations with the United States, which had been tolerably cordial since the late 1920s, cooled. But Cárdenas reassured the United States that oil was a special case, that further nationalizations were not contemplated, and that an adequate indemnity would be paid. And President Roosevelt, pilloried by big business at home and alarmed by the rise of fascism overseas, was reluctant either to champion the companies or to offend a friendly, anti-fascist Mexico. Indeed, with his condemnation of fascist aggression in Europe, Abyssinia (now Ethiopia), and China and his vigorous support of the Spanish Republic (a policy that elicited strong criticism from pro-Franco Mexicans), Cárdenas now appeared as a stalwart ally of the democratic powers. The United States therefore refrained from political or military reprisals and entered negotiations over the proposed oil indemnity, which was agreed to in 1942.

The oil crisis, followed by an oil company boycott of PEMEX, harmed the Mexican economy. Exports, the peso, and business confidence declined. Inflation quickened. Workers in the nationalized industries were required to tighten their belts and Cárdenas spent much of his final two years in office wrestling with the problems of the oil and railroad industries. Meanwhile, the presidential succession began to absorb political attention. International tensions—in particular, the global fascist–popular front confrontation—affected domestic politics. Right-wing groups, on the defensive since the Depression, staged a comeback. The National Sinarquista Union (UNS), a popular, Catholic, quasi-fascist movement founded in 1937, inveighed against Cardenista collectivism and "atheism." Conservative elements also mobilized behind dissident caudillos, on the right of the PRM, and in the pro-business, pro-Catholic National Action Party (PAN), founded in 1939. Some working-class Cardenistas broke ranks. Fearing destabilization, Cárdenas tacked to the center, reining in his radical policies and opting for a right-of-center successor, Ávila Camacho, rather than the radical Francisco Múgica. In the July 1940 presidential election Ávila Camacho easily defeated the challenge of the conservative

Peasants expound their demands face to face with President Cárdenas, ca. 1937. ARCHIVO GENERAL DE LA NACIÓN, MEXICO.

caudillo Juan Andréu ALMAZÁN, but did so amid scenes of fraud and violence. The Cárdenas presidency, which had indelibly marked Mexican political life, thus ended in dissent and controversy.

After 1940, the rightward drift of official policy was accelerated. Agrarian reform slowed, socialist education ended, détente with the church and the United States advanced. The structures set in place by Cárdenas—PEMEX, the corporate party, the collective *ejido*—remained, but they now contributed to a national project dedicated to industrialization and capital accumulation, goals that Cárdenas had neither set nor endorsed. The ex-president, however, remained loyal to the system he had helped create. He served as minister of war in 1942–1945, reassuring nationalist sentiment as Mexico collaborated increasingly closely with the United States. During the 1950s and 1960s he headed two major regional development projects, working, as in the past, for the material betterment of the poorer regions of southern and southwestern Mexico, thereby reinforcing his popular and populist reputation (a factor that would prove significant with the rise of "neo-Cardenismo" the leftist movement headed by Cárdenas's son, Cuauhtémoc Cárdenas, in the late 1980s). Loyalty to the system did not, however, prevent him from exercising significant influence: against the proposed reelection of President Miguel Alemán in 1951–1952; against the Vietnam War and U.S. policy toward Cuba in the 1960s; and in favor of political dissidents within Mexico. At the time of his death in 1970, Cárdenas was criticized by some as an authoritarian populist and a dangerous fellow-traveler, and revered by others, particularly in the Cardenista countryside, as the greatest constructive radical of the Mexican Revolution.

LUIS GONZÁLEZ, *Historia de la Revolución Mexicana: Los días del presidente Cárdenas* (1979) is a deft, sensitive narrative of the Cárdenas presidency; NORA HAMILTON, *The Limits of State Au-*

tonomy: Post-revolutionary Mexico (1982) gives a perceptive Marxist analysis of the postrevolutionary state, focusing on the 1930s; ALAN KNIGHT, "The Rise and Fall of Cardenismo, c. 1930–c. 1946," *Mexico Since Independence*, edited by Leslie Bethell (1991), provides a recent general overview and contains a bibliography; ENRIQUE KRAUZE, *General misionero: Lázaro Cárdenas* (1987) is an intelligent popular biography, critical of Cárdenas and well illustrated. A hagiographic biography by a United States admirer of Cárdenas is WILLIAM CAMERON TOWNSEND, *Lázaro Cárdenas: Mexican Democrat* (1952). For a succinct, sympathetic analysis of Cardenista politics and philosophy see TZVÍ MEDÍN, *Ideología y praxis política de Lázaro Cárdenas* (1972).

ALAN KNIGHT

*See also* **Mexico: Political Parties.**

**CÁRDENAS SOLORZANO, CUAUHTÉMOC** (*b.* 1 May 1934), Mexican politician and presidential candidate. Cárdenas's presidential candidacy, representing a coalition of opposition parties in the 1988 election, provoked the strongest support against the Institutional Revolutionary Party (PRI) since 1952. Cárdenas's parties, which included the Partido Popular Socialista, the Partido Auténtico de la Revolución Mexicana, the Partido Mexicano Socialista, and the Partido del Frente Cardenista de Reconstrucción Nacional, won four senate seats in Michoacán and the Federal District and captured most of the congressional seats in the key state of México, the Federal District, Michoacán, and Morelos. Cárdenas himself received a reported 31 percent of the vote to Carlos SALINAS GORTARI's reported 51 percent. Most observers believe extensive fraud took place, and some analysts assert that Cárdenas actually defeated Salinas.

Born in Mexico City, Cardenas is the son of General Lázaro CÁRDENAS, without doubt Mexico's most popular president of the twentieth century. This fact accounts in part for his own political popularity, especially among the *campesinos*, who considered Cárdenas Senior an agrarian savior. The son studied at the Colegio de San Nicolás in Morelia and graduated from the National School of Engineering 22 January 1957. Cárdenas then studied abroad on a Bank of Mexico fellowship, interning in France and for Krupp in Germany (1957–1958).

Cárdenas got his first taste of electoral politics in 1951, when as a preparatory student he supported the candidacy of General Miguel Henríquez Guzmán, who—as Cárdenas would later do—left the government's fold to oppose the official party presidential candidate. Later he joined the Movimiento de Liberación Nacional, a loosely constituted leftist opposition movement supported by his father, serving on the national committee with Heberto Castillo, who would join him in the 1988 presidential campaign.

After engaging in private practice in the 1960s, Cárdenas began holding various public positions. In 1970 he became subdirector of the Las Truchas steel complex, a decentralized federal agency, and in 1973 served as director of the public trust fund of Lázaro Cárdenas City. In 1976 he was elected senator from his home state, but he left his post that same year to serve as undersecretary of forest resources and fauna in the secretariat of agriculture and livestock. In 1980 he resigned this position to run for governor of Michoacán as the PRI candidate. Elected, he served until 1986, when he began his efforts to reform the official party. He and other reformers advocated democratizing the internal structure of the PRI and the electoral system in general. Their economic policies were populist, focused on debt renegotiation, deficit spending, and an increased state role in the economy. When the government leadership refused to accept their views, Cárdenas, Porfirio Muñóz Ledo (a former president of the PRI), and other leaders bolted the party in 1987. Not all the reformists followed their lead. Some, who call themselves the Critical Current, remained within the PRI.

Following the 1988 elections, Cárdenas's coalition reorganized itself as the Partido de la Revolución Democrática and offered intensive opposition in races for mayor and state legislative and gubernatorial posts. The strength of Cárdenas's opposition movement, and its persistence after the 1988 presidential elections, contributed significantly to the pressure for electoral reform and internal change within the government party. Cárdenas used his personal stature within Mexico and abroad to appeal for honesty in the electoral process.

LÁZARO CÁRDENAS, *Obras* 2 vols. (1973); and WAYNE A. CORNELIUS, ed., *Mexico's Alternative Political Futures* (1989).

RODERIC AI CAMP

**CARDIM, FREI FERNÃO** (*b.* 1540; *d.* 27 January 1625), Portuguese Jesuit and writer. Cardim accompanied the visitador Cristóvão de Gouveia to Brazil. Arriving in Bahia on 9 May 1584, Cardim described their activities in a report on the JESUITS entitled *Narrativa epistolar, ou Informação da missão do padre Cristóvão de Gouveia às partes do Brasil.* The two had visited the captaincies of Bahia, Ilhéus, Porto Seguro, Pernambuco, Espírito Santo, Rio de Janeiro, and São Vicente. Cardim was nominated dean of the Jesuit *colégio* in the city of Salvador, where he served until 1593, and then as dean in Rio de Janeiro in 1596. Returning from a 1598 mission to Rome, he was captured by Flemish pirates and kept in England until 1601.

By 1604 Cardim was provincial of the Jesuits in Brazil, and in 1607 he was nominated for the second time as dean of the Bahian *colégio,* the position he occupied when the Dutch attacked Salvador in 1624. The Jesuits took refuge in the Indian village of Espírito Santo, where Cardim died in 1625. He summarized his Brazilian experiences in two treatises: *Do princípio e origem dos índios do Brasil e de seus costumes e cerimônias* and *Do clima e terra do Brasil e de algumas coisas notáveis que se acham*

*assim na terra como no mar,* both published anonymously in Samuel Purchas's *Purchas his Pilgrimes* (London, 1625).

JOÃO CAPISTRANO DE ABREU, *Ensaios e estudos: Crítica e história* (1st and 2d ser., 1975, 1976); JOSÉ HONÓRIO RODRIGUES, *História da história do Brasil,* vol. 1, *Historiografia colonial* (1979).

MARIA BEATRIZ NIZZA DA SILVA

**CARDOSO, FELIPE SANTIAGO** (*b.* 1 May 1773; *d.* 17 September 1818), Uruguayan politician. Cardoso played an important role in the period of the revolution of the Provincia Oriental, known today as Uruguay. He was elected representative for Canelones to the CONGRESS OF APRIL 1813, which produced the famous Instructions of 1813—the first expression of federalist thought of the eastern caudillo José ARTIGAS. Cardoso acted as a confidential agent of Artigas in Buenos Aires, attempting to win the inclusion of representatives from the Provincia Oriental in the constituent assembly, which the government of Buenos Aires opposed. The representatives were finally rejected for technical reasons, the real reason being their federalist ideas, which ran contrary to the centralism of the capital. Cardoso was a member of the town council of Montevideo in 1815, a time during which Artigas, from his camp in Purificación on the Uruguay River, exercised a protectorate over the provinces of the Argentine littoral.

JOHN STREET, *Artigas and the Emancipation of Uruguay* (1959); WASHINGTON REYES ABADIE and ANDRÉS VÁZQUEZ ROMERO, *Crónica general del Uruguay,* vol. 2 (1984).

JOSÉ DE TORRES WILSON

**CARDOSO, FERNANDO HENRIQUE** (*b.* 18 June 1931), Brazilian sociologist and politician. Cardoso studied sociology with Roger Bastide and Florestan Fernandes at the University of São Paulo and taught there until the 1964 coup. In exile in Santiago, Chile, Cardoso contributed signally to dependency analysis at a moment when import-substitution industrialization (ISI) seemed to have failed. The structuralist economist Celso FURTADO had already hypothesized the connection between development and underdevelopment and argued that economic phenomena had to be understood in a historical framework. In the mid-1960s Cardoso and his collaborator Enzo Faletto extended the analysis to social relations. Pessimistic about development directed by "national bourgeoisies" as a result of his earlier research, Cardoso saw dependency not solely as a historical situation determined by a dynamic capitalist "center," but one in which there also exists a complex internal dynamic of class conflict in dependent countries of the less-industrialized "periphery." He accepted the structuralists' argument that the center gains more from exchange than the periphery through the latter's deteriorating terms-of-trade. But he stressed mutual interests among social classes across the international system—in particular, those of the bourgeoisies of the center and periphery. Cardoso and Faletto linked the failure of populism with the stagnation of ISI, viewing authoritarian regimes as necessary to secure political demobilization of the masses.

But unlike some other contributors to dependency (notably Andre Gunder Frank and Ruy Mauro Marini), Cardoso emphasized shifting alliances and a range of historical possibility. For Latin American economies controlled by local bourgeoisies, he saw the option of "associated dependent" development. Like other dependency writers, he saw the international system, not the nation-state, as the proper unit of analysis; development and underdevelopment were *locations* in the international economic system, not stages. Cardoso also denied that dependency (for him, a region of Marxism) could be operationalized as a quantitative methodology but rather saw it as a framework for concrete historical analysis of a specific dialectical process.

Cardoso returned to Brazil in 1968, opposed the military dictatorship, and was elected to the Brazilian Senate in 1986. In 1988 he helped form the Partido da Social Democracia Brasileira (PSDB).

On the impeachment of President Fernando COLLOR DE MELLO, Cardoso became foreign minister in the cabinet of Itamar FRANCO, Collor's successor, in October 1992. In May 1993 Cardoso was named finance minister, the most powerful cabinet post. The following year he ran for the presidency. His campaign was helped greatly by the fact that the policies ("Plano Real"), which he had introduced as finance minister, were sharply reducing the rate of inflation. In October 1994 Cardoso was elected president by direct popular vote, but he publicly disavowed many of his theses about dependency. Cordoso was inaugurated in January 1995.

FERNANDO HENRIQUE CARDOSO, *Empresário industrial e desenvolvimento econômico no Brasil* (1964), and "Associated-Dependent Development," in *Authoritarian Brazil*, edited by Alfred Stepan (1973), pp. 142–178; FERNANDO HENRIQUE CARDOSO and ENZO FALETTO, *Dependency and Development in Latin America*, translated by Marjory Urquidi (1979); JOSEPH KAHL, *Modernization, Exploitation, and Dependency in Latin America*, 2d ed. (1988); JOSEPH L. LOVE, "The Origins of Dependency Analysis," *Journal of Latin American Studies* 22, 1 (1990): 143–168.

JOSEPH L. LOVE

*See also* **Dependency Theory.**

**CARDOZA Y ARAGÓN, LUIS** (*b.* 21 June 1904; *d.* 4 September 1992), Guatemalan poet, essayist, and art critic. Widely recognized for his book *Guatemala: Las líneas de su mano* (1955), Cardoza y Aragón was one of modern Guatemala's most important literary figures. Following the surrealist tradition of the 1920s, he used experiences in Europe to nourish his aesthetic and social preoccupations through poetic works such as *Luna Park*

(1923) and *Maelstrom* (1926). With the French anthropologist Georges Raynaud he translated a pre-Columbian Maya-Quiché drama, *Rabinal Achí* (1928).

In 1931 Cardoza chose exile in Mexico over a return to Guatemala, which was entering one of the most brutal and repressive periods of its modern history under the dictatorship of Jorge UBICO Y CASTAÑEDA (1931–1944). He continued to publish his poetry—*Soledad* (1936) and *El sonámbulo* (1937)—and began to write critical essays on contemporary Mexican art, including the controversial volume *La nube y el reloj* (1940).

Cardoza returned to Guatemala in October 1944, on the eve of the revolution. He was cofounder of *Revista de Guatemala* (1945) and continued his artistic and political commitment to the revolution until its defeat in 1954.

Cardoza returned to Mexico, where he completed and published *Guatemala: Las líneas de su mano* (1955), in which he underscores his personal experiences through a presentation of Guatemala's cultural and political heritage. His poetic account of Guatemala, and the hopes of the October Revolution, establish this work as essential reading for understanding Guatemala and its people as well as Cardoza y Aragón's life. He died in Mexico City.

A brief overview and a selected bibliography are in FRANCISCO ALBIZÚREZ PALMA and CATALINA BARRIOS Y BARRIOS, *Historia de la literatura guatemalteca*, vol. 2 (1986), pp. 205–213. A collection of critical essays, including articles by Arturo Arias, Augusto Monterroso, and José Emilio Pacheco, is in *Homenaje a Luis Cardoza y Aragón* (1987). Most of Cardoza's poetry, and some prose, with an excellent prologue by José Emilio Pacheco, is in *Poesías completas y algunas prosas* (1977). For further information on Cardoza's life, see his autobiography, *El río: Novelas de caballería* (1986).

SHELLY JARRETT BROMBERG

**CARDOZO, EFRAÍM** (*b.* 16 October 1906; *d.* 10 April 1973), Paraguayan diplomat and historian. Born in Villarrica, Efraím Cardozo was the son of noted educator and journalist Ramón I. Cardozo and Juana Sosa. Given his parents' interest in the study of history, it is little wonder that Cardozo became a professional historian, one of Paraguay's best. He received a doctorate in law and social sciences at the National University of Asunción in 1932, and set off immediately on a diplomatic career, participating in the cease-fire negotiations that ended the CHACO WAR (1932–1935) and in the 1938 signing of the final peace treaty with Bolivia.

Cardozo was a Liberal, and on several occasions, officially (1970–1972) as well as unofficially, was president of the Liberal Radical Party. His political affiliations brought him considerable hardships during the Higinio MORÍNIGO dictatorship (1940–1948), including exile to Argentina on eight occasions. He later served in the Chamber of Deputies and in the Senate, while simultaneously working as a professor at the National University and the Catholic University in Asunción.

Cardozo is best remembered for his many historical

studies, which were scrupulously researched and which betrayed none of the partisan fanaticism so common in Paraguayan historiography. His thoroughly documented *El imperio del Brasil y el Río de la Plata: Antecedentes y estallido de la guerra del Paraguay* (1961) won the Alberdi-Sarmiento prize for its incisive analysis of South American diplomacy prior to the WAR OF THE TRIPLE ALLIANCE (1864–1870). His other publications include *Paraguay independiente* (1949), *Vísperas de la guerra del Paraguay* (1954), *El Paraguay colonial: Las raíces de la nacionalidad* (1959), *Historiografía paraguaya* (1959), and *Hace cien años: Crónicas de la guerra 1864–1870* (13 vols., 1967–1976).

DENNIS JOSEPH VODARSIK, "Efraím Cardozo (1906–1973)," in *Hispanic American Historical Review* 54, no. 1 (1974): 116; JACK RAY THOMAS, *Biographical Dictionary of Latin American Historians and Historiography* (1984); EFRAÍM CARDOZO, *Paraguay independiente* (Asunción, 1987).

MARTA FERNÁNDEZ WHIGHAM

**CARÍAS ANDINO, TIBURCIO** (*b.* 15 March 1876; *d.* 23 December 1969), president of Honduras (1933–1948).

Carías was born in Tegucigalpa, the youngest son of General Calixto Carías and Sara Andino de Carías. An excellent student, he received his law degree from the Central University of Honduras in 1898; later he taught mathematics at the National Institute as well as night classes for poor children and workers. Standing six feet, two inches in height, unusually tall for a Central American, Carías developed natural leadership ability. As early as 1891 he was campaigning for the dominant Liberal Party, in which his father was active. Thereafter he became involved in the military conflicts related to Central American politics.

In 1903 Carías left the Liberals to support Manuel BONILLA in founding the National Party, a successor to the nineteenth-century Conservative Party. Although his part in a 1907 revolt earned him the rank of brigadier general, he was not primarily a military man but rather a skillful politician who used the military to build an effective political machine. As a congressman and governor of several departments, Carías became the National Party leader and in 1923 its presidential candidate. He won a plurality but lacked the required majority, and when the Congress failed to resolve the stalemate, his armed forces seized Tegucigalpa in 1924. Subsequent elections, assisted by United States mediation, elected Carías's running mate, Miguel PAZ BARAONA, as president. When, in 1928, Carías lost to the Liberals by twelve thousand votes, many of his supporters called for revolt, but Carías accepted the official results, a move that won him wide respect.

Honduran politics of the 1920s were closely related to the rise of the U.S. banana companies, which were responsible for much of the political turbulence of the era. Samuel Zemurray's CUYAMEL FRUIT COMPANY supported the Liberals, while the UNITED FRUIT COMPANY backed Carías's National Party. In 1932 Carías won a convincing victory over José Ángel Zúñiga Huete and took office in 1933 after putting down an opposition revolt. Revisions of the constitution in 1939 allowed Carías to remain in office, first to 1944 and later through 1949. When he finally stepped down on 31 December 1948, having ruled his country longer than any other president in Honduran history, he turned over power to his protégé and minister of war, Juan Manuel GÁLVEZ DURÓN, following the first presidential election in the country since 1932.

Carías has been compared to contemporary dictators in the other Central American states: Jorge UBICO in Guatemala, Maximiliano HERNÁNDEZ MARTÍNEZ in El Salvador, and Anastasio SOMOZA in Nicaragua. His regime had similar fascist tendencies, and he achieved order and a measure of economic growth at the cost of civil liberties and the general welfare. Ángel Zúñiga kept up a propaganda campaign against Carías from exile in Mexico and there was an occasional revolt attempted from within, but Carías's firm control of the military assured his continued rule. He also cooperated closely with American business and government interests, including support of the Allies in World War II. Although he promoted modernization and made his country the leader in the development of Central American commercial aviation, Honduras continued to be the least developed of the isthmian states.

Unlike his "Dictators' League" counterparts in one important respect, Carías abandoned the Liberal Party. Although he had come from a Liberal Party background, his National Party retained some of the nineteenth-century Conservative Party philosophy, which defended a curious alliance of the leading families of the elite with the masses and adopted a somewhat friendlier attitude toward the Roman Catholic church than had the Liberals. While all of the Central American dictators were repressive and often brutal, Carías was somewhat more benign than the others, and he was the only one of them to step down gracefully. The overthrow of Hernández and Ubico by popular uprisings in 1944 probably contributed to Carías's decision to leave the presidency in 1948, for he, too, began to face student and labor unrest in 1944. In reality, his National Party, still a force in Honduras today, represented a union of nineteenth-century Liberal and Conservative elitist attitudes, allowing the Honduran Liberal Party of today to become more closely identified with middle-class interests. The major role of the military in modern Honduran politics was another legacy of Carías's dictatorship.

In the election of 1954, the seventy-nine-year-old Carías sought unsuccessfully to return to the presidency. A subsequent coup reduced his political influence even more, although he continued to live in Honduras until his death.

MARIO ARGUETA, *Tiburcio Carías: Anatomía de una época, 1923–1948* (1989); FILANDER DÍAZ CHÁVEZ, *Carías, el último caudillo frutero* (1982); GILBERTO GONZÁLEZ Y CONTRERAS, *El último cau-*

dillo (*ensayo biográfico*) (1946); JAMES A. MORRIS, *Honduras: Caudillo Politics and Military Rulers* (1984), which reviews his regime in some detail. See also WILLIAM S. STOKES, *Honduras: An Area Study in Government* (1950); JAMES D. RUDOLF, ed., *Honduras: A Country Study* (1984); and FRANKLIN DALLAS PARKER, *The Central American Republics* (1964).

RALPH LEE WOODWARD, JR.

*See also* **Banana Industry; Honduras: Political Parties.**

**CARIBBEAN ANTILLES.** The Caribbean can be defined in several different ways. What is commonly referred to as the Caribbean Basin is a multicultural group of twenty-six states (thirteen insular and thirteen littoral) plus assorted territories. It can also be defined in terms of its cultural-linguistic subgroups, including Spanish-speaking Cuba, the Dominican Republic, and U.S.-controlled Puerto Rico; an expanding English-speaking bloc of ten insular and two littoral states plus five insular territories; a French-speaking bloc made up of Haiti, the French departments of Martinique, Guadeloupe, and French Guiana, plus half of the island of Saint Martin; a Dutch-speaking section comprising independent Suriname on the South American littoral, Aruba, and the Netherlands Antilles (including Bonaire, Curaçao, Saba, Saint Eustatius, and the remaining half of Saint Martin, known as Sint Maarten). The last definition, and the focus of this essay, is that of the multicultural insular Caribbean that includes the Greater and Lesser Antilles (along with other scattered islands and the French, Dutch, and British littoral territories that have been historically grouped with their island counterparts).

The Greater Antilles is composed of Cuba; Hispaniola, which is divided between the Dominican Republic and Haiti; the Commonwealth of Puerto Rico; and Jamaica. The Lesser Antilles arcs southward from the Bahamas toward Trinidad and includes the Leeward and Windward island groupings that together form a majority of the states and colonies of the Commonwealth Caribbean, the U.S. Virgin Islands, plus French and Dutch possessions. Most have common features. In addition to their European colonization and the general replacement of eradicated native Arawaks and CARIBS by African slaves and a much lesser number of indentured workers from Asia and Europe, they share small size, restricted resources, and, in general, irregularly performing economies that remain highly dependent on metropolitan markets and goods. Except for Cuba, all adopted elected governments by 1995.

Haiti, although culturally rich, remains the most economically disadvantaged state in the Americas and one of the poorest globally. The Dominican Republic, which since the 1970s has been a democratic success story, frequently suffers strikes and food riots and now faces additional controversy resulting from the sentencing of its president, Salvador Jorge Blanco (1982–1986) for corruption in office. Along with Haiti and most of the larger Commonwealth Caribbean states, the Dominican Republic has severe economic problems, including restructuring imposed by the International Monetary Fund (IMF). Cuba, which is not eligible for IMF or World Bank assistance—or its conditionalities—also faces severe economic dislocations in the face of major cutbacks in economic and political assistance from Russia and Eastern Europe as well as rising frustration with the slowness of democratization in this Communist bastion. In the Commonwealth Caribbean, only Belize and a few of the smaller islands, especially the Commonwealth Dependencies most oriented to offshore banking (the Cayman Islands, the British Virgin Islands, and the Turks and Caicos Islands), have escaped the economic downturn of the 1990s. Cases of corruption and drug trafficking have followed the economic adversities in much of the region, requiring increased vigilance from all area governments.

Considerable regional change may accompany the Commonwealth Caribbean countries and Suriname, all of which are small and weak. Most have relatively open societies with memories of earlier good times promoting a sense of relative deprivation that is increased in intensity by the reality of popular demonstrations or coup attempts in several during the 1980s and 1990s. The authoritarian governments of Cuba and Haiti, the two exceptions to open societies in the insular Caribbean, are besieged with even greater anxieties as Cuba faces a probable revolution-altering economic and political crisis, and Haiti must cope with post-1994 intervention changes that included the restoration of President Jean-Bertrand ARISTIDE and another attempt at electoral democracy.

Greater emphasis on regionalism must be part of the answer in the post–Cold War era, in view of the fact that both Russia and the United States appear preoccupied with internal domestic problems and higher-priority concerns in eastern Europe and Asia. Regional solutions in the Caribbean include a deepening and widening of the CARIBBEAN COMMON MARKET (CARICOM); possible confederation of the Windward Islands (whose members currently hold individual memberships in both the Organization of Eastern Caribbean States [OECS] and CARICOM); and expansion of the NORTH AMERICAN FREE TRADE ASSOCIATION (NAFTA) as outlined at the end of 1994 by President William Clinton; plus a possible enhancement of trade and economic assistance by regional intermediate powers such as Canada, Venezuela, Colombia, and Mexico, the latter following resolution of its own domestic troubles.

Caricom membership, now restricted to the Commonwealth Caribbean, has been sought by Venezuela, the Dominican Republic, Suriname, Haiti, and Cuba. The potential for such expansion is strengthened by increased democratization in Haiti and Suriname, and eventually, it would appear, in Cuba, a status that will enhance the desirability of their membership. The deepening of integrative ties in the Windward Islands

(Grenada, Saint Lucia, Dominica and Saint Vincent and the Grenadines) has been impaired, ironically, by electoral democracy, since each time a plebiscite is planned one or another of the nations is facing a national election. The Leeward Islands have temporarily opted out of increased integration as the result of growth in their economies, especially in Antigua-Barbuda. The interests of the United States and the intermediate powers would be served by their attention to the integration processes in the Windward Islands and in the region in general. Finally, expansion of NAFTA is also possible, although fraught with perceived difficulties for local manufacturing and overall industrialization by Jamaica and other regional entities.

Latin America and Caribbean Contemporary Record is an annual reference work (from 1983). Caribbean Insight is the most current and accurate updated volume on the multicultural insular Caribbean. See also CHARLES AMERINGER, Political Parties of the Americas, 1980s to 1990s (1992) and ROBERT J. ALEXANDER, ed., Biographical Dictionary of Latin American and Caribbean Political Leaders (1988). FRANKLIN KNIGHT, The Caribbean (1978, rev. ed. 1990), is one of the best one-volume histories. GORDON K. LEWIS, The Growth of the Modern West Indies (1968) and Main Currents in Caribbean Thought (1983), remain near classics. CARL STONE, Power in the Caribbean Basin (1986), is the best cross-cultural comparison of political economies. HOWARD WIARDA, The Dominican Republic: Nation in Transition (1969), and WIARDA and MICHAEL J. KRYZANEK, The Dominican Republic: A Caribbean Crucible (1992), are among the better works on that troubled country. JORGE I. DOMÍNGUEZ, Cuba: Order and Revolution (1978), though dated, remains a front-running assessment of this Marxist regime. ANDRES SERBIN, "The CARICOM States and the Group of Three," in Journal of Interamerican and World Affairs 33, no. 2 (1991): 53–89, is of high value.

W. MARVIN WILL

**CARIBBEAN BASIN INITIATIVE (CBI),** a twelve-year program that went into effect on 1 January 1984, under which designated Caribbean and Central American countries could ship a wide range of products duty-free to the United States. First proposed by President Ronald Reagan in February 1982, the program was not approved by Congress until July 1983. Reagan's original proposal called for an emergency appropriation of $350 million for currency support; duty-free entry into the United States for exports, except textiles and apparel; and tax incentives for U.S. firms investing in manufacturing plants in the region. When approved by Congress, only the emergency appropriation remained unchanged. The duty-free list was altered to exclude footwear, handbags, luggage, flat goods (cloth materials), work gloves, leather apparel, canned tuna, petroleum and petroleum products, and certain watches and parts. Bowing to U.S. labor group pressure, Congress jettisoned the investment tax incentives. Communist-ruled countries—a clear reference to Cuba and Nicaragua—were denied any benefits under the plan.

From the outset the CBI was fraught with problems.

More than half of the initial emergency allocation went to Costa Rica and El Salvador, the two countries most affected by Reagan's efforts to dislodge the Sandinistas from power in Nicaragua. The Bahamas and the Cayman Islands refused to participate in the CBI because the program required them to share tax information with the United States (an attempt to discourage offshore banking). Heads of Caribbean states immediately began to pressure Reagan to expand the duty-free list. The only concessions included the admission of garments manufactured with fabrics made in the United States and the implementation of a "twin plant" program by the Commonwealth of Puerto Rico, by which Puerto Rican–based industries could establish subsidiary operations in other Caribbean countries to produce products that would be sent back to Puerto Rico for final assembly. By 1990 the CBI had not generated broad-based economic growth, alleviated debt problems, generated lasting employment opportunities, or improved trade relations with the United States. Efforts by Reagan and his successor, George Bush, to expand and extend the program until 2007 failed to win congressional approval.

"The Reagan Caribbean Basin Initiative," Congressional Digest 62 (1983): 69–96; U.S. CONGRESS. HOUSE. COMMITTEE ON WAYS AND MEANS, SUBCOMMITTEE ON OVERSIGHT, Review of the Impact and Effectiveness of the Caribbean Basin Initiative, 99th Congress, 2d session, February 1986; PETER D. WHITNEY, Five Years of the Caribbean Basin Initiative (1990).

THOMAS M. LEONARD

**CARIBBEAN COMMON MARKET (CARIFTA AND CARICOM).** The search for economic viability through some form of economic integration began in 1965 when Guyana invited Barbados and Antigua to join in an initiative on economic integration. The proposal was modeled on the European customs union, the European Free Trade Association (EFTA). By May 1968 all the other English-speaking Caribbean nations joined in the creation of the Caribbean Free Trade Association (CARIFTA). The ultimate goals of the union were, first and foremost, to encourage the kind of economic development that would provide the highest rates of employment and, second, reduce the region's external economic dependence. More immediately, CARIFTA called for the immediate removal of customs duties on some items and a five-year phasing out of other duties. A year later the Caribbean Development Bank was established to help CARIFTA fulfill its mission. Also in 1968 the Eastern Caribbean Common Market began operating as a parallel organization.

In October 1972 Jamaica, Trinidad and Tobago, Guyana, and Barbados (called the "more developed countries" within CARIFTA) agreed to deepen the integration process, forming the Caribbean Community and Common Market (CARICOM). This agreement called for the establishment of a common external tariff, the harmonization of fiscal incentives for industry, double-taxation agreements, and the formation of a Caribbean Investment Corporation (CIC). The latter was geared toward helping the "less developed countries" (LDCs) of the area. By 1974 the other eight members of CARIFTA had joined.

From an institutional point of view, the English-speaking Caribbean nations had agreed to a very comprehensive structure that went beyond economics. The highest decision-making body is the annual Heads of Government Conference. Its decisions are given shape by the Common Market Council and implemented by the Caribbean Community Secretariat based in Georgetown, Guyana. The ministers of education jointly are in charge of the UNIVERSITY OF THE WEST INDIES, with campuses in Jamaica, Trinidad, and Barbados; the University of Guyana; the Caribbean Examination Council; and the Council of Legal Education. A law school is located on the Barbados campus of UWI. Finances, specifically the Caribbean Development Bank and the Caribbean Investment Corporation, are under the purview of the ministers of finance and their administrative arm, the Council of Central Banks and Monetary Authorities.

Whatever the potential of such a structure for future political integration, the fact remains that CARICOM will stand or fall on the basis of its economic performance. Using the best single measure of economic success, the rates of growth of intraregional trade as a share of total trade, the record appears mixed. In 1967 the rate was 8 percent; in 1973 it had risen to 11 percent, but by 1976 it had declined to 7 percent, where it has remained. By the late 1980s little had been done to harmonize industrial planning, especially in terms of incentives for foreign investments. Each territory appears to be going its own way, a repeat of the history of the WEST INDIES FEDERATION. With the NORTH AMERICAN FREE TRADE AGREEMENT and the Interprise of the Americas already on the horizon, the nations of the Caribbean will have to either move toward regional integration or face an uncertain global economy as individual ministates.

ANTHONY P. MAINGOT

**CARIBBEAN LEGION,** a term applied to a conglomerate of exile groups that actively opposed the dictatorial regimes in the Caribbean during the period 1946 to 1950. Though the legion never existed as a specific military unit, certain personalities and matériel were common elements in a series of filibustering expeditions. Among the most prominent of these were Cayo Confites (1947), an ill-fated attempt to invade the Dominican Republic from Cuba; Costa Rica (1948), where Cayo Confites remnants based in Guatemala and augmented by Nicaraguan exiles aided José FIGUERES FERRER (1906–1990) in his War of National Liberation; and Luperón (1949), wherein Dominican exiles, primarily using Guatemala as a base, carried out an unsuccessful raid on their homeland. Although each of these events was under

distinct leadership and sponsorship, none boasted a coherent military force, such as the term "Caribbean Legion" would imply. Supported by the presidents of Cuba (Ramón GRAU SAN MARTÍN and Carlos PRÍO SOCARRÁS, successively) and Guatemala (Juan José ARÉVALO BERMEJO), these armed bands were comprised principally of Cubans and by Dominican, Honduran, Nicaraguan, and Salvadoran exiles at one time or another.

The core unit of these expeditions was the Liberation Army of America, founded in 1946 by General Juan Rodríguez García, as the military arm of a coalition of Dominican exiles opposing the dictator Rafael TRUJILLO MOLINA. The first use of the term "Caribbean Legion," however, occurred during the Costa Rican civil war, when it was used to designate a small force of exiles airlifted from Guatemala to seize Puerto Limón. The name caught on. Even Trujillo and Anastasio SOMOZA DEBAYLE utilized it in the hope of depicting their adversaries as adventurers and mercenaries.

The phantom army ceased to exist altogether in 1950, after the ORGANIZATION OF AMERICAN STATES imposed on Caribbean governments a series of "principles and standards" that severely restricted the activities of political exiles. The involvement of certain Central American exiles in Guatemalan affairs, particularly the implication of the Honduran Miguel Francisco MORAZÁN in the 1949 assassination of Francisco Javier ARANA, chief of the Guatemalan armed forces, also accounted for the eventual disappearance of the so-called Caribbean Legion.

ALBERTO BAYO, *Tempestad en el Caribe* (1950); ENRIQUE V. COROMINAS, *In the Caribbean Political Areas,* translated by L. Charles Foresti (1954); ROSENDO ARGÜELLO, JR., *By Whom We Were Betrayed . . . And How* (1955); HORACIO ORNES, *Desembarco en Luperón* (1956); JOHN PATRICK BELL, *Crisis in Costa Rica: The 1948 Revolution* (1971); CHARLES D. AMERINGER, *The Democratic Left in Exile: The Antidictatorial Struggle in the Caribbean, 1945–1959* (1974) and *Don Pepe: A Political Biography of José Figueres of Costa Rica* (1978).

CHARLES D. AMERINGER

**CARIBBEAN SEA.** Defined geographically, the Caribbean Sea is the body of water surrounding the islands of the West Indies that also washes the mainland, Antilles-facing shores of Belize, Honduras, Nicaragua, Costa Rica, Panama, Colombia, and Venezuela. As a cultural designation, the word "Caribbean" may also be used to identify not only the diverse peoples who inhabit the territory outlined above but also the population of Guyana.

The term "Caribbean" has long suffered from lack of precision. Carl O. Sauer put the matter succinctly: "The whole of the Caribbean area came to be known in English as the Spanish Main, including the sea. Thus, sailing *to* the Spanish Main became called sailing *on* the Spanish Main." For two decades after Columbus made landfall, what the Spaniards called the Ocean Sea was thought to be a vast, unbroken expanse lying to the west between Europe and Asia. After Balboa traversed Darién, the Ocean Sea was divided in two, with the Pacific Ocean called the Mar del Sur (South Sea) and the Atlantic, with its Caribbean indentation, called the Mar del Norte (North Sea). In the English-language world, the designation dates to the eighteenth century and is attributed by Sauer to Thomas Jefferys, whose introduction to the *West-India Atlas* (1775) states that "it has been sometimes called the Caribbean-Sea, which name would be better to adopt, than to leave this space quite anonymous." "'Caribbean'' derives from CARIB, the name given to a group of people originally from mainland South America who later island-hopped their way across the Lesser Antilles, displacing other cultures as they went and raiding eastern Puerto Rico until Spanish intrusion halted their expansion.

The best account of the tragedy that befell the native peoples of the Caribbean, a bitter experience of enslavement, exploitation, demographic collapse, and cultural extinction, is CARL O. SAUER's masterly reconstruction *The Early Spanish Main* (1966; 2d ed. 1992.) Also authoritative is MARY W. HELMS's "The Indians of the Caribbean and Circum-Caribbean at the End of the Fifteenth Century," in *The Cambridge History of Latin America*, edited by Leslie Bethell, vol. 1 (1984), pp. 37–58. A more controversial depiction of the encounter between natives and newcomers is KIRKPATRICK SALE, *The Conquest of Paradise: Christopher Columbus and the Columbian Legacy* (1990). An enduring classic is the textbook by ROBERT C. WEST and JOHN P. AUGELLI, *Middle America: Its Lands and Peoples* (1966; 3d ed. 1989).

W. GEORGE LOVELL

*See also* individual countries and islands.

## CARIBBEAN SEA: COMMONWEALTH STATES.

The Commonwealth Caribbean encompasses twelve independent states and six British colonies with a total population of approximately 6 million. Spread throughout the insular and littoral Caribbean Basin, this assemblage stretches from the Bahamas in the north, an archipelago of 2,700 islands, cays, and reefs that extends to within 50 miles of Florida, to the South American state of Guyana (formerly British Guiana), which shares a disputed border with Venezuela plus boundaries with Brazil and Dutch-speaking Suriname. The Commonwealth includes the states of Jamaica, just 90 miles south of Cuba; Belize (formerly British Honduras) on the Central American littoral, sandwiched between Mexico and a border now under negotiation with Guatemala; Trinidad and Tobago, within eyesight of Venezuela; and insular Barbados, on the Atlantic rim of the Caribbean. The remaining six independent states and four of the six colonies are found in the Lesser Antilles of the eastern Caribbean. This chain of islands includes the Leewards east of Puerto Rico, among which are found the two-island states of Saint Christopher (Kitts)–Nevis and An-

tigua and Barbuda, and the Windwards, which include the states of Dominica (between the French departments of Guadeloupe and Martinique), Saint Lucia, Saint Vincent, Grenada, and Bermuda.

In the seventeenth and eighteenth centuries these Caribbean territories served as pawns in power struggles between a weakening Spain and the emerging empire of Britain. As British Foreign Secretary George Canning bragged, probably from hindsight, "I called the New World into existence to redress the balance of the Old!" Almost all of these territories were ruled consecutively by two or three colonial masters, especially Britain and France—with some passed from hand to hand up to fourteen times, as in the case of Saint Lucia. According to James Pope-Hennessy, a former governor, these "pieces in Elizabethan schemes of empire, objects of Caroline and Cromwellian enterprise [and] loot of eighteenth century wars . . . have been prized with an excessive enthusiasm in one century and left to decay . . . in the next." These alternating patterns of metropolitan attention and neglect have not been limited to past centuries. After World War II, their primary perceived interest to the major actors shifted to a strategic level, an emphasis that is severely diminishing in the post–Cold War era.

A special period of neglect by the metropolitan colonial powers occurred in the years before World War II. By the 1930s and early 1940s these colonies, which had developed as slave-powered, plantation-organized appendages of European mercantilism, had not yet engendered strong support among the primarily black masses for the transplanted political or economic British structures nor for the importance of effective mass participation. With severe commodity price downturns related to the Great Depression plus continued low social expenditures and restrictions on suffrage, a period of insurrection among workers throughout the Caribbean led to political-economic mobilization and a stress-adaptation reaction by the British, highlighted by an official investigation and, ultimately, increased economic, social, and political assistance from the European metropole. British-sanctioned experimentation with self-governance was initiated in Jamaica, then in Barbados and Trinidad, and eventually in the other territories. The independence movement in the British Caribbean gathered momentum after World War II and received support from Whitehall, in the form of federations in the late 1950s and early 1960s and then through declarations of independence, beginning in 1962 with Jamaica and Trinidad and Tobago, the most populous territories in the Anglophone group both then and now: 2.5 and 1.2 million, respectively (1992). The state to gain independence most recently is St. Kitts–Nevis (1983). The decolonization process continues: Montserrat (population 12,000) is presently seeking independence. Colonies with relatively high per capita incomes that perceive it to be in their best interest to remain British dependencies for the foreseeable future include Anguilla, which opted to return to colonial status after its

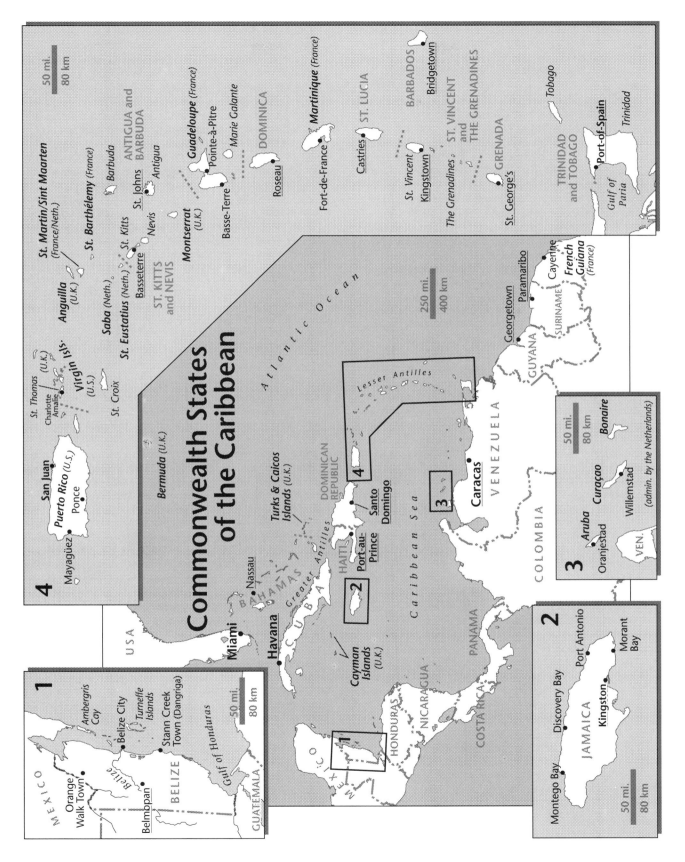

# Commonwealth States of the Caribbean

**4**

50 mi.
80 km

St. Martin/Sint Maarten *(France/Neth.)*

**St. Barthélemy** *(France)*

Barbuda

ANTIGUA and BARBUDA

St. Johns • Antigua

**Anguilla** *(U.K.)*

Nevis • St. Kitts
Basseterre

Saba *(Neth.)*

**Montserrat** *(U.K.)*

ST. KITTS and NEVIS

St. Eustatius *(Neth.)*

**Guadeloupe** *(France)*
Pointe-à-Pitre •
Basse-Terre •
*Marie Galante*

DOMINICA
Roseau •

**Martinique** *(France)*
Fort-de-France •

ST. LUCIA
Castries •

BARBADOS
Bridgetown •

ST. VINCENT and THE GRENADINES
St. Vincent
Kingstown
*The Grenadines*

GRENADA
St. George's •

*Tobago*

**Port-of-Spain** •
*Trinidad*

TRINIDAD and TOBAGO

*Gulf of Paria*

St. Thomas *(U.K.)*
Charlotte
Amalie
Virgin Isls.
*(U.S.)*
St. Croix

San Juan •
**Puerto Rico** *(U.S.)*
Mayagüez • • Ponce

*Bermuda (U.K.)*

*Atlantic Ocean*

250 mi.
400 km

Lesser Antilles

VENEZUELA
Caracas •

Cayenne •
*French Guiana (France)*

Georgetown • Paramaribo •
GUYANA SURINAME

COLOMBIA

**3**
50 mi.
80 km
*Bonaire*
**Aruba** *Curaçao*
Oranjestad • • Willemstad
VEN.
*(admin. by the Netherlands)*

Miami •
USA

Havana •
C U B A
BAHAMAS
Nassau •
*Greater Antilles*

*Turks & Caicos Islands (U.K.)*

HAITI
Port-au-Prince •
DOMINICAN REPUBLIC
Santo Domingo •

**4**

**2**

*Cayman Islands (U.K.)*

*Caribbean Sea*

MEXICO

HONDURAS
NICARAGUA

COSTA RICA
PANAMA

**1**
Ambergris Cay
Belize City •
*Turneffe Islands*
Stann Creek Town (Dangriga) •
MEXICO
Orange Walk Town •
Belmopan •
BELIZE
*Belize*
GUATEMALA
*Gulf of Honduras*
50 mi.
80 km

**2**
Port Antonio •
Discovery Bay •
Morant Bay •
JAMAICA
Kingston •
Montego Bay •
50 mi.
80 km

formal break from Saint Kitts–Nevis in 1971; the British Virgin Islands; the Cayman Islands, once ruled by Jamaica; and the Turks and Caicos Islands, located south of the Bahamas archipelago, with which they were once associated.

All of the independent states have elected governments, and since the 1992 elections, all but the Bahamas and Guyana have alternated the party elected to power. The Bahamas and Barbados led the independent states of geopolitical Latin America in 1989 with per capita GDPs of US$8,205 and $6,673, respectively. Despite their considerable political, social, and economic developmental advantages, these small states find their options for economic development severely restricted and their socioeconomic-political vulnerability exacerbated by their initial limited natural resource bases and an often negative international economic climate. Systematic vulnerability is induced by the high degree of political openness these states enjoy, an openness that at the same time contributes positively to both the democratic process and the political legitimacy of governance.

Most Commonwealth Caribbean states have faced a rising tide of debt and International Monetary Fund (IMF) conditionalities since the late 1970s, while the 1980s and early 1990s have seen sharp international pricing declines for many regional commodities, including petroleum, which only Trinidad and Tobago produce in sufficient quantity for export; bauxite/alumina, plentiful in both Guyana and Jamaica; sugar, still a multiterritorial mainstay (especially important to Barbados), which in the late 1980s failed to command a world price commensurate with the cost of production; and coffee, which is produced in Jamaica. As a result, both Trinidad and Tobago and Guyana have ended the decade of the 1980s with approximately half their per capita GDP level of 1980. Jamaica and several other states have experienced only marginal growth and little real development following major economic declines during the 1970s. Unemployment and underemployment remain at very high levels in most states.

When political participation outraces a political system's ability to respond satisfactorily, especially in crisis situations, the vulnerability of the regime escalates dramatically. These open political systems appear extremely vulnerable to such stress, especially when periods of sustained economic growth have become part of the national memory—as was the case in Trinidad and Tobago, Jamaica, and Guyana. This situation may explain the bloody coup attempt in Trinidad in 1990 and the earlier violence in Trinidad, Jamaica, and Guyana. After periods of regional leadership in economic growth, even the Bahamas and Barbados have had major economic downturns, accelerating debt and labor unrest and increasing voters' apathy during the 1980s. These problems among the "Big Five" states of the Caribbean Community (CARICOM) have severely affected regional trade, which declined 50 percent during the decade, and overall cooperation.

Partly because of production and trading problems, especially since 1987, a new spirit of integration has appeared within CARICOM and its subunit, the Organization of Eastern Caribbean States (OECS). Plans have been formulated for a true common market within CARICOM, while the four Windward group members of the OECS, which already shares economically, politically (including international representation), and militarily, have held talks on the possibility of confederating. The role of the United States and other metropolitan actors is vital if this region is to remain democratically stable.

HECTOR BOLITHO, ed., The British Empire (1947); JAMES POPE-HENNESSY, Verandah: Some Episodes in the Crown Colony, 1867–1889 (1964); GORDON K. LEWIS, The Growth of the Modern West Indies (1968); CARL STONE, Power in the Caribbean Basin: A Comparative Study of Political Economy (1986); ROBERT ALEXANDER, ed., Biographical Dictionary of Latin American and Caribbean Political Leaders (1988); LESTER D. LANGLEY, The United States and the Caribbean in the Twentieth Century (1989); CARIBBEAN DEVELOPMENT BANK, Annual Report 1990 (1991); W. MARVIN WILL, "A Nation Divided: The Quest for Caribbean Integration," in Latin American Research Review 26, no. 2 (1991): 3–37; CHARLES AMERINGER, ed., Political Parties of the Americas, 1980s to 1990s (1992).

W. MARVIN WILL

**CARIBS,** the European name for some of the American INDIANS first of the Lesser Antilles, and later in the Orinoco and Amazon basins of South America. It came to be used more generally to mean "wild," "untamed," "fierce," and was sometimes applied to indigenous peoples elsewhere in the world. Most properly today it refers to a language family, but also designates an indigenous South American culture and, increasingly, a modern South American ethnic entity. Ironically, those Antillean peoples who sometimes today identify themselves as Caribs bear little resemblance either to the Caribs of South America or to their ancestors of the "encounter" period, who apparently were not actually Caribs in the ethnographic sense. Only the Garifuna, or Black Caribs of Central America, have preserved recognizable patterns of the original island culture and language, which was fundamentally Arawak with a Carib overlay.

To understand this apparent set of contradictions, one must consider the politics and the state of racial and ethnic thinking in Europe in the sixteenth century. Some scholars believe the early distinction made by Europeans between "Arawak" and "Carib" groups in the Caribbean was spurious—the latter term coming to refer to those Indians whose resistance to European incursions took a violent form, and were difficult to subdue because they were more mobile than the TAINO.

At the time of Columbus's 1492 landing, the Greater Antilles were dominated by the Arawak-speaking Taino, who had developed a populous, agricultural society with permanent settlements. Led by chieftains and priests, they created a distinctive art style known archaeologically in ceramic and carved stone artifacts. Their settlements were continually at risk of raids by seafaring marauders—also Arawak-speakers—from the more southern islands, who called themselves by various names, including Galibi, from which the Europeans may have derived the term Carib (Spanish, *Caribe*).

Accounts by Europeans throughout the sixteenth and seventeenth centuries contain contrasting descriptions of Caribs and Tainos. While the latter were depicted as peaceful and civilized, the former were accused of cannibalism and other atrocities, and came to be greatly feared by Europeans, at the same time that they were respected for their military prowess. These so-called Caribs lived in small settlements, usually on the leeward coastlines or along inland rivers. Their culture was based on slash-and-burn manioc cultivation carried out primarily by the women, and fishing and trading by the men, who combined the latter with raiding. Linguistic analyses of historical documents suggest that, like the Tainos, their language was Arawak, although the men also used a pidgin based on Carib in their raiding and trading forays, probably to enhance communication with South American Carib-speakers.

In their fierce opposition to European settlement, the so-called Caribs of the Lesser Antilles raided European plantations and carried off many slaves, later adopting them into their own society. Other blacks, fleeing their masters, were either shipwrecked near or purposely sought refuge among the native islanders. After some two centuries of miscegenation, a new racial and ethnic type developed, phenotypically and culturally distinct from both ancestral strains. Europeans called them Black Caribs, and came to consider them even more dangerous than their lighter-skinned brethren.

St. Vincent became known to both Europeans and African slaves as the site where the largest group of Black Caribs resided and prospered from about 1700 onward. In 1797, after a generation of intermittent violence and two years of concentrated warfare, the British forcibly removed most of the Black Caribs—some two thousand individuals—from St. Vincent, sending them across the Caribbean to Roatán, an island in the Bay of Honduras. Unable to live there, they contrived to have the Spanish remove them to mainland Trujillo, where they helped the latter in fighting off would-be British invaders and, later, Creole insurgents. Some of them moved up the coast to the British colony of Belize (later known as British Honduras), where as free laborers they cut and transported mahogany for the British settlers, much to the distress of government authorities, who feared them because of their reputation for aggressiveness, and because they assumed they might provide haven for escaped Belizean slaves.

During the nineteenth century the Black Caribs settled nearly one hundred small communities along the Caribbean coast of Central America between Bluefields, Nicaragua, and Belize City. Their Amerindian culture, preserved and somewhat modified by the African in-

Chief of the Caribs and wife, 1917. Roseau, Dominica. LATIN AMERICAN LIBRARY, TULANE UNIVERSITY.

flux on St. Vincent, also survived the deportation. In Central America, in addition to their traditional fishing and horticulture, the latter carried on almost exclusively by the women, they worked for wages along the coast, becoming known for their facility in several languages, their resistance to tropical diseases, and their reliable labor in various enterprises. Before World War II they provided most of the coastwise transportation facilities in that area, with reputations as skillful seamen and manufacturers of small, but seaworthy craft. Some of their "canoes" were as long as 30 feet and could hold up to 100 people. During the first half of the twentieth century they were in demand as stevedores for the large fruit companies in Honduras, Guatemala, and Belize.

While adopting bits and pieces of European culture, the Black Caribs have continued to preserve their own traditions, including their language, religious beliefs and practices, musical expressions, oral literature, and fishing and horticultural technology. Some of what they have come to consider exclusively their own was adopted from French, British, and Spanish cultural patterns; other traits they shared with neighboring Amerindians in Central America, especially the Miskito, an

African hybrid people living primarily in Nicaragua and Honduras.

During World War II the men emigrated to work on ships and docks in the United States and Great Britain. That tradition continued after the war, and beginning in the mid-1960s, more women also left their coastal villages, seeking jobs either in the highland cities of their home countries or in the United States. At first, children were left in the villages, to be raised by their grandmothers during their parents' overseas residence, but increasingly they are being brought to the United States in their teens or even before.

In the 1970s intellectuals and activists pushed the name "Garifuna," which is more properly an adjective referring to the culture and the language, but which has now largely replaced Black Carib. There are large Garifuna communities in New York, Chicago, Los Angeles, and New Orleans, with many thousands scattered in other American cities. Many have achieved considerable economic, social, and psychological security in their new country and have little desire to return to Central America. Others dream of retiring to their beachside homes, and many have done this, especially in Honduras. In Nicaragua they have become largely incorporated into the larger black coastal population known as *criollos*, their characteristic cultural patterns attenuated or forgotten. In Belize, Guatemala, and Honduras they are ubiquitous, many having achieved professional status as schoolteachers, doctors, nurses, and engineers.

In the diaspora, their transnational identities are increasingly labeled in national, regional, or racial classificatory terms, reflecting the fact that both their traditional culture and their sense of peoplehood are in jeopardy. In the United States some Garifuna have formed organizations aimed at celebrating and preserving both; these give them a vehicle for continuing social interaction, but the culture has not necessarily been preserved in that process. In New York and Los Angeles the local Belizean Garifuna communities celebrate Settlement Day, a national holiday in Belize commemorating the arrival of the first Garifuna there. Honduran Garifuna celebrate a similar holiday. Both occasions are modern creations designed to enhance ethnic pride and prestige. Most of the dances and songs, like the "punta rock" popular in 1990s California, bear little resemblance to those practiced by their ancestors. Perhaps because of the salience of other African culture elements in the United States, the Garifuna heritage from that continent has taken precedence.

Over the centuries some "true" Caribs, i.e. Carib-speaking American Indians of the Amazon and Orinoco basins, also survived the European conquest, as well as the colonial and independence periods. Their defense, like that of neighboring Arawak-speaking groups, was to retreat more deeply into the interior tropical forest, where they remained largely unknown to Western civilization until the twentieth century.

In some South American countries there is today a revival of pride in the Carib heritage, where the emphasis is on those psychological characteristics celebrating ferocity, tenacity, and love of independence. As everywhere in the Americas, the remnants of isolated Amerindian groups have suffered cultural and physical losses which may never be rectified, despite the emergence of ethnic identity as an accepted way of defining minorities within national borders.

ELLEN B. BASSO, ed., *Carib-Speaking Indians: Culture, Society, and Language* (1977); DOUGLAS M. TAYLOR and BEREND J. HOFF, "The Linguistic Repertory of the Island Carib in the Seventeenth Century: The Men's Language—a Carib Pidgin?" in *International Journal of American Linguistics* 46, no. 4 (1980): 301–312; IRVING B. ROUSE, *Migrations in Prehistory* (1987); NANCIE L. GONZÁLEZ, *Sojourners of the Caribbean: Ethnogenesis and Ethnohistory of the Garifuna* (1988); NEIL LANCELOT WHITEHEAD, *Lords of the Tiger Spirit: A History of the Caribs in Colonial Venezuela and Guyana 1498–1820* (1988).

NANCIE L. GONZÁLEZ

**CARIMBÓ,** a type of *atabaque* (conical single-headed drum) and the African-derived dance performed with it in the north of Brazil. The instrument is made of a hollowed trunk with an animal-skin drumhead. The drummer sits on the trunk and strikes the skin with his hands. Historically, the *carimbó* was used in the *batuque*, a dance brought from Africa by enslaved Africans. In the *carimbó*, men and women dance in a circle. Often dressed as a *Bahiana*, a woman then leaves the circle, dances into the center and, in a teasing manner, throws her flared skirt over the head of a male dancer. *Carimbó* can be found among the peasants and fishermen of the state of Pará.

DAVID P. APPLEBY, *The Music of Brazil* (1983); LUIS DA CAMARA CASCUDO, *Dicionário do folclore brasileiro*, 5th ed. (1984).

BERNADETTE DICKERSON

*See also* **Musical Instruments.**

**CARIOCA,** anyone or anything from or pertaining to the city of Rio de Janeiro; thus, residents of Rio de Janeiro are called Cariocas, just as people from São Paulo are known as Paulistas. The name comes from the Carioca River, which originates in the valley between the Tijuca and Paineiras mountains, flows through the neighborhoods of Laranjeiras and Catete, and empties into Guanabara Bay at Flamengo and Glória beaches. Today almost entirely subterranean and extremely polluted, due to the emptying of raw sewage into it, the Carioca River was once famed for the purity and pleasant temperature of its water, which was believed to have medicinal qualities. The Tamoio, a Tupí community that lived on the margins of Guanabara Bay in the sixteenth century, believed the Carioca's waters sacred and inspirational for musicians and poets. Until the late nineteenth century, the river was the city's major source of potable water. A monumental aqueduct built in the early eighteenth century brought water from the Carioca to public fountains in the center of the city. Part of this Roman-style aqueduct, built in stone and mortar, which is today called the Arcos de Lapa, is one of Rio de Janeiro's most striking man-made landmarks.

SUEANN CAULFIELD

**CARLÉS, MANUEL** (*b*. 30 May 1872; *d*. 25 October 1946), Argentine politician, teacher, and president of the anti-leftist Argentine Patriotic League (1919–1946).

Carlés was born in Rosario, Santa Fe, to a prominent family. Although he never joined the Radical Civic Union (Unión Cívica Radical), he favored efforts to reform politics and participated in the Radical revolt of 1893. He served as national deputy from 1898 to 1912 and supported President Roque SÁENZ PEÑA (1910–1914), who helped institute electoral democracy. After 1912 he devoted himself to the law and to his teaching at several schools, including the COLEGIO MILITAR de la Nación and Escuela Superior de Guerra, where he influenced many future military officers. He initially sympathized with the government of the Radical leader Hipólito YRIGOYEN (1916–1922, 1928–1930), who appointed him *interventor* (temporary administrator) in Salta in 1918. The next president, the Radical Marcelo T. de ALVEAR (1922–1928), appointed him *interventor* in San Juan in 1922.

Nevertheless, Carlés, like other middle- and upper-class Argentines, thought that the Yrigoyen government was not doing enough to repress leftism. During the SEMANA TRÁGICA (Tragic Week) disturbances between labor and the forces of order in Buenos Aires in 1919, military officers and civilians, including Carlés, formed militias to protect bourgeois neighborhoods and attack worker areas. Militias spread throughout the country. On 20 January 1919 these groups united to form the Argentine Patriotic League and on 5 April, Carlés was elected its president, a post he retained until his death. In the early postwar years, the League violently suppressed strikes and leftist groups. In 1923 an anarchist unsuccessfully attempted to kill Carlés. Fearing a leftist resurgence and disorder, Carlés influenced the League and the public to turn against Yrigoyen in 1930 and thus helped inspire the coup of that year. General José F. URIBURU's (1930–1932) antidemocratic excesses, however, led Carlés to denounce this administration and return to his Radical roots. While he continued to criticize leftism, during the 1930s Carlés opposed electoral fraud and supported Marcelo Alvear's efforts to unite and strengthen Radical forces.

PEDRO P. MAGLIONE JAIMES, "Una figura señera—Manuel Carlés," *La Nación*, 12 January 1969; DAVID ROCK, *Politics in Argentina, 1890–1930: The Rise and Fall of Radicalism* (1975); SANDRA MC GEE DEUTSCH, *Counterrevolution in Argentina, 1900–1932: The Argentine Patriotic League* (1986).

SANDRA MCGEE DEUTSCH

*See also* **Argentina: Organizations.**

**CARLOS, ROBERTO** (*b*. 1943), Brazilian pop singer and songwriter. Carlos has been one of Latin America's most popular recording artists throughout his career. He started out singing rock and roll, cowriting songs with Erasmo Carlos (no relation), and gained fame singing the 1963 hits "Calembeque" and "Splish Splash" (a cover of the American hit). In 1965, he and Erasmo led the *jovem guarda* movement, a post–BOSSA-NOVA manifestation of domestic rock by several young Brazilian musicians. Roberto and Erasmo hosted the "Jovem Guarda" show on the TV Record network from 1965 to 1968, and cowrote hit songs like "Parei na contramão" (I Parked the Wrong Way), "É proibido fumar" (No Smoking), and "Garota do baile" (Dance Girl).

In the 1970s, Roberto transformed himself into a romantic interpreter of ballads and boleros, although he and Erasmo continued their songwriting partnership. During that decade, Roberto was the top-selling recording artist in Brazil, selling an annual average of one million records (quadruple-platinum) with each new album. With recordings frequently hitting the top ten in numerous Latin American and European countries, he also became an international star. In the 1980s, Carlos recorded hits in Portuguese, Spanish, French, and English, but was supplanted as Brazil's number-one recording artist in the late 1980s by the children's music singer XUXA.

*Rock, a música do século XX*, edited by Pedro Paulo Popovic Consultores Editorias Ltda. (1983); RITA CAÚRIO, ed., *Brasil Musical* (1988); CHRIS MC GOWAN and RICARDO PESSANHA, *The Brazilian Sound: Samba, Bossa Nova, and the Popular Music of Brazil* (1991).

CHRIS MCGOWAN

**CARLOTA** (Carlota Joaquina de Borbón y Parma; *b*. 25 April 1775; *d*. 7 January 1830), Spanish princess, queen consort of Portugal, and royalist leader in South America. Daughter of King Carlos IV and Queen María Luisa of Spain, Princess Carlota Joaquina consummated her arranged marriage to Prince João, heir to the Portuguese throne, in 1790. The royal pair thoroughly disliked each other and were constantly at odds over political and personal matters; nevertheless, they produced nine children, including Pedro, who became emperor of Brazil, and Miguel, who usurped the Portuguese throne—although the paternity of the latter as well as that of two of his sisters is in doubt. Carlota reluctantly joined the emigration of the Portuguese court to Brazil in 1807, when Portugal was invaded by France in alliance with Spain.

In Rio de Janeiro, after the French had deposed her brother, King Fernando VII of Spain, Carlota in 1808 set out to establish herself as the regent of Spain's empire in the Americas in the name of her imprisoned brother. Carlota enlisted the aid of her good friend, British admiral Sir Sidney Smith, and initially had her husband's acquiescence in the regency project. But Prince João, regent of Portugal for the insane Queen MARIA I, perceived a united Spanish America ruled by his wife as a threat to his own domains. His concern was shared by the British government, which, in 1809, recalled Admiral Smith and forestalled his scheme to sail with Carlota to Buenos Aires and install her there as Spanish regent.

A new opportunity for Carlota arose with the revolution in Buenos Aires in May 1810. From Rio she established contact with members of the Buenos Aires junta, offering herself as their leader. João was disconcerted by his wife's willingness to deal with revolutionaries to further her ambitions. In the end, however, Carlota's royal absolutism found few partisans in Spanish America and Fernando's return to the throne in Spain in 1814 obviated any need for a regency in his name.

In 1821 Carlota returned with her husband, now King JOÃO VI, to Portugal, where she continued to conspire against him. In 1824 she and her favorite son, Miguel, seized the government in Lisbon and forced João to seek refuge on a British warship. The British demanded and got João's restoration. After João's death in 1826, Carlota vigorously supported Miguel as king of Portugal, denying the claim of MARIA II, Pedro's daughter. With Miguel seemingly secure on the Portuguese throne, Carlota died in 1830.

JULIÁN MARÍA RUBIO, *La infanta Carlota Joaquina y la política de España en América, 1808–1812* (1920); MARCUS CHEKE, *Carlota Joaquina, Queen of Portugal* (1947).

NEILL MACAULAY

**CARMELITES (DISCALCED),** a religious order of the Roman CATHOLIC CHURCH with separate branches for men and women. The order was founded in the Holy Land during the Crusades of the twelfth century when Albert, patriarch of Jerusalem, wrote a rule for the purpose of organizing the hermits living on the slopes of Mount Carmel into one community. Carmelites look to the Old Testament prophet Elijah as their spiritual father, for he is said to have inspired their life-style of silence, solitary prayer, and contemplation. With an invasion of the Holy Lands in 1238, the Carmelites dispersed, bringing the rule with them to Europe. From that time until the sixteenth century there was a general relaxation of the strict rule, but Saint Teresa of Ávila then succeeded in reversing the trend. This sixteenth-century Spanish mystic traveled throughout her country founding communities of Carmelites, for men and for women, based on a return to the strict rule. Those who chose to adopt this life of silence, contemplation, and abstinence from eating meat became known as Discalced (Barefoot) Carmelites. It is this branch of the order that first went to the Americas.

Carmelites had traveled to the New World as early as 1527, but not with the intention of founding monasteries. It was not until Quivira (a mythical town) and New Mexico became slated for colonization that there was an opportunity for the Carmelites to join in the missionary activities of the Spanish church. In 1585 the order petitioned the king's council for permission to establish a monastery for men in New Spain. The request was granted, and in September of that year eleven Carmelites arrived. This settlement led eventually to the founding of the province of San Alberto of New Spain by 1590. In the sixteenth century, there were Carmelite communities in Mexico City, Puebla, Atlixco, Morelia, Guadalajara, and Celaya, which were followed by other foundations throughout the colonial period.

A characteristic discipline of the order is the building of a "desert," a monastery of individual cells designed to accommodate a reclusive life. One such desert, El Desierto de los Leones, was founded in 1606 near Mexico City. At its peak in the middle of the eighteenth century, the order counted over 500 members. The Reform Laws of the nineteenth century all but extinguished the order, though in 1884 a novitiate opened and Carmelites began to be trained once again. The province of San Alberto, however, was not restored until 1960.

In the seventeenth century monasteries were erected elsewhere in Latin America, including Colombia (Bogotá, 1606), Argentina (Córdoba, 1628), Peru (Lima, 1643), Ecuador (Quito, 1653), Bolivia (Sucre, 1665), and Chile (Santiago, 1690). In Brazil there were six monasteries by the end of the sixteenth century, and three separate provinces by 1720. At present there are nearly one hundred Carmelite houses in fifteen countries of Latin America, with new foundations as recent as 1980.

The first community of Discalced Carmelite nuns in the Americas was established in Puebla in 1604, with four Spanish women under the direction of the Carmelite frairs. In the colonial period and nineteenth century, eleven convents were founded in Mexico. Spanish women also founded communities in Argentina, Bolivia, Chile, Colombia, Ecuador, Peru, and Cuba; convents were established by Portuguese women in Brazil. These are cloistered, contemplative communities. Currently there are Carmelite convents in eight Latin American countries.

LEÓN LOPETEGUI and FELIX ZUBILLAGA, *Historia de la Iglesia en la América Española*, vol. 1 (1965); AGUSTÍN DE LA MADRE DE DIOS, *Tesoro escondido en el Santo Carmelo Mexicano* (1984); ALFONSO MARTÍNEZ ROSALES, *El gran teatro de un pequeño mundo: El Carmen de San Luis Potosí, 1732–1859* (1985).

BRIAN C. BELANGER

*See also* **Anticlericalism.**

**CARNEIRO DE CAMPOS, JOSÉ JOAQUÍM** (Caravelas, Marquês de; *b.* 4 March 1768; *d.* 8 September 1836), Brazilian statesman. Campos first pursued a religious career as a Benedictine monk, but then abandoned the ecclesiastic life to study law in Coimbra, Portugal. After receiving a doctor of jurisprudence degree, Campos began his political career in the kingdom of Portugal. He followed the royal family into exile in Brazil in 1807, shortly before the Napoleonic invasion. As aide to Prince Regent Dom João (later JOÃO VI), Campos rose quickly within the court. After independence in September 1822, Campos was elected to the constituent assembly, where he was one of the principal authors of the constitution of the monarchy. By 1823 Campos was already a cabinet member. In 1826 he was elected to the Senate from Bahia and ennobled by Emperor PEDRO I. Subsequently, he served twice more in the cabinet during the First Empire (1822–1831).

José Campos and his brother Francisco, also a senator and cabinet officer, were as politically prominent as the ANDRADA BROTHERS of São Paulo and the Cavalcanti brothers from Pernambuco. In April 1831, when PEDRO I abdicated and retreated to Portugal, Campos was one of the three provisional regents elected to govern Brazil in the name of the child emperor, PEDRO II. In June 1831 Campos was elected one of the three permanent regents who ruled in Pedro's name until 1835.

SACRAMENTO AUGUSTO VICTORINO ALVES BLAKE, *Diccionario bibliographico brasileiro*, 7 vols. (1897); EUL-SOO PANG, *In Pursuit of Honor and Power: Noblemen of the Southern Cross in Nineteenth-Century Brazil* (1988).

EUL-SOO PANG

*See also* **Brazil: First Empire; Brazil: Regency.**

**CARNEY, JAMES "GUADALUPE"** (*b.* 28 October 1924; *d.* probably 16 September 1983), U.S. Catholic missionary in Honduras, revolutionary priest. Carney, a native of Chicago, entered the JESUIT seminary in 1948 and was ordained a priest in 1961. He was sent to Honduras, where he served as chaplain for the National Association of Honduran Peasants (ANACH), championed land reform, and helped establish CHRISTIAN BASE COMMUNITIES in the department of Yoro. Expelled from the country in 1979, he was assigned to rural Nicaragua, where he was impressed by Sandinista social programs. After writing his autobiography and declaring himself a Christian Marxist, he resigned from the Jesuits and then crossed into Honduras in July 1983 with ninety-six Honduran guerrillas. Although U.S. and Honduran authorities claim he died in the jungle from starvation, subsequent investigations have led some scholars to conclude that he had been captured, tortured, and executed by the Honduran military. His body was never found.

J. GUADALUPE CARNEY, *To Be a Revolutionary* (1985); DONNA WHITSON BRETT and EDWARD T. BRETT, *Murdered in Central America: The Stories of Eleven U.S. Missionaries* (1988), pp. 38–66.

EDWARD T. BRETT

**CARNIVAL,** Brazil's major popular festival. Occurring in full summer, almost always in the month of February, Carnival is considered one of the major components of Brazil's national identity. The three days of Carnival are also known as the Reign of Momo. The festival is evocative of two ancient traditions: the beginning of Christian Lent on Ash Wednesday and the combined influences of pagan Egyptian, Greek, and Roman feasts. From a historical perspective, Brazil has made this festival its own as a result of a long process of transformation with exotic cultural influences. In this sense Carnival, like the SAMBA, is almost always considered derived from Afro-Brazilian slaves. But indigenous influences were also significant; similar celebrations exist in Peru, Bolivia, Argentina, and elsewhere.

The urban atmosphere of Brazil's former capital, Rio de Janeiro, was the source of two celebrations prototypical of Carnival. One took place in the streets, the other in the salons. The year 1853 can be considered the date of redefinition of the Brazilian Carnival. The old celebrations, of Portuguese origin and known as the *entrudo*, were banned in that year because a French architect, Grandjean de Montigny, visiting Rio de Janeiro to work on some city development projects, died of pneumonia "after having received one of those water baths." After the incident, the police and the state felt obligated to intervene and discipline perpetrators of public meetings that might "disturb the public peace."

With the abolition of slavery, a large group of former slaves amassed in the hills around Rio. These Afro-Brazilians brought about a return to some of their cultural observances and went through an internal reorganization, part of which could be seen in the recurrence of the celebrations banned since 1853. In addition, the bourgeois celebration of the festival attracted members of Rio's elite to carnivalesque encounters first in the hotels and later in the clubs.

For a long time the two forms of Carnival—in the streets and in the salons—remained separate. They grew closer in the twentieth century, however, and reached a climax during the first Vargas administration (1930–1945). In the 1930s, Carnival became a street festival, with a tendency to attract the well-to-do. The example of the capital spread throughout Brazil. The festival became structured around the SAMBA SCHOOLS and from the beginning received a lot of attention from the press.

When Brazil's period of modernization got under way in the 1960s, and especially during the military dictatorship begun in 1964, Carnival began to be used as a tool for political propaganda. Foreign capital was being courted, and the parades in Rio seen on television provided an image of a happy, organized, and orderly Brazilian people. The dominance of the Rio style of Carnival awakened reactions in some regions of the country that formed their own styles and began to compete with Rio's. Salvador in Bahia, Olinda and Recife in Pernambuco, Ouro Prêto in Minas Gerais, and Florianópolis in

Carnival in Rio de Janeiro, 1940s. JUCA MARTINS / PULSAR IMAGENS E EDITORA.

Santa Catarina are some of the many Carnivals that take place in Brazil.

JOSÉ CARLOS SEBE BOM MEIHY, *Carnaval, carnavais* (1986); ROBERTO DA MATTA, *Carnivals, Rogues, and Heroes,* translated by John Drury (1991).

JOSÉ CARLOS SEBE BOM MEIHY

**CARO, JOSÉ EUSEBIO** (*b.* 5 March 1817; *d.* 28 January 1853), Colombian Conservative publicist and romantic poet. Caro was born in Ocaña, Norte de Santander. His mother's amorous relationships with Simón BOLÍVAR, Francisco de Paula SANTANDER, and José Ignacio de MÁRQUEZ shadowed his impoverished youth. He received his doctorate in law in 1837 and became a government clerk (1838). A political libertarian, Caro wrote articles for the press and started composing verse. Among his best-loved poems are "El bautismo" and "Estar contigo." The violence of the WAR OF THE SUPREMES (1839–1842), in which he served sporadically but with distinction, caused Caro to move to more conservative political ground. He rose in the bureaucracy to chief of a section in the Secretariat of Interior and Foreign Relations (1843), and expounded his increasingly authoritarian ideas in *El Granadino*, which appeared sporadically between 1840 and 1845. A partisan, he deplored the bipartisanship (after 1846) of Tomás Cipri-

ano de MOSQUERA's administration, though he did serve briefly as finance minister (1848). Caro's vehement opposition to the Liberal José Hilario LÓPEZ (1849–1853) caused his removal from government service (September 1849). With Mariano OSPINA RODRÍGUEZ, he fashioned the first Conservative Party platform (1849) and was an editor of the newspaper *La Civilización* (1849–1850), whose editorials were a devastating indictment of López's presidency that resulted in Caro's exile (1850–1853) to New York. Upon returning to Colombia, Caro died of yellow fever in Santa Marta.

FERNANDO GALVIS SALAZAR, *José Eusebio Caro* (1956); JOSÉ LUIS MARTÍN, *La poesía de José Eusebio Caro . . . Contribución estilística al estudio del romanticismo hispanoamericano* (1966); ROBERT HENRY DAVIS, "Acosta, Caro, and Lleras: Three Essayists and Their Views of New Granada's National Problems, 1832–1853" (Ph.D. diss., Vanderbilt University, 1969), pp. 243–299; LUCIO PABÓN NÚÑEZ, ed., *Poesías completas. José Eusebio Caro* (1973); SIMÓN ALJURE CHALELA, comp., *Artículos y escritos histórico-políticos de José Eusebio Caro* (1981).

J. LEÓN HELGUERA

**CARO, MIGUEL ANTONIO** (*b.* 10 November 1843; *d.* 5 August 1909), Colombian president (1894–1898). Miguel Antonio Caro lived his entire life in the area of Bogotá, where he was born, and was a staunch defender of traditional Catholic and Hispanic values. A professor of Latin at the Universidad Nacional and expert in Spanish grammar and linguistics, Caro achieved distinction as a scholar (collaborating with Rufino José CUERVO) but is chiefly remembered as one of the architects of the REGENERATION that put an end to Liberal hegemony in Colombia. He was the principal author of the centralist, proclerical Constitution of 1886. As a "Nationalist" Conservative he became vice president under Rafael NÚÑEZ in 1892 but in reality was acting president, completing the term (1894–1898) after Núñez's death. His doctrinaire rigidity alienated both Liberals and the "Historical" faction of Conservatives, thus contributing to the outbreak of the WAR OF THE THOUSAND DAYS that began shortly after he left the presidency.

GUILLERMO TORRES GARCÍA, *Miguel Antonio Caro, su personalidad política* (1956); JAIME JARAMILLO URIBE, *El pensamiento colombiano en el siglo XIX* (1964), chap. 19; CHARLES W. BERGQUIST, *Coffee and Conflict in Colombia, 1886–1910* (1978), pp. 42–47 and passim.

DAVID BUSHNELL

**CARONDELET, FRANÇOIS-LOUIS HECTOR,** Baron de (*b.* 27 July 1747; *d.* 10 December 1807), governor of San Salvador and Louisiana; president of the Audiencia of Quito. A prototype of the bureaucratic *ilustrados* who staffed the late eighteenth-century Spanish colonies, Carondelet trod an ambiguous path between progress and reaction. Born at Cambray or Flanders, in what is the present-day French department of Nord, he entered the military service of Charles III of Spain at fifteen and saw brief action at the conclusion of the Seven Years' War. After serving at Algiers in 1775 and writing a book on infantry training and strategy, he was assigned to the Caribbean, where he fought with Bernardo de GÁLVEZ against the British at PENSACOLA (1781).

In 1789 Carondelet became governor–intendant of SAN SALVADOR, an indigo-producing region on the Pacific coast of the Audiencia of Guatemala. He strove to rationalize dye production and marketing, and to establish settlements for those displaced by expanding commercial agriculture. Two years later, he was promoted to the governorship of Louisiana and West Florida.

The succeeding five years severely tested Carondelet's determination to keep the lower Mississippi watershed under permanent Spanish sovereignty. With paltry resources, he bluffed and badgered the local French Jacobins, the region's mercurial Indian groups, land-hungry American frontiersmen, free colored, a slave population equaling that of the free, including Europeans, and intriguers of many stripes. He deftly outmaneuvered a range of antimonarchical forces and challenged American use of the Mississippi and the right of deposit at New Orleans.

Carondelet was reassigned to the presidency of the remote Audiencia of Quito (where he was also governor-general) late in 1798. There he found a declining textile trade, widespread native unrest, and bickering among the clerical orders. Although at a loss to cope with internal issues of an unfamiliar society, Carondelet managed to complete a road to the north coast and to facilitate the expedition of Alexander von HUMBOLDT. He died in Quito.

ARTHUR PRESTON WHITAKER, *The Spanish-American Frontier, 1763–1795* (1927); THOMAS M. FIEHRER, "The Baron de Carondelet as Agent of Bourbon Reform" (Ph.D. diss., Tulane University, 1977); CARLOS MANUEL LARREA, *El barón de Carondelet* (1978); ERIC BEERMAN, "Baron de Carondelet," in *The Louisiana Genealogical Register* 29, no. 1 (March 1982): 5–19.

THOMAS FIEHRER

**CARPENTIER, ALEJO** (*b.* 26 December 1904; *d.* 24 April 1980), Cuban novelist and short-story writer. Carpentier was born in Havana and studied music with his mother, through whom he developed a love of music that became central to his life and work. In 1921 he studied architecture at the University of Havana and that same year began writing for local newspapers and magazines. Together with the noted Cuban composer Amadeo ROLDÁN he organized concerts of "new music," bringing to Cuba the works of Stravinsky, Poulenc, Satie, and Malipiero. He also wrote the librettos for two ballets with music by Roldán.

In 1928, with the help of Cuban poet and then-diplomatic official Mariano Brull, Carpentier moved to Paris, where he met André Breton, Paul Éluard, Ives Tanguy, Arthur Honegger, and Pablo Picasso, among others. With the 1933 publication of his first novel, *¡Ecue-Yamba-O!*, in Madrid, he traveled to Spain, where he met the celebrated Spanish poets Federico García Lorca, Rafael Alberti, Pedro Salinas, and José Bergamín. In 1937, along with fellow Cuban writers Juan MARINELLO, Nicolás GUILLÉN, and Félix PITA RODRÍGUEZ, he represented Cuba at the Second Congress for the Defense of Culture, held in Madrid and Valencia.

In 1939 Carpentier returned to Cuba to work for the Ministry of Education and to teach the history of music at the National Conservatory, where he later conducted research that led to the rediscovery of neglected Cuban composers Esteban Salas and Manuel Saumell. In 1945 he moved to Venezuela to work in radio and advertising. While there, he traveled extensively in 1947–1948 through the Amazon region, an area vividly evoked in his novel *Los pasos perdidos* (1953; *The Lost Steps*, 1956). After the Cuban Revolution in 1959 Carpentier returned to Cuba, where he was appointed vice-president of the National Council on Culture. He was also a vice-president of the powerful Cuban Union of Writers and Artists (UNEAC) and from 1963 to 1968 the director of the Cuban National Publishing House. He traveled widely as a representative of the Cuban government on both cultural and political missions. In 1968 he was named Ministerial Counsel for Cultural Affairs at the Cuban embassy in Paris, a post he occupied until his death in 1980.

Carpentier's novels and short stories have been greatly acclaimed both in Cuba and abroad. He received many national honors as well as the international prizes Cino del Duca and Alfonso Reyes (1975). His work frequently evokes a particular historical period and is characterized by an ornate, meticulous, and rhythmical prose in which his love of music and architecture is evident. Among his other well-known works are *El reino de este mundo* (1949; *The Kingdom of This World*, 1957); *El siglo de las luces* (1962; *Explosion in a Cathedral*, 1963); and *El recurso del método* (1974; *Reasons of State*, 1976).

ROBERTO GONZÁLEZ ECHEVARRÍA, *Alejo Carpentier: The Pilgrim at Home* (1977) and *Alejo Carpentier: Bibliographical Guide* (1983); ARACELI GARCÍA-CARRANZA, *Bibliografía de Alejo Carpentier* (1984); KLAUS MÜLLER-BERGH, "Alejo Carpentier," in *Latin American Writers*, edited by Carlos A. Solé and Maria Isabel Abreu (1989), pp. 1019–1031; SIMON GIKANDI, *Writing in Limbo: Modernism and Caribbean Literature* (1992); BARBARA J. WEBB, *Myth and History in Caribbean Fiction* (1992).

ROBERTO VALERO

**CARPINTERÍA, BATTLE OF,** a conflict between the troops of Uruguayan President Manuel ORIBE and revolutionaries under General Fructuoso RIVERA that took place on 19 September 1836 in the department of Durazno. It was the first time the colors white (*blanco*, for Oribe) and red (*colorado*, for Rivera) were used to distinguish the combatants. These two colors later became identified with the major political parties in Uruguay, the Blanco (National) Party and the Colorado Party. Once the uprising had begun, President Oribe ordered the use of a white ribbon bearing the inscription "defenders of the laws." In order to differentiate themselves, Rivera's troops began using a blue ribbon, but later changed to red. In Uruguay, "whites" and "reds" generally refer to "conservatives" and "liberals," respectively, the former associated with Spanish tradition and the latter more open to the liberal influences of England, France, and North America.

ALFREDO CASTELLANOS, *La Cisplatina: La independencia y la república caudillesca, 1820–1838* (1974); WASHINGTON REYES ABADIE and ANDRÉS VÁZQUES ROMERO, *Crónica general del Uruguay*, vol. 2 (1984).

JOSÉ DE TORRES WILSON

*See also* **Uruguay: Political Parties.**

**CARPIO NICOLLE, JORGE** (*b.* 1932), Guatemalan journalist and politician. Born in Guatemala City, he received his degree in political science from the University of San Carlos in 1980. In 1963, he began publishing the newspaper *El Gráfico*, which has the second largest circulation in the country, and in 1984 he founded the political party Union of the National Center (Unión del Centro Nacional—UCN), which he serves as secretary general. He belongs to the Liberal International and has been the Secretary General of its Central American branch. He has twice been a candidate for the presidency of Guatemala, finishing second in 1985 and 1990. He has long been an avid supporter of cycling and is the author of *La ideología centrista* (1989).

FERNANDO GONZÁLEZ DAVISON

**CARRANZA, VENUSTIANO** (*b.* 29 December 1859; *d.* 21 May 1920), first chief of the Constitutionalist forces during the MEXICAN REVOLUTION (1913–1917), president of Mexico (1917–1920), Carranza was born at Cuatro Ciénegas in the northeastern frontier state of Coahuila, son of a well-to-do landed proprietor who had supported Benito Juárez. After a conventional liberal education in Saltillo and Mexico City, Carranza returned to Coahuila, where, during the PORFIRIATO (1876–1911), he farmed and engaged in politics. After election as mayor of his hometown in 1887, Carranza was ousted by the autocratic state governor, José María Garza Galán, against whom he successfully rebelled (1893). Porfirio DÍAZ acquiesced in the installation of a state government congenial to the Carranza family and sympathetic to the great caudillo of the northeast, Bernardo REYES of Nuevo León. Carranza, a loyal Reyista, served as mayor, state deputy, and federal senator, combining cautious political advancement with the acquisition of land and other property.

During the 1900s, political opposition to Díaz mounted and Reyes became a major contender for power. As the Reyista movement boomed (1908–1909), Carranza ran for the governorship of Coahuila. However, Díaz, resentful of overly powerful subjects, froze Reyes out of national politics and ensured Carranza's defeat. In retaliation, Carranza then forged an alliance of expedience with fellow Coahuilan Francisco MADERO, who dared challenge Díaz for the presidency. Although he was linked to the Madero family by old political ties and shared Madero's liberal philosophy, Carranza lacked Madero's naïve optimism; he was, rather, a crafty and hardened practitioner of realpolitik. Thus, while Carranza supported the successful Madero revolution (1910–1911), he did so with typical caution, exercising his role as revolutionary commander of the northeast from the sanctuary of Texas. He also criticized Madero for being too generous to the defeated Porfiristas when he signed the Treaty of Ciudad Juárez (May 1911).

During Madero's presidency (November 1911–February 1913) Carranza served as governor of Coahuila, adhering to a moderate liberal program that stressed municipal democracy, educational and fiscal reform, and temperance. He also built an independent state military, which defended Coahuila against rebel incursions, afforded the state government a certain political autonomy, and gave rise to serious wrangles between himself and Madero. Indeed, there were rumors that Carranza and some like-minded northern governors—"hawks" who rejected Madero's dovish conciliation of conservative opponents—flirted with outright rebellion.

In February 1913, when military rebels ousted and killed Madero, installing General Victoriano HUERTA in power, Carranza refused to recognize the coup. While his admirers depict this as an act of immediate outrage, the truth was more complex. For two weeks after the coup the telegraph wires between Coahuila and the capital hummed. Carranza negotiated with Huerta, whose characteristic bullheadedness prevented a deal from being made. Instead, Carranza marshaled his forces and declared himself in revolt. His military fortunes soon faltered. A rebel attack on Saltillo was a costly failure; during the summer of 1913 he was forced to flee to the northwestern state of Sonora, where a similar rebellion had begun with greater success.

However, Carranza's stand was politically decisive. As the senior Maderista rebel, he became the figurehead—and to some extent the actual leader—of a broad anti-Huerta movement. On 26 March 1913, Carranza and his entourage drew up and promulgated the PLAN OF GUADALUPE, in which they repudiated Huerta and promised the return of constitutional rule. (Hence Carranza became "First Chief of the Constitutionalist Army.") However—at Carranza's insistence and to the disgust of some young radicals—the Plan made no reference to broader socioeconomic reforms.

During 1913–1914, as the revolt against Huerta spread, Carranza established an alternative government in the north. He decreed, taxed, issued currency, dealt with foreign powers, and tried to control the heterogeneous Constitutionalist forces. He succeeded, to the extent that Huerta was forced from power; and he succeeded, too, in securing U.S. backing without ceding an iota of Mexican sovereignty. (Indeed, his prickly nationalism made him, in American eyes, a difficult ingrate.) But his relations with Emiliano ZAPATA, in the distant south, were tenuous and mutually suspicious. Francisco "Pancho" VILLA, the charismatic caudillo of Chihuahua, who was victorious in the campaigns against Huerta in 1914, chafed under Carranza's persnickety authority. He resented Carranza's interference in Chihuahua and applauded the U.S. occupation of Veracruz—which tightened the noose around Huerta's neck—even as Carranza outspokenly condemned it. Differences were patched up until the fall of Huerta in July 1914.

Thereafter, the Constitutionalist revolution fragmented. The Zapatistas of Morelos had little time for Carranza, an elderly Porfirian politico whose commitment to agrarian reform was suspect. Villa, too, regarded Carranza with suspicion and personal dislike; when Villa and Zapata met in December 1914, they broke the ice by trading insults about Carranza. More important, the grand revolutionary convention that met at AGUASCALIENTES in October 1914 proved incapable of reconciling the major caudillos of the Revolution—Carranza spurned it, and Villa effectively hijacked it. Mexico's many lesser caudillos were forced to choose, and the forces that had been briefly united against Huerta now split apart and embarked on a bloody internecine conflict.

The civil war resolved itself into a struggle between Villa, loosely allied to Zapata, and Carranza, whose chief ally was the Sonoran general Álvaro OBREGÓN. For some historians, this last great bout of revolutionary warfare was a clear-cut conflict between a popular and peasant coalition led by Villa and Zapata and the "bourgeois" forces of Carranza. However, this interpretation overlooks the sameness of the two sides' social makeup (nationwide, the Carrancistas included many "peasants," just as the Villistas included landlords and bourgeoisie) and political programs (the rival programs differed little).

But the struggle was not irrelevant to Mexico's future. For while a victory of Villa and Zapata would probably have resulted in a weak, fragmented state, a collage of revolutionary fiefs of varied political hues presided over by a feeble central government, a victory by Carranza and his Sonoran allies would—and did—lay the foundations of a more ambitious, centralizing state dedicated to national integration and nationalist self-assertion. In this respect, Carranza, a product of Porfirian politics, helped lend a "neo-Porfirian" coloration to the revolutionary regime after 1915; he served, as Enrique Krauze observes, as the bridge between two centuries.

Carranza's triumph over Villa and Zapata, like his previous successes, owed more to political shrewdness than to military prowess. During 1914–1915 he overcame his ingrained political caution and promised agrarian and social reforms, legitimizing the efforts of his more radical supporters and undercutting the popular appeal of his enemies. He allowed Obregón to form an alliance with the workers of Mexico City and dispatched "proconsuls" to the states of southern Mexico, compelling those states to enter the revolutionary fold and—in Yucatán—skimming off valuable export revenues.

All this would have been in vain had not Obregón, triumphed on the battlefield, repeatedly defeating Villa in a series of battles between April and June 1915, forcing him to relinquish claims to national power. Carranza was therefore recognized as de facto president by the United States in October 1915, establishing his administration in Mexico City, and, following elections, inaugurated as constitutional president in May 1917.

Carranza's three years as president were difficult. Rebellion still simmered. Large areas of the country remained ungovernable. The economy was in disarray, the currency had collapsed, and 1917 became known, in popular memory, as the "year of hunger." Over two-thirds of government expenditures went to the military, on whose bayonets Carranza depended. Politics remained the preserve of the Carrancista faction (their enemies were proscribed) and elections, though boisterous, were rigged and unrepresentative. A constituent congress, summoned by Carranza, produced a new constitution (1917) embracing radical measures: labor and agrarian reform, anticlericalism, and economic nationalism. (Carranza probably wanted a more moderate document, but was content to go with the tide.) Implementation came slowly. Land reform remained minimal, while Carranza ordered the wholesale restitution of haciendas seized during the revolution. The brief alliance with the Mexico City workers ended and, in 1916, when he was de facto president, a general strike was ruthlessly crushed. When, in 1918, a new national labor confederation (the Confederación Regional Obrera Mexicana [CROM]; Mexican Regional Labor Confederation) was established, Obregón, rather than Carranza, was the chief political sponsor—and beneficiary.

As in the past, Carranza displayed more skill and consistency in the international arena. After Villa's defeat, the U.S. government grudgingly recognized the Carranza administration, without extracting any quid pro quo from the obstinate Mexican leader. When, in 1916–1917, U.S. troops entered Mexico in pursuit of Villa, Carranza demanded their unconditional withdrawal, ultimately successfully. He flirted with Germany, the better to keep the United States at bay; but he spurned the offer of an alliance, communicated in the notorious ZIMMERMAN TELEGRAM. He also made a determined, if unsuccessful, attempt to enforce the provisions of the new constitution that claimed subsoil deposits (including petroleum) as the patrimony of the state. The booming oil companies were obliged to yield vital additional revenue to the penurious state, but they refused to acknowledge their new constitutional status. The impasse remained a source of serious contention into the 1920s.

Carranza thus stoutly defended the integrity of Mexico and the principles of the revolution in the face of foreign pressure. But domestically, Carranza soft-pedaled reform and displayed a poor grasp of the populist politics the Revolution had ushered in. After 1918 his authority waned. As the presidential election of 1920 neared, and Obregón launched a powerful campaign, Carranza attempted to impose a chosen successor, a little-known diplomat named Ignacio Bonillas. The military balked; the CROM backed Obregón; and the Sonoran leaders initiated a coup that swiftly drove Carranza from Mexico City into the Puebla sierra. There, in May 1920, he was killed at Tlaxcalantongo or, as Krauze hypothesizes, he committed suicide rather than give his enemies the satisfaction of killing him. This was to be the last successful rebellion of Mexico's revolutionary history. Obregón and the Sonorans, the architects of Carranza's rise and fall, shared his hardheaded opportunism, but they displayed a better grasp of the mechanisms of popular mobilization, allied to social reform, that would form the bases of a durable revolutionary regime after 1920. For this reason, Carranza has often been regarded as a conservative revolutionary who was overtaken by events and outflanked by younger, more "populist" revolutionaries. He did, however, forge a winning revolutionary coalition, defeating both Huerta and Villa and sponsoring the 1917 Constitution. In ad-

dition, most critics concede, he was a strenuous and successful defender of Mexican sovereignty against the United States.

DOUGLAS W. RICHMOND, *Venustiano Carranza's Nationalist Struggle, 1893–1920* (1983), is the fullest recent biography; well researched, it is uncritically charitable toward its subject. ENRIQUE KRAUZE, *Puente entre siglos: Venustiano Carranza* (1987), is brief, intelligent, and replete with illustrations. Of several older Mexican studies, ALFONSO JUNCO, *Carranza y los orígenes de su rebelión* (1955), is a telling critique of Carranza's conduct toward Madero and Huerta. Detailed general histories of the revolution, which necessarily give much attention to Carranza and the Constitutionalists, are CHARLES C. CUMBERLAND, *The Mexican Revolution: The Constitutionalist Years* (1972); ALAN KNIGHT, *The Mexican Revolution* (1986), vol. 2, *Counterrevolution and Reconstruction;* and RAMÓN EDUARDO RUÍZ, *The Great Rebellion: Mexico 1905–1924* (1980), which sharply contrasts with Richmond's laudatory biography. Carranza's important international role has been analyzed in several good studies, including MARK T. GILDERHUS, *Diplomacy and Revolution: U.S.-Mexican Relations Under Wilson and Carranza* (1977); P. EDWARD HALEY, *Revolution and Intervention: The Diplomacy of Taft and Wilson with Mexico 1910–17* (1970); and an outstanding piece of research, FRIEDRICH KATZ, *The Secret War in Mexico: Europe, the United States and the Mexican Revolution* (1981). ROBERT FREEMAN SMITH, *The United States and Revolutionary Nationalism in Mexico, 1916–1932* (1972), offers a cogent analysis of economic nationalism during the Carranza years and after.

ALAN KNIGHT

**CARRANZA FERNÁNDEZ, EDUARDO** (b. 23 July 1913; d. 13 February 1985), Colombian poet, born in Apiay. Carranza started to achieve recognition in 1934 through the publication of his poetry and his collaboration on the journal *Revista de las Indias*. His first sonnets, written between 1937 and 1944 and collected in *Azul de ti* (1947), made him famous. Carranza was an important member of the Piedra y Cielo group, influenced by the poetry of Juan Ramón Jiménez and, to a lesser extent, Pablo NERUDA. The works of Jiménez, Rafael Alberti, and Gerardo Diego were the models for Carranza's poetry, which is metaphorical, musical, and reminiscent of traditional Spanish styles. In the early 1940s his aesthetic confronted the modernist poet Guillermo VALENCIA, who was then the model of Colombian poets. While Valencia cultivates the perfection of the meter and shows preference for exotic landscapes, Carranza prefers intimate and vernacular landscapes. Carranza's work is also marked by a purity of language and faithfulness to love, Catholicism, and country, and is untouched by Colombia's political violence of the 1950s and 1960s. In the 1940s and 1950s, his poetry circulated widely in Spain and Chile, countries in which he traveled and resided because of his work in the Colombian diplomatic service. Other collections of his poetry are *Los pasos cantados* (1975), *Los días que ahora son sueños* (1973), and *Veinte poemas* (1980).

GLORIA SERPA DE DE FRANCISCO, *Gran reportaje a Eduardo Carranza* (1978); TERESA ROZO DE MOORHOUSE, *La evolución del ha-*

*blante lírico en Eduardo Carranza* (1985); GIOVANNI QUESSEP, *Eduardo Carranza* (1990).

JUAN CARLOS GALEANO

**CARRASQUILLA, TOMÁS** (*b.* 1858; *d.* 1940), Colombian fiction writer. One of Colombia's greatest classic prose writers, Carrasquilla is best known for two novels, *Frutos de mi tierra* (1896) and *La Marquesa de Yolombó* (1926); between the publication of these two novels and afterward, he published several other novels, short novels, and numerous short stories with folkloric, psychological, fantastic, and symbolic perspectives. Carrasquilla believed that themes of rural, provincial life in Colombia were enough to make for good fiction; as such, his writings fall within the category of *costumbrista* (local color), which consists of providing vivid descriptions of popular customs and recreating the language of the popular classes. Nevertheless, Carrasquilla's fiction transcends the moralizing tone and didactic goal of *costumbrista*.

In one sense, his narrative success lies in his ability to draw upon such literary traditions of Spanish literature as the picaresque novel and stories portraying Spanish customs. While *Frutos de mi tierra* is a Cinderella story, it relies on local color, proverbs, legends, and the oral tradition to provide anecdotes that focus on hypocrisy in small, provincial towns. Carrasquilla does not just extol the good life in the provinces but also exposes moral issues centered on bigotry and cruelty. *La Marquesa de Yolombó* is Carrasquilla's most ambitious effort. The action takes place during the Spanish American colonial period of the late nineteenth century and criticizes the colonial government for inefficiency, corruption, and waste.

KURT LEVY, *Tomás Carrasquilla* (1980).

DICK GERDES

**CARREÑO, MARIO** (*b.* 24 June 1913), Cuban-born painter. Born in Havana, Carreño trained at the Academy of San Alejandro in Havana, the Academy of San Fernando in Madrid, and the École des Arts Appliques in Paris. During the 1920s he worked as a political cartoonist for *Revista de Havana* and *Diario de la Marina*, both in Cuba. In the 1930s Carreño lived in Spain, where he designed revolutionary posters (1932–1935). After meeting the Mexican muralists in 1936, he returned to Paris, where he met the surrealist Oscar Domínguez and Pablo Picasso (1937). His paintings from the late 1930s combined traditional European painting techniques with the influence of the school of Paris and classical Picasso.

At the outbreak of World War II Carreño fled first to Italy, then to New York City, returning to Cuba in 1941. Influenced by David Alfaro SIQUEIROS, he experimented with industrial paint, a medium he had tried in the late 1930s (*Cane Cutters*, 1943). In 1946 he was appointed professor of painting at the New York School for Social Research and in the late 1940s turned to a late cubist vocabulary with distinctively Afro-Cuban themes (*Caribbean Enchantment*, 1949). He moved to Chile and became a citizen in 1951. For a brief period he worked on an abstract geometric style. In the late 1950s Carreño began to paint surrealist petrified and fragmented human figures in volcanic landscapes.

In the 1960s he collaborated with Chilean architects in the design of three-dimensional murals. The most distinguished examples are a freestanding, double-faced wall designed with glazed bricks for the Central Plaza of the University of Concepción (1962); an exterior wall for the Saint Ignatius Loyola School in Santiago (1960); and a freestanding wall and pool monument designed for the United Nations Regional Building, also in Santiago (1963–1964).

JOSÉ GÓMEZ SICRE, *Carreño* (1947); MARTA TRABA et al., eds., *Museum of Modern Art of Latin America: Selections from the Permanent Collection* (1985), pp. 172–173; EVA COCKROFT, ''The United States and Socially Concerned Latin American Art: 1920–1970,'' in Luis Cancel et al., *The Latin American Spirit: Art and Artists in the United States, 1920–1970* (1989), pp. 195–199.

MARTA GARSD

**CARRERA, JOSÉ MIGUEL** (*b.* 15 October 1785; *d.* 4 September 1821), Chilean patriot and revolutionary. Carrera came from an old and distinguished family. A troublesome youth, he was sent in 1806 by his father to Spain, where he fought in at least thirteen actions in the Peninsular War. In July 1811 he returned to Chile and immediately immersed himself in the struggle for independence, using his sway over the military to seize power (15 November 1811). Handsome and personable, Carrera was a popular leader. During his dictatorship Chile's first newspaper, *La Aurora de Chile*, was published and the first national flag created. However, no declaration of independence was forthcoming.

With the arrival of a royalist expedition from Peru early in 1813, Carrera took command of the patriot forces in the south, leaving the government in the hands of a junta, over which his adversaries later assumed control. Given his limited military success, the junta transferred command to Bernardo O'HIGGINS (1778–1842), thereby opening up a serious rift between the two men. Soon afterward Carrera was captured by the royalists, but he escaped and returned to Santiago, where he staged a second coup d'état 23 July 1814. Civil war between the followers of O'Higgins and Carrera was averted only by the arrival of a new and powerful royalist expedition under the command of General Mariano Osorio (1777–1819). Carrera's failure to send relief to O'Higgins's valiant defense against Osorio at RANCAGUA (1–2 October 1814), resulted in a complete royalist triumph and the collapse of patriot Chile.

Carrera and two thousand others fled across the

Andes to Mendoza, where the governor of Cuyo, José de SAN MARTÍN, preferring the more reliable support of O'Higgins, ordered Carrera on to Buenos Aires. In November 1815 Carrera traveled to the United States, procured two warships, and then returned to Buenos Aires. Denied a part in the liberation of Chile now underway, he moved to Montevideo and launched a propaganda war against the new O'Higgins government.

Temperamentally incapable of remaining inactive for long, he next involved himself in the fighting then raging in the Argentine interior, lending support to various provincial caudillos. He was finally captured and executed at Mendoza, where his brothers Juan José (1782–1818) and Luis (1792–1818) had been shot three years earlier. These executions roused resentment against the O'Higgins regime in Chile. The remains of the three Carreras were repatriated in 1828. Following in his father's footsteps, Carrera's son, José Miguel Carrera Fontecilla (1820–1860), fought in the Chilean rebellions of 1851 and 1859.

JULIO ALEMPARTE ROBLES, *Carrera y Freire, fundadores de la República* (1963); SIMON COLLIER, *Ideas and Politics of Chilean Independence* (1967), chap. 3.

SIMON COLLIER

**CARRERA, JOSÉ RAFAEL** (*b.* 24 October 1814; *d.* 14 April 1865), chief of state of Guatemala (1844–1848, 1851–1865). Born to poor parents in Guatemala City, Carrera joined the Central American federal army as a drummer at age twelve, and rose rapidly in the ranks during the civil war of 1826–1829. The army, dominated by the Guatemalan conservative elite, not only provided military training but also indoctrinated him in conservative ideology. After Francisco MORAZÁN defeated this army in 1829, Carrera drifted for several years, eventually settling in Mataquescuintla, where he became a swineherd. Father Francisco Aqueche influenced him there and was instrumental in Carrera's marriage to Petrona García, the daughter of a local landowner.

Carrera emerged as a natural leader of the peasants and landowners of eastern Guatemala against the liberal reforms of the Guatemalan governor, Dr. Mariano GÁLVEZ. The rural population, spurred on by the clergy, opposed his anticlericalism, taxes, judicial reforms, and land, labor, and immigration policies that appeared to favor foreigners over natives. With these grievances already strong, the Gálvez government's efforts to check the cholera epidemic that broke out in 1837 led to uprisings, especially in eastern Guatemala. Although Carrera did not instigate the 1837 revolt, and in fact had accepted assignment as commander of a government quarantine patrol, local residents soon persuaded him to join the revolt. At Santa Rosa, on 9 June 1837, he led a ragged band of insurgents to a stunning victory, sending government troops fleeing back to the capital.

José Rafael Carrera. BENSON LATIN AMERICAN COLLECTION, UNIVERSITY OF TEXAS AT AUSTIN.

Aided by serious divisions between Gálvez and José Francisco BARRUNDIA, Carrera's peasant army took Guatemala City on 1 February 1838, bringing down the Gálvez government. This resulted temporarily in a more liberal government under Lieutenant Governor Pedro Valenzuela, who succeeded in persuading Carrera to leave the capital in return for promised reform and military command of the district of Mita. Resurgent strength of the conservative elite of the capital, however, and failure of the Valenzuela government to move fast enough with the reforms caused Carrera to resume the war in March 1838. President Morazán brought federal troops from El Salvador into the struggle, but on 13 April 1839 Carrera once more took the capital, this time installing a conservative government under Mariano Rivera Paz. In March 1840 Carrera decisively defeated Morazán at Guatemala City, effectively ending the Central American national government. From this point until his death, except briefly in 1848–1849, Carrera was the military master of Guatemala. He consolidated the power of his army during the early 1840s, especially by the CONVENIO OF GUADALUPE on 11 March 1844.

In December 1844 Carrera assumed the presidency of Guatemala. Although his policies were conservative, during this period he sometimes supported moderate liberal political leaders as a check against the pretensions of the conservative ecclesiastical and economic elite of the capital. On 21 March 1847 Carrera completed the process of Guatemalan secession from the defunct Central American union by establishing the Republic of Guatemala.

Liberal opposition, combined with continued rebel activity in eastern Guatemala, led to Carrera's resignation and exile in Mexico in August 1848. The new Liberal government, however, failed to achieve unity or solve the country's problems, and Carrera reentered the country in March 1849 at the head of an "army of restoration" composed heavily of Indians. When Carrera took Quetzaltenango, several generals defected to him and an agreement was reached in June that made him a lieutenant general in the Guatemalan army, followed in August by his appointment once more as commanding general of the army. Thereafter he strengthened the army as he carried out campaigns against continuing rebellions within Guatemala and against the liberals' attempts to revive the Central American union in El Salvador, Honduras, and Nicaragua. He dealt those forces a major blow with a stunning victory against the "national army" at San José la ARADA on 2 February 1851. This victory assured the dominance of the conservatives in Guatemala for many years to come.

After 1850 Carrera allied himself closely with the conservative and ecclesiastical elite of Guatemala City. His government restored close relations with Spain and signed a concordat with the Vatican guaranteeing the clergy a major role in the regime. Although Carrera was often described as reactionary by his opponents, Guatemala enjoyed considerable economic growth during the next twenty years as coffee began to replace cochineal as its leading export. Carrera once more became president of Guatemala on 6 November 1851. He consolidated his strength and greatly increased his power when he became president for life, a virtual monarch, on 21 October 1854.

As the most powerful caudillo in mid-nineteenth-century Central America, Carrera affected the development of neighboring states as well, frequently intervening to assure conservative rule in El Salvador and Honduras. When the North American filibuster William WALKER came to the aid of Nicaraguan liberals and subsequently became president of Nicaragua, Carrera provided substantial aid to the combined Central American force that routed Walker in 1857. Although he declined an invitation to command the Central American army, leaving that to Costa Rica's Juan Rafael Mora, Carrera sent more troops than any other state in the "National Campaign."

In 1863 Carrera challenged the rise in El Salvador of Gerardo BARRIOS, who had begun to pursue liberal, anticlerical reforms. Although initially repulsed at Coatepeque in February, he returned to conquer San Salvador later in the year, removing Barrios from office.

When he died in 1865, probably from dysentery, Carrera had achieved considerable stability and economic growth for Guatemala, but had also established a stifling political dictatorship that had reserved many of the benefits of the regime for a small elite in Guatemala City. At the same time, Carrera deserves credit for protecting the rural Indian masses of the country from increased exploitation of their land and labor and for bringing Indians and mestizos into positions of political and military leadership. Perhaps the most lasting legacy of his long rule, however, was the establishment of the military as the dominant political institution in the country.

LUIS BELTRANENA SINIBALDI, *Fudación de la República de Guatemala* (1971); KEITH L. MICELI, "Rafael Carrera: Defender and Promoter of Peasant Interest in Guatemala, 1837–1848," in *The Americas* 31, no. 1 (1974): 72–95; RALPH LEE WOODWARD, JR., *Rafael Carrera and the Emergence of the Republic of Guatemala, 1821–1871* (1993).

RALPH LEE WOODWARD, JR.

*See also* **Central America.**

**CARRERA ANDRADE, JORGE** (*b.* 18 September 1903; *d.* 11 November 1978). Possibly Ecuador's greatest poet of the twentieth century, Carrera Andrade was also a diplomat and anthropologist who traveled extensively both inside and outside his native land. In constant evolution throughout Carrera Andrade's life, his literary works comprise more than two dozen books of poetry spanning fifty years, numerous prose works, translations, and several literary studies of Ecuadorian, French, and Japanese literature. In his poetry, the luscious, diverse land of Ecuador and its strong telluric magnetism symbolize, in the vein of the European romantics and French symbolists, the origins of cosmic man and woman. Carrera Andrade's verse is a vehicle that constantly takes him back to the center of his poetic world: Ecuador.

Early on, his poetry reads like a carefully crafted, melodious song dedicated to his native land and the American landscape, and it continues to impart a musical quality to the land through innovative visual imagery and metaphor. Through his poetry, Carrera Andrade rediscovers his identity in the beauty and order of nature, which gives rise to certain constants in his poetry: optimism, despite growing world problems throughout his long career; social concern for the less fortunate in the world; and a search for ways to deal with solitude. *Hombre planetario* (1957–1963) is his best book of poetry, for in it he reconfirms his long-standing conviction concerning the need to understand our relationship with the land and with each other. Carrera

Andrade also pioneered the adaptation of haiku to the Spanish language.

ENRIQUE OJEDA CASTILLO, *Jorge Carrera Andrade: Introducción al estudio de su vida y de su obra* (1972); PETER R. BEARDSELL, *Winds of Exile: The Poetry of Jorge Carrera Andrade* (1977).

DICK GERDES

**CARRERA DEL PARAGUAY.** For 400 years the only practical outlet of Paraguay to the rest of Spanish America, and then to the outside world, was by means of the PARAGUAY-PARANÁ RIVER system. Colonial exports, mainly high-bulk, low-profit commodities as TOBACCO, timber, and yerba MATÉ flowed south to Santa Fe for transshipment to the interior, or on to the estuary.

Paraguayan-built and -crewed river craft dominated the Carrera to the early 1800s, as did Paraguayan-produced products. In the Bay of Asunción flat-bottomed craft for the one-way trip south were constructed. Elsewhere along the Paraguay River or the multitude of tributaries, rafts and log-booms were gathered. Skilled pilots and helmsmen guided these boats through the treacherous mud shoals of the Paraná, bound for their destination at Sante Fe or Las Conchas, a delta settlement serving Buenos Aires. Salaried peons from the Paraguayan countryside supplied the necessary muscle for rowing and lightering. For the return trip, small sailing vessels loaded with passengers and finished goods made the four-month voyage north to Asunción from Las Conchas. By the viceregal era, a complex web of credit from Buenos Aires merchants held this commercial network together.

After a twenty-year hiatus during the tenure of José Gaspar de FRANCIA, the Carrera again served Paraguay well during the era of Don Carlos Antonio LÓPEZ (1844–1862). However, after the destructive WAR OF THE TRIPLE ALLIANCE (1864–1870), Argentine entrepreneurs and their steamers captured control of commerce on the Carrera. It remained the primary external transport for Paraguay into the twentieth century.

JERRY W. COONEY, *Economía y sociedad en la Intendencia del Paraguay* (1990); THOMAS WHIGHAM, *The Politics of River Trade: Tradition and Development in the Upper Plata, 1780–1870* (1991).

JERRY W. COONEY

*See also* **Transportation.**

**CARRILLO, JULIÁN [ANTONIO]** (*b.* 28 January 1875; *d.* 9 September 1965), Mexican composer, theorist, conductor, violinist, and teacher. Born in Ahualulco, San Luis Potosí, Carrillo studied at the National Conservatory in Mexico City, where he took violin with Pedro Manzano, composition with Melesio MORALES, and acoustics with Francisco Ortega y Fonseca. He went to Europe in 1899, remaining there until 1905 and studying at the Leipzig Conservatory with Salomon Jadassohn (composition), Carl Reinecke (theory), Jean Becker (violin), and Arthur Nikisch and Sitt (conducting). He also studied violin with Albert Zimmer at the Ghent Conservatory. In Leipzig he led the Gewandhaus Orchestra. During that epoch Carrillo started to develop his new musical theory about dividing a violin string in such a way as to create a ratio of 1:1–007246. Carrillo divided the octave into microtones (intervals smaller than the semitone), calling his system "Sonido 13"—the "thirteenth sound." He also developed a method of music notation for the microtonal system. Carrillo's Symphony no. 1 (1902) was premiered under his baton by the Leipzig Conservatory Orchestra. In it he used what he called "ideological unity and tonal variety." He continued to experiment and began using an excessively complex musical vocabulary, even though one third of his works are written without microtones.

Carrillo returned to Mexico and was appointed professor of composition at the National Conservatory (1906), inspector general of music for Mexico City (1908), and director of the National Conservatory (1913–1915, 1920–1924). Beginning in 1926 Carrillo's musical works and theoretical writings were very much praised abroad, by the New York League of Composers, the Philadelphia Orchestra, in Belgium and in France. In 1961 the Lamoureux Orchestra of Paris recorded twenty of his microtonal and tonal works. A special piano for use with Carrillo's new system was built by the firm of Carl Sauter. Carrillo composed two operas as well as several symphonies, orchestral works, chamber music, and works for guitar, violin, and piano, and published numerous essays about his musical theory. He died in San Ángel.

JULIAN CARRILLO, *Julian Carrillo: Su vida y su obra* (1945); GERALD R. BENJAMIN, "Julian Carrillo and 'sonido 13,' " in *Yearbook, Inter-American Institute for Musical Research*, vol. 3 (1967), pp. 33–68; JUAN A. ORREGO-SALAS, ed., *Music from Latin America Available at Indiana University* (1971), p. 168; *New Grove Dictionary of Music and Musicians*, vol. 3 (1980).

SUSANA SALGADO

**CARRILLO COLINA, BRAULIO** (*b.* 20 March 1800; *d.* 15 May 1845), president and later dictator of Costa Rica (1835–1837; 1838–1842). Carrillo was an opponent of the Central American Federation as led by Francisco MORAZÁN, in whose execution he was implicated. However, he followed essentially radical liberal policies in internal economic affairs. He was most strongly identified with the supremacy of coffee-growing interests and of the new national capital of SAN JOSÉ. After studying law in León, Nicaragua, he returned to serve as deputy from his native city of Cartago (1827–1829), San José's principal rival as capital. He was chosen as a compromise chief of state in 1835 and then deposed his successor, Manuel Aguilar, to become virtual dictator in 1838. He was overthrown by Morazán's expeditionary force in 1842. Later, after engineering Morazán's capture and execution, he was forced into exile in El Salvador and assassinated near San Miguel.

During his first term Carrillo forcefully resolved the question of the site of the new capital by ending the system of "ambulatory," or rotating, capitals in favor of San José. When challenged in revolt (Guerra de la Liga) in 1835, he defeated the anti–San José forces despite his forces being outnumbered nearly three to one. This was followed by an abortive invasion of exiles (led by Manuel Quijano) from Nicaragua to Guanacaste, in June 1836, with even less success.

During his dictatorship Carrillo abrogated the 1825 Constitution and replaced it with the Ley de Bases y Garantías in 1841, which named him ruler for life. Although that provision was short-lived, the larger document proved more significant, greatly influencing the Constitution of 1871 in further strengthening the central government and liquidating the power of local municipal authorities. He also convened a Constituent Assembly in 1838 which declared Costa Rica's independence from the collapsing Central American Federation. Severely tested by Morazán's occupation, this policy was reaffirmed in 1848.

Carrillo's policies were consistently in favor of coffee exports and the city of San José, despite his origins in the rival city of Cartago. He ordered municipalities to provide coffee seedlings to all who would plant them, as well as terms for purchase or rental of public lands for coffee cultivation. He also abolished the collection of the tithe on coffee production after 1835, a policy of great importance in both stimulating production and undermining the power of the church thereafter.

Basic material on Carrillo can be found in CARLOS MONGE ALFARO, *Historia de Costa Rica,* 16th ed. (1980), pp. 193–199, 223–227. The most detailed examination of his policies is found in RODOLFO CERDAS CRUZ, *Formación del estado de Costa Rica,* 2d ed. (1978). A more recent study with some new information is CLOTILDE OBREGÓN, *Carrillo: Una época y un hombre, 1835–1842* (1989). See also VICTOR HUGO ACUÑO ORTEGA and IVAN MOLINA JIMÉNEZ, *El desarrollo económico y social de Costa Rica: De la colonia a la crisis de 1930* (1986); JORGE SÁENZ CARBONELL, *El despertar constitucional de Costa Rica* (1985); JOSÉ LUIS VEGA CARBALLO, *Orden y progreso: La formación del estado nacional en Costa Rica* (1981); and ALBERTO SÁENZ MAROTO, *Braulio Carrillo, reformador agrícola de Costa Rica* (1987).

LOWELL GUDMUNDSON

**CARRILLO FLORES, ANTONIO** (*b.* 23 June 1909; *d.* 20 March 1986), leading political figure in Mexican financial affairs since 1952. Born in Mexico City, he was the son of a famous musician Julián Carrillo. With Miguel Alemán, Carrillo Flores was a member of the 1929 law school graduating class at the National University. From 1946 to 1970 he held a succession of influential political posts, including secretary of the treasury (1952–1958), ambassador to the United States (1958–1964), and secretary of foreign relations (1964–1970). Through his public service

and teaching careers he trained two generations of disciples who became mentors to Mexico's new political technocrats of the 1980s and 1990s. He was the brother of the distinguished scientist Nabor Carrillo Flores.

*Diccionario biográfico de México,* vol. 1 (1968), pp. 121–122; and *Excélsior,* 1 March 1980, p. 4A.

RODERIC AI CAMP

**CARRILLO FLORES, NABOR** (*b.* 23 February 1911; *d.* 19 February 1967), educator, scientist, and intellectual. Born in Mexico City, he was the younger brother of Antonio Carrillo Flores, and the son of the musician Julián Carrillo. He received a civil engineering degree from the National University in 1938 and a doctorate from Harvard in 1942. Internationally renowned for his work in subsoil mechanics, Carrillo Flores studied with Sotero Prieto before receiving a Guggenheim fellowship (1940). He directed various scientific research projects at the National University, and served as its rector from 1952 to 1961. He received the National Prize in Sciences in 1957 and pioneered the use of atomic energy in Mexico. He died in Mexico City.

"Presente y futuro de la UNAM," in *Hispano Americano* 22 (27 February 1953): 35–37; and *Excélsior,* 21 August 1971, p. 7A.

RODERIC AI CAMP

**CARRILLO PUERTO, FELIPE** (*b.* 8 November 1874; *d.* 3 January 1924), one of the MEXICAN REVOLUTION's most radical agrarian leaders. During his short-lived governorship of Yucatán (1922–1923), Carrillo Puerto presided over what was arguably the Americas' first attempted transition to socialism. Assassinated in January 1924 by insurgent federal troops allied with powerful members of Yucatán's HENEQUEN oligarchy, he has since become one of the most enduring martyrs of Mexico's twentieth-century revolution.

Carrillo Puerto was born in Motul—the heart of Yucatán's henequen zone—the second of fourteen children of a modest mestizo retail merchant. As a young man he was a *ranchero* (small land-holder), mule driver, petty trader, and railroad conductor during Yucatán's henequen export boom, which descendants of the original MAYA fieldworkers still recall as the *época de esclavitud* (age of slavery). Carrillo Puerto learned the Maya vernacular as part of his daily life, and developed close ties to Yucatán's rural underclass in the process. An autodidact who read a bit of Marx and other leftist European thinkers along with the more standard fare of mainstream Mexican liberalism, Carrillo Puerto was jailed several times for his political activities against the local oligarchical machine. Following the fall of the PORFIRIATO in 1911, his political aspirations within the state were frustrated by his backing of the wrong Maderista politician, and he left Yucatán for Morelos in late 1914 to volunteer his services to the celebrated agrarian movement of Emiliano ZAPATA. Six months later, however, he was back on his native soil, determined to work with the new populist governor, General Salvador ALVARADO, to bring AGRARIAN REFORM to Yucatán.

Carrillo Puerto proved both too popular and too radical for the authoritarian Alvarado, who kept him on a short leash prior to departing the peninsula in 1918. Once Carrillo Puerto assumed control of Alvarado's Socialist Party of the Southwest (Partido Socialista del Sureste—PSS) later that year, the Mexican Revolution moved steadily to the left in Yucatán. Whereas Alvarado had been reluctant to let the rural masses participate in the political process, Carrillo Puerto encouraged them to accept responsibility for their political destiny. And while Alvarado had been prepared to initiate only a limited agrarian reform, under Carrillo Puerto's leadership, the pace of agrarian reform accelerated to the point that Yucatán distributed more land than any other state, save perhaps Zapata's Morelos. By the time of his death, Carrillo Puerto had made sure that virtually every one of the state's major pueblos had received at least a basic ejidal grant. His regime and life were snuffed out just as he seemed ready to initiate a more sweeping agrarian reform, one that would have expropriated the region's henequen plantations and turned them into collective farms owned and operated by the workers.

Under Carrillo Puerto the Mexican Revolution in Yucatán became a genuinely Yucatecan movement. He used locally trained cadres of agrarian agitators and activist schoolteachers, and allied with local CACIQUES (power brokers). Moreover, Carrillo Puerto reinforced the regional character of his revolution in a variety of symbolic ways, most of which sought to wean the Maya campesino away from the institutions and passive attitudes of the old regime and to develop a sense of ethnic pride as a prelude to class consciousness. He encouraged the speaking of Maya and the teaching of Maya culture and art forms, began earnest restoration of the great archaeological sites of Chichén Itzá and Uxmal, and made every effort to recall the great revolutionary tradition of protest to which the campesinos were heir.

Ultimately, Carrillo Puerto's homegrown variant of "Yucatecan socialism" proved threatening, not only to the regional oligarchy, but also to the more moderate regime then consolidating its control over the republic under the leadership of Sonoran caudillos Alvaro OBREGÓN SALIDO and Plutarco Calles. When, under cover of the DE LA HUERTA rebellion, insurgent federal troops were contracted by the henequen kings to expunge "bolshevism," Mexico City abandoned Carrillo Puerto. Yucatán's socialist experiment ended tragically when Felipe Carrillo Puerto and many of his closest supporters in Mérida were hunted down and summarily executed by a firing squad on 3 January 1924. Following the defeat of the de la Huerta rebellion, the remnants of the PSS were absorbed by the new corporatist structure in Mexico City. Only the outer trappings of the Americas' first attempted socialist transition—the

red shirts, the radical slogans, the formal organization of the PSS—survived its leader's untimely death.

FRANCISCO J. PAOLI BOLIO and ENRIQUE MONTALVO, El socialismo olvidado de Yucatán (1977); GILBERT M. JOSEPH, Revolution from Without: Yucatán, Mexico, and the United States, 1880–1924, rev. ed. (1988).

GILBERT M. JOSEPH

**CARRIÓN, ALEJANDRO** (b. 11 March 1915; d. 1991), Ecuadorian writer. Born in Loja, Alejandro Carrión is known in Ecuador principally as a political journalist. Many of his writings were signed with the pseudonym "Juan sin Cielo." Carrión also wrote poetry and narrative fiction. Among his most cited works are La manzana dañada (1948), a collection of short stories that depicts the sordid aspects of a school system controlled by the Catholic church in southern Ecuador, and La espina (1959), a novel of solitude in which the protagonist tries to reconstruct the image of his mother, who had died during his birth. Because of his political views, which ran the gamut from socialism in his early life to conservatism in his later years, Carrión was a controversial figure in Ecuador. During the government of León FEBRES CORDERO (1984–1988), many accused Carrión of being the president's principal apologist; in his journalism, Carrión defended the government's neoliberal economic policies and its conservative political agenda. In 1985, President Febres awarded Carrión the Eugenio Espejo Prize for Literature.

MICHAEL HANDELSMAN

**CARRIÓN, JERÓNIMO** (b. 6 July 1801; d. 5 May 1873), president of Ecuador (1865–1867). Carrión served as governor of Azuay province (1845–1847), deputy (1845, 1852) and senator (1847–1849) from Loja province, and vice president of Ecuador in 1859 during the administration of Francisco ROBLES (1856–1859). In 1865 he accepted the invitation of archconservative dictator Gabriel GARCÍA MORENO (1861–1865, 1869–1875) to succeed him. The retiring president arranged a landslide electoral victory for Carrión, who, to García Moreno's dismay, proved unwilling to be a puppet ruler. He chose his own cabinet, naming several liberals, and dispatched García Moreno on a diplomatic mission to Chile.

Yet on policy matters Carrión did not diverge significantly from the García Moreno agenda, save for his unwillingness to savage political opponents with violent repression. Under Carrión freedom of expression returned, bringing the reemergence of a lively—if often reckless and irresponsible—opposition press. In 1867 his leading minister, Manuel Bustamante, angered powerful Liberal elements then ascendant in Congress. In the ensuing political showdown with Senate president Pedro CARBO Y NOBOA, Congress censured Carrión. He was overthrown and replaced by Pedro José Arteta in

1867. Lacking support, Carrión agreed. Contemporaries generally regarded him as honest if not especially bright or energetic.

On nineteenth-century Ecuadorian politics, see OSVALDO HURTADO's interpretive *Political Power in Ecuador*, translated by Nick D. Mills, Jr. (1985); and FRANK MAC DONALD SPINDLER's descriptive *Nineteenth Century Ecuador: An Historical Introduction* (1987). For a brief analysis of Ecuadorian political economy in the nineteenth century, consult DAVID W. SCHODT, *Ecuador: An Andean Enigma* (1987).

RONN F. PINEO

*See also* **Espinosa y Espinosa, Javier.**

**CARRIÓN, MANUEL BENJAMÍN** (*b.* 20 April 1897; *d.* 8 March 1979), Ecuadorian essayist. Originally from Loja, Benjamín Carrión spent his life writing about the major social, political, and cultural problems of both his native Ecuador and the rest of Latin America. During his youth, he was one of the early founders of Ecuador's Socialist Party (1925). His contributions to the continent's many democratic causes were formally recognized when the Mexican government awarded him in 1968 the prestigious Benito Juárez Prize. In 1944, Carrión founded Ecuador's Casa de la Cultura Ecuatoriana (House of Ecuadorian Culture), which through the years has become one of the country's principal institutions charged with developing among all Ecuadorians the many forms of cultural and intellectual expression. In Ecuador, Carrión is revered for his efforts to stimulate and guide others in their creative endeavors. His most celebrated works are *Atahuallpa* (1934) and *Cartas al Ecuador* (1943). In 1975 he received the Eugenio Espejo Prize, Ecuador's highest literary and cultural honor.

MICHAEL HANDELSMAN

**CARTAGENA,** the northern province of the New Kingdom of Granada, whose capital, Cartagena de Indias, was the principal Spanish port and defense center on the northern Caribbean littoral.

Located on the Caribbean coast of modern-day Colombia between the Magdalena and Sinú rivers and extending southward to the town of Mompós, Cartagena was an eminent colonial jurisdiction dominated by activity in the port of Cartagena de Indias. When the Spanish explorers Juan de la Cosa and Rodrigo de BASTIDAS first reconnoitered the area in 1502, they recognized the potential afforded by a large bay reminiscent of the bay at Cartagena, Spain. Cosa and others, however, did not return to the site until 1509.

As in 1502, they confronted Caramari, Turbaco, and other Indians who resisted the Spanish incursion. In a February 1510 battle, for example, Turbaco warriors killed Cosa and seventy others, dealing Spanish troops their worst defeat yet in the Caribbean conquest. Cosa's compatriot, Alonso de OJEDA, and recently arrived reinforcements commanded by Diego de NICUESA successfully counterattacked, but they abandoned the field for territories farther south and west. Modern scholarship continues to examine the origins and cultural affinities of these Indians, but sixteenth-century Spaniards knew them to be stout fighters, skillful archers, and active merchants, trading salt, fish, and cotton hammocks for gold and clothing.

Not until 1533 did Spanish colonists, led by Pedro de HEREDIA, establish a permanent settlement at Cartagena. Because of continuing Indian hostility at Turbaco and the island of Tierra Bomba, upon their arrival, Heredia selected a deserted Caramari village site for his new town. Heredia's efforts paid off in great dividends for imperial Spain. Within the decade, Cartagena de Indias developed into a major imperial entrepôt for the ship-

*Vista de Cartagena* (View of Cartagena). Engraving based on drawing of E. Therond, ca. 1872.

ment of American bullion to Spain as well as for slaves and manufactures intended for northern South American markets. In turn, this commerce energized economic life within the city itself.

Foreigners, too, recognized the significance of Cartagena de Indias and so sought to appropriate its wealth and deal Spain a military and political blow. French pirates sacked the city in 1544 and 1559. A decade later (1568), John HAWKINS took the port, as did Francis DRAKE in 1586. French troops captured Cartagena in 1697. British forces twice besieged the port, in 1727 and 1741, the second time with a force of twenty thousand men and nearly two hundred ships under the command of Admiral Edward Vernon.

Because of the commercial and strategic prominence of the port, Spanish authorities ordered substantial fortifications for the city, raising there some of the best and most impressive colonial military architecture. Highlighted by walls eight feet thick and the looming fortress of San Felipe de Barajas, these defenses—constructed between 1560 and 1780—demonstrated royal resolve, declared imperial pretensions and power, and marked the colonial greatness of the port. The battlements remain even today a constant reminder of one of the most celebrated historical events in Colombian historiography: the defeat of Vernon's 1741 assault on the city. Aided by tropical disease, which devasted the English forces, and guided by Viceroy Sebastián de Eslava (1740–1749) and naval commander Blas de Lezo (1689–1741), the defenders withstood the British attacks and thus earned the port the appellation "heroic."

Cartagena de Indias was also an ecclesiastical and political hub, rivaled only in New Granada by Santa Fe de BOGOTÁ. It was an episcopal see and possessed one of three American offices of the Inquisition (established in 1610), charged with responsibility for northern South America, Panama, and the Spanish Caribbean. It contained four monasteries, two convents, and the San Juan de Dios hospital. Moreover, one of the most famous Jesuit missionaries of the colonial period, Saint Pedro CLAVER, labored there among Africans between 1610 and 1654, when the city was a major slave distribution center for the Caribbean. Governors and treasury officials also served in Cartagena, and, in the eighteenth century, viceroys occasionally ruled from there.

The fame of Cartagena de Indias notwithstanding, more people lived in the provincial hinterlands than in the city, especially in times of foreign hostilities. Whereas in the eighteenth century, for example, the population of the port generally fluctuated between ten and sixteen thousand, as many as nine times that many people lived in the rest of the province. The commercial milieu that dominated port life also characterized activity in and around Mompós (founded 1537) and Tolú, two towns known for their contraband fairs and centrality in regional trade networks.

For a representative sampling of works available in English see JAMES NELSON GOODSELL, "Cartagena de Indias: Entrepôt for a New World (1533–1597)" (Ph.D. diss., Harvard University, 1966); LINDA L. GREENOW, *Family, Household, and Home: A Microgeographic Analysis of Cartagena (New Granada) in 1777* (1976); and LANCE R. GRAHN, "Cartagena and Its Hinterland in the Eighteenth Century," in *Atlantic Port Cities: Economy, Culture, and Society in the Atlantic World, 1650–1850*, edited by Franklin W. Knight and Peggy K. Liss (1991), pp. 168–195. Essential, however, are these books in Spanish: ENRIQUE MARCO DORTA, *Cartagena de Indias: Puerto y plaza fuerte* (1960), which is unsurpassed in its survey of the military architecture of the port; EDUARDO LEMAITRE ROMÁN, *Cartagena colonial* (1973), a fine general history; DONALDO BOSSA HERRAZO's guide to the geography and place-names of the city and province, *Nomenclatur cartagenero* (1981); and ORLANDO FALS-BORDA's ongoing multivolume study of the provincial hinterlands of Cartagena, *Historia doble de la costa*, 4 vols. (1979–1986).

LANCE R. GRAHN

**CARTAGENA MANIFESTO.** The first major political statement of Simón BOLÍVAR, at the time a relatively obscure fugitive from the collapse of Venezuela's First Republic, was the "manifesto" that he published at Cartagena in neighboring New Granada (1812). In the form of a pamphlet titled *Memoria dirigida a los ciudadanos de la Nueva Granada por un caraqueño*, it contained Bolívar's analysis of the reasons for the recent failure of the Venezuelan patriots and anticipated many of the themes of his later writings. He placed particular emphasis on the errors of doctrinaire theorists whose infatuation with foreign ideas and with federalist forms of organization—which Bolívar considered unsuited to Spanish American conditions—had caused them to ignore the need for a strong central executive. He urged New Granadans both to avoid repetition of the same mistakes and to support a new campaign to liberate Venezuela.

*Selected Writings of Bolívar*, compiled by Vicente Lecuna, edited by Harold A. Bierck, Jr., translated by Lewis Bertrand (1951), vol. 1, pp. 18–26; GERHARD MASUR, *Simón Bolívar* (1948; rev. ed. 1969), chap. 9.

DAVID BUSHNELL

**CARTAGO,** capital of the province of Cartago, the second most densely populated Costa Rican province after San José. Cartago competes with Heredia and Alajuela for the distinction of being the second city of the *meseta central*, the Costa Rican heartland. As the site of the basilica of the "Black Virgin" (Nuestra Señora de los Angeles), it retains an unrivaled place in the religious sentiments of the people and is the destination of an impressive annual pilgrimage. Cartago and its residents played pivotal roles in the watershed 1948 revolution. Costa Ricans always remember Cartago for the devastating earthquake it suffered in 1910 and its sporadic episodes with the nearby Irazú volcano.

Cartago's greatest glory came in the colonial period. From the time of its foundation in 1564, it was the capital and most important city in one of Spain's most isolated and neglected colonies. By the independence era (ca. 1821) the city had a scant seven thousand residents. In 1823 Cartago was defeated by the more dynamic and republican San José in the struggle to be the new nation's capital city.

For the independence period, see RICARDO FERNÁNDEZ GUARDIA, *La independencia: historia de Costa Rica* (1971); for the role of Cartago in the crisis of the 1940s, see JOHN PATRICK BELL, *Crisis in Costa Rica* (1971); for the impact of coffee production and its aftermath, see CAROLYN HALL, *Costa Rica: A Geographical Interpretation in Historical Perspective* (1985); and for its place in Costa Rican society over the years, see RICHARD BIESANZ, KAREN ZUBRIS BIESANZ, and MAVIS HILTUNEN BIESANZ, *The Costa Ricans* (1982; rev. ed. 1988).

JOHN PATRICK BELL

**CARTAVIO,** a SUGAR-producing landed estate in northern Peru dating from Spanish colonial times. In 1882 this 1,447-acre HACIENDA was surrendered by its Peruvian owner, Guillermo Alzamora, to the U.S. commercial firm W. R. GRACE and Company in payment of its accumulated debt. In the 1890s the Grace firm formed the Cartavio Sugar Company as a subsidiary corporation. A pioneering U.S. direct investment of 200,000 pounds sterling was used to modernize the estate and build a sugar mill. In this way the Grace interests contributed to a process of land consolidation by giant estates (Cartavio, CASA GRANDE, and Laredo) which displaced smaller landowners in the northern Chicama valley of Peru. In the 1970s, during the implementation of the agrarian reform sponsored by the military regime, the Cartavio estate's ownership and administration were transferred to an agrarian cooperative.

PETER KLARÉN, *Modernization, Dislocation, and Aprismo* (1973); MICHAEL GONZÁLEZ, *Plantation Agriculture and Social Control in Northern Peru, 1875–1933* (1985).

ALFONSO W. QUIROZ

**CARTOGRAPHY.** The mapping of the lands that are known as Latin America predates their discovery by the Europeans, perhaps by many centuries. Upon landing on the mainland, Spanish and Portuguese found amazingly rich and diverse traditions of cartography among the native inhabitants of the Americas. Generally, the most developed of these traditions was that of the indigenous peoples of MESOAMERICA. They regularly drew very detailed maps of large areas, some reflecting their view of the world and its creation, as well as smaller-area topographical maps and city plans.

Because of their apparent fragility and the harshness and religious zeal of the European conquerors, very few of these indigenous maps (e.g., the Mixtec Nuttall "screenfold" Codex) have survived, and those that have, are difficult to date precisely. The techniques and the technology of indigenous mapmaking are, therefore, also difficult to determine with much specificity.

However, a large number of Spanish descriptions of Amerindian maps from the era of first contact that survive in the writings of Hernán CORTÉS, Bernal DÍAZ DEL CASTILLO, Peter MARTYR, and others, make possible a better understanding of the distinguishing characteristics of the indigenous cartography at that time.

During the period of the conquests, indigenous and European cultures and cartographic styles fused; thus, surviving maps (e.g., Codex Xolotl, ca. 1530) exhibit both styles. In the process, earlier Amerindian maps yielded valuable information that was reflected on later European maps of Latin America.

The Spanish and Portuguese mapping of the Americas progressed abreast of, and was to a large extent determined by, discovery, exploration, conquest, and settlement. Three untitled maps of the Indies, derived from the text, but not drawn by Christopher COLUMBUS, illustrated the first published version (1493) of his letter about the voyage to Ferdinand and Isabella. The only extant map drawn by Columbus is a sketch of the northwest coast of HISPANIOLA done in December 1492. The first map that distinctly shows the New World as found by Columbus, the CABOTS, and others is a world map drawn in 1500 by Juan de la Cosa, a navigator who had sailed with Columbus in 1492–1493, now preserved in the Museo Naval, Madrid. The Cantino world map (1502) recorded the results of Portuguese voyages to the Americas and indicated the LINE OF DEMARCATION, established by the Treaty of TORDESILLAS (1494), which divided the New World between Spain and Portugal and excluded all others from it. The Contarini-Roselli world map (1506) was the first printed map to show the American discoveries, including CUBA, Hispaniola, and the northern coast of South America.

The Americas were named by a cartographer from Lorraine, Martin Waldseemüller (who seemed to be ignorant of Columbus), on the world and New World maps in his edition of Ptolemy's *Universalis cosmographia* (1507), after the explorer-geographer Amerigo VESPUCCI, whose works Waldseemüller had previously published. On four voyages to the New World in 1499–1502, Vespucci explored more than 6,000 miles of coastline; he wrote an account of them, *Quaturo navigationes*, which Waldseemüller published in 1507. Beginning with the 1513 edition of these maps (the "Admiral's maps," after Columbus), Waldseemüller gave Columbus due credit. However, other cartographers, such as Gerard Mercator, had already popularized the designation "America," and so it held. In the same year, Johannes Ruysch's world map (1507) still showed the New World discoveries as part of Asia.

Columbus's discovery led to the establishment of the CASA DE CONTRATACIÓN, centered in Seville and Cádiz, which, with the COUNCIL OF THE INDIES, created in 1524, was in charge of Spanish America. It not only directed exploration and settlement but also functioned as the official collation center and clearinghouse for information about the New World. It also possessed the most accurate map of Spanish America, the master map, the *padrón real*. It was constantly updated by incoming reports from the New World and was used to prepare maps and charts for future ventures there. It survives only in fragmented copies, the earliest of which is the Castiglione world map of 1525.

The Spanish treated the geographical knowledge of the Americas, especially of the interior, as a state secret. It was closely guarded and rarely disseminated publicly, and then only inaccurately. Hence, when early Spanish maps of the New World were published, they were like those in Antonio de HERRERA Y TORDESILLAS's four-volume *Historia general de los hechos de los Castillanos en las yslas y tierra firme del mar Oceano* (1601), depicting only generalized coastal outlines and the vague locations of inland major towns like Mexico City.

In 1416, a year after playing a leading role in the conquest of Muslim Ceuta to the west of the Straits of Gibraltar in Morocco, Prince Henry the Navigator, third son of King John I, began gathering around him, in Sagres and the nearby port of Lagos in the far southwest of Portugal, experts in seamanship and cartography. His goal was to further his country's knowledge of what lay to the south along the African coast. By the time of his death in 1460, his captains, motivated by profit and their master's crusading zeal, had explored and mapped as far as present-day Sierra Leone. Henry's personal patronage helped to pioneer the sea routes that would eventually lead to Brazil and around Africa to India. He also laid the groundwork for the navigational and cartographic skills and geographic knowledge that were necessary to the establishment of the Iberian empires in Africa, Asia, and the Americas in the sixteenth century.

The Europeans mapped Latin America as they encountered it: the coasts and islands of the Gulf of Mexico and the Caribbean Sea; the Atlantic coast of South America; the interior of Mesoamerica; the Pacific coast of Middle, North, and South America; and the interiors of North and South America. Mapping usually proceeded from the coasts inland, often via rivers, especially large ones like the Mississippi, the Orinoco, and the Amazon. But it frequently was hampered by the vastness and diversity of New World geography. Over time, mapping was necessitated by economic, military, and political demands. The last areas to be mapped were in Amazonia and the Andes in South America, and the North American Southwest. The mapping of the New World was hampered by simple ignorance, the striving for fortune and glory, faulty science and technology, and Old World mind-sets.

The sixteenth century was the century of coasting expeditions, conquests, and ENTRADAS; the geography they revealed was depicted on maps. The first rough chart of the coast of the Gulf of Mexico from Florida to Mexico near Veracruz, including the mouths of the Mississippi, the Rio Grande, and other important rivers, the "Piñeda Chart," came from an expedition led by Alonso ÁLVAREZ DE PIÑEDA in 1519. The "Cortés map" of the Gulf of Mexico, which included a plan of Mexico City (1524) and was the first European printed map of an American city, illustrated the published account of the conquest of the Aztecs.

Although elaborate coastal representations of the Americas were produced throughout the sixteenth century, among the most impressive were the portolans (manuscript charts and atlases) of the Genoese cartographer Battista Agnese, who worked in Venice. Beginning in 1543, he published a series of beautiful world maps presenting a relatively accurate view of much of the Western Hemisphere separate from Asia and often showing the route of Ferdinand MAGELLAN's global circumnavigation in 1519–1522 and the similar route of the MANILA GALLEON treasure fleets from the Far East to Spain that followed.

Printed world maps showing the Americas and based on Agnese's charts and other manuscript maps began appearing in Europe at about the same time. Giambattista Ramusio's *Carta universale* (1534) showed mainly the east coasts of the Americas, the Gulf of Mexico, the Caribbean Sea, the Straits of Magellan, and the mouths of the great rivers; the Andes were the principal interior detail. Sebastian Münster's map, *Die nüw Welt* (1540), the first printed map of the Americas alone, was an illustration in his edition of the third-century *Geographia* of Ptolemy; it was less accurate and showed the island of "Zipangri" not very far off the coast of California.

The crowning achievement in this genre was the New World map, *Americae sive Novi orbis nova descriptio*, in Abraham Ortelius's atlas, *Theatrum orbis terrarum* (1570), consisting of seventy maps in fifty-three sheets printed from superbly worked and designed copperplate engravings. It reflected knowledge from numerous expeditions, maps, and charts, including the conquests of Mexico, Yucatán, and Peru, and the great *entradas* of Pánfilo de NARVÁEZ and Alvar Núñez CABEZA DE VACA (1527–1537), Fray Marcos de NIZA and Francisco Vázquez de CORONADO (1539–1542), and Hernando de SOTO and Luis de Moscoso (1539–1543), as well as from Amerindian sources. With every successive edition of this map through 1587, its accuracy increased, especially with regard to outline and interior detail of South America. Ortelius also produced a series of regional maps of the New World—such as *La Florida; Guastecan; Peruvial auriferae regiones typus* (1584–1612), individual maps of Florida, Guasteca in northern Mexico on the Gulf, and the gold-rich regions of Peru on one sheet—for the later editions of his *Theatrum orbis terrarum*.

In the early seventeenth century, with the failure to find new wealth as readily accessible as that of the Aztecs and Incas, Spain consolidated its New World empire. By the end of the century however, European rivals had begun to strongly challenge Spain for these holdings. Consequently, the mapping of the interior, especially of the American Southwest, proceeded slowly, and information from exploration continued to be kept secret. As always, published Spanish maps revealed lit-

Sixteenth-century map of North and South America, from the 1570 Ortelius atlas. LIBRARY OF CONGRESS.

tle. Maps produced in other nations were derived from earlier maps and charts and from those captured from the Spanish by French, Dutch, and English spies, expeditions, and pirates.

At the beginning of the seventeenth century, Edward Wright's chart of the world on Mercator's projection was a typical synthesis of existing maps, especially with regard to the depiction of Latin America. Published in the second edition of Richard Hakluyt's *The Principall Navigations, Voiages, Traffiques, and Discoueries of the English Nation* (3 vols., 1598–1600), it was one of the first engravings to appear in England that was based on Mercator's projection as modified by Wright. John Speed's *America* (1627) was the first printed English map of the Americas, and although better than Wright's on the interior detail of Latin America, it was replete with mistakes such as showing California as an island (based on Henry Briggs's North American map of 1625).

Many navigators since the days of Cortés had erroneously estimated Baja California's insularity. To help satisfy European audiences' growing hunger for more and more information about the New World, the borders of Speed's highly decorative map were punctuated with inserts showing plans of various cities ("Havan,"

"Cartagena," "Mexico," etc.) and pictures of natives ("Peruviane," "Brasiliane," "Magellanican," etc.) of Latin America.

The equivalent of Ortelius's achievement in Latin American cartography in the seventeenth century was produced by the Blaeus, a family of cartographers, publishers, and scientific instrument makers who lived in Amsterdam when the city was the center of global commerce and of the map trade in Europe. Willem Janszoon Blaeu's great *Theatrum orbis terrarum sive Novus atlas* (1635) shows more coastal and interior detail more accurately than Wright's and Speed's maps; Baja California is clearly attached to the mainland oriented southward off the west coast of Mexico. The family's efforts with regard to Latin America culminated in the very fine and decorative continental and more localized maps in the eleven-volume *Atlas major* (1662), published in various languages by Willem's son, Joan, who was the official cartographer for the Dutch East India Company.

Between 1666 and 1680, João Teixeira Albernas II, working in Lisbon, produced four beautiful and informative manuscript atlases of Bahia and Brazil. They were superb for coastal detail and the courses of rivers like the Amazon, but sketchy on interior locations, except for the sites of some military outposts. And in the closing decades of the century, Vincenzo Maria Coronelli, cosmographer of the Republic of Venice, published his *planisfero del mondo nuovo* (1688). Although it shows California as an extremely large island, this major map presents a very accurate configuration of South America and many of its rivers.

For more than three centuries after the Treaty of Tordesillas, the Portuguese tried, through warfare, aggressive exploration and colonization, and tireless negotiations, to have the Atlantic meridian of the Line of Demarcation set as far to the west as possible to maximize their hold over Brazil and its wealth. It was only with the treaties of Madrid (1750) and San Ildefonso (1777) that Spain came reluctantly to recognize the more extensive areas of Portuguese control in South America. But a lack of geographic knowledge about the interior and ongoing boundary disagreements continued to make the mapping of western Brazil and its inland political boundaries difficult. Like so many other boundary disputes in Latin America, these and the resulting cartographic vagueness were carried well into the twentieth century.

The maps of Latin America in the eighteenth century reflected the competition for empire among the European powers and the decline of Spain in this region. With the gaining of the ability to measure time precisely (1773), and thereby to determine longitude accurately, the maps of the later part of the century marked the dawn of the age of scientific cartography. Henry Abraham Chatelain's lavishly decorated world map (1719) and Herman Moll's map of South America (1717) reflect the heightened imperial rivalries in Latin America. For example, the British geographer Moll's two-sheet map, *A New & Exact Map of the Coasts, Countries and Islands within ye Limits of ye South Sea Company* . . . , from his folio atlas *The World Described* . . . (1717–1754), depicted the newly established British South Sea Company's claimed economic sphere in South America and the southeastern Pacific. In anticipation of never-realized trade, this map was particularly detailed for the west coast and offshore islands of South America.

The best early examples of the scientific mapping of Latin America are in the various atlases of the New World published by the German scientist-geographer Alexander von Humboldt (1805–1834). Beginning in 1799, he spent more than five years exploring the New World, taking exact measurements and making many geographic and other scientific discoveries. His maps of Mexico and New Spain were standards for almost a century.

The nineteenth century was the period of the revolutions for national independence from Spain throughout most of Latin America. With the emergence of the new nation-state system in the southern part of the hemisphere came national mapping, principally to establish boundaries and territorial claims. However, most of these first national maps of the region were not made by the new nations themselves but by the European powers and the United States, largely as parts of hemispheric and global atlases.

In the twentieth century, with the growing economic, political, and strategic importance of Latin America, the mapping of the region was fully integrated into contemporary global cartography. This is especially true after the development of modern surveying (e.g., use of lasers) and remote sensing (aerial photography and earth satellite multiple-spectrum imaging) techniques. Currently, much of this high-tech mapping of Latin America is motivated by such critical ecological issues as overpopulation, agricultural production, and rain forest decimation.

SEYMOUR I. SCHWARTZ and RALPH E. EHRENBERG, *The Mapping of America* (1980), esp. pp. 14–155; TONY CAMPBELL, *Early Maps* (1981), esp. pp. 24–67; RODNEY W. SHIRLEY, *The Mapping of the World: Early Printed Maps 1472–1700* (1983); JAMES C. MARTIN and ROBERT SIDNEY MARTIN, *Maps of Texas and the Southwest 1513–1900* (1984); PIERLUIGI PORTINARO and FRANCO KNIRSCH, *The Cartography of North America 1500–1800* (1987); CHARLES BRICKER, *Landmarks of Mapmaking* (1989), esp. pp. 191–242; DAVID BUISSERET, ed., *From Sea Charts to Satellite Images: Interpreting North American History Through Maps* (1990), esp. pp. 3–141; JOHN GOSS, *The Mapping of North America: Three Centuries of Map-making 1500–1860* (1990), esp. pp. 7–137; JOHN BRIAN HARLEY, *Maps and the Columbian Encounter* (1990); KATHERINE R. GOODWIN and DENNIS REINHARTZ, *Terra Tabula Nova* (1992); SANDRA SIDER, ANITA ANDREASIAN, and MITCHELL CODDING, *Maps, Charts, Globes: Five Centuries of Exploration* (1992); HANS WOLFF, *America: Early Maps of the New World* (1992).

DENNIS REINHARTZ

*See also* **Explorers and Exploration.**

### The Spanish Borderlands

Spanning the 300-year colonial era, mapping of the Spanish Borderlands began with efforts to understand the discovery of the New World, advanced with attempts to define competing claims, and culminated in surveys to determine international boundaries.

The first cartographic efforts were accomplished with primitive technology, which militated against accuracy. Latitude determination, with astrolabe or cross-staff, was imprecise; there was no dependable means of computing longitude. As data accrued from the early discoveries, King Ferdinand designated the CASA DE CONTRATACIÓN in Seville as the repository for geographical data. Cosmographers there kept a master chart, called the *padrón real*. As reports came in, cartographers drafted the data into finished maps. Crown policy kept this knowledge from other nations, and each copy of the *padrón real* was destroyed when superseded. Hence, mapmakers of other nations, using whatever Spanish data were at their disposal, shaped Europeans' concepts of the Spanish discoveries.

Following Juan PONCE DE LEÓN's discovery of FLORIDA in 1513, Spanish North America was mapped in three chronological stages: (1) the Gulf coast, (2) the Atlantic coast from Florida northward, and (3) the Pacific coast.

From a 1519 voyage dispatched by Francisco de GARAY, governor of Jamaica, came the first crude map sketch of the Gulf of Mexico. This expedition, commanded by Alonso ÁLVAREZ DE PINEDA, explored the coast from Ponce's Florida landing to Hernán CORTÉS's new settlement of Villa Rica on the Veracruz coast. It discovered the mouth of the Mississippi River (named Río del Espíritu Santo) and proved there was no strait linking the Gulf with the Pacific. The "Pineda sketch," preserved in the Archivo General de Indias in Seville, was a cartographic cornerstone. Its Gulf configuration, with data from Atlantic coast explorations north of Florida by Lucas VÁZQUEZ DE AYLLÓN's pilots in 1520–1521 and by Estevão Gomes in 1525, enabled cosmographers to present a portion of the continent in recognizable outline. It aided especially the 1529 world maps by Diogo Ribeiro, chief cosmographer in the Casa de Contratación, which became prototypes.

Not until the coastlines were roughly established did maps begin to show significant interior detail. The so-called De Soto map, found among the papers of the cosmographer Alonso de Santa Cruz about 1572, was the first to supply information on rivers and native towns. Although most of the information was derived from Hernando de SOTO's expedition (1539–1543), the map also drew from other explorers: Ponce de León and Vasquez de Ayllón in the East and Alvar Núñez CABEZA DE VACA and Francisco Vázquez de CORONADO in the Southwest. It influenced Borderlands cartography for half a century.

Influenced by Coronado's march onto the Great Plains, voyages around 1540, including those of Francisco de Ulloa, Hernando de Alarcón, and Juan RODRÍGUEZ CABRILLO, focused on the Pacific Coast. Domingo del Castillo, a pilot with both Ulloa and Alarcón, drew a map showing the results of these two voyages, which traced 2,000 miles of coastline, proved California was not an island, and discovered the Colorado River. By 1570 Abraham Ortelius, with his landmark *Americae sive novi orbis nova descriptio*, was able to portray North America to its far limits, using the Mercator projection introduced the previous year.

Maps of the seventeenth century reflected little new knowledge of the Borderlands. Spanish secrecy continued to deny the most accurate data to cartographic centers in other European countries. The French explorer René-Robert LA SALLE, in descending the Mississippi River from Illinois to the Gulf of Mexico in 1682, had no reliable map to guide him. The lack of geographical data and faulty cartography have been blamed for his subsequent landing in Texas while seeking the mouth of the Mississippi from the Gulf.

The Spaniards' three-year search for La Salle's Gulf Coast colony constituted a rebirth of exploration. The pilot Juan Enríquez Barroto, on a 1686–1687 search voyage that circumnavigated the Gulf, mapped the shoreline and named its features. Although his maps have been lost, his diary survives, revealing the source of many place names appearing on a host of non-Spanish maps, including those of the French geographer Guillaume Delisle.

Delisle and his father, Claude, brought to the mapping of America a level of scholarship not previously attained, as is evident in the 1703 *carte du Mexique et de la Floride*. This joint effort utilized sources from Pánfilo de NARVÁEZ and Cabeza de Vaca to Louisiana founder Pierre Le Moyne d'Iberville. Delisle's 1718 *Carte de la Louisiane et du cours du Mississippi* utilized information from explorers such as Louis Juchereau de Saint-Denis and small-area maps like those of François Le Maire.

In the Far West, Jesuit Father Eusebio KINO settled, with his 1702 map, confusion that since Ulloa's time had made California an island. Later in the eighteenth century, military inspections of New Spain's interior provinces brought a new dimension to Borderlands cartography, notably the series of six maps by Francisco Álvarez Barreiro, engineer with Pedro de RIVERA's inspection team (1724–1727), and the 1771 map by Nicolás de Lafora, engineer with the Marqués de RUBÍ's visit of 1766–1768. Both these examples extended from the Gulf of California to Louisiana.

With the end of the SEVEN YEARS' WAR in 1763, both England and Spain faced the need to explore and map their new territories. Thus came into play the work of cartographers in English service such as George Gauld, Philip Pittman, and Bernard Romans along the Gulf coast and the Mississippi.

A lack of accurate coastal mapping was recognized by Bernardo de GÁLVEZ, campaigning against the British on the Gulf Coast during the American Revolution. Having reclaimed the Floridas, Gálvez sent José de Evía to explore and map the Gulf coast from Florida to Tampico, in 1785–1786. Evía's work served as the basis for subsequent maps by the Spanish Hydrographic Service and contributed to José Antonio Pichardo's 1811 map of New Mexico and adjacent regions, meant to be used in the settlement of the Louisiana-Texas boundary dispute. The Hydrographic Office charts, in turn, provided the Gulf of Mexico configuration for Alexander von HUMBOLDT's map of New Spain (1811). Zebulon M. Pike's *A Map of the Internal Provinces of New Spain,* based in part on his own military reconnaissance, and Aaron Arrowsmith's *A New Map of Mexico,* both showing the western Borderlands, drew on Humboldt's data.

Philadelphia publisher John Melish facilitated the eventual division of lands between the United States and Mexico under the 1819 Adams–Onís Treaty with his 1816 *Map of the United States.* In its six sheets this map epitomized the state of cartographic knowledge as Florida passed to the United States, and Spain, in 1821, yielded the rest of the Borderlands to independent Mexico.

Anglo-American colonization of Mexican Texas brought forth maps by Stephen F. AUSTIN (1830) and

David H. Burr (1833), showing Texas and adjacent Mexican states, north to the Arkansas River. Pertinent to the question of annexation of Texas to the United States, after it gained independence from Mexico, was William H. Emory's 1844 *Map of Texas and the Countries Adjacent*, which embraced the territory west to the Pacific Ocean.

Texas was annexed in 1845, and the Treaty of Guadalupe Hidalgo, ending the Mexican-American War, gave the United States title to the present states of Arizona, California, Nevada, New Mexico, and Utah. Mapping of the former Spanish Borderlands from Texas to California was carried out by the U.S. Topographical Engineers and the Boundary Commission.

JEAN DELANGLEZ, *El Río del Espíritu Santo: An Essay on the Cartography of the Gulf Coast and the Adjacent Territory During the Sixteenth and Seventeenth Centuries* (1945); WILLIAM PRATT CUMMING, R. A. SKELTON, and D. B. QUINN, *The Discovery of North America* (1972); SEYMOUR J. SCHWARTZ and RALPH E. EHRENBERT, *The Mapping of America* (1980); JAMES C. MARTIN and ROBERT SIDNEY MARTIN, *Maps of Texas and the Southwest, 1513–1900* (1984); ROBERT S. WEDDLE, *Spanish Sea: The Gulf of Mexico in North American Discovery, 1500–1685* (1985), pp. 103–104, 232–233; HENRY G. TALIAFERRO, JANE A. KENAMORE, and ULI HALLER, *Cartographic Sources in the Rosenberg Library* (1988), esp. pp. 3–36; ROBERT S. WEDDLE, *The French Thorn: Rival Explorers in the Spanish Sea, 1682–1762* (1991).

ROBERT S. WEDDLE

**CARVAJAL, LUIS DE** (*b.* 1566; *d.* 8 December 1596), prominent crypto-Jew (secret Jew) in Mexico. Carvajal was born in Benavente, Castile, and studied at the Jesuit school in Medina del Campo. In 1580 he and his family emigrated to Mexico at the invitation of Luis's uncle, Luis de Carvajal y de la Cueva, conquistador and governor of Nuevo León, who was unaware that his relatives secretly practiced Judaism. Carvajal tried his hand at a variety of trades, raising sheep, and working as an itinerant merchant. The Carvajals established extensive contacts with other crypto-Jews and became the cynosure of the INQUISITION's first major campaign against Judaizers. On 9 May 1589 agents of the Inquisition arrested Carvajal and his mother. While in prison, Carvajal had several dreams that convinced him that God had chosen him to sustain the Jewish community in Mexico. He therefore feigned repentance, formally abjured his heresy, and was reconciled to the Catholic church. But he continued to practice Judaism in secret and persuaded other members of his family to do the same.

While serving in the Colegio de Santiago de Tlatelolco as part of his penance, he used the library to further his knowledge of the Old Testament and correct Jewish practice. In early 1595 Carvajal wrote his *Memoirs*, a mystical autobiography in which he referred to himself as Joseph Lumbroso ("the Enlightened"). Shortly after, he was again arrested by the Inquisition and condemned as a relapsed heretic. He and several other family members were burned at the stake in the century's largest auto-da-fé. According to some reports,

Carvajal made a last-minute conversion to Christianity and was garroted before being burned.

LUIS DE CARVAJAL, *The Enlightened: The Writings of Luis de Carvajal, el Mozo*, edited and translated by Seymour B. Liebman (1967); MARTIN A. COHEN, *The Martyr: The Story of a Secret Jew and the Mexican Inquisition in the Sixteenth Century* (1973).

R. DOUGLAS COPE

*See also* **Jews.**

**CARVALHO, ANTÔNIO DE ALBUQUERQUE COELHO DE** (*b.* 1655; *d.* 25 April 1725), Portuguese colonial administrator. Born in Lisbon and baptized on 14 September 1655, Carvalho was the son of the governor of Maranhão (1667–1671) of the same name; the nephew of Feliciano Coelho de Carvalho, the first lord-proprietor of the captaincy of Camutá (also known as Cametá); the grandson of Francisco Coelho de Carvalho, first governor-general (1626–1636) of the newly established state of Maranhão and Grão-Pará; and the great-grandson of Feliciano Coelho de Carvalho, Indian fighter and governor of Paraíba in the 1590s. He accompanied his father to America, leaving Portugal in 1666 and returning in 1671. In 1678 young Carvalho returned to Maranhão to serve as *capitão-mor* of his family's captaincy of Camutá until 1682. That same year, he fathered by Angela de Bairros, whose parents were said to be *pardos* from Pernambuco, the bastard Antônio de Albuquerque Coelho (1682–1746), who later gained fame as the one-armed governor and captain-general of Macau. From 1685 to 1690 Carvalho served as governor and *capitão-mor* of Grão-Pará. On 17 May 1690, he became governor and captain-general of the state of Maranhão, Grão-Pará, and Rio Negro, administering that vast territory until 1701.

After returning to Portugal, Carvalho served in the WAR OF SPANISH SUCCESSION. For his services in Portuguese America, Carvalho, already a knight in the Order of Christ, was awarded a commandery worth 300 milreis and the post of *alcaide-mor*. Since there was no single commandery available with annual receipts for that amount, he was given the commandery of Santo Ildefonso de Val de Telhas in the Order of Christ, two other commanderies in Setúbal, and the post of *alcaide-mor* of Sines—the latter three in the Order of Santiago.

In March 1709, Carvalho was named governor of Rio de Janeiro. He arrived in June 1709, departed for Minas Gerais in July, and spent the next few months pacifying the area in the wake of the War of the Emboabas, the civil conflict between the Paulistas who had discovered the area's mineral wealth and the newcomers from Portugal and coastal Brazil. In the late fall he returned to Rio de Janeiro, where he remained until his appointment as governor of the newly created captaincy of São Paulo and Minas do Ouro. Installed in São Paulo in June 1710, he remained in the captaincy, erecting new townships and strengthening crown authority, until late September 1711. Upon hearing that an armada of eighteen ships under the French corsair René Duguay-Trouin had arrived at Rio de Janeiro, he quickly mobilized six thousand men from the mining areas and marched to the city's rescue. But it was too late: Rio had already been occupied and plundered by the French, and most of the ransom they had demanded had been paid. After the French departed on 13 November 1711, Carvalho helped restore order and rebuild Rio de Janeiro, holding the post of governor (October 1711–June 1713) while he continued to hold his governorship of São Paulo and Minas do Ouro.

Late in 1713 he set sail for Portugal. Enroute he spent eighteen days in Recife's harbor in the aftermath of Pernambuco's War of the Mascates and, upon his return to Portugal, he lobbied for the planter faction.

Carvalho married Dona Luisa Antônia de Mendonça, daughter of Dom Francisco de Melo and Dona Joana de Abreu e Melo. From this marriage, a son, Francisco de Albuquerque Coelho de Carvalho, was born. On 22 March 1722, Carvalho took office as governor of Angola, where he died.

The best treatment to date of Antônio de Albuquerque Coelho de Carvalho's Brazilian experience is found in C. R. BOXER, *The Golden Age of Brazil, 1695–1750* (1962). Also useful is the same author's *Fidalgos in the Far East, 1550–1770* (repr. 1968). There is a short biography in Portuguese by AURELIANO LEITE, *Antônio de Albuquerque Coelho de Carvalho: Capitão-General de São Paulo de Minas do Ouro, no Brasil* (1944). For Carvalho's services in Angola, see the late-eighteenth-century account of his governorship by ELIAS ALEXANDRE SILVA CORREIA, *História de Angola*, vol. 1 (1937), pp. 353–357.

FRANCIS A. DUTRA

**CARVALHO E MELLO, SEBASTIÃO JOSÉ DE.** *See* **Pombal, Marquês de.**

**CASA DA INDIA.** *See* **Portuguese Overseas Administration.**

**CASA DA SUPLICAÇÃO,** a Portuguese High Court of Appeal that served as a model for the Brazilian High Court. It was originally joined with the Casa do Cível, from which it was separated at the end of the fourteenth century. The main body of the Casa da Suplicação consisted of *desembargadores* (high court magistrates), including *desembargadores extravagantes* (unassigned judges) and *desembargadores dos agravos* (appellate judges). The *desembargadores* were divided into two chambers, or *mesas*, one for civil cases and one for criminal cases. Each was directed by a *desembargador dos agravos*, who bore the title of *corregedor*. A plenary session, called a *mesa grande*, could be convened for matters of great importance. A chancellor served as a kind of chief justice and assigned judges to hear litigation, issued sentences, and reviewed decisions to avoid conflict with existing statutes.

The Casa da Suplicação heard appeals in criminal cases, in civil cases involving sums of money above the amount established for the Casa de Cível, and in appeals of judicial decisions made in the colonies. Because it was the highest court of appeal, the Casa da Suplicação made some of the most important decisions affecting life in colonial Brazil.

STUART B. SCHWARTZ, *Sovereignty and Society of Colonial Brazil* (1973).

ROSS WILKINSON

**CASA DA TORRE,** a dynasty of northeastern Brazilian cattle barons founded in 1549 by Garcia d'Avila, a protégé of Governor Tomé de SOUSA. The name "Casa da Torre" came from the family seat at Tatuapara, Bahia, a fortified tower citadel. Garcia d'Avila and his grandson, Colonel Francisco Dias d'Avila, expanded into the backlands of Pernambuco, Piauí, and Sergipe, winning a series of land grants from the crown in the seventeenth century for their efforts in organizing mining expeditions, defending Bahia against the Dutch, and "pacifying" (massacring) Amerindians. By 1700 the Casa possessed nearly the entire interior of Pernambuco. In 1711 João Antônio ANDREONI recorded that it controlled 260 leagues (league = 6,600 meters) along the Rio São Francisco and another 70 leagues between the São Francisco and the Parnaíba.

JOÃO CAPISTRANO DE ABRUE, *Capítulos de história colonial, 1500–1800*, 4th ed. (1954), p. 215; PEDRO CALMON, *História da Casa da Tôrre, uma dinastia de pioneiros*, 2d ed. (1958); *Nôvo dicionário de história do Brasil* (1971); and JOHN HEMMING, *Red Gold: The Conquest of the Brazilian Indians, 1500–1760* (1978), pp. 346–354.

JUDY BIEBER FREITAS

**CASA DE CONTRATACIÓN.** The "House of Trade," was established by the crown in Seville in 1503, initially with the limited but vital brief of overseeing the purchase, transport, warehousing, and sale of merchandise exported to and imported from Spain's newly discovered American territories. As discovery and conquest spread during the next two decades from Hispaniola to Cuba and Jamaica, Venezuela, Central America, and Mexico, the Casa's commercial and financial responsibilities multiplied. Moreover, as the only crown agency competent in this period to deal with American affairs as a whole, it also regulated the flow of passengers and assumed a wide range of additional responsibilities, including the training of pilots, the preparation and provision of maps and charts, the exercise of probate in respect of the estates of Spaniards who died in America, and the resolution of legal disputes concerning commerce.

The broader administrative responsibilities of the Casa were curtailed by the creation of the Council of the Indies in 1524. Thereafter, the Casa functioned primarily as a Board of Trade. It was headed by three key

589

officials: a FACTOR, responsible for the provisioning and inspection of shipping and the purchase on behalf of the crown of strategic commodities required in America, including arms, munitions, and mercury; a treasurer, entrusted with the registration and safe custody of all bullion and jewels landed in Seville; and an accountant-secretary, responsible for maintaining accounts relating to the Casa's internal and external activities. These functions were exercised from the body's splendid headquarters in the Alcázar of Seville, a prestigious base that emphasized the importance to the monarchy of the regulation of imperial commerce, not only in terms of the provision of revenue—the Casa oversaw the collection of the ALMOJARIFAZGO, or tax on maritime trade, the AVERÍA, or defense tax, and other taxes—but also as a means of preserving America as a uniquely Spanish, Catholic environment.

In this and related matters, including the control of contraband, the Casa, like other Hapsburg organs of government, tended by the seventeenth century to become obsessed with bureaucratic detail, losing sight of the broader need to adjust commercial policies and practices to take account of the changing economic conditions in America. Its registers of shipping, passengers, and cargoes were meticulously maintained, for example (and constitute a source of fundamental importance for historians of imperial trade), but little consistent effort was made to curb widespread fraud and contraband even within Seville, let alone in American ports.

The history of the Casa is closely related to the role of Seville as the only Spanish port licensed to trade with America for the greater part of the Hapsburg period. By the end of the seventeenth century this monopoly had been transferred, in effect, to Cádiz, which enjoyed easier access to the sea (and, thus, to the foreign manufactures required for re-export to America), although administrative inertia delayed the transfer of the Casa to Cádiz until 1717. It functioned there with diminishing efficiency until 1790, when it was abolished in the wake of the radical restructuring of imperial trade undertaken in 1778–1789.

EDUARDO TRUEBA, *Sevilla marítima (siglo XVI)* (1986); ANTONIA HEREDIA HERRERA, *Sevilla y los hombres del comercio (1700–1800)* (1989); JOSÉ MIGUEL DELGADO BARRADO, ''Las relaciones comerciales entre España e Indias durante el siglo XVI: Estado de la cuestión,'' in *Revista de Indias* 50, no. 188 (1990): 139–150.

JOHN R. FISHER

*See also* **Commercial Policy.**

**CASA DE LAS AMÉRICAS.** Founded in Havana, Cuba, in 1960, it is one of the major institutions for the publication and dissemination of scholarly, cultural, and political studies in the Caribbean. Since CASTRO's rise to power it has become a powerful center for promoting national culture, Marxism, and the reinterpretation of history. Casa de las Américas publishes books by authors from throughout the Western Hemisphere as well as a bimonthly review guide. It also is a principal forum for Latin Americans' intellectual exploration of Third World issues. The most prestigious Cuban literary award is given annually by this organization to promising Latin American novelists, playwrights, and poets.

JUDITH A. WEISS, *Casa de las Américas: An Intellectual Review in the Cuban Revolution* (1977).

DARIÉN DAVIS

**CASA DEL OBRERO MUNDIAL,** an anarcho-syndicalist organization advocating working-class control of the means of production that led the way in mobilizing Mexican labor between 1911 and 1916. While violence grew in the countryside, Mexican workers joined unions on an unprecedented scale. Enabled by revolutionary zeal, unrest, and the weakness of the new state, they confronted employers and the new government of Francisco MADERO with strikes, boycotts, sit-ins, and violence. The Casa grew out of small groups of anarchist intellectuals and artisans, such as the Mexican Typographic Confederation, and anarcho-syndicalist industrial workers to mobilize the working class. Formed in Mexico City in 1912 as the Casa del Obrero, by 1914 it could claim national standing and had adopted its formal name, becoming one of the most important entities of the revolutionary era.

The formation by 5,000 or more Casa members of the Red Battalions, which joined with the undermanned Constitutionalist Army during the Revolution, proved instrumental in the critically important victory over the forces of Francisco VILLA in the battle of El Ebano, fought in late 1914 for control of Mexico's oil fields along the Gulf Coast. Fifteen hundred women members of the Casa, many of them textile workers, adopted the name Acratas (those opposed to all authority) and formed military nursing units offering essential support to the male combat units. By agreement with the Constitutionalist government, the Casa was to have an independent command staff and the exclusive right to organize workers in the areas that came under government control.

While never becoming part of the independent officer corps, the Casa did grow rapidly and comprised 150,000 members by early 1916. Following the Constitutionalist victory over the Villistas in 1915, the Casa and the new government quickly came into conflict. Military demobilization of the Casa in 1915 presaged general strikes in the spring and summer of 1916, before the Constitutionalist government of Venustiano CARRANZA used the regular army to crush and disband the Casa.

JOHN M. HART, *Anarchism and the Mexican Working Class, 1860–1931* (1978), and *Revolutionary Mexico: The Coming and Process of the Mexican Revolution* (1987).

JOHN MASON HART

*See also* **Anarchism and Anarchosyndicalism; Mexico: Revolutionary Movements.**

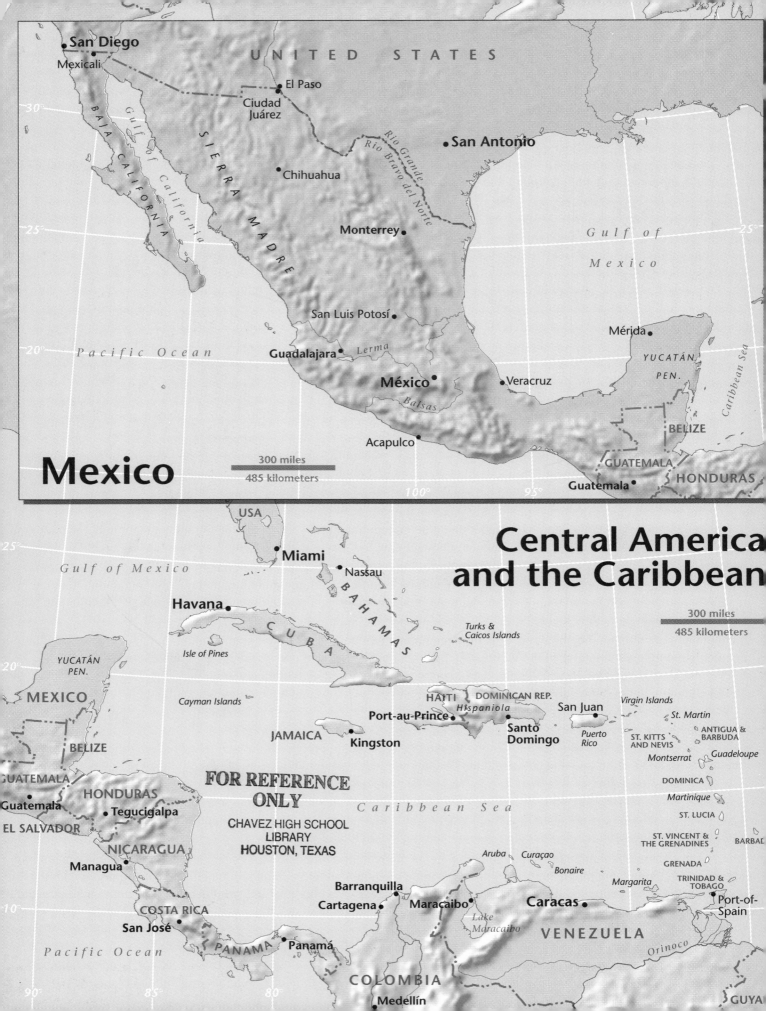

# Mexico

UNITED STATES

San Diego
Mexicali
El Paso
Ciudad Juárez
San Antonio
Chihuahua
Rio Grande
Rio Bravo del Norte
Monterrey

BAJA CALIFORNIA

Gulf of California

SIERRA MADRE

Pacific Ocean

San Luis Potosí
Guadalajara
Lerma
México
Balsas
Veracruz
Acapulco

Gulf of Mexico

Mérida
YUCATÁN PEN.
Caribbean Sea

BELIZE
GUATEMALA
Guatemala
HONDURAS

30
25
20

100°
95°

300 miles
485 kilometers

# Central America and the Caribbean

USA

Gulf of Mexico

Miami
Nassau

Havana
Isle of Pines
CUBA
BAHAMAS

Turks & Caicos Islands

YUCATÁN PEN.

MEXICO

BELIZE

Cayman Islands

JAMAICA
Kingston

HAITI
Port-au-Prince
Hispaniola

DOMINICAN REP.
Santo Domingo

San Juan
Puerto Rico

Virgin Islands
St. Martin
ANTIGUA & BARBUDA
ST. KITTS AND NEVIS
Montserrat
Guadeloupe
DOMINICA
Martinique
ST. LUCIA
ST. VINCENT & THE GRENADINES
GRENADA
BARBAD...

GUATEMALA
Guatemala
HONDURAS
Tegucigalpa
EL SALVADOR

FOR REFERENCE ONLY
CHAVEZ HIGH SCHOOL LIBRARY
HOUSTON, TEXAS

Caribbean Sea

NICARAGUA
Managua

COSTA RICA
San José

Pacific Ocean

PANAMA
Panamá

Barranquilla
Cartagena
Maracaibo
Lake Maracaibo

Aruba
Curaçao
Bonaire

Margarita

Caracas

TRINIDAD & TOBAGO
Port-of-Spain

VENEZUELA

COLOMBIA
Medellín

Orinoco

GUY...

300 miles
485 kilometers

90°
85°
80°
25
20
10